Frommer's®

American Southwest

4th Edition

by Lesley S. King & Karl Samson

Colorado & Utah coverage by Don & Barbara Laine

Las Vegas coverage by Mary Herczog

Wiley Publishing, Inc.

Published by:

WILEY PUBLISHING, INC.

111 River St.
Hoboken, NJ 07030-5774

ISBN 978-0-470-50465-9

Editor: Matthew Brown with Anuja Madar
Production Editor: Katie Robinson
Cartographer: Tim Lohnes
Photo Editor: Richard Fox
Production by Wiley Indianapolis Composition Services

Front cover photo: Arizona: View from John Ford's Point, Monument Valley 3
© Jon Bower USA/Alamy Images
Back cover photo: San Miguel Mission (oldest church in USA), Santa Fe, New Mexico, USA
© Walter Bibikow/Jon Arnold Images Ltd./Alamy Images

For information on our other products and services or to obtain technical support, please contact our Customer Care Department within the U.S. at 877/762-2974, outside the U.S. at 317/572-3993 or fax 317/572-4002.

Wiley also publishes its books in a variety of electronic formats. Some content that appears in print may not be available in electronic formats.

Manufactured in the United States of America

5 4 3 2 1

CONTENTS

4 SUGGESTED SOUTHWEST ITINERARIES 52

5 THE ACTIVE VACATION PLANNER 67

6 THE FOUR CORNERS AREA 82

7 SANTA FE 138

8 TAOS 201

9 ALBUQUERQUE 237

10 NORTHERN NEW MEXICO 270

11 SOUTHERN NEW MEXICO 297

12 TUCSON 347

13 PHOENIX & THE VALLEY OF THE SUN 400

LIST OF MAPS

ABOUT THE AUTHORS

Lesley S. King (New Mexico coverage, plus chapters 1, 2, 3, 4, 5, and 19) grew up on a ranch in northern New Mexico, where she still returns on weekends. A freelance writer and photographer, she has written for the *New York Times, Audubon Magazine,* United Airlines *Hemispheres* magazine, and *La Vie Claire,* and she pens a monthly travel column in *New Mexico Magazine.* She is also author of *King of the Road* (a book of her travel essays and photographs); *Frommer's Santa Fe, Taos & Albuquerque;* and *Frommer's New Mexico.*

Karl Samson (Arizona coverage, plus chapters 2 and 3) lives in Oregon, where he spends his time juggling his obsessions with traveling, gardening, outdoor sports, and wine. Each winter, to dry out his webbed feet, he flees the soggy Northwest to update the *Frommer's Arizona* guide. Karl is also the author of *Frommer's Seattle* and *Frommer's Washington State.*

Residents of northern New Mexico for close to 40 years, **Don** and **Barbara Laine** (Colorado and Utah coverage) have traveled extensively throughout the Rocky Mountains and the Southwest, exploring the mountains and deserts with their always-curious dogs. They (the Laines, not their dogs) are the lead authors of *Frommer's National Parks of the American West* and have also authored *Frommer's Zion & Bryce Canyon National Parks* and other Frommer's travel guides. The Laines have also written *Little-Known Southwest, New Mexico & Arizona State Parks,* and *Best Short Hikes in Arizona* for The Mountaineers Books; and *The New Mexico Guide* for Fulcrum Publishing.

Mary Herczog (Las Vegas coverage) lives in Los Angeles and works in the film industry. She is the author of *Frommer's New Orleans* and *Las Vegas For Dummies,* and has contributed to *Frommer's Los Angeles.* She still isn't sure when to hit and when to hold when playing blackjack.

HOW TO CONTACT US

In researching this book, we discovered many wonderful places—hotels, restaurants, shops, and more. We're sure you'll find others. Please tell us about them, so we can share the information with your fellow travelers in upcoming editions. If you were disappointed with a recommendation, we'd love to know that, too. Please write to:

Frommer's American Southwest, 4th Edition
Wiley Publishing, Inc. • 111 River St. • Hoboken, NJ 07030-5774

AN ADDITIONAL NOTE

Please be advised that travel information is subject to change at any time—and this is especially true of prices. We therefore suggest that you write or call ahead for confirmation when making your travel plans. The authors, editors, and publisher cannot be held responsible for the experiences of readers while traveling. Your safety is important to us, however, so we encourage you to stay alert and be aware of your surroundings. Keep a close eye on cameras, purses, and wallets, all favorite targets of thieves and pickpockets.

FROMMER'S STAR RATINGS, ICONS & ABBREVIATIONS

Every hotel, restaurant, and attraction listing in this guide has been ranked for quality, value, service, amenities, and special features using a **star-rating system.** In country, state, and regional guides, we also rate towns and regions to help you narrow down your choices and budget your time accordingly. Hotels and restaurants are rated on a scale of zero (recommended) to three stars (exceptional). Attractions, shopping, nightlife, towns, and regions are rated according to the following scale: zero stars (recommended), one star (highly recommended), two stars (very highly recommended), and three stars (must-see).

In addition to the star-rating system, we also use **eight feature icons** that point you to the great deals, in-the-know advice, and unique experiences that separate travelers from tourists. Throughout the book, look for:

Finds	Special finds—those places only insiders know about
Fun Facts	Fun facts—details that make travelers more informed and their trips more fun
Kids	Best bets for kids, and advice for the whole family
Moments	Special moments—those experiences that memories are made of
Overrated	Places or experiences not worth your time or money
Tips	Insider tips—great ways to save time and money
Value	Great values—where to get the best deals
Warning!	Warning—traveler's advisories are usually in effect

The following **abbreviations** are used for credit cards:

AE	American Express	DISC	Discover	V	Visa
DC	Diners Club	MC	MasterCard		

TRAVEL RESOURCES AT FROMMERS.COM

Frommer's travel resources don't end with this guide. Frommer's website, **www.frommers.com,** has travel information on more than 4,000 destinations. We update features regularly, giving you access to the most current trip-planning information and the best airfare, lodging, and car-rental bargains. You can also listen to podcasts, connect with other Frommers.com members through our active-reader forums, share your travel photos, read blogs from guidebook editors and fellow travelers, and much more.

1

The Best of the Southwest

Planning a trip to a region as large and diverse as the American Southwest involves a lot of decision making, so in this chapter we've tried to give you some direction. We've chosen what we feel is the very best the region has to offer—the places and experiences you won't want to miss. Although the sights and activities listed here are written up in more detail elsewhere in this book, this chapter gives you an overview of the highlights and gets you started.

1 THE BEST OF THE NATURAL SOUTHWEST

- **Monument Valley Buttes at Sunset** (UT and AZ): These stark sentinels of the desert are impressive at any time, but they take on a particularly dignified aura when the setting sun casts its deep colors over them, etching their profiles against a darkening sky. Although the park generally closes before sunset, you can arrange a sunset tour—it's well worth the cost. See p. 115.
- **Rio Grande Gorge** (NM): A hike into this dramatic gorge is unforgettable. You'll first see it as you come over a rise heading toward Taos. It's a colossal slice in the earth, formed during the late Cretaceous period (130 million years ago) and the early Tertiary period (about 70 million years ago). Drive about 35 miles north of Taos, near the village of Cerro, to the **Wild Rivers Recreation Area.** From the lip of the canyon, you descend through land inhabited by Indians since 16,000 B.C. If you're visiting during spring or early summer and like an adrenaline rush, be sure to find a professional guide and raft the Taos Box, a 17-mile stretch of Class IV white water. See "Other Outdoor Activities," in chapter 8.
- **Carlsbad Caverns National Park** (NM): One of the world's largest and most complex cave systems is in southeastern New Mexico. The 80 known caves have spectacular stalagmite and stalactite formations. Explore the Big Room on a 1-mile self-guided tour, then catch the massive bat flight from the cave entrance at sunset. See p. 319.
- **White Sands National Monument** (NM): Located 15 miles southwest of Alamogordo, White Sands National Monument preserves the best part of the world's largest gypsum dune field. For a truly unforgettable experience, camp overnight so that you can watch the sun rise on the smooth, endless dunes. See p. 304.
- **Arizona–Sonora Desert Museum** (AZ): The name is misleading—this is more zoo and botanical garden than museum. Naturalistic settings house dozens of species of desert animals, including a number of critters you wouldn't want to meet in the wild (rattlesnakes, tarantulas, scorpions, black widows, and Gila monsters). See p. 374.
- **Saguaro National Park** (AZ): Lying both east and west of Tucson, this park

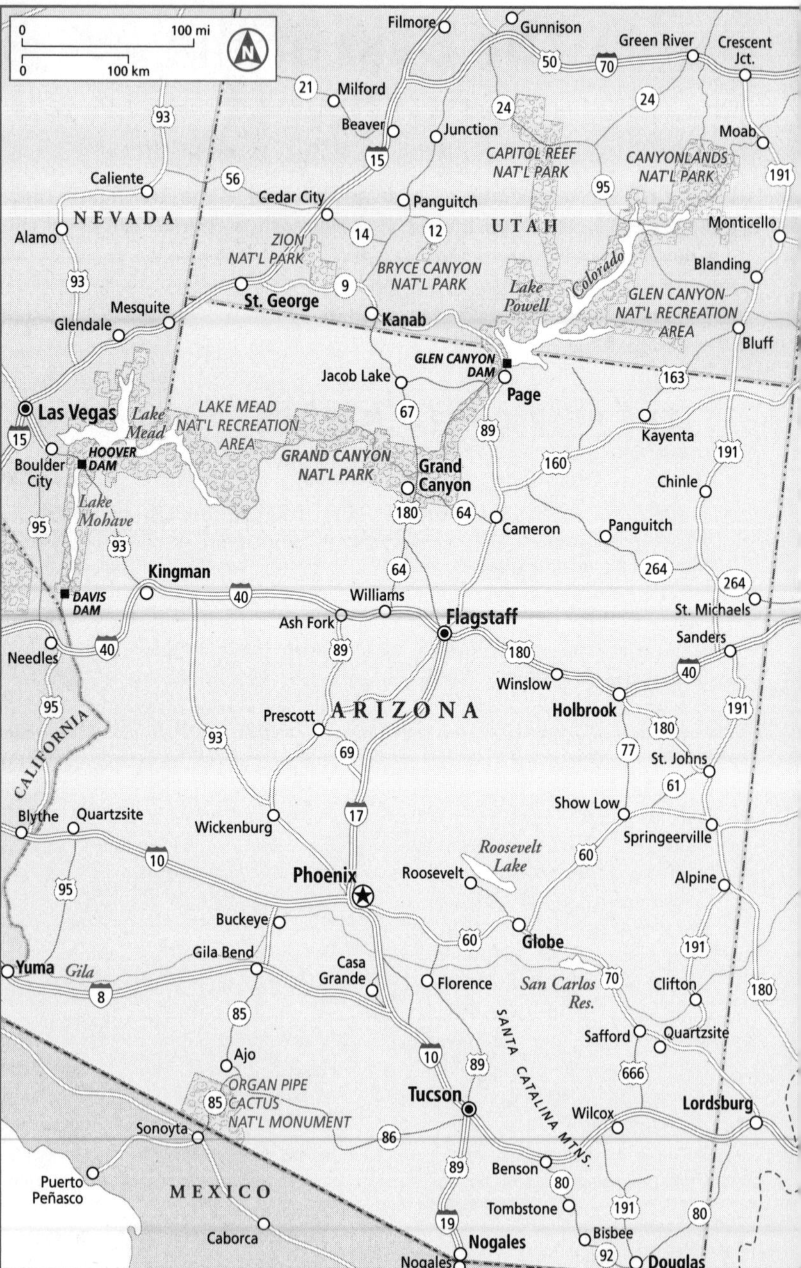
0 100 mi
0 100 km
N
NEVADA
UTAH
ARIZONA
CALIFORNIA
MEXICO
Filmore
Gunnison
Green River
Crescent Jct.
Milford
Beaver
Junction
Moab
CAPITOL REEF NAT'L PARK
CANYONLANDS NAT'L PARK
Caliente
Cedar City
Panguitch
Alamo
Monticello
ZION NAT'L PARK
BRYCE CANYON NAT'L PARK
Blanding
Lake Powell
Colorado
GLEN CANYON NAT'L RECREATION AREA
Mesquite
St. George
Kanab
Glendale
Bluff
GLEN CANYON DAM
Jacob Lake
Page
Las Vegas
Lake Mead
LAKE MEAD NAT'L RECREATION AREA
Kayenta
HOOVER DAM
Boulder City
GRAND CANYON NAT'L PARK
Grand Canyon
Chinle
Lake Mohave
Cameron
Panguitch
Kingman
DAVIS DAM
Williams
St. Michaels
Ash Fork
Flagstaff
Needles
Sanders
Winslow
Holbrook
Prescott
St. Johns
Show Low
Blythe
Quartzsite
Wickenburg
Springeerville
Roosevelt Lake
Phoenix
Roosevelt
Alpine
Buckeye
Globe
Gila Bend
Casa Grande
Yuma
Gila
Florence
San Carlos Res.
Clifton
SANTA CATALINA MTNS.
Safford
Quartzsite
Ajo
ORGAN PIPE CACTUS NAT'L MONUMENT
Tucson
Lordsburg
Wilcox
Sonoyta
Benson
Puerto Peñasco
Tombstone
Bisbee
Caborca
Nogales
Nogales
Douglas

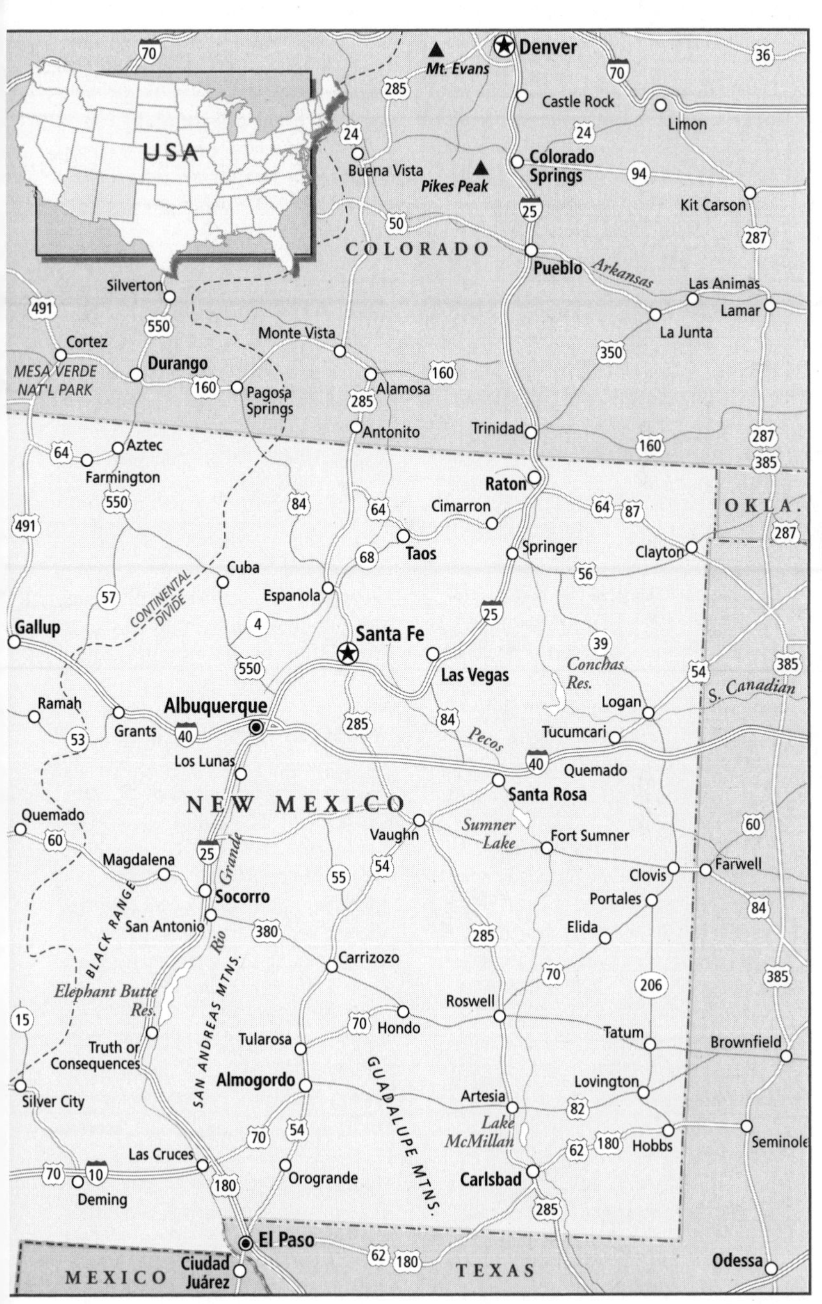
USA
Denver
Mt. Evans
Castle Rock
Limon
Buena Vista
Colorado Springs
Pikes Peak
Kit Carson
COLORADO
Pueblo
Arkansas
Las Animas
Lamar
La Junta
Silverton
Monte Vista
Cortez
Durango
MESA VERDE NAT'L PARK
Pagosa Springs
Alamosa
Antonito
Trinidad
Aztec
Farmington
Raton
Cimarron
OKLA.
Taos
Springer
Clayton
Cuba
Espanola
CONTINENTAL DIVIDE
Gallup
Santa Fe
Las Vegas
Conchas Res.
S. Canadian
Ramah
Grants
Albuquerque
Logan
Tucumcari
Pecos
Los Lunas
Quemado
Santa Rosa
NEW MEXICO
Quemado
Vaughn
Sumner Lake
Fort Sumner
Magdalena
Grande
Farwell
Clovis
Socorro
Portales
BLACK RANGE
San Antonio
Rio
Elida
Carrizozo
SAN ANDREAS MTNS.
Elephant Butte Res.
Roswell
Hondo
Tatum
Tularosa
Brownfield
Truth or Consequences
GUADALUPE MTNS.
Almogordo
Lovington
Silver City
Artesia
Lake McMillan
Hobbs
Seminole
Las Cruces
Orogrande
Carlsbad
Deming
El Paso
Ciudad Juárez
MEXICO
TEXAS
Odessa

preserves "forests" of saguaro cactuses and is the very essence of the desert as so many people imagine it. You can hike it, bike it, or drive it. See p. 375.

- **Desert Botanical Garden** (AZ): There's no better place to learn about the plants of Arizona's Sonoran Desert and the many other deserts of the world. Displays at this Phoenix botanical garden explain plant adaptations and how indigenous tribes once used many of this region's wild plants. See p. 434.
- **Zion National Park** (UT): At the Narrows in Zion, sheer 1,000-foot-high walls enclose you in a 20-foot-wide world of hanging gardens, waterfalls, and sculpted sandstone arches, with the Virgin River beneath your feet. This is one of the park's many awe-inspiring experiences. See p. 567.

2 THE BEST OUTDOOR ACTIVITIES

- **Hiking** (throughout the region): What's unique about hiking in the Southwest is the variety of terrain, from desert to alpine forest to badlands to canyons. In Utah, you can hike right past all three stone formations at Natural Bridges National Monument (p. 95) or explore the hoodoo formations in Bryce Canyon National Park (p. 573). Some of our favorite places for a hike in New Mexico are the El Morro National Monument (p. 279), the hauntingly sculpted rock formations at Abiquiu that artist Georgia O'Keeffe made famous in her paintings (p. 164), and White Sands National Monument (p. 304).

  In Arizona, a hike down into the Grand Canyon or Havasu Canyon is not for the unfit or the faint of heart, but it will take you on a journey through millions of years set in stone. This trip takes plenty of planning and requires some strenuous hiking. See "The Grand Canyon South Rim" and "Havasu Canyon & Grand Canyon West," in chapter 16.
- **Ballooning** (NM and AZ): With the International Balloon Fiesta in Albuquerque bringing more than 750 balloons to the area, Albuquerque has become the sport's world capital. Fortunately, visitors can let loose the tethers and float free, too. Most of the operators are in Albuquerque; see p. 75 for recommendations. Ballooning is also popular in Arizona; see "Organized Tours," in chapter 12, "Organized Tours & Excursions," in chapter 13, and "Organized Tours," under "Sedona & Oak Creek Canyon," in chapter 15, for information on companies in Tucson, Phoenix, and Sedona.
- **Horseback riding** (NM and AZ): New Mexico's history is stamped with the hoof, dating from the Spanish conquistadors' introduction of horses to the New World. Riding in New Mexico still has that Old West feel, with trails that wind through wilderness, traversing passes and broad meadows. Some of the best rides are near Santa Fe, on Taos Pueblo land, and in Southern New Mexico. See p. 176, 229, and 300.

  Cowboys still ride ranges all over Arizona, and so can you, if you book a stay at one of the state's many guest ranches (formerly known as dude ranches). You might even get to drive some cattle down the trail. After a long or short day in the saddle, you can soak in a hot tub, go for a swim, or play tennis before chowing down. See chapters 12, 14, and 15.
- **Mountain Biking** (NM and AZ): Almost anywhere you go in New Mexico, you'll find trails. We've hooked onto some fun single-track near Cloudcroft down south and explored sage

forest on the rim of the Taos Gorge in the north. See the "Biking" sections in each New Mexico chapter, especially chapter 8.

In Arizona, among the red rocks of Sedona, you can pedal through awesome scenery on some of the most memorable single-track trails in the Southwest. There's even plenty of slickrock. See "Getting Outside," under "Sedona & Oak Creek Canyon," in chapter 15.

- **River Rafting** (NM and AZ): Whether you go for 3 days or 2 weeks, no other active vacation in the region comes close to matching the excitement of a raft trip. In Arizona, nothing beats a Colorado River rafting trip through the Grand Canyon. Sure, the river is crowded with groups in the summer, but the grandeur of the canyon more than makes up for it. See "Other Ways of Seeing the Canyon," under "The Grand Canyon South Rim," in chapter 16. In New Mexico, the wild **Taos Box,** a steep-sided canyon south of the Wild Rivers Recreation Area, offers a series of Class IV rapids that rarely lets up for some 17 miles, providing one of the most exciting 1-day white-water tours in the West. See "Other Outdoor Activities," in chapter 8.

3 THE BEST SCENIC DRIVES

- **Monument Valley Navajo Tribal Park** (UT and AZ): This valley of sandstone buttes and mesas is one of the most photographed spots in America and, due to appearances in countless movies, TV shows, and commercials, is familiar to people all over the world. A 17-mile dirt road winds through the park, giving visitors close-up views of such landmarks as Elephant Butte, the Mittens, and Totem Pole. See "Monument Valley Navajo Tribal Park," in chapter 6.
- **High Road to Taos** (Santa Fe, NM): One of New Mexico's primo experiences, this road traverses the mountains from Santa Fe to Taos, passing by chili and apple farms in old Hispanic villages. Stop in Chimayo to see unique wool weaving, in Cordova to find lovely woodcarvings, and in renegade Truchas, where life remains much as it did a century ago. Most important, the route crosses the base of New Mexico's grandest peaks. See "Taking the High Road to Taos," in chapter 7.
- **Turquoise Trail** (Albuquerque, NM): Meandering through the broad Galisteo basin, this scenic route winds from Albuquerque to Santa Fe. The two-lane road runs through piñon-studded hills and old mining towns, such as Madrid and Cerrillos, where 2,000 years ago Native Americans hammered turquoise and silver from the hills. Today artists and craftspeople have revived the towns. See "En Route to Santa Fe: Along the Turquoise Trail," in chapter 9.
- **Lincoln Loop** (Ruidoso, NM): Elegant art, ancient petroglyphs, and Billy the Kid memorabilia draw road warriors to this 162-mile loop in southeastern New Mexico. It begins in the mountain resort town of Ruidoso and cruises to Lincoln, where travelers can "walk in the footsteps" of the notorious punk Billy the Kid. Next it passes imaginative petroglyphs, through the Mescalero Apache Reservation, and back to Ruidoso. See "A Scenic Drive Around the Lincoln Loop," in chapter 11.
- **Mount Lemmon** (Tucson, AZ): The views of Tucson from the city's northern foothills are great, but the vistas from Mount Lemmon are even better. With a ski area at its summit, Mount Lemmon rises from the desert like an island

emerging from the sea. Along the way, the road climbs from cactus country to cool pine forests. See "Getting Outside," in chapter 12.

- **The Apache Trail** (east of Phoenix, AZ): Much of this winding road, which passes just north of the Superstition Mountains, is unpaved and follows a rugged route once ridden by Apaches. This is some of the most remote country in the Phoenix area, with far-reaching desert vistas and lots to see and do along the way. See "A Side Trip from Phoenix: The Apache Trail," in chapter 13.
- **Oak Creek Canyon** (Sedona, AZ): Slicing down from the pine country outside Flagstaff to the red rocks of Sedona, Oak Creek Canyon is a cool oasis. From the scenic overlook at the top of the canyon to the swimming holes and hiking trails at the bottom, this canyon road provides a rapid change in climate and landscape. See "Sedona & Oak Creek Canyon," in chapter 15.

4 THE BEST NATIVE AMERICAN SITES

- **Ute Mountain Tribal Park** (CO): These ruins differ from others in Colorado because they're on the Ute Mountain Indian Reservation, and the only way to see the reservation is on a guided tour conducted by members of the tribe. You'll see ruins and petroglyphs similar to those in Mesa Verde, but with an informed personal guide and without crowds. See p. 86
- **Mesa Verde National Park** (CO): Home to the most impressive prehistoric cliff dwellings in the Southwest, Mesa Verde (Spanish for "green table") overwhelms you with its size and complexity. The first national park set aside to preserve works created by humans, it covers some 52,000 acres just outside Cortez. Among the most compelling sites are Spruce Tree House, Square Tower House, and Cliff Palace, a four-story, apartment-style dwelling. See p. 88.
- **Hovenweep National Monument** (UT): This deserted valley contains some of the most striking and most isolated archaeological sites in the Four Corners area—the remains of curious sandstone towers built more than 700 years ago by the Ancestral Puebloans. These mysterious structures still keep archaeologists guessing. See p. 87.
- **Canyon de Chelly National Monument** (AZ): Small cliff dwellings up and down the length of Canyon de Chelly are visible from overlooks, while a trip into the canyon itself offers a chance to see some of these ruins up close. See p. 109.
- **Navajo National Monument** (AZ): Keet Seel and Betatakin are some of the finest examples of Ancestral Puebloan cliff dwellings in the state. Although the ruins are at the end of long hikes, their size and state of preservation make the sites well worth the effort you'll expend to see them. See p. 114.
- **Monument Valley Navajo Tribal Park** (UT and AZ): For most of us, Monument Valley is the Old West. We've seen it dozens of times in movie theaters, on TV, in magazine advertisements, and on billboards. The Old West may be gone, but many Navajos still call this home. A Navajo guide will give you the Navajo perspective on this majestic land and take you into areas not otherwise open to visitors. See p. 115.
- **Chaco Culture National Historical Park** (NM): A combination of a stunning setting and well-preserved ruins makes the long drive to Chaco Canyon an incredible adventure into Ancestral

Puebloan culture. Many good hikes and bike rides are found in the area, and there's also a campground. See p. 135.

- **Bandelier National Monument** (NM): These ruins provide a spectacular peek into the lives of the Ancestral Puebloan culture, which flourished in the area between A.D. 1100 and 1550. The most dramatic site is a dwelling and kiva (a room used for religious activities) in a cave 140 feet above the canyon floor—reached by a climb up long pueblo-style ladders. See p. 193.
- **Indian Pueblo Cultural Center** (NM): Owned and operated as a nonprofit organization by the 19 pueblos of New Mexico, this is a fine place to begin an exploration of Native American culture. The Albuquerque museum is modeled after Pueblo Bonito, a spectacular 9th-century ruin in Chaco Culture National Historic Park, and contains art and artifacts old and new. See p. 250.
- **Heard Museum** (AZ): This Phoenix institution is one of the nation's premier museums devoted to Native American cultures. In addition to historical exhibits, a huge kachina collection, and an excellent store, it has annual exhibits of contemporary Native American art as well as dance performances and demonstrations of traditional skills. See p. 434.
- **Tonto National Monument** (AZ): Reached via the Apache Trail scenic road, this historic site has one of Arizona's few easily accessible cliff dwellings that still allows visitors to walk around inside the ruins; you don't have to observe from a distance. See p. 462.
- **Montezuma Castle National Monument** (AZ): Located just off I-17, this is the easiest cliff dwelling to get to in Arizona, but visitors cannot go inside the ruins. Nearby Montezuma Well also has some small ruins. See p. 502.

5 THE BEST FAMILY EXPERIENCES

- **Santa Fe Children's Museum** (NM): Designed for the whole family to experience, this museum offers interactive exhibits and hands-on activities in the arts, humanities, science, and technology. Most notable is a 16-foot climbing wall that kids can scale when outfitted with helmets and harnesses. A 1-acre Southwestern horticulture garden features animals, wetlands, and a greenhouse. *Family Life* magazine named this one of the 10 hottest children's museums in the nation. See p. 172.
- **Albuquerque Aquarium** (NM): For those of us born and raised in the desert, this attraction quenches years of soul thirst. Exhibits focus on sea areas fed by the Rio Grande River. You'll pass by many large tanks and within an eels' den. The culminating show is a 285,000-gallon shark tank, where many species of fish and 15 to 20 sand, tiger, brown, and nurse sharks swim around looking ominous. See p. 252.
- **Rio Grande Zoo** (NM): More than 250 species live on 64 acres of riverside bosk among ancient cottonwoods. Open-moat exhibits with animals in naturalized habitats are a treat for zoo-goers. Major exhibits include the polar bears, the giraffes, the sea lions (with underwater viewing), the cat walk, the bird show, and ape country, with its gorilla and orangutans. See p. 254.
- **Carlsbad Caverns National Park** (NM): Truly one of the world's natural wonders, these caverns swallow visitors as they embark on what feels like a journey to the center of the earth. Nocturnal creatures thrive, and water drips onto your body. Kids won't like the fact that they can't climb on the formations,

but they'll be too fascinated to complain much. See p. 319.

- **Arizona–Sonora Desert Museum** (AZ): This Tucson attraction is actually a zoo featuring the animals of the Sonoran Desert. It has rooms full of snakes, a prairie-dog town, bighorn sheep, mountain lions, and an aviary full of hummingbirds. Kids and adults love this place. See p. 374.
- **Shootouts at the O.K. Corral** (AZ): Tombstone may be "the town too tough to die," but poor Ike Clanton and his buddies, the McLaury boys, have to die over and over at frequent reenactments of the famous gunfight. See p. 479.
- **The Grand Canyon Railway** (AZ): Not only is this train excursion a fun way to get to the Grand Canyon, but it also lets you avoid wearisome parking problems and congestion. Shootouts and train robberies are to be expected in this corner of the Wild West. See p. 540.
- **Zion National Park** (UT): The Junior Ranger/Explorers program, available at most national parks, is particularly extensive here. Morning and afternoon activities all summer are geared toward teaching kids what makes this natural wonder so special. They'll have so much fun, they won't even notice they're learning. See p. 567.

6 THE BEST LUXURY HOTELS & RESORTS

- **Inn of the Five Graces** (Santa Fe, NM; ✆ **505/992-0957;** www.fivegraces.com): This inn offers an exotic Southwest-meets-the-Orient experience right in Santa Fe. Ornately carved beds, elaborate tile work, and cozy linens add up to an especially sumptuous stay. See p. 144.
- **La Posada de Santa Fe Resort and Spa** (Santa Fe, NM; ✆ **800/727-5276** or 505/986-0000; www.laposadadesanta fe.com): With the feel of a meandering adobe village but the service of a fine hotel, this has become one of New Mexico's premier resorts. It has an elegant spa and pool and spacious spa rooms. Most rooms lack views but have outdoor patios, and most are tucked back into the quiet compound. See p. 145.
- **Bishop's Lodge** (Santa Fe, NM; ✆ **505/983-6377;** www.bishopslodge.com): More than a century ago, Bishop Jean Baptiste Lamy often escaped clerical politics by hiking into a valley north of town called Little Tesuque. He built a retreat and chapel that years later have become the Bishop's Lodge. All rooms are spacious and feature handcrafted furniture and local artwork. Activities include horseback riding, hiking, tennis, swimming, and spa treatments. See p. 149.
- **Rancho de San Juan** (Española, NM; ✆ **505/753-6818;** www.ranchodesan juan.com): Located in the enchanting country near Ojo Caliente, this award-winning inn offers complete luxury and the quiet of the country. Private casitas set among the hills are decorated with antiques and have spectacular views. See p. 199.
- **El Monte Sagrado** (Taos, NM; ✆ **800/828-TAOS** [8267] or 575/758-3502; www.elmontesagrado.com): With guest rooms and casitas set around a grassy "Sacred Circle," this ecoresort is the quintessence of luxury. Every detail, from the waterfalls and chemical-free pool and hot tubs to the authentic theme decor in the rooms, has been created with conscious care. See p. 204.
- **Hyatt Regency Tamaya Resort and Spa** (Bernalillo, NM; ✆ **800/55-HYATT** [554-9288] or 505/867-1234; www.tamaya.hyatt.com): Situated on Santa Ana Pueblo land, this grand resort has

everything a person might need to get away from the world. Three swimming pools, a 16,000-square-foot full-service spa and fitness center, the 18-hole Twin Warriors Championship Golf Course designed by Gary Panks, and views of the Sandia Mountains make for plenty to do. It's only 25 minutes from Albuquerque and 45 minutes from Santa Fe. See p. 244.

- **Loews Ventana Canyon Resort** (Tucson, AZ; ✆ **800/234-5117** or 520/299-2020; www.loewshotels.com/hotels/tucson): With the Santa Catalina Mountains rising in the backyard and an almost-natural waterfall only steps away from the lobby, this is Tucson's most dramatic resort. Contemporary styling throughout makes constant reference to the desert setting. See p. 357.
- **Hyatt Regency Scottsdale Resort & Spa at Gainey Ranch** (Scottsdale, AZ; ✆ **800/55-HYATT** [554-9288] or 480/444-1234; www.scottsdale.hyatt.com): Contemporary desert architecture, dramatic landscaping, a water playground with its own beach, a staff that's always ready to assist you, several good restaurants, and even gondola rides—it all adds up to a lot of fun at one of the best run resorts in Arizona. See p. 408.
- **The Phoenician** (Scottsdale, AZ; ✆ **800/888-8234** or 480/941-8200; www.thephoenician.com): This Xanadu of the resort world brims with marble, crystal, and art. With staff members seemingly around every corner, the hotel offers its guests impeccable service. For the utmost in luxury, there are the Canyon Suites, a boutique hotel within the resort. See p. 408.
- **Four Seasons Resort Scottsdale at Troon North** (Scottsdale, AZ; ✆ **888/207-9696;** www.fourseasons.com/scottsdale): Located in north Scottsdale, this is the most luxurious resort in Arizona. The setting is dramatic, the accommodations are spacious, and one of Arizona's top golf courses is next door. See p. 412.
- **Arizona Biltmore Resort & Spa** (Phoenix, AZ; ✆ **800/950-0086** or 602/955-6600; www.arizonabiltmore.com): Combining discreet service and the architectural styling of Frank Lloyd Wright, the Biltmore has long been one of Arizona's most prestigious resorts. This is a thoroughly old-money place, but it continues to keep pace with the times. See p. 413.
- **El Portal Sedona** (Sedona, AZ; ✆ **800/313-0017;** www.elportalsedona.com): Built of hand-cast adobe blocks, and incorporating huge wooden beams salvaged from a railroad trestle, this inn is a work of art both inside and out. The mix of Arts and Crafts and Santa Fe–styling conjures up haciendas of old. See p. 513.
- **Enchantment Resort** (Sedona, AZ; ✆ **800/826-4180** or 928/282-2900; www.enchantmentresort.com): A dramatic setting in a red-rock canyon makes this the most memorably situated resort in the state. If you want to feel as though you're vacationing in the desert, this place fits the bill. Guest rooms are constructed in Pueblo architectural style, and the spa is one of Arizona's finest. See p. 513.

7 THE BEST BED & BREAKFASTS

- **Casa Blanca** (Farmington, NM; ✆ **800/550-6503** or 505/327-6503; www.casablancanm.com): This inn offers patios, fountains, and lush gardens set on a ridge overlooking Farmington. The rooms have elegant furnishings rich in Native American and world folk art.

The full breakfast included with the room is always gourmet. See p. 133.

- **Kokopelli's Cave** (Farmington, NM; ✆ **505/326-2461;** www.bbonline.com/nm/kokopelli): This is an actual cave, but it's like no other cave you've ever seen. Carved deep into the side of a cliff, it's a three-room luxury apartment complete with carpet, VCR, kitchen, and space enough for a family. See p. 133
- **Don Gaspar Inn** (Santa Fe, NM; ✆ **888/986-8664** or 505/986-8664; www.dongaspar.com): Composed of a cluster of Southwestern-style homes set in a historic Santa Fe neighborhood, this inn feels both elegant and friendly. Rooms boast fireplaces and are set around lively gardens, with breakfast served under a peach tree in summer. See p. 146.
- **Casa de las Chimeneas** (Taos, NM; ✆ **877/758-4777** or 575/758-4777; www.visittaos.com): This 1925 adobe home has been a model of Southwestern elegance since it opened as a B&B in 1988. The inn has lovely gardens, comfortable rooms, and a spa, as well as complete massage and facial treatments. The newest rooms have heated Saltillo tile floors, gas kiva fireplaces, and jetted tubs. See p. 207.
- **Bear Mountain Lodge** (Silver City, NM; ✆ **877/620-BEAR** [2327] or 575/538-2538; www.bearmountainlodge.com): This lodge, owned and managed by the Nature Conservancy, offers a nature-lover's paradise. The inn itself was built in 1928, but the grounds show evidence of visitors that dates from 6000 B.C. Nature Conservancy staff members are on hand to guide visitors in their bird-, wildlife-, and plant-viewing pursuits. Rooms are large, with maple floors, high ceilings, and French windows. See p. 342.
- **The Royal Elizabeth** (Tucson, AZ; ✆ **877/670-9022** or 520/670-9022; www.royalelizabeth.com): In downtown Tucson, just a block from the Temple of Music and Art, this Territorial-style historic home is filled with beautiful Victorian antiques and architectural details. Guest rooms have lots of touches not often seen in historic B&Bs, including "vintage" phones, TVs, fridges, and safes. See p. 354
- **La Zarzuela** (Tucson, AZ; ✆ **888/848-8225;** www.zarzuela-az.com): Perched high on a hill on the west side of Tucson, this luxurious B&B boasts great views, colorful decor, and loads of outdoor spaces where guests can relax in the warmth of the desert. See p. 359.
- **Across the Creek at Aravaipa Farms** (Winkelman, AZ; ✆ **520/357-6901;** www.aravaipafarms.com): This is the quintessential desert B&B experience, though it isn't for everyone. To reach this inn, you have to drive *through* Aravaipa Creek (or have the innkeeper shuttle you across). Exploring the nearby wilderness area is the main activity in this remote locale. See p. 361.
- **Rocamadour Bed & Breakfast for (Rock) Lovers** (Prescott, AZ; ✆ **888/771-1933** or 928/771-1933): Set amid the rounded boulders of the Granite Dells just north of Prescott, this inn combines a spectacular setting with French antiques and luxurious accommodations. You won't find a more memorable setting in the state. See p. 497.
- **Briar Patch Inn** (Sedona, AZ; ✆ **888/809-3030** or 928/282-2342; www.briarpatchinn.com): Oak Creek Canyon, near Sedona, where you'll find this collection of luxurious cottages, is an oasis in the desert. Few experiences are more restorative than breakfast on the shady banks of the creek. See p. 514.
- **The Inn at 410** (Flagstaff, AZ; ✆ **800/774-2008** or 928/774-0088; www.inn410.com): This restored 1907 bungalow offers a convenient location in

downtown Flagstaff, pleasant surroundings, comfortable rooms, and delicious breakfasts. Rooms feature distinctive themes, and eight of them have their own fireplaces. See p. 560.

- **Cochise Stronghold B&B** (Cochise County, AZ; ✆ **877/426-4141** or 520/826-4141; www.cochisestrongholdbb.com): Surrounded by the national forest and mountainsides strewn with giant boulders, this B&B is one of the state's remotest inns. The passive solar building was built from straw bales and is not only energy-efficient but also quite beautiful. See p. 487.

8 THE BEST MODERATELY PRICED HOTELS

- **La Posada** (Winslow, AZ; ✆ **928/289-4366;** www.laposada.org): Designed by Mary Jane Colter, who also designed buildings on the South Rim of the Grand Canyon, La Posada opened in 1930 and was the last of the great Santa Fe Railroad hotels. Today, La Posada has been restored to its former glory and is again one of the finest hotels in the West. See p. 99.
- **Santa Fe Motel and Inn** (Santa Fe, NM; ✆ **800/930-5002** or 505/982-1039; www.santafemotel.com): Rooms at this inn are walking distance from the plaza and provide ambience of the Southwest—bold colors and some handmade furniture—with a standard motel price tag. See p. 148.
- **El Rey Inn** (Santa Fe, NM; ✆ **800/521-1349** or 505/982-1931; www.elreyinnsantafe.com): If old-style court motels awaken the road warrior in you, this is your place. Built in the 1930s and expanded over the years, this place has various styles of rooms, all nicely appointed. See p. 152.
- **Old Taos Guesthouse Bed & Breakfast** (Taos, NM; ✆ **800/758-5448** or 575/758-5448; www.oldtaos.com): Set in a 190-year-old adobe dwelling, this inn offers acres of quiet within minutes of downtown Taos. Rooms range from atmospheric to very practical, all with comfortable beds. A family-run business, its owners take good care of their guests. See p. 209.
- **Nativo Lodge** (Albuquerque, NM; ✆ **888/628-4861** or 505/798-4300; www.nativolodge.com.): Utilizing a Native American theme, this hotel on the north end of town offers standard-size rooms with a bit of designer flair and plenty of amenities, all at a reasonable price. See p. 243.
- **Inn on the Santa Fe Trail** (Las Vegas, NM; ✆ **888/448-8438** or 505/425-6791; www.innonthesantafetrail.com): This 1920s court motel, set around a grassy courtyard, has been restored to provide comfortable Southwestern-style rooms, with nice accents such as handcrafted furniture and light fixtures. See p. 291.
- **Hotel Encanto de Las Cruces** (Las Cruces, NM: ✆ **866/383-0443** or 575/522-4300; www.hhandr.com). This hotel exudes colonial elegance while offering reasonable prices. A tiered fountain in the lobby, colorful tiles throughout the hotel, and old-world furnishings make this one of our favorite spots in the region. A cafe and nightclub add to the experience. See p. 334.
- **Windmill Suites at St. Philip's Plaza** (Tucson, AZ; ✆ **800/547-4747** or 520/577-0007; www.windmillinns.com): With large suites and a great location in a shopping plaza that's home to a couple of good restaurants, this hotel midway between downtown Tucson and the foothills is convenient and economical.

Bikes are available for guests to ride on the adjacent bike path. See p. 358.

- **Crowne Plaza San Marcos Golf Resort** (Chandler, AZ; ✆ **800/528-8071** or 480/812-0900; www.sanmarcosresort.com): Opened in 1912, this is the oldest golf resort in Arizona. The resort is right on the pretty central plaza of the booming city of Chandler, 30 minutes southeast of downtown Scottsdale. See p. 418.
- **Letson Loft Hotel** (Bisbee, AZ; ✆ **877/432-3210** or 520/432-3210; www.letsonlofthotel.com): In southeastern Arizona's historic former copper-mining town of Bisbee, the Letson Loft has the prettiest hotel rooms in town. The building has loads of historic character, and front rooms have bay windows overlooking Main Street. See p. 483.
- **Forest Houses** (Sedona, AZ; ✆ **928/282-2999;** www.foresthousesresort.com): Set in the shady depths of Oak Creek Canyon, this collection of handmade cabins is right on the banks of Oak Creek. In fact, you have to drive through the creek to get to the cabins.

9 THE BEST FLAVORS OF THE SOUTHWEST

- **The Turquoise Room** (Winslow, AZ; ✆ **928/289-2888;** http://theturquoiseroom.net): Located in the little-visited town of Winslow in the restored La Posada historic hotel, this restaurant conjures up the days when the wealthy still traveled by railroad. Rarely will you find such excellent meals in such an off-the-beaten-path locale. See p. 99.
- **The Compound** (Santa Fe, NM; ✆ **505/982-4353;** www.compoundrestaurant.com): This reincarnation of one of Santa Fe's classic restaurants serves daring contemporary American food in a soulful setting. Such delicacies as monkfish chorizo with watercress or grilled beef tenderloin with Italian potatoes will please sophisticated palates—and probably simpler ones, too. See p. 156.
- **Geronimo** (Santa Fe, NM; ✆ **505/982-1500;** www.geronimorestaurant.com): Set in the 1756 Borrego House on Canyon Road, this restaurant offers brilliant flavors in a serene adobe atmosphere. The elk tenderloin here is Santa Fe's most prized entree. See p. 158.
- **Santacafé** (Santa Fe, NM; ✆ **505/984-1788;** www.santacafe.com): This restaurant, an all-time favorite, borrows from an international menu of preparations and offerings. The minimalist decor accentuates the beautiful architecture of the 18th-century Padre Gallegos House. One of the best dishes is the Alaskan halibut with English peas and saffron couscous. See p. 159.
- **The Shed** (Santa Fe, NM; ✆ **505/982-9030;** www.sfshed.com): The Shed, a Santa Fe luncheon institution since 1953, occupies a rambling hacienda that was built in 1692. The sauces here have been refined over the years, creating amazing flavors in basic dishes such as enchiladas, burritos, and stuffed *sopaipillas.* The mocha cake is renowned. Its sister restaurant, **La Choza,** is just as good and has a similar menu. See p. 162.
- **De La Tierra** (Taos, NM; ✆ **800/828-TAOS** [8267] or 575/758-3502; www.elmontesagrado.com): Located at the ecoresort El Monte Sagrado, this elegant restaurant serves imaginative regional American food. The pan roasted East Coast cod served with truffle Persian potatoes is delectable. An

expansive wine list completes the experience. See p. 211.

- **Joseph's Table** (Taos, NM; ✆ **575/751-4512;** www.josephstable.com): Located on Taos Plaza, this font of creativity serves delightful dishes with plenty of flair. Try the steak au poivre over mashed potatoes with a Madeira mushroom sauce. See p. 212.
- **Diane's Bakery & Cafe** (Silver City, NM; ✆ **575/538-8722**): Diane Barrett, once a pastry chef at both La Traviata and Eldorado in Santa Fe, has brought refined flavors to the little mining town of Silver City. Come here to feast on sumptuous baked goods and sophisticated meals such as rack of lamb. See p. 343.
- **Café Poca Cosa** (Tucson, AZ; ✆ **520/622-6400;** http://cafepocacosatucson.com): Forget the gloppy melted cheese and flavorless red sauces. This place treats south-of-the-border ingredients with the respect they deserve. It's Mexican food the likes of which you'll never find at your local Mexican joint. See p. 363.
- **El Charro Café** (Tucson, AZ; ✆ **520/622-1922;** www.elcharrocafe.com): Nothing sums up Tucson-style Mexican food quite like the *carne seca* at this, the oldest family-run Mexican restaurant in Tucson. *Carne seca,* which is a bit like shredded beef jerky in a spicy sauce, is made from strips of beef that air-dry on the roof of this restaurant. See p. 366.
- **Janos/J Bar** (Tucson, AZ; ✆ **520/615-6100;** www.janos.com): Serving a combination of regional and Southwestern dishes, Janos for many years has been one of Tucson's premier restaurants. It's just outside the front door of the Westin La Paloma resort, and is as formal a place as you'll find in this city. J Bar is Janos's less-formal bar and grill. See p. 370 and 371.
- **Fry Bread House** (Phoenix, AZ; ✆ **602/351-2345**): Unless you've traveled in the Southwest before, you've probably never had a fry-bread taco. This stick-to-your-ribs dish is a staple on Indian reservations throughout Arizona, but the fry-bread tacos at this Phoenix restaurant are the best I've had anywhere in the state. See p. 432.

2

The Southwest in Depth

In the Hopi creation myth, the Spider Woman fashioned from clay all the birds and beasts, men and women. With Tawa, the sun god, she sang a song and brought forth life. In the American Southwest, the magic of that story is apparent. An elephant, camel, or medicine man fashioned from stone might dominate the landscape; great canyons cut through the earth's crust, laying bare centuries of rock-layer stories. And human artifacts tell their own stories: spear points left some 9,000 years ago, centuries-old cliff dwellings where the scent of smoke still lingers, and grand missions and fortresses where Catholicism once ruled. It's a land with its own song, one the traveler can't help getting caught up in, stepping to the Spider Woman's ancient rhythm.

1 MORE THAN DESERT & CACTUSES

Those who have never visited the American Southwest tend to have some misconceptions. The most common one is that the whole place is a hot desert studded with saguaro cactuses. In fact, the Southwest has varied terrain, encompassing all seven of the earth's life zones, from the low Sonoran cactus country, through the higher plateaus marked with piñon and juniper, to the rich forested sections and even high alpine country. And rather than year-round heat, the Southwest has a range of temperatures, including blistering desert climes, midland regions with warm summers and cold winters, and high mountains where the air is always cool and winter brings world-class skiing.

Major landforms traverse the region. The southern Rocky Mountains cut down through central Colorado and northern New Mexico. The Grand Canyon slices across northern Arizona, as do other prominent canyons, which stretch into Utah. Dramatic stone formations carved by weather and erosion stud this region, including those you've likely seen in movies filmed in Monument Valley, as well as others such as Shiprock and Natural Bridges National Monument. In the south, volcanic mountains, called "sky islands," dot the desert and are home to abundant wildlife, especially bird populations.

Water is the language of the region, enunciating the fate of what grows and what dies here. Rain is scarce. Rivers are scarcer. The Rio Grande cuts New Mexico nearly in half, barely feeding the towns and cities along its banks. The Colorado River snakes from its namesake state across Utah, Arizona, and Nevada before heading south to the Gulf of California. Over the years, it's been heavily dammed, resulting in grand lakes that supply the desert with electricity and irrigation.

What water there is feeds a remarkable array of plant and animal life. In the Sonoran Desert, the notable saguaro cactus, which can reach 40 feet tall and weigh several tons, stands as a symbol for the entire region. Many other kinds of cactuses thrive here as well, as does a range of vegetation, from delicate wildflowers, such the deep-pink sand verbena and bright-yellow brittlebush, to hearty pines such as

Teddy's Tip

Do nothing to mar its grandeur . . . keep it for your children, your children's children, all who come after you, as the one great sight which every American should see.

—President Theodore Roosevelt, after visiting the Grand Canyon in 1903

blue spruce and ponderosa. They help feed and house a broad variety of animal life, from tropical birds such as the elegant trogon to hearty mammals such as pronghorn antelopes, brown bears, and mountain lions. But the desert's most notorious creatures are those that crawl and creep: scorpions, tarantulas, and rattlesnakes. You should avoid these, but don't lose sleep over them—generally, if you leave them alone, they'll do the same to you.

2 LOOKING BACK AT THE SOUTHWEST

IN THE BEGINNING Archaeologists say that humans first migrated to the Southwest, moving southward from the Bering Land Bridge, around 12,000 B.C. Sites such as Sandia Cave and Folsom—where weapon points were discovered that clearly established that our prehistoric ancestors hunted now-extinct mammals, such as woolly mammoths—are internationally known. When large-prey animals died off during the late Ice Age (about 8000 B.C.), people turned to hunting smaller game and gathering wild food.

Stable farming settlements, evidenced by the remains of domestically grown maize, date from around 3000 B.C. As the nomadic peoples became more sedentary, they built permanent residences, known as pit houses, and made pottery. Cultural differences began to emerge in their choice of architecture and decoration: The Mogollon people, in the southwestern part of modern New Mexico, created brown and red pottery and built large community lodges; the Anasazi (also called Ancestral Puebloans), in the Four Corners region, made gray pottery and smaller lodges for extended families. In Arizona, the Sinagua and Hohokam cultures farmed the land, creating extensive irrigation systems.

By about A.D. 700, and perhaps a couple of centuries earlier, the Ancestral Puebloans had built villages throughout what is now known as the Four Corners region (where New Mexico, Arizona, Utah, and Colorado come together). Chaco Culture National Historic Park and Aztec Ruins National Monument in New Mexico; Mesa Verde National Park in Colorado; and Betatakin, Keet Seel, and Canyon de Chelly in Arizona, among other sites, all exhibit an architectural excellence and skill, and a scientific sensitivity to nature, that marks this as one of America's classic pre-Columbian civilizations.

The sites include condominium-style communities of stone and mud adobe bricks, three and four stories high. The villages incorporated circular spiritual chambers called kivas. The Anasazi also developed the means to irrigate their fields of corn, beans, and squash by controlling the flow of water from area's rivers. From Chaco Canyon, they built a complex system of well-engineered roads leading in four directions to other towns or ceremonial centers. Artifacts found during excavation, such as seashells and macaw feathers, indicate that they had a far-reaching trade network. The incorporation of solar alignments into some of their architecture has led modern archaeoastronomers to speculate on the importance of the equinoxes to the Anasazi religion.

The diminishing of the Ancestral Puebloan culture, and the emergence of the Pueblo culture in its place, is something of a mystery today. Scholars disagree about why the Anasazi left their villages around the 13th century. Some suggest drought or soil exhaustion; others, invasion, epidemic, or social unrest. But by the time the first Spanish explorers arrived in the 1500s, the Anasazi were long gone and the Pueblo culture was well established throughout northern and western New Mexico, from Taos to Zuni, near Gallup. The Hopi had also established their home in northeastern Arizona.

Certain elements of the Anasazi civilization had clearly been kept alive by the Pueblos, including the apartmentlike adobe architecture, the creation of rather elaborate pottery, and the use of irrigation or flood-farming in their fields. Agriculture, and especially corn, was the economic mainstay.

Each village fiercely guarded its independence. When the Spanish arrived, there were no alliances between villages, even among those with a common language or dialect. No more than a few hundred people lived in any one pueblo, an indication that the natives had learned to keep their population down in order to preserve their soil and other natural resources. But not all was peaceful: They alternately fought and traded with each other, as well as with nomadic Apaches.

THE ARRIVAL OF THE SPANISH The Spanish controlled the Southwest for 300 years, from the mid–16th to the mid–19th century—longer than the United States has. The Hispanic legacy in language and culture is still strong in the region.

The spark that sent the first European explorers into the region was a fabulous medieval myth that seven Spanish bishops had fled the Moorish invasion of the 8th century, sailed westward to the legendary isle of Antilia, and built themselves seven cities of gold. Hernán Cortés's 1519 discovery and conquest of the Aztecs' treasure-laden capital of Tenochtitlán, now Mexico City, fueled belief in the myth. Twenty years later, when a Franciscan friar, on a reconnaissance mission for the viceroyalty, claimed to have sighted, from a distance, "a very beautiful city," in a region known as Cíbola, the gates were open.

Francisco Vásquez de Coronado, the ambitious young governor of New Spain's western province of Nueva Galicia, was commissioned to lead an expedition to the "seven cities." Several hundred soldiers, accompanied by servants and missionaries, marched overland to Cíbola with him in 1540, along with a support fleet of three ships in the Gulf of California. What they discovered, after 6 hard months on the trail, was a bitter disappointment: Instead of a city of gold, they found a rock-and-mud pueblo at Hawikku, the westernmost of the Zuni towns. The expedition wintered at Tiguex, on the Rio Grande near modern Santa Fe, before proceeding to the Great Plains, seeking more treasure at Quivira, in what is now Kansas. The grass houses of the Wichita Indians were all they found.

Coronado returned to New Spain in 1542, admitting failure. Historically, though, his expedition was a great success, contributing the first widespread knowledge of the Southwest and Great Plains, and encountering the Grand Canyon.

By the 1580s, after important silver discoveries in the mountains of Mexico, the Spanish began to wonder if the wealth of the Pueblo country might lie in its land and people rather than in its cities. They were convinced that they had been divinely appointed to convert the natives of the New World to Christianity. And so a northward migration began, orchestrated and directed by the royal government. It was a mere trickle in the late 16th century. Juan de Oñate established a capital in 1598 at San Gabriel, near Ohkay Owinge in New Mexico, but a variety of factors led to its failure. Then in 1610, under Don Pedro de Peralta, the migration began in earnest.

It was not dissimilar to America's schoolbook stereotype. Bands of armored conquistadors did troop through the desert, humble robed friars striding by their sides. But most of the pioneers came up the valley of the Rio Grande with oxcarts and mule trains rather than with armor, intent on transplanting their Hispanic traditions of government, religion, and material culture to this new world.

RELIGION & REVOLT The 17th century in the Southwest was essentially a missionary era, as Franciscan priests attempted to turn the Indians into model Christian peasants. Their churches became the focal point of every pueblo, with Catholic schools a mandatory adjunct. By 1625, there were an estimated 50 churches in the Rio Grande valley; and by 1670, the Franciscans had founded several missions among the Hopi pueblos. But the Native Americans weren't enthused about doing "God's work"—building new adobe missions, tilling fields for the Spanish, and weaving garments for export to Mexico. To solve the problem, soldiers backed the church in extracting labor, a system known as *repartimiento.* Simultaneously, the *encomienda* system mandated that a yearly tribute in corn and blankets be levied upon each Indian. The Pueblos were willing to take part in Catholic religious ceremonies and proclaim themselves converts. To them, spiritual forces were actively involved in the material world. If establishing harmony with the cosmos meant absorbing Jesus Christ and various saints into their hierarchy of *kachinas* and other spiritual beings, so much the better. But the Spanish friars demanded that they do away with their traditional singing and masked dancing, as well as with other "pagan practices." When the Pueblo religion was violently crushed and driven literally underground, resentment toward the Spanish grew. In 1680, the Pueblo Revolt erupted.

Popé, a San Juan shaman, catalyzed the revolt. Assisted by other Pueblo leaders, he unified the far-flung Native Americans, who had never confederated before. They pillaged and burned the province's outlying settlements, then turned their attention to Santa Fe, besieging the citizens who had fled to the Palace of the Governors. After 9 days, having reconquered Spain's northernmost American province, they let the refugees retreat south to Mexico.

Popé ordered that the Pueblos return to the lifestyle they had led before the arrival of the Spanish. All Hispanic items, from tools to livestock to fruit trees, were to be destroyed, and the blemish of baptism was to be washed away in the river. But the shaman misjudged the influence of the Spanish upon the Pueblos. They were not the people they had been a century earlier, and they *liked* much of the material culture they had absorbed from the Europeans. What's more, they had no intention of remaining confederated; their independent streak was too strong.

In 1692, led by newly appointed Gov. Don Diego de Vargas, the Spanish recaptured Santa Fe without bloodshed. Popé had died, and without a leader to reunify them, the Pueblos were no match for the Spanish. Vargas pledged not to punish them, but to pardon and convert. Still, when he returned the following year with 70 families to recolonize the city, he used force. And for the next several years, bloody battles persisted throughout the Pueblo country.

By the turn of the 18th century, the Southwest was firmly in Spanish hands. This time, however, the colonists seemed to have learned from some of their errors.

They were more tolerant of other religions, and less ruthless in their demands and punishments.

ARRIVAL OF THE ANGLOS In 1739, the first French trade mission entered Santa Fe, welcomed by the citizenry but not by the government. For 24 years, until 1763, a black-market trade thrived between Louisiana and New Mexico. It ended only when France lost its toehold on its North American claims during the French and Indian War against Great Britain.

The Native Americans were more fearsome foes. Apache, Comanche, Ute, and Navajo launched repeated raids against each other and the Rio Grande settlements for most of the 18th century, which led the Spanish and Pueblos to pull closer together for mutual protection. Pueblo and Hispanic militias fought side by side in campaigns against the invaders. But, by the 1770s, the attacks had become so savage and destructive that the viceroy in Mexico City created a military jurisdiction in the province, and Gov. Juan Bautista de Anza led a force north to Colorado to defeat the most feared of the Comanche chiefs, Cuerno Verde ("Green Horn"), in 1779. Seven years later, the Comanche and Ute signed a lasting treaty with the Spanish and thereafter helped keep the Apache in check.

France sold the Louisiana Territory to the young United States in 1803, and the Spanish suddenly had a new intruder to fear. The Lewis and Clark expedition of 1803 progressed unchallenged by the Spanish government. But, in 1807, when Lt. Zebulon Pike built a stockade on a Rio Grande tributary in Colorado, he and his troops were taken prisoner by Spanish troops from Santa Fe. Pike was transported to the New Mexico capital, where he was interrogated extensively, and then to Chihuahua, Mexico. The report he wrote upon his return was the United States' first inside look at Spain's frontier province.

At first, pioneering American merchants—excited by Pike's observations of the region's economy—were summarily expelled from Santa Fe or jailed, and their goods confiscated. But after Mexico gained independence from Spain in 1821, traders were welcomed. The wagon ruts of the Santa Fe Trail soon extended from Missouri to New Mexico, and from there to Chihuahua. (Later, it became the primary southern highway to California.)

As the merchants hastened to Santa Fe, Anglo-American and French Canadian fur trappers headed into the wilderness. Their commercial hub became Taos, a tiny village near a large pueblo a few days' ride north of Santa Fe. Many married into native or Hispanic families. Perhaps the best known was Kit Carson (1809–68), a sometime federal agent and sometime scout whose legend is inextricably interwoven with that of the early Southwest.

In 1846, the Mexican–American War broke out and New Mexico (which included Arizona) became a territory of the United States. There were several causes of the war, including the U.S. annexation of Texas in 1845, disagreement over the international boundary, and unpaid claims owed to American citizens by the Mexican government. But foremost was the prevailing U.S. sentiment of "manifest destiny," the belief that the Union should extend "from sea to shining sea." Gen. Stephen Kearny marched south from Colorado; on the plaza in Las Vegas, New Mexico, he announced that he had come to take possession of the area for the United States. His arrival in Santa Fe on August 18, 1846, went unopposed.

An 1847 revolt in Taos resulted in the slaying of the new governor of New Mexico, Charles Bent, but U.S. troops defeated the rebels and executed their leaders. That was the last threat to American sovereignty in the territory. In 1848, the Treaty of Guadalupe Hidalgo officially transferred title of New Mexico, along with Texas, Arizona, and California, to the United States.

Kearny promised that the United States would respect religion and property rights and would safeguard homes and possessions from hostile Indians. His troops behaved with rigid decorum. The United States upheld Spanish policy toward the Pueblos, assuring the survival of their ancestral lands, their traditional culture, and their old religion—which even 3 centuries of Hispanic Catholicism could not do away with.

Meanwhile, on a broad valley of what is now southeastern Nevada, Spanish explorers found a new route to Los Angeles. Named Las Vegas (the meadows), the place had abundant wild grasses and plentiful water. It was also the home to the Paiute Indians. With hopes of teaching the Paiute to farm, in 1855, Brigham Young assigned 30 Mormon missionaries to build a fort in the valley. It was raided and left in ruins just a few years later, but a precedent was established. By the 1880s, precious minerals had been found, bringing miners to the area. And the land itself proved fertile, attracting farmers. The phenomenon that would become Las Vegas had begun.

THE CIVIL WAR As conflict between the North and South flared east of the Mississippi, the Southwest found itself caught in the debate over slavery. Southerners wanted to expand slavery to the western territories, but abolitionists fought a bitter campaign to prevent that from happening. In 1861, the Confederacy, after seceding from the Union, laid plans to make the region its own as a first step toward capturing the West.

In fact, southern New Mexicans, including those in Tucson (Arizona was still part of the New Mexico Territory), were disenchanted with the attention paid them by Santa Fe and already were threatening to form their own state. So when Confederate Lt. Col. John Baylor captured Fort Fillmore, near Mesilla, and on August 1, 1861, proclaimed all of New Mexico south of the 34th parallel to be the new territory of Arizona, there were few complaints.

The following year, Confederate Gen. Henry Sibley assembled three regiments of 2,600 Texans and moved up the Rio Grande. They defeated Union loyalists in a bloody battle at Valverde, near Socorro; easily took Albuquerque and Santa Fe, which were protected only by small garrisons; and proceeded toward the federal arsenal at Fort Union, 90 miles east of Santa Fe. Sibley planned to replenish his supplies there before continuing north to Colorado, then west to California.

On March 27 and 28, 1862, the Confederates were met head-on in Glorieta Pass, about 16 miles outside Santa Fe, by regular troops from Fort Union supported by a regiment of Colorado Volunteers. By the second day, the rebels were in control, until a detachment of Coloradoans circled behind the Confederate troops and destroyed their poorly defended supply train. Sibley was forced into a rapid retreat back down the Rio Grande. A few months later, Mesilla was reclaimed for the Union, and the Confederate presence in the New Mexico Territory ended.

THE LAND WARS The various tribes had not missed the fact that whites were fighting among themselves, and they took advantage of this weakness to step up their raids on border settlements. As retaliation, in 1864, the government interned the Navajo; in what is known in tribal history as "The Long Walk," they were relocated to the new Bosque Redondo Reservation on the Pecos River at Fort Sumner, in east-central New Mexico. Militia Col. Kit Carson led New Mexico troops in this venture, and was a moderating influence between the Navajo and those who called

Reflections

I wasn't the leader of any gang. I was for Billy all the time.

—Billy the Kid to a Las Vegas, New Mexico, reporter, after his capture at Stinking Springs

for their unconditional surrender or extermination. The experiment failed, and within 5 years the Navajo were returned to their homeland, though they were forced to live on a reservation.

Corralling the rogue Apache in the south presented the territory with its biggest challenge. Led by chiefs Victorio, Nana, and Geronimo, these bands wreaked havoc upon the mining towns. Eventually they succumbed, and the capture of Geronimo in 1886 was the final chapter in the region's long history of Indian wars.

As the Native American threat decreased, more and more livestock and sheep ranchers established themselves on the vast plains east of the Rio Grande, in the San Juan basin of the northwest, and in the area around present-day Phoenix. Cattle drives up the Pecos Valley, on the Goodnight-Loving Trail, are the stuff of legend; so, too, is Roswell cattle baron John Chisum, whose 80,000 head of beef probably represented the largest herd in America in the late 1870s.

Mining grew as well. Albuquerque blossomed in the wake of a series of major gold strikes in the Madrid Valley, close to ancient turquoise mines. Other gold, silver, and copper discoveries through the 1870s gave birth to boomtowns—infamous for their gambling halls, bordellos, and shootouts in the streets. Tombstone and Bisbee, in Arizona; Silver City, in New Mexico; and Leadville and Cripple Creek, in Colorado, remain legendary.

In the late 1870s, the railroads arrived. Now linked by rail to the great markets of America, the region enjoyed an economic boom period. In 1905, the main railway connecting southern California with Salt Lake City was completed. Las Vegas, Nevada, became an important refueling point and rest stop on the route.

But ranching invites cattle rustling and range wars, mining beckons feuds and land fraud, and the construction of railroads has often been tied to political corruption and swindles. The Southwest had all of this, especially during the latter part of the 19th century. One of the central figures was William "Billy the Kid" Bonney, a headstrong youth (b. 1858) who became probably the best-known outlaw of the American West. He blazed a trail of bloodshed from Silver City to Lincoln to Fort Sumner, where he was finally killed by Sheriff Pat Garrett in July 1881.

By the turn of the 20th century, most of the violence had been checked. The mineral lodes were drying up, and ranching was taking on increased importance. Economic and social stability were coming.

AGRICULTURE & ATOMS In the late 19th and early 20th century, official statehood came to the Southwest: Nevada in 1864, Colorado in 1876, Utah in 1896, and New Mexico and Arizona in 1912. This was an exciting era for the West. Theodore Roosevelt set aside great tracts of land as national forests and established what is now called the Theodore Roosevelt Dam on the Salt River in Arizona, which enabled large-scale agriculture to take root.

In 1931, the state of Nevada legalized gambling, a decision that forever changed the face of the one-time agricultural and railroad town, Las Vegas.

But the most dramatic development in 20th century occurred during World War II. In 1943, the U.S. government sealed off a tract of land on the Pajarito Plateau, west of Santa Fe, which had been an exclusive boys' school. On this site, in utter secrecy, it built the Los Alamos National Laboratory, otherwise known as Project Y of the Manhattan Engineer District—the "Manhattan Project." Its goal: to split the atom and develop the world's first nuclear weapons.

Under the direction of J. Robert Oppenheimer, later succeeded by Norris E. Bradbury, a team of 30 to 100 scientists and hundreds of support staff lived and worked in almost complete seclusion for 2 years. Their effort resulted in the atomic bomb, tested for the first time at the Trinity Site, north of White Sands, on July 16, 1945. The bombings of Hiroshima and Nagasaki, Japan, 3 weeks later, signaled to the world that the nuclear age had arrived.

3 THE SOUTHWEST TODAY

GROWING PAINS The Southwest is experiencing a reconquest of sorts, as the Anglo population soars, and outside money and values make their way in. The process continues to transform the region's many distinct cultures and their unique ways of life, albeit in a less violent manner than during the Spanish conquest.

Certainly, the new arrivals—many of them from large cities—add a cosmopolitan flavor. The variety of restaurants has greatly improved, as have entertainment options. For their small size, towns such as Taos, Santa Fe, and Flagstaff offer a broad variety of restaurants and cultural events. Santa Fe, Tucson, and Phoenix have developed strong dance and drama scenes, with such treats as flamenco and opera that you'd expect to find in cosmopolitan centers such as New York and Los Angeles. Albuquerque and Tucson have exciting nightlife scenes with a wealth of jazz, rock, country, and alternative music.

Yet many newcomers, attracted by the exotic feel, often bring only a loose appreciation for the area. Some tend to romanticize the lifestyle of other cultures and trivialize their beliefs. Native American symbology, for example, is employed in ever-popular Southwestern decorative motifs; New Age groups appropriate valued rituals, such as sweats (in which believers sit in a very hot, enclosed space to cleanse their spirits). The effects of cultural and economic change are even apparent throughout the countryside, where land is being developed at an alarming rate, often as lots for new million-dollar homes.

Transformation of the local way of life and landscape is also apparent in the retail stores continually springing up in the area. For some of us, these are a welcome relief from Western clothing stores and provincial dress shops. The downside is that city plazas, which once contained pharmacies and grocery stores frequented by residents, now overflow with T-shirt shops and galleries appealing to tourists. Many locals in these cities now rarely visit their downtown areas except during special events such as fiestas.

The region's biggest addition is the $225-million Airport America spaceport near Truth or Consequences, in southern New Mexico. Still in its early stages, it will eventually include one or more runways, hangars, a control building, and launch pads. Test flights have already begun, with plans for Virgin Galactic to send tourists into space from here in 2010.

Environmental threats are another regional reality. Nuclear-waste issues form part of an ongoing conflict affecting the entire Southwest, and a section of southern New Mexico has been designated a nuclear-waste site. Colorado has its own nuclear-waste woes; cleanup of Rocky Flats nuclear weapons facility has been an ongoing problem.

Still, new ways of thinking have brought positive changes, and many locals have directly benefited from the influx of newcomers and the region's popularity as a tourist destination. Businesses and industries large and small have come to the area. Today, electronics manufacturing, aerospace engineering, and other high-tech industries employ thousands. Local artists and artisans also benefit from growth. Many craftspeople—furniture makers, silversmiths, and weavers—have expanded their businesses. The influx of people has broadened the sensibility of a fairly provincial region. You'll find a level of creativity and tolerance here that you would generally find in very large cities but not in smaller communities.

CULTURAL QUESTIONS Faced with new challenges to their ways of life, both Native Americans and Hispanics are marshaling forces to protect their cultural identities. A prime concern is language. Through the years, many Native Americans have begun to speak more and more English, with their children getting little exposure to their native tongue. To counter the effects, a number of villages have implemented language classes.

Some of the pueblos have introduced programs to conserve the environment, preserve ancient seed strains, and protect religious rites. Because their religion is tied closely to nature, a loss of natural resources would threaten the entire culture. Some area pueblos have limited outsider access to their villages and ceremonies. Jemez Pueblo, for instance, no longer allows visitors, while Zuni has limited the access to their notable Shalako ceremonies.

Hispanics, through art and observance of cultural traditions, are also embracing their roots. Throughout the region, murals depicting important historic events, such as the Treaty of Guadalupe Hidalgo of 1848, adorn walls. The Spanish Market in Santa Fe has expanded into a grand celebration of traditional arts, from tin working to *santo* carving. Public schools have bilingual education programs, allowing young people to embrace their Spanish-speaking roots.

Hispanics are also making their voices heard, insisting on more conscientious development of their neighborhoods and rising to positions of power in government. The region's best example of a prominent Hispanic citizen is Bill Richardson, who was appointed U.S. ambassador to the United Nations and left that post to become energy secretary in President Clinton's cabinet. Now he is New Mexico's governor.

GAMBLING WINS & LOSSES Gambling, a fact of life and a source of much-needed revenue for Native American populations across the country, has been a center of controversy in the Southwest for a number of years, and now is well entrenched throughout the region.

Many are concerned about the tone gambling sets, fearing a fate similar to that of Las Vegas, Nevada: Since World War II, Las Vegas has expanded rapidly to become a world center for gambling, with attendant problems such as corruption and what some see as lax moral standards.

The Native American casinos aren't as flashy as those in Las Vegas, though they are, for the most part, large and unsightly. The neon-bedecked buildings stand out sorely on some of the region's most picturesque land. Though most residents appreciate the boost that gambling can ultimately bring to the Native American economies, many critics wonder where gambling profits actually go—and if the casinos can possibly be a good thing for the pueblos and tribes.

A number of pueblos and tribes, however, are showing signs of prosperity, and they are using newfound revenues to buy firefighting and medical equipment and to invest in local schools.

4 ART & ARCHITECTURE

Many artists claim that the crystalline light draws them to the Southwest. In truth, the light is only part of the attraction: Nature in this part of the country, with its awe-inspiring thunderheads, endless expanse of blue skies, and rugged desert, is itself an artwork. To record the wonders of earth and sky, early natives imprinted images (in the form of petroglyphs and pictographs) on the walls of caves and on stones, as well as on the sides of pots they shaped from clay dug in the hills.

Today's Native American tribes carry on that legacy, as do the other cultures that have settled here. Life is shaped by the arts. Everywhere you turn, you'll see pottery, paintings, jewelry, and weavings. You're liable to meet an artist whether you're having coffee in a Sedona cafe or walking along Canyon Road in Santa Fe.

The area is full of little villages that maintain their own artistic specialties. Each Indian pueblo has a trademark design, such as **Santa Clara's** and **San Ildefonso's** black pottery and the **Navajo's** geometric emblazoned weavings. Bear in mind that the images often have profound meaning. When purchasing art, you may want to talk with the maker about what the symbols signify.

Hispanic and Native American villagers take their goods to the cities, where, for centuries, people have bought and traded. Under the portals along plazas, you'll find a variety of works in silver, stone, and pottery for sale. In the cities, you'll find streets lined with galleries, both slick and modest. Trading posts, most notably Arizona's Hubbell Trading Post in Ganado and Cameron Trading Post in Cameron, offer excellent variety and quality. At major markets, such as the **Spanish Market** and **Indian Market** in Santa Fe and the **Heard Museum Indian Fair and Market** in Phoenix, some of the top artists from the area sell their works. Smaller shows at the pueblos also attract artists and artisans. The **Northern Pueblo Artists and Craftsman Show,** revolving each July to a different New Mexico pueblo, continues to grow.

Drawn by the beauty of the local landscape and respect for indigenous art, artists from all over have flocked here, particularly during the 20th century. They have established locally important art societies; one of the most notable is the **Taos Society of Artists.** Santa Fe has its own art society, begun in the 1920s by a nucleus of five painters who became known as **Los Cinco Pintores.** Meanwhile, Scottsdale, Tucson, Sedona, Tubac, and Jerome have developed into rich founts for Southwestern and Western art.

Impressions

[Sun-bleached bones] were most wonderful against the blue—that blue that will always be there as it is now after all man's destruction is finished.

—Georgia O'Keeffe, on the desert skies of New Mexico

The visitor interested in art should exercise some caution, however; there's a lot of schlock out there targeting tourists. But if you persist, you're likely to find many inspiring works as well. The museums and many of the galleries are excellent repositories of local art. Their offerings range from small-town folk art to works by major artists who show internationally.

A RICH ARCHITECTURAL MELTING POT Nowhere else in the United States are you likely to see such extremes of architectural style as in the Southwest. The region's distinctive architecture reflects the diversity of cultures that have left their imprint on the region.

The first people to build in the area were the Anasazi (Ancestral Puebloans), who made stone and mud homes at the bottoms of canyons and inside caves. **Pueblo-style adobe architecture** evolved and became the basis for traditional homes: sun-dried clay bricks mixed with grass for strength, mud-mortared, and covered with additional protective layers of mud. Roofs are supported by a network of vigas—long beams with ends that protrude through the outer facades—and *latillas,* smaller stripped branches layered between the vigas. Other adapted Pueblo architectural elements include plastered adobe-brick kiva fireplaces, *bancos* (adobe benches that protrude from walls), and *nichos* (small indentations within a wall that hold religious icons). These adobe homes are characterized by flat roofs and soft, rounded contours.

Spaniards wedded many elements to Pueblo style, such as portals (porches held up with posts, often running the length of a home) and enclosed patios, as well as the simple, dramatic sculptural shapes of Spanish mission arches and bell towers. They also brought elements from the Moorish architecture found in southern Spain: heavy wooden doors and elaborate corbels—carved wooden supports for the vertical posts.

The next wave of building came with the opening of the Santa Fe Trail in 1821 and the 1860s gold boom, both of which brought more Anglo settlers. New arrivals contributed architectural elements such as neo-Grecian and Victorian influences popular in the middle part of the United States at the time. Distinguishing features of what came to be known as **Territorial-style** architecture can be seen today; they include brick facades and cornices as well as porches, often placed on the second story. You'll also note millwork on doors and wood trim around windows and doorways, double-hung windows, and Victorian bric-a-brac.

Santa Fe Plaza is an excellent example of the convergence of these early architectural styles. On the west side is a Territorial-style balcony, while Pueblo-style vigas and oversize Spanish/Moorish doors mark the Palace of Governors. Outside Tucson, one of the most noted examples of Mission-style architecture still stands at **Mission San Xavier del Bac.**

In the mid–20th century, architect Frank Lloyd Wright designed several buildings in the Phoenix area, ushering in innovative building concepts. In the desert north of Phoenix, one of his students, Paolo Soleri, built an environmentally sensitive, ideal city called Arcosanti, which is open to the public.

5 THE SOUTHWEST IN BOOKS, FILMS & MUSIC

BOOKS

FICTION Many well-known writers made their homes in the Southwest. In the 1920s, the most celebrated were **D. H. Lawrence** and **Willa Cather,** both short-term Taos residents. Lawrence's *Mornings in Mexico* and *Etruscan Places* capture the flavor of the region. Inspired by her stay in the region, Cather, a Pulitzer Prize winner famous for her depictions of the pioneer spirit, penned *Death Comes for the Archbishop.* It's a fictionalized account of the 19th-century Santa Fe bishop Jean Baptiste Lamy.

Many contemporary authors also live in and write about the region. John Nichols, of Taos, whose *Milagro Beanfield War* (Henry Holt, 2000) was made into a Robert Redford movie in 1987, writes insightfully about the problems of poor Hispanic farming communities. For the past 2 decades, Albuquerque's Tony Hillerman has woven mysteries around Navajo tribal police in books such as *Listening Woman* (HarperCollins, 1990) and *A Thief of Time* (HarperCollins, 2004). Of the desert environment and politics, no one wrote better than the late Edward Abbey; *The Monkey Wrench Gang* (HarperPerennial, 2000) tells of an unlikely gang of ecoterrorists, and helped inspire the founding of the radical Earth First! movement. Zane Grey fans should pick up a copy of *Riders of the Purple Sage* (Pocket Books, 1974). Set in southern Utah toward the end of the 19th century, it explores polygamy and the restraints it placed on women.

NONFICTION Marshall Trimble and Joe Beeler's *Roadside History of Arizona* (Mountain Press Publishing, 1986) is an ideal book to take along on a driving tour of the Grand Canyon State. For general histories of New Mexico, try Myra Ellen Jenkins and Albert H. Schroeder's *A Brief History of New Mexico* (University of New Mexico Press, 1974), and Marc Simmons's *New Mexico: An Interpretive History* (University of New Mexico Press, 1988). If you like road trips to small towns, check out *King of the Road* (New Mexico Magazine Press, 2007), by Frommer's author Lesley S. King. It's a compilation of articles and photographs from her monthly column in *New Mexico Magazine.* Get some Colorado history from the short, easy-to-read *Colorado: Bicentennial and History Guide* (W.W. Norton, 1996), by Marshall Sprague. John Wesley Powell's 1869 diary, the first account of travels through the Grand Canyon, offers an exciting viewpoint of the canyon. You can read a recent republication of it, titled *The Exploration of the Colorado River and Its Canyons* (Penguin, 1997), with an introduction by Wallace Stegner. For an interesting account of the recent human history of the canyon, read Stephen J. Pyne's *How the Canyon Became Grand* (Viking Penguin, 1999).

To catch the mood of southern Utah, read Abbey's *Desert Solitaire* (New York: Ballantine, 1968), a nonfiction work based on time Abbey spent in Arches National Monument, before it gained national park status.

MOVIES

Hundreds of movies have been filmed in the region. One of the most notable classics is director John Ford's *Stagecoach* (1939), filmed in Monument Valley. The valley has also shown up in such non-Western films as *2001: A Space Odyssey, Thelma and Louise,* and *Forrest Gump.* Many films have been made in Tucson at what's now called Old Tucson Studios, including *Arizona, Tombstone,* John Wayne's *Rio Lobo,* Clint Eastwood's *The Outlaw Josey Wales,* Kirk Douglas's *Gunfight at the*

O.K. Corral, and Paul Newman's *The Life and Times of Judge Roy Bean.* New Mexico landscapes have set the scene for Westerns such as *The Cowboys, Silverado, Young Guns, City Slickers,* and *Wyatt Earp,* as well as two miniseries based on popular Larry McMurtry novels, *Lonesome Dove* and *Buffalo Girls.* The science fiction movies *Armageddon* and *Contact* were shot in New Mexico as well.

In recent years, the Coen Brothers produced one of the most offbeat films to have been shot in Arizona. *Raising Arizona,* starring Nicholas Cage and Holly Hunter, is a bizarre story of a childless couple who kidnap a baby. Other contemporary films that have been shot in the state include *Broken Arrow* (starring John Travolta and Christian Slater), *Nurse Betty* (with Morgan Freeman, Renée Zellweger, Chris Rock, and Greg Kinnear), *Days of Thunder* (starring Tom Cruise, Nicole Kidman, and Robert Duvall), and *Traffic* (with Michael Douglas and Catherine Zeta-Jones).

MUSIC

The American Southwest has a soundtrack. You hear it in hotel lobbies and gift shops, in restaurants and national park visitor centers. It is the sound of Native American flute music. The haunting melodies are the perfect accompaniment to a long drive across the wide-open spaces of the region. R. Carlos Nakai, who was born in Flagstaff, Arizona, and is of Navajo and Ute heritage, is considered the preeminent Native American flutist, and you'll find his music for sale in gift shops all over the region. Also listen for flute playing by Robert Mirabal, which is informed by the ceremonial music he grew up with at Taos Pueblo in New Mexico. Check out his 2006 Grammy Award–winning album *Sacred Ground.*

Tucson, home to April's annual Tucson International Mariachi Conference, is called the mariachi capital of America, and year-round you can hear this lively south-of-the-border music in Mexican restaurants. Also in Tucson, you can sometimes catch a bit of indigenous *waila* music. This is the music of southern Arizona's Tohono O'odham tribe and is a mix of polka, waltz, and various Mexican influences.

Such musical legends as Bo Diddley, Buddy Holly, Roy Orbison, and the Fireballs basked in New Mexico's light for parts of their careers. More recent musicians whose music really reflects the region include Mansanares, two brothers who grew up in Abiquiu, New Mexico, and are known for their Spanish guitar and soulful vocals. Look for their album *Nuevo Latino.* Using New Mexico as his creative retreat since the 1980s, Michael Martin Murphey often plays live in the state, where fans always cheer for his most notable song, "Wildfire." *The Best of Michael Martin Murphey* offers a good taste of his music. Country music superstar Randy Travis calls Santa Fe home. His newest release, *Around the Bend,* is a treasure, as are his classics. A favorite resident musician in Santa Fe is Ottmar Liebert and his band the Luna Negra. All of their flamenco-inspired music is rich with the region's tones. Check out their CD *Leaning into the Night.*

Utah's most notable music contribution is the Mormon Tabernacle Choir, which has released many albums since its founding in 1910. Some of our favorite musicians hailing from Colorado include the late John Denver, who sang poignantly about the Rocky Mountains in many albums, including in his hit single "Rocky Mountain High," and Big Head Todd and the Monsters, with their most notable 1993 album *Sister Sweetly.*

6 EATING & DRINKING IN THE SOUTHWEST

FOOD

With its mix of cultures—Anglo, Hispanic, Native American—the Southwest's culinary scene offers rich diversity. Of course, you'll find plenty of fast-food restaurants as well as restaurants following the latest trends, but you'll also find Native American foods little changed in hundreds of years and an astonishingly wide variety of Mexican food, from Baja-style fish tacos to Nuevo Latino preparations that seem lifted from the pages of *Like Water for Chocolate.*

If you have an adventurous palate, be sure to search out some of the region's Southwestern restaurants. Although many of these can be rather expensive, the flavors, which mix the spices of Mexico with the fruit-and-meat pairings of nouvelle cuisine, are deliciously distinctive.

Southwestern cuisine combines elements from various parts of Mexico, such as sauces from the Yucatán Peninsula, and fried bananas served with bean dishes, typical of Costa Rica and other Central American locales. You'll also find Asian elements mixed in. Don't worry, for the most part the cuisine isn't spicy. Expect pistachio-crusted meats, fruit salsas, cream sauces made with smoky chipotle peppers, and the likes of duck tamales and cassoulet made with indigenous tepary beans.

There is also the simple fare favored by the Southwest's Native Americans. On reservations throughout the region, you'll usually find fry bread on the menu. These deep-fried disks of dough are similar to that county-fair staple the elephant ear (only without the sugar and cinnamon). Fry bread is eaten as a side or is used to make fry-bread (or Indian) tacos (called Navajo tacos on the Navajo reservation).

These tacos are made by piling shredded lettuce, ground beef, pinto beans, and cheese on top of a circle of fry bread. The best we've eaten are in Phoenix, at the Fry Bread House (p. 432), and in Albuquerque, at the Indian Pueblo Cultural Center. The biggest are at the Cameron Trading Post restaurant near the east entrance to Grand Canyon National Park. One regular fry-bread taco there is enough for two people.

Other than fry-bread tacos, authentic Native American fare is hard to come by in the Southwest. At the Chihootso Indian Market, in the Navajo Nation capital of Window Rock, and at the Gallup Flea Market (p. 280), you can sample such traditional dishes as mutton stew and steam corn (a soup made with whole corn kernels). Also, if you should happen to see a roadside sign for kneel-down bread, be sure to buy some. This traditional Navajo corn bread is similar to a tamale, only sweeter. Wherever you sample Navajo food, ask whether Navajo tea is available. This is a mild herbal tea made from a plant that grows in the Four Corners region.

No discussion of Southwestern cuisine would be complete without mentioning Mexican food. Yes, we know that Mexican food is ubiquitous in the U.S., but Mexican restaurants in the Southwest have far more to offer than most other places. Even within the region, the food varies greatly. Although Mexican restaurants around Arizona serve a variety of regional styles, the state is best known for its Sonoran-style food. This is the Mexican food of the desert, and while much of it will be familiar to fans of Mexican food, there are some distinctive regional specialties. You might find a Sonoran hot dog, for instance. These, available at El Guero Canelo (p. 367), in Tucson, are hot dogs wrapped in bacon and slathered with beans and salsa. For another distinctive Sonoran dish, sample the *carne seca* at Tucson's El Charro Café

(p. 366). The English translation of this dish (dry meat) may not sound too appetizing, but, trust us, this stuff is great. Because the Sonoran Desert extends all the way to the Gulf of California, you'll also find seafood dishes on the menus of many Mexican restaurants in Arizona. Keep an eye out for fat Guaymas shrimp. At the other end of the Mexican spectrum are the flavorful and creative dishes concocted by Chef Suzana Davila at her Tucson restaurant Café Poca Cosa (p. 363).

New Mexico is renowned for its flavorful chile sauces, whether brilliant red or green and with various levels of spicy bite. Chile forms the base for these sauces that top most dishes such as enchiladas and burritos. One is not necessarily hotter than the other; spiciness depends on the type, and where and during what kind of season (dry or wet) the chiles were grown. Any of the New Mexico restaurants recommended in this book offer these sauces,. Possibly the most renowned sauces are in Santa Fe, at The Shed (p. 162) and its sister restaurant La Choza (p. 162).

Even if you're familiar with Mexican cooking, the dishes you know and love are likely to be prepared differently here. The following is a rundown of some regional dishes, a number of which aren't widely known outside the Southwest:

albondigas Meatballs—often in a broth soup.

biscochito A cookie made with anise.

carne adovada Tender pork marinated in red-chile sauce, herbs, and spices, and then baked.

ceviche Raw seafood marinated in lime juice, usually with tomatoes, chiles, green onions, garlic, and cilantro.

cheese crisp Basically a Mexican pizza of cheese melted on top of a large flour tortilla.

chile rellenos Peppers stuffed with cheese, deep-fried, and then covered with green chile sauce.

chorizo burrito (also called "breakfast burrito") Mexican sausage, scrambled eggs, potatoes, and scallions wrapped in a flour tortilla with red- or green-chile sauce and melted Jack cheese.

elote Roasted corn on the cob sprinkled with lime juice, salt, and white cheese, and smeared with spicy mayonnaise.

empanada A fried turnover with nuts and currants and sometimes meat.

enchiladas Tortillas either rolled or layered with chicken, beef, or cheese, topped with chile sauce.

green-chile stew Locally grown chiles, cooked in a stew, with chunks of meat, beans, and potatoes.

huevos rancheros Fried eggs on corn tortillas, topped with cheese and red or green chile, served with pinto beans.

nopalitos Sliced prickly-pear cactus pads, often pickled.

pan dulce A sweet Native American bread.

posole A corn soup or stew (called hominy in other parts of the south), sometimes prepared with pork and chile.

sopaipilla A lightly fried puff pastry, served with honey as a dessert or stuffed with meat and vegetables as a main dish. *Sopaipillas* with honey have a cooling effect on your palate after you've eaten a spicy dish.

tacos Spiced chicken or beef served either in soft tortillas or crispy shells.

tamales A dish made from cornmeal dough stuffed with chile-seasoned meat, and wrapped in husks and steamed.

DRINK

Margaritas are among the most popular drinks in the region, and they come in a wide range of flavors. Although you might be a traditional on-the-rocks-with-salt person, you might try a prickly-pear margarita. These cocktails, prepared with syrup

Fun Facts You Say Chili, We Say Chile

You'll never see "chili" on a menu in New Mexico. New Mexicans are adamant that *chile* (the Spanish spelling) is the only way to spell it. And as one of the world's largest chile producers, we think we ought to *know!*

Virtually anything you order in a restaurant is likely to be topped with a chile sauce. If you're not accustomed to spicy foods, certain varieties will make your eyes water, your sinuses drain, and your palate feel as if it's on fire. ***Warning:*** No amount of water or beer will alleviate the sting. (Drink milk. A *sopaipilla* drizzled with honey is also helpful.)

But the pleasure of eating them far outweighs the pain. Start slowly, with salsas and chile sauces first, perhaps rellenos (stuffed peppers) next. Before long, you'll be buying chile *ristras* (chiles strung on rope).

from the fruit of the prickly-pear cactus, are pink and surprisingly good.

The Southwest produces some excellent wines. Some of the vineyards in the region are centuries old—the vines brought with the first missionaries who arrived here some 400 years ago. Wineries are found in southern Arizona in and near the small town of Sonoita, and in central Arizona near Sedona and Cottonwood. New Mexico vineyards dot the Rio Grande Valley from Albuquerque north and can also be found in parts of southern New Mexico.

3

Planning Your Trip to the Southwest

You may find the Southwest very different from what you expected. Travelers often envision only desert, saguaro cactuses, and intense heat. In fact, much of the area lies upwards of 5,000 feet in elevation, which means that four full seasons act upon the land. The sun can indeed be scorching, so come prepared with a hat and plenty of sunscreen.

Also note the often-significant distances between cities. Your best bet is to travel by car here, as many of the "must see" attractions are located off the main thoroughfares traversed by the few public transportation options available. Besides, there are few enjoyments as great as driving in the sparkling light through farming villages and past ancient ruins, around plazas and over mountain passes, finding your own road to nowhere, and then taking that attitude home.

We also suggest that you do some advance planning if you want to see any special shows in Las Vegas, Nevada, or to visit any of the national parks during the high summer season. For additional help in planning your trip and for more on-the-ground resources in the Southwest, please turn to "Fast Facts: American Southwest," on p. 607.

1 WHEN TO GO

THE CLIMATE The climate in the Southwest is, overall, a great pleasure. Though the low humidity can dry your skin, the same aridness makes the heat and cold easier to handle and promises lots of sunny days. Summers are hot throughout most of the region, though distinctly cooler at higher elevations. Winters are relatively mild in the south, harsher in the north and in the mountains. Spring and fall have pleasant temperatures, though spring winds blow throughout the region. Rainfall is sparse except in the higher mountains; summer afternoon thunderstorms and winter snows account for most precipitation.

WHEN TO GO The Southwest is a year-round destination, although people head to different parts at different times of year. In Phoenix, Tucson, and other parts of the desert, the high season runs from October to mid-May, with the highest hotel rates during the holidays. Wintertime is also high season in the mountain areas of northern New Mexico and southern Colorado, where skiing is popular.

Summer is high season at most national parks, particularly Grand Canyon and Carlsbad Caverns, though the latter receives much less traffic than the former. In late summer, monsoon rains cool the region in afternoons. But beware: These storms can cause flash floods that make roads briefly impassable. Avoid entering low areas if it's raining anywhere nearby.

Spring and autumn are the best times to visit the region. Temperatures are cool in the mountains and warm in the desert, without extreme temperatures on either end. Still, snow can fall in the high regions well into spring, and in fall, thunderstorms can pound the desert.

New Mexico Average High/Low Temperatures in °F (°C) & Precipitation

	Jan	Apr	July	Oct	Annual Rainfall (inches)
Santa Fe	47 (8)/18 (–8)	64 (18)/33 (1)	85 (29)/56 (13)	67 (19)/38 (3)	11.4
Las Cruces	56 (13)/29 (–2)	79 (26)/48 (9)	96 (36)/68 (20)	78 (26)/50 (10)	8.6

Arizona Average High/Low Temperatures in °F (°C) & Precipitation

	Jan	Apr	July	Oct	Annual Rainfall (inches)
Flagstaff	42 (5)/15 (–9)	58 (14)/27 (–2)	82 (27)/50 (10)	64 (17)/31 (0)	22.1
Phoenix	66 (18)/41 (5)	84 (28)/55 (12)	105 (40)/80 (26)	88 (31)/61 (16)	7.7

CALENDAR OF EVENTS

For an exhaustive list of events beyond those listed here, check http://events.frommers.com, where you'll find a searchable, up-to-the-minute roster of what's happening in cities all over the world.

January

New Year's Day. King's Day transfer of canes to new officials and various dances at all eight northern New Mexico pueblos. Turtle Dance at Taos Pueblo (no photography allowed). Call ✆ **575/758-1028,** or go to www.taospueblo.com. January 1.

Tostitos Fiesta Bowl Football Classic, University of Phoenix Stadium, Glendale, AZ. This college bowl game usually sells out nearly a year in advance. Call ✆ **800/635-5748** or 480/350-0911, or go to www.tostitosfiestabowl.com. Early January.

Wings over Willcox, Willcox, AZ. You can take part in birding tours, workshops, and, of course, watching the tens of thousands of sandhill cranes that gather in the Sulphur Springs Valley near Willcox. Call ✆ **800/200-2272,** or go to www.wingsoverwillcox.com. Mid-January.

February

Tubac Festival of the Arts, Tubac, AZ. Exhibits by North American artists and craftspeople. Call ✆ **520/398-2704,** or go to www.tubacaz.com/festival.asp. Early February.

World Championship Hoop Dance Contest, Phoenix, AZ. Native American dancers from around the nation take part in this colorful competition held at the Heard Museum. Call ✆ **602/252-8848,** or go to www.heard.org. Early February.

Arizona Renaissance Festival, Apache Junction, AZ. Patterned after a 16th-century English country fair, this festival features costumed participants and tournament jousting. Call ✆ **520/463-2700,** or go to www.royalfaires.com/arizona. Weekends from early February to late March or early April.

Tucson Gem and Mineral Show, Tucson, AZ. This huge show at the Tucson Convention Center offers seminars, museum displays from around the world, and hundreds of dealers selling just about any kind of rock you can imagine. For information, visit www.tucsonshowguide.com. You may also call ✆ **520/322-5773,** or go to www.tgms.org. Mid-February.

Mt. Taylor Winter Quadrathlon, near Grants, NM. Hundreds of athletes come from all over to bicycle, run, cross-country ski, and snowshoe up and down this mountain. Call ✆ **800/748-2142,** or go to www.mttaylorquad.org. Mid-February.

O'odham Tash, Casa Grande, AZ. This is one of the largest annual Native American festivals in the country, attracting dozens of tribes that participate in rodeos, arts-and-crafts exhibits, and dance performances. Call ✆ **800/916-1515** or 520/836-4723. Mid-February.

Bryce Canyon Winter Festival, Bryce, UT. A winter celebration amid the colorful rock formations of the Bryce Canyon National Park area. Call ✆ **866/866-6616,** or check www.utah.com/nationalparks/bryce.htm. Mid-February.

La Fiesta de los Vaqueros, Tucson, AZ. This cowboy festival and rodeo at the Tucson Rodeo Grounds includes the Tucson Rodeo Parade, which claims to be the world's largest nonmotorized parade. Call ✆ **800/964-5662** or 520/741-2233, or go to www.tucsonrodeo.com. Late February.

Parada del Sol Parade and Rodeo, Scottsdale, AZ. The state's largest horse-drawn parade includes a street dance and rodeo. Call ✆ **480/990-3179,** or go to www.scottsdalejaycees.com. Late February to early March.

Sedona International Film Festival, Sedona, AZ. View various new indie features, documentaries, and animated films before they (it is hoped) get picked up for wider distribution. Call ✆ **928/282-1177,** or go to www.sedonafilmfestival.com. Late February to early March.

MARCH

Heard Museum Guild Indian Fair & Market, Phoenix, AZ. Indian cultural and dance presentations and one of the largest selections of Native American crafts in the Southwest make this a fascinating festival. Go early to avoid the crowds. Call ✆ **602/252-8848,** or go to www.heard.org. Early March.

Rio Grande Arts and Crafts Festival, Albuquerque, NM. A juried show that features 200 artists and craftspeople from around the country takes place at the State Fairgrounds. Call ✆ **505/292-7457,** or visit www.riograndefestivals.com. Second week of March.

Rockhound Roundup, Deming, NM. Gems, jewelry, tools, and crafted items are displayed and sold at the Southwest New Mexico State Fairgrounds. Contact ✆ **575/543-8915** or 575-267-4399, or go to www.dgms.bravehost.com. Second weekend in March.

Festival of the West, Chandler, AZ. A celebration of all things cowboy, from cowboy poetry to Western music and movies. There's a chuck-wagon cook-off, a mountain-man rendezvous, and historic shootout reenactments. Call ✆ **602/996-4387,** or go to www.festivalofthewest.com. Mid-March.

Ostrich Festival, Chandler, AZ. Give the carnival a miss and head straight for the ostrich races. Although brief, these unusual races are something you ought to see at least once in your lifetime. Call ✆ **480/963-4571,** or go to www.ostrichfestival.com. Mid-March.

Wa:k Pow Wow, Tucson, AZ. Tohono O'odham celebration at Mission San Xavier del Bac, featuring many Southwestern Native American groups. Call ✆ **520/294-5727.** Second weekend in March.

APRIL

Chimayo Pilgrimage. On Good Friday, thousands of pilgrims trek on foot to the Santuario de Chimayo, a small church north of Santa Fe that's believed to aid in miracles. Call ✆ **505/351-4889.**

Easter Weekend Celebration, at most New Mexico pueblos celebrations including masses, parades, Corn Dances, and other dances, such as the Bow and Arrow Dance at Nambé. Call ✆ **505/843-7270,** or go to www.indianpueblo.org. Easter weekend.

St. George Art Festival, St. George, UT. This outdoors fine-arts festival draws artists and visitors from all over the American West. Call ✆ **435/627-4500** or go to www.sgcity.org/artfestival. Friday and Saturday of Easter weekend.

Gathering of Nations Powwow, University Arena, Albuquerque, NM. Dance competitions, arts-and-crafts exhibitions, and Miss Indian World contest. Call ✆ **505/836-2810** or visit www.gatheringofnations.com for more information. Late April.

Tucson International Mariachi Conference, Tucson, AZ. Mariachi bands from all over the world come to compete before standing-room-only crowds. Call ✆ **520/838-3908,** or go to www.tucsonmariachi.org. Late April.

May

Taos Spring Arts Festival, Taos, NM. Contemporary visual, performing, and literary arts are highlighted for 2 weeks at venues throughout Taos and Taos County. For dates and ticket info contact ✆ **800/732-TAOS** [8267] or 575/758-3873, or visit www.taoschamber.com. Month of May.

Cinco de Mayo Fiestas, across the region. Celebrations of the restoration of the Mexican republic (from French occupation 1863–67) occur in, among other places, Phoenix, AZ (call ✆ **602/279-4669;** www.arvizu.com); Tucson, AZ (✆ **520/292-9326**); and Las Cruces, NM, at Old Mesilla Plaza (✆ **575/524-3262,** ext. 117; www.oldmesilla.org). First weekend in May.

Taste of Santa Fe, Santa Fe, NM. Sample the city's best chefs' recipes, including appetizers, entrees, and desserts at La Fonda Hotel. Call ✆ **505/982-6366,** ext. 112. Held in May or June.

Wyatt Earp Days, Tombstone, AZ. Gunfights are reenacted in memory of the shootout at the O.K. Corral. Call ✆ **888/457-3929** or 520/457-3929, or go to www.tombstonechamber.com. Memorial Day weekend.

Phippen Museum Western Art Show & Sale, Prescott, AZ. This is the state's premier Western-art sale. Call ✆ **928/778-1385,** or go to www.phippenartmuseum.org. Memorial Day weekend.

Iron Horse Bicycle Classic, Durango, CO. Mountain bikers race against a steam train from Durango to Silverton. Call ✆ **970/259-4621,** or visit www.ironhorsebicycleclassic.com. Memorial Day weekend.

World Series of Poker, Las Vegas, NV. This famed event, now held at the **Rio Hotel and Casino,** features high-stakes gamblers and showbiz personalities competing for six-figure purses. To enter the World Championship Event (purse: $1 million), players must pony up $10,000. It costs nothing to crowd around the tables and watch the action, however. Visit www.worldseriesofpoker.com. Late May to mid-July.

June

Telluride Bluegrass Festival, Telluride, CO. This major international gathering features bluegrass, folk, and country music played among mountain splendor. Call ✆ **800/624-2422,** or see www.telluridebluegrass.com. Late June.

Utah Shakespearean Festival, Cedar City, UT. This professional theater festival produces several plays by William Shakespeare, plus a few contemporary offerings. Call ✆ **800/752-9849,** or check out www.bard.org. Late June through August.

Taos Solar Music Festival, Taos, NM. Sit on the grass at Kit Carson Municipal Park and listen to major players at this event celebrating the summer solstice. The event has a stage powered by a solar generator and educational displays within a "Solar Village." Call ✆ **575/758-9191,** or go to www.solarmusicfest.com. Late June.

Rodeo de Santa Fe, Santa Fe, NM. This 4-day event features a Western parade, a rodeo dance, and five rodeo performances. For tickets and information, call ✆ **505/471-4300,** or go to www.rodeodesantafe.org. Late June.

New Mexico Arts and Crafts Fair, Albuquerque, NM. A tradition for 43 years, this juried show offers work from more than 200 New Mexico artisans, accompanied by nonstop entertainment for the whole family. Call ✆ **505/884-9043,** or check www.nmartsandcraftsfair.org. Last full weekend in June.

July

Santa Fe Opera, Santa Fe, NM. The world-class Santa Fe Opera season runs from the beginning of July to the end of August. Call ✆ **800/280-4654,** or go to www.santafeopera.org.

Hopi Festival of Arts and Culture, Flagstaff, AZ. This exhibition and sale is held at the Museum of Northern Arizona and includes cultural events. Call ✆ **928/774-5213,** or go to www.musnaz.org. Early July.

Fourth of July Celebrations. Parades, fireworks, and various other events are held all over the region. Call the chamber of commerce in each city or town for more information.

Prescott Frontier Days/World's Oldest Rodeo, Prescott, AZ. This is one of the state's two rodeos that claim to be the nation's oldest. Call ✆ **800/358-1888** or 928/445-3103, or go to www.worldsoldestrodeo.com. Early July.

Pancake Breakfast on the Plaza, Santa Fe, NM. Rub elbows with Santa Fe residents at this locals' event on the plaza. Call ✆ **505/982-2002,** or visit www.santafe.org. July 4.

UFO Festival, Roswell, NM. Celebrate all manner of extraterrestrial oddity that has sprung to life since the alleged 1947 alien crash here. More than 7,000 visitors fill the town to attend lectures and participate in a costume contest and parade. Contact ✆ **575/625-8607,** or visit www.roswellufofestival.com. Early July.

Santa Fe International Folk Art Market, Santa Fe, NM. This has fast become one of the city's most popular summer events. Artisans from all over the world come to display and sell works ranging from basketry to textiles outside the International Museum of Folk Art. Concerts, dance performances, and children's programs charge the air, while the scent of delectable food wafts about. For tickets call ✆ **505/988-1234,** or visit www.folkartmarket.org. Early July.

Eight Northern Pueblos Artist and Craftsman Show, NM. More than 600 Native American artists exhibit their work at one of the eight northern pueblos. There are traditional dances and food booths. Call ✆ **505/747-1593,** or go to www.indianpueblo.org for exact dates and the location, which varies. Mid-July.

Bat Flight Breakfast, Carlsbad Caverns National Park, NM. An early-morning buffet breakfast is served while participants watch the bats return to the cave. Contact ✆ **575/785-2232,** or go to www.nps.gov/cave. Mid- to late-July or early August.

Fiestas de Santiago y Santa Ana, Taos, NM. The fiestas feature candlelight processions, special Masses, music, dancing, parades, crafts, and food booths. For information, contact the Taos Fiesta Council (✆ **800/732-8267;** www.fiestasdetaos.com). Third weekend in July.

Spanish Market, Santa Fe Plaza, Santa Fe, NM. More than 300 Hispanic artists from New Mexico and southern Colorado exhibit and sell their work in this lively community event. For information, contact the Spanish Colonial Arts Society (✆ **505/982-2226;** www.spanishcolonial.org). Last full weekend in July.

Navajo Festival of Arts and Culture, Flagstaff, AZ. This exhibition and sale at the Museum of Northern Arizona includes cultural events. Call ✆ **928/774-5213,** or go to www.musnaz.org. Late July to early August.

Intertribal Indian Ceremonial, near Gallup, NM. Thirty tribes from the United States and Mexico participate in rodeos, parades, dances, athletic competitions, and an arts-and-crafts show at Red Rock State Park, east of Gallup. Call ✆ **800/242-4282,** or go to www.gallupnm.org. Late July or early to mid-August.

Old Lincoln Days and Billy the Kid Pageant, Lincoln, NM. The main attraction is a reenactment of Billy the Kid's escape from the Lincoln jail. There are also a fiddling contest and living-history demonstrations (such as weaving and blacksmithing). Contact ✆ **575/653-4372,** or go to www.nmmonuments.org. Last weekend in July or first weekend in August.

August

Southwest Wings Birding and Nature Festival, Sierra Vista, AZ. Spotting hummingbirds and looking for owls and bats keep participants busy. Includes lectures and field trips throughout southeastern Arizona. Call ✆ **520/678-8237,** or go to www.swwings.org. Early August.

The Indian Market, Santa Fe, NM. The largest all–Native American market in the country, this event hosts about 1,000 artisans who display their baskets, blankets, jewelry, pottery, and other arts. Sales are brisk. The market is free, but hotels book up months in advance. Contact the Southwestern Association for Indian Art (✆ **505/983-5220;** www.swaia.org). Third weekend in August.

World's Oldest Continuous Rodeo, Payson, AZ. The second of Arizona's rodeos claiming to be the country's oldest. Call ✆ **800/672-9766** or 928/474-4515. Third weekend in August.

Great American Duck Race, Deming, NM. Devised in a bar in 1979, this event has grown to include a parade, a tortilla toss, an outhouse race, ballooning, dances, and, of course, the duck race. It takes place on the courthouse lawn ("Duck Downs"). Call ✆ **888/345-1125,** or visit www.demingduckrace.com. Fourth weekend in August.

September

Artist Studio Tours take place all over northern New Mexico in the fall. For specific details, see "High on Art" box, on p. 194.

Navajo Nation Fair, Window Rock, AZ. This fair features traditional music and dancing, a fry-bread contest, and more. Call ✆ **928/871-6478,** or go to www.navajonationfair.com. Early September.

New Mexico State Fair and Rodeo, Albuquerque, NM. This is one of America's top state fairs; it features parimutuel horse racing, a nationally acclaimed rodeo, entertainment by top country artists, Native American and Spanish villages, the requisite midway, livestock shows, and arts and crafts. Call ✆ **505/265-1791,** or visit www.exponm.com for tickets. Early September.

Telluride Film Festival, Telluride, CO. This influential international festival celebrates the art of film and has featured the premieres of some of the finest independent films. Call ✆ **510/665-9494,** or see www.telluridefilmfestival.org. Labor Day weekend.

Chile Festival, Hatch, NM. New Mexicans celebrate their favorite fiery food item with a festival in the "Chile Capital of the World." Call ✆ **575/267-5050,** or visit www.hatchchilefest.com. Labor Day weekend.

La Fiesta de Santa Fe, Santa Fe, NM. An exuberant combination of spirit, history, and general merrymaking, La Fiesta is the oldest community celebration in the United States. Zozobra, "Old Man Gloom," a 40-foot-tall effigy of wood, canvas, and paper, is burned at dusk on Thursday to revitalize the community. Call ✆ **505/988-7575.** Weekend after Labor Day.

Moab Music Festival, Moab, UT. Live classical, jazz, bluegrass, and other types of music, presented in a stunning red-rock amphitheater and at other locations. Call ✆ **435/259-7003,** or visit www.moabmusicfest.org. Early to mid-September.

Grand Canyon Music Festival, Grand Canyon Village, AZ. For more than a quarter of a century, this festival has been bringing classical music to the South Rim of the Grand Canyon. Call ✆ **800/997-8285** or 928/638-9215, or go to www.grandcanyonmusicfest.org. Early to mid-September.

Stone Lake Fiesta, Jicarilla Reservation, 19 miles south of Dulce, NM. Apache festival with rodeo, ceremonial dances, and footrace. Call ✆ **575/759-4276,** or go to www.jicarillaonline.com. Mid-September.

Taos Fall Arts Festival, Taos, NM. Highlights include arts-and-crafts exhibitions and competitions, studio tours, gallery openings, lectures, concerts, dances, and stage plays. Simultaneous events include the **Old Taos Trade Fair,** the **Wool Festival,** and **San Geronimo Day** at Taos Pueblo. Held throughout Taos and Taos County. Contact the Taos County Chamber of Commerce (✆ **800/732-8267** or 575/751-8800; www.taoschamber.com). Mid-September (or the third weekend) to the first week in October.

Santa Fe Wine & Chile Fiesta, Santa Fe, NM. This lively celebration boasts 5 days of wine and food events. It takes place at many venues in downtown Santa Fe. Tickets go on sale in early July and sell out quickly. Call ✆ **505/438-8060,** or go to www.santafewineandchile.org. Last Wednesday through Sunday in September.

Sedona Jazz on the Rocks, Sedona, AZ. Jazz festival held amid the red rocks of Sedona. Call ✆ **928/282-1985,** or go to www.sedonajazz.com. Late September.

The Whole Enchilada Fiesta, Las Cruces, NM. The world's biggest enchilada (sometimes over 7 ft. wide) is created and eaten. Call ✆ **575/524-1968,** or go to www.enchiladafiesta.com. Late September or early October.

OCTOBER

Cowboy Gathering, Durango, CO. Cowboy poetry, Western art, a motorless parade, a dance, historical lectures, and demonstrations. Call ✆ **970/382-7494,** or go to www.durangocowboygathering.org. Early October.

Sedona Arts Festival, Sedona, AZ. One of the top arts festivals in the state. Call ✆ **928/204-9456,** or go to www.sedonaartsfestival.org. Early to mid-October.

Albuquerque International Balloon Fiesta, Albuquerque, NM. The world's largest balloon rally, this 9-day festival brings together more than 750 colorful balloons and includes races and contests. Balloons lift off from Balloon Fiesta Park (at I-25 and Alameda Blvd. NE) on Albuquerque's northern city limits. Call ✆ **800/733-9918,** or visit www.balloonfiesta.com. Second week in October.

Arizona Exposition & State Fair, Phoenix, AZ. Featured are rodeos, top-name entertainment, and ethnic food. Call ✆ **602/252-6771,** or go to www.azstatefair.com. Mid-October to early November.

Helldorado Days, Tombstone, AZ. Attendants of this festival can check out an 1880s fashion show, beard contest, reenactments, and street entertainment. Call ✆ **888/457-3929** or 520/457-3929, or go to www.tombstonechamber.com. Third full weekend in October.

Cowboy Artists of America Annual Sale & Exhibition, Phoenix, AZ. The Phoenix Art Museum hosts the most prestigious and best-known Western-art show in the region. Call ✆ **602/257-1222,** or go to www.phxart.org. Late October to mid-November.

Moab Ho-Down Festival, Moab, UT. Mountain-bike races, hill climbs, and related events are featured. Call ✆ **888/677-4688.** Late October to early November.

November

The Comedy Festival, Las Vegas, NV. Some of the world's top comics and comedy troupes perform at this festival, and the event also includes workshops, film festivals, and more. The primary host hotel is Caesars Palace. Call ✆ **800/634-6661,** or go to www.thecomedyfestival.com. Mid-November.

Festival of the Cranes, Bosque del Apache National Wildlife Refuge, NM. People come from all over the world to attend this bird-watching event just an hour and a half south of Albuquerque, near Socorro. Call ✆ **575/835-1828,** or go to www.friendsofthebosque.org. Weekend before Thanksgiving.

Christmas on the Pecos, Carlsbad, NM. Pontoon-boat rides take place each evening, past a fascinating display of Christmas lights on riverside homes and businesses. Call ✆ **800/221-1224** or 575/877-6516, or visit www.christmasonthepecos.com. Thanksgiving to New Year's Eve (except Christmas Eve).

Yuletide in Taos, Taos, NM. This holiday event emphasizes northern New Mexican traditions, cultures, and arts, with carols, festive classical music, Hispanic and Native American songs and dances, historic walking tours, art exhibitions, dance performances, candlelight dinners, and more. Call ✆ **800/732-8267,** or visit www.taoschamber.com. From Thanksgiving through New Year's Day.

December

National Finals Rodeo, Las Vegas, NV. The Super Bowl of rodeos is held at 17,000-seat Thomas & Mack Center of the University of Nevada, Las Vegas (UNLV), and attended by about 200,000 people. On the line is $5 million in prize money. In connection with this event, hotels book country stars into their showrooms, and a cowboy shopping spree—the **NFR Cowboy Christmas Gift Show,** a trade show for Western gear—is held at Cashman Field. Order tickets as far in advance as possible (✆ **702/895-3900;** www.nfrexperience.com). First 2 weeks of December.

Pueblo Grande Museum Indian Market, Phoenix, AZ. This is the largest market of its kind in the state, with more than 300 Native American artisans. Call ✆ **877/706-4408** or 602/495-0901, or go to www.pueblogrande.com. Second full weekend in December.

Festival of Lights, Sedona, AZ. Thousands of *luminarias* are lit at dusk at the Tlaquepaque Arts and Crafts Village. Call ✆ **928/282-4838,** or go to www.tlaq.com. Mid-December.

Canyon Road Farolito Walk, Santa Fe, NM. Locals and visitors bundle up and stroll Canyon Road, where streets and rooftops are lined with *farolitos* (candle lamps). Musicians play and carolers sing around *luminarias* (little fires). Though it's not responsible for the event, the **Santa Fe Convention and Visitors Bureau** (✆ **505/955-6200;** www.santafe.org) can help direct you there; or ask your hotel concierge. Christmas Eve at dusk.

Christmas Native American Celebrations, near Albuquerque, NM. Many of the pueblos have winter dances, including the Matachine and buffalo. For more information, contact the **Indian Pueblo Cultural Center** at ✆ **866/855-7902** or 505/843-7270, or go online to www.indianpueblo.org. December 24 and 25.

Torchlight Procession, Taos Ski Valley, NM. Brave skiers carve down a steep run, named Snakedance, in the dark, while carrying golden fire. Call ✆ **800/992-7669** or 575/776-2291, or visit www.skitaos.org. December 31.

New Year's Eve Celebration, Las Vegas, NV. This is a biggie in Vegas, *baby* (reserve your hotel room early), downtown, on the Fremont Street. Enjoy a big block party with two dramatic countdowns to midnight (the first is at 9pm, midnight on the East Coast). The Strip is usually closed to street traffic, and hundreds of thousands of people pack the area for the festivities. Of course, there are fireworks. December 31.

2 ENTRY REQUIREMENTS

PASSPORTS

See "Passports," under "Fast Facts: American Southwest," (p. 607) for more information.

Virtually every air traveler entering the U.S. is required to show a passport. All persons, including U.S. citizens, traveling by air between the United States and Canada, Mexico, Central and South America, the Caribbean, and Bermuda are required to present a valid passport. U.S. and Canadian citizens entering the U. S. at land and sea ports of entry from within the western hemisphere will need to present government-issued proof of citizenship, such as a birth certificate, along with a government issued photo ID, such as a driver's license. A passport is not required for U.S. or Canadian citizens entering by land or sea, but it is highly encouraged to carry one.

VISAS

For information on obtaining a Visa, please see "Visas," on p. 610.

The U.S. State Department has a **Visa Waiver Program (VWP)** allowing citizens of the following countries to enter the United States without a visa for stays of up to 90 days: Andorra, Australia, Austria, Belgium, Brunei, Denmark, Finland, France, Germany, Iceland, Ireland, Italy, Japan, Liechtenstein, Luxembourg, Monaco, the Netherlands, New Zealand, Norway, Portugal, San Marino, Singapore, Slovenia, Spain, Sweden, Switzerland, and the United Kingdom. Citizens of Czech

Republic, Estonia, Hungary, Latvia, Lithuania, Malta, Republic of Korea, and Slovakia are soon to be admitted to the VWP. (***Note:*** This list was accurate at press time; for the most up-to-date list of countries in the VWP, consult http://travel.state.gov/visa.) Even though a visa isn't necessary, in an effort to help U.S. officials check travelers against terrorist watch lists before they arrive at U.S. borders, visitors from VWP countries must register online through the Electronic System for Travel Authorization (ESTA) before boarding a plane or a boat to the U.S. Travelers will complete an electronic application providing basic personal and travel eligibility information. The Department of Homeland Security recommends filling out the form at least 3 days before traveling. Authorizations will be valid for up to 2 years or until the traveler's passport expires, whichever comes first. Currently, there is no fee for the online application. ***Note:*** Any passport issued on or after October 26, 2006, by a VWP country must be an **e-Passport** for VWP travelers to be eligible to enter the U.S. without a visa. Citizens of these nations also need to present a round-trip air or cruise ticket upon arrival. E-Passports contain computer chips capable of storing biometric information, such as the required digital photograph of the holder. If your passport doesn't have this feature, you can still travel without a visa if it is a valid passport issued before October 26, 2005, and includes a machine-readable zone, or between October 26, 2005, and October 25, 2006, and includes a digital photograph. For more information, go to **http://travel.state.gov/visa**. Canadian citizens may enter the United States without visas; however, they will need to show passports (if traveling by air) and proof of residence.

Citizens of all other countries must have (1) a valid passport that expires at least 6 months later than the scheduled end of their visit to the U.S., and (2) a tourist visa.

CUSTOMS

What You Can Bring into the U.S.

Every visitor more than 21 years of age may bring in, free of duty, the following: (1) 1 liter of wine or hard liquor; (2) 200 cigarettes, 100 cigars (but not from Cuba), or 3 pounds of smoking tobacco; and (3) $100 worth of gifts. These exemptions are offered to travelers who spend at least 72 hours in the United States and who have not claimed them within the preceding 6 months. It is forbidden to bring into the country almost any meat products (including canned, fresh, and dried meat products such as bullion, soup mixes, and so on). Generally, condiments including vinegars, oils, spices, coffee, tea, and some cheeses and baked goods are permitted. Avoid rice products, as rice can often harbor insects. Bringing fruits and vegetables is not advised, though not prohibited. Customs will allow produce depending on where you got it and where you're going after you arrive in the U.S. International visitors may carry in or out up to $10,000 in U.S. or foreign currency with no formalities; larger sums must be declared to U.S. Customs on entering or leaving, which includes filing form CM 4790. For details regarding U.S. Customs and Border Protection, consult your nearest U.S. embassy or consulate, or **U.S. Customs** (www.customs.gov).

What You Can Take Home from the U.S.

For information on what you're allowed to bring home, contact one of the following agencies:

Canadian Citizens: Canada Border Services Agency (✆ **800/461-9999** in Canada, or 204/983-3500; www.cbsa-asfc.gc.ca).

U.K. Citizens: HM Customs & Excise at ✆ **0845/010-9000** (from outside the U.K., 020/8929-0152), or consult their website at **www.hmce.gov.uk**.

Australian Citizens: Australian Customs Service at © **1300/363-263,** or log on to **www.customs.gov.au**.

New Zealand Citizens: New Zealand Customs, The Customhouse, 17–21 Whitmore St., Box 2218, Wellington (© **04/473-6099** or 0800/428-786; www.customs.govt.nz).

MEDICAL REQUIREMENTS

Unless you're arriving from an area known to be suffering from an epidemic (particularly cholera or yellow fever), inoculations or vaccinations are not required for entry into the United States.

3 GETTING THERE & GETTING AROUND

GETTING TO THE SOUTHWEST

By Plane

Deciding where to touch down in the Southwest is a bit tricky. Where you land will depend on what part of the region you intend to focus on. For instance, Albuquerque, New Mexico, is closest to the Four Corners region, but if you also intend to visit the Grand Canyon, you may be better off flying in and out of Phoenix, which would allow you to visit Sedona, Arizona, as well. However, if you intend to only visit the northernmost part of the region, you may want to fly into Las Vegas, Nevada, and possibly save on airfare. Meanwhile, if you want to experience some mountain country en route to the mostly desert attractions of the Southwest, you could fly into Durango, Colorado. Your best bet is to take out a map, pinpoint where you want to focus your travel time, and find the closest airport. Alternatively, check out the suggested itineraries described in chapter 4.

Many airlines flying to both Phoenix and Tucson serve Arizona from around the United States. The Phoenix **Sky Harbor Airport** (PHX; © **602/273-3300;** www.phxskyharbor.com) is the more centrally located of the two airports and is closer to the Grand Canyon. However, if you're planning to explore the southern part of the state or are going to visit both Phoenix and Tucson, you might want to fly into **Tucson International Airport** (TUS; © **520/573-8100;** www.tucsonairport.org), which is smaller and charges lower taxes on its car rentals. Both airports are serviced by all major airlines.

The **Albuquerque International Sunport** (ABQ; © **505/842-4366;** www.cabq.gov/airport) is the hub for travel to most parts of New Mexico. A secondary hub, for southern New Mexico, is **El Paso International Airport** (ELP; © **915/780-4700;** www.elpasointernationalairport.com), in western Texas. Both airports are served by all major airlines.

McCarran International Airport (LAS: © **702/261-5211;** www.mccarran.com), in Las Vegas, Nevada, is a good option if you plan to visit northern Arizona and southern Utah. Budget-conscious travelers may find good deals on airfares and rental cars from there.

Colorado Springs Airport (COS; © **719/550-1900;** www.coloradospringsairport.com), in the southeast corner of Colorado Springs, handles over 100 flights each day, with connections to most major U.S. cities. Even more convenient to the region is the **Durango/La Plata County Airport** (DRO; © **970/247-8143;** www.flydurango.com), with direct daily nonstop service from Denver and Phoenix.

Those whose destination is western Colorado can make connections to Grand Junction's **Walker Field** (GJT; © **970/244-9100;** www.walkerfield.com) from Denver, Phoenix, or Salt Lake City.

To find out which airlines travel to the Southwest, please see "Airlines," p. 612.

By Car

Three interstate highways cross the Southwest. The north–south I-25 bisects New Mexico, passing through Albuquerque and Las Cruces. The east–west I-40 follows the path of the old Route 66 through Kingman and Flagstaff, in Arizona, and Gallup, Albuquerque, and Tucumcari in New Mexico. I-10 from San Diego crosses the southern part of the region, passing through Yuma and Tucson in Arizona, and intersecting I-25 at Las Cruces, New Mexico. I-15 crosses the region at the southwest corner of Utah. These major routes help provide easy access to the many sights in the region that are on much smaller state highways and roadways.

The distance to Phoenix from Los Angeles is approximately 369 miles; from San Francisco, 778 miles; from Albuquerque, 455 miles; from Salt Lake City, 660 miles; from Las Vegas, 287 miles; and from Santa Fe, 516 miles.

Your biggest concern is weather. In winter, be sure your car has front-wheel drive or four-wheel drive and good tires, because roads can become snowpacked and icy.

For more information on negotiating roads in this region, see "Getting Around," below.

International visitors should note that insurance and taxes are almost never included in quoted rental-car rates in the U.S. Be sure to ask your rental agency about additional fees for these. They can add a significant cost to your car rental.

By Train

Amtrak (© **800/USA-RAIL** [872-7245]; www.amtrak.com) has two routes through the region. The *Southwest Chief,* which runs between Chicago and Los Angeles, passes through once daily in each direction, with Arizona stops in Kingman, Grand Canyon, Williams, Flagstaff, and Winslow; in New Mexico in Gallup, Grants, Albuquerque, Lamy (for Santa Fe), Las Vegas, and Raton; and in Colorado in Trinidad, La Junta, and Lamar. A second train, the *Sunset Limited,* skims through the southern part of the region three times weekly in each direction between Los Angeles and New Orleans, with stops in Arizona in Yuma, Maricopa, Tucson, and Benson; in New Mexico in Lordsburg and Deming; and in Texas in El Paso. Greyhound/Trailways bus lines provide through-ticketing for Amtrak between Albuquerque and El Paso and other destinations. You can get a copy of Amtrak's national timetable from any Amtrak station, from travel agents, or by contacting the number above.

GETTING AROUND

By Car

The broad expanses of the American Southwest make driving the best means of getting around, and they also necessitate some precautions. If you plan to drive your own vehicle to and around the region, give it a thorough road check before starting out. There are lots of wide-open desert and wilderness spaces here, and it is not fun to be stranded in the heat or cold with a vehicle that doesn't run. Check your lights, windshield wipers, horn, tires, battery, drive belts, fluid levels, alignment, and other possible trouble spots. Make sure your driver's license, vehicle registration, safety-inspection sticker, and auto-club membership (if you have one) are valid. Check with your auto-insurance company to make sure you're covered when out of state, or when driving a rental car. A breakdown in the desert can be serious. Always carry water with you in the car.

Gasoline is readily available at service stations throughout the region. However, keep close tabs on your gauge, and in more remote areas fill up whenever you can. It's not unusual to drive 60 miles without seeing a gas station. Prices are cheapest in major cities and 10% to 15% more expensive in more-isolated communities. All prices are subject to the same fluctuations as elsewhere in the United States.

If you're visiting from abroad and plan to rent a car in the United States, keep in mind that foreign driver's licenses are usually recognized in the U.S., but you may want to consider obtaining an international driver's license.

CAR RENTALS Car rentals are available in every sizable town and city in the region, always at the local airport, and usually also downtown. All the major car-rental companies have offices in the Southwest. See chapter 19, "Fast Facts: American Southwest," for phone numbers and websites.

Drivers who need wheelchair-accessible transportation should call **Wheelchair Getaways** (✆ **800/642-2042;** www.wheelchair-getaways.com); the company rents vans by the day, week, or month.

Check out **Breezenet.com,** which offers domestic car-rental discounts with some of the most competitive rates around.

DRIVING RULES Unless otherwise posted, the **speed limits** on open roads are 65 mph to 75 mph on interstate highways and 55 mph on state highways. The minimum age for drivers is 16. Safety belts are required for drivers and all passengers ages 5 and over; children under age 5 must be in an approved child seat secured by the seat belt.

Indian reservations are considered sovereign nations, and they enforce their own laws. For instance, the Navajo reservation (the region's largest) prohibits transporting alcoholic beverages, leaving established roadways, and traveling without a seat belt. Motorcyclists must wear helmets.

EMERGENCIES State Highway and Transportation departments provide up-to-the-hour information on road closures and conditions through their toll-free road-advisory hot lines: Arizona (✆ **888/411-7623;** www.azdot.gov); Colorado (✆ **303/639-1111;** www.cotrip.org); New Mexico (✆ **800/432-4269;** www.nmshtd.state.nm.us); and Utah (✆ **866/511-8824;** http://commuterlink.utah.gov).

Members of the **American Automobile Association (AAA)** can get free emergency road service by calling AAA's emergency number (✆ **800/AAA-HELP** [222-4357]).

PARKING The relatively vast amount of space available in the American Southwest makes parking less problematic than in many U.S. cities. Most of the hotels listed in this book offer free parking, except for those in the middle of major cities, where parking garages prevail. In those cases, parking generally runs around $10 per day. Also, in cities, look for metered on-street parking as well as municipal parking garages, where costs will run approximately $1 to $2 per hour.

MAPS Excellent state highway maps are available from departments of tourism (see "Visitor Information," under "Fast Facts: American Southwest," on p. 611). The American Automobile Association (AAA) supplies detailed state and city maps free to members (see "Emergencies," above).

By Plane

This is a broad region, so if your time is short, you might want to consider flying between cities, though your options are limited. **US Airways** (✆ **800/428-4322;** www.usairways.com) serves Phoenix, Tucson, Flagstaff, Yuma, Las Vegas, Albuquerque, El Paso, Durango, and Telluride. Also, **Great Lakes Airlines** (✆ **800/554-5111;** www.flygreatlakes.com) flies between Phoenix and Prescott, Show Low, and Page/Lake Powell. The airline also flies from Albuquerque to Farmington and Grant County Airport near Silver City. **Scenic Airlines** (✆ **800/634-6801;** www.scenic.com) flies between Las Vegas and the Grand Canyon.

New Mexico Airlines (✆ **888/564-6119;** www.pacificwings.com/nma) provides daily flights between Albuquerque and **Cavern City Air Terminal,** near Carlsbad. The airline also serves Alamogordo and El Paso, Texas.

Some large airlines offer transatlantic or transpacific passengers special discount tickets under the name **Visit USA,** which allows mostly one-way travel from one U.S. destination to another at very low prices. Unavailable in the U.S., these discount tickets must be purchased abroad in conjunction with your international fare. This system is the easiest, fastest, cheapest way to see the country.

By Train

Due to limited options, the train is not the best way of getting around the region. **Amtrak** (✆ **800/USA-RAIL** [872-7245]; www.amtrak.com) has two routes through the region. See "By Train," under "Getting to the Southwest," above.

If you're headed to the Grand Canyon, you can get to the town of Williams, 30 miles west of Flagstaff, Arizona, on Amtrak, and transfer to the Grand Canyon Railway excursion train, which runs to Grand Canyon Village at the South Rim of the Grand Canyon. Be aware, however, that the Williams stop is on the outskirts of town; you'll have to arrange in advance to be picked up.

You can get a copy of Amtrak's national timetable from any Amtrak station, from travel agents, or by contacting Amtrak.

International visitors can buy a **USA Rail Pass,** good for 15, 30, or 45 days of unlimited travel on Amtrak (✆ **800/USA-RAIL** [872-7245]; www.amtrak.com). The pass is available online or through many overseas travel agents. See Amtrak's website for the cost of travel within the western, eastern, or northwestern United States. Reservations are generally required and should be made as early as possible. Regional rail passes are also available.

By Bus

The long distances between destinations in the Southwest makes riding the bus a pretty grueling prospect. **Greyhound** (✆ **800/231-2222;** www.greyhound.com) does traverse the region and can be a good option for those on a tight budget. International visitors can obtain information about the **Greyhound North American Discovery Pass.** The pass, which offers unlimited travel and stopovers in the U.S. and Canada, can be obtained from foreign travel agents or through www.discovery pass.com.

4 MONEY & COSTS

The Value of the U.S. Dollar vs. Other Popular Currencies

US$	C$	UK£	Euro €	A$	NZ$
1	1.24	.70	.75	1.44	1.76

Frommer's lists exact prices in the local currency. The currency conversions quoted above were correct at press time. However, rates fluctuate; before departing consult a currency exchange website such as **www.oanda.com/convert/classic** to check up-to-the-minute rates.

The most common U.S. bills are the $1 (a "buck"), $5, $10, and $20 denominations. There are also $2 bills (seldom encountered), $50 bills, and $100 bills (the last two are usually not welcome as payment for small purchases).

What Things Cost in the Southwest

	US$
Weekly compact car rental (with taxes)	531.00
Local telephone call	0.50
Double room in high season at Santa Fe Motel and Inn	130.00
Double room at El Tovar Hotel, Grand Canyon	174.00
Dinner for two at Santa Fe's La Choza, without alcohol, tax, or tip	25.00
Dinner for two at Cowboy Ciao, Scottsdale, without alcohol, tax, or tip	80.00
Pint of beer in a restaurant	4.00
Double latte	3.25
Adult admission to the Museum of International Folk Art	8.00
Admission to the Grand Canyon (per vehicle)	25.00

It's always advisable to bring money in a variety of forms on a vacation: a mix of cash, credit cards, and traveler's checks. You should also exchange enough petty cash to cover airport incidentals, tipping, and transportation to your hotel before you leave home, or withdraw money upon arrival at an airport ATM.

Prices in the Southwest vary greatly. You can find world-class resorts, if that's your bent, or a cheap roadside motel and a diner, if you like to pinch pennies. If you come from a major city such as New York or London, you may find prices overall fairly inexpensive, though the major cities will be closer in price to what you're accustomed to. Exceptions are major tourist destinations such as the Grand Canyon, Zion National Park, and Carlsbad Caverns, where one or two concessionaires often have a monopoly and charge premium prices.

Nationwide, the easiest and best way to get cash away from home is from an ATM (automated teller machine), sometimes referred to as a "cash machine," or "cashpoint." In the Southwest, ATMs are ubiquitous but possibly not as plentiful as city dwellers are accustomed to, simply because there is so much space here between towns.

5 HEALTH

STAYING HEALTHY

One thing that sets the Southwest apart from most other regions is its elevation. Much of the region is above 4,000 feet, and many heavily traveled areas, including the Four Corners region, the Grand Canyon, and Santa Fe, are at 7,000 feet or above. Getting plenty of rest, avoiding large meals, and drinking lots of nonalcoholic fluids (especially water) can help make the adjustment easier for flatlanders.

General Availability of Health Care

The best medical facilities in the region are in Arizona, in Phoenix, Scottsdale, and Tucson; in New Mexico, in Albuquerque and Santa Fe; and in Las Vegas, Nevada.

COMMON AILMENTS

HIGH DESERT CHALLENGES One of the most common ailments in the region is acute mountain sickness. In its early stages, you might experience headaches, shortness of breath, loss of appetite and/or nausea, tingling in the fingers or toes, lethargy, and insomnia. The condition can usually be treated by taking aspirin as well as by getting plenty of rest, avoiding large meals, and drinking lots of nonalcoholic fluids (especially water). If the condition persists or worsens, return to a lower altitude. Other dangers of higher elevations include hypothermia and sun exposure, and these should be taken seriously. To avoid dehydration, drink water as often as possible.

Limit your exposure to the sun, especially during the first few days of your trip and, thereafter, between 11am and 2pm. Liberally apply sunscreen with a high protection factor. Remember that children need more protection than adults do. It's important to monitor your children's health while in the region. They are just as susceptible to mountain sickness, hypothermia, sunburn, and dehydration as you are.

DIETARY RED FLAGS Though some places in the Southwest can have the feel of towns in our neighboring Mexico, the food and water here are safe. A broad range of food is available, so that even vegetarians can usually find something to eat; small cafes often offer beans and rice. One of the few dietary concerns is the spicy chile, so be sure to ask how hot it is before ordering.

BUGS, BITES & OTHER WILDLIFE CONCERNS If you're spending time outdoors, be on the lookout for snakes—particularly rattlers. Avoid them. Don't even get close enough to take a picture (unless you have a very good zoom lens). Also watch for black widow spiders, which have a bulbous body and an hourglass image on their belly; a bite from this spider can make you very sick. The same goes for scorpions, which are crablike arachnids with a curled, stinging tail. If you get bitten by a snake or spider, or stung by a scorpion, seek professional medical help immediately.

This is also home to a large poisonous lizard called the Gila monster. These black-and-orange lizards are far less common than rattlesnakes, and your chances of meeting one are very slight.

Visitors to the region should also be careful of contracting the plague and hantavirus, as a few cases of each are reported annually in the region. Both diseases can be fatal, and both are transmitted through exposure to infected rodent droppings. Though it's unlikely that you'll be exposed to such things while traveling, be careful anytime you note the presence of mice or other rodents.

WEATHER CONCERNS You'll also want to be wary of arroyos, or creek beds, in the desert where flash floods can occur without warning. If water is flowing across a road, *do not* try to drive through it because chances are the water is deeper and flowing faster than you think. Just wait it out. Arroyo floods don't last long.

WHAT TO DO IF YOU GET SICK AWAY FROM HOME

We list **hospitals** and **emergency numbers** under "Fast Facts," in each major city chapter.

If you suffer from a chronic illness, consult your doctor before your departure. Pack **prescription medications** in your carry-on luggage, and carry them in their original containers, with pharmacy labels—otherwise they won't make it through airport security. Visitors from outside the U.S. should carry generic names of prescription drugs. For U.S. travelers, most reliable health-care plans provide coverage if you get sick away from home. Foreign visitors may have to pay all medical costs up front and be reimbursed later.

6 SAFETY

While tourist areas as a rule are safe, urban areas may not be at night. You should always stay alert. Check with your hotel's front-desk staff if you are in doubt about which neighborhoods are safe. Avoid deserted areas, especially at night, and avoid public parks at night. Women in particular should follow these guidelines. With purse snatchings a reality at tourist spots in the country, it's best not to carry valuables.

Remember that hotels are open to the public, and in a large hotel, security may not be able to screen everyone who enters. Always lock your room door; don't assume that once inside your hotel you are automatically safe and no longer need to be aware of your surroundings.

7 SPECIALIZED TRAVEL RESOURCES

In addition to the destination-specific resources listed below, please visit www.frommers.com/planning for additional specialized travel resources.

GAY & LESBIAN TRAVELERS

In general, gay and lesbian travelers will find they are treated just like any other visitors in the Southwest. At gay bars around Phoenix and Tucson, Arizona, you can pick up various gay-oriented local publications, including **Echo Magazine** (© **602/266-0550;** www.echomag.com).

For information on gay- and lesbian-friendly businesses in the Phoenix metro area, contact the **Greater Phoenix Gay & Lesbian Chamber of Commerce** (© **888/4GPGLCC** [447-4522] or 602/266-5055; www.gpglcc.org). **Wingspan,** 425 E. Seventh St., Tucson (© **520/624-1779;** www.wingspan.org), is southern Arizona's lesbian, gay, bisexual, and transgender community center. *The Tucson Observer* (© **520/622-7176;** www.tucsonobserver.com) is a local Tucson gay newspaper available at Wingspan and **Antigone** (411 N. Fourth Ave.; © **520/792-3715;** www.antigonebooks.com) bookstores.

Common Bond (© **505/891-3647**) provides information and outreach services for Albuquerque's gay and lesbian community as well as referrals for other New Mexico cities. Another good New Mexico resource is **www.gaynm.com**, a website that provides news, resources, and lists of events. In Colorado, contact **Gay, Lesbian, and Bisexual Community Services Center of Colorado** (© **303/733-7743;** www.coloradoglbt.org) in Denver; the organization provides information on services, events, and venues of interest to gay and lesbian visitors. The **Utah Pride Center,** 361 N. 300 West, in Salt Lake City (© **801/539-8800;** www.glccu.com), is home to a community center, coffeehouse, and information center for Utah.

In Las Vegas, Nevada, head to **The Center,** 953 E. Sahara, Ste. B-31 (© **702/733-9800;** www.thecenter-lasvegas.com), for support and information. Another source is **www.lasvegaspride.org**, with lists of activities for the Las Vegas area.

TRAVELERS WITH DISABILITIES

If you have no intention of letting your disability prevent you from having the adventure of a lifetime, contact **Arizona River Runners,** P.O. Box 47788, Phoenix, AZ 85068 (© **800/477-7238;** www.arizonariverrunners.com), or **Arizona Raft Adventures,** 4050 E. Huntington Dr., Flagstaff, AZ 86004 (© **800/786-7238;**

www.azraft.com), both of which offer Grand Canyon rafting trips for people with disabilities. In the northwest corner of the state, **Stagecoach Trails Guest Ranch,** 19985 S. Doc Holiday Rd. (P.O. Box 580), Yucca, AZ 86438 (✆ **866/444-4471** or 928/727-8270; www.stagecoachtrailsranch.com), is a dude ranch designed with the needs of persons with disabilities in mind. All the ranch buildings are accessible, and there are horseback riding programs for persons with disabilities.

The **Information Center for New Mexicans with Disabilities** (✆ **800/552-8195** or 505/272-8549) accesses a database with lists of services ranging from restaurants and hotels to wheelchair rentals. It's a service of the **Developmental Disabilities Planning Council** (✆ **800/311-2229**). The ***Access New Mexico*** guide lists accessible hotels, attractions, and restaurants throughout the state. For more information, contact the **Governor's Commission on Disabilities,** 491 Old Santa Fe Trail, Lamy Building Room 117, Santa Fe, NM 87503 (✆ **505/827-6465;** www.gcd.state.nm.us).

The Utah information and referral line for people with disabilities is ✆ **800/333-8824;** or visit www.accessut.org.

The **America the Beautiful—National Park and Federal Recreational Lands Pass—Access Pass** (formerly the **Golden Access Passport**) gives travelers with visual impairments or those with permanent disabilities (regardless of age) free lifetime entrance to federal recreation sites administered by the National Park Service, including the Fish and Wildlife Service, the Forest Service, the Bureau of Land Management, and the Bureau of Reclamation. This may include national parks, monuments, historic sites, recreation areas, and national wildlife refuges.

The America the Beautiful Access Pass can only be obtained in person at a National Park Service facility that charges an entrance fee, including Grand Canyon National Park, Saguaro National Park, Petrified Forest National Park, Organ Pipe Cactus National Monument, Montezuma Castle National Monument, Wupatki National Monument, Casa Grande Ruins National Monument, Tonto National Monument, Tumacácori National Monument, and a handful of others. You need to show proof of a medically determined disability. Besides free entry, the pass also offers a 50% discount on some federal-use fees charged for such facilities as camping, swimming, parking, boat launching, and tours. For more information, go to www.nps.gov/fees_passes.htm, or call the United States Geological Survey (USGS), which issues the passes, at ✆ **888/275-8747.**

For more on organizations that offer resources to travelers with disabilities, go to frommers.com/planning.

FAMILY TRAVEL

With its robust mix of outdoorsy activities and cultural attractions, the Southwest lends itself to family vacations. That said, the drives between the activities and attractions can be rather long, and they don't always lead to the sort of juicy theme-park treats that you find in other states. Sure, you may stumble across a water park or a video arcade here and there, but the real attractions are the natural and cultural ones and the adventurous ways you can experience them: hiking along the Grand Canyon, white-water rafting down the Rio Grande, riding a horse through the cathedrals of Monument Valley, or climbing a wooden ladder up to a cliff dwelling, to name just a few.

If you're not traveling with an adventure-oriented brood, don't worry. Many of the hotels and resorts listed in this book have inviting pools around which you can lounge, or on-site activities planned especially for kids. But keep in mind that the Southwest can truly offer your children a new perspective on life by exposing them to ancient ruins, zesty cuisine, and unique cultures.

To locate accommodations, restaurants, and attractions that are particularly kid-friendly, look for the "Kids" icon throughout this guide.

SENIOR TRAVEL

Senior travelers tend to enjoy the Southwest's mild climate. However, they are often more susceptible to changes in elevation and may experience heart or respiratory problems. Consult your physician before your trip.

The U.S. National Park Service offers an **America the Beautiful—National Park and Federal Recreational Lands Pass—Senior Pass** (formerly the **Golden Age Passport**), which gives seniors 62 years or older lifetime entrance to all properties administered by the National Park Service for a one-time processing fee of $10. Besides free entry, the American the Beautiful Senior Pass also offers a 50% discount on some federal-use fees charged for such facilities as camping, swimming, parking, boat launching, and tours. For more information, see the "Travelers with Disabilities" section, above, and visit www.frommers.com/planning.

TRAVELING WITH PETS

The Southwest is increasingly accepting of animals as travel companions. Many of the major chain hotels, such as Motel 6 and most Best Westerns, allow pets in the rooms. Your biggest concern when traveling with a pet in the region is the heat. In fact, during the warm months, it's best to leave your pet at home. Though some attractions, such as Carlsbad Caverns and the Grand Canyon, have kennels available, most do not.

That said, during the cooler seasons, few places are more fun to bring a pet than the Southwest. Hiking abounds in the region, as does space to throw a stick. In accommodations listings throughout the book, look for the note that states whether the establishment allows pets and if it charges a fee. Some websites worth checking out include www.petswelcome.com, www.pettravel.com, and www.travelpets.com.

8 SUSTAINABLE TOURISM

It's hard to be green in the desert. The desert simply is not a place to build very sustainable major cities. High temperatures and lack of water long impeded the development of arid landscapes. However, with the use of giant dams, wells, and canals that can transport huge amounts of water hundreds of miles across the desert, cities such as Phoenix, Tucson, Albuquerque, and Las Vegas have been able to grow into the sprawling metropolises of today. Unfortunately, in places where it often tops 120°F (49°C) in the summer, massive amounts of energy must be used to keep cool.

For decades, resort hotels in the region have been criticized for their profligate water usage, and such criticism has yet to eliminate the vast acres of lawns that surround some of the resorts. Arizona and Las Vegas are well known for their many golf courses, but those courses use up an inordinate amount of water. The region's dude ranches make great family destinations, but cattle ranching can be very damaging to the desert environment.

There are, however, some things you can do to make your Southwest vacation a little bit greener. Stay at a resort that uses native desert landscaping rather than one surrounded by vast lawns. Play golf on a water-conserving "desert-style" course; while these courses can be very challenging, they preserve the natural desert environment and save water. Some courses have even been certified by the Audubon

General Resources for Green Travel

In addition to the resources for the American Southwest listed above, the following websites provide valuable wide-ranging information on sustainable travel. For a list of even more sustainable resources, as well as tips and explanations on how to travel greener, visit www.frommers.com/planning.

- **Responsible Travel** (www.responsibletravel.com) is a great source of sustainable travel ideas; the site is run by a spokesperson for ethical tourism in the travel industry. **Sustainable Travel International** (www.sustainabletravelinternational.org) promotes ethical tourism practices, and manages an extensive directory of sustainable properties and tour operators around the world.
- In the U.K., **Tourism Concern** (www.tourismconcern.org.uk) works to reduce social and environmental problems connected to tourism. The **Association of Independent Tour Operators (AITO)** (www.aito.co.uk) is a group of specialist operators leading the field in making holidays sustainable.
- In Canada, **www.greenlivingonline.com** offers extensive content on how to travel sustainably, including a travel and transport section and profiles of the best green shops and services in Toronto, Vancouver, and Calgary.
- In Australia, the national body that sets guidelines and standards for ecotourism is **Ecotourism Australia** (www.ecotourism.org.au). **The Green Directory** (www.thegreendirectory.com.au), **Green Pages** (www.thegreenpages.com.au), and **Eco Directory** (www.ecodirectory.com.au) offer sustainable travel tips and directories of green businesses.
- **Carbonfund** (www.carbonfund.org), **TerraPass** (www.terrapass.org), and **Carbon Neutral** (www.carbonneutral.org) provide info on "carbon offsetting," or offsetting the greenhouse gas emitted during flights.
- **Greenhotels** (www.greenhotels.com) recommends green-rated member hotels around the world that fulfill the company's stringent environmental requirements. **Environmentally Friendly Hotels** (www.environmentallyfriendlyhotels.com) offers more green accommodation ratings. The **Hotel Association of Canada** (www.hacgreenhotels.com) has a Green Key Eco-Rating Program, which audits the environmental performance of Canadian hotels, motels, and resorts.
- **Sustain Lane** (www.sustainlane.com) lists sustainable eating and drinking choices around the U.S.; also visit **www.eatwellguide.org** for tips on eating sustainably in the U.S. and Canada.
- For information on animal-friendly issues throughout the world, visit **Tread Lightly** (www.treadlightly.org). For information about the ethics of swimming with dolphins, visit the **Whale and Dolphin Conservation Society** (www.wdcs.org).
- **Volunteer International** (www.volunteerinternational.org) has a list of questions to help you determine the intentions and the nature of a volunteer program. For general info on volunteer travel, visit **www.volunteerabroad.org** and **www.idealist.org**.

Society as wildlife sanctuaries. See the Golf & The Environment website www.golfand environment.org. If you're heading to Grand Canyon National Park, take the train and then use the park's free, environmentally friendly compressed-natural-gas buses to get around.

For more ideas on how to green your Southwest vacation, visit the Arizona Office of Tourism's website (www.arizonaguide.com) and click on "What to Know," and then "Special Interests." This will take you to pages focusing on agritourism, ecotourism, and volunteer tourism.

9 STAYING CONNECTED

Generally, hotel surcharges on long-distance and local calls are astronomical, so you're better off using your **cellphone** or a **public pay telephone.** Many convenience and grocery stores sell **prepaid calling cards** in denominations up to $50; for international visitors these can be the least expensive way to call home. Many public pay phones now accept American Express, MasterCard, and Visa credit cards. **Local calls** made from pay phones in most locales cost roughly 50¢ (pennies not accepted).

The majority of long-distance and international calls can be dialed directly from any phone. **For calls within the U.S. and to Canada,** dial 1 followed by the area code and the seven-digit number. **For other international calls,** dial 011 followed by the country code, the city code, and the number you are calling.

Calls to area codes **800, 888, 877,** and **866** are toll-free. However, calls to area codes **700** and **900** (chat lines, bulletin boards, "dating" services, and so on) can be very expensive—usually a charge of 95¢ to $3 or more per minute, and they sometimes have minimum charges that can run as high as $15 or more.

For **reversed-charge** or **collect calls,** and for **person-to-person calls,** dial the number 0, then the area code and number; an operator will come on the line, and you should specify whether you are calling collect, person-to-person, or both. If your operator-assisted call is international, ask for the overseas operator.

For **local directory assistance** ("information"), dial 411; for long-distance information, dial 1, then the appropriate area code and 555-1212.

CELLPHONES

It's a good bet that your phone will work in the Southwest's major cities, but take a look at your wireless company's coverage map on its website before heading out. If you need to stay in touch in a destination where you know your phone won't work, **rent** a phone that does from **InTouch USA** (© **800/872-7626;** www.intouchusa.us) or from a rental-car location, but beware that you'll pay $1 a minute or more for airtime. And you may or may not be able to send SMS (text messaging) home.

You can rent a cellphone from **Roberts rent-a-phone** (© **800/964-2468;** www.roberts-rent-a-phone.com). If you're heading down into the Grand Canyon and want to rent a satellite phone, contact **Professional River Outfitters** (© **800/648-3236** or 928/779-1512; www.proriver.com).

INTERNET & E-MAIL

More and more hotels, resorts, airports, cafes, and retailers throughout the Southwest are offering **Wi-Fi** (wireless fidelity). Wi-Fi is even found in some of the region's campgrounds, RV parks, and even entire towns. To find public Wi-Fi hot spots at your destination, go to **www.jiwire.com**;

its Hotspot Finder holds the world's largest directory of public wireless hot spots. For information on electric current, see "Electricity," in chapter 19. To locate cybercafes and other establishments where you can go for Internet access, visit **www.cybercaptive.com** and **www.cybercafe.com**.

10 TIPS ON ACCOMMODATIONS

The Southwest has a broad enough range of accommodations to satisfy even the most eccentric adventurer. If you long to be pampered, you'll find swanky resorts, with a variety of the luxury options such as pool and exercise facilities, golf, tennis, horseback riding, and spa treatments. Of course none of it comes cheap.

If you're looking to really savor the flavor of the region, you may want to opt for one of its historic hotels. They include hacienda-style inns—adobe one- or two-story structures often built around a courtyard. You'll also find some Victorian inns that have a frontier flavor. Amenities vary from places with antique but workable plumbing and no television, to those with hot tubs and Wi-Fi in rooms. Cost-conscious travelers will find plenty of chain motels in the region.

When making your reservations during shoulder seasons, such as spring and fall, be sure to ask when hotel rates change (in the desert, for instance, they drop for the summer or go up in the fall).

4

Suggested Southwest Itineraries

Because the Southwest is such an amazingly diverse region, planning a route through it can be overwhelming. The itineraries suggested here should help guide you to the highlights, and, with any luck, your trip won't be too hectic. The most important thing to keep in mind when planning a trip to the Southwest is that this is a vast region. Distances always turn out to be much greater than they seem when you're scanning a map in the comfort of your living room. Be prepared to do a lot of driving, and you won't be too surprised by the number of miles you put on your rental car.

1 THE REGIONS IN BRIEF

THE FOUR CORNERS This region is the bull's-eye for this book. Containing some of the world's most cherished archaeological sites, the Four Corners area is the home not only to such ancient cultures as the Anasazi (Ancestral Puebloans) but also to their modern-day descendants and other Native American peoples such as the Navajo and Apache. This region's other claim to fame is that it's the only place in the U.S. where four states—Colorado, Utah, New Mexico, and Arizona—meet. Each state has its own treasures. To name only a few, Colorado has Mesa Verde National Park, Utah has Monument Valley, New Mexico has Chaco Culture National Historic Park, and Arizona has Canyon de Chelly National Monument and the Hopi and Navajo reservations. These spectacular landmarks are set among painted canyons and poetic buttes, the perfect ambience to fulfill Southwestern fantasies.

SANTA FE, TAOS & ALBUQUERQUE Besides the Four Corners region, the starring role in New Mexico goes to its major art and cultural center, Santa Fe, with Taos and Albuquerque playing supporting roles. Santa Fe is a hip, arty city that wears its 400-year-old mores on its sleeve. Nestled on the side of the Sangre de Cristo Mountains, it's an adobe showcase of centuries-old buildings that hug the earth. Many of these are artist studios and galleries set on narrow streets, ideal for desultory browsing. And then there's upstart Taos, the little arts town and ski center of just 5,000 people that lies wedged between the 13,000-foot Sangre de Cristo Mountains and the 700-foot-deep Rio Grande Gorge. Albuquerque is New Mexico's big city, a place with good restaurants and fun attractions such as a tramway to the top of the Sandia Mountains and lava flows covered with petroglyphs.

NORTHERN NEW MEXICO In this region, the lush Rocky Mountains rise directly out of parched plateaus, with the Rio Grande nourishing rich cultures. Woven throughout this terrain are 19 settlements and numerous ruins of the Native American Pueblo culture, an incredible testament to the resilience of a proud people. The Hispanic culture also has a legacy here; its cathedrals and missions, small mountain villages, and iconographic artwork date back over 400 years. Relics of the Old West are also prevalent, in mountain towns such as Chama and on the open plains of the northeast.

SOUTHERN NEW MEXICO A land of wide-open spaces, this region is rich with natural wonders and Wild West and Native American history. To the east, the United States' first designated wilderness, the Gila, was once home to the Mogollon Indians; the Gila Cliff Dwellings National Monument preserves their past. The once-booming mining town of Silver City is at the heart of the region. Las Cruces, New Mexico's second-largest city, sits at the foot of the Organ Mountains, and not far east of there stand the blazing dunes of White Sands National Monument. At Carlsbad Caverns National Park, one of the nation's most elaborate cave systems offers the opportunity for underground exploration.

TUCSON, PHOENIX, SCOTTSDALE & THE VALLEY OF THE SUN These cities, which form a backbone across Arizona, offer desert beauty and sophisticated lifestyles. Tucson is in the lushest part of the Sonoran Desert and has all the highlights of a major city—excellent arts and culture, and plenty more. Encircled by mountain ranges, this desert oasis offers world-class golf resorts; historical treasures with Native American, Hispanic, and Anglo roots; and some of the Southwest's best hiking in Saguaro National Park. North of Tucson, Phoenix, Scottsdale, and the Valley of the Sun sprawl across the Sonoran Desert. Twenty cities and communities nestle among several mountain ranges. Resorts and golf courses abound here, as do retirement communities. But the sprawl has a positive note: The area boasts world-class shopping; museums; culture, such as opera, dance, and theater; and professional sports.

SOUTHERN & EASTERN ARIZONA Southern Arizona is a region of great contrasts, from desert lowlands to "sky islands," volcanic mountain ranges that seem to rise up from nowhere. The desert climate here attracts many retirees, and also many rare birds, which travel up from the tropics. To the southwest, along the U.S.–Mexico border, lies Organ Pipe Cactus National Monument, home to outlandish desert plant, bird, and animal life and one of the nation's best-kept secrets. To the north, what's known as eastern Arizona is a world apart from these desert lands. Made up of the Mogollon Rim, an escarpment that rises some 2,000 feet off the desert floor, as well as the White Mountains, this region offers tall forests and clear streams. It's home to the Sunrise Park Resort ski area on the White Mountain Apache Indian Reservation.

CENTRAL & WESTERN ARIZONA At the center of Arizona, desert predominates. Parts of it are the desolate desert of Wile E. Coyote, but it has stunning variety. This region is home to the red-rock country of Sedona, which hosts a thriving arts scene and recreational opportunities, from hiking to hot-air ballooning. In the higher regions lie the quaint city of Prescott and the old mining town of Jerome, now an arts community. Arizona's West Coast region has miles of waterfront, and Lakes Mead and Mohave provide the state with plenty of watersports.

THE GRAND CANYON & NORTHERN ARIZONA Few sights inspire as many superlatives as Grand Canyon National Park, which dominates this region. One of the world's natural wonders, the Grand Canyon is not only beautiful but expansive, with numerous canyons stretching across hundreds of miles. The neighboring cities of Flagstaff, Williams, and Tusayan accommodate and feed millions of visitors each year. North of the Grand Canyon lies the state's most remote and untracked region, the Arizona Strip.

LAS VEGAS In high contrast to the nature-oriented Southwest is this glittery city in the desert, noted for its art, cuisine, and shows. Yeah, right. Most people, of course, come to gamble. In recent years this city has become a master of illusion, with hotels posing as pyramids or Italian palaces, their structures providing whole worlds of fantasy. Some find Las Vegas a fun and convenient entryway to their Southwest vacation.

SOUTHERN UTAH All five of Utah's national parks are in this region, and for good reason—it's undeniably beautiful. Ancient geologic forces, erosion, oxidation, and other natural processes have carved spectacular rock sculptures—delicate and intricate, bold and stately—and painted them in a riot of color. This is where you'll find Zion National Park, with its undulating landscapes; Bryce Canyon National Park, with its marvelous stone sculptures, called hoodoos; and the stunning red-rock country of Arches and Canyonlands National Parks. It's also the home of the bulk of Lake Powell and Glen Canyon National Recreation Area, a scenic play land for nearly every type of boater.

2 THE SOUTHWEST IN 1 WEEK

A week really isn't long enough to do justice to this vast and sprawling landscape, but if that's all the time you have, you can definitely hit the highlights. The following is just such an itinerary. You'll gaze in awe at the Grand Canyon, marvel at the play of light on the buttes and mesas of Monument Valley, ponder the mysterious cliff dwellings of Mesa Verde, and stroll the streets of Santa Fe. ***Note:*** If you take this trip in the summer, try to get an early start each day in order to avoid the heat. During the middle of the day, it's best to be in an air-conditioned car or hotel room.

Day ❶: Sedona ★★★

Fly into **Phoenix.** Before leaving town to head north to Sedona, stop at the **Desert Botanical Garden** (p. 434) or the **Heard Museum** (p. 434). Just be sure you make it to Sedona in time to watch the sunset from either **Airport Mesa** or **Crescent Moon Picnic Area** (p. 507).

Day ❷: Sedona to Grand Canyon National Park ★★★

In Sedona in the morning, do a **Jeep tour** (p. 510) or a hike. Then head north to the **Grand Canyon** by way of scenic **Oak Creek Canyon** (p.508). Take US 89 from Flagstaff to the east entrance of Grand Canyon National Park. Be sure to stop at the **Cameron Trading Post** (p. 105) to see the gallery of Native American artifacts in the historic stone building. Stop at **Desert View,** just inside the park entrance, and also at **Lipan Point,** and catch the sunset over the Grand Canyon.

Day ❸: Canyon de Chelly National Monument ★★★

If you can, get up early enough to catch sunrise from one of the Grand Canyon overlooks. Then head east out of the park to Cameron, and go north to **Tuba City.** Be sure to check out the dinosaur footprints in the bedrock just west of Tuba City. Continue east through the villages of the Hopi mesas. Here, you can tour **Walpi village** (p. 102) with a guide and shop for Hopi crafts and jewelry at the many roadside crafts shops. When you reach **Canyon de Chelly National Monument** (p. 109), take one of the Rim Drives before it gets dark.

Day ❹: Canyon de Chelly to Monument Valley Navajo Tribal Park ★★★

Do a half-day truck tour of Canyon de Chelly in the morning. After lunch, drive to **Monument Valley Navajo Tribal Park**

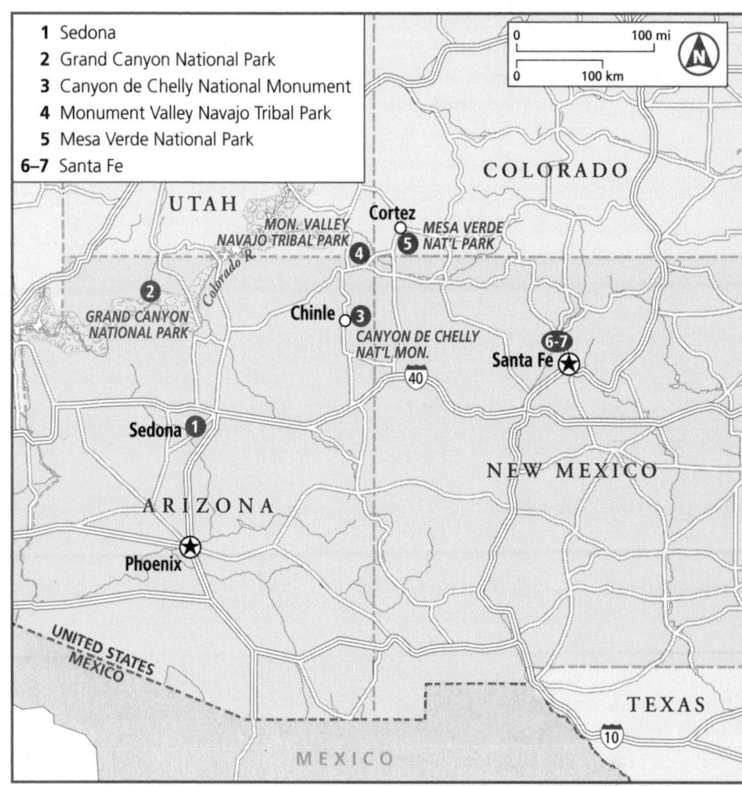

(p. 115). Make sure that you get there in time to catch the sunset. If you arrive early enough in the day, do a Jeep tour of the valley. Alternatively, go for a horseback ride; there is no more scenic spot in the Southwest to connect with your inner cowboy or cowgirl. Whether at lunch or dinner, be sure to try some Navajo fry bread.

Day 5: Monument Valley to Mesa Verde National Park ★★★

Today, do a morning **Jeep tour** (p. 116) of Monument Valley before heading east to Mesa Verde. En route, be sure to stop at **Four Corners Monument Navajo Tribal Park** (p. 91), the only place in the country where four states meet. At **Mesa Verde National Park** (p. 88), sign up for a ranger-led tour so you can see Balcony House, Cliff Palace, and Long House. Spend the night in Cortez.

Days 6 & 7: Santa Fe ★★★

After so many days in the desert, you'll find an oasis in Santa Fe. Spend a little time wandering the **plaza** and visiting the **Palace of the Governors** (p. 164). If you're interested in shopping for Southwestern jewelry, peruse the offerings under the Palace of the Governors portal. Next, head to the **St. Francis Cathedral** (p. 166) and, if you have time, the **Loretto Chapel Museum** (p. 169), with its "magical" staircase. If it's summer, take in a performance at the **Santa Fe Opera** or the **Santa Fe Chamber Music Festival** (p. 185).

The next day, start at the **Museum of International Folk Art** (p. 168), then visit the **Museum of Indian Arts & Culture** (p. 167). Have lunch at the **Museum Hill Café** (p. 167), and then see either the **Wheelwright Museum of the American Indian** (p. 168) or the **Museum of Spanish Colonial Art** (p. 168). Spend the late afternoon exploring and shopping along **Canyon Road** (p. 178), where you can also eat dinner.

3 THE SOUTHWEST IN 2 WEEKS

If you have 2 weeks to explore the Southwest, consider yourself fortunate. You'll not only be able to hit the highlights, but you'll also be able to spend time getting to know such places as Tucson, Santa Fe, and the Grand Canyon. Additionally, you'll have time to visit some of the region's more out-of-the-way attractions, such as Carlsbad Caverns National Park and White Sands National Monument.

Days ❶ & ❷: Tucson ★★

Head straight for the pool at your resort—after all, lounging in the sun is one of the main reasons to visit Arizona. If you're a hiker, head to one of the trails in the foothills of the Santa Catalina Mountains. **Sabino Canyon** (p. 375) is just about the best place in the city for a quick hike. If you're more interested in culture, head to **Mission San Xavier del Bac** (p. 379), a Spanish mission church that is known as the "White Dove of the Desert." The next day, go west to the **Arizona–Sonora Desert Museum** (p. 374), which is more a zoo than a museum. After you've hung out with the hummingbirds and communed with the coatis, drive a few miles to **Saguaro National Park** (p. 375). Be sure to check out the petroglyphs at Signal Hill.

Day ❸: White Sands National Monument ★★★

Spend the morning driving east across the Sonoran and Chihuahuan deserts. You'll see the lovely Chiricahua Mountains and the Gila National Forest en route. Stop for lunch in Las Cruces, on **Old Mesilla Plaza.** Spend the afternoon exploring **White Sands** (p. 304), the world's largest gypsum dune field, where you'll want to take the 16-mile Dunes Drive, stopping along the way to hike on the sand. Stay in the mountains at the **Lodge at Cloudcroft** (p. 304).

Day ❹: Carlsbad Caverns National Park ★★★

Today you'll drive farther, through forest and more Chihuahuan Desert to **Carlsbad Caverns National Park** (p. 319). Be sure to take the 1-mile self-guided walk down along the Natural Entrance route, following the original explorers' path deep into the earth. In the evening, visit the **Living Desert Zoo & Gardens State Park** (p. 316) to see some 50 species of (rescued) desert animals and 500 varieties of plants. Stay the night in Carlsbad.

Days ❺ & ❻: Santa Fe ★★★

It's a hearty drive to Santa Fe; once there, you'll enjoy the sophistication of the City Different. See "The Southwest in 1 Week: Days 6–7," above.

Day ❼: Mesa Verde National Park ★★★

Head north on one of the region's prettiest drives, US 84, to Pagosa Springs, Colorado, then across to Cortez. Spend the afternoon touring **Mesa Verde National Park** (p. 88), the largest archaeological

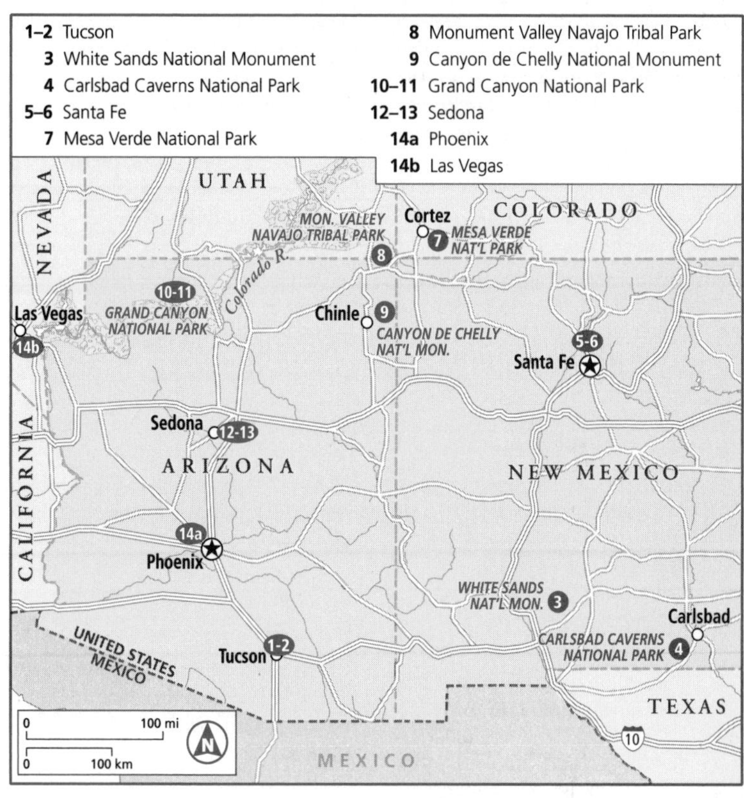

preserve in the U.S. See "The Southwest in 1 Week: Day 5," above. Spend the night in Cortez.

Day 8: Monument Valley Navajo Tribal Park ★★★

From Mesa Verde, head to **Monument Valley Navajo Tribal Park** (p. 115). On the way, stop at **Four Corners Monument Navajo Tribal Park** (p. 91). Just be sure you reach Monument Valley early enough for a **Jeep tour** (p. 116) of the valley with a Navajo guide. Stick around to take pictures of sunset on the Mitten Buttes. This is also the best place in Arizona to go for a horseback ride. You'll feel as if you've ridden into a scene from a John Ford movie.

Day 9: Canyon de Chelly National Monument ★★★

The next day, drive to **Canyon de Chelly National Monument** (p. 109), which Navajo families still inhabit in summer, farming and raising sheep in much the same way that their ancestors did. Make a reservation in advance for a half-day **"shake-and-bake" truck tour** (p. 112) of the canyon, or hire a Navajo guide to take you into the canyon by Jeep or on horseback. Alternatively, drive one of the rim drives. The **South Rim Drive** (p. 111) is our favorite because it provides the opportunity to hike down into the canyon on the **White House Ruins** trail (p. 111).

Days ⑩ & ⑪: Grand Canyon National Park ★★★

From Canyon de Chelly, head south to Ganado and visit the historic **Hubbell Trading Post National Historic Site.** Then head west across the Hopi Reservation and stop in the village of **Walpi** (p. 102). You can take a guided tour of the ancient mesa-top pueblo. Also be sure to stop at the **Cameron Trading Post** (p. 105). At the Grand Canyon, stop at **Desert View,** just inside the park entrance, and at **Lipan Point,** and catch the sunset. The next day, get up for the sunrise, then do a day hike or **mule ride** (p. 540) down into the canyon. If you plan ahead, you can even spend the night down in the canyon at **Phantom Ranch.** If you're not a hiker, spend the day exploring along **Hermit Road,** where there are numerous overlooks.

Days ⑫ & ⑬: Sedona ★★★

Sedona may be touristy, but the red-rock cliffs, buttes, and mesas that surround the city make it one of the most beautiful communities in America. To get out amid the red rocks, take a **Jeep tour** (p. 510) or hike the 4- to 5-mile loop trail around **Bell Rock** and **Courthouse Butte** (p. 506). Although this trail sees a lot of hikers, it is just about the best introduction to the area's amazing hiking. Head up on **Airport Mesa** for the sunset. If you arrive too late for a Jeep tour, plan to do one the next day.

On your second day in Sedona, in the morning either take a Jeep tour or visit the fascinating **V Bar V petroglyph site** (p. 508). In the afternoon, head west of town to **Palatki Ruins** (p. 507) and go for a hike in the area, perhaps up **Boynton Canyon.** Head to the **Crescent Moon Picnic Area** (p. 507) for sunset.

Day ⑭ (Option 1): Phoenix ★★

Heading south from Sedona, you can stop at the cliff dwellings at **Montezuma Castle National Monument** (p. 502). Then spend the end of your trip lounging at a resort or playing a round of golf on one of the Phoenix area's many top-rated courses. Also, before catching your flight out of town, be sure to stop at the **Heard Museum** (p. 434) or the **Desert Botanical Garden** (p. 434).

Day ⑭ (Option 2): Las Vegas ★★

If your interests lean more toward casinos and neon lights, head west to Las Vegas, where you can marvel at the nation's foremost city of excess. See chapter 18.

4 THE SOUTHWEST FOR FAMILIES IN 2 WEEKS

Though the Southwest lacks the major theme-park variety of attractions, it makes up for it by offering experiences that have a deeper impact. This trip takes families to the region's most notable sights, including Grand Canyon National Park and White Sands National Monument, and offers some poolside lounging and a hike through an archaeological site. While you're planning this trip, keep in mind that in the Southwest, many miles can stretch between spectacular sights. Parents who like to drive with their kids (some we know actually do) can choose this journey. Those who find long drives with their kids difficult might want to vacation at a guest ranch or resort, or focus in on one area with lots of family attractions.

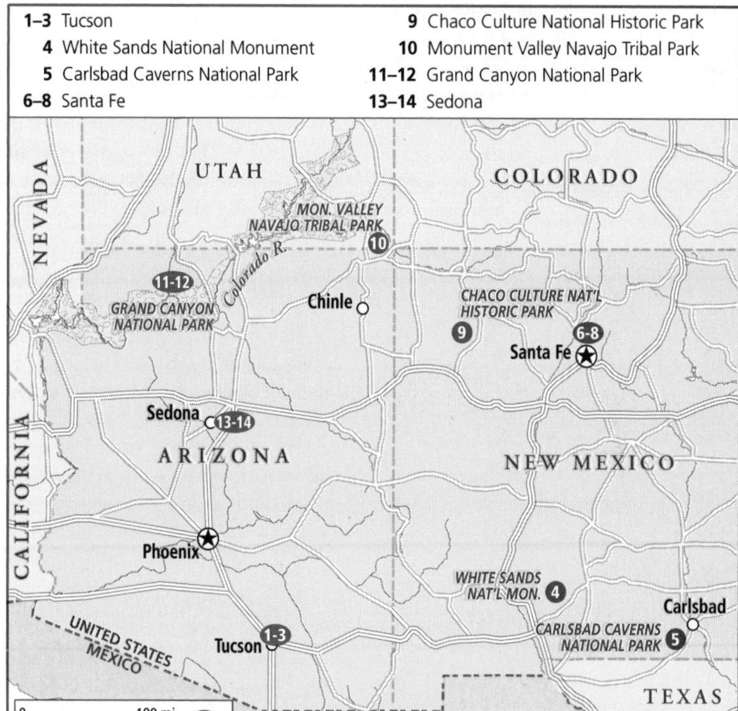

Days 1–3: Tucson ★★

Spend your first couple of days in Tucson, where you can learn all about the desert and the kids can pet snakes and tarantulas at the **Arizona–Sonora Desert Museum** (p. 374). Spend the morning at this amazing place, then after lunch head to **Old Tucson Studios** (p. 379), a one-time movie set that is now a sort of Wild West amusement park, albeit without any thrill rides. On one of your nights in town, have dinner at a cowboy steakhouse. Alternatively, you could just spend a couple of days at a guest ranch (the Tucson area has two). On your third day in Tucson, do a day trip to **Tombstone** (p. 478). Yes, there is a Tombstone, and it's where Wyatt Earp and Doc Holliday shot it out with the bad guys at the O.K. Corral. Sure, it's touristy, but you owe it to your kids to bring them to this icon of the American west. On the way back from Tombstone, be sure to head underground at **Kartchner Caverns State Park** (p. 475). The caverns here are second only to Carlsbad Caverns for impressiveness.

Day 4: White Sands National Monument ★★★

Head east from Tucson, stopping at **Old Mesilla Plaza** in Las Cruces for lunch. **White Sands National Monument** (p. 304) is a kid's dream—a giant sandbox to play in all afternoon. The world's largest gypsum dune field supplies plenty of fun hiking and sand sliding for the kids and panoramic beauty for adults. Be sure to take the 16-mile **Dunes Drive.** In the afternoon, head up to Cloudcroft, where you can cool down in the forest and enjoy a lavish night at the **Lodge at Cloudcroft** (p. 304).

Day 5: Carlsbad Caverns National Park ★★★

Another kids' play land, **Carlsbad Caverns National Park** (p. 319) is especially appealing if you hike down into the caves from the Natural Entrance, the route the original spelunkers took. The late afternoon offers an opportunity to see Gila monsters and bobcats at the **Living Desert Zoo & Gardens State Park** (p. 316). After dinner, take a stroll along or swim in the **Pecos River** (p. 175). Spend the night in Carlsbad.

Days 6–8: Santa Fe ★★★

Head north, stopping to stretch your legs at the **International UFO Museum** (p. 313) in Roswell, which will challenge—or confirm—your belief in what's "out there." In the gift shop, your kids can stock up on the latest alien kitsch. Then head to Santa Fe, passing through the lovely Galisteo Basin. Wander the **Plaza** and explore the **Palace of the Governors** (p. 164) and **St. Francis Cathedral** (p. 166).

Begin your seventh day at the **Museum of International Folk Art** (p. 168), which displays works from over 100 countries. Kids enjoy the hundreds of toys on display. A morsel for the parents, the **Museum of Indian Arts & Culture** (p. 167) is like a journey into another world, with vivid displays of ancient Native American life. Alternatively, head to the **Santa Fe Children's Museum** (p. 172), where kids can rock climb and visit a horticulture garden. Spend the late afternoon wandering **Canyon Road** (p. 178), where parents will find world-class art and kids will find fun works such as mobiles and rocking horses.

Take your last Santa Fe day to explore New Mexico's outdoors. If it's winter, head up to **Ski Santa Fe** (p. 176). In spring or early summer, take a white-water (or flat-water if you have small children) raft trip down the **Rio Grande** (p. 77) in Pilar. If it's summer or fall, hike in the Santa Fe National Forest. You can enjoy a **chairlift ride** (p. 175) to the Ski Santa Fe summit (panoramic views!) and then hike down.

Day 9: Chaco Culture National Historical Park ★★★

There's plenty of space for kids to stretch their legs after the long drive to **Chaco Culture National Historic Park** (p. 135). With its stunning desert setting and awesome ruins, the site offers opportunities to peek into dwellings and climb down into kivas. Be sure to hike up the **Pueblo Alto Trail** to see the ruins from above and get a view of the entire canyon. Spend the night in Farmington or Aztec.

Day 10: Monument Valley Navajo Tribal Park ★★★

From Farmington, head to **Monument Valley Navajo Tribal Park** (p. 115). On the way, be sure to stop at **Four Corners Monument Navajo Tribal Park** (p. 91), the only place in the country where four states meet. Because you can stand simultaneously in Colorado, Utah, Arizona, and New Mexico, this is one of the Southwest's premier family photo ops. Just be sure you reach Monument Valley early enough to go for a horseback ride. We recommend **Dineh Trail Rides** (p. 117), which leads its rides from a point deep within the valley. Alternatively, do a **Jeep tour** (p. 116). Be sure to try some fry bread or a Navajo taco while you're here.

Days 11 & 12: Grand Canyon National Park ★★★

From Monument Valley, head for the east entrance of **Grand Canyon National Park** (p. 528). En route, be sure to check out the cool **dinosaur footprints** (p. 105) just west of Tuba City. **Cameron Trading Post** (p. 105) is a good place to stop for lunch; it has a huge selection of Native American crafts as well as souvenirs that will appeal to the kids. Just be sure you make it to the Grand Canyon in time for sunset. In the evening, you may be able to catch an interesting interpretive program.

Spend the next day hiking a little way into the canyon, riding a mule down into the canyon (if your kids are old enough), or exploring along Hermit Road. The historic little Hermit's Rest is a good place to get cocoa and hang out by the fireplace.

Days ⓭ & ⓮: Grand Canyon to Sedona ★★★

Head back out the east entrance of the park and then drive south toward Flagstaff and Sedona. You can dawdle along the way, perhaps by stopping at **Wupatki National Monument** (p. 560). From Flagstaff, drive down through Oak Creek Canyon and stop at **Slide Rock State Park** (p. 508), where you and the kids can cool off in the waters of Oak Creek and have a blast on the natural water slide. The next morning, do a Jeep tour so you can get out in the famous red rocks of Sedona. In the afternoon, head back to Slide Rock.

5 A MULTISPORT TOUR OF THE SOUTHWEST

Anyone who hikes, mountain bikes, or rafts knows that the Southwest's offerings for outdoors enthusiasts are unsurpassed. The Grand Canyon has the world's greatest rafting adventure, and Moab, Utah, is legendary among mountain bikers. Hikers are in awe of the canyonlands of southern Utah—not only for their bizarre and beautiful rock formations but also for their narrow slot canyons. In a 2-week adventure, you can take in the best this region has to offer. ***Note:*** Because Grand Canyon rafting trips are so popular and need to be booked up to a year in advance, this itinerary is workable only if you first book your raft trip.

Days ❶ & ❷: Zion National Park ★★

Fly into Las Vegas and immediately head out of Sin City bound for **Zion National Park** (p. 567), a sort of paradise amid the rugged cliffs of southwestern Utah. Hiking trails abound; weather permitting, plan a day hike up the spectacular Narrows. This route follows the Virgin River, and you will get your feet wet, but it's the perfect introduction to the slot canyons of the Southwest. You can hike as far up the canyon as your stamina allows. The next day, try the **Lower Emerald Pools Trail** or the **Angel's Landing Trail.** Stay at Zion Lodge (p. 572).

Day ❸: Bryce Canyon National Park ★★★

From Zion, head north to **Bryce Canyon National Park** (p. 573), which is not a canyon but rather a series of bizarrely eroded natural amphitheaters. A maze of trails meanders amid the hoodoos and forests of the national park. For a quick, moderately strenuous hike, take the **Navajo Loop Trail** between Sunrise Point and Sunset Point. Spend the night at Bryce Canyon Lodge (p. 575).

Days ❹ & ❺: Moab & Arches National Park ★★★

After 3 days of hiking in Zion and Bryce Canyon, you'll probably appreciate the chance to sit for a while as you make the long drive to Moab, the mountain-biking capital of the Southwest. In Moab, rent a

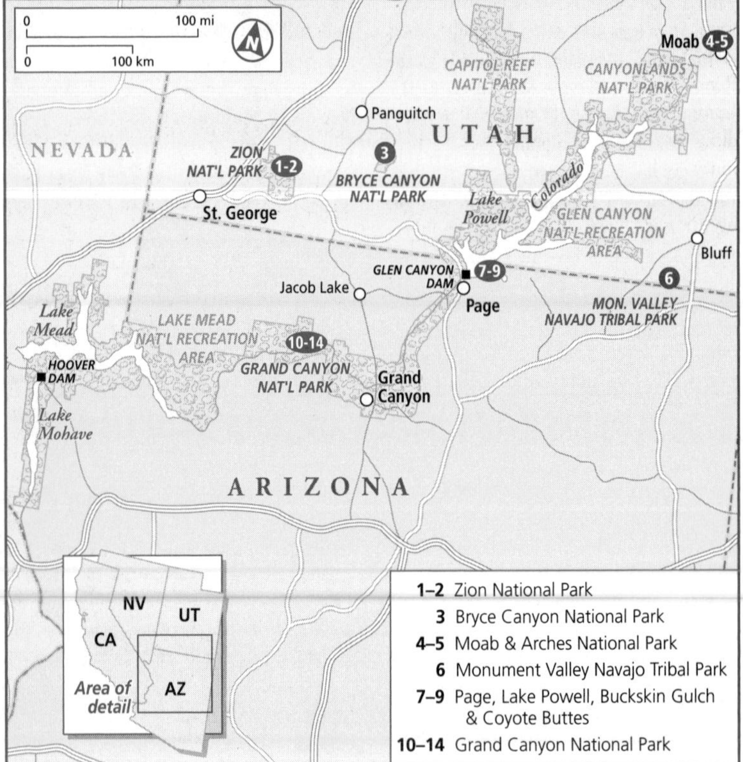

bike, get your hands on a map, and head out on the slickrock trails of this wonderland of rock. In between bike rides, consider driving to **Arches National Park** (p. 583) to see some of its incredible sandstone arches.

Day 6: Moab to Monument Valley

Get up early for one last bike ride in Moab. Then head south to **Monument Valley Navajo Tribal Park** (p. 115). Although this park isn't known specifically as an outdoor-sports destination, the scenery is too awesome to ignore. To burn off some calories, you can hike the 3.2-mile Wildcat Trail or hire a Navajo guide to take you on a hike deeper into the park. However, if you aren't already too saddle-sore from biking in Moab, you should really saddle up a palomino and ride off into the sunset. No other place in the West will give you such a feeling of having ridden right into a classic Hollywood western. Stay at **The View Hotel** (p. 119) inside the park, or **Goulding's Lodge** (p. 118) just outside the park.

Day 7: Page & Lake Powell ★★

The next day, drive west to Page. Just before you reach town, you can stop at **Antelope Canyon** (p. 122) and hike into one of the Southwest's most photographed slot canyons. It's beautiful but is also often crowded, which will give you a greater appreciation for the permit systems in effect at some of the region's other slot canyons. Now for something completely different: Although the Lake Powell reservoir is best known to houseboaters and water-skiers, it also offers the most spectacular **sea kayaking** in the Southwest. Rent a boat and head out to Antelope Canyon again. This time, you'll be paddling up from the mouth. If there isn't too much quicksand where the water gives way to land, you can even get out and hike up the slot canyon.

Days 8 & 9: Buckskin Gulch & Coyote Buttes ★★★

Using Page as a base, spend the next 2 days exploring some of the most famous slot canyons in the Southwest. The 37-mile **Paria Canyon** (p. 124) is a 3- to 4-day backpacking trip, but you can day hike into **Buckskin Gulch,** one of its tributaries. The hike starts at the Wire Pass Trailhead, about 30 miles west of Page. From this same trailhead, you can also hike into **Coyote Buttes** (p. 554), but only if you managed to get a permit, which can be difficult. If you have a permit, spend one day at Coyote Buttes and one day in Buckskin Gulch. Spend your second night in Page or at Lees Ferry, depending on where your rafting trip starts.

Days 10–14: Grand Canyon National Park ★★★

Rafting the Grand Canyon (p. 541) is the adventure of a lifetime. Although it's possible to spend less than a week rafting through a portion of the canyon, such trips are in big motorized rafts that detract from the wilderness experience of floating through the canyon. You owe it to yourself to make the most of the trip and go by oar-powered raft or dory. Talk about a thrill ride! If you opt for a trip that puts in at Lee's Ferry and ends at Phantom Ranch, you'll get to hike up out of the canyon at the end of your trip, adding one last great segment to an unforgettable 2 weeks in the Southwest. Spend your last night at one of the lodges on the park's South Rim, and the next day drive back to Las Vegas. You'll have to arrange through your rafting company to have your car shuttled to the national park.

6 THE NATIVE AMERICAN & CONQUISTADOR TRAIL

The Native American presence in the American Southwest stretches back as far as 3000 B.C. That history intersects with the Spanish conquistadors, whose culture has transformed over 4 centuries into its own unique way of life. Visitors encounter ancient ruins and artifacts, formidable mission churches, and poetic Spanish villages, set against the backdrop of stunning scenery. Those who want to travel back in time will find plenty of adventure here. Though you can take this trip anytime, it's best in spring, summer, or fall.

Day 1: Albuquerque ★★

Enjoy a relaxing day. Stroll **Old Town** (p. 251), wandering some of the narrow back streets in search of shops displaying Native American and Spanish artifacts. Nearby is the **Indian Pueblo Cultural Center** (p. 250), where you can get acquainted with the cultures that you'll encounter throughout the New Mexico portion of your trip. If you have the energy, head west of town to the **Petroglyph National Monument** (p. 251) to hike and watch the sunset.

Days 2–4: Santa Fe ★★★

In the morning of day 2, drive the **Turquoise Trail** (p. 268) to Santa Fe. You'll pass through old mining towns and hills where Native Americans and others once mined turquoise. See "The Southwest in 1 Week: Days 6–7," above, for pointers on how to spend days 2 and 3. On day 4, head north to explore **Bandelier National Monument** (p. 193), or take the **High Road to Taos** (p. 193) for a visit to **Taos Pueblo** (p. 220). Your choice will depend on whether you prefer to see ancient ruins or Native Americans' current lifestyles.

Day 5: Acoma Pueblo ★★★

Today you'll head south and then west to **Acoma Pueblo** (p. 274). Take the bus and walking tour, but then hike down on your own to get a good sense of this mesa-top village, where people still live as their ancestors did hundreds of years ago. If you have energy and time afterward, visit **El Morro National Monument** (p. 279) to see inscriptions left by visitors for hundreds of years. Be sure to climb up to the Anasazi (Ancestral Puebloan) ruins. Spend the night in Grants.

Day 6: Chaco Culture National Historic Park ★★★

Though it's a long, dusty drive to **Chaco Culture National Historic Park** (p. 135), the combination of a stunning setting and expansive ruins makes the park worthwhile. Chaco is the Holy Grail for Southwest history buffs. Be sure to hike up the **Pueblo Alto Trail** to get a full view of the grand kivas and amazing network of dwellings. Spend the night in Farmington at **Casa Blanca** (p. 133).

Day 7: Mesa Verde National Park & Monument Valley Navajo Tribal Park ★★★

Though similar to Chaco, **Mesa Verde** (p. 88) presents an entirely different style of living and architecture. Sign up for a ranger-led tour to get a close-up view of some of the best ruins. When you've finished wandering, head for **Monument Valley Navajo Tribal Park** (p. 115), arriving in time to see the sun set on Mitten Buttes. Stay the night at **Goulding's Lodge** (p. 118).

Day 8: Canyon de Chelly National Monument ★★★

Get an early start and drive to **Canyon de Chelly National Monument** (p. 109). See "The Southwest in 2 Weeks: Day 9," above.

Day 9: The Hopi Mesas

After leaving Canyon de Chelly, head south to Ganado and visit the historic **Hubbell Trading Post National Historic Site.** Then head west across the Hopi Reservation and stop in the village of **Walpi** (p. 102), where you can take a guided tour of the ancient mesa-top pueblo. Also be sure to stop at **Tsakurshovi** (p. 104), a tiny crafts shop that specializes in traditional Hopi kachina dolls. Continue south to Winslow and stay at the historic **La Posada** hotel (p. 99).

Day 10: Sedona ★★★

Although Sedona is best known for its red-rock scenery and art galleries, the area has several small Sinagua ruins and an impressive rock-art site. Get an early start and head first to **Montezuma Castle National Monument** (p. 502), a Sinagua cliff dwelling. From there, head north to **Montezuma Well** (p. 502), then continue to the **V Bar V Petroglyph Site** (p. 508), which has a small rock wall covered with fascinating petroglyphs. After a picnic on the banks of Beaver Creek or lunch in Sedona, visit the remote cliff dwellings at **Palatki Ruins** (p. 507). If you have time, visit the partially reconstructed hilltop ruins at **Tuzigoot National Monument** (p. 503), in nearby Clarkdale.

Day 11: Phoenix ★★

Today, head south to Phoenix and visit the **Heard Museum** (p. 434), Arizona's foremost museum of Native American art and culture. This museum can help you make sense of what you've been seeing during

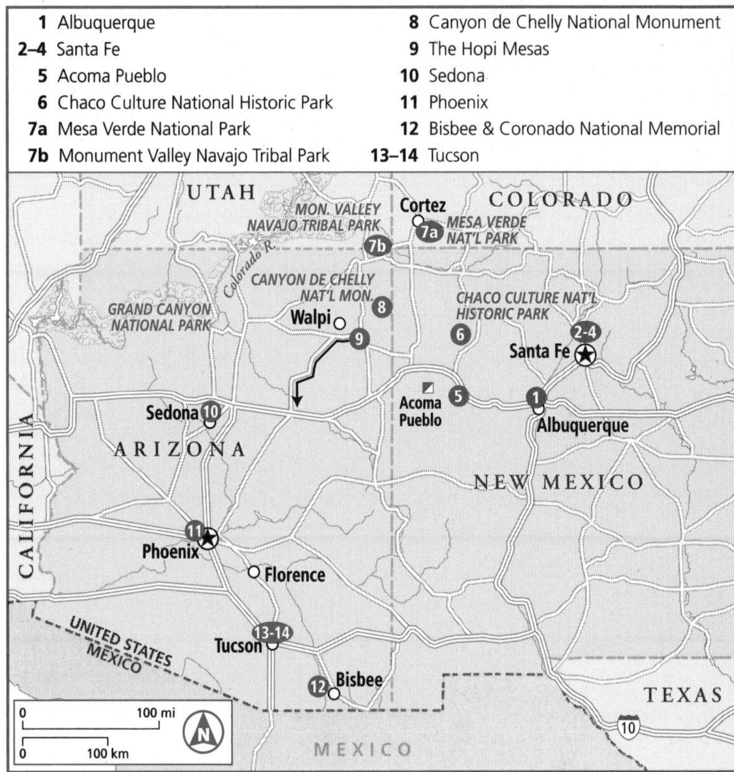

your trip. If you want to see more petroglyphs, visit **Deer Valley Rock Art Center** (p. 434). Alternatively, you can see a partially reconstructed Hohokam village at **Pueblo Grande Museum and Archaeological Park** (p. 435). In the evening, stroll the grounds of the **Desert Botanical Garden** (p. 434), which has an ethnobotanical garden.

Day ⓬: Bisbee & Coronado National Memorial ★

Today, head south through Tucson to the historic copper-mining town of Bisbee. It makes a good base for exploring the nearby **Coronado National Memorial** (p. 476). This memorial commemorates the 16th-century expedition of Spanish explorer Francisco Vásquez de Coronado. As you drive south from Phoenix to Bisbee, detour to visit **Casa Grande Ruins National Monument** (p. 463), which preserves a huge 650-year-old earth-walled Hohokam building that may have been an astronomical observatory.

Days ⓭ & ⓮: Tucson ★★

From Bisbee, head west on scenic back roads to the historic Spanish mission now preserved as **Tumacácori National Historical Park** (p. 467). Nearby you can tour more Spanish ruins at **Tubac Presidio State Historic Park** (p. 467). Be sure to stop at Wisdom's Café for a fruit burrito. As you drive north from Tubac, you'll come to **Mission San Xavier del Bac** (p. 379). This Spanish mission church, known as the White Dove of the Desert, is the most beautiful and best preserved of all the Spanish churches in the Southwest. The next day, stroll around the Barrio Viejo and El Presidio historic districts to get a feel for Spanish and Mexican days in Tucson. Several of the historic buildings in the Presidio neighborhood are part of the Tucson Museum of Art and are open to the public.

5

The Active Vacation Planner

You may be pleasantly surprised at the range of outdoor fun available in the Southwest. From the deserts of the southern regions to the mountains and canyons of the north, diversity reigns. Whether you're interested in a short day hike or an overnight horse trip, groomed ski trails or backcountry adventures, you won't be disappointed.

For more in-depth coverage of the activities that follow, contact some of the local outfitters or organizations that appear in the "Outdoor Activities" sections, later in this book.

1 BICYCLING

It's inspiring to pedal out into the dry southwest air and see not only incredible terrain but also ancient history. Just about the entire region is conducive to the sport, making it one of the most popular places in the United States for avid cyclers, especially mountain bikers.

For road warriors, many miles of pavement traverse the area. Rides range greatly in length and difficulty; all provide beautiful scenery, and most have decent pavement with good shoulders. In northern New Mexico, try biking the Enchanted Circle (see chapter 8); and, in southern New Mexico, try Silver City to Glenwood (see chapter 11). Road biking is highly recommended in Utah's Zion National Park as well (see chapter 17).

Few can think of mountain biking without Moab, Utah, coming to mind. Moab and many other parts of southern Utah hold hundreds of miles of trails, a wide variety of terrain, and spectacular scenery. In addition to the mountain-biking possibilities on four-wheel-drive roads in the national parks, abundant trails on Bureau of Land Management and national forest lands are much less trafficked than national park routes. Moab's most famous trail is undoubtedly the **Slickrock Bike Trail,** a scenic but challenging 9.6-mile loop that crosses a mesa of heavily eroded pale orange Navajo sandstone just a few minutes from downtown Moab (see chapter 17 for information about Moab).

In New Mexico, bikers will find excellent trails in **Albuquerque** at the base of the Sandia Mountains (see chapter 9). In **Santa Fe,** you'll find some very rugged and steep mountain trails, most accessed off the road to Ski Santa Fe (see chapter 7). **Taos** is a rider's paradise, with lots of extreme mountain trails, as well as some that are purely scenic, such as the west rim of the Rio Grande Gorge (see chapter 8). In northwestern New Mexico, you can ride around El Malpais National Monument in the **Grants** area (see chapter 10). You can also take your bike with you to Chaco Culture National Historical Park and tour the Anasazi ruins (see chapter 6). In the southwestern region, bikes are not allowed in the Gila Wilderness, but they are permitted in other parts of Gila National Forest; you'll find terrific trails that originate in **Silver City,** particularly the Continental Divide Trail. In the southeast region, the **Cloudcroft** area has some excellent trails; there are a few that explore history as well as natural terrain, most notably the 17-mile Rim Trail (see chapter 11).

Some of the best biking in the area is in Arizona. With its wide range of climates, this sunny state offers good pedaling somewhere in the state every month of the year. In summer, the **Kaibab National Forest** (btw. Flagstaff and Grand Canyon National Park; see chapter 16) offers good mountain biking. There's also excellent biking at several Phoenix parks. Our favorite trail is the **Desert Classic,** in South Mountain Park (see chapter 13). Tucson is one of the most bicycle-friendly cities in the country. Check out the **Bajada Loop Drive** in the Saguaro National Park (see chapter 12). One of the best spots in the region is Sedona; head to the **Bell Rock Pathway** (see chapter 15).

Known World Guides, in Velarde (✆ **800/983-7756** or 575/983-7756; www.knownworldguides.com), offers single-day and multiday trips all over New Mexico, with options such as 3 days in the Jemez Mountains, west of Santa Fe, or 5 days in the Gila National Forest in Silver City. **Mellow Velo,** in Santa Fe (✆ **505/982-8986;** www.mellowvelo.com), runs bike tours to some of the most spectacular spots in northern New Mexico. Trips range from the easy Train Tour south of Santa Fe, to a challenging Borrego Bust ride in the Santa Fe National Forest. **Bicycle Adventures** (✆ **800/443-6060** or 360/786-0989) offers tours to northern New Mexico. Riders get to experience some of the region's most lovely routes such as the High Road to Taos and the Enchanted Circle. Participants visit major sights such as Santa Fe's Canyon Road and Taos Pueblo and can even opt for a river trip. In business for over 2 decades, this company knows how to put together a good tour.

Backroads (✆ **800/462-2848** or 510/527-1555; www.backroads.com) offers 7-day multisport trips through southern Utah and the Grand Canyon for $1,998 to $2,498. There's also a similar 9-day cycling trip ($3,098). **Sojourn Bicycling & Active Vacations** (✆ **800/730-4771** or 802/425-4771; www.gosojourn.com) offers 6-day bike tours of the Sonoran Desert near Tucson. Tours are $2,395. **Western Spirit Cycling Adventures** (✆ **800/845-2453** or 435/259-8732; www.westernspirit.com) has a number of interesting mountain-bike tours, including trips to both the North and South rims of the Grand Canyon and through the desert south of Tucson. This company also offsets its carbon emissions and consequently is a carbon-neutral company. Each trip lasts 5 days and costs $1,185.

Arizona Outback Adventures (✆ **866/455-1601** or 480/945-2881; www.aoa-adventures.com) does 5-day Sonoran Desert single-track mountain bike tours for $999 and 3-day trips for $599. **WomanTours** (✆ **800/247-1444** or 585-256-9807; www.womantours.com) offers a couple of different Arizona bike tours that are exclusively for women. You'll pay $1,690 for a 7-day tour.

For the multisport fan, **The World Outdoors** (✆ **800/488-8483** or 303/413-0938; www.theworldoutdoors.org) offers a variety of trips, including Utah adventures with mountain biking, hiking, horseback riding, and rafting to the Canyonlands area, plus hiking/biking trips in the vicinities of Bryce Canyon, Zion, and the North Rim of the Grand Canyon.

Some books to check out are *Mountain Biking Moab* (Falcon Press) and *Mountain Biking New Mexico* (Falcon Press). To research Arizona trails, pick up a copy of *Fat Tire Tales and Trails,* by Cosmic Ray.

2 BIRD-WATCHING

Bird-watchers know that the Southwest is directly on the Central Flyway, which makes it a great spot for this activity all year long. Each region offers refuge to a wide variety of birds, including everything from doves, finches, bluebirds, and roadrunners (the New Mexico state bird) to the rare and wonderful whooping crane. The bald eagle is also frequently spotted during winter and spring migrations. A good place to pull out your binoculars is southeastern Arizona, where many species found primarily south of the border come to visit. Birding hot spots include **Ramsey Canyon Preserve** (known for its many species of hummingbirds), **Cave Creek Canyon** (nesting site for elegant trogons), **Patagonia–Sonoita Creek Preserve** (home to 22 species of flycatchers, kingbirds, and phoebes, as well as Montezuma quails), **Buenos Aires National Wildlife Refuge** (home to masked bob-white quail and gray hawks), and the sewage ponds outside the town of **Willcox** (known for avocets and sandhill cranes). For further information on these birding spots, see chapter 14. If you're into eclectic bird-watching, head to the **Vermilion Cliffs,** in northern Arizona, where you'll likely catch a glimpse of the noble California condor, which the California Condor Recovery Plan has brought to the area in the hope that it can flourish there (see chapter 16). To find out which birds have been spotted lately, call the **Tucson Audubon Society's Bird Report** (✆ **520/798-1005;** www.tucsonaudubon.org).

Though not quite as renowned a birding spot as southern Arizona, New Mexico does host plenty of feathered friends. Check out the wildlife refuge centers in New Mexico, most notably the **Bosque del Apache National Wildlife Refuge,** 93 miles south of Albuquerque (see chapter 11). Others include the **Las Vegas National Wildlife Refuge,** 5 miles southeast of Las Vegas (see chapter 10), and **Bitter Lake National Wildlife Refuge,** 13 miles northeast of Roswell (see chapter 11). The Gila National Forest is renowned for its bird sightings, with the Nature Conservancy's **Bear Mountain Lodge** serving as an excellent base (see chapter 11). Some common sightings at these areas might include sandhill cranes, snow geese, a wide variety of ducks, and falcons. New Mexico is also home to an amazing variety of hummingbirds. If you're interested in bird-watching during your trip to New Mexico, contact the state office of **Audubon New Mexico** (✆ **505/983-4609;** http://nm.audubon.org), in Santa Fe.

In Utah, head to **Zion National Park,** where the rare peregrine falcon sometimes nests in the Weeping Rock area. Also in the park are golden eagles, hummingbirds, and road-runners (see chapter 17).

Serious birders eager to add lots of rare birds to their life lists may want to visit south-eastern Arizona on a guided tour. These are available through **High Lonesome Ecotours,** 570 S. Little Bear Trail, Sierra Vista, AZ 85635 (✆ **800/743-2668** or 520/458-9446; www.hilonesome.com), which charges $1,140 per person for a 5-day trip, $1,470 for a 6-day trip, and $2,050 to $2,225 for an 8-day trip. **WingsWest Bird Watching Tours** (✆ **800/583-6928;** http://home.earthlink.net/~wingswestnm) offers customized birding tours in New Mexico and Sonora, Mexico.

3 FISHING

The variety of terrain in the Southwest, from deserts to canyons to mountains, makes for a diverse year-round fishing experience. In such places as the San Juan River and Navajo

Lake, Lees Ferry and Lake Powell, cold-water fishing and warm-water fishing are separated by yards rather than by miles, thanks to dams set between these and many other rivers and lakes.

Warm-water lakes and streams are home to large- and small-mouth bass, walleye, stripers, catfish, crappie, and bluegill. In cold-water lakes and streams, look for the Rio Grande cutthroat, as well as kokanee salmon and rainbow, brown, lake, and brook trout.

Two of the best places for fishing in New Mexico are the San Juan River, near Farmington, and Elephant Butte Lake, not far from Truth or Consequences. The San Juan River offers excellent trout fishing and is extremely popular with fly fishers. Elephant Butte is great for bass fishing; in fact, it is considered one of the top 10 bass fishing locations in the United States.

Arizona offers good trout fishing on the Mogollon Rim and in the White Mountains there, as well as in the Grand Canyon and the more easily accessible sections of the free-running Colorado River between Glen Canyon Dam and Lees Ferry. In fact, this latter area is among the country's most fabled stretches of trout water. Near there, Lake Powell also offers abundant lake fishing within its many finger canyons.

Colorado has many cold-water species living in lakes and streams, including seven kinds of trout (native cutthroat, rainbow, brown, brook, lake, kokanee, and whitefish), walleye, yellow perch, northern pike, tiger muskie, and bluegill. Warm-water sport fish (especially in eastern Colorado and in large rivers) include catfish, crappie, and bass (largemouth, smallmouth, white, and wiper). Both lake and stream fishing are available in the Durango area.

We recommend Taylor Streit's *Fly Fishing New Mexico* (David Communications). It provides important details about 20 of the state's most notable waterways. Also of note are *49 Trout Streams in New Mexico* (University of New Mexico Press) and *Flyfisher's Guide to Arizona* (Wilderness Adventures Press). They include information about regulations and descriptions of the types and varieties of fish you're likely to catch.

For information on obtaining fishing licensing, contact the **New Mexico Game and Fish Department** (✆ **505/476-8000;** www.wildlife.state.nm.us), the **Arizona Game and Fish Department** (✆ **602/942-3000;** www.azgfd.com), the **Utah Division of Wildlife Resources** (✆ **801/538-4700;** www.wildlife.utah.gov), or the **Colorado Division of Wildlife** (✆ **800/244-5613** or 303/297-1192; http://wildlife.state.co.us).

It is not necessary to have a fishing license in order to fish on Native American reservation land, but you must receive written permission and an official tribal document before setting out on any fishing trips. Phone numbers for individual tribes and pueblos are listed separately in the regional and city chapters later in this book.

4 GOLF

Many come to this region specifically to play golf. The Southwest's hundreds of golf courses range from easy public layouts to PGA championship links that have challenged the best.

In Phoenix and Tucson, greens fees, like room rates, are seasonal. In the popular winter months, fees at resort courses range from about $100 to $250 for 18 holes, which usually includes mandatory cart rental. In summer, fees often drop more than 50%. Almost all resorts offer special golf packages as well. Municipal courses charge about $40, with cart rental an additional $20 or so. In New Mexico, fees range from $20 to $145, with most averaging about $60, and with reduced rates in winter. (Cart rentals run about $15.)

For more information on golfing in Arizona, contact the **Arizona Golf Association** (✆ **800/458-8484** or 602/944-3035; www.azgolf.org), which publishes a directory listing all the courses in the state. You can also access the directory online. In addition, you can pick up the *Phoenix Golf Guide* and the *Tucson Golf Guide* (www.azgolfguides.com) at visitor centers, golf courses, and many hotels and resorts. Also check that website to find Web pages for the Arizona resorts listed below.

For spectacular scenery at a resort course, it's just plain impossible to beat the **Boulders** (✆ **480/488-9028**), north of Scottsdale in the town of Carefree. Elevated tee boxes beside giant balanced boulders are enough to distract anyone. Way over on the east side of the valley, in Apache Junction, the **Gold Canyon Golf Resort** (✆ **480/982-9449**) has what have been rated as three of the best holes in the state: the 2nd, 3rd, and 4th holes on the Dinosaur Mountain course. Jumping over to Litchfield Park, on the far west side of the valley, you'll find the **Wigwam Golf Resort & Spa** (✆ **800/327-0396** or 623/935-9414) and its three 18-hole courses; the Gold Course here is legendary. The **Phoenician Golf Club** (✆ **800/888-8234** or 480/423-2449) is another noteworthy resort course in the area. It has a mix of traditional and desert-style holes. The semiprivate **Troon North Golf Club** (✆ **480/585-7700**), a course that seems only barely carved out of raw desert, garners the most local accolades (and charges some of the highest green fees in the state). If you want to swing where the pros do, beg, borrow, or steal a tee time on the Stadium Course at the **Tournament Players Club (TPC) of Scottsdale** (✆ **888/400-4001** or 480/585-4334). The area's favorite municipal course is Phoenix's **Papago Golf Course** (✆ **602/275-8428**), which has a killer 17th hole.

Tucson may not have as many golf courses as the Valley of the Sun, but the courses here are every bit as challenging and memorable. Among the city's resort courses, the Mountain Course at the **Ventana Canyon Golf and Racquet Club** (✆ **520/577-4015**) is legendary, especially the spectacular 107-yard, par-3 3rd hole. The 8th hole on the Sunrise Course at **El Conquistador Country Club** (✆ **520/544-1800**) is another of the area's more memorable par-3 holes. If you want to play where the pros have played, reserve a tee time at the **Omni Tucson National Resort** (✆ **520/575-7540**), which, for many years, was home to the Tucson Open. **Randolph Golf Course** (✆ **520/791-4161**), Tucson's best municipal course, has been the site of the city's annual LPGA tournament. The **Silverbell Golf Course** (✆ **520/791-5235**) boasts a bear of a par-5 17th hole; and, at **Fred Enke Golf Course** (✆ **520/791-2539**), you'll find the city's only desert-style municipal golf course.

Courses worth trying in other parts of the state include **Los Caballeros Golf Club** (✆ **928/684-2704**), which is part of a luxury guest ranch outside Wickenburg. *Golf Digest* has rated this course one of Arizona's top 10. For concentration-taxing scenery, few courses compare with the **Sedona Golf Resort** (✆ **877/733-6630**), which has good views of the red rocks; try to get a sunrise or twilight tee time. Way up in the Four Corners region, in the town of Page, you'll find the 27-hole **Lake Powell National Golf Course** (✆ **928/645-2023**), which is one of the most spectacular in the state. The fairways here wrap around the base of the red-sandstone bluff atop which sits the town of Page. South of Tucson, the **Tubac Golf Resort** (✆ **520/398-2211**) has cows grazing along its fairways for a classic Wild West feel. For dramatic views near the Colorado River in western Arizona, check out the **Emerald Canyon Golf Course** (✆ **928/667-3366**), a municipal course in Parker that plays up and down small canyons and offers the sort of scenery usually associated only with the most expensive desert resort courses.

New Mexico provides the clear air and oft-cool climates that draw many golfers. In northern New Mexico, you'll find great packages for nine respected courses from **Golf on the Santa Fe Trail** (✆ **866/465-3660;** www.santafetrailgolf.com). ***Golf New Mexico*** magazine is a good source of information, and the website lists all New Mexico golf courses (✆ **505/480-8687;** www.golfnewmexico.com).

The most challenging course in the state is the **University of New Mexico Championship Golf Course** in Albuquerque (✆ **505/277-4546;** www.unmgolf.com); one of the most scenic is the **Cochiti Lake Golf Course,** at Cochiti Lake (✆ **505/465-2239;** www.pueblodecochiti.org). If you're in the Farmington area, check out **Piñon Hills Golf Course** (✆ **505/326-6066;** www.fmtn.org), a few years ago rated by *Golf Digest* as the "best public golf course" in New Mexico. In the south, you can enjoy views, a challenging course, and cool climes, even in summer, at the **Links at Sierra Blanca,** in Ruidoso (✆ **800/854-6571** or 575/258-5330; www.thelinksatsierrablanca.com). See individual chapters for more suggestions.

If you can break away from the gambling tables long enough to play golf in Las Vegas, you'll be well rewarded. The city offers excellent courses. Three notable ones are **Bear's Best,** which offers dramatic views on a Jack Nicklaus–designed course. The **Las Vegas Paiute Golf Resort** has impeccable fairways on a challenging course, and **Dragon Ridge** offers play for many skill levels in natural desert mountain surroundings. Fees range from about $65 to $300, with summer and evening rates often half that. You can book any of these and see course overviews with photographs at www.lasvegasgolf.com; or call ✆ **866/456-9912.**

Utah's and Colorado's golf courses are known for their beautiful scenery and variety of challenging terrain. They range from mountain courses set among beautiful forests to desert courses with scenic views of red rock country. The warm climate of St. George, in Utah's southwest corner, makes it a perfect location for year-round golf, and it has become the premier destination for visiting golfers—**St. George's Sunbrook Golf Course** (✆ **435/627-4400;** www.sgcity.org) is probably Utah's best. Durango has two public courses worth checking out: **Hillcrest Golf Course** (✆ **970/247-1499;** www.golfhillcrest.com) and **Dalton Ranch & Golf Club** (✆ **970/247-8774;** www.daltonranch.com). These areas of Utah and Colorado are beyond the scope of this book, so call the numbers listed above for more information.

For information on Colorado's major golf courses, check with the **Colorado Golf Association** (✆ **800/228-4675** or 303/366-4653; www.cogolf.org). Another information resource is ***Colorado Golf*** (www.golfcolorado.com), an annual magazine published jointly by several statewide golf organizations and available free at state welcome centers. Contact the **Utah Office of Tourism** (✆ **800/200-1160** or 801/538-1030; www.utah.com) for information on any of Utah's 100-plus courses.

5 HIKING

Everywhere you go in the region, you'll find opportunities for hiking. The terrain and climate vary from the heat and relative flatness of the desert to the cold, forested alpine areas. You can visit both (from 3,000–13,000 ft. in elevation) and anything in between in the same day without much trouble. Each part of the region is covered below. See later chapters for details about outfitters, guides, llama-trekking services, and whom to contact for maps and other information.

In the Santa Fe area, one of the most pleasant hikes is the **Aspen Vista Trail.** It's an easy hike through aspen forests that offers long views of New Mexico's broad eastern plains. See chapter 7 for details. If you're looking for something more challenging in the north-central region of the state, head up to Taos and give **Wheeler Peak** your best shot. The hike up New Mexico's highest peak is about 15 miles round-trip. If you want a much less difficult hike in the Taos area, try hiking down into **Rio Grande Gorge.** It's beautiful and can be hiked year-round. See chapter 8 for details on these two. In the northeastern region of New Mexico, try the 1-mile loop around **Capulin Volcano.** The crater rim offers stunning views, and you can look down into the dormant caldera (see chapter 10). If you're heading to the northwestern region of the state, try hiking the **Bisti/De-Na-Zin Wilderness,** 37 miles south of Farmington. Though there are no marked trails, the hiking is easy in this area of low, eroded hills and fanciful rock formations. See chapter 6 for details. This region is also home to **El Malpais National Monument,** where you can hike into great lava tubes (see chapter 10). In the southwestern region is the **Gila National Forest,** which has more than 1,400 miles of trails with varying ranges of length and difficulty. One favorite day hike in the forest is the **Catwalk National Recreation Trail,** a moderately strenuous hike along a series of steel bridges and walkways suspended over Whitewater Canyon. See chapter 11 for details. In the southeastern region, you'll find one of New Mexico's cherished places: **White Sands National Monument.** Hiking the white-sand dunes is easy, if sometimes awkward, and the magnificence of the view is unsurpassed. See chapter 11 for more information.

Arizona also has fascinating and challenging hiking. In northern Arizona, there are good day hikes in **Grand Canyon National Park** and in the **San Francisco Peaks** north of Flagstaff (see chapter 16). Hiking is the order of the day in Sedona, where such places as **Boynton Canyon** offer red-rock beauty and ancient ruins (see chapter 15). In the Phoenix area, popular day hikes include the trails up **Camelback Mountain** and **Squaw Peak** and the many trails in **South Mountain Park** (see chapter 13). In the Tucson area, there are good hikes on **Mount Lemmon** and in **Saguaro National Park, Sabino Canyon,** and **Catalina State Park** (see chapter 12). In the southern part of the state, there are good day hikes in Chiricahua National Monument, most notably the **Heart of Rocks Loop,** which meanders through formations that could have been created by Dr. Seuss. Also in the south are the **Coronado National Forest,** the Nature Conservancy's **Ramsey Canyon Preserve** and **Patagonia–Sonoita Creek Preserve, Cochise Stronghold,** and **Organ Pipe Cactus National Monument** (see chapter 14).

The state's two most unforgettable overnight backpack trips are the hike down to Phantom Ranch at the bottom of the Grand Canyon and the hike into Havasu Canyon, a side canyon of the Grand Canyon. See chapter 16.

Hiking is the best—and sometimes the only—way to see many of Utah's most beautiful and exciting areas, and the state is interlaced with hiking trails. In particular, check out **Natural Bridges National Monument,** where numerous trails take hikers through magical stone formations (see chapter 6). At Zion, the **Lower Emerald Pools Trail** takes you along emerald-colored pools, and at Bryce, the **Navajo Loop/Queen's Garden Trail** is an intermediate trail that traverses the park's magical beauty. (See chapter 17.)

The **Continental Divide Trail Alliance (CDTA)** (✆ **888/909-2382** or 303/838-3760; www.cdtrail.org) is building a trail—using volunteers—along the mountains of the Great Divide, from Canada to Mexico, and that means right through the middle of

Colorado and New Mexico. Each year, the CDTA publishes a project schedule for the next summer, complete with volunteer needs, project description, and difficulty rating.

Guided backpacking trips of different durations and difficulty levels are offered by the **Grand Canyon Field Institute** (✆ **866/471-4435** or 928/638-2485; www.grandcanyon.org/fieldinstitute) and **Discovery Treks** (✆ **888/256-8731;** www.discoverytreks.com). **Backroads** (✆ **800/462-2848** or 510/527-1555; www.backroads.com), better known for its bike trips, also offers a 7-day hiking/biking trip to Grand Canyon, Bryce Canyon, and Zion national parks for between $1,998 and $2,498. Vermont-based **Country Walkers** (✆ **800/464-9255** or 802/244-1387; www.countrywalkers.com), has a 6-day hiking-oriented trip that takes in the Grand Canyon and Sedona, as well as a similar tour for women only. Either trip costs $2,798.

The highly respected **Colorado Mountain School** (✆ **800/836-4008;** www.totalclimbing.com) leads climbs in various parts of Colorado. **The Colorado Trail Foundation** (✆ **303/384-3729;** www.ColoradoTrail.org) assembles volunteers to maintain the Colorado Trail, and offers supported treks and outdoor workshops on the Colorado Trail.

You can choose from hundreds of other hikes. Consider purchasing a hiking book or contacting the National Park Service, National Forest Service, Bureau of Land Management, or other appropriate agencies directly. The best guides for the region are *50 Hikes in Northern New Mexico: From Chaco Canyon to the High Peaks of the Sangre de Cristos* (Countryman), by Kai Huschke, and *100 Hikes in New Mexico,* 2nd Edition, by Craig Martin (the Mountaineers). *Hiking Arizona,* by Bruce Grubbs (Falcon), outlines many excellent excursions.

6 HORSEBACK RIDING

Adventurers come from all over the world to horseback ride in the Southwest. Some of the most notable Western historic moments took place here, and many Westerns have been filmed. There's a great variety in the types of riding a person can do in the Southwest, so do some research and choose carefully.

If you're content with a nose-to-tail kind of ride, you'll be happiest riding in such mountainous regions as the White Mountains or in more controlled environments such as through Monument Valley. But if you'd prefer to really ride—to trot and canter your horse—you'll want to go to places where the terrain allows for such riding. The Wickenburg, Arizona, area offers plenty of open-trail riding. Check out the **Kay El Bar Guest Ranch** (✆ **800/684-7583** or 928/684-7593; www.kayelbar.com; see chapter 15). Some good riding spots include Canyon de Chelly National Monument (see chapter 6), and the red-rock country around Sedona (see chapter 15).

Among the most popular guided adventures in Arizona are the mule rides down into the Grand Canyon. These trips vary in length from 1 to 2 days; for reservations and more information, contact **Grand Canyon National Park Lodges/Xanterra Parks & Resorts** (✆ **888/297-2757,** 303/297-2757, or, for last-minute reservations, 928/638-2631; www.grandcanyonlodges.com). You'll need to make mule-ride reservations many months in advance. However, if at the last minute (1 or 2 days before you want to ride) you decide you want to go on a mule trip into the Grand Canyon, contact Grand Canyon National Park Lodges at its last-minute reservations phone number (see above), or stop by the **Bright Angel Transportation Desk,** in Grand Canyon Village. Spaces sometimes open up at the last minute.

It's also possible to do overnight horseback rides in various locations around the state. For information on day or overnight rides into the Superstition Mountains east of Phoenix, contact **Don Donnelly Horseback Adventures** (✆ **602/810-7029;** www.don donnelly.com).

Want to kick it up a notch? At the **Arizona Cowboy College,** in Scottsdale (✆ **888/330-8070** or 480/471-3151; www.cowboycollege.com), you can literally learn the ropes and the brands and how to say "Git along little doggie" like you really mean it. This is no city slicker's staged roundup; this is the real thing. You actually learn how to be a real cowboy. Six-day programs cost $2,250.

What's unique about much of New Mexico's horseback riding is its variety. You'll find a broad range of riding terrain, from open plains to high mountain wilderness. In the Santa Fe area, you can ride across the plains of the spectacular Galisteo basin with **Santa Fe Detours,** 54½ E. San Francisco St. (✆ **800/338-6877** or 505/983-6565; www.sfdetours.com). In Taos, you can explore secluded Taos Pueblo land with the **Taos Indian Horse Ranch,** on Pueblo land off Ski Valley Road, just before Arroyo Seco (✆ **800/659-3210** or 575/758-3212; www.taosindianhorseranch.com). In the southeast, try **Inn of the Mountain Gods,** Carrizo Canyon Road (✆ **800/545-9011** or 575/464-4100; www.innofthemountaingods.com). If you're looking for a resort horseback riding experience, contact **Bishop's Lodge,** in Santa Fe (✆ **800/732-2240** or 505/983-6377; www.bishops lodge.com). If you want an authentic cowpoke experience, check out the **Double E Guest Ranch** (✆ **866/242-3500** or 575/535-2048; www.doubleeranch.com), in the Silver City area.

Utah's most notable place to ride is Monument Valley Navajo Tribal Park. **Sacred Monument Tours** (✆ **435/727-3218;** www.monumentvalley.net) offers horseback trips ranging from 1 to 8 hours. See chapter 6.

7 HOT-AIR BALLOONING

Renowned for hot-air ballooning, the Southwest boasts the annual **Albuquerque International Balloon Fiesta,** in early October (see the "Calendar of Events," in chapter 3), which draws thousands of people from all over the world. It is possible to charter hot-air balloon rides in many parts of the region, particularly Taos and Albuquerque (see chapters 8 and 9), in New Mexico, and Tucson and Phoenix, in Arizona (see chapters 12 and 13). One of the best spots for scenic floating is Sedona (see chapter 15). Most companies offer a variety of packages, from the standard flight to a more elaborate all-day affair that includes meals. For more information, see the individual chapters.

8 HOUSEBOATING

With the Colorado River turned into a long string of lakes, Arizona's "West Coast" provides excellent houseboat vacations. Although this doesn't have to be an active vacation, fishing, hiking, and swimming are usually part of a houseboat stay. Rentals are available on Lake Mead, Lake Mohave, and Lake Havasu (see chapter 15). The canyonlands scenery of Lake

Powell makes it great for a houseboat vacation—reserve well in advance for a summer trip. Houseboats provide all the comforts of home—toilets, showers, sleeping quarters, and full kitchens—but in somewhat tighter quarters. Some of the larger houseboats have facilities for up to a dozen people. You don't have to be an accomplished boater to drive one: Houseboats are easy to maneuver and can't go very fast. No boating license is required, but you'll need to reserve your houseboat well in advance, especially in summer, and send in a sizable deposit.

9 SKIING & SNOWBOARDING

The Southwest has some of the best snow skiing and snowboarding in the United States. With most alpine areas above 10,000 feet and many above 12,000 feet, several ski areas offer vertical drops of over 2,000 feet. Average annual snowfall ranges from 100 to 300 inches. Many areas, aided by vigorous snow-making efforts, open around Thanksgiving, and most open by mid-December, making this a popular vacation spot around the holidays. As a result, you'll see a definite rise in hotel room rates in and around ski areas during the holiday season. The ski season runs through March and often into the first week in April.

Some of the best skiing in the region is at **Taos Ski Valley** (© **575/776-2291;** www.skitaos.org). Taos challenges skiers and snowboarders with plenty of vertical runs, and beginners can take advantage of one of the best ski schools in the country. Nearby, the resort town of **Angel Fire Resort** (© **800/633-7463** or 575/377-6401; www.angelfireresort.com) offers interesting terrain and excellent facilities. **Red River Ski Area** (© **800/331-7669** or 575/754-2223; www.redriverskiarea.com) is an excellent family mountain. See chapter 8.

Arizona has a couple of decent ski areas: the **Arizona Snowbowl** (© **928/779-1951;** www.arizonasnowbowl.com), outside Flagstaff, and **Sunrise Park Resort** (© **800/772-7669** or 928/735-7669; www.sunriseskipark.com), on the Apache Reservation outside the town of McNary in the White Mountains. When it's a good snow year, Tucsonans head up to **Mount Lemmon Ski Valley** (© **520/576-1400**), the southernmost ski area in the U.S. Snows here aren't as reliable as they are farther north, so be sure to call first to make sure the ski area is operating. All ski areas in the region offer rentals and lessons. Prices for an adult all-day ticket range from about $34 to $66.

Some of the best **cross-country skiing** in the region can be found at the Enchanted Forest, near Red River, and in Chama, New Mexico (see chapter 10); and outside Flagstaff, Arizona (see chapter 16). Other great areas in Arizona include Sunrise Park, outside the town of McNary, at the South Rim of the Grand Canyon; in the White Mountains, around Greer and Alpine; outside Payson, on the Mogollon Rim; and on Mount Lemmon, outside Tucson (see chapter 12). In Utah, head to Bryce Canyon National Park to ski trails along the rim (see chapter 17).

10 TENNIS

Tennis is one of the most popular winter sports in the desert, and resorts all over the region have courts. Although there may be better courts, none can match the views you'll have from those at Enchantment Resort, outside Sedona. Other noteworthy tennis-oriented resorts include, in the Phoenix/Scottsdale area, the Phoenician, Copperwynd Resort and Club, the Fairmont Scottsdale, the Arizona Grand Resort, and the Pointe Hilton Tapatio Cliffs Resort; and, in Tucson, the Lodge at Ventana Canyon, the Hilton Tucson El Conquistador Golf & Tennis Resort, the Westin La Paloma Resort & Spa, the Westward Look Resort, and the Omni Tucson National Resort. See the individual chapters for contact information for these resorts.

Although New Mexico's high and dry climate is ideal for tennis much of the year, the sport is somewhat underdeveloped in the state. Certainly each of the major cities has municipal courts, information about which you'll find in the city and regional chapters of this book. If you're looking for a tennis resort experience, try **Bishop's Lodge** in Santa Fe (© **800/732-2240** or 505/983-6377; www.bishopslodge.com).

Las Vegas is a nearly ideal spot to play tennis (except in the scorching heat of summer). One popular resort with a good spa and tennis facility is the **Flamingo Las Vegas** (© **800/732-2111** or 702/733-3444; www.flamingolasvegas.com). The **Las Vegas Hilton** (© **800/732-7117;** www.lvhilton.com) also has good courts. See chapter 18.

11 WATERSPORTS

Watersports in the Southwest? Absolutely! You'll find a variety of activities, ranging from white-water rafting to pleasure boating.

WHITE-WATER RAFTING The most notable white-water rafting experience is down the Colorado River through the Grand Canyon. If it's one of your dreams, plan well ahead. Companies and trips are limited, and they tend to fill up early. For a discussion and list of companies that run trips down the canyon, see chapter 16. For 1-day rafting trips on the Colorado below the main section of the Grand Canyon, contact **Hualapai River Runners** (© **888/255-9550** or 928/769-2219; www.destinationgrandcanyon.com). For a half-day float on the Colorado above the Grand Canyon, contact **Colorado River Discovery** (© **888/522-6644** or 928/645-9175; www.raftthecanyon.com), which runs trips between Glen Canyon Dam and Lees Ferry.

Rafting trips are also available on the upper Salt River east of Phoenix. **Wilderness Aware Rafting** (© **800/462-7238;** www.inaraft.com), **Canyon Rio Rafting** (© **800/272-3353;** www.canyonrio.com), and **Mild to Wild Rafting** (© **800/567-6745;** www.mild2wildrafting.com) all run trips of varying lengths down this river (conditions permitting).

New Mexico offers good opportunities for white-water rafting and kayaking. The waters in the Chama River and the Rio Grande are generally at their best during the spring and summer (May–July). Most notable is the 1-day trip down the Taos Box Canyon, offering an almost nonstop series of Class IV rapids. Many reputable companies run the Box, including **Los Rios River Runners** (© **800/544-1181** or 575/776-8854; www.losriosriverrunners.com) and **Native Sons Adventures** (© **800/753-7559** or 575/758-9342; www.nativesonsadventures.com). In addition to calling outfitters, you can contact the **Bureau of Land Management** (© **575/758-8851**) for information.

In Utah, the town of Moab, along the Colorado River, is rapidly becoming a major boating center. You can travel down the river in a canoe, kayak, large or small rubber raft (with or without motor), or speedy, solid jet boat. A worthwhile and lesser-known river trip is along the San Juan River in Bluff. This relaxing excursion will take you to relatively unknown archaeological sites and striking rock formations. A complete list of outfitters is available at the Moab Information Center or through the **Moab Area Travel Council** (✆ **800/635-6622** or 435/259-8825; www.discovermoab.com).

Opportunities for **pleasure boating** are available on many of the region's lakes and reservoirs. Lake Mead, Lake Mohave, and Lake Havasu, what many call Arizona's "West Coast," offer plenty of water fun (see chapter 15). In New Mexico, Elephant Butte Lake is one of the best and most beautiful spots for boating (see chapter 11).

FLAT-WATER CANOEING & KAYAKING Okay, so maybe these sports don't jump to mind when you think of the desert, but there are indeed rivers and lakes here (and they happen to be some of the best places to see wildlife). By far the most memorable place for a flat-water kayak tour is Lake Powell. Multiday kayak tours are offered by **Hidden Canyon Kayak** (✆ **800/343-3121** or 928/645-8866; www.diamondriver.com/kayak), which charges $760 to $1,000 for 4- to 6-day trips. Guided kayak trips are also offered by **Kayak Powell** (✆ **888/854-7862;** www.kayaklakepowell.com), which charges $495 for a 2-day tour, $695 for a 3-day tour, $795 for a 4-day tour, and $895 for a 5-day tour.

There are also a couple of companies that rent canoes and offer trips on the Colorado River south of Lake Mead. See chapter 15.

12 SPECIAL-INTEREST TRIPS

The Southwest is in the process of developing a network of special-interest trips that we're certain will expand even more in upcoming years.

ACADEMIC TRIPS

Those who like a scholarly bent to their vacations can hook up with **Southwest Seminars** (✆ **505/466-2775;** www.southwestseminars.org) and their "Travels with a Scholar" program. This organization offers tours throughout the Southwest, led by museum directors, historians, geologists, archaeologists, anthropologists, and authors. Southwest Seminars is able to arrange visits to sites that are not open to the general public, such as archaeological sites, petroglyph panels, volcanic calderas, contemporary Indian pueblos, and Native artists' homes and studios. Each Monday at 6pm, they offer a talk given by a regional scholar, well worth checking out.

Learning Expeditions, a program run by the **Arizona State Museum,** occasionally offers scholar-led archaeological tours, including a trip to Navajo and Hopi country. For information, contact the marketing department at the **Arizona State Museum** (✆ **520/626-8381;** www.statemuseum.arizona.edu). Through its Ventures program, the **Museum of Northern Arizona,** in Flagstaff (✆ **928/774-5213;** www.musnaz.org), offers educational camping, backpacking, and hotel-based tours primarily in the Colorado Plateau region of northern Arizona. Trips range in length from 1 day to 1 week.

Old Pueblo Archaeology Center, in Tucson (✆ **520/798-1201;** www.oldpueblo.org), is a nonprofit educational and scientific organization that, throughout the years, has led numerous archaeology-oriented trips around Arizona. **Crossing Worlds Journeys & Retreats,** in Sedona (✆ **800/350-2693** or 928/203-0024; www.crossingworlds.com), offers tours throughout the Four Corners region. Trips visit the Hopi mesas as well as backcountry ruins on the Navajo reservation. Journeys of self-discovery are a specialty of this company.

The **Nature Conservancy** (✆ **520/622-3861;** www.nature.org), in both Tucson and Santa Fe (✆ **505/988-3867;** www.nature.org), has preserved some of the Southwest's finest land, parts of which are open to the public for hiking, bird-watching, and nature study. The organization operates educational field trips.

ADVENTURE & ART TRIPS

One excellent operator is **Santa Fe Mountain Adventures** (✆ **800/965-4010** or 505/988-4000; www.santafemountainadventures.com), which combines such outdoor adventures as hiking and river running with cultural activities such as visits to pueblos or museums. A collaborative effort in conjunction with *Outside* magazine, the business is ecoconscious.

If you'd like to turn a trip to the Grand Canyon into an educational experience, the **Grand Canyon Field Institute** (✆ **866/471-4435** or 928/638-2485; www.grand canyon.org/fieldinstitute) offers a variety of programs from early spring to late fall. Examples include day hikes, photography and painting classes, backpacking trips for women, mule-assisted treks, archaeology trips, and guided hikes and backpacking trips with a natural-history or ecological slant.

If you'd like to pursue an artistic adventure, check out the week-long classes in such media as painting, Native American pottery making, and weaving offered by **Taos Art School** (✆ **575/758-0350;** www.taosartschool.org). This organization is especially known for its weaving and horseback-riding creative "odyssey." Open since 1989, the school is a virtual campus in which classes go where they need to be. For instance, a painting class on Georgia O'Keeffe is held in Abiquiu, a Pueblo pottery class at Taos Pueblo, and a class on the churches in New Mexico is held at five different churches in the region. The fees vary from class to class and include lodging and meals.

Some of the world's most outstanding photographers convene in Santa Fe at various times during the year for the **Santa Fe Workshops,** held at a delightful campus in the hills on the east side of town (✆ **505/983-1400;** www.santafeworkshops.com). Most courses are full time, lasting a week. Food and lodging packages are available.

Great Expectations (✆ **800/663-3364;** www.greatexpectations.com) offers an "Opera in Santa Fe" trip, which focuses on more than the opera, but also partakes of this world-class entertainment.

FOOD & WINE TRIPS

Jane Butel Cooking School, in Albuquerque (✆ **800/473-8226** or 505/243-2622; www.janebutel.com), offers week-long and weekend packages with a hotel stay and full-participation classes. The weekend classes are held in noted chef and television personality Jane Butel's home kitchen in Corrales, a village along the Rio Grande on the edge of Albuquerque. The week-long classes are in Santa Fe.

If you'd like to learn how to cook Southwestern cuisine while you're in Arizona, consider taking a cooking class from celebrated Tucson chef Janos Wilder. The 2-hour classes are offered at his eponymously named restaurant at the Westin La Paloma Resort, and cost $50 each. Contact **Janos** in Tucson (✆ **520/615-6100;** www.janos.com). In Phoenix, you can take 1-day cooking classes at the **JW Marriott Desert Ridge Resort** (✆ **800/835-6206** or 480/293-3976; www.jwdesertridge.com). Classes cost $45.

Sedona's luxurious **Enchantment Resort** (✆ **800/826-4180** or 928/282-2900; www.enchantmentresort.com) offers cooking demonstrations several days a week. Cooking classes are also offered at the **Cottage Place Restaurant** in Flagstaff (✆ **928/774-8431;**

www.cottageplace.com). Classes here are quite broad in scope (Mediterranean, smoking and grilling, seafood), cost $50, and last 3½ hours.

VOLUNTEER & WORKING TRIPS

Sierra Club Outings (✆ **415/977-5522;** www.sierraclub.org/outings/national/service.asp) organizes working vacations all over the world, with some work to the Southwest. The Sierra Club also offers hiking, camping, and other adventure trips to various destinations in Arizona. **Global Citizens Network** offers volunteer vacations to worldwide destinations as well, including, at times, to the Southwest. To check their schedule, contact (✆ **800/644-9292;** www.globalcitizens.org).

You can also join a work crew organized by the **Arizona Trail Association** (✆ **602/252-4794;** www.aztrail.org). These crews spend 1 to 2 days building and maintaining various portions of the Arizona Trail, which will eventually stretch from the Utah state line to the Mexico border.

Another type of service trip is offered by the National Park Service. It accepts volunteers to pick up garbage left by thoughtless visitors to Glen Canyon National Recreation Area. In exchange for picking up trash, you'll get to spend 5 or 7 days on a houseboat called the Trash Tracker, cruising through the gorgeous canyonlands of Lake Powell, Arizona. Volunteers must be at least 18 years old and in good physical condition, and must provide their own food, sleeping bag, and transportation to the marina. For information, contact **Glen Canyon National Recreation Area,** Attn: Trash Tracker, P.O. Box 1507, Page, AZ 86040 (✆ **928/608-6350;** www.nps.gov/glca/supportyourpark/trashtracker.htm).

Finally, if you're interested in architecture or the ecology of urban design, you may want to help out on the continued construction of **Arcosanti,** the slow realization of Paolo Soleri's dream of a city that merges architecture and ecology. Located 70 miles north of Phoenix, Arcosanti offers 5-week learning-by-doing workshops ($1,350 per person) and 1-week seminars ($485 per person). Contact Arcosanti Workshop Coordinator (✆ **928/632-6233;** www.arcosanti.org).

13 ESCORTED GENERAL-INTEREST TOURS

Some reliable tours for those with broader interests include **Gray Line Tours Phoenix** (✆ **800/777-3484** or 602/437-3484; www.graylinephoenix.com), which offers a 3-day tour to the Grand Canyon by way of Sedona and Oak Creek Canyon. **Maupintour** (✆ **800/255-4266;** www.maupintour.com), one of the largest tour operators in the world, offers an 8-day Arizona itinerary that covers the Grand Canyon, the Four Corners region, Phoenix, and Scottsdale. **Open Road Tours** (✆ **800/766-7117;** www.openroadtours.com) offers a variety of 2- to 5-day tours around Arizona. Most of these focus on the Grand Canyon.

Detours (✆ **866/438-6877;** www.detoursaz.com) specializes in small-group tours throughout Arizona and other parts of the Southwest. One of its tours, **Hillerman Country,** is a 5-day journey through northern Arizona with a focus on spots that have been mentioned in Tony Hillerman novels about Navajo Tribal Police officers Jim Chee and Joe Leaphorn.

The British tour company **Trek America** (✆ **800/TREK-USA** [873-5872]; www.trekamerica.com) specializes in off-the-beaten-path, small-group adventure travel and offers lots of tours of the American Southwest; most include stops at the Grand Canyon and other scenic locations in Arizona.

Tauck World Discovery (✆ **800/788-7885;** www.tauck.com) offers weeklong cultural trips to New Mexico. **Destination Southwest, Inc.,** in Albuquerque (✆ **800/999-3109** or 505/766-9068; www.destinationsouthwest.com), offers an escorted tour to the Albuquerque International Balloon Fiesta.

Twice a year, **Canyon Calling, Adventures for Women,** in Sedona (✆ **928/282-0916;** www.canyoncalling.com), offers a 10-day women-only tour that visits Sedona, Canyon de Chelly, Lake Powell, the Grand Canyon, and Havasu Canyon. The cost is $2,595 per person. There are also twice-yearly 5-day tours of the Sedona area for $1,595.

For more information on escorted general-interest tours, including questions to ask before booking your trip, see www.frommers.com/planning.

6 The Four Corners Area

The major archaeological center of the United States, the Four Corners area—where the borders of Colorado, New Mexico, Arizona, and Utah meet—is surrounded by a vast complex of ancient villages that dominated this entire region a thousand years ago. Here among the reddish-brown rocks, abandoned canyons, and flat mesas, you'll discover another world, once ruled by the Ancestral Puebloans (also known as Anasazi), and today largely the domain of the Navajo, but also home to the Hopi and Zuni tribes.

Wander among the stunning formations of Monument Valley, where the Navajo still tend their sheep and weave their rugs, and then step back in time to discover a civilization that vanished more than 7 centuries ago, leaving behind more questions than answers. The two best places to explore this ancient culture are Mesa Verde National Park and Chaco Culture National Historic Park. Also, along the Colorado-Utah border is one of America's newest national monuments, Canyon of the Ancients, created by presidential proclamation in June of 2000.

This region is sparsely populated, and you might not find your favorite chain motel around every corner. That's assuming you can even *find* a corner. Therefore many travelers discover a place they like, rent a room or campsite for a few days, and take day trips. In this chapter, we give you a gateway town for each state and also mention places to stay throughout the region.

1 CORTEZ: COLORADO'S FOUR CORNERS GATEWAY

45 miles W of Durango; 203 miles S of Grand Junction

Most visitors to Cortez won't be spending much time in the city, but will use it as a home base. This area is an important archaeological center, and Cortez is surrounded by a vast complex of ancient villages that dominated the Four Corners region—where Colorado, New Mexico, Arizona, and Utah's borders meet—1,000 years ago. Mesa Verde National Park, 10 miles east, is certainly the most prominent nearby attraction, drawing hundreds of thousands of visitors annually. In addition, archaeological sites such as those at Canyons of the Ancients and Hovenweep national monuments as well as Ute Mountain Tribal Park are an easy drive from the city. Its elevation is 6,200 feet.

ESSENTIALS

GETTING THERE **By Car** Cortez is located at the junction of north–south US 491 and east–west US 160.

As it enters Cortez from the east, US 160 crosses Dolores Road (CO 145, which goes north to Telluride and Grand Junction), then runs due west through town for about 2 miles as Main Street. The city's main thoroughfare, Main Street intersects US 491 (Broadway) at the west end of town.

By Plane **Cortez Airport,** off US 160 and 491, southwest of town (✆ **970/565-7458;** www.cityofcortez.com), is served by **Great Lakes Airlines** (✆ **800/554-5111** or 970/565-9510), with direct daily flights to Denver.

Budget (✆ **800/527-0700** or 970/564-9012) and **Hertz** (✆ **800/654-3001** or 970/565-2001) provide car rentals at the airport.

VISITOR INFORMATION Stop at the **Colorado Welcome Center at Cortez,** Cortez City Park, 928 E. Main St. (✆ **970/565-3414**), open daily from 8am to 6pm in summer and from 8am to 5pm the rest of the year; or contact the **Mesa Verde Country Visitor Information Bureau,** P.O. Box HH, Cortez, CO 81321 (✆ **800/253-1616;** www.mesaverdecountry.com), or the **Cortez Area Chamber of Commerce,** P.O. Box 968, Cortez, CO 81321 (✆ **970/565-3414;** www.cortezchamber.org).

FAST FACTS The local hospital is **Southwest Memorial Hospital,** 1311 N. Mildred Rd. (✆ **970/565-6666;** 970/564-2025 24-hr. emergency room; www.swhealth.org). The **post office** is at 35 S. Beech St.; contact the U.S. Postal Service (✆ **800/275-8777;** www.usps.com) for hours and additional information.

NEARBY ARCHAEOLOGICAL SITES

Anasazi Heritage Center ★

When the Dolores River was dammed and the McPhee Reservoir was created in 1985, some 1,600 ancient archaeological sites were threatened. Four percent of the project costs were set aside for archaeological work, and over two million artifacts and other prehistoric items were rescued. Most are displayed in this museum. Located 10 miles north of Cortez, it is set into a hillside near the remains of 12th-century sites.

Operated by the Bureau of Land Management, the center emphasizes visitor involvement. Children and adults are invited to examine corn-grinding implements, a loom and other weaving materials, and a re-created pit house. You can touch artifacts 1,000 to 2,000 years old, examine samples through microscopes, use interactive computer programs, and engage in video lessons in archaeological techniques. During summer there are lectures and other programs on Sunday afternoons.

A half-mile wheelchair-accessible trail leads from the museum to the small **Dominguez Pueblo Ruins,** atop a low hill, with a beautiful view across the Montezuma Valley. It was probably home to a family of four to six people and has low walls marking four rooms. Nearby are ruins of the much larger **Escalante Pueblo** ★★, with about 28 rooms surrounding a kiva. Archeologists say that Escalante Pueblo was one of the northernmost settlements influenced by the Chaco culture.

The center also serves as the visitor center for Canyons of the Ancients National Monument (see below). It is located 10 miles north of Cortez at 27501 Colorado 184, Dolores (✆ **970/882-5600;** www.co.blm.gov/ahc). It's open March through October, daily from 9am to 5pm; November through February, daily from 10am to 4pm. An admission fee of $3 for adults is charged March through October only; admission is free for those 17 and under. Allow 2 hours.

Canyons of the Ancients National Monument

Among the country's more recent national monuments, Canyons of the Ancients was created by presidential proclamation in June 2000. The 164,000-acre national monument contains over 6,000 archaeological sites—what some claim is the highest density of archaeological sites in the United States—including the remains of villages, cliff dwellings,

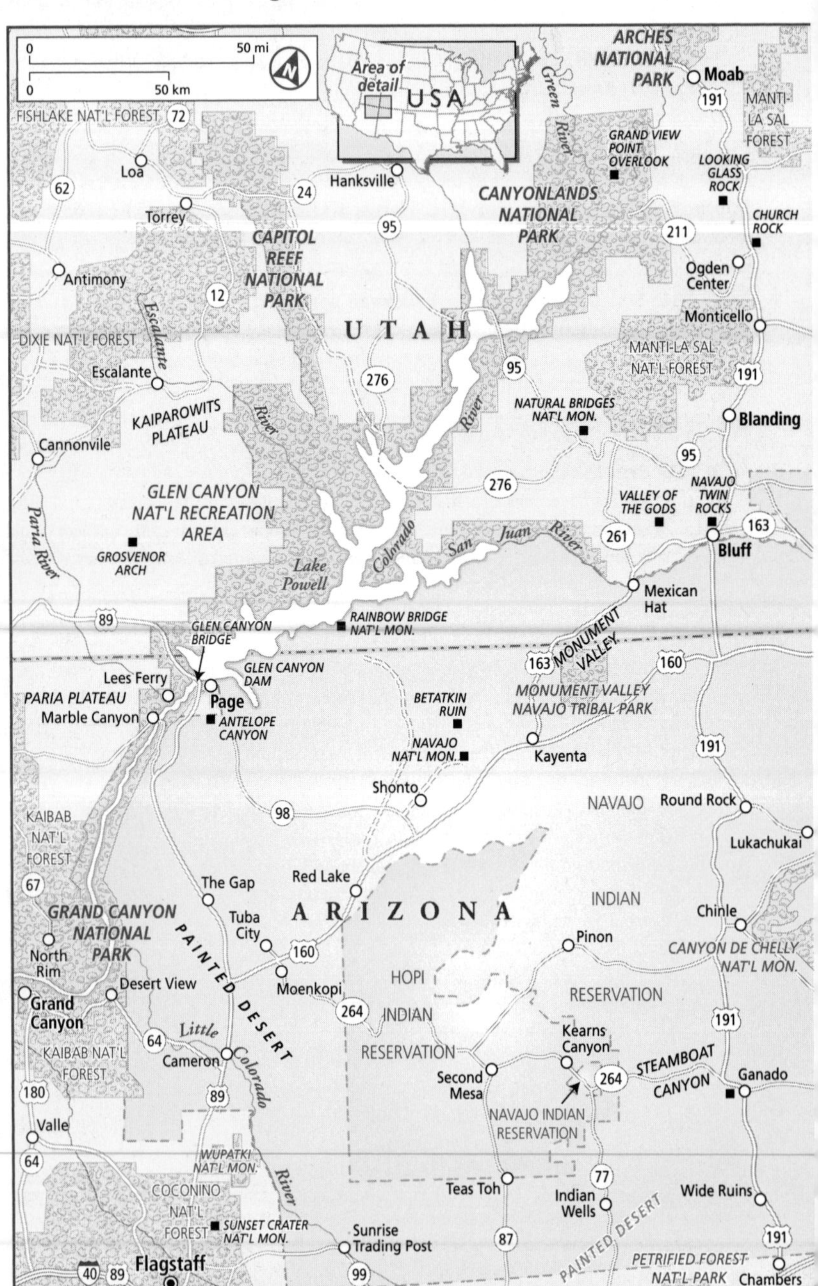
0 50 mi
0 50 km
Area of detail
USA
ARCHES NATIONAL PARK
Moab
MANTI-LA SAL FOREST
FISHLAKE NAT'L FOREST
Loa
Torrey
Hanksville
Green River
GRAND VIEW POINT OVERLOOK
LOOKING GLASS ROCK
CANYONLANDS NATIONAL PARK
CHURCH ROCK
CAPITOL REEF NATIONAL PARK
Ogden Center
Antimony
Monticello
UTAH
Escalante
DIXIE NAT'L FOREST
MANTI-LA SAL NAT'L FOREST
Escalante
KAIPAROWITS PLATEAU
River
NATURAL BRIDGES NAT'L MON.
Blanding
Cannonvile
GLEN CANYON NAT'L RECREATION AREA
VALLEY OF THE GODS
NAVAJO TWIN ROCKS
Paria River
GROSVENOR ARCH
Lake Powell
Colorado
San Juan River
Bluff
Mexican Hat
RAINBOW BRIDGE NAT'L MON.
GLEN CANYON BRIDGE
MONUMENT VALLEY
GLEN CANYON DAM
Lees Ferry
PARIA PLATEAU
Page
Marble Canyon
ANTELOPE CANYON
BETATKIN RUIN
MONUMENT VALLEY NAVAJO TRIBAL PARK
NAVAJO NAT'L MON.
Kayenta
Shonto
NAVAJO
Round Rock
KAIBAB NAT'L FOREST
Lukachukai
Red Lake
The Gap
INDIAN
GRAND CANYON NATIONAL PARK
Tuba City
ARIZONA
Chinle
North Rim
PAINTED DESERT
Pinon
CANYON DE CHELLY NAT'L MON.
Moenkopi
HOPI
Desert View
RESERVATION
Grand Canyon
INDIAN
Little Colorado
Kearns Canyon
KAIBAB NAT'L FOREST
Cameron
RESERVATION
STEAMBOAT CANYON
Second Mesa
Ganado
NAVAJO INDIAN RESERVATION
Valle
WUPATKI NAT'L MON.
River
Teas Toh
Indian Wells
Wide Ruins
COCONINO NAT'L FOREST
SUNSET CRATER NAT'L MON.
Sunrise Trading Post
PAINTED DESERT
PETRIFIED FOREST NAT'L PARK
Chambers
Flagstaff
72 62 24 95 12 276 95 211 191 191 95 276 261 163 89 163 160 191 98 67 160 264 191 64 264 180 89 64 77 87 191 40 89 99

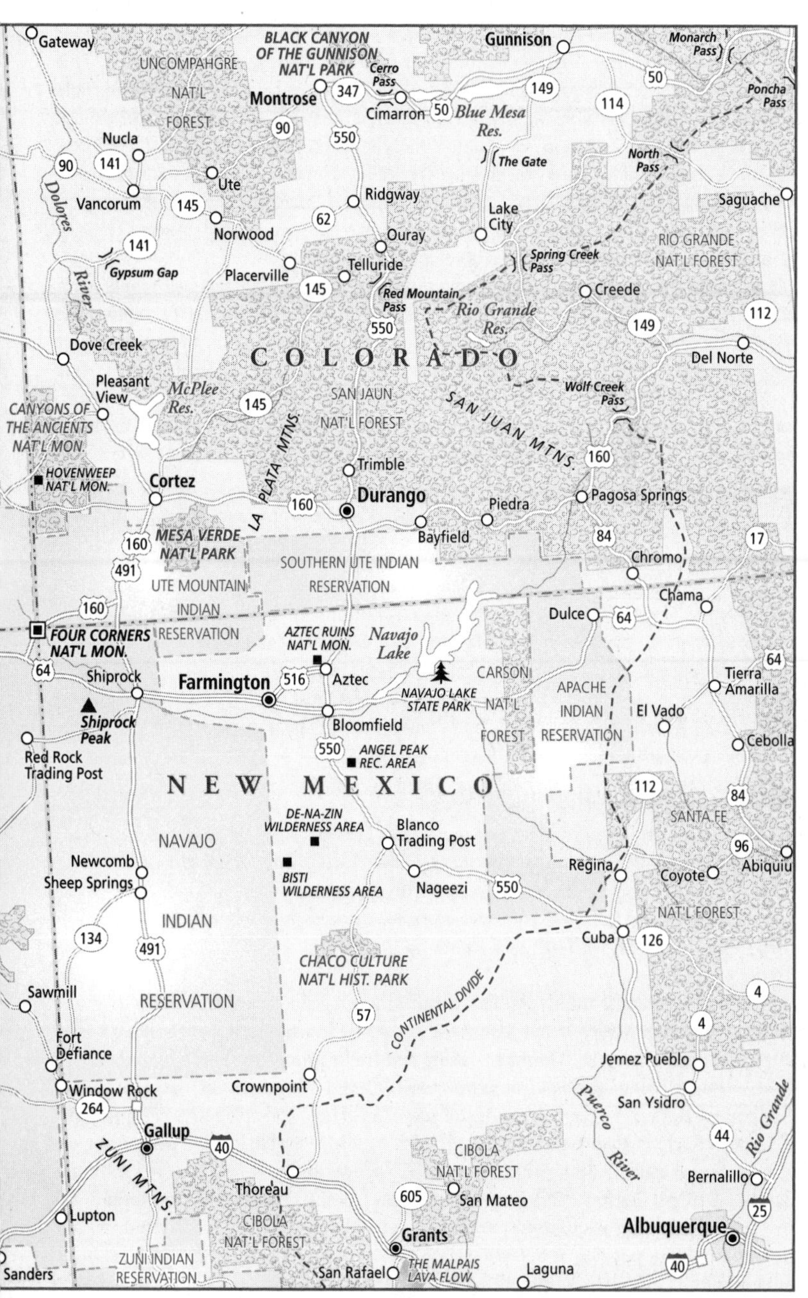

THE FOUR CORNERS AREA

6

CORTEZ: COLORADO'S FOUR CORNERS GATEWAY

sweat lodges, and petroglyphs at least 700 years old, and possibly as much as 10,000 years old.

It's primary excavated site is **Lowry Pueblo,** a prehistoric village that is located about 27 miles west of Cortez via US 491, on C.R. CC, 9 miles west of Pleasant View. This pueblo, built about 1060 and likely abandoned by 1200, is believed to have housed some 100 people. It has standing walls from 40 rooms plus 9 kivas (circular underground ceremonial chambers). A short, self-guided interpretive trail leads past a kiva and continues to the remains of a great kiva, which, at 54 feet in diameter, is among the largest ever found. Hiking is permitted throughout the monument, but hikers are asked to stay on developed trails. The area offers a picnic area, drinking water, and toilets. There is primitive, dispersed camping but no developed campsites.

Canyons of the Ancients is overseen by the Bureau of Land Management, and as yet has no onsite visitor center or even a contact station. Those wishing to explore the monument are strongly advised to contact, or preferably stop first at, the visitor center located at **Anasazi Heritage Center** (see above) for information, especially current road conditions and directions. Information is also available online at www.co.blm.gov/canm, and from the welcome center in Cortez (see the Cortez section, above). Allow at least 2 hours.

Cortez Cultural Center

The center, 25 N. Market St., Cortez (✆ **970/565-1151;** www.cortezculturalcenter.org), includes a museum with exhibits on both prehistoric and modern American Indians, an art gallery with displays of regional art, and a good gift shop offering crafts by local tribal members. A variety of programs is offered year-round, ranging from guided kids' hikes to photo exhibits; and, from late May through early September, there are American Indian dances and cultural programs most evenings, starting at 7:30pm. The center is open daily from 10am to 10pm from June through August, with shorter hours the rest of the year. Admission is free and you should plan to spend at least an hour in the museum (more if there are dances or other programs).

Ute Mountain Tribal Park ★★

Set aside by the Ute Mountain tribe to preserve its heritage, the 125,000-acre Ute Mountain Tribal Park, P.O. Box 109, Towaoc, CO 81334 (✆ **800/847-5485** or 970/565-3751, ext. 330; www.utemountainute.com/tribalpark.htm)—which abuts Mesa Verde National Park—includes wall paintings and ancient petroglyphs as well as hundreds of surface sites and cliff dwellings that are similar in size and complexity to those in Mesa Verde.

Access to the park is strictly limited to guided tours. Full- and half-day tours begin at the Ute Mountain Museum and Visitor Center, at the junction of US 491 and US 160, 20 miles south of Cortez. Mountain-biking and backpacking trips are also offered. No food, water, lodging, gasoline, or other services are available within the park. Some climbing of ladders is necessary on the full-day tour. There's one primitive **campground** ($12 per vehicle; reservations required). Cabins are also available for $10 per person.

Charges for tours in your vehicle start at $27 per person for a half-day, $45 for a full day; it's $10 per person extra to go in the tour guide's vehicle, and reservations are required. Special private tours to remote sections of the park are also offered, with a minimum of four persons, at $60 per person per day. Credit cards are not accepted (cash or checks only), dogs are not permitted on the property, and professional photography is not allowed. Allow from a half- to a full day here.

Hovenweep National Monument ★

Preserving some of the most striking and isolated archaeological sites in the Four Corners area, this national monument straddles the Colorado-Utah border, 40 miles west of Cortez.

Hovenweep is the Ute word for "deserted valley," appropriate because its inhabitants apparently left around 1300. The monument contains six separate sites, and is noted for mysterious, 20-foot-high sandstone towers, some square, others oval, circular, or D-shaped. Archaeologists have suggested their possible function as everything from guard or signal towers, celestial observatories, and ceremonial structures to water towers or granaries.

A ranger station, with exhibits, restrooms, and drinking water, is located at the **Square Tower Site** ★, in the Utah section of the monument, the most impressive and best preserved of the sites. The **Hovenweep Campground,** which contains 28 sites, is open year-round. Sites are fairly small—most appropriate for tents or small pickup-truck campers—but a few sites can accommodate RVs up to 36 feet long. The campground has flush toilets, drinking water, picnic tables, and fire pits, but no showers or RV hookups. Cost is $10 per night; reservations are not accepted, but the campground rarely fills.

From Cortez, take US 160 south to C.R. G (McElmo Canyon Rd.), and follow signs into Utah and the monument. The other five sites are difficult to find, and you'll need to obtain detailed driving directions and check on current road conditions before setting out. Summer temperatures can reach over 100°F (38°C), and water supplies are limited—so take your own and carry a canteen, even on short walks. Bug repellent is advised, as gnats can be a nuisance in late spring.

The visitor center/ranger station is open daily 8am to 6pm from April through September and from 8am to 5pm the rest of the year; it's closed New Year's Day, Thanksgiving, and Christmas. Admission for up to a week costs $6 per vehicle or $3 per person on bike or foot. For advance information, contact Hovenweep National Monument, McElmo Route, Cortez, CO 81321 (✆ **970/562-4282;** www.nps.gov/hove).

WHERE TO STAY

Lodging in Cortez is generally adequate but not very exciting, although you probably will just use Cortez as a base for exploring the area, so this may not matter. We recommend that you stay in your favorite chain. Summer is the busy season here, and that's when you'll pay the highest rates. Among those offering clean, comfortable, and reasonably priced rooms (ranging from about $65–$135 double) in Cortez (zip code 81321) are **Best Western Turquoise Inn & Suites,** 535 E. Main St. (✆ 800/547-3376 or 970/565-3778); **Comfort Inn,** 2321 E. Main St. (✆ 800/424-6423 or 970/565-3400); **Econo Lodge,** 2020 E. Main St. (✆ 800/553-2666 or 970/565-3474); **Holiday Inn Express,** 2121 E. Main St. (✆ 888/465-4329 or 970/565-6000); and **Super 8,** 505 E. Main St. (✆ 800/800-8000 or 970/565-8888). Room tax adds about 8% to lodging bills.

WHERE TO DINE

Homesteaders Restaurant ★ AMERICAN/MEXICAN A rustic, Old West atmosphere pervades this popular family restaurant, which is decorated with historic photos and memorabilia. The menu has a good selection of home-style American basics, such as burgers, T-bones, and top sirloins. Those wanting a bit more zip might try the Southwestern steak—top sirloin smothered with salsa, green chile, and cheese. We also suggest the barbecued baby back ribs and the old-fashioned dinners, such as thin-sliced roast beef or deep-fried catfish filet. Several Mexican standards are also offered, as well as salads and vegetarian items.

45 E. Main St. ✆ **970/565-6253.** www.thehomesteaders.com. Main courses $5.95–$9.95 lunch, $7.95–$20 dinner. AE, DISC, MC, V. Mon–Sat 11am–9:30pm; summer also Sun 4–9:30pm.

Main St. Brewery and Restaurant ★ AMERICAN Fans slice the air under a stamped-tin ceiling, and fanciful murals splash color above subdued wood paneling. The pleasant contrasts found in the decor carry over to the menu. In addition to brewpub staples, such as fish and chips, pizza, and bratwurst, this restaurant offers steaks and prime rib—dry aged Angus beef from its own herd of Angus cattle, raised with no artificial growth stimulants or antibiotics—plus a vegetarian stir-fry plate and Rocky Mountain trout. The beers brewed here go well with everything. We especially recommend the hoppy, slightly bitter Pale Export and the Munich-style Pale Bock.

21 E. Main St., Cortez. ✆ **970/564-9112.** Main courses $6.95–$24. AE, MC, V. Daily 3:30pm–close.

Nero's ★★ ITALIAN/AMERICAN This is our top choice in this area when we're craving something unique. The innovative entrees, prepared by Culinary Institute of America chef Richard Gurd, include house specialties such as the Cowboy Steak (a charbroiled 12-ounce sirloin seasoned with a spicy rub and served with pasta or fries); our favorite, the mushroom ravioli served with an Alfredo sauce, sautéed spinach, sun-dried tomatoes, and pecans; and shrimp Alfredo (sautéed shrimp, with spinach, served over fettuccine with Alfredo sauce and Romano cheese). There's an excellent selection of beef, plus seafood, fowl, pork, veal, and lots of homemade pasta. A small, homey restaurant with a Southwestern art-gallery decor, Nero's also offers pleasant outdoor seating in warm weather.

303 W. Main St. ✆ **970/565-7366.** www.subee.com/neros/home.html. Reservations recommended in summer. Entrees $8.95–$21. AE, MC, V. Daily 5–9:30pm. Closed Sun in winter.

Pippo's Cafe AMERICAN This friendly, down-home cafe is great for those seeking a casual ambience, good, basic American cooking, and reasonable prices. Located along busy Main Street, Pippo's serves only breakfast and lunch—the former, the restaurant's specialty, is served during all open hours. We especially like the omelets and the homemade hash browns, but then we wouldn't turn down the steak and eggs, either. The lunch menu includes the usual burger and fries, along with homemade soups, Navajo tacos, and fried chicken with mashed potatoes and gravy.

100 W. Main St. ✆ **970/565-6039.** Main courses $1.90–$5.90. MC, V. Mon–Sat 6:30am–3pm, Sun 6:30am–2pm.

2 MESA VERDE NATIONAL PARK ★★★

125 miles E of Bluff; 390 miles SE of Salt Lake City

Mesa Verde is the largest archaeological preserve in the United States, with some 4,000 known sites dating from A.D. 550 to 1300, including the most impressive cliff dwellings in the Southwest.

The earliest known inhabitants of Mesa Verde (Spanish for "green table") built subterranean pit houses on the mesa tops. During the 13th century, they moved into shallow caves and constructed complex cliff dwellings. Despite being a massive construction project, these homes were only occupied for about a century; their residents left in about 1300 for reasons as yet undetermined.

Seeing the Highlights in a Day

If you have only a day to spend at the park, stop first at the Far View Visitor Center to buy tickets for a late-afternoon tour of either Cliff House or Balcony House—visitors are not allowed to tour both on the same day. Then travel to the Chapin Mesa archeological museum for a look at the history behind the sites you're about to see. From here, walk down the trail behind the museum to Spruce Tree House. Then drive the Mesa Top Loop Road. Cap your day with the guided tour.

The area was little known until ranchers Charles and Richard Wetherill chanced upon it in 1888. Looting of artifacts followed their discovery until a Denver newspaper reporter's stories aroused national interest in protecting the site. The 52,000-acre site was declared a national park in 1906—it's the only U.S. national park devoted entirely to the works of humans.

Fires have plagued the park in recent years, and burned trees and blackened ground are evident today. Two lightning-induced fires blackened about 40% of the park during the summer of 2000, closing the park for about 3 weeks. Officials said that although the park's piñon-juniper forests were severely burned, none of the major archaeological sites were damaged; in fact, the fires revealed some sites that they were not aware existed. Then a lightning-induced fire struck again in the summer of 2002, closing the park for about 10 days. It destroyed several employees' homes, a sewage treatment plant, and phone and power lines, and also damaged a water storage tank. Officials said that the only damage to archaeological sites was the scorching of the wall of one ruin.

ESSENTIALS

ENTRY The park entrance is located on US 160, 10 miles east of Cortez and 6 miles west of Mancos.

FEES & REGULATIONS Admission to the park for up to 1 week for private vehicles costs $15 from Memorial Day weekend through Labor Day weekend and $10 the rest of the year; rates for motorcyclists are $8 and $5, respectively. Tours of Cliff Palace, Balcony House, and Long House are $3; ranger-guided tours of other areas are free. To protect the many archaeological sites, the Park Service has outlawed backcountry camping and off-trail hiking. It's also illegal to enter cliff dwellings without a ranger present. The Wetherill Mesa Road cannot accommodate vehicles longer than 25 feet. Cyclists must have lights to pedal through the tunnel on the entrance road.

VISITOR CENTERS & INFORMATION **Chapin Mesa,** site of the park headquarters, museum, and a post office, is 20 miles from the park entrance on US 160. The **Far View Visitor Center,** site of Far View Lodge, a restaurant, gift shop, and other facilities, is 15 miles off US 160. For a park brochure, contact Mesa Verde National Park, P.O. Box 8, Mesa Verde, CO 81330 (✆ **970/529-4465;** www.nps.gov/meve).

HOURS & SEASONS The park is open daily year-round, but full interpretive services are available only from mid-June to Labor Day. In winter, the Mesa Top Road and museum remain open, but many other facilities are closed. The **Far View Visitor Center** is open from mid-April through mid-October only, from 8am to 5pm daily. The **Chapin**

Tips Keeping Fido Safe & Happy

While there's plenty for human visitors to do in Mesa Verde National Park, the U.S. Park Service is not very welcoming to our canine friends, and prohibits them on all trails (the only exceptions are for service dogs, such as Seeing Eye dogs). This means that if you want to explore the park, you'll need to leave your dogs behind. Fortunately, there are several kennels in the area, including **The Dog Hotel,** 33350 CO 184, Mancos, CO 81328 (✆ **970/882-5416**), which is a well-run facility, open 7 days a week, that also offers accommodations for cats. Appointments are required, and pet owners must have proof of current vaccinations.

Mesa Archeological Museum is open daily from 8am to 6:30pm from early April through early October, daily from 8am to 5pm the rest of the year.

AVOIDING THE CROWDS With close to half a million visitors annually, Mesa Verde seems packed at times, but the numbers are much lower just before and after the summer rush, usually from mid-June through mid-August. Another way to beat the crowds is to make the 12-mile drive to Wetherill Mesa, which attracts only a small percentage of park visitors.

RANGER PROGRAMS In addition to guided tours to the cliff dwellings (see below), rangers give nightly campfire programs at Morefield Campground in summer.

EXPLORING THE PARK

Cliff Palace ★★, the park's largest and best-known site, is a four-story apartment complex with stepped-back roofs forming porches for the dwellings above. Accessible by guided tour only, it is reached by a quarter-mile downhill path. Its towers, walls, and kivas (large circular rooms used for ceremonies) are all set back beneath the rim of a cliff. Another ranger-led tour takes visitors up a 32-foot ladder to explore the interior of **Balcony House.** Each of these tours is given only in summer and into fall (call for exact dates). Guided tours are also offered by Far View Lodge (see "Where to Stay & Dine," below).

Two other important sites—**Step House** and **Long House,** both on Wetherill Mesa—can be visited in summer only. Rangers lead free tours to **Spruce Tree House,** another of the major cliff-dwelling complexes, only in winter, when other park facilities are closed. Visitors can also explore Spruce Tree House on their own at any time.

Although none of the trails to the Mesa Verde sites are strenuous, the 7,000-foot elevation can make the treks tiring for visitors who aren't used to the altitude. For those who want to avoid hiking and climbing, the 12-mile **Mesa Top Road** makes a number of pit houses and cliffside overlooks easily accessible by car. **Chapin Mesa Archeological Museum** houses artifacts and specimens related to the history of the area, including other nearby sites.

OUTDOOR ACTIVITIES Though this isn't an outdoor-recreation park per se—the reason to come here is to see the cliff dwellings and other archaeological sites—you'll find yourself hiking and climbing to get to the sites. Several longer hikes into scenic Spruce Canyon let you stretch your legs and get away from the crowds. Hikers must register at the ranger's office before setting out.

CAMPING Open from early May to mid-October, **Morefield Campground,** c/o Aramark, P.O. Box 277, Mancos, CO 81328 (✆ **866/292-8295;** www.visitmesaverde.com), 4 miles south of the park entrance, has 435 sites, including 15 with full RV hookups. The campground is set in rolling hills in a grassy area with scrub oak and brush. The attractive sites are fairly well spaced, and mostly separated by trees and other foliage, and have picnic tables and grills. Facilities include modern restrooms, coin-operated showers (not within easy walking distance of most campsites), a convenience store, and an RV dump station. Programs on the area's human and natural history and other subjects are presented nightly at the campground amphitheater from Memorial Day weekend through Labor Day weekend. Campsites cost $23, or $31 with hookups. Reservations are strongly recommended for hookup sites, available for other sites. There are also several commercial campgrounds along US 160, just outside the park entrance.

WHERE TO STAY & DINE

There is only one lodging facility in the park, Far View Lodge (see below), which contains two restaurants and a bar. The company that runs the lodge also operates two other restaurants in the park—one near the campground and another near Chapin Mesa Museum. None of the restaurants accept reservations. For additional information on the in-park restaurants, see www.visitmesaverde.com. There are also numerous lodging and dining possibilities in nearby Cortez (see above).

Far View Lodge Located in the heart of Mesa Verde National Park, Far View Lodge offers not only the most convenient location for visiting the park but also the best views of any accommodations in the area. The facility lodges guests in 17 separate buildings spread across a hilltop. Rooms aren't fancy, and some are a bit on the small side, but they are well maintained and more than adequate, with Southwestern decor. The upscale "Kiva" rooms boast handcrafted furniture, one king- or two double beds, bathrobes, CD players, and other amenities. Most standard rooms have one queen-size bed or two doubles, although a variety of bed combinations are available. For a couple, we prefer the rooms with one bed—they seem less cramped than rooms with two beds. There are no TVs, but each unit has a private balcony, and the views are magnificent in all directions. All rooms are smoke-free.

The **lodge restaurants** serve three meals daily, and during the warmer months guided tours of the park are scheduled. Call for the current schedule and rates.

Mesa Verde National Park (P.O. Box 277), Mancos, CO 81328. ✆ **866/292-8295.** Fax 970/564-4311. www.visitmesaverde.com. 150 units. $116–$150 double. AE, DC, DISC, MC, V. Closed mid-Oct to mid-Apr. Pets accepted in standard rooms only with $50 deposit and $10 nonrefundable fee per pet per night. **Amenities:** 2 restaurants; Wi-Fi (in lobby). *In room:* A/C (Kiva rooms only), CD player (Kiva rooms only), fridge, hair dryer.

3 FOUR CORNERS MONUMENT

This is the only place in the United States where you can stand in four states at once. There's a flat monument marking the spot where Utah, Colorado, New Mexico, and Arizona meet, on which visitors can perch for photos. Official seals of the four states are displayed, along with the motto FOUR STATES HERE MEET IN FREEDOM UNDER GOD. Surrounding the monument are the flags of the four states, the Navajo Nation and Ute tribes, and the United States.

There are often crafts demonstrations here, and jewelry, pottery, sand paintings, and other crafts are for sale, along with T-shirts and other souvenirs. In addition, traditional Navajo food, such as fry bread, is available, and there's a small visitor center with information on visiting the Navajo Nation.

Located a half-mile northwest of US 160, the monument is open daily from 7am to 8pm from June through September and from 8am to 5pm the rest of the year. Entry costs $3 per person. For information, contact the **Navajo Parks and Recreation Department,** Four Corners Park Manager, P.O. Box 2520, Window Rock, AZ 86515 (© **928/871-6647;** www.navajonationparks.org). Allow half an hour.

4 BLUFF: UTAH'S FOUR CORNERS GATEWAY

100 miles S of Moab; 338 miles SE of Salt Lake City

We particularly enjoy the tiny and friendly village of Bluff, which sits near the intersection of US 191 and US 163, with roads leading off toward all the attractions of the Four Corners. With a population of about 300, Bluff (elevation 4,320 ft.) is one of those comfortable little places with most basic services, but not a lot more. Founded by Mormon pioneers in 1880, the town's site had already been home to both Ancestral Puebloan and Navajo peoples. Local businesses distribute a free historic walking- and biking-tour guide that shows where ancient rock art and archaeological sites are located, as well as pointing out the locations of some of Bluff's handsome stone homes and other historic sites from the late 19th century.

There is no visitor center in Bluff, but most motels and restaurants have visitor information brochure racks. For information on Bluff before you go, see the website for the **Business Owners of Bluff** (www.bluffutah.org). You can also get information on Bluff, as well as on the other southeast Utah communities of Blanding, Monticello, Mexican Hat, and Monument Valley, from **Utah's Canyon Country,** P.O. Box 490, Monticello, UT 84535 (© **800/574-4386** or 435/587-3235, ext. 4139; www.utahscanyoncountry.com).

WHITE-WATER RAFTING & OTHER ORGANIZED TOURS

Situated along the San Juan River, Bluff is a center for river rafting. **Wild Rivers Expeditions,** 101 Main St. (Box 118), Bluff, UT 84512 (© **800/422-7654** or 435/672-2244; www.riversandruins.com), offers river trips on the San Juan that are both fun and educational. Boaters see dozens of American Indian sites along the river, such as the spectacular Butler Wash Petroglyph Panel—a 250-yard-long wall of petroglyphs—plus spectacular rock formations. Trips, offered from March through October, range from a full day to more than a week, with rates starting at $165 per adult and $123 per child under 13, including lunch.

To really see the scenery and cultural resources here we suggest a trip with **Far Out Expeditions** ★★. This local company specializes in hiking tours to the abundant archaeological sites in the region, offering custom full or half-day hikes or multiday backpacking trips to the spectacular scenery and fascinating rock art and ruins left by ancient inhabitants. Rates are based on the number of participants. Far Out Expeditions also offers lodging: The **Far Out Bunkhouse** is cozy, fun lodging for groups of up to 12 people. Offering two bedrooms—each sleeping up to six, with private bathroom and shower (only)—there is also a fully equipped kitchen, a screened porch, and a comfortable living room. Rates per night are $90 for one or two people, $100 for three or four people, $110 for five or six, and $195 for the entire house. For information on both the tours and lodging, contact Far Out Expeditions, 7th East St. and Mulberry Ave. (P.O. Box 307), Bluff, UT 84512 (✆ **435/672-2294;** www.faroutexpeditions.com).

Note that both of the above companies also collect per-person user fees charged by the Bureau of Land Management (BLM).

MORE TO SEE & DO

About 2 miles west of town is **Sand Island Recreation Site,** operated by the BLM. Located along the San Juan River among cottonwoods, Russian olives, and salt cedar, this area offers boating (there's a boat ramp) and fishing. Boaters must obtain river permits in advance, which are awarded through a lottery. Permits are free for river trips from November through February, but fees are charged the rest of the year, based on the section of river and number of people in your party. There is a lottery for permits in early February, so applications should be submitted by February 1. After the lottery has been held, you may still get a permit if there are cancellations or vacant time periods. Contact the Bureau of Land Management, 435 N. Main St. (P.O. Box 7), Monticello, UT 84535 (✆ **435/587-1500;** 435/587-1544, 8am–noon Mon–Fri for permits and applications; www.ut.blm.gov). Nestled between the river and a high rock bluff are picnic tables, vault toilets, and graveled campsites; camping is $10 per night and drinking water is available. Head west from the boat launch to see a number of petroglyphs; some can be seen easily on foot, others are glimpsed only from a boat. Unfortunately, you must have your own boat, as there are no nearby rentals.

Goosenecks State Park, set on a rim high above the San Juan, offers spectacular views over the twisting, turning river some 1,000 feet below. It's named for the sharp turns in the river, which meanders more than 5 miles to progress just 1 linear mile, and provides a look straight down through 300 million years of geologic history. (The park also has some Hollywood history: It served as the location for the climactic scene in *Thelma & Louise*.) You'll find picnic tables, trash cans, vault toilets, and an observation shelter, but no drinking water, in a gravelly open area at the end of the paved road. It is often very hot in summer, and there is practically no shade. The park is open around the clock, and admission is free; primitive camping is permitted at no charge. The park is about 23½ miles from Bluff, just off the route to Monument Valley Navajo Tribal Park. Head west on US 163 for about 20 miles, turn north (right) on Utah 261 for about a mile, and then west (left) on Utah 316 for 2½ miles. For information, contact Goosenecks State Park, c/o Edge of the Cedars State Park Museum, 600 W. 400 North, Blanding, UT 84511 (✆ **435/678-2238;** www.stateparks.utah.gov).

WHERE TO STAY

Lodging tax adds just over 10% to room bills in Bluff. Far Out Expeditions (see above) also offers accommodations in its guesthouse.

Desert Rose Inn and Cabins ★★ You can't miss this imposing lodge-style building on Bluff's main drag, and if you're looking for upscale accommodations with a decidedly Western flavor, this is it. The spacious and attractively decorated motel rooms have log headboards, pottery-style lamps, solid-wood furnishings, and Native American artwork. In addition there are five pleasant cabins, a bit more rustic in appearance, each with a large walk-in shower (no tubs), one queen bed, refrigerators and microwaves, porches, and cathedral ceilings with exposed beams. There is also an attractive cabin suite with a wraparound porch, king-size bed, and separate living room. All units are nonsmoking.

701 W. Main St. (US 191, P.O. Box 148), Bluff, UT 84512. ✆ **888/475-7673** or 435/672-2303. Fax 435/672-2217. www.desertroseinn.com. 37 units. Summer $99–$119 double; winter $69–$89 double. $139 suite. AE, DISC, MC, V. *In room:* A/C, fridge and microwave (cabins only), Wi-Fi.

Recapture Lodge ★ (Value) This property may be older, but we appreciate its quiet, clean, and inexpensive rooms, and this is our first choice when staying in Bluff. A well-kept motel located near the center of town, Recapture Lodge has an attractive Western decor and a nature trail that follows the San Juan River along the back of the property. Rooms contain two double beds or one queen, and shower/tub combinations; several budget units, with shower only and one double bed, are also available. Guests enjoy the heated pool and hot tub.

US 191 (P.O. Box 309), Bluff, UT 84512. ✆ **435/672-2281.** Fax 435/672-2284. www.recapturelodge.com. 28 units. Summer $60 double; winter $40 double. Pets welcome. AE, DISC, MC, V. **Amenities:** Outdoor pool; hot tub. *In room:* A/C, TV, Wi-Fi, no phone.

Camping

Campgrounds include **Cadillac Ranch RV Park,** US 191 (P.O. Box 157), Bluff, UT 84512 (✆ **800/538-6195** or 435/672-2262), a down-home sort of place on the east side of town with sites around a small fishing lake, where there's no license needed and no extra charge for fishing. There are 20 RV sites—all large pull-throughs—and 10 tent sites, as well as restrooms with showers. The campground is open year-round, but water is turned off in winter. Cost per site is $16 for tents and $23 to $25 for RVs; paddleboats can be rented at $4 per half hour. There is free Wi-Fi access.

WHERE TO DINE

Cottonwood Steakhouse ★★ STEAK/AMERICAN Set up like the main street of an old tumbleweed town, this Old West–style restaurant knows what to do with beef. The solid fare includes a 16-ounce T-bone steak, barbecued chicken or ribs, and 12-ounce rib-eye steak, accompanied by large salads and potatoes or baked beans; there's also a vegetarian plate. Diners sit at picnic tables, both inside the restaurant and outside under cottonwood trees. Beer (including Utah microbrew on tap) is available.

US 191, on the west side of Bluff. ✆ **435/672-2282.** www.cottonwoodsteakhouse.com. Main courses $13–$25. MC, V. Daily from 5:30–9:30pm Mar to mid-Oct. Closed mid-Oct to Feb.

Twin Rocks Cafe AMERICAN/SOUTHWESTERN In the shadow of the prominent Twin Rocks formation, this cafe has the best breakfast in town and does a good job with lunch and dinner as well. The open, airy dining room has large picture windows offering views of the surrounding red rock walls. The American and Southwestern selections range from half-pound burgers to fried chicken and steaks. But the most popular items by far are the regional dishes—the sheepherder's sandwich (roast beef on fry bread with cheddar cheese), Navajo taco (available with meat or vegetarian), and Navajo fry bread. Microbrewed beers are available with meals. You can surf the Internet here; and, while you're here, check out the museum-quality American Indian arts and crafts at Twin Rocks Trading Post, under the same management, next door.

913 E. Navajo Twins Dr. (off US 191, on the east end of Bluff). ✆ **435/672-2341.** www.twinrockscafe.com. Breakfast $4.30–$8.90; lunch and dinner main courses $7.80–$20. AE, DC, DISC, MC, V. Daily 7am–9pm in summer; reduced hours in winter.

5 NATURAL BRIDGES NATIONAL MONUMENT ★

60 miles NW of Bluff, 360 miles south of Salt Lake City

Utah's first National Park Service area—and the world's first "International Dark Sky Park"—Natural Bridges was designated primarily to show off and protect its three outstanding natural rock bridges, carved by streams and other forms of erosion beginning some 10,000 to 15,000 years ago. You can see the bridges from roadside viewpoints, take individual hikes to each one, or hike a loop trail that connects all three.

Giant **Sipapu Bridge** is considered a "mature" bridge. It's 220 feet high, with a span of 268 feet, and is believed to be the second-largest natural bridge in the world, after Rainbow Bridge in nearby Glen Canyon National Recreation Area. **Owachomo Bridge,** which appears to be on the brink of collapse (then again, it could stand for centuries), is the smallest of the three at 106 feet high, with a span of 180 feet. **Kachina Bridge,** 210 feet high, with a span of 204 feet, is the thickest of the monument's bridges, at 93 feet. All three bridges were given Hopi names: Sipapu means the "gateway to the spirit world" in Hopi legend; Owachomo is Hopi for "rock mound," so called for a rounded sandstone formation atop one side of the bridge; and Kachina was given its name because rock art on the bridge resembles decorations found on traditional Hopi kachina dolls.

The monument also offers a short walk to an overlook where you can see a prehistoric cliff dwelling.

ESSENTIALS

Natural Bridges National Monument is about 40 miles west of Blanding, 60 miles northwest of Bluff, 43 miles north of Mexican Hat, and about 50 miles east of Glen Canyon National Recreation Area's Hite or Halls Crossing marinas.

GETTING THERE The national monument is located in southeast Utah, off scenic Utah 95 via Utah 275. From Monument Valley, follow US 163 north to Utah 261 (just past Mexican Hat); at Utah 95, go west to Utah 275 and the Monument. Beware, though—Utah 261, although a very pretty drive, has 3 miles with 10% grades and numerous steep switchbacks. It's not recommended for motor homes, those towing trailers, or anyone who's afraid of heights. The less adventurous and RV-bound should stick to approaching from the east, via Utah 95.

Take note: Make sure you have enough fuel for the trip to Natural Bridges; the closest gas stations are at least 40 miles away, in Mexican Hat or Blanding. In fact, there are no services of any kind within 40 miles of the monument.

INFORMATION/VISITOR CENTER For a park brochure and other information, contact **Natural Bridges National Monument,** HC 60 Box 1, Lake Powell, UT 84533 (✆ **435/692-1234;** www.nps.gov/nabr).

A **visitor center** at the park entrance is open daily from 8am to 5pm with some seasonal variations, and closed New Year's Day, Thanksgiving, and Christmas. It has exhibits and a video program on bridge formation, the human history of the area, and the monument's plants and wildlife. Rangers are available to advise you about hiking trails and scheduled activities. The visitor center is the only place in the monument where you can get drinking water.

FEES & REGULATIONS Entry to the monument is $6 per vehicle or $3 per person on foot, bicycle, or motorcycle. Regulations are similar to those in most areas administered by the National Park Service, with an emphasis on protecting the natural resources. Be especially careful not to damage any of the fragile archaeological sites in the monument; climbing on the natural bridges is prohibited. Overnight backpacking is not permitted within the monument, and vehicles may not be left unattended overnight. Because parking at the overlooks and trail heads is limited, anyone towing trailers or extra vehicles is asked to leave them at the visitor center parking lot. Pets must be leashed and are not allowed on trails or in buildings.

RANGER PROGRAMS Guided hikes and walks, evening campground programs, and talks at the visitor-center patio are presented from spring through fall. Schedules are posted at the visitor center.

SEEING THE HIGHLIGHTS

Natural Bridges National Monument probably won't be your major vacation destination, but you can easily spend a half- or full-day here (or possibly even 2 days). For those who want to take a quick look and move on to the other, larger national park lands in southern Utah, stop at the visitor center for a brief introduction, and then take the 9-mile (one-way) loop drive to the various natural bridge overlooks. Those with the time and the inclination might also take an easy hike down to Owachomo Bridge; it's a half-hour walk.

OUTDOOR PURSUITS

Hiking is the number-one activity here. From the trail heads, you can hike separately to each of the bridges, or start at one and do a loop hike to all three. Be prepared for summer afternoon thunderstorms, which can cause flash flooding. Although the possibility of encountering a rattlesnake is very small, you should still watch carefully. During the hot summers, all hikers should wear hats and other protective clothing, use sunscreen, and carry a gallon of water per person for all but the shortest walks.

The easiest hike—more of a walk—leads to **Owachomo Bridge** (.4 mile round-trip), with an elevation gain of 180 feet. Look toward the eastern horizon to see the twin buttes named Bear's Ears. Allow a half-hour.

The Sipapu and Kachina Bridge trails are both considered moderately strenuous—allocate about 1 hour for each. On the trek to **Sipapu Bridge,** you'll have a 500-foot elevation change, climbing two flights of stairs with three ladders and handrails on a 1.2-mile round-trip trail. This is the steepest trail in the park, and you'll have a splendid view of the bridge about halfway down. The hike takes about 1 hour.

The 1.4-mile round-trip hike to massive **Kachina Bridge** has a 400-foot elevation change, descending steep slickrock with handrails. Under the bridge, you'll notice a pile of rocks that fell in June 1992, slightly enlarging the bridge opening. Allow about 1 hour.

Those planning to hike the **loop to all three bridges** ★★ can start at any of the trail heads, although rangers recommend starting at Owachomo. The round-trip, including your walk back across the mesa, is 8.6 miles. Although the trails from the rim to the canyon bottom can be steep, the walk along the bottom is easy.

For a view of an Ancestral Puebloan cliff dwelling take the short **Horsecollar Ruin Overlook Trail.** This easy, mostly level walk meanders across a mesa to the edge of the canyon where there is an overlook. The ruin gets its name from the oddly shaped doors on two adjacent granaries that resemble horse collars. The trail is about .6 mile round-trip. Allow a half-hour.

CAMPING

A primitive 13-site campground has pit toilets, tables, tent pads, and fire grates, but no drinking water, showers, or other facilities. It's limited to vehicles no more than 26 feet long, and only one vehicle is allowed per site. Cost is $10; sites are allotted on a first-come, first-served basis. (***Note:*** Free drinking water is available from a spigot in the visitor center's parking lot, but there's a five-gallon limit.)

6 WINSLOW: ARIZONA'S FOUR CORNERS GATEWAY

55 miles E of Flagstaff; 70 miles S of Second Mesa; 33 miles W of Holbrook

It's hard to imagine a town that could build most of its tourist fortunes on a mention in a pop song, but that is exactly what Winslow has done ever since the Eagles sang about "standin' on a corner in Winslow, Arizona," in their hit song "Take It Easy." On the corner of Second Street and Kinsley Avenue, the town has even built an official Standin' on the Corner Park (complete with a mural of a girl in a flatbed Ford).

Popular songs aside, Winslow can claim a couple of more significant attractions. Right in town is one of the Southwest's historic railroad hotels, La Posada, which, over recent years, has been restored to its original glory. Twenty miles west of town is mile-wide Meteor Crater. And east of town is Homolovi Ruins State Park, which has ancient ruins as well as extensive petroglyphs.

Winslow makes a good home base for visiting some of Arizona's four corners attractions, but we've found some great places to stay scattered across the region; they're mentioned in the sections below. In particular, if you're hoping to spend some time at Canyon de Chelly National Monument, you should consider spending a night or two at one of the Chinle accommodations recommended in that section.

ESSENTIALS

GETTING THERE Winslow is on I-40 at the junction with Arizona 87, which leads north to the Hopi mesas and south to Payson. **Amtrak** (✆ **800/872-7245**) trains stop in Winslow at La Posada hotel, 501 E. Second Street.

VISITOR INFORMATION Contact the **Winslow Chamber of Commerce,** 101 E. Second St. (✆ **928/289-2434;** www.winslowarizona.org).

ONE BIG HOLE IN THE GROUND

Meteor Crater ★★ At 550 feet deep and 2½ miles in circumference, the Barringer Meteorite Crater is the best-preserved meteorite impact crater on earth. The meteorite, which estimates put at roughly 150 feet in diameter, was traveling at 40,000 mph when it slammed into the earth 50,000 years ago. Within seconds, more than 175 million tons of rock had been displaced, leaving a gaping crater and a devastated landscape. Today, you can stand on the rim of the crater (there are observation decks and a short trail) and marvel at the power, equivalent to 20 million tons of TNT, which created this otherworldly setting. In fact, so closely does this crater resemble craters on the surface of the moon that in the 1960s, NASA came here to train Apollo astronauts.

Fred Harvey & His Girls

Unless you grew up in the Southwest and can remember back to pre–World War II days, you may have never heard of Fred Harvey and the Harvey Girls. But if you spend much time in northern Arizona, you're likely to run into quite a few references to the Harvey Girls and their boss.

Fred Harvey was the Southwest's most famous mogul of railroad hospitality and was an early promoter of tourism in the Grand Canyon State. Harvey, who was working for a railroad in the years shortly after the Civil War, developed a distaste for the food served at railroad stations. He decided he could do a better job and in 1876 opened his first Harvey House railway-station restaurant for the Santa Fe Railroad. By the time of his death in 1901, Harvey operated 47 restaurants, 30 diners, and 15 hotels across the West.

The women who worked as waitresses in the Harvey House restaurants came to be called Harvey Girls. Known for their distinctive black dresses, white aprons, and black bow ties, Harvey Girls had to adhere to very strict behavior codes. In fact, in the late 19th century, they were considered the only real "ladies" in the West, aside from schoolteachers. So celebrated were they in their day that in the 1940s, Judy Garland starred in a Technicolor MGM musical called *The Harvey Girls.* Garland played a Harvey Girl who battles the evil town dance-hall queen (played by Angela Lansbury) for the soul of the local saloon-keeper.

On the rim of the crater, there's a small museum that features exhibits on astrogeology and space exploration, as well as a film on meteorites. On display are a 1,400-pound meteorite and an Apollo space capsule. Throughout the day, there are 1-hour hiking tours along the rim of the crater.

20 miles west of Winslow (exit 233 off I-40). ✆ **800/289-5898** or 928/289-5898. www.meteorcrater.com. Admission $15 adults, $13 seniors, $6 children 6–17. Memorial Day to mid-Sept daily 7am–7pm; mid-Sept to Memorial Day daily 8am–5pm. Closed Christmas.

OTHER AREA ATTRACTIONS

In downtown Winslow, near that famous corner, you'll find the little **Old Trails Museum,** 212 Kinsley Ave., at Second Street (✆ **928/289-5861;** www.oldtrailsmuseum.org), which is something of a community attic and has exhibits on Route 66 and the Harvey Girls (who once worked in the nearby La Posada hotel; see the box "Fred Harvey & His Girls," above). The museum is open Tuesday through Saturday from 10am to 4pm. Admission is free.

Even if you aren't planning on staying the night at the restored **La Posada,** 303 E. Second St. (✆ **928/289-4366**), be sure to stop by just to see this historic railway hotel. Self-guided tours are available for a $3 donation.

On the windswept plains north of Winslow, 1¼ miles north of I-40, at exit 257, is **Homolovi Ruins State Park** (✆ **928/289-4106;** www.azstateparks.com), which preserves more than 300 Ancestral Puebloan archaeological sites, several of which have been partially excavated. Although these ruins are not nearly as impressive as those at Wupatki or Walnut Canyon, a visit here will give you a better understanding of the interrelationship of the many ancient pueblos of this region. Also in the park are numerous petroglyphs; ask for directions at the visitor center. Admission is $5 per vehicle. The ruins are open daily during daylight hours, but the visitor center is open only from 8am to 5pm. There's also a campground, charging $10 to $15 per site.

Continuing north from the state park, you'll find the little-known and little-visited **Little Painted Desert ★**, a 660-acre county park. To reach the park and its viewpoint overlooking the painted hills of this stark yet colorful landscape, continue north on Ariz. 87 from Homolovi Ruins State Park for another 12 miles.

If you're in the market for some Route 66 memorabilia, drop by **Roadworks,** 101 W. Second St. (✆ **928/289-5423;** www.roadworksroute66.com). Also, be sure to check out the **SNOWDRIFT Art Space,** 120 W. Second St. (✆ **928/289-8201;** www.snowdriftart.com), an art gallery/studio owned by artist Daniel Lutzick, who was one of the people who helped get the historic La Posada hotel up and running again.

WHERE TO STAY

In addition to the following historic hotel, you'll find lots of budget chain motels in Winslow.

La Posada ★★ (Finds) What an unexpected beauty this place is! Designed by Mary Elizabeth Jane Colter, architect of many of the buildings on the South Rim of the Grand Canyon, this railroad hotel first opened in 1930. Colter gave La Posada the feel of an old Spanish hacienda and even created a fictitious history for the building. In the lobby are numerous pieces of original furniture as well as reproductions of pieces once found in the hotel. The nicest rooms are the large units named for famous guests—Albert Einstein, Howard Hughes, Harry Truman, and Charles Lindbergh. The hotel's Turquoise Room (see "Where to Dine," below) is by far the best restaurant in the entire Four Corners region. La Posada is in the process of being slowly but completely restored and is reason enough to overnight in Winslow.

303 E. Second St. (Rte. 66), Winslow, AZ 86047. ✆ **928/289-4366.** Fax 928/289-3873. www.laposada.org. 51 units. $99–$169 double. AE, DC, DISC, MC, V. Pets accepted ($10 fee). **Amenities:** Restaurant; lounge; concierge; access to nearby health club; room service. *In room:* A/C, TV, hair dryer, Wi-Fi, no phone.

WHERE TO DINE

The Turquoise Room ★★ (Value) NEW AMERICAN/SOUTHWESTERN When Fred Harvey began his railroad hospitality career, his objective was to provide decent meals to the traveling public. (See "Fred Harvey & His Girls," on p. 98.) Here, in La Posada's reincarnated dining room, chef/owner John Sharpe prepares not just decent meals, but superb meals the likes of which you won't find anywhere else in northern Arizona. In summer, herbs and vegetables often come from the hotel's own gardens, and wild game is a specialty. Be sure to start your meal with the sweet-corn and black-bean soup, which is actually two soups served side by side in the same bowl to create a sort of yin-yang symbol. On top of all this, you can watch the trains rolling by just outside the window while you dine.

At La Posada, 303 E. Second St. ✆ **928/289-2888.** www.theturquoiseroom.net. Reservations recommended. Main courses $9–$13 lunch, $16–$31 dinner. AE, DISC, MC, V. Daily 7am–2pm and 5–9pm.

7 THE HOPI RESERVATION

67 miles N of Winslow; 250 miles NE of Phoenix; 100 miles SW of Canyon de Chelly; 140 miles SE of Page/ Lake Powell

The Hopi Reservation, often referred to as Hopiland or just Hopi, is completely encircled by the Navajo Reservation and has at its center a grouping of mesas upon which the Hopi have lived for nearly 1,000 years. This remote region, with its flat-topped mesas and barren landscape, is the center of the universe for the Hopi people. Here the Hopi follow their ancient customs, and many aspects of pueblo culture remain intact. However, much of the culture is hidden from the view of visitors, and although the Hopi perform elaborate religious and social dances throughout the year, many of these dances are not open to outsiders.

The mesas are home to two of the oldest continuously inhabited villages in North America—Walpi and Old Oraibi. Although these two communities show their age and serve as a direct tie to the pueblos of the Ancestral Puebloan culture, most of the villages on the reservation are scattered collections of modern homes. These villages are not destinations unto themselves, but along Ariz. 264 numerous crafts shops and studios sell kachinas, baskets, pottery, and silver jewelry. The chance to buy crafts directly from the Hopi is the main reason for a visit to this area, although you can also take a guided tour of Walpi village.

Important note: When visiting the Hopi pueblos, remember that you are a guest and your privileges can be revoked at any time. Respect all posted signs at village entrances, and remember that ***photographing, sketching, and recording are prohibited in the villages and at ceremonies.*** Also, kivas (ceremonial rooms) and ruins are off-limits.

ESSENTIALS

GETTING THERE This is one of the state's most remote regions. Distances are great, but highways are generally in good condition. Ariz. 87 leads from Winslow to Second Mesa, and Ariz. 264 runs from Tuba City in the west to the New Mexico state line in the east.

VISITOR INFORMATION For advance information, contact the **Hopi Cultural Preservation Office,** P.O. Box 123, Kykotsmovi, AZ 86039 (© **928/734-3612;** www.nau.edu/~hcpo-p).

THE VILLAGES

With the exception of Upper and Lower Moenkopi, which are near the Navajo town of Tuba City, and the recently settled Yuh Weh Loo Pah Ki community, east of Keams Canyon, the Hopi villages are scattered along roughly 20 miles of Ariz. 264. Although Old Oraibi is the oldest, there are no tours of this village, and visitors are not likely to feel very welcome here. Consequently, Walpi, the only village with organized tours, is the best place for visitors to learn more about life in the Hopi villages. We mention all of the Hopi villages below to provide a bit of history and perspective on this area, but for the most part, these villages (with the exception of Walpi and Old Oraibi) are not at all picturesque. However, most do have quite a few crafts galleries and stores selling silver jewelry.

FIRST MESA At the top of First Mesa is the village of **Walpi,** parts of which today still look much like the ruins of Ancestral Puebloan villages in such locations as Canyon de

Chelly, Navajo National Monument, and Wupatki National Monument. Small stone houses seem to grow directly from the rock of the mesa top, and ladders jut from the roofs of kivas. The view from the village stretches for hundreds of miles, and it is easy to see why the Hopi settled on this spot. Walpi was originally located lower on the slopes of First Mesa, but after the Pueblo Revolt of 1680 brought on fear of reprisal from the Spanish, villagers moved to the top of the mesa so that they could better defend themselves in the event of a Spanish attack.

Immediately adjacent to Walpi are the two villages of **Sichomovi,** which was founded in 1750 as a colony of Walpi, and **Hano,** which was founded by Tewa peoples who were most likely seeking refuge from the Spanish after the Pueblo Revolt. Neither of these villages has the ancient character of Walpi. At the foot of First Mesa is **Polacca,** a settlement founded in the late 1800s by Walpi villagers who wanted to be closer to the trading post and school.

SECOND MESA Second Mesa is today the center of tourism in Hopiland and is where you'll find the Hopi Cultural Center. Villages on Second Mesa include **Shungopavi,** which was moved to its present site after Old Shungopavi was abandoned in 1680 following the Pueblo Revolt. Old Shungopavi is said to be the first Hopi village and was founded by the Bear Clan. Shungopavi is notable for its silver jewelry and its coiled plaques (flat baskets).

Mishongnovi, which means "place of the black man," is named for the leader of a clan that came here from the San Francisco Peaks around 1200. The original Mishongnovi village, located at the base of the mesa, was abandoned in the 1690s, and the village was reestablished at the current site atop the mesa. The Snake Dance is held here during odd-numbered years. It is doubtful that these dances will be open to non-Hopis, although you could check with the Hopi Cultural Preservation Office (see "Visitor Information," above).

Sipaulovi, which is located on the eastern edge of the mesa, was founded after the Pueblo Revolt of 1680.

THIRD MESA **Oraibi,** which the Hopi claim is the oldest continuously occupied town in the United States, is located on Third Mesa. The village dates from 1150 and, according to legend, was founded by people from Old Shungopavi. A Spanish mission was established in Oraibi in 1629, and the ruins are still visible north of the village. Today, Oraibi is a mix of old stone houses and modern ones, usually of cinder block. Wander around Oraibi, and you'll likely be approached by village women and children offering to sell you various local crafts and the traditional blue-corn *piki* bread. You may also be invited into someone's home to see the crafts they have to offer. For this reason, Old Oraibi is the most interesting village in which to shop for local crafts.

For centuries, Oraibi was the largest of the Hopi villages, but in 1906, a schism arose due to Bureau of Indian Affairs policies, and many of the villagers left to form **Hotevilla.** This is considered the most conservative of the Hopi villages and has had frequent confrontations with the federal government. **Kykotsmovi,** also known as Lower Oraibi or New Oraibi, was founded in 1890 by villagers from Oraibi who wanted to be closer to the school and trading post. This village is the seat of the Hopi Tribal Government. **Bacavi** was founded in 1907 by villagers who had helped found Hotevilla but who later decided that they wanted to return to Oraibi. The people of Oraibi would not let them return, and rather than go back to Hotevilla, they founded a new village.

MOENKOPI This village is 40 miles to the west of the Hopi mesas. Founded in 1870 by people from Oraibi, Moenkopi sits in the center of a wide green valley where plentiful water makes farming more reliable. Moenkopi is only a few miles from Tuba City off U.S. 160 and is divided into the villages of Upper Moenkopi and Lower Moenkopi.

EXPLORING THE WORLD OF THE HOPI

Start your visit to the Hopi pueblos at the **Hopi Cultural Center,** on Ariz. 264 in Second Mesa (✆ **928/734-6650**). This combination museum, motel, and restaurant is the tourism headquarters for the area. The museum is open Monday through Friday from 8am to 5pm and Saturday and Sunday from 9am to 3pm. Admission is $3 for adults and $1 for children 13 and under.

From here, it's just a few miles to the Second Mesa village of Sipaulovi and the **Sipaulovi Visitor Center** (✆ **928/737-5426;** www.sipaulovihopiinformationcenter.org). At the visitor center, you can watch a 20-minute video about the Hopi culture and arrange for a 1-hour walking tour of Sipaulovi. Tours are offered Monday through Friday from 9am to 4pm (Sat–Sun by reservation) and cost $15.

The most rewarding Hopi village to visit is **Walpi** ★, on First Mesa. Guided tours of this tiny village are offered daily between 10am and 3pm (shorter hours in winter). Admission is $13 for adults, $10 for youths age 14 to 17, and $5 for children 5 to 13. To sign up for a tour, drive to the top of First Mesa (in Polacca, take the road that says FIRST MESA VILLAGE) and continue through the village to **Ponsi Hall Visitor Center** (✆ **928/737-2262**), where you'll see signs for the tours. The tours, which last 1 hour, are led by Hopis who will tell you the history of the village and explain a bit about the local culture.

About 1½ miles north of the community of Keams Canyon, in the pretty little canyon for which this historic community is named, you'll find, carved into the stone walls of the canyon, an inscription left by Colonel "Kit" Carson. It was Carson who led the war on the Navajos during the summer of 1863 and who, to defeat the tribe, burned their crops, effectively leaving the Navajos with no winter supplies. The inscription reads simply, "1st Regt. N.M. Vols. Aug 13th 1863 Col. C. Carson Com." To find the inscription, turn off Ariz. 264 in Keams Canyon and drive north on the main road through the community. You'll also find some picnic tables along this road.

CULTURAL TOURS

To get the most out of a visit to the Hopi mesas, it is best to book a guided tour. With a guide, you will learn much more about this rather insular culture than you ever could on your own. Tour companies frequently use local guides and stop at the homes of working artisans. This all adds up to a more in-depth and educational visit to one of the oldest cultures on the continent.

Bertram Tsavadawa at **Ancient Pathways Tours** (✆ **928/797-8145;** www.experience hopi.com/tourcompanies.html) specializes in tours to Hopi petroglyph sites. These are sites that are not open to the public unless you are with a Hopi guide. Three-hour tours cost $75 for adults and $35 for children under 18; 6-hour tours cost $165 for adults and $80 for children. One-hour tours of Old Oraibi ($15 for adults and $7.50 for children) can also be arranged.

DANCES & CEREMONIES

The Hopi have developed the most complex religious ceremonies of any of the Southwest tribes. The masked kachina dances for which they are most famous are held from January to July. However, most kachina dances are closed to the non-Hopi public. Social dances (usually open to the public) are held August through February. If you're on the reservation during these months, ask if any dances are taking place. Who knows? You might get lucky. Snake Dances (usually closed to the non-Hopi public) are held August through December.

Kachinas, whether in the form of dolls or masked dancers, are representative of the spirits of everything from plants and animals to ancestors and sacred places. More than 300 kachinas appear on a regular basis in Hopi ceremonies, and another 200 appear occasionally. The kachina spirits are said to live in the San Francisco Peaks to the southwest and at Spring of the Shadows in the east. According to legend, the kachinas lived with the Hopi long ago, but the Hopi people made the kachinas angry, causing them to leave. Before departing, though, the kachinas taught the Hopi how to perform their ceremonies.

Today, the kachina ceremonies, performed by men wearing elaborate costumes and masks, serve several purposes. Most important, they bring clouds and rain to water the all-important corn crop, but they also ensure health, happiness, long life, and harmony in the universe. As part of the kachina ceremonies, dancers often bring carved wooden kachina dolls to village children to introduce them to the various spirits.

The kachina season lasts from the winter solstice until shortly after the summer solstice. The actual dates for dances are usually announced only shortly before the ceremonies are to be held. Preparations for the dances take place inside kivas that are entered from the roof by means of a ladder; the dances themselves are usually held in a village square or street.

With ludicrous and sometimes lewd mimicry, clowns known as *koyemsi, koshares,* and *tsukus* entertain spectators between the dances, bringing a lighthearted counterpoint to the very serious nature of the kachina dances. Non-Hopis attending dances have often become the focus of attention for these clowns.

Despite the importance of the kachina dances, it is the **Snake Dance** that has captured the attention of many non-Hopis. The Snake Dance involves the handling of poisonous and nonpoisonous snakes alike. The ceremony takes place over 16 days, with the first 4 days dedicated to collecting snakes from the four cardinal directions. Later, footraces are held from the bottom of the mesa to the top. On the last day of the ceremony, the actual Snake Dance is performed. Men of the Snake Society form pairs of dancers—one to carry the snake in his mouth and the other to distract the snake with an eagle feather. When all the snakes have been danced around the plaza, they are rushed down to their homes at the bottom of the mesa to carry the Hopi prayers for rain to the spirits of the underworld.

Due to the disrespectful attitude of some past visitors, many ceremonies and dances are now closed to non-Hopis. However, a couple of Hopi villages do allow visitors to attend some of their dances. The best way to find out about attending dances is to contact the **Hopi Cultural Preservation office** (see "Visitor Information," above).

SHOPPING

Most visitors come to the reservation to shop for Hopi crafts. Across the reservation, dozens of small shops sell crafts and jewelry of different quality, and some homes, especially at the foot of First Mesa, have signs indicating that they sell crafts. Shops often sell the work of only a few individuals, so you should stop at several to get an idea of the variety of work available. Also, if you tour Walpi or wander around in Oraibi, you will likely be approached by villagers selling various crafts, including kachina dolls. The quality will not be as high as that in shops, but then, neither are the prices.

At Keams Canyon, almost 30 miles east of the cultural center, you'll find **McGee's Indian Art Gallery** (✆ **928/738-2295;** www.hopiart.com), which is the best place on the reservation to shop for high-quality contemporary kachina dolls. This shop is adjacent to a grocery store and has been a trading post for more than 100 years.

If you're in the market for Hopi silver jewelry, stop in at **Hopi Fine Arts** (✆ **928/737-2222**), which is at the foot of Second Mesa at the junction of Ariz. 264 and Ariz. 87. This shop also has a good selection of kachina dolls and some beautiful coil and wicker plaque baskets.

One of the best places to get a quick education in Hopi art and crafts is **Tsakurshovi** ★ (✆ **928/734-2478**), a tiny shop 1½ miles east of the Hopi Cultural Center on Second Mesa. This shop has a huge selection of traditional kachina dolls and also has lots of jewelry. Janice and Joseph Day, the owners, are very friendly and are always happy to share their expertise with visitors. This is also where you can buy a "Don't Worry Be Hopi" T-shirt.

If you're interested in kachina dolls, be sure to visit Oraibi's **Monongya Gallery** (✆ **928/734-2344**), a big building right on Ariz. 264 outside of Oraibi. It usually has one of the largest selections of kachina dolls in the area. Also in Oraibi is **Hamana So-o's Arts & Crafts** (✆ **928/206-6392**), which is in an old stone house from which owner Sandra Hamana sells primarily artwork and crafts based on kachina images.

WHERE TO STAY & DINE

If you've brought your food along, you'll find picnic tables just east of Oraibi on top of the mesa. These tables have an amazing view!

Hopi Cultural Center Restaurant & Inn Although it isn't much, this simple motel makes the best base for anyone planning to spend a couple of days shopping for crafts in the area. Because it is the only lodging for miles around, be sure you have a reservation before heading up for an overnight visit. Guest rooms are comfortable enough, though the grounds are quite desolate. The restaurant has a salad bar and serves American and traditional Hopi meals, including *piki* bread (a paper-thin bread made from blue corn) and Hopi stew, which is made with hominy, lamb, and green chili. There's also a small museum.

P.O. Box 67, Second Mesa, AZ 86043. ✆ **928/734-2401.** Fax 928/734-6651. www.hopiculturalcenter.com. 30 units. Mar 15–Oct 15 $101–$105 double; Oct 16–Mar 14 $81–$85 double. Children 12 and under stay free in parent's room. AE, DISC, MC, V. **Amenities:** Restaurant. *In room:* A/C, TV, free local calls.

EN ROUTE TO OR FROM THE HOPI MESAS

On the west side of the reservation, in Tuba City, is the **Tuba City Trading Post,** Main Street and Moenave Avenue (✆ **928/283-5441**). This octagonal trading post was built in 1906 of local stone and is designed to resemble a Navajo hogan or traditional home (there's also a real hogan on the grounds). The trading post sells Native American crafts, with an emphasis on books, music, and jewelry. Across the parking lot from the trading post, you'll find **Hogan Espresso,** Main Street and Moenave Avenue (✆ **800/644-8383** or 928/283-4545), one of the few places on the reservation where you can get espresso. Behind the trading post, you'll find the **Explore Navajo Interactive Museum,** 10 N. Main St. (✆ **928/640-0684**), a small museum in a tentlike structure that was used at the 2002 Salt Lake City Olympics. Although small, the museum provides a good introduction to Navajo culture. There is also a good Navajo code talkers exhibit here. The museum is open Monday through Friday 9am to 5pm; Saturday 9am to 4pm. Admission is $9 for adults, $7 for seniors, and $6 for children ages 7 to 12.

On the western outskirts of Tuba City, on U.S. 160, you'll find **Van's Trading Co.** (✆ **928/283-5343;** vanstradingcompany.com), in the corner of a large grocery store. Van's has a dead-pawn auction on the 15th of each month at 3pm (any pawned item not reclaimed by the owner by a specified date is considered "dead pawn"). The auction provides opportunities to buy older pieces of Navajo silver-and-turquoise jewelry.

West of Tuba City and just off U.S. 160, you can see **dinosaur footprints** ★ preserved in the stone surface of the desert. There are usually a few people waiting at the site to guide visitors to the best footprints (these guides will expect a tip of $1–$2). The scenery out your car window is some of the strangest in the region—you'll see lots of red-rock sandstone formations that resemble petrified sand dunes.

The **Cameron Trading Post** ★ (✆ **800/338-7385** or 928/679-2231; www.camerontradingpost.com), 16 miles south of the junction of U.S. 160 and U.S. 89, is well worth a visit. The main trading post is filled with souvenirs but has large selections of rugs and jewelry as well. In the adjacent stone-walled gallery are museum-quality Native American artifacts (with prices to match). The trading post includes a motel (p. 546), convenience store, and gas station.

Where to Stay

Quality Inn Navajo Nation Located in the bustling Navajo community of Tuba City (where you'll find gas stations, fast-food restaurants, and grocery stores), this modern hotel is adjacent to the historic Tuba City Trading Post and is actually a more attractive place to stay in this region than the Hopi Cultural Center. The hotel offers comfortable rooms of average size, but the green lawns, shade trees, and old trading post (complete with hogan) are what really set this place apart. This hotel is also adjacent to the Explore Navajo Interactive Museum (see above).

Main St. and Moenave Ave. (P.O. Box 247), Tuba City, AZ 86045. ✆ **800/644-8383** or 928/283-4545. Fax 928/283-4144. www.qualityinntubacity.com. 80 units. Apr–Oct $108–$140 double; Nov–Mar $88–$118 double. Rates include full breakfast. Children 17 and under stay free in parent's room. AE, DC, DISC, MC, V. Pets accepted ($10 per day). **Amenities:** Restaurant. *In room:* A/C, TV, hair dryer, Wi-Fi.

8 THE PETRIFIED FOREST ★

25 miles E of Holbrook; 90 miles E of Flagstaff; 118 miles S of Canyon de Chelly; 180 miles N of Phoenix

Petrified wood has long fascinated people, and although it can be found in almost every state, the "forest" of downed logs in northeastern Arizona is by far the most extensive. But don't head out this way expecting to see standing trees of stone with leaves and branches intact. Although there is enough petrified timber scattered across this landscape to fill a forest, it is, in fact, in the form of broken logs and not standing trees. Many a visitor has shown up expecting to find some sort of national forest of stone trees. The reality is much less impressive than the petrified forest of the imagination.

However, this area is still unique. When, in the 1850s, this vast treasure-trove of petrified wood was discovered, scattered like kindling across the landscape, enterprising people began exporting it wholesale to the East. Within 50 years, so much had been removed that in 1906 several areas were set aside as the Petrified Forest National Monument, which, in 1962, became a national park. A 27-mile scenic drive winds through the petrified forest (and a small corner of the Painted Desert), providing a fascinating high-desert experience.

It may be hard to believe as you drive across this arid landscape, but at one time this area was a vast steamy swamp. That was 225 million years ago, when dinosaurs and huge amphibians ruled the earth and giant now-extinct trees grew on the high ground around the swamp. Fallen trees were washed downstream, gathered in piles in quiet backwaters, and eventually were covered over with silt, mud, and volcanic ash. As water seeped through this soil, it dissolved the silica in the volcanic ash and redeposited the silica inside the cells of the logs. Eventually, the silica recrystallized into stone to form petrified wood, with minerals such as iron, manganese, and carbon contributing the distinctive colors.

This region was later inundated with water, and thick deposits of sediment buried the logs ever deeper. Eventually, the land was transformed yet again as a geologic upheaval thrust the lake bottom up above sea level. This upthrust of the land cracked the logs into the segments we see today. Wind and water gradually eroded the landscape to create the Painted Desert, and the petrified logs were once again exposed on the surface of the land.

ESSENTIALS

GETTING THERE The north entrance to Petrified Forest National Park is 25 miles east of Holbrook on I-40. The south entrance is 20 miles east of Holbrook on U.S. 180.

FEES The entry fee is $10 per car. Between late May and early September, the park is open from 7am to 7pm; other months it is open from 8am to 5pm.

VISITOR INFORMATION For further information on the Petrified Forest or the Painted Desert, contact **Petrified Forest National Park,** P.O. Box 2217, Petrified Forest, AZ 86028 (© **928/524-6228;** www.nps.gov/pefo). For information on Holbrook and the surrounding region, contact the **Holbrook Chamber of Commerce Visitor Center & Museum,** 100 E. Arizona St. (© **800/524-2459** or 928/524-6558; www.gotouraz.com/holbrook).

EXPLORING A UNIQUE LANDSCAPE

Petrified Forest National Park has both a north and a south entrance. If you are coming from the west, it's better to start at the southern entrance and work your way north along the park's 27-mile scenic road, which has more than 20 overlooks. This way, you'll see the most impressive displays of petrified logs early in your visit and save the Painted Desert vistas for last. If you're coming from the east, start at the northern entrance and work your way south.

The **Rainbow Forest Museum** (© **928/524-6228**), just inside the south entrance to the park, is the best place to begin your tour. Here you can learn all about petrified wood, watch an introductory film, and otherwise get oriented. Exhibits chronicle the area's geologic and human history. There are also displays on the reptiles and dinosaurs that once inhabited this region. The museum sells maps and books and also issues free backpacking permits. It's open daily from 8am to 5pm (7am–7pm in summer). Adjacent to the museum is a snack bar.

The **Giant Logs self-guided trail** starts behind the museum. The trail winds across a hillside strewn with logs that are 4 to 5 feet in diameter. Almost directly across the parking lot from the museum is the entrance to the **Long Logs** and **Agate House** areas. On the 1.6-mile Long Logs trail, you can see more big trees, while at Agate House, a 2-mile round-trip hike will lead you to the ruins of a pueblo built from colorful petrified wood. These two trails can be combined into a 2.5-mile hike.

> **Fun Facts** **Rock Talk**
>
> Gift shops throughout this region sell petrified wood in all sizes and colors, natural and polished. This petrified wood does not come from the national park, but is collected on private land in the area. No piece of petrified wood, no matter how small, may be removed from Petrified Forest National Park.

Heading north, you'll pass by the unusual formations known as the **Flattops.** These structures were caused by the erosion of softer mineral deposits from beneath a harder and more erosion-resistant layer of sandstone. The Flattops is one of the park's wilderness areas. The **Crystal Forest** is the next stop to the north, named for the beautiful amethyst and quartz crystals once found in the cracks of petrified logs. Concern over the removal of these crystals was what led to the protection of the petrified forest. A .75-mile loop trail winds past the logs that once held the crystals.

At the **Jasper Forest Overlook,** you can see logs that include petrified roots, and a little bit farther north, at the **Agate Bridge** stop, you can see a petrified log that forms a natural agate bridge. Continuing north, you'll reach **Blue Mesa,** where pieces of petrified wood form capstones over easily eroded clay soils. As wind and water wear away at the clay beneath a piece of stone, the balance of the stone becomes more and more precarious until it eventually comes toppling down. A 1-mile loop trail here leads into the park's badlands.

Erosion has played a major role in the formation of the Painted Desert, and to the north of Blue Mesa you'll see some of the most interesting erosional features of the area. It's quite evident why these hills of sandstone and clay are known as the **Teepees.** The layers of different color are due to manganese, iron, and other minerals in the soil.

By this point, you've probably seen as much petrified wood as you'd ever care to see, so be sure to stop at **Newspaper Rock,** where instead of staring at more ancient logs, you can see a dense concentration of petroglyphs left by generations of Native Americans. Unfortunately you can no longer get close to these petroglyphs, so you'll have to be content to observe them from a distance. At nearby **Puerco Pueblo,** the park's largest archaeological site, you can view the remains of homes built by the people who created the park's petroglyphs. This pueblo was probably occupied around A.D. 1400. Don't miss the petroglyphs on its back side.

North of Puerco Pueblo, the road crosses I-40. From here to the Painted Desert Visitor Center, there are eight overlooks onto the southernmost edge of the **Painted Desert.** Named for the vivid colors of the soil and stone that cover the land here, the Painted Desert is a dreamscape of pastels washed across a barren expanse of eroded hills. The colors are created by minerals dissolved in sandstone and clay soils that were deposited during different geologic periods. There's a picnic area at Chinde Point overlook. At Kachina Point, you'll find the **Painted Desert Inn,** a renovated historic building that is operated as a bookstore and museum. From here, there's access to the park's other wilderness area. The inn, which was built in 1924 and expanded by the Civilian Conservation Corps, is noteworthy for both its architecture and the Fred Kabotie murals on the interior walls. Hours are 9am to 5pm daily. Between Kachina Point and Tawa Point, you can do an easy 1-mile round-trip hike along the rim of the Painted Desert. An even more interesting route leads down into the Painted Desert from behind the Painted Desert Inn.

Just inside the northern entrance to the park is the **Painted Desert Visitor Center** (✆ **928/524-6228**), open daily 8am to 5pm (7am–7pm in summer), where you can watch a short film that explains the process by which wood becomes fossilized. Adjacent to the visitor center are a cafeteria, a bookshop, and a gas station.

OTHER REASONS TO LINGER IN HOLBROOK

Although the Petrified Forest National Park is the main reason for visiting this area, you might want to stop by downtown Holbrook's **Old West Museum,** 100 E. Arizona St. (✆ **928/524-6558**), which also houses the Holbrook Chamber of Commerce visitor center. This old and dusty museum has exhibits on local history but is most interesting for its old jail cells. It's open Monday through Friday from 8am to 5pm and Saturday and Sunday from 8am to 4pm; admission is free. On weekday evenings between June and July, the Holbrook Chamber sponsors Native American dances on the lawn in front.

Although it is against the law to collect petrified wood inside Petrified Forest National Park, there are several rock shops in Holbrook where you can buy legally collected pieces of petrified wood in all shapes and sizes. You'll find them lined up along the main street through town and out on U.S. 180, the highway leading to the south entrance of Petrified Forest National Park. The biggest and best of these rock shops is **Jim Gray's Petrified Wood Co.,** 147 Hwy. 180 (✆ **928/524-1842;** www.petrifiedwoodco.com), which has everything from raw rocks to $24,000 petrified-wood coffee tables. This store also has a fascinating display of minerals and fossils. It's open daily from 7:30am to 7pm (longer hours in summer) and is well worth a stop.

If you're interested in petroglyphs, you may want to schedule a visit to the **Rock Art Ranch** ★ (✆ **928/288-3260** or 928/386-5047), southwest of Holbrook, on part of the old Hashknife Ranch, which was the largest ranch in the country during the late 19th century. Within the bounds of this ranch, pecked into the rock walls of Chevelon Canyon, are hundreds of Ancestral Puebloan petroglyphs. The setting, a narrow canyon that is almost invisible until you are right beside it, is enchanting, making this the finest place in the state to view petroglyphs. Tours (reservations required) are available Monday through Saturday at 9 and 11am (call to get rate information and directions to the ranch).

WHERE TO STAY & DINE

Holbrook, the town nearest to Petrified Forest National Park, offers lots of budget chain motels charging very reasonable rates.

While there are plenty of inexpensive restaurants in Holbrook, none is particularly memorable or recommendable. Your best bet is to drive over to Winslow to the Turquoise Room at La Posada hotel.

Wigwam Motel (Finds) If you're willing to sleep on a saggy mattress for the sake of reliving a bit of Route 66 history, don't miss this collection of concrete wigwams (tepees, actually). This unique motel was built in the 1940s, when unusual architecture was springing up all along famous Route 66. The motel has been owned by the same family since it was built and still has the original rustic furniture. Old cars are kept in the parking lot for an added dose of Route 66 character.

811 W. Hopi Dr., Holbrook, AZ 86025. ✆ **928/524-3048.** Fax 928/524-3048. www.galerie-kokopelli.com/wigwam. 15 units. $52–$58 double. MC, V. Pets accepted. *In room:* A/C, TV.

9 CANYON DE CHELLY NATIONAL MONUMENT ★★★

68 miles NW of Window Rock; 222 miles NE of Flagstaff; 110 miles SE of Navajo National Monument; 110 miles SE of Monument Valley Navajo Tribal Park

It's hard to imagine narrow canyons less than 1,000 feet deep being more spectacular than the Grand Canyon, but in some ways Canyon de Chelly National Monument is just that. Gaze down from the rim at an ancient cliff dwelling as the whinnying of horses and clanging of goat bells drift up from far below, and you'll be struck by the continuity of human existence. For more than 2,000 years, people have called these canyons home, and today the canyon is the site of not only prehistoric dwelling sites, but also the summer homes of Navajo farmers and shepherds.

Canyon de Chelly National Monument consists primarily of two major canyons—Canyon de Chelly (which is pronounced "Canyon duh Shay" and is derived from the Navajo word *tsegi,* meaning "rock canyon") and Canyon del Muerto (Spanish for "Canyon of the Dead"). The canyons extend for more than 100 miles through the rugged slickrock landscape of northeastern Arizona, draining the seasonal snowmelt runoff from the Chuska Mountains.

In summer, Canyon de Chelly's smooth sandstone walls of red and yellow contrast sharply with the greens of corn, pastures, and cottonwoods on the canyon floor. Vast stone amphitheaters form the caves in which the Ancestral Puebloans built their homes, and as you watch shadows and light paint an ever-changing canyon panorama, it's easy to see why the Navajo consider this sacred ground. The many mysteriously abandoned cliff dwellings and the breathtaking natural beauty make Canyon de Chelly as worthy of a visit as the Grand Canyon.

ESSENTIALS

GETTING THERE From Flagstaff, the easiest route to Canyon de Chelly is I-40 to U.S. 191 to Ganado. At Ganado, drive west on Ariz. 264 and pick up U.S. 191 N. to Chinle. If you're coming down from Monument Valley or Navajo National Monument, Indian Rte. 59, which connects U.S. 160 and U.S. 191, is an excellent road with plenty of beautiful scenery.

FEES Monument admission is free.

VISITOR INFORMATION Before leaving home, you can contact **Canyon de Chelly National Monument,** P.O. Box 588, Chinle, AZ 86503 (✆ **928/674-5500;** www.nps.gov/cach), for information. The monument itself is open daily from sunrise to sunset. The visitor center is open daily 8am to 5pm (closed Christmas day). Remember that the Navajo Nation observes daylight saving time.

SPECIAL EVENTS The annual **Central Navajo Fair** is held in Chinle in August.

EXPLORING THE CANYON

Your first stop should be the **visitor center** (see above), in front of which is an example of a traditional crib-style hogan, a hexagonal structure of logs and earth that Navajos use as both a home and a ceremonial center. Inside the visitor center, a small museum explores the history of Canyon de Chelly, and there's often a silversmith demonstrating Navajo jewelry-making techniques. Interpretive programs are offered at the monument

Taking Photos on the Reservations

Before taking a photograph of a Navajo, always ask permission. If it's granted, a tip of $1 or more is expected. Photography is not allowed at all in Hopi villages.

from Memorial Day to Labor Day. Check at the visitor center for daily activities, such as campfire programs and natural-history programs.

From the visitor center, most people tour the canyon by car. Very different views of the monument's system of canyons are provided by the 15-mile North Rim and 16-mile South Rim drives. The North Rim Drive overlooks Canyon del Muerto, while the South Rim Drive overlooks Canyon de Chelly. With stops, the drive along either rim road can easily take 2 to 3 hours. If you have time for only one, make it the South Rim Drive, which provides both a dramatic view of Spider Rock and the chance to hike down into the canyon on the only trail you can explore without hiring a guide. If, on the other hand, you're more interested in the history and prehistory of this area, opt for the North Rim Drive, which overlooks several historically significant sites within the canyon.

The North Rim Drive

The first stop on the North Rim is the **Ledge Ruin Overlook.** On the opposite wall, about 100 feet up from the canyon floor, you can see the Ledge Ruin. This site was occupied by the Ancestral Puebloans between 1050 and 1275. Nearby, at the unmarked Dekaa Kiva Viewpoint, you can see a lone kiva (circular ceremonial building). This structure was reached by means of toeholds cut into the soft sandstone cliff wall.

The second stop is the **Antelope House Overlook,** which is the all-around most interesting overlook in the monument. Not only do you get to hike .25 mile over the rugged rimrock landscape, but you also get to view ruins, rock art, and impressive cliff walls. The Antelope House ruin takes its name from the antelope paintings, believed to date back to the 1830s, on a nearby cliff wall. Beneath the ruins of Antelope House, archaeologists have found the remains of an earlier pit house dating from A.D. 693. Although most of the Ancestral Puebloan cliff dwellings were abandoned sometime after a drought began in 1276, Antelope House had already been abandoned by 1260, possibly because of damage caused by flooding. Across the wash from Antelope House, an ancient tomb, known as the Tomb of the Weaver, was discovered by archaeologists in the 1920s. The tomb contained the well-preserved body of an old man wrapped in a blanket of golden eagle feathers and accompanied by cornmeal, shelled and husked corn, pine nuts, beans, salt, and thick skeins of cotton. Also visible from this overlook is Navajo Fortress, a red-sandstone butte that the Navajo once used as a refuge from attackers. A steep trail once led to the top of Navajo Fortress, and by using log ladders that could be pulled up into the refuge, the Navajo were able to escape their attackers.

The third stop is **Mummy Cave Overlook,** named for two mummies found in burial urns below the ruins. Archaeological evidence indicates that this giant amphitheater consisting of two caves was occupied for 1,000 years, from A.D. 300 to 1300. In the two caves and on the shelf between are 80 rooms, including three kivas. The central structure between the two caves includes an interesting three-story building characteristic of the architecture in Mesa Verde in New Mexico. Archaeologists speculate that a group of Ancestral Puebloans migrated here from New Mexico. Much of the original plasterwork is still intact and indicates that the buildings were colorfully decorated.

The fourth and last stop on the North Rim is the **Massacre Cave Overlook,** which got its name after an 1805 Spanish military expedition killed more than 115 Navajo at this site. The Navajo at the time had been raiding Spanish settlements that were encroaching on their territory. Accounts of the battle at Massacre Cave differ. One version claims there were only women, children, and old men taking shelter in the cave, but the official Spanish records claim 90 warriors and 25 women and children were killed. Also visible from this overlook is Yucca Cave, which was occupied about 1,000 years ago.

The South Rim Drive

The South Rim Drive climbs slowly but steadily, and at each stop you're a little bit higher above the canyon floor. Near the mouth of the canyon is the **Tunnel Overlook,** where a short narrow canyon feeds into Chinle Wash, a wash formed by the streams that cut through the canyons of the national monument. *Tsegi* is a Navajo word meaning "rock canyon," and at the nearby **Tsegi Overlook,** that's just what you'll see when you gaze down from the viewpoint.

The next stop is the **Junction Overlook,** so named because it overlooks the junction of Canyon del Muerto and Canyon de Chelly. Here you can see the Junction Ruin, which has 10 rooms and a kiva. Ancestral Puebloans occupied this ruin during the Great Pueblo Period, which lasted from around 1100 until shortly before 1300. First Ruin, which is perched precariously on a long narrow ledge, is also visible. There are 22 rooms and two kivas in this ruin. Good luck picking out the two canyons in this maze of curving cliff walls.

The third stop is **White House Overlook,** from which you can see the 80-room White House Ruins, which are among the largest ruins in the canyon. These buildings were inhabited between 1040 and 1275. From this overlook, you have your only opportunity to descend into Canyon de Chelly without a guide or ranger. The **White House Ruins Trail ★★** descends 600 feet to the canyon floor and crosses Chinle Wash before reaching the White House Ruins. The buildings of this ruin were constructed both on the canyon floor and 50 feet up the cliff wall in a small cave. Although you cannot enter the ruins, you can get close enough to get a good look. Do not wander off this trail, and please respect the privacy of the Navajo living here. The 2.5-mile round-trip hike takes about 2 hours. Be sure to carry water.

Notice the black streaks on the sandstone walls above the White House Ruins. These streaks, known as desert varnish, are formed by seeping water, which reacts with iron in the sandstone (iron is what gives the walls their reddish hue). To create the canyon's many petroglyphs, Ancestral Puebloan artists would chip away at the desert varnish. Later, the Navajo used paints to create pictographs of animals and historical events, such as the Spanish military expedition that killed 115 Navajo at Massacre Cave. Many of these petroglyphs and pictographs can be seen if you take a guided tour into the canyon.

The fifth stop is **Sliding House Overlook.** These ruins were built on a narrow shelf and appear to be sliding down into the canyon. Inhabited from about 900 until 1200, Sliding House contained between 30 and 50 rooms. This overlook is already more than 700 feet above the canyon floor, with sheer walls giving the narrow canyon a very foreboding appearance.

On the last access road to the canyon rim, you'll come to the **Face Rock Overlook,** which provides yet another dizzying glimpse of the ever-deepening canyon. Here you gaze 1,000 feet down to the bottom. However, it is the next stop—**Spider Rock Overlook ★★**—that offers the monument's most spectacular view. This viewpoint overlooks the junction of Canyon de Chelly and Monument Canyon. The monolithic pinnacle known as Spider Rock rises 800 feet from the canyon floor, its two free-standing towers forming a natural monument. Across the canyon from Spider Rock is the similarly striking **Speaking Rock,** which is connected to the far canyon wall.

Other Ways to See the Canyon

Access to the floor of Canyon de Chelly is restricted; unless you're on the White House Ruins Trail (see "The South Rim Drive," above), you must be accompanied by an authorized guide in order to enter the canyon. **Navajo guides** usually charge $15 per hour with a 3-hour minimum and will lead you into the canyon on foot or in your own four-wheel-drive vehicle. **De Chelly Tours** (© **928/674-3772** or 928/814-5396; www.acanyondechellytour.com) charges $125 for a 3-hour guided Jeep tour for up to three people. Similar tours are offered by **Canyon de Chelly Tours** (© **928/674-5433** or 928/349-1600; www.canyondechellytours.com), which will take you into the canyon in a Jeep or a Unimog truck (a powerful four-wheel-drive off-road vehicle). Unimog tours are $60 to $66 for adults and $40 to $44 for children 12 and under; Jeep tours are $175 to $193 for 3-hour tours for up to three people. Tours depart from the Holiday Inn parking lot. Reservations are recommended. The monument visitor center also maintains a list of guides.

Another way to see Canyon de Chelly and Canyon del Muerto is on what locals call **shake-and-bake tours** ★, via a six-wheel-drive truck. In summer, these excursions really live up to the name. (In winter, the truck is enclosed to keep out the elements.) The trucks operate out of **Thunderbird Lodge** (© **800/679-2473;** www.tbirdlodge.com) and are equipped with seats in the bed. Tours make frequent stops for photographs and to visit ruins, Navajo farms, and rock art. Half-day trips cost $46 per person ($35 for children 12 and under), while full-day tours cost $74 for all ages. Full-day tours, offered spring through fall, leave at 9am and return at 5pm.

If you'd rather use a more traditional means of transportation, you can go on a guided horseback ride. To leave the crowds behind, drive east along South Rim Drive to **Totsonii Ranch** ★ (© **928/755-2037;** www.totsoniiranch.com), which is 1¼ miles past the end of the paved stretch of this road. Rides from here visit a remote part of the canyon (including the Spider Rock area) and cost $15 per group per hour for the guide and $15 per person per hour. Totsonii Ranch also offers overnight rides for $335 per person and 2-night rides for $515 per person.

If you're physically fit and like hiking, consider hiring a guide to lead you into the canyon. Hikes can start at the White House Ruin trail, near the Spider Rock overlook, or from near the Antelope House overlook. These latter two starting points are trails that are not open to the public without a guide and should be your top choices. The hike from Antelope House gets our vote for best option for a hike. Guides can often be hired at the monument visitor center. Guides charge $15 per hour for up to 15 people.

SHOPPING

The **Thunderbird Lodge Gift Shop,** in Chinle (© **800/679-2473**), is well worth a stop while you're in the area. It has a large collection of rugs, as well as a good selection of pottery and plenty of souvenirs. In the canyon wherever visitors gather (at ruins and petroglyph sites), you're likely to encounter craftspeople selling jewelry and other types of handwork. These craftspeople accept cash, personal checks, traveler's checks, and sometimes credit cards.

Forget About Wine with Dinner

Alcohol is prohibited on both the Navajo and the Hopi reservations. Unfortunately, however, despite this prohibition, drunk drivers are a problem on the reservation, so stay alert.

WHERE TO STAY & DINE

Other than a handful of fast-food restaurants in Chinle, the only places to eat in town are hotel dining rooms. While the cafeteria at the Thunderbird Lodge has a memorable setting in a historic trading post, the food is forgettable. The food at the Holiday Inn's dining room is quite a bit better. If you need an espresso, stop by **Changing Woman Tours & Gourmet Coffee** (✆ **928/674-5260;** changingwomancafe.com), which is in a hogan under the trees across from the national monument's Cottonwood Campground. The coffee is organic, and the cafe owner, Victoria Begay, also offers a variety of four-wheel-drive, hiking, and camping tours.

Holiday Inn–Canyon de Chelly ★ Between the town of Chinle and the national monument entrance, this modern hotel is on the site of the old Garcia Trading Post, which has been incorporated into the restaurant and gift-shop building (although the building no longer has any historical character). All guest rooms have patios or balconies, and most face the cottonwood-shaded pool courtyard. Because Canyon de Chelly truck tours leave from the parking lot here, and because the restaurant serves the best food in town, this should be your top choice for a room in Chinle.

Indian Rte. 7 (P.O. Box 1889), Chinle, AZ 86503. ✆ **888/465-4329** or 928/674-5000. Fax 928/674-8264. www.holiday-inn.com/chinle-garcia. 108 units. $89–$129 double. Children 17 and under stay free in parent's room; children 12 and under eat free. AE, DC, DISC, MC, V. **Amenities:** Restaurant; concierge; exercise room; outdoor pool; room service. *In room:* A/C, TV, fridge, hair dryer, Wi-Fi.

Thunderbird Lodge Built on the site of an early trading post right at the mouth of Canyon de Chelly, the Thunderbird Lodge is the closest hotel to the national monument. The red-adobe construction of the lodge itself is reminiscent of ancient pueblos, and the presence on the property of an old stone-walled trading post gives this place lots of character. However, the rooms here are not quite as modern or as comfortable as those at the nearby Holiday Inn. The old trading post now serves as a cafeteria that serves a few Navajo dishes. There's also a shop that sells Navajo rugs.

P.O. Box 548, Chinle, AZ 86503. ✆ **800/679-2473** or 928/674-5841. Fax 928/674-5844. www.tbirdlodge.com. 74 units. Mar–Oct $106–$111 double, $152 suite; Nov–Feb $69 double, $95 suite. Children 2 and under stay free in parent's room. AE, DC, DISC, MC, V. Pets accepted ($25 fee). **Amenities:** Restaurant. *In room:* A/C, TV, free local calls, Wi-Fi.

Campgrounds

Adjacent to the Thunderbird Lodge is the free **Cottonwood Campground,** which has around 100 sites but does not take reservations. On South Rim Drive 10 miles east of the Canyon de Chelly visitor center is another option, the private **Spider Rock Campground** (✆ **928/674-8261;** www.spiderrockcampground.com), which has more than 30 spaces and charges $10 to $15 per night. This campground also has a couple of hogans for rent for $29 to $39 per night.

10 NAVAJO NATIONAL MONUMENT ★

110 miles NW of Canyon de Chelly; 140 miles NE of Flagstaff; 60 miles SW of Monument Valley; 90 miles E of Page

Navajo National Monument, 30 miles west of Kayenta and 60 miles northeast of Tuba City, encompasses three of the largest and best-preserved Ancestral Puebloan cliff dwellings in the region—Betatakin, Keet Seel, and Inscription House. It's possible to visit both Betatakin and Keet Seel, but, due to its fragility, Inscription House is closed to the public. The name Navajo National Monument is a bit misleading. Although the Navajo do inhabit the area now, the cliff dwellings were built by Kayenta Ancestral Puebloans, who were the ancestral Hopi and Pueblo peoples. The Navajo did not arrive in this area until centuries after the cliff dwellings had been abandoned.

For reasons unknown, the well-constructed cliff dwellings here were abandoned around the middle of the 13th century. Tree rings suggest that a drought in the latter part of the 13th century prevented the Ancestral Puebloans from growing sufficient crops. In Tsegi Canyon, however, there's another theory for the abandonment. The canyon was usually flooded each year by spring and summer snowmelt, which made farming quite productive, but in the mid-1200s, weather patterns changed and streams began cutting deep into the soil, forming narrow little canyons called arroyos, which lowered the water table and made farming much more difficult.

ESSENTIALS

GETTING THERE Navajo National Monument can be reached by taking US 89 north to US 160 to Ariz. 564 north.

FEES Monument admission is free.

VISITOR INFORMATION For information, contact **Navajo National Monument,** HC 71, Box 3, Tonalea, AZ 86044 (✆ **928/672-2700;** www.nps.gov/nava). Late May through mid-September, the visitor center is open daily from 8am to 6pm; in winter the visitor center is open daily from 9am to 5pm. The monument is open daily from sunrise to sunset.

EXPLORING THE MONUMENT

A visit to Navajo National Monument is definitely not a point-and-shoot experience. You're going to have to expend some energy if you want to see what this monument is all about. The shortest distance you'll have to walk is 1 mile, which is the round-trip from the visitor center to the Betatakin overlook. However, if you want to actually get close to these ruins, you're looking at strenuous day or overnight hikes.

Your first stop should be the **visitor center,** which has informative displays on the Ancestral Puebloan and Navajo cultures, including numerous artifacts from Tsegi Canyon. You can also watch a couple of short films or a slide show.

The only one of the monument's three ruins that can be seen easily is **Betatakin** ★, which means "ledge house" in Navajo. Built in a huge amphitheater-like alcove in the canyon wall, Betatakin was occupied only from 1250 to 1300 and may have housed 125 people. A 1-mile round-trip paved trail from the visitor center leads to overlooks of Betatakin. The strenuous 5-mile round-trip hike to Betatakin itself is led by a ranger, takes 3 to 5 hours, and involves descending more than 700 feet to the floor of Tsegi

Canyon and later returning to the rim. Between late May and early September, these guided hikes are offered twice a day and leave the visitor center at 8:15 and 10am (remember, daylight saving time *is* observed here on the Navajo Nation). Other months, tours leave weekends at 10am, but call to make sure the tour will be going out. These hikes are offered on a first-come, first-served basis. All participants should carry 1 to 2 quarts of water. While this is a fascinating hike, you will be hiking with a large group.

Keet Seel ★, which means "broken pieces of pottery" in Navajo, has a much longer history than Betatakin, with occupation beginning as early as A.D. 950 and continuing until 1300. At one point, Keet Seel may have housed 150 people. The 17-mile round-trip hike is quite strenuous. During the summer, hikers usually stay overnight at a primitive campground near the ruins, but in the winter, the hike is done as a day hike. You must carry enough water for your trip—up to 2 gallons in summer—because none is available along the trail. These hikes are offered daily between Memorial Day and Labor Day, and sometimes on weekends in other months.

WHERE TO STAY

There is no lodge at the national monument, but there are two free campgrounds that have a total of 48 campsites. Sunset View Campground is open all year, while Canyon View Campground is open only between April and September. Both campgrounds are free, and neither takes reservations. The nearest reliable motels are 30 miles away in Kayenta. See the section on Monument Valley, below, for details.

11 MONUMENT VALLEY NAVAJO TRIBAL PARK ★★★

60 miles NE of Navajo National Monument; 110 miles NW of Canyon de Chelly; 200 miles NE of Flagstaff; 150 miles E of Page

In its role as sculptor, nature has, in the north central part of the Navajo Reservation, created a garden of monoliths and spires unequaled anywhere on earth. Whether you've been here or not, you've almost certainly seen images of Monument Valley before. This otherworldly landscape has been an object of fascination for years, and since Hollywood director John Ford first came here in the 1930s, it has served as backdrop for countless movies, TV shows, and commercials.

Located 30 miles north of Kayenta and straddling the Arizona-Utah state line (you actually go into Utah to get to the park entrance), Monument Valley is a vast flat plain punctuated by natural sandstone cathedrals. These huge monoliths rise up from the sagebrush with sheer walls that capture the light of the rising and setting sun and transform it into fiery hues. Evocative names including the Mittens, Three Sisters, Camel Butte, Elephant Butte, the Thumb, and Totem Pole reflect the shapes the sandstone has taken under the erosive forces of nature.

While it may at first seem as if this strange landscape is a barren wasteland, it is actually still home to a few hardy Navajo families. The Navajo have been living in the valley for generations, herding their sheep through the sagebrush scrublands, and some families continue to reside here today. In fact, human habitation in Monument Valley dates back hundreds of years. Within the park are more than 100 Ancestral Puebloan archaeological sites, ruins, and petroglyphs dating from before 1300.

ESSENTIALS

GETTING THERE Monument Valley Navajo Tribal Park is 200 miles northeast of Flagstaff. Take U.S. 89 north to U.S. 160 to Kayenta, which is 23 miles south of Monument Valley and 29 miles east of Navajo National Monument. Then drive north on U.S. 163.

FEES Admission to the park is $5 per person (free for children 9 and under). ***Note:*** Because this is a tribal park and not a federal park, America the Beautiful passes are not valid here.

VISITOR INFORMATION For information, contact **Monument Valley Navajo Tribal Park** (© **435/727-5874** or 435/727-5875; www.navajonationparks.org). May through September, the park is open daily from 6am to 8:30pm; between October and April, it's open daily from 8am to 4:30pm. The park is closed on Thanksgiving and Christmas.

EXPLORING THE PARK

This is big country and, like the Grand Canyon, is primarily a point-and-shoot experience for most visitors. Because this is reservation land and people still live in Monument Valley, most backcountry and off-road travel is prohibited unless you're with a licensed guide. So basically, with one exception, your options for seeing the park are limited. You can take a few pictures from the overlook beside the visitor center and the View Hotel, drive the park's Valley Drive (a scenic but very rough 17-mile dirt road), take a Jeep or van tour, or go on a guided hike or horseback ride. At the visitor center, you'll find a small museum, a large gift shop, and a restaurant with a knockout view. A quarter-mile away from the visitor center there's a picnic area.

Although Valley Drive is best driven in a high-clearance vehicle, plenty of people drive the loop in rental cars and other standard passenger vehicles. Take it slow, and you should do fine. However, if the first stretch of rocky, rutted road convinces you to change your mind about the drive, just return to the visitor center and book a Jeep or van tour and let someone else pay the repair bills. Along the loop drive, you'll pass 11 very scenic viewpoints that provide ample opportunities for photographing the valley's many natural monuments. At many of these viewpoints, you'll also encounter Navajos selling jewelry and other crafts. At John Ford's Point, so named because it was a favorite shooting location for film director John Ford, you may even get the chance to photograph a Navajo on horseback posed in front of all that spectacular scenery. He'll expect a tip.

If you're trying to decide whether to take a tour, here's some little-publicized information that might help you with your decision. Most tours don't just drive the 17-mile loop; they go off into a part of the valley that is closed to anyone who is not on a tour. This part of the valley is, in our opinion, the most beautiful. You'll get close-up looks at several natural arches and stop at some beautiful petroglyphs. Before booking a tour, make sure that the tour will go to this "closed" section of the valley. There are always plenty of Jeep-tour companies waiting for business in the park's main parking lot. If you're staying at Goulding's Lodge, then your best bet is to go out with **Goulding's Tours** (© **435/727-3231;** www.gouldings.com), which has its office right at the lodge (see "Where to Stay & Dine," below), just a few miles from the park entrance. Goulding's offers 2½-hour tours ($40 for adults, $27 for children 7 and under), 3½-hour tours ($50 for adults, $30 for children), 5½-hour tours ($70 for adults, $55 for children), and all-day tours ($90 for adults, $70 for children). This company also offers full-moon tours (Sept and Oct are the best months for these). **Monument Valley Simpson's Trailhandler Tours** (© **877/**

Moments **Monumental Sunsets**

Be sure to save some storage space on the memory card of your digital camera (or keep plenty of film in your camera) for sunset at Monument Valley. Sure, these rocks are impressive at noon, but as the sun sets and the shadows lengthen, they are positively enchanting—definitely one of the most spectacular sites in America.

686-2848 or 435/727-3362; www.trailhandlertours.com), another reliable company to try, charges $62 to $86 for a 2½-hour tour ($31 for children 6–12). **Sacred Monument Tours** (✆ **435/727-3218** or 928/380-4527; www.monumentvalley.net) charges $73 for a 2½-hour Jeep tour ($58 for children 11 and under). A variety of other tours are also available.

The traditional way to explore this quintessentially Wild West landscape, however, is from the back of a horse, a la John Wayne. We recommend going out with **Dineh Trail Rides** (✆ **435/419-0135**), which starts its rides from John Ford's Point, about halfway around Valley Drive. Trail rides range in price from $35 to $45 for a half-hour ride to $125 for a 6-hour ride. Alternatively, try **Sacred Monument Tours** (✆ **435/727-3218** or 928/380-4527; www.monumentvalley.net), which charges from $68 for a 1-hour horseback ride up to $286 for an all-day ride.

Because the Jeep and van tours are such a big business here, there's a steady stream of the vehicles on Valley Drive throughout the day. One way to get away from the rumble of engines is to go out on a guided hike. These are offered by **Sacred Monument Tours** (✆ **435/727-3218** or 928/380-4527; www.monumentvalley.net), which charges between $57 and $166 per person for hikes of different lengths. **Kéyah Hózhóní Tours** (✆ **928/309-7440;** www.monumentvalley.com) also offers hiking tours ($100 per person) and overnight camping trips ($300 for 1 or 2 people). Keep in mind that summers can be very hot here.

There are two exceptions to the no-traveling-off-road rule. The 3.3-mile **Wildcat Trail ★★** is a loop trail that circles West Mitten Butte and provides the only opportunity to get close to this picturesque butte. As you circle the butte, you'll get all kinds of different perspectives, even one that completely eliminates the "thumb." Because this is the park's only option for unguided hiking, it's a not-to-be-missed excursion and one of the most memorable hikes in the state. In summer, be sure to carry plenty of water. The other trail open without a guide is the Mesa Rim Trail, a .5-mile trail along the mesa above the View Hotel.

ACTIVITIES OUTSIDE THE PARK

Before leaving the area, you might want to visit **Goulding's Museum & Trading Post,** at Goulding's Lodge (see "Where to Stay & Dine," below). This old trading post was the home of the Gouldings for many years and is set up as they had it back in the 1920s and 1930s. There are also displays about the many movies that have been shot here. The trading post hours vary with the seasons; admission is by donation.

Inside Kayenta's Burger King, which is next door to the Hampton Inn, there's an interesting exhibit on the Navajo code talkers of World War II. The code talkers were Navajo soldiers who used their own language to transmit military messages, primarily in the South Pacific.

WHERE TO STAY & DINE

In addition to the lodgings listed here, you'll find several budget motels north of Monument Valley in the Utah towns of Mexican Hat and Bluff. When it's time for a meal, try the View Restaurant, which is in the park's visitor center and more than lives up to its name. Alternatively, try the Stagecoach Dining Room at Goulding's. The Navajo steak, served atop fry bread, is great. If you need a latte to get you on down the road, stop by **Shepherd's Eyes** (✆ **928/697-3368**), an espresso bar and Internet cafe a quarter-mile west of the junction of U.S. 160 and U.S. 163. This cafe also serves Navajo tea, which is made from a wild plant that grows in the area.

Best Western Wetherill Inn Located in Kayenta a mile north of the junction of U.S. 160 and U.S. 163, and 20 miles south of Monument Valley, the Wetherill Inn doesn't look like much from the outside, but guest rooms were all redone in 2008 and are now the most modern rooms in Kayenta. While the hotel offers neither the convenience of the View Hotel or Goulding's Lodge nor the amenities of the nearby Holiday Inn or Hampton Inn, if you just want a nice room for the night, this is a good bet. A cafe next door serves Navajo and American food.

U.S. 163 (P.O. Box 175), Kayenta, AZ 86033. ✆ **800/528-1234** or 928/697-3231. Fax 928/697-3233. www.bestwestern.com/wetherillinn. 54 units. May 1–Oct 15 $129 double; Oct 16–Nov 15 and Apr $87 double; Nov 16–Mar 31 $72 double. Children 12 and under stay free in parent's room. Rates include continental breakfast. AE, DC, DISC, MC, V. Pets accepted in winter ($50 deposit). **Amenities:** Indoor pool. *In room:* A/C, TV, hair dryer, Wi-Fi.

Goulding's Lodge ★ For decades, this was the only lodge actually located in Monument Valley; and, although you can now stay inside the park at the Navajo-owned View Hotel, Goulding's is still a good bet. Because this is one of the most popular hotels in the area, be sure to make your reservation well in advance. Goulding's offers great views from the private balconies of its large guest rooms (especially at sunrise). The restaurant serves Navajo and American dishes, and also boast views that are enough to make any meal an event. Unfortunately, although the setting is memorable, the service in the restaurant can be somewhat lacking. The lodge also has a museum and a video library that includes a few films that have been shot in Monument Valley.

P.O. Box 360001, Monument Valley, UT 84536. ✆ **435/727-3231.** Fax 435/727-3344. www.gouldings.com. 62 units. Mar 15–Nov 15 $123–$180 double; Nov 16–Mar 14 $73–$83 double. Children 5 and under stay free in parent's room. AE, DC, DISC, MC, V. Pets accepted ($20 fee). **Amenities:** Restaurant; exercise room; indoor pool. *In room:* A/C, TV/DVD, fridge, hair dryer, Wi-Fi.

Hampton Inn–Navajo Nation In the center of Kayenta, this is the most modern lodging in the area and, as such, should be your first choice if you can't get a room in Monument Valley itself. The Hampton Inn is built in a contemporary Santa Fe style and has spacious, comfortable guest rooms. In the hotel's dining room, you can get a few Navajo dishes. Adjacent to the hotel, you'll find the Navajo Cultural Center and a Burger King that has an interesting display on the Navajo code talkers of World War II.

U.S. 160 (P.O. Box 1217), Kayenta, AZ 86033. ✆ **800/426-7866** or 928/697-3170. Fax 928/697-3189. www.hamptoninn.com. 73 units. $89–$156 double. Rates include continental breakfast. Children 18 and under stay free in parent's room. AE, DC, DISC, MC, V. Pets accepted ($20 fee). **Amenities:** Restaurant; small outdoor pool. *In room:* A/C, TV, hair dryer, Wi-Fi.

Holiday Inn–Kayenta (Kids) This Holiday Inn, right in the center of Kayenta, is very popular with tour groups and is almost always crowded. Although the grounds are dusty and a bit run-down, the rooms are spacious and clean. We like the poolside units best.

Part of the hotel's dining room is designed to look like an Ancestral Puebloan ruin, and the menu offers both American and Navajo cuisine.

U.S. 160 and U.S. 163 (P.O. Box 307), Kayenta, AZ 86033. ✆ **888/465-4329** or 928/697-3221. Fax 928/697-3349. www.holidayinnkayenta.com. 164 units. Nov–Apr $69–$109 double, $79–$119 suite; May–June and Sept–Oct $139–$169 double, $159–$189 suite; July–Aug $159–$189 double, $179–$209 suite. Children 18 and under stay free in parent's room; children 12 and under eat free. AE, DC, DISC, MC, V. **Amenities:** Restaurant; exercise room; small outdoor pool; room service. *In room:* A/C, TV, hair dryer, Wi-Fi.

The View Hotel ★★ This Navajo-owned hotel inside Monument Valley Navajo Tribal Park is the newest and most luxurious hotel in the region, and it's the only hotel actually inside the park. As such, it should be your first choice for accommodations in the area. The hotel's name, as appropriate as it is, does little to convey how breathtaking the views are from windows and balconies of this hotel. With the park's most famous and picturesque buttes right there, you need do nothing more than sit back and watch the play of light on red rock pinnacles. The rooms themselves are also quite comfortable and sport Native American touches in their decor.

P.O. Box 360457, Monument Valley Tribal Park, UT 84436. ✆ **435/727-5556.** Fax 435/727-4545. www.monumentvalleyview.com. 96 units. Mid-Mar to Nov $75–$215 double, $185–$350 suite; Dec to mid-Mar $50–$115 double, $135–$195 suite. Children 8 and under stay free in parent's room. AE, DISC, MC, V. **Amenities:** Restaurant; exercise room; Wi-Fi. *In room:* A/C, TV, fridge.

Campgrounds

If you're headed to Monument Valley Navajo Tribal Park, you can camp at **Goulding's Campground** (✆ **435/727-3231;** www.gouldings.com), which charges $25 to $42 per night. There are also small cabins that go for $74 per night. This campground is open year-round (limited services Nov to mid-Mar) and has an indoor pool, hot showers, a playground, a coin-op laundry, and Wi-Fi.

12 LAKE POWELL ★★ & PAGE

272 miles N of Phoenix; 130 miles E of Grand Canyon North Rim; 130 miles NE of Grand Canyon South Rim

Had the early Spanish explorers of Arizona suddenly come upon Lake Powell after traipsing for months across desolate desert, they would have either taken it for a mirage or fallen to their knees and rejoiced. Imagine the Grand Canyon filled with water, and you have a pretty good picture of Lake Powell. Surrounded by hundreds of miles of parched desert, this reservoir, created by the damming of the Colorado River at Glen Canyon, seems unreal when first glimpsed. Yet real it is, and it draws everyone in the region toward its promise of relief from the heat.

Construction of the Glen Canyon Dam came about despite the angry outcry of many who felt that this canyon was even more beautiful than the Grand Canyon and should be preserved in its natural state. Preservationists lost the battle, and construction of the dam began in 1960, with completion in 1963. It took another 17 years for Lake Powell to fill to capacity. Today, the lake is a watery powerboat playground, and houseboats and water-skiers cruise where once only bird songs and the splashing of waterfalls filled the canyon air. These days most people seem to agree, though, that Lake Powell is as amazing a sight as the Grand Canyon, and it draws almost as many visitors each year as its downriver neighbor. In the past few years, however, Lake Powell has lost some of its luster as a prolonged drought in the Southwest has left the lake's water level down by almost 100 feet. Although this has left a bathtub-ring effect on the shores of the lake, it has also exposed wide expanses of beach in the Wahweap area.

While Lake Powell is something of a man-made wonder of the world, one of the natural wonders of the world—Rainbow Bridge—can also be found on its shores. Called by the Navajo *nonnozhoshi,* or "the rainbow turned to stone," this is the largest natural bridge on earth and stretches 275 feet across a side canyon off Lake Powell.

The town of Page, originally a camp constructed to house the workers who built the dam, has many motels and inexpensive restaurants, and is the main base for many visitors who come to explore Lake Powell.

ESSENTIALS

GETTING THERE Page is connected to Flagstaff by U.S. 89. Ariz. 98 leads southeast onto the Navajo Indian Reservation and connects with U.S. 160 to Kayenta and Four Corners. The Page Airport is served by **Great Lakes Airlines** (✆ **800/554-5111** or 307/433-2899; www.greatlakesav.com), which flies from Phoenix. Round-trip airfares start around $198.

FEES Admission to Glen Canyon National Recreation Area is $15 per car (good for 1 week). There is also a $16-per-week boat fee if you bring your own boat.

VISITOR INFORMATION For further information on the Lake Powell area, contact the **Glen Canyon National Recreation Area** (✆ **928/608-6404;** www.nps.gov/glca); the **Page-Lake Powell Chamber of Commerce,** 608 Elm St., Ste. C, Page (✆ **888/261-7243** or 928/645-2741; www.pagelakepowellchamber.org); or the **John Wesley Powell Memorial Museum,** 6 N. Lake Powell Blvd., Page (✆ **888/597-6873** or 928/645-9496; www.powellmuseum.org). You can also go to www.powellguide.com.

GETTING AROUND Rental cars are available at the Page Airport from **Avis** (✆ **800/331-1212** or 928/645-2024).

GLEN CANYON NATIONAL RECREATION AREA

Until the flooding of Glen Canyon formed Lake Powell, this area was one of the most remote regions in the contiguous 48 states. However, because the construction of Glen Canyon Dam at a spot where the canyon of the Colorado River was less than a third of a mile wide, this remote and rugged landscape has become one of the country's most popular national recreation areas. Today, the lake and much of the surrounding land is designated the Glen Canyon National Recreation Area and attracts around two million visitors each year. The otherworldly setting amid the slickrock canyons of northern Arizona and southern Utah is a tapestry of colors, the blues and greens of the lake contrasting with the reds and oranges of the surrounding sandstone cliffs. This interplay of colors and vast desert landscapes easily makes Lake Powell the most beautiful of Arizona's many reservoirs.

Built to provide water for the desert communities of the Southwest and West, **Glen Canyon Dam** stands 710 feet above the bedrock and contains almost 5 million cubic yards of concrete. The dam also provides hydroelectric power, and deep within its massive wall of concrete are huge power turbines. Although most Lake Powell visitors are more interested in water-skiing and powerboating than they are in drinking water and power production, there would be no lake without the dam, so any visit to this area ought to start at the **Carl Hayden Visitor Center** (✆ **928/608-6404**), which is located beside the dam on U.S. 89 just north of Page. Here you can tour the dam and learn about its construction. Between mid-May and mid-September, the visitor center is open daily from 8am to 6pm; November to February, it's open daily 8:30am to 4:30pm; other months, it's open daily 8am to 5pm (it's closed Thanksgiving, Christmas, and New Year's Day).

More than 500 feet deep in some places, and bounded by nearly 2,000 miles of shoreline, **Lake Powell** is a maze of convoluted canyons where rock walls often rise hundreds of feet straight out of the water. In places, the long, winding canyons are so narrow there isn't even room to turn a motorboat around. The only way to truly appreciate this lake is from a boat, whether a houseboat, a runabout, or a sea kayak. Water-skiing, riding personal watercrafts, and fishing have long been the most popular on-water activities, and consequently, you'll be hard-pressed to find a quiet corner of the lake if you happen to be a solitude-seeking sea kayaker. However, with so many miles of shoreline, you're bound to find someplace to get away from it all. Your best bet for solitude is to head up-lake from Wahweap Marina. This will get you away from the crowds and into some of the narrower reaches of the lake.

In addition to the Carl Hayden Visitor Center mentioned above, there's the **Bullfrog Visitor Center,** in Bullfrog, Utah (✆ **435/684-7420**). It's open intermittently from May to early October; call for hours.

Boat & Air Tours

There are few roads penetrating the Glen Canyon National Recreation Area, so the best way to appreciate this rugged region is by boat. If you don't have your own boat, you can at least see a small part of the lake on a boat tour. A variety of tours depart from **Wahweap Marina** (✆ **888/896-3829** or 928/645-2433; www.lakepowell.com). Your best bet is either the 1½-hour **Antelope Canyon Cruise** ($35 for adults, $23 for children) or the 3-hour **Navajo Tapestry Cruise** ($66 for adults, $42 for children). To see more of the lake, opt for the full-day tour to Rainbow Bridge (see below for details). Breakfast and evening cruises are also offered.

The Glen Canyon National Recreation Area covers an immense area, much of it only partially accessible by boat. If you'd like to see more of the area than is visible from car or boat, consider taking an air tour with **Westwind Scenic Air Tours** (✆ **800/245-8668** or 928/645-2494; www.westwindairservice.com), which offers several tours of northern Arizona and southern Utah, including flights over Rainbow Bridge and Monument Valley. Sample rates are $125 for a 30-minute flight over Rainbow Bridge and $263 for a 75-minute flight over Monument Valley. Children 12 and under get a 10% discount.

RAINBOW BRIDGE NATIONAL MONUMENT

Roughly 40 miles up Lake Powell from Wahweap Marina and Glen Canyon Dam, in a narrow side canyon of the lake, rises **Rainbow Bridge** ★★★, the world's largest natural bridge and one of the most spectacular sights in the Southwest. Preserved in Rainbow Bridge National Monument, this natural arch of sandstone stands 290 feet high and spans 275 feet. Carved by wind and water over the ages, Rainbow Bridge is an awesome reminder of the powers of erosion that have sculpted this entire region into the spectacle it is today.

Rainbow Bridge is accessible only by boat or on foot (a hike of 14 miles minimum), and, of course, going by boat is by far the more popular method. **Lake Powell Resorts and Marinas** (✆ **888/896-3829** or 928/645-2433; www.lakepowell.com) offers full-day tours ($144 for adults, $89 for children) that not only get you to Rainbow Bridge in comfort, but also cruise through some of the most spectacular scenery on earth. Tours include a box lunch and a bit more exploring after visiting Rainbow Bridge. Currently, because the lake's water level is so low from years of drought, the boat must stop a mile from Rainbow Bridge, so if you aren't able to walk this distance, you won't even be able to see the sandstone arch. During the summer, there are also half-day trips ($104 for adults and $64 for children).

Rainbow Bridge National Monument (© **928/608-6200;** www.nps.gov/rabr) is administered by Glen Canyon National Recreation Area. For information on hiking to Rainbow Bridge, contact the **Navajo Parks and Recreation Department,** P.O. Box 2520, Window Rock, AZ 86515 (© **928/871-6647;** www.navajonationparks.org). The hike to Rainbow Bridge is about 25 miles round-trip and should be done as an overnight backpacking trip. It requires a Navajo Nation permit, which is available through the Navajo Parks and Recreation Department, at the **Cameron Visitor Center** (© **928/679-2303**), in the community of Cameron near the turnoff for the Grand Canyon, and at the **Lake Powell Navajo Tribal Park Office** (© **928/698-2808**), 3 miles south of Page on Navajo Rte. 20 (beside the LeChee Chapter House).

ANTELOPE CANYON

If you've spent any time in Arizona, chances are you've noticed photos of a narrow sandstone canyon only a few feet wide. The walls of the canyon seem to glow with an inner light, and beams of sunlight slice the darkness of the deep slot canyon. Sound familiar? If you've seen such a photo, you were probably looking at Antelope Canyon (sometimes called Corkscrew Canyon). Located 2½ miles southeast of Page off Ariz. 98 (at milepost 299), this photogenic canyon comprises the **Lake Powell Navajo Tribal Park ★★★** (© **928/698-2808;** www.navajonationparks.org/htm/antelopecanyon.htm), which is on the Navajo Reservation and is divided into upper and lower canyons. The entry fee is $6, and children 7 and under enter free. March through October, Antelope Canyon is open daily from 8am to 5pm; November through February, hours vary and closures are common.

There are currently two options for visiting Antelope Canyon. The most convenient and reliable way is to take a 1½-hour tour with **Antelope Canyon Tours** (© **866/645-9102** or 928/645-9102; www.antelopecanyon.com), which charges $32 per adult for a basic tour. Photographic tours cost $50. If you don't want to deal with crowds of tourists ogling the rocks and snapping pictures with their point-and-shoots, we recommend heading out with **Overland Canyon Tours,** 48 S. Lake Powell Blvd. (© **928/608-4072;** www.overlandcanyontours.com), to nearby Canyon X, which is much less visited than Antelope Canyon and is a good choice for serious photographers who want to avoid the crowds. One other option for avoiding the crowds is to book a tour with **Slot Canyon Hummer Adventures,** 12 N. Lake Powell Blvd. (© **928/645-2266;** www.lakepowell hummertours.com), which leads tours to several other little-visited area slot canyons. A 3-hour tour is $79 and a 5-hour tour is $149.

Alternatively, at both the upper and lower canyons, you'll find Navajo guides collecting park entry fees and fees for guide services. At Lower Antelope Canyon, these guides charge $20 ($12 for children ages 6–12). At Upper Antelope Canyon, guides charge $25 ($10 for children ages 6–12). Upper Antelope Canyon is a short drive up a sandy streambed from the highway, while Lower Antelope Canyon is a short walk from the parking area just off the highway. You'll get more out of your experience if you go on one of the guided tours mentioned above, but you'll save a little money by visiting the canyon on your own. For more information, contact **Antelope Canyon Navajo Tours** (© **928/698-3384;** www.navajotours.com).

Just remember that if there's even the slightest chance of rain in the region, you should not venture into this canyon, which is subject to flash floods. In the past, people who have ignored bad weather predictions have been killed by such floods.

WATERSPORTS

While simply exploring the lake's maze of canyons on a narrated tour is satisfying enough for many visitors, the most popular activities are still houseboating, water-skiing, riding personal watercrafts, and fishing. Five marinas (only Wahweap is in Ariz.) help boaters explore the lake. At the **Wahweap Marina** (✆ **888/896-3829** or 928/645-2433; www.lakepowell.com), you can rent various types of boats, along with personal watercrafts and water skis. Rates in summer range from about $375 to $695 per day, depending on the type of boat. Personal watercrafts go for $335 per day, and sea kayaks rent for $46 per day. For information on renting houseboats, see "Where to Stay," below. A variety of boats, including ski boats and kayaks, can also be rented at **Antelope Point Marina,** 537 Marina Pkwy., Navajo Rte. 22B (✆ **928/645-5900;** antelopepointlakepowell.com). Expect to pay $375 to $425 per day for a ski boat and $30 to $45 per day for a kayak.

If roaring engines aren't your speed, you might want to consider exploring Lake Powell by sea kayak. While afternoon winds can sometimes make paddling difficult, mornings are often quiet. With a sea kayak, you can even explore canyons too narrow for powerboats. Rentals are available at **Twin Finn Diving,** 811 Vista Ave. (✆ **928/645-3114;** www.twinfinn.com). Sea kayaks rent for $45 to $55 per day, and sit-on-top kayaks for $35 to $45. Multiday kayak tours are operated by **Hidden Canyon Kayak** (✆ **800/343-3121** or 928/645-8866; www.diamondriver.com/kayak), which charges $760 to $1,000 for 4- to 6-day trips. Guided kayak trips are also offered by **Kayak Powell** (✆ **888/854-7862;** www.kayaklakepowell.com), which charges $95 for a half-day tour, multiday tours range from $495 for a 2-day tour to $895 for 5-day tour.

While most of Glen Canyon National Recreation Area consists of the impounded waters of Lake Powell, the recreation area also contains a short stretch of the Colorado River that still flows swift and free. If you'd like to see this stretch of river, try a float trip from Glen Canyon Dam to Lees Ferry. These trips are operated by **Colorado River Discovery** (✆ **888/522-6644** or 928/645-9175; www.raftthecanyon.com) between March and November. Half-day trips in motorized rafts cost $80 for adults and $70 for children ages 4 to 11. Try to reserve at least 2 weeks in advance. Spring and fall, this company also offers full-day oar-powered raft trips ($161 for adults and $151 for children). **Kayak Powell** (see above) offers self-guided kayak trips ($99) on this stretch of the Colorado River.

If you have a boat (your own or a rental), avail yourself of some excellent year-round fishing. Smallmouth, largemouth, and striped bass, as well as walleye, catfish, crappie, and carp, are all plentiful. Because the lake lies within both Arizona and Utah, you'll need to know which state's waters you're fishing in whenever you cast your line out, and you'll need the appropriate license. (Be sure to pick up a copy of the Ariz. and Utah state fishing regulations, or ask about applicable regulations at any of the marinas.) In Wahweap, you can arrange licenses to fish the entire lake at **Lake Powell Resorts and Marinas** (✆ **928/645-2433**), which also sells bait and tackle and can provide you with advice on fishing this massive reservoir. Other marinas on the lake also sell licenses, bait, and tackle. The best season is March through November, but walleye are most often caught during the cooler months. If you'd rather try your hand at catching enormous rainbow trout, try downstream of the Glen Canyon Dam, where cold waters provide ideal conditions for trophy trout. Unfortunately, there isn't much access to this stretch of river. You'll need a

Finds Acrophobes, Beware!

If you have a fear of heights, there are a couple of places in the Page area that you should never visit. On the other hand, if you want some great views, then don't miss the following two scenic vistas.

As you drive down the hill from Page on Lake Powell Boulevard (the road toward Glen Canyon Dam from Page), go straight through the intersection instead of turning right toward the dam. Here you'll find a parking area and a short path to a viewing platform perched on the edge of sheer cliff walls. Below lie the clear green waters of the Colorado River, while upstream looms Glen Canyon Dam.

If you're up for a short hike, grab the camera and head to the **Horseshoe Bend** ★ viewpoint. Horseshoe Bend is a huge loop of the Colorado River, and the viewpoint is hundreds of feet above the water on the edge of a cliff. It's about a half-mile to the viewpoint from the trail head, which is 5 miles south of the Carl Hayden Visitor Center on U.S. 89 just south of milepost 545.

trout stamp to fish for the rainbows. If you want a guide to take you where the fish are biting, contact Bill McBurney at **Ambassador Guide Service** (✆ **800/256-7596;** www.ambassadorguides.com).

If you're just looking for a good place for a swim near Lake Powell Resort, take the Coves Loop just west of the marina. Of the three coves, the third one, which has a sandy beach, is the best. The Chains area, another good place to jump off the rocks and otherwise lounge by the lake, is outside Page down a rough dirt road just before you reach Glen Canyon Dam. Although the desert may not immediately jump to mind when considering a scuba-diving vacation, the view underwater at Lake Powell is as scenic as the view above it. To explore the underwater regions of the canyon, contact **Twin Finn Diving Center,** 811 Vista Ave. (✆ **928/645-3114;** www.twinfinn.com), which charges $45 a day for scuba gear and also rents snorkeling equipment.

OTHER OUTDOOR PURSUITS

If you're looking for a quick, easy hike with great views, head north on North Navajo Drive from downtown Page. At the end of this street is the main trail head for Page's **Rimview Trail.** This trail runs along the edge of Manson Mesa, upon which Page is built, and has views of Lake Powell and miles of red-rock country. The entire loop trail is 8 miles long, but if you want to do a shorter hike, we recommend the stretch of trail heading east (clockwise) from the trail head. If you happen to have your mountain bike with you, the trail is a great ride.

At Lees Ferry, a 39-mile drive from Page at the southern tip of the national recreation area, you'll find three short trails (Cathedral Wash, River, and Spencer). The 2-mile **Cathedral Wash Trail** is the most interesting of the three day hikes and follows a dry wash through a narrow canyon with unusual rock formations. The trail head is at the second turnout after turning off U.S. 89A. Be aware that this wash is subject to flash floods. The **River Trail** is a 2-mile round-trip hike along the river and starts at the boat ramp. The **Spencer Trail,** which begins along the River Trail, leads up to the top of a 1,700-foot cliff for spectacular views of Marble Canyon. Lees Ferry is also the southern trail head for famed **Paria Canyon** ★, a favorite of canyoneering backpackers. This trail is between 38 and 47 miles long (depending on where you start) and follows the meandering route of a narrow slot canyon for much of its length. Most hikers start from the northern trail head, which is in Utah on U.S. 89. For more information on hiking in Paria Canyon, contact the **Arizona Strip Interpretive Association/Interagency Visitor Center,** 345 E. Riverside Dr., St. George, UT 84790 (✆ **435/688-3200;** www.blm.gov/az/st/en/fo/arizona_strip_field.html).

The 27-hole **Lake Powell National Golf Course** ★, 400 Clubhouse Dr. (✆ **928/645-2023;** www.golflakepowell.com), is one of the most spectacular in the state. The fairways wrap around the base of the red-sandstone bluff atop which sits the town of Page. The views stretch on forever, and in places, eroded sandstone walls come right down to the greens and fairways. Greens fees are $69 ($44 for twilight play).

OTHER AREA ATTRACTIONS

Between April and October, you can learn about Navajo culture at **Navajo Village Heritage Center** (✆ **928/660-0304;** www.navajo-village.com), a living-history center on the northeast corner of Ariz. 98 and Coppermine Road (on the south side of Page). Evening performances here center on programs of Native American dancing, but there are also demonstrations by weavers, silversmiths, and other artisans. Tours, which last 2½ hours, cost $50 ($30 for children) and include dinner and traditional dances. Reservations are required. Although this is definitely a tourist attraction, you will come away with a better sense of Navajo culture. For $10 per person, you can attend a Native American dance performance.

John Wesley Powell Memorial Museum In 1869, one-armed Civil War veteran John Wesley Powell and a small band of men spent more than 3 months fighting the rapids of the Green and Colorado rivers to become the first people to travel the length of the Grand Canyon. It is for this intrepid—some said crazy—adventurer that Lake Powell is named and to whom this small museum is dedicated. Besides documenting the Powell expedition with photographs, etchings, artifacts, and dioramas, the museum displays Native American artifacts ranging from Ancestral Puebloan pottery to contemporary Navajo and Hopi crafts. The museum also acts as an information center for Page, Lake Powell, and the surrounding region.

6 N. Lake Powell Blvd. ✆ **888/597-6873** or 928/645-9496. www.powellmuseum.org. Admission $5 adults, $3 seniors, $1 children 5–12, free for children 4 and under. Mid-Feb to Nov Mon–Fri 9am–5pm (sometimes open Sat–Sun in summer, but call to be sure). Closed Dec to mid-Feb.

WHERE TO STAY

Houseboats

Antelope Point Resort & Marina ★★ (Kids) At this marina, you can rent some of the newest and most luxurious houseboats on the lake (the larger ones even have outdoor hot tubs). There are both 59-foot and 70-foot boats available, ranging in quality from deluxe to luxury. Speedboats ($375–$425 per day), personal watercraft ($375 per day), and sea kayaks ($30 per day) can also be rented and are a great way to explore smaller waterways that your houseboat can't navigate. To reach the marina, head east out of Page on Ariz. 98 and drive 5 miles to the signposted Antelope Point Marina turnoff.

Antelope Point Marina, P.O. Box 4180, Page, AZ 86040. ✆ **800/255-5561.** Fax 480/998-7399. www.antelopepointlakepowell.com. Early June to early Sept $7,494–$9,595 per week; lower rates other months. 3-, 4-, and 5-night rates also available. AE, DISC, MC, V. Pets accepted ($100 fee). **Amenities:** Watersports equipment/rentals. *In room:* A/C, TV/DVD, kitchen.

Lake Powell Resorts & Marinas ★ Kids This is the original houseboat-rental operation on Lake Powell, and houseboats here range in size from 46 to 75 feet, sleep anywhere from 8 to 22 people, and come complete with showers and a fully equipped kitchen. For deluxe on-the-water accommodations, opt for one of the 62-foot "Journey" houseboats. If you're coming in the summer, splurge on a boat with some sort of cooling system.

100 Lakeshore Dr., Page, AZ 86040. ✆ **888/486-4665** or 602/278-8888. Fax 602/331-5258. www.lakepowell.com. Early June to late Sept $3,200–$12,000 per week; lower rates other months. 3-, 4-, 5-, and 6-night rates also available on most houseboats. AE, DC, DISC, MC, V. Pets accepted ($10). *In room:* Kitchen, no phone.

Hotels & Motels

Best Western Arizonainn Perched right at the edge of the mesa on which Page is built, this modern motel has a fine view across miles of desert. While the guest rooms are unremarkable and are basically just standard motel rooms, about half have lake views. Be sure to ask for one of these. If you can't get a room with a view, you can at least hang out by the pool; it's got that same 100-mile view.

716 Rimview Dr. (P. O. Box 250), Page, AZ 86040. ✆ **800/826-2718** or 928/645-2466. Fax 928/645-2053. www.bestwestern.com. 102 units. $85–$110 double. Rates include continental breakfast. Children 17 and under stay free in parent's room. AE, DC, DISC, MC, V. Pets accepted ($10 per night). **Amenities:** Free airport transfers; exercise room; Jacuzzi, small outdoor pool. *In room:* A/C, TV, hair dryer, Wi-Fi.

Courtyard by Marriott ★ Located at the foot of the mesa on which Page is built and adjacent to the Lake Powell National Golf Course, this is the top in-town choice. It's also the closest you'll come to a golf resort in this corner of the state. Although you'll pay a premium for views of the golf course or lake, it's a worthwhile investment. Guest rooms are larger than those at most area lodgings. Moderately priced meals are served in a casual restaurant that has a terrace overlooking the distant lake. The 18-hole golf course has great views of the surrounding landscape.

600 Clubhouse Dr. (P.O. Box 4150), Page, AZ 86040. ✆ **800/321-2211** or 928/645-5000. Fax 928/645-5004. www.marriott.com/pgacy. 153 units. $89–$189 double. Children 17 and under stay free in parent's room. AE, DC, DISC, MC, V. **Amenities:** Restaurant; lounge; exercise room; 18-hole golf course; Jacuzzi; outdoor pool; room service. *In room:* A/C, TV, hair dryer, Wi-Fi.

Lake Powell Resort ★ This hotel at the sprawling Wahweap Marina 5 miles north of Page should be your first lodging choice in the area. As the biggest hotel in the area, the Lake Powell Resort features lots of resort amenities and activities, but it is often overwhelmed by busloads of tour groups. Consequently, don't expect very good service. Guest rooms are arranged in several long two-story wings, and every unit has either a balcony or a patio. Half of the rooms have lake views; those in the west wing have the better vantage point, as the east wing overlooks a coal-fired power plant. The resort also offers EcoRooms, which have bathroom floors and counters made from recycled glass, and carpets made with recycled materials. The Rainbow Room (see "Where to Dine," below) offers fine dining. Because of all the tour groups that stay here, getting a reservation can be difficult.

100 Lakeshore Dr. (P.O. Box 1597), Page, AZ 86040. ✆ **888/486-4665** or 602/278-8888. Fax 928/645-1031. www.lakepowell.com. 348 units. May–Sept $119–$189 double, $249 suite; Oct–Apr $89–$129 double, $149 suite. Children 17 and under stay free in parent's room. AE, DC, DISC, MC, V. Pets accepted ($20). **Amenities:** 2 restaurants; snack bar; 2 lounges; free airport transfers; concierge; exercise room; Jacuzzi; 2 outdoor pools; room service; sauna; watersports equipment/rentals. *In room:* A/C, TV, fridge, hair dryer.

Campgrounds

There are campgrounds at **Wahweap** and **Lees Ferry** in Arizona, and at Bullfrog, Hite, and Halls Crossing in Utah. Some scrubby trees provide a bit of shade at the Wahweap site, but the wind and sun make this a rather bleak spot in summer. Nevertheless, because of the lake's popularity, these campgrounds stay packed for much of the year. Wahweap (✆ **800/528-6154** or 928/645-2433) charges $19 to $37 per night (reservations are accepted for RV sites) and Lees Ferry charges $12 (reservations are not accepted).

WHERE TO DINE

The Dam Bar & Grille Kids AMERICAN This theme restaurant is a warehouse-size space designed to conjure up images of the interior of Glen Canyon Dam. Inside, cement walls, hard hats, and a big transformer that sends out bolts of neon "electricity" will put you in a "dam" good mood. Sandwiches, pastas, and steaks dominate the menu, but the slow-roasted chicken is excellent and well worth ordering. The lounge area is a popular local hangout, and next door is the affiliated Gunsmoke Saloon nightclub. Kids will love the cool dam decor and old boats inside the restaurant.

644 N. Navajo Dr. ✆ **928/645-2161.** www.damplaza.com. Reservations recommended in summer. Main courses $7–$25. AE, DISC, MC, V. Daily 11am–9pm (until 10pm in summer).

Ja' di' Tooh ★ AMERICAN Even if this wasn't the only floating restaurant on Lake Powell, we'd tell you to be sure to have a meal here while you're in the area. With big walls of glass (some of which roll up like garage doors) and a large patio off the bar, this place is the perfect spot for lingering over a meal and drinks, especially on a hot summer day. The water lapping at the floats and the sandstone rising all around make this the quintessential Lake Powell dining experience. Okay, so the menu isn't creative (a few pizzas, sandwiches, and wraps at lunch and primarily steaks at dinner), but the setting can't be beat.

Antelope Point Marina, 537 Marina Pkwy., Navajo Rte. 22B. ✆ **928/645-5900.** www.antelopepointlakepowell.com. Main courses $7–$12 lunch, $11–$32 dinner. AE, MC, V. Daily 11am–9pm (Fri–Mon 11am–9pm in winter).

Rainbow Room AMERICAN/SOUTHWESTERN With sweeping vistas of Lake Powell through the walls of glass, the Rainbow Room is both Page's top restaurant and its most touristy. The menu is short and includes a few dishes with Southwestern flavor, and many of the ingredients are organic. We like the southwestern buffalo osso buco. Be prepared for a wait; this place regularly feeds busloads of tourists. The adjacent bar has a knock-out view through a long wall of glass.

At Lake Powell Resort, 100 Lakeshore Dr. ✆ **928/645-1162.** Reservations recommended. Main courses $8–$10 lunch, $9–$34 dinner. AE, DISC, MC, V. Daily 6am–2pm and 5–9pm.

13 NEW MEXICO'S FOUR CORNERS GATEWAYS

Farmington has historic and outdoor finds that can keep you occupied for at least a day or two. It sits at the junction of the San Juan, Animas, and La Plata rivers. Adorned with arched globe willow trees, it's a lush place by New Mexico standards. A system of five parks along the San Juan River and its tributaries is its pride and joy. What's most notable for me, however, is the quaint downtown area, where century-old buildings still house thriving businesses and some trading posts with great prices. The town is also an industrial center (coal, oil, natural gas, and hydroelectricity) and a shopping center for people within a 100-mile radius.

For visitors, Farmington is a takeoff point for explorations of the Navajo Reservation and Chaco Culture National Historical Park. For outdoors lovers, it's the spot to head to the Bisti/De-Na-Zin Wilderness; world-class fly-fishing on the San Juan River; lovely scenery at the Angel Peak Recreation Area; and even a trip up to Durango to enjoy some rafting, kayaking, skiing, and mountain biking. The nearby towns of **Aztec** and Bloomfield offer a variety of attractions as well.

ESSENTIALS

GETTING THERE From Albuquerque, take US 550 (through Cuba) from the I-25 Bernalillo exit, and then head west on US 64 at Bloomfield (45 min.). From Gallup, take US 491 north to Shiprock, and then head east on US 64 (2¼ hr.). From Taos, follow US 64 all the way (4½ hr.). From Durango, Colorado, take US 500 south (1 hr.).

All commercial flights arrive at busy **Four Corners Regional Airport** on West Navajo Drive (✆ **505/599-1395**). The principal carrier is **Great Lakes Airlines** (✆ **800/554-5111;** www.flygreatlakes.com).

Car-rental agencies at Four Corners Regional Airport include **Avis** (✆ **800/331-1212** or 505/327-9864), **Budget** (✆ **505/327-7304**), and **Hertz** (✆ **800/654-3131** or 505/327-6093).

VISITOR INFORMATION The **Farmington Convention and Visitors Bureau,** 3041 E. Main St. (✆ **800/448-1240** or 505/326-7602; www.farmingtonnm.org), is the clearinghouse for tourist information for the Four Corners region. For more information, contact the **Farmington Chamber of Commerce,** 100 W. Broadway (✆ **505/325-0279;** www.gofarmington.com).

SEEING THE SIGHTS IN THE AREA

In Farmington

Farmington Museum and Gateway Center (Kids) Small-town museums can be completely precious, and this one and its neighbor in Aztec (see below) typify a tiny part of the world, but the truths they reveal span continents. Here you get to see the everyday struggle of a people to support themselves within a fairly inhospitable part of the world, spanning boom and bust years of agriculture, oil and gas production, and tourism. Located in the slick Gateway Visitor Center, exhibits vary, utilizing over 7,000 objects. You may walk through displays of a 1930s trading post, with an old enameled scale, cloth bolts, and vintage saddles. Next, you can tour the Dinosaurs to Drill Bits exhibit, exploring the region's rich oil and gas history, including a 7-minute ride in the **Geovator,** which simulates a trip 7,285 feet into an oil well. Kids enjoy this! Excellent changing exhibits rotate through as well. A gift shop sells fun local art and some nice New Mexico–made crafts.

3041 E. Main St. ✆ **505/599-1174.** Fax 505/326-7572. www.farmingtonmuseum.org. Free admission. Mon–Sat 8am–5pm.

In Nearby Aztec

VISITOR INFORMATION The **Aztec Chamber of Commerce,** 110 N. Ash St. (✆ **505/334-9551;** www.aztecchamber.com), is a friendly place with a wealth of information about the area.

Aztec Museum and Pioneer Village (Kids) A real treat for kids, this museum and village transport visitors back over a century to a place populated by strangely ubiquitous mannequins. The museum is crammed with memorabilia, but the outer **Pioneer Village** of replicas and real buildings, with all the trimmings, is what will hold interest. You'll walk through the actual 1912 Aztec jail—nowhere you'd want to live—into the sheriff's office, where a stuffed Andy of Mayberry look-alike is strangely lethargic. The blacksmith shop has an anvil and lots of dusty, uncomfortable-looking saddles, even some oddly shaped burro shoes. The Citizens Bank has a lovely oak cage and counter, and it's run by attentive mannequin women. You'll see an authentic 1906 church and a schoolhouse where mannequins Dick and Jane lead a possibly heated discussion. New additions include a farmhouse and historic drilling rigs. The second Saturday in September, the museum celebrates Founders' Day, with live exhibits, food, and games.

125 N. Main Ave., Aztec. ✆ **505/334-9829.** www.aztecmuseum.org. Admission $3 adults, $1 children 11–17, free for children 10 and under. Summer Wed–Sat 10am–4pm; winter hours vary (see website).

In Nearby Bloomfield

Salmon Ruins ★ (Kids) What really marks the 150 rooms of these ruins 11 miles west of Farmington near Bloomfield is their setting on a hillside, surrounded by lush San Juan River bosk. You'll begin in the museum, though, where a number of informative displays range from one showing the variety of types of Ancestral Puebloan vessels, from pitchers to canteens, to wild plants. Like the ruins at Aztec, two strong architectural influences are visible here. First the Chacoan, who built the village around the 11th century, with walls of an intricate rubble-filled core with sandstone veneer. The more simple Mesa Verde masonry was added in the 13th century. A trail guide will lead you to each site.

Built in 1990, **Heritage Park,** on an adjoining plot of land, comprises a series of reconstructed ancient and historic dwellings representing the area's cultures, from a paleoarchaic sand-dune site to an Anasazi pit house, from Apache wickiups and tepees to Navajo hogans, and an original pioneer homestead. Visitors are encouraged to enter the re-creations.

In the visitor center, you'll find a gift shop and a scholarly research library.

6131 US 64 (P.O. Box 125), Bloomfield, NM 87413. ✆ **505/632-2013.** Fax 505/632-8633. www.salmonruins.com. Admission $3 adults, $1 children 6–16, $2 seniors, free for children 5 and under. Summer Mon–Fri 8am–5pm, Sat–Sun 9am–5pm; winter Mon–Fri 8am–5pm, Sat 9am–5pm, and Sun noon–5pm.

AZTEC RUINS NATIONAL MONUMENT ★

Aztec Ruins is best known for its Great Kiva, the only completely reconstructed Anasazi great kiva in existence. Visitors can enter and sit within it, sensing the site's ancient history. The ruins of this 450-room Native American pueblo, left by the Ancestral Puebloans 7 centuries ago, are 14 miles northeast of Farmington, in the town of Aztec on the Animas River. Early Anglo settlers, convinced that the ruins were of Aztec origin, misnamed the site. Despite the fact that this pueblo was built long before the Aztecs of central Mexico lived, the name persisted.

The influence of the Chaco culture is strong at Aztec, as evidenced in the preplanned architecture, the open plaza, and the fine stone masonry in the old walls. But a later occupation shows the influence of Mesa Verde (which flourished 1200–75). This second group of settlers remodeled the old pueblo and built others nearby, using techniques less elaborate and decorative than those of the Chacoans. Visiting Aztec Ruins National Monument will take you approximately 1 hour, even if you take the .25-mile self-guided trail and spend some time in the visitor center, which displays some outstanding

Historic Art Stroll

Northwestern New Mexico's lush green fields and (mostly) mild climate are attracting more and more artists. A great place to sample some of the lively work is **Artifacts Gallery,** 302 E. Main St. (✆ **505/327-2907;** www.artifacts-gallery.com) in Farmington. Set in a Victorian-style lumber building is a collection of art studios whose artists are often on hand to discuss their work. Just down the street, step into **Andrea Kristina's Bookstore & Kafé,** 218 W. Main St. (✆ **505/327-3313;** www.andreakristinas.com). This lively place, in a historic building with tables set amid bookshelves, has a great selection of books and offers live music, poetry, and films on Friday and Saturday nights from 7 to 9pm. A range of coffee drinks and soups, salads, sandwiches, and pizza dress the menu. It's open Monday to Friday 7am to 9pm and Saturday 8am to 10pm. In nearby Aztec, stop in at **Feat of Clay,** 107 S. Main St. (✆ **505/334-4335**). A cooperative gallery, it holds the work of 14 local artists and has great prices. Look for "Molten Treasures," glass jewelry by Jinx Bolli. While in Aztec be sure to take some time to stroll through the town's newly renovated 19th-century **historic district.**

examples of Anasazi ceramics and basketry. Add another half-hour if you plan to watch the video that imaginatively documents the history of native cultures in the area.

Essentials

GETTING THERE Aztec Ruins is approximately a half-mile north of US 550, on Ruins Road (C.R. 2900), on the north edge of the city of Aztec. Ruins Road is the first street immediately west of the Animas River Bridge, on NM 516 in Aztec.

VISITOR INFORMATION For more information, contact **Aztec Ruins National Monument,** 84 C.R. 2900, Aztec, NM 87410-0640 (✆ **505/334-6174,** ext. 30; www.nps.gov/azru).

ADMISSION FEES & HOURS Admission is $5 for adults; children under 17 are admitted free. The monument is open daily from 8am to 6pm Memorial Day through Labor Day and 8am to 5pm the rest of the year; it's closed Thanksgiving, Christmas, and New Year's Day.

Camping

Camping is not permitted at the monument. Nearby, **Bloomfield KOA,** on Blanco Boulevard (✆ **800/562-8513** or 505/632-8339; www.koa.com), offers 83 sites, 73 full hookups, tenting, cabins, laundry and grocery facilities, picnic tables, grills, and firewood. Recreation facilities include arcade games, a heated swimming pool, a basketball hoop, a playground, horseshoes, volleyball, and a hot tub.

Camping is also available at **Navajo Lake State Park** (✆ **505/632-2278**).

SHOPPING

Downtown Farmington shops are generally open from 10am to 6pm Monday through Saturday. Native American arts and crafts are best purchased at trading posts, either downtown on Main or Broadway streets, or west of Farmington on US 64 toward Shiprock. You may want to check out one of the best in the city: **Fifth Generation Trading Company** ★, 232 W. Broadway (✆ **505/326-3211;** www.tannertrading.com), which has been trading since 1875. The Tanner family offers jewelry, Navajo rugs, pottery, alabaster sculptures, old pawn, and katsinas (kachinas). **Bob French Navajo Rugs,** on US 64, 18 miles west of Farmington (✆ **505/598-5621;** www.bobfrenchnavajorugs.com), sells silver and turquoise jewelry and a range of antique and new rugs. **Hogback Trading Company,** 3221 US 64, Waterflow, 17 miles west of Farmington (✆ **505/598-5154**), has large displays of Indian jewelry, rugs, and folk art. And **Navajo Trading Company,** 126 E. Main St. (✆ **505/325-1685**), is an actual pawnshop, with lots of exquisite old jewelry; you can peruse bracelets and necklaces while listening to clerks speaking Navajo.

GETTING OUTSIDE: NEARBY PARKS & RECREATION AREAS

Shiprock Peak

This distinctive landmark, on the Navajo Indian Reservation southwest of Shiprock, 29 miles west of Farmington via US 64, is known to the Navajo as *Tse bidá hi,* "Rock with wings." Composed of igneous rock flanked by long upright walls of solidified lava, it rises 1,700 feet off the desert floor to an elevation of 7,178 feet. There are scenic viewing points off US 491, 6 to 7 miles south of the town of Shiprock. You can get closer by taking the tribal road to the community of Red Rock, but you must have permission to get any nearer to this sacred Navajo rock. Climbing is not permitted.

The town named after the rock is a gateway to the Navajo reservation and the Four Corners region. There's a tribal visitor center here.

From Shiprock, you may want to make the 32-mile drive west on US 64 to Teec Nos Pos, Arizona, and then north on US 160, to the **Four Corners Monument** (✆ **928/871-6647;** www.navajonationsparks.org). A concrete slab here sits astride the only point in the United States where four states meet: New Mexico, Colorado, Utah, and Arizona. Kids especially like the idea of standing at the center and occupying four states at once. There's no view here, but vendors sell crafts and food. Some people find a visit here not worth the trip or cost. The monument is open daily 7am to 8pm Memorial Day to Labor Day and 8am to 5pm the rest of the year. The cost is $3 per person for all ages.

Navajo Lake State Park

The **San Juan River, Pine River,** and **Sims Mesa recreation sites,** all with camping, fishing, and boating, make this the most popular watersports destination for residents of northwestern New Mexico. Trout, northern pike, largemouth bass, and catfish are caught in lake and river waters, and the surrounding hills attract hunters seeking deer and elk. A visitor center at Pine River Recreation Area has interpretive displays on natural history and on the construction and use of the dam.

Navajo Lake, with an area of 15,000 acres, extends from the confluence of the San Juan and Los Pinos rivers 25 miles north into Colorado. Navajo Dam, an earthen embankment, is three-quarters of a mile long and 400 feet high. It provides Farmington-area cities, industries, and farms with their principal water supply. It's also the main storage reservoir for the Navajo Indian Irrigation Project, designed to irrigate 110,000 acres.

Anglers come from all over the world to fish the San Juan below the dam, a pastoral spot bordered by green hills, where golden light reflects off the water. Much of the water is designated "catch and release" and is teeming with rainbow, brown, and cutthroat trout. Experts will be heartily challenged by these fish that are attuned to the best tricks, while amateurs may want to hire a guide. For more information, see "Getting Outside in

Northern New Mexico," p. 272. The park is 40 miles east of Farmington on NM 511. Call ✆ **505/632-2278** for more information.

Not far from the park, **Wines of the San Juan,** 233 NM 511 at Turley (✆ **505/632-0879;** www.winesofthesanjuan.com), offers wine tastings and sells bottles of wines ranging from merlot to malvasia bianca. Call ahead to find out about the Sunday programs offered spring through fall, which might include flamenco guitar. The last weekend in September, the winery holds a festival featuring several bands and arts-and-crafts booths. The tasting room is open Monday to Saturday 10am to 6pm and Sunday noon to 6pm. Closed Tuesday.

Angel Peak Recreation Area

The distinctive pinnacle of 6,991-foot Angel Peak can often be spotted from the hillsides around Farmington. The area offers a short nature trail and a variety of unusual, colorful geological formations and canyons to explore on foot. The Bureau of Land Management has developed a primitive campground with nine campsites and provided picnic tables in a few spots (no drinking water provided). The park is about 35 miles south of Farmington on US 550; the last 6 miles of access, after turning off US 550, are over a graded dirt road. For park information, call ✆ **505/599-8900.**

Bisti/De-Na-Zin Wilderness

Often referred to as Bisti Badlands (pronounced Bist-*eye*), this barren region may merit that name today, but it was once very different. Around 70 million years ago, large dinosaurs lived near what was then a coastal swamp bordering a retreating inland sea. Today, their bones, and those of fish, turtles, lizards, and small mammals, are eroding slowly from the low shale hills.

Kirtland Shale, containing several bands of color, dominates the eastern part of the wilderness and caps the mushroom-shaped formations found there. Along with the spires and fanciful shapes of rock, hikers may find petrified wood sprinkled in small chips throughout the area, or even an occasional log. ***Note:*** Removing petrified wood, fossils, or anything else from the wilderness is prohibited.

Hiking in the Bisti is fairly easy; from the small parking lot, follow an arroyo east 2 or 3 miles into the heart of the formations, which you'll see on your right (aim for the two red hills). The De-Na-Zin Wilderness to the east requires more climbing and navigational skills. It has no designated trails, bikes and motorized vehicles are prohibited, and it has no water or significant shade. The hour just after sunset or, especially, just before sunrise is a pleasant and quite magical time to see this starkly beautiful landscape. Primitive camping is allowed (bring plenty of water and supplies).

Bisti/De-Na-Zin Wilderness is just off NM 371, 37 miles south of Farmington. For more information, call the **Bureau of Land Management** at ✆ **505/599-8900.**

WHERE TO STAY IN & AROUND FARMINGTON & AZTEC

Courtyard by Marriott ★ Kids This newer hotel provides elegant rooms and all the amenities of a full-service inn, with the consistency you'd expect from Marriott. The expansive lobby overlooking Riverwalk Park is decorated in a Southwestern style. Just off it is a quiet lounge and a restaurant. The style carries into the rooms. They are spacious with comfortable beds and medium-size bathrooms with outer vanities. Southwestern landscape paintings adorn the walls. The suites are large and contain one bedroom and a living room with a foldout couch, wet bar, and microwave—a good choice for small families.

560 Scott Ave., Farmington, NM 87401. ✆ **800/228-9290** or 505/325-5111. Fax 505/325-5588. www.marriott.com. 125 units. $89–$105 double; $125–$130 suite. AE, DC, DISC, MC, V. **Amenities:** Restaurant; bar; indoor pool w/sun deck; exercise room; Jacuzzi; room service. *In room:* A/C, TV, hair dryer, Wi-Fi.

Soaring Eagle Lodge ★ Finds This lodge offers basic and clean cabins on a poetic bend of the San Juan River. It's mostly a place for fishing enthusiasts, who come to ply these world-renowned waters, but those seeking to escape to the quiet of a lovely river would like it too. Each cabin has a kitchenette, partitioned-off bedroom space, and a front room with two easy chairs. Beds are comfortable and bathrooms very clean. An on site restaurant serves tasty breakfasts and dinners. Be sure to reserve a cabin on the river edge where the views couldn't be finer. The lodge can set you up with a guide, and you may fish for free from shore on the lodge's private waters.

48 C.R. 4370, off NM 511, Navajo Dam, NM, 87419. ✆ **800/866-2719** or 505/632-5621. www.soaringeaglelodge.net. 11 units. $156 per person, double. Price includes a full breakfast and fishing privileges. MC, V. **Amenities:** Restaurant; guide service; Wi-Fi (in conference room). *In room:* A/C, TV, fridge, microwave.

Bed & Breakfasts

Casa Blanca ★★★ Finds Kids This B&B offers such nice rooms, it's a travel destination. In a quiet residential neighborhood just a few blocks from the shops and restaurants of Main Street, this inn, built in the 1940s, was once the home of a wealthy family that traded with the Navajos. In 2004, new owners expanded it, adding patios and fountains, creating a lovely oasis. The large rooms, decorated in an elegant Southwestern style, have original artwork and plenty of amenities. Our favorite room is the Chaco, with red-brick floors, authentic Navajo rugs, and antique furnishings. Also of note is the Vista Grande, a large upstairs room with views in every direction. Travelers with disabilities are treated especially well here (there are two large suites especially for them), as are business travelers. The full breakfast is always gourmet. Ask about their lovely two-bedroom, two-bathroom cottage, with a full kitchen, a great place for families, marked by the same elegance as the rest of the inn.

505 E. La Plata St., Farmington, NM 87401. ✆ **800/550-6503** or 505/327-6503. Fax 505/326-5680. www.casablancanm.com. 8 units. $125–$215 double; $20 single-traveler discount. Rates include full breakfast. AE, MC, V. *In room:* A/C, TV, fridge, hair dryer, microwave; Wi-Fi.

Kokopelli's Cave ★★ Retired geologist Bruce Black wanted to build a cave, so he gave some laid-off Grants miners $20,000 to bore as deeply as they could into the side of a cliff face. This luxury apartment was the result. Built in a semicircle, both the entry hall and the bedroom have wide sliding-glass doors leading to little balconies beyond which the cliff face drops hundreds of feet below. This really is a cliff dwelling, and you must hike a bit down to it, though good guardrails guide you. The apartment is laid out around a broad central pillar, and the ceilings and walls are thick, undulating stone. A grill is outside, as are chairs where you can relax in the mornings and evenings. Fruit, juice, coffee, and pastries make up a self-serve breakfast.

3204 Crestridge Dr., Farmington, NM 87401. ✆ **505/326-2461.** Fax 505/325-9671. www.bbonline.com/nm/kokopelli. 1 unit. $240 double; $280 for 3–4 people. Closed Dec–Feb. AE, MC, V. **Amenities:** Jacuzzi. *In room:* TV/VCR, kitchen, hair dryer.

Camping

Mom and Pop RV Park (✆ **505/327-3200**) has 36 sites, 35 of them with full hookups, tenting, a bathhouse, and a toy soldier shop. The sites are a bit desolate, around an asphalt central area, but a little grassy spot at the office has an incredible electric train set that Pop runs at certain times during the day. Mom and Pop RV Park is at 901 Illinois Ave., in Farmington (just off US 64).

WHERE TO DINE IN FARMINGTON & AZTEC

The Bluffs ★★ Finds SANDWICHES/SEAFOOD/STEAKS Ten minutes east of town center, the Bluffs serves inventive food with attention to detail. A large room is sectioned off by wooden partitions crowned with elegantly glazed glass shaped like the bluffs prominent in the surrounding area. It's a comfortable atmosphere with roomy booths and stacked sandstone accents. Service is efficient. The outdoor patio is a nice spot on not-so-hot days. For lunch, our pick is the turkey-bacon club, served on ciabatta bread. The Thai beef salad is also tasty. At dinner, try your favorite steak cut of Angus beef or sesame-crusted ahi tuna. Dinners come with salad and a choice of vegetable or potato. A full bar accompanies the menu.

3450 E. Main St. ✆ **505/325-8155.** Reservations recommended Fri–Sat nights. Main courses $8–$12 lunch, $15–$39 dinner. AE, DISC, MC, V. Mon–Fri 11am–2pm, Mon–Sat 5–9pm; lounge daily 4–9 or 10pm.

Main Street Bistro ★ BAKERY/CAFE This imaginative little cafe in Aztec, with brightly colored floors and walls, offers tasty housemade breakfasts, sandwiches, soups, and salads. Order at the counter and the friendly waitstaff will bring your food to the table. Be aware that the place bustles during peak hours; so if you want quiet time, go midmorning or later in the afternoon. At breakfast, you might order the egg-centric—two eggs, hash browns, English muffin, and fruit. For lunch, you can't go wrong with the daily soup special, a salad, or sandwich (try the Ultimate—turkey, bacon, avocado, and sprouts), or the quiche, made fresh daily. Wash it all down with a full range of coffee drinks or their delicious raspberry iced tea.

122 N. Main St., Aztec. ✆ **505/334-0109.** All menu items under $9. DISC, MC, V. Mon–Fri 7am–4pm; Sat 7am–noon.

3 Rivers Eatery & Brewhouse ★★ Kids AMERICAN This brewpub on an elegant corner in the center of downtown serves some of the region's best food and beer. After our first sip of their Arroyo Amber Ale, we were sold. The restaurant is set in a big two-story brick building that once housed the Farmington Drug Store and the Farmington *Times-Hustler* newspaper. Hardwood floors and vintage items, such as period bottles and posters found in the renovation, complete the experience. It's a comfortable place where the owner might just sit down in one of the comfy booths with you and chat about his passion, beer brewing. I recommend the burgers, which come in a variety of flavors, from grilled onion and Swiss to jack and green chile. You'll also find barbecue pork ribs, steaks, and seafood. Families enjoy the spacious booths in the back and a kid's menu.

101 E. Main St., Farmington. ✆ **505/324-2187.** www.threeriversbrewery.com. Main courses $6–$25. AE, DISC, MC, V. Mon–Thurs 11am–10pm; Fri–Sat 11am–11pm; Sun 11am–9pm.

FARMINGTON AFTER DARK

Sandstone Production's **Summer Outdoor Theater ★** stages two fun shows each year. Presented in the Lions Wilderness Park Amphitheater (off College Blvd.) against a sandstone backdrop, the offerings are usually a dramatic piece and a musical. For information and advance ticket sales, contact ✆ **505/599-1148** (www.fmtn.org/sandstone). Shows are Wednesday through Saturday from mid-June through July, with dinner at 6:30pm and the performance at 8pm.

If you're looking for a pub, **3 Rivers Tap & Game Room,** 113 E. Main St. (✆ **505/325-6605;** www.threeriversbrewery.com), is a big hit with locals. This brewpub/game room has wood floors, high ceilings, and lots of laughter and brew flowing. Pool tables, foosball, and shuffleboard fill patrons' time while they munch on popcorn and peanuts, and, some nights, listen to live music jam. Patrons can order food from the next-door brewpub/restaurant of the same name (see above).

14 CHACO CULTURE NATIONAL PARK ★★★

A stunning setting and well-preserved ruins make the long drive to **Chaco Culture National Historic Park,** often referred to as Chaco Canyon, worthwhile. Whether you come from the north or south, you drive in on a dusty (and sometimes muddy) road that adds to the authenticity and adventure of this remote New Mexico experience. When you finally arrive, you walk through stark desert country that seems perhaps ill suited as a center of culture. However, the Ancestral Puebloan (Anasazi) people successfully farmed the lowlands and built great masonry towns, which connected with other towns over a wide-ranging network of roads crossing this desolate place.

What's most interesting here is how changes in architecture—beginning in the mid-800s, when the Anasazi started building on a larger scale than they had previously—chart the area's cultural progress. The Anasazi used the same masonry techniques that tribes had used in smaller villages in the region (walls one stone thick, with generous use of mud mortar), but they built stone villages of multiple stories with rooms several times larger than in the previous stage of their culture. Within a century, six large pueblos were underway. This pattern of a single large pueblo with oversize rooms, surrounded by conventional villages, caught on throughout the region. New communities built along these lines sprang up. Old villages built similarly large pueblos. Eventually there were more than 75 such towns, most of them closely tied to Chaco by an extensive system of roads. Aerial photos show hundreds of miles of roads connecting these towns with the Chaco pueblos, one of the longest running 42 miles straight north to Salmon Ruins and the Aztec Ruins. It is this road network that leads some scholars to believe that Chaco was the center of a unified Anasazi society.

This progress led to Chaco becoming the economic center of the San Juan Basin by A.D. 1000. As many as 5,000 people may have lived in some 400 settlements in and around Chaco. As masonry techniques advanced through the years, walls rose more than four stories in height. Some of these are still visible today.

Chaco's decline after 1½ centuries of success coincided with a drought in the San Juan Basin between A.D. 1130 and 1180. Scientists still argue vehemently over why the site was abandoned and where the Chacoans went. Many believe that an influx of outsiders may have brought new rituals to the region, causing a schism among tribal members. Most agree, however, that the people drifted away to more hospitable places in the region and that their descendants are today's Pueblo people.

This is an isolated area, and there are **no services** available within or close to the park—no food, gas, auto repairs, firewood, lodging (besides the campground), or drinking water (other than at the visitor center) are available. Overnight camping is permitted year-round. If you're headed toward Santa Fe after a day at the park and looking for a place to spend the night, one nice option is the **Cañon del Rio–A Riverside Inn,** 16445 Scenic Hwy. 4, Jemez Springs, NM 87025 (✆ **575/829-4377;** www.canondelrio.com).

ESSENTIALS

GETTING THERE To get to Chaco from Santa Fe, take I-25 south to Bernalillo and then US 550 northwest. Turn off US 550 at CR 7900 (3 miles southeast of Nageezi and about 50 miles west of Cuba at mile 112.5). Follow the signs from US 550 to the park boundary (21 miles). This route includes 8 miles of paved road (CR 7900) and 13 miles of rough dirt road (CR 7950). This is the recommended route. NM 57 from Blanco Trading Post is closed. The trip takes about 3½ to 4 hours. Farmington is the nearest population center, a 1½-hour drive away. The park can also be reached from Grants via I-40 west to NM 371, which you follow north to Indian Route 9, east, and north again on NM 57 (IR 14), with the final 19 miles ungraded dirt. This route is rough to impassable and is not recommended for RVs.

Call ahead to inquire about **road conditions** (✆ **505/786-7014**) before leaving the paved highways. The dirt roads can get extremely muddy and dangerous after rain or snow, and afternoon thunderstorms are common in late summer.

VISITOR INFORMATION Ranger-guided walks and campfire talks are available in the summer at the visitor center, where you can get self-guiding trail brochures and permits for the overnight campground (see "Camping," below). If you want information before you leave home, contact the Superintendent, Chaco Culture National Historical Park, 1808 County Rd. 7950, Nageezi, NM 87037 (✆ **505/786-7014;** www.nps.gov/chcu).

ADMISSION FEES & HOURS Admission is $8 per car; a campsite is $10 extra. The visitor center is open daily from 8am to 5pm. Trails are open from sunrise to sunset.

SEEING THE HIGHLIGHTS

Exploring the ruins and hiking are the most popular activities here. A series of pueblo ruins stands within 5 or 6 miles of each other on the broad, flat, treeless canyon floor. Plan to spend at least 3 to 4 hours here driving to and exploring the different pueblos. A one-way road from the visitor center loops up one side of the canyon and down the other. Parking lots are scattered along the road near the various pueblos; from most, it's only a short walk to the ruins.

You may want to focus your energy on seeing **Pueblo Bonito,** the largest prehistoric Southwest Native American dwelling ever excavated. It contains giant kivas and 800 rooms covering more than 3 acres. The **Pueblo Alto Trail** is a nice hike that takes you up on the canyon rim so that you can see the ruins from above—in the afternoon, with thunderheads building, the views are spectacular. If you're a cyclist, stop at the visitor center to pick up a map outlining ridable trails.

WHERE TO STAY & DINE

If you're driving from the northwest, your best bet is to stay in the Farmington/Aztec area (see above). However, if you're driving on US 550 from Albuquerque, you have limited options. The town of Cuba (pop. 600) offers good dining and okay accommodations. You may want to plan your drive to stop for lunch at **El Bruno's Restaurante y Cantina,** 6453 Main St. (US 550), in the center of Cuba (✆ **575/289-9429**). Within an adobe building with ceiling vigas, Mexican leather furniture, and a lovely patio, this place serves good New Mexican food and steaks. It's open daily 11am to 10pm. Diners can order from a full bar.

Meanwhile, the lodging situation in this little town isn't quite so bright. Your only option here, really, is the **Frontier Motel,** on US 550 (✆ **505/289-3474**). This place straddling both sides of the highway offers clean rooms to travelers. Be sure to get one on the south side of the highway, which is more upscale. Rooms have decent furnishings, fairly comfortable beds, and small bathrooms. Most units have fridges and microwaves. Prices range from $45 to $60.

Camping

Gallo Campground is quite popular with hikers. It's about 1 mile east of the visitor center; fees are $10 per night. Gallo has 48 sites, with fire grates (bring your own wood or charcoal), central toilets, and nonpotable water. Drinking water is available only at the visitor center. The campground cannot accommodate trailers over 30 feet. There's no place to stock up on supplies after you start the arduous drive to the canyon, so make sure you're well supplied, especially with water, before you head out.

7

Santa Fe

A city of 70,000 people living 7,000 feet above sea level, Santa Fe is an exotic and sophisticated place. The Native Americans enlighten the area with viewpoints and lifestyles deeply tied to nature and completely contrary to the American norm. Many of the Hispanics here still live within extended families and practice a devout Catholicism; they bring a slower pace to the city and an appreciation for deep-rooted ties. Meanwhile, a strong cosmopolitan element contributes cutting-edge cuisine, world-class opera, first-run art films, and some of the finest artwork in the world, seen easily while wandering on foot from gallery to gallery, museum to museum.

The city's history is told through its architecture. For its first 2 centuries, it was constructed mainly of adobe bricks. When the U.S. took over the territory from Mexico in 1846 and trade began flowing from the eastern states, new tools and materials began to change the face of the city. The old adobe took on brick facades and roof decoration in what became known as the Territorial style. But the flat roofs were retained so that the city never lost its unique, low profile, creating a sense of serenity found in no other U.S. city.

Bishop Jean Baptiste Lamy, the inspiration for the character of Bishop Latour in Willa Cather's *Death Comes for the Archbishop,* built the French Romanesque St. Francis Cathedral shortly after he was appointed to head the diocese in 1851. Other structures still standing include what is claimed to be the oldest house in the United States. The San Miguel Mission is the oldest mission church in the country, while the state capitol, built in the circular form of a ceremonial Indian kiva, is among the newest in the U.S.

The city was originally named La Villa Real de la Santa Fe de San Francisco de Asis (the Royal City of the Holy Faith of St. Francis of Assisi) by its founder, Spanish governor Don Pedro de Peralta. He built the Palace of the Governors as his capitol on the central plaza; today it's an excellent museum of the city's 4 centuries of history. It is one of the major attractions in the Southwest, and under its portico, Native Americans sell their crafts to eager travelers, as they have done for decades.

The plaza is the focus of numerous bustling art markets and Santa Fe's early September fiesta, celebrated annually since 1770. The fiesta commemorates the time following the years of the Pueblo revolt, when Spanish governor Don Diego de Vargas reconquered the city in 1692. The plaza was also the terminus of the Santa Fe Trail from Missouri, and of the earlier Camino Real (Royal Rd.) from Mexico, when the city thrived on the wool and fur of the Chihuahua trade. Today, a central gazebo makes a fun venue for summer concerts.

What captures the eye most, though, is the city's setting, backed by the rolling hills and the blue peaks of the Sangre de Cristo Mountains. In the summer, thunderheads build into giant swirling structures above those peaks and move over the city, dropping cool rain. In the winter, snow often covers the many flat-roofed adobe homes, creating a poetic abstraction that at every glance convinces you that the place itself is exotic art.

1 ORIENTATION

Part of the charm of Santa Fe is that it's so easy to get around. Like most cities of Hispanic origin, it was built around a parklike central plaza. Centuries-old adobe buildings and churches still line the narrow streets; many of them house shops, restaurants, art galleries, and museums.

Santa Fe sits high and dry at the foot of the Sangre de Cristo range. Santa Fe Baldy, a mere 12 miles northeast of the plaza, rises to more than 12,600 feet. The city's downtown straddles the Santa Fe River, a tiny tributary of the Rio Grande that is little more than a trickle for much of the year. North is the Española Valley and about 70 miles beyond that is the village of Taos (see chapter 8). South are ancient Indian turquoise mines in the Cerrillos Hills; southwest is metropolitan Albuquerque, 58 miles away (see chapter 9). To the west, across the Caja del Rio Plateau, is the Rio Grande, and beyond that, the 11,000-foot Jemez Mountains and Valle Grande, an ancient and massive volcanic caldera. Native American pueblos dot the entire Rio Grande valley; they're an hour's drive in any direction.

ARRIVING

BY PLANE Many people choose to fly into the Albuquerque International Sunport. However, if you want to save time and don't mind paying a bit more, you can fly into the **Santa Fe Municipal Airport** (SAF; ✆ **505/955-2900;** www.santafenm.gov), just outside the southwestern city limits on Airport Road. In conjunction with American Airlines, commuter flights are offered by **American Eagle** (✆ **800/433-7300;** www.aa.com). Delta Airlines (✆ **800/221-1212;** www.delta.com) is planning to begin service in the near future.

If you do fly into Albuquerque, you can rent a car or take one of the bus services. See "Getting There & Getting Around," in chapter 3, for details.

From the Santa Fe Municipal Airport, **Roadrunner Shuttle** (✆ **505/424-3367**) meets every commercial flight and takes visitors anywhere in Santa Fe. From the Albuquerque Sunport to Santa Fe, **Sandia Shuttle Express** (✆ **888/775-5696** or 505/474-5696; www.sandiashuttle.com) runs shuttles from 8:45am to 10:45pm.

BY TRAIN & BUS For detailed information about train and bus service to Santa Fe, see "Getting There & Getting Around," in chapter 3.

BY CAR I-25 skims past Santa Fe's southern city limits, connecting it along one continuous highway from Billings, Montana, to El Paso, Texas. I-40, the state's major east–west thoroughfare, which bisects Albuquerque, affords coast-to-coast access to Santa Fe. (From the west, motorists leave I-40 in Albuquerque and take I-25 north; from the east, travelers exit I-40 at Clines Corners and continue 52 miles to Santa Fe on US 285. ***Note:*** Diesel is scarce on US 285, so be sure to fill up before you leave Clines Corners.) For those coming from the northwest, the most direct route is via Durango, Colorado, on US 160, entering Santa Fe on US 84.

For a list of car-rental agencies, see "Fast Facts," on p. 613; for agencies in Santa Fe, see "Getting Around," below.

VISITOR INFORMATION

The **Santa Fe Community Convention Center and Visitors Bureau** is located downtown at 201 W. Marcy St. (P.O. Box 909), Santa Fe, NM 87504-0909 (✆ **800/777-CITY** [2489] or 505/955-6200). You can also log on to the bureau's website, **www.santafe.org**.

CITY LAYOUT

MAIN ARTERIES & STREETS The limits of downtown Santa Fe are demarcated on three sides by the horseshoe-shaped Paseo de Peralta and on the west by St. Francis Drive, otherwise known as US 84/285. Alameda Street follows the north side of the Santa Fe River through downtown, with the State Capitol and other government buildings on the south side of the river, and most buildings of historic and tourist interest on the north, east of Guadalupe Street.

The plaza is Santa Fe's universally accepted point of orientation. Its four diagonal walkways meet at a central monument, around which a strange and wonderful assortment of people of all ages, nationalities, and lifestyles can be found at nearly any hour of the day or night.

If you stand in the center of the plaza looking north, you'll be gazing directly at the Palace of the Governors. In front of you is Palace Avenue; behind you, San Francisco Street. To your left is Lincoln Avenue, and to your right is Washington Avenue, which divides the downtown avenues into east and west. St. Francis Cathedral is the massive Romanesque structure a block east, down San Francisco Street. Alameda Street is 2 full blocks behind you.

Near the intersection of Alameda Street and Paseo de Peralta, you'll find Canyon Road running east toward the mountains. Much of this street is one-way. The best way to see it is to walk up or down, taking time to explore shops and galleries and even have lunch or dinner.

Running to the southwest from the downtown area, beginning opposite the state office buildings on Galisteo Avenue, is Cerrillos Road. Once the main north–south highway connecting New Mexico's state capital with its largest city, Albuquerque, it is now a 6-mile-long motel and fast-food strip. St. Francis Drive, which crosses Cerrillos Road 3 blocks south of Guadalupe Street, is a far less tawdry byway, linking Santa Fe with I-25, 4 miles southwest of downtown. The Old Pecos Trail, on the east side of the city, also joins downtown and the freeway. St. Michael's Drive connects the three arteries.

FINDING AN ADDRESS The city's layout makes it difficult to know exactly where to look for a particular address. It's best to call ahead for directions.

MAPS Free city and state maps can be obtained at tourist information offices. An excellent state highway map is published by the **New Mexico Department of Tourism,** 491 Old Santa Fe Trail, Lamy Building, Santa Fe, NM 87503 (✆ **800/733-6396** or 505/827-7400; www.newmexico.org; to receive a tourism guide call ✆ **800/777-CITY** [2489]). There's also a Santa Fe visitor center in the same building. More specific county and city maps are available from the **State Highway and Transportation Department,** 1120 Cerrillos Rd., Santa Fe, NM 87504 (✆ **505/827-5100**). Members of the **American Automobile Association (AAA),** 1644 St. Michael's Dr. (✆ **505/471-6620;** www.aaa.com), can obtain free maps from the AAA office. Other good regional maps can be purchased at area bookstores.

2 GETTING AROUND

The best way to see downtown Santa Fe is on foot. Free **walking-tour maps** are available at the **tourist information center,** 201 W. Marcy St. (✆ **800/777-CITY** [2489] or 505/955-6200), and several guided walking tours, as well as two self-guided tours, are included later in this chapter.

BY BUS

In 1993, Santa Fe opened **Santa Fe Trails** (✆ **505/955-2001;** www.santafenm.gov), its first public bus system. There are seven routes, and visitors can pick up a map from the Community Convention Center and Visitors Bureau. Most buses operate Monday to Friday 6am to 11pm and Saturday 8am to 8pm. There is some service on Sunday and holidays. Call for a current schedule and fare information.

BY CAR

Cars can be rented from any of the following firms in Santa Fe: **Avis,** Santa Fe Airport (✆ **505/471-5892**); **Budget,** 1946 Cerrillos Rd. (✆ **505/984-1596**); **Enterprise,** 2641A Cerrillos Rd., and 4450 Cerrillos Rd. (at the Auto Park; ✆ **505/473-3600**); and **Hertz,** Santa Fe Airport (✆ **505/471-7189**).

Note: In 2002, the Santa Fe City Council imposed a law prohibiting use of cellphones while driving within the city limits, with strict fines imposed. If you need to make a call, be sure to pull off the road.

Street parking is difficult to find during summer months. There's a metered parking lot near the federal courthouse, 2 blocks north of the plaza; a city lot behind Santa Fe Village, a block south of the plaza; and another city lot at Water and Sandoval streets. If you stop by the Santa Fe Community Convention Center and Visitors Bureau, at 201 W. Marcy St., you can pick up a wallet-size guide to Santa Fe parking areas. The map shows both street and lot parking.

BY TAXI

Cabs are difficult to flag from the street, but you can call for one. Expect to pay a standard fee of $4 for the service and an average of about $2.75 per mile. **Capital City Cab** (✆ **505/438-0000**) is the main company in Santa Fe.

BY BICYCLE

Riding a bicycle is a good way to get around town, though you'll have to ride cautiously because there are few designated bike paths. Check with **Mellow Velo,** 638 Old Santa Fe Trail (✆ **505/982-8986;** www.mellowvelo.com); **Bike-N-Sport,** 524 Cordova Rd. (✆ **505/820-0809;** www.nmbikensport.com), or **Santa Fe Mountain Sports,** 607 Cerrillos Rd. (✆ **505/988-3337;** www.santafemountainsports.com), for rentals.

FAST FACTS

ABQ Health Partners, 465 St. Michaels Dr. (✆ **505/995-2400**), is open Monday to Thursday 8am to 6pm and Friday 8am to 5pm. For physician and surgeon referral and information services, call the **American Board of Medical Specialties** (✆ **866/275-2267**). **St. Vincent Hospital,** 455 St. Michaels Dr. (✆ **505/983-3361,** or 505/995-3934 for emergency services), is a 248-bed regional health center. Patient services include urgent and emergency-room care and ambulatory surgery. Health services are also available at the

Women's Health Services Family Care and Counseling Center (✆ **505/988-8869**). **Ultimed,** 707 Paseo de Peralta (✆ **505/989-8707**), an urgent-care facility near the plaza, offers comprehensive health care.

See also "Fast Facts: American Southwest" on p. 607.

3 WHERE TO STAY

The City Different offers a broad range of accommodations. From downtown hotels to Cerrillos Road motels, ranch-style resorts to quaint bed-and-breakfasts, the standard is almost universally high.

Be aware of the seasonal nature of the tourist industry in Santa Fe: Accommodations are often booked solid through the summer months, and most places raise their prices accordingly. Rates increase even more during Indian Market, the third weekend of August. During these periods, it's essential to make reservations well in advance.

RESERVATIONS SERVICES Year-round reservation assistance is available from **SantaFeHotels.com** (✆ 800/745-9910), the **Accommodation Hot Line** (✆ 800/338-6877), **All Santa Fe Reservations** (✆ 877/737-7366), and **Santa Fe Stay,** which specializes in casitas (✆ 800/995-2272). **Emergency Lodging Assistance** is available free after 4pm daily (✆ 505/986-0038). All of the above are private companies and may have biases toward certain properties. Do your own research before calling.

HOTELS/MOTELS

Downtown

Everything within the horseshoe-shaped Paseo de Peralta and east a few blocks along either side of the Santa Fe River is considered downtown Santa Fe. All these accommodations are within walking distance of the plaza.

Very Expensive

Eldorado Hotel & Spa ★★ Since its opening in 1986, the Eldorado has been a model hotel for the city. In a large structure, the architects managed to meld pueblo revival style with an interesting cathedral feel, inside and out. The lobby has a high ceiling that continues into the court area and the cafe, all adorned with well over a million dollars' worth of Southwestern art. The spacious, quiet rooms received a makeover in 2006, maintaining an artistic motif, with a warm feel created by custom-made furniture in all units (and kiva fireplaces in many). You'll find families, businesspeople, and conference-goers staying here. Most of the rooms have views of downtown Santa Fe, many from balconies. If you're really indulging, join the ranks of Mick Jagger, Geena Davis, and King Juan Carlos of Spain, and try the penthouse five-room presidential suite for $1,500 per night. The Nidah Spa offers a full range of treatments, including a turquoise gemstone therapy, worth sampling. The Eldorado also manages the nearby Zona Rosa condominiums, which are two-, three-, and four-bedroom suites with full kitchens. The hotel's innovative and elegant restaurant, the **Old House**, serves creative American cuisine.

309 W. San Francisco St., Santa Fe, NM 87501. ✆ **800/955-4455** or 505/988-4455. Fax 505/995-4544. www.eldoradohotel.com. 219 units. $139–$389 double. Seasonal package rates are available. AE, DC, DISC, MC, V. Valet parking $18 per night. Pets accepted. **Amenities:** 2 restaurants; bar; concierge; gym (w/ view); Jacuzzi; heated rooftop pool; room service; his-and-hers saunas and steam baths; spa. *In room:* A/C, TV, hair dryer, minibar, Wi-Fi.

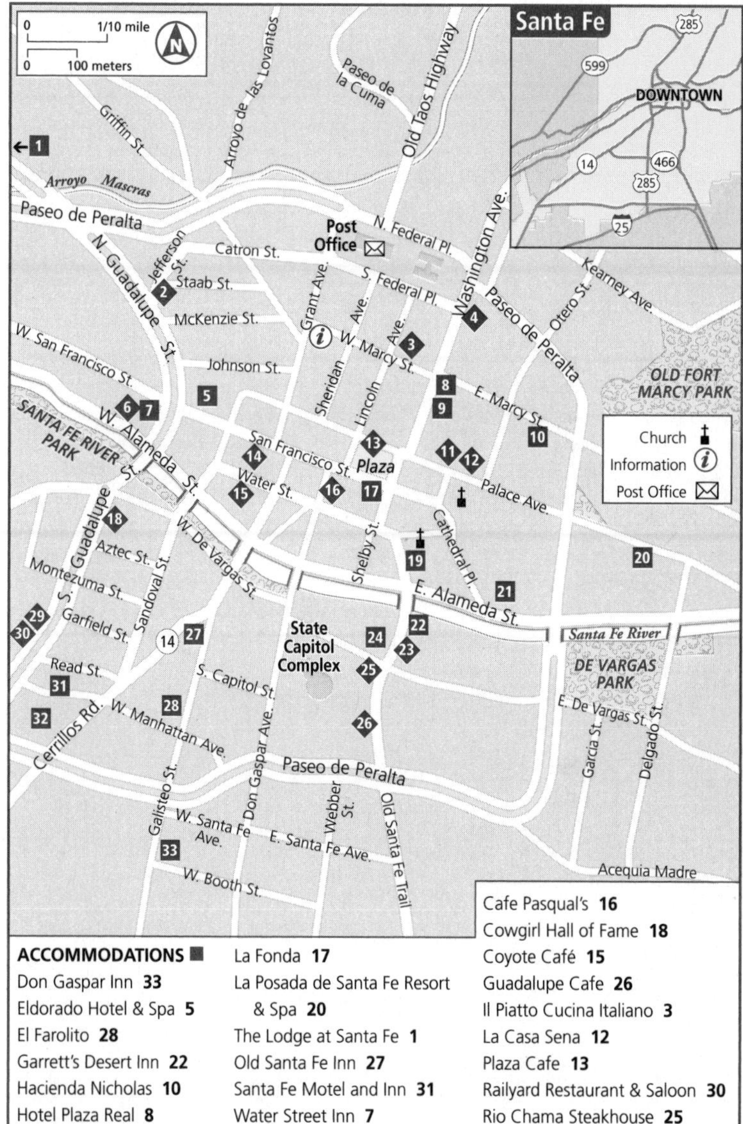

ACCOMMODATIONS ■

Don Gaspar Inn **33**
Eldorado Hotel & Spa **5**
El Farolito **28**
Garrett's Desert Inn **22**
Hacienda Nicholas **10**
Hotel Plaza Real **8**
Hotel Santa Fe **32**
Inn & Spa at Loretto **19**
Inn of the Anasazi **9**
Inn of the Five Graces **24**
Inn on the Alameda **21**
La Fonda **17**
La Posada de Santa Fe Resort & Spa **20**
The Lodge at Santa Fe **1**
Old Santa Fe Inn **27**
Santa Fe Motel and Inn **31**
Water Street Inn **7**

DINING ◆

Aqua Santa **6**
Blue Corn Café **14**
Bumble Bee's Baja Grill **2**
Cafe Pasqual's **16**
Cowgirl Hall of Fame **18**
Coyote Café **15**
Guadalupe Cafe **26**
Il Piatto Cucina Italiano **3**
La Casa Sena **12**
Plaza Cafe **13**
Railyard Restaurant & Saloon **30**
Rio Chama Steakhouse **25**
Santacafé **4**
The Shed **11**
Tomasita's Cafe **29**
Upper Crust Pizza **23**
315 **23**

Encantado ★★★ Santa Fe recently witnessed the opening of this Auberge Resort, an architectural artwork. About 15 minutes north of the plaza, the resort resides where the old Rancho Encantado was, though all the former buildings of that historic property have been razed. The new resort, set in the pink foothills of the Sangre de Cristo Mountains, offers 65 elegant casitas, an artfully kiva-shaped spa, and gourmet dining. The resort melds contemporary architecture with traditional Pueblo style, utilizing textured art and earth tones to add warmth to the design. Broad windows blur the boundary between indoor and out, with views from nearly every vantage point. In the casitas, polished concrete floors, kiva fireplaces, vaulted ceilings, and patios with stunning vistas facing west toward the Jemez Mountains add to the "mystical" quality the resort touts. Encantado's **Terra** offers three meals daily in a glass-walled dining room accented with stone and wood.

198 NM 592. ✆ **877/262-4666.** Fax 505/946-5888. www.encantadoresort.com. 65 units. $275–$650 double; $675–$1,050 suite. AE, DC, DISC, MC, V. **Amenities:** Restaurant; bar; concierge; gym; Jacuzzi; heated outdoor pool; room service; sauna; spa. *In-room:* A/C, TV, fridge, hair dryer, Wi-Fi.

Inn of the Anasazi ★★★ The designers of this fine luxury hotel have crafted a feeling of grandness in a very limited space. A 2006 remodel added even finer touches, including new bedding and decor in the rooms, with bold splashes of color from artwork and weavings. Flagstone floors and vigas create a warm and welcoming ambience that evokes the feeling of an Anasazi cliff dwelling. Oversize cacti complete the look. Accents are appropriately Navajo, in a nod to the fact that the Navajo live in the area the Anasazi once inhabited. A half-block off the plaza, this hotel was built in 1991 to cater to travelers who know their hotels. On the ground floor are a living room and library with oversize furniture and replicas of Anasazi pottery and Navajo rugs. The rooms range from medium-size to spacious, with pearl-finished walls, comfortable four-poster beds, and novelties such as iron candle sconces, gaslit kiva fireplaces (in some), and humidifiers. All the rooms are quiet and comfortable, though none have dramatic views. Though this is still a great hotel, a recent visit left me asking if it was worth the price. The **Anasazi Restaurant** serves creative Southwestern cuisine.

113 Washington Ave., Santa Fe, NM 87501. ✆ **800/688-8100** or 505/988-3030. Fax 505/988-3277. www.innoftheanasazi.com. 57 units. Jan 5–Feb 26 $269–$469; Feb 27–Apr 28 $325–$525; Apr 29–Jan 4 $325–$525 double. AE, DC, DISC, MC, V. Valet parking $15 per day. **Amenities:** Restaurant; concierge; room service. *In room:* A/C, TV/DVD, hair dryer, Wi-Fi.

Inn of the Five Graces ★★ Finds In the historic Barrio de Analco, just a few blocks from the Plaza, this inn holds true to its stated theme: "Here the Orient and the Old West meet, surprisingly at home in each other's arms." With floral-decked courtyards, elaborately decorated suites with kilim rugs, ornately carved beds, and often beautiful mosaic tile work in the bathrooms, this is truly a "sheik" place. All but a few suites are medium size, most with small bathrooms, and some with fireplaces. The lower-priced rooms are smaller. Request one of the suites in the buildings on the north side of East de Vargas Street; they're more spacious and substantially built. Travelers seeking an exotic stay will like this place; it's of the same caliber as Inn of the Anasazi, but with more flair. The inn's biggest news is the purchase of the **Pink Adobe** next door, which they've turned into their restaurant. Wine-and-cheese hour is offered every other day. This is a non-tipping property and all amenities are included with the room rate.

150 E. de Vargas St., Santa Fe, NM 87501. ✆ **505/992-0957.** www.fivegraces.com. 23 units. $400–$900 double, depending on the season and type of room. Price includes full breakfast with specialty items and afternoon treats. AE, MC, V. Free parking. Pets welcome with fee and deposit. **Amenities:** Restaurant; bar; concierge; Wi-Fi (in lobby). *In room:* A/C, TV, CD player, fridge, hair dryer, microwave.

Inn & Spa at Loretto ★★ This much-photographed hotel, just 2 blocks from the plaza, was built in 1975 to resemble Taos Pueblo. Light and shadow dance upon the five-level structure as the sun crosses the sky. After a multimillion-dollar renovation in 2008, this is a comfortable and elegant place to stay. The medium-size rooms employ a Navajo motif, with comfortable beds and fine linens, while the medium-size bathrooms have fine tiling and robes. Be aware that the Loretto likes convention traffic, so sometimes service lags for travelers. Overall, it is fairly quiet and has nice views—especially on the northeast side, where you'll see both the historic St. Francis Cathedral and the Loretto Chapel (with its "miraculous" spiral staircase; see "More Attractions," later in the chapter). The Spa Terre offers a range of treatments, from facials to massages, in intimate, Southwest-meets-Asia rooms.

211 Old Santa Fe Trail (P.O. Box 1417), Santa Fe, NM 87501. ✆ **800/727-5531** or 505/988-5531. Fax 505/984-7968. www.innatloretto.com. 134 units. Jan–Mar $179–$279 double; Apr–June $189–$349 double; July–Oct $199–$499 double; Nov–Dec $179–$299 double. Additional person $30. Children 17 and under stay free in parent's room. Resort fee of $10 per night. AE, DC, DISC, MC, V. Valet parking $16 per night. **Amenities:** Restaurant; bar; concierge; health club; outdoor pool (heated year-round); room service; spa. *In room:* A/C, TV, hair dryer, Wi-Fi.

La Fonda ★ Whether you stay in this hotel or not, it's worth strolling through just to get a sense of how Santa Fe once was—and in some ways still is. Located right on the plaza, this was the inn at the end of the Santa Fe Trail; it saw trappers, traders, and merchants, as well as notables such as President Rutherford B. Hayes and General Ulysses S. Grant. The original inn was dying of old age in 1920 when it was razed and replaced by the current La Fonda. Its architecture is pueblo revival: imitation adobe with wooden balconies and beam ends protruding over the tops of windows. Inside, the lobby is rich and slightly dark, with people bustling about, sitting in the cafe, and buying jewelry from Native Americans.

The hotel has seen some renovation through the years, as well as a whole new wing to the east, where you'll find deluxe suites and new meeting spaces. If you want a feel of the real Santa Fe, this is the place to stay. Overall, however, this hotel isn't the model of refinement. No two rooms are the same here, and while each has its own funky touch, some are more kitsch than quaint. A recently added spa offers a variety of treatments ranging from massages to salt glows, as well as a sauna and Jacuzzi. The Bell Tower Bar is the highest point in downtown Santa Fe—a great place for a cocktail and a view of the city.

100 E. San Francisco St. (P.O. Box 1209), Santa Fe, NM 87501. ✆ **800/523-5002** or 505/982-5511. Fax 505/988-2952. www.lafondasantafe.com. 167 units. $219–$319 standard double; $239–$319 deluxe double; $349–$549 suite. Additional person $15. Children 11 and under stay free in parent's room. AE, DC, DISC, MC, V. Parking $10 per day in a covered garage. **Amenities:** Restaurant; 2 bars; concierge; health club; Jacuzzi; outdoor pool; room service; spa. *In room:* A/C, TV, fridge (in some), hair dryer, fireplace (in some), private balcony (in some), Wi-Fi.

La Posada de Santa Fe Resort and Spa ★★ If you're in the mood to stay in a little New Mexico adobe village, you'll enjoy this luxury hotel just 3 blocks from the plaza. It's especially nice in the summer, when surrounded by acres of green grass. Here, you get to experience squeaky maple floors, vigas and *latillas,* and, in many rooms, kiva fireplaces. Be aware that unless you've secured a suite, most rooms tend to be fairly small. Fortunately, the hotel benefited from major remodels in recent years, including a $6-million one in 2008, so all the bathrooms are modern and the rooms have fine linens and comfortable beds. Most notable are the Zen-Southwestern–style spa rooms, as well as a few "gallery suites," appointed with original artwork from some of the region's most prestigious artists. Travelers who are reluctant to trust the whims of older adobe construction should reserve one of the spa rooms or any of the other 40 newer rooms. Most rooms lack views but do have outdoor patios, and most are tucked back into the quiet compound. The top-notch on-site restaurant, **Fuego** (p. 157), serves artfully prepared international cuisine in a romantic, Spanish-colonial dining room. The Rockresorts Spa offers a full range of treatments.

330 E. Palace Ave., Santa Fe, NM 87501. ✆ **800/727-5276** or 505/986-0000. Fax 505/982-6850. www.rockresorts.com. 157 units. $239–$359 double; suites $449 and way up, depending on the season. Various spa packages available. AE, DC, DISC, MC, V. $30 resort fee per day includes parking. **Amenities:** 2 restaurants; bar; babysitting; concierge; health club; Jacuzzi; outdoor pool; room service; spa w/full treatments. *In room:* A/C, TV/DVD, CD player, hair dryer, minibar, Wi-Fi.

Expensive

Don Gaspar Inn ★★ (Finds) If you'd like to pretend that you live in Santa Fe, that you're blessed with your very own Southwestern-style home—in a historic neighborhood—full of artful touches such as Native American tapestries and a kiva fireplace, this is your inn. A 10-minute walk from the plaza, Don Gaspar occupies three homes connected by brilliant gardens and brick walkways. Rooms vary in size, though all are plenty spacious, most with patios, some with kitchenettes, and there's even a full house for rent. Travelers looking for an adventure beyond a hotel stay, but without the close interaction of a B&B, enjoy this place. Though the rooms don't have views, all are quiet. The Courtyard Casita, with a kitchenette and a sleeper couch in its own room, is nice for a small family. The Territorial Suite, with carpet throughout and Italian marble in the bath, is perfect for a romantic getaway. All rooms have bathrobes and fireplaces. The friendly and dedicated staff serves a full breakfast—such as green-chile stew with fresh baked items—on the patio under a peach tree (the fruit from which they make cobbler); in winter, guests eat in the atrium.

623 Don Gaspar Ave., Santa Fe, NM 87505. ✆ **888/986-8664** or 505/986-8664. Fax 505/986-0696. www.dongaspar.com. 12 units. $118–$165 double; $165–$205 suite; $185–$245 casita; $295–$355 house. Rates include full breakfast. AE, MC, V. Free parking. **Amenities:** Babysitting. *In room:* A/C, TV/DVD, hair dryer, Internet.

Hotel Plaza Real ★ (Value) This New Orleans–meets–Santa Fe Territorial–style hotel, built in 1990, provides comfortable rooms near the plaza. The construction and decor of the lobby are rustically elegant, built around a fireplace with balconies perched above. Clean and attractively decorated rooms have Southwestern-style furniture, many with French doors opening onto balconies or terraces that surround a quiet courtyard decorated with *ristras* (strung chiles). Beds are comfortably soft and baths small but with an outer sink vanity. The junior suites have an especially nice layout, with a sitting area near a fireplace and good light from the north and south. In recent years, the hotel has been receiving some needed upgrades.

125 Washington Ave., Santa Fe, NM 87501. ✆ **877/901-7666** or 505/988-4900. Fax 505/983-9322. www.hhandr.com. 56 units. $119–$149 double; $149–$289 suite, depending on time of year and type of room. Additional person $20. Children 11 and under stay free in parent's room. AE, DC, DISC, MC, V. Parking $12 per day. Pets $50 per stay. **Amenities:** Lounge. *In room:* A/C, TV, hair dryer, Wi-Fi.

Hotel St. Francis ★ If you long for the rich fabrics, fine antiques, and slow pace of a European hotel, this is your place. The building was first constructed in the 1880s; it became fairly dilapidated but was renovated in 1986. Now elegantly redecorated, the lobby is crowned by a Victorian fireplace with hovering cherubs, a theme repeated throughout the hotel. The small rooms continue the European decor, each with its own unique bent. You'll find a fishing room, a golf room, a garden room, and a music room, with each motif evoked by the furnishings: a vintage set of golf clubs here, a sheet of music in a dry-flower arrangement there. The hotel, which attracts individual travelers as well as families and many Europeans, is well cared for by a concierge who speaks six languages. Enjoy high tea in the lobby from 3 to 5:30pm daily. Request a room facing east, and you'll wake each day to a view of the mountains, seen through lovely lace.

210 Don Gaspar Ave., Santa Fe, NM 87501. ✆ **800/529-5700** or 505/983-5700. Fax 505/989-7690. www.hotelstfrancis.com. 82 units. $99–$349 all rooms, depending on the season. Children 11 and under stay free in parent's room. AE, DC, DISC, MC, V. Parking $5 per day. **Amenities:** Restaurant; bar; concierge; health club; room service. *In room:* A/C, TV, fridge, hair dryer (in some), Wi-Fi.

Hotel Santa Fe ★ Finds About a 10-minute walk south of the plaza you'll find this newer three-story establishment, the only Native American–owned hotel in Santa Fe. It is a good choice for consistent, well-planned lodgings. Picuris Pueblo is the majority stockholder here, and part of the pleasure of staying here is the culture the Picuris bring to your visit. This is not to say that you'll get any sense of the rusticity of a pueblo in your accommodations—this sophisticated hotel, built in the late 1980s, is decorated in Southwestern style, with a few novel aspects such as an Allan Houser bronze buffalo dancer watching over the front desk and a fireplace surrounded by comfortable furniture in the lobby. The rooms are medium size, with clean lines and comfortable beds, the decor accented with pine Taos-style furniture. Rooms on the north side get less street noise from Cerrillos Road and have better views of the mountains, but they don't have the sun shining onto their balconies. You will get a strong sense of the Native American presence on the patio during the summer, when Picuris dancers come to perform and bread bakers uncover the *horno* (oven) and prepare loaves for sale. Wireless Internet access is available in the lobby.

1501 Paseo de Peralta, Santa Fe, NM 87501. ✆ **800/825-9876** or 505/982-1200. Fax 505/984-2211. www.hotelsantafe.com. 163 units. $129–$199 double; $239–$459 suite, depending on the season. Hacienda rooms and suites $199–$459. Additional person $20. Children 17 and under stay free in parent's room. AE, DC, DISC, MC, V. Free parking. Pets accepted with $20 fee. **Amenities:** Restaurant; babysitting; concierge; Jacuzzi; outdoor pool; room service. *In room:* A/C, TV, hair dryer, minibar, Wi-Fi.

Inn on the Alameda ★★ Just across the street from the bosk-shaded Santa Fe River sits the Inn on the Alameda, a cozy stop for those who like the services of a hotel with the intimacy of an inn. Built in 1986, with additions over the years, it's now a little like a village, with a number of buildings and casitas. All are Pueblo-style adobe, ranging in age, but most were built in the late 1980s. The owner, Joe Schepps, appreciates traditional Southwestern style; he's used red brick in the dining area and Mexican *equipae* (wicker) furniture in the lobby, as well as thick vigas and shiny *latillas* in a sitting area set around a grand fireplace. The rooms follow a similar good taste, some with refrigerators, CD players, and kiva fireplaces. All rooms have comfortable beds, good linens, robes, and well-planned bathrooms with tile. The trees surrounding the inn—cottonwoods and aspens—add a bit of a rural feel to the property. If you're an art shopper, this is an ideal spot because it's a quick walk to Canyon Road. A full-service bar is open nightly. Breakfast is delicious, with bakery items and always a hot dish.

303 E. Alameda, Santa Fe, NM 87501. ✆ **800/289-2122** or 505/984-2121. Fax 505/986-8325. www.innonthealameda.com. 71 units. $125–$240 queen; $140–$245 king; $255–$390 suites (reduced off-season rates available). Additional person $25. Rates include breakfast and afternoon wine-and-cheese reception. AE, DC, DISC, MC, V. Free parking. Small pets under 30 pounds welcome with $30 fee. **Amenities:** Bar; babysitting; concierge; medium-size health club; 2 open-air Jacuzzis. *In room:* A/C, TV, hair dryer, Internet.

Moderate

Garrett's Desert Inn (Value) Completion of this hotel in 1957 prompted the Historic Design Review Board to implement zoning restrictions throughout downtown. Apparently, residents were appalled by the huge air conditioners on the roof. Though they're still unsightly, the hotel offers decent accommodations just 3 blocks from the plaza. It's a clean, two-story, concrete-block building around a broad parking lot. The hotel underwent a complete remodel in 1994, with touch-ups through the years, though new carpet and updated furnishings are now needed. It has managed to maintain some '50s touches, such as Art Deco tile in the bathrooms and plenty of space in the rooms. If you're traveling in winter, ask for a south-facing room and you might be able to sunbathe under the portal. The outdoor pool here is one of the nicest in town.

311 Old Santa Fe Trail, Santa Fe, NM 87501. ✆ **800/888-2145** or 505/982-1851. Fax 505/989-1647. www.garrettsdesertinn.com. 83 units. $89–$169, depending on season and type of room. AE, DISC, MC, V. **Amenities:** Restaurant; outdoor pool heated year-round. *In room:* A/C, TV, fridge (in minisuites), hair dryer, microwave (in minisuites), Wi-Fi.

Old Santa Fe Inn ★ (Finds) Want to stay downtown and savor Santa Fe–style ambience without wearing out your plastic? This is your hotel. A multimillion-dollar renovation to this 1930s court motel has created a comfortable, quiet inn just a few blocks from the plaza. Rooms verge on small but are decorated with such lovely handcrafted colonial-style furniture. All have small Mexican-tiled bathrooms, and some have gas fireplaces. King, queen, and twin bedrooms are available, as are suites. Breakfast is served in an atmospheric dining room next to a comfortable library. This inn jacks prices *way* up during special events such as the Indian Market.

320 Galisteo St., Santa Fe, NM 87501. ✆ **800/745-9910** or 505/995-0800. Fax 505/995-0400. www.oldsantafeinn.com. 43 units. $90–$450 depending on type of room and season. Rates include continental breakfast. AE, DC, DISC, MC, V. *In room:* A/C, TV, DVD (in some), Wi-Fi.

Santa Fe Motel and Inn ★ If you like walking to the plaza and restaurants but don't want to pay big bucks, this little compound is a good choice. Rooms here are larger than at the Old Santa Fe Inn and have more personality than those at Garrett's Desert Inn. Ask for one of the casitas in back—you'll pay more but get a little turn-of-the-20th-century charm, plus more quiet and privacy. Some have vigas; others have skylights, fireplaces, and patios. The main part of the motel, built in 1955, is two-story Territorial style, with upstairs rooms that open onto a portal with a bit of a view. All guest rooms are decorated with a Southwest motif and some have antique furnishings. All have medium-size bathrooms and comfortable beds. Some rooms have kitchenettes, with refrigerators, microwaves, stoves, coffeemakers, and toasters. A full breakfast is served each morning in the Southwest-style dining room or on a quaint patio.

510 Cerrillos Rd., Santa Fe, NM 87501. ✆ **800/930-5002** or 505/982-1039. Fax 505/986-1275. www.santafemotel.com. 23 units. $80–$149, depending on the season and type of room. Additional person $10. Rates include full breakfast. AE, DC, MC, V. Free parking. *In room:* A/C, TV, hair dryer, Internet.

Family-Friendly Hotels

Bishop's Lodge Ranch Resort & Spa (see below) Riding lessons, tennis courts with instruction, a pool with a lifeguard, a stocked trout pond just for kids, a summer daytime program, horseback trail trips, and more make this a veritable day camp for all ages.

El Rey Inn (p. 152) A picnic area and playground in a courtyard set back away from the street make this a nice place for families to commune in summer.

The Lodge at Santa Fe (p. 152) Built above the city, with a bit of a country-club feel, this place offers a nice outdoor pool and condo units that serve family needs well.

Santa Fe Sage Inn (p. 149) With its fenced-in pool and reasonable prices, this is a good spot for families.

Inexpensive

Santa Fe Sage Inn (Value) (Kids) If you're looking for a convenient, almost-downtown location at a reasonable price, this is one of your best bets. This two-story stucco adobe motel with portals is spread through three buildings and is about a 10-minute walk from the plaza. Built in 1985, it was remodeled in 2005. The smallish rooms have Southwestern furnishings, with comfortable beds and small baths. There's a park in the back and an outdoor pool set in a secluded fenced area, a good place for kids. To avoid street noise, ask for a room at the back of the property.

725 Cerrillos Rd., Santa Fe, NM 87501. ✆ **866/433-0335** or 505/982-5952. Fax 505/984-8879. www.santafesageinn.com. 160 units. $58–$95 double. Rates include continental breakfast. Additional person $10. AE, DC, DISC, MC, V. Free parking. **Amenities:** Outdoor pool. *In room:* A/C, TV, hair dryer, Wi-Fi.

The Northside

Within easy reach of the plaza, the north side encompasses the area that lies north of the loop of Paseo de Peralta.

Very Expensive

Bishop's Lodge Ranch Resort & Spa ★★★ (Moments) (Kids) This is a place rich with history. More than a century ago, when Bishop Jean-Baptiste Lamy was the spiritual leader of northern New Mexico's Roman Catholic population, he often escaped clerical politics by hiking into this valley called Little Tesuque. He built a retreat and a humble chapel (now on the National Register of Historic Places) with high-vaulted ceilings and a hand-built altar. Today, Lamy's 450-acre getaway has become Bishop's Lodge.

In recent years, a $17-million renovation spruced up the place and added a spa and 8,000 square feet of meeting space. The guest rooms, spread through many buildings, feature handcrafted furniture and regional artwork. The traditional rooms are medium size with the rustic feel of the historic buildings they occupy; many have balconies or patios. The newer Ridge Rooms are spacious, with high ceilings, vigas, gas fireplaces, patios or balconies, and most with views. All rooms have comfortable beds with fine

ATTRACTIONS ●

College of Santa Fe **20**
El Rancho de las Golondrinas **22**
Museum of Indian Arts & Culture **15**
Museum of International Folk Art **16**
Museum of Spanish Colonial Art **14**
Randall Davey Audubon Center **10**
Santa Fe Children's Museum **13**
Santa Fe Opera **1**
Santa Fe River Park **6**
Santa Fe Southern Railway **4**
Skateboard Park **5**
Wheelwright Museum of the American Indian **17**

DINING ◆

The Compound **7**
El Farol **9**
Geronimo **8**
La Choza **11**
mu du noodles **18**

ACCOMMODATIONS ■

Bishop's Lodge Ranch Resort & Spa **3**
El Rey Inn **19**
Encantado **2**
La Quinta Inn **23**
Los Campos RV Resort **21**
Rancheros de Santa Fe Campground **24**
Santa Fe KOA **24**
Santa Fe Sage Inn **12**

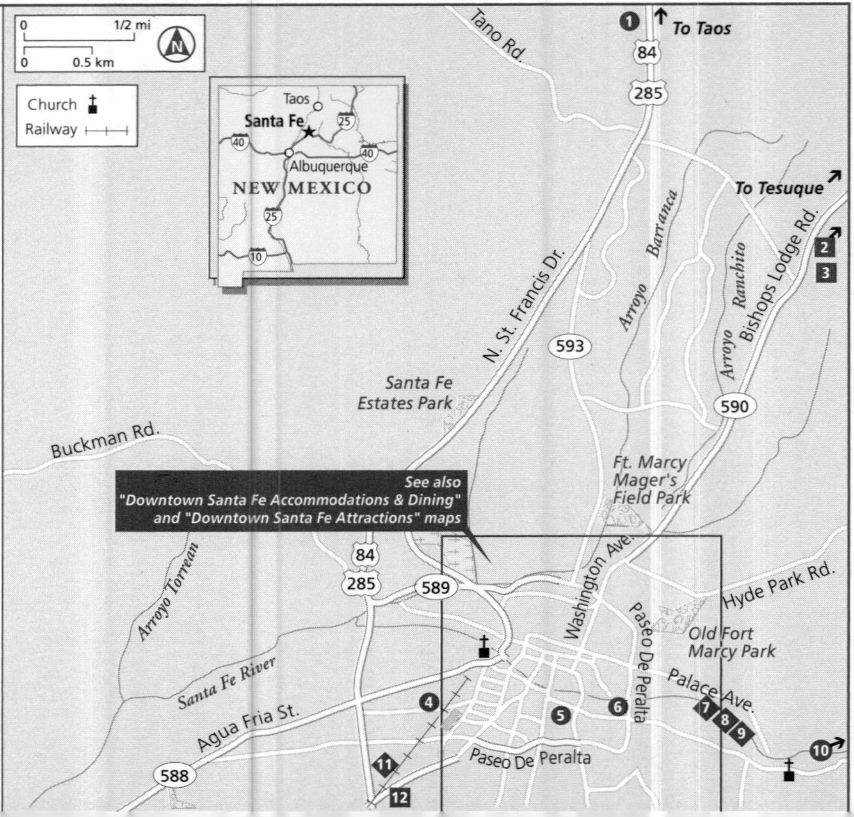

0 1/2 mi
0 0.5 km
N
Church
Railway
Taos
Santa Fe
Albuquerque
NEW MEXICO
40
25
10
To Taos
To Tesuque
Tano Rd.
84
285
593
590
589
588
N. St. Francis Dr.
Arroyo Barranca
Arroyo Ranchito
Bishops Lodge Rd.
Santa Fe Estates Park
Buckman Rd.
Ft. Marcy Mager's Field Park
See also "Downtown Santa Fe Accommodations & Dining" and "Downtown Santa Fe Attractions" maps
Arroyo Torreon
Washington Ave.
Hyde Park Rd.
Old Fort Marcy Park
Paseo De Peralta
Palace Ave.
Santa Fe River
Agua Fria St.
Paseo De Peralta

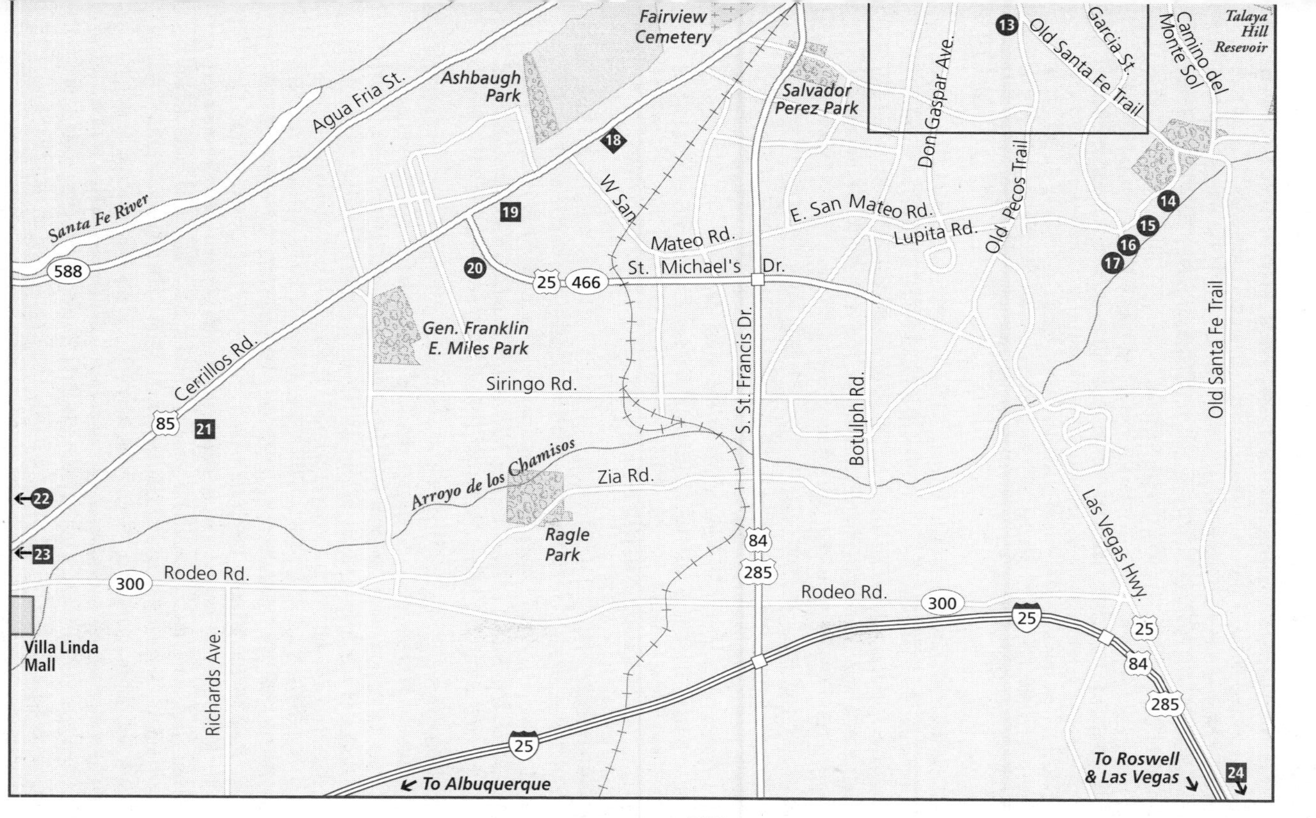
Fairview Cemetery
Talaya Hill Reservoir
Camino del Monte Sol
Garcia St.
Old Santa Fe Trail
Agua Fria St.
Ashbaugh Park
Salvador Perez Park
Don Gaspar Ave.
Old Pecos Trail
Santa Fe River
W San Mateo Rd.
E. San Mateo Rd.
Lupita Rd.
St. Michael's Dr.
588
25
466
Gen. Franklin E. Miles Park
Cerrillos Rd.
Siringo Rd.
S. St. Francis Dr.
Botulph Rd.
Old Santa Fe Trail
85
Arroyo de los Chamisos
Zia Rd.
Ragle Park
84
285
Las Vegas Hwy.
Rodeo Rd.
300
Villa Linda Mall
Richards Ave.
To Albuquerque
To Roswell & Las Vegas
13
14
15
16
17
18
19
20
21
22
23
24

linens and tile bathrooms with the hotel's own signature bath products. The newest addition are villas: spectacular two- and three-bedroom town houses, filled with amenities, including full kitchens, fireplaces, patios, and views, a great option for families or couples who travel together. The Bishop's Lodge is an active resort three seasons of the year, with activities such as horseback riding, nature walks, and cookouts; in the winter, it takes on the character of a romantic country retreat. A children's program keeps kids busy for much of the day. This place offers excellent service.

Bishop's Lodge Rd. (P.O. Box 2367), Santa Fe, NM 87504. ✆ **505/983-6377.** Fax 505/989-8939. www.bishopslodge.com. 111 units. Summer $399–$489 double; fall and spring $299–$399 double; midwinter $189–$269 double. Villas $550–$1,500. Resort fee $15 per person per day. Additional person $15. Children 3 and under stay free in parent's room. Ask about packages that include meals. AE, DC, DISC, MC, V. Free parking. **Amenities:** Restaurant; bar; babysitting; concierge; Jacuzzi; outdoor pool; room service; spa; tennis courts; Wi-Fi (in lobby). *In room:* A/C, TV, fridge, hair dryer, high-speed Internet.

Expensive

The Lodge at Santa Fe ★ Kids Set on a hill as you head north toward the Santa Fe Opera, this three-story hotel is a convenient and relaxing place to stay. The theme here is Native American, with Anasazi-style stacked sandstone throughout the lobby and dining room, a theme that carries into the guest rooms. They are medium size, decorated in earth tones with bold prints, some with views of the mountains, others overlooking the pool. Premium rooms are more spacious, some with large living rooms and private balconies. Each parlor suite has a Murphy bed and kiva fireplace in the living room, a big dining area, a wet bar and refrigerator, and a jetted bathtub. The condo units nearby come with fully equipped kitchens, fireplaces, and private decks.

750 N. St. Francis Dr., Santa Fe, NM 87501. ✆ **800/LODGESF** (563-4373) or 505/992-5800. Fax 505/992-5856. www.lodgeatsantafe.com. 135 units. $89–$179 double; $129–$199 suite; $200–$300 condo. AE, DC, DISC, MC, V. Free parking. **Amenities:** Bar; outdoor pool. *In room:* A/C, TV, hair dryer, Wi-Fi.

Southside

Santa Fe's major strip, Cerrillos Road, is US 85, the main route to and from Albuquerque and the I-25 freeway. It's about 5¼ miles from the plaza to the Santa Fe Place, which marks the southern boundary of the city. Most motels are on this strip, although several of them are to the east, closer to St. Francis Drive (US 84) or the Las Vegas Highway.

Moderate

El Rey Inn ★ Finds Kids Staying at "the King" makes you feel as if you're traveling the old Route 66 through the Southwest. The white stucco buildings of this court motel are decorated with bright trim around the doors and hand-painted Mexican tiles on the walls. Opened in the 1930s, it received additions in the 1950s, and remodeling is ongoing. No two rooms are alike. The oldest section, nearest the lobby, feels a bit cramped, though the rooms have style, with Art Deco tile in the bathrooms and vigas on the ceilings. Some have little patios. Be sure to request a room as far back as possible from Cerrillos Road. The two stories of suites around the Spanish colonial courtyard are sweet deals. These rooms make you feel as if you're at a Spanish inn, with carved furniture and cozy couches. Some rooms have kitchenettes. To the north sit 10 deluxe units around the courtyard. These rooms offer more upscale amenities and gas log fireplaces, as well as distinctive furnishings and artwork. A complimentary continental breakfast is served in a sunny room or on a terrace in the warmer months. There's also a sitting room with a library and games tables, as well as a picnic area, a playground, and an exercise room.

1862 Cerrillos Rd. (P.O. Box 4759), Santa Fe, NM 87502. ✆ **800/521-1349** or 505/982-1931. Fax 505/989-9249. www.elreyinnsantafe.com. 86 units. $99–$165 double; $125–$225 suite. Rates include continental breakfast. AE, DC, DISC, MC, V. Free parking. **Amenities:** Health club; 2 Jacuzzis; outdoor pool; sauna; Wi-Fi (in lobby). *In room:* A/C, TV, fridge, hair dryer.

Inexpensive

La Quinta Inn (Value) Though it's a good 15-minute drive from the plaza, this is my choice of economical Cerrillos Road chain hotels. Built in 1986, it has had ongoing remodeling to keep the rooms comfortable and tasteful. The rooms within the three-story building have an unexpectedly elegant feel, with lots of deep colors and Art Deco tile in the bathrooms. There's plenty of space in these rooms, and they're lit for mood as well as for reading. A complimentary continental breakfast is served in the intimate lobby. The outdoor kidney-shaped pool has a nice lounging area and is open and heated May to October. The hotel is just across a parking lot from the Santa Fe Place mall, which shoppers and moviegoers appreciate. The Flying Tortilla coffee shop is adjacent.

4298 Cerrillos Rd., Santa Fe, NM 87507. ✆ **800/531-5900** or 505/471-1142. Fax 505/438-7219. www.lq.com. 130 units. June to mid-Oct $92–$115 double; late Oct to May $79–$89 double. Children 18 and under stay free in parent's room. Discount for AAA members. Rates include continental breakfast. AE, DC, DISC, MC, V. Free parking. Maximum 2 pets stay free. **Amenities:** Executive-level rooms; outdoor heated pool. *In room:* A/C, TV, hair dryer, Wi-Fi.

BED & BREAKFASTS

If you prefer a homey, intimate setting to the sometimes-impersonal ambience of a large hotel, one of Santa Fe's bed-and-breakfast inns may be right for you. All those listed here are in or close to the downtown area and offer comfortable accommodations at expensive to moderate prices.

El Farolito ★★ The owners of this inn, which is within walking distance of the plaza, have created an authentic theme experience for guests in each room. The themes include the Native American Room, decorated with rugs and pottery; the South-of-the-Border Room, with Mexican folk art with a full-size sleeper sofa; and the elegant Santa Fe–style Opera Room, with hand-carved, lavishly upholstered furniture. A two-room suite has been added in the main building, with a queen-size iron bed and Southwestern decor. The walls of most of the rooms are rubbed with beeswax during plastering to give them a smooth, golden finish. All rooms have kiva fireplaces and private patios. The common area displays works by notable New Mexico artists. Part of the inn was built before 1912, and the rest is new, but the old-world elegance carries through. For breakfast, the focus is on healthy food with a little decadence thrown in. You'll enjoy fresh fruit and home-baked breads and pastries. Under the same stellar ownership (but a little less expensive) is the nearby **Four Kachinas Inn ★** (✆ **888/634-8782;** www.fourkachinas.com), where Southwestern-style rooms sit around a sunny courtyard. A little less lavish than those at El Farolito, these rooms are sparkly clean, all with patios.

514 Galisteo St., Santa Fe, NM 87501. ✆ **888/634-8782** or 505/988-1631. Fax 505/988-4589. www.farolito.com. 8 units. $150–$280 casita. Rates include hot entree breakfast buffet. AE, DISC, MC, V. Free parking. **Amenities:** Babysitting by appointment. *In room:* A/C, TV, fridge, hair dryer.

Hacienda Nicholas ★★ This inn, a few blocks from the plaza, has a delightful Southwest hacienda feel. Rooms surround a sunny patio; my favorite is the bright Cottonwood, with a serene feel created by the sunshine-colored walls, wood floors, and a kiva fireplace. Even more luxurious, the Sunflower has French doors, plenty of space, and a fireplace. The rooms off the sitting room in the house are more modest but also have a warm "Southwest meets Provence" feel. All beds are comfortable and bathrooms range from small (with showers only) to larger (with tub/shower combinations). A full breakfast—including such delicacies as homemade granola and red-and-green chile breakfast burritos—and afternoon wine and cheese are served in the lovely Great Room or on the patio, both with fireplaces. Service in this inn is excellent. Under the same ownership, **Alexander's Inn** (✆ **888/321-5123** or 505/986-1431; www.alexanders-inn.com) has long been one of the city's finest B&Bs. In recent years, the inn itself has closed, but the same managers now rent four casitas in the older district of Santa Fe. Each is a fully equipped home, with a kitchen, including fridge, range, and microwave. All have unique Southwestern furnishings and plenty of charm.

320 E. Marcy St., Santa Fe, NM 87501. ✆ **888/284-3170** or 505/992-8385. Fax 505/982-8572. www.haciendanicholas.com. 7 units. $120–$240 double. Additional person $25. Rates include breakfast and afternoon wine and cheese. AE, DISC, MC, V. Free parking. Pets accepted with $20 fee. **Amenities:** Concierge. *In room:* A/C, TV, hair dryer, Wi-Fi.

Water Street Inn ★★ An award-winning adobe restoration 4 blocks from the plaza, this friendly inn features elegant Southwestern-style rooms with antique furnishings and several with kiva fireplaces. Rooms are medium size to large, some with four-poster beds; all are comfortable with fine linens and well-planned Mexican-tiled baths. Four suites have elegant contemporary Southwestern furnishings and outdoor private patios with fountains. Most rooms have balconies or patios. In the afternoons, a happy hour, with quesadillas and margaritas (on Friday), is offered in the living room or on the upstairs portal, where an extended continental breakfast is also served.

427 W. Water St., Santa Fe, NM 87501. ✆ **800/646-6752** or 505/984-1193. Fax 505/984-6235. www.waterstreetinn.com. 12 units. $150–$250 double. Rates include continental breakfast and afternoon hors d'oeuvres and refreshments. AE, DISC, MC, V. Free parking. Children and pets welcome with prior approval. **Amenities:** Concierge; Jacuzzi; room service. *In room:* A/C, TV/DVD/VCR, hair dryer, Wi-Fi.

RV PARKS & CAMPGROUNDS

RV Parks

At least four private camping areas, mainly for recreational vehicles, are located within a few minutes' drive of downtown Santa Fe. Typical rates are $30 for full RV hookups, $20 for tents. Be sure to book ahead at busy times.

Los Campos RV Resort The resort has 95 spaces with full hookups, picnic tables, and covered pavilion for use with reservation at no charge. It's just 5 miles south of the plaza, so it's plenty convenient, but keep in mind that it is surrounded by the city. The campground honors a variety of discounts.

3574 Cerrillos Rd., Santa Fe, NM 87507. ✆ **800/852-8160.** Fax 505/471-9220. $28–$33 daily; $172–$212 weekly; $450 monthly/winter; $500 monthly/summer. MC, V. Pets welcome. **Amenities:** Outdoor pool; concierge; grills; restrooms; showers; free cable TV; vending machines; Wi-Fi (available in half the park).

Rancheros de Santa Fe Campground ★ Tents, motor homes, and trailers requiring full hookups are welcome here. The park's 127 sites are situated on 22 acres of piñon and juniper forest. Cabins are also available. About 6 miles southeast of Santa Fe, it's open March 15 to October 31.

736 Old Las Vegas Hwy. (exit 290 off I-25), Santa Fe, NM 87505. ✆ **800/426-9259** or 505/466-3482. www.rancheros.com. Tent site $20–$22; RV hookup $24–$36. AE, DISC, MC, V. **Amenities:** Outdoor pool; fireplaces; grills; grocery store; free nightly movies May–Sept; nature trails; playground; propane; recreation room; restrooms; showers; picnic tables; public telephones; cable TV hookups; Wi-Fi (available throughout the park).

Santa Fe KOA This campground, about 11 miles northeast of Santa Fe, sits among the foothills of the Sangre de Cristo Mountains, an excellent place to enjoy northern New Mexico's pine-filled high desert. It offers full hookups, pull-through sites, and tent sites.

934 Old Las Vegas Hwy. (exit 290 or 294 off I-25), Santa Fe, NM 87505. ✆ **800/KOA-1514** [562-1514], or 505/466-1419 for reservations. www.koa.com. Tent site $22–$25; RV hookup $29–$40. MC, V. **Amenities:** Dumping station; restrooms; playground; picnic tables; propane; recreation room; showers; store/gift shop; Wi-Fi (available throughout the park).

Campgrounds

There are three forested sites along NM 475 on the way to Ski Santa Fe. All are open from May to October. Overnight rates start at about $12.

Hyde Memorial State Park ★ About 8 miles from the city, this pine-surrounded park offers a quiet retreat. Seven RV pads with electrical pedestals and an RV dumping station are available. There are nature and hiking trails and a playground as well as a small winter skating pond.

740 Hyde Park Rd., Santa Fe, NM 87501. ✆ **505/983-7175.** www.nmparks.com. **Amenities:** Shelters; picnic tables; vault toilets; water.

Santa Fe National Forest ★★ You'll reach Black Canyon campground, with 44 sites, before you arrive at Hyde State Park. It's one of the only campgrounds in the state for which you can make a reservation (✆ **877/444-6777;** www.reserveusa.com). The sites sit within thick forest, with hiking trails nearby. Big Tesuque, a first-come, first-served campground with 10 newly rehabilitated sites, is about 12 miles from town. The sites here are closer to the road and sit at the edge of aspen forests. Both Black Canyon and Big Tesuque campgrounds, along the Santa Fe Scenic Byway, NM 475, are equipped with vault toilets.

1474 Rodeo Rd., Santa Fe, NM 87505. ✆ **505/438-7840** or 505/753-7331 (Española District). www.fs.fed.us/r3/sfe. **Amenities:** Vault toilets; water.

4 WHERE TO DINE

Santa Fe abounds in dining options, with hundreds of restaurants in all categories. Competition among them is steep, and spots are continually opening and closing. Locals watch closely to see which ones will survive. Some chefs create dishes that incorporate traditional Southwestern foods with ingredients not indigenous to the region; their restaurants are referred to in the listings as "Southwestern." There is also regional New Mexican cuisine, which has its own unique blend of sauces and uses elements from the Native American tribes of the region. Beyond that, diners can opt for excellent steak and seafood, as well as Continental, European, Asian, and, of course, Mexican menus. On the south end of town, Santa Fe has the requisite chain establishments such as **Outback Steakhouse,** 2574 Camino Entrada (✆ **505/424-6800**), **Olive Garden,** 3781 Cerrillos Rd. (✆ **505/438-7109**), and **Red Lobster,** 4450 Rodeo Rd. (✆ **505/473-1610**).

Especially during peak tourist seasons, dinner reservations may be essential. Reservations are always recommended at better restaurants.

DOWNTOWN

This area includes the circle defined by the Paseo de Peralta and St. Francis Drive, as well as Canyon Road.

Expensive

Aqua Santa ★★★ Finds NEW AMERICAN This is one of my favorite Santa Fe restaurants. Tucked into a little nook along the Santa Fe River, it could easily go unnoticed, but it already has a strong following of locals who enjoy the serene environment and fresh artesanal food. The atmosphere is like a quaint country hacienda with a touch of elegance created by hardwood floors, a kiva fireplace, cream-colored walls, and fine art. Service is excellent, though cooking times run a little long. The chef employs organic meats and seasonal vegetables. At lunch, I've enjoyed the local lamb braised with rapini greens and pistachios. At dinner, a great start is the escarole salad with feta and grapefruit, and one of many exquisite entrees is the sautéed sea scallops in duck fat with shitake mushrooms and lemon. For dessert, try the buttermilk panna cotta or espresso mascarpone parfait. A carefully chosen beer and wine list compliments the menu. In warmer months, you might want to request a table on the patio, where you can sit under a cherry tree. If you want a peaceful and delectable meal out, this is the spot to have it.

451 W. Alameda St. ✆ **505/982-6297.** Reservations recommended. Main courses $10–$15 lunch, $11–$29 dinner. AE, MC, V. Wed–Fri noon–2pm; Tues–Sat 5:30–9pm.

Cafe Pasqual's ★★ SOUTHWESTERN/MEXICAN "You have to become the food, erase the line between it as an object and you," says Pasqual's owner Katharine Kagel, who uses mostly organic ingredients in her dishes. Her attitude is apparent in this restaurant, where the walls are lined with murals depicting voluptuous villagers playing guitars, drinking, and even flying. Needless to say, it's a festive place, though it's also excellent for a romantic dinner. Service is jovial and professional. My favorite dish for breakfast or lunch is the *huevos motuleños* (two eggs, over easy, on blue-corn tortillas, and black beans topped with sautéed bananas, feta cheese, salsa, and green chile). Soups and salads are also served for lunch, and there's a delectable grilled-salmon burrito with herbed goat cheese and cucumber salsa. The frequently changing dinner menu offers grilled meats and seafood, plus vegetarian specials. Start with the Mexican prawn cocktail with lime, tomato, and avocado, and move on to the chicken mole enchiladas with cilantro rice and orange-jicama salad or "flame-kissed" ahi tuna with caramelized onions and sautéed spinach. There's a communal table for those who would like to meet new people over a meal. Pasqual's offers imported beers and wine by the bottle or glass. Try to go at an odd hour—late morning or afternoon—or make a reservation for dinner; otherwise, you'll have to wait.

121 Don Gaspar Ave. ✆ **505/983-9340.** www.pasquals.com. Reservations recommended for dinner. Main courses $8–$15 breakfast, $9–$17 lunch, $19–$39 dinner. AE, MC, V. Mon–Sat 7am–3pm; Sun–Thurs 5:30–9:30pm; Fri–Sat 5:30–10pm; summer daily 5:30–10:30pm. Brunch Sun 8am–2pm.

The Compound ★★★ NEW AMERICAN This reincarnation of one of Santa Fe's classic restaurants serves some of the most flavorful and daring food in the Southwest. Inside, it's an elegant old adobe with white walls often offset by bold splashes of flowers. Outside, during warm months, a broad patio shelters diners from the city bustle. With friendly, efficient service, this is an excellent place for a romantic dinner or a relaxing lunch. Chef and owner Mark Kiffin (a James Beard award winner and the former chef at Coyote Café; see below), lets his creativity soar. For lunch, monkfish chorizo with watercress is outrageously tasty. At dinner, you might start off with tuna tartare topped with Osetra caviar. For an entree, a signature dish is the grilled beef tenderloin with Italian potatoes and foie gras hollandaise, the beef so tender you won't quite believe it. Finish with a warm bittersweet liquid chocolate cake. A carefully selected beer and wine list accompanies the menu.

653 Canyon Rd. ✆ **505/982-4353.** www.compoundrestaurant.com. Reservations recommended. Main courses $12–$20 lunch, $25–$44 dinner. AE, DC, DISC, MC, V. Mon–Sat noon–2pm; daily 6–9pm; bar opens nightly at 5pm.

Coyote Café ★★ SOUTHWESTERN World-renowned chef and cookbook author Mark Miller put this place on the map decades ago. Now under new ownership, it has gained new popularity as a place for innovative food in a festive environment. The atmosphere blends warm colors and creative lighting to make for a memorable meal. The waitstaff is efficient and friendly. The menu changes seasonally, so the dishes I mention may not be available. Past favorites have included sautéed Italian porcinis or prawns over corn cakes with chipotle butter and guacamole. For a main course, look for delights such as pan-seared white miso halibut with roasted lobster jus, wasabi mashed potatoes, and braised baby bok choy; or the "Cowboy Cut," a rib-eye with "borracho" beans, red chile onion rings, and roasted fingerling potatoes. You can order drinks from the full bar or wine by the glass.

Coyote Café has an adjunct establishment. In summer, the place to be seen is **La Nueva Cantina,** where light Mexican fare and cocktails are served on a festively painted terrace. Try the guacamole and chips, the crispy calamari strips, or the jalapeño rellenos with buttermilk roasted-garlic sauce.

132 Water St. ✆ **505/983-1615.** www.coyotecafe.com. Reservations highly recommended. Main courses $6–$16 (Nueva Cantina), $19–$36 (Coyote Café). AE, DC, DISC, MC, V. Nueva Cantina: Daily 11:30am–9:30pm. Dining room: Daily 5:30–10pm.

El Farol ★★ SPANISH This is the place to head for local ambience and flavors of Spain, Santa Fe, and Mexico. El Farol (the Lantern), set in an 1835 adobe building, is the Canyon Road artists' quarter's original neighborhood bar. The restaurant has cozy low ceilings and hand-smoothed adobe walls. Thirty-five varieties of tapas are offered, including such delicacies as *gambas al ajillo* (shrimp with chile, garlic, Madeira, and lime) and *pinchos morunos* (grilled pork skewers with harissa sauce). You can make a meal out of two or three tapas shared with your friends, or order a full dinner such as the paella or the mixed grill, with lamb, chorizo, and shrimp over delectable potatoes. There is live entertainment 7 nights a week—including jazz/swing, folk, and Latin guitar music—starting at 9:30pm. In summer, two outdoor patios are open to diners. Call ahead to find out about their flamenco dinner shows. The restaurant offers some of the finest wines and sherries in the world.

808 Canyon Rd. ✆ **505/983-9912.** www.elfarolsf.com. Reservations recommended. Tapas $8; main courses $8.75–$18 lunch, $26–$33 dinner. AE, DC, DISC, MC, V. Daily 11:30am–3pm and 5:30–10pm. Bar until 2am Mon–Sat; until midnight Sun.

Fuego ★★★ (Moments) INTERNATIONAL This is one of Santa Fe's most stylish and sophisticated dining experiences. The restaurant offers the ambience of a traditional Southwestern hacienda, accented with colorful paintings from local galleries, grand iron chandeliers hanging from high ceilings, and comfortable couches, along with a broad dining patio that's one of Santa Fe's best. Service is excellent. Some locals consider the "Rancher's Brunch" one of the town's finest. It includes favorites such as eggs Benedict, along with inventive items such as a shellfish-and-brie omelet. Lunch might start with a seafood platter or Caesar salad and move onto duck leg confit, cooked for 10 hours and served with sautéed potatoes. Dinner might start with lobster medallions, followed by a Kobe New York strip steak with truffles and braised potatoes. For dessert, try selections from a world-class artisanal farmhouse cheese cart or variety of sweets. An excellent wine list accompanies the menu. Bring your heaviest plastic; this is one of the most expensive spots in Santa Fe, but a well-worth-it, memorable choice for special occasions.

330 E. Palace Ave. (at La Posada de Santa Fe Resort and Spa). ✆ **800/727-5276** or 505/954-9670. www.rockresorts.com. Reservations recommended. Main courses $45 adults, $25 children 12 and under brunch; $15–$28 lunch; $25–$45 dinner. Prix-fixe tasting menus at dinner $75–$125. AE, DC, DISC, MC, V. Breakfast daily 6:30–11am; lunch Mon–Sat 11:30am–1:30pm; brunch Sun 11:30am–2pm; dinner daily 6–9:30pm.

Geronimo ★★★ CONTINENTAL This elegant restaurant offers one of Santa's Fe's most delectable and atmospheric dining experiences. Occupying an old adobe structure known as the Borrego House—which was built by Geronimo Lopez in 1756 but has since been completely restored—it retains the feel of an old Santa Fe home. And now, with Chef Martin Rios at the helm, its food is simply fantastic, always utilizing seasonal produce. If you enjoy dining outside, reserve a spot on the porch and watch the action on Canyon Road. You might start with Hawaiian tuna, smoked salmon and avocado tartare, served with chive buttermilk pancakes, and then move onto Alaskan halibut with red and yellow peppers, baby fennel, and saffron risotto. If you want to try one of Santa Fe's most renowned entrees, order the peppery elk tenderloin with applewood smoked bacon served with fork-mashed Yukon gold potatoes. For dessert try the Jivara chocolate Palet d'Or, a flourless cake with apricot cream and caramelized Rice Krispies. The menu changes seasonally, and there's an excellent wine list.

724 Canyon Rd. ✆ **505/982-1500.** www.geronimorestaurant.com. Reservations recommended. Main courses $30–$50 dinner. AE, MC, V. Daily 5:45–9:30pm.

La Casa Sena ★★ SOUTHWESTERN Combining alluring ambience and tasty food, this is one of Santa Fe's favorite restaurants, though the food here isn't as precise and flavorful as at Santacafé or Geronimo. It sits within the Sena compound, a prime example of a Spanish hacienda, in a Territorial-style adobe house built in 1867 by Civil War–hero Major José Sena. The house, which surrounds a garden courtyard, is today a veritable art gallery, with museum-quality landscapes on the walls and Taos-style handcrafted furniture. During the warm months, this restaurant has the best patio in town. The cuisine might be described as northern New Mexican with a continental flair. One of my favorite lunches is the fish tacos with achiote-corn rice. In the evening, diners might start with a salad of garden greens and grilled mushrooms, and then move on to a pork loin with roasted sweet potatoes and a peach prickly pear sauce.

In the adjacent **La Cantina,** waitstaff sing Broadway show tunes as they carry platters from the kitchen to the table. The more moderately priced Cantina menu offers the likes of enchiladas with black beans and Mexican rice. Both restaurants have exquisite desserts; try the black-and-white bittersweet chocolate terrine with raspberry sauce. The award-winning wine list features more than 850 selections.

125 E. Palace Ave. ✆ **505/988-9232.** www.lacasasena.com. Reservations recommended. La Casa Sena main courses $11–$23 lunch, $24–$42 dinner; 5-course chef's tasting menu $58, with wine $82; La Cantina main courses $13–$28. AE, DC, DISC, MC, V. Mon–Sat 11:30am–3pm; Sun brunch 11am–3pm; daily 5:30–10pm.

Rio Chama Steakhouse ★★ STEAK/SEAFOOD Serving up tasty steaks in a refined ranch atmosphere, this is one of Santa Fe's most popular restaurants. It's a good spot for a business lunch or a fun-filled evening, and the patio is a bright spot during warm months. Service is efficient, and there's a full bar. I suggest sticking to the meat dishes here, though the fish and pasta dishes can be quite good too. At lunch or dinner you might start with the Capitol salad, with lots of fresh greens, piñon nuts, and

 Family-Friendly Restaurants

Blue Corn Café (p. 161) A relaxed atmosphere and their own menu pleases kids, while excellent brewpub beer pleases parents.

Bumble Bee's Baja Grill (p. 161) A casual atmosphere allows parents to relax while their kids chow down on quesadillas and burritos.

Cowgirl Hall of Fame (p. 187) Children can enjoy the "kid's corral," while their parents take in live music.

Upper Crust Pizza (p. 163) Many people feel it has the best pizza in town, and it'll deliver it to tired tots and their families at downtown hotels.

blue-cheese crumbles. My favorite for lunch is the half BLT with soup or salad, best when ordered with their green-chile stew. Lunch also brings more formal dishes such as a lumpy crab over angel hair pasta. At dinner, the prime rib is a big hit, as is the filet mignon, both served with a potato and vegetable. For dessert, try chocolate cake. The bar here romps during happy hour, when the booths fill up, martinis nearly overflow, and reasonably priced menu items sate post-work appetites.

414 Old Santa Fe Trail. ✆ **505/955-0765.** www.riochamasteakhouse.com. Reservations recommended Fri–Sat nights. Main courses $8.50–$24 lunch, $18–$39 dinner. AE, DC, DISC, MC, V. Daily 11am–3pm and 5–10pm; patio bar 5pm–closing.

Santacafé ★★★ (Moments) NEW AMERICAN/SOUTHWESTERN This is where my mother and I go to celebrate birthdays and other special occasions because the place exudes unique charm, both in its food and ambience. The food combines the best of many cuisines, from Asian to Southwestern, served in an elegant setting with minimalist decor that accentuates the graceful architecture of the 18th-century Padre Gallegos House, 2 blocks from the plaza. The white walls are decorated only with deer antlers, and each room contains a fireplace. In warm months you can sit under elm trees in the charming courtyard. Beware that on busy nights the rooms are noisy. The dishes change to take advantage of local and seasonal specialties, each served with precision. Their Sunday brunch menu offers such delights as a mascarpone-stuffed French toast and poached eggs with corned beef. For a lunch or dinner starter, try the shiitake and cactus spring rolls with Southwestern ponzu. One of my favorite main courses at lunch is the baby spinach niçoise salad with tuna seared to perfection. At dinner I've enjoyed the grilled rack of lamb with potato-leek gratin. A lighter eater might try the sautéed Diver scallops with kalamata olive linguine and wild mushrooms. There's an extensive wine list. Desserts, as elegant as the rest of the food, are made in-house; try the warm chocolate upside-down cake with vanilla ice cream.

231 Washington Ave. ✆ **505/984-1788.** www.santacafe.com. Reservations recommended. Main courses $9–$15 lunch, $22–$40 dinner. AE, DISC, MC, V. Mon–Sat 11:30am–2pm; daily 5:30–10pm. Sun brunch served in summer, Easter Sunday, and Mother's Day.

315 ★★ FRENCH This classy French bistro enjoyed instant success when it opened in 1995 because the food is simply excellent. The elegant atmosphere provides a perfect setting for a romantic meal, and during warm months the patio is a popular place to people-watch, with little white lights setting the whole place aglow. Service is excellent.

The menu changes seasonally; on one of my visits, I started with a smooth and flavorful lobster bisque and moved on to lamb chops served with a tart mustard sauce and mashed potatoes. My favorite dessert here is the flourless chocolate cake: not too sweet, and luscious. The wine list includes over 250 offerings from France to California to Australia.

315 Old Santa Fe Trail. ✆ **505/986-9190.** www.315santafe.com. Reservations essential. Main courses $9–$17 lunch, $20–$29 dinner. AE, DISC, MC, V. Summer Mon–Sat 11:30am–2pm, Sun–Thurs 5:30–9pm, Fri–Sat 5:30–9:30pm; winter 5:30–9pm daily.

Moderate

Cowgirl Hall of Fame ★ (Kids) BARBECUE/CAJUN/NEW MEXICAN This raucous bar/restaurant serves decent food in a festive atmosphere. The main room is a bar—a hip hangout spot, and a good place to eat. The back room offers more quiet, with wood floors and tables and plenty of cowgirl memorabilia. The brick patio provides the best setting, lit with strings of white lights during the warm season. Service can be brusque, and the food varies. In winter, my favorite is a big bowl of gumbo or crawfish étoufée, and the rest of the time, I order Jamaican jerk chicken or pork tenderloin when it's a special. Careful, both can be hot. The daily blue-plate special is a real buy, especially on Tuesday nights, when it's chile rellenos. There's even a special "kid's corral" that has horseshoes, a rocking horse, a horse-shaped rubber tire swing, hay bales, and a beanbag toss. Happy hour is from 3 to 6pm. There is also live music almost every night, a pool hall, and a deli.

319 S. Guadalupe St. ✆ **505/982-2565.** www.cowgirlsantafe.com. Reservations recommended. Main courses $7–$13 lunch, $8–$23 dinner. AE, DISC, MC, V. Mon–Fri 11am–midnight; Sat 8:30am–midnight; Sun 8:30am–11pm. Bar Mon–Sat until 2am; Sun until midnight.

Il Piatto Cucina Italiano ★★ (Value) NORTHERN ITALIAN This simple Italian cafe brings innovative flavors to thinner wallets. It's simple and elegant, with contemporary art on the walls—nice for a romantic evening. Service is efficient, though on a busy night, overworked. The menu changes seasonally, complemented by a few perennial standards. For a starter, try the grilled calamari with shaved fennel and aioli. Among entrees, my favorite is the pancetta-wrapped trout with grilled polenta and wild mushrooms, though you can't go wrong with the jumbo scampi risotto with sweet peppers. The Gorgonzola-walnut ravioli is a favorite of many, though not quite enough food to fill me up, so I order an appetizer. A full wine and beer menu is available.

95 W. Marcy St. ✆ **505/984-1091.** Reservations recommended. Main courses $15–$22. AE, DISC, MC, V. Mon–Fri 11:30am–2pm; daily 5:30–9pm. Closed July 4.

Railyard Restaurant & Saloon ★★ (Finds) NEW AMERICAN Santa Fe locals' most talked-about newer spot, the Railyard is a fun and thoughtful addition to the restaurant scene. Set in one of the city's old railroad buildings, the place offers a comfortable ambience and imaginative food at not-too-steep prices. The space has clean lines, with maroon walls and spacious booths and tables set under an industrial ceiling with visible ductwork. Service is friendly and knowledgeable. This is the creation of Louis Moskow, who put 315 (see above) on the map. Here, he's offering a slice of Americana, with creative twists. At lunch you might try shrimp tacos with black beans and rice or one of the excellent burgers or salads. Dinner might start with crispy calamari and move on to dishes such as an outstanding rib-eye and tasty pan-fried pork chop, but also some less American fare such as, my favorite, sesame-and-panko-crusted tuna. All menu items are a la carte, but the side portions you'll order separately are large enough to share. Select from a carefully considered wine list or from the full bar. An excellent but more limited selection of food is available all day at the bar. The patio is a lively place to hang in the warm months.

530 S. Guadalupe St. (1/4 block north of Paseo de Peralta). ✆ **505/989-3300.** www.railyardrestaurantandsaloon.com. Reservations recommended Fri–Sat nights. Main courses $7.50–$23 lunch, $9–$25 dinner. Mon–Sat 11:30am–2:30pm; Mon–Thurs 5:30–9:30pm; Fri–Sat 5:30–10pm; Sun 5–9:30pm. Bar Mon–Sat 11:30am–close; Sun 5pm–close.

Inexpensive

Blue Corn Café ★ (Kids) NEW MEXICAN/AMERICAN If you're ready for a fun and inexpensive night out to eat decent New Mexican food, this is your place. Within a clean and breezy decor—wooden tables and abstract art—you'll find a raucous and buoyant atmosphere; it's a good place to bring kids. The overworked waitstaff may be slow, but they're friendly. I recommend sampling dishes from the combination menu. You can get two to five items served with your choice of rice, beans, or one of the best *posoles* (hominy and chile) that I've tasted. I had the chicken enchilada, which I recommend, and the chalupa, which I don't because it was soggy. You can have tacos, tamales, and rellenos, too. Kids have their own menu and crayons to keep them occupied. Nightly specials include the tasty shrimp fajitas, served with a nice guacamole and the usual toppings. Because this is also a brewery, you might want to sample the High Altitude Pale Ale or Sleeping Dog Stout. My beverage choice is the prickly-pear iced tea (black tea with enough cactus juice to give it a zing). The Spanish flan is tasty and large enough to share. The **Blue Corn Cafe & Brewery** (4056 Cerrillos Rd., Ste. G; ✆ **505/438-1800**), on the south side at the corner of Cerrillos and Rodeo roads, has similar fare and atmosphere.

133 W. Water St. ✆ **505/984-1800.** Reservations accepted for parties of 6 or more. www.bluecorncafe.com. Main courses $10–$12. AE, DC, DISC, MC, V. Daily 11am–10pm.

Bumble Bee's Baja Grill ★ (Finds) (Kids) MEXICAN This "beestro" offers a refreshing twist on fast food: It's actually healthy! The secret? Tacos are made Mexican style, with a tortilla folded around quality meat, fish, and poultry grilled with veggies. You pick from an array of salsas. Waist watchers can sample from a selection of salads, including one with grilled chicken and avocado. Rotisserie chicken and various burritos round out the main menu, while kids have their own options, such as the quesadillas. Diners order at a counter, and a waiter brings the food. The decor is a bit Formica-esque for my tastes, though the primary colors are fun. During warm months, I try to nab a patio table. Evenings often offer live jazz music, when folks sit back and sip beer and wine. There's also a drive-through window. There's another **Bumble Bee's Baja Grill** (3777 Cerrillos Rd.; ✆ **505/988-3278**), with similar decor and offerings, on the south side of town.

301 Jefferson St. (from W. San Francisco St., take Guadalupe 2 blocks north). ✆ **505/820-2862.** www.bumblebeesbajagrill.com. Main courses $7–$12. AE, MC, V. Daily 11am–9pm.

Guadalupe Cafe ★★ NEW MEXICAN When I want New Mexican food, I go to this restaurant, and like many Santa Feans, I go there often. This casually elegant cafe is in a white stucco building that's warm and friendly and has a nice-size patio for dining in warmer months. Service is friendly and conscientious. For breakfast, try the spinach-mushroom burritos or huevos rancheros, and for lunch, the chalupas or stuffed *sopaipillas.* Any other time, I'd start with fresh roasted ancho chiles (filled with a combination of Montrachet and Monterey Jack cheeses and piñon nuts, and topped with your choice of chile) and move on to the sour-cream chicken enchilada or any of the other Southwestern dishes. Order both red and green chile ("Christmas") so that you can sample some of the best sauces in town. Beware, though: The chile here can be hot, and the chef won't put it on the side. Diners can order from a choice of delicious salads, such as a Caesar with chicken. Daily specials are available, and don't miss the famous chocolate-amaretto adobe pie for dessert. Beer and wine are served.

422 Old Santa Fe Trail. ✆ **505/982-9762.** Breakfast $5.50–$9.75; lunch $6–$12; dinner $8–$17. DISC, MC, V. Tues–Fri 7am–2pm; Sat–Sun 8am–2pm; Tues–Sat 5:30–9pm.

La Choza ★★ NEW MEXICAN This sister restaurant of the Shed (below) offers some of the best New Mexican food in town at a convenient location near the intersection of Cerrillos Road and St. Francis Drive. When other restaurants are packed, you'll only wait a little while here. It's a warm, casual eatery with vividly painted walls; it's especially popular on cold days, when diners gather around the wood-burning stove and fireplace. The patio is delightful in summer. Service is friendly and efficient. The menu offers enchiladas, tacos, and burritos, as well as green-chile stew, chile con carne, and carne adovada. The portions are medium size, so if you're hungry, start with guacamole or nachos. For years, I've ordered the cheese or chicken enchilada, two dishes I will always recommend, served with *posole.* You can't leave without trying the mocha cake (chocolate cake with a mocha pudding filling, served with whipped cream). Vegetarians and children have their own menus. Beer and wine are available.

905 Alarid St. ✆ **505/982-0909.** Lunch or dinner $8.95–$12. AE, DISC, MC, V. Summer Mon–Sat 11am–9pm; winter Mon–Thurs 11am–8pm, Fri–Sat 11am–9pm.

Plaza Cafe ★ AMERICAN/DELI/NEW MEXICAN/GREEK Santa Fe's best example of diner-style eating, this cafe has excellent food in a bright and friendly atmosphere right on the plaza. A restaurant since the turn of the 20th century, it's been owned by the Razatos family since 1947. The decor has changed only enough to stay comfortable and clean, with red upholstered banquettes, Art Deco tile, and a soda fountain–style service counter. Service is always quick and conscientious, and only during the heavy tourist seasons will you have to wait long for a table. Breakfasts are excellent and large, and the hamburgers and sandwiches at lunch and dinner are good. I also like the soups and New Mexican dishes, such as the bowl of green-chile stew, or, if you're more adventurous, the pumpkin *posole.* Check out the Greek dishes, such as vegetable moussaka or beef and lamb gyros. Wash it down with an Italian soda, in flavors from vanilla to amaretto. Alternatively, you can have a shake, a piece of coconut cream pie, or Plaza Cafe's signature dessert, *cajeta* (apple and pecan pie with Mexican caramel). Beer and wine are available.

54 Lincoln Ave. (on the plaza). ✆ **505/982-1664.** www.thefamousplazacafe.com. No reservations. Main courses $8–$17. AE, DISC, MC, V. Daily 7am–9pm.

The Shed ★★ NEW MEXICAN This longtime locals' favorite is so popular that, during lunch, lines often form outside. Half a block east of the plaza, it's been a luncheon institution since 1953, occupying several rooms and the patio of a rambling hacienda that was built in 1692. Festive folk art adorns the doorways and walls. The food is delicious, some of the best in the state, and a compliment to traditional Hispanic and Pueblo cooking. The red-chile cheese enchilada is renowned in Santa Fe. Tacos, and burritos are good, too. The green-chile stew is a local favorite. Vegetarian and low-fat Mexican foods have been added to the menu, along with a variety of soups and salads and grilled chicken and steak. Don't leave without trying the mocha cake, possibly the best dessert you'll ever eat. In addition to wine and a number of beers, there's full bar service. The cantina-style bar is a fun place to schmooze, and the brick patio is well shaded.

113½ E. Palace Ave. ✆ **505/982-9030.** www.sfshed.com. Reservations accepted at dinner. Lunch $5.75–$9.50, dinner $8–$17. AE, DC, DISC, MC, V. Mon–Sat 11am–2:30pm and 5:30–9pm.

Tomasita's Cafe ★ NEW MEXICAN When I was in high school, I used to eat at Tomasita's, a little dive on a back street. It's now in a modern building near the train station, and its food has become renowned. The atmosphere is simple—hanging plants and wood accents—with lots of families sitting at booths or tables and a festive spillover from the bar, where many come to drink margaritas. Service is quick, even a little rushed, which is my only gripe. Sure, the food is still tasty, but unless you go at some odd hour, you'll wait for a table, and once you're seated, you may eat and be out again in less than an hour. The burritos are still excellent, though you may want to try the chile rellenos, a house specialty. Vegetarian dishes, burgers, steaks, and daily specials are also offered. There's full bar service.

500 S. Guadalupe St. ✆ **505/983-5721.** No reservations; large parties call ahead. Lunch $6–$15, dinner $6.25–$16. AE, DISC, MC, V. Mon–Sat 11am–10pm.

Upper Crust Pizza ★ Kids PIZZA Upper Crust serves some of Santa Fe's best pizzas, in an adobe house near the old San Miguel Mission. The atmosphere is plain, with wooden tables; in summer, the outdoor patio overlooking Old Santa Fe Trail is more inviting. Meals-in-a-dish include the Grecian gourmet pizza (feta and olives) and the whole-wheat vegetarian pizza (topped with sesame seeds). You can either eat here or request free delivery (it takes about 30 min.) to your downtown hotel. Beer and wine are available, as are salads, calzones, sandwiches, and stromboli.

329 Old Santa Fe Trail. ✆ **505/982-0000.** www.uppercrustpizza.com. Pizzas $7.95–$18. DISC, MC, V. Summer daily 11am–midnight; winter Sun–Thurs 11am–10pm, Fri–Sat 11am–11pm.

SOUTHSIDE

Santa Fe's motel strip and other streets south of Paseo de Peralta have their share of good, reasonably priced restaurants. Note that the Blue Corn Café and Bumble Bee's Baja Grill have southside locations (see above).

mu du noodles ★★ PACIFIC RIM If you're ready for a light, healthy meal with lots of flavor, head to this small restaurant, about an 8-minute drive from downtown. The two rooms have brightly painted walls, pine tables and chairs and sparse Asian prints on the walls. The carpeted back room is cozier, and a woodsy-feeling patio is definitely worth requesting during the warmer months. The waitstaff is friendly and unimposing. I almost always order the Malaysian *laksa,* thick rice noodles in a blend of coconut milk, hazelnuts, onions, and red curry, stir-fried with chicken or tofu and julienned vegetables and sprouts. If you're eating with others, you may each want to order a different dish and share. The pad Thai is lighter and spicier than most, served with a chile-vinegar sauce. A list of beers, wines, and sakes is available, tailored to the menu. I'm especially fond of the ginseng ginger ale. Menu items change seasonally.

1494 Cerrillos Rd. ✆ **505/983-1411.** www.mudunoodles.com. Reservations for parties of 3 or larger only. Main courses $9–$18. AE, DC, DISC, MC, V. Tues–Sat 5:30–9pm (sometimes to 10pm in summer).

5 WHAT TO SEE & DO

One of the oldest cities in the United States, Santa Fe has long been a center for the creative and performing arts, so it's not surprising that most of the city's major sights are related to local history and the arts. The city's Museum of New Mexico, art galleries and studios, historic churches, and cultural sights associated with local Native American and Hispanic communities all merit a visit. It would be easy to spend a full week sightseeing in the city, without ever heading out to any nearby attractions.

THE TOP ATTRACTIONS

Georgia O'Keeffe Museum ★★ The Georgia O'Keeffe Museum, inaugurated in July 1997, contains the largest collection of O'Keeffes in the world: currently 1,149 paintings, drawings, and sculptures, and 1,851 works by other artists of note. It's the largest museum in the United States dedicated solely to an internationally known woman artist. You can see such remarkable O'Keeffes as *Jimson Weed,* painted in 1932, and *Evening Star No. VII,* from 1917. The museum presents special exhibitions that are either devoted entirely to O'Keeffe's work or combine examples of her art with works by her American modernist contemporaries. My favorite in recent years brought together works of O'Keeffe and photographer Ansel Adams. The rich and varied collection adorns the walls of a cathedral-like, 13,000-square-foot space—a former Baptist church with adobe walls. O'Keeffe's images are tied inextricably to local desert landscapes. She first visited New Mexico in 1917 (though the museum film says 1929) and returned for extended periods from the '20s through the '40s. In 1949, she moved here permanently. An excellent film at the museum depicts her life. Plan to spend 1 to 2 hours here.

217 Johnson St. ✆ **505/946-1000.** www.okeeffemuseum.org. Admission $8, free for students and youth 18 and under, free for all Fri 5–8pm. June–Oct daily 10am–5pm (Fri until 8pm). Closed Tues Nov–May.

New Mexico History Museum & the Palace of the Governors ★★★ Open in 2009, the New Mexico History Museum presents the state's unique role in world history. Set in 96,000 square feet of exhibit space, the museum offers visitors an interactive experience exploring a region occupied by Pueblo, Navajo, and Apache people, followed by the arrival of the Spanish in the 1500s, and, finally, the present day.

A part of the museum, the Palace of the Governors, offers a glimpse into the Pueblo Revolt of 1680. Prior to the uprising, this was the local seat of power, and after Don Diego de Vargas reconquered the natives, it resumed that position. Built in 1610 as the original capitol of New Mexico, the palace has been in continuous public use longer than any other structure in the United States. Out front, Native Americans sell jewelry, pottery, and some weavings under the protection of the portal. This is a good place to buy, and it's a fun place to shop, especially if you take the time to visit with the artisans about their work. When you buy a piece, you may learn its history, a treasure often as valuable as the piece itself. Plan to spend 2 or more hours exploring the museum and shopping here.

Two shops are of particular interest. One is the bookstore/gift shop, which has an excellent selection of art, history, and anthropology books. The other is the print shop and bindery, where limited-edition works are produced on hand-operated presses. The museum offers walking tours April through October. Call for the schedule.

North plaza. ✆ **505/476-5100.** www.museumofnewmexico.org. Admission $8 adults, free for children 16 and under, free for all Fri 5–8pm. 4-day passes (good at all 4 branches of the Museum of New Mexico and the Museum of Spanish Colonial Art) $18 for adults. Tues–Sun 10am–5pm. Closed New Year's Day, Thanksgiving, Christmas.

New Mexico Museum of Art ★ Opposite the Palace of the Governors, this was one of the first pueblo revival–style buildings constructed in Santa Fe (in 1917). The museum's permanent collection of more than 20,000 works emphasizes regional art and

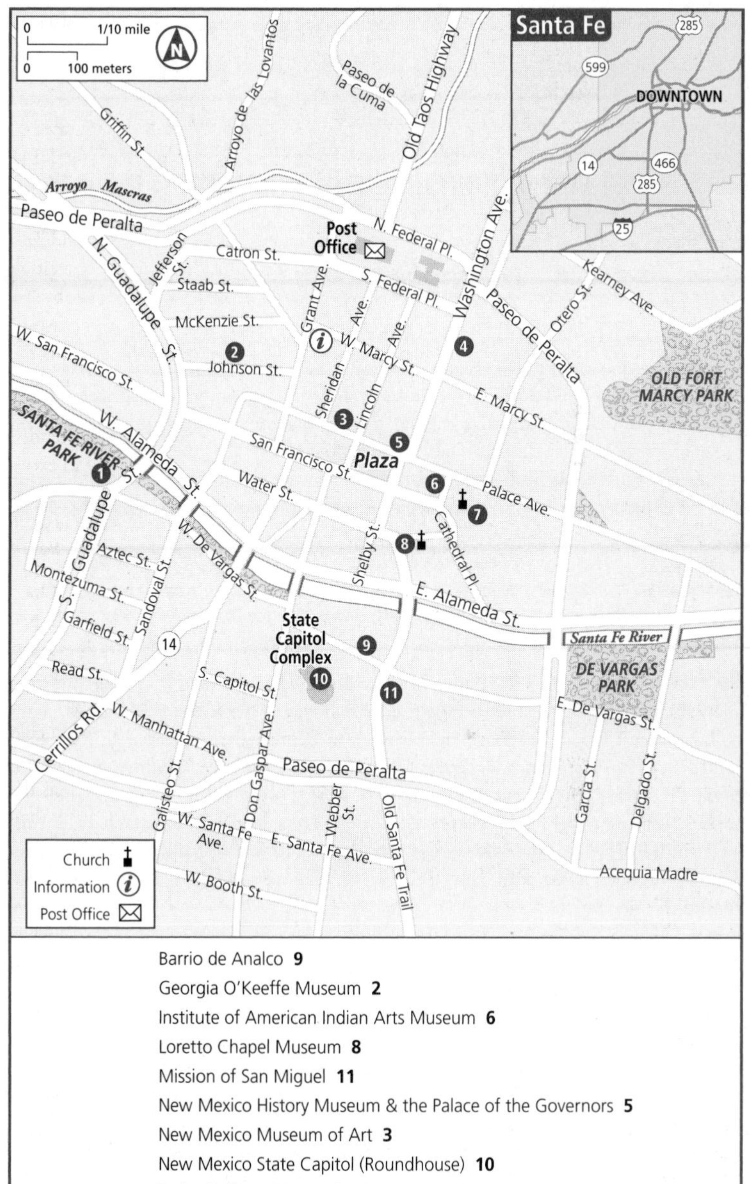

Barrio de Analco **9**

Georgia O'Keeffe Museum **2**

Institute of American Indian Arts Museum **6**

Loretto Chapel Museum **8**

Mission of San Miguel **11**

New Mexico History Museum & the Palace of the Governors **5**

New Mexico Museum of Art **3**

New Mexico State Capitol (Roundhouse) **10**

Padre Gallegos House **4**

Santuario de Nuestra Señora de Guadalupe **1**

St. Francis Cathedral **7**

Museum Bingeing

If you're a museum buff, pick up one of **Museum of New Mexico's 4-day passes.** It's good at all five branches of the Museum of New Mexico: the Palace of the Governors, the Museum of Fine Arts, the Museum of International Folk Art, and the Museum of Indian Arts & Culture, with the Museum of Spanish Colonial Art thrown in for good measure. The cost is $18 for adults. Also ask about the new **Culture Pass,** good for 1 year, to visit museums all over the state for $25.

includes landscapes and portraits by all the Taos masters, *los Cincos Pintores* (a 1920s organization of Santa Fe artists), and contemporary artists. The museum also has a collection of photographic works by such masters as Ansel Adams and Elliot Porter. Modern artists are featured in temporary exhibits throughout the year. Two sculpture gardens present a range of three-dimensional art, from the traditional to the abstract.

Graceful **St. Francis Auditorium,** patterned after the interiors of traditional Hispanic mission churches, adjoins the art museum. A museum shop sells gifts, art books, prints, and postcards of the collection. Plan to spend 1 hour here.

107 W. Palace (at Lincoln Ave.). ✆ **505/476-5072.** www.museumofnewmexico.org. Admission $8 adults, free for seniors Wed, free for children 16 and under, free for all Fri 5–8pm. 4-day passes (good at all 4 branches of the Museum of New Mexico and the Museum of Spanish Colonial Art) $18 for adults. Tues–Sun 10am–5pm; Fri 10am–8pm. Closed New Year's Day, Easter, Thanksgiving, Christmas.

St. Francis Cathedral ★ Santa Fe's grandest religious structure is an architectural anomaly in Santa Fe because its design is French. Just a block east of the plaza, it was built between 1869 and 1886 by Archbishop Jean-Baptiste Lamy in the style of the great cathedrals of Europe. French architects designed the Romanesque building—named after Santa Fe's patron saint—and Italian masons assisted with its construction. The small adobe Our Lady of the Rosary chapel on the northeast side of the cathedral has a Spanish look. Built in 1807, it's the only portion that remains from Our Lady of the Assumption Church, founded along with Santa Fe in 1610. The new cathedral was built over and around the old church.

A wooden icon set in a niche in the wall of the north chapel, Our Lady of Peace, is the oldest representation of the Madonna in the United States. Rescued from the old church during the 1680 Pueblo Rebellion, it was brought back by Don Diego de Vargas on his (mostly peaceful) reconquest 12 years later—thus, the name. Today, Our Lady of Peace plays an important part in the annual Feast of Corpus Christi in June and July.

The cathedral's front doors feature 16 carved panels of historic note and a plaque memorializing the 38 Franciscan friars who were martyred during New Mexico's early years. There's also a large bronze statue of Archbishop Lamy himself; his grave is under the main altar of the cathedral. Touring the cathedral will take a half-hour to an hour.

Cathedral Place at San Francisco St. ✆ **505/982-5619.** Donations appreciated. Daily. Visitors may attend Mass Mon–Sat 7am and 5:15pm; Sun 8, 10am, noon, and 5:15pm. Free parking in city lot next to the cathedral to attend church services.

Santa Fe Plaza ★★ (Moments) This square has been the heart and soul of Santa Fe, as well as its literal center, since its concurrent establishment with the city in 1610.

Originally designed as a meeting place, it has been the site of innumerable festivals and other historical, cultural, and social events. Long ago the plaza was a dusty hive of activity as the staging ground and terminus of the Santa Fe Trail. Today, those who congregate around the central monument enjoy the best people-watching in New Mexico. Live music and dancing are often staged on the gazebo/bandstand in summer. At Christmastime, the plaza is decked with lights. Santa Feans understandably feel nostalgic for the days when the plaza, now the hub of the tourist trade, still belonged to locals rather than to outside commercial interests.

At the corner of San Francisco St. and Lincoln Ave. Daily 24 hr.

MORE ATTRACTIONS

Museums

Institute of American Indian Arts Museum ★ A visit to this museum (with over 7,000 works, often called the "national collection of contemporary Native American art") offers a profound look into the lives of a people negotiating two worlds: traditional and contemporary. Here, you'll see cutting-edge art that pushes the limits of many media, from creative writing to textile manufacturing to painting. Much of the work originates from artists from the Institute of American Indian Arts (IAIA), the nation's only congressionally chartered institute of higher education devoted solely to the study and practice of the artistic and cultural traditions of all American Indian and Alaskan native peoples.

Exhibits change periodically, while a more permanent collection of Allan Houser's monumental sculpture is on display in the museum's Art Park. The museum store offers a broad collection of contemporary jewelry, pottery, and other crafts, as well as books and music.

108 Cathedral Place. ✆ **505/983-8900.** www.iaia.edu. Admission $5 adults, $2.50 seniors and students, free for children 16 and under. Mon–Sat 10am–5pm; Sun noon–5pm.

Museum of Indian Arts & Culture ★★ An interactive permanent exhibit here has made this one of the most exciting Native American museum experiences in the Southwest. "Here, Now and Always" takes visitors through thousands of years of Native American history. More than 70,000 pieces of basketry, pottery, clothing, carpets, and jewelry—much of it quite old—are on continual rotating display. You begin by entering through a tunnel that symbolizes the *sipapu,* the Ancestral Puebloan (Anasazi) entrance into the upper worlds; you're greeted by the sounds of trickling water, drums, and Native American music. Videos show Native Americans telling creation stories. Visitors can reflect on the lives of modern-day Native Americans by juxtaposing a traditional Pueblo

Cultural Chow

If you get hungry while visiting the Museum of Indian Arts & Culture, the Museum of International Folk Art, the Wheelwright Museum of the American Indian, or the Museum of Spanish Colonial Art (all located together, southeast of the plaza), you can now feast on more than your fingernails. The **Museum Hill Café ★** (✆ **505/820-1776**) opens Tuesday through Saturday for beverages and snacks at 10am, and a tasty lunch from 11am to 3pm; it serves brunch on Sunday from 11am to 3pm.

 kitchen with a modern kitchen. You can step into a Navajo hogan (log and mud hut) and stroll through a trading post. The rest of the museum houses a lovely pottery collection as well as changing exhibits. There's always a contemporary show.

710 Camino Lejo. ✆ **505/476-1250.** www.miaclab.org. Admission $8 adults, free for kids 16 and under. 4-day passes (good at all 4 branches of the Museum of New Mexico and the Museum of Spanish Colonial Art) $18 for adults. Tues–Sun 10am–5pm. Closed New Year's Day, Easter, Thanksgiving, and Christmas. Drive southeast on Old Santa Fe Trail (***Note:*** Old Santa Fe Trail takes a left turn; if you find yourself on Old Pecos Trail, you missed the turn). Look for signs pointing right onto Camino Lejo.

Museum of International Folk Art ★★★ Kids This branch of the Museum of New Mexico may not seem quite as typically Southwestern as other Santa Fe museums, but it's the largest of its kind in the world. With a collection of some 130,000 objects from more than 100 countries, it's my favorite city museum, well worth an hour or two of perusing. It was founded in 1953 by the Chicago collector Florence Dibell Bartlett, who said, "If peoples of different countries could have the opportunity to study each other's cultures, it would be one avenue for a closer understanding between men." That's the basis on which the museum operates today.

The special collections include Spanish colonial silver, traditional and contemporary New Mexican religious art, Mexican tribal costumes and majolica ceramics, Brazilian folk art, European glass, African sculptures, and East Indian textiles. Particularly delightful are numerous dioramas of people around the world at work and play in typical town, village, and home settings, which kids love.

The Hispanic Heritage Wing houses a fine collection of Spanish colonial and contemporary Hispanic folk art. Folk-art demonstrations, performances, and workshops are often presented here. The 80,000-square-foot museum also has a lecture room, a research library, and two gift shops, where a variety of folk art is available for purchase.

706 Camino Lejo. ✆ **505/476-1200.** www.moifa.org. Admission $8 adults, free for kids 16 and under. 4-day passes (good at all 4 branches of the Museum of New Mexico and at the Museum of Spanish Colonial Art) $18 for adults. Memorial Day to Labor Day daily 10am–5pm; rest of the year Tues–Sun 10am–5pm. Closed New Year's Day, Easter, Thanksgiving, and Christmas. The museum is about 2 miles southeast of the plaza. Drive southeast on Old Santa Fe Trail (***Note:*** Old Santa Fe Trail takes a left turn; if you find yourself on Old Pecos Trail, you missed the turn). Look for signs pointing right onto Camino Lejo.

Museum of Spanish Colonial Art ★ Beauty often follows in the wake of imperialism. A good example of this is Spanish colonial art, which has flourished from Europe across the Americas and even in the Philippines. This museum, located in the same compound as the Museum of International Folk Art, the Museum of Indian Arts & Culture, and the Wheelwright Museum of the American Indian, celebrates this art with a collection of 3,000 devotional and decorative works and utilitarian artifacts. Housed in a home built by noted architect John Gaw Meem, the museum displays *retablos* (religious paintings on wood), *bultos* (free-standing religious sculptures), furniture, metalwork, textiles, and, outside, an 18th-century wooden colonial house from Mexico.

750 Camino Lejo. ✆ **505/982-2226.** www.spanishcolonial.org. Admission $8 adults, free for kids 16 and under. 4-day passes (good at all 4 branches of the Museum of New Mexico and at this one) $18 for adults. Tues–Sun 10am–5pm. Closed New Year's Day, Easter, Thanksgiving, and Christmas. The museum is located about 2 miles southeast of the plaza. Drive southeast on Old Santa Fe Trail (***Note:*** Old Santa Fe Trail takes a left turn; if you find yourself on Old Pecos Trail, you missed the turn). Look for signs pointing right onto Camino Lejo.

Wheelwright Museum of the American Indian ★ Kids Next to the Museum of International Folk Art, this museum resembles a Navajo hogan, with its doorway facing east (toward the rising sun) and its ceiling formed in the interlocking "whirling log" style. It was founded in 1937 by Boston scholar Mary Cabot Wheelwright, in collaboration with a Navajo medicine man, Hastiin Klah, to preserve and document Navajo ritual beliefs and practices. In 1976, the museum's focus was altered to include the living arts of all Native American cultures. The museum offers three or four exhibits per year. You may see a basketry exhibit, mixed-media Navajo toys, or amazing contemporary Navajo rugs. An added treat here is the Case Trading Post, an arts-and-crafts shop built to resemble the typical turn-of-the-20th-century trading post found on the Navajo reservation. Best of all here are the **storytelling sessions ★★** given by Joe Hayes, scheduled in July and August on Saturday and Sunday evenings at 7pm. Check the website for more details.

704 Camino Lejo. ✆ **800/607-4636** or 505/982-4636. Fax 505/989-7386. www.wheelwright.org. Donations appreciated. Mon–Sat 10am–5pm; Sun 1–5pm. Closed New Year's Day, Thanksgiving, Christmas. Drive southeast on Old Santa Fe Trail (***Note:*** Old Santa Fe Trail takes a left turn; if you find yourself on Old Pecos Trail, you missed the turn). Look for signs pointing right onto Camino Lejo.

Churches

Loretto Chapel Museum ★★ Though no longer consecrated for worship, the Loretto Chapel remains an important site in Santa Fe. Patterned after the famous Sainte-Chapelle church in Paris, it was constructed in 1873—by the same French architects and Italian masons who were building Archbishop Lamy's cathedral—as a chapel for the Sisters of Loretto, who had established a school for young women in Santa Fe in 1852.

The chapel has an especially notable spiral staircase: It makes two complete 360-degree turns, with no central or other visible support. The structure is steeped in legend. The building was nearly finished in 1878, when workers realized the stairs to the choir loft wouldn't fit. Hoping for a solution more attractive than a ladder, the sisters made a novena (9-day prayer) to St. Joseph—and were rewarded when a mysterious carpenter appeared astride a donkey and offered to build a staircase. Armed with only a saw, a hammer, and a T-square, the master constructed this work of genius by soaking slats of wood in tubs of water to curve them and holding them together with wooden pegs. Then he disappeared without bothering to collect his fee.

207 Old Santa Fe Trail (btw. Alameda and Water sts.). ✆ **505/982-0092.** www.lorettochapel.com. Admission $2.50 adults, $2 children 7–12 and seniors 65 and over, free for children 6 and under. Mon–Sat 9am–5pm; Sun 10:30am–5pm.

Mission of San Miguel If you really want to get the feel of colonial Catholicism, visit this church. Better yet, attend Mass here. You won't be disappointed. Built in 1610, the church has massive adobe walls, high windows, an elegant altar screen (erected in 1798), and a 780-pound San José bell (now found inside), which was cast in Spain in 1356. If that doesn't impress you, perhaps the buffalo-hide and deerskin Bible paintings (used in 1630 by Franciscan missionaries to teach the Native Americans) will. Anthropologists have excavated near the altar, down to the original floor that some claim to be part of a 12th-century pueblo. A small store just off the sanctuary sells religious articles.

401 Old Santa Fe Trail (at E. de Vargas St.). ✆ **505/983-3974.** Admission $1 adults, free for children 6 and under. Mon–Sat 9am–5pm; Sun 9am–4pm. Summer hours start earlier. Mass Sun 5pm.

Santuario de Nuestra Señora de Guadalupe ★ This church, built between 1776 and 1796 at the end of El Camino Real by Franciscan missionaries, is believed to be the oldest shrine in the United States honoring the Virgin of Guadalupe, the patron saint of Mexico. Better known as Santuario de Guadalupe, the shrine's adobe walls stand almost 3-feet thick, and the deep-red plaster wall behind the altar was dyed with oxblood in traditional fashion when the church was restored early in the 20th century.

It is well worth a visit to see photographs of the transformation of the building over time; its styles have ranged from flat-topped pueblo to New England town meeting and today's northern New Mexico style. On one wall hangs a famous oil painting, *Our Lady of Guadalupe,* created in 1783 by the renowned Mexican artist José de Alzibar. Painted expressly for this church, it was brought from Mexico City by mule caravan.

100 S. Guadalupe St. ✆ **505/983-8868.** Donations appreciated. Mon–Sat 9am–4pm; Labor Day–Memorial Day till 6pm. Mass held Mon–Fri 6:30am, Sat 8am, Sun noon.

Other Attractions

El Rancho de las Golondrinas ★★ Kids This 200-acre ranch, about 15 miles south of the plaza via I-25, was once the last stopping place on the 1,000-mile El Camino Real from Mexico City to Santa Fe. Today, it's a living 18th- and 19th-century Spanish village, composed of a hacienda, a village store, a schoolhouse, and several chapels and kitchens. There's also a working molasses mill, wheelwright and blacksmith shops, shearing and weaving rooms, a threshing ground, a winery and vineyard, and four water mills, as well as dozens of farm animals. A walk around the entire property is 1¾ miles in length, with amazing scenery and plenty of room for the kids to romp.

334 Los Pinos Rd. ✆ **505/471-2261.** www.golondrinas.org. Admission $5 adults, $4 seniors and teens, $2 children 5–12, free for children 4 and under. Festival weekends $7 adults, $5 seniors and teens, $3 children 5–12. June–Sept Wed–Sun 10am–4pm; Apr–May and Oct by advance arrangement. Closed Nov–Mar. From Santa Fe, drive south on I-25, taking exit 276; this will lead to NM 599 going north; turn left on W. Frontage Rd.; drive ½ mile; turn right on Los Pinos Rd.; travel 3 miles to the museum.

New Mexico State Capitol (Roundhouse) Some are surprised to learn that this is the only round capitol building in the U.S. Built in 1966, it's designed in the shape of a Zia Pueblo emblem (or sun sign, which is also the state symbol). It symbolizes the Circle of Life: four winds, four seasons, four directions, and four sacred obligations. Surrounding the capitol is a lush 6½-acre garden boasting more than 100 varieties of plants, including roses, plums, almonds, nectarines, Russian olive trees, and sequoias. Inside you'll find standard functional offices, with New Mexican art hanging on the walls. Check out the Governor's Gallery and the Capitol Art Collection. Self-guided tours are available 8am to 5pm Monday through Friday year-round; Memorial Day to Labor Day guided tours are available Monday through Saturday at 10am and 2pm. All tours and self-guided brochures are free to the public.

Paseo de Peralta and Old Santa Fe Trail. ✆ **505/986-4589.** www.legis.state.nm.us. Free admission. Mon–Sat 8am–5pm. Free parking.

Santa Fe Southern Railway ★ "Riding the old Santa Fe" always referred to riding the Atchison, Topeka & Santa Fe railroad. Ironically, the main route of the AT&SF bypassed Santa Fe, which probably forestalled some development for the capital city. A spur was run off the main line to Santa Fe in 1880, and today, an 18-mile ride along that spur offers views of some of New Mexico's most spectacular scenery.

Inside the restored coach, passengers enjoy aged mahogany paneling and faded velvet seats. The train snakes through Santa Fe and into the Galisteo Basin, broad landscapes spotted with piñon and chamisa, with views of the Sandia and Ortiz mountains. Arriving in the small track town of Lamy, you get another glimpse of a Mission-style station, this one surrounded by spacious lawns where passengers picnic. Check out the sunset rides on weekends and specialty trains throughout the year.

410 S. Guadalupe St. ✆ **888/989-8600** or 505/989-8600. Fax 505/983-7620. www.thetraininsantafe.com. Tickets range from $18 (children) to $30 (adults), $30–$80 Fri–Sat evening rides (May–Oct). Discounts available. Depending on the season, trains depart the Santa Fe Depot (call to check schedule) Mon–Sat 9:30am–1pm. Rides also available Fri–Sat evening and Sun afternoon.

PARKS & REFUGES

Old Fort Marcy Park Marking the 1846 site of the first U.S. military reservation in the Southwest, this park overlooks the northeast corner of downtown. Only a few mounds remain from the fort, but the Cross of the Martyrs, at the top of a winding brick walkway from Paseo de Peralta near Otero Street, is a popular spot for bird's-eye photographs. The cross was erected in 1920 by the Knights of Columbus and the Historical Society of New Mexico to commemorate the Franciscans killed during the Pueblo Rebellion of 1680. It has since played a role in numerous religious processions. The park's open daily 24 hours, though it's dark and not likely safe at night.

617 Paseo de Peralta (or travel 3 blocks up Artist Rd. and turn right).

Randall Davey Audubon Center ★ Named for the late Santa Fe artist who willed his home to the National Audubon Society, this wildlife refuge occupies 135 acres at the mouth of Santa Fe Canyon. Just a few minutes' drive from the plaza, it's an excellent escape. More than 100 species of birds and 120 types of plants live here, and varied mammals have been spotted—including black bears, mule deer, mountain lions, bobcats, raccoons, and coyotes. Trails winding through more than 100 acres of the nature sanctuary are open to day hikers (but not to dogs). There's also a natural history bookstore on site.

1800 Upper Canyon Rd. ✆ **505/983-4609.** http://nm.audubon.org. Trail admission $2 adults, $1 children. Daily 9am–5pm. House tours conducted Mon and Fri at 2pm, $5 per person. Gift shop daily 10am–4pm (call for winter hours). Free 1-hr. guided bird walk every Fri at 2pm.

Santa Fe River Park This is a lovely spot for an early-morning jog, a midday walk beneath the trees, or perhaps a sack lunch at a picnic table. The green strip follows the midtown stream for about 4 miles as it meanders along Alameda from St. Francis Drive upstream beyond Camino Cabra, near its source. It's open daily 24 hours, but it's not a safe place to linger at night.

Alameda St. ✆ **505/955-6977.**

COOKING & ART CLASSES

If you're looking for something to do that's a little off the beaten tourist path, you might consider taking a class.

You can master the flavors of Santa Fe with an entertaining 3-hour demonstration cooking class at the **Santa Fe School of Cooking and Market ★**, on the upper level of the Plaza Mercado, 116 W. San Francisco St. (✆ **505/983-4511;** fax 505/983-7540; www.santafeschoolofcooking.com). The class teaches about the flavors and history of traditional New Mexican and contemporary Southwestern cuisines. "Cooking Light" classes are available as well.

If Southwestern art has you hooked, you can take a drawing and painting class led by Santa Fe artist Jane Shoenfeld. Contact her at **Sketching Santa Fe ★**, P.O. Box 5912, Santa Fe, NM 87502 (✆ **505/986-1108;** www.skyfields.net).

WINE TASTINGS

If you enjoy sampling regional wines, consider visiting the wineries within easy driving distance of Santa Fe: **Santa Fe Vineyards,** with a retail outlet at 235 Don Gaspar Ave., in Santa Fe (✆ **505/982-3474**), or the vineyard itself about 20 miles north of Santa Fe on US 84/285 (✆ **505/753-8100**); **Madison Vineyards & Winery,** in Ribera (✆ **505/421-8028**), about 45 miles east of Santa Fe on I-25 North; and the **Black Mesa Winery,** 1502 Hwy. 68, in Velarde (✆ **800/852-6372**), north on US 84/285 to NM 68 (about 1-hr. drive). Be sure to call in advance to find out when the wineries are open for tastings and to get specific directions.

ESPECIALLY FOR KIDS

Don't miss taking the kids to the **Museum of International Folk Art** (p. 168), where they'll love the international dioramas and the toys. Also visit the tepee at the **Wheelwright Museum of the American Indian** (p. 168), where storyteller Joe Hayes spins traditional Spanish *cuentos,* Native American folk tales, and Wild West tall tales on weekend evenings. **The Bishop's Lodge Ranch Resort and Spa** has extensive children's programs during the summer. These include horseback riding, swimming, arts-and-crafts programs, and special activities, such as archery and tennis. Kids are sure to enjoy **El Rancho de las Golondrinas** (p. 170), a living 18th- and 19th-century Spanish village that includes a hacienda, a village store, a schoolhouse, and several chapels and kitchens.

The **Genoveva Chavez Community Center** is a full-service family recreation center on the south side of Santa Fe (3221 Rodeo Rd.). The complex includes a 50m pool, a leisure pool, a therapy pool, an ice-skating rink, three gyms, a workout room, racquetball courts, and an indoor running track, as well as a spa and sauna. For hours and more information, call ✆ **505/955-4001,** or visit www.gccommunitycenter.com.

Santa Fe Children's Museum ★ This museum offers interactive exhibits and hands-on activities in the arts, humanities, and science. The most notable features include a 16-foot climbing wall that kids—outfitted with helmets and harnesses—can scale, and a 1-acre Southwestern horticulture garden, complete with animals, wetlands, and a greenhouse. This fascinating area serves as an outdoor classroom for ongoing environmental educational programs. Special performances and hands-on sessions with artists and scientists are regularly scheduled. *Family Life* magazine named this as one of the 10 hottest children's museums in the nation.

1050 Old Pecos Trail. ✆ **505/989-8359.** www.santafechildrensmuseum.org. Admission $8 for nonresidents; $4 New Mexico residents; $4 children 12 and under, must be accompanied by an adult. Wed–Sat 10am–5pm; Sun noon–5pm.

Skateboard Park Split-level ramps for daredevils, park benches for onlookers, and climbing structures for youngsters are located at this park near downtown.

At the intersection of de Vargas and Sandoval sts. ✆ **505/955-2100.** Free admission. 24 hr.

6 ORGANIZED TOURS

BUS TOURS

Loretto Line ★ For an open-air tour of the city covering history and sights, contact this company that has been running tours for 17 years. Tours last 1¼ hours and are offered daily from April to October. They depart at 10am, noon, and 2pm—and sometimes more frequently in summer.

At the Inn & Spa at Loretto, 211 Old Santa Fe Trail. Tours depart from the Loretto Chapel. ✆ **505/983-3701.** www.toursofsantafe.com. Tours $14 adults, $10 children 12 and under.

WALKING TOURS

Walking Tour of Santa Fe ★ One of Santa Fe's best walking tours begins under the T-shirt tree at Tees & Skis, 107 Washington Ave., near the northeast corner of the plaza (at 9:30am and 1:30pm). It lasts about 2½ hours. From November through March, the tour runs by reservation only.

54½ E. San Francisco St. (tour meets at 107 Washington Ave.). ✆ **800/338-6877** or 505/983-6565. Tours $10 adults, free for children 12 and under.

MISCELLANEOUS TOURS

Pathways Customized Tours ★ Don Dietz offers several planned tours, including a downtown Santa Fe walking tour, a full city tour, a trip to the cliff dwellings and native pueblos, a "Taos adventure," and a trip to Georgia O'Keeffe country (with a focus on the landscape that inspired the art now viewable in the O'Keeffe Museum). He will try to accommodate any special requests you might have. These tours last anywhere from 2 to 9 hours. Don has extensive knowledge of the area's culture, history, geology, and flora and fauna, and will help you make the most of your precious vacation time.

161-F Calle Ojo Feliz. ✆ **505/982-5382.** www.santafepathways.com. Tours $60–$200 (or more) per day, covers up to 2 people. No credit cards.

Rain Parrish ★ A Navajo (or *Diné*) anthropologist, artist, and curator, Rain Parrish offers custom guide services focusing on cultural anthropology, Native American arts, and the history of the Native Americans of the Southwest. Some of these are true adventures to insider locations. Parrish includes visits to local Pueblo villages.

704 Kathryn St. ✆ **505/984-8236.** Tours $135 for up to 2 people for 4 hr.

Rojo Tours & Services Customized and private tours are arranged to pueblos, cliff dwellings, ruins, hot-air ballooning, backpacking, or white-water rafting. Rojo also provides planning services for groups.

P.O. Box 15744. ✆ **505/474-8333.** Fax 505/474-2992. www.rojotours.com.

Santa Fe Detours ★ Santa Fe's most extensive tour-booking agency accommodates almost all travelers' tastes, from bus and rail tours to river rafting, backpacking, and cross-country skiing. The agency can also facilitate hotel reservations, from budget to high end.

54½ E. San Francisco St. (summer tour desk, 107 Washington Ave.). ✆ **800/338-6877** or 505/983-6565. www.sfdetours.com.

Southwest Safaris ★★ This tour is one of the most interesting Southwestern experiences available. You'll fly in a small plane 1,000 feet off the ground to various destinations while pilot Bruce Adams explains millions of years of geologic history. En route to the Grand Canyon, for instance, you may pass by the ancient ruins of Chaco Canyon, over the vivid colors of the Painted Desert, and then, of course, over the spectacular Grand Canyon itself. Trips to many Southwestern destinations are available.

Departs from Santa Fe Airport. ✆ **800/842-4246** or 505/988-4246. www.southwestsafaris.com. Tours $89–$699 per person.

7 GETTING OUTSIDE

Set between the granite peaks of the Sangre de Cristo Mountains and the subtler volcanic Jemez Mountains, and with the Rio Grande flowing through, the Santa Fe area offers outdoor enthusiasts many opportunities to play. This is the land of high desert, where temperatures vary with the elevation, allowing for a full range of activities throughout the year.

BIKING

You can cycle along main roadways and paved country roads year-round in Santa Fe, but be aware that traffic is particularly heavy around the plaza—and all over town, motorists are not particularly attentive to bicyclists, so you need to be especially alert. Mountain-biking interest has exploded here and is especially popular in the spring, summer, and fall; the high-desert terrain is rugged and challenging, but mountain bikers of all levels can find exhilarating rides. The Santa Fe Community Convention Center and Visitors Bureau can supply you with bike maps.

I recommend the following trails: The **railroad tracks south of Santa Fe** provide wide-open biking on beginner-to-intermediate technical trails; and the **Borrego Trail** up toward the Santa Fe Ski Area is a challenging technical ride that links in with the **Windsor Trail,** a nationally renowned technical romp with plenty of verticality.

In Santa Fe bookstores, or online at such sites as Amazon.com, look for *Mountain Biking Northern New Mexico: A Guide to Taos, Santa Fe, and Albuquerque Areas' Greatest Off-Road Bicycle Rides,* by Bob D'Antonio. The book details 40 rides ranging in difficulty from beginner to advanced. **Santa Fe Mountain Sports,** 606 Cerrillos Rd. (✆ **505/988-3337;** www.santafemountainsports.com), rents hard-tail mountain bikes for $20 per half-day and $25 per full day; full-suspension bikes are available for $35 for a full day. **Mellow Velo Bikes,** 638 Old Santa Fe Trail (✆ **505/982-8986;** www.mellowvelo.com), rents front-suspension mountain bikes for $23 for a half-day and $30 for a full day. Town cruisers run $23 per half-day and $30 per full day; full-suspension bikes run $43 per day. Add $7, and Mellow Velo will deliver to and pick up from your hotel (in the Santa Fe area). Multiday rentals can be arranged. Both shops supply accessories such as helmets, locks, maps, and trail information, usually at an additional cost. Mellow Velo also runs a private guided tour service, which includes back-country guided adventures starting from $60 to $95 per person. On their guided train tour, clients cycle to Lamy and take a train back.

BIRD-WATCHING

Bird-watchers flock to the **Randall Davey Audubon Center** ★ (see "Parks & Refuges," above), 1800 Upper Canyon Rd. (✆ **505/983-4609**), to see more than 100 species of birds and many other animals. For guided bird-watching tours all over the region, contact **Wings West** (✆ **800/583-6928;** http://home.earthlink.net/~wingswestnm). Bill West guides half-day tours to local spots such as the Santa Fe Mountains and Cochiti Lake ($105 for 1–2 people) and full-day ones farther afield ($195 for 1–2 people).

FISHING

In the lakes and waterways around Santa Fe, anglers typically catch trout (there are five varieties in the area). Other local fish include bass, perch, and kokanee salmon. The most popular fishing holes are Cochiti and Abiquiu lakes as well as the Rio Chama, Pecos River, and the Rio Grande. A world-renowned fly-fishing destination, the **San Juan River,** near Farmington, is worth a visit and can make for an exciting 2-day trip in combination with a tour around **Chaco Culture National Historic Park** (see chapter 6). Check with the **New Mexico Game and Fish Department** (✆ **505/476-8000;** www.wildlife.state.nm.us) for information (including maps of area waters), licenses, and fishing proclamations. **High Desert Angler,** 453 Cerrillos Rd. (✆ **505/988-7688;** www.highdesertangler.com), specializes in fly-fishing gear and guide services.

GOLF

There are three courses in the Santa Fe area: the 18-hole **Santa Fe Country Club,** on Airport Road (✆ **505/471-2626;** www.santafecountryclub.com); the often-praised 18-hole **Cochiti Lake Golf Course,** 5200 Cochiti Hwy., Cochiti Lake, about 35 miles southwest of Santa Fe via I-25 and NM 16 and 22 (✆ **505/465-2239;** www.pueblodecochiti.org); and Santa Fe's newest 18-hole course, **Marty Sanchez Links de Santa Fe,** 205 Caja del Rio (✆ **505/955-4400;** www.linksdesantafe.com). Both the Santa Fe Country Club and the Marty Sanchez Links offer driving ranges as well. North of Santa Fe on Pojoaque Pueblo land, the **Towa Golf Resort** (Buffalo Thunder Resort, 12 miles north of Santa Fe on US 285/84; ✆ **877/465-3489** or 505/455-9000; www.towagolf.com), offers 36 holes, 27 of them designed by Hale Irwin and William Phillips, set with views of the Jemez and Sangre de Cristo mountains.

HIKING

It's hard to decide which of the 1,000 miles of nearby national forest trails to tackle. Four wilderness areas are nearby, most notably **Pecos Wilderness,** with 223,000 acres east of Santa Fe. Also visit the 58,000-acre **Jemez Mountain National Recreation Area.** Information on these and other wilderness areas is available from the **Santa Fe National Forest,** P.O. Box 1689 (1474 Rodeo Rd.), Santa Fe, NM 87504 (✆ **505/438-7840;** www.fs.fed.us).

If you're looking for company on your trek, contact the Santa Fe branch of the **Sierra Club,** 1807 Second St. (✆ **505/983-2703;** www.riogrande.sierraclub.org). A hiking schedule can be found in the local newsletter; you can pick one up outside the office. Some people enjoy taking a chairlift ride to the summit of the **Santa Fe Ski Area** (✆ **505/982-4429;** www.skisantafe.com) and hiking around up there during the summer. A popular guide with Santa Feans is *Day Hikes in the Santa Fe Area,* put out by the local branch of the Sierra Club. The most popular hiking trails are the **Borrego Trail,** a moderate 4-mile jaunt through aspens and ponderosa pines, ending at a creek, and **Aspen Vista,** an easy 1- to 5-mile hike through aspen forest with views to the east. Both are easy to find; simply head up Hyde Park Road toward Ski Santa Fe. The Borrego Trail is 8¼ miles up, while Aspen Vista is 10 miles. In recent years an energetic crew has cut the **Dale Ball Trails** (✆ **505/955-6977**), miles of hiking/biking trails throughout the Santa Fe foothills. The easiest access is off Hyde Park Road toward Ski Santa Fe. Drive 2 miles from Bishop's Lodge Road and watch for the trail head on the left. If you're looking for "outspiration" (versus inspiration) on a guided day-hiking experience, call **Outspire** (✆ **505/660-0394;** www.outspire.com). They'll set you up with a guide and design just the hike for your ability level and interest. A 3- to 4-hour hike runs at a flat rate of $150, with prices going up from there. Outspire also guides snowshoeing trips.

HORSEBACK RIDING

Trips ranging in length from a few hours to overnight can be arranged by **Santa Fe Detours,** 54½ E. San Francisco St. (summer tour desk, 107 Washington Ave.; ✆ **800/338-6877** or 505/983-6565; www.sfdetours.com). You'll ride with "experienced wranglers," and they can even arrange a trip that includes a cookout or brunch. Rides are also major activities at the **Bishop's Lodge** (see earlier). The **Broken Saddle Riding Company** (✆ **505/424-7774**) offers rides through the stunning Galisteo Basin, south of Santa Fe.

RIVER RAFTING & KAYAKING

Although Taos is the real rafting center of New Mexico, several companies serve Santa Fe during the April-to-October white-water season. They include **New Wave Rafting,** 70 County Rd. 84B, Santa Fe, NM 87506 (✆ **800/984-1444** or 505/984-1444; www.newwaverafting.com); and **Santa Fe Rafting Co.,** 1000 Cerrillos Rd., Santa Fe, NM 87505 (✆ **888/988-4914** or 505/988-4914; www.santaferafting.com). You can expect the cost of a full-day trip to range from about $110 to $125 per person before tax and the 3% federal land use fee. The day of the week (Mon–Fri are less expensive) and group size may also affect the price.

RUNNING

Despite its elevation, Santa Fe is popular with runners and hosts numerous competitions, including the annual **Old Santa Fe Trail Run** on Labor Day. The website **Santa Fe Striders** (www.santafestriders.org) lists various runs during the year, as well as weekly runs. This is a great opportunity for travelers to find their way and to meet some locals.

SKIING

Every ability level can enjoy **Ski Santa Fe,** about 16 miles northeast of Santa Fe via Hyde Park (Ski Basin) Road. Lots of locals ski here, particularly on weekends; if you can, go on weekdays. It's a good family area and fairly small, so it's easy to split off from and later reconnect with your party. Built on the upper reaches of 12,000-foot Tesuque Peak, the area has an average annual snowfall of 225 inches and a vertical drop of 1,725 feet. Seven lifts, including a 5,000-foot triple chair and a quad chair, serve 69 runs and 660 acres of terrain, with a total capacity of 7,800 riders an hour. Base facilities, at 10,350 feet, center on **La Casa Mall,** with a cafeteria, lounge, ski shop, and boutique. A restaurant, **Totemoff's,** has a midmountain patio.

The ski area is open daily from 9am to 4pm; the season often runs from Thanksgiving to early April, depending on snow conditions. Rates for all lifts are $58 for adults, $46 for teens (13–20 years old), $40 for children 12 and under and seniors 62 to 71 years old; half-day tickets run $42. Tickets are free for kids less than 46 inches tall (in their ski boots), and for seniors 72 and older. For more information, contact **Ski Santa Fe,** 2209 Brothers Rd., Ste. 220 (✆ **505/982-4429;** www.skisantafe.com). For 24-hour reports on snow conditions, call ✆ **505/983-9155. Ski New Mexico** (✆ **505/585-2422**) gives statewide reports. Ski packages are available through **SantaFeHotels.com** (✆ **800/745-9910**).

Cross-country skiers find seemingly endless miles of snow to track in the **Santa Fe National Forest** (✆ **505/438-7840;** www.fs.fed.us). A favorite place to start is at the Black Canyon campground, about 9 miles from downtown en route to the Ski Santa Fe. In the same area are the **Borrego Trail** (high intermediate), **Aspen Vista Trail,** and the **Norski Trail,** all en route to Ski Santa Fe as well. Other popular activities at the ski area

Getting Pampered: The Spa Scene

If traveling, skiing, or other activities have left you weary, Santa Fe has a number of relaxation options. The **Absolute Nirvana Spa & Gardens** ★★ (✆ **505/983-7942;** www.absolutenirvana.com), voted one of the three best spas in town by the *Santa Fe Reporter,* offers imaginative Indo-Asian spa "experiences" as well as massages and facials. The spa is open Sunday to Thursday 10am to 6pm, and Friday and Saturday 10am to 8pm. Prices range from $105 to $240.

Another option with a more Japanese bent is **Ten Thousand Waves** ★★, a spa about 3 miles northeast of Santa Fe on Hyde Park Road (✆ **505/982-9304;** www.tenthousandwaves.com). This serene retreat, nestled in a grove of piñons, offers hot tubs, saunas, and cold plunges, plus a variety of massage and other bodywork techniques. If you call far enough in advance, you may be able to find lodging at Ten Thousand Waves as well. The spa is open Monday, Wednesday, and Thursday from 10:30am to 10:30pm; Tuesday from 2 to 10:30pm; and Friday through Sunday from 9am to 10:30pm (winter hours are shorter, so be sure to call). Reservations are recommended, especially on weekends.

The City Different's newest retreat, **Shánah Spa and Wellness Center** ★★ (✆ **800/732-2240;** www.bishopslodge.com), at Bishop's Lodge Ranch Resort & Spa (p. 149), offers a full range of treatments in a serene Native American–style ambience surrounded by lush grounds 10 minutes north of Santa Fe. Their signature natural stone massage features warmed river-smoothed rocks from northern New Mexico. A hot tub and outdoor treatments—even one in a tepee—add to the allure. Plan a trip there to include a meal at **Las Fuentes** ★★, where you'll sample some of the region's best New American fare.

Another luxurious option is **Rockresorts Spa** ★★, at La Posada de Santa Fe Resort and Spa (✆ **505/986-0000;** www.rockresorts.com; p. 145). Offering a range of treatments from massage to salt glows, this spot offers free use of a steam room, hot tub, and grass-surrounded pool.

in winter include snowshoeing, snowboarding, sledding, and inner tubing. Ski, snowboard, and snowshoe rentals are available at a number of downtown shops and the ski area.

SWIMMING

There's a public pool at the **Fort Marcy Complex,** on Camino Santiago, off Bishop's Lodge Road (✆ **505/955-2500;** www.santafenm.gov). In summer, the public **Bicentennial Pool,** 1121 Alto St. (✆ **505/955-4778**), offers outdoor swimming. Admission to both is less than $2 for all ages.

TENNIS

Santa Fe has 44 public tennis courts and four major private facilities. The **City Recreation Department** (✆ **505/955-2100;** www.santafenm.gov) can help you locate indoor, outdoor, and lighted public courts.

8 SHOPPING

Santa Fe offers a broad range of art, from very traditional Native American crafts and Hispanic folk art to extremely innovative contemporary work. Some locals call Santa Fe one of the top art markets in the world. Galleries speckle the downtown area, and as an artists' thoroughfare, Canyon Road is preeminent. The greatest concentration of Native American crafts is displayed beneath the portal of the Palace of the Governors.

Any serious arts aficionado should try to attend one or more of the city's great arts festivals—the Spring Festival of the Arts, in May; the Spanish Market, in July; the Indian Market, in August; and the Fall Festival of the Arts, in October.

Few visitors to Santa Fe leave the city without acquiring at least one item from the Native American artisans at the Palace of the Governors. You can also peruse one of the outstanding **gallery catalogs** for an introduction to local dealers. They're available for free in many galleries and hotels. They include *The Collector's Guide to Art in Santa Fe and Taos* (www.collectorsguide.com), *The Essential Guide* (www.essentialguide.com), and others. For a current listing of gallery openings, with recommendations on which ones to attend, purchase a copy of the monthly magazine the *Santa Fean* (www.santafean.com). Also check in the "Pasatiempo" section of the local newspaper, the *New Mexican* (www.santafenewmexican.com), every Friday.

THE TOP GALLERIES

Contemporary Art

Canyon Road Contemporary Art This gallery represents some of the finest emerging U.S. contemporary artists, as well as internationally known artists. You'll find figurative, landscape, and abstract paintings, as well as raku pottery. 403 Canyon Rd. ✆ **505/983-0433.**

Hahn Ross Gallery Owners Tom Ross and Elizabeth Hahn, a children's book illustrator and surrealist painter, respectively, specialize in representing artists who create colorful, fantasy-oriented works. Check out the sculpture garden here. 409 Canyon Rd. ✆ **505/984-8434.** www.hahnross.com.

La Mesa of Santa Fe ★ Finds Step into this gallery and let your senses dance. Dramatically colored ceramic plates, bowls, and other kitchen items fill one room. Contemporary katsinas by Gregory Lomayesva—a real buy—line the walls, accented by steel lamps and rag rugs. 225 Canyon Rd. ✆ **505/984-1688.** www.lamesaofsantafe.com.

LewAllen Contemporary ★★ Finds This is one of Santa Fe's most prized galleries. You'll find bizarre and beautiful contemporary works in a range of media, from granite to clay to twigs. There are always exciting works on canvas. 129 W. Palace Ave. ✆ **505/988-8997.** www.lewallencontemporary.com.

Linda Durham Contemporary Art ★ The opening of this broad and bright art space in summer 2004 marked the return of one of Santa Fe's best galleries. Longtime gallery owner Linda Durham had moved her gallery 25 miles south of town, but now she's back, with a strong roster of talent, including Greg Erf and Judy Tuwaletstiwa. 1101 Paseo de Peralta. ✆ **505/466-6600.** www.lindadurham.com.

Patina Gallery Finds Selling functional objects and sculptural art, including jewelry, fiber, clay and wood pieces, this gallery exhibits the work of more than 100 leading

American and European artists. Look for silver work by Harold O'Connor. 131 W. Palace Ave. ✆ **877/877-0827.** www.patina-gallery.com.

Peyton Wright Gallery ★ Housed within the Historic Spiegelberg House (a refurbished Victorian adobe), this excellent gallery offers contemporary, American Modernism, Spanish Colonial, Russian, and 18th-century New Mexico *bultos* and *santos.* In addition to representing such artists as Orlando Leyba, Roni Stretch, and Tim Murphy, the gallery features monthly exhibitions—including contemporary paintings, sculptures, and works on paper. 237 E. Palace Ave. ✆ **800/879-8898** or 505/989-9888. www.peytonwright.com.

Shidoni Foundry, Gallery, and Sculpture Gardens ★★ **Moments** Shidoni Foundry is one of the area's most exciting spots for sculptors and sculpture enthusiasts. At the foundry, visitors may take a tour through the facilities to view casting processes. In addition, Shidoni Foundry includes a 5,000-square-foot contemporary gallery, a bronze gallery, and a wonderful sculpture garden—a great place for a picnic. Bishop's Lodge Rd., Tesuque. ✆ **505/988-8001.** www.shidoni.com.

Waxlander Gallery Primarily featuring the whimsical acrylics and occasional watercolors of Phyllis Kapp, this is the place to browse if you like bold color. 622 Canyon Rd. ✆ **800/342-2202** or 505/984-2202. www.waxlander.com.

Native American & Other Indigenous Art

Andrea Fisher Fine Pottery ★ This expansive gallery is a wonderland of authentic Southwestern Indian pottery. You'll find real showpieces here, including the work of renowned San Ildefonso Pueblo potter Maria Martinez. 100 W. San Francisco St. ✆ **505/986-1234.** www.andreafisherpottery.com.

Frank Howell Gallery If you've never seen the wonderful illustrative hand of the late Frank Howell, you'll want to visit this gallery. You'll find a variety of works by contemporary American Indian artists. The gallery also features sculpture, jewelry, and graphics. 103 Washington Ave. ✆ **505/984-1074.** www.frankhowellgallery.com.

Morning Star Gallery ★★ **Finds** This is one of my favorite places to browse. Throughout the rambling gallery are American Indian art masterpieces, all elegantly displayed. You'll see a broad range of works, from late-19th-century Navajo blankets to 1920s Zuni needlepoint jewelry. 513 Canyon Rd. ✆ **505/982-8187.** www.morningstargallery.com.

Ortega's on the Plaza A hearty shopper could spend hours here, perusing inventive turquoise and silver jewelry and especially fine strung beadwork, as well as rugs and pottery. An adjacent room showcases a wide array of clothing, all with a hip Southwestern flair. 101 W. San Francisco St. ✆ **505/988-1866.**

Sherwoods ★ Set in the historic Bandelier House, this gallery features museum-quality Plains Indians antiquities such as an 1870 Nez Perce beaded dress and a Crow war shirt. Some paintings hang here as well, including works by Santa Fe masters such as J. H. Sharp and Gene Kloss. Firearm buffs will go ballistic over the gun room here. 1005 Paseo de Peralta. ✆ **505/988-1776.** www.sherwoodsspirit.com.

Photography

Andrew Smith Gallery ★ I'm always amazed when I enter this gallery and notice works I've seen reprinted in major magazines for years. There they are, photographic prints, large and beautiful, hanging on the wall. Here, you'll see famous works by Edward

 Curtis, Henri Cartier-Bresson, Ansel Adams, Annie Leibovitz, and others. A new gallery at the corner of Grant and Johnson streets extends this collection. 203 W. San Francisco St. ✆ **505/984-1234.** www.andrewsmithgallery.com.

Lisa Kristine Gallery ★★ With galleries here in Santa Fe and in the California cities of Sausalito, Sonoma, and Mendocino, Lisa Kristine's work gets around, and it's no wonder. These richly colored portraits and landscapes of Asian and African culture will have you gaping in wonderment. 204 W. San Francisco St. ✆ **505/820-6330.** www.lisakristine.com.

Photo-Eye Gallery You're bound to be surprised each time you step into this gallery a few blocks off Canyon Road. Dealing in contemporary photography, the gallery represents internationally renowned and emerging artists alike. 370 Garcia St. ✆ **505/988-5152.** www.photoeye.com.

Traditional Art

Altermann Galleries This is a well of interesting traditional art, mostly 19th-, 20th-, and 21st-century American paintings and sculpture. The gallery represents Remington and Russell, in addition to Taos founders, Santa Fe artists, and members of the Cowboy Artists of America and the National Academy of Western Art. Stroll through the sculpture garden among whimsical bronzes of children and dogs. 225 Canyon Rd. ✆ **505/983-1590.** www.altermann.com.

Gerald Peters Gallery ★★ Displayed throughout a graceful pueblo-style building, the works here are so fine you'll feel as though you're in a museum. You'll find 19th-, 20th-, and 21st-century American painting and sculpture, featuring the art of Georgia O'Keeffe, William Wegman, and the founders of the Santa Fe and Taos artist colonies, as well as more contemporary works. 1011 Paseo de Peralta. ✆ **505/954-5700.** www.gpgallery.com.

The Mayans Gallery Ltd. Established in 1977, this is one of the oldest galleries in Santa Fe. You'll find 20th-century American and Latin American paintings, photography, prints, and sculpture. 601 Canyon Rd. ✆ **505/983-8068.**

Nedra Matteucci Galleries ★★ As you approach this gallery, note the elaborately crafted stone and adobe wall that surrounds it, merely a taste of what's to come. The gallery specializes in 19th-, 20th-, and 21st-century American art. Inside, you'll find a lot of high-ticket works, such as those of early Taos and Santa Fe painters, as well as classic American Impressionism, historical Western modernism, and contemporary Southwestern landscapes and sculpture. Another excellent gallery, Nedra Matteucci Fine Art, is located at 555 Canyon Rd. While there, look for the fabulous impressionist works by Evelyne Boren. 1075 Paseo de Peralta. ✆ **505/982-4631.** www.matteucci.com.

Owings-Dewey Fine Art ★ These are treasure-filled rooms. You'll find 19th-, 20th-, and 21st-century American painting and sculpture, including works by Georgia O'Keeffe, Robert Henri, Maynard Dixon, Fremont Ellis, and Andrew Dasburg, as well as antique works such as Spanish colonial *retablos, bultos,* and tin works. Look for the exciting bird sculptures by Peter Woytuk. 76 E. San Francisco St., upstairs, and a second shop at 120 E. Marcy St. ✆ **505/982-6244.**

Zaplin Lampert Gallery ★★ Art aficionados, as well as those who just like a nice landscape, will enjoy this gallery, one of Santa Fe's classics. Hanging on old adobe walls are works by some of the region's early masters, including Bert Phillips, Gene Kloss, and Gustauve Baumann. 651 Canyon Rd. ✆ **505/982-6100.** www.zaplinlampert.com.

MORE SHOPPING A TO Z

Antiques

El Paso Import Company ★ Whenever I'm in the vicinity of this shop, I always stop in. It's packed—and I mean packed—with colorful, weathered colonial and ranchero furniture. The affordable home furnishings and folk art here are imported from Mexico, India, and Romania. 418 Sandoval St. ✆ **505/982-5698.** www.elpasoimportco.com.

Jackalope ★ Value Kids Spread over 7 acres of land, this is a wild place to spend a morning or an afternoon browsing through exotic furnishings from India and Mexico, as well as imported textiles, pottery, jewelry, and clothing. It's a great place to find gifts. Kids will love the prairie-dog village. 2820 Cerrillos Rd. ✆ **505/471-8539.** www.jackalope.com.

Books

Borders With close to 200 stores nationwide, this chain provides a broad range of books, music, and videos, and it hosts in-store appearances by authors, musicians, and artists. 500 Montezuma Ave. ✆ **505/954-4707.** www.borders.com.

Collected Works Bookstore This is a good downtown book source, with carefully recommended books up front, in case you're not sure what you want, and shelves of Southwest, travel, nature, and other books. 202 Galisteo St. ✆ **505/988-4226.** www.collectedworksbookstore.com.

Garcia Street Books One of Santa Fe's best shops for perusing, this gem stocks a broad range of titles on the Southwest and collectibles. Not sure what to read? The knowledgeable staff here will help you decide. 376 Garcia St. ✆ **866/986-0151** or 505/986-0151. www.garciastreetbooks.com.

Children

Gypsy Baby This shop sells bright clothes, beaded slippers, and mustang rocking horses, all mindful of the slogan "Born to be spoiled." 318 S. Guadalupe St. ✆ **505/820-1898.** www.gypsybabies.com.

Crafts

Nambé ★ Finds The cooking, serving, and decorating pieces here are fashioned from an exquisite sand-cast and handcrafted alloy. These items are also available at the Nambé store at 104 W. San Francisco St. (✆ **505/988-3574**), and at the one in Taos at 113A Paseo del Pueblo Norte (✆ **575/758-8221**). 924 Paseo de Peralta. ✆ **505/988-5528.** www.nambe.com.

Fashions

Back at the Ranch ★ This shop has chic western wear and what it calls the "largest selection of handmade cowboy boots in the country." 209 E. Marcy St. ✆ **888/962-6687** or 505/989-8110; www.backattheranch.com.

Origins ★ Moments A little like a Guatemalan or Turkish marketplace, this store is packed with wearable art, folk art, and the work of local designers. Look for good buys on ethnic jewelry. Throughout the summer there are trunk shows, which offer opportunities to meet the artists. 135 W. San Francisco St. ✆ **505/988-2323.** www.originssantafe.com.

Overland Sheepskin Company The rich smell of leather will draw you in the door and possibly hold onto you until you purchase a coat, blazer, hat, or other finely made leather item. 74 E. San Francisco St. ✆ **505/983-4727.** www.overland.com.

Food

The Chile Shop This store has too many cheap trinkets for me, but many people find some novelty items to take back home. You'll find everything from salsas to cornmeal and tortilla chips. The shop also stocks cookbooks and pottery. 109 E. Water St. ✆ **505/983-6080.** www.thechileshop.com.

Señor Murphy Candy Maker Unlike any candy store you'll find in other parts of the country—everything here is made with local ingredients. The chile piñon-nut brittle is a taste sensation! Señor Murphy has another shop in the Santa Fe Place mall (✆ **505/471-8899**). 100 E. San Francisco St. (La Fonda Hotel). ✆ **505/982-0461.** www.senormurphy.com.

Furniture

Southwest Spanish Craftsmen The Spanish colonial and Spanish provincial furniture, doors, and home accessories in this store are a bit too elaborate for my tastes, but if you find yourself dreaming of carved wood, this is your place. 314 S. Guadalupe St. ✆ **505/982-1767.** www.nussbaumerfineart.com.

Taos Furniture Here you'll find classic Southwestern furnishings handcrafted in solid ponderosa pine—both contemporary and traditional. Prices are a little better here than in downtown shops. 217 Galisteo St. ✆ **800/443-3448** or 505/988-1229. www.taosfurniture.com.

Gifts & Souvenirs

El Nicho (Value) If you want to take a little piece of Santa Fe home with you, you'll likely find it at this shop. You'll find handcrafted Navajo folk art as well as jewelry and other items by local artisans, including woodcarvings (watch for the *santos!*) by the renowned Ortega family. 227 Don Gaspar Ave. ✆ **505/984-2830.**

Hats

Montecristi Custom Hat Works ★ This fun shop hand-makes fine Panama and felt hats in a range of styles, from Australian outback to Mexican bolero. 322 McKenzie St. ✆ **505/983-9598.** www.montecristihats.com.

Jewelry

Packards ★ Opened by a notable trader, Al Packard, and later sold to new owners, this store on the plaza is worth checking out to see some of the best jewelry available. You'll also find exquisite rugs and pottery. 61 Old Santa Fe Trail. ✆ **505/983-9241.** www.packards-santafe.com.

Tresa Vorenberg Goldsmiths You'll find some wildly imaginative designs in this jewelry store, where more than 40 artisans are represented. All items are handcrafted, and custom commissions are welcomed. 656 Canyon Rd. ✆ **505/988-7215.** www.tvgoldsmiths.com.

Malls & Shopping Centers

de Vargas Center There are approximately 50 merchants and restaurants in this mall just northwest of downtown. This is Santa Fe's small, more intimate mall, with anchors Ross Dress for Less and Office Depot. Open Monday to Friday 10am to 7pm, Saturday 10am to 6pm, and Sunday noon to 5pm. N. Guadalupe St. and Paseo de Peralta. ✆ **505/982-2655.** www.devargascenter.com.

Fashion Outlets of Santa Fe Outlet shopping fans will enjoy this open-air mall on the south end of town. Anchors include Brooks Brothers, Jones New York, and Coach. Open Monday to Saturday 10am to 7pm, Sunday 11am to 6pm. 8380 Cerrillos Rd. ✆ **505/474-4000.** www.fashionoutletssantafe.com.

Sanbusco Market Center ★ Unique shops and restaurants occupy this remodeled warehouse near the old Santa Fe Railyard. Many of the shops are overpriced, but it's a fun place to window-shop. Borders is here as well. Open Monday to Saturday 10am to 6pm, Sunday noon to 5pm. 500 Montezuma St. ✆ **505/989-9390.** www.sanbusco.com.

Santa Fe Place Santa Fe's largest mall is near the southwestern city limits, not far from the I-25 on-ramp. If you're from a major city, you'll probably find shopping here very provincial. Anchors include JCPenney, Sears, Dillard's, and Mervyn's. Open Monday to Saturday 10am to 9pm, Sunday noon to 6pm. 4250 Cerrillos Rd. (at Rodeo Rd.). ✆ **505/473-4253.** www.shopsantafeplace.com.

Markets

Santa Fe Farmers' Market ★★ Finds This farmers' market has everything from fruits, vegetables, and flowers to cheeses, cider, and salsas. Great local treats! If you're an early riser, stroll through and enjoy good coffee, excellent breakfast burritos, and music ranging from flute to fiddle. In 2008, the market moved into a beautiful new building in the railyard district. Open April to mid-November, Tuesday and Saturday 7am to noon. In winter, an abbreviated version takes place indoors. In the Santa Fe Railyard, off Paseo de Peralta. ✆ **505/983-4098.** www.santafefarmersmarket.com.

Tesuque Flea Market ★ Moments If you're a flea-market hound, you'll be happy to discover this one. More than 500 vendors sell everything from used cowboy boots (you might find some real beauties) to clothing, jewelry, books, and furniture, all against a big northern New Mexico view. Open March to late November, Friday to Sunday. Vendors start selling at about 7:30am and stay open until about 6:30pm, weather permitting. US 84/285 (about 8 miles north of Santa Fe). No phone. www.tesuquepueblofleamarket.com.

Natural Art

Mineral & Fossil Gallery of Santa Fe ★ You'll find ancient artwork here, from fossils to geodes in all sizes and shapes. Natural mineral jewelry and decorative items for the home, including lamps, wall clocks, furniture, art glass, and carvings are also on hand. Mineral & Fossil also has galleries in Taos, and in Scottsdale and Sedona, Arizona. 127 W. San Francisco St. ✆ **800/762-9777** or 505/984-1682. www.mineralgallery.com.

Stone Forest ★★ Finds Proprietor Michael Zimber travels to China and other Asian countries every year to collaborate with the stone carvers who create the fountains, sculptures, and bath fixtures that fill this inventive shop and garden not far from the plaza. 213 St. Francis Dr. ✆ **505/986-8883.** www.stoneforest.com.

Pottery & Tiles

Artesanos Imports Company ★ Moments Coming here is like taking a trip south of the border, with all the scents and colors you'd expect on such a journey. You'll find a wide selection of Talavera tile and pottery, as well as light fixtures and many other accessories for the home. 1414 Maclovia St. ✆ **505/471-8020.** www.artesanos.com.

Santa Fe Pottery at Double Take The work of more than 120 master potters from New Mexico and the Southwest is on display here; you'll find everything from mugs and lamps to home furnishings. 323 S. Guadalupe St. ✆ **505/989-3363.** www.santafepottery.com.

Rugs

Seret & Sons Rugs, Furnishings, and Architectural Pieces ★ If you're like me and find Middle Eastern decor irresistible, you'll want to wander through this shop. You'll find kilims and Persian and Turkish rugs, as well as some of the Moorish-style ancient doors and furnishings that you see around Santa Fe. 224 Galisteo St. ✆ **505/988-9151** or 505/983-5008. www.seretandsons.com.

9 SANTA FE AFTER DARK

Santa Fe is a city committed to the arts, so it's no surprise that the Santa Fe night scene is dominated by highbrow cultural events, beginning with the world-famous Santa Fe Opera. The club and popular music scene runs a distant second.

Information on all major cultural events can be obtained from the **Santa Fe Community Convention Center and Visitors Bureau** (✆ **800/777-CITY** [2489] or 505/955-6200) or from the **City of Santa Fe Arts Commission** (✆ **505/955-6707**). Current listings are published each Friday in the "Pasatiempo" section of the *New Mexican* (www.santafenewmexican.com), the city's daily newspaper, and in the *Santa Fe Reporter* (www.sfreporter.com), published every Wednesday.

You can also order tickets to events from **Ticketmaster** (✆ **505/883-7800;** www.ticketmaster.com). Discount tickets may be available on the night of a performance; for example, the opera offers standing-room tickets on the day of the performance. Sales start at 10am.

A variety of free concerts, lectures, and other events are presented in the summer, cosponsored by the City of Santa Fe and the Chamber of Commerce. Many of these musical and cultural events take place on the plaza; check in the "Pasatiempo" section for current listings and information.

THE PERFORMING ARTS

At least two dozen performing-arts groups flourish in this city of 70,000. Many of them perform year-round, but some are seasonal. The acclaimed Santa Fe Opera, for instance, has just a 2-month summer season.

Note: Many companies below perform at locations other than their listed addresses—call or check the websites for details.

Major Performing Arts Companies

Opera & Classical Music

Santa Fe Opera ★★★ Many rank the Santa Fe Opera second only to the Metropolitan Opera of New York in the United States. Established in 1957, it consistently attracts famed conductors, directors, and singers. At the height of the season, the company is 500 strong. It's noted for its performances of the classics, little-known works by classical European composers, and American premieres of 21st-century works. The theater, completed for the 1998 season, sits on a wooded hilltop 7 miles north of the city, off US 84/285. It's partially open-air, with open sides.

The 8-week, 40-performance opera season runs from late June through late August. All performances begin at 9pm, until the end of July, when performances start at 8:30pm, and the last week of the season, when performances begin at 8pm. A small screen in front of each seat shows the libretto during the performance. A gift shop has been added, as has additional parking. The entire theater is wheelchair accessible. P.O. Box 2408. ✆ 800/280-4654 or 505/986-5900. www.santafeopera.org. Tickets $28–$180; standing room $10; Opening Night Gala $1,750–$3,000. Backstage tours June–Aug Mon–Sat at 9am; $5 adults, free for children ages 5–17.

Orchestral & Chamber Music

Santa Fe Pro Musica Chamber Orchestra & Ensemble ★ Recently nominated for a Grammy Award, this chamber ensemble performs everything from Bach to Vivaldi to contemporary masters. During Holy Week, the Santa Fe Pro Musica presents its annual Mozart and Hayden Concert at the St. Francis Cathedral. Christmas brings candlelight chamber ensemble concerts. Pro Musica's season runs September to May. 430 Manhattan, Ste. 10. ✆ **505/988-4640.** www.santafepromusica.com. Tickets $15–$50.

Santa Fe Symphony Orchestra and Chorus ★ This 60-piece professional symphony orchestra has grown rapidly in stature since its founding in 1984. Matinee and evening performances of classical and popular works are presented in a subscription series at the Lensic Performing Arts Center from August to May. There's a preconcert lecture before each performance. During the spring, the orchestra presents music festivals (call for details). P.O. Box 9692. ✆ **800/480-1319** or 505/983-1414. www.sf-symphony.org. Tickets $18–$65.

Music Festivals & Concert Series

Santa Fe Chamber Music Festival ★★ An extraordinary group of international artists comes to Santa Fe every summer for this festival. Its 6-week season runs mid-July to mid-August and is held in the St. Francis Auditorium and the Lensic Performing Arts Center. Each festival features chamber-music masterpieces, new music by a composer in residence, jazz, free youth concerts, preconcert lectures, and open rehearsals. Performances are Monday, Tuesday, Thursday, and Friday at 8pm; Saturday at various evening times; and Sunday at 6pm. Open rehearsals, youth concerts, and preconcert lectures are free to the public. 239 Johnson St., Ste. B (P.O. Box 2227). ✆ **505/983-2075** or 505/982-1890 for box office (after June 22). www.sfchambermusic.com. Tickets $16–$125.

Santa Fe Concert Association Founded in 1937, this oldest musical organization in northern New Mexico has a September-to-May season that includes a 6-performance series. Among them are a "Great Performances" series and an "Adventures" series, which feature renowned instrumental and vocal soloists and chamber ensembles. The association also hosts special holiday concerts around Christmas and New Year's. Performances are held at the Lensic Performing Arts Center; tickets are available at the Lensic box office (✆ **505/988-1234**) and at ✆ 800/905-3315 (www.tickets.com), or ✆ 505/984-8759; www.santafeconcerts.org. 210 E. Marcy St., Ste. 15. Tickets $20–$85.

Theater Companies

Greer Garson Theater Center In this graceful, intimate theater, the College of Santa Fe's Performing Arts Department produces four plays annually, with six presentations of each, given between October and May. Usually, the season consists of a comedy, a drama, a musical, and a classic. The college also sponsors studio productions and various contemporary music concerts. College of Santa Fe, 1600 St. Michaels Dr. ✆ **505/473-6511.** www.csf.edu. Tickets $10–$20 adults, $5 students.

Major Concert Halls & All-Purpose Auditoriums

Center for Contemporary Arts and Cinematheque, 1050 Old Pecos Trail. ✆ **505/982-1338.** www.ccasantafe.org.

Lensic Performing Arts Center, 211 W. San Francisco St. ✆ **505/988-7050.** www.lensic.com.

St. Francis Auditorium, Museum of Fine Arts, Lincoln and Palace aves. ✆ **505/476-5072.**

Santa Fe Playhouse ★ Founded in the 1920s, this is the oldest extant theater group in New Mexico. Still performing in a historic adobe theater in the Barrio de Analco, it attracts thousands for its dramas, avant-garde theater, and musical comedy. Its popular one-act melodramas call on the public to boo the sneering villain and swoon for the damsel in distress. 142 E. de Vargas St. ✆ **505/988-4262.** www.santafeplayhouse.org. Tickets from "Pay What You Wish" to $20, depending on the show.

Theater Grottesco ★★ **Finds** This troupe combines the best of comedy, drama, and dance in its original productions performed each spring, summer, or fall, at whatever venue suits the performance. Expect to be romanced, shocked, intellectually stimulated, and, above all, struck silly with laughter. Look for upcoming winter shows as well. 551 W. Cordova Rd., #8400. ✆ **505/474-8400.** www.theatergrottesco.org. Tickets $10–$25.

Theaterwork Studio ★ This community theater goes out of its way to present refreshing, at times risky, plays. In an intimate space on the south end of town, Theaterwork offers seven main-stage productions a year, a broad variety including new plays and classics by regional and national playwrights. Expect to see works by such names as Brecht, Shakespeare, and Victor Hugo. 1336 Rufina Circle (P.O. Box 842). ✆ **505/471-1799.** www.theaterwork.org. Tickets $10–$18. Call for performance times.

Dance Companies

Aspen Santa Fe Ballet ★ In its second decade, the Aspen Santa Fe Ballet brings classically trained dancers to Santa Fe and Aspen. Performances are an eclectic repertoire by some of the world's foremost choreographers. The season is year-round, with performances at the Lensic Performing Arts Center. 550-B St. Michaels Dr. ✆ **505/983-5591;** www.aspensantafeballet.com. Purchase tickets at the Lensic ✆ **505/988-1234.** Tickets $20–$58.

María Benitez Teatro Flamenco ★★ **Finds** You won't want to miss this cultural treat. True flamenco is one of the most thrilling of dance forms, displaying the inner spirit and verve of the gypsies of Spanish Andalusia, and María Benitez, trained in Spain, is a fabulous performer. The Benitez Company's "Estampa Flamenca" summer series is performed nightly except Monday from late June to early September. The María Benitez Theater at the Lodge at Santa Fe is modern and showy, and yet it's intimate enough so you're immersed in the art. Institute for Spanish Arts, P.O. Box 8418. For tickets call ✆ **888/435-2636,** or the box office (June 16–Sept 3; ✆ **505/982-1237**). www.mariabenitez.com. Tickets $30–$50.

THE CLUB & MUSIC SCENE

In addition to the clubs and bars listed below, there are a number of hotels whose bars and lounges feature some type of entertainment (see "Where to Stay," earlier in this chapter).

Country, Jazz & Latin

Chispa! ★ A tapas bar with the *chispa,* or "spark," of fun entertainment and dancing, this hot spot next to the dining room at El Meson draws locals of all types. Music ranges from guitar duos to jazz combos and Brazilian music, with flamenco dancers performing on some Saturday nights. On Tango Tuesdays, locals turn out in their tightest dance clothes to party. The tapas are excellent. Open Tuesday to Saturday. 213 Washington Ave. ✆ **505/983-6756.** www.elmeson-santafe.com. Cover charge for select performances.

Cowgirl Hall of Fame ★ It's difficult to categorize what goes on in this bar and restaurant, but there's live entertainment nightly. Some nights there's blues guitar, others folk music; you might also find "progressive rock," comedy, or cowboy poetry. In the summer, this is a great place to sit under the stars and listen to music. 319 S. Guadalupe St. ✆ **505/982-2565.** No cover for music Sun, Mon, and Wed. Tues and Thurs–Sat $3–$4 cover. Special performances $10.

Eldorado Hotel ★ In a grand lobby-lounge full of fine art, classical guitarists and pianists perform nightly. 309 W. San Francisco St. ✆ **505/988-4455.** www.eldoradohotel.com.

El Farol ★ This original neighborhood bar of the Canyon Road artists' quarter (its name means "the lantern") is the place to head for local ambience. Its low ceilings and brown walls are home to Santa Fe's largest and most unusual selection of tapas (bar snacks and appetizers). Jazz, swing, folk, and, most notably, salsa and flamenco musicians (and dancers)—some of national note—perform most nights. 808 Canyon Rd. ✆ **505/983-9912.** www.elfarolsf.com. Cover $7.

La Fiesta Lounge ★ Set in the notable La Fonda hotel on the plaza, this nightclub offers excellent country bands on weekends, with old- and new-timers two-stepping across the floor. This lively lobby bar offers cocktails, an appetizer menu, and live entertainment nightly. It's a great authentic Santa Fe spot. La Fonda Hotel (p. 145), 110 E. San Francisco St. ✆ **505/982-5511.** www.lafondasantafe.com.

THE BAR SCENE

The Dragon Room ★ A number of years ago, *International Newsweek* named the Dragon Room at the Pink Adobe one of the top 20 bars in the world. The reason is its spirited but comfortable ambience, which draws students, artists, politicians, and even an occasional celebrity. The decor theme is dragons, which you'll find carved on the front doors as well as depicted on the walls, all within low-lit, aged elegance. Live trees also

Snub Out the Smokes

In 2006, smoking in Santa Fe bars and restaurants, including outdoor-dining areas, became illegal. The law was instituted mainly to protect entertainment and hospitality workers from secondhand smoke, but it will likely protect many others as well.

grow through the roof. In addition to the tempting lunch and bar menu, there's always a complimentary bowl of popcorn close at hand. 406 Old Santa Fe Trail. ✆ **505/983-7712.**

El Paseo Bar and Grill You can almost always catch live music at this casual, unpretentious place (yet it's not a "sports bar"). The crowd here is somewhat younger than at most other downtown establishments; and, on certain nights, the bar is completely packed. In addition to the open-mic night on Tuesdays, a variety of local bands play here regularly—cranking out many types of music, from blues to rock to jazz to bluegrass. 208 Galisteo St. ✆ **505/992-2848.** www.elpaseobar.com. Cover $3–$5 Fri–Sat.

Evangelo's A popular downtown hangout, with tropical decor and a mahogany bar, this place can get raucous at times. It's a bit seedy, but more than 200 varieties of imported beer are available, and pool tables are an added attraction. On Friday and Saturday nights starting at 9pm and Wednesdays at 7:30pm, live bands play (jazz, rock, or reggae). Evangelo's is extremely popular with the local crowd. You'll find your share of businesspeople, artists, and even bikers here. Open Monday to Saturday noon to 1:30am and Sundays until midnight. 200 W. San Francisco St. ✆ **505/982-9014.** Cover for special performances only.

Vanessie of Santa Fe ★ This is unquestionably Santa Fe's most popular piano bar. The talented Doug Montgomery and Charles Tichenor have a loyal local following. Their repertoire ranges from Bach to Billy Joel, Gershwin to Barry Manilow. They play nightly from 8pm until closing, which could be anywhere from midnight to 2am. There's an extra microphone, so if you're daring (or drunk), you can stand up and accompany the piano and vocals (though this is *not* a karaoke scene). National celebrities have even joined in—including Harry Connick, Jr. Vanessie's offers a great bar menu. 434 W. San Francisco St. ✆ **505/982-9966.** www.vanessiesantafe.com.

10 TOURING SOME PUEBLOS AROUND SANTA FE

Of the eight northern pueblos, Tesuque, Pojoaque, Nambe, San Ildefonso, San Juan, and Santa Clara are within about 30 miles of Santa Fe. Picuris (San Lorenzo) is on the High Road to Taos (see "Taking the High Road to Taos," later in this chapter), and Taos Pueblo is just outside the town of Taos (p. 220).

Pueblo Etiquette

When you visit pueblos, it is important to observe certain rules of etiquette. These are personal dwellings and/or important historic sites and must be respected as such. Don't climb on the buildings or peek into doors or windows. Don't enter sacred grounds, such as cemeteries and kivas. If you attend a dance or ceremony, remain silent while it is taking place and refrain from applause when it's over. Many pueblos prohibit photography or sketches; others require you to pay a fee for a permit. If you don't respect the privacy of the Native Americans who live at the pueblo, you'll be asked to leave.

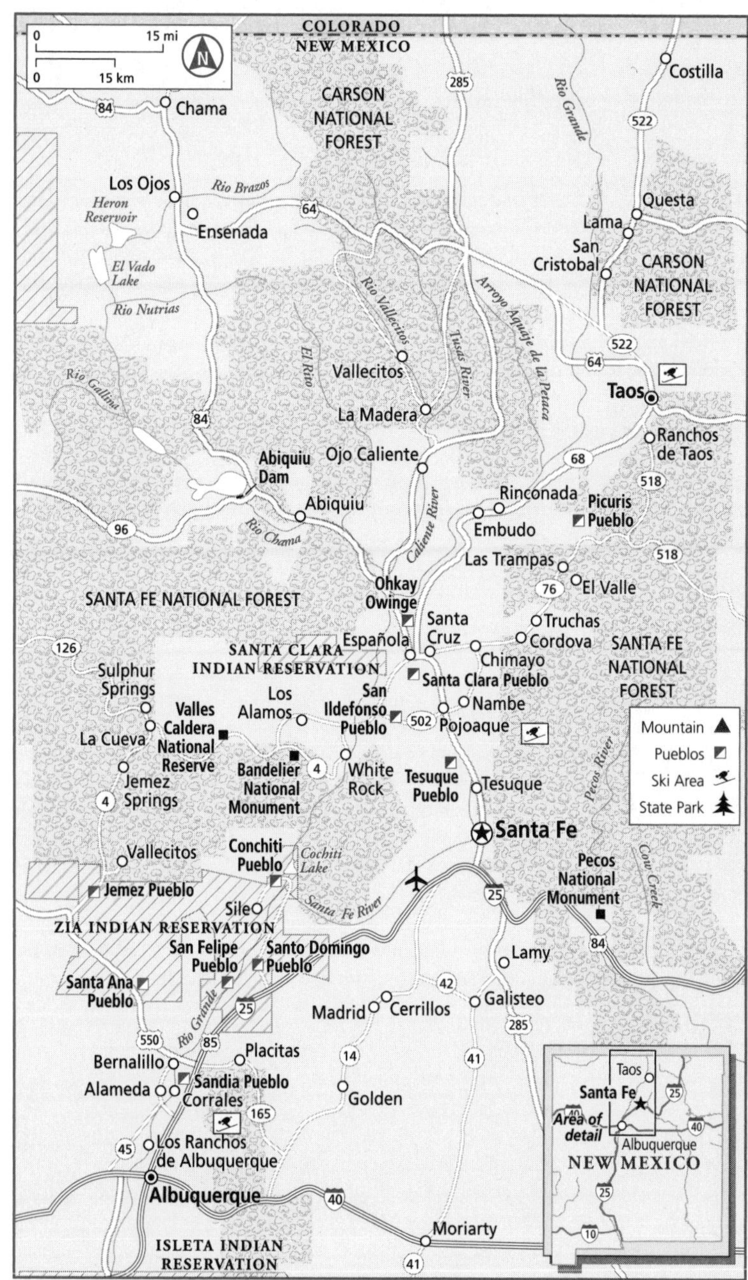
COLORADO
NEW MEXICO
0 15 mi
0 15 km
N
Chama
Costilla
CARSON NATIONAL FOREST
Rio Grande
Los Ojos
Rio Brazos
Heron Reservoir
Ensenada
Questa
Lama
San Cristobal
CARSON NATIONAL FOREST
El Vado Lake
Rio Nutrias
Rio Vallecitos
Arroyo Aguaje de la Petaca
El Rito
Tusas River
Vallecitos
Taos
Rio Gallina
La Madera
Ranchos de Taos
Abiquiu Dam
Ojo Caliente
Rinconada
Picuris Pueblo
Abiquiu
Embudo
Rio Chama
Caliente River
Las Trampas
El Valle
SANTA FE NATIONAL FOREST
Ohkay Owinge
Santa Cruz
Truchas
Española
Cordova
SANTA FE NATIONAL FOREST
SANTA CLARA INDIAN RESERVATION
Chimayo
Santa Clara Pueblo
Sulphur Springs
Los Alamos
San Ildefonso Pueblo
Nambe
Valles Caldera National Reserve
Pojoaque
La Cueva
Mountain
Pueblos
Ski Area
State Park
Bandelier National Monument
White Rock
Tesuque Pueblo
Tesuque
Pecos River
Jemez Springs
Santa Fe
Vallecitos
Conchiti Pueblo
Cochiti Lake
Pecos National Monument
Cow Creek
Jemez Pueblo
Santa Fe River
Sile
ZIA INDIAN RESERVATION
San Felipe Pueblo
Santo Domingo Pueblo
Lamy
Santa Ana Pueblo
Madrid
Cerrillos
Galisteo
Rio Grande
Placitas
Bernalillo
Sandia Pueblo
Alameda
Corrales
Golden
Taos
Santa Fe
Area of detail
Albuquerque
NEW MEXICO
Los Ranchos de Albuquerque
Albuquerque
Moriarty
ISLETA INDIAN RESERVATION

Pojoaque Pueblo's New Resort

Owned by Pojoaque Pueblo, the new **Hilton Santa Fe Buffalo Thunder Resort** ★★ (✆ **800/HILTONS** [445-8667]; www.hiltonworldresorts.com/resorts/SantaFe/index.html) opened in 2008. The structure itself is gigantic, though designers have managed to impart an intimate feel through the use of art—pottery, basketry, sculpture, and paintings—from many of New Mexico's pueblos. The resort features a number of restaurants and lounges, including an elaborate buffet, and a contemporary nightclub. In addition, the resort offers duffers 36 holes at the Towa Golf Course, gamblers 1,200 slots, and spa-fans 16,000 square feet of relaxation. With some 66,000 square feet of meeting space, the resort views itself as a convention center, but the services still attend to travelers. Room prices range from $149 to $299 double, $249 to $399 suite.

The four pueblos described in this section can easily be visited in a single day's round-trip from Santa Fe, though I suggest visiting just the two that really give a feel of the ancient lifestyle: **San Ildefonso,** with its broad plaza, and **Ohkay Owinge,** with its setting along the Rio Grande. In an easy day trip from Santa Fe you can take in both, with some delicious New Mexican food in Española en route. If you're in the area at a time when you can catch certain rituals, that's when you should see some of the other pueblos.

TESUQUE PUEBLO

Tesuque (te-*soo*-keh) Pueblo is about 9 miles north of Santa Fe on US 84/285. You'll know that you're approaching the pueblo when you see a large store near the highway. If you're driving north and you get to the unusual Camel Rock and a large roadside casino, you've missed the pueblo entrance.

The 800 pueblo dwellers at Tesuque are faithful to their traditional religion, rituals, and ceremonies. Excavations confirm that a pueblo has existed here at least since the year A.D. 1200; accordingly, this pueblo is now on the National Register of Historic Places. When you come to the welcome sign at the pueblo, turn right, go a block, and park on the right. You'll see the plaza off to the left. There's not a lot to see; in recent years renovation has brought a new look to some of the homes around it. There's a big open area where dances are held and the **San Diego Church,** completed in 2004 on the site of an 1888 structure that burned down recently. It's the fifth church on the pueblo's plaza since 1641. Visitors are asked to remain in this area.

Some Tesuque women are skilled potters; Ignacia Duran's black-and-white and red micaceous pottery and Teresa Tapia's miniatures and pots with animal figures are especially noteworthy. You'll find many crafts at a gallery on the plaza's southeast corner. The **San Diego Feast Day,** which may feature harvest, buffalo, deer, flag, or Comanche dances, is November 12.

The Tesuque Pueblo's address is Route 5, Box 360-T, Santa Fe, NM 87501 (✆ **505/983-2667**). Admission to the pueblo is free; however, there is a $20 charge for use of still cameras; special permission is required for filming, sketching, and painting. The pueblo is open daily from 9am to 5pm. **Camel Rock Casino** (© **505/984-8414;** www.camelrockcasino.com) is open Sunday to Wednesday from 8am to 4am, and Thursday to Saturday for 24 hours; it has a snack bar on the premises.

SAN ILDEFONSO PUEBLO ★★

Pox Oge, as San Ildefonso Pueblo is called in its own Tewa language, means "place where the water cuts down through," possibly so-named because of the way the Rio Grande cuts through the mountains nearby. Turn left on NM 502 at Pojoaque, and drive about 6 miles to the turnoff. This pueblo has a broad, dusty plaza, with a kiva on one side, ancient dwellings on the other, and a church at the far end. It's nationally famous for its matte-finish, black-on-black pottery, developed by tribeswoman María Martinez in the 1920s. One of the most visited pueblos in northern New Mexico, San Ildefonso (pop. 1,524) attracts more than 20,000 visitors a year.

The San Ildefonsos could best be described as rebellious because this was one of the last pueblos to succumb to the reconquest spearheaded by Don Diego de Vargas in 1692. Within view of the pueblo is the volcanic Black Mesa, a symbol of the San Ildefonso people's strength. Through the years, each time San Ildefonso felt itself threatened by enemy forces, the residents, along with members of other pueblos, would hide out up on the butte, returning to the valley only when starvation set in. Today, a visit to the pueblo is valuable mainly in order to see or buy rich black pottery. A few shops surround the plaza, and there's the **San Ildefonso Pueblo Museum** tucked away in the governor's office beyond the plaza. I especially recommend visiting during ceremonial days. **San Ildefonso Feast Day,** on January 23, features the buffalo and Comanche dances in alternate years. **Corn dances,** held in late August or early September, commemorate a basic element in pueblo life, the importance of fertility in all creatures—humans as well as animals—and plants.

The pueblo has a 4½-acre fishing lake that is surrounded by bosk (or *bosque,* which is Spanish for "forest"), open April to October. Picnicking is encouraged, though you may want to look at the sites before you decide to stay; some are nicer than others. Camping is not allowed.

The pueblo's address is Route 5, Box 315A, Santa Fe, NM 87506 (© **505/455-3549**). The admission charge is $5 per car. The charge for taking photographs is $10; you'll pay $20 to film and $25 to sketch. If you plan to fish, the charge is $10 for adults and $5 for seniors and children 11 and under, but you'll want to call to be sure the lake is open. The pueblo is open daily in the summer from 8am to 5pm; call for weekend hours. In the winter, it's open Monday to Friday from 8am to 4:30pm. It's closed for major holidays and tribal events.

OHKAY OWINGE (SAN JUAN PUEBLO) ★

If you continue north on US 84/285, you will reach San Juan Pueblo, now renamed in Tewa language Ohkay Owinge, via NM 74, a mile off NM 68, about 4 miles north of Española.

The largest (pop. 6,748) and northernmost of the Tewa-speaking pueblos, and headquarters of the Eight Northern Indian Pueblos Council, San Juan is on the east side of the Rio Grande—opposite the 1598 site of San Gabriel, the first Spanish settlement west of the Mississippi River and the first capital of New Spain. In 1598, the Spanish, impressed with the openness and helpfulness of the people of San Juan, decided to establish a capital there (it was moved to Santa Fe 10 years later), making San Juan Pueblo the first to be subjected to Spanish colonization. The Indians were generous, providing food, clothing, shelter, and fuel—they even helped sustain the settlement when its leader, conquistador Juan de Oñate, became preoccupied with his search for gold and neglected the needs of his people.

The past and present cohabit here. Though many of the tribe members are Catholics, most of the San Juan tribe still practice traditional religious rituals. Thus, two rectangular kivas flank the church in the main plaza, and *caciques* (pueblo priests) share power with civil authorities. The annual **San Juan Fiesta** is held June 23 and 24; it features buffalo and Comanche dances. Another annual ceremony is the **turtle dance** on December 26. The **Matachine dance,** performed here Christmas Day, vividly depicts the subjugation of the Native Americans by the Catholic Spaniards.

The address of the pueblo is P.O. Box 1099, San Juan Pueblo, NM 87566 (✆ **505/852-4400** or 505/852-4210). Admission is free. Photography or sketching may be allowed for a fee, with prior permission from the governor's office. For information, call the number above. The charge for fishing is $8 for adults and $5 for children and seniors. The pueblo is open every day during daylight hours.

The **Eight Northern Indian Pueblos Council** (✆ **505/747-1593**) is a sort of chamber of commerce and social-service agency.

Fishing and picnicking are encouraged at the **San Juan Tribal Lakes,** open year-round. **Ohkay Casino** (✆ **505/747-1668;** www.ohkay.com) offers table games and slot machines, as well as live music nightly Tuesday through Saturday. It's open 24 hours on weekends.

SANTA CLARA PUEBLO

Close to Española (on NM 5), Santa Clara, with a population of about 1,944, is one of the largest pueblos. You'll see the village sprawling across the river basin near the beautiful Black Mesa, with rows of tract homes surrounding an adobe central area. Although it's in an incredible setting, the pueblo itself is not much to see; however, a trip through it will give a real feel for the contemporary lives of these people. Though stories vary, the Santa Clarans teach their children that their ancestors once lived in cliffside dwellings named Puye and migrated down to the river bottom in the 13th century. This pueblo is noted for its language program. Artisan elders work with children to teach them their native Tewa language, on the brink of extinction because so many now speak English. This pueblo is also the home of noted potter Nancy Youngblood, who comes from a long line of famous potters and now does alluring contemporary work.

Follow the main route to the old village, where you come to the visitor center, also known as the neighborhood center. There you can get directions to small shops that sell distinctive black incised Santa Clara pottery, red burnished pottery, baskets, and other crafts. One stunning sight here is the cemetery. Stop on the west side of the church and look over the 4-foot wall. It's a primitive site, with plain wooden crosses and some graves adorned with plastic flowers.

There are corn and harvest dances on **Santa Clara Feast Day** (Aug 12); information on other special days (including the corn or harvest dances, as well as children's dances) can be obtained from the pueblo office.

The famed **Puye Cliffs National Historic Landmark,** on the Santa Clara reservation, recently reopened to visitors. This spectacular ruin, where nearly 2,000 people lived from about A.D. 1200 to A.D. 1580, offers a unique glimpse into the past. Currently visitors must book tours at least one week in advance at a cost of $25 per person, though in the future drop-in visits may be welcome. Call ✆ **505/901-0681.**

The pueblo's address is P.O. Box 580, Española, NM 87532 (✆ **505/753-7326**). Admission is free. The charge for taking photographs is $5; filming and sketching are not allowed. The pueblo is open every day from 9am to 4pm.

11 LOS ALAMOS & BANDELIER NATIONAL MONUMENT

Los Alamos spreads over the colorful, fingerlike mesas of the Pajarito Plateau, between the Jemez Mountains and the Rio Grande Valley. It's the home of Los Alamos National Laboratory, established here during World War II, the origin of the first atomic bomb. Still the home of a world-renowned science laboratory, the town hosts the **Bradbury Science Museum,** 15th Street and Central Avenue (✆ **505/667-4444;** www.lanl.gov/museum), a great place to get acquainted with what goes on at a weapons production facility after nuclear proliferation. As NM 502 enters Los Alamos from Santa Fe, it follows Trinity Drive, where accommodations, restaurants, and other services are located.

Bandelier National Monument ★★★ Less than 15 miles south of Los Alamos along NM 4, this National Park Service area contains stunningly preserved ruins of the ancient cliff-dwelling Ancestral Puebloan (Anasazi) culture within 46 square miles of canyon-and-mesa wilderness. The national monument is named after the Swiss-American archaeologist Adolph Bandelier, who explored here in the 1880s. During busy summer months, head out early; there can be a waiting line for cars to park.

After an orientation stop at the visitor center and museum to learn about the culture that flourished here between 1100 and 1550, most visitors follow a trail along Frijoles Creek to the principal ruins. The pueblo site, including an underground kiva, has been stabilized. The biggest thrill for most folks is climbing hardy ponderosa pine ladders to visit an alcove—140 feet above the canyon floor—that was once home to prehistoric peoples. Tours are self-guided or led by a National Park Service ranger. Be aware that dogs are not allowed on trails.

NM 4 (HCR 1, Box 1, Ste. 15, Los Alamos). ✆ **505/672-3861,** ext 517. www.nps.gov/band. Admission $12 per vehicle. Daily during daylight hours. No pets allowed on trails. Closed Christmas and New Year's Day.

12 TAKING THE HIGH ROAD TO TAOS ★★

Unless you're in a hurry to get from Santa Fe to Taos, the High Road—also called the Mountain Road or the King's Road—is by far the most fascinating route between the two cities. It begins in lowlands of mystically formed pink and yellow stone, passing by apple and peach orchards and chile farms in the weaving village of **Chimayo.** Then it climbs

Fun Facts High on Art

If you really like art and want to meet artists, check out one of the **Art Studio Tours** held in the fall in the region. Artists spend months preparing their best work, and then open their doors to visitors. Wares range from pottery and paintings to furniture and woodcarvings to ristras and dried-flower arrangements. The most notable tour is the **High Road Studio Art Tour** (www.highroadnewmexico.com) in mid- to late September. If you're not in the region during that time, watch the newspapers (such as the *Santa Fe New Mexican's* Friday edition "Pasatiempo") for notices of other art-studio tours. Good ones are held in **Galisteo** (in mid-Oct; www.galisteostudiotour.com); **Abiquiu** (early Sept; www.abiquiustudiotour.org); **El Rito** (mid-Oct; www.elritolibrary.org/studiotour.html); and **Dixon** (early Nov; www.dixonarts.org). If you're not here during those times, you can still visit many of the galleries listed on the websites.

toward the highlands to the village of **Cordova,** known for its woodcarvers, and higher still to **Truchas,** a renegade arts town where Hispanic traditions and ways of life continue much as they did a century ago. Though I've described this tour from south to north, the most scenic way to see it is from north to south, when you travel down off the mountains rather than up into them. This way, you see more expansive views.

CHIMAYO

About 28 miles north of Santa Fe on NM 76/285 is the historic weaving center of Chimayo. It's approximately 16 miles past the Pojoaque junction, at the junction of NM 520 and NM 76 via NM 503. In this small village, families still maintain the tradition of crafting hand-woven textiles initiated by their ancestors seven generations ago, in the early 1800s. One such family is the Ortegas, and **Ortega's Weaving Shop** (✆ **505/351-4215;** www.ortegasweaving.com) and **Galeria Ortega** ★ (✆ **505/351-2288;** www.galeriaortega.com), both at the corner of NM 520 and NM 76, are fine places to take a close look at this ancient craft. A more humble spot is **Trujillo Weaving Shop** (✆ **505/351-4457**), on NM 76. If you're lucky enough to find the proprietors in, you might get a weaving history lesson. You can see a 100-year-old loom and an even older shuttle carved from apricot wood. The weavings you'll find are some of the best of the Rio Grande style, with rich patterns, many made from naturally dyed wool. Also on display are some fine Cordova woodcarvings. You'll also want to check out **Centinela Traditional Arts,** 946 NM 76 (✆ **877/351-2180** or 505/351-2180; www.chimayoweavers.com), for a good selection of rugs made by weavers from up and down the Rio Grande Valley. Watch for the chenille shawls by Scarlet Rose.

One of the best places to shop in Chimayo, **Chimayo Trading and Mercantile** ★ (✆ **505/351-4566**), on NM 76, is a richly cluttered store carrying local arts and crafts as well as select imports. It has a good selection of katsinas and Hopi corn maidens, as well as specialty items such as elaborately beaded cow skulls. Look for George Zarolinski's "smoked porcelain."

Many people come to Chimayo to visit **El Santuario de Nuestro Señor de Esquipulas (the Shrine of Our Lord of Esquipulas)** ★★ (✆ **505/351-4360;** holyfamily@cybermesa.com), better known simply as "El Santuario de Chimayo." Ascribed with miraculous powers of healing, this church has attracted thousands of pilgrims since its construction in 1814–16. Up to 30,000 people participate in the annual Good Friday pilgrimage, many of them walking from as far away as Albuquerque.

Although only the earth in the anteroom beside the altar is presumed to have the gift of healing powers, the entire shrine radiates true serenity. A National Historic Landmark, the church has five beautiful *reredos* (panels of sacred paintings)—one behind the main altar and two on each side of the nave. The Santuario is open daily March to September 9am to 6pm, and October to February 9am to 5pm. Please remember that this is a place of worship, so quiet is always appreciated.

A good place to stop for a quick bite, **Leona's Restaurante de Chimayo** (✆ **505/351-4569**) is right next door to the Santuario de Chimayo. Leona herself presides over this little taco and burrito stand with plastic tables inside and, during warm months, out. Burritos and soft tacos made with chicken, beef, or veggie-style with beans will definitely tide you over en route to Taos or Santa Fe. Open Thursday through Monday 11am to 5pm.

Where to Stay

Casa Escondida ★ On the outskirts of Chimayo, this inn offers a lovely retreat and a good home base for exploring the Sangre de Cristo Mountains and their many soulful farming villages. This hacienda-feeling place has a cozy living room with a large kiva fireplace. Decor is simple and classic, with Mission-style furniture lending a colonial feel. The breakfast room is a sunny atrium with French doors that open out in summer to a grassy yard spotted with apricot trees. The rooms are varied; all my favorites are within the main house. The Sun Room catches all that passionate northern New Mexico sun upon its red brick floors and on its private flagstone patio as well; it has an elegant feel and connects with a smaller room, so it's a good choice for families. The Vista is on the second story. Its dormer windows give it an uniquely shaped roofline. It has a wrought-iron queen-size bed as well a twin, and it opens out onto a large deck offering spectacular sunset views. The casita adjacent to the main house has a kiva fireplace, a stove, and a minifridge, as well as nice meadow views.

P.O. Box 142, Chimayo, NM 87522. ✆ **800/643-7201** or 505/351-4805. Fax 505/351-2575. www.casaescondida.com. 8 units. $95–$155 double. Rates include full breakfast. MC, V. Pets welcome in 4 rooms for a small fee; prearrangement required. **Amenities:** Jacuzzi.

Where to Dine

Restaurante Rancho de Chimayo ★ NEW MEXICAN For as long as I can remember, my family and many of my friends' families have scheduled trips into northern New Mexico to coincide with lunch or dinner at this fun restaurant. In an adobe home built by Hermenegildo Jaramillo in the 1880s, it's now run as a restaurant by his descendants. Unfortunately, over the years the restaurant has become so famous that tour buses now stop here. However, the food has suffered only a little. In the warmer months, request to dine on the terraced patio. During winter, you'll be seated in one of a number of cozy rooms with thick viga ceilings. The food is native New Mexican, prepared from generations-old Jaramillo family recipes. You can't go wrong with the enchiladas, served layered, northern New Mexico style, rather than rolled. For variety you might want to try the *combinación picante* (carne adovada, tamale, enchilada, beans, and posole). Each plate comes with a *sopaipilla*. With a little honey, who needs dessert? The full bar serves delicious margaritas.

300 County Rd. 98 (1/4 mile west of the Santuario), Chimayo, NM 87522. © **505/351-4444.** www.ranchodechimayo.com. Reservations recommended. Lunch $7.50–$13; dinner $11–$21. AE, DC, DISC, MC, V. Daily May–Oct 11:30am–9pm; Sat–Sun breakfast 8:30–10:30am. Nov 1–Apr 30 closed Mon.

CORDOVA

Just as Chimayo is famous for its weaving, the village of Cordova, about 7 miles east on NM 76, is noted for its woodcarving. It's easy to whiz by this village, nestled below the High Road, but don't. Just a short way through this truly traditional northern New Mexico town is a gem: The **Castillo Gallery** ★ (© **505/351-4067**), a mile into the village of Cordova, carries moody and colorful acrylic paintings by Paula Castillo, as well as her metal welded sculptures. It also carries the work of Terry Enseñat Mulert, whose contemporary woodcarvings are treasures of the high country. En route to the Castillo, you may want to stop in at two other local carvers' galleries. The first you'll come to is that of **Sabinita Lopez Ortiz;** the second belongs to her cousin, **Gloria Ortiz.** Both are descendants of the well-noted José Dolores Lopez. Carved from cedar wood and aspen, their works range from simple statues of saints *(santos)* to elaborate scenes of birds.

TRUCHAS

Robert Redford's 1988 movie *The Milagro Beanfield War* featured the town of Truchas (which means "trout"). A former Spanish colonial outpost built on top of an 8,000-foot mesa, 4 miles east of Cordova, it was chosen as the site for the film in part because traditional Hispanic culture is still very much in evidence. Subsistence farming is prevalent here. The scenery is spectacular: 13,101-foot Truchas Peak dominates one side of the mesa, and the broad Rio Grande Valley dominates the other.

Look for the **High Road Marketplace** ★ (© **866/343-5381** or 505/351-1078), an artists' co-op gallery with a variety of offerings ranging from jewelry to landscape paintings to a broad range of crosses made from tin, rusted metal, and nails. Be sure to find your way into the **Cordovas' Handweaving Workshop** (© **505/689-1124**). In the center of town, this tiny shop is run by Harry Cordova, a fourth-generation weaver with a unique style. His works tend to be simpler than many Rio Grande weavings, utilizing mainly stripes in the designs.

Just down the road from Cordovas' is **Hand Artes Gallery** (© **800/689-2441** or 505/689-2443), a definite surprise in this remote region. Here you'll find an array of contemporary as well as representational art from noted regional artists. Look for Sheila Keeffe's worldly painted panels, and Norbert Voelkel's colorful paintings and monoprints.

About 6 miles east of Truchas on NM 76 is the small town of **Las Trampas,** noted for its 1780 **San José de Gracia Church,** which, with its thick walls and elegant lines, might possibly be the most beautiful of all New Mexico churches built during the Spanish colonial period.

PICURIS (SAN LORENZO) PUEBLO

Not far from the regional education center of Peñasco, about 24 miles from Chimayo, near the intersection of NM 75 and NM 76, is the Picuris (San Lorenzo) Pueblo (© **505/587-2519;** www.picurispueblo.net). The 375 citizens of this 15,000-acre mountain pueblo, native Tewa speakers, consider themselves a sovereign nation: Their forebears

Georgia O'Keeffe & New Mexico: A Desert Romance

In June 1917, during a short visit to the Southwest, the painter Georgia O'Keeffe (born 1887) visited New Mexico for the first time. She was immediately enchanted by the stark scenery; even after her return to the energy and chaos of New York City, her mind wandered frequently to New Mexico's arid land and undulating mesas. However, not until coaxed by the arts patron and "collector of people" Mabel Dodge Luhan 12 years later did O'Keeffe return to the multihued desert of her daydreams.

O'Keeffe was reportedly ill, both physically and emotionally, when she arrived in Santa Fe in April 1929. New Mexico seemed to soothe her spirit and heal her physical ailments almost magically. Two days after her arrival, Mabel Dodge Luhan persuaded O'Keeffe to move into her home in Taos. There, she would be free to paint and socialize as she liked.

In Taos, O'Keeffe began painting what would become some of her best-known canvases—close-ups of desert flowers and objects such as cow and horse skulls. "The color up there is different . . . the blue-green of the sage and the mountains, the wildflowers in bloom," O'Keeffe once said of Taos. "It's a different kind of color from any I've ever seen—there's nothing like that in north Texas or even in Colorado." Taos transformed not only her art but her personality as well. She bought a car and learned to drive. Sometimes, on warm days, she ran naked through the sage fields. That August, a new, rejuvenated O'Keeffe rejoined her husband, photographer Alfred Stieglitz, in New York.

The artist returned to New Mexico year after year, spending time with Mabel Dodge Luhan as well as staying at the isolated Ghost Ranch. She drove through the countryside in her snappy Ford, stopping to paint in her favorite spots along the way. Until 1949, O'Keeffe always returned to New York in the fall. Three years after Stieglitz's death, though, she relocated permanently to New Mexico, spending each winter and spring in Abiquiu and each summer and fall at Ghost Ranch. Georgia O'Keeffe died in Santa Fe in 1986.

A great way to see Ghost Ranch is on a hike that climbs above the mystical area. Take US 84 north from Española about 36 miles to Ghost Ranch and follow the road to the Ghost Ranch office. The ranch is owned by the Presbyterian Church, and the staff will supply you with a primitive map for the **Kitchen Mesa** and **Chimney Rock** hikes. If you hike there, be sure to check in at the front desk, which is open Monday to Saturday from 8am to 5pm. For more information, contact **Ghost Ranch,** 401 Old Taos Hwy., Santa Fe (✆ **505/685-4333;** www.ghostranch.org).

never made a treaty with any foreign country, including the United States. Thus, they observe a traditional form of tribal council government. A few of the original mud-and-stone houses still stand, as does a lovely church. A striking aboveground ceremonial kiva called "the Roundhouse," built at least 700 years ago, and some historic excavated kivas and storerooms are on a hill above the pueblo and are open to visitors. The **annual feast days** at San Lorenzo Church are August 9 and 10.

The people here are modern enough to have fully computerized their public showcase operations as Picuris Tribal Enterprises, and they run the Hotel Santa Fe in the state capital. Fishing permits ($11 for all ages) are available, as are permits to camp ($8) at Tu-Tah Lake, which is regularly stocked with trout.

You might want to plan your High Road trip to include a visit to **Sugar Nymphs Bistro** ★★, 15046 NM 75 (✆ **575/587-0311**) for some inventive food. Inside a vintage theater in the little farming village of Peñasco, Kai Harper, former executive chef at Greens in San Francisco, prepares contemporary bistro cuisine, using local and seasonal ingredients. Lunch brings imaginative pizza, salads, and burgers, while dinner includes a full range of entrees. Yaki Udon is a favorite at lunch and dinner: Grilled chicken is combined with red bell peppers, poblano chiles, carrots, and snap peas in a soy-ginger sauce. In summer, the cafe is open Tuesday to Saturday 11:30am to 3pm, and Thursday to Saturday 5:30 to 7:30 or 8pm, with Sunday brunch from 11am to 2pm. In winter, spring, and fall, the schedule is abbreviated. Call ahead to be sure it's open.

DIXON & EMBUDO

Taos is about 24 miles north of Peñasco via NM 518, but day-trippers from Santa Fe can loop back to the capital by taking NM 75 west from Picuris Pueblo. Dixon, approximately 12 miles west of Picuris, and its twin village Embudo, a mile farther on NM 68 at the Rio Grande, are home to many artists and craftspeople who exhibit their works during the annual **autumn show** sponsored by the Dixon Arts Association.

To taste the local grape, follow signs to **La Chiripada Winery** (✆ **505/579-4437;** www.lachiripada.com), whose product is surprisingly good, especially to those who don't know that New Mexico has a long winemaking history. Local pottery is also sold in the tasting room. The winery is open Monday to Saturday 10am to 6pm, Sunday noon to 6pm.

ESPAÑOLA

The commercial center of Española (pop. 9,688) no longer has the railroad that led to its establishment in the 1880s, but it may have New Mexico's greatest concentration of **low riders.** These are late-model customized cars, so called because their suspension leaves them sitting quite close to the ground. Watch for them as you pass through town.

Sights of interest in Española include the **Bond House Museum** (✆ **505/747-8535**), a Victorian-era adobe home that exhibits local history and art, and the **Santa Cruz Church,** built in 1733 and renovated in 1979, which houses many fine examples of Spanish colonial religious art. The **Convento,** built to resemble a colonial cathedral, on the Española Plaza (at the junction of NM 30 and US 84), houses a variety of shops, including a trading post and an antiques gallery, as well as a display room for the Historical Society.

Complete information on Española and the vicinity can be obtained from the **Española Valley Chamber of Commerce,** #1 Calle de Las Españolas, NM 87532 (✆ **505/753-2831;** www.espanolanmchamber.com).

If you admire the work of Georgia O'Keeffe, try to plan a short trip to **Abiquiu,** a tiny town at a bend of the Rio Chama, 14 miles south of Ghost Ranch and 22 miles north of Española on US 84. When you see the surrounding terrain, it will be clear that this was the inspiration for many of her startling landscapes. **O'Keeffe's adobe home ★** (where she lived and painted) is open for public tours. A reservation must be made in advance; the fee for adults is $30 (some discounts apply) for a 1-hour tour. A number of tours are given each week—on Tuesday, Thursday, and Friday (mid-Mar to late Nov only)—and a limited number of people are accepted per tour. Visitors are not permitted to take pictures. Fortunately, O'Keeffe's home remains as it was when she lived there (until 1986). Call several months in advance for reservations (✆ **505/685-4539**).

Where to Stay & Dine

El Paragua ★ NORTHERN NEW MEXICAN This Española restaurant is a great place to stop en route to Taos, though some Santa Feans make a special trip here. Every time I enter El Paragua (which means "the umbrella"), with its red-tile floors and colorful Saltillo-tile trimmings, I feel as though I've stepped into Mexico. The restaurant opened in 1958 as a small taco stand owned by two brothers, and through the years it has flourished. It has received praise from many sources, including *Gourmet Magazine* and N. Scott Momaday, writing for the *New York Times.* You can't go wrong ordering the Enchilada Suprema, a chicken and cheese enchilada with onion and sour cream. Also on the menu are fajitas and a variety of seafood dishes and steaks, including the *churrasco Argentino.* Served at your table in a hot brazier, it's cooked in a green herb *salsa chimichurri.* There's a full bar from which you may want to try Don Luis's Italian coffee, made with a coffee-flavored liquor called Tuaca. For equally excellent but faster food, skip next door to the kin restaurant **El Parasol ★** and order a chicken taco—the best ever.

603 Santa Cruz Rd., Española (off the main drag; turn east at Long John Silver's). ✆ **505/753-3211.** www.elparagua.com. Reservations recommended. Main courses $11–$22. AE, DISC, MC, V. Daily 11am–8:30pm.

Rancho de San Juan ★★★ **Moments** Just 38 miles from Santa Fe, set between Española and Ojo Caliente, this inn provides an authentic northern New Mexico desert experience with the comforts of a luxury hotel and the ease of staying with friends. In 2006, this place received some serious recognition; it was listed on the *Condé Nast Traveler* Gold List and named as one of the top six inns in the United States by *Executive Traveler.* It's the passion of architect and chef John Johnson, responsible for the design and cuisine, and interior designer David Heath, responsible for the elegant interiors. The original part of the inn comprises four recently renovated and enlarged rooms around a central courtyard. Additional casitas with kitchens are in the outlying hills. Rooms here are open, bright, and very elegant—stylishly decorated with a creative mix from the owners' personal art collections including contemporary paintings, tribal masks, and European antiques. From private patios, you'll have spectacular views of desert landscapes and distant, snow-capped peaks. The Kiva suite is the most innovative, with a round bedroom and a skylight just above the bed, perfect for stargazing.

Meals here are some of the best in the state. The weekly seasonal menus are original, flavorful, and beautifully presented. The selection of appetizers, entrees ($38), and desserts often take a French-inspired twist on local Southwest ingredients.

US 285 (en route to Ojo Caliente), P.O. Box 4140, Fairview Station, Española, NM 87533. ✆ **505/753-6818.** www.ranchodesanjuan.com. 13 units. $285–$685 double. AE, MC, V. **Amenities:** Restaurant; concierge. *In room:* A/C, CD player, fridge w/stocked beverages, hair dryer.

OJO CALIENTE

Many locals from the area like to rejuvenate at **Ojo Caliente Mineral Springs,** Ojo Caliente, NM 87549 (✆ **800/222-9162** or 505/583-2233; http://ojocalientesprings.com); it's on US 285, 50 miles (a 1-hr. drive) northwest of Santa Fe and 50 miles southwest of Taos. This National Historic Site was considered sacred by prehistoric tribes. When Spanish explorer Cabeza de Vaca discovered and named the springs in the 16th century, he called them "the greatest treasure that I found these strange people to possess." No other hot springs in the world has Ojo Caliente's combination of iron, soda, lithium, sodium, and arsenic. If the weather is warm enough, the outdoor mud bath is a treat. The dressing rooms are in fairly good shape; however, the whole place has an earthy feel. If you're a fastidious type, you won't be comfortable here. The resort offers herbal wraps and massages, lodging, and meals. It's open daily 8am to 10pm.

Taos

New Mexico's favorite arts town sits in a masterpiece setting. It's wedged between the towering peaks of the Rocky Mountains and the plunging chasm of the Rio Grande Gorge.

About 70 miles north of Santa Fe, this town of 5,000 residents combines 1960s hippiedom (thanks to communes set up in the hills back then) with the ancient culture of Taos Pueblo (some people still live without electricity and running water, as their ancestors did 1,000 years ago). It can be an odd place, where some completely eschew materialism and live "off the grid" in half-underground houses called earthships. But there are plenty of more mainstream attractions as well—Taos boasts some of the best restaurants in the state, a hot and funky arts scene, and incredible outdoors action, including world-class skiing.

Its history is rich. Throughout the Taos valley, ruins and artifacts attest to a Native American presence dating back 5,000 years. The Spanish first visited this area in 1540, colonizing it in 1598. In the last 2 decades of the 17th century, they put down three rebellions at Taos Pueblo. During the 18th and 19th centuries, Taos was an important trade center: New Mexico's annual caravan to Chihuahua, Mexico, couldn't leave until after the annual midsummer **Taos Fair.** French trappers began attending the fair in 1739. Even though the Plains tribes often attacked the pueblos at other times, they would attend the market festival under a temporary annual truce. By the early 1800s, Taos had become a meeting place for American mountain men, the most famous of whom, Kit Carson, made his home in Taos from 1826 to 1868.

Taos remained loyal to Mexico during the U.S.–Mexican War of 1846. The town rebelled against its new U.S. landlord in 1847, even killing newly appointed Governor Charles Bent in his Taos home. Nevertheless, the town was eventually incorporated into the Territory of New Mexico in 1850. During the Civil War, Taos fell into Confederate hands for 6 weeks; afterward, Carson and two other men raised the Union flag over Taos Plaza and guarded it day and night. Since that time, Taos has had the honor of flying the flag 24 hours a day.

Taos's population declined when the railroad bypassed it in favor of Santa Fe. In 1898, two East Coast artists—Ernest Blumenschein and Bert Phillips—discovered the dramatic, varied effects of sunlight on the natural environment of the Taos valley and depicted them on canvas. By 1912, thanks to the growing influence of the **Taos Society of Artists,** the town had gained a worldwide reputation as a cultural center. Today, it's estimated that more than 15% of the population are painters, sculptors, writers, or musicians, or in some other way earn their income from artistic pursuits.

The town of Taos is merely the focal point of the rugged 2,200-square-mile Taos County. Two features dominate this sparsely populated region: the high desert mesa, split in two by the 650-foot-deep chasm of the **Rio Grande;** and the **Sangre de Cristo** range, which tops out at 13,161-foot Wheeler Peak, New Mexico's highest mountain. From the forested uplands to the sage-carpeted mesa, the county is home to a large variety of wildlife.

Taos is also inhabited by many people who have chosen to retreat from, or altogether drop out of, mainstream society. Most Taoseños live here to play here—and that means outdoors. Many work at the ski area all winter (skiing whenever they can) and work for raft companies in the summer (to get on the river as much as they can). Others are into rock climbing, mountain biking, and backpacking. That's not to say that Taos is just a resort town. With the Hispanic and Native American populations' histories in the area, there's a richness and depth here that most resort towns lack.

1 ORIENTATION

ARRIVING

BY PLANE The **Taos Regional Airport** (✆ **575/758-4995**) is about 8 miles northwest of town on US 64. Most people opt to fly into Albuquerque International Sunport, rent a car, and drive up to Taos from there. The drive takes approximately 2½ hours. If you'd rather be picked up at Albuquerque International Sunport, call **Faust's Transportation, Inc.** (✆ **575/758-3410**), which offers daily service, as well as taxi service between Taos and Taos Ski Valley.

BY BUS The **Taos Bus Center** is 5 miles south of the plaza at 710 Paseo del Pueblo Sur (✆ **575/758-1144**). **TNM&O** arrives and departs from this depot several times a day. For more information on this and other bus services to and from Albuquerque and Santa Fe, see "Getting There & Getting Around," in chapter 3.

BY CAR Most visitors arrive in Taos via either NM 68 or US 64. Northbound travelers should take exit I-25 at Santa Fe, follow US 285 as far as Española, and then continue on the divided highway when it becomes NM 68. Taos is about 79 miles from the I-25 junction. Southbound travelers from Denver on I-25 should exit about 6 miles south of Raton at US 64 and then follow it about 95 miles to Taos. Another major route is US 64 from the west (214 miles from Farmington).

VISITOR INFORMATION

The **Taos County Chamber of Commerce,** at 108 F Kit Carson Rd., Taos, NM 87571 (✆ **575/751-8800;** www.taoschamber.com), is open in summer, daily 9am to 5pm. It's closed on major holidays.

CITY LAYOUT

The **plaza** is a short block west of Taos's major intersection—where US 64 (Kit Carson Rd.) from the east joins NM 68, **Paseo del Pueblo Sur.** US 64 proceeds north from the intersection as **Paseo del Pueblo Norte. Camino de la Placita (Placita Rd.)** circles the west side of downtown, passing within a block of the other side of the plaza. Many of the streets that join these thoroughfares are winding lanes lined by traditional adobe homes, many of them over 100 years old.

Most of the art galleries are located on or near the plaza, which was paved over with bricks several years ago, and along neighboring streets. Others are in the **Ranchos de Taos** area, a few miles south of the plaza.

MAPS To find your way around town, pick up a free Taos map from the **Town of Taos Visitor Center,** 1139 Paseo del Pueblo Sur (✆ **800/732-TAOS** [8267] or 575/758-3873). Good, detailed city maps can be found at area bookstores as well. **Carson National Forest** information and maps are available in the same building.

With offices at the Taos airport, **Enterprise** (✆ **575/751-7490**) is reliable and efficient. Other car-rental agencies are available out of Albuquerque. See "Getting Around," in chapter 9, for details.

PARKING Parking can be difficult during the summer rush, when the stream of tourists' cars moving north and south through town never ceases. If you can't find parking on the street or in the plaza, check out some of the nearby roads (Kit Carson Rd., for instance); there are plenty of metered and unmetered lots in Taos.

ROAD CONDITIONS Information on highway conditions throughout the state can be obtained from the **State Highway Department** (✆ **800/432-4269**).

BY BUS & TAXI

If you're in Taos without a car, you're in luck because there's local bus service, provided by **Chile Line Town of Taos Transit** (✆ **575/751-4459**). It operates every half-hour Monday to Saturday 7am to 7pm in summer, 7am to 6pm in winter, and on the hour Sunday 8am to 5pm. Two simultaneous routes run southbound from Taos Pueblo and northbound from the Ranchos de Taos Post Office. Each route makes stops at the casino and various hotels in town, as well as at Taos RV Park. Bus fares are 50¢ one-way, $1 round-trip, $5 for a 7-day pass, and $20 for a 31-day pass.

In addition, **Faust's Transportation** (✆ **575/758-3410**) has a taxi service linking town hotels and Taos Ski Valley. Faust's Transportation also offers shuttle service and on-call taxi service daily from 8am to 5pm (special arrangements made for after hours; Sun by appointment only), with fares of about $10 anywhere within the city limits for up to two people.

BY BICYCLE

Bicycle rentals are available from **Gearing Up Bicycle Shop,** 129 Paseo del Pueblo Sur (✆ **575/751-0365**); daily rentals run $35 for a full day and $25 for a half-day for a mountain bike with front suspension. From April to October, **Native Sons Adventures,** 1334 Paseo del Pueblo Sur (✆ **800/753-7559** or 575/758-9342; www.nativesonsadventures.com), rents front-suspension bikes for $25 for a half-day and $35 for a full day. It also rents car racks for $5. Each shop supplies helmets and water bottles with rentals.

Warning for Drivers

En route to many recreation sites, reliable paved roads often give way to poorer forest roads. When you get off the main roads, you don't find gas stations or cafes. Four-wheel-drive vehicles are recommended on snow and much of the unpaved terrain of the region. If you're doing some off-road adventuring, it's wise to go with a full gas tank, extra food and water, and warm clothing—just in case. At the higher-than-10,000-foot elevations of northern New Mexico, sudden summer snowstorms are not unheard of.

Members of the **Taos Medical Group,** on Weimer Road (✆ **575/758-2224**), are highly respected. Also recommended are **Family Practice Associates of Taos,** 630 Paseo del Pueblo Sur, Ste. 150 (✆ **575/758-3005**). **Holy Cross Hospital,** 1397 Weimer Rd., off Paseo del Canyon (✆ **575/758-8883**), has 24-hour emergency service. Serious cases are transferred to Santa Fe or Albuquerque. Gross receipts tax for the city of Taos is 7.5%, and for Taos County it's 6.3%. There is an additional lodgers' tax of 5% in both the city of Taos and in Taos County. If you're looking to connect to the Internet with your laptop, head for the plaza, which offers free wireless access anywhere you sit.

See also "Fast Facts: American Southwest," on p. 607.

3 WHERE TO STAY

A tiny town with a big tourist market, Taos has thousands of rooms in hotels, motels, condominiums, and bed-and-breakfasts. Many new properties have recently opened, turning this into a buyer's market. In the slower seasons—January through early February and April through early May—when competition for travelers is steep, you may even want to try bargaining your room rate down. Most of the hotels and motels are on Paseo del Pueblo Sur and Norte, with a few scattered just east of the town center, along Kit Carson Road. The condos and bed-and-breakfasts are generally scattered throughout Taos's back streets.

During peak seasons, visitors without reservations may have difficulty finding vacant rooms. **Taos Chamber of Commerce,** 108 F Kit Carson Rd. (✆ **575/751-8800**), might be able to help.

Southern Rockies Reservations (✆ **866/250-7313;** www.taosskitrips.com) will help you find accommodations ranging from bed-and-breakfasts to home rentals, hotels, and cabins throughout Taos, Taos Ski Valley, and the rest of northern New Mexico. It'll also help you arrange package trips for outdoor activities such as skiing, horseback riding, hot-air ballooning, and snowmobiling.

TAOS & VICINITY

Hotels/Motels

Expensive

El Monte Sagrado ★★★ (Moments) New to Taos in 2003, this resort near the center of town offers a feast for the senses. Water running over falls, lush landscaping, and delicious food and drink lull guests into a sweet *samadhi,* or state of relaxation, while the eyes luxuriate in the beauty of rooms impeccably decorated. These range in theme from the Caribbean casita, a medium-size room with a medium-size bathroom, which evokes the feel of an African jungle, to the Argentina global suite, a huge two-bedroom decorated in cowboy-contemporary style with wood floors, leather furniture, iron and copper accents, and two large bathrooms featuring stone and glass mosaic-decorated shower and tub, not to mention its own patio and outdoor hot tub. In 2007, the inn nearly doubled in size with a series of new, more reasonably priced rooms and an elegant meeting center. All rooms are quiet and lovely, with patios or balconies and views. In line with the resort owner Tom Worrell's plan to preserve the earth's environment through responsible development and sustainable technologies, the resort recycles its water, using it to irrigate the grassy cottonwood-shaded "Sacred Circle," at the resort's center. The intimate spa, with

ACCOMMODATIONS ■

Best Western Kachina Lodge & Meeting Center **8**
Carson National Forest **1**
Casa de las Chimeneas **16**
El Monte Sagrado **13**
Hacienda del Sol **2**
The Historic Taos Inn **10**
Hotel La Fonda de Taos **11**
Little Tree Bed & Breakfast **1**
Old Taos Guesthouse Bed & Breakfast **17**
Taos Hampton Inn **18**
Taos Valley RV Park and Campground **18**

DINING ◆

De La Tierra **13**
Doc Martin's **9**
El Meze **6**
Graham's Grille **12**
Gutiz **5**
Joseph's Table **11**
Lambert's of Taos **15**
Lula's **14**
Old Blinking Light **3**
Orlando's New Mexican Café **4**
Stakeout Grill & Bar **19**
Taos Cow **3**
Taos Pizza Out Back **7**
Trading Post Café **19**

 Family-Friendly Hotels

Best Western Kachina Lodge (p. 207) A picnic area in a courtyard set back away from the street and an outdoor pool make this a nice place for families to commune in summer.

Old Taos Guesthouse Bed & Breakfast (p. 209) With a country setting, friendly dogs, and some rooms with kitchenettes, this inn serves family needs well.

Taos Hampton Inn (p. 207) Fairly spacious, predictable rooms and an indoor pool make this a family oasis in Taos.

a waiting area that resembles a greenhouse filled with plants, offers a full range of excellent treatments, and the Living Spa Program offers classes such as yoga and T'ai Chi free for guests. The **Anaconda Bar** (p. 235) and **De La Tierra** restaurant (p. 211) combine a contemporary feel with elegant Asian touches.

317 Kit Carson Rd., Taos, NM 87571. ✆ **800/828-TAOS** (8267) or 575/758-3502. www.elmontesagrado.com. 84 units. $159–$369 historic 1-bedroom casita; $179–$399 Taos Mountain Room; $199–$439 Native American suite; $219–$479 Bali and Tibet premier suite; $419–$839 2-bedroom global suite. AE, DC, DISC, MC, V. Valet parking $12. **Amenities:** Restaurant; bar; concierge; health club; Jacuzzi; indoor pool; spa. *In room:* A/C, TV, CD player, hair dryer, minibar, Wi-Fi.

The Historic Taos Inn ★ It's rare to see a hotel that has withstood the years with grace, but the Historic Taos Inn has done just that. Here, you'll be surrounded by 21st-century luxury without ever forgetting that you're within the thick walls of a number of 19th-century Southwestern homes once owned by Dr. Thomas Paul Martin, the town's first physician, who purchased the complex in 1895. It's now listed on both the State and National Registers of Historic Places.

The lobby doubles as the **Adobe Bar** (p. 235), a popular local gathering place, with adobe *bancos* (benches) and a sunken fireplace, all surrounding a wishing well that was once the old town well. A number of rooms open onto a balcony that overlooks this area. I don't recommend these rooms, as they can be noisy. All the other rooms sit among a number of "houses" separated by walkways and grass. Some have more modest style, with lower ceilings and Spanish Colonial furnishings, while others are more chic. My favorites are no. 204 in the Sandoval House, decorated with antiques, and any room in the recently built **Helen House ★★**. These rooms, with saltillo tile floors, kiva fireplaces and stylish furnishings made from interesting things such as saguaro cactus, in one, will appeal to travelers who don't appreciate the whims of an older building, but still enjoy character. When reserving here, be sure to discuss your needs with the reservation service.

Doc Martin's (p. 212), serving nouveau Southwestern and international cuisine, some of it organic, is a good bet for any meal.

125 Paseo del Pueblo Norte, Taos, NM 87571. ✆ **800/TAOS-INN** (826-7466) or 575/758-2233. Fax 575/758-5776. www.taosinn.com. 44 units. $85–$275, depending on the type of room and season. AE, DISC, MC, V. **Amenities:** Restaurant; bar; Jacuzzi; room service; Wi-Fi (in lobby). *In room:* A/C, TV, DVD on request.

Hotel La Fonda de Taos ★ Finally, Taos has a recommendable hotel on the plaza. A $3-million renovation to this historic property built in 1880 has turned it into a comfortable, fun spot with a stellar location. The charismatic Taos figure Saki Kavaras put this hotel on the society map in the 1930s, when, most notably, British author D. H. Lawrence frequented it. His legacy is preserved in a unique D. H. Lawrence Forbidden Art Museum, where some of his risqué paintings hang—a must-see even if you don't stay here (free for guests; $3 for nonguests). Rooms are set off broad hallways, each styled in earth tones, Southwestern furnishings, and tile bathrooms. Standards are small, each with a queen-size bed. Your better bet is to reserve a plaza or deluxe plaza room, or a suite. These are larger, with king beds. My favorite rooms are nos. 201 and 301, which overlook the plaza. Groups can rent the whole top floor (or the whole hotel), which includes a full kitchen suite. **Joseph's Table** (p. 212), one of Taos's finest restaurants, is off the lobby.

108 South Plaza, Taos, NM 87571. ✆ **800/833-2211** or 575/758-2211. Fax 575/758-8508. www.lafondataos.com. 24 units. $109–$149 standard double; $139–$209 plaza and deluxe plaza double; $199–$239 suite. AE, DC, DISC, MC, V. Free parking. **Amenities:** Restaurant; bar; coffee shop. *In room:* A/C, TV, hair dryer, Internet.

Moderate

Taos Hampton Inn ★ Kids The most reliable moderately priced hotel in town, the Hampton was built in the mid-1990s and is about 5 minutes (by car) from the plaza. Rooms are medium-size with either two queens or one king bed, a few with Jacuzzis and mountain views. All have nice pine furnishings, quality bedding, and a hint of Southwestern decor, some with desks, others with a table and chair. The beds are comfortable and the bathrooms very clean and functional. The indoor pool keeps kids entertained year-round.

1515 Paseo del Pueblo Sur, Taos, NM 87571. **800/HAMPTON** (426-7866) or 575/737-5700. Fax 575/737-5701. www.hampton.com. 71 units. $109–$149. Rates include full hot breakfast and afternoon snack. AE, DC, DISC, MC, V. **Amenities:** Indoor pool; Jacuzzi. *In room:* A/C, TV, hair dryer, Wi-Fi.

Inexpensive

Best Western Kachina Lodge & Meeting Center Kids Built in the early 1960s, this lodge on the north end of town, in walking distance of the plaza, has a lot of charm despite the fact that it's a motor hotel. Unfortunately, with an aging owner who's looking to sell the property, it's in dire need of remodeling right now, so only stay here if you don't mind crumbling sidewalks and frayed carpeting and furnishings. The Southwestern-style rooms—some have couches and most have Taos-style *trasteros* (armoires) that hold the TVs—have comfortable beds and small but functional and clean baths. Rooms sit around a grassy courtyard studded with huge blue spruce trees, allowing kids room to run. In the center is a stage where a family from Taos Pueblo builds a bonfire and dances nightly in the summer, and explains the significance of the dances—a real treat for anyone baffled by the Pueblo rituals. A full, hot breakfast is served in a retro kiva-shaped cafe.

413 Paseo del Pueblo Norte (P.O. Box NM), Taos, NM 87571. ✆ **800/522-4462** or 575/758-2275. Fax 575/758-9207. www.kachinalodge.com. 118 units. $59–$159 double. Rates include full breakfast. Additional person $10. Children 11 and under stay free in parent's room. AE, DISC, MC, V. **Amenities:** 2 restaurants; bar; outdoor pool. *In room:* A/C, TV, hair dryer, Wi-Fi.

Bed & Breakfasts

Expensive

Casa de las Chimeneas ★★★ This 82-year-old adobe home set on spacious grounds has, since its opening as a luxury inn in 1988, been a model of Southwestern elegance. Adding to its appeal is a spa with a small fitness room and sauna, as well as complete massage and facial treatments for an additional charge. I recommend the Rio Grande and Territorial rooms, which are spacious and air-conditioned. Both of these rooms have heated Saltillo-tile floors, gas kiva fireplaces, and Jacuzzi tubs. If you prefer a more antique-feeling room, try the delightful older section, especially the Library Suite. Each room in the inn is decorated with original works of art and has elegant bedding, a private entrance, and robes. All rooms have kiva fireplaces, and most look out on flower and herb gardens. Breakfasts are delicious. Specialties include an artichoke-heart and mushroom omelet or ricotta cream-cheese blintz. In the evenings the inn offers a full dinner, which may include corn-crusted tilapia or roasted chicken served with vegetables from a local organic farm. End the day at the large hot tub in the courtyard. Ask about the spa specials. A courtesy computer with Internet is available for guest use.

405 Cordoba Rd., at Los Pandos Rd. (5303 NDCBU), Taos, NM 87571. ✆ **877/758-4777** or 575/758-4777. Fax 575/758-3976. www.visittaos.com. 8 units. $180–$320 double; $325 suite. Rates include breakfast and light evening supper. AE, DC, DISC, MC, V. **Amenities:** Concierge; small health club; computer w/ Internet; Jacuzzi; sauna; spa. *In room:* TV/VCR, hair dryer, free stocked non-alcoholic minibar, Wi-Fi.

Hacienda del Sol ★★ What's unique about this bed-and-breakfast is its spectacular view of Taos Mountain. Because the 1¼-acre property borders Taos Pueblo, the land is pristine. The inn also has a rich history. It was once owned by arts patron Mabel Dodge Luhan, and it was here that author Frank Waters wrote *The People of the Valley.* You'll find bold splashes of color from the gardens—where, in summer, tulips, pansies, and flax bloom—to the rooms themselves—where woven bedspreads and original art lend a Mexican feel. The main house is 204 years old, so it has the wonderful curves of adobe as well as thick vigas. Some guest rooms are in this section. Others range from 9 to 27 years in age. These newer rooms are finely constructed, and I almost recommend them over the others because they're a little more private and the bathrooms are more refined. All rooms have robes and CD players, most have fireplaces, three have private Jacuzzis, and four have private steam showers. Some have minifridges. A full and delicious breakfast is served in the Spanish-hacienda-style dining area. The outdoor hot tub has a mountain view and is available for private guest use in half-hour segments. A courtesy computer with Internet is available for guest use.

109 Mabel Dodge Lane (P.O. Box 177), Taos, NM 87571. ✆ **575/758-0287.** Fax 575/758-5895. www.taoshaciendadelsol.com. 11 units. $135–$325 double. Rates include full breakfast and evening sweets. AE, DISC, MC, V. **Amenities:** Concierge; computer w/Internet; Jacuzzi. *In room:* CD player, fridge (in some), hair dryer, minibar, Wi-Fi.

Little Tree Bed & Breakfast ★★ Finds Little Tree is one of my favorite Taos bed-and-breakfasts, partly because it's in a beautiful, secluded setting, and partly because it's constructed with real adobe that's been left in its raw state, lending the place an authentic hacienda feel. Two miles down a country road, about midway between Taos and the ski area, it's surrounded by sage and piñon. The charming and cozy rooms have radiant heat under the floors, queen-size beds (one with a king-size), nice medium-size bathrooms, and access to the portal and courtyard garden, at the center of which is the little tree for which the inn is named. The Piñon (my favorite) and Juniper rooms are equipped with fireplaces and private entrances. The Piñon and Aspen rooms offer sunset views. The Spruce Room has a private patio and outdoor hot tub. Visiting hummingbirds enchant guests as they enjoy a scrumptious breakfast on the portal during warmer months. On arrival, guests are treated to refreshments. A courtesy computer with Internet is available for guest use.

County Road B-143 (P.O. Box 509), Arroyo Hondo, NM 87513. ✆ **800/334-8467** or 575/776-8467. www.littletreebandb.com. 4 units. $135–$195 double. Rates include breakfast and afternoon snack. MC, V. **Amenities:** Courtesy computer w/Internet. *In room:* TV/VCR.

Moderate

Old Taos Guesthouse Bed & Breakfast ★ Kids Once a farmer's home and later an artist's estate, this 190-year-old adobe hacienda has been restored by owners and incorrigible ski bums Tim and Leslie Reeves, who, for more than 18 years, have carefully maintained the country charm: Mexican tile in the bathrooms, vigas on the ceilings, and kiva-style fireplaces in most of the rooms. Each room has an entrance from the outside, some off the broad portal that shades the front of the hacienda, some from a grassy lawn in the back, with a view toward the mountains. Some rooms are more utilitarian, some quainter, so make a request depending on your needs. One of my favorites is the Taos Suite, with a king-size bed, a big picture window, and a full kitchen that includes an oven, a stove, a minifridge, and a microwave. Less than 2 miles from the plaza, this inn sits on 7$^1/_2$ acres and provides a cozy northern New Mexico rural experience, complete with an *acequia* (irrigation system), birds galore, and a healthy breakfast. Kids enjoy the inn's dogs and plenty of space to run free.

1028 Witt Rd., Taos, NM 87571. ✆ **800/758-5448** or 575/758-5448. www.oldtaos.com. 10 units. $90–$175 double. Rates include a full breakfast. Ask about seasonal rates. DISC, MC, V. Pets accepted in some rooms with $25 flat fee. **Amenities:** Babysitting; concierge; Jacuzzi; Wi-Fi. *In room:* Hair dryer.

TAOS SKI VALLEY

For information on skiing and the facilities at Taos Ski Valley, see "Skiing Taos," later in this chapter.

A Lodge

Alpine Village Suites ★★ Alpine Village is a small village within Taos Ski Valley, a few steps from the lift. Owned by John and Barbara Cottam, the complex also houses a ski shop and bar/restaurant. The Cottams began with seven rooms, still nice rentals, above their ski shop. Each has a sleeping loft for the agile who care to climb a ladder, as well as sunny windows. The newer section has elegantly decorated rooms, with attractive touches such as Mexican furniture and inventive tile work done by locals. Like most other accommodations at Taos Ski Valley, the rooms are not especially soundproof. Fortunately, most skiers go to bed early. All rooms have VCRs and small kitchenettes equipped with stoves, microwaves, and minifridges. In the newer building, rooms have fireplaces and private balconies. Request a south-facing room for a view of the slopes. The Jacuzzi sits below a lovely mural and has a fireplace and a view of the slopes.

100 Thunderbird Rd. (P.O. Box 98), Taos Ski Valley, NM 87525. ✆ **800/576-2666** or 575/776-8540. Fax 575/776-8542. www.alpine-suites.com. 29 units. Ski season $150–$215 suite for 2, $216–$347 suite for 4, $216–$391 suite for up to 6; summer $66–$172 suite for 2 (includes continental breakfast). AE, DISC, MC, V. Covered valet parking $10 per night. **Amenities:** Jacuzzi; sauna. *In room:* TV/VCR, kitchenette, Wi-Fi (available in all but 2 units).

Condominiums

Expensive

Edelweiss Lodge & Spa ★★ Opened in 2005, this lodge at the base of the mountain took the place of a 1960s classic chalet. Now, it's a brand new condo-hotel. The condominiums are upscale, each with a flagstone fireplace and full kitchen with marble countertops, stainless steel appliances, and many with nice views of the slopes. All have luxury furnishings decorated in earth tones. For those looking for an upscale stay, this is your choice. Hotel rooms follow with the same luxury as the condos. Rooms are medium size with comfortable beds and medium-size bathrooms. Check the website for a glimpse of the rooms and other facilities. Underground parking, a full spa, an excellent restaurant, and valet service for your skis add to the appeal.

106 Sutton Place, Taos Ski Valley, NM 87525. ✆ **800/I-LUV-SKI** (458-8754) or 575/737-6900. Fax 575/737-6995. www.edelweisslodgeandspa.com. 31 units. Hotel room winter $220–$440 double; summer $125 double; condo winter $275–$1,156, summer $198–$375 (ranges cover 1 bedroom/1 bathroom to 3 bedrooms/3 bathrooms). AE, DISC, MC, V. Free parking. **Amenities:** Restaurant; bar; concierge; health club; 2 Jacuzzis; sauna; spa; Wi-Fi (in lobby). *In room:* TV, hair dryer, Internet.

Powderhorn Suites and Condominiums ★ (Value) A cozy, homelike feel and Euro-Southwestern ambience make this condo-inn one of the best buys in Taos Ski Valley, just a 2-minute walk from the lift. You'll find consistency and quality here, with clean medium-size rooms, mountain views, vaulted ceilings, well-planned bathrooms, and comfortable beds. The larger suites have stoves, balconies, and fireplaces. Adjoining rooms are good for families. Like almost all the accommodations in Taos Ski Valley, Powderhorn has been "condo-ized" so each suite has a distinct owner; thus the service isn't what you would find at a full-service hotel, though it is still conscientious. There's no elevator, so if stairs are a problem for you, make sure to ask for a room on the ground floor.

5 Ernie Blake Rd. (P.O. Box 69), Taos Ski Valley, NM 87525. ✆ **800/776-2346** or 575/776-2341. Fax 575/776-2341, ext. 103. www.taoswebb.com/powderhorn. 17 units. Ski season $99–$165 double, $130–$200 suite, $195–$400 condo; summer $69–$129. 2- to 6-person occupancy. MC, V. Valet parking. **Amenities:** 2 Jacuzzis. *In room:* TV, kitchenette, Wi-Fi.

Sierra del Sol Condominiums ★ I have wonderful memories of these condominiums, which are just a 2-minute walk from the lift; family friends used to invite me to stay with them when I was young. I'm happy to say that the units, built in the 1960s, with additions through the years, have been well maintained. Though they're privately owned, and therefore decorated at the whim of the owners, management does inspect them every year and make suggestions. They're smartly built and come in a few sizes: studio, one-bedroom, and two-bedroom. The one- and two-bedroom units have big living rooms with fireplaces and porches that look out on the ski runs. The bedrooms are spacious, and some have sleeping lofts. Each has a full kitchen, with a dishwasher, stove, oven, microwave, and refrigerator. Two-bedroom units sleep up to six. Grills and picnic tables on the grounds sit near a mountain river.

13 Thunderbird Rd. (P.O. Box 84), Taos Ski Valley, NM 87525. ✆ **800/523-3954** or 575/776-2981. Fax 575/776-2347. www.sierrataos.com. 32 units. Prices range from $79 for studio in summer to $414 for 2-bedroom condo in high season. DISC, MC, V. Free parking. **Amenities:** Babysitting; 2 Jacuzzis; 2 saunas; Wi-Fi (in conference room). *In room:* TV/DVD, hair dryer, kitchen.

Snakedance Condominiums and Spa ★★ A $3.5-million renovation has transformed the rooms of this former hotel into elegant condominiums. Skiers appreciate the inn's location, just steps from the lift, as well as amenities such as ski storage and boot dryers. The original structure that stood on this site was known as the Hondo Lodge. Before there was a Taos Ski Valley, Hondo Lodge served as a refuge for fishermen, hunters, and artists. The Snakedance Condominiums today are privately owned units, so each may differ some, though they are consistent in quality. All are bright, comfortable spaces, with French-door-accessible balconies and kitchens with granite counters, ranges, fridges, dishwashers, and microwaves. All have gas fireplaces. The hotel also offers shuttle service to and from nearby shops and restaurants, and, at certain times, to Albuquerque and Santa Fe.

110 Sutton Place (P.O. Box 89), Taos Ski Valley, NM 87525. ✆ **800/322-9815** or 575/776-2277. Fax 575/776-1410. www.snakedancecondos.com. 33 units. 1-bedroom condo $225–$400 double in winter, in summer $95; 2-bedroom condo $285–$600 for 4 people in winter, $120 in summer; 2-bedroom loft condo $345–$725 for 6 people in winter, $150 in summer. Extra person $30 in winter, $10 in summer. Rates include a complimentary continental breakfast. AE, DC, DISC, MC, V. Free parking at Taos Ski Valley parking lot. Closed mid-Apr to Memorial Day and mid-Oct to mid-Nov. **Amenities:** Restaurant; bar; health club; Jacuzzi; spa. *In room:* TV, hair dryer, kitchen, Wi-Fi.

Moderate

Taos Mountain Lodge (Value) These loft suites (which can each accommodate up to six) provide airy, comfortable lodging for a good price. Built in 1990, about a mile west of Taos Ski Valley on the road from Taos, the place has undergone some renovation over the years. Don't expect a lot of privacy in these condominiums, but they're good for a romping ski vacation. The beds are comfortable and the bathrooms are small but functional. Each unit has a small bedroom downstairs and a loft bedroom upstairs, as well as a fold-out or futon couch in the living room. Regular rooms have kitchenettes, with minifridges and stoves; deluxe rooms have full kitchens, with full refrigerators, stoves, and ovens.

Taos Ski Valley Rd. (P.O. Box 202), Taos Ski Valley, NM 87525. ✆ **866/320-8267** or 575/776-2229. Fax 575/776-3982. www.taosmountainlodge.com. 10 units. Ski season $119–$280 suite; May–Oct $80–$100 suite. AE, DISC, MC, V. *In room:* TV, kitchen or kitchenette, hair dryer.

RV Parks & Campgrounds

Carson National Forest There are nine national forest camping areas within 20 miles of Taos; these developed areas are open from Memorial Day to Labor Day. They range from woodsy, streamside sites on the road to Taos Ski Valley to open lowlands with lots of sage. Call the Forest Service to discuss the best location for your needs.

208 Cruz Alta Rd., Taos, NM 87571. ✆ **575/758-6200.** www.fs.fed.us/r3/carson. Fees range from $7–$15 per night. No credit cards.

Taos Valley RV Park and Campground ★ Just 2½ miles south of the plaza, this lovely, well-maintained campground is surrounded by sage and offers views of the surrounding mountains. Each site has a picnic table and grill. The place has a small store, a laundry room, a playground, and tent shelters, as well as a dump station and very clean restrooms. Pets are welcome. Wireless Internet access is available throughout the park.

120 Este Rd., off NM 68 (7204 NDCBU), Taos, NM 87571. ✆ **800/999-7571** or 575/758-4469. Fax 575/758-4469. www.camptaos.com/rv. 95 spaces. $22 without RV hookup; $30–$39 with RV hookup. AE, DISC, MC, V.

4 WHERE TO DINE

Taos is not a late-night place; most restaurants finish serving at about 9pm. For the locations of these restaurants, see the map "Central Taos Accommodations & Dining," on p. 205.

EXPENSIVE

De La Tierra ★★★ NEW AMERICAN Located in the eco-resort El Monte Sagrado (p. 204), this restaurant offers delectably inventive American cuisine in an old-world Orient ambience, with a high ceiling, comfortable black silk chairs, and elegant contemporary art on the walls. Service is excellent. The chef utilizes seasonal and local ingredients, including organic ones when he can. For starters, you might have winter squash raviolis in a caramel orange broth, or a Caesar salad with tamale croutons. For a main course, the beef tenderloin is very juicy, served with potato enchiladas and Swiss chard. The pan roasted East Coast cod served with truffle Persian potatoes is delectable. Kids have their own menu here. Excellent food, including Sunday brunch, is served during the day at the Gardens, a more casual spot, with lots of exotic plants and a lovely patio. Meals are also served at the **Anaconda Bar** (p. 235).

In the El Monte Sagrado hotel (p. 204), 317 Kit Carson Rd. ✆ **800/828-TAOS** (8267) or 575/758-3502. www.elmontesagrado.com/dining/de_la_tierra.asp. Reservations recommended. The Gardens breakfast $7–$12; lunch $8–$16; De La Tierra dinner $19–$39. AE, DC, DISC, MC, V. The Gardens daily 7am–3pm; De La Tierra Sun–Thurs 6–9pm, Fri–Sat 6–10pm.

Doc Martin's ★ NEW AMERICAN Doc Martin's serves innovative food in a historic setting. The chef uses local and organic ingredients, and wild game, when available. In the rich atmosphere of a thick-walled adobe home with a kiva fireplace, diners feast on Southwestern breakfast fare such as a grilled organic buffalo patty and eggs, with wild mushroom gravy and home fries or blue corn and blueberry hotcakes. Lunch might include the house specialty, Doc's Chile relleno or a turkey, avocado, bacon, and green chile sandwich. For dinner, a good bet is the almond-dusted ruby trout with posole (hominy) or the rack of red deer with roasted potatoes. If you still have room, there's always a nice selection of desserts—try the chocolate-mousse cake or the *capirotada* (New Mexican bread pudding). The **Adobe Bar** (p. 235) has live jazz with no cover charge. Brunch is served on Saturdays and Sundays from 7:30am to 2:30pm.

In the Historic Taos Inn (p. 206), 125 Paseo del Pueblo Norte. ✆ **575/758-1977.** www.taosinn.com. Reservations recommended. Breakfast $5–$10; lunch $7–$15; dinner $18–$30. AE, DISC, MC, V. Daily 7:30–11am, 11:30am–2:30pm, and 5:30–9pm.

El Meze ★★ Finds SPANISH/MEDITERRANEAN Meaning "table" in Arabic, El Meze offers delicious Spanish/Mediterranean food with Moorish influences. The creation of Fred Muller, who for years ran the popular Fred's Place, this new restaurant is set in El Torreon, an 1847 hacienda with the vigas (wooden beams), walls painted orange and green, a gold fireplace, and bright contemporary art on the walls. A classically trained chef, Muller puts much thought into his food and its preparation. Service is helpful and efficient. Dinner might begin with grilled prawns with lemon and Moroccan spices, and move onto a butternut squash and chick pea soup with smoked ham hock. For an entree I've enjoyed a terrific Chilean sea bass with sweet potatoes, fennel, and andouille sausage in a rich broth. Another excellent offering is the grilled double cut lamb chops cooked with lavender and served with vegetable jus and fried garlic chips. For dessert, the chocolate truffle soufflé is as good as it sounds. A thoughtful beer and wine list accompanies the menu.

1017 Paseo del Pueblo Norte. ✆ **575/751-3337.** www.elmeze.com. Reservations recommended. Main courses $18–$32. AE, DISC, MC, V. Mon–Sat 5:30–9:30pm in summer; winter hours vary, call ahead.

Joseph's Table ★★★ Finds NEW AMERICAN/MEDITERRANEAN This notable eatery, in the Hotel La Fonda de Taos on the plaza, serves some of the most imaginative and precisely prepared food in northern New Mexico. The ambience is something like old-west saloon meets sophisticated artist's home. Hand-painted pastel flowers decorate the walls and pussy-willow-and-iron chandeliers hang between hand-hewn vigas on the ceiling. There are hardwood floors and some Asian-style tables with pillow seating along the back. Chef/owner Joseph Wrede (once selected as one of the 10

"Best New Chefs" in America by *Food & Wine Magazine*) creates such delicacies as a juicy green-chile buffalo cheeseburger served with a mixed green salad for lunch. Dinner is equally inventive. It might start with mussels and move on to pepper-crusted beef tenderloin over butter mashed potatoes or a soy-cured duck breast with a sweet potato tamal. There's typically a vegetarian option as well. Be aware that Wrede likes complex flavors, so those who prefer more conservative food might opt for the Stakeout (see below). The friendly and attentive servers can help guide you through the menu, so be sure to ask. An eclectic selection of beers and wines by the bottle and glass is available.

In the Hotel La Fonda de Taos (p. 207), 108-A S. Taos Plaza. ✆ **575/751-4512.** www.josephstable.com. Reservations recommended. Main courses $8–$18 lunch, $18–$35 dinner. AE, DISC, MC, V. May–Aug Mon–Sat 11:30am–2:30pm and daily 5:30–10pm; Sun brunch 10:30am–2:30pm. Hours are abbreviated in winter; call first.

Lambert's of Taos ★★ CONTINENTAL Set in the historic Randall Home, this restaurant offers the fine touch of new owner Joseph Wrede (see above review for Joseph's Table), while maintaining a more continental tradition reminiscent of its founder, Zeke Lambert. It's a sparsely decorated hacienda with wood floors and lacy curtains—a nice spot for a romantic evening. The service is good. You might start with roasted rock shrimp dusted with red chile, or the spinach salad with sautéed mushrooms and bacon in a walnut raspberry dressing, which is excellent. For an entree, the pepper-crusted lamb—very peppery—served with garlic pasta is a signature dish, but you might opt for one of the fresh fish specials, such as seared ahi tuna, or a game special such as buffalo tenderloin. A full bar, with an interesting wine and beer list and espresso coffee, is available. The restaurant also has a cozy lounge with its own menu.

309 Paseo del Pueblo Sur. ✆ **575/758-1009.** www.lambertsoftaos.com. Reservations recommended. Main courses $15–$35. AE, DC, DISC, MC, V. Daily 5pm–closing, usually 9pm or so.

Stakeout Grill & Bar ★★ CONTINENTAL/STEAKS/SEAFOOD This is one of northern New Mexico's most adventurous dining experiences. You drive about a mile up a dirt road toward the base of the Sangre de Cristo Mountains to reach the restaurant, and dine looking down on the Taos gorge while the sun sets over the Jemez Range. The warm, rustic decor of this sprawling hacienda with a broad patio (a great place to sit in summer) includes creaking hardwood floors—and a crackling fireplace in the winter. The fare, which focuses on steak and seafood, is fresh and thoughtfully prepared. Start with baked brie with sliced almonds and apples, or green-chile crab cakes with citrus aioli. Move on to a filet mignon served with béarnaise sauce, or sample one of the chef's excellent pasta specials. Recently, I had shrimp over linguini with goat cheese that was a bowl of pure joy. This is also the place to come if you have a craving for lobster. Try to time your reservation so you can see the sunset. A full bar, an extensive wine list, and cigars are available.

101 Stakeout Dr. (9 miles south of Taos, just off Hwy. 68). ✆ **575/758-2042.** www.stakeoutrestaurant.com. Reservations recommended. Main courses $20–$70. AE, DC, DISC, MC, V. Daily 5–9:30pm.

MODERATE

Graham's Grille ★★ NEW AMERICAN This restaurant opened in 2007 and offers comfort food with a Southwestern flair. It's set in a long, narrow space just off the plaza, a cozy urban atmosphere with hanging halogen lamps and a long bench along one wall. Meals might start with delectable flour tortilla crisps. The must-have appetizer is the baked mac and cheese with green chile and bacon, but if that sounds too rich, the grilled artichokes served with lemon aioli will also please. Lunches offer soup, salad, and

 Family-Friendly Restaurants

Lula's (p. 215) A relaxed atmosphere and lots of sandwich choices, as well as soups, are sure to please here.

Orlando's New Mexican Café (p. 216) The relaxed atmosphere and playfully colorful walls will please the kids almost as much as the tacos and quesadillas made especially for them.

Taos Cow (p. 216) Pot pies and sandwiches will fill kids up before they dive into the all-natural ice cream at this cafe north of town.

Taos Pizza Out Back (see below) The pizza will please parents and kids alike, and so will all the odd decorations, such as the chain with foot-long links hanging over the front counter.

sandwich combinations. The town is buzzing about the salmon BLT, which is just what it sounds, salmon with good bacon, lettuce, and tomato. Burritos, tamale pie, and burgers—even veggie, buffalo, and lamb ones—come on house-made buns. For dinner, the spice-crusted grilled salmon with Israeli cous cous is the most popular dish here; the Moroccan chicken, also served with cous cous, runs a close second. For dessert, the chocolate nachos are a real novelty, but my favorite is the mango coconut cake. A select beer and wine list accompanies the menu.

106 Paseo del Pueblo Norte. ✆ **575/751-1350.** www.grahamsgrille.com. AE, MC, V. Reservations recommended at dinner. Main courses $7–$11 lunch; $14–$20 dinner. Mon–Sat 11am–2pm and 5–9pm.

Old Blinking Light ★ AMERICAN This restaurant on the Ski Valley Road provides tasty American food in a casual atmosphere. It's named for the blinking yellow light that was once the marker Taoseños used to give directions ("turn left at the blinking light," and so on), now replaced by a stoplight. Decorated with brightly painted furniture, this restaurant is a good place to stop after skiing or for a romping night of music. The service is friendly and efficient. To accompany the free chips and homemade salsa, order a margarita—preferably their standard, made with Sauza Gold Tequila—and sip it next to the patio bonfire, open evenings year-round. The menu is broad, ranging from salads and burgers to steaks, seafood, and Mexican food. I say head straight for the fajitas, especially the jumbo shrimp wrapped in bacon and stuffed with poblano peppers and jack cheese. Leave room for the Old Blinking Light mud pie, made with local Taos Cow ice cream. Live music plays on Monday and Friday nights.

US 150, mile marker 1. ✆ **575/776-8787.** Reservations recommended Fri–Sat and Mon nights. Main courses $9–$26. AE, MC, V. Wine shop daily noon–10pm. Restaurant daily 5–10pm.

Taos Pizza Out Back ★ Kids PASTA/PIZZA My kayaking buddies always go here after a day on the river. That will give you an idea of the level of informality (very), as well as the quality of the food and beer (great), and the size of the portions (large). It's a raucous old hippie-decorated adobe restaurant, with a friendly and eager waitstaff. What to order? I have one big word here: PIZZA. Sure the spicy Greek pasta is good, as is the Veggie Zone (a calzone filled with stir-fried veggies and two cheeses)—but, why? The pizzas are incredible. All come with a delicious thin crust (no sogginess here) that's folded over on the edges and sprinkled with sesame seeds. The sauce is unthinkably tasty, and the variations are broad. There's the Killer, with sun-dried tomatoes, Gorgonzola, green chile, and black olives; and my favorite, pizza Florentine (spinach, basil, sun-dried tomatoes, chicken breast, mushrooms, capers, and garlic, sautéed in white wine). Check out the small selection of wines and large selection of microbrews.

712 Paseo del Pueblo Norte (just north of Allsup's). ✆ **575/758-3112.** Reservations recommended Sat–Sun and holidays. Pizzas $13–$28; pastas and calzones $10–$13. MC, V. Summer daily 11am–10pm; winter Sun–Thurs 11am–9pm, Fri–Sat 11am–10pm.

Trading Post Café ★★ Finds NORTHERN ITALIAN/INTERNATIONAL One of my tastiest writing assignments was when I did a profile of this restaurant for the *New York Times.* Chef/owner René Mettler spent 3 hours serving course after course of dishes prepared especially for us. If you think this gastronomical orgy might color my opinion, just ask anyone in town where he or she most likes to eat. Even notables such as Dennis Hopper and Gene Hackman will likely name the Trading Post. What draws the crowds here is a gallery atmosphere, where rough plastered walls washed with an orange hue are set off by sculptures, paintings, and photographs. If you show up without reservations, be prepared to wait for a table, and don't expect quiet romance: The place bustles. A bar encloses an open-exhibition kitchen. If you're dining alone or just don't feel like waiting for a table, the bar is a fun place to sit. Although the focus is on the fine food, diners can feel comfortable here, even if trying three appetizers and skipping the main course. The outstanding Caesar salad has an interesting twist—garlic chips. You'll find a nice variety of pastas on the menu; the fettuccine alla carbonara is tasty, as is the seafood pasta. Heartier appetites might like the New Zealand lamb chops with tomato-mint sauce. A good list of beers and wines rounds out the experience.

4179 Paseo del Pueblo Sur, Ranchos de Taos. ✆ **575/758-5089.** Reservations recommended. Menu items $8–$30. AE, DC, DISC, MC, V. Tues–Sat 11:30am–9:30pm; Sun 4–9:30pm.

INEXPENSIVE

Gutiz ★★ Finds FRENCH/NUEVO LATINO Between azure walls hung with bright contemporary art, this restaurant, the creation of Chef Eduardo Gutiz, serves some of Taos's most unique and flavorful cuisine. Born in Spain, raised in France, he traveled in Peru and Bolivia. From these locales, he's combined flavors using organic greens and fresh meats and fish, and a broad variety of chile peppers. Service is friendly and efficient. Breakfast brings delicacies such as my favorite, the Taoseño (some mornings I wake up in Santa Fe and want to drive to Taos just to eat this!)—rice, potatoes, chile, cheese, and fresh herbs baked in a ceramic dish and then topped with scrambled eggs. The French toast is thick, made with home-baked bread. Lunch might begin with a niçoise salad made with fresh tuna, French beans, veggies, potatoes, and niçoise olives. Another favorite is the tilapia, cooked with white wine. The many, varied sandwiches come on homemade bread. Alongside the great food, sip from a variety of coffees and chai tea.

812-B Paseo del Pueblo Norte. ✆ **575/758-1226.** Main courses $6.50–$15. No credit cards. Tues–Sun 7am–4pm (3pm in winter). In summer, call to see if the chef is serving dinner.

Lula's ★★ Kids AMERICAN/LIGHT FARE A few blocks south of the plaza, this new deli is run by the same folks as the excellent Taos Pizza Out Back (see above), and offers gourmet soups and sandwiches and a select few diner-style meals between sun-colored walls, as well as meals to go. Most of the tables here, tall and glass, with stools, don't quite match the comfort level of the food, so diners tend to grab the few regular wooden ones, which you should try to do, too. You order at a counter and the food is served at your table relatively quickly. Paninis are a big draw here, the one with roasted eggplant, roasted red bell peppers, zucchini, spinach, provolone, and pesto a real favorite, as is the Wellington sandwich, which has sliced roast beef, caramelized onions, and sharp cheddar on a ciabatta roll. The nightly blue-plate specials served after 4pm on weekdays and all day Saturday may include all-American meat loaf with a twice-baked potato or veggie lasagna, to name a few. A kids menu pleases the tots, and lots of good teas and coffees wash it all down.

316 Paseo del Pueblo Sur. ✆ **575/751-1280.** Main courses lunch and dinner $5–$13. MC. V. Mon–Sat in summer 11am–9pm; in winter Mon–Fri 11am–8pm, Sat 11am–6pm.

Orlando's New Mexican Café ★ **Kids** NEW MEXICAN Festivity reigns in this spicy little cafe on the north end of town. Serving some of northern New Mexico's best chile, this place has colorful tables set around a bustling open kitchen and airy patio dining during warmer months. Service is friendly but minimal. Try the Los Colores, their most popular dish, with three enchiladas (chicken, beef, and cheese) smothered in chile and served with beans and *posole* (a Mexican stew). The taco salad is another favorite. Portions are big here, and you can order a Mexican or microbrew beer, or a New Mexican or California wine.

114 Don Juan Valdez Ln. (1¾ miles north of the plaza, off Paseo del Pueblo Norte). ✆ **575/751-1450.** Reservations not accepted. Main courses under $12. MC, V. Daily 10:30am–3pm and 5–9pm.

NORTH OF TOWN

Taos Cow ★ **Kids** DELI/DESSERT Set in one of my favorite villages, Taos Cow offers fun breakfast and lunch fare in a relaxed atmosphere—and, of course, ice cream! Diners order and pick up at a counter. A variety of sandwiches and soups are made with fresh ingredients ranging from black forest ham to portobello mushrooms. The real reason to come here is the hormone-free ice cream in a variety of flavors. My favorite is the Cherry Ristra, with piñon nuts and chocolate chunks. Kids love their shakes. On chillier afternoons, there's espresso, cappuccino, and hot chocolate to warm you after a day on the slopes.

485 Hwy. 150, Arroyo Seco. ✆ **575/776-5640.** All menu items under $12. AE, DISC, MC, V. Daily 7am–7pm in summer; 7am–6pm in winter.

5 WHAT TO SEE & DO

With a history shaped by pre-Columbian civilization, Spanish colonialism, and the Wild West; outdoor activities that range from ballooning to world-class skiing; and a clustering of artists, writers, and musicians, Taos has something to offer almost everybody. Its pueblo is the most accessible in New Mexico, and its museums represent a world-class display of regional history and culture. In addition to the "Taos Attractions" map in this section, see also "The Taos Area (Including Enchanted Circle)" map, on p. 227.

THE TOP ATTRACTIONS

Millicent Rogers Museum ★ This museum offers a glimpse of some of the finest Southwestern arts and crafts anywhere, but it's small enough to avoid being overwhelming. It was founded in 1953 by Millicent Rogers's family members after her death. Rogers was a wealthy Taos émigré who, in 1947, began acquiring a magnificent collection of

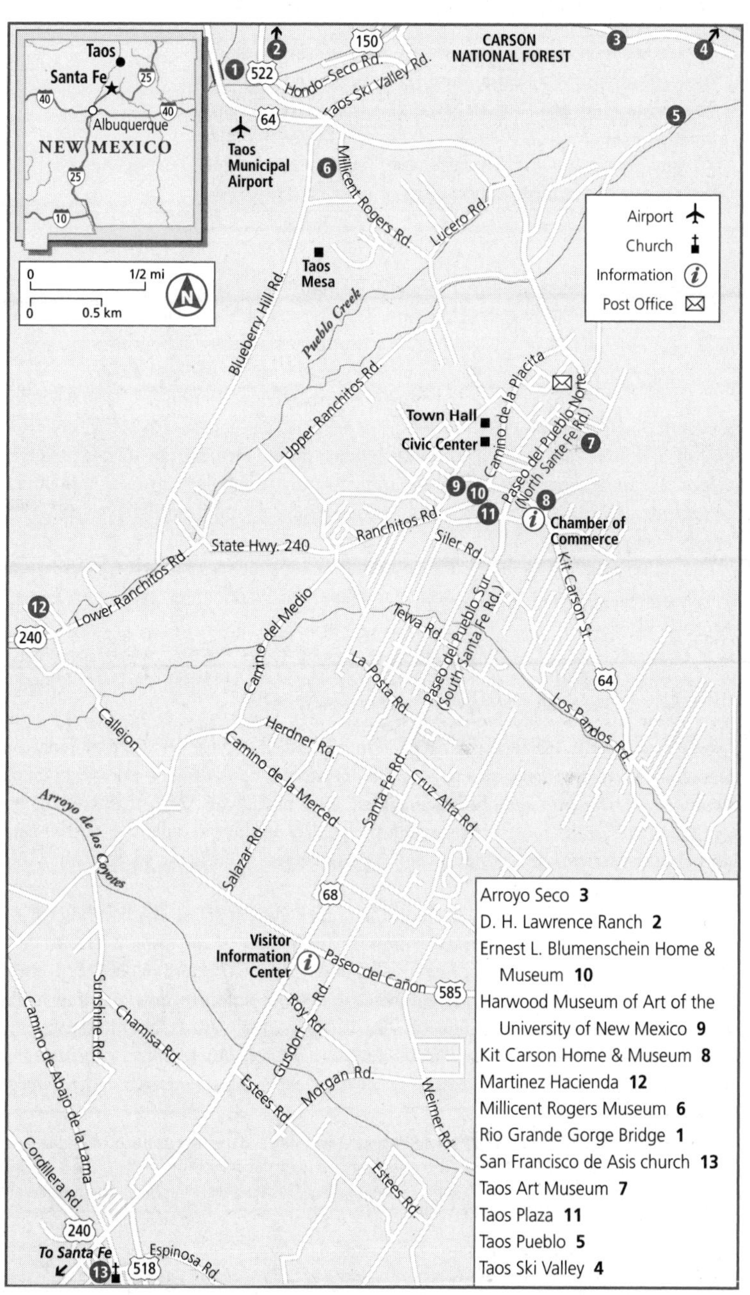

Taos
Santa Fe
Albuquerque
NEW MEXICO
CARSON NATIONAL FOREST
Taos Municipal Airport
Taos Mesa
Town Hall
Civic Center
Chamber of Commerce
Visitor Information Center
To Santa Fe
Airport
Church
Information
Post Office
Arroyo Seco 3
D. H. Lawrence Ranch 2
Ernest L. Blumenschein Home & Museum 10
Harwood Museum of Art of the University of New Mexico 9
Kit Carson Home & Museum 8
Martinez Hacienda 12
Millicent Rogers Museum 6
Rio Grande Gorge Bridge 1
San Francisco de Asis church 13
Taos Art Museum 7
Taos Plaza 11
Taos Pueblo 5
Taos Ski Valley 4

Tips A Tip for Museumgoers

If you'd like to visit five museums that make up the Museum Association of Taos—Blumenschein Home, Martinez Hacienda, Harwood Museum, Millicent Rogers Museum, and Taos Art Museum—you'll save money by purchasing a combination ticket for $25. The ticket allows one-time entry to each museum during a 1-year period and is fully transferable. You may purchase the pass at any of the five museums. For more information, call ✆ **575/758-0505.**

beautiful Native American arts and crafts. Included are Navajo and Pueblo jewelry, Navajo textiles, Pueblo pottery, Hopi and Zuni katsina (kachina) dolls, paintings from the Rio Grande Pueblo people, and basketry from a wide variety of Southwestern tribes. The museum also presents exhibitions of Southwestern art, crafts, and design.

Since the 1970s, the scope of the museum's permanent collection has been expanded to include Anglo arts and crafts and Hispanic religious and secular arts and crafts, from Spanish and Mexican colonial to contemporary times. Included are *santos* (religious images), furniture, weavings, *colcha* embroideries, and decorative tinwork. Agricultural implements, domestic utensils, and craftspeople's tools dating from the 17th and 18th centuries are also displayed.

The museum gift shop has a fine collection of superior regional art. Classes, workshops, lectures, and field trips are held throughout the year. Plan to spend 1 to 2 hours exploring the museum.

Off US 64, 4 miles north of Taos Plaza, on Millicent Rogers Rd. ✆ **575/758-2462.** www.millicentrogers.org. Admission $10 adults, $8 students and seniors, $2 children 6–16, $18 family rate. Daily 10am–5pm. Closed Mon Nov–Mar, Easter, Thanksgiving, Christmas, New Year's Day.

San Francisco de Asis church ★★ On NM 68, about 4 miles south of Taos, this famous church appears as a modern adobe sculpture with no doors or windows, an image that has often been photographed and painted, most notably by Ansel Adams and Georgia O'Keeffe. Visitors must walk through the garden on the east side to enter the two-story church and get a full perspective of its massive walls, authentic adobe plaster, and beauty.

A video presentation is given in the church office every hour on the half-hour. Also, displayed on the wall is an unusual painting, *The Shadow of the Cross,* by Henri Ault (1896). Under ordinary light, it portrays a barefoot Christ, at the Sea of Galilee; in darkness, however, the portrait becomes luminescent, and the perfect shadow of a cross forms over the left shoulder of Jesus' silhouette. The artist reportedly was as shocked as everyone else to see this. The reason for the illusion remains a mystery. A few crafts shops surround the square. Plan to spend a half-hour to an hour exploring the church and shopping here.

Ranchos de Taos Plaza. ✆ **575/758-2754.** Admission $3 for video and mystery painting. Mon–Sat 9am–4pm. Visitors may attend Mass Mon–Fri 5pm, Sat 6pm (Mass rotates from this church to the 3 mission chapels), Sun 7 (in Spanish), 9, and 11:30am. Closed to the public 1st 2 weeks in June, when repairs are done (however services still take place).

Taos Art Museum ★ Finds Set in the home of Russian artist Nicolai Fechin (*Feh-shin*), this collection displays works of the Taos Society of Artists, which give a sense of what Taos was like in the late 19th and early 20th centuries. The works are rich and varied, including panoramas and images of the Native American and Hispanic villagers. The setting in what was Fechin's home from 1927 until 1933 is truly unique. The historic building commemorates his career. Born in Russia in 1881, Fechin came to the United States in 1923, already acclaimed as a master of painting, drawing, sculpture, architecture, and woodwork. In Taos, he renovated the home and embellished it with hand-carved doors, windows, gates, posts, fireplaces, and other features of a Russian country home. Fechin died in 1955. Though the collection and home are interesting, some visitors balk at the price. If you're one of those, you can at least see Fechin's studio, which is attached to the gift shop, for free. Also, bear in mind that this museum is privately funded, so your dollars are a real help. Plan to spend 1 hour here.

227 Paseo del Pueblo Norte. ✆ **575/758-2690.** www.taosmuseums.org. Admission $8 adults, $7 seniors, $4 children 6–12, free for children 5 and under. Summer Thurs–Sun 10am–5pm; call for winter hours.

Taos Historic Museums ★★ Two historical homes are operated as museums, affording visitors a glimpse of early Taos lifestyles. The Martinez Hacienda and Ernest Blumenschein home each has unique appeal.

The **Martinez Hacienda,** Lower Ranchitos Road, Highway 240 (✆ **575/758-1000**), is one of the only Spanish colonial haciendas in the United States that's open to the public year-round. This was the home of the merchant, trader, and *alcalde* (mayor) Don Antonio Severino Martinez, who bought it in 1804 and lived here until his death in 1827. His eldest son was Padre Antonio José Martinez, northern New Mexico's controversial spiritual leader from 1826 to 1867. Located on the west bank of the Rio Pueblo de Taos, about 2 miles southwest of the plaza, the museum is remarkably beautiful, with thick, raw adobe walls. The hacienda has no exterior windows—this was to protect against raids by Plains tribes.

Twenty-one rooms were built around two *placitas,* or interior courtyards. They give you a glimpse of the austerity of frontier lives, with only a few pieces of modest period furniture in each. You'll see bedrooms, stables, a kitchen, and a large fiesta room. Exhibits tell the story of the Martinez family and life in Spanish Taos between 1598 and 1821, when Mexico gained control. Taos Historic Museums has developed the Martinez Hacienda into a living museum with weavers, blacksmiths, and wood carvers. Demonstrations are scheduled daily.

The **Ernest L. Blumenschein Home & Museum,** 222 Ledoux St. (✆ **575/758-0505**), 1½ blocks southwest of the plaza, re-creates the lifestyle of one of the founders of the Taos Society of Artists (founded 1915). An adobe home with garden walls and a courtyard, parts of which date from the 1790s, it became the home and studio of Blumenschein (1874–1960) and his family in 1919. Period furnishings include European antiques and handmade Taos furniture in Spanish colonial style.

Blumenschein was born and raised in Cincinnati. In 1898, after training in New York and Paris, he and fellow painter Bert Phillips were on assignment for *Harper's* and *McClure's* magazines of New York when a wheel of their wagon broke 30 miles north of Taos. Blumenschein drew the short straw and thus was obliged to bring the wheel by horseback to Taos for repair. He later recounted his initial reaction to the valley he entered: "No artist had ever recorded the New Mexico I was now seeing. No writer had ever written down the smell of this air or the feel of that morning sky. I was receiving . . . the first great unforgettable inspiration of my life. My destiny was being decided."

That spark later led to the foundation of Taos as an art colony. An extensive collection of works by early-20th-century Taos artists, including some by Blumenschein's wife,

Mary, and daughter, Helen, are on display in several rooms of the home. Wandering through the home takes about an hour.

222 Ledoux St. © **575/758-0505** (information for both museums can be obtained at this number). www.taoshistoricmuseums.org. Admission for each museum $8 adults, $4 children ages 6–16, free for children 5 and under. Summer daily 9am–5pm; call for winter hours.

Taos Pueblo ★★★ It's amazing that in our frenetic world more than 100 Taos Pueblo residents still live much as their ancestors did 1,000 years ago. When you enter the pueblo, you'll see two large buildings, both with rooms piled on top of each other, forming structures that echo the shape of Taos Mountain (which sits to the northeast). Here, a portion of Taos residents live without electricity and running water. The remaining 2,000 residents of Taos Pueblo live in conventional homes on the pueblo's 95,000 acres.

The main buildings' distinctive flowing lines of shaped mud, with a straw-and-mud exterior plaster, are typical of Pueblo architecture throughout the Southwest. It's architecture that blends in with the surrounding land. Bright blue doors are the same shade as the sky that frames the brown buildings.

The northernmost of New Mexico's 19 pueblos, Taos Pueblo has been home to the Tiwa tribes for more than 900 years. Many residents here still practice ancestral rituals. The center of their world is still nature; women use hornos to bake bread, and most still drink water that flows down from the sacred Blue Lake. Meanwhile, arts and crafts and other tourism-related businesses support the economy, along with government services, ranching, and farming.

The village looks much the same today as it did when a regiment from Coronado's expedition first came upon it in 1540. Though the Tiwa were essentially a peaceful agrarian people, they are perhaps best remembered for spearheading the only successful revolt by Native Americans in history. Launched by Pope (poh-*pay*) in 1680, the uprising drove the Spanish from Santa Fe until 1692, and from Taos until 1698.

As you explore the pueblo, you can visit the residents' studios, sample homemade bread, look into the **San Geronimo Chapel,** and wander past the fascinating ruins of the old church and cemetery. You're expected to ask permission from individuals before taking their photos; some will ask for a small payment. Do not trespass into kivas (ceremonial rooms) and other areas marked as restricted.

The **Feast of San Geronimo** (the patron saint of Taos Pueblo), on September 29 and 30, marks the end of the harvest season. The feast day is reminiscent of an ancient trade fair for the Taos Indians, when tribes from as far south as South America and as far north as the Arctic would come and trade for wares, hides, clothing, and harvested crops. The day is filled with foot races, pole climbing done by traditional Indian clowns, and artists and craftspeople mimicking the early traders. Dances are performed the evening of September 29. Other annual events include a **turtle dance** on New Year's Day, **deer or buffalo dances** on Three Kings Day (Jan 6), **corn dances** on Santa Cruz Day (May 3), San Antonio Day (June 13), San Juan Day (June 24), Santiago Day (July 25), and Santa Ana Day (July 26). The annual **Taos Pueblo Powwow,** a dance competition and parade that brings together tribes from throughout North America, is held the second weekend of July on tribal lands off NM 522 (see "Calendar of Events," in chapter 3). The pueblo Christmas celebration begins on Christmas Eve, with bonfires and a procession with children's dances. On Christmas day, the deer or **Matachine dances** take place (p. 38).

During your visit to the pueblo you will have the opportunity to purchase traditional fried and oven-baked bread as well as a variety of arts and crafts. If you would like to try traditional feast-day meals, the **Tiwa Kitchen,** near the entrance to the pueblo, is a good place to stop. Close to Tiwa Kitchen is the **Oo-oonah Children's Art Center,** where you can see the creative works of pueblo children.

As with many of the other pueblos in New Mexico, Taos Pueblo has opened a casino. **Taos Mountain Casino** (✆ **888/WIN-TAOS** [946-8267]; www.taosmountaincasino.com) is on the main road to Taos Pueblo and features slot machines, blackjack, and poker.

Note: To learn more about the pueblo and its people, I highly recommend taking a 30-minute guided tour. Ask upon arrival when the next one will be given and where you should meet your guide. Plan to spend 2 or more hours here.

Veterans Hwy. (P.O. Box 1846), Taos Pueblo. (From Paseo del Pueblo Norte, travel north 2 miles on Veterans Hwy.) ✆ **575/758-1028.** www.taospueblo.com. Admission cost, as well as camera, video, and sketching fees, subject to change on a yearly basis; be sure to ask about telephoto lenses and digital cameras; photography not permitted on feast days. Daily 8am–4:30pm, with a few exceptions. Guided tours available. Closed for 45 consecutive days every year late winter or early spring (call ahead). Also, because this is a living community, you can expect periodic closures.

MORE ATTRACTIONS

D. H. Lawrence Ranch A trip to this ranch north of Taos leads you into odd realms of devotion for the controversial early-20th-century author who lived and wrote in the area in the early '20s. A short uphill walk from the ranch home (not open to visitors) is the D. H. Lawrence Memorial, a little white shrine, adorned inside by his favorite symbol, a rising phoenix. The guest book is interesting: One couple wrote of trying for 24 years to get here from England.

NM 522, San Cristobal. ✆ **575/776-2245.** Free admission. Daily 8am–5pm. To reach the site, head north from Taos about 15 miles on NM 522, and then another 6 miles east into the forested Sangre de Cristo Range via a well-marked dirt road.

Harwood Museum of Art of the University of New Mexico ★ With its high ceilings and broad wood floors, this museum is a lovely place to wander among New Mexico–inspired images. A cultural and community center since 1923, the museum displays paintings, drawings, prints, sculpture, and photographs by Taos-area artists from 1800 to the present. Featured are paintings from the early days of the art colony by members of the Taos Society of Artists, including Oscar Berninghaus, Ernest Blumenschein, Herbert Dunton, Victor Higgins, Bert Phillips, and Walter Ufer. Also included are works by Emil Bisttram, Andrew Dasburg, Agnes Martin, Larry Bell, and Thomas Benrimo.

Upstairs are 19th-century pounded-tin pieces and *retablos,* religious paintings of saints that have traditionally been used for decoration and inspiration in the homes and churches of New Mexico. The permanent collection includes sculptures by Patrociño Barela, one of the leading Hispanic artists of 20th-century New Mexico. It's well worth seeing, especially his 3-foot-tall *Death Cart,* a rendition of Doña Sebastiana, the bringer of death.

The museum also schedules more than eight changing exhibitions a year, many of which feature works by celebrated artists currently living in Taos.

238 Ledoux St. ✆ **575/758-9826.** www.harwoodmuseum.org. Admission $7, $6 seniors, free for children 11 and under. Tues–Sat 10am–5pm; Sun noon–5pm.

Kit Carson Home & Museum If you want a glimpse into the modest lifestyle of Taos's frontiersmen, head to this 3-room adobe home, a block east of the plaza. Built in 1825 and purchased in 1843 by Carson—the famous mountain man, Indian agent, and scout—it was a wedding gift for his young bride, Josefa Jaramillo. It remained their home for 25 years, until both died (exactly a month apart) in 1868. Rooms have sparse displays, such as buffalo hide and sheepskin bedding, a wooden chest, basic kitchen utensils, and a cooking fireplace. The museum also includes a film on Carson produced by the History Channel. The price of a visit here is a bit steep for what you see, but if you decide to come, plan on spending about a half-hour. If you'd like to see more of Carson's possessions, visit the Martinez Hacienda (see above).

113 Kit Carson Rd. ✆ **575/758-4613.** www.kitcarsonhome.com. Admission $5 adult, $4 seniors 65 years and older, $3 teens 13–18, $2 children 6–12. Daily 9am–6pm.

Kit Carson Park and Cemetery Major community events are held in the park in summer. The cemetery, established in 1847, contains the graves of Carson, his wife, Governor Charles Bent, the Don Antonio Martinez family, Mabel Dodge Luhan, and many other noted historical figures and artists. Their lives are described briefly on plaques.

Paseo del Pueblo Norte. ✆ **575/758-8234.** Free admission. Daily 24 hr.

Rio Grande Gorge Bridge ★ Kids This impressive bridge, west of the Taos airport, spans the Southwest's greatest river. At 650 feet above the canyon floor, it's one of America's highest bridges. If you can withstand the vertigo, it's interesting to come more than once, at different times of day, to observe the way the changing light plays tricks with the colors of the cliff walls. A curious aside: The wedding scene in the movie *Natural Born Killers* was filmed here.

US 64, 10 miles west of Taos. Free admission. Daily 24 hr.

ORGANIZED TOURS

An excellent opportunity to explore the historic downtown area of Taos is offered by **Taos Historic Walking Tours** (✆ **575/758-4020**). Tours cost $12 and take 1½ to 2 hours, leaving from the Kit Carson Cemetery at 10am Monday to Saturday (June–Aug). Closed Sundays and holidays. Call to make an appointment during the off season.

If you'd really like a taste of Taos history and drama, call **Enchantment Dreams Walking Tours ★** (✆ **575/776-2562**). Roberta Courtney Meyers, a theater artist, dramatist, and composer, will guide you through Taos's history while performing a number of characters, such as Georgia O'Keeffe and Kit Carson. Walking tours cost $25 per person.

6 SKIING TAOS ★★★

DOWNHILL SKIING

Five alpine resorts are within an hour's drive of Taos; all offer complete facilities, including equipment rentals. Although exact opening and closing dates vary according to snow conditions, the season usually begins around Thanksgiving and continues into early April.

Ski clothing can be purchased, and ski equipment can be rented or bought, from several Taos outlets. Among them are **Cottam's Ski & Outdoor Shops,** with four locations (call ✆ **800/322-8267** or 575/758-2822 for the one nearest you;

Kids Skiing with Kids

With its children's ski school, Taos Ski Valley has always been an excellent choice for skiing families, but with the 1994 addition of an 18,000-square-foot children's center (Kinderkäfig Center), skiing with your children in Taos is even better. Kinderkäfig offers many services, from equipment rental for children to babysitting services. Call ahead for more information.

www.cottamsoutdoor.com), and **Taos Ski Valley Sportswear, Ski & Boot Co.,** in Taos Ski Valley (✆ **575/776-2291**).

Taos Ski Valley ★★★, P.O. Box 90, Taos Ski Valley, NM 87525 (✆ **866/968-7386** or 575/776-2291; www.skitaos.org), is the preeminent ski resort in the southern Rocky Mountains. It was founded in 1955 by a Swiss-German immigrant, Ernie Blake. According to local legend, Blake searched for 2 years in a small plane for the perfect location for a ski resort comparable to what he was accustomed to in the Alps. He found it at the abandoned mining site of Twining, high above Taos. Today, under the management of two younger generations of Blakes, the resort has become internationally renowned for its light, dry powder (as much as 320 in. annually), its superb ski school, and its personal, friendly service.

Taos Ski Valley can best be appreciated by the more experienced skier and snowboarder. It offers steep, high-alpine, high-adventure skiing. The mountain is more intricate than it might seem at first glance, and it holds many surprises and challenges—even for the expert. The *London Times* called the valley "without any argument the best ski resort in the world. Small, intimate, and endlessly challenging, Taos simply has no equal." The quality of the snow here (light and dry) is believed to be due to the dry Southwestern air and abundant sunshine. ***Note:*** In 2008, Taos Ski Valley began allowing snowboarders onto its slopes.

Between the 11,819-foot summit and the 9,207-foot base, there are 72 trails and bowls, more than half of them designated for expert and advanced skiers. Most of the remaining trails are suitable for advanced intermediates; there is little flat terrain for novices to gain experience and mileage. However, many beginning skiers find that after spending time in lessons they can enjoy the **Kachina Bowl,** which offers spectacular views as well as wide-open slopes.

The area has an uphill capacity of 15,000 skiers per hour on its five double chairs, one triple, four quads, and one surface tow. Full-day lift tickets, depending on the season, cost $40 to $66 for adults, $30 to $55 for teens ages 13 to 17, $25 to $40 for children 12 and under, $40 to $50 for seniors ages 65 to 79, and are free for seniors 80 and over and for children 6 and under with an adult ticket purchase. Full rental packages are $29 for adults and $20 for children. Taos Ski Valley is open daily 9am to 4pm from Thanksgiving to around the second week of April. ***Note:*** Taos Ski Valley has one of the best ski schools in the country, specializing in teaching people how to negotiate steep and challenging runs.

Taos Ski Valley has many lodges and condominiums, with nearly 1,500 beds. (See "Taos Ski Valley," under "Where to Stay," earlier in this chapter.) All offer ski-week packages; three of them have restaurants. There are three restaurants on the mountain in addition to the many facilities of Village Center at the base. Call the **Taos Ski Valley** (✆ **800/776-1111** or 575/776-2233).

Not far from Taos Ski Valley is **Red River Ski & Snowboard Area,** P.O. Box 900, Red River, NM 87558 (✆ **800/331-7669** for reservations; 575/754-2223 for information; www.redriverskiarea.com). One of the bonuses of this ski area is that lodgers at Red River can walk out their doors and be on the slopes. Two other factors make this almost 50-year-old, family-oriented area special: First, most of its 58 trails are geared toward the intermediate skier, though beginners and experts also have some trails; and second, good snow is guaranteed early and late in the year by snowmaking equipment that can work on 87% of the runs, more than any other in New Mexico. However, be aware that this human-made snow tends to be icy, and the mountain is full of inexperienced skiers, so you really have to watch your back. Locals in the area refer to this as "Little Texas" because it's so popular with Texans and other Southerners. A very friendly atmosphere, with a touch of redneck attitude, prevails.

There's a 1,600-foot vertical drop here to a base elevation of 8,750 feet. Lifts include four double chairs, two triple chairs, and a surface tow, with a capacity of 7,920 skiers per hour. The cost of a lift ticket for all lifts is $55 for adults for a full day, $40 half-day; $48 for teens 13 to 19 for a full day, $35 half-day; and $39 for children ages 4 to 12 and seniors 60 through 69 for a full day, $28 half-day. Free for seniors 70 and over. All rental packages start at $20 for adults, $13 for children. Lifts run daily 9am to 4pm Thanksgiving to about March 28. Ask about their lesson packages.

Also quite close to Taos (approx. 20 miles) is **Angel Fire Resort** ★, P.O. Drawer B, Angel Fire, NM 87710 (✆ **800/633-7463** or 575/377-6401; www.angelfireresort.com). If you (or your kids) don't feel up to skiing steeper Taos Mountain, Angel Fire is a good choice. The 73 trails are primarily oriented to beginner and intermediate skiers and snowboarders, with a few runs for more advanced skiers and snowboarders. The mountain has received over $7 million in improvements in past years. This is not an old village like you'll find at Taos and Red River. Instead, it's a Vail-style resort, built in 1960, with a variety of activities other than skiing. The snowmaking capabilities here are excellent, and the ski school is good, though I hear it's so crowded that it's difficult to get in during spring break. Two high-speed quad lifts whisk you to the top quickly. There are also three double lifts and one surface lift. A large snowboard park contains a banked slalom course, rails, jumps, and other obstacles. Cross-country skiing, snowshoeing, and snowbiking are also available. All-day lift tickets cost $59 for adults, $49 for teens (ages 13–17), and $39 for children (ages 7–12). Kids 6 and under and seniors 70 and over ski free. It's open from approximately mid-December to March 29 (depending on the weather) daily 9am to 4pm.

The oldest ski area in the Taos region, founded in 1952, **Sipapu Ski and Summer Resort,** HC 65, Rte. Box 29, Vadito, NM 87579 (✆ **575/587-2240;** www.sipapunm.com), is 25 miles southeast of Taos, on NM 518 in Tres Ritos Canyon. It prides itself on being a small local ski area, especially popular with schoolchildren. It has two triple chairs and two surface lifts, with a vertical drop of 1,025 feet to the 8,200-foot base elevation. There are 31 trails, half classified as intermediate, and two terrain park trails have been added. It's a nice little area, tucked way back in the mountains, with excellent lodging rates. Be aware that because the elevation is fairly low, runs can be icy. Lift tickets are $40 for adults for a full day, $26 half-day; $26 for children 12 and under for a full day, $22 half-day; $22 for seniors (ages 60–69) for a half- or full day; and free for seniors 70 and over, as well as for children 5 and under. A package including lift tickets, equipment rental, and a lesson costs $53 for adults and $42 for children. Sipapu is open from about the end of November to April 1, and lifts run daily from 9am to 4pm.

CROSS-COUNTRY SKIING

Just east of Red River, with 16 miles of groomed trails (in addition to 6 miles of trails strictly for snowshoers), in 400 acres of forestlands atop Bobcat Pass, is the **Enchanted Forest Cross Country Ski Area** ★ (✆ **575/754-6112;** www.enchantedforestxc.com). Full-day trail passes, good from 9am to 4:30pm, are $14 for adults, $10 for teens 13 to 17 and seniors 62 to 69, $6 for children age 7 to 12, and free for seniors age 70 and over, as well as for children 6 and under. In addition to cross-country ski and snowshoe rentals, the ski area rents pulk sleds—high-tech devices in which children are pulled by their skiing parents. The ski area offers a full snack bar. Equipment rentals and lessons can be arranged either at Enchanted Forest or at **Miller's Crossing** ski shop at 417 W. Main St., in Red River (✆ **575/754-2374**). Nordic skiers can get instruction in cross-country classic as well as freestyle skating. **Taos Mountain Outfitters,** 114 S. Plaza (✆ **575/758-9292;** www.taosmountainoutfitters.com), offers telemark and cross-country sales, and rentals.

7 OTHER OUTDOOR ACTIVITIES

Taos County's 2,200 square miles embrace a great diversity of scenic beauty, from New Mexico's highest mountain, 13,161-foot **Wheeler Peak,** to the 650-foot-deep chasm of the **Rio Grande Gorge** ★★. Carson National Forest, which extends to the eastern city limits of Taos and cloaks a large part of the county, contains several major ski facilities as well as hundreds of miles of hiking trails through the Sangre de Cristo range.

Recreation areas are mainly in the national forest, where pine and aspen provide refuge for abundant wildlife. Forty-eight areas are accessible by road, including 38 with campsites. There are also areas on the high desert mesa, carpeted by sagebrush, cactus, and, frequently, wildflowers. Two beautiful areas within a short drive of Taos are the **Valle Vidal Recreation Area,** north of Red River, and the **Wild Rivers Recreation Area,** near Questa. For complete information, contact **Carson National Forest,** 208 Cruz Alta Rd. (✆ **575/758-6200;** www.fs.fed.us/r3/carson), or the **Bureau of Land Management,** 226 Cruz Alta Rd. (✆ **575/758-8851;** www.blm.gov.nm/st/en.html).

BALLOONING

As in many other towns throughout New Mexico, hot-air ballooning is a top attraction. Recreational trips over the Taos Valley and Rio Grande Gorge are offered by **Paradise Hot Air Balloon Adventure** (✆ **575/751-6098;** www.taosballooning.com). The company also offers ultra-light rides.

The **Taos Mountain Balloon Rally,** P.O. Box 3096 (✆ **575/751-1000;** www.taosballoonrally.com), is held each year in late October. (See "Calendar of Events," in chapter 3.)

BIKING

Even if you're not an avid cyclist, it won't take long for you to realize that getting around Taos by bike is preferable to driving. You won't have the usual parking problems, and you won't have to sit in the line of traffic as it snakes through the center of town. If you feel like exploring the surrounding area, Carson National Forest rangers recommend several biking trails in the greater Taos area. Head to the **West Rim Trail** for a scenic and easy ride. To reach the trail, travel US 64 to the Taos Gorge Bridge, cross it and find the trail head on your left; or head south on NM 68 for 17 miles to Pilar, and then turn west onto

NM 570. Travel along the river for 6¼ miles, cross the bridge, and drive to the top of the ridge. Watch for the trail marker on your right. The **U.S. Forest Service** office, 208 Cruz Alta Rd. (✆ **575/758-6200**), has excellent trail information. Also look for the *Taos Trails* map (created jointly by Carson National Forest, Native Sons Adventures, and Trails Illustrated) at area bookstores.

Bicycle rentals are available from the **Gearing Up Bicycle Shop,** 129 Paseo del Pueblo Sur (✆ **575/751-0365;** www.gearingupbikes.com); daily rentals run $35 for a mountain bike with front suspension.

FISHING

In many of New Mexico's waters, fishing is possible year-round, though, due to conditions, many high lakes and streams are fishable only during the warmer months. Overall, the best fishing is in the spring and fall. Naturally, the Rio Grande is a favorite fishing spot, but there is also excellent fishing in the streams around Taos. Taoseños favor the Rio Hondo, Rio Pueblo (near Tres Ritos), Rio Fernando (in Taos Canyon), Pot Creek, and Rio Chiquito. Rainbow, cutthroat, German brown trout, and kokanee (a freshwater salmon) are commonly stocked and caught. Pike and catfish have been caught in the Rio Grande as well. Jiggs, spinners, or woolly worms are recommended as lure, or worms, corn, or salmon eggs as bait; many experienced anglers prefer fly-fishing.

Licenses are required, of course, and are sold, along with tackle, at several Taos sporting-goods shops. For backcountry guides, try **Deep Creek Wilderness Outfitters and Guides,** P.O. Box 721, El Prado, NM 87529 (✆ **575/776-8423** or 575/776-5901), or **Taylor Streit Flyfishing Service,** 405 Camino de la Placita (✆ **575/751-1312;** www.streitflyfishing.com).

FITNESS FACILITIES

The **Taos Spa and Tennis Club,** 111 Dona Ana Dr. (across from Sagebrush Inn; ✆ **575/758-1980;** www.taosspa.com), is a fully equipped fitness center that rivals any you'd find in a big city. It has a variety of cardiovascular machines, bikes, and weight-training machines, as well as saunas, indoor and outdoor Jacuzzis, a steam room, and indoor and outdoor pools. Classes range from yoga to Pilates to water fitness. In addition, it has tennis and racquetball courts. Therapeutic massage, facials, and physical therapy are available daily by appointment. Children's programs include a tennis camp and swimming lessons, and babysitting programs are available in the morning and evening. The spa is open Monday to Friday 4am to 9pm; Saturday and Sunday 7am to 8pm. Monthly memberships are available for individuals and families, as are summer memberships and punch cards. For visitors, there's a daily rate of $12.

The **Northside Health and Fitness Center,** at 1307 Paseo del Pueblo Norte (✆ **575/751-1242**), is also a full-service facility, featuring top-of-the-line Cybex equipment, free weights, and cardiovascular equipment. Aerobics classes are scheduled daily (Jazzercise classes weekly), and there are indoor/outdoor pools and four tennis courts, as well as children's and seniors' programs. Open weekdays 6am to 9pm, weekends 8am to 8pm. The daily visitors' rate is $11. Also of note, with classes daily, is **Taos Pilates Studio,** 1103 Paseo del Pueblo Norte (✆ **575/758-7604;** www.taospilates.net).

GOLF

Since the summer of 1993, the 18-hole golf course at the **Taos Country Club,** 54 Golf Course Dr., Ranchos de Taos (✆ **800/758-7375** or 575/758-7300), has been open to the public. Located on Country Road 110, just 6 miles south of the plaza, it's a first-rate

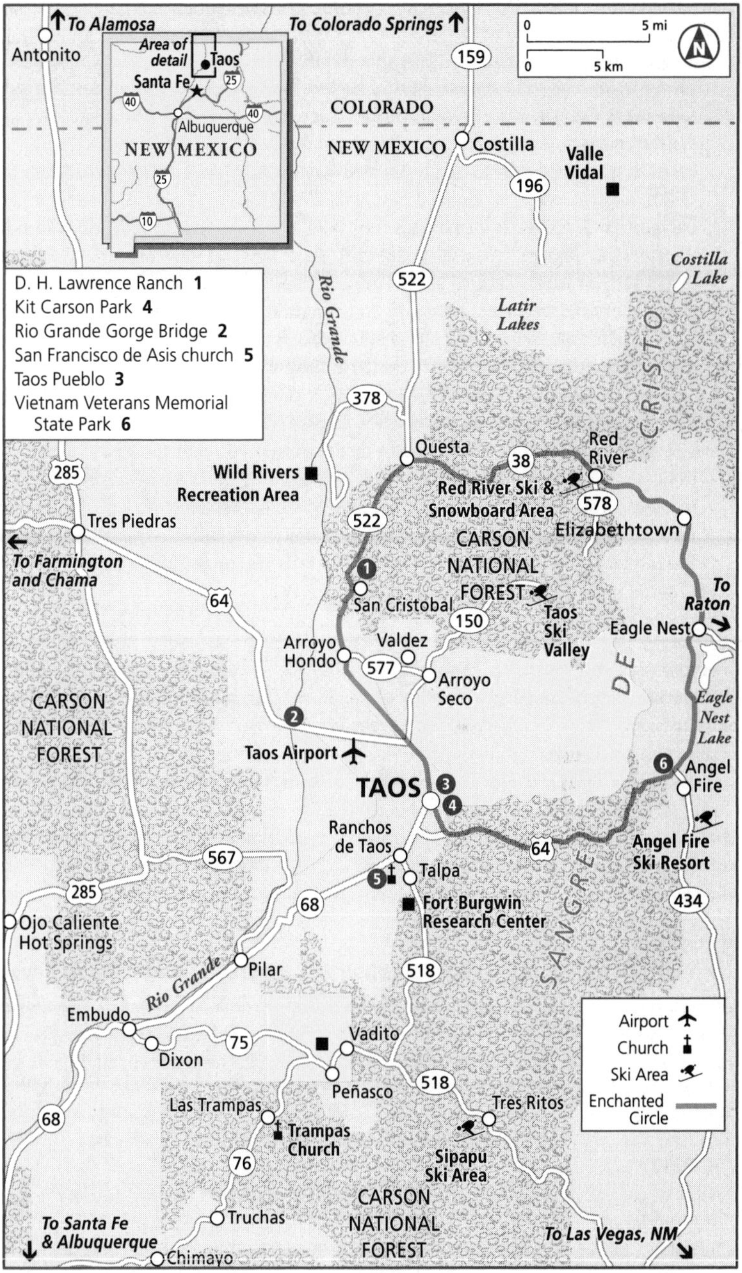

D. H. Lawrence Ranch **1**
Kit Carson Park **4**
Rio Grande Gorge Bridge **2**
San Francisco de Asis church **5**
Taos Pueblo **3**
Vietnam Veterans Memorial State Park **6**

Airport
Church
Ski Area
Enchanted Circle

0 5 mi
0 5 km

Area of detail
Taos
Santa Fe
Albuquerque
NEW MEXICO

To Alamosa
Antonito
To Colorado Springs
COLORADO
NEW MEXICO
Costilla
Valle Vidal
Costilla Lake
Latir Lakes
Rio Grande
Questa
Red River
Red River Ski & Snowboard Area
Elizabethtown
Wild Rivers Recreation Area
Tres Piedras
To Farmington and Chama
CARSON NATIONAL FOREST
San Cristobal
Taos Ski Valley
To Raton
Eagle Nest
Valdez
Arroyo Hondo
Arroyo Seco
SANGRE DE CRISTO
Eagle Nest Lake
Taos Airport
TAOS
Angel Fire
Angel Fire Ski Resort
Ranchos de Taos
Talpa
Fort Burgwin Research Center
CARSON NATIONAL FOREST
Ojo Caliente Hot Springs
Pilar
Rio Grande
Embudo
Dixon
Vadito
Peñasco
Las Trampas
Trampas Church
Tres Ritos
Sipapu Ski Area
Truchas
CARSON NATIONAL FOREST
To Santa Fe & Albuquerque
Chimayo
To Las Vegas, NM

Moments Exploring the Enchanted Circle ★★

Longing for a little road trip? Few places offer more white-stripe adventure than the 90-mile loop around northern New Mexico's Enchanted Circle. The road leads through old Hispanic villages such as Arroyo Hondo and Questa. About 3 miles north of the latter, you can turn west of NM 522 onto NM 378 and travel 8 miles on a paved road to **Wild Rivers Recreation Area** (✆ **575/770-1600**), a great place to begin a hike into the Rio Grande Gorge. Next, the Enchanted Circle heads into a pass the Plains Indians once used, to the Wild West mining town of Red River, along the base of some of New Mexico's tallest peaks, to the resort village of Angel Fire, and back to Taos along the meandering Rio Fernando de Taos. Although you can drive the entire loop in 2 hours from Taos, most folks prefer to take a full day, and some take several days. If you get hungry along the way, stop for lunch at **Mountain Treasures** (212 W. Main St., Red River, NM 87558; ✆ **575/754-2700**), a gallery, bistro, and espresso coffee bar that offers excellent sandwiches. To drive the loop, travel north on NM 522 10 miles to Arroyo Hondo. Then drive another 13 miles to Questa. Turn right on NM 38, traveling 12 miles to Red River. Stay on NM 38 and drive 16 miles to Eagle Nest. From there you come to US 64, which goes west for 12 miles to Angel Fire. The final leg is a lovely 21-mile jaunt on US 64 back to Taos. See "The Taos Area (Including Enchanted Circle)" map, on p. 227.

championship golf course designed for all levels of play. It has open fairways and no hidden greens. The club also features a driving range, practice putting and chipping greens, and instruction by PGA professionals. Greens fees are seasonal and start at $49; cart and club rentals are available.

The par-72, 18-hole course at the **Angel Fire Resort Golf Course** (✆ **800/633-7463** or 575/377-3055) is PGA endorsed. Surrounded by stands of ponderosa pine, spruce, and aspen, at 8,500 feet, it's one of the highest regulation golf courses in the world. It also has a driving range and putting green. Carts and clubs can be rented at the course, and the club pro provides instruction. Greens fees range from $47 to $99.

HIKING

There are hundreds of miles of hiking trails in Taos County's mountain and high-mesa country. The trails are especially well traveled in the summer and fall, although nights turn chilly and mountain weather may be fickle by September.

Free materials and advice on all **Carson National Forest** trails and recreation areas can be obtained from the **Forest Service Building,** 208 Cruz Alta Rd. (✆ **575/758-6200**), open Monday to Friday 8am to 4:30pm. Detailed USGS topographical maps of backcountry areas can be purchased from **Taos Mountain Outfitters,** South Plaza (✆ **575/758-9292**).

One of the easiest hikes to access is the **West Rim Trail,** aptly named because it runs along the rim of the Rio Grande Gorge. Access this 9-mile-long trail by driving west from Taos on US 64, crossing the Rio Grande Gorge Bridge and turning left into the picnic area. The 19,663-acre **Wheeler Peak Wilderness** is a wonderland of alpine tundra, encompassing New Mexico's highest peak (13,161 ft.). A favorite (though rigorous) hike to Wheeler Peak's summit (15 miles round-trip with a 3,700-ft. elevation gain) makes for a long but fun day. The trail head is at Taos Ski Valley. For year-round hiking, head to the **Wild Rivers Recreation Area** ★ (✆ **575/770-1600**), near Questa (see "Exploring the Enchanted Circle" box, below).

The sage meadows and pine-covered mountains around Taos make it one of the West's most romantic places to ride. **Taos Indian Horse Ranch** ★★, on Pueblo land off Ski Valley Road, just before **Arroyo Seco** (✆ **575/758-3212;** www.taosindianhorseranch.com), offers a variety of guided rides. Open by appointment, the ranch provides horses for all types of riders (English, Western, Australian, and bareback) and ability levels. Call ahead to reserve and for prices, which will likely run about $100 for a 2-hour trail ride.

Horseback riding is also offered by **Rio Grande Stables,** P.O. Box 2122, El Prado (✆ **575/776-5913;** www.lajitasstables.com/taos.htm), with rides taking place during the summer months at Taos Ski Valley. Most riding outfitters offer lunch trips and overnight trips. Call for prices and further details.

HUNTING

Hunters in **Carson National Forest** bag deer, turkey, grouse, band-tailed pigeons, and elk by special permit. Hunting seasons vary year to year, so it's important to inquire ahead with the New Mexico **Game and Fish Department** in Santa Fe (✆ **575/476-8000;** www.wildlife.state.nm.us).

JOGGING

The paved paths and grass of Kit Carson Park (see "More Attractions," earlier in this chapter) provide a quiet place to stretch your legs.

LLAMA TREKKING

For a taste of the unusual, you might want to try letting a llama carry your gear and food while you walk and explore, free of any heavy burdens. They're friendly, gentle animals that have keen senses of sight and smell. Often, other animals, such as elk, deer, and mountain sheep, are attracted to the scent of the llamas and will venture closer to hikers if the llamas are present.

Wild Earth Llama Adventures ★★ (✆ **800/758-LAMA** [5262] or 575/586-0174; www.llamaadventures.com) offers a "Take a Llama to Llunch" day hike—a full day of hiking into the Sangre de Cristo Mountains, complete with a gourmet lunch for $89. Wild Earth also offers a variety of custom multiday wilderness adventures tailored to trekkers' needs and fitness levels for $125 per person per day. Children under 12 receive discounts. **El Paseo Llama Expeditions** ★ (✆ **800/455-2627** or 575/758-3111; www.elpaseollama.com) utilizes U.S. Forest Service–maintained trails that wind through canyons and over mountain ridges. The llama expeditions are scheduled March to November, and day hikes are scheduled year-round. The rides are for all ages and kids can ride, too. Gourmet meals are provided. Half-day hikes cost $74 and $84, day hikes $94, and 2- to 8-day hikes run $299 to $1,199.

RIVER RAFTING

Half- or full-day white-water rafting trips down the Rio Grande and Rio Chama originate in Taos and can be booked through a variety of outfitters in the area. The wild **Taos Box** ★★★, a steep-sided canyon south of the Wild Rivers Recreation Area, offers a series of Class IV rapids that rarely let up for some 17 miles. The water drops up to 90

Getting Pampered: The Spa Scene

Taos doesn't have the spa scene that Tucson and Phoenix do, but you can get pampered with treatments ranging from body polishes to mud wraps to massages at **Estrella Massage & Day Spa,** 601 Callejon Rd. (✆ **575/751-7307;** www.estrellamassage.com). **Taos Spa and Tennis Club** (see "Fitness Facilities," above) also offers massages.

If you'd like to stay at a spa, **El Monte Sagrado,** 317 Kit Carson Rd. (✆ **800/828-TAOS** [8267] or 575/758-3502; www.elmontesagrado.com), and **Casa de las Chimeneas,** 405 Cordoba Rd. (✆ **877/758-4777** or 575/758-4777; www.visittaos.com), offer a variety of treatments to their guests (see "Where to Stay," earlier in this chapter).

feet per mile, providing one of the most exciting 1-day white-water tours in the West. May and June, when the water is rising, is a good time to go. Experience is not required, but you will be required to wear a life jacket (provided), and you should be willing to get wet.

Most of the companies listed run the **Taos Box** ($104–$115 per person) and **Pilar Racecourse** ($45–$56 per person for a half-day) on a daily basis.

I highly recommend **Los Rios River Runners** ★ in Taos, P.O. Box 2734 (✆ **800/544-1181** or 575/776-8854; www.losriosriverrunners.com). Other safe bets are **Native Sons Adventures,** 1033-A Paseo del Pueblo Sur (✆ **800/753-7559** or 575/758-9342; www.nativesonsadventures.com), and **Far Flung Adventures,** P.O. Box 707, El Prado (✆ **800/359-2627** or 575/758-2628; www.farflung.com).

Safety warning: Taos is not the place to experiment if you're not an experienced rafter. Do yourself a favor and check with the **Bureau of Land Management** (✆ **575/758-8851**) to make sure that you're fully equipped to go white-water rafting without a guide. Have them check your gear to make sure that it's sturdy enough—this is serious rafting!

ROCK CLIMBING

Mountain Skills, P.O. Box 206, Arroyo Seco, NM 87514 (✆ **575/776-2222;** www.climbingschoolusa.com), offers rock-climbing instruction for all skill levels, from beginners to more advanced climbers who would like to fine-tune their skills or just find out about the best area climbs.

SKATEBOARDING

Try your board at **Taos Youth Family Center,** 406 Paseo del Cañon, 2 miles south of the plaza and about 3/4 of a mile off Paseo del Pueblo Sur (✆ **575/758-4160**), where there is an in-line-skate and skateboarding park, open when there's no snow or ice. Admission is free.

SNOWMOBILING & ATV RIDING

Native Sons Adventures, 1335 Paseo del Pueblo Sur (✆ **800/753-7559** or 575/758-9342; www.nativesonsadventures.com), runs fully guided tours in the Sangre de Cristo Mountains. Rates run $67 to $150. Advance reservations required.

SWIMMING

The **Taos Swimming Pool,** Civic Plaza Drive at Camino de la Placita, opposite the Convention Center (✆ **575/758-4160**), admits swimmers 8 and over without adult supervision.

TENNIS

Taos Spa and Tennis Club (see "Fitness Facilities," above) has four courts, and the **Northside Health and Fitness Center** (see "Fitness Facilities," above) has three tennis courts. In addition, there are four free public courts in Taos, two at **Kit Carson Park,** on Paseo del Pueblo Norte, and two at **Fred Baca Memorial Park,** on Camino del Medio, south of Ranchitos Road.

8 SHOPPING

Given the town's historical associations with the arts, it isn't surprising that many visitors come to Taos to buy fine art. Some 50-odd galleries are within walking distance of the plaza, and a couple dozen more are just a short drive from downtown. Galleries and shops are generally open 7 days a week during summer and closed Sundays during winter. Hours vary but generally run from 10am to 5 or 6pm. Some artists show their work by appointment only.

The best-known artist in modern Taos is the late R. C. Gorman, a Navajo from Arizona who made his home in Taos for more than 2 decades. He was internationally acclaimed for his bright, somewhat surrealistic depictions of Navajo women. His **Navajo Gallery,** at 210 Ledoux St. (✆ **575/758-3250;** www.rcgormangallery.com), is a showcase for his widely varied work: acrylics, lithographs, silk screens, bronzes, tapestries, hand-cast ceramic vases, etched glass, and more.

ART

Act I Gallery This gallery has a broad range of works in a variety of media. You'll find watercolors, *retablos,* furniture, paintings, Hispanic folk art, pottery, jewelry, and sculpture. 218 Paseo del Pueblo Norte. ✆ **800/666-2933** or 575/758-7831. www.actonegallery.com.

Fenix Gallery The Fenix Gallery focuses on Taos artists with national and/or international collections and reputations who live and work in Taos. The work is primarily nonobjective and very contemporary. Some "historic" artists are represented as well. 208A Ranchitos Rd. ✆ **575/758-9120.** www.fenixgallery.com.

Inger Jirby Gallery ★ Finds The word *expressionist* could have been created to define the work of internationally known artist Inger Jirby. Full of bold color and passionate brush strokes, Jirby's oils record the lives and landscapes of villages from the southwestern U.S. to Guatemala to Bali. This gallery, which meanders back through a 400-year-old adobe house, is a feast for the eyes and soul. 207 Ledoux St. ✆ **575/758-7333.**

Lumina Contemporary Art ★★ Finds North of Taos (about 8 min.) outside the village of Arroyo Seco, this gallery, a new version of the notable gallery that was in Taos, offers a tranquil museum-quality experience. Set within a 3-acre Japanese garden, it has a water cascade and Buddhist teahouse accented with large stone sculptures. Inside, works offer a refreshing look at the world. Open in summer Thursday to Monday 11am to 6:30pm; winter Friday to Monday 11am to 5pm. 11 NM 230, Arroyo Seco. ✆ **877/5LUMINA** (558-6462) or 575/758-7282. www.luminagallery.com.

Michael McCormick Gallery ★ Finds Nationally renowned artists dynamically play with Southwestern themes in the works hanging at this gallery, steps from the plaza. Especially notable are the bright portraits by Miguel Martinez. If the gallery's namesake is in, strike up a conversation about art or poetry. 106C Paseo del Pueblo Norte. ✆ **800/279-0879** or 575/758-1372. www.mccormickgallery.com.

Nichols Taos Fine Art Gallery Here you will find traditional works in all media, including Western and cowboy art. 403 Paseo del Pueblo Norte. ✆ **575/758-2475.** www.nicholsgallery.com.

Parks Gallery ★ Some of the region's finest contemporary art decks the walls of this gallery just off the plaza. Some of the top artists here include Melissa Zink, Jim Wagner, Susan Contreres, and Erin Currier. 127 Bent St. ✆ **575/751-0343.** www.parksgallery.com.

Philip Bareiss Gallery The works of some 30 leading Taos artists, including sculptor and painter Ron Davis, painter Norbert Voelkel, and watercolorist Patricia Sanford, are exhibited here, along with early Taos modernists. 15 Rt. 150. ✆ **575/776-2284.** www.taosartappraisal.com.

R. B. Ravens A trader for many years, including 25 on the Ranchos Plaza, R. B. Ravens is skilled at finding incredible period artwork. Here, you'll see (and have the chance to buy) Navajo rugs and pottery, all in the setting of an old home with raw pine floors and hand-sculpted adobe walls. 4146 NM 68 (across from the St. Francis Church Plaza), Ranchos de Taos. ✆ **575/758-7322.** www.rbravens.com.

BOOKS

Moby Dickens Bookshop ★ This is Taos's best bookstore, with comfortable places to sit and read. You'll find children's and adults' collections of Southwest, Native American, and out-of-print books. 124A Bent St. ✆ **888/442-9980** or 575/758-3050. www.mobydickens.com.

CRAFTS

Taos Artisans Cooperative Gallery Value This seven-member cooperative gallery, owned and operated by local artists, sells local handmade jewelry, wearables, clay work, glass, leather work, and garden sculpture. You'll always find an artist in the shop. 107C Bent St. ✆ **575/758-1558.** www.taosartisanscooperative.com.

Taos Blue This gallery has fine Native American and contemporary handicrafts. 101A Bent St. ✆ **575/758-3561.** www.taosblue.com.

Weaving Southwest Contemporary tapestries by New Mexico artists, as well as one-of-a-kind rugs, blankets, and pillows, are the woven specialties found here. 216B Paseo del Pueblo Norte. ✆ **575/758-0433.** www.weavingsouthwest.com.

FASHIONS

Artemisia ★ Advertising "one-of-a-kind artwear and accessories," this shop delivers, with wearable art in bold colors, all hand-woven or hand-sewn, all for women. 115 Bent St. ✆ **575/737-9800.** www.artemisiataos.com.

Overland Sheepskin Company ★ Finds You can't miss the romantically weathered barn sitting on a meadow north of town. Inside, you'll find anything you can imagine in leather: coats, gloves, hats, slippers. The coats here are exquisite, from oversize ranch styles to tailored blazers in a variety of leathers, from sheepskin to buffalo hide. NM 522 (a few miles north of town). ✆ **575/758-8820.** www.overland.com.

FOOD

Cid's Food Market This store has the best selection of natural and gourmet foods in Taos. It's a great place to stock your picnic basket with such items as roasted chicken and barbecued brisket, or with lighter fare, such as sushi, Purple Onion–brand sandwiches, black-bean salad, and fresh hummus and tabbouleh. 623 Paseo del Pueblo Norte. ✆ **575/758-1148.** www.cidsfoodmarket.com.

FURNITURE

Country Furnishings of Taos Here you'll find unique hand-painted folk-art furniture. The pieces are as individual as the styles of the local folk artists who make them. There are also home accessories, unusual gifts, clothing, and jewelry. 534 Paseo del Pueblo Norte. ✆ **575/758-4633.**

The Taos Company This interior-design showroom specializes in unique Southwestern and contemporary furniture and decorative accessories. Especially look for graceful stone fountains, iron-and-wood furniture, and custom jewelry. 124K John Dunn Plaza, Bent St. ✆ **800/548-1141** or 575/758-1141. www.thetaoscompany.com.

GIFTS & SOUVENIRS

Chimayo Trading del Norte Specializing in Navajo weavings, pueblo pottery, and other types of pottery, this is a fun spot to peruse on the Ranchos de Taos Plaza. Look especially for the Casas Grandes pottery from Mexico. #1 Ranchos de Taos Plaza. ✆ **575/758-0504.**

El Rincón Trading Post (Finds) This shop has a real trading-post feel. It's a wonderful place to find turquoise jewelry, whether you're looking for contemporary or antique. In the back of the store is a museum full of Native American and Western artifacts. 114 Kit Carson Rd. ✆ **575/758-9188.**

San Francisco de Asis Gift Shop Local devotional art fills this funky little shop behind the San Francisco de Asis church. *Retablos* (altar paintings), rosary beads, and hand-carved wooden crosses appeal to a range of visitors, from the deeply religious to the pagan power shopper. Ranchos de Taos Plaza. ✆ **575/758-2754.**

JEWELRY

Artwares Contemporary Jewelry The gallery owners here call their contemporary jewelry "a departure from the traditional." True to this slogan, each piece here offers a new twist on traditional Southwestern and Native American design, by artists such as Roberto Coin, John Hardy, Diane Malouf, Judith Ripka, and Alex Sepkus. 129 N. Plaza. ✆ **800/527-8850** or 575/758-8850. www.artwaresjewelry.com.

Taos Gems & Minerals In business for over 30 years, Taos Gems & Minerals is a fine lapidary showroom. This is a great place to explore; you can buy jewelry, carvings, and antique pieces at reasonable prices. 637 Paseo del Pueblo Sur. ✆ **575/758-3910.**

MUSICAL INSTRUMENTS

Taos Drum Company ★ Taos Drums has one of the largest selections of Native American log and hand drums in the world. In addition to drums, the showroom displays Southwestern and wrought-iron furniture, cowboy art, and more than 60 styles of rawhide lampshades. To find Taos Drum Company, look for the tepees and drums off NM 68. Ask about the tour that demonstrates the drum-making process. 5 miles south of Taos Plaza (off NM 68). ✆ **575/758-3796.** www.taosdrums.com.

POTTERY

Stephen Kilborn Pottery Visiting this shop in town is a treat, but for a real adventure, go 17 miles south of Taos toward Santa Fe to Stephen Kilborn's studio in Pilar, open Monday to Saturday 11am to 5pm and noon to 4pm on Sunday. There, you'll see where the pottery is made. 136A Paseo del Pueblo Norte. ✆ **800/758-0136** or 575/758-5760. www.kilbornpottery.com.

9 TAOS AFTER DARK

For a small town, Taos has its share of top entertainment. The resort atmosphere and the arts community attract performers, and the city enjoys annual programs in music and literary arts. State troupes, such as the New Mexico Repertory Theater and New Mexico Symphony Orchestra, make regular visits.

Many events are scheduled by the **Taos Center for the Arts (TCA),** 133 Paseo del Pueblo Norte (✆ **575/758-2052;** www.taoscenterforthearts.org), at the Taos Community Auditorium. The TCA imports local, regional, and national performers in theater, dance, and concerts (Robert Mirabal, among others, has performed here). Also, look for a weekly film series offered year-round.

You can obtain information on current events in the *Taos News,* published every Thursday. The **Taos County Chamber of Commerce** (✆ **800/732-TAOS** [8267] or 575/758-3873; www.taoschamber.com) publishes semiannual listings of *Taos County Events,* as well as the annual *Taos Vacation Guide* that also lists events and happenings around town.

THE PERFORMING ARTS

Fort Burgwin This historic site (of the 1,000-year-old Pot Creek Pueblo), located about 10 miles south of Taos, is a summer campus of Dallas's Southern Methodist University. From mid-May through mid-August, the SMU-in-Taos curriculum (including studio arts, humanities, and sciences) includes courses in music and theater. There are regularly scheduled orchestral concerts, guitar and harpsichord recitals, and theater performances available to the community, without charge, throughout the summer. 6580 NM 518, Ranchos de Taos. ✆ **575/758-8322.**

Music from Angel Fire This acclaimed program of chamber music begins in mid-August, with weekend concerts, and continues up to Labor Day. Based in the small resort community of Angel Fire (located about 21 miles east of Taos, off US 64), it also presents numerous concerts in Taos, Las Vegas, and Raton. P.O. Box 502, Angel Fire. ✆ **575/377-3233** or 888/377-3300. www.musicfromangelfire.org.

Taos School of Music ★ Founded in 1963, this music summer school, located at the Hotel St. Bernard in Taos Ski Valley, offers excellent concerts by notable artists. From mid-June to mid-August there is an intensive 8-week study and performance program for advanced students of violin, viola, cello, and piano. The 8-week **Chamber Music Festival,** an important adjunct of the school, offers 16 concerts and seminars for the public; performances are given by pianist Robert McDonald; the Borromeo, St. Lawrence, and Brentano String quartets; and the international young student artists. Performances are held at the Taos Community Auditorium and the Hotel St. Bernard. P.O. Box 1879. ✆ **575/776-2388.** www.taosschoolofmusic.com. Tickets for chamber music concerts $15 for adults, $10 for children 16 and under.

The Major Concert & Performance Halls

Taos Convention Center, 121 Civic Plaza Dr. (✆ **575/758-5792**). This convention space has an exhibit center where presentations, lectures, and concerts are held.

Taos Community Auditorium, Kit Carson Memorial State Park (✆ **575/758-4677**). A comfortable, small-town space, this community auditorium makes a nice venue for films, concerts, and lectures.

THE CLUB & MUSIC SCENE

Adobe Bar ★ A favorite gathering place for locals and visitors, the Adobe Bar is known for its live music series (nights vary) devoted to the eclectic talents of Taos musicians. The schedule offers a little of everything—classical, jazz, folk, flamenco, and world music. The Adobe Bar features a wide selection of international beers, wines by the glass, light New Mexican dining, desserts, and an espresso menu. Their margarita consistently wins the "Best of Taos" competition in *Taos News.* In the Historic Taos Inn (p. 206), 125 Paseo del Pueblo Norte. ✆ **575/758-2233.**

Alley Cantina ★ Moments This bar that touts its location as the oldest house in Taos has become the hot late-night spot. The focus is on interaction, as well as TV sports, but there's also a cozy outdoor patio. Patrons playing shuffleboard, pool, chess, and backgammon listen to live music 4 to 5 nights a week. Burgers, fish and chips, and other informal dishes are served until 11pm. 121 Teresina Lane. ✆ **575/758-2121.** Cover for live music only.

Anaconda Bar ★★ Set in the eco-resort El Monte Sagrado, this is Taos's most happening nightspot, with live entertainment—jazz, blues, Native American flute, or country—playing Thursday through Saturday. An anaconda sculpture snaking across the ceiling and an 11,000-gallon fish tank set the contemporary tone of the place, where a variety of the hotel's signature dishes are served. In the El Monte Sagrado hotel (p. 204), 317 Kit Carson Rd. ✆ **575/758-3502.** www.elmontesagrado.com.

Caffe Tazza ★ This cozy three-room cafe, with a summer patio, attracts local community groups, artists, performers, and poets. Plays, films, comedy, and musical performances are given here on weekends (and some weeknights in summer). The food—soups and sandwiches—is quite good. Pastries, which are imported from many bakeries around the region, are almost as big a draw here as the Taos Cow ice cream. Choose from 15 flavors. 122 Kit Carson Rd. ✆ **575/758-8706.**

Eske's Brew Pub and Eatery ★ I have a fondness for this place that one might have for an oasis in the desert. The first time I ate here, I'd been on assignment ice climbing and just spent 8 hours in the shadow of a canyon, hacking my way up an 80-foot frozen waterfall. I sat down at one of the high tables in the main room, dipped into a big bowl of Wanda's green-chile turkey stew, and felt the blood return to my extremities. Owner, Steve "Eske" Eskeback, designs all the beers here, which are excellent. At times, this can be a rowdy place, but mostly it's just fun, with lots of ski patrollers and mountain guides showing up to swap stories. In summer, you can eat on picnic tables outside. March to

September, and peak times such as spring and winter breaks, it's open daily 11:30am to 10pm; the rest of winter Friday to Sunday 11:30am to 10pm. 106 Des Georges Lane. ✆ 575/758-1517.

Sagebrush Inn ★ This is a real hot spot for locals. The atmosphere is Old West, with a rustic wooden dance floor and plenty of rowdiness. Dancers generally two-step to country music nightly, year-round, starting at 9pm. Paseo del Pueblo Sur (P.O. Box 557). ✆ 575/758-2254.

9

Albuquerque

Albuquerque is the gateway to New Mexico, the portal through which most domestic and international visitors pass before traveling on to other towns. But it's worth stopping for a day or two in order to get a feel for the history of this area.

From the rocky crest of Sandia Peak at sunset, one can see the lights of this city spread out across 16 miles of high desert grassland. As the sun drops beyond the western horizon, it reflects off the Rio Grande, flowing through Albuquerque more than a mile below. This waterway is the bloodline for the area, what allowed a city to spring up in this vast desert, and it continues to be at the center of the area's growth.

The railroad, which set up a major stop here in 1880, prompted much of Albuquerque's initial growth, but that economic explosion was nothing compared with what has happened since World War II. Designated a major national center for military research and production, Albuquerque became a trading center for New Mexico, whose populace is spread widely across the land. That's why the city may strike visitors as nothing more than one big strip mall. Look closely, and you'll see ranchers, Native Americans, and Hispanic villagers stocking up on goods to take home.

Mornings are always unique in this city, when the clear blue sky often fills with hot-air balloons. The Albuquerque International Balloon Fiesta celebrates the sport in October, but now visitors can partake of the city's airy legacy any time at the new Balloon Museum on the north end of town.

Climbing out of the valley is **Route 66,** well worth a drive, if only to see the rust that time has left. Old court motels still line the street, many with their funky '50s signage. One enclave on this route is the **University of New Mexico district,** with a number of hippie-ish cafes and shops.

Farther downhill, you'll come to **downtown Albuquerque.** During the day, this area is all suits and heels, but at night it boasts a hip nightlife scene. People from all over the state come to Albuquerque to check out the live music and dance clubs, most within walking distance from each other.

The section called **Old Town** is worth a visit. Though it's the most touristy part of town, it's also a unique Southwestern village with a beautiful and intact plaza. Also in this area are Albuquerque's aquarium and botanical gardens, as well as its zoo.

Indian pueblos in the area welcome tourists, and, along with other pueblos throughout New Mexico, have worked to create the Pueblo Cultural Center, a showplace of Indian crafts of both past and present. The country's longest aerial tramway takes visitors to the top of Sandia Peak, which protects the city's eastern flank. To the west run a series of volcanoes; the Petroglyph National Monument there is an amazing tribute to the area's ancient Native American past.

1 ORIENTATION

ARRIVING

Albuquerque is the transportation hub for New Mexico, so getting in and out of town is easy. For more detailed information, see "Getting There & Getting Around," in chapter 3.

BY PLANE The **Albuquerque International Sunport** (ABQ; ✆ **505/842-4366;** www.cabq.gov/airport) is in the south-central part of the city, between I-25 on the west and Kirtland Air Force Base on the east, just south of Gibson Boulevard. Sleek and efficient, the airport is served by most national airlines and two local ones. It offers free Wi-Fi.

Most hotels have courtesy vans to meet their guests and take them to their respective destinations. In addition, **Airport Shuttle of Albuquerque** (✆ **505/765-1234;** www.airportshuttleabq.com) runs services to and from city hotels. **ABQ Ride** (✆ **505/243-7433;** www.cabq.gov/transit/index.html), Albuquerque's public bus system, also makes airport stops. There is efficient taxi service to and from the airport, and there are numerous car-rental agencies.

BY TRAIN **Amtrak's** "Southwest Chief" arrives and departs daily to and from Los Angeles and Chicago. The station is at the Alvarado Transportation Center, 300 Second St. SW (at the corner of Lead and Second; ✆ **800/USA-RAIL** [872-7245] or 505/842-9650; www.amtrak.com).

BY BUS **Greyhound/Trailways** (✆ **800/231-2222;** www.greyhound.com) and **TNM&O** (✆ **505/243-4435;** www.tnmo.com) arrive and depart from the Alvarado Transportation Center, 300 Second St. SW (at the corner of Lead and Second).

BY CAR If you're driving, you'll probably arrive via either the east–west I-40 or the north–south I-25. Exits are well marked. For information and advice on driving in New Mexico, see "Getting There & Getting Around," in chapter 3.

VISITOR INFORMATION

The main office of the **Albuquerque Convention and Visitors Bureau** is at 20 First Plaza NW (✆ **800/284-2282** or 505/842-9918; www.itsatrip.org). It's open Monday to Friday 8am to 5pm. There are information centers at the airport, on the lower level at the bottom of the escalator, open daily 9:30am to 8pm; and in Old Town at 303 Romero St. NW, Ste. 107, open daily 10am to 5pm. Tape-recorded information about current local events is available from the bureau after 5pm weekdays and all day Saturday and Sunday. Call ✆ **800/284-2282.**

CITY LAYOUT

The city's sprawl takes awhile to get used to. A visitor's first impression is of a grid of arteries lined with shopping malls and fast-food eateries, with residences tucked behind on side streets.

If you look at a map of Albuquerque, you'll notice that it lies at the crossroads of I-25 north–south and I-40 east–west. Focus your attention on the **southwest quadrant:** Here, you'll find both downtown Albuquerque and Old Town, site of many tourist attractions. Lomas Boulevard and Central Avenue, the old Route 66 (US 66), flank downtown on the north and south. They come together 2 miles west of downtown near

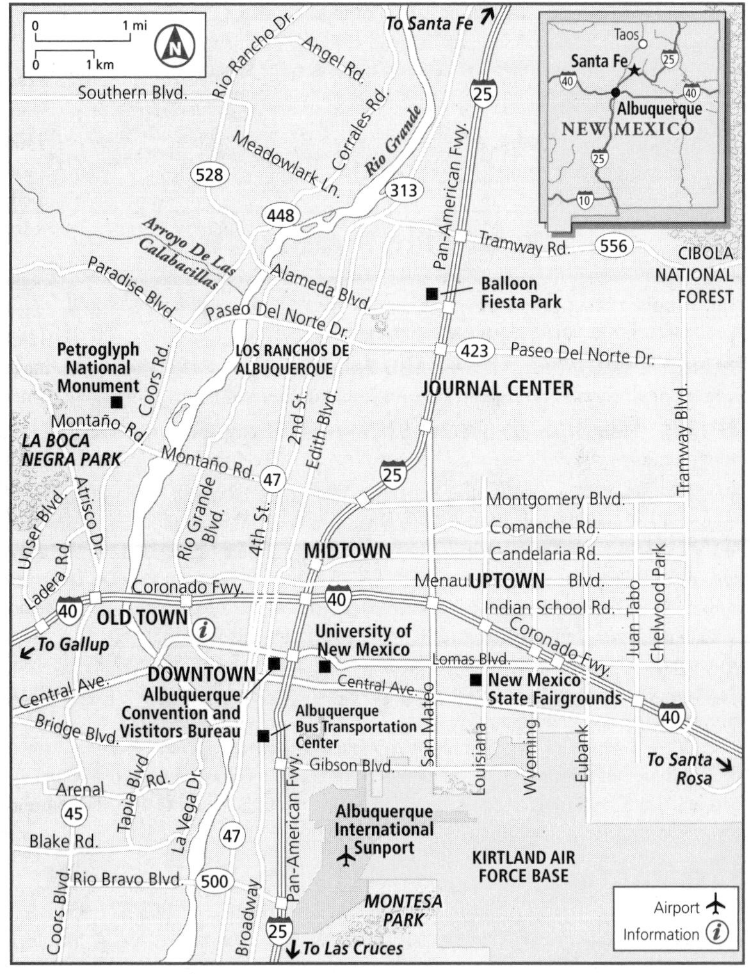

Old Town Plaza, the historical and spiritual heart of the city. Lomas and Central continue east across I-25, staying about half a mile apart as they pass by the University of New Mexico and the New Mexico State Fairgrounds. The airport is directly south of the UNM campus, about 3 miles via Yale Boulevard. Kirtland Air Force Base—site of Sandia National Laboratories—is an equal distance south of the fairgrounds, on Louisiana Boulevard.

Roughly paralleling I-40 to the north is Menaul Boulevard, the focus of midtown and uptown shopping, as well as the hotel districts. As Albuquerque expands northward, the Journal Center business park area, about 4½ miles north of the freeway interchange, is expanding. Near there is home to the Albuquerque International Balloon Fiesta and the new Balloon Museum. East of Eubank Boulevard lie the Sandia Foothills, where the alluvial plain slants a bit more steeply toward the mountains.

When looking for an address, it is helpful to know that Central Avenue divides the city into north and south, and the railroad tracks—which run just east of First Street downtown—are the dividing line between east and west. Street names are followed by a directional: NE, NW, SE, or SW.

MAPS The most comprehensive Albuquerque street map is distributed by the Convention and Visitors Bureau, 20 First Plaza NW (✆ **800/284-2282** or 505/842-9918).

2 GETTING AROUND

Albuquerque is easy to get around, thanks to its wide thoroughfares and grid layout, combined with its efficient transportation systems.

BY PUBLIC TRANSPORTATION **ABQ Ride** (✆ **505/243-7433**) cloaks the arterials with its city bus network. Call for information on routes and fares.

BY TAXI **Yellow Cab** (✆ **505/247-8888**) serves the city and surrounding area 24 hours a day.

BY CAR The Yellow Pages lists more than 30 car-rental agencies in Albuquerque. Among them are the following well-known national firms: **Alamo,** 3400 University Blvd. SE (✆ 505/842-4057; www.alamo.com); **Avis,** at the airport (✆ 505/842-4080; www.avis.com); **Budget,** at the airport (✆ 505/247-3443; www.budget.com); **Dollar,** at the airport (✆ 505/842-4224; www.dollar.com); **Hertz,** at the airport (✆ 505/842-4235; www.hertz.com); **Rent-A-Wreck,** 2001 Ridegecrest Dr. SE (✆ 505/232-7552; www.rentawreck.com/nm.htm); and **Thrifty,** 2039 Yale Blvd. SE (✆ 505/842-8733; www.thrifty.com). Those not located at the airport itself are close by and can provide rapid airport pickup and delivery service.

Parking is generally not difficult in Albuquerque. Meters operate weekdays 8am to 6pm and are not monitored at other times. Only the large downtown hotels charge for parking. Traffic is a problem only at certain hours. Avoid I-25 and I-40 at the center of town around 8am and 5pm.

FAST FACTS

You can reach the **Greater Albuquerque Medical Association** at ✆ **505/821-4583.** The major hospital facilities are **Presbyterian Hospital,** 1100 Central Ave. SE (✆ **505/841-1234,** or 505/841-1111 for emergency services), and **University of New Mexico Hospital,** 2211 Lomas Blvd. NE (✆ **505/272-2111,** or 505/272-2411 for emergency services). In Albuquerque, the sales tax is 6.875%. An additional hotel tax of 6% will be added to your bill.

See also "Fast Facts: American Southwest," on p. 607.

3 WHERE TO STAY

Albuquerque's hotel glut is good news for travelers looking for quality rooms at a reasonable cost. Except during peak periods—specifically, the New Mexico Arts and Crafts Fair (late June), the New Mexico State Fair (Sept), and the Albuquerque International Balloon

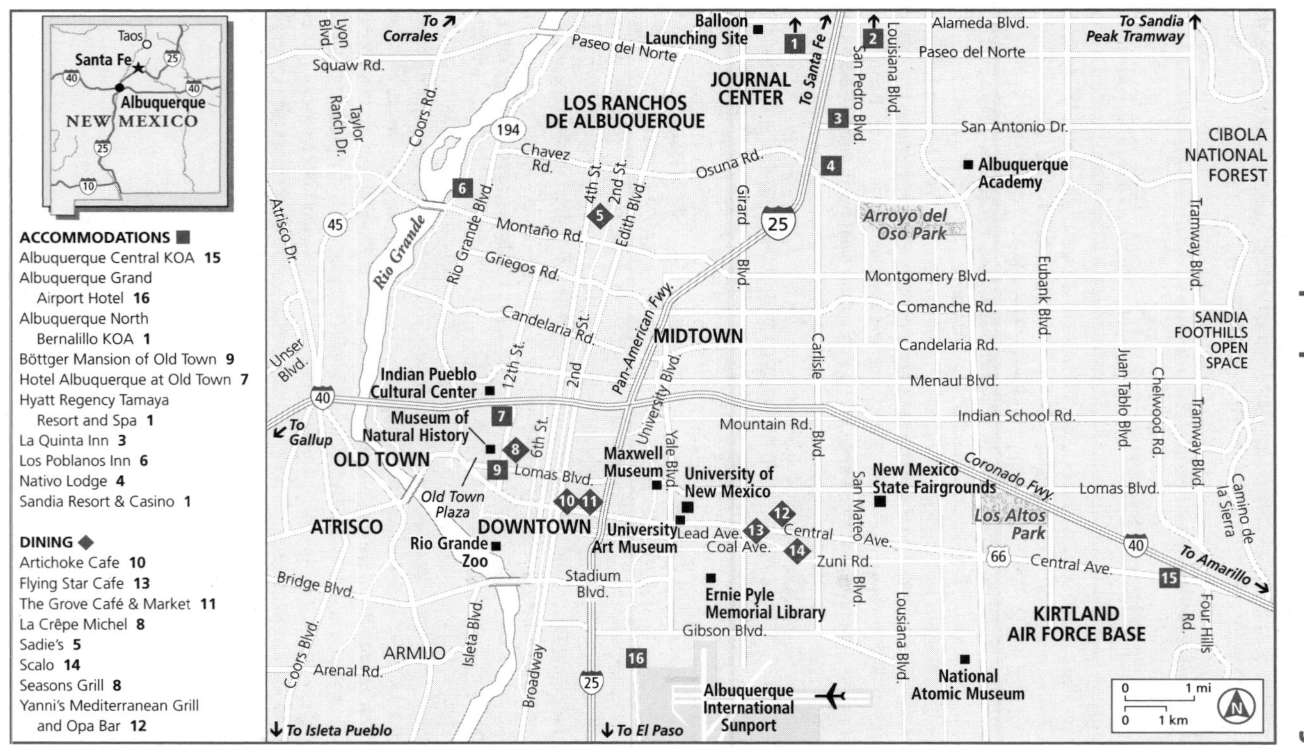
Taos
Santa Fe
Albuquerque
NEW MEXICO
ACCOMMODATIONS ■
Albuquerque Central KOA 15
Albuquerque Grand Airport Hotel 16
Albuquerque North Bernalillo KOA 1
Böttger Mansion of Old Town 9
Hotel Albuquerque at Old Town 7
Hyatt Regency Tamaya Resort and Spa 1
La Quinta Inn 3
Los Poblanos Inn 6
Nativo Lodge 4
Sandia Resort & Casino 1
DINING ◆
Artichoke Cafe 10
Flying Star Cafe 13
The Grove Café & Market 11
La Crêpe Michel 8
Sadie's 5
Scalo 14
Seasons Grill 8
Yanni's Mediterranean Grill and Opa Bar 12
Lyon Blvd.
To Corrales
Balloon Launching Site
To Santa Fe
Alameda Blvd.
To Sandia Peak Tramway
Paseo del Norte
Squaw Rd.
JOURNAL CENTER
San Pedro Blvd.
Louisiana Blvd.
LOS RANCHOS DE ALBUQUERQUE
Taylor Ranch Dr.
Coors Rd.
San Antonio Dr.
CIBOLA NATIONAL FOREST
Chavez Rd.
4th St.
2nd St.
Edith Blvd.
Osuna Rd.
Albuquerque Academy
Atrisco Dr.
Montaño Rd.
Rio Grande
Rio Grande Blvd.
Girard Blvd.
Arroyo del Oso Park
Griegos Rd.
Tramway Blvd.
Montgomery Blvd.
Eubank Blvd.
Comanche Rd.
Candelaria Rd.
MIDTOWN
Pan-American Fwy.
SANDIA FOOTHILLS OPEN SPACE
Unser Blvd.
12th St.
2nd
Carlisle Blvd.
Juan Tablo Blvd.
Chelwood Rd.
Indian Pueblo Cultural Center
Menaul Blvd.
University Blvd.
To Gallup
Museum of Natural History
6th St.
Mountain Rd.
Indian School Rd.
OLD TOWN
Lomas Blvd.
Maxwell Museum
Yale Blvd.
University of New Mexico
New Mexico State Fairgrounds
Coronado Fwy.
Camino de la Sierra
Old Town Plaza
San Mateo Ave.
Los Altos Park
ATRISCO
DOWNTOWN
University Art Museum
Lead Ave.
Coal Ave.
Central Ave.
Rio Grande Zoo
Zuni Rd.
Central Ave.
To Amarillo
Bridge Blvd.
Stadium Blvd.
Ernie Pyle Memorial Library
Four Hills Rd.
Gibson Blvd.
KIRTLAND AIR FORCE BASE
Coors Blvd.
ARMIJO
Isleta Blvd.
Arenal Rd.
Broadway
National Atomic Museum
Albuquerque International Sunport
0 1 mi
0 1 km
To Isleta Pueblo
To El Paso

Fiesta (early Oct)—most of the city's hotels have vacant rooms, so guests can frequently request and get lower room rates than the ones posted.

A tax of 12.875% is added to every hotel bill. All hotels and bed-and-breakfasts listed offer rooms for nonsmokers and travelers with disabilities.

HOTELS/MOTELS

Expensive

Hotel Albuquerque at Old Town ★★ This completely renovated hotel just 5 minutes from Old Town offers artfully decorated rooms with views and excellent service. No Albuquerque hotel is closer to top tourist attractions than the Hotel Albuquerque. Constructed in 1975, it existed for years under the Sheraton banner. Now a Heritage Hotel, it has received a $16-million makeover. The cathedral-style lobby has Spanish colonial furnishings and art, a theme that carries into the guest rooms. They're medium size, with comfortable beds and medium-size bathrooms with outer vanities. Request a south-side room, and you'll get a balcony with a view over Old Town. A north-side room yields mountain views but no balconies (this is the side to request during the Balloon Fiesta). The lovely grounds have a long portal and a quaint chapel. The **Q Bar** (p. 262) is one of Albuquerque's chicest night spots, with a good tapas menu and billiards.

800 Rio Grande Blvd. NW, Albuquerque, NM 87104. ✆ **800/237-2133** (reservations only), or 505/843-6300. Fax 505/842-8426. www.hotelabq.com. 188 units. $99–$209 double; $149–$350 jr. suite double. Children stay free in parent's room. AE, DC, DISC, MC, V. Free parking. **Amenities:** 2 restaurants; bar; concierge; executive-level rooms; Jacuzzi; outdoor pool (in summer); room service. *In room:* A/C, TV, hair dryer, Wi-Fi.

Sandia Resort & Casino ★★★ On the Sandia Reservation, at the north end of town, in a grand nine-story Pueblo-style structure, this resort offers plenty of fun activities in a scenic setting. The hotel has spectacular views of the Sandia Mountains and the Albuquerque skyline. The lobby, constructed in a majestic mission-church style, offers space for lounging, and just off it, there's a casino, with 1,800 slots, Vegas-style gambling, and all the blinking lights that a gambler could want. Each spacious guest room, decorated in an elegant Native American motif, has a very comfortable bed, a lounge chair, a desk, and louvered blackout blinds, as well as many amenities. The bathrooms are large, with Italian tile throughout, and robes. The suites are even more spacious, of course. The Green Reed Spa offers a full range of treatments, and the Scott Miller–designed 18-hole golf course wraps around the hotel, giving a sense of lush green to the desert. The **Bien Shur restaurant,** on the ninth floor, offers excellent cuisine and city and mountain views. Be aware that this resort best serves people who like to play into the night. If you're looking for a more relaxing stay, you might choose the Hyatt Tamaya (see below).

30 Rainbow Rd. NE, Albuquerque, NM 87113. www.sandiaresort.com. ✆ **877/272-9199** (reservations only), 800/526-9366, or 505/798-3930. Fax 505/796-7606. 228 units. $139–$299 double; $319–$389 1-bedroom suite; $699 2-bedroom suite. AE, DC, DISC, MC, V. Free valet parking. **Amenities:** 3 restaurants; bar; concierge; golf course; health club; Jacuzzi; large outdoor pool; room service; spa. *In room:* A/C, TV, hair dryer, Wi-Fi.

Moderate

Albuquerque Grand Airport Hotel ★★ This 15-story hotel right at the airport provides spacious rooms with a touch of elegance. The lobby, grill, and lounge areas employ a lot of sandstone, wood, copper, and tile to lend an Anasazi feel, which carries into the rooms, each with a broad view from a balcony. A recent remodel brought new, comfortable mattresses and bright pine furnishings. Air travelers enjoy this hotel's location, but because it has good access to freeways and excellent views, it could also be a wise choice for a few days of browsing around Albuquerque. Of course, you will hear some jet noise. The Rojo Grill serves a variety of American and Southwestern dishes.

2910 Yale Blvd. SE, Albuquerque, NM 87106. ✆ **800/227-1117** or 505/843-7000. Fax 505/843-6307. www.albuquerquegrandairporthotel.com. 276 units. $79–$176 double. AE, DC, DISC, MC, V. Free parking. Small pets (15 lb. or less) welcome with prior approval. **Amenities:** Restaurant; bar; concierge; access to golf course; outdoor pool; 2 tennis courts. *In room:* A/C, TV, hair dryer, Wi-Fi.

Nativo Lodge ★ This full-service hotel provides comfortable rooms with a Native American theme, utilizing high-tech elements as well. It's part of the Heritage Hotels & Resorts group, which, in recent years, has renovated a number of New Mexico hotels such as the Hotel Encanto in Las Cruces and Hotel Albuquerque at Old Town. The five-story building, renovated in 2004, has tan walls throughout the two-tiered lobby and standard-size guest rooms. The rooms are tastefully decorated with Native American geometric patterns creating a cozy feel, with comfortable beds and good linens, desks and small balconies. The bathrooms are small but functional. Be sure to request a room well away from the lounge area, which can be noisy on weekend nights. The service is thoughtful and efficient. This is a good home base for the Balloon Fiesta, as well as to explore the city. The property even has a tepee used for special events.

6000 Pan American Fwy. NE, Albuquerque, NM 87109. ✆ **888/628-4861** or 505/798-4300. Fax 505/798-4305. www.nativolodge.com. $79–$139 double. AE, DC, DISC, MC, V. Free parking. **Amenities:** Restaurant; bar; health club; Jacuzzi; indoor/outdoor pool; room service. *In room:* A/C, TV, hair dryer, Wi-Fi.

Inexpensive

La Quinta Inn La Quinta offers reliable, clean rooms at a decent price. Rooms are tastefully decorated, fairly spacious, and comfortable, each with a table and chairs and a shower-only bathroom big enough to move around in. Each king room has a recliner, and two-room suites are available. If you're headed to the Balloon Fiesta, this is a good choice because it's not far from the launch site, though you'll have to reserve as much as a year in advance.

There's another La Quinta near the airport (La Quinta Airport Inn, 2116 Yale Blvd. SE); you can make reservations for either branch at the toll-free number.

5241 San Antonio Dr. NE, Albuquerque, NM 87109. ✆ **800/531-5900** or 505/821-9000. Fax 505/821-2399. www.lq.com. 130 units. $72–$79 double (higher during Balloon Fiesta). Children stay free in parent's room. AE, DC, DISC, MC, V. Free parking. Pets welcome (free). **Amenities:** Heated outdoor pool (May–Oct). *In room:* A/C, TV, hair dryer, Wi-Fi.

BED & BREAKFASTS

Böttger Mansion of Old Town ★★ Decorated with antiques but not overdone with chintz, this Victorian inn situated right in Old Town is an excellent choice. It offers a sweet taste of a past era. My favorite room is the Carole Rose, with lots of sun; also lovely is the Rebecca Leah, with pink marble tile and a Jacuzzi tub. All rooms are medium-size and have excellent beds; most have small bathrooms. The rooms facing south let in the most sun but pick up a bit of street noise from nearby Central Avenue and a nearby elementary school (both quiet down at night). Breakfast (such as green-chile quiche) is elaborate enough to keep you going through the day, at the end of which you can enjoy treats from the guest snack bar (try the chocolate cookies with a little chile in them). During warm months, the patio is lovely.

110 San Felipe NW, Albuquerque, NM 87104. ✆ **800/758-3639** or 505/243-3639. www.bottger.com. 8 units. $99–$179 double. Rates include full breakfast and snack bar. AE, DISC, MC, V. *In room:* A/C, TV/VCR, hair dryer, Wi-Fi.

Los Poblanos Inn ★★ Lushness in the desert city of Albuquerque? It's no mirage. Nestled among century-old cottonwoods, this bed-and-breakfast sits on 25 acres of European-style gardens and peasantlike vegetable and lavender fields, providing one of the state's richest country-living experiences. Notable architect John Gaw Meem built the structure, a 7-minute drive from Old Town, in the 1930s. All six guest rooms, most arranged around a poetically planted courtyard with a fountain, have unique touches such as hand-carved doors, traditional tin fixtures, fireplaces, and views across the lushly landscaped grounds. The rooms vary in size. All are comfortable, tastefully decorated with good linens, and offer organic shampoo and soap scented with lavender from the inn's garden. At breakfast, you might feast on eggs Florentine made with eggs from the inn's chickens, spinach from the garden, and artisanal bread made locally, while watching peacocks preen outside the windows of the very Mexican-feeling, boldly decorated cantina. Light sleepers should be aware that the peacocks may caw at night. Fortunately, the inn provides earplugs. A copy of the *New York Times* arrives on each doorstep in the morning.

4803 Rio Grande Blvd. NW, Albuquerque, NM 87107. ✆ **866/344-9297** or 505/344-9297. Fax 505/342-1302. www.lospoblanos.com. 7 units. $150–$265 double. Rates include full breakfast. AE, MC, V. Free parking. **Amenities:** Bikes; outdoor pool (in summer); walking trails. *In room:* A/C, hair dryer, Wi-Fi.

NEAR ALBUQUERQUE

Hyatt Regency Tamaya Resort and Spa ★★★ This is the spot for a get-away-from-it-all luxury vacation. Set in the hills above the lush Rio Grande Valley on the Santa Ana Pueblo, this Pueblo-style resort offers a 16,000-square-foot full-service spa and fitness center, an 18-hole Twin Warriors Championship Golf Course designed by Gary Panks, and views of the Sandia Mountains. Rooms are spacious, with large tile bathrooms. Request one that faces the mountains for one of the state's more spectacular vistas. Other rooms look out across a large courtyard, where the pools and hot tub are. Though the resort is surrounded by acres of quiet countryside, it's only 20 minutes from Albuquerque and 50 minutes from Santa Fe. The concierge offers trips to attractions daily, as well as on-site activities such as hot-air balloon rides, horseback rides, and nature/cultural walks or carriage rides by the river. Plan at least one dinner at the innovative Corn Maiden.

1300 Tuyuna Trail, Santa Ana Pueblo, NM 87004. ✆ **800/55-HYATT** (554-9288) or 505/867-1234. www.tamaya.hyatt.com. 350 units. May–Oct $245–$415; Nov–Apr $199–$305, depending on the type of room. Suite rates available upon request. Inquire about spa, horseback riding, golf, and family packages. AE, DC, DISC, MC, V. Free parking. From I-25 take exit 242, following US 550 west to Tamaya Blvd.; drive 1½ miles to the resort. **Amenities:** 2 restaurants; 2 snack bars; bar; children's programs; concierge; golf course; health club; 3 pools (heated year-round); room service; spa; 2 tennis courts. *In room:* A/C, TV, fridge, hair dryer, Wi-Fi.

RV PARKS

Albuquerque Central KOA This RV park, in the foothills east of Albuquerque, is a good choice for those who want to be close to town. It offers some shade trees, lots of amenities, and convenient freeway access. Cabins are available. A fenced dog park offers space for Fido to roam.

12400 Skyline Rd. NE, Albuquerque, NM 87123. ✆ **800/562-7781** or 505/296-2729. www.koa.com. $30–$47 tent site; $35–$65 RV site, depending on hookup; $45–$85 1-room cabin; $48–$95 2-room cabin. All prices valid for up to 2 people. Additional adult $5, child $3. AE, DISC, MC, V. Free parking. Pets welcome. **Amenities:** Bathhouse; bike rentals; Jacuzzi; miniature golf; playground; outdoor pool (summer only); store; Wi-Fi.

Albuquerque North Bernalillo KOA ★ More than 1,000 cottonwood and pine trees shade this park, and you'll see many flowers in the warm months. At the foot of the mountains, 14 miles from Albuquerque, this campground has plenty of amenities. Guests enjoy a free pancake breakfast daily. Reservations are recommended. Six Kamping Kabins are also available.

555 Hill Rd., Bernalillo, NM 87004. ✆ **800/562-3616** or 505/867-5227. www.koa.com. $21–$23 tent site; $30–$36 RV site, depending on hookup; $38 1-bedroom cabin; $48 2-bedroom cabin. Rates include pancake breakfast and are valid for up to 2 people. Additional person $4. Children 5 and under free with parent. AE, DISC, MC, V. Free parking. Pets welcome. **Amenities:** Restaurant; playground; outdoor pool (summer only); store, Wi-Fi.

4 WHERE TO DINE

For the locations of these restaurants, see the map "Central Albuquerque Accommodations & Dining," on p. 241.

IN & AROUND OLD TOWN

Expensive

Seasons Grill ★★ NEW AMERICAN Between sunshine-colored walls and under an arched ceiling, this restaurant serves sophisticated flavors just steps from Old Town. It's a sweet oasis at midday and a romantic spot in the evening. The upstairs cantina bustles at sundown, with folks drinking margaritas. Service is excellent. At lunch you can't go wrong with the Angus burger with lemon aioli and roasted poblano chiles, served with herb fries. For the lighter eater, a number of salads head the menu. Dinner brings more sophisticated offerings. The grilled pork chop with goat cheese and roasted potatoes is tasty, as is the hoisin-glazed Atlantic salmon with jasmine rice. A full bar and an imaginative wine and beer list accompany the menu. On Saturday and Sunday evenings in summer, live jazz plays.

2031 Mountain Rd. NW. ✆ **505/766-5100.** Reservations recommended at dinner. Main courses $7–$14 lunch, $16–$40 dinner. AE, DC, DISC, MC, V. Mon–Fri 11:30am–2:30pm; daily 5–10:30pm. Cantina daily 4pm–midnight.

Moderate

La Crêpe Michel ★★ FRENCH Locals love this small cafe, tucked away in a secluded walkway not far from the plaza, where the food is fun and imaginatively prepared. Run by Chef Claudie Zamet-Wilcox, from France, it has a cozy, informal European feel, with checked table coverings and simple furnishings. Service is friendly and calm, which makes this a good place for a romantic meal. You can't miss with any of the crepes. The *crêpe aux fruits de mer* (blend of sea scallops, bay scallops, and shrimp in a velouté sauce with mushrooms) is especially nice, as is the *crêpe à la volaille* (chunks of chicken in a cream sauce with mushrooms and Madeira wine). For a heartier meal, try one of the specials listed on the board on the wall, such as the beef filet (tenderloin

Kids Family-Friendly Restaurants

Flying Star Cafe (p. 248) With a huge selection, a relaxed atmosphere, and a number of locations, the whole family can enjoy this place.

Sadie's (p. 246) Kids like the quesadillas, tacos, and *sopaipillas* drizzled with honey; parents like the casual atmosphere, where kid noise isn't scorned.

finished with either black peppercorn–brandy cream sauce or Roquefort-brandy cream sauce) or the *saumon au champagne* (filet of salmon with a white-wine and cream sauce). Both are served with vegetables cooked just enough to leave them crisp and tasty. For dessert, don't leave without having a *crêpe aux fraises* (strawberry crepe). To accompany your meal, choose from a carefully planned beer and wine menu.

400 San Felipe C2. ✆ **505/242-1251.** www.lacrepemichel.com. Main courses $6–$24. AE, DISC, MC, V. Tues–Sun 11:30am–2pm; Tues–Sat 6–9pm.

Inexpensive

Sadie's ★ Kids NEW MEXICAN Many New Mexicans lament the lost days when this restaurant was in a bowling alley. It's true that you can no longer hear the pins fall, and the main dining room is a little too big and the atmosphere a little too bright, but something is still drawing crowds: It's the food—simply some of the best in New Mexico, with tasty sauces and large portions. I recommend the enchilada, either chicken or beef. The stuffed *sopaipilla* dinner is also delicious and is one of the signature dishes. All meals come with chips and salsa, beans, and *sopaipillas.* There's a full bar, with excellent margaritas (and TV screens for you sports lovers). A casual atmosphere where kids can be themselves makes this a nice spot for families.

6230 Fourth St. NW. ✆ **505/345-5339.** Main courses $8–$17. AE, DC, DISC, MC, V. Mon–Sat 11am–10pm; Sun 10am–9pm.

DOWNTOWN

Expensive

Artichoke Cafe ★★ CONTINENTAL An art gallery as well as a restaurant, this popular spot has modern paintings and sculptures, offering bursts of color set against calm earth tones, a hint at the innovative dining experience offered here. Set in three rooms, this is a nice romantic place. The service is friendly and efficient. At lunch, a number of gourmet sandwiches top the menu, along with salads. One of my favorites is the grilled Greek lamb salad, with tomatoes, capers, feta, and grilled eggplant. At dinner, you might start with roasted garlic with Montrachet goat cheese, and then move on to the housemade pumpkin ravioli with hazelnut-sage butter sauce, or sea scallops wrapped in proscuitto served with green beans and small potatoes. A carefully selected beer and wine (*Wine Spectator* award-winning) list accompanies the menu. Recently the Artichoke has opened a wine bar on the premises, a fun, cozy spot.

424 Central Ave. SE. ✆ **505/243-0200.** www.artichokecafe.com. Reservations recommended. Main courses $9–$15 lunch, $18–$31 dinner. AE, DC, DISC, MC, V. Mon–Fri 11am–2:30pm; Mon 5:30–9pm; Tues–Sat 5:30–10pm; Sun 5–9 pm.

Moderate

The Grove Café & Market ★★ **Finds** CAFE/LIGHT FARE Albuquerque's hippest new dining spot in the EDo district (east of downtown) offers fresh breakfasts and lunches utilizing organic and locally grown produce in a fun and open space. Colorful nature paintings hang on sky-blue walls, and a patio opens during warm months. Order at a counter and a very friendly server brings your food to the table. The menu offers creative twists on standards, such as French-style pancakes with fruit and crème fraiche, but the real winner here is the croque madame—black forest ham, tomato, and Gruyère cheese on rustic farm loaf, topped with a sunny-side-up egg. Wash it all down with good coffees and teas. This is also an excellent place to stock a picnic basket and purchase specialty teas and cookies in the Market portion of the restaurant.

600 Central Ave. SE (just west of I-25). ✆ **505/248-9800.** www.thegrovecafemarket.com. All main courses under $10. AE, MC, V. Tues–Sat 7am–4pm; Sun 8am–3pm.

UNIVERSITY & NOB HILL

Moderate

Scalo ★★ INTERNATIONAL/ITALIAN This Nob Hill restaurant is a local favorite, so it's usually crowded, a good sign of the food's quality. The place has a simple, bistro-style elegance, with white-linen-clothed tables indoors, plus outdoor tables in a covered, temperature-controlled patio. Service is decent. The kitchen, which makes its own pasta and breads, offers an international menu with excellent selections for lunch and dinner. Seasonal menus focus on New Mexico–grown produce. At lunch you can select from salads, wood-fired pizzas, and paninis. Their *panini con salsiccia* has sausage, caramelized onions, and mozzarella. The varied dinner menu offers soups, salads, pizza, pasta, and meat and fish entrees. The *bianchi e neri al capesante* has black and white linguine, shrimp, salmon, and peas in a cream sauce. For dinner a standing favorite is the veal scallopine with sautéed mushrooms. The wine list won a *Wine Spectator* award; from it you can sample 30 wines by the glass. Or you may order from the full bar.

3500 Central Ave. SE. ✆ **505/255-8781.** www.scalonobhill.com. Reservations recommended. Lunch $6–$10, dinner $8–$29. AE, DC, DISC, MC, V. Mon–Thurs 11:30am–10pm; Fri 11:30am–11pm; Sat 11:30am–11pm; Sun 11am–9pm.

Yanni's Mediterranean Grill and Opa Bar ★★ MEDITERRANEAN With bright blue and white decor, Athenian-style pillars, and Mediterranean paintings on the walls, this is a great place for a festive meal. Locals crowd the cafe any time they can, including the patio with big windows looking out on Central Avenue. Service is friendly, though overworked during peak hours. All food is made fresh, with specials daily. You might start with jumbo sea scallops seared and served with grilled tomato, and then move on to one of the excellent specials such as wild opa roasted with oranges, wild halibut seared crispy with lemon and thyme, or, my favorite, oven-roasted lamb. The menu hosts a variety of pasta dishes and, of course, moussaka. Entrees come with a salad, bread, vegetable, and a potato or rice side. An international wine list featuring Greek offerings and a full bar accompany the menu. And the attached Opa! Bar provides live entertainment on weekends.

3109 Central Ave. NE. ✆ **505/268-9250.** www.yannisandopabar.com. Reservations recommended. Main courses $7–$14 lunch, $13–$27 dinner. AE, DISC, MC, V. Mon–Thurs 11am–10pm; Fri–Sat 11am–11pm; Sun noon–9pm.

Inexpensive

Flying Star Cafe ★ Kids CAFE/BAKERY The Flying Star Cafe makes good on its promise of uptown food with down-home ingredients. It's a fun and friendly place with excellent contemporary international food. But beware: During mealtime, the university location on Central Avenue gets packed and rowdy. The selections range broadly, all made with local and organic produce, when possible. You can choose from 16 different breakfast options ranging from homemade soups and salads to sandwiches and pasta (and pizza at the Juan Tabo and Rio Grande locations). Try the Rancher's Melt (New Zealand sirloin sautéed with green chile, with provolone and horseradish on sourdough) or the Buddha's Bowl (sautéed vegetables, in ginger sauce, with tofu over jasmine rice). Flying Star also has locations at 4501 Juan Tabo Blvd. NE (✆ **505/275-8311**); 8001 Menaul Blvd. NE (✆ **505/293-6911**); and 4026 Rio Grande Blvd. NW (✆ **505/344-6714**). They don't serve alcohol, but they do brew up plenty of espresso and cappuccino. Kids enjoy the relaxed atmosphere and their own selections from the menu. Though hours vary for each location, they are all open daily for breakfast, lunch, and dinner.

3416 Central Ave. SE. ✆ **505/255-6633.** www.flyingstarcafe.com. All menu items under $15. AE, DISC, MC, V. Daily 6am–11:30pm.

5 WHAT TO SEE & DO

Albuquerque's original town site, known today as **Old Town,** is the central point of interest for visitors. Here, grouped around the plaza, are the venerable Church of San Felipe de Neri and numerous restaurants, art galleries, and crafts shops. Several important museums are close by. Within a few blocks are the 25,000-square-foot Albuquerque Aquarium and the 50-acre Rio Grande Botanic Garden (near Central Ave. and Tingley Dr. NW), both well worth a visit.

But don't get stuck in Old Town. Elsewhere, you'll find the Sandia Peak Tramway, the new Balloon Museum, and a number of natural attractions. Within day-trip range are several pueblos and significant monuments (see "Touring the Jemez Mountain Trail," later in this chapter).

Albuquerque Museum of Art and History ★★ Kids Take an interesting journey into New Mexico's present and past in this museum on the outskirts of Old Town. An expansion has brought new gallery space, filled with impressive changing exhibits. Most notable for me are works from the museum's art collection, which includes canvases by Fritz Scholder, Peter Hurd, Ernest Blumenshein, and Georgia O'Keeffe, as well as contemporary woodwork by Luis Tapia. Downstairs take a trip through history, represented by an impressive collection of Spanish colonial artifacts. Displays include Don Quixote–style helmets, swords, and horse armor, a 19th-century house compound and chapel, and gear used by *vaqueros,* the original cowboys who came to the area in the 16th century. In an old-style theater, two films on Albuquerque history are shown. An **Old Town walking tour** originates here at 11am Tuesday to Sunday during spring, summer, and fall. A gift shop sells books and jewelry, and a cafe serves upscale sandwiches and soups. Plan to spend 1 to 2 hours here.

2000 Mountain Rd. NW. ✆ **505/243-7255.** www.albuquerquemuseum.com. Admission $4 adults, $2 seniors 65 and older, $1 children 4–12. Tues–Sun 9am–5pm. Closed major holidays.

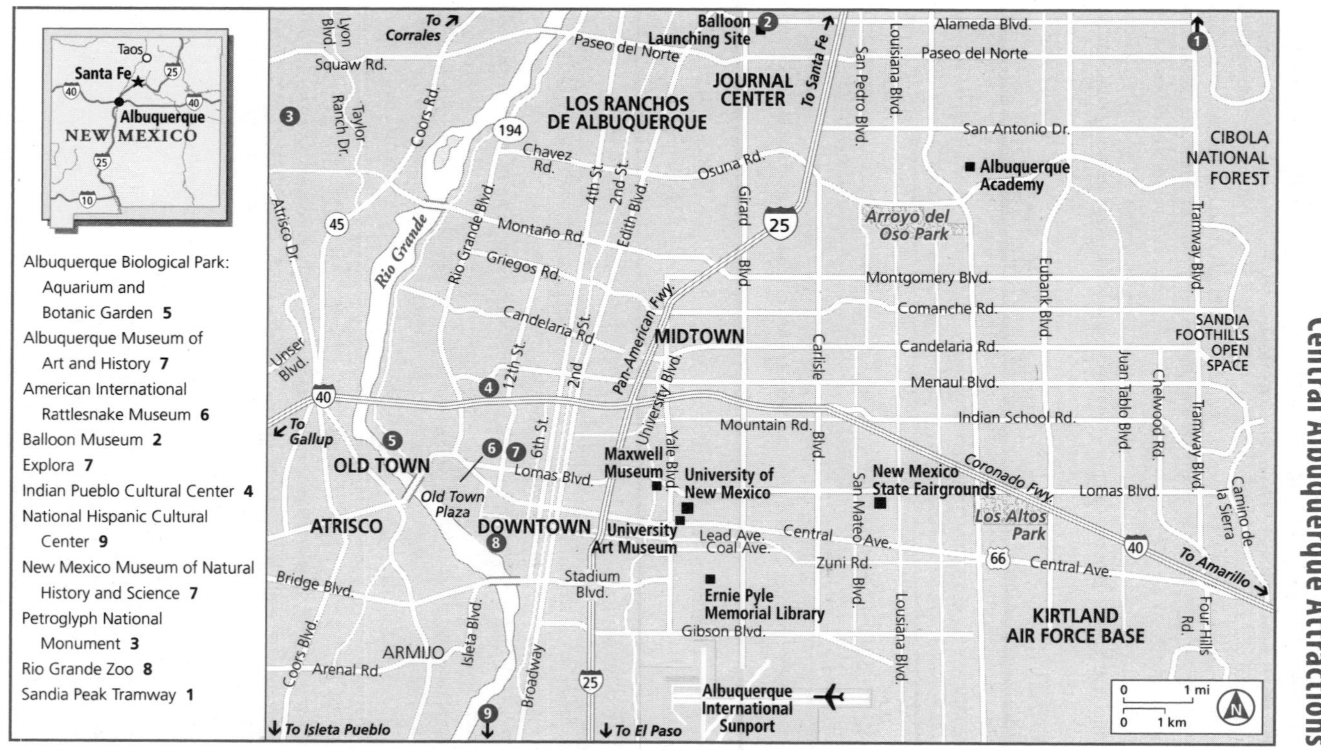
Taos
Santa Fe
Albuquerque
NEW MEXICO
Albuquerque Biological Park:
Aquarium and Botanic Garden 5
Albuquerque Museum of Art and History 7
American International Rattlesnake Museum 6
Balloon Museum 2
Explora 7
Indian Pueblo Cultural Center 4
National Hispanic Cultural Center 9
New Mexico Museum of Natural History and Science 7
Petroglyph National Monument 3
Rio Grande Zoo 8
Sandia Peak Tramway 1
Lyon Blvd.
To Corrales
Balloon Launching Site
Paseo del Norte
Alameda Blvd.
Squaw Rd.
Taylor Ranch Dr.
Coors Rd.
LOS RANCHOS DE ALBUQUERQUE
JOURNAL CENTER
To Santa Fe
San Pedro Blvd.
Louisiana Blvd.
San Antonio Dr.
CIBOLA NATIONAL FOREST
Chavez Rd.
4th St.
2nd St.
Edith Blvd.
Osuna Rd.
Girard Blvd.
Albuquerque Academy
Atrisco Dr.
Rio Grande
Rio Grande Blvd.
Montaño Rd.
Griegos Rd.
Arroyo del Oso Park
Tramway Blvd.
Montgomery Blvd.
Eubank Blvd.
Comanche Rd.
SANDIA FOOTHILLS OPEN SPACE
Candelaria Rd.
MIDTOWN
Pan-American Fwy.
Carlisle Blvd.
Unser Blvd.
12th St.
2nd St.
Menaul Blvd.
Juan Tablo Blvd.
Chelwood Rd.
To Gallup
University Blvd.
Mountain Rd.
Indian School Rd.
6th St.
OLD TOWN
Old Town Plaza
Lomas Blvd.
Maxwell Museum
Yale Blvd.
University of New Mexico
New Mexico State Fairgrounds
Coronado Fwy.
Camino de la Sierra
ATRISCO
DOWNTOWN
University Art Museum
Lead Ave.
Coal Ave.
Central Ave.
San Mateo Blvd.
Los Altos Park
Zuni Rd.
To Amarillo
Bridge Blvd.
Stadium Blvd.
Ernie Pyle Memorial Library
Gibson Blvd.
KIRTLAND AIR FORCE BASE
Four Hills Rd.
Coors Blvd.
Arenal Rd.
ARMIJO
Isleta Blvd.
Broadway
Albuquerque International Sunport
To Isleta Pueblo
To El Paso
0 1 mi
0 1 km

Balloon Museum ★★ Kids The Anderson-Abruzzo Albuquerque International Balloon Museum holds special significance for me, as my parents owned part of the first hot-air balloon in Albuquerque over 40 years ago. Today, with the Albuquerque International Balloon Fiesta drawing hundreds of brilliantly colored and imaginatively shaped balloons to the city each October (p. 37), this museum's time has come. It tells the history of ballooning, from the first flight in France in 1783, with a rooster, sheep, and duck as passengers, to the use of balloons in military, science, and aerospace research. Most poignant are displays of Albuquerque balloonists Maxie Anderson and Ben Abruzzo, who, with Larry Newman, completed the first manned crossing of the Atlantic Ocean in 1978. Originals and replicas of various historic crafts dot the three-story-tall space, and windows look out at the Sandia Mountains and Rio Grande Valley. Kids will enjoy the flight simulator, which tests their ability to fly and land a balloon on target. Plan on spending at least an hour here.

9201 Balloon Museum Dr. NE. ✆ **505/768-6020.** www.cabq.gov/balloon.com. Admission $4 adults, $2 seniors 65 and older, $1 children 4–12, free for children 3 and under. Tues–Sun 9am–5pm. Closed New Year's Day, Thanksgiving, Christmas, and city holidays.

Indian Pueblo Cultural Center ★ Kids Owned and operated as a nonprofit organization by the 19 pueblos of New Mexico, this is a fine place to begin an exploration of Native American culture. About a mile northeast of Old Town, this museum—modeled after Pueblo Bonito, a spectacular 9th-century ruin in Chaco Culture National Historic Park—consists of several parts.

You'll want to spend 1 to 2 hours here. Begin above ground, where you'll find changing shows of contemporary Puebloan arts and crafts. Next, head to the basement, where a permanent exhibit depicts the evolution of the various pueblos from prehistory to present, including displays of the distinctive handicrafts of each community. Note especially how pottery differs in concept and design from one pueblo to the next. On the first floor is an enormous (10,000-sq.-ft.) **gift shop,** featuring fine pottery, rugs, sand paintings, katsinas (kachinas), drums, and jewelry, among other things. Southwestern clothing and souvenirs are also available. Prices here are quite reasonable.

Throughout the year, **Native American dancers** perform in an outdoor arena that is surrounded by original murals. Dances are at noon in winter, and at 11am and 2pm in spring. In summer, dances are scheduled at 2pm on Thursday and Friday, and at 11am and 2pm on Saturday. Often, artisans demonstrate their crafts there as well. During certain weeks of the year, such as the Balloon Fiesta, dances are performed daily.

The restaurant serves traditional Native American foods. It's a good place for some Indian fry bread and a bowl of *posole.*

2401 12th St. NW. ✆ **866/855-7902** or 505/843-7270. www.indianpueblo.org. Admission $6 adults, $5.50 seniors, $1 students, free for children 4 and under. AE, DISC, MC, V. Daily 9am–5:30pm; restaurant Mon–Fri 8am–3pm; Fri–Sat 8am–10pm. Closed New Year's Day, July 4, Labor Day, Thanksgiving, and Christmas.

National Hispanic Cultural Center ★ In the historic Barelas neighborhood on the Camino Real, this gem of Albuquerque museums offers a rich cultural journey through hundreds of years of history and across the globe. It explores Hispanic arts and lifeways with visual arts, drama, music, dance, and other programs. I most enjoy the 11,000-square-foot gallery space, which exhibits exciting contemporary and traditional works, as well as changing exhibits. A restaurant offers New Mexican and American food for breakfast and lunch. It's a good spot to sample authentic regional dishes such as tacos, enchiladas, and the rich custard dessert called flan. The shop offers a broad range of fun gifts from Latin America and New Mexico. Plan to spend 1 to 2 hours here.

1701 Fourth St. SW (corner of Fourth St. and Av. Cesar Chavez). ✆ **505/246-2261.** Fax 505/246-2613. www.nhccnm.org. Admission Tues–Sat $3 adults, $2 seniors 60 and over, free for children 16 and under; Sun free for adults and seniors. MC, V. Tues–Sun 10am–5pm; restaurant Tues–Fri 7:30am–3pm; Sat 8am–3pm; Sun 9am–3pm. Closed New Year's Day, Easter, Memorial Day, Labor Day, and Christmas.

Old Town ★★ A maze of cobbled courtyard walkways leads to hidden patios and gardens, where many of Old Town's 150 galleries and shops are located. Adobe buildings, many refurbished in the pueblo-revival style of the 1950s, are grouped around the tree-shaded plaza, created in 1780. Pueblo and Navajo artisans often display their pottery, blankets, and silver jewelry on the sidewalks lining the plaza.

The buildings of Old Town once served as mercantile shops, grocery stores, and government offices, but the importance of Old Town as Albuquerque's commercial center declined after 1880, when the railroad came through 1¼ miles east of the plaza, and businesses relocated to be closer to the trains. Old Town clung to its historical and sentimental roots, but the quarter fell into disrepair until the 1930s and 1940s, when artisans and other shop owners rediscovered it and the tourism industry burgeoned.

When Albuquerque was established in 1706, the first building erected by the settlers was the **Church of San Felipe de Neri,** which faces the plaza on its north side. It's a cozy church with wonderful stained-glass windows and vivid *retablos* (religious paintings). This house of worship has been in almost continuous use for nearly 300 years.

Though you'll wade through a few trinket and T-shirt shops on the plaza, don't be fooled: Old Town is an excellent place to shop. Look for good buys from the Native Americans selling jewelry on the plaza, especially silver bracelets and strung turquoise. If you want to take something fun home and spend very little money, buy a dyed corn necklace. Your best bet when wandering around Old Town is to peek into shops, but there are a few places you'll definitely want to spend time. See "Shopping," later in this chapter, for a list of recommendations. An excellent Old Town historic walking tour originates at the Albuquerque Museum of Art and History (see above) at 11am Tuesday to Sunday during spring, summer, and fall. Plan to spend 2 to 3 hours strolling around.

Northeast of Central Ave. and Rio Grande Blvd. NW. Old Town Visitor Center: 303 Romero St. NW, Albuquerque, NM 87104 (across the street from the Church of San Felipe de Neri). ✆ **505/243-3215.** Visitor Center summer daily 10am–5pm; rest of the year daily 10am–4:30pm.

Petroglyph National Monument ★★ (Kids) These lava flows were once a hunting and gathering area for prehistoric Native Americans, who left a chronicle of their beliefs etched on the dark basalt boulders. Some 25,000 petroglyphs provide a nice outdoor adventure after a morning in a museum. You'll want to stop at the visitor center to get a map and check out the interactive computer. From there, you can drive north to the Boca Negra area, where you'll have a choice of three trails. Take the Mesa Point Trail (30 min.) that climbs quickly up the side of a hill, offering many petroglyph sightings as well as an outstanding view of the Sandia Mountains. If you're traveling with your dog, you can bring her along on the Rinconada Trail. Hikers can have fun searching the rocks for more petroglyphs; there are many yet to be found. This trail (a few miles south of the visitor center) runs for miles around a huge *rincon* (corner) at the base of the lava flow. Camping is not permitted in the park; it's strictly for day use, with picnic areas, drinking water, and restrooms provided. Visitors can see many petroglyphs in 30 minutes, while hikers may want to spend 1 to 2 hours here.

6001 Unser Blvd. NW (3 miles north of I-40 at Unser and Western Trail). ✆ **505/899-0205.** Fax 505/899-0207. www.nps.gov/petr. Admission spring, fall, and winter $1 per vehicle; summer $2 per vehicle. DISC, MC, V. Visitor Center and Boca Negra area daily 8am–5pm. Closed New Year's Day, Thanksgiving, and Christmas.

Sandia Peak ★★ Kids This fun and exciting half-day or evening outing allows incredible views of the Albuquerque landscape and wildlife. The Sandia Peak Tram is a "jigback"; in other words, as one car approaches the top, the other nears the bottom. The two pass halfway through the trip, in the midst of a 1½-mile "clear span" of unsupported cable between the second tower and the upper terminal.

Several hiking trails are available on Sandia Peak, and one of them—La Luz Trail—takes you on a steep and rigorous trek from the base to the summit. The views in all directions are extraordinary. ***Note:*** The trails on Sandia may not be suitable for children. If you'd like to enjoy a meal during your trip, you can eat lunch (salads, burgers, and pasta dishes) or dinner (steaks, seafood, and pasta) at the **High Finance Restaurant and Tavern** at the top of the tram. Recently opened at the base of the of the tram, **Sandiago's Mexican Grill** serves lunch and dinner. Special tram rates apply with dinner reservations. Be aware that the tram does not operate on very windy days. The ride takes 15 minutes each way. Plan to spend 1 to 2 hours here, more if you're a hiker.

10 Tramway Loop NE. ✆ **505/856-7325.** Fax 505/856-6335. www.sandiapeak.com. Admission $18 adults, $15 seniors and teens 13–20, $10 children 5–12, free for children 4 and under. Memorial Day–Labor Day daily 9am–9pm; spring and fall Wed–Mon 9am–8pm, Tues 5–8pm; ski season Wed–Mon 9am–8pm, Tues noon–8pm. Closed 2 weeks each spring and fall for maintenance; check the website for details. Parking $1 daily. AE, DISC, MC, V. To reach the base of the tram, take I-25 north to Tramway Rd. (exit 234), then proceed east about 5 miles on Tramway Rd. (NM 556); or take Tramway Blvd., exit 167 (NM 556), north of I-40 approximately 8½ miles.

6 ESPECIALLY FOR KIDS

Albuquerque Biological Park: Aquarium and Botanic Garden ★★ Kids For those of us born and raised in the desert, this attraction quenches years of soul thirst. The self-guided aquarium tour begins with a beautifully produced 9-minute film that describes the course of the Rio Grande from its origin to the Gulf Coast. Then, you'll move on to the "touch pool," where at certain times of day you can gently touch hermit crabs and starfish. Next comes the eel tank, an arched aquarium you get to walk through and a colorful coral-reef exhibit. Finally, culminating the show, is a 285,000-gallon shark tank.

Within a state-of-the-art 10,000-square-foot conservatory, you'll find the botanical garden, split into two sections. The smaller one houses the desert collection and features plants from the lower Chihuahuan and Sonoran deserts, including unique species from Baja, California. The larger pavilion exhibits the Mediterranean collection and includes many exotic species native to the Mediterranean climates of southern California, South Africa, Australia, and the Mediterranean Basin. Allow at least 2 hours to see both parks. There is a restaurant on the premises. May to September, the PNM Butterfly Pavilion fills with the colors of several hundred North American butterflies.

In December, you can see the "River of Lights Holiday Light Display" Tuesday through Sunday; and June through August, you can attend Thursday evening concerts.

2601 Central Ave. NW. ✆ **505/764-6200.** www.cabq.gov/biopark. Admission $7 adults ($12 with Rio Grande Zoo admission), $3 seniors 65 and over and children 12 and under ($5 with Rio Grande Zoo admission). Ticket sales stop a half-hour before closing. MC, V. Tues–Sun 9am–5pm (June–Aug Sat–Sun until 6pm). Closed New Year's Day, Thanksgiving, and Christmas.

American International Rattlesnake Museum ★ Finds Kids This unique museum, just off Old Town Plaza, has living specimens of common, uncommon, and very rare rattlesnakes of North, Central, and South America, in naturally landscaped habitats. Such oddities as albino and patternless rattlesnakes are included, as is a display of baby rattlesnakes, popular with youngsters. More than 30 species can be seen, followed by a 7-minute film on this contributor to the ecological balance of our hemisphere. Throughout the museum are rattlesnake artifacts from early American history, Native American culture, medicine, the arts, and advertising. You'll also find a gift shop that specializes in Native American jewelry, T-shirts, and other memorabilia related to the natural world and the Southwest, all with an emphasis on rattlesnakes.

202 San Felipe St. NW. ✆ **505/242-6569.** www.rattlesnakes.com. Admission $5 adults, $4 seniors, $3 children 3–12. AE, DISC, MC, V. Summer Mon–Sat 10am–6pm, Sun 1–5pm; winter Mon–Sat 11:30am–5:30pm, Sun 1–5pm.

Explora ★ Kids As a center for lifelong learning, Explora houses more than 250 hands-on transactive exhibits in science, technology, and art. Visitors of all ages make their way through the mazelike museum exploring topics as diverse as water, the Rio Grande, light and optics, biological perception, and energy. The museum features exhibits utilizing technology that is creatively accessible to the public and exhibits that engage visitors in creating all kinds of art. My favorite is the Laminar Flow Fountain in which water leaps across spaces, seeming to come alive. Younger kids especially enjoy the arts and crafts workshop, where they can make art to take home. You could spend anywhere from an hour and a half to a full day here.

1701 Mountain Rd. NW. ✆ **505/224-8300.** Fax 505/224-8325. www.explora.us. Admission $7 ages 12–64, $5 seniors 65 and over, $3 children 1–11, free for children under 1. Mon–Sat 10am–6pm; Sun noon–6pm.

New Mexico Museum of Natural History and Science ★★ Kids A trip through this museum will take you through 12 billion years of natural history, from the formation of the universe to the present day. Begin by looking at a display of stones and gems, and then stroll through the "Age Jurassic Super Giants" display, where you'll find dinosaur skeletons cast from the real bones. See the latest display "Triassic: Dawn of the Dinosaur." You can ride the Evolator (kids love this!), a simulated time-travel experience that moves and rumbles, taking you 1¼ miles up (or down) and through 38 million years of history; soon, you'll find yourself in the age of the mammoths and moving through the Ice Age. Be sure to check out the museum's Planetarium. That exhibit, as well as the DynaTheater, which surrounds you with images and sound, costs an additional fee. A gift shop on the ground floor sells imaginative nature games and other curios. Plan to spend 1 to 2 hours here, more if you take in extra attractions.

1801 Mountain Rd. NW. ✆ **505/841-2800.** www.nmnaturalhistory.org. Admission $7 adults, $6 seniors, $4 children 3–12, free for children 2 and under. DynaTheater, Planetarium, and Virtual Voyages cost extra, with prices in the $7 range for adults and $4 range for children. Buying ticket combinations qualifies you for discounts. Daily 9am–5pm. Jan and Sept closed Mon except major holidays, when it's open Mon; also closed New Year's Day, Thanksgiving, and Christmas.

Rio Grande Zoo ★ Kids Some 250 species live on 64 acres of riverside bosk here among ancient cottonwoods. Open-moat exhibits with animals in naturalized habitats are a treat for zoo-goers. Major exhibits include polar bears, giraffes, sea lions (with underwater viewing), the cat walk, the bird show, and ape country, with gorillas and orangutans. The zoo has an especially fine collection of elephants, koalas, polar bears, reptiles, and native Southwestern species. The Thunderbird Express Train operates in a nonstop loop around the zoo, except on Mondays. The Rio Line operates between the zoo and the Albuquerque Biological Park (see above). There are numerous snack bars on the zoo grounds, and La Ventana Gift Shop carries souvenirs. Check out the seal and sea lion feeding at 10:30am and 3:30pm daily, and the summer Zoo Music Concert Series. Plan to spend 2 hours exploring.

903 10th St. SW. ✆ **505/764-6200.** www.cabq.gov/biopark/zoo. Admission $7 adults ($10 with Aquarium and Botanic Garden admission), $3 seniors and children 3–12 ($5 with Aquarium and Botanic Garden admission), free for children 2 and under. MC, V. Daily 9am–5pm (6pm summer Fri–Sat). Closed New Year's Day, Thanksgiving, and Christmas.

7 OUTDOOR ACTIVITIES

BALLOONING

Visitors have a choice of several hot-air balloon operators; rates start at about $160 per person per hour. Call **Rainbow Ryders,** 5601 Eagle Rock Ave. NE (✆ **505/823-1111;** www.rainbowryders.com), or **World Balloon Corporation,** 1103 La Poblana NW (✆ **505/293-6800;** www.worldballoon.com).

If you'd rather just watch, go to the annual **Albuquerque International Balloon Fiesta** ★★, which begins the first weekend and continues through the second weekend of October (see "Calendar of Events," in chapter 3, for details).

BIKING

Albuquerque is a major bicycling hub in the summer, for road racers and mountain bikers alike. For an excellent map of Albuquerque bicycle routes, call the **Albuquerque Parks & Recreation Department** at ✆ **505/768-3550.** You can also find links to many recreation opportunities for adults and kids at **www.cabq.gov/visiting.html**. A great place to bike is **Sandia Peak** (✆ **505/242-9133;** www.sandiapeak.com) in Cíbola National Forest. You can't take your bike on the tram, but chairlift no. 1 is available for up- or downhill transportation with a bike. Bike rentals are available at the top and bottom of the chairlift. They cost $40 for adult bikes and $30 for junior ones. The lift costs $16 and runs on Saturday and Sunday, with Friday added in July and August, though you'll want to call ahead to confirm. Helmets are mandatory. Bike maps are available; the clearly marked trails range from easy to very difficult.

Down in the valley, a **bosk trail** runs along the Rio Grande, accessed through the Rio Grande Nature Center (see "Especially for Kids," above). To the east, the **Foothills Trail** runs along the base of the mountains. It's a fun 7-mile-long trail that offers excellent views. Access it by driving east from downtown on Montgomery Boulevard, past the intersection with Tramway Boulevard. Go left on Glenwood Hills Drive and head north about a half-mile before turning right onto a short road that leads to the Embudito trail head.

Northeast Cyclery, 8305 Menaul Blvd. NE (✆ **505/299-1210**), rents bikes at the rate of $25 per day for front-suspension mountain bikes and $35 per day for road bikes. Multiday discounts are available. Unfortunately, the shop doesn't rent children's bikes. Rentals come with helmets.

BIRD-WATCHING

Bosque del Apache National Wildlife Refuge ★★ (✆ **505/835-1828;** www.fws.gov/southwest/refuges/newmex/bosque/index.html) is a haven for migratory waterfowl such as snow geese and cranes. It's 90 miles south of Albuquerque on I-25, and it's well worth the drive. See chapter 11 for more details. Closer to town, check out the **Rio Grande Nature Center State Park** ★ (✆ **505/344-7240;** www.nmparks.com). It spans 270 acres of riverside forest and meadows that include stands of 100-year-old cottonwoods and a 3-acre pond, attracting some 260 bird species.

FISHING

Albuquerque's most notable fishing spot, **Tingley Beach** (✆ **505/768-2000;** www.cabq.gov/biopark/tingley), is stocked weekly with trout, bass, and catfish. It's open daily and is free. To access Tingley from Rio Grande Boulevard, head west to Tingley Drive (Parkway) and turn south. Another option is **Shady Lakes** (✆ **505/898-2568**). Nestled among cottonwood trees, it's near I-25 on Albuquerque's north side. The most common catches are rainbow trout, black bass, bluegill, and channel catfish. To reach Shady Lakes, take I-25 north to the Tramway exit. Follow Tramway Road west for a mile and then go right on NM 313 for a half-mile. **Sandia Lakes Recreational Area** (✆ **505/897-3971;** www.sandiapueblo.nsn.us), also on NM 313, is another popular fishing spot. There is a bait and tackle shop there.

GOLF

There are quite a few public courses in the Albuquerque area. The **Championship Golf Course at the University of New Mexico,** 3601 University Blvd. SE (✆ **505/277-4546;** www.unmgolf.com), is one of the best in the Southwest and was rated one of the country's top 25 public links by *Golf Digest.* **Desert Greens Golf Course,** 10035 Country Club Lane NW (✆ **505/898-7001;** www.desertgreens.com), is a popular 18-hole golf course on the west side of town.

Other Albuquerque courses to check with for tee times are **Arroyo del Oso,** 7001 Osuna Rd. NE (✆ **505/884-7505;** www.cabq.gov/golf/arroyo-del-oso); **Ladera,** 3401 Ladera Dr. NW (✆ **505/836-4449**); **Los Altos,** 9717 Copper Ave. NE (✆ **505/298-1897;** www.cabq.gov/golf/los-altos); **Puerto del Sol,** 1800 Girard Blvd. SE (✆ **505/265-5636;** www.cabq.gov/golf/puerto-del-sol); and **Sandia Golf Club** (✆ **505/798-3990;** www.sandiagolf.com), located at Sandia Resort and Casino on the north end of town.

If you're willing to drive a short distance just outside Albuquerque, you can play at the **Santa Ana Golf Club at Santa Ana Pueblo,** 288 Prairie Star Rd., Bernalillo, NM 87004 (✆ **505/867-9464;** www.santaanagolf.com), which was rated by the *New York Times* as one of the best public golf courses in the country. Club rentals are available (call for information). In addition, **Isleta Pueblo,** 4001 Hwy. 47 (✆ **505/869-0950;** www.isletapueblo.com), south of Albuquerque, has an 18-hole course.

HIKING

The 1½-million-acre **Cíbola National Forest** offers ample hiking opportunities. Within town, the best hike is the **Embudito Trail,** which heads up into the foothills, with spectacular views down across Albuquerque. The 5.5-mile one-way hike is moderate to difficult. Allow 1 to 8 hours, depending on how far you want to go. Access it by driving east from downtown on Montgomery Boulevard past the intersection with Tramway Boulevard. Go left on Glenwood Hills Drive and head north about a half-mile before turning right onto a short road that leads to the trail head. The premier Sandia Mountain hike is **La Luz Trail,** a very strenuous journey from the Sandia foothills to the top of the Crest. It's a 15-mile round-trip jaunt, and it's half that if you take the Sandia Peak Tramway (see "The Top Attractions," earlier in this chapter) either up or down. Allow a full day for this hike. Access is off Tramway Boulevard and Forest Service Road 333. For more details, contact **Sandia Ranger Station,** Highway 337 south toward Tijeras (✆ **505/281-3304;** www.fs.fed.us/r3/cibola).

HORSEBACK RIDING

If you have a hankering to get in a saddle and eat some trail dust, call the **Hyatt Regency Tamaya Resort and Spa,** 1300 Tuyuna Trail, Santa Ana Pueblo (✆ **505/771-6037;** www.tamaya.hyatt.com). The resort offers 2½-hour-long rides near the Rio Grande for $75 per person. Children must be over 7 years of age and over 4 feet tall. The resort is about 15 miles north of Albuquerque. From I-25, take exit 242, following US 550 west to Tamaya Boulevard, and drive 1½ miles to the resort. See p. 244.

SKIING

Sandia Peak Ski Area is a good place for family skiing. There are plenty of beginner and intermediate runs. (However, if you're looking for more challenge or more variety, head north to Santa Fe or Taos.) The ski area has twin base-to-summit chairlifts to its upper slopes at 10,360 feet and a 1,700-foot vertical drop. There are 30 runs (35% beginner, 55% intermediate, 10% advanced) above the day lodge and ski-rental shop. Four chairs and two pomas accommodate 3,400 skiers an hour. All-day lift tickets are $48 for adults, $38 for ages 13 to 20, $35 for children ages 6 to 12 and seniors (ages 62–71), and free for children 46 inches tall or less (in ski boots) and seniors ages 72 and over; rental packages are available. The season runs mid-December to mid-March. Contact the ski area, 10 Tramway Loop NE (✆ **505/242-9052;** www.sandiapeak.com), for more information, or call the hot line for ski conditions (✆ **505/857-8977**).

Cross-country skiers can enjoy the trails of the Sandia Wilderness from the ski area, or they can go an hour north to the remote Jemez Wilderness and its hot springs.

TENNIS

Albuquerque has 29 public parks with tennis courts. Because of the city's size, your best bet is to call the **Albuquerque Convention and Visitors Bureau** (✆ **800/284-2282;** www.itsatrip.org) to find out which park is closest to your hotel.

8 SPECTATOR SPORTS

BASEBALL

The **Albuquerque Isotopes** (AAA affiliate of the Los Angeles Dodgers) play 72 home games as part of the Pacific Coast League in their stadium, Isotopes Park. Tickets range in price from $6 to $24. For information, contact ✆ **505/924-2255;** www.albuquerquebaseball.com. Isotopes Park is at 1601 Av. Cesar Chavez SE. Take I-25 south of town to

Avenida Cesar Chavez and go east; the stadium is at the intersection of Avenida Cesar Chavez and University Boulevard.

BASKETBALL

The **University of New Mexico Lobos** play an average of 16 home games from late November to early March. Capacity crowds cheer the team at the 17,121-seat University Arena (fondly called "the Pit"), at University and Stadium boulevards. For tickets and information, call © **505/925-LOBO** [5626] or visit www.golobos.com.

FOOTBALL

The **UNM Lobos** football team plays a September-to-November season, usually with five home games, at the 30,000-seat University of New Mexico Stadium, opposite both Albuquerque Sports Stadium and University Arena at University and Stadium boulevards. For tickets and information, call © **505/925-LOBO** [5626] or visit www.golobos.com.

HOCKEY

The **New Mexico Scorpions** play in the Western Professional Hockey League. Their home is at the **Rio Rancho Events Center,** 3001 Civic Center, Rio Rancho (© **505/881-7825;** www.scorpionshockey.com).

HORSE RACING

The **Downs at Albuquerque Racetrack and Casino,** New Mexico State Fairgrounds (© **505/266-5555** for post times; www.abqdowns.com), is near Lomas and Louisiana boulevards NE. Racing and betting—on thoroughbreds and quarter horses—take place August 16 through November 16 (including the New Mexico State Fair, in Sept). The Downs has a glass-enclosed grandstand and exclusive club seating. General admission is free. Simulcast racing happens year-round daily, except Christmas. The 340-slot casino is open daily 10am to 2am, with drinks and dining in the Jockey Club. ***Note:*** The Downs is planning to move east of Albuquerque, so call before setting out.

9 SHOPPING

Visitors seeking regional specialties will find many **local artists** and **galleries** of interest in Albuquerque, although not as many as in Santa Fe and Taos. The galleries and regional fashion designers around the plaza in Old Town are a kind of a shopping center for travelers, with more than 40 merchants represented. The Sandia Pueblo runs its own **crafts market** at the reservation, off I-25 at Tramway Road, just beyond Albuquerque's northern city limits.

Albuquerque has three of the largest **shopping malls** in New Mexico, two within 2 blocks of each other on Louisiana Boulevard just north of I-40—Coronado Center and Winrock Center. The other is the Cottonwood Mall, on the west mesa, at 10000 Coors Blvd. NW (© **505/899-SHOP** [7467]). But the city's best mall is the new **ABQ Uptown ★★**, at Louisiana Boulevard NE and Indian School Road NE (© **505/883-7676;** www.abquptown.com), an outdoor mall with such anchors as Williams-Sonoma, Pottery Barn, Sharper Image, Chicos, and Ann Taylor.

Best Buys

The best buys in Albuquerque are Southwestern regional items, including **arts and crafts** of all kinds—traditional Native American and Hispanic, as well as contemporary works. In local Native American art, look for silver and turquoise jewelry, pottery, weavings, baskets, sand paintings, and Hopi katsina (kachina) dolls. Hispanic folk art—hand-crafted furniture, tinwork, and *retablos*—is worth seeking out. The best contemporary art is in paintings, sculpture, jewelry, ceramics, and fiber art, including weaving. Other items of potential interest are Southwestern fashions, gourmet foods, and unique local Native American and Hispanic creations.

By far, the most **galleries** are in Old Town; others are spread around the city, with smaller groupings in the university district and the Nob Hill area.

Business hours vary, but shops are generally open Monday to Saturday 10am to 6pm; many have extended hours; some have reduced hours; and a few, especially in shopping malls or during the high tourist season, are open on Sunday.

In Albuquerque the sales tax is 6.875%.

ARTS & CRAFTS

Amapola Gallery ★ Fifty artists and craftspeople show their talents at this lovely cooperative gallery, upstairs in the historic 1849 Romero House. You'll find pottery, paintings, textiles, carvings, baskets, jewelry, and other items. 205 Romero St. ✆ **505/242-4311.**

Andrews Pueblo Pottery ★ Carrying pueblo pottery that ranges from the black firings of San Ildefonso to the sand-colored Acoma, this gallery is a place for rich perusing as well as serious buying. Also of note here are Zuni stone fetishes and Hopi katsinas (kachinas). 303 N. Romero NW, Old Town. ✆ **877/606-0543** or 505/243-0414. www.andrewspueblopottery.com.

Bien Mur Indian Market Center ★ Sandia Pueblo's crafts market, on the reservation, sells turquoise and silver jewelry, pottery, baskets, katsina (kachina) dolls, hand-woven rugs, sand paintings, and other arts and crafts. The market is open Monday through Saturday from 9:30am to 5:30pm and Sunday from 11am to 5pm. I-25, at Tramway Road NE. ✆ **800/365-5400** or 505/821-5400.

Gallery One This gallery features folk art, jewelry, contemporary crafts, cards and paper, and natural-fiber clothing. In the Nob Hill Shopping Center, 3500 Central Ave. SE. ✆ **505/268-7449.**

Hispaniae in Old Town ★ **Finds** Day of the Dead people and Frida Kahlo faces greet you at this wild shop with everything from kitschy Mexican tableware to fine Oaxacan woodcarvings. 410 Romero St. NW, Old Town. ✆ **505/244-1533.** www.hispaniae.com.

Mariposa Gallery ★★ **Value** Eclectic contemporary art, jewelry, blown glass, and sculpture fill this Nob Hill shop, with prices that even a travel writer can afford. In the Nob Hill Shopping Center, 3500 Central Ave. SE. ✆ **505/268-6828.** www.mariposa-gallery.com.

Ortega's Indian Arts and Crafts An institution in Gallup, adjacent to the Navajo Reservation, Ortega's now has this Albuquerque store. It sells, repairs, and appraises silver and turquoise jewelry. 6600 Menaul Blvd. NE, no. 359. ✆ **505/881-1231.**

R. C. Gorman Nizhoni Gallery Old Town ★ The painting and sculpture of the late Navajo artist Gorman, who was a resident of Taos, are shown here. Most works are available in limited-edition lithographs. 323 Romero St. NW, Ste. 1, and another shop at 400 Romero St. NW, Ste. 3, Old Town. ✆ **505/843-7666.** www.rcgorman-nizhoni.com.

Skip Maisel's (Value) If you want a real bargain in Native American arts and crafts, this is the place to shop. You'll find a broad range of quality and price here, in goods such as pottery, weavings, and katsinas (kachinas). ***Take note:*** Adorning the outside of the store are murals painted in 1933 by notable Navajo painter Harrison Begay and Pueblo painter Pablita Velarde. 510 Central Ave. SW. ✆ **505/242-6526.**

Tanner Chaney Galleries ★ In business since 1875, this gallery has fine jewelry, pottery, rugs, and more. 323 Romero St. NW, Ste. 4, Old Town. ✆ **800/444-2242** or 505/247-2242. www.tannerchaney.com.

Wright's Collection of Indian Art This gallery, first opened in 1907, features a free private museum and carries fine handmade Native American arts and crafts, both contemporary and traditional. 1100 San Mateo Blvd. NE. ✆ **505/266-0120.** www.wrightsgallery.com.

BOOKS

Barnes & Noble On the west side, just north of Cottonwood Mall, this huge bookstore offers plenty of browsing room and a Starbucks Cafe for lounging. The store is known for its large children's section and weekly story-time readings. 3701 Ellison Dr. NW #A. ✆ **505/792-4234.** Or at the Coronado Center, 6600 Menaul Blvd. NE. ✆ **505/883-8200.** www.barnesandnoble.com.

Bookworks ★ Selling both new and used books, Bookworks has one of the most complete Southwestern nonfiction and fiction sections in the region. A good place to linger, the store has a coffee bar and an area for readings. It also carries CDs and books on tape. 4022 Rio Grande Blvd. NW. ✆ **505/344-8139.** www.bkwrks.com.

Borders This branch of the popular chain provides a broad range of books, music, and videos, and hosts in-store appearances by authors, musicians, and artists. Uptown Center, 2240 Q St. NE. ✆ **505/884-7711.** www.borders.com.

FASHION

Albuquerque Pendleton Cuddle up in a large selection of blankets and shawls, and haul them away in a handbag. 1100 San Mateo NE Blvd., Stes. 2 and 4. ✆ **505/255-6444.**

Gertrude Zachary ★★ This large well of imagination has beaded velvet scarves and elaborate antique furniture, but the real buy here is jewelry, ranging from traditional Native American bracelets and necklaces to wildly kitschy butterfly concho belts. From purses to beaded lamps, this place has anything that a contemporary gal could want. 3300 Central Ave. SE (in the Nob Hill area at Wellsley). ✆ **505/766-4700.** www.gertrudezachary.com.

FOOD

The Candy Lady Having made chocolate for over 30 years, the Candy Lady is especially known for 21 varieties of fudge, including jalapeño flavor. 524 Romero St. NW, Old Town. ✆ **800/214-7731** or 505/243-6239. www.thecandylady.com.

GIFTS/SOUVENIRS

Jackalope International ★★ Wandering through this vast shopping area is like an adventure to another land—to many lands, really. You'll find Mexican *trasteros* (armoires) next to Balinese puppets. The store sells sculpture, pottery, and Christmas ornaments as well. 834 US 550, Bernalillo. ✆ **505/867-9813.** www.jackalope.com.

HOME FURNISHINGS

A ★ Offering contemporary furnishings and colorful kitchenware, this shop is a fun place to browse and buy. As well as home furnishings, it offers eclectic soaps and even men's ties. 3500 Central SE, in the Nob Hill Shopping Center. ✆ **505/266-2222.**

El Paso Import Company ★ Advertising "unique furnishings from around the world," this place in the Nob Hill Shopping Center is packed with all manner of tables, *trasteros,* and chairs, most with aged and chipped paint, for those who love the worn look. It's a fun place to browse even if you don't buy. 3500 Central SE, Nob Hill. ✆ **505/265-1160.** www.elpasoimportco.com.

Strictly Southwestern You'll find nice, solid pine and oak Southwestern-style furniture here. Lighting, art, pottery, and other interior items are also available. 1321 Eubank Blvd. NE. ✆ **505/292-7337.** www.strictlysouthwestern.com.

MARKETS

Flea Market Every Saturday and Sunday, year-round, the fairgrounds host this market from 8am to 5pm. It's a great place to browse for turquoise and silver jewelry and locally made crafts, as well as newly manufactured inexpensive goods such as socks and T-shirts. The place takes on a fair atmosphere, with the smell of cotton candy filling the air. There's no admission charge. New Mexico State Fairgrounds. For information, call the Albuquerque Convention and Visitors Bureau, ✆ **800/284-2282.** www.abqfleamarket.com.

10 ALBUQUERQUE AFTER DARK

Albuquerque has an active performing-arts and nightlife scene, as befits a city of half a million people. The performing arts are multicultural, with Hispanic and (to a lesser extent) Native American productions sharing stage space with Anglo works, including theater, opera, symphony, and dance. Albuquerque also attracts many national touring companies. Nightclubs run the gamut, with rock, jazz, and country predominant.

Complete information on all major cultural events can be obtained from the **Albuquerque Convention and Visitors Bureau** (✆ **800/284-2282** for recorded information after 5pm). Current listings appear in the two daily newspapers; detailed weekend arts calendars can be found in Friday's *Journal.* The monthly *On the Scene* also carries entertainment listings.

Tickets for nearly all major entertainment and sporting events can be obtained from **Ticketmaster,** 4004 Carlisle Blvd. NE (✆ **505/883-7800**). Discount tickets are often available for midweek and matinee performances; check with individual theater or concert hall box offices.

The Major Concert & Performance Halls

- **Journal Pavilion,** 5601 University Blvd. NE (✆ **505/452-5100**).
- **Keller Hall,** University of New Mexico, Cornell Street at Redondo Drive South NE (✆ **505/277-4569**).
- **KiMo Theatre,** 423 Central Ave. NW (✆ **505/768-3544**).
- **Popejoy Hall,** University of New Mexico, Cornell Street at Redondo Drive South NE (✆ **505/277-3824**).
- **South Broadway Cultural Center,** 1025 Broadway Blvd. SE (✆ **505/848-1320**).

THE PERFORMING ARTS

Classical Music

New Mexico Symphony Orchestra ★ The NMSO first played in 1932 and has continued as a strong cultural force throughout the state. The symphony performs classics and pops, as well as family and neighborhood concerts. It plays for more than 20,000 grade-school students and visits communities throughout the state in its annual tour program. Concert venues are generally Popejoy Hall on the University of New Mexico campus, the National Hispanic Cultural Center, and the Rio Grande Zoo, all of which are accessible to people with disabilities. Guillermo Figueroa is the music director and conductor. I recommend going to one of the outdoor concerts at the band shell at the Rio Grande Zoo. 4407 Menaul Blvd. NE. ✆ **800/251-6676** for tickets and information, or 505/881-9590. www.nmso.org. Ticket prices vary with concert; call for details.

Dance

New Mexico Ballet Company Founded in 1972, the state's oldest ballet company holds most of its performances at Popejoy Hall. A typical season includes a fall production, such as *Dracula;* a holiday one, such as *The Nutcracker* or *A Christmas Carol;* and a contemporary spring production. 4200 Wyoming Blvd. NE, Ste. B2 Albuquerque, NM 87154-1518. ✆ **505/292-4245.** www.nmballet.org. Tickets $15–$40 adults, depending on the performance and venue.

Theater

Albuquerque Little Theatre The Albuquerque Little Theatre has been offering a variety of productions ranging from comedies to dramas to musicals since 1930. Eight plays are presented here annually during a July-to-June season. Located across from Old Town, the theater offers plenty of free parking. The box office is open Monday to Friday from 9am to 6pm. 224 San Pasquale Ave. SW. ✆ **505/242-4750.** www.albuquerquelittletheatre.org. Tickets $22 adults, $18 seniors; $10 for student rush-tickets purchased 30 min. before showtime.

Musical Theatre Southwest From February to January, this theater presents six major Broadway musicals, in addition to several smaller productions, at either Popejoy Hall or the MTS's own 890-seat Hiland Theater. Most productions are staged for 3 consecutive weekends, including some Sunday matinees. 2401 Ross. SE. ✆ **505/265-9119.** www.musicaltheatresw.com. Tickets $15–$30 adults; students and seniors receive a $2 discount.

Vortex Theatre ★ A 35-year-old community theater known for its innovative productions, the Vortex is Albuquerque's "Off-Broadway" theater, presenting a range of plays from classics to originals. You'll see such plays as *I Hate Hamlet,* by Paul Rudnik, and *Death & the Maiden,* by Ariel Dorfman. Performances take place on Friday and Saturday at 8pm and on Sunday at 6pm. The black-box theater seats 90. 2004½ Central Ave. SE. ✆ **505/247-8600.** www.vortexabq.org. All tickets $12.

THE CLUB & MUSIC SCENE

Comedy Clubs/Dinner Theater

Laffs Comedy Cafe This club offers top acts from each coast, including comedians who have appeared on *The Late Show with David Letterman* and HBO. Shows Wednesday through Sunday nights. San Mateo Blvd. and Osuna Rd., in the Fiesta del Norte Shopping Center. ✆ **505/296-5653.** www.laffscomedy.com. $8 per person, with a 2-item minimum purchase. Call for showtimes.

Mystery Cafe ★ **Finds** If you're in the mood for a little interactive dinner theater, the Mystery Cafe might be just the ticket. You'll help the characters in this ever-popular, delightfully funny show solve the mystery as they serve you a four-course meal. Reservations are a must. Performances Friday and Saturday evenings at 7:30pm; doors open at 7pm. P.O. Box 11433. Performances held at Sheraton Uptown (at Menaul Blvd. and Louisiana Blvd.). ✆ **505/237-1385.** www.abqmystery.com. Approximately $38, plus tip.

Rock/Jazz

Burt's Tiki Lounge This club won the weekly paper *Alibi's* award for the best variety of drinks. The club offers live music Thursday to Sunday and charges no cover. 313 Gold Ave. ✆ **505/247-2878.** www.burtstikilounge.com.

Kelly's BYOB Near the university, Kelly's is a local brewpub, set in a renovated autobody shop. The place has tasty pub fare, excellent brew specials, and live music for special events. 3222 Central SE. ✆ **505/262-2739.** www.kellysbrewpub.com.

Martini Grille ★ On the eastern side of the Nob Hill district, this is the place for young professionals and the gay crowd, who lush out on more than 30 flavors of martinis within a seductive Batman cave atmosphere. Live entertainment plays most weekends and some weeknights. 4200 Central SE. ✆ **505/255-4111.**

Q Bar ★ With sophisticated decor—lots of plush couches and comfy chairs in muted tones—this lounge in the Hotel Albuquerque at Old Town offers innovative cuisine, jazz piano entertainment, and media and billiards rooms. 800 Rio Grande Blvd. NW. ✆ **505/843-6300.**

MORE ENTERTAINMENT

Albuquerque's best nighttime attraction is the **Sandia Peak Tramway,** from which you can enjoy a view nonpareil of the Rio Grande Valley and the city lights.

Many travelers like to include a little dice-throw and slot-machine play in their trip to New Mexico. Those who do are in luck, with the expansive **Sandia Resort & Casino,** north of I-25 and a quarter-mile east on Tramway Boulevard (✆ **800/526-9366;** www.sandiacasino.com). The $80-million structure sits on Sandia Pueblo land and has outstanding views of the Sandia Mountains. Built in pueblo architectural style, the graceful casino has a 3,650-seat outdoor amphitheater, three restaurants (one, **Bien Shur,** has excellent food), a lounge, more than 1,800 slot and video poker machines, the largest poker room in the state, and blackjack, roulette, and craps tables. It's open from 8am to 4am Sunday to Wednesday and 24 hours Thursday to Saturday.

11 TOURING THE JEMEZ MOUNTAIN TRAIL ★

Ten Native American pueblos are within an hour's drive of central Albuquerque. One of them, Acoma, is discussed in chapter 10. If you'd like to combine a tour of the archaeological sites and inhabited pueblos, consider driving the **Jemez Mountain Trail** ★. Head north on Interstate 25 to Bernalillo, where you can visit the Coronado State Monument. Continue west on US 550 to Zia Pueblo. Six miles farther on US 550 takes you to NM 4, where you'll turn north and drive through orchards and along narrow cornfields of Jemez Pueblo. Farther north on NM 4, you'll find another archaeological site, the Jemez State Monument. You'll also find Jemez Springs, where you can stop for a hot soak. The road continues to the Los Alamos area, where you can see the spectacular ruins at Bandelier National Monument. From there you have the option of returning the way you came or via Santa Fe.

ZIA PUEBLO

Zia Pueblo, 135 Capitol Square Dr., Zia Pueblo, NM, 87053 (✆ **505/867-3304**), which has 720 inhabitants, blends in so perfectly with the soft tans of the stone and sand of the desertlike land around it that it's very hard to see—it's like a chameleon on a tree trunk. The pueblo is best known for its famous sun symbol—now the official symbol of the state of New Mexico—adapted from a pottery design showing three rays going in each of the four directions from a sun, or circle. It is hailed in the pledge to the state flag as "a symbol of perfect friendship among united cultures."

Zia has a reputation for excellence in pottery making. Its pottery is identified by its unglazed terra-cotta coloring, traditional geometric designs, and plant and animal motifs painted on a white slip. Paintings, weaving, and sculptures are also prized products of the artists of the Zia community. Their work can be viewed at the **Zia Cultural Center** located at the pueblo. Our Lady of the Assumption, the patron saint, is given a celebratory corn dance on her day, August 15.

The pueblo is about 17 miles northwest of Bernalillo, just off of US 550. It's open to visitors daily during daylight hours, and admission is free. Photography is not permitted.

JEMEZ PUEBLO

The more than 2,500 **Jemez Pueblo** natives—including descendants of the Pecos Pueblo, east of Santa Fe, abandoned in 1838—are the only remaining people to speak the Towa dialect of the Tanoan group. The Jemez are famous for their excellent dancing and feast-making; their feast days attract residents from other pueblos, turning the celebrations into multitribal fairs. Two rectangular kivas are central points for groups of dancers. However, in recent years the pueblo has been closed to visitors, though visitors are allowed on dance days. However, visitors can partake of the crafts at local shops along NM 4 and at the Walatowa Visitor Center (see box below). The primary craft is Jemez pottery.

On weekends April through mid-October, weather permitting, arts and crafts and traditional foods are sold across the street from the visitor center at the **Jemez Red Rocks Open-Air Market.**

Pueblo Etiquette: Do's & Don'ts

Those who are not Native American are welcome to visit Indian pueblos and reservations; however, there are some guidelines you should follow as a guest on tribal land.

Native American reservations and pueblos have their own systems of government and, therefore, their own laws and regulations. If you don't follow their laws, you will be subject to punishment as outlined by the American Indian government. The best thing that could happen is that you'd simply be asked to leave.

Stay out of cemeteries and ceremonial rooms, such as kivas, as these are sacred grounds. Remember, these are not museums or tourist attractions in their own right; they are people's homes. Don't peek into doors and windows, and don't climb on top of buildings.

Most pueblos require a permit to carry a camera or to sketch or paint on location, and many prohibit photography at any time. If you want to take pictures, make a video, or sketch anything on pueblo or reservation land, find out about permits and fees in advance.

Do not wander around on your own if the residents have asked that you visit the pueblo only by guided tour. If, on a guided tour, you are asked not to take pictures of something, or are asked to stay out of a certain area, please follow the guidelines. If you don't have to visit by guided tour, don't go into private buildings without being escorted by someone who lives there or who has the authority to take you inside.

Be respectful of ceremonial dances. Do not speak during dances or ceremonies and don't applaud at the end of the dance—they aren't dancing for your amusement; they are dancing as part of their ceremony.

In short, be courteous and don't do anything you wouldn't do in your own mother's house.

A STATE MONUMENT IN THE AREA

Coronado State Monument ★ When the Spanish explorer Coronado traveled through this region in 1540–41 while searching for the Seven Cities of Cíbola, he wintered at a village on the west bank of the Rio Grande—probably one on the ruins of the ancient Anasazi Pueblo known as Kuaua. Those excavated ruins have been preserved in this state monument.

Hundreds of rooms can be seen, and a kiva has been restored so that visitors can descend a ladder into the enclosed space, once the site of sacred rites. Unique multicolored murals, depicting human and animal forms, were found on successive layers of wall plaster in this and other kivas here; some examples are displayed in the monument's small archaeological museum.

485 Kuaua Rd., Bernalillo. ✆ **505/867-5351.** Admission $3 adults, free for children 16 and under. Wed–Mon 8:30am–5pm. Closed Easter, Thanksgiving, Christmas, New Year's. To get to the site (20 miles north of Albuquerque), take I-25 to Bernalillo and US 550 west for 1$^{3}/_{4}$ miles.

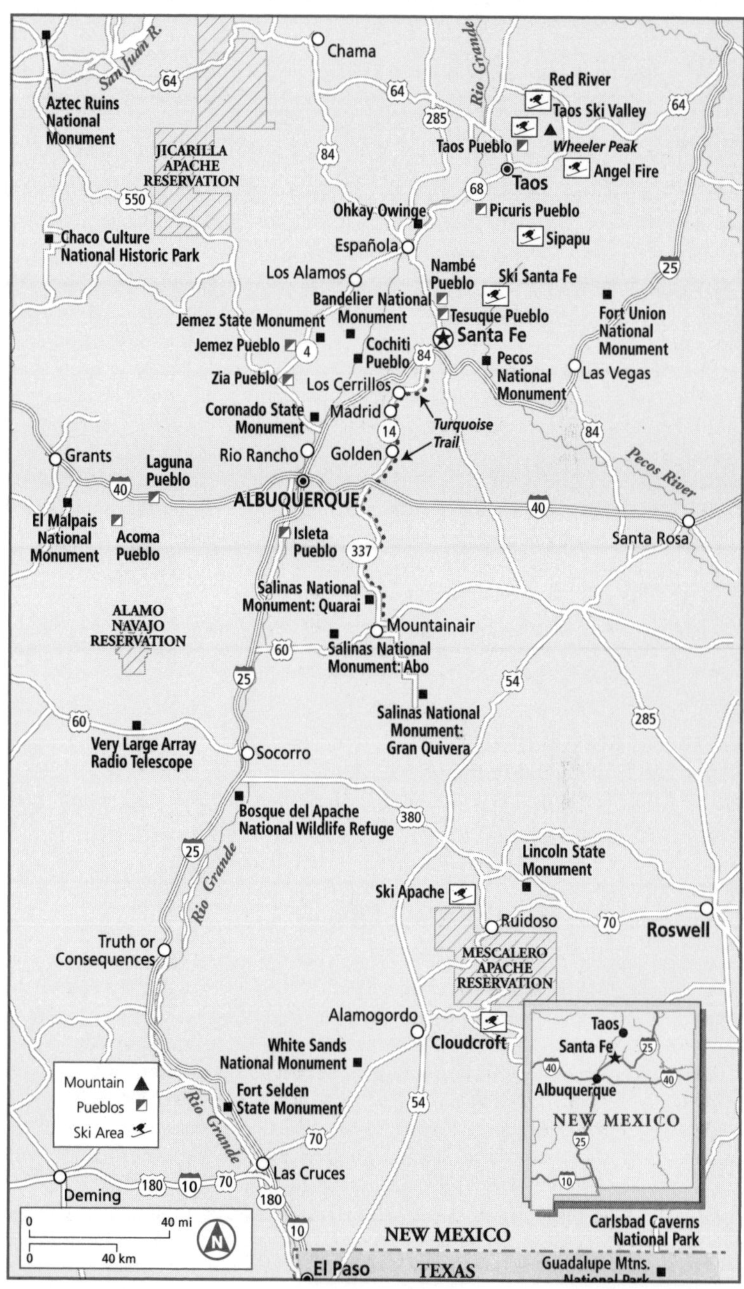
Chama
Aztec Ruins National Monument
San Juan R.
JICARILLA APACHE RESERVATION
Rio Grande
Red River
Taos Ski Valley
Taos Pueblo
Wheeler Peak
Angel Fire
Taos
Picuris Pueblo
Sipapu
Ohkay Owinge
Española
Chaco Culture National Historic Park
Los Alamos
Nambé Pueblo
Ski Santa Fe
Bandelier National Monument
Tesuque Pueblo
Jemez State Monument
Fort Union National Monument
Santa Fe
Jemez Pueblo
Cochiti Pueblo
Pecos National Monument
Zia Pueblo
Los Cerrillos
Las Vegas
Coronado State Monument
Madrid
Turquoise Trail
Grants
Laguna Pueblo
Rio Rancho
Golden
Pecos River
ALBUQUERQUE
El Malpais National Monument
Acoma Pueblo
Isleta Pueblo
Santa Rosa
Salinas National Monument: Quarai
ALAMO NAVAJO RESERVATION
Mountainair
Salinas National Monument: Abo
Salinas National Monument: Gran Quivera
Very Large Array Radio Telescope
Socorro
Bosque del Apache National Wildlife Refuge
Lincoln State Monument
Ski Apache
Ruidoso
Roswell
Truth or Consequences
MESCALERO APACHE RESERVATION
Alamogordo
Cloudcroft
White Sands National Monument
Fort Selden State Monument
Las Cruces
Deming
Mountain
Pueblos
Ski Area
0 40 mi
0 40 km
NEW MEXICO
TEXAS
El Paso
Carlsbad Caverns National Park
Guadalupe Mtns. National Park
Taos
Santa Fe
Albuquerque
NEW MEXICO

JEMEZ SPRINGS

Getting to this village along the Jemez River is half the fun. You'll drive the **Jemez Mountain Trail ★** into the Jemez Mountains, a trip that can provide a relaxing retreat and/or an exhilarating adventure. In the area are historic sites and relaxing hot springs, as well as excellent stream fishing, hiking, and cross-country skiing. You may want to combine a drive through this area with a visit to Los Alamos and Bandelier National Monument (see chapter 7).

North of town you'll come to the **Soda Dam,** a strange and beautiful mineral mass formed by travertine deposits—minerals that precipitate out of geothermal springs. Considered a sacred site by Native Americans, it has a gushing waterfall and caves. During the warm months, it's a popular swimming hole.

Jemez State Monument ★ A stop at this small monument takes you on a journey through the history of the Jemez people. The journey begins in the museum, which tells the tale of Giusewa, "place of boiling waters," the original Tewa name of the area. Then it moves out into the mission ruins, whose story is told on small plaques that juxtapose the first impressions of the missionaries against the reality of the Jemez life. The missionaries saw the Jemez people as barbaric and set out to civilize them. Part of the process involved hauling up river stones and erecting 6-foot-thick walls of the Mission of San José de los Jemez (founded in 1621) in the early 17th century. Excavations in 1921–22 and 1935–37 unearthed this massive complex, through which you may wander. You enter through a broad doorway to a room that once held elaborate fresco paintings, the room tapering back to the nave, with a giant bell tower above. The setting is startling—next to a creek, with steep mountains rising behind.

18160 NM 4 (P.O. Box 143), Jemez Springs. ✆ **505/829-3530.** www.nmmonuments.org. Admission $3 adults, free for children 17 and under. Wed–Mon 8:30am–5pm. Closed New Year's Day, Easter, Thanksgiving, and Christmas. From Albuquerque, take NM 550 (NM 44) to NM 4 and then continue on NM 4 for about 18 miles.

Where to Stay & Dine

Cañon del Rio–Riverside Inn ★ "Eventually the watcher joined the river, and there was only one of us. I believe it was the river," wrote Norman Maclean in *A River Runs Through It.* That was my experience while sitting on a cottonwood-shaded bench at

Historic Culture with a Hint of Honey

Jemez Pueblo, home to more than 3,000, no longer welcomes visitors except on selected days. However, visitors can get a taste of the Jemez culture at the **Walatowa Visitor Center,** on NM 4, 8 miles north of the junction with US 550 (✆ **877/733-5687** or 505/834-7235; www.jemezpueblo.org). A museum and shop highlight the center, which also offers information about hiking and scenic tour routes. While in the area, you may encounter Jemez people sitting under ramadas (thatch-roofed lean-tos) selling home-baked bread, cookies, and pies. If you're lucky, they may also be making fry bread, which you can smother with honey for one of New Mexico's more delectable treats.

Moments **Bath Time**

If you like to soak in warm springs, head to Jemez. The waters running through the area are high in mineral content. In fact, the owner of **Jemez Springs Bath House,** 62 NM 4, on the Jemez Springs Plaza (✆ **505/829-3303;** www.jemezspringsbathhouse.com), says they are so healing, more than once she's had to run after visitors who walked off without their canes. This bathhouse was one of the first structures to be built in what is now Jemez Springs. It is open daily 10am to 8pm.

Another option in town is the **Giggling Springs** ★ (✆ **505/829-9175;** www.gigglingsprings.com), across the street from the Laughing Lizard Inn & Cafe (see above). A small outdoor pool, surrounded by sandstone and funky art, highlights this place. The Jemez River acts as a cold plunge. It's open Wednesday to Sunday 11am to 8pm, with an abbreviated schedule in winter. Reservations are recommended.

Cañon del Rio, on a long bow of the Jemez River, a small, fast-flowing stream lined with cottonwoods. Built in 1994, the inn has clean lines and comfortable rooms, each named after a Native American tribe. Each has a sliding glass door that opens out to a patio, where there's a fountain. Located on the river are decks for enjoying nature, and there's a heated pool. The beds are comfortable, with good reading lights. The Great Room has a cozy, welcoming feel, with a big-screen TV, as well as a large table where breakfast is served family style. Smoking is not allowed.

16445 (Scenic) NM 4, Jemez Springs, NM 87025. ✆ **505/829-4377.** www.canondelrio.com. 7 units. $119–$200 double, depending on the season; house $125–$150. Rates include full breakfast with inn room. AE, DISC, MC, V. **Amenities:** Jacuzzi; outdoor pool. *In room:* A/C, hair dryer, Wi-Fi.

The Laughing Lizard Inn & Cafe ★ AMERICAN This is the kind of small-town cafe that doesn't need to try to have a personality. It already has thick adobe walls, wood floors, and a wood-burning stove for its innate charm. Added touches are the brightly painted walls and funky old tables. If there were a Western version of the Whistle Stop Cafe, this would be it. The menu is somewhat eclectic—most dishes have a bit of an imaginative flair. The burritos come in a variety of types, such as fresh spinach with black beans, mushrooms, jack cheese, salsa, and guacamole. The homemade pizzas, made with blue-corn crusts, feature ingredients such as pesto, sun-dried tomatoes, and feta, or more basic ones with red sauce as well. Beer and wine are served, and there are daily dessert treats such as piñon pie, chocolate mousse, and berry cobbler. The staff is friendly and accommodating. A small inn attached to the cafe provides **inexpensive rooms** that are clean but a bit timeworn.

17526 NM 4, Jemez Springs, NM 87025. ✆ **505/829-3108.** www.thelaughinglizard.com. Main courses lunch $5–$10, dinner $6–$13. DISC, MC, V. May–Nov Tues–Sat 11am–8pm, Sun 11am–6pm; Dec–Apr Thurs–Sat 11am–8pm, Sun 11am–6pm.

THE TURQUOISE TRAIL ★★

Known as "the Turquoise Trail," NM 14 begins about 16 miles east of downtown Albuquerque, at I-40's Cedar Crest exit, and winds some 46 miles to Santa Fe along the east side of the Sandia Mountains. This state-designated scenic and historic route traverses the revived ghost towns of Golden, Madrid, and Cerrillos, where gold, silver, coal, and turquoise were once mined in great quantities. Modern-day settlers, mostly artists and craftspeople, have brought a renewed frontier spirit to the old mining towns.

SANDIA CREST As you start along the Turquoise Trail, you may want to turn left onto Sandia Crest Road and drive about 5 minutes to the **Tinkertown Museum** ★, 121 Sandia Crest Rd. (✆ **505/284-5233;** www.tinkertown.com). The creation of Ross Ward, who took 40 years to carve, collect, and construct the place, it is mostly a miniatures museum, featuring dollhouse-type exhibits of a mining town, a circus, and other venues, with push buttons to make the little characters move. The building itself is constructed of glass bottles, wagon wheels, and horseshoes, among other ingredients. Great fun for the kids here. It's open daily, April 1 to November 1, from 9am to 6pm. Admission is $3 for adults, $1 for children 4 to 16.

GOLDEN Golden is approximately 10 miles north of the Sandia Park junction on NM 14. Its sagging houses, with their missing boards and the wind whistling through the broken eaves, make it a purist's ghost town. There's a general store widely known for its large selection of well-priced jewelry, as well as, across the street, a bottle seller's "glass garden." Be sure to slow down and look for the village church, a great photo opportunity, on the east side of the road. Nearby are the ruins of a pueblo called **Paako,** abandoned around 1670.

MADRID Madrid (pronounced *mah*-drid) is about 12 miles north of Golden. This town, along with neighboring Cerrillos, was in a fabled turquoise-mining area dating back to prehistory. Gold and silver mines followed, and when they faltered, there was coal. The Turquoise Trail towns supplied fuel for the locomotives of the Santa Fe Railroad until the 1950s, when the railroad converted to diesel fuel. Madrid used to produce 100,000 tons of coal a year and was a true "company town," but the mine closed in 1956. Today, this is a village of artists and craftspeople seemingly stuck in the 1960s: Its funky, ramshackle houses have many counterculture residents who operate several crafts stores and import shops.

The **Old Coal Mine Museum and Old West Photography** (✆ **505/438-3780**) invites visitors to peek into a mine that was saved when the town was abandoned. You can see the old mine's offices, steam engines, machines, and tools. It's open daily; admission is $5 for adults, $3 for seniors, and free for children 5 and under. You might want to have a picture taken in one of the 1,000 costumes at Old West Photography, $3 per person, $25 for one 8x10 or two 5x7s.

Next door, the **Mine Shaft Tavern** (✆ **505/473-0743**) continues its colorful career by offering a variety of burgers (try the green-chile cheeseburger) and presenting live music Saturday nights and Sunday afternoons; it's open for meals in summer Monday to Thursday 11am to 6pm and Friday to Sunday 11am to 8pm. In winter, meals are served Monday to Thursday from noon to 4pm and Friday to Sunday noon to 8pm. The bar is open in summer Sunday to Thursday 11am to 11pm and Friday to Saturday 11am to 1am. In winter, the bar is open from Sunday to Thursday noon to 10pm and Friday to Saturday noon to 1am. Next door is the **Madrid Engine House Theater** (**© 505/438-3780**), offering melodrama during the summer. Its back doors open out so a steam locomotive can take center stage. The place to eat is **Mama Lisa's Café** ★, 2859 NM 14 (**© 505/471-5769**). You'll find salads, sandwiches, and New Mexican specialties, all prepared with fresh ingredients. During the summer, it's open Wednesday to Monday from 11am to 4:30pm. In winter, it's open intermittently, so call ahead.

CERRILLOS AND GALISTEO Cerrillos, about 3 miles north of Madrid, is a village of dirt roads that sprawls along Galisteo Creek. It appears to have changed very little since it was founded during a lead strike in 1879; the old hotel, the saloon, and even the sheriff's office look very much like parts of an Old West movie set. You may want to stop in at **Casa Grande Trading Post,** 17 Waldo St. (**© 505/438-3008**), a shop that was featured on PBS's *Antiques Roadshow.* You'll find lots of jewelry and rocks, as well as the **Cerrillos Turquoise Mining Museum,** full of artifacts from this region's mining era.

A good horseback-riding outfitter in this beautiful area is **Broken Saddle Riding Company.** A 1¼-hour ride is $55 a person, a 2-hour ride is $75, and a 3-hour ride is $95; riders are grouped according to skill level. For more information, call **© 505/424-7774** and listen to the recorded message, or go to www.brokensaddle.com.

If you're getting hungry on the way back to Santa Fe, stop by the **San Marcos Café** ★, 3877 NM 14, near Lone Butte (**© 505/471-9298**). Set next to a feed store, in a curvaceous old adobe with wood-plank floors and lots of Southwest ambience, this cafe serves creative fare such as cinnamon rolls and their special eggs San Marcos—tortillas stuffed with scrambled eggs and topped with guacamole, pinto beans, jack cheese, and red chile. Open daily 8am to 2pm (cafe stops serving at 1:50pm).

10 Northern New Mexico

If the humdrum of contemporary American life has you longing for excitement, this is the place to get your adrenaline flowing. Not only can you travel to a "foreign land"—namely Gallup, what locals call "Indian Country"—but you can also sample a history of Wild West shootouts and exploding volcanoes.

The biggest presence in the northwest is Native American culture, old and new. The Pueblo, Navajo, and Apache inhabit the area. They are the majority and set the pace and tone of the place. The Zuni, Acoma, and Laguna pueblos are within a short distance of I-40. **Acoma's "Sky City"** has been continually occupied for more than 9 centuries. Part of the Navajo Reservation—the largest in America—takes up a huge chunk of the northwest, and the Jicarilla Apache Reservation stretches 65 miles south from the Colorado border.

Three main towns provide launching points for adventures. **Grants** (pop. 8,900) is a boom-and-bust town on Route 66, and **Gallup** (pop. 20,000) is a mecca for silver jewelry shoppers. Outdoor adventurers head to **Chama** (pop. 1,000), where many enjoy a ride on the Cumbres & Toltec Railroad.

Two other national monuments in northwestern New Mexico also speak of the region's history. **El Morro** is a sandstone monolith known as "Inscription Rock," where travelers and explorers documented their journeys for centuries, and **El Malpais** is a volcanic badland with spectacular cinder cones, ice caves, and lava tubes.

Meanwhile, the northeast is a place of wide-open plains once traversed by wagon trains on the Santa Fe Trail—a 19th-century trade route that ran from Missouri to Santa Fe. In **Cimarron** you'll see evidence of the holdings of cattle baron Lucien Maxwell, who controlled most of these prairies as his private empire in the latter half of the 19th century. Cimarron attracted nearly every gunslinger of the era, from Butch Cassidy to Clay Allison, Black Jack Ketchum to Jesse James.

Established long before its Nevada namesake, **Las Vegas** was the largest city in New Mexico at the turn of the 20th century, with a fast-growing, cosmopolitan population. Doc Holliday, Bat Masterson, and Wyatt Earp walked its wild streets in the 1880s. A decade later, it was the headquarters of Teddy Roosevelt's Rough Riders, and early in the 20th century, it was a silent film capital. Today, with a population of approximately 17,000, it is the region's largest city and the proud home of 900 historic properties. **Raton** (pop. 7,500), on I-25 in the Sangre de Cristo foothills, is the gateway to New Mexico from the north. **Clayton** (pop. 2,500), **Tucumcari** (pop. 6,831), and **Santa Rosa** (pop. 2,500) are all transportation hubs and ranching centers.

Two national monuments are particular points of interest. **Fort Union,** 24 miles north of Las Vegas, was the largest military installation in the Southwest in the 1860s and 1870s. **Capulin Volcano,** 33 miles east of Raton, last erupted 60,000 years ago; visitors can now walk inside the crater.

Drained by the Pecos and Canadian rivers, northeastern New Mexico is notable for the number of small lakes that afford opportunities for fishing, hunting, boating, camping—even scuba diving. Eleven state parks and about a half dozen designated wildlife areas are within the region.

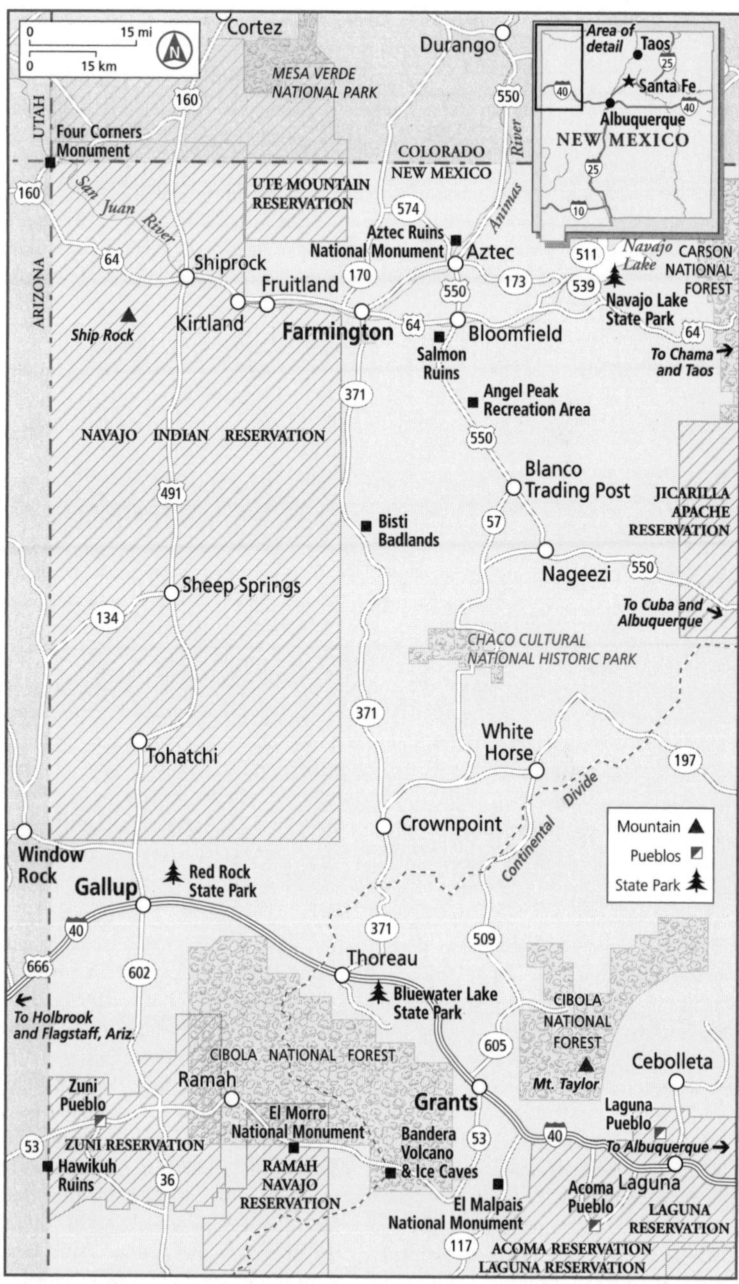
0 15 mi
0 15 km
Cortez
Durango
MESA VERDE NATIONAL PARK
UTAH
Four Corners Monument
COLORADO
NEW MEXICO
UTE MOUNTAIN RESERVATION
San Juan River
Animas River
Area of detail
Taos
Santa Fe
Albuquerque
NEW MEXICO
ARIZONA
Aztec Ruins National Monument
Aztec
Navajo Lake
CARSON NATIONAL FOREST
Navajo Lake State Park
Shiprock
Fruitland
Kirtland
Farmington
Bloomfield
Ship Rock
Salmon Ruins
To Chama and Taos
Angel Peak Recreation Area
NAVAJO INDIAN RESERVATION
Blanco Trading Post
JICARILLA APACHE RESERVATION
Bisti Badlands
Nageezi
Sheep Springs
To Cuba and Albuquerque
CHACO CULTURAL NATIONAL HISTORIC PARK
White Horse
Tohatchi
Continental Divide
Crownpoint
Mountain
Pueblos
State Park
Window Rock
Gallup
Red Rock State Park
Thoreau
Bluewater Lake State Park
To Holbrook and Flagstaff, Ariz.
CIBOLA NATIONAL FOREST
Mt. Taylor
Cebolleta
Zuni Pueblo
Ramah
Grants
Laguna Pueblo
El Morro National Monument
ZUNI RESERVATION
To Albuquerque
Hawikuh Ruins
Bandera Volcano & Ice Caves
RAMAH NAVAJO RESERVATION
Acoma Pueblo
Laguna
LAGUNA RESERVATION
El Malpais National Monument
ACOMA RESERVATION
LAGUNA RESERVATION

1 GETTING OUTSIDE IN NORTHERN NEW MEXICO

BIKING Some of the best biking is in Farmington, which is where the "Durangatangs" come during the winter to train and ride (Durango is a mountain-biking mecca). **Bicycle Express,** 103 N. Main Ave. (✆ **505/334-4354**), in Aztec, will give trail directions, as will **Cottonwood Cycles,** 4370 E. Main (✆ **505/326-0429;** www.cottonwoodcycles.com), in Farmington. Cottonwood also rents bikes. Be sure to check out the **Lions Wilderness Park,** where you'll find its renowned **Road Apple Trail** on the north end of town. Bikers are also welcome at the **Bureau of Land Management Conservation Area,** just off NM 117 near **El Malpais National Monument** (see "Acoma Pueblo," below). At Chaco Canyon, check out the Wijiji Ruin trail, nice and easy but through beautiful country leading to an Anasazi ruin.

BIRD-WATCHING **Las Vegas National Wildlife Refuge** (✆ **505/425-3581**), 5 miles southeast of Las Vegas, is a great place for bird-watching. Species spotted year-round include prairie falcons and hawks; during late fall and early winter, migratory birds such as sandhill cranes, snow geese, Canada geese, and bald and golden eagles frequent the refuge. In all, more than 240 species can be sighted in the area. The **Maxwell National Wildlife Refuge** (✆ **575/375-2331**), near Raton, also boasts a rich population of resident and migratory birds, including raptors and bald eagles.

BOATING If you're towing a boat, good places to stop are **Bluewater Lake State Park** (✆ **505/876-2391**), a reservoir between Gallup and Grants, and **Navajo Lake State Park** (✆ **505/632-2278**), about 25 miles east of Bloomfield. Both of these state parks have boat ramps, and Navajo Lake has several marinas (from which visitors can rent boats), picnic areas, a visitor center, and groceries for those who plan to make a day of it. To find information on New Mexico state parks, go to **www.nmparks.com**. **Zuni Lakes,** six bodies of water operated by the Zuni tribe, also offers opportunities for boating, although you're not allowed to use gasoline motors and you must receive a permit (✆ **505/782-5851**) before setting out. You'll find opportunities for boating, windsurfing, and swimming throughout this region. Two of the most popular boating areas are **Storrie Lake State Park** (✆ **505/425-7278**), 6 miles north of Las Vegas, and **Conchas Lake State Park** (✆ **575/868-2270**), near Tucumcari. Storrie Lake is especially popular among **windsurfers,** who favor its consistent winds.

FISHING **Bluewater Lake State Park** (mentioned above for boating) is one of the best places to fish in the area. In fact, some people believe it has the highest catch rate of all New Mexico lakes. Look to catch trout here. A world-renowned fishing destination, the **San Juan River ★★**, just below Navajo Dam, was named the best fishing spot in the United States by *Field & Stream.* The scenery is outstanding and excellent guides in the area can help you find the choicest spots. **Navajo Lake State Park** (see "Boating," above) features about 150 miles of shoreline, where fishers go to catch trout, bass, catfish, and pike. Navajo Lake is one of the largest lakes in New Mexico, and the park is very heavily trafficked, so if crowds aren't your thing, look for another fishing hole. Just 4 miles south of Kirtland is **Morgan Lake,** a quiet spot for largemouth bass and catfish. If you need fishing gear or want to hire a guide while in the area, contact **Abe's Motel and Fly Shop,** 1791 US 173, Navajo Dam (✆ **505/632-2194**). In Farmington, contact **Dad's Boat Parts and Backyard Boutique,** 210 E. Piñon St. (✆ **505/326-1870**), or **Zia Sporting**

Goods, 500 E. Main (✆ **505/327-6004;** www.ziasportinggoods.com). Isolated and primitive **Morphy Lake State Park** is a favorite destination for serious anglers. The lake is regularly stocked with rainbow trout. **Cimarron Canyon State Park** is also popular with fishers. Lake Alice in **Sugarite Canyon State Park,** just north of Raton at the Colorado border, is a good spot for fly-fishing.

GOLF In this region, greens fees range from $20 to $55, with most averaging about $25; winter rates are lower. Cart rentals run about $15. In 2002, *Golf Digest* rated **Piñon Hills Golf Course,** 2101 Sunrise Pkwy., in Farmington (✆ **505/326-6066;** www.fmtn.org), the "best municipal course" in the United States. Also in Farmington is the **Civitan Golf Course,** 2100 N. Dustin (✆ **505/599-1194**). In Kirtland (approx. 7 miles west of Farmington), your golf option is **Riverview Golf Course,** on US 64 (✆ **505/598-0140**). In Grants, tee off at the 18-hole Coyote del Malpais Golf Course, at the base of Mount Taylor (✆ **505/285-5544;** http://coyotedelmalpaisgolfcourse.com). Duffers in northeast New Mexico can get in a few holes in or near virtually every town covered in this section. I recommend the following courses: **Raton Municipal Golf Course,** 510 Country Club Rd., Raton NM 87740 (✆ **575/445-8113**); **Pendaries Village Mountain Resort,** in Rociada (✆ **505/425-3561;** www.pendaries.net), 13 miles south of Mora and 27 miles northwest of Las Vegas; and **Tucumcari Municipal Golf Course,** Route 66 Boulevard, Tucumcari, NM 88401 (✆ **575/461-1849**).

HIKING This part of the state has some great hiking trails. You'll get to see ancient archaeological ruins in places such as Aztec Ruins and Chaco Canyon. In **Cíbola National Forest** (✆ **505/287-8833;** www.fs.fed.us/r3/cibola), the hike to the summit of Mount Taylor is excellent. In cooler months, but not winter, try hiking around **El Malpais National Monument** (✆ **505/285-4641;** www.nps.gov/elma). Two good hikes to try in El Malpais are the Zuni–Acoma Trail (this one is extremely taxing, so if you're not in shape, don't expect to make the 15-mile round-trip hike) and the Big Lava Tubes Trail (1 mile round-trip). My favorite hike in the region is to the top of **El Morro National Monument** ★★ (✆ **505/285-4641;** www.nps.gov/elma), which takes you to some Anasazi ruins. For quiet hiking on fairly level ground, head to **Bluewater Lake State Park** (✆ **505/876-2391**), **Red Rock Park** (✆ **505/722-3839**), or **Angel Peak Recreation Area** (✆ **505/599-8900**).

Sporting goods stores where you can get hiking gear include **REI-Albuquerque,** 1550 Mercantile Ave. NE, in Albuquerque (✆ **505/247-1191;** www.rei.com), **Frontier Sports,** 300 NE Aztec Blvd., in Aztec (✆ **505/334-0009**), and **Zia Sporting Goods,** 500 E. Main, in Farmington (✆ **505/327-6004;** www.ziasportinggoods.com).

Northeastern New Mexico abounds in great places to hike, including the trails at Capulin Volcano; however, the best places are in the mountains to the north of Las Vegas and west of Santa Fe and Taos. The region's premier hike takes you to the top of **Hermit's Peak,** a lovely but strenuous 8-mile round-trip foray onto a stunning precipice. Take NM 65 about 15 miles northwest of Las Vegas to the El Porvenir Campground. It's probably best to acquire equipment and supplies in Albuquerque before you set out.

SCUBA DIVING There couldn't possibly be scuba diving in this dry, landlocked state, could there? Yes, there is, with the best at Santa Rosa, where you'll find the **Blue Hole,** an 81-foot-deep artesian well that's a favorite of divers from around the world. The best place to rent equipment is at the **Santa Rosa Dive Center,** on Blue Hole Road, open only on weekends (✆ **575/472-3370**).

SKIING Some of the best cross-country skiing in the state is in the Chama area. Lots of broad bowls make the area a favorite of backcountry skiers as well as day-touring skiers. If you're up for an overnight adventure, contact **Southwest Nordic Center** (© **575/758-4761;** www.southwestnordiccenter.com), a company that rents yurts (Russian-style huts). The season is from mid-November to April, depending on snow conditions. Some like to ski the old logging roads of Mount Taylor in **Cíbola National Forest** near Grants. Contact the Ranger Station in Grants at © **505/287-8833** for more information.

SWIMMING Good swimming is available at **Navajo Lake State Park** (© **505/632-2278**). Before diving in at other lakes in state parks, make sure swimming is permitted. Swimming is best (although chilly) at **Clayton, Conchas, Morphy, Storrie,** and **Ute lakes.** (You can find directions to and specifics about these lakes at various points in the rest of this chapter.) In addition, though it's an indoor rather than outdoor experience, the **Las Vegas Recreation Center**'s swimming pool, at 1751 N. Grand Ave. (© **505/426-1739**), is an especially good place to take kids. It's Olympic-size and has a fun slide that will keep kids busy for hours. Call for more information.

2 ACOMA PUEBLO ★★★

30 miles SE of Grants; 90 miles SE of Gallup; 150 miles SE of Farmington

The spectacular Acoma Sky City, a walled adobe village perched high atop a sheer rock mesa 367 feet above the 6,600-foot valley floor, is said to have been inhabited at least since the 11th century—it's the longest continuously occupied community in the United States. Native history says it has been inhabited since before the time of Christ. Both the pueblo and its mission church of **San Esteban del Rey** are National Historic Landmarks. When Coronado visited in 1540, he suggested that Acoma was "the greatest stronghold in the world"; those who attempt to follow the cliffside footpath down after their guided tour, rather than take the bus back down, may agree.

About 50 to 75 Keresan-speaking Acoma (pronounced *Ack*-oo-mah) reside year-round on the 70-acre mesa top. Many others maintain ancestral homes and occupy them during ceremonial periods. The terraced three-story buildings face south for maximum exposure to the winter sun. Most of Sky City's permanent residents make their living off the throngs of tourists who flock here to see the magnificent church, built in 1639 and containing numerous masterpieces of Spanish colonial art, and to purchase the thin-walled white pottery with brown-and-black designs for which the pueblo is famous.

Many Acomas work in Grants, 15 miles west of the pueblo, in Albuquerque; or for one of Acoma's business enterprises, such as Sky City Casino. Others are cattle ranchers and farm individual family gardens.

ESSENTIALS

GETTING THERE To reach Acoma from Grants, drive east 15 miles on I-40 to McCartys, and then south 13 miles on paved tribal roads to the visitor center. From Albuquerque, drive west 65 miles to the Acoma–Sky City exit (102), and then 15 miles southwest.

VISITOR INFORMATION Contact the Sky City Cultural Center and Pueblo of Acoma (© **800/747-0181;** www.acomaskycity.org).

ADMISSION FEES & HOURS Admission is $12 for adults, $11 for seniors 60 and over, $9 for children 6 to 17, and free for children 5 and under. There's a discount for Native American visitors. The photography charge is $10; tripods are prohibited, telephoto lenses are restricted, and no video cameras are allowed. No cellphones, binoculars, sketching, or painting are allowed, except by special permission. The pueblo is open daily in the summer from 8am to 6:30pm; daily in the spring, fall, and winter from 8am to 5pm. One-hour tours begin every 30 minutes, depending on the demand; the last tour is scheduled 1 hour before closing. The pueblo is closed June 24 and 29; July 10 through July 13 and July 25; the first or second weekends in October; and the first Saturday in December. It's best to call ahead to confirm that the tour is available when you're visiting.

SEEING THE HIGHLIGHTS

You absolutely cannot wander freely around Acoma Pueblo, but you can start your tour there at the 40,000-square-foot museum and peruse their gallery, which offers art and crafts for sale, and have a meal at the Yaak'a Café.

You'll begin the tour by boarding the tour bus, which climbs through a rock garden of 50-foot sandstone monoliths and past precipitously dangling outhouses to the mesa's summit. With no running water or electricity in this medieval-looking village, it's a truly unique place. A small reservoir collects rainwater for most uses, and drinking water is transported up from below. Wood-hole ladders and mica windows are prevalent among the 300-odd adobe structures. As you tour the village, you'll have many opportunities to buy pottery and other pueblo treasures. Pottery is expensive here, but you're not going to find it any cheaper anywhere else, and you'll be guaranteed that it's authentic if you buy it directly from the craftsperson. Along the way, be sure to sample some Indian fry bread topped with honey.

DANCES & CEREMONIES

The annual San Esteban del Rey feast day is September 2, when the pueblo's patron saint is honored with a morning Mass, a procession, an afternoon corn dance, and an arts-and-crafts fair. The Governor's Feast is held annually in February; and 4 days of Christmas festivals run from December 25 to 28. Guided tours do not operate on the mesa during feast days, and cameras are not permitted then.

Other celebrations are held in nearby low-lying pueblo villages at Easter (in Acomita), the first weekend in May (Santa Maria feast at McCartys), and August 10 (San Lorenzo Day in Acomita).

WHERE TO STAY & DINE

The **Sky City Hotel & Casino,** off I-40, at exit 102 (✆ **888/759-2489;** www.skycity.com), offers good, basic accommodations, with prices ranging from $79 to $129 for a double. The hotel has a restaurant, snack bar, night club, casino, and RV park.

3 GRANTS

If you've ever wondered what a "boom-and-bust town" looks like, come to Grants and find out. Grants first boomed with the coming of the railroad in the late 19th century, when 4,000 workers descended on the tiny farm town. When the railroad was completed, the workers left, and the town was bust. Next, Grants saw high times in the 1940s, growing carrots and sending them to the East Coast; but when packaging became more advanced, Grants lost its foothold in the market and busted again. Then came the 1950s, when a Navajo sheep rancher named Paddy Martinez discovered some strange yellow rocks near Haystack Mountain, northwest of town. The United States was in need of uranium, and his find led to the biggest boom in the area. By the early 1980s, demand for uranium had dropped, and so went the big wages and big spenders that the ore's popularity had produced. However, recent demand may just revive that industry once again. Today, the city on a segment of Route 66 is a jumping-off point for outdoor adventures.

The city is the seat of expansive Cíbola County, which stretches from the Arizona border nearly to Albuquerque. For more information, contact the **Grants/Cíbola County Chamber of Commerce** at 100 N. Iron Ave. (P.O. Box 297), Grants, NM 87020 (✆ **800/748-2142** or 505/287-4802; www.grants.org). It's in the same building as the New Mexico Mining Museum.

WHAT TO SEE IN GRANTS

New Mexico Mining Museum ★ (Kids) This enormously interesting little museum primes you for the underground adventure of traveling into a re-creation of a mine shaft by showing you, on ground level, some geology, such as a fossilized dinosaur leg bone and a piece of Malpais lava. The world's only underground uranium-mining museum also gives you a sense of the context within which uranium was mined, through photos of the uranium-mining pioneers. Thus, the stage is set for your walk into a mine shaft–like doorway adorned with rusty metal hats. An elevator takes you down into a spooky, low-lit place with stone walls. You begin in the station where uranium was loaded and unloaded and travel through the earth to places defined on wall plaques. While exploring, you get a sense of the dark and dirty work that mining can be. Those with claustrophobia may have to content themselves with visiting the exhibits *above* ground.

100 N. Iron Ave., at Santa Fe Ave. ✆ **800/748-2142** or 505/287-4802. www.grants.org. Admission $3 adults, $2 seniors 60 and over and children 7–18; free for children 6 and under. Mon–Sat 9am–4pm.

Northwest New Mexico Visitor Center ★ East of Grants, this center sits within an expansive pueblo-style building with a broad atrium showing off views of the Malpais. It offers fliers and films on the region's parks, forests, and Indian country. A real treat here is a series of suggested driving tours displayed with large color photos and free cards describing the routes. One tour takes visitors along the volcanoes of the Malpais, another through the abandoned logging communities of the Zuni Mountains Historical Loop, and another to the stunning geologic formations of the Cabezon and Rio Puerco area. A fun shelf of Southwest book titles is worth perusing.

1900 Santa Fe Ave. ✆ **505/876-2783.** Free admission. Daily 9am–6pm during daylight saving time; 8am–5pm during Mountain Standard Time.

WHERE TO STAY IN GRANTS

Grants hotels are all on or near Route 66, with major properties near I-40 interchanges, and smaller or older motels nearer downtown. Lodger's tax is 5%, which is added to the gross receipts tax of 7.50%, for a total room tax of 12.5%. Parking is usually free.

Holiday Inn Express This two-story motel, just off the interstate, provides large, well-conceived rooms with a comfortable atmosphere. Ground-floor rooms open both off an inner corridor and from an outside door where your car is parked. Rooms are spacious, with high ceilings, comfortable beds, and large bathrooms.

1496 E. Santa Fe Ave., Grants, NM 87020. ✆ **800/HOLIDAY** [465-4329] or 505/285-4676. Fax 505/285-6998. www.hiexpress.com. 58 units. $119 double. Rates include hot breakfast. AE, DC, DISC, MC, V. Pets welcome. **Amenities:** Jacuzzi; small indoor pool. *In room:* A/C, TV, hair dryer, Wi-Fi.

Camping

Grants has two decent campgrounds with both tent and RV facilities. All range in price from $12 to $15 for tent camping and $15 to $20 for full hookups. **Blue Spruce RV Park** (✆ **505/287-2560**) has 25 sites and 16 full hookups and is open year-round. It has enough trees to block the wind, some grass, and the roads and parking spaces are gravel, so dust is minimized. Cable television hookups are available, as are laundry facilities and a recreation room. To reach the park, take I-40 to exit 81 and then go a quarter-mile south on NM 53.

Lavaland RV Park (✆ **505/287-8665;** www.lavalandrvpark.com), the closest site to Grants, has 51 sites and 39 full hookups. Near a lava outcropping, the site is clean, though a little desolate and dusty, with a few pine trees to block the wind. Air-conditioning and heating hookups are available, as are some free cable and telephone hookups. In addition, you'll find cabins, laundry, limited grocery facilities, picnic tables and grills, and recreation facilities. Lavaland is open year-round. From I-40, get off at exit 85 and continue 100 yards south on Access Road.

WHERE TO DINE IN GRANTS

In general, you won't find much to eat at pueblos or national monuments, so you're best off looking for a restaurant in Grants.

El Cafecito (Value) (Kids) AMERICAN/MEXICAN This real locals' spot serves up tasty food in a relaxed atmosphere. At mealtime, the brightly lit space with Saltillo tile floors bustles with families eating huevos rancheros (eggs over tortillas, smothered in chile) for breakfast, and enchiladas, stuffed *sopaipillas,* and burgers for lunch and dinner. All meals are large and inexpensive. Kids enjoy their own menu selections.

820 E. Santa Fe Ave. ✆ **505/285-6229.** Main courses $4–$8 breakfast, $6–$12 lunch or dinner. AE, DISC, MC, V. Mon–Fri 7am–9pm; Sat 7am–8pm.

La Ventana NEW MEXICAN/STEAKS Grants locals come here for a special lunch or dinner out. With one large room that seats about 50 people, the restaurant has a Southwestern decor, with a two-horse sculpture and some dancing katsinas (kachinas). Ironically, despite it name—which means "the window" and refers to the natural arch south of town—the place is dark. If you can catch Grants on a nonwindy day, opt for the patio. Service is friendly and varies in its efficiency. Recommended dishes include chicken fajita salad and prime rib. You'll also find sandwiches such as turkey and guacamole served on seven-grain bread. You can order from a full bar.

110½ Geis St., Hillcrest Center. ✆ **505/287-9393.** Reservations recommended. Main courses $5–$12 lunch, $8–$20 dinner. AE, DC, DISC, MC, V. Mon–Sat 11am–11pm.

4 EL MALPAIS & EL MORRO NATIONAL MONUMENTS

El Malpais: 15 miles S of Grants; 75 miles SE of Gallup; 135 miles S of Farmington. El Morro: 30 miles SW of Grants; 45 miles SE of Gallup; 149 miles S of Farmington

Northwestern New Mexico has two national monuments that are must-sees for anyone touring this region: El Malpais and El Morro. The region is also home to the Cíbola National Forest, with its stately Mount Taylor, visible from miles away and an excellent place to hike and backcountry ski.

EL MALPAIS: EXPLORING THE BADLANDS ★

Designated a national monument in 1987, El Malpais (Spanish for "badlands") is an outstanding example of the volcanic landscapes in the United States. El Malpais contains 115,000 acres of cinder cones, vast lava flows, hundreds of lava tubes, ice caves, sandstone cliffs, natural bridges and arches, Anasazi ruins, ancient Native American trails, and Spanish and Anglo homesteads.

Essentials

GETTING THERE You can take one of two approaches to El Malpais, via NM 117 or NM 53. NM 117 exits I-40 7 miles east of Grants.

VISITOR INFORMATION Admission to El Malpais is free (unless you're visiting the privately owned Ice Caves), and it's open to visitors year-round. The **visitor center,** off Route 53 between mile markers 63 and 64, is open daily from 8:30am to 4:30pm. Here you can pick up maps of the park, leaflets on specific trails, and other details about exploring the monument. For more information, contact **El Malpais National Monument,** NPS, P.O. Box 939, Grants, NM 87020 (✆ **505/285-4641;** www.nps.gov/elma).

Seeing the Highlights

From **Sandstone Bluffs Overlook** (10 miles south of I-40 off NM 117), many craters are visible in the lava flow, which extends for miles along the eastern flank of the Continental Divide. The most recent flows are only 1,000 years old; Native American legends tell of rivers of "fire rock." Seventeen miles south of I-40 is **La Ventana Natural Arch,** the largest accessible natural arch in New Mexico.

From NM 53, which exits I-40 just west of Grants, visitors have access to the **Zuni–Acoma Trail,** an ancient Pueblo trade route that crosses four major lava flows in a 7.5-mile (one-way) hike. A printed trail guide is available. **El Calderon,** a forested area 20 miles south of I-40, is a trail head for exploring a cinder cone, lava tubes, and a bat cave. (***Warning:*** Hikers should not enter the bat cave or otherwise disturb the bats.)

The largest of all Malpais cinder cones, **Bandera Crater** is on private property 25 miles south of I-40. The National Park Service has plans to absorb this commercial operation, known as **Ice Caves Resort** (✆ **888/ICE-CAVE** [423-2283] or 505/783-4303; www.icecaves.com). For a fee ($9 for adults and $4 for children 5–12), visitors hike up the crater or walk to the edge of an ice cave. It's open daily from 8am to 7pm in summer and from 8am to 4pm in winter (generally closing 1 hr. before sunset).

Perhaps the most fascinating phenomenon of El Malpais is the lava tubes, formed when the outer surface of a lava flow cooled and solidified. When the lava river drained, tunnel-like caves were left. Ice caves within some of the tubes have delicate ice-crystal ceilings, ice stalactites, and floors like ice rinks.

Hiking & Camping

El Malpais has several hiking trails, including the above-mentioned Zuni–Acoma Trail. Most are marked with rock cairns; some are dirt trails. The best times to hike this area are during spring and fall, when it's not too hot. You're pretty much on your own when you explore this area, so prepare accordingly. Carry plenty of water with you; do not drink surface water. Carrying first-aid gear is always a good idea because the lava rocks can be extremely sharp and inflict nasty cuts. Never go into a cave alone. The park service advises wearing hard hats, boots, protective clothing, and gloves, and carrying three sources of light when entering lava tubes. The weather can change suddenly, so be prepared; if lightning is around, move off the lava as quickly as possible.

Primitive camping is allowed in the park, but you must first obtain a free backcountry permit from the visitor center.

EL MORRO NATIONAL MONUMENT ★★

Travelers who like to look history straight in the eye are fascinated by "Inscription Rock," 43 miles west of Grants along NM 53. Looming up out of the sand and sagebrush is a bluff 200 feet high, holding some of the most captivating messages in North America. Its sandstone face displays a written record of the many who inhabited and traveled through this land, beginning with the ancestral Puebloans, who lived atop the formation around 1200. Carved with steel points are the signatures and comments of almost every explorer, conquistador, missionary, army officer, surveyor, and pioneer who passed this way between 1605, when Gov. Don Juan de Oñate carved the first inscription, and 1906, when it was preserved by the National Park Service. Oñate's inscription, dated April 16, 1605, was perhaps the first graffiti any European left in America.

A paved walkway makes it easy to walk to the writings, and a stone stairway leads up to other treasures. One entry reads: "Year of 1716 on the 26th of August passed by here Don Feliz Martinez, Governor and Captain General of this realm to the reduction and conquest of the Moqui." Confident of success as he was, Martinez actually got nowhere with any "conquest of the Moqui," or Hopi, peoples. After a 2-month battle, they chased him back to Santa Fe.

Another special group to pass by this way was the U.S. Camel Corps, trekking past on their way from Texas to California in 1857. The camels worked out fine in mountains and deserts, outlasting horses and mules 10 to 1, but the Civil War ended the experiment. When Peachy Breckinridge, fresh out of the Virginia Military Academy, came by with 25 camels, he noted the fact on the stone here.

El Morro was at one time as famous as the Blarney Stone of Ireland: Everybody had to stop by and make a mark. But when the Santa Fe Railroad was laid 25 miles to the north, El Morro was no longer on the main route to California, and from the 1870s, the tradition began to die out.

If you like to hike, be sure to take the full loop to the top of Inscription Rock. It's a spectacular trip that takes you along the rim of this mesa—offering 360-degree views—culminating in an up-close look at Anasazi ruins, which occupy an area 200 by 300 feet. Inscription Rock's name, Atsinna, suggests that carving one's name here is a very old custom indeed: The word, in Zuni, means "writing on rock."

Essentials

GETTING THERE El Morro is 43 miles west of Grants on NM 53.

VISITOR INFORMATION For information, contact **El Morro National Monument,** HC61, Box 43, Ramah, NM 87321-9603 (✆ **505/783-4226;** www.nps.gov/elmo). Admission to El Morro is $3 per person 16 and older. Self-guided trail booklets are available at the visitor center (turn off NM 53 at the El Morro sign and travel approximately a half-mile), open year-round from 9am to 5pm. Trails are also open year-round; check with the **visitor center** for hours. A **museum** at the visitor center features exhibits on the 700 years of human activity at El Morro. A 15-minute video gives a good introduction to the park. Also within the visitor center is a **bookstore** where you can pick up souvenirs and informational books. It takes approximately 2 hours to visit the museum and hike the trails. The park is closed on Christmas and New Year's Day.

Camping

Though it isn't necessary to camp here in order to see most of the park, a nine-site campground at El Morro is open year-round, with a fee of $5 per night charged from approximately April to November. No supplies are available within the park, so if you're planning on spending a night or two, be sure to arrive well equipped.

One nearby private enterprise, **El Morro RV Park, Cabins & Cafe,** HC 61, Box 44, Ramah, NM 87321 (© **505/783-4612;** www.elmorro-nm.com), has cabins, RV and tent camping, and a cafe (see below). The cabins are well appointed, and the bathrooms clean.

5 GALLUP: GATEWAY TO INDIAN COUNTRY ★

62 miles NW of Grants; 118 miles NW of Albuquerque; 164 miles W of Santa Fe

Gallup has always been a mysterious place, home to many Native Americans, with dust left from its Wild West days, and with an unmistakable Route 66 architectural presence; it just doesn't seem to exist in this era. The best way to get a sense of the place is by walking around downtown, wandering through the trading posts and pawnshops and by the historic buildings. In doing so, you'll probably encounter many locals and get a real feel for this "Heart of Indian Country."

Gallup began as a town when the railroad from Arizona reached this spot in 1881. At that time, the town consisted of a stagecoach stop and a saloon, the Blue Goose. Within 2 years, coal mining had made the town boom, and some 22 saloons (including the Bucket of Blood) and an opera house filled the town, most of which was inhabited by immigrants from mining areas in eastern Europe, England, Wales, Germany, and Italy.

When the popularity of the railroads declined, Gallup turned briefly to the movie business as its boom ticket. The area's red-rock canyons and lonely deserts were perfect for Westerns of the era, such as *Big Carnival,* with Kirk Douglas; *Four Faces West,* with Joel McCrea; and *The Bad Man,* starring Wallace Beery, Lionel Barrymore, and Ronald Reagan. These stars and many others stayed in a Route 66 hotel built by R. E. Griffith in 1937. Today, the El Rancho Hotel and Motel is one of Gallup's most notable landmarks and worth strolling through (see "Where to Stay in Gallup," and "Where to Dine in Gallup," below). Gallup now relies on trade and tourism, due to its central location within the Navajo Reservation and the Zuni lands, as well as its proximity to the ancient ruins at Chaco.

Gallup's most notable special event is the **Inter-Tribal Indian Ceremonial,** held every August. Native Americans converge on the town for a parade, dances, and an all-Indian rodeo east of town, at Red Rock State Park. It's a busy time in Gallup, so make reservations far in advance. If you're not in town for the Ceremonial, try visiting on a Saturday, when many Native Americans come to town to trade. Best of all on this day is the **flea market,** north of town just off US 491. Here you can sample fry bread, Zuni bread, and Acoma bread; eat real mutton stew; and shop for anything from jewelry to underwear. After the flea market, most Gallup-area residents, native and nonnative alike, go to Earl's (see "Where to Dine in Gallup," below) to eat.

ESSENTIALS

GETTING THERE From Albuquerque, take I-40 west (2½ hr.). From Farmington, take US 64 west to Shiprock, and then US 491 south (2½ hr.). From Flagstaff, Arizona, take I-40 east (3 hr.). Gallup is not served by any commercial airlines at this time.

VISITOR INFORMATION The **Gallup–McKinley County Chamber of Commerce,** 103 W. US 66, Gallup, NM 87301 (✆ **800/242-4282** or 505/722-2228; www.thegallupchamber.com), is just south of the main I-40 interchange for downtown Gallup.

WHAT TO SEE & DO

Exploring Gallup

Gallup has 20 buildings that are either listed on or have been nominated to the National Register of Historic Places. Some hold trading posts worth visiting. A good place to start is at the **Santa Fe Railroad Depot,** which also houses the **Gallup Cultural Center ★**, at East 66 Avenue and Strong Street (✆ **505/863-4131**). Built in 1923 in modified Mission style, it has been renovated into a community transportation and cultural center, with a museum worth visiting, as well as a gift shop and diner. Note especially the exhibits on regional history and the Master's Exhibit of paintings, pottery, and basketry from area Native Americans (for more activities see "Sunset Dances," below). The center is open weekdays from 9am to 5pm, often with extended hours in the summer. Across the street, the **Drake Hotel** (later the Turquoise Club but now abandoned), built of blond brick in 1919, had the Prohibition-era reputation of being controlled by bootleggers, with wine running in the faucets in place of water.

The 1928 **White Cafe,** 100 W. 66 Ave., is an elaborate decorative brick structure that catered to the early auto tourist traffic. Now it's a jewelry store. Down the street, the **Eagle Café,** 220 W. 66 Ave. (✆ **505/722-3220**), open since 1920, serves diner food in an authentic atmosphere. A few doors down, **Richardson's Trading Company,** 222 W. 66 Ave. (✆ **505/722-4762;** www.richardsontrading.com), has been selling good Native American arts and crafts since 1913.

The **Rex Hotel,** 300 W. 66 Ave., constructed of locally quarried sandstone, was once known for its "ladies of the night." It's now the **Rex Museum** (✆ **505/863-1363**), a somewhat random display of items from the Gallup Historical Society Collection, but fun for history buffs. It's open daily but with unpredictable hours. Call before setting out.

Gallup's architectural gems include the **Chief Theater,** 228 W. Coal Ave. This structure was built in 1920; in 1936, it was completely redesigned in Pueblo-Deco style, with zigzag relief and geometric form, by R. E. "Griff" Griffith (who also built the El Rancho Hotel), brother of Hollywood producer D. W. Griffith. Now this is **City Electric Shoe Shop** (✆ **505/863-5252;** www.cityelectricshoe.com), where Native Americans go to buy feathers, leather, and other goods to make ceremonial clothing. It's known to locals simply as City Electric because it was the first shop in town to have an automated shoe-repair machine. It also has a good selection of moccasins and hats. Also visit the 1928 **El Morro Theater,** 207 W. Coal Ave., built in Spanish colonial revival style with Spanish baroque plaster carving and bright polychromatic painting; it's where locals come to see movies and dance performances.

Shopping

Nowhere are the jewelry and crafts of Navajo, Zuni, and Hopi tribes less expensive than in Gallup. The most intriguing places to shop are the trading posts and pawnshops, which provide a surprising range of services for their largely Native American clientele and have little in common with the pawnshops of large U.S. cities.

Navajoland **pawnbrokers** in essence are bankers, at least from the Navajo and Zuni viewpoint. Pawnshops provide safekeeping of valuable personal goods and make small-collateral loans. The trader will hold on to an item for months or even years before deeming it "dead" and putting it up for sale. Fewer than 5% of items ever go unredeemed, but over the years traders do accumulate a selection, so the shops are worth perusing.

Most shops are open Monday through Saturday from 9am to 5pm. For a look at everything from pawn jewelry to Pendleton robes and shawls to enamel and cast-iron kitchenware, visit **Ellis Tanner Trading Company** (✆ **505/863-4434;** www.etanner.com), NM 602 Bypass, south from I-40 on NM 602 about 2 miles; it's at the corner of Nizhoni Boulevard. Also try **Perry Null–Tobe Turpen's Indian Trading Company,** 1710 S. Second St. (✆ **505/722-3806**), a big free-standing brick building full of jewelry, rugs, katsinas, and pottery.

Sunset Dances

Every evening Memorial Day to Labor Day, dancers from a variety of area tribes sing, drum, and twirl in a stunning display of ritual from 7 to 8pm. The dances take place at the **Gallup Cultural Center,** on East 66 Avenue and Strong Street (✆ **505/863-4131**). Admission to the center and dances is free.

WHERE TO STAY IN GALLUP

Virtually all accommodations options in Gallup are somewhere along Route 66, either near the I-40 interchanges or on the highway through downtown.

El Rancho Hotel and Motel ★ This historic hotel owes as much to Hollywood as to Gallup. Built in 1937 by R. E. "Griff" Griffith, brother of movie mogul D. W. Griffith, it became the place for film companies to set up headquarters when filming here. Between the 1940s and 1960s, a who's who of Hollywood stayed here. Their autographed photos line the walls of the hotel's cafe. Spencer Tracy and Katharine Hepburn stayed here during production of *The Sea of Grass;* Burt Lancaster and Lee Remick were guests when they made *The Hallelujah Trail.* The list goes on and on: Gene Autry, Lucille Ball, Jack Benny, Humphrey Bogart, James Cagney, Errol Flynn, Henry Fonda, the Marx Brothers, Ronald Reagan, Rosalind Russell, James Stewart, John Wayne, and Mae West all stayed here.

In 1986, Gallup businessman Armand Ortega, a longtime jewelry merchant, bought the then run-down El Rancho and restored it to its earlier elegance. The lobby staircase rises to the mezzanine on either side of an enormous stone fireplace, while heavy ceiling beams and railings made of tree limbs give the room a hunting-lodge ambience. The hotel is on the National Register of Historic Places.

Rooms in El Rancho differ from one to the next and are named for the stars that stayed in them. Most are long and medium size, with wagon-wheel headboards and good, heavy pine furniture stained dark. The beds are comfortable. The bathrooms can be small; some have showers only, while others have tub/shower combos. All have lovely white hexagonal tiles. Many rooms have balconies. Two suites with kitchenettes are also available. My favorite rooms are on the ground floor, which is the quietest part of the hotel. Light sleepers should be aware that the train can be heard from rooms in the upper stories.

1000 E. 66 Ave., Gallup, NM 87301. ✆ **800/543-6351** or 505/863-9311. Fax 505/722-5917. www.elranchohotel.com. 99 units. $84–$92 double; $130 suite. AE, DISC, MC, V. Pets welcome. **Amenities:** Restaurant (p. 283); bar; courtesy computer; outdoor pool (in summer); Wi-Fi (in lobby). *In room:* A/C, TV.

La Quinta ★ The challenge in Gallup is to find a quiet place to sleep. With busy train tracks running right through town, most accommodations stay noisy through the night. Sitting east of town, this is one of the quietest places I've found, but you'll have to reserve carefully. The trick here is to ask for a room on the side of the hotel that faces *away* from the tracks and you'll get a good night's sleep. Rooms are medium size, with high ceilings and the calming green decor for which this chain is known. The rooms are new and have comfortable beds and fairly spacious bathrooms. A hot breakfast adds to the appeal.

675 Scott Ave., Gallup, NM 87401. ✆ **800/531-5900** or 505/327-4706. Fax 505/325-6583. www.laquinta.com. 66 units. $102 double; $138 suite. Rates include hot breakfast. AE, DC, DISC, MC, V. **Amenities:** Jacuzzi; outdoor pool. *In room:* A/C, TV, fridge, hair dryer, Internet.

Camping

As in the rest of the state, the Gallup area offers plenty of places to pitch a tent or hook up your RV. **USA RV Park** (✆ **505/863-5021;** www.usarvpark.com) has 145 sites, 50 full hookups, and cabins, as well as grocery and laundry facilities. Recreation facilities include arcade games, a seasonal heated swimming pool, and a playground. An outdoor breakfast and dinner are served at an extra cost. Sites range from $21 for tents to $28 for full hookups (cable TV costs extra). Cabins are $37. To reach the campground, take I-40 to the US 66/Business I-40 junction (exit 16); go 1 mile east on US 66/Business I-40.

Red Rock Park campground (✆ **505/722-3839**) has 106 sites—50 with no hookups and 56 with water and electricity. Tent sites are available. Sites range from $20 for tents to $25 for full hookups. The sites are right against the buttes, though in the spring they will surely be dusty because of little protection from the wind. Also accessible are a convenience store, picnic tables, and grills.

WHERE TO DINE IN GALLUP

Earl's ★ (Kids) AMERICAN/NEW MEXICAN This is where the locals come to eat, particularly on weekends, en route to and from trading in Gallup. The place fills up with a variety of clientele, from college students to Navajo grandmothers. A Denny's-style diner, with comfortable booths and chairs, the restaurant allows Native Americans to sell their wares to you while you eat; however, you have the option of putting up a sign asking not to be disturbed. Often on weekends, vendors set up tables out front, so the entire place takes on a bustling bazaar atmosphere. And the food is good. I recommend the New Mexican dishes such as huevos rancheros, the enchilada plate, or the smothered grande burrito. Earl's offers a kids' menu and half-portion items for smaller appetites, as well as some salads and a "baked potato meal." Open since 1947, Earl's continues to please.

1400 E. 66 Ave. ✆ **505/863-4201.** Reservations accepted except Fri–Sat. Most menu items under $10. AE, MC, V. Mon–Sat 6am–9pm; Sun 7am–9pm.

El Rancho ★ (Moments) (Kids) AMERICAN/NEW MEXICAN Set in the historic El Rancho Hotel (see above), this restaurant has fans all across the Southwest. They come to experience the Old West decor—with well-spaced, heavy wooden furniture and movie memorabilia on the walls—and the sense of the many movie stars who once ate here. The food is fine-diner style, with dishes such as steak and eggs or hot cakes for breakfast, as well as regional delights, such as *atole* (hot blue-corn cereal) or a breakfast taco. At lunch you can always count on a good burger here or select from a cast of sandwiches, such as the Doris Day (sirloin steak on French bread), or salads. At dinner, steaks are a big hit, as is the grilled salmon, both served with soup or salad, vegetable, and your choice of potato or rice. The New Mexican food is also good. Kids can select from the "little buckaroos" menu. A full bar is available.

In the El Rancho Hotel and Motel, 1000 E. 66 Ave. ✆ **800/543-6351** or 505/863-9311. www.historicelranchohotel.com. Reservations not accepted. Main courses $5–$12 breakfast, $8–$13 lunch, $9–$20 dinner. AE, DISC, MC, V. Daily 6:30am–10pm.

6 CHAMA

59 miles NW of Taos; 91 miles NW of Santa Fe; 95 miles E of Farmington

This pioneer village of 1,250 people at the base of the 10,000-foot Cumbres Pass is New Mexico's undiscovered playland. Now, with some new additions, the town is really looking up. A park, clock tower, and—drumroll, please—sidewalks (!) give it a friendlier tone.

Bordered by three wilderness areas, the Carson, Rio Grande, and Santa Fe national forests, the area is indeed prime for hunting, fishing, cross-country skiing, snowmobiling, snowshoeing, and hiking.

Another highlight here is America's longest and highest narrow-gauge coal-fired steam line, the **Cumbres & Toltec Scenic Railroad,** which winds 64 miles through valleys and mountain meadows between Chama and Antonito, Colorado. The village of Chama boomed when the railroad arrived in 1881. A rough-and-ready frontier town, the place still maintains that flavor, with lumber and ranching making up a big part of the economy.

Landmarks to watch for are the **Brazos Cliffs** and waterfall and **Heron and El Vado lakes.** Tierra Amarilla, the Rio Arriba County seat, is 14 miles south, and is at the center—along with Los Ojos and Los Brazos—of a wool-raising and weaving tradition where local craftspeople still weave masterpieces. Dulce, governmental seat of the Jicarilla Apache Indian Reservation, is 27 miles west.

ESSENTIALS

GETTING THERE From Santa Fe, take US 84 north (2 hr.). From Taos, take US 64 west (2½ hr.). From Farmington, take US 64 east (2¼ hr.).

VISITOR INFORMATION The **New Mexico Visitor Information Center,** P.O. Box 697, Chama, NM 87520 (✆ **575/756-2235**), is at 2372 US 17. It's open daily from 8am to 6pm in the summer, from 8am to 5pm in the winter. At the same address is the **Chama Valley Chamber of Commerce** (✆ **800/477-0149** or 575/756-2306; www.chamavalley.com).

ALL ABOARD THE HISTORIC C&T RAILROAD

Cumbres & Toltec Scenic Railroad ★★ (Moments) If you have a passion for the past and for incredible scenery, climb aboard America's longest and highest narrow-gauge steam railroad, the historic C&T. It operates on a 64-mile track between Chama and Antonito, Colorado. Built in 1880 as an extension of the Denver and Rio Grande line to serve the mining camps of the San Juan Mountains, it is perhaps the finest surviving example of what once was a vast network of remote Rocky Mountain railways.

The C&T passes through forests of pine and aspen, past striking rock formations, and over the magnificent Toltec Gorge of the Rio de los Pinos. It crests at the 10,015-foot Cumbres Pass, the highest in the United States used by scheduled passenger trains.

Steam Power Shopping

After sitting on the steam train, you may want to stroll for a while, hitting a few of the shops in Chama. One of note is the **Local Color Gallery,** 567 Terrace Ave. (✆ **888/756-2604** or 575/756-2604), in the center of town. Here you'll find all kinds of locally made arts and crafts, from pottery to moody candles painted with petroglyph symbols to picturesque watercolors of the Chama area.

Halfway through the route, at Osier, Colorado, the *New Mexico Express,* from Chama, meets the *Colorado Limited,* from Antonito. They stop to exchange greetings, engines, and through passengers. A lunch of roast turkey, mashed potatoes, gravy, and other offerings is served in a big, barnlike dining hall in Osier. From there, through passengers continue on to Antonito and return by van, while round-trip passengers return to their starting point. Be aware that both trips are nearly full-day events. Those who find it uncomfortable to sit for long periods may instead want to opt for hiking or skiing in the area. Ask about their Parlor Car, a more luxurious alternative to coach seating.

A walking-tour brochure, describing 23 points of interest in the Chama railroad yards, can be picked up at the 1899 depot in Chama. These yards are a living, working museum, which fascinates history buffs. A registered National Historic Site, the C&T is owned by the states of Colorado and New Mexico. Special cars with lifts for people with disabilities are available with a 7-day advance reservation.

500 Terrace Ave., Chama, NM 87520. ✆ **888/CUMBRES** [286-2737] or 575/756-2151. Fax 575/756-2694. www.cumbrestoltec.com. Lunch is included with all fares. Round-trip to Osier: Adults $70, children 11 and under $35. Through trip to Antonito, return by van (or to Antonito by van, return by train): Adults $80, children $40. Reservations highly recommended. Memorial Day to mid-Oct trains leave Chama daily at 10am; vans depart for Antonito at 8:30am.

WHERE TO STAY IN CHAMA

Most accommodations in this area are found on NM 17 or south of the US 64/84 junction, known as the "Y."

Hotels/Lodges

Chama Station Inn ★ Set in downtown Chama, right across the street from the Cumbres & Toltec Scenic Railroad station, this inn offers clean, atmospheric rooms in a 1920s building. Wood floors, high ceilings, and quilts on the comfortable beds create a cozy atmosphere. Bathrooms are small, with only a shower, but functional. A portal on the two-story building allows a nice place to lounge next to an elaborate garden. Best of all, you can climb out of bed and walk to the train. The only drawback here is that the inn is only open from late May to mid-October, when the train is running. Two of the rooms have kiva fireplaces. Next door, a coffee shop offers breakfast.

423 Terrace Ave., Chama, NM 87520. ✆ **888/726-8150** or 505/756-2315. www.chamastationinn.com. 9 units. $75–$85 double. AE, DISC, MC, V. *In room:* TV, hair dryer.

River Bend Lodge (Kids) Set on a bend of the Chama River, this lodging offers the best cabins in town and clean motel rooms. Though they're prefab cabins, they're better than some of the more authentic and overly rustic ones at nearby lodgings. If you can reserve cabin no. 40, 50, or 60 at the back of the property, you'll have a sweet riverside stay. Some of these are split level, with a queen-size sleeping loft and a bedroom—not great for privacy, but good for a family that doesn't mind sharing space. Others are similar, but without the loft. Every cabin has a fold-out futon in the living room, an efficient little kitchen, and a small bathroom. The motel rooms are medium size, with basic furnishing and a long portal to relax under in the afternoons. Guests may fish and wade in the river flowing through the property.

2625 US 84/64, Chama, NM 87520. ✆ **800/288-1371** or 505/756-2264. Fax 505/756-2664. www.chamariverbendlodge.com. 21 units. Motel rooms $68–$89 double; cabins $115–$135 double. Children 12 and under stay free in parent's room. AE, DC, DISC, MC, V. Pets accepted with $10 fee. **Amenities:** Coffee and microwave in lobby; Jacuzzi. *In room:* A/C, TV, fridge.

Camping

At **Rio Chama RV Campground** (✆ **575/756-2303**), you're within easy walking distance of the Cumbres & Toltec Scenic Railroad depot. This shady campground with 94 sites along the Rio Chama is ideal for RVers and tenters who plan to take train rides. The campground also offers great photo opportunities of the old steam trains leaving the depot. Hot showers, a dump station, and complete hookups are available. It's open from May to mid-October only. The campground is 2¼ miles north of the US 84/64 junction on NM 17.

Twin Rivers Trailer Park (✆ **575/756-2218;** www.twinriversonline.net) has 50 sites and 40 full hookups; phone hookups are offered. Tenting is available, as are laundry facilities and ice and picnic tables. River swimming and fishing are popular activities; other sports facilities include basketball, volleyball, badminton, and horseshoes. Twin Rivers is open from April 15 to November 15 and is 100 yards west of the junction of NM 17 and US 84/64.

WHERE TO DINE IN CHAMA

High Country Restaurant and Saloon ★ STEAKS/SEAFOOD/NEW MEXICAN This is definitely a country place, with functional furniture, orange vinyl chairs, brown carpet, and a big stone fireplace. But it's *the* place innkeepers recommend, and one traveling couple I spoke to had eaten lunch and dinner here every day of their weeklong stay. The steaks are a big draw here. More sophisticated appetites may like the *trucha con piñon,* trout dusted in flour and cooked with pine nuts, garlic, and shallots. Meals are served with a salad and choice of potato. The New Mexican food is also good. The attached saloon has a full bar and bustles with people eating peanuts and throwing the shells on the floor. Breakfast on Sunday is country-style, with offerings such as steak and eggs and biscuits and gravy topping the menu, as well as omelets, pancakes, and huevos rancheros (eggs atop tortillas smothered in chile sauce).

Main St. (1/10 mile north of the Y), Chama. ✆ **575/756-2384.** Breakfast $4–$10; lunch $6–$12; dinner $5–$20; Sun breakfast buffet $8.95. AE, DISC, MC, V. Mon–Sat 11am–10pm; Sun 8am–10pm. Closed Easter, Thanksgiving, Christmas.

ON THE ROAD: WHAT TO SEE & DO ON US 84 SOUTH

Distinctive yellow earth provided a name for the town of **Tierra Amarilla,** 14 miles south of Chama at the junction of US 84 and US 64. Throughout New Mexico, this name is synonymous with a continuing controversy over the land-grant rights of the descendants of the original Hispanic settlers. But the economy of this community of 1,000 is dyed in the wool—literally.

The organization *Ganados del Valle* (Livestock Growers of the Valley) is at work to save the longhaired Spanish churro sheep from extinction, to introduce other unusual wool breeds to the valley, and to perpetuate a 200-year-old tradition of shepherding, spinning, weaving, and dyeing. Many of the craftspeople work in conjunction with **Tierra Wools ★**, P.O. Box 229, Los Ojos, NM 87551 (✆ **505/588-7231;** www.handweavers.com), which has a showroom and workshop in a century-old mercantile building just north of Tierra Amarilla. One-of-a-kind blankets and men's and women's apparel are among the products displayed and sold. Just down the street, across from the Los Ojos General Store, is an interesting little art studio worth checking out. **Yellow Earth Studio** (✆ **575/588-7807**), the passion of Paul Trachtman, the resident artist, is a great place to see and purchase enchanting scenes of the Los Ojos area.

Two state parks are a short drive west from Tierra Amarilla. **El Vado Lake State Park,** 14 miles southwest on NM 112 (✆ **575/588-7247;** www.nmparks.com), offers boating and water-skiing, fishing, and camping in summer; cross-country skiing and ice fishing in winter. **Heron Lake State Park,** 11 miles west on US 64 and NM 95 (✆ **575/588-7470;** www.nmparks.com), has a no-wake speed limit for motor vessels, adding to its appeal for fishing, sailing, windsurfing, canoeing, and swimming. The park has an interpretive center, plus camping, picnic sites, hiking trails, and cross-country skiing in the winter. The 5.5-mile Rio Chama trail connects the two lakes.

East of Tierra Amarilla, the Rio Brazos cuts a canyon through the Tusas Mountains and around 11,403-foot Brazos Peak. Just north of Los Ojos, NM 512 heads east 7½ miles up the **Brazos Box Canyon.** High cliffs that rise straight from the valley floor give it a Yosemite-like appearance—which is even more apparent from an overlook on US 64, 18 miles east of Tierra Amarilla en route to Taos. **El Chorro,** an impressive waterfall at the mouth of the canyon, usually flows only from early May to mid-June. Several resort lodges are in the area.

About 37 miles south of Tierra Amarilla on US 84, and 3 miles north of Ghost Ranch, is **Echo Canyon Amphitheater** (✆ **575/684-2486**), a U.S. Forest Service campground and picnic area. The "theater," hollowed out of sandstone by thousands of years of erosion, is a natural work of art with layers of stone ranging from pearl-color to blood red. The walls send back eerie echoes and even clips of conversations. It's just a 10-minute walk from the parking area. The fee is $2 per car. Some 13 miles west of here, via the dirt Forest Service road 151 into the Chama River Canyon Wilderness, is the isolated **Monastery of Christ in the Desert** (www.christdesert.org), built in 1964 by Benedictine monks. The brothers produce crafts, sold at a small gift shop, and operate a guesthouse.

Along the same road (FS 151) is access to the Chama River, a good place to hike, mountain bike, kayak, and camp. The **Rim Vista Trail** will take you to the top of the rim, with vast views out across Abiquiu Lake and Ghost Ranch. Primitive campsites can be found all along the river.

A 3-mile drive from there is **Ghost Ranch,** a collection of adobe buildings that make up an adult study center maintained by the United Presbyterian Church. A number of hauntingly memorable hikes originate from this place, which gets its name from the *brujas,* or witches, said to inhabit the canyons. Most popular among the hikes is spectacular **Chimney Rock,** but even more notable, in my opinion, is **Kitchen Mesa.** Directions for the hikes can be obtained at the visitor center. World-renowned painter Georgia O'Keeffe spent time at Ghost Ranch painting these canyons and other land formations. Eventually she bought a portion of the ranch and lived in a humble adobe house there. The ranch now offers seminars on a variety of topics, ranging from art to literature to religion, that are open to all. For information, contact **Ghost Ranch,** 401 Old Taos Hwy., Santa Fe (✆ **505/982-8539;** www.ghostranch.org).

The **Florence Hawley Ellis Museum of Anthropology** has interpretative exhibits of a Spanish ranch house and Native American anthropology, and the **Ruth Hall Paleontology Museum** (both museums ✆ **505/685-4333;** www.ghostranch.org) displays fossils of the early dinosaur named coelophysis found on the ranch. A lightly built creature, it was very fast when chasing prey. It roamed the area 250 million years ago, making it the oldest dinosaur found in New Mexico.

Many dinosaur skeletons have been found in rocks along the base of cliffs near **Abiquiu Reservoir** (✆ **505/685-4371**), a popular boating and fishing spot formed by the Abiquiu Dam.

A good place to stay and dine in the area is the **Abiquiu Inn** ★, a small country inn, restaurant, art gallery, and gift shop, a half-mile north of the village of Abiquiu (✆ **505/685-4378**). The casitas are especially nice. Rates are $139 to $199.

Heading south from Abiquiu, watch for **Dar al Islam** (✆ **505/685-4515**), a spiritual center with a circular Middle Eastern–style mosque made of adobe; the small community of **Mendanales,** is the home of renowned weaver Cordelia Coronado; and **Hernandez,** the village immortalized in Ansel Adams's famous 1941 photograph *Moonrise, Hernandez, New Mexico.* **Rancho de San Juan** (p. 199) is a wonderful nearby place to stay and dine.

7 LAS VEGAS & ENVIRONS ★★

21 miles E of Santa Fe; 59 miles SE of Taos; 141 miles NE of Albuquerque

Once known as the "gateway to New Mexico," Las Vegas, a pleasant town in the foothills of the Sangre de Cristo Mountains, was founded with a land grant from the Mexican government in 1835. A group of 29 Spanish colonists planted crops in the area and built a central plaza, which started out as a meeting place and a defense against Indian attack but soon became a main trading center on the Santa Fe Trail. Las Vegas boomed with the advent of the Atchison, Topeka, and Santa Fe Railway in 1879; almost overnight the town became the most important trading center and gathering place in the state and one of the largest towns in the Rocky Mountain West, rivaling Denver, Tucson, and El Paso in size.

Town settlers who arrived by train in the late 19th century shunned the indigenous adobe architecture, favoring instead building styles more typical of the Midwest or New England. They put up scores of fancy Queen Anne– and Victorian-style houses and hotels, and the town is noted to this day for its dazzling diversity of architectural styles. Some 900 buildings in Las Vegas are on the National Register of Historic Places.

ESSENTIALS

GETTING THERE From Santa Fe, take I-25 northeast 60 miles (1¼ hr.); from Raton, take I-25 south 105 miles (1¾ hr.); from Taos, follow NM 518 southeast 78 miles through Mora (2 hr.); from Tucumcari, follow NM 104 west 112 miles (2 hr.). Las Vegas Municipal Airport handles private flights and charters but has no regularly scheduled commercial service.

VISITOR INFORMATION The **Las Vegas & San Miguel County Chamber of Commerce** is at 503 Sixth St. (P.O. Box 128), Las Vegas, NM 87701 (✆ **800/832-5947** or 505/425-8631; www.lvsmchamber.org). It's open weekdays from 9am to 5pm.

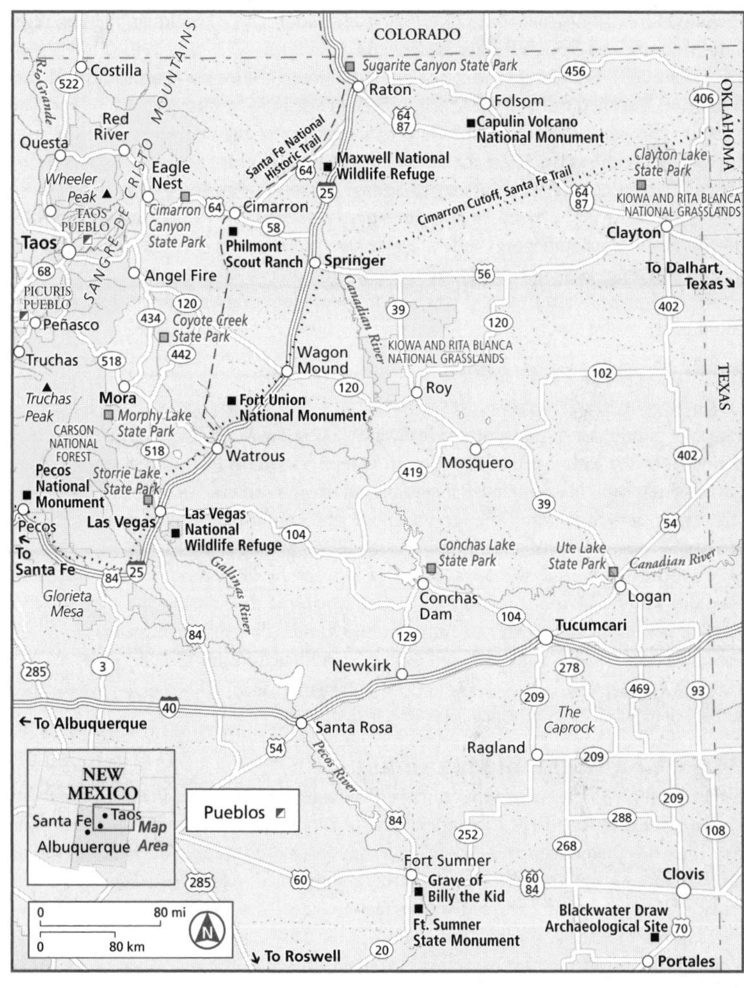

EXPLORING LAS VEGAS'S HISTORIC DISTRICT

The chamber of commerce on Grand Avenue (see "Essentials," above) has a map of a self-guided tour of this area. What's most notable is the town's early Spanish history; adobe buildings dating back to the first Spanish visits in the 16th century are still standing alongside the ornate structures of the late 1800s. In addition, it's hard to find such a well-preserved collection of Territorial-style buildings. Most of the interesting structures can be found in the Plaza–Bridge Street area.

In particular, don't miss the **Plaza Hotel,** 230 Old Town Plaza, the finest hotel in the New Mexico Territory back in 1881. Its three-story facade, topped with a fancy broken pediment decoration, was the town's pride and joy, and it has been happily restored. (See "Where to Stay in Las Vegas," below.)

Housed in a 1940s-era Work Projects Administration (WPA) building, the **Las Vegas City Museum and Rough Riders Memorial Collection,** 727 Grand Ave. (✆ **505/454-1401,** ext. 283), is a fun spot to spend about an hour. The largest contingent of Rough Riders was recruited from New Mexico to fight in the 1898 Spanish-American War. This museum chronicles their contribution to U.S. history and also contains artifacts relating to the history of the city. Another exhibit documents the history of Las Vegas. Admission is free. The museum is open Tuesday to Sunday 10am to 4pm, and by appointment.

In the plaza area, the **Santa Fe Trail Interpretive Center,** 127 Bridge St. (✆ **505/425-8803;** www.lvsmchamber.org), offers a glimpse into efforts to restore the town's 918 historic buildings as well as information about the Santa Fe Trail. Set in the 1890s Winternitz Building, it's a fun stop, if you find it open. Hours vary greatly, as it is staffed by volunteers.

EXPLORING THE AREA

La Cueva National Historic Site and Salman Ranch ★ Finds Each fall, I make a bit of a pilgrimage to this spot in a lush valley along the Mora River. Its history is rich, dating from the early 1800s, when a man named Vicente Romero began farming and raising sheep here. He completed an elegant two-story northern New Mexico home that still stands, as well as a mill that ground flour and supplied electricity for the area (the real draw). Just north of these historic sites is the San Rafael Mission Church, with exquisite French Gothic windows. Recently restored by local people, it's now painted blue and white. The trip through these sites is worth the time during any season, but in the fall, the raspberries ripen and turn this into a must-do trip to sample berries by the basket or crate, as well as in jams and over soft vanilla ice cream. Delicious.

NM 518, 6 miles east of Mora, Buena Vista, NM 87712. ✆ **505/387-2900.** Free admission. Summer Mon–Sat 9am–5pm, Sun 10am–5pm; winter hours limited (call first).

Fort Union National Monument ★

Established in 1851 to defend the Santa Fe Trail against attacks from Plains Indians, Fort Union was expanded in 1861 in anticipation of a Confederate invasion, which was subsequently thwarted at Glorieta Pass, 20 miles southeast of Santa Fe. Fort Union's location on the Santa Fe Trail made it a welcome way station for travelers, but when the railroad replaced the trail in 1879, the fort was on its way out. It was abandoned in 1891. Today, Fort Union, the largest military installation in the 19th-century Southwest, is in ruins. Though it offers little to see but adobe walls and chimneys, the very scope of the fort is impressive. Santa Fe Trail wagon ruts can still be seen nearby. Follow the 1.5-mile self-guided interpretive trail that wanders through the ruins and imagine yourself a weary 19th-century wagon traveler stopping for rest and supplies.

The national monument has a small visitor center and museum with exhibits and booklets on the fort's history. Visitors should allow 2 hours to tour the ruins.

JUST THE FACTS To reach the site from Las Vegas, drive 18 miles north on I-25 to the Watrous exit, and then another 8 miles northwest on NM 161. Admission is $3 per person. Fort Union National Monument is open Memorial Day to Labor Day daily from 8am to 6pm; during the rest of the year, it is open daily from 8am to 4pm. It's closed Thanksgiving, Christmas, and New Year's Day.

A gift shop carries a wide selection of books on New Mexico history and women's history, and frontier military books. Camping is not available at the monument, but facilities are available in nearby Las Vegas.

For more information on the monument, contact Fort Union National Monument, P.O. Box 127, Watrous, NM 87753 (✆ **505/425-8025;** www.nps.gov/foun).

WHERE TO STAY IN LAS VEGAS

Most motels are on US 85 (Grand Ave.), the main north–south highway through downtown Las Vegas. (An exception is the Plaza Hotel, below.)

Inn on the Santa Fe Trail ★ Built in the 1920s as a court motel, this inn has been remodeled in a hacienda style, with all rooms looking out onto the central courtyard, creating a quiet retreat just off busy Grand Avenue. Although it's not as historical as the Plaza Hotel (see below), the rooms are a bit more up-to-date and functional, and you can park your car right outside. Rooms are medium size with nice accents, such as handcrafted iron light fixtures and hand-carved pine furniture—including *trasteros* (armoires) to conceal the televisions. The beds are comfortably firm, and each room has a table with two chairs and a desk. The bathrooms are small but very clean. Suites have sofa beds and minifridges. **Blackjack's Grill** (see below) is a great spot for dinner. The heated outdoor pool, open seasonally, is lovely.

1133 Grand Ave., Las Vegas, NM 87701. ✆ **888/448-8438** or 505/425-6791. www.innonthesantafetrail.com. 42 units. $82 double. Rates include continental breakfast. Extra person $5. AE, DISC, MC, V. Pets permitted for $5 fee. **Amenities:** Restaurant; outdoor heated pool. *In room:* A/C, TV, fridge (in suites), Wi-Fi.

Plaza Hotel ★ A stay in this hotel offers a romantic peek into the past, with a view of the plaza. The inn was built in Italianate bracketed style in 1882, in the days when Western towns vied with one another in constructing fancy "railroad hotels." Considered the finest hotel in the New Mexico Territory when it was built, it underwent a $2-million renovation exactly 100 years later. Stately walnut staircases frame the lobby and conservatory (with its piano); throughout the hotel, the architecture is true to its era. Don't expect to see the elegance of the Ritz. Instead, expect a more frontier style, with Old West antiques. Rooms vary in size, but most are average size, with elegantly high ceilings, antique furnishings, comfortably firm beds, and armoires concealing the televisions. The bathrooms also range in size; most are small, with lots of original tile but up-to-date fixtures. The rooms either have windows facing outward toward the plaza and surrounding streets or inward toward an atrium. The inward-facing rooms are quieter but a bit claustrophobic. All rooms open onto spacious hallways with casual seating areas.

The hotel offers three meals daily and limited room service from its **Landmark Grill** (see below). Byron T's 19th-century saloon often features live music on Friday evenings.

230 Plaza, Las Vegas, NM 87701. ✆ **800/328-1882** or 505/425-3591. Fax 505/425-9659. www.plazahotel-nm.com. 36 units. $109–$130 double; $154–$180 suite. Rates include cooked-to-order breakfast. AE, DC, DISC, MC, V. **Amenities:** Restaurant; bar. *In room:* A/C, TV, Wi-Fi.

Camping

There's plenty of camping available in and around Las Vegas. I recommend the **Las Vegas KOA** (✆ **800/562-3423** or 505/454-0180; www.koa.com), which has 65 sites, 15 with full hookups, 26 with water and electricity. Laundry, grocery, ice, and recreational facilities (including a pool) are available, as is a large gift shop. Seasonal cookouts are offered.

 From I-25, go 1 block southeast on US 84, and then half a mile southwest on Frontage Road (also called Sheridan Rd.).

WHERE TO DINE IN LAS VEGAS

Blackjack's Grill ★★ SEAFOOD/STEAKS Set in the Inn on the Santa Fe Trail, this restaurant serves tasty food with a bit of flair. The main dining room is small and cozy, done in bright colors with moody lighting. In the warmer months, diners can sit on a patio under white cloth umbrellas. As befits the area, it's a fairly informal restaurant that does fill up, so try to make reservations. Each night the chef serves some special dishes. Most are fairly traditional. I've enjoyed beef medallions in wine sauce served with garlic mashed potatoes. The pasta dishes, such as fettuccine Alfredo, can also be good. Most meals come with bread, a choice of salad or soup, and a vegetable. A variety of dessert specials are available. Beer and wine are served.

At the Inn on the Santa Fe Trail (see above), 1133 Grand Ave. ✆ **888/448-8438** or 505/425-6791. Reservations recommended. Main courses $15–$22. AE, MC, V. Daily 5:30–9pm.

Plaza Hotel's Landmark Grill ★★ Finds AMERICAN/NEW MEXICAN Lately this has become my favorite place to dine while looking out upon the graceful Las Vegas plaza, with its towering elm trees. The restaurant, set in the historic 1882 Plaza Hotel, has good food, especially the New Mexican and the grilled dishes. It has a sunny dining room, with tables well spaced, adorned by the original 19th-century stenciling along the walls. Service is good. At breakfast you might have egg and pancake dishes, and on Sunday for brunch, eggs Florentine (poached eggs, spinach, grilled tomato, and hollandaise sauce on an English muffin), served with hash browns. Lunch brings salads, sandwiches, burgers, pasta, and New Mexican food. I've enjoyed a grilled turkey with Swiss cheese and green chile on rye. At dinner, you might enjoy a filet with bleu-cheese mushroom sauce, or grilled pecan crusted trout with pecan butter, each served with salad, vegetable, and choice of starch. Beer and wine accompany the menu. Byron T's 19th-century saloon next door offers food daily from 2 to 5pm.

230 Plaza. ✆ **800/328-1882** or 505/425-3591. www.plazahotel-nm.com. Reservations recommended on Fri–Sat nights. Main courses breakfast/brunch and lunch $5–$15; dinner $8–$25. AE, DC, DISC, MC, V. Daily 7am–2pm and 5–9pm.

8 CIMARRON & RATON: ON THE SANTA FE TRAIL

Cimarron: 35 miles E of Taos; 23 miles NE of Las Vegas; 76 miles NE of Santa Fe. Raton: 67 miles NE of Taos; 93 miles NE of Las Vegas; 111 miles NE of Santa Fe

CIMARRON ★

Few towns in the American West have as much lore or legend attached to them as Cimarron, 41 miles southwest of Raton on US 64. Nestled against the eastern slope of the Sangre de Cristo Mountains, the town (its name is Spanish for "wild" or "untamed") achieved its greatest fame as a wild and woolly outpost on the Santa Fe Trail from the 1850s to 1880s. It was a gathering place for area ranchers, traders, gamblers, gunslingers, and other characters. Frontier personalities, such as Kit Carson and Wyatt Earp, Buffalo Bill Cody and Annie Oakley, Bat Masterson and Doc Holliday, Butch Cassidy and Jesse

James, painter Frederic Remington and novelist Zane Grey, all passed through and stayed in Cimarron—most of them at the **St. James Hotel,** 17th Street and Collinson (✆ **866/472-5019** or 505/376-2664). Even if you're not planning an overnight stay, it's a fun place to visit for an hour or two. The **Old Mill Museum** (✆ **575/376-2417**), a grand, three-story stone structure that's well worth visiting, houses an interesting collection of early photos, as well as memorabilia including a saddle that belonged to Kit Carson. It's open in May and September, Saturday from 10am to noon and 1 to 5pm, and Sunday from 1 to 5pm; Memorial Day to Labor Day, Friday through Wednesday from 10am to noon and 1 to 5pm. It's closed October through April. Admission is by donation. Ask for a historic walking-tour map at the Old Mill Museum.

The **Cimarron Chamber of Commerce,** 104 N. Lincoln Ave. (✆ **575/376-2417;** www.cimarronnm.com), has complete information on the region. It is open June to August daily 9am to 5pm, and November to April Monday through Saturday 10am to 3pm; the rest of the year 10am to 4pm.

RATON

Raton was founded in 1879 at the site of Willow Springs, a watering stop on the Santa Fe Trail. Mountain man "Uncle Dick" Wooton, a closet entrepreneur, had blasted a pass through the Rocky Mountains just north of the spring, and he began charging tolls. When the railroad bought Wooton's road, Raton developed as the railroad, mining, and ranching center for this part of the New Mexico Territory. Today it has a well-preserved historic district. The tourist information center is at the **Raton Chamber and Economic Development Council,** 100 Clayton Rd., at the corner of 2nd Street (P.O. Box 1211), Raton, NM 87740 (✆ **800/638-6161** or 575/445-3689; www.raton.info). Memorial Day to Labor Day, the center is open daily from 8am to 6pm; hours are 8am to 5pm during the rest of the year.

East of Raton is Capulin Mountain, home to **Capulin Volcano National Monument ★★**, which offers visitors the rare opportunity to walk inside a volcanic crater. A 2-mile road spirals up from the visitor center more than 600 feet to the crater of the 8,182-foot peak. Two self-guided trails leave from the parking area: an energetic and spectacular 1-mile hike around the crater rim, and a 100-foot descent into the crater to the ancient volcanic vent. One of the most interesting features here is the symmetry of the main cinder cone. The volcano was last active about 60,000 years ago. The monument is 30 miles east of Raton; take US 64/87 and go north 3 miles on NM 325. The visitor center, at the base of the western side of the volcano, is open daily Memorial Day to Labor Day from 7:30am to 6:30pm, the rest of the year daily from 8am to 4pm. An audiovisual program discusses volcanism, and park personnel will answer questions. Admission is $5 per car. For more information, contact **Capulin Volcano National Monument** (✆ **575/278-2201;** www.nps.gov/cavo).

9 THE I-40 CORRIDOR

The 216 freeway miles on I-40 from Albuquerque to the Texas border cross featureless prairie and very few towns. But the valleys of the Pecos River (site of **Santa Rosa**) and the Canadian River (**Tucumcari** is on its banks) have several attractions, including natural lakes. There's not a lot to explore here unless you're a bird-watcher or a fisher, but both towns can make a day's stopover worthwhile.

ESSENTIALS

GETTING THERE Travel time from Albuquerque to Tucumcari via I-40 is about 2 hours, 40 minutes; to Santa Rosa, 1 hour, 45 minutes. There's no regularly scheduled commercial service into either Tucumcari or Santa Rosa. Private planes can land at **Tucumcari Municipal Airport** (✆ **575/461-3229**).

VISITOR INFORMATION Contact the **Tucumcari–Quay County Chamber of Commerce,** 404 W. Rte. 66 Blvd. (P.O. Drawer E), Tucumcari, NM 88401 (✆ **575/461-1694;** www.tucumcarinm.com), or the **Santa Rosa City Information Center,** 244 S. Fourth St., Santa Rosa, NM 88435 (✆ **575/472-3763;** www.santarosanm.org).

WHERE TO STAY

Major chain hotels are at I-40 interchanges in both Tucumcari and Santa Rosa. Smaller ma-and-pa motels can be found along the main streets through town that were once segments of legendary Route 66—still bearing that historic name.

In Tucumcari

Hampton Inn This hotel provides a bit of an oasis in this part of the state. It's located near I-40, but has some very quiet rooms. Each is medium size with earth-tone decor and comfortable beds with luxury bedding. Some have microwaves and fridges. The baths are standard size with floor tiles. The west-side rooms offer the most quiet and a bit of a view out across meadows and ponds.

3409 E. Rte. 66 (at I-40 exit 335), Tucumcari, NM 88401. ✆ **800/HAMPTON** [426-7866] or 575/461-1111. Fax 575/461-0000. www.hamptoninn.hilton.com. 58 units. $99–$115. Price includes hot breakfast. AE, DC, DISC, MC, V. **Amenities:** Jacuzzi; indoor pool; sauna. *In room:* A/C, TV, fridge (in some), hair dryer, Wi-Fi.

Camping near Tucumcari

Tucumcari KOA (✆ **800/562-1871** or 575/461-1841; www.koa.com) has 111 sites, laundry and grocery facilities, RV supplies, picnic tables, and grills. It also offers a recreation hall with video games, a heated swimming pool, a basketball hoop, a playground, horseshoes, and shuffleboard. From I-40, get off the interstate at exit 335, and then go a quarter-mile east on South Frontage Road.

In Santa Rosa

La Quinta ★ Perched on a hill above Santa Rosa, this newer whitewashed chain hotel offers clean and very functional rooms. All are medium size, decorated in tasteful earth tones. Each has an extremely small bathroom with an outer sink/vanity. Beds are comfy and are accompanied by a table and chairs. The place is inventively landscaped with a rock grotto patio where the hot tub sits.

1701 Will Rogers Dr., Santa Rosa, NM 88435. ✆ **800/531-5900** or 575/472-4800. Fax 575/472-4809. www.laquinta.com. 60 units. $75–$95 double. Rates include continental breakfast. AE, DC, DISC, MC, V. **Amenities:** Outdoor Jacuzzi; indoor pool. *In room:* A/C, TV, hair dryer, Wi-Fi.

Camping near Santa Rosa

The **Santa Rosa Campground** (✆ **575/472-3126**) offers 94 sites, 33 full hookups, laundry and grocery facilities, fire rings, grills, a heated swimming pool, and a playground for the kids. Situated in a piñon and juniper forest near town, the campground has a few small elm trees on the grounds. Coming from the east on I-40, take exit 277 and go 1 mile west on Business Loop; coming from the west on I-40, take exit 275 and go a quarter-mile east on Business Loop.

Moments Route 66 Revisited: Rediscovering New Mexico's Stretch of the Mother Road

The highway that once stretched from Chicago to California was hailed as the road to freedom. During the Great Depression, it was the way west for farmers escaping Dust Bowl poverty out on the plains. If you found yourself in a rut in the late 1940s and 1950s, all you had to do was hop in the car and head west on Route 66. Built in the late 1920s and paved in 1937, it was the lifeblood of communities in eight states. Nowadays, however, US 66 is as elusive as the fantasies that once carried hundreds of thousands west in search of a better life. Replaced by other roads, covered up by interstates (mostly I-40), and just plain out of use, Route 66 still exists in New Mexico, but you'll have to do a little searching and take some extra time to find it.

Motorists driving west from Texas can take a spin (make that a slow spin) on a 20-mile gravel stretch of the original highway running from Glenrio (Texas) to San Jon. From San Jon to Tucumcari, you can enjoy nearly 24 continuous paved miles of vintage 66. In Tucumcari, the historic route sliced through the center of town along what is now Route 66 Boulevard. Santa Rosa's Historic Route 66 is that city's 4-mile claim to the Mother Road. In Albuquerque, US 66 follows Central Avenue for 18 miles, from the 1936 State Fairgrounds, past original 1930s motels and the historic Nob Hill district, on west through downtown.

One of the best spots to pretend you are a 1950s road warrior crossing the desert is along NM 124, which winds 25 miles from Mesita to Acoma in northwestern New Mexico. You can next pick up old Route 66 in Grants, along the 6-mile Santa Fe Avenue. In Gallup, a 9-mile segment of US 66 is lined with restaurants and hotels reminiscent of the city's days as a Western film capital from 1929 to 1964. Just outside Gallup, the historic route continues west to the Arizona border as NM 118.

For more information about Route 66, contact the **Grants/Cíbola County Chamber of Commerce** (✆ **800/748-2142**) or the **New Mexico Department of Tourism** (✆ **800/545-2040**).

Also in the area is **Santa Rosa Lake State Park** (✆ **575/472-3110**), with year-round camping, featuring 75 sites (about a third with electric hookups) as well as grills, boating, fishing, and hiking trails. Swimming in the lake is permitted but not encouraged because of the lake's uneven bottom and lack of beaches; children would be safer swimming in Park Lake in Santa Rosa.

TWO GOOD PLACES TO EAT IN THE AREA

Del's Family Restaurant AMERICAN/NEW MEXICAN The big cow atop Del's neon sign is not only a Route 66 landmark, but it also points to the fine steaks inside. It's a casual, diner-style eatery with lots of plants. Breakfast brings big plates of dishes such as scrambled eggs and pancakes. At lunch, sample sandwiches and salads. The roast beef is a big seller here at dinnertime, served with a scoop of mashed potatoes and a trip to the salad bar. You can also order a grilled chicken breast. The New Mexican food is good but not great. Del's is not licensed for alcoholic beverages.

1202 E. Rte. 66, Tucumcari. © **575/461-1740.** Reservations not accepted. Main courses $5–$8 breakfast, $5–$10 lunch, $8–$16 dinner. MC, V. Mon–Sat 7am–9pm.

Joseph's Restaurant & Cantina ★ AMERICAN/NEW MEXICAN You may want to plan your drive so you can eat a meal at "Joe's," a real Route 66 diner, with linoleum tables, comfortable booths, and plenty of memorabilia. The locals all eat here: You'll see Hispanic grandmothers, skinny cowboys in straw hats, and dusty farmhands just in from the fields. The varied menu offers excellent fare. Breakfast brings eggs and bacon or omelets. At lunch, I've enjoyed a salad topped with tender grilled chicken. The New Mexican dishes are large and chile smothered; and the burgers are juicy, with a variety of toppings—from the Rio Pecos, topped with green chile, to the Acapulco, with guacamole. Steaks are a big seller, also at a good price. For dessert, try a piece of pie or a shake. Also on the premises are a bakery, a full-service bar, and a gift shop.

865 Historic Rte. 66, Santa Rosa. © **575/472-3361.** Reservations not accepted. Main courses $4–$8 breakfast, $6–$9 lunch, $7–$15 dinner. AE, DC, DISC, MC, V. Summer daily 7am–10pm; winter daily 7am–9pm.

11

Southern New Mexico

If your idea of fun is road-tripping across exotic landscapes, delving into ancient cultures, peering into outer space, and chatting up an alien or two, southern New Mexico is your destination. Here you'll find an astonishing array of singular landscapes and unusual attractions, from the rolling gypsum sand dunes of White Sands National Monument to the underground natural cathedrals of Carlsbad Caverns National Park.

Wildness abounds at places such as the Bosque del Apache National Wildlife Refuge and the 3.3-million-acre Gila National Forest, both known for great bird-watching. Within the forest lies Gila Cliff Dwellings National Monument, home to the Mogollon people 1,000 years ago. The final frontier is also present in this region, at places such as the International UFO Museum and Research Center in Roswell, the area where aliens may have landed, and the Very Large Array, the world's most powerful radio telescope.

Between the sights lie more miles of open country than most people can imagine. Though on first glance it may appear desolate, it's actually filled with petroglyphs and lava fields, hot springs and ghost towns, places where legends such as Geronimo and Billy the Kid once roamed.

The big city in the area is Las Cruces, New Mexico's second largest, with a population of 73,600. Set at the foot of the dramatic Organ Mountains, it is an agricultural and education center. To the east lies Ruidoso, a booming resort town with good skiing in winter. To the west is Silver City, a charming mining town that's been revived in recent years. The Rio Grande slices a green swath through the center of the region, nourishing many communities along its banks.

With such long distances to cover, you'll need a reliable car to get around. Flip on the tunes, keep a close eye on the gas gauge, and enjoy the ride.

1 GETTING OUTSIDE IN SOUTHERN NEW MEXICO

Rugged, remote, forested, and fascinating all describe southwestern New Mexico, where few tourists venture—lucky for you if you're looking for backcountry adventure.

BIKING Several forest roads and single-track trails in this region are favorites with mountain bikers. In the Ruidoso area, near Cloudcroft, the **Rim Trail,** a 17-mile intermediate trail that offers views of White Sands, is considered one of the top 10 trails in the nation. To reach the trail, take NM 130 from Cloudcroft to NM 6563, turn right, and look for the Rim Trail signs. The Cloudcroft area offers three other good trails: La Luz Canyon, Silver Springs Loop, and Pumphouse Canyon. For directions, contact the Cloudcroft Ranger Station (✆ **575/682-2551**). The paved road up to **Carlsbad Caverns National Park** is scenic, and the auto traffic drives slowly, but it's very hot in the summer. Bikes are not allowed in the Gila Wilderness, but they are permitted on trails in other parts of **Gila National Forest** (✆ **575/388-8201;** www.fs.fed.us/r3/gila). Refer to "Other Adventures in Gila National Forest," later in this chapter, for some specific ride suggestions; also contact **Gila Hike and Bike** (✆ **575/388-3222**) in Silver City for rentals as well as guidebooks to riding in the Gila National Forest.

BIRD-WATCHING **Bitter Lake National Wildlife Refuge** (✆ 575/622-6755), northeast of Roswell, is particularly good for watching migratory waterfowl, and **Bluff Springs** (✆ 575/682-2551), south of Cloudcroft, is popular with turkeys and hummingbirds. If you find turkey vultures particularly fascinating, **Rattlesnake Springs** (✆ 575/785-2232), south of Carlsbad, is the place to go. **Bosque del Apache National Wildlife Refuge** (✆ 575/835-1828) is a refuge for migratory waterfowl such as snow geese and cranes. It's 16 miles south of Socorro. **North Monticello Point** (✆ 575/744-5421), on Elephant Butte Lake, is a great place to see pelicans, bald eagles, and a variety of waterfowl, while **Water Canyon** (✆ 575/854-2281), 14 miles west of Socorro, in the **Cíbola National Forest,** is home to golden eagles. In recent years, the **Gila National Forest** (✆ 575/388-8201) has become quite popular with birders. Guests at the **Bear Mountain Lodge** (✆ 877/620-BEAR [2327] or 575/538-2538; www.bearmountainlodge.com) benefit from an on-site naturalist and occasional birding tours. In the Gila, my favorite birding spot is **Lake Roberts,** where hummingbirds abound.

BOATING Boating, water-skiing, jet-skiing, and sailing are permitted at **Carlsbad Municipal Park,** which runs through town for just over a mile along the west bank of Lake Carlsbad. The lake also has a beach that's open to swimmers. **Brantley Lake State Park** (✆ **575/457-2384**), 15 miles north of Carlsbad, is popular with windsurfers, who favor its consistent desert winds. In the Gila National Forest, both **Lake Roberts** (✆ **575/536-2250**), about 40 miles north of Silver City, on NM 15, and **Snow Lake** (✆ **575/533-6231**), north on US 180 from Silver City, and then east on NM 159, allow boating. Lake Roberts features motorboat rentals, whereas Snow Lake only permits canoes, rowboats, and other boats without gas motors. **Elephant Butte Lake State Park** (✆ **575/744-5923**) boasts the largest body of water in New Mexico. The lake is 43 miles long and popular with boating enthusiasts. Three ramps provide boating access to the lake, and there are launching areas for smaller vessels. (To find information on New Mexico state parks, go to www.nmparks.com.)

FISHING **Bonito Lake** and **Rio Ruidoso** are popular destinations for trout fishing. The scenic **Oasis State Park** (✆ **575/356-5331**) just north of Portales, also offers fishing. **Caballo Lake State Park** (✆ **575/743-3942**), about 18 miles south of Truth or Consequences, offers smallmouth and largemouth bass, stripers, bluegill, crappie, catfish, and walleye fishing in its 11,500-acre lake. **Elephant Butte Lake State Park** (✆ **575/744-5923**), also near Truth or Consequences, is another great fishing location. Look to catch white bass, black bass, catfish, walleye, crappie, and stripers here. **Lake Roberts** (✆ **575/536-2250**), about 40 miles north of Silver City in the Gila National Forest, is prime rainbow trout fishing waters. A fishing license and habitat stamp are both required. You'll find fly-fishing in the **Gila River** year-round, but the best seasons are spring and fall. Mainly rainbow trout swim these waters, with catfish on the lower Gila. For more information, contact the **New Mexico Game and Fish Department** (✆ **505/476-8000;** www.wildlife.state.nm.us).

GOLF This region has plenty of golfing opportunities. In Ruidoso, **Cree Meadows Country Club,** Country Club Drive, off Sudderth Drive (✆ 575/257-5815; www.playcreemeadows.com), is an 18-hole public course. Also public in the Ruidoso area are the 18-hole courses at the **Inn of the Mountain Gods Resort & Casino,** 287 Carrizo Canyon Rd. (✆ 800/545-6040 or 575/464-4100; www.innofthemountaingods.com);

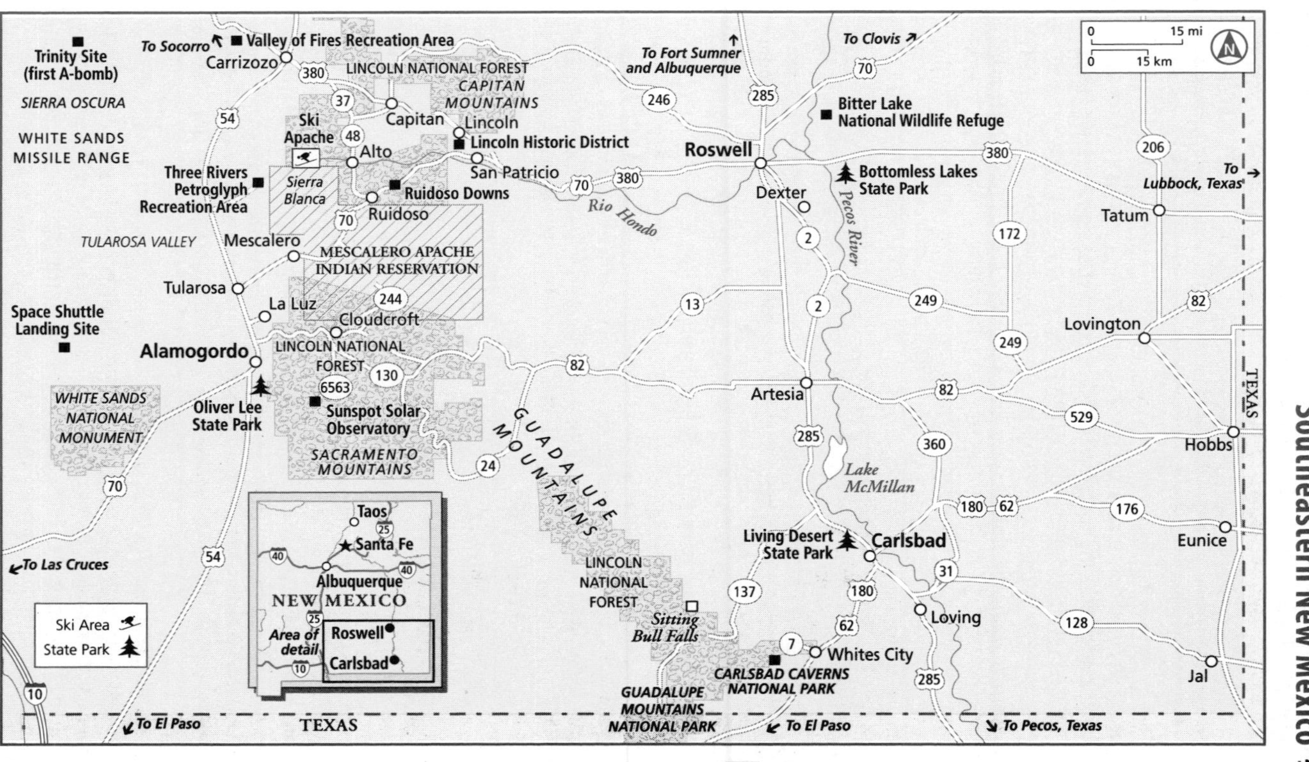

SOUTHERN NEW MEXICO

11

GETTING OUTSIDE IN SOUTHERN NEW MEXICO

and the **Links at Sierra Blanca,** 105 Sierra Blanca Dr. (✆ 575/258-5330; www.thelodgeatsierrablanca.com). In Cloudcroft, the 9-hole **Lodge at Cloudcroft Golf Course** (✆ 800/395-6343 or 575/682-2566; www.thelodgeresort.com) boasts an elevation of 9,200 feet; it's one of the highest courses in the world and one of the oldest in the United States. Alamogordo's **Desert Lakes Golf Course** (✆ 575/437-0290; www.desertlakesgolf.com) has views of Sierra Blanca and the Sacramento Mountains. In Socorro, the 18-hole **New Mexico Tech Golf Course** (✆ 575/835-5335; www.nmt.edu) offers tree-lined fairways and water on more than half of its holes. The **Truth or Consequences Golf Course** (✆ 575/894-2603) offers 9 fairly traditional holes in a desert setting. The new **Sierra del Rio Golf Course** at Turtleback Mountain Resort (✆ 575/744-4653; www.sierradelrio.com), opened in 2007, offers 18 holes that area golfers are talking about. Another contemporary course is in Las Cruces, at the 18-hole **Sonoma Ranch Golf Course** (✆ 575/521-1818; www.sonomaranchgolf.com), which opened in 2000. Las Cruces also has the **New Mexico State University Golf Course** (✆ 575/646-3219; www.nmsu.edu/golf), built with collegiate golf in mind. With wide-spanning views and undulating terrain, this Cal Olsen–designed course has much to offer. Deming has the 18-hole **Rio Mimbres Country Club** (✆ 575/546-9481), while Silver City golfers go to the 18-hole **Silver City Golf Course** (✆ 575/538-5041; www.silvercity.org), home to the annual Billy Casper Golf Tournament.

HIKING More than 225 miles of trails weave a web through the Smokey Bear Ranger District of the **Lincoln National Forest.** From Ruidoso, a favorite destination of hikers is the White Mountain Wilderness, with nine trails, and the Capitan Mountains Wilderness, with 11 trails. **Smokey Bear Ranger District office,** 901 Mechem Dr., Ruidoso (✆ **575/257-4095**), has excellent and inexpensive maps of each wilderness area. Monjeau Lookout is a popular destination off Ski Run Road (NM 532). **Carlsbad Caverns National Park** has an extensive trail system as well (outside the caves, of course). There's great hiking in the **Gila National Forest** (✆ **575/388-8201**), which has approximately 1,500 miles of trails, ranging in length and difficulty. Your best bet for hiking in the area is to purchase a guidebook devoted entirely to hiking the Gila National Forest; popular areas include the Crest Trail, the West Fork Trail, and the Aldo Leopold Wilderness. One favorite day hike in the forest is the Catwalk, a moderately strenuous hike along a series of steel bridges and walkways suspended over Whitewater Canyon. See "Other Adventures in Gila National Forest," later in this chapter, for more hiking suggestions. Whenever and wherever you go hiking, be sure to carry plenty of water.

HORSEBACK RIDING Horseback riding is popular in Ruidoso. Try the **Inn of the Mountain Gods Resort & Casino** (✆ **800/545-6040** or 575/464-4100; www.innofthemountaingods.com) or **Cowboys Riding Stables** (✆ **575/378-8217;** www.cowboysridingstables.com). The **Double E Guest Ranch** (✆ **575/535-2048;** www.doubleeranch.com) offers authentic ranch riding in the southwestern New Mexico desert and forest lands. The ranch does not have a separate children's program but does accept kids.

SKIING Southern New Mexico's premier ski resort is **Ski Apache** (✆ **575/257-9001** for snow reports, 575/336-4356 for information; www.skiapache.com), only 20 miles northwest of Ruidoso in the Mescalero Apache Indian Reservation. Situated on an 11,500-foot ridge of the 12,003-foot Sierra Blanca, the resort boasts a gondola, two quad chairs, five triple chairs, one double chair, a day lodge, a sport shop, a rental shop, a ski school, a first-aid center, four snack bars, and a lounge. Ski Apache has 55 trails and slopes (20% beginner, 35% intermediate, and 45% advanced), with a vertical drop of

1,900 feet and a total skier capacity of 16,500 an hour. Though its location seems remote, skiers often fill this mountain during weekends and holidays. Because the mountain is owned and run by the Apaches, you can experience another culture while skiing. All-day lift tickets cost $51 for adults, $45 for seniors, $43 for teens (13–17), $25 for children 12 and under. The mountain is open Thanksgiving to Easter daily from 8:45am to 4pm. Lift-and-lodging packages can be booked through the **Inn of the Mountain Gods Resort & Casino** (✆ **800/545-6040** or 575/464-4100; www.innofthemountaingods.com).

SWIMMING Swimming is permitted at **Elephant Butte Lake State Park** (✆ **575/744-5923**) and **Caballo Lake State Park** (✆ **575/743-3942**), but not at some others. Be sure to ask first.

2 ALAMOGORDO

60 miles NE of Las Cruces; 83 miles SW of Roswell; 146 miles SE of Albuquerque

Famous for its leading role in America's space research and military technology industries, Alamogordo (pop. 35,582) achieved worldwide fame on July 16, 1945, when the first atomic bomb was exploded at nearby Trinity Site. Today, it is home of the New Mexico Museum of Space History, White Sands National Monument, and Holloman Air Force Base. While traveling in this area, I came to jokingly call it "Alamageddin," mostly because the town itself is fairly desolate, without many amenities, although it is improving. Twenty miles east and twice as high, the resort village of Cloudcroft (elevation 8,650 ft.) attracts vacationers to the forested heights of the Sacramento Mountains.

ESSENTIALS

GETTING THERE From Albuquerque, take I-25 south 87 miles to San Antonio; turn east on US 380, go 66 miles to Carrizozo; then turn south on US 54 for 58 miles (4 hr.). From Las Cruces, take US 70 northeast (1½ hr.). (***Note:*** US 70 may be closed for up to 2 hr. during tests on White Sands Missile Range.) From El Paso, take US 54 north (1½ hr.).

The nearest major airport is **El Paso International.** The local airport, Alamogordo–White Sands Regional Airport (✆ **575/439-4110**) does not offer commercial service.

VISITOR INFORMATION The **Alamogordo Chamber of Commerce** and visitor center is at 1301 N. White Sands Blvd., Alamogordo, NM 88311 (✆ **800/826-0294** or 575/437-6120; www.alamogordo.com).

CITY LAYOUT Alamogordo is on the eastern edge of the Tularosa Valley, at the foot of the Sacramento Mountains. US 54 (White Sands Blvd.) is the main street, extending several miles north and south. The downtown district is actually a few blocks east of White Sands Boulevard, off 10th Street.

WHAT TO SEE & DO

New Mexico Museum of Space History ★ The New Mexico Museum of Space History comes in two parts: the International Space Hall of Fame and the Clyde W. Tombaugh IMAX Dome Theater. Both are on the lower slopes of the Sacramento Mountains, 2 miles east of US 54, and just above New Mexico State University's Alamogordo branch campus.

Trinity Site

The world's first atomic bomb was exploded in this desert never-never land on July 16, 1945. It is strictly off-limits to civilians—except twice a year, on the first Saturday of April and October. A small lava monument commemorates the explosion, which left a crater a quarter-mile across and 8 feet deep, and transformed the desert sand into a jade-green glaze called "Trinitite" that remains today. The McDonald House, where the bomb's plutonium core was assembled 2 miles from ground zero, has been restored to its 1945 condition. The site is on the west slope of Sierra Oscura, 90 air miles northwest of Alamogordo. For more information, call the public affairs office of **White Sands Missile Range** (✆ **575/678-1134;** www.wsmr.army.mil).

The **Space Hall of Fame** occupies the "Golden Cube," a five-story building with walls of golden glass. Visitors are encouraged to start on the top floor and work their way down. En route, they recall the accomplishments of the first astronauts and cosmonauts, including America's Mercury, Gemini, and Apollo programs, and the early Soviet orbital flights. Spacecraft and a lunar exploration module are exhibited. Displays tell the history and purposes of rocketry, missiles, and satellites and provide an orientation to astronomy and other planets.

At **Tombaugh Theater,** IMAX projection and Spitz 512 Planetarium Systems create earthly and cosmic experiences on a 2,700-square-foot dome screen.

Located at the top of NM 2001. ✆ **877/333-6589** outside New Mexico, or 575/437-2840. Fax 575/434-2245. www.spacefame.org. Admission to International Space Hall of Fame $6 adults, $5 seniors 60 and older and military, $4 children 4–12, free for children 3 and under. IMAX Theater $6 adults, $5.50 seniors, $4.50 children age 4–12, free for children 3 and under; additional charge for double feature. Daily 9am–5pm.

EXPLORING THE SURROUNDING AREA

Cloudcroft ★ is a picturesque mountain village (pop. 765) high in the Sacramento Mountains, surrounded by Lincoln National Forest. Though only about 20 miles east of Alamogordo via US 82, it is twice as high, overlooking the Tularosa Valley from a dizzying elevation of almost 9,000 feet. It was founded in 1899 when railroad surveyors reached the mountain summit and built a lodge for Southern Pacific Railroad workers. Today, the Lodge is Cloudcroft's biggest attraction and biggest employer (see "Nearby Places to Stay & Dine," below). Other accommodations are also available in town, as are lots of recreational opportunities and community festivals. For information, contact the **Cloudcroft Chamber of Commerce,** P.O. Box 1290, Cloudcroft, NM 88317 (✆ **866/874-4447** or 575/682-2733; www.cloudcroft.net). It's in a log cabin in the center of town, on the south side of US 82.

If you'd like a tasty meal in this mountain town, head to where the locals eat, **Dave's Café,** 300 Burro Ave. (✆ **575/682-2127**). You can order from an array of sandwiches and salads. Try the Coney-style burger with grilled onions, or the grilled chicken salad with lots of veggies and bacon. For dessert, pick up truffles or ice cream from the attached sweets shop. Dave's is open Sunday to Thursday 10:30am to 5pm and Friday and Saturday 10:30am to 7pm.

WHERE TO STAY IN ALAMOGORDO

All accommodations in Alamogordo are centered on White Sands Boulevard, the north-south highway through town.

Holiday Inn Express ★ This newer hotel on the south end of town provides what you'd expect from this chain—clean, comfortable rooms with a bit of flair. The hotel is steps above the Best Western (though it's also more expensive). Rooms are medium size, with high ceilings, and come in standards and suites. All are spacious, decorated in natural hues, with comfortable beds, while the bathrooms are medium size with granite countertops. A full, hot breakfast comes with the room.

100 Kerry Ave. ✆ **800/465-4329** or 575/434-9773. Fax 575/434-3279. www.hiexpress.com. 80 units. $105 double; $119–$149 suite. Rates include breakfast. AE, DC, DISC, MC, V. **Amenities:** Health club; indoor pool. *In room:* A/C, TV, fridge, hair dryer, Internet, microwave.

Camping

The **Alamogordo Roadrunner** (✆ **877/437-3003** or 575/437-3003; www.roadrunner campground.com) has laundry and grocery facilities, as well as a recreation room/area, swimming pool, playground, shuffleboard, and planned group activities in winter. The campground is on 24th Street in Alamogordo, just east of the US 54/70/82 junction. **Oliver Lee State Park,** 15 miles southeast of Alamogordo via US 54 and Dog Canyon Road (✆ **575/437-8284**), is a good choice, with 44 sites, 10 full hookups, picnic tables, grills, tenting availability, a playground, and hiking trails.

WHERE TO DINE IN ALAMOGORDO

Memories Restaurant ★ Finds AMERICAN Set in a 1907 Victorian home in a residential neighborhood right on the edge of historic downtown, this restaurant serves excellent food in an old-world setting. Functional tables sit on Brazilian-oak floors within what was once the living room and den, creating a casual, comfortable atmosphere, which is a good thing because the service can be overworked. Diners come to sample salads and croissant sandwiches for lunch and grilled steaks and seafood for dinner. Basically, the place is packed nonstop while it's open. I recommend the crab salad served over avocado, or the turkey and avocado croissant sandwich. For dinner, a big seller is the prime rib, which comes with salad or soup, bread, a side dish, and vegetable. The grilled shrimp is also good. Beer and wine are available.

1223 New York Ave. (corner of 13th St.). ✆ **575/437-0077.** Reservations recommended. Main courses $6–$13 lunch, $13–$21 dinner. AE, DISC, MC, V. Mon–Sat 11am–9pm.

Nearby Places to Stay & Dine

Casa de Sueños ★ Kids NEW MEXICAN For tasty New Mexican fare, with a good dose of the whimsy of Mexico, check out this fun restaurant about 15 miles north of Alamogordo, outside Tularosa. Decorated with Mexican folk paintings and a country-home mural, it exudes a fiesta atmosphere. Outside, the broad patio is lit with little Christmas lights and has chile peppers printed on the tablecloths. For breakfast, try the huevos rancheros. A lunch buffet provides a good sampling of enchiladas and beans. To start your meal, try the guacamole, made with red onions. For an entree, order anything with the green-chile sauce, made with fresh chiles and well seasoned. Vegetarian and children's selections round out the menu. You can order from a variety of beers and wines.

35 St. Francis Dr., Tularosa, NM. ✆ **575/585-3494.** Reservations recommended Fri–Sat. Main courses $5–$8 breakfast, $7–$15 lunch and dinner. AE, DISC, MC, V. Mon–Fri and Sat–Sun 11am–8pm.

The Lodge at Cloudcroft ★★ This lodge is an antique jewel, a well-preserved relic of another era. From the grand fireplace in the lobby to the homey Victorian decor in the guest rooms, it exudes gentility and class. Its 9-hole golf course, one of the nation's highest, challenges golfers across rolling hills between 8,600 and 9,200 feet of elevation. Most rooms in the Lodge have views, and all are filled with antiques, from sideboards and lamps to mirrors and steam radiators. The standard rooms are small, so you may want to reserve one of their suites, which have a bedroom and a sitting room with a sofa bed. Some suites have Jacuzzi tubs. Guests are greeted by a stuffed bear sitting on the bed with a sampler of homemade fudge from the Lodge Mercantile. In 1991, more rooms were added in the form of the Pavilion and the Retreat, which were built adjacent to the Lodge. These are most often rented out in blocks and are less desirable than those in the main hotel. The hotel's new Spirit of the Mountain Spa offers a variety of massage treatments.

Rebecca's (✆ **575/682-2566**), the lodge's restaurant, is named for the resident ghost, believed to have been a chambermaid in the 1930s who was killed by her lumberjack lover. Three meals, plus a midday snack menu, are served daily. Service is friendly and very efficient, and the atmosphere is elegant, with bright sunshine during the day and romantic lighting at night. I recommend the roasted duck with Madeira wine sauce and rice. For dessert, try one of their tableside flambé desserts. The champagne Sunday brunch is a must here, offering a prime-rib serving station and an array of side selections.

1 Corona Place (P.O. Box 497), Cloudcroft, NM 88317. ✆ **800/395-6343** or 575/682-2566. Fax 575/682-2715. www.thelodgeresort.com. 59 units. $109–$159 double; $169–$329 suite. AE, DC, DISC, MC, V. Free parking. **Amenities:** Restaurant; bar; babysitting; golf course; health club; Jacuzzi; outdoor heated pool; sauna; spa; access to nearby tennis courts. *In room:* A/C, TV, hair dryer upon request, Wi-Fi.

3 WHITE SANDS NATIONAL MONUMENT ★★★

15 miles SW of Alamogordo; 46 miles NE of Las Cruces; 150 miles S of Albuquerque

Arguably the most memorable natural area in this part of the Southwest, White Sands National Monument preserves the best part of the world's largest gypsum dune field, an area of 275 square miles of pure white gypsum sand reaching out over the floor of the Tularosa Basin in wavelike dunes. Plants and animals have evolved in special ways to adapt to the bright white environment here. Some creatures have a bleached coloration to match the whiteness all around them, and some plants have evolved means for surviving against the smothering pressures of the blowing sands.

Warning! Safety Tips

The National Park Service emphasizes that (1) tunneling in this sand can be dangerous because it collapses easily and could suffocate a person; (2) sand-surfing down the dune slopes, although permitted, can also be hazardous, so it should be undertaken with care, and never near an auto road; and (3) hikers can get lost in a sudden sandstorm if they stray from marked trails or areas.

The surrounding mountains—the Sacramentos to the east, with their forested slopes, and the serene San Andres to the west—are composed of sandstone, limestone, sedimentary rocks, and pockets of gypsum. Over millions of years, rains and melting snows dissolved the gypsum and carried it down into Lake Lucero. Here, the hot sun and dry winds evaporate the water, leaving the pure white gypsum to crystallize. Then the persistent winds blow these crystals, in the form of minuscule bits of sand, in a northeastern direction, adding them to growing dunes. As each dune grows and moves farther from the lake, new ones form, rank after rank, in what seems an endless procession.

The dunes are especially enchanting at sunrise and under the light of a full moon, but you'll have to camp here to experience this extraordinary sight (see "Camping," below). If you're not camping, you'll probably want to spend only a couple of hours here. Refreshments and snacks can be purchased at the visitor center, along with books, maps, posters, and other souvenirs; however, no dining or grocery facilities are available here.

ESSENTIALS

GETTING THERE The visitor center is 15 miles southwest of Alamogordo on US 70/82. (***Note:*** Due to missile testing on the adjacent White Sands Missile Range, this road is sometimes closed for up to 2 hr. at a time.) The nearest major airport is **El Paso International,** 90 miles away.

VISITOR INFORMATION For more information, contact **White Sands National Monument,** P.O. Box 1086, Holloman AFB, NM 88330-1086 (✆ **575/479-6124;** www.nps.gov/whsa). When driving near or in the monument, tune your radio to 1610 AM for information on what's happening.

ADMISSION FEES & HOURS Admission is $3 (free for children 15 and under). Memorial Day to Labor Day, the visitor center is open daily from 8am to 7pm, and Dunes Drive is open daily from 7am to 9pm. Ranger talks and sunset strolls are given nightly at 7 and 8:30pm during summer. During the rest of the year, the visitor center is open daily from 8am to 5pm, and Dunes Drive is open daily from 7am to sunset.

SEEING THE HIGHLIGHTS

The 16-mile **Dunes Drive** loops through the "heart of sands" from the visitor center. Information available at the center tells you what to look for on your drive. Sometimes the winds blow the dunes over the road, which must then be rerouted. All the dunes are in fact moving slowly to the northeast, pushed by prevailing southwest winds, some at the rate of as much as 20 feet per year.

In the center of the monument, the road itself is made of hard-packed gypsum. (***Note:*** It can be especially slick after an afternoon thunderstorm, so drive cautiously!) Visitors are invited to get out of their cars at established parking areas and explore a bit; some like to climb a dune for a better view of the endless sea of sand. If you'd rather experience the park by hiking than on the long drive, try the Big Dune Trail, a good trail right near the entrance. It takes you on a 45-minute loop along the edges of the dunes and then into their whiteness, ending atop a 60-foot-tall one. In summer, ranger-guided nature walks and evening programs take place in the dunes.

CAMPING

I recommend camping here, especially to see the dunes at sunrise or under a full moon. The park closes at dusk, and you'll have to leave if you're not camping. It doesn't reopen until after dawn, so you'll have no way to see the sunrise unless you camp. White Sands has no facilities, however, so this is strictly a backcountry adventure. Only tent camping is allowed, and you'll hike three-quarters of a mile to the campsite where you can pitch a tent. On a full moon, the campsites go quickly; you may want to arrive early in the morning. At other times, availability shouldn't be a problem. You must register at the visitor center, get clearance, and pay a small fee. Call © **575/479-6124** for information.

If backcountry camping isn't your speed, try one of the other campgrounds in nearby Alamogordo or Las Cruces (see "Alamogordo," earlier in this chapter, and "Las Cruces," later in this chapter).

4 RUIDOSO ★ & ENVIRONS

33 miles NE of Alamagordo; 62 miles W of Roswell; 125 miles SE of Albuquerque

Ruidoso (most New Mexicans pronounce it "Ree-uh-*do*-so") is situated at 6,900 feet in the timbered Sacramento Mountains, the southernmost finger of the Rockies. It is a mountain resort town most famous for the nearby Ruidoso Downs racetrack, where the world's richest quarter-horse race is run for a $2.5-million purse. Outdoors lovers, hikers, horseback riders, fishers, and hunters are drawn to the surrounding Lincoln National Forest. Southern New Mexico's most important ski resort, Ski Apache, is just out of town. The nearby **Mescalero Apache Indian Reservation** includes the Inn of the Mountain Gods Resort & Casino. Not far away, the historic village of **Lincoln** recalls the Wild West days of Billy the Kid. Be aware that during those busiest of months, Ruidoso seems to live up to its Spanish name—which translates as "noisy," although the name originally referred to the sound of the river running through town.

ESSENTIALS

GETTING THERE From Albuquerque, take I-25 south 87 miles to San Antonio; turn east on US 380 and travel 74 miles; then head south on NM 37/48 (4 hr.). From Alamogordo, take US 70 northeast via Tularosa (1 hr.). From Roswell, take US 70 west (1½ hr.). No commercial service is available to **Sierra Blanca Regional Airport** (© **575/336-8111**), 17 miles north, near Alto.

VISITOR INFORMATION The **Ruidoso Valley Chamber of Commerce** and visitor center is at 720 Sudderth Dr. (© **800/253-2255** or 575/257-7395; www.ruidosonow.com).

EXPLORING RUIDOSO

Gallery Hopping

Many noted artists—among them Peter Hurd, Henriette Wyeth, and Gordon Snidow—made their homes in Ruidoso and the surrounding Lincoln County. Dozens of other art-world hopefuls have followed them here, resulting in a proliferation of galleries in town. Most are open Monday to Saturday from 10am to 5pm, except where noted. Among my favorites are **De Carol Designs,** 2616 Sudderth Dr. (© **575/257-5024**); **McGary Studios,** a bronze foundry at 2002 Sudderth Dr. (© **575/257-1000**); and **Hurd–La Rinconada** (© **575/653-4331**), in San Patricio, 20 miles east of Ruidoso on US 70 (see "A Scenic Drive Around the Lincoln Loop," later in this chapter), open Monday through Saturday from 9am to 5pm.

Kids Family Fun

Families enjoy the excitement at **Funtrackers Family Fun Center,** 101 Carrizo Canyon Rd. (© **575/257-3275**), which offers go-kart courses, bumper boats, bull riding, and miniature golf. ***Beware:*** It can be crammed with people midsummer. It's open Memorial Day to Labor Day from 10am to 10pm; from September to May it's open weekends only, with limited hours.

Ruidoso's best shopping is at 2801 Sudderth Dr., where a cluster of shops fulfill many desires. Slip on sassy sandals and other contemporary shoes at **Steppin' Out** (© **575/257-5924**). Next door, tots and teens can find upscale duds at **Klassy Kids** (© **575/257-3857**). Meanwhile, wine lovers may want to sample the grape and artisanal cheeses at **End of the Vine** (© **575/630-WINE** [9463]). And finally, foodies will like the kitchen selection at **House of Kelham** (© **575/257-2492**).

Ruidoso Downs

In a stunning setting surrounded by green grass and pine trees, the famous **Ruidoso Downs racetrack** and **Billy the Kid Casino** (© **575/378-4431;** www.ruidosodownsracing.com), 2 miles east of Ruidoso on US 70, is home to the world's richest quarter-horse race, the $2.5 million **All American Futurity,** run each year on Labor Day. Many other days of quarter-horse and thoroughbred racing lead up to the big one, beginning in May and running to Labor Day. Post time is 1pm Thursday through Sunday. Grandstand admission is free; call about reserved seating prices, which range from $5 to $42.

The on-site casino has all the neon, noise, and smoke gamblers love. Though you'll find only slots at this casino (for more variety, head to Inn of the Mountain Gods Resort & Casino, p. 309), bonuses here include simulcast racing on big-screen TVs in the bar and a well-priced buffet with tables overlooking the track. It's open Saturday through Thursday from 11am to 11pm, and Friday from noon to midnight.

An Interesting Museum

The Hubbard Museum of the American West ★ This museum contains a collection of thousands of horse-related items, including saddles from all over the world, a Russian sleigh, a horse-drawn "fire engine," and an 1860 stagecoach. Several great American artists, including Frederic Remington and Charles M. Russell, are represented in the museum's permanent collection. A gift shop has some interesting books and curios.

841 W. US 70, Ruidoso Downs, NM 88346. © **575/378-4142.** Fax 575/378-4166. www.hubbardmuseum.org. Admission $8 adults, $6 seniors and military, $3 children 6–16, free for children 5 and under. Mon–Fri 10am–5pm. Closed Thanksgiving and Christmas.

Ruidoso After Dark: Spencer Theater for the Performing Arts ★★

The dream of Alto, New Mexico, residents Dr. A. N. and Jackie Spencer, the 514-seat Spencer Theater, on Sierra Blanca Airport Hwy. 220, 4½ miles east of NM 48 (© **888/818-7872** or 575/336-4800; www.spencertheater.com), is a model performance space that cost more than $20 million to construct. Opened in 1997, the theater has drawn such talents as Ottmar Liebert and Chuck Mangione. Free tours are offered at 10am Tuesday and Thursday. Performances take place on weekends and during the week. The theater runs two seasons year-round, and tickets cost from $30 to $70.

MESCALERO APACHE INDIAN RESERVATION

Immediately south and west of Ruidoso, the Mescalero Apache Indian Reservation covers over 460,000 acres (719 sq. miles) and is home to about 2,800 members of the Mescalero, Chiricahua, and Lipan bands of Apaches. Established by order of President Ulysses S. Grant in 1873, it sustains a profitable cattle-ranching industry and the Apache-run logging firm of Mescalero Forest Products.

Seeing the Highlights

Even if you're not staying or dining here, be sure to visit the **Inn of the Mountain Gods Resort & Casino,** a luxury resort owned and operated by the tribe (see below); it's the crowning achievement of Wendell Chino, former president of the Mescalero Apache tribe.

Also on the reservation, on US 70, about 17 miles southwest of Ruidoso, is the **Mescalero Cultural Center** (**© 575/671-4494**), open weekdays from 8am to 4:30pm. Photos, artifacts, clothing, crafts, and other exhibits demonstrate the history and culture of the tribe.

St. Joseph's Apache Mission ★ (**© 575/464-4473**), just off US 70 in Mescalero, on a hill overlooking the reservation, is a grand Romanesque-style stone structure that stands 103 feet tall and has walls 4 feet thick. Built between 1920 and 1939, the mission church also contains an icon of the Apache Christ, with Christ depicted as a Mescalero holy man, as well as other Apache religious art. Local arts and crafts and religious items are for sale at the parish office. The church is open daily during daylight hours.

WHERE TO STAY IN & AROUND RUIDOSO

If you're looking for a budget stay in Ruidoso, the **Motel 6** on the outskirts of town has clean, reliable rooms. Call **© 800/466-8356** for reservations.

Escape Resort ★★★ *(Finds)* For years Ruidoso has needed a really upscale lodging option, one with elegance and functionality. Now, finally, it has one. This cluster of five casitas, set within town a little off the main road and surrounded by pine trees, offers

A Silver Dollar Dinner

One of the region's most cherished relics has been restored. **Tinnie Silver Dollar Steakhouse and Saloon,** on US 70, 43 miles west of Roswell and 28 miles east of Ruidoso (**© 575/653-4177;** http://tinniesilverdollar.com), offers excellent food and fine accommodations. The elegant 1870s Victorian structure provides a perfect backdrop for frontier-style dining. A meal here might start with coconut shrimp and move on to a filet mignon with green-chile au gratin potatoes or roasted chicken with mashed potatoes and a light gravy. Tinnie also serves Sunday champagne brunch, including such traditional favorites as eggs Benedict and prime rib. The steakhouse is open Monday to Thursday from 5 to 9pm, and Friday and Saturday from 5 to 10pm, with the saloon opening at 4pm. While eating, enjoy the view of the gardens and water fountain from the veranda, and the original Peter Hurd paintings that hang in each room of the restaurant.

The same location has a deli (Mon–Sat 10am–9pm; Sun 10am–8pm), offering packaged liquor sales, a gift shop, and two suites for overnight guests. The suites range in price from $89 to $175, depending on the season.

accommodations of a level one would find in Santa Fe. They come in 1- and 2-bedroom sizes and have large rooms with high ceilings, comfortable beds with fine linens, contemporary furnishings in muted earth tones, and gas fireplaces fashioned from stacked sandstone. The tiled bathrooms are large, with Jacuzzi tubs and steam-showers. All have fully equipped kitchens with stainless steel appliances. Calling this a "resort" is a bit of a stretch, as it has few amenities, but all else here is stellar.

1016 Mechem Rd., Ruidoso, NM 88345. ✆ **888/762-8551** or 575/258-1234. www.theescaperesort.com. 5 units. $229 1-bedroom casita; $279 2-bedroom casita. Rates include complimentary wine. AE, DISC, MC, V. **Amenities:** Outdoor pool (seasonal). *In room:* A/C, TV, hair dryer, kitchen, Wi-Fi.

Hotel Ruidoso ★★ Value This new hotel, set in the center of town, but a little back from the main street and surrounded by pines, offers clean, contemporary rooms with a bit of flair. Currently, it's one of the town's best values. It's a big, blocky-looking three-story building, but it has well-appointed accommodations. Rooms are medium size and come in standards or minisuites. All have comfortable beds and are decorated in earth tones, with medium-size bathrooms with granite sinks and tilework in the tubs. Minisuites have a sofa bed, a good option for small families. Service is good. The breakfast room is a comfortably airy place to spend the morning.

110 Chase St. Ruidoso, NM 88345 ✆ **866/734-5197** or 575/257-2007. Fax 575/257-2008. www.hotelruidoso.net. 55 units. $79–$99 Mon–Fri; $119–$169 Sat–Sun. Rates include continental breakfast. AE, DISC, MC, V. **Amenities:** Exercise room; Jacuzzi; medium-size indoor pool. *In room:* A/C, TV, fridge, hair dryer, microwave; Wi-Fi.

Inn of the Mountain Gods Resort & Casino ★★ What's most impressive about this resort is its location, set on a grassy slope above a mountain lake on the Mescalero Apache Indian Reservation, 3½ miles southwest of Ruidoso. In 2004, the original resort was leveled and a new one built, much in the style of a Lake Tahoe casino, with glossy gaming rooms, a variety of restaurants, and a golf course. Though the architecture has a cold modernity, the rooms are comfortable, with luxurious touches. You're greeted outside by an impressive Crown Dancer fountain, and inside by banks of windows looking out on the lake. The rooms come in a few sizes, though standard ones are pretty spacious, all with quality bedding, very comfortable beds, and medium-size bathrooms. I recommend paying a little more for a lakeside view. **Wendell's,** with a mountain and lake view, features steak and seafood, with extensive wine offerings. The resort also has a sports bar, a nightclub with live music Friday and Saturday nights, and a casino with more than 1,000 slot machines and 34 table games.

287 Carrizo Canyon Rd., Mescalero, NM 88340. ✆ **800/545-9011** or 575/464-7777. www.innofthemountaingods.com. 273 units. $129–$209 forest-view double, $169–$289 lake-view double; $269–$349 suite, depending on the season and type of room. Golf and ski packages available. AE, DC, DISC, MC, V. **Amenities:** 3 restaurants; 2 bars; golf course; Jacuzzi; indoor pool; room service; watersports equipment/rentals. *In room:* A/C, TV, hair dryer, Wi-Fi.

The Lodge at Sierra Blanca ★★ Surrounded by a golf course and plenty of quiet, this hotel offers clean, reliable rooms in a picturesque setting. However, if you find convention traffic daunting, you'll want to ask what's scheduled at the next-door convention center before reserving. When I visited, the hotel was quiet and serene. The lobby is centered on an Anasazi-style stacked sandstone fireplace, creating an elegance that carries into the rooms. The rooms are medium size, decorated in a contemporary Southwestern style, with comfortable beds and medium-size bathrooms. The suites, which are large, have sofa beds, fireplaces, and balconies. Many of the rooms have two-person Jacuzzi tubs. The hotel offers golf packages.

107 Sierra Blanca Dr., Ruidoso, NM 88345. ✆ **866/211-7727** or 575/258-5500. Fax 575/258-2419. www.thelodgeatsierrablanca.com. 120 units. $149–$169 double; $169–$189 suite. Rates include full breakfast. AE, DISC, MC, V. Take Mechem Dr. 5 min. north of Sudderth. Pets allowed ($50 per stay). **Amenities:** Golf course; exercise room; courtesy computer; Jacuzzi; indoor pool. *In room:* A/C, TV, fridge, microwave, Wi-Fi.

Camping

Lincoln National Forest has more than a dozen campgrounds in the region; four of them are within the immediate area. The **Smokey Bear Ranger Station,** 901 Mechem Dr., Ruidoso (✆ **575/257-4095**), is open Memorial Day to Labor Day from 7:30am to 4:30pm Monday through Saturday; closed on Saturday the rest of the year.

Where to Dine in Ruidoso

Casa Blanca ★ Kids NEW MEXICAN/TEX-MEX This is a real locals' favorite for the margaritas and fun Tex-Mex and New Mexican food. You can count on a good meal here, as the food is made with fresh ingredients. The decor is casual—four rooms in a sprawling house on a hill within town, each with brick or tile floors and colorful art on the walls. The garden room and patio are my choices. All of them can get a little noisy from the many kids who like the menu selections here. Your efficient and friendly server will start you out with complimentary chips and salsa. The best bet here is the chicken enchiladas with sour cream, or the beef or chicken fajitas. Recently I enjoyed some excellent chicken tacos as well. For dessert? Try the chocolate flan cake.

501 Mechem Dr. ✆ **575/257-2495.** Main courses $5–$10. AE, MC, V. Mon–Sat 11am–9pm; Sun 11am–8pm. Closed Thanksgiving and Christmas.

Cattle Baron Steak House ★ SEAFOOD/STEAK This is the place to go if you really have an appetite. It's a casually elegant restaurant, part of a chain with six locations around the Southwest, that may not serve the best steaks and seafood you've tasted, but it still provides good-quality food. It's decorated in an opulent Western style with lots of burgundy upholstery and brass. Often the place is busy and festive, so it's not ideal for a romantic getaway. Service is efficient and friendly. For lunch, try the turkey and avocado sandwich or the teriyaki kabob. For dinner, I usually order the filet mignon or the shrimp scampi. An extensive salad bar dominates the main dining room, and a comfortable lounge sits near the entryway.

657 Sudderth Dr. ✆ **575/257-9355.** Reservations recommended for 6 or more. Main courses $8–$12 lunch, $12–$22 dinner. AE, DC, DISC, MC, V. Mon–Thurs and Sun 11am–10pm; Fri–Sat 11am–10:30pm.

Le Bistro ★★ FRENCH In some kind of alchemistic feat, Chef Richard Girot has transformed casual into elegant in this downtown cafe set in an oddly round building. Decorated with French posters, the place is laid-back enough for folks walking in off the street, but the food is more refined—bistro-style fare similar to what you might find at a streetside cafe in France. Still, it's usually a quiet place, and it's a good spot for a romantic dinner. The service is friendly, though at times overworked. Try the pork tenderloin with rosemary and whipped potatoes, or one of the daily specials, such as seafood-stuffed sea bass. All dinners come with baguette-style bread and a salad. Finish with a chocolate or strawberry crepe. Wine and beer accompany the menu. The patio offers a front-row view of the busy downtown Ruidoso scene.

2800 Sudderth Dr. ✆ **575/257-0132.** Reservations recommended for dinner. Main courses $6–$10 lunch, $9–$18 dinner. AE, MC, V. Mon–Sat 11am–2pm and 5–9pm.

Moments A Scenic Drive Around the Lincoln Loop

An enjoyable way to see many of the sights of the Ruidoso area is a 1- or 2-day 162-mile loop tour. Heading east from Ruidoso on US 70, about 18 miles past Ruidoso Downs, is the small community of **San Patricio,** where you'll find the **Hurd–La Rinconada Gallery** (watch for signs; ✆ **575/653-4331;** www.wyethartists.com). Late artist Peter Hurd, a Roswell native, flunked out of West Point before studying with artist N. C. Wyeth and marrying Wyeth's daughter, Henriette, eventually returning with her to New Mexico. This gallery shows and sells works by Peter Hurd, Henriette Wyeth, their son Michael Hurd, Andrew Wyeth, and N. C. Wyeth. Many of the works capture the ambience of the landscape in the San Patricio area. In addition to original works, signed reproductions are available. The gallery is open Monday through Saturday from 9am to 5pm and Sunday from 10am to 4pm. Several rooms and guesthouses are also available by the night or for longer periods.

From San Patricio, continue east on US 70 for 4 miles to the community of Hondo, at the confluence of the Rio Hondo and Rio Bonito, and turn west onto US 380. From here it's about 10 miles to **Lincoln,** a fascinating little town that is also a National Historic Landmark (see "Lincoln Historic District: A Walk in the Footsteps of Billy the Kid," above). Heading west takes you to **Carrizozo,** the Lincoln County seat since 1912. The **Outpost,** 415 Central Ave. (✆ **575/648-9994**), serves one of the best green-chile cheeseburgers in the Southwest. To continue the loop tour, turn south onto US 54 and go about 28 miles to the turnoff to **Three Rivers Petroglyph National Recreation Area** (✆ **575/525-4300**), about 5 miles east on a paved road. Some 20,000 individual rock art images are here, carved by Mogollon peoples who lived in the area centuries ago. A trail about .75 mile long links many of the most interesting petroglyphs, and the view surrounding the area, with mountains to the east and White Sands to the southwest, is outstanding. The day-use fee is $2 per vehicle. Overnight camping is $10. The U.S. Forest Service also has a campground in the area, about 5 miles east on a gravel road.

Continuing south on US 54, drive about 2 miles to Tularosa and turn east onto US 70, which you take for about 16 miles to the village of **Mescalero** on the Mescalero Apache Indian Reservation. From US 70, take the exit for the Bureau of Indian Affairs and follow the signs to the imposing **St. Joseph's Apache Mission** (see "Mescalero Apache Indian Reservation," p. 308). After you return to US 70, it's about 19 miles back to Ruidoso.

LINCOLN HISTORIC DISTRICT: A WALK IN THE FOOTSTEPS OF BILLY THE KID ★★

One of the last historic yet uncommercialized 19th-century towns remaining in the American West, the tiny community of Lincoln lies 37 miles northeast of Ruidoso on US 380, in the valley of the Rio Bonito. Few people live here today, but it was once the seat of the largest county in the United States, and the focal point of the notorious Lincoln County War of 1878–79. Though the town contains a number of museums today, a single ticket will get you entry into all of them.

The bloody Lincoln County War was fought between various ranching and merchant factions over the issue of beef contracts for nearby Fort Stanton. A sharpshooting teenager named William Bonney—soon to be known as "Billy the Kid"—took sides in this issue with "the good guys," escaping from the burning McSween House after his employer and colleague were shot and killed. Three years later, after shooting down a sheriff, he was captured in Lincoln and sentenced to death by hanging. But he shot his way out of his cell in what is now the **Lincoln County Courthouse Museum,** which still has a hole made by a bullet from the Kid's gun. Of special note here is a letter handwritten by Billy defending himself to Governor Lew Wallace.

Many of the original structures from that era have been preserved and restored by the Museum of New Mexico, the Lincoln County Historical Society, and an organization called **Historic Lincoln** (✆ **575/653-4025;** www.nmmonuments.org), a subsidiary of the Lincoln State Monument.

JUST THE FACTS At the **Visitor Center,** on NM 380 on the east side of town (✆ **575/653-4025**), exhibits explain the role in Lincoln's history of Apaches, Hispanics, Anglo cowboys, and the black Buffalo Soldiers, and detail the Lincoln County War. A 12-minute film on Lincoln history is presented in an old-fashioned theater. Start your visit here and join a tour given every hour by docents in period costumes, included in the admission cost. Across the courtyard is the **Luna Museum Store.** Also of note in the town is the short, round **Torreon** fortress, which served as protection from Apache raids; the **Montaño Store,** once a saloon and boarding house; **Dr. Wood's House,** filled with pre-1920s furnishings, books, and instruments; and the **Tunstall Store Museum,** with late 19th- and early-20th-century clothes, hardware, and butter churns.

An annual **folk pageant,** *The Last Escape of Billy the Kid,* has been presented outdoors since 1949 as a highly romanticized version of the Lincoln County War. It's staged Friday and Saturday night and Sunday afternoon during the first full weekend in August as part of the **Old Lincoln Days** celebration. The festival also includes living-history demonstrations of traditional crafts, musical programs, and food booths throughout the village.

The historic district is open year-round daily 8:30am–4:30pm. Admission is $5 for adults (includes entry to 6 buildings during summer and 4 in winter). It's free for children 16 and under. For more information, write to P.O. Box 36, Lincoln, NM 88338, or call ✆ **575/653-4025.**

5 ROSWELL

62 miles E of Ruidoso; 83 miles NE of Alamagordo; 158 miles SE of Albuquerque

Best known as a destination for UFO enthusiasts and conspiracy theorists, Roswell has become a household name thanks to old Mulder and Scully. And even if you're not glued to your set for reruns of *The X-Files,* you may remember Roswell as the setting for major scenes from the 1996 blockbuster *Independence Day.* Government cover-ups, alien autopsies, and cigarette-smoking feds . . . come along as we venture into the UFO capital of the world.

Fun Facts The Incident at Roswell

In July 1947, something "happened" in Roswell. What was it? Debate still rages. On July 8, 1947, a local rancher named MacBrazel found unusual debris scattered across his property. The U.S. military released a statement saying the debris was wreckage from a spaceship crash. Four hours later, however, the military retracted the statement, claiming what fell from the sky was "only a weather balloon." Most of the community didn't believe the story, although some did suspect that the military was somehow involved—Robert Goddard had been working on rockets in this area since the 1930s, and the Roswell Air Base was nearby. Eyewitnesses to the account, however, maintain the debris "was not of this world."

Theorists believe that the crash actually involved two spacecraft. One disintegrated, hence the debris across the MacBrazel ranch, and the other crash-landed, hence the four alien bodies that were also claimed to have been discovered.

UFO believers have remained dissatisfied with the U.S. Air Force's weather balloon story and have insisted on an explanation for the "alien bodies." The most recent comment from the Air Force came in 1997, 2 weeks before the 50th anniversary of the "crash." The Air Force said that the most likely explanation for the unverified alien reports was that people were simply remembering and misplacing in time a number of life-size dummies dropped from the sky during a series of experiments in the 1950s.

The main place to go in Roswell to learn more about the incident is the **International UFO Museum and Research Center** (✆ **575/625-9495;** www.roswellufomuseum.com), in the old Plains Theater on Main Street. Staffers will be more than happy to discuss the crash and the alleged military cover-up. As well as displaying an hour-by-hour timeline of the "incident," the museum has photographs of bizarre and elaborate crop circles, and a videotape in which an alleged witness tells his account. The museum is open daily from 9am to 5pm; admission is $5 for adults, $2 for those 5 to 15, and free for children 4 and under.

Roswell hosts a **UFO Festival** every year during the first week in July. Some of the events include guest speakers, celebrity appearances, an Alien Village, and a parade. For details on the event, call ✆ **575/625-8607** or go to www.roswellufofestival.com.

—Su Hudson

ESSENTIALS

GETTING THERE From Albuquerque, take I-40 east 59 miles to Clines Corners; turn south on US 285, and travel 140 miles to Roswell (4 hr.). From Las Cruces, take US 70 east (4 hr.). From Carlsbad, take US 285 north (1½ hr.).

Roswell Airport, at Roswell Industrial Air Center on South Main Street (✆ **575/347-5703**), is served commercially, twice daily, by **American Eagle Airlines** (✆ **800/433-7300;** www.aa.com), directly from Dallas.

VISITOR INFORMATION The **Roswell Chamber of Commerce** is at 131 W. Second St. (P.O. Box 70), Roswell, NM 88202 (✆ **575/623-5695;** www.roswellnm.org). The **Roswell Convention and Visitors Center** is at 912 N. Main (✆ **575/624-6860**).

WHAT TO SEE

Roswell Museum and Art Center ★ This highly acclaimed small museum is a good place to stop and get a sense of this area before heading out to explore. The art center contains an excellent collection of works by Peter Hurd and his wife, Henriette Wyeth, many of which depict the gentry-ranching lifestyle in this area. You'll also find works by Georgia O'Keeffe, Ernest Blumenschein, Joseph Sharp, and others famed from the early-20th-century Taos and Santa Fe art colonies. The museum has an early historical section, but its pride and joy is the **Robert Goddard Collection,** which presents actual engines, rocket assemblies, and specialized parts developed by Goddard in the 1930s, when he lived and worked in Roswell. Goddard's workshop has been re-created for the exhibit.

100 W. 11th St., Roswell, NM 88201. ✆ **575/624-6744.** Fax 575/624-6765. www.roswellmuseum.org. Free admission. Mon–Sat 9am–5pm; Sun and holidays 1–5pm. Closed Thanksgiving, Christmas Eve, Christmas Day, and New Year's Day.

WHERE TO STAY IN ROSWELL

Fairfield Inn & Suites by Marriott ★ This inn at the center of town offers bright rooms with plenty of amenities. The lobby and breakfast area have a living room feel, and the whole place offers the convenience and good prices one can expect from a Fairfield. Such elements as marble and tile in the bathrooms and a nice pool further enhance the place. The suites offer an interesting angled two-room configuration, with a big TV and a CD player; the standard rooms are medium size, each with a desk. All rooms have comfortable beds.

1201 N. Main St., Roswell, NM 88201. ✆ **800/228-2800** or 575/624-1300. www.marriott.com. 67 units. $90–$139 double. Rates include continental breakfast. AE, DC, DISC, MC, V. **Amenities:** Health club; outdoor pool; Wi-Fi (in lobby). *In room:* A/C, TV, hair dryer, Internet, microwave.

Camping

Town and Country RV Park (✆ **800/499-4364** or 575/624-1833; www.roswell-usa.com/tandcrv), south of Roswell, is your best bet for camping, with some grass and cottonwood and elm trees for shade. The campground has 75 sites, most with full hookups. Prices range from $33 to $39. Tent campers can set up here as well. Bathrooms are clean and convenient, as is the large pool. The campground is at 331 W. Brasher Rd. Head south on Main Street for 3 miles; turn west on West Brasher Road.

WHERE TO DINE IN ROSWELL

Tia Juana's Mexican Grille & Cantina ★★ Kids NEW MEXICAN On the north end of town, this spot serves tasty New Mexican fare in a festive Mexican-cantina ambience. Red-chile lights and photos of Oaxaca accent the large dining area, which is made intimate with booths and tables nicely spaced. Service is friendly and on the mark. The food is prepared with fresh ingredients and good chile—the restaurant even makes its own tortillas daily. You can't go wrong with the enchiladas, served rolled or stacked, or the tacos, served soft or crisp. Finish your meal with the Kahlúa sombrero cake, made with liqueur and topped with toffee whipped cream. Kids have plenty of menu options, as well as crayons to draw with, and adults can enjoy a full bar.

3601 N. Main St. ✆ **575/627-6113.** http://tiajuanas.net. Main courses $6–$20. AE, DC, DISC, MC, V. Mon–Thurs 11am–9:30pm; Fri–Sat 11am–10pm; Sun 11am–9pm.

6 CARLSBAD & ENVIRONS

65 miles S of Roswell; 98 miles SE of Alamogordo; 139 miles E of Las Cruces

Carlsbad, named for a spa in Bohemia, offers almost 3 miles of beaches and paths along the tree-shaded Pecos River. Founded in the late 1800s, its back streets have many elegant homes, and its town square encircles a Pueblo-style courthouse designed by New Mexico architect John Gaw Meem. Besides getting a good tourist business from Carlsbad Caverns, the town thrives on farming, with irrigated crops of cotton, hay, and pecans.

The caverns (see "Carlsbad Caverns National Park," later in this chapter) are the big attraction, having drawn more than 33 million visitors since opening in 1923. A satellite community, White's City (www.whitescity.com), was created 20 miles south of Carlsbad at the park entrance junction. The family of Jack White, Jr., owns all its motels, restaurants, gift shops, and other attractions.

ESSENTIALS

GETTING THERE From Albuquerque, take 1-40 east 59 miles to Clines Corners; turn south on US 285, and travel 216 miles to Carlsbad via Roswell (6 hr.). From El Paso, take US 62/180 east (3 hr.).

New Mexico Airlines (✆ **888/564-6119;** www.pacificwings.com/nma) provides commercial service, with daily flights between Albuquerque and **Cavern City Air Terminal** (✆ **575/887-3060**), 4 miles south of the city via National Parks Highway (US 62/180). You can rent a car from **Enterprise,** 609 N. Canal St. (✆ **575/887-3039**); with an advance reservation they will pick you up at the airport.

VISITOR INFORMATION The **Carlsbad Chamber of Commerce** and the **Carlsbad Convention and Visitors Bureau,** both at 302 S. Canal St. (US 285), P.O. Box 910, Carlsbad, NM 88220 (✆ **800/221-1224** or 575/887-6516; www.carlsbadchamber.com), are open Monday from 9am to 5pm and Tuesday through Friday from 8am to 5pm.

EXPLORING CARLSBAD

Carlsbad's pride and joy is the broad Pecos River, with a $3^1/_2$-mile **riverwalk** along the tree-shaded banks, beginning near the north end of Riverside Drive. This is a lovely place for a picnic, and if you'd like to cool off, a municipal beach at the north end has changing rooms and showers. Annual **Christmas on the Pecos** ★★ pontoon boat rides take place each evening from Thanksgiving to New Year's Eve (except Christmas Eve), past a fascinating display of Christmas lights on riverside homes and businesses. Advance reservations, available from the chamber of commerce, are required.

The **Carlsbad Museum and Art Center,** 418 W. Fox St., 1 block west of Canal Street (✆ **575/887-0276**), contains Apache relics, pioneer artifacts, and an impressive art collection. The museum's store has a small but fine selection of jewelry and books at reasonable prices. The museum is open Monday through Saturday from 10am to 5pm; admission is free, although donations are welcome. If you're looking to shop, check out the **Artist Gallery,** 120 S. Canyon St. (✆ **575/887-1210**), selling local and regional art. Look especially for Helen Gwinn's mixed-media pieces.

OUTDOOR ACTIVITIES

Recreational facilities in the Carlsbad area include some two dozen parks, several golf courses, numerous tennis courts and swimming pools, a municipal beach, and a shooting and archery range. Contact the **City of Carlsbad Recreation Department** (✆ **575/887-1191**).

Living Desert Zoo & Gardens State Park ★ Kids Situated within 1,200 acres of authentic Chihuahuan Desert, this park contains more than 50 species of desert mammals, birds, and reptiles, and almost 500 varieties of plants. Even for someone like me, who cringes at the thought of zoos, this is a pleasant 1.3-mile walk. You pass through displays with plaques pointing out vegetation, such as mountain mahogany, and geologic formations such as gypsum sinkholes. In addition to a nocturnal exhibit, you're likely to see lizards and other wild creatures, as well as captive ones.

Rehabilitation programs provide for the park's animals, which have been sick or injured and are no longer able to survive in the wild. You'll see golden eagles and great horned owls among the birds of prey in the aviary, and large animals such as deer and elk in outdoor pastures. The view from the park, high atop the Ocotillo Hills on the northwest side of Carlsbad, is superb.

1504 Miehls Dr. (P.O. Box 100), Carlsbad, NM 88221-0100. ✆ **575/887-5516.** www.emnrd.state.nm.us/prd/livingdesert.htm. Admission $5 adults, $3 children 7–12, free for children 6 and under. Group rates are available. Memorial Day weekend to Labor Day 8am–8pm, last park entry by 6:30pm; rest of year 9am–5pm, last park entry by 3:30pm. Gift shop closes 45 min. prior to zoo. Closed Christmas. Take Miehls Dr. off US 285 west of town and proceed just over a mile.

WHERE TO STAY IN & AROUND CARLSBAD

Most properties are along the highway south toward Carlsbad Caverns National Park (see "Carlsbad Caverns National Park," below). Only the Best Western Cavern Inn is near the National Park. The downside to staying there is that your restaurant and activity options are limited.

Best Western Cavern Inn If you'd like to be close to the caverns, this hotel is there, but it's not my choice. This whole complex could use updating, but seems to survive because it's the only lodging near the caverns. The lobby is within an Old West storefront, and the accommodations are across the street. The staff here seems to be overworked, so you may not get the service you would in Carlsbad. The motel has two main sections. The best is the Cavern Inn. This section is built around a courtyard, and rooms have an updated feel, with vigas on the ceilings and Southwestern pine furniture. Bathrooms are roomy enough, and the beds are comfortably firm. Next door, the two-story Walnut Canyon Inn provides 1970s rooms that are large, though the small bathrooms with jetted tubs could use sprucing up.

The White's City Arcade contains a post office, a grocery store, a gift shop, and the Million Dollar Museum of various antiques and paraphernalia. The hotel's two restaurants serve three meals in an ambience that could also use updating.

17 Carlsbad Cavern Hwy. at NM 7 (P.O. Box 128), White's City, NM 88268. ✆ **800/CAVERNS** [228-3767] or 575/785-2291. Fax 575/785-2283. www.bestwestern.com. 63 units. May 15–Sept 15 $104 double; Sept 16–May 14 $85 double. Rates include breakfast. AE, DC, DISC, MC, V. Pets welcome, with $10 fee. **Amenities:** 2 restaurants; bar; outdoor pool. *In room:* A/C, TV, hair dryer, Wi-Fi.

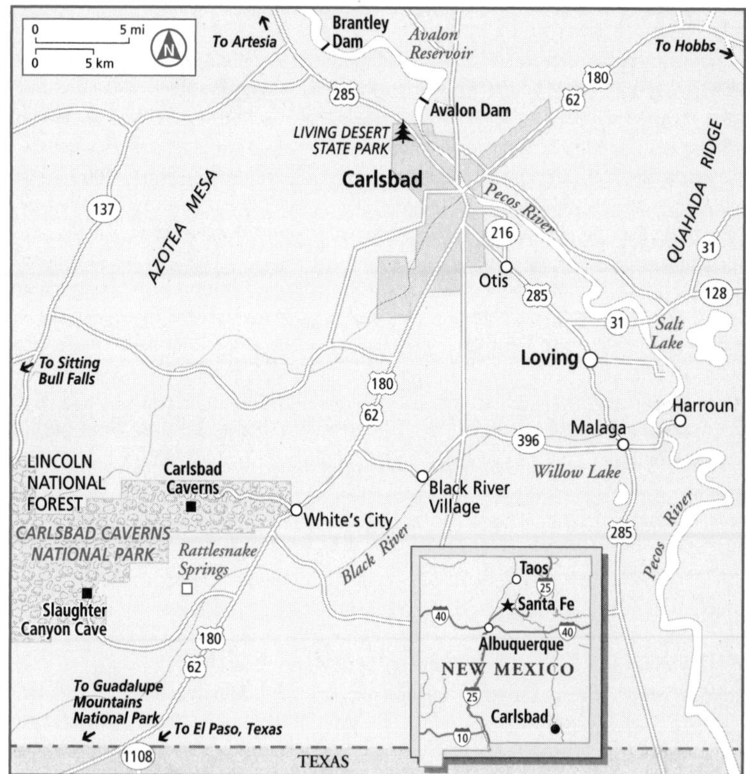

Best Western Stevens Inn ★ This is a comfortable and welcoming place after the rigor of traveling in this part of the state, where there are miles between stops. The grounds are carefully landscaped, and the inn offers numerous types of rooms built in different eras. Some need to be upgraded, so be sure to request a remodeled one; or, better yet, request one of the newest rooms at the south end of the property, which are large and have large bathrooms, a fridge and microwave, and some have full kitchens. The rooms in the 400 and 600 numbered buildings are also updated. All the rooms are medium size, decorated in a Southwestern print, and have firm beds. Bathrooms are small but have outer double-sink vanities. **The Flume** (see below) is one of the better restaurants in town.

1829 S. Canal St., Carlsbad, NM 88220. ✆ **800/730-2851,** 800/528-1234, or 575/887-2851. Fax 575/887-6338. www.bestwestern.com. 221 units. $62–$89 double; $70–$99 suite. Rates include breakfast buffet. AE, DISC, MC, V. Small pets allowed, with $25 deposit. **Amenities:** 2 restaurants; bar; health club; large outdoor pool; room service. *In room:* A/C, TV, fridge, hair dryer, microwave, Wi-Fi.

Camping

Brantley Lake State Park (✆ **575/457-2384;** www.nmparks.com) in Carlsbad has RV hookups as well as tent campsites. Picnic tables, grills, and recreational facilities are available.

Boating and lake fishing are popular here. **Carlsbad RV Park and Campground,** on the south end of town at 4301 National Parks Hwy. (✆ **888/878-7275** or 575/885-6333; www.carlsbadrvpark.com), is a large, full-service campground with a swimming pool and playground.

WHERE TO DINE IN & AROUND CARLSBAD

Blue House ★ Finds BAKERY/CAFE In a quest to find good coffee in even the smallest of New Mexico towns, I now rate Carlsbad high. On a quiet residential street just north of historic downtown is this gem, set in a Queen Anne–style blue house with morning-glory vines adorning the front fence. Inside, Parisian colors warm the walls, contrasting with brightly painted chairs and small round tables. The fare is simple, fresh, and imaginative, with espresso, lattes, and Italian sodas the biggest draws, along with special sandwiches and soups daily. Excellent baked goods top the breakfast menu, including homemade cinnamon rolls. For lunch, try any of the fresh organic salads such as the grilled chicken or Oriental. For something sweeter, order the cream cheese–raspberry coffee cake.

609 N. Canyon Rd. ✆ **575/628-0555.** All menu items under $8. DISC, MC, V. Mon–Fri 6am–2pm; Sat 6am–noon (lunch served Tues–Fri 11am–1pm). Take Canal St. to Church St. east, and then south on Canyon Rd.

The Flume ★ AMERICAN Named for the irrigation ditch that brings water to the region's farmers, the Flume serves reliable beef, pork, and chicken dishes in a comfortable atmosphere. This is where Carlsbad locals come for their special nights out. The decor in the two-room dining area, separated by arches, has a bit of a 1970s feel, but includes comfortable chairs. Service is good. Breakfast brings standard egg and pancake offerings. For lunch you might try one of their sandwiches such as the smoked turkey with Swiss cheese and avocado. The salads and burgers are also tasty. At dinner, I've enjoyed a nice grilled chicken here, and my mother liked her fettuccine Alfredo with shrimp. Others order the rib-eye or prime rib, which is served on Friday and Saturday nights. Entrees come with a trip to the salad bar, a vegetable, and choice of a starch. Diners can order from a full bar. A seniors' menu is available.

1829 S. Canal St. ✆ **575/887-2851.** www.bestwestern.com. Breakfast and lunch $5–$12; dinner $13–$23. AE, DISC, MC, V. Daily 6am–10pm.

Lucy's ★ Kids MEXICAN When you walk in the door of this busy restaurant with festive Mexican decor, Lucy is likely to wave you toward the dining room and tell you to find a seat. Such is the casual nature of the place—and a sign of the good home-style food to come. Since 1974, Lucy and Justo Yanez's restaurant has been dedicated to the words of a Mexican proverb printed on the menu: *El hambre es un fuego, y la comida es fresca* (Hunger is a burning, and eating is a coolness). You'll probably want to start with a margarita or Mexican beer. The food is tasty, with Lucy's personal adaptations of old favorites, often invented by requests from regulars. I recommend the chicken fajita burrito or the combination plate. Finish with a dessert of *buñelos* (fritters), sprinkled with cinnamon sugar. Children's plates are available; diners can choose mild or hot chile. A second Lucy's restaurant is in Hobbs, at 4428 Lovington Hwy.

701 S. Canal St. ✆ **575/887-7714.** Reservations recommended Fri–Sat. Main courses $6–$15. AE, DC, DISC, MC, V. Mon–Sat 11am–9pm.

7 CARLSBAD CAVERNS NATIONAL PARK ★★★

23 miles SW of Carlsbad; 81 miles S of Roswell; 150 miles NE of El Paso

One of the largest and most spectacular cave systems in the world, Carlsbad Caverns comprise some 100 known caves that snake through the porous limestone reef of the Guadalupe Mountains. Fantastic and grotesque formations fascinate visitors, who find every shape imaginable (and unimaginable) naturally sculpted in the underground world—from frozen waterfalls to strands of pearls, from soda straws to miniature castles, from draperies to ice-cream cones.

Although Native Americans had known of the caverns for centuries, they were not discovered by Anglos until about a century ago, when settlers were attracted by sunset flights of bats from the cave. Jim White, a guano miner, began to explore the main cave in the early 1900s and to share its wonders with tourists. By 1923, the caverns had become a national monument, upgraded to national park status in 1930.

ESSENTIALS

GETTING THERE Take US 62/180 from either Carlsbad (see "Essentials," under "Carlsbad & Environs," earlier in this chapter), which is 23 miles to the northeast, or El Paso, Texas, which is 150 miles to the west. The scenic entrance road to the park is 7 miles long and originates at the park gate at White's City. Van service to Carlsbad Caverns National Park from White's City, south of Carlsbad, is provided by **Sun Country Tours/White's City Services** (✆ **575/785-2291**).

VISITOR INFORMATION For more information about the park, contact **Carlsbad Caverns National Park,** 3225 National Parks Hwy., Carlsbad, NM 88220 (✆ **800/967-CAVE** [2283] for tour reservations, 575/785-2232 for information about guided tours, and 575/785-3012 for bat flight information; www.nps.gov/cave).

ADMISSION FEES & HOURS General admission to the park is $6 for adults, free for children under age 15. Admission is good for 3 days and includes entry to the two self-guided walking tours. Guided tours range in price from $7 to $20, depending on the type of tour, and reservations are required. The visitor center and park are open daily from Memorial Day to mid-August from 8am to 7pm; the rest of the year they're open from 8am to 5pm. They're closed Christmas.

TOURING THE CAVES

Two caves, **Carlsbad Cavern** and **Slaughter Canyon Cave,** are open to the public. The National Park Service has provided facilities, including elevators, to make it easy for everyone to visit the cavern, and a kennel for pets is available. Visitors in wheelchairs are common.

In addition to the tours described below, inquire at the visitor center information desk about other ranger-guided tours, including climbing and crawling "wild" cave tours. Be sure to call days in advance because some tours are offered only 1 day per week. Spelunkers who seek access to the park's undeveloped caves require special permission from the park superintendent.

Carlsbad Cavern Tour Tips

Wear flat shoes with rubber soles and heels because of the slippery paths. A light sweater or jacket feels good in the constant temperature of 56°F (13°C), especially when it's 100°F (38°C) outside in the sun. The cavern is well lit, but you may want to bring along a flashlight as well. Rangers are stationed in the cave to answer questions.

Carlsbad Cavern Tours

You can tour Carlsbad Cavern in one of three ways, depending on your time, interest, and level of ability. The first, and least difficult, option is to take the elevator from the visitor center down 750 feet to the start of the self-guided tour of the Big Room. More difficult and time-consuming, but vastly more rewarding, is the 1-mile self-guided tour along the Natural Entrance route, which follows the traditional explorer's route, entering the cavern through the large historic natural entrance. The paved walkway through the natural entrance winds into the depths of the cavern and leads through a series of underground rooms; this tour takes about an hour. Parts of it are steep. At its lowest point, the trail reaches 750 feet below the surface, ending finally at an underground rest area.

Visitors who take either the elevator or the Natural Entrance route begin the self-guided tour of the spectacular Big Room near the rest area. The floor of this room covers 14 acres; the tour, over a relatively level path, is 1.25 miles long and takes about an hour.

The third option is the 1½-hour ranger-guided Kings Palace tour, which also departs from the underground rest area. This tour descends 830 feet beneath the surface of the desert to the deepest portion of the cavern open to the public. Reservations are required, and an additional fee is charged.

Other Guided Tours

Be sure to ask about the Slaughter Canyon Cave, Left Hand Tunnel, Lower Cave, Hall of the White Giant, and Spider Cave tours. These vary in degree of difficulty and adventure, from Left Hand, which is an easy half-mile lantern tour; to Spider Cave, where you can expect tight crawlways and canyonlike passages; to Hall of the White Giant, a strenuous tour in which you're required to crawl long distances, squeeze through tight crevices, and climb up slippery flow-stone-lined passages. Call in advance for times of each tour. All these tours depart from the visitor center.

BAT FLIGHTS

Every sunset from May to October, a crowd gathers at the natural entrance of the cave to watch a quarter-million bats take flight for a night of insect feasting. (The bats winter in Mexico.) All day long, the Mexican free-tailed bats sleep in the cavern; at night, they strike out on an insect hunt. A ranger program is offered around 7:30pm (verify the time at the visitor center) at the outdoor Bat Flight Amphitheater. Midsummer, the park sponsors a **Bat Flight Breakfast,** beginning at 5am, during which visitors watch the bats return to the cavern. The cost is $7 for adults and $3 for children 12 and under. For information and specific date, call ✆ **575/785-2232,** ext. 0; or check www.nps.gov/cave.

OTHER PARK ACTIVITIES

Aside from the caves, the park offers a 10-mile one-way scenic loop drive through the Chihuahuan Desert to view Rattlesnake and Upper Walnut canyons. Picnickers can head for Rattlesnake Springs Picnic Area, on C.R. 418 near Slaughter Canyon Cave, a water source for hundreds of years for the Native Americans, and a primo birding spot. Back-country hikers must register at the visitor center before going out on any of the trails in the park's 46,766 acres.

DINING

A cafe at the base of the caverns serves refreshments. Otherwise, your best bet is to eat in Carlsbad. If you are hungry while in the area, head to the **Velvet Garter Saloon & Restaurant** and **Jack's,** 26 Carlsbad Cavern Hwy. (✆ **575/785-2291**). Both are part of White's City. The food is decent, with the Velvet Garter serving steaks and pasta in the evenings, and Jack's offering basic breakfasts and lunches. Dinner reservations are recommended in summer. The saloon is unmistakable, with longhorns mounted over the door. Main courses are $10 to $21 (Velvet Garter); $5.50 to $10 breakfast or lunch (Jack's). Velvet Garter is open daily 4 to 9pm (8:30pm in winter); Jack's daily 7am to 4pm.

8 SOCORRO

62 miles NE of Truth or Consequences; 69 miles S of Albuquerque; 112 miles N of Las Cruces

Socorro, a quiet, pleasant town of about 9,000 residents, is an unusual mix of the 19th, 20th, and 21st centuries. Established as a mining settlement and ranching center, Socorro has a downtown area dominated by numerous mid-1800s buildings and the 17th-century San Miguel Mission. **The New Mexico Institute of Mining and Technology** (New Mexico Tech) is a major research center. Socorro is also the gateway to a vast and varied two-county region that includes the **Bosque del Apache National Wildlife Refuge,** the **Very Large Array National Radio Astronomy Observatory (VLA),** and three national forests.

ESSENTIALS

GETTING THERE From Albuquerque, take I-25 south (1¼ hr.). From Las Cruces, take I-25 north (2¾ hr.).

VISITOR INFORMATION The **Socorro County Chamber of Commerce,** which is also the visitor information headquarters, is at 101 Plaza (P.O. Box 743), Socorro, NM 87801 (✆ **575/835-0424;** www.socorro-nm.com).

EXPLORING SOCORRO

The best introduction to Socorro is a walking tour of the historic district. A brochure with a map and guidebook, available at the chamber of commerce on the **plaza,** where the tour begins, points out several historic buildings, many on the National Register of Historic Places.

You'll definitely want to check out the old **Val Verde Hotel.** The horseshoe-shaped Val Verde, a National Historic Landmark, was built in 1919 in California Mission style. It's been converted to apartments. Another interesting spot is the **Fullingim-Isenhour-Leard Gallery,** 113-C W. Abeyta St., just off the plaza (✆ **575/835-4487;** www.figalleries.com). In a historic building, four artists share their bronze-work, paintings, and etchings.

If you're craving a cappuccino or latte while in Socorro, head to the **Manzanares Coffee House** ★, 110 Manzanares St. (✆ **575/838-0809**). As well as coffee drinks, the shop offers good sandwiches on foccacia bread, salads, and house-made gelato and sorbet. Manzanares also offers Wi-Fi access.

OTHER ATTRACTIONS

El Camino Real International Heritage Center ★ This museum, opened in 2005, tells the story of El Camino Real, the 1,500-mile international trade route from Mexico to San Juan Pueblo, near Santa Fe. The impressive $5-million, 20,000-square-foot structure, set in the middle of the desert, is an award-winning building, perched like a ship above Sheep Canyon, between Socorro and Truth or Consequences. In fact, the center is designed with ship elements, including a bowsprit on the helm. "The journey across the Jornada del Muerto reminded travelers of crossing the sea, with its tufts of grass, mirages, and overwhelming silence," says Monument Ranger Dave Wunker. The real fun starts in the exhibit hall, where visitors get to travel the trail themselves, beginning at Zacatecas Plaza in Mexico, one of many stops along the road. Artifacts from the Camino days—*a caja fuerte* (strong box) and an Apache water jug—help tell the story, though my one complaint about the museum is that it's a bit short on artifacts, which may be remedied as it matures. Excellent period photos and some high-tech displays help fill the gap.

C.R. 1598, 30 miles south of Socorro. From I-25, take exit 115 and follow the signs. ✆ **575/854-3600.** www.caminorealheritage.org. Admission $5 adults; free for children 15 and under. Daily 8:30am–5pm.

Old San Miguel Mission ★★ Built from 1615 to 1626, but abandoned during the Pueblo Revolt of 1680, this graceful church was subsequently restored, and a new wing was added in 1853. It boasts thick adobe walls, large carved vigas (rafters), and supporting corbel arches. English-language Masses are Saturday at 6pm and Sunday at 9:30 and 11am.

403 El Camino Real NW, 2 blocks north of the plaza. ✆ **575/835-1620.** Free admission. Summer Mon–Fri 8am–7:30pm; winter Mon–Fri 8am–6:30pm.

SEEING THE SIGHTS NEAR SOCORRO

SOUTH OF SOCORRO The village of **San Antonio,** the boyhood home of Conrad Hilton, is 10 miles from Socorro via I-25. During the financial panic of 1907, his merchant father, Augustus Hilton, converted part of his store into a rooming house. This gave Conrad his first exposure to the hospitality industry, and he went on to worldwide fame as a hotelier. Only ruins of the store/boardinghouse remain.

WEST OF SOCORRO US 60, running west to Arizona, is the avenue to several points of interest. **Magdalena,** 27 miles from Socorro, is a mining and ranching town that preserves an 1880s Old West spirit. In mid-November, this little town holds its Fall Festival, which includes a variety of studio tours, artist demonstrations, and a silent auction.

Fifty-four miles west of Socorro, via US 60, is the **Very Large Array National Radio Astronomy Observatory (VLA)** ★★. (The Socorro office is at 1003 Lopezville Rd. NW; ✆ **575/835-7000;** www.nrao.edu.) Here, 27 dish-shaped antennas, each 82 feet in diameter, are spread across the plains of San Agustin, forming a single gigantic radio telescope. Many recognize the site from the 1997 movie *Contact,* starring Jodie Foster. Photographs taken with this apparatus are similar to those taken with the largest optical telescopes, except that radio telescopes are sensitive to low-frequency radio waves. All

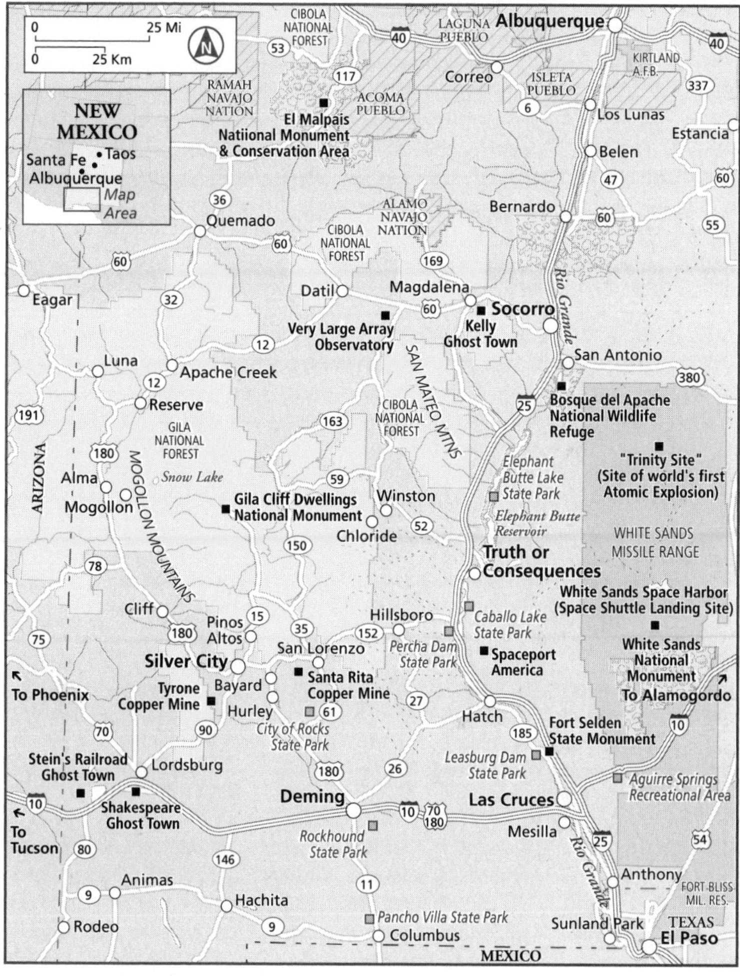

types of celestial objects are photographed, including the sun and its planets, stars, quasars, galaxies, and even the faint remains of the "big bang" that scientists believe occurred some 10 billion years ago. On the outdoor, self-guided walking tour, you'll have a chance to get a closer look at the massive antennas. Admission is free, and visitors are welcomed daily from 8:30am to sunset.

WHERE TO STAY IN THE SOCORRO AREA

Most accommodations are along California Street, the main highway through town, or the adjacent I-25 frontage road. Most lodgings provide free parking.

Casa Blanca ★ The ideal situation in this part of the world is to be just a few minutes away from the Bosque del Apache. That way, you only have to get out of bed a half-hour or so before sunup in order to get to the wildlife refuge and see the morning flight (see "Oasis in the Desert: Bosque del Apache National Wildlife Refuge," below). Casa Blanca is the place to stay for this reason. It's a cozy Victorian farmhouse and home to proprietor Phoebe Wood, a former schoolteacher. The place has a genuine homelike quality—comfortable and well maintained. The best room is the Heron, with a queen-size bed and private bathroom with a whirlpool tub. A morning snack and coffee are offered for those leaving early to the Bosque, and later, upon your return a full breakfast is available. Fruit, cereals, eggs and home-baked muffins are served in a homey kitchen. Smoking is not permitted.

13 Montoya St. (P.O. Box 31), San Antonio, NM 87832. ✆ **575/835-3027.** www.casablancabedandbreakfast.com. 3 units. $80–$100 double. Rates include generous breakfast. MC, V. Closed June–Sept. Pets welcome.

Holiday Inn Express ★ (Kids) Opened in 2007, this new hotel right within town, with good access to I-25, offers the region's best lodgings. Rooms come in kings, two queens, and suites. All are medium size, with lounge chairs and/or desks and/or two chairs and tables. The rooms, decorated in earth tones, have comfortable beds and nice linens. The suites have sofa beds, a good option for those traveling with children. Bathrooms are medium size, with granite countertops. Service here is courteous and efficient. A hot breakfast is served in the sunny breakfast room or on the patio.

1040 California St. NE, Socorro, NM 87801. ✆ **800/HOLIDAY** [465-4329] or 575/838-4600. Fax 575/838-4700. www.hiexpress.com/socorronm. 77 units. $105 double; $135 suite. Rates include breakfast. AE, DISC, MC, V. **Amenities:** Health club; Jacuzzi; indoor pool. *In room:* A/C, TV, fridge, hair dryer, microwave, Wi-Fi.

Camping

Casey's Socorro RV Park (✆ **800/674-2234** or 575/835-2234) offers mountain and valley views and plenty of shade, as well as 100 sites and 30 full hookups. Tenting is available, as are picnic tables, grills, and ice. A playground and swimming pool are open year-round. To reach Casey's, take I-25 to exit 147, go 1 block west on Business I-25 and then 1 block south on West Frontage Road.

WHERE TO DINE IN THE SOCORRO AREA

Manny's Buckhorn Tavern ★★ AMERICAN For years, the cafe across the street from this place in San Antonio (10 miles south of town), the Owl Bar, held the state's title for the best green-chile cheeseburger. More recently, this spry contender has come to dominate the ring. With the title has come a slew of press, including *GQ* magazine naming its burgers on their national top-20 burger list. *Travel + Leisure* and the *New York Times* have also written about this charming place that's full of local color. It has hardwood floors, beer neons, and memorabilia on the walls—a Christ crucifix, antelope antlers—set above cozy booths. Order their specialty, a Buckhorn Burger, made with hand-patted 80% lean beef topped with green chile and cheese. On the side, choose fries or onion rings, both good and crispy. If you're not a burger fan, try the tacos or tamales. Wash your meal down with a beer or margarita from the full bar.

Building 68, NM 380, San Antonio (10 miles south of Socorro). ✆ **575/835-4423.** All menu items under $8. MC, V. Mon–Sat 11am–8pm.

Stage Door Grill ★★ STEAKS/SEAFOOD/CAJUN Set in the historic 1850 Elfego Baca building, with adobe walls, a viga ceiling, and bright paintings, this new restaurant serves tasty steaks, seafood, burgers, pasta, and Cajun dishes. A little dark inside, the restaurant rambles through three rooms and is anchored by a classic wooden bar in the back. Service is good. For lunch, locals seem to prefer burgers in a variety of types or salads such as the Asian chicken, with mandarin oranges, chow mein noodles, and sesame vinaigrette. At dinner, the steaks are a good choice, served with soup or salad, vegetable, and potato or rice, as are the Cajun dishes (the restaurant owner's relations cook at many venues in Louisiana, so he's pulled recipes from them). The shrimp étoufée is quite nice. A brief but international wine list and a selection of brew pub beers accompany the menu. Thursday through Saturday nights, live music—ranging from folk to country to blues to jazz—plays.

Bernard and Abeyta (just north of Plaza). ✆ **575/835-2403.** www.stagedoorgrill.net. Reservations recommended Fri–Sat. Main courses $7–$20. AE, DISC, MC, V. Daily 11am–10pm.

9 BOSQUE DEL APACHE ★★

16 miles S of Socorro; 85 miles S of Albuquerque; 100 miles N of Las Cruces

By Ian Wilker

The barren lands to either side of I-25 south of Albuquerque seem hardly fit for rattlesnakes, much less one of the Southwest's greatest concentrations of wildlife. The plants that do find purchase in the parched washes and small canyons along the road—forbiddingly named hardies such as creosote bush, tarbush, and white thorn—serve notice that you are indeed within the northernmost finger of the great Chihuahuan Desert, which covers southern New Mexico and southwestern Texas, and runs deep into Mexico.

However, to the east of the interstate is the green-margined Rio Grande. In the midst of such a blasted landscape, the river stands out as an inviting beacon to wildlife, and nowhere does it shine more brightly than at Bosque del Apache's 7,000 acres of carefully managed riparian habitat, which includes marshlands, meadows, agricultural fields, arrow-weed thickets on the riverbanks, and big old-growth cottonwoods lining what were once the oxbows of the river. The refuge supports a riot of wildlife, including all the characteristic mammals and reptiles of the Southwest (mule deer, jackrabbits, and coyotes are common), and about 377 species of birds.

A visit here during the peak winter season—from November to March—is one of the most consistently thrilling wildlife spectacles you can see anywhere in the lower 48 states, especially if you're an avid bird-watcher. Bosque del Apache is, you might say, the LAX of the Central Flyway, one of four paths that migratory birds follow every year between their summer breeding grounds in the tundral north and wintering grounds in the southern United States, Mexico, and even as far away as South America—and many of these birds either stop over here to recharge their batteries or settle down for the winter.

It's not enough to say that hundreds of species of birds are on hand. The wonder is in the sheer numbers of them. In early December the refuge may harbor as many as 45,000 snow geese, 57,000 ducks of many different species, and 18,000 sandhill cranes—huge, ungainly birds that nonetheless have a special majesty in flight, pinkish in the sun at dawn or dusk. Plenty of raptors are also about—numerous red-tailed hawks and northern harriers (sometimes called marsh hawks), Cooper's hawks and kestrels, and even bald and golden eagles—as well as Bosque del Apache's many year-round avian residents: pheasants and quail, wild turkeys, and much-mythologized roadrunners (*El Paisano,* in Mexican folklore). Everyone will be mesmerized by the huge societies of sandhills, ducks, and geese, going about their daily business of feeding, gabbling, quarreling, honking, and otherwise making an immense racket.

The refuge has a 12-mile auto tour loop, which you should drive very slowly; the south half of the loop travels past numerous water impoundments, where the majority of the ducks and geese hang out, and the north half has the meadows and farmland, where you'll see the roadrunners and other land birds, and where the cranes and geese feed from midmorning through the afternoon.

A few special experiences bear further explanation. Dawn is definitely the best time to be here—songbirds are far more active in the first hours of the day, and the cranes and geese take flight en masse. This last is not to be missed. Dusk, when the birds return to the water, is also a good time. At either dawn or dusk, find your way to one of the observation decks and wait for what birders call the "fly out" (off the water to the fields) or "fly in" (from the fields to the water).

Don't despair if you can't be at the Bosque del Apache during the prime winter months, for it's a special place any time of year. By April, the geese and ducks have flown north, and the refuge drains the water impoundments to allow the marsh plants to regenerate; the resulting mud flats are an ideal feeding ground for the migrating shorebirds that arrive in April and May.

If you'd like to stretch your legs a bit, check out the **Chupadera Peak Trail,** which follows a 2.5-mile loop or a 10-mile loop to a high point overlooking the refuge. Ask for directions at the visitor center.

JUST THE FACTS The Bosque del Apache National Wildlife Refuge is about a 1½-hour drive from Albuquerque. Follow I-25 for 9 miles south of Socorro, and then take the San Antonio exit. At the main intersection of San Antonio, turn south onto NM 1. In 3 miles, you'll be on refuge lands, and another 4 miles will bring you to the excellent visitor center, which has a small museum with interpretive displays and a large shelf of field guides, natural histories, and other books of interest for visitors to New Mexico. The visitor center is open from 7:30am to 4pm weekdays, and from 8am to 4:30pm weekends. The refuge itself is open daily year-round, from 1 hour before sunrise to 1 hour after sunset. Admission is $3 per vehicle. For more information, contact **Bosque del Apache National Wildlife Refuge,** P.O. Box 1246, Socorro, NM 87801 (✆ **575/835-1828;** www.fws.gov/southwest/refuges/newmex/bosque).

10 TRUTH OR CONSEQUENCES

58 miles N of Las Cruces; 62 miles SW of Socorro; 131 miles S of Albuquerque

Originally known as Hot Springs, after the therapeutic mineral springs bubbling up near the river, the town took the name Truth or Consequences—usually shortened to "T or C"—in 1950. That was the year that Ralph Edwards, producer of the popular radio and television program *Truth or Consequences,* began his weekly broadcast with these words: "I wish that some town in the United States liked and respected our show so much that it would like to change its name to Truth or Consequences." The reward to any city willing to do so was to become the site of the 10th-anniversary broadcast of the program, which would put it on the national map in a big way. The locals voted for the name change, which has survived three protest elections over the years.

Although the TV program was canceled decades ago, Ralph Edwards continued to return for the annual **Truth or Consequences Fiesta,** the first weekend of May. He died

Fun Facts Next Stop: Space

Fasten your seat belt and settle back for an orbit or two of Earth—that's what space-minded folks, such as New Mexico Governor Bill Richardson and British tycoon Richard Branson foresee as a reality soon. Space tourists would take off from the proposed $225-million Airport America near Truth or Consequences. In its embryonic stages now, the spaceport will include one or more runways, hangars, a control building, and launch pads. The first test flights took place in 2007, while the completion date for some facilities at the spaceport is 2010.

When it's complete, Branson plans to headquarter Virgin Galactic here. Currently Virgin is selling tickets for $200,000 apiece for a 2½-hour flight, including 5 minutes of weightlessness. The first of these flights will likely fly out of the Mojave Airport in California, where SpaceShipOne became the first privately manned rocket to reach space in 2004. Virgin Galactic has contracted to build a fleet of rockets called SpaceShipTwo, with hopes of initiating tourist flights in the upcoming years. For updates, log onto www.virgingalactic.com or www.edd.state.nm.us.

in 2005. Another popular annual festival is **Geronimo Days,** the second weekend of October. Despite its festive roots, T or C seems to have an identity crisis—perhaps a consequence of giving up your name for the fame and fortune of television. The city displays a forlorn quality, possibly due to the struggling economy. However, in recent years, a few of the bathhouses have undergone renovation, and a number of galleries and restaurants have opened up, bringing new life to the town.

ESSENTIALS

GETTING THERE From Albuquerque, take I-25 south (2½ hr.). From Las Cruces, take I-25 north (1¼ hr.). Though no commercial flight service exists, those who fly themselves may contact the **Truth or Consequences Municipal Airport,** Old North Hwy. 85 (✆ **575/894-6199**).

VISITOR INFORMATION The **visitor information center** is at the corner of Main (Business Loop 25) and Foch streets in downtown Truth or Consequences. Also there is the **Truth or Consequences & Sierra County Chamber of Commerce,** P.O. Box 31, Truth or Consequences, NM 87901 (✆ **575/894-3536;** www.truthorconsequencesnm.net).

CITY LAYOUT This year-round resort town and retirement community of 7,500 is spread along the Rio Grande, between the Elephant Butte and Caballo reservoirs, two of the three largest bodies of water in the state. Business Loop 25 branches off from I-25 to wind through the city, splitting into Main Street (one-way west) and South Broadway (one-way east) in the downtown area. Third Avenue connects T or C with the Elephant Butte resort community, 5 miles east.

TAKING THE WATERS AT THE HISTORIC HOT SPRINGS

The town's "original" attraction is its hot springs. The entire downtown area is located over a table of odorless hot mineral water, 98° to 115°F (37°–46°C), that bubbles to the surface through wells or pools. The first bathhouse was built in the 1880s; most of the half-dozen historic spas operating today date from the 1930s. Generally open from morning to early evening, these spas welcome visitors for soaks and massages. Baths of 20 minutes or longer start at $7 per person.

The chamber of commerce has information on all the local spas (see "Essentials," above). Among them is **Sierra Grande Lodge & Spa ★★**, 501 McAdoo St. (✆ **575/894-6976;** www.sierragrandelodge.com), where Geronimo himself is rumored to have taken a break. (See "Where to Stay in & Around Truth or Consequences," below.) **Artesian Bath House,** 312 Marr St. (✆ **575/894-2684**), is quite clean and has an RV park on the premises.

I highly recommend the **Hay-Yo-Kay Hot Springs ★**, 300 Austin St. (✆ **575/894-2228;** www.hay-yo-kay.com). It has natural-flow pools (versus tubs filled with spring water). The tub rooms are private and gracefully tiled. The Long House, a cooler tub, is the largest in town and can hold up to 20 people. Hay-Yo-Kay is open Wednesday through Sunday 11am to 7pm. Massages and reflexology are also available.

A MUSEUM & MORE

Geronimo Springs Museum Outside this museum is Geronimo's Spring, where the great Apache shaman is said to have taken his warriors to bathe their battle wounds. Turtleback Mountain, looming over the Rio Grande east of the city, is believed to have been sacred to Native Americans.

Exhibits include prehistoric Mimbres pottery (A.D. 950–1250); the Spanish Heritage Room, updated and renovated, featuring artifacts of the first families of Sierra County; and artists' work, including historical murals and sculptured bronzes. An authentic miner's cabin has been moved here from the nearby mountains. The Ralph Edwards Wing contains the history and highlights of the annual fiestas and celebrates the city's name change, including television footage from the shows filmed in T or C.

211 Main St. ✆ **575/894-6600.** Admission $4 adults, $2 students; family rates available. DISC, MC, V. Mon–Sat 9am–5pm; Sun 11am–4pm.

SOUTH OF TRUTH OR CONSEQUENCES Thirty-two miles from Truth or Consequences, via I-25 south to NM 152, then west, is **Hillsboro ★**, another ghost town that's fast losing its ghosts to a small invasion of artists and craftspeople, antiques shops, and galleries. This town boomed after an 1877 gold strike nearby, and, during its heyday, it produced $6 million in silver and gold. It was the county seat from 1884 to 1938. You may want to plan your drive to include breakfast or lunch at **Hillsboro General Store & Country Café ★**, on NM 152 in the center of town (✆ **575/895-5306**). Serving excellent burgers and burritos in a historic general store ambience, this spot also has some of the best pie in the region; it's called bumbleberry and combines many berries in a flaky crust. Open daily for breakfast and lunch.

WHERE TO STAY IN & AROUND TRUTH OR CONSEQUENCES

Elephant Butte Inn ★ For a comfortable stay and a unique experience, try Elephant Butte Inn. It sits above Elephant Butte Lake and has panoramic views as well as a relaxing resortlike feel. Recent years have brought a face-lift to many of the rooms. It caters to boaters, fishers, and other relaxation lovers. Rooms are standard size, furnished with medium-firm king- or queen-size beds. Bathrooms are small but functional, with an outer sink vanity. I recommend the lakeside view, where a big grassy lawn stretches down to tennis courts. These rooms are a bit more upscale, with unique decor in each, and are equipped with plasma TVs, fridges, and microwaves. For golfers, packages are available that include greens fees at the new Sierra del Rio Golf Course at Turtleback Mountain Resort. The new Ivory Spa here offers a full range of treatments, including reasonably priced spa packages.

401 NM 195 (P.O. Box 996), Elephant Butte, NM 87935. © **575/744-5431.** Fax 575/744-5044. www.elephantbutteinn.com. 45 units. Mid-Sept to Apr $90–$129 double; May to early Sept $80–$100 double. Golf and spa packages available. AE, DC, DISC, MC, V. Pets welcome $15–$20 per visit. **Amenities:** Restaurant; bar; courtesy computer; outdoor pool; room service; spa; tennis courts; . *In room:* A/C, TV, hair dryer, Wi-Fi.

Sierra Grande Lodge & Spa ★★ Prepare yourself for a sensual oasis at this resort in southern New Mexico. The biggest draw is the springs. Nowhere else in the state can you stay in luxury while partaking of warm, healing waters rich in minerals. The medium-size rooms in this renovated 1920s lodge have handcrafted furnishings, and many have balconies. All have comfortable beds with good linens. Bathrooms are small but functional. Suites have in-room Jacuzzis. A special casita, with its own outdoor tub, is so popular that it's reserved months in advance. The spa offers a full range of treatments. The Sierra Grande Restaurant opened to wide acclaim, but has since only remained open sporadically.

501 McAdoo St., Truth or Consequences, NM 87901. © **575/894-6976.** www.sierragrandelodge.com. 18 units. $99–$129 double Sun–Thurs; $129–$159 double Fri–Sat; $259 suite. AE, DISC, MC, V. **Amenities:** Restaurant; spa. *In room:* A/C, TV, DVD player upon request, hair dryer, Wi-Fi (on guest room balcony as well as in lobby and on patio).

Camping

Elephant Butte Lake State Park (© **575/744-5923**) welcomes backpackers and RVs alike, with 200 developed campsites, 150 RV hookups, picnic tables, and access points for swimming, hiking, boating, and fishing. Kids love the playground.

Not far from Elephant Butte Lake is **Monticello Point RV Park** (© **575/894-6468**), which offers tenting and 69 sites with full hookups. Laundry and grocery facilities are also on the premises, as are restrooms with showers. To reach Monticello Point, take I-25 to exit 89, and proceed 5½ miles east on the paved road—follow the signs.

Lakeside RV Park and Lodging (© **575/744-5996**), also near Elephant Butte, has 50 sites, two overflow sites (all 52 are full hookups), as well as a recreation room with cable and laundry facilities. When you are headed south on I-25, the RV park is 4 miles southeast of the I-25 and NM 195 junction (exit 83) on NM 195. To reach the RV park when you're headed north on I-25, take exit 79, go half a mile east on the paved road, 1½ miles north on NM 181, then 1½ miles east on NM 171, and finally a quarter-mile south on NM 195.

Camping is also available at **Caballo Lake State Park** and **Percha Dam State Park.** For information on either park, call © **575/743-3942** or visit **www.nmparks.com**.

WHERE TO DINE IN & AROUND TRUTH OR CONSEQUENCES

Café Bella Luca ★★ TUSCAN/ITALIAN Set in a historic building renovated to have a clean look, with high ceilings, stained concrete floors, and warm earth tones, this new restaurant serves some of the best food in the region. Chef Byron Harrel hand-makes all the sauces and breads here, and the seafood is flown in fresh. For breakfast, locals fill the place to drink espresso, eat pastries, and check e-mail (the restaurant has Wi-Fi). Lunch or dinner might start with crispy fried calamari or a crab cake. At lunch, one of the many sandwiches is a good bet. I've enjoyed the turkey pancetta on foccacia, with house-made fries or a salad. The pasta Alfredo with grilled shrimp is also nice. At dinner, the seafood *puttanesca* has a nice bite, and the roasted grouper is delectable. An extensive wine and beer list, with organic options, accompanies the menu, as do a variety of house-made desserts.

303 Jones St. ✆ **575/894-9866.** Reservations recommended Fri–Sat. Main courses $6–$10 lunch; $10–$23 dinner. AE, DISC, MC, V. Wed–Mon 11am–4pm; Wed–Thurs and Sun–Mon 5–9pm; Fri–Sat 5–10pm.

La Cocina Kids AMERICAN/NEW MEXICAN A real locals' place, this restaurant serves decent New Mexican food in a festive atmosphere. The *tostadas* (crispy tortillas covered with beans and meat) and chile rellenos are tasty, but my favorite is the cheese enchiladas. For dessert, try the *sopaipillas.* Kids like the big booths and their own quesadillas and tacos.

1 Lakeview Dr. (at Date St.). ✆ **575/894-6499.** Reservations recommended Fri–Sat. Main courses $8–$20 lunch and dinner. DISC, MC, V. Mon–Thurs 10:30am–9pm; Fri–Sun 10:30am–10pm.

Los Arcos Steak & Lobster ★ AMERICAN This spacious hacienda-style restaurant, fronted by a lovely desert garden, is intimate and friendly in atmosphere, as if you're at an old friend's home. Its steaks are regionally famous; my choice is always the filet mignon, served with salad and your choice of potato or rice. The fish dishes are also good. You may want to try a fresh catch, such as walleye pike or catfish, served on weekends. The restaurant also has a fine dessert list and cordial selection. During warmer months, diners enjoy the outdoor patio.

1400 Date St. ✆ **575/894-6200.** Main courses $11–$40. AE, DC, DISC, MC, V. Sun–Thurs 5–9:30pm; Fri–Sat 5–10:30pm.

11 LAS CRUCES

60 miles SW of Alamogordo; 112 miles S of Socorro; 180 miles S of Albuquerque

Picture a valley full of weathered wooden crosses marking graves of settlers brutally murdered by Apaches, and behind them mountains with peaks so jagged they resemble organ pipes. Such was the scene that caused people to begin calling this city Las Cruces, meaning "the crosses." Even today, the place has a mysterious presence, its rich history haunting it still. Reminders of such characters as Billy the Kid, who was sentenced to death in this area, and Pancho Villa, who spent time here, are present throughout the region.

Established in 1849 on El Camino Real, the "royal highway" between Santa Fe and Mexico City, Las Cruces became a supply center for miners prospecting the Organ Mountains, and for soldiers stationed at nearby Fort Selden. Today, it's New Mexico's second-largest urban area, with 86,268 people. It's noted as an agricultural center, especially for its cotton, pecans, and chiles; as a regional transportation hub; and as the gateway to the White Sands Missile Range and other defense installations.

Las Cruces manages to survive within a desert landscape that gets only 8 inches of moisture a year, pulling enough moisture from the Rio Grande, which runs through, to irrigate a broad swath of valley.

ESSENTIALS

GETTING THERE From Albuquerque, take I-25 south (4 hr.). From El Paso, take I-10 north (3/4 hr.). From Tucson, take I-25 east (5 hr.).

Las Cruces International Airport (✆ **575/541-2471;** www.las-cruces.org/facilities/airport), 8 miles west of the city, offers no commercial flights at this time. **El Paso International Airport** (✆ **915/772-4271;** www.elpasointernationalairport.com), 47 miles south, has daily flights to Albuquerque, Phoenix, Dallas, and Houston, among other cities. The **Las Cruces Shuttle Service,** P.O. Box 3172, Las Cruces, NM 88003 (✆ **800/288-1784** or 575/525-1784; www.lascrucesshuttle.com), provides service between the El Paso airport and Las Cruces. It leaves Las Cruces 12 times daily between 5am and 9:30pm for a charge of $40 one-way or $70 round-trip per person, with large discounts for additional passengers traveling together. A $9 charge is added for pickup or drop-off at places other than its regular stops at major hotels. Connections can also be made three times a day from Las Cruces to Deming and Silver City.

VISITOR INFORMATION The **Las Cruces Convention and Visitors Bureau** is at 211 N. Water St., Las Cruces, NM 88001 (✆ **877/266-8252** or 575/541-2444; www.lascrucescvb.org). The **Greater Las Cruces Chamber of Commerce,** 760 W. Picacho Ave., can be reached at P.O. Drawer 519, Las Cruces, NM 88005 (✆ **575/524-1968;** www.lascruces.org).

WHAT TO SEE & DO IN LAS CRUCES

On a hot day, when the church bells are ringing and you're wandering the brick streets of **Mesilla** ★★, you may, for a moment, slip back into the late 16th century—or certainly feel as though you have. This village on Las Cruces's southwestern flank was established in the late 1500s by Mexican colonists. It became the crossroads of El Camino Real and the Butterfield Overland Mail route. The Gadsden Purchase, which annexed Mesilla to the United States and fixed the current international boundaries of New Mexico and Arizona, was signed here in 1854.

Mesilla's most notorious resident, William Bonney, otherwise known as Billy the Kid, was sentenced to death at the county courthouse here. He was sent back to Lincoln, New Mexico, to be hanged, but escaped before the sentence was carried out. Legendary hero Pat Garrett eventually tracked down and killed the Kid at Fort Sumner; later, Garrett was mysteriously murdered in an arroyo just outside Las Cruces. He is buried in the local Masonic cemetery.

Thick-walled adobe buildings, which once protected residents against Apache attacks, now house art galleries, restaurants, museums, and gift shops. Throughout Mesilla, colorful red-chile *ristras* decorate homes and businesses. On Sundays during the summer, locals sell crafts and baked goods, and mariachi bands play.

Places of Note in Mesilla

For a fun and easy jaunt that will familiarize you with the history and architecture of this interesting village, purchase the booklet *A Walking Tour of Mesilla, NM,* sold at shops around the plaza and at the **J. Paul Taylor Visitor Center,** in the Mesilla Town Hall, 2231 Avenida de Mesilla (✆ **575/524-3262,** ext. 117), where you'll also find period photos and plenty of brochures on the area, as well as clean public restrooms. A good source for Mesilla events is **www.oldmesilla.org**.

Other Attractions

Las Cruces Museum of Art This museum houses galleries, art studios, and classrooms, with frequently changing exhibitions of contemporary art in a variety of media. It offers art classes year-round. Two recent exhibitions included traveling shows by Salvador Dalí and Auguste Rodin.

490 N. Water St. ✆ **575/541-2137.** http://museums.las-cruces.org. Free admission. Mon–Fri 9am–4pm; Sat 9am–1pm.

Las Cruces Museum of Natural History (Kids) This small city-funded museum offers a variety of exhibits, changed quarterly, that emphasize science and natural history. The museum features live animals of the Chihuahuan Desert, hands-on science activities, and a small native plant garden. The Cenozoic Shop offers scientific toys and books about the region. Exhibits, such as "Insects and Bugs" and "Every Body Eats," change every few months. This museum has plans to move to a new venue in the downtown mall, though at press time an opening date had not been set.

Mesilla Valley Mall, 700 S. Telshor Blvd. ✆ **575/522-3120.** http://museums.las-cruces.org. Free admission. Mon–Thurs and Sat 10am–5pm; Fri 10am–8pm; Sun 1–5pm.

New Mexico Farm and Ranch Heritage Museum ★★ This 47-acre interactive museum brings to life the 3,000-year history of farming, ranching, and rural living in New Mexico. It's housed within a huge structure that's designed to look like a hacienda-style barn, with a U-shaped courtyard in back and exhibits surrounding it on expansive grounds. The museum displays such relics as a 1937 John Deere tractor and a number of examples of how ranchers "make do," ingeniously combining tools such as a tractor seat with a milk barrel to come up with a chair. Visitors can watch a cow being milked, stroll along corrals filled with livestock, enjoy several gardens, and drop by the blacksmith shop. Annual events at the museum are the La Fiesta de San Ysidro in May and Cowboy Days the third weekend in October.

4100 Dripping Springs Rd. (follow University Ave. east beyond the edge of town). ✆ **575/522-4100.** www.frhm.org. Admission $5 adults, $3 seniors 60 and over, $2 children 5–17; free for children 4 and under. Mon–Sat 9am–5pm; Sun noon–5pm.

San Albino Church ★★ This is one of the oldest churches in the Mesilla valley. The present structure was built in 1906 on the foundation of the original church, constructed in 1851. It was named for St. Albin, a medieval English bishop of North Africa, on whose day an important irrigation ditch from the Rio Grande was completed. The church bells date from the early 1870s; the pews were made in Taos of Philippine mahogany.

North side of Old Mesilla Plaza. ✆ **575/526-9349.** Free admission; donations appreciated. Usually Mon–Sat 1–3pm (call ahead). English-language Mass Sat 5:30pm and Sun 11am; Spanish Mass Sun 8am, Mon–Fri 7am.

Shopping

Shoppers should be aware that in Las Cruces, Monday is a notoriously quiet day. Some stores close for the day, so it's best to call ahead before heading to a specific store.

For art, visit **Lundeen's Inn of the Arts ★**, 618 S. Alameda Blvd. (✆ **575/526-3326;** www.innofthearts.com), displaying the works of about 30 Southwest painters, sculptors, and potters; **Rising Sky Artworks,** 415 E. Foster (✆ **575/525-8454;** www.risingsky pottery.com), which features works in clay by local and Western artists; and the **William Bonney Gallery,** 2060 Calle de Parian, just off the southeast corner of Old Mesilla Plaza (✆ **575/526-8275**), with a variety of Southwestern art.

For books, try **Mesilla Book Center,** in an 1856 mercantile building on the west side of Old Mesilla Plaza (✆ **575/526-6220**).

For native crafts and jewelry, check out **Silver Assets ★**, 1948 Calle de Santiago (✆ **575/523-8747;** www.silverassetsonline.com), 1½ blocks east of San Albino Church in Mesilla. Set back from the plaza itself, look for **Galeri Azul,** Mesilla Plaza (✆ **575/523-8783**), where you'll find colorful handmade altars by Ernie Bean, whimsical T-shirts and sun hats, and kitschy jewelry.

Mesilla Valley Mall is a full-service shopping center at 700 S. Telshor Blvd., just off the I-25 interchange with Lohman Avenue (✆ **575/522-1001;** www.mesillavalleymall.com), with well over 100 stores. The mall is open Monday through Saturday from 10am to 9pm and Sunday from noon to 6pm.

LAS CRUCES AFTER DARK

National recording artists frequently perform at NMSU's **Pan Am Center** (✆ **575/646-1420;** www.nmsu.edu). The **NMSU Music Department** (✆ **575/646-2421**) offers free jazz, classical, and pop concerts from August to May, and the **Las Cruces Symphony Orchestra** (✆ **575/646-3709;** www.lascrucessymphony.com) often performs here as well.

If you'd like a cocktail in a fun atmosphere, a new option has opened up. **Azul Nightclub** ★, in the Hotel Encanto, 705 S. Telshor Blvd. (✆ **866/383-0443** or 575/522-4300; www.hhandr.com). In a contemporary setting reminiscent of a Spanish nightclub, the city's youngish business set has drinks and hors 'd oeuvres.

EXPLORING THE AREA

NORTH OF LAS CRUCES The town of **Hatch,** 39 miles north via I-25 or 34 miles north via NM 185, calls itself the "chile capital of the world." It's the center of a 22,000-acre agricultural belt that grows and processes more chile than anywhere else in the world. The annual Hatch Chile Festival, over Labor Day weekend, celebrates the harvest. For information, call the **Hatch Chamber of Commerce** (✆ **575/267-5050**).

Fort Selden State Monument is 15 miles north of Las Cruces between I-25 (exit 19) and NM 185. Founded in 1865, Fort Selden housed the famous Black Cavalry, the "Buffalo Soldiers," who protected settlers from marauding natives. It was subsequently the boyhood home of Gen. Douglas MacArthur, whose father, Arthur, was in charge of troops patrolling the U.S.-Mexico border in the 1880s. The fort closed permanently in 1891. Today, elegantly eroded ruins remain. The monument is open from 8:30am to 5pm Wednesday to Monday; admission is $3 for adults and free for children age 16 and under. For more information, call ✆ **575/526-8911** or visit **www.nmmonuments.org**. Adjacent to the state monument, **Leasburg Dam State Park** (✆ **575/524-4068**) offers picnicking, camping, canoeing, and fishing.

SOUTH OF LAS CRUCES **Stahmann Farms,** 10 miles south of La Mesilla on NM 28, is one of the world's largest single producers of pecans. Several million pounds are harvested, mostly during November, from orchards in the bed of an ancient lake. **Stahmann's Country Store** ★ (✆ **800/654-6887** or 575/525-3470; www.stahmanns.com) sells pecans, pecan candy, ice cream, and other specialty foods, and it has a small cafe. It's open Monday through Saturday from 9am to 6pm, Sunday from 11am to 5pm. If you'd like to stay south of Las Cruces, book a night or two at **Casa de Sueños** ★, 405 Mountain Vista Rd., La Union, NM 88021 (✆ **575/874-9166;** www.casaofdreams.com). Set high on a plain overlooking the Rio Grande River Valley, with the Franklin Mountains in the distance, it offers atmospheric Southwest-style rooms about a half-hour south of Las Cruces, with good access to El Paso.

EAST OF LAS CRUCES The **Organ Mountains,** so-called because they resemble the pipes of a church organ, draw inevitable comparisons to Wyoming's Grand Tetons. Organ Peak, at 9,119 feet, is the highest point in Doña Ana County.

The **Aguirre Springs Recreation Area** (✆ **575/525-4300;** www.blm.gov.nm), off US 70, on the western slope of the Organ Mountains, is one of the most spectacular places I've ever camped. Operated by the Bureau of Land Management, the camping and picnic sites sit at the base of the jagged Organ Mountains. Visitors to the area can hike, camp, picnic, or ride horseback (no horse rentals on site). If you'd like to hike, don't miss the **Baylor Pass** trail, which crosses along the base of the Organ peaks, up through a pass, and over to the Las Cruces side. Though the hike is 6 miles one-way, just over 2 miles will get you to the pass, where there's a meadow with amazing views.

WHERE TO STAY IN & AROUND LAS CRUCES

Hotel Encanto de Las Cruces ★★★ Spanish Colonial elegance defines this seven-story hotel on the east side of town, about a 15-minute drive from Mesilla, with an incredible view of the city and the Organ Mountains. The hotel was built in 1986, and implemented a major remodel in 2006, including new bedding and furnishings, all with a lovely old-world Mexican/colonial motif. The lobby has a tiered fountain, colorful tile, and museum-quality furnishings. Rooms are spacious and outfitted with hand-crafted furniture and comfortable beds with good linens. Photography by the noted artist Miguel Gandert dresses the walls. Bathrooms are medium size, with granite countertops and Aveda bath products. Some rooms flank the pool and have little patios. The service here is excellent. **Café España** serves breakfast, lunch, and dinner, in an elegant Spanish Colonial ambience, and the Azul Nightclub offers drinks with a contemporary Southwest flair.

705 S. Telshor Blvd., Las Cruces, NM 88011. ✆ **866/383-0443** or 575/522-4300. Fax 575/521-4707. www.hhandr.com. 203 units. $109–$159 double; $179–$199 suite. AE, DC, DISC, MC, V. Pets welcome ($15 per night). **Amenities:** Restaurant; bar; health club; Jacuzzi; heated outdoor pool; room service. *In room:* A/C, TV, hair dryer, Wi-Fi.

La Quinta ★ Five minutes from Old Mesilla, this chain hotel provides relatively quiet and very comfortable rooms with plenty of amenities. The clean and well-designed rooms range from medium to large, all with desks and medium-size bathrooms. An outdoor pool sits within a comfortable courtyard, an important addition in this warm climate. Guests eat their continental breakfast in a bright garden room off the lobby. When you reserve here, ask for one of the "annex" rooms, which are the largest and newest. Also, be aware that trains pass near this area at night. A few new casual dining restaurants have opened across the street.

790 Av. de Mesilla, Las Cruces, NM 88005. ✆ **800/531-5900** or 575/524-0331. Fax 575/525-8360. www.laquinta.com. $78–$97 double. Rates include continental breakfast. AE, DISC, MC, V. Pets welcome (free). **Amenities:** Health club; outdoor pool. *In room:* A/C, TV, hair dryer, Wi-Fi.

A Bed & Breakfast

The Lundeen Inn of the Arts ★★ This inn is a late-1890s adobe home, with whitewashed walls, narrow alleys, and arched doorways. It's a composite of rooms stretching across 10,000 square feet of floor space. There's a wide range of rooms, each named for an artist. My favorites are in the main part of the house, set around a two-story garden room, with elegant antiques and arched windows. Most rooms are medium size with comfortably firm beds dressed in good linens. Bathrooms are generally small and simple but clean. The inn is also an art gallery, displaying the works of about 30 Southwestern painters, sculptors, and potters. Breakfast includes fresh fruit and such specialties as pumpkin pancakes and huevos rancheros.

618 S. Alameda Blvd., Las Cruces, NM 88005. ✆ **888/526-3326** or 575/526-3326. Fax 575/647-1334. www.innofthearts.com. 7 units. $85–$99 double; $85–$105 suite. Rates include full breakfast. AE, DC, DISC, MC, V. Pets welcome. *In room:* A/C, TV, hair dryer, Wi-Fi.

Camping

Quite a few campgrounds are within or near Las Cruces. All the ones listed here include full hookups for RVs, tenting areas, and recreation areas. **Best View RV Park** (✆ **575/526-6555**) also offers cabins and laundry and grocery facilities. From the junction of I-10 and US 70 (exit 135), go 1½ miles east on US 70, and then half a block south on Weinrich Road.

Another option is **Dalmont's RV Park** (✆ **575/523-2992**). If you're coming from the west, when you reach the junction of I-25 and I-10, go 2½ miles northwest on I-10 to the Main Street exit, and then go 2 blocks west on Valley Drive. If you're coming from the east, at the junction of I-10 and Main Street, go a quarter-mile north on Main Street and then 1 block west on Valley Drive. To reach **Siesta RV Park** (✆ **575/523-6816**), at the junction of I-10 and NM 28, take exit 140 and go half a mile south on NM 28. **Leasburg Dam State Park** (✆ **575/524-4068**) is a smaller park that also offers RV and tent camping, but it has no laundry or grocery facilities. A general country store is about 1 mile down the road, and hiking and fishing are available.

WHERE TO DINE IN & AROUND LAS CRUCES

Expensive

Double Eagle ★★ CONTINENTAL When I was a kid, whenever we went to Las Cruces, we always made a special trip to this elegant restaurant imbued with Old West style. I'm pleased to say that it's still a quality place to dine. This 150-year-old Territorial-style hacienda, once the governor's mansion, is on the National Register of Historic Places. Built around a central courtyard, it has numerous rooms, one of which is said to be frequented by a woman's ghost. Another room has a 30-foot-long bar with Corinthian columns in gold leaf, Gay Nineties oil paintings, and 18-armed brass chandeliers hung with Baccarat crystals. The menu is quite varied and includes pasta, chicken, fish, and steak dishes. My favorite is the filet mignon bordelaise, served on a French rusk with a rich red-wine sauce. The Columbia River salmon, served with a triple citrus-chipotle-chile sauce, is also delicious. All entrees come with salad, vegetable, and choice of potato or pasta. There's a full bar, from which you might want to order a mango margarita, and for dessert you can end it all with the Death by Chocolate Cake.

2355 Calle de Guadalupe, on the east side of Mesilla Plaza. ✆ **575/523-6700.** www.double-eagle-messilla.com. Reservations recommended. Main courses $8–$15 lunch, $14–$36 dinner. AE, DC, DISC, MC, V. Mon–Sat 11am–10pm; Sun 11am–9pm.

Inexpensive

La Posta de Mesilla (Kids) NEW MEXICAN/STEAKS If you're on the Mesilla Plaza and want to eat New Mexican food for not much money, walk in here. The restaurant occupies a mid-18th-century adobe building that is the only surviving stagecoach station of the Butterfield Overland Mail route from Tipton, Missouri, to San Francisco. Kit Carson, Pancho Villa, Gen. Douglas MacArthur, and Billy the Kid were all here at one time. The entrance leads through a jungle of tall plants beneath a Plexiglas roof, past a tank of piranhas and a noisy aviary of macaws and Amazon parrots, to nine dining rooms with bright, festive decor. (Kids love this and their own menu selections.) The tables are basic, with vinyl and metal chairs. Try the enchiladas, which come with a nice chile sauce.

Avoid the dry rellenos and the soggy tacos. The tostadas (tortilla cups filled with beans and topped with chile and cheese) are a house specialty. There's a full-service bar.

2410 Calle de San Albino (southeast corner of Old Mesilla Plaza). ✆ **575/524-3524.** Reservations recommended. Main courses $6–$17. AE, DC, DISC, MC, V. Sun and Tues–Thurs 11am–9pm; Fri–Sat 11am–9:30pm.

Lorenzo's Restaurante Italiano de Old Mesilla ★★ SICILIAN In a spirited building with lots of brick and with murals depicting rural scenes on the walls, the restaurant offers the feel of a Sicilian village cafe, a good indication of the quality of the food here. Rather than fancy Italian food like you find in many cities, this restaurant serves traditional Sicilian meals, with lots of red sauces and homemade pasta. It's big with locals, and it fills up, so you may want to make reservations. The atmosphere is jovial and the service is good, though it can be a bit slow because the food is cooked in-house. You can't go wrong with standards such as spaghetti marinara or lasagna; for something more adventurous, try the linguini and clams. Meals are served with bread and a salad of freshly tossed greens. Wash it down with a carafe of Chianti or your favorite beer.

1750 Calle de Mercado #4 (Onate Plaza, a block from Old Mesilla Plaza). ✆ **575/525-3174.** Reservations recommended. Main courses $8–$16. AE, DISC, MC, V. Mon–Thurs 11am–9pm; Fri–Sat 11am–9:30pm; Sun 11–8:30pm.

12 DEMING & LORDSBURG

Deming: 44 miles SE of Silver City, 52 miles W of Las Cruces, 193 miles SW of Albuquerque; Lordsburg: 52 miles W of Deming, 36 miles SW of Silver City

New Mexico's least populated corner is this one, which includes the "boot heel" of the Gadsden Purchase, poking 40 miles down toward Mexico (a great place for backpacking). These two railroad towns, an hour apart on I-10, see a lot of traffic; but whereas **Deming** (pop. 14,500) is thriving as a ranching and retirement center, **Lordsburg** has had a steady population of about 3,379 for years. This is a popular area for rockhounds, aficionados of ghost towns, and history buffs. **Columbus,** 32 miles south of Deming, was attacked by the Mexican bandit-revolutionary Pancho Villa in 1916. The U.S. military retaliated by sending 10,000 troops into Mexico to find him, to no avail.

ESSENTIALS

GETTING THERE From Las Cruces, take I-10 west (1 hr. to Deming, 2 hr. to Lordsburg). From Tucson, Arizona, take I-10 east (3 hr. to Lordsburg, 4 hr. to Deming).

Great Lakes Airlines (✆ **575/388-4115**) flies daily to **Grant County Airport** (✆ **575/388-4554**), 15 miles south of Silver City, near Hurley. The **Las Cruces Shuttle Service,** P.O. Box 3172, Las Cruces, NM 88003 (✆ **800/288-1784** or 575/525-1784; www.lascrucesshuttle.com), runs several times daily between Deming and the El Paso airport by way of Las Cruces.

VISITOR INFORMATION The **Deming–Luna County Chamber of Commerce** is at 800 E. Pine St., Deming (✆ **800/848-4955** or 575/546-2674; www.demingchamber.com). The **Greater Hidalgo Area Chamber of Commerce** is at 117 E. 2nd St., Lordsburg, NM 88045 (✆ **575/542-9864**).

WHAT TO SEE & DO IN & AROUND DEMING

Deming Luna Mimbres Museum ★ Deming was the meeting place of the second east-west railroad to connect the Pacific and Atlantic coasts, and that heritage is recalled in this museum, run by the Luna County Historical Society. It has a military room that contains exhibits from the Indian wars, Pancho Villa's raid, WWI and WWII, and the Korean and Vietnam wars; a room featuring the John and Mary Alice King Collection of Mimbres pottery; and a doll room with more than 800 dolls. A 5,000-square-foot adjacent space displays transportation-related exhibits, including a replica of a railroad depot, a Harvey House, and vintage firetrucks. Across the street is the Custom House, a turn-of-the-20th-century adobe home that has been turned into a walk-through exhibit.

301 S. Silver Ave., Deming. ✆ **575/546-2382.** Fax 575/544-0121. Free admission; donations encouraged. Mon–Sat 9am–4pm; Sun 1:30–4pm.

Getting Outside

At **Rockhound State Park ★**, 14 miles southeast of Deming via NM 11, visitors are encouraged to pick up and take home with them as much as 15 pounds of minerals—jasper, agate, quartz crystal, flow-banded rhyolite, and others. At the base of the Little Florida Mountains, the park is a lovely, arid, cactus-covered land with paths leading down into dry gullies and canyons. (You may have to walk a bit, as the more accessible minerals have been largely picked out.)

The campground ($10 for nonelectric hookup; $14 with electric hookup), which has shelters, restrooms, and showers, offers a distant view of mountain ranges all the way to the U.S.-Mexico border. The park also has one marked hiking trail and a playground. Admission is $5 per vehicle, and the park is open year-round from dawn to dusk. For more information, call ✆ **575/546-6182.**

Some 35 miles south of Deming is the tiny border town of **Columbus,** which looks across at Mexico. The **Pancho Villa State Park ★** here marks the last foreign invasion of American soil. A temporary fort, where a tiny garrison was housed in tents, was attacked in 1916 by 600 Mexican revolutionaries, who cut through the boundary fence at Columbus. Eighteen Americans were killed, 12 wounded; an estimated 200 Mexicans died. The Mexicans immediately retreated across their border. An American punitive expedition, headed by Gen. John J. Pershing, was launched into Mexico but got nowhere. Villa restricted his banditry to Mexico after that, and was assassinated in 1923.

The state park includes ruins of the old fort and a new visitor center and 7,000-square-foot museum offering exhibits and a film. The park also has a strikingly beautiful desert botanical garden (worth the trip alone), plus campsites, restrooms, showers, an RV dump station, and a playground. There's a $5-per-vehicle entrance fee; the park is staffed from 8am to 5pm daily. For more information, call ✆ **575/531-2711.**

Across the street from the state park is the old Southern Pacific Railroad Depot, which has been restored by the Columbus Historical Society and now houses the **Columbus Historical Museum** (✆ **575/531-2620**), which contains railroad memorabilia and exhibits on local history. Call for hours, which vary.

If you'd like to stay in Columbus, call **Martha's Place Bed & Breakfast,** Main and Lima streets (✆ **575/531-2467**). It's a two-story stucco Pueblo-style adobe painted cream and green, with Victorian touches inside. The medium-size rooms have comfortable beds and French doors leading to a balcony. Prices are $70 double. Rates include breakfast. Pets are welcome.

WHAT TO SEE & DO NEAR LORDSBURG

Visitors to Lordsburg can go **rockhounding** in this area rich in minerals of many kinds. Desert roses can be found near Summit, and agate is known to exist in many abandoned mines locally. Mine dumps, southwest of Hachita, contain lead, zinc, and gold; the Animas Mountains have manganese. Volcanic glass can be picked up in Coronado National Forest, and you can pan for gold in Gold Gulch.

Shakespeare Ghost Town (Kids) A national historic site, Shakespeare was once the home of 3,000 miners, promoters, and dealers of various kinds. Under the name Ralston, it enjoyed a silver boom in 1870. This was followed by a notorious diamond fraud in 1872, in which a mine was salted with diamonds in order to raise prices on mining stock; many notables were sucked in, particularly William Ralston, founder of the Bank of California. It enjoyed a mining revival in 1879 under its new name, Shakespeare. It was a town with no church, no newspaper, and no local law. Some serious fights resulted in hangings, from the roof timbers in the Stage Station. Since 1935, it's been privately owned by the Hill family, which has kept it uncommercialized, with no souvenir hype or gift shops. Six original buildings and two reconstructed buildings survive in various stages of repair. Two-hour guided tours are offered on a limited basis, and reenactments and living history are staged on the fourth weekends of April, June, August, and October, if performers are available. Phone to confirm the performances.

2½ miles south of Lordsburg (no street address; P.O. Box 253), Lordsburg, NM 88045. ✆ **575/542-9034.** www.shakespeareghostown.com. Admission $4 adults, $3 children 6–12; for shoot-outs and special events $5 adults, $4 children. 10am–2pm on the 2nd Sun and preceding Sat of each month. Special tours by appointment. To reach Shakespeare, drive 1½ miles south from I-10 on Main St. Just before the town cemetery, turn right, proceed a half-mile, and turn right again. Follow the dirt road another half-mile into Shakespeare.

WHERE TO STAY

In Deming

La Quinta Inn ★ True to its origins, this new whitewashed hotel provides consistent and comfortable rooms at a decent price. Each is medium size with high ceilings, redwood furniture, and earth-tone decor. The beds are comfortable and the bathrooms are spacious enough and have granite countertops. This is a good option if you like a newer-style hotel than the Holiday Inn next door.

4300 E. Pine St., Deming, NM 88030. ✆ **800/531-5900** or 575/546-0600. Fax 575/544-8207. www.laquinta.com. 58 units. $79–$105 double. Rates include continental breakfast. AE, DC, DISC, MC, V. **Amenities:** Health club; outdoor heated pool (summer). *In room:* A/C, TV, fridge, hair dryer, microwave, Wi-Fi.

In Lordsburg

Holiday Inn Express ★ This hotel remains true to the Holiday Inn Express name, providing clean and comfortable rooms at a reasonable price. This is a motel-style property, allowing you to park right outside your room. All accommodations are medium size with earth-tone-colored decor and comfortable beds. The bathrooms are small but have an outer sink vanity. Four of the rooms offer fridges and microwaves.

1408 S. Main St., Lordsburg, NM 88045. ✆ **800/HOLIDAY** [465-4329] or 575/542-3666. Fax 575/542-3665. www.hiexpress.com. 40 units. $89 double. Rates include continental breakfast. AE, DC, DISC, MC, V. Pets $20 fee. **Amenities:** Outdoor pool. *In room:* A/C, TV, hair dryer, Wi-Fi.

Camping In & Around Deming & Lordsburg

City of Rocks State Park, in Deming (✆ **575/536-2800**), has 52 campsites, 10 with electric hookups; tenting is available, and picnic tables and a hiking trail are nearby. **Dreamcatcher RV Park** (✆ **575/544-4004**), also in Deming (take exit 85, Motel Dr., off I-10 and go 1 block south on Business I-10), has 92 sites, all with full hookups. It also offers free access to a nearby swimming pool and on-site laundry facilities. **Little Vineyard RV Park** (✆ **575/546-3560**), in Deming (from I-10 take exit 85 and go 1 mile southwest on Business I-10 toward Deming), is larger than those mentioned above. It offers the same facilities as Dreamcatcher RV Park, with the addition of limited groceries, an indoor pool and hot tub, cable TV hookups, e-mail access, and a small RV parts store. The campground at **Rockhound State Park** (✆ **575/546-6182**) is picturesque and great for rockhounds who can't get enough of their hobby. RV sites (with hookups) and tenting are both available, as are shelters, restrooms, and showers.

If you'd rather camp near Lordsburg, try **Lordsburg KOA** (✆ **800/562-5772** or 575/542-8003; www.koa.com). It's in a desert setting but with shade trees, and tenting is permitted. Grocery and laundry facilities are available, in addition to a recreation room/area, a swimming pool, a playground, and horseshoes. To reach the campground, take I-10 to exit 22, and then go 1 block south; next, turn right at the Chevron station and follow the signs to the campground.

WHERE TO DINE

In Deming

Si Señor ★ NEW MEXICAN Locals crowd this downtown cafe to eat platters full of tasty New Mexican food. The interior has functional furniture and a lovely tile floor. At breakfast, try the huevos rancheros (eggs over corn tortillas, smothered in chile). The big seller here, for lunch and dinner, is the deluxe combination, with a chile relleno, a tamale, a cheese enchilada, a taco, refried beans, Spanish rice, and red or green chile. The menu also sports salads, hamburgers, and chicken and fish dishes. All come with chips and salsa, and wine and beer are served.

200 E. Pine, Deming. ✆ **575/546-3938.** Main courses $6–$10 breakfast, $5–$12 lunch and dinner. DISC, MC, V. Mon–Sat 9am–8 pm; Sun 1–10pm.

In Lordsburg

Kranberry's Family Restaurant AMERICAN/MEXICAN A friendly, casual Denny's-style family restaurant decorated with Southwestern art, Kranberry's offers American favorites, including eggs and pancakes for breakfast; and burgers, chicken, beef, and salads, as well as Mexican selections for lunch and dinner. Baked goods are made on the premises daily. My favorite is the corn bread, served with the soup special.

1405 S. Main St., Lordsburg. ✆ **575/542-9400.** Main courses $4–$7 breakfast, $6–$17 lunch and dinner. AE, DC, DISC, MC, V. Daily 6am–10pm.

13 SILVER CITY

44 miles NW of Deming; 57 miles SW of Truth or Consequences; 170 miles SW of Albuquerque

Silver City (pop. 12,500) is an old mining town, in the foothills of the Pinos Altos Range of the Mogollon Mountains, and gateway to the Gila Wilderness and the Gila Cliff Dwellings. Early Native Americans mined turquoise from these hills; and by 1804, Spanish settlers were digging for copper. In 1870, a group of prospectors discovered silver, and the rush was on. In 10 short months, the newly christened Silver City grew from a single cabin to more than 80 buildings. Early visitors included Billy the Kid, Judge Roy Bean, and William Randolph Hearst.

This comparatively isolated community kept pace with every modern convenience: telephones in 1883, electric lights in 1884 (only 2 years after New York City installed its lighting), and a water system in 1887. The town should have busted with the crash of silver prices in 1893. But unlike many Western towns, Silver City did not become a picturesque memory. It capitalized on its high, dry climate to become today's county seat and trade center. Copper mining and processing are still the major industry. But Silver City also can boast a famous son: The late Harrison (Jack) Schmitt, the first civilian geologist to visit the moon, and later a U.S. senator, was born and raised in nearby Santa Rita.

ESSENTIALS

GETTING THERE From Albuquerque, take I-25 south, 15 miles past Truth or Consequences; then west on NM 152 and US 180 (5 hr.). From Las Cruces, take I-10 west to Deming, and then north on US 180 (2 hr.).

Great Lakes Airlines (✆ **575/388-4115**) flies daily to **Grant County Airport** (✆ **575/388-4554**), 15 miles south of Silver City, near Hurley. **Silver Stage Lines** (✆ **800/522-0162**) offers daily shuttle service to the El Paso airport, and charter service to Tucson, Arizona. The **Las Cruces Shuttle Service** (✆ **800/288-1784** or 575/525-1784; www.lascrucesshuttle.com) runs several times daily from Silver City to the El Paso airport, by way of Las Cruces.

VISITOR INFORMATION The **Murray Ryan Visitor Center,** at 201 N. Hudson St., Silver City, NM 88061 (✆ **800/548-9378** or 575/538-3785; www.silvercity.org), also houses the Silver City Grant County Chamber of Commerce and is a good source of information. The chamber produces extremely useful tourist publications. Also of note at this site is a replica 1870s log cabin donated to the city by movie producer Ron Howard. It was built for the filming of the 2005 movie *The Missing.* A plaque on it says that Billy the Kid likely lived in one similar to it when he was a young resident of this town.

WHAT TO SEE & DO IN SILVER CITY

Silver City's downtown **Historic District** ★, the first such district to receive National Register recognition, is a must for visitors. The downtown core is marked by the extensive use of brick in construction: Brick clay was discovered in the area soon after the town's founding in 1870, and an 1880 ordinance prohibited frame construction within the town limits. Mansard-roofed Victorian houses, Queen Anne and Italianate residences, and commercial buildings show off the cast-iron architecture of the period. Some are still undergoing restoration.

An 1895 flood washed out Main Street and turned it into a gaping chasm, which was eventually bridged over; finally, the **Big Ditch,** as it's called, was made into a green park in the center of town. Facing downtown, in the 500 block of North Hudson Street, was a famous red-light district from the turn-of-the-century until the late 1960s.

Billy the Kid lived in Silver City as a youth. You can see his cabin site a block north of the Broadway Bridge, on the east side of the Big Ditch. The Kid (William Bonney) waited tables at the Star Hotel, at Hudson Street and Broadway. He was jailed (at 304 N.

Way Beyond Silver

Silver City has become an artists' mecca, as creative people retreat to the small town for the peace it offers. You can spend a fun day wandering the streets. Some of my favorite shops and galleries include **Silver City Trading Company's Antique Mall,** 205 W. Broadway (✆ **575/388-8989**), which is packed with a range of items, from fun junk to Western antiques. **Copper Quail Gallery,** 211-A N. Texas St. (✆ **575/388-2646**), offers wonderful regional paintings and pottery. Imaginative fiber art adorns the walls at **Yello on Yankee,** 108 W. Yankie St. (✆ **575/534-4968;** www.susanszajer.com). Meanwhile **Elemental Arts,** 106 W. Yankie St. (✆ **575/590-7554;** www.gourdweb.com), offers fabulous folk art, much of it made out of gourds, by Valerie M. Milner. Also look for oil paintings here by Chris Alvarez.

Hudson St.) in 1875 at the age of 15, after being convicted of stealing from a Chinese laundry, but he escaped—a first for the Kid. The grave of Bonney's mother, Catherine McCarty, is in Silver City Cemetery, east of town on Memory Lane, off US 180. She died of tuberculosis about a year after the family moved here in 1873.

Silver City Museum ★ This very well-presented museum of city and regional history contains collections relating to southwestern New Mexico history, mining, Native American pottery, and early photographs. Exhibits include a southwestern New Mexico history timeline, a parlor displaying Victorian decorative arts, and a chronicle of commerce in early Silver City. A local history research library is available to visitors also. The main gallery features changing exhibits. The museum is lodged in the 1881 H. B. Ailman House, a former city hall and fire station, remarkable for its cupola and Victorian mansard roof. Ailman came to Silver City penniless in 1871, made a fortune in mining, and went on to start the Meredith and Ailman Bank. Guided historic district walking tours are offered on Memorial Day and Labor Day. There's also a museum store. Take a fun trip up into the cupola for a nice view of the city.

312 W. Broadway. ✆ **575/538-5921.** Fax 575/388-1096. Free admission. Tues–Fri 9am–4:30pm; Sat–Sun 10am–4pm. Closed Mon except Memorial Day and Labor Day.

EXPLORING THE AREA

NORTH OF SILVER CITY The virtual ghost town of **Pinos Altos ★**, straddling the Continental Divide, is 6 miles north of Silver City on NM 15. Dubbed "Tall Pines" when it was founded in the gold- and silver-rush eras, Apache attacks and mine failures took their toll.

The adobe **Methodist-Episcopal Church** was built with William Randolph Hearst's money in 1898 and now houses the Grant County Art Guild. The town also has the **Log Cabin Curio Shop and Museum,** set in an 1866 cabin (✆ **575/388-1882**), and the **Buckhorn Saloon and Opera House** (see below).

SOUTH OF SILVER CITY **City of Rocks State Park ★** (✆ **575/536-2800**), 25 miles from Silver City via US 180 and NM 61, is an area of fantastically shaped volcanic rock formations, formed in ancient times from thick blankets of ash that hardened into tuff. This soft stone, eroded by wind and rain, was shaped into monolithic blocks reminiscent of Stonehenge. For some, the park resembles a medieval village; for others, it's a collection of misshapen, albeit benign, giants. Complete with a desert garden, the park offers excellent camping and picnic sites. It's also a renowned spot for *bouldering,* a type of rock climbing in which participants don't use ropes. Day use is allowed from 6am to 9pm for $5 per vehicle; a campsite costs $8 to $18. The visitor center is typically open from 10am to 4pm, but its hours vary, depending on volunteer staffing.

WEST OF SILVER CITY US 180, heading northwest from Silver City, is the gateway to Catron County and most of the Gila National Forest, including the villages of Glenwood, Reserve, and Quemado. For details on this area, see "Other Adventures in Gila National Forest," later in this chapter.

WHERE TO STAY IN & AROUND SILVER CITY

Silver City now offers a full range of chain hotels, many with reasonable prices, so if you have a favorite, call their toll-free number to see if it's represented. Most lodgings in town provide free parking.

Bear Mountain Lodge ★★★ Set on 160 acres just 3½ miles northwest of downtown Silver City, this lodge, owned and operated by the Nature Conservancy, is ideal for outdoors enthusiasts, from birders to bicyclers. The 1920s inn offers large rooms with old-world charm, accented by maple floors and high ceilings, and with such details as authentic Navajo rugs and original art on the walls. Beds are very comfortable, and bathrooms are medium size with elegant tile work. Four rooms have private balconies. On-site naturalist staff members inform visitors about the flora and fauna of the area, and they also conduct guided trips. Breakfasts are hearty and healthy, with treats such as muffins and quiche. Dinner is served for guests nightly for an extra fee. It's a gourmet buffet-style affair that changes seasonally, with such offerings as poached salmon and a Thai dinner. What's best here is that you can count on complete quiet.

2251 Cottage San Rd., Silver City, NM 88061 (P.O. Box 1163, Silver City, NM 88062). ✆ **877/620-BEAR** (2327) or 575/538-2538. www.bearmountainlodge.com. 11 units. $125–$185 double. 2-night minimum stay. Rates include full breakfast. Box lunches available for an extra charge. Horse boarding $15 per night. AE, MC, V. Turn north off US 180 on Alabama St. (½ mile west of NM 90 intersection). Proceed 3 miles (Alabama becomes Cottage San Rd.) to dirt road turnoff to left; the lodge is another ½ mile. No children 9 or under. **Amenities:** Concierge; mountain bikes; hiking trails; computer w/Internet access. *In room:* A/C, hair dryer, Wi-Fi.

Holiday Inn Express ★ Kids East of downtown, this hotel offers clean and quiet rooms with standards you expect from the brand name. Rooms are medium size, decorated with earth tones, and have high ceilings and large windows letting in lots of sunlight. Beds are comfortable. The medium-size bathrooms are very clean. Be sure *not* to book room no. 121, which has noisy pipes playing tunes through the night.

1103 Superior St., Silver City, NM 88061. ✆ **800/HOLIDAY** [465-4329] or 575/538-2525. Fax 575/538-2525. 60 units. $110 double. AE, DC, DISC, MC, V. Pets allowed in some rooms. **Amenities:** Health club; Jacuzzi; indoor pool; Wi-Fi (in lobby and breakfast bar). *In room:* A/C, TV, hair dryer, Internet.

Camping

Silver City KOA (✆ **800/562-7623** or 575/388-3351; www.koa.com) has 82 sites and 42 full hookups, and it offers groceries, laundry facilities, and a pool. The campground is 5 miles east of the NM 90/US 180 junction on US 180. **Silver City RV Park** (✆ **575/538-2239;** www.silvercityrv.com) has 48 sites (45 with full hookups), showers, laundry facilities, and picnic tables. It's downtown on Bennett Street, behind Food Basket supermarket. Camping is also available at the Gila Cliff Dwellings (see "Gila Cliff Dwellings National Monument," below).

WHERE TO DINE IN & AROUND SILVER CITY

Buckhorn Saloon and Opera House ★ BURGERS/SEAFOOD/STEAKS Seven miles north of Silver City in Pinos Altos, the Buckhorn offers fine dining in 1860s decor. It's completely authentic, with vigas on the ceiling and thick adobe walls, but be aware that the dining room has very low light. The restaurant is noted for its Western-style steaks, seafood, homemade desserts, and excellent wine list. If you've got a big appetite, try the New York strip with green chile and cheese. I like the shrimp and chicken kabobs. Entrees are served with a salad (try the blue-cheese dressing) or soup and choice of potatoes or rice. Live entertainment is offered nightly. The high-personality saloon offers big round tables and a great wooden bar. Many come to this saloon to have excellent burgers and hear live music on selected nights. While waiting for your food, take a moment to peruse the attached opera house, where good melodrama theater is presented seasonally. Enjoy a drink from the full bar.

32 Main St., Pinos Altos. ✆ **575/538-9911.** Reservations highly recommended. Main courses $10–$46. MC, V. Mon–Sat 6–10pm; saloon Mon–Sat 3–10pm.

Diane's Bakery & Cafe ★★ NEW AMERICAN This is a wonderful find in such a small town. Diane Barrett, who was once a pastry chef at La Traviata and Eldorado in Santa Fe, has brought refined city food to this small town. At lunch, the atmosphere is bustling, usually with a slight wait for a table. At dinner, the tone is more romantic and low key, with more nouvelle specialties. The service is friendly and adequate. You can't go wrong with any of the baked goods here. At brunch, try the hatch Benedict, a version of eggs Benedict made with home-baked chile cheddar toast. At lunch, I suggest the spanokopita, a baked spinach pastry, served with a salad; the quiche of the day is also delicious. At dinner, you may want to order the pork loin, with apricot brandy demi-glace, served with red potatoes and seasonal vegetables, or the seafood Thai coconut curry. Diane's also serves great steaks. There's a small but creative wine and beer menu. Don't leave without sampling one of the desserts, such as the four-layer chocolate cake.

510 N. Bullard St., Silver City. ✆ **575/538-8722.** Reservations recommended for dinner. Main courses $6–$9 breakfast and lunch, $15–$25 dinner. MC, V. Tues–Sat 11am–2pm and 5:30–9pm; brunch Sat–Sun 9am–2pm.

Jalisco's ★ (Kids) NEW MEXICAN Set within an enchanting brick building in the historic district, this festive restaurant serves big portions of good food. Three dining rooms fill the old structure, which has been Latinized with arched doorways and bold Mexican street-scene calendars on the walls. The combination plates are large and popular, as are the enchiladas. There are also burgers and a children's menu. Whatever you do, be sure to order a *sopaipilla* for dessert. They're delicious and huge. Beer and wine are served.

103 S. Bullard St., Silver City. ✆ **575/388-2060.** Reservations not accepted. Main courses $6–$12. DISC, MC, V. Mon–Sat 11am–8:30pm.

SILVER CITY AFTER DARK

Some of southwestern New Mexico's most passionate performances are held at the **Pinos Altos Melodrama Theater,** 30 Main St., Pinos Altos (in the Pinos Altos Opera House, next to the Buckhorn Saloon; ✆ **575/388-3848;** www.pinosaltos.org). Local actors fight the forces of good and evil in such productions as *The Legend of Billy the Kid* or *It's Just a Little Gun Play.* Productions are on Friday and Saturday nights from February to November. **Silver City Brewing Co. ★**, 101 E. College (✆ **575/534-2739;** www.swnmbeer.com), the town's new brewpub, offers tasty beer and a brewpub menu including pizza, pasta, sandwiches, and salads. Best of all here, during warm months, live music plays on the patio on weekends. It's open Tuesday to Friday 11am to 8pm and Saturday noon to 8pm. **Isaac's Bar & Grill** ★ offers live entertainment on Saturday nights. See "Where to Dine in & Around Silver City," above.

14 GILA CLIFF DWELLINGS ★★

44 miles N of Silver City

It takes 1½ to 2 hours to reach the Gila Cliff Dwellings from Silver City, but it's definitely worth the trip. First-time visitors are inevitably awed by the remains of an ancient civilization set in the mouths of caves, abandoned for 7 centuries. You reach the dwellings on a 1-mile moderate hike along which you catch glimpses of the ruins. This walk is an elaborate journey into the past. It winds its way into a narrow canyon, from which you first spot the poetic ruins perched in six caves 180 feet up on the canyon wall, stone shiny and hard as porcelain. Then the ascent begins up innumerable steps and rocks until you're standing face-to-face with these ancient relics, which offer a glimpse into the lives of Native Americans who lived here from the late 1270s through the early 1300s. Tree-ring dating indicates their residence didn't last longer than 30 to 40 years.

What's remarkable about the journey through the cliff dwellings is the depth of some of the caves. At one point, you'll climb a ladder and pass from one cave into the next, viewing the intricate little rooms (42 total) and walls that once made up a community dwelling. Probably not more than 10 to 15 families (about 40–50 people) lived in the cliff dwellings at any one time. The inhabitants were excellent weavers and skilled potters.

The cliff dwellings were discovered by Anglo settlers in the early 1870s, near where the three forks of the Gila River rise. Once you leave the last cave, you'll head down again traversing some steep steps to the canyon floor. Pets are not allowed within the monument, but they can be taken on trails within the Gila Wilderness. Be sure to pick up a trail guide at the visitor center.

ESSENTIALS

GETTING THERE From Silver City, take NM 15 north 44 miles to the Gila Cliff Dwellings. Travel time from Silver City is approximately 2 hours. You won't find any gas stations between Silver City and Gila Cliff Dwellings, so plan accordingly. Also know that at the monument, vehicles are permitted on paved roads only.

VISITOR INFORMATION For more information, contact **Gila Cliff Dwellings National Monument,** HC 68, Box 100, Silver City, NM 88061 (✆ **575/536-9461;** www.nps.gov/gicl).

ADMISSION FEES & HOURS Admission to the monument is $3 per person, with children age 12 and under admitted free. The visitor center, where you can pick up detailed brochures, is open from 8am to 5pm Memorial Day to Labor Day and from 8am to 4:30pm the rest of the year. The cliff dwellings are open from 8am to 6pm in the summer and from 9am to 4pm the rest of the year.

SEEING THE HIGHLIGHTS

Today, the dwellings allow a rare glimpse inside the homes and lives of prehistoric Native Americans. About 75% of what is seen is original, although the walls have been capped and the foundations strengthened to prevent further deterioration. It took a great deal of effort to build these homes: The stones were held in place by mortar, and all the clay and water for the mortar had to be hand-carried up from the stream, as the Mogollon did not have any pack animals. The vigas for the roof were cut and shaped with stone axes or fire.

The people who lived here were farmers, as shown by the remains of beans, squash, and corn in their homes. The fields were along the valley of the west fork of the Gila River and on the mesa across the canyon. No signs of irrigation have been found.

Near the visitor center, about a mile away, the remains of an earlier pit house (A.D. 100–400), built below ground level, and later pit houses (up to A.D. 1000), aboveground structures of adobe or wattle, have been found.

CAMPING

Camping and picnicking are encouraged in the national monument, with four developed campgrounds. Camping is free and some sites are RV accessible, though there are no hookups. Overnight lodging can be found in Silver City and in the nearby town of Gila Hot Springs, which also has a grocery store, horse rentals, and guided pack trips. For information, contact the visitor center (© **575/536-9461**).

15 OTHER ADVENTURES IN GILA NATIONAL FOREST

Gila National Forest, which offers some of the most spectacular mountain scenery in the Southwest, comprises 3.3 million acres in four counties. Nearly one-fourth of that acreage (790,000 acres) is composed of the **Gila, Aldo Leopold,** and **Blue Range wildernesses.** Its highest peak is Whitewater Baldy, at 10,892 feet. Within the forest, six out of seven life zones can be found, so the range of plant and wildlife is broad. You may see mule deer, elk, antelope, black bear, mountain lion, and bighorn sheep. Nearly 400 miles of streams and a few small lakes sustain healthy populations of trout as well as bass, bluegill, and catfish. Anglers can head to Lake Roberts, Snow Lake, and Quemado Lake.

JUST THE FACTS For more information on the national forest, contact the **U.S. Forest Service,** Forest Supervisor's Office, 3005 E. Camino del Bosque, Silver City, NM 88061 (© **575/388-8201;** www.fs.fed.us).

The national forest has 29 campgrounds, all with toilets, six with drinking water. Car and backpack camping are also permitted throughout the forest.

GETTING OUTSIDE

The forest has 1,490 miles of trails for hiking and horseback riding, and, in winter, cross-country skiing. Outside the wilderness areas, trail bikes and off-road vehicles are permitted. Hiking trails in the Gila Wilderness, especially the 41-mile Middle Fork Trail, with its east end near Gila Cliff Dwellings, are among the most popular in the state and can sometimes be crowded. If you are more interested in communing with nature than with fellow hikers, you will find plenty of trails to suit you, both in and out of the officially designated wilderness areas.

Most of the trails are maintained and easy to follow. Trails along river bottoms have many stream crossings (so be prepared for hiking with wet feet) and may be washed out by summer flash floods. It's best to inquire about trail conditions before you set out. More than 50 trail heads provide roadside parking.

Some of the best hikes in the area are the Frisco Box, Pueblo Creek, Whitewater Baldy, the Catwalk and Beyond, the Middle Fork/Little Bear Loop, and the Black Range Crest Trail. The Gila National Forest contains several wilderness areas that are off-limits to mountain bikes, including the Gila, Aldo Leopold, and the Blue Range Primitive Area. However, cyclists can access quite a few trails. Some to look for are the Cleveland Mine trail, Silver City Loop, Continental Divide, Signal Peak, Pinos Altos Loop, Fort Bayard Historical Trails, and Forest Trail 100.

The Catwalk National Recreation Trail ★ (**✆ 575/539-2481**), 68 miles north of Silver City on US 180, then 5 miles east of Glenwood via NM 174, is a great break after a long drive. Kids are especially thrilled with this hike. It follows the route of a pipeline built in 1897 to carry water to the now-defunct town of Graham and its electric generator. About a quarter-mile above the parking area is the beginning of a striking 250-foot metal causeway clinging to the sides of the boulder-choked Whitewater Canyon, which, in spots, is 20 feet wide and 250 feet deep. Along the way, you'll find water pouring through caves and waterfalls spitting off the cliff side. Farther up the canyon, a suspension bridge spans the chasm. Picnic facilities are near the parking area. There's a $3 fee per car.

12

Tucson

Encircled by mountain ranges and bookended by the two units of Saguaro National Park, Tucson is Arizona's second-largest city, and for the vacationer it has everything that Phoenix has to offer, plus a bit more. There are world-class golf resorts, excellent restaurants, art museums and galleries, an active cultural life, and, of course, plenty of great weather. Tucson also has a long history that melds Native American, Hispanic, and Anglo roots. And with a national park, a national forest, and other natural areas just beyond the city limits, Tucson is a city that celebrates its Sonoran Desert setting.

At Saguaro National Park, you can marvel at the massive cactuses that have come to symbolize the desert Southwest, while at the Arizona–Sonora Desert Museum (actually a zoo), you can acquaint yourself with the flora and fauna of this region. Take a hike or a horseback ride up one of the trails that leads into the wilderness from the edge of the city, and you may even meet up with a few desert denizens on their own turf. Look beyond the saguaros and prickly pears, and you can find a desert oasis, complete with waterfalls and swimming holes, and, a short drive from the city, a pine forest that's home to the southernmost ski area in the country.

Founded by the Spanish in 1775, Tucson was built on the site of a much older Native American village. The city's name comes from the Pima Indian word *chukeson,* which means "spring at the base of black mountain," a reference to the peak now known simply as "A Mountain." From 1867 to 1877, Tucson was the territorial capital of Arizona, but eventually the capital was moved to Phoenix. Consequently, Tucson did not develop as quickly as Phoenix and still holds on to some of its Hispanic and Western heritage.

Tucson has a history of valuing quality of life over development, which sets it apart from the Phoenix area. Back in the days of urban renewal, its citizens turned back the bulldozers and managed to preserve at least some of the city's old Mexican character. Likewise, today, in the face of the sort of sprawl that has given Phoenix the feel of a landlocked Los Angeles, advocates for controlled growth are fighting hard to preserve both Tucson's desert environment and the city's unique character. However, the inevitable sprawl has now ringed much of Tucson with vast suburbs, though as yet, the city is far from becoming another Phoenix.

The struggle to retain an identity distinct from other Southwestern cities is ongoing, and despite long, drawn-out attempts to breathe life into the city's core, downtown Tucson has little to offer visitors other than an art museum, a convention center, a couple of historic neighborhoods, and a couple of good restaurants.

Despite this minor shortcoming, Tucson remains Arizona's most beautiful and most livable city. With the Santa Catalina Mountains for a backdrop, Tucson boasts one of the most dramatic settings in the Southwest, and whether you're taking in the mountain vistas from the tee box of the 12th hole, the saddle of a palomino, or a table for two, I'm sure you'll agree that Tucson makes a superb vacation destination.

1 ORIENTATION

ARRIVING

BY PLANE Located 6 miles south of downtown, **Tucson International Airport,** 7250 S. Tucson Blvd. (© 520/573-8000; www.tucsonairport.org), is served by the following major airlines: **Alaska Airlines/Horizon Air** (© 800/252-7522; www.alaskaair.com), **American** (© 800/433-7300; www.aa.com), **Continental** (© 800/523-3273; www.continental.com), **Delta** (© 800/221-1212; www.delta.com), **Frontier** (© 800/432-1359; www.flyfrontier.com), **Northwest/KLM** (© 800/225-2525; www.nwa.com), **Southwest** (© 800/435-9792; www.southwest.com), **Sun Country Airlines** (© 800/359-6786; www.suncountry.com), **United** (© 800/864-8331; www.ual.com), and **US Airways** (© 800/428-4322; www.usairways.com).

Visitor centers in both baggage-claim areas can give you brochures and reserve a hotel room if you haven't done so already.

Many resorts and hotels in Tucson provide free or competitively priced airport shuttle service. **Arizona Stagecoach** (© **520/889-1000;** www.azstagecoach.com) operates 24-hour van service to downtown Tucson and the foothills resorts. Fares to downtown are around $21 one-way and $42 round-trip ($24 and $48 for a couple), and to the foothills resorts around $42 one-way and $78 round-trip ($48 and $88 for a couple). It takes between 45 minutes and 1 hour to reach the foothills resorts. To return to the airport, it's best to call at least a day before your scheduled departure.

You'll also find taxis waiting outside baggage claim, or you can call **Yellow Cab** (© **520/624-6611;** www.yellowcabtucson.com) or **Allstate Cab** (© **520/798-1111**). The flag-drop rate at the airport is $4.50, and then $2.50 per mile. A taxi to downtown costs around $25, to the foothills resorts about $30 to $50.

Sun Tran (© **520/792-9222;** www.suntran.com), the local public transit system, operates bus service to and from the airport. The fare is $1. Route no. 6, to downtown, runs Monday through Friday from about 4:50am to 10:50pm, Saturday from about 6:15am to 8:15pm, and Sunday from about 6:15am to 7:15pm. Departures are every 30 to 60 minutes on weekdays and every hour on weekends. It takes 40 to 50 minutes to reach downtown. Route no. 11 operates on a similar schedule and travels along Alvernon Road to the midtown area.

BY CAR **I-10,** the main east-west interstate across the southern United States, passes through Tucson and connects to Phoenix. **I-19** connects Tucson with the Mexican border at Nogales. **Ariz. 86** heads southwest into the Tohono O'odham Indian Reservation, and **Ariz. 79** leads north toward Florence and eventually connects with **U.S. 60** into Phoenix.

If you're headed downtown, take the Congress Street exit off I-10. If you're coming from the north and going to one of the foothills resorts north of downtown, you'll probably want to take the Ina Road exit off I-10.

BY TRAIN Tucson is served by **Amtrak** (© **800/872-7245;** www.amtrak.com) passenger rail service. The *Sunset Limited,* which runs between Orlando and Los Angeles, stops in Tucson, as does the *Texas Eagle,* which runs between Los Angeles and Chicago. The **train station** is at 400 E. Toole Ave. (© **520/623-4442**), in the heart of downtown and within walking distance of the Tucson Convention Center, El Presidio Historic District, and a few hotels. You'll see taxis waiting to meet the train; see "Getting Around," below, for more info.

BY BUS **Greyhound** (✆ **800/231-2222** or 520/792-3475; www.greyhound.com) connects Tucson to the rest of the United States through its extensive system. The bus station is at 471 W. Congress St.

VISITOR INFORMATION

The **Metropolitan Tucson Convention & Visitors Bureau (MTCVB),** 100 S. Church Ave. (at Broadway) (✆ **800/638-8350** or 520/624-1817; www.visittucson.org), is an excellent source of information on Tucson and its environs. The visitor center is open Monday through Friday from 8am to 5pm, Saturday and Sunday from 9am to 4pm.

CITY LAYOUT

MAIN ARTERIES & STREETS Tucson is laid out on a grid that's fairly regular in the downtown areas but becomes less orderly the farther you go from the city center. In the flatlands, major thoroughfares are spaced at 1-mile intervals, with smaller streets filling in the squares created by the major roads. In the foothills, where Tucson's most recent growth has occurred, the grid system breaks down completely because of the hilly terrain.

The main **east-west roads** are (from south to north) 22nd Street, Broadway Boulevard, Speedway Boulevard, Grant Road (with Tanque Verde Rd. as an extension), and Ina Road/Skyline Drive/Sunrise Road. The main **north-south roads** are (from west to east) Miracle Mile/Oracle Road, Stone/Sixth Avenue, Campbell Avenue, Country Club Road, Alvernon Road, and Swan Road. **I-10** cuts diagonally across the Tucson metropolitan area from northwest to southeast.

In **downtown Tucson,** Congress Street and Broadway Boulevard are the main east-west streets; Stone Avenue, Sixth Avenue, and Fourth Avenue are the main north-south streets.

FINDING AN ADDRESS Because Tucson is laid out on a grid, finding an address is relatively easy. The zero (or starting) point for all Tucson addresses is the corner of Stone Avenue, which runs north and south, and Congress Street, which runs east and west. From this point, streets are designated either north, south, east, or west. Addresses usually, but not always, increase by 100 with each block, so an address of 4321 E. Broadway Blvd. should be 43 blocks east of Stone Avenue. In the downtown area, many of the streets and avenues are numbered, with numbered streets running east and west, and numbered avenues running north and south.

2 GETTING AROUND

BY CAR

Unless you plan to stay by the pool or on the golf course, you'll want to rent a car. Luckily, rates are fairly economical. At press time, Alamo was charging $180 per week ($230 with taxes and surcharges included) for an economy car with unlimited mileage in Tucson. See "Getting to Arizona," in chapter 3, for general tips on car rentals in Arizona.

The following agencies have offices at or near Tucson International Airport as well as other locations in the area. Because taxes and surcharges add up to between 25% and 30% on car rentals at the airport, you may want to consider renting at some other location, where you can avoid paying some of these fees. Among the Tucson car-rental agencies are **Alamo** (✆ 800/462-5266 or 520/573-4740), **Avis** (✆ 800/331-1212 or

520/294-1494), **Budget** (© 800/527-0700 or 520/889-8800), **Dollar** (© 800/800-3665 or 866/434-2226), **Enterprise** (© 800/261-7331 or 520/573-5250), **Hertz** (© 800/654-3131 or 520/573-5201), **National** (© 800/227-7368 or 520/573-8050), and **Thrifty** (© 800/847-4389 or 877/283-0898).

Downtown Tucson is still a relatively easy place to find a parking space, and parking fees are low. There are two huge parking lots on the south side of the Tucson Convention Center, a couple of small lots on either side of the Tucson Museum of Art (one at Main Ave. and Paseo Redondo, south of El Presidio Historic District, and one at the corner of Council St. and Court Ave.), and parking garages beneath the main library (101 N. Stone Ave.) and El Presidio Park (on Alameda St.). You'll find plenty of metered parking on the smaller downtown streets. Almost all Tucson hotels and resorts provide free parking.

Lanes on several major avenues in Tucson change direction at rush hour to facilitate traffic flow, so pay attention to signs that tell you the time and direction of traffic.

BY PUBLIC TRANSPORTATION

BY BUS Covering much of the Tucson metropolitan area, **Sun Tran** (© **520/792-9222;** www.suntran.com) public buses are $1 for adults and students, 40¢ for seniors, and free for children 5 and under. Day passes are available on buses for $2.

The **Ronstadt Transit Center,** 215 E. Congress St., is served by about 30 regular and express bus routes to all parts of Tucson. The bus system does *not* extend to such tourist attractions as the Arizona–Sonora Desert Museum, Old Tucson, Saguaro National Park, or the foothills resorts, and thus is of limited use to visitors. However, Sun Tran does provide a shuttle for sports games and special events. Call the above phone number for information.

BY TROLLEY Although they don't go very far, the restored electric streetcars of **Old Pueblo Trolley** (© **520/792-1802;** www.oldpueblotrolley.org) are a fun way to get from the Fourth Avenue shopping district to the University of Arizona. The trolleys operate on Friday from 6 to 10pm, Saturday from noon to midnight, and Sunday from noon to 6pm. The fare is $1 for adults and 50¢ for children 6 to 12. The fare on Sunday is only 25¢ for all riders. Friday and Saturday all-day passes are $2.50 for adults and $1.25 for children.

BY TAXI

If you need a taxi, you'll have to phone for one. **Yellow Cab** (© **520/624-6611;** www.yellowcabtucson.com) and **Discount Cab** (© **520/388-9000;** www.discountcab.com) provide service throughout the city. The flag-drop rate is between $2.50 and $2.95, and after that it's $1.95 to $2 per mile. Although distances in Tucson are not as great as those in Phoenix, it's still a good 10 or more miles from the foothills resorts to downtown Tucson, so expect to pay at least $10 or $12 for a taxi. Most resorts have shuttle vans or can arrange taxi service to major attractions.

ON FOOT

Downtown Tucson is compact and easily explored on foot, and many old streets in the downtown historic neighborhoods are narrow and much easier to appreciate if you leave your car in a parking lot. Also, although several major attractions—including the Arizona–Sonora Desert Museum, Old Tucson Studios, Saguaro National Park, and Sabino Canyon—can be reached only by car, they require quite a bit of walking once you arrive.

These attractions often have uneven footing, so be sure to bring a good pair of walking shoes.

FAST FACTS

For a doctor referral, ask at your hotel or call Northwest Medical Center (✆ **866/694-9355**). For a dentist referral, call the Arizona Dental Association (✆ **800/866-2732**).

Local hospitals are the **Tucson Medical Center,** at 5301 E. Grant Rd. (✆ **520/327-5461**), and the **University Medical Center,** at 1501 N. Campbell Ave. (✆ **520/694-0111**).

In addition to the 5.6% sales tax levied by the state, Tucson levies a 2% city sales tax. Car-rental taxes, surcharges, and fees add up to around 30%. The hotel tax in the Tucson area is approximately 12%.

3 WHERE TO STAY

Although Phoenix still holds the title of Resort Capital of Arizona, Tucson is not far behind, and this city's resorts boast much more spectacular settings than most comparable properties in Phoenix and Scottsdale. As far as nonresort accommodations go, Tucson has a wider variety than Phoenix—partly because there are numerous bed-and-breakfast inns both in historic neighborhoods and in the desert on the outskirts of the city. The presence of two guest ranches within a 20-minute drive of Tucson also adds to the city's diversity of accommodations. Business and budget travelers are well served with all-suite and conference hotels, as well as plenty of budget chain motels.

At the more expensive hotels and resorts, summer rates, usually in effect from May to September, are often less than half what they are in winter. Surprisingly, temperatures usually aren't unbearable in May or September, which makes these good times to visit if you're looking to save money. When making late-spring or early-fall reservations, always be sure to ask when rates are scheduled to go up or down. If you aren't coming to Tucson specifically for the winter gem and mineral shows, then you'll save quite a bit if you avoid the last week in January and the first 2 weeks in February, when hotels around town generally charge exorbitant rates.

Most hotels offer special packages, weekend rates, various discounts (such as for AARP or AAA members), and free accommodations for children, so it helps to ask when you reserve. Nearly all hotels have smoke-free and wheelchair-accessible rooms.

BED & BREAKFASTS If you're looking to stay in a B&B, several agencies can help. The **Arizona Association of Bed & Breakfast Inns** (www.arizona-bed-breakfast.com) has several members in Tucson. **Mi Casa Su Casa** (✆ **800/456-0682** or 480/990-0682; www.azres.com) can book you into one of its many B&Bs and homestays in the Tucson area or elsewhere in the state, as will **Arizona Trails Travel Services** (✆ **888/799-4284** or 480/837-4284; www.arizonatrails.com), which also books tour and hotel reservations.

DOWNTOWN & THE UNIVERSITY AREA

Very Expensive

Arizona Inn ★★★ Kids With its pink-stucco buildings and immaculately tended flower gardens, the Arizona Inn is an oasis of tranquility. Gracious and welcoming, it's an unforgettable place to spend a vacation. Opened in 1930 by Isabella Greenway, Arizona's

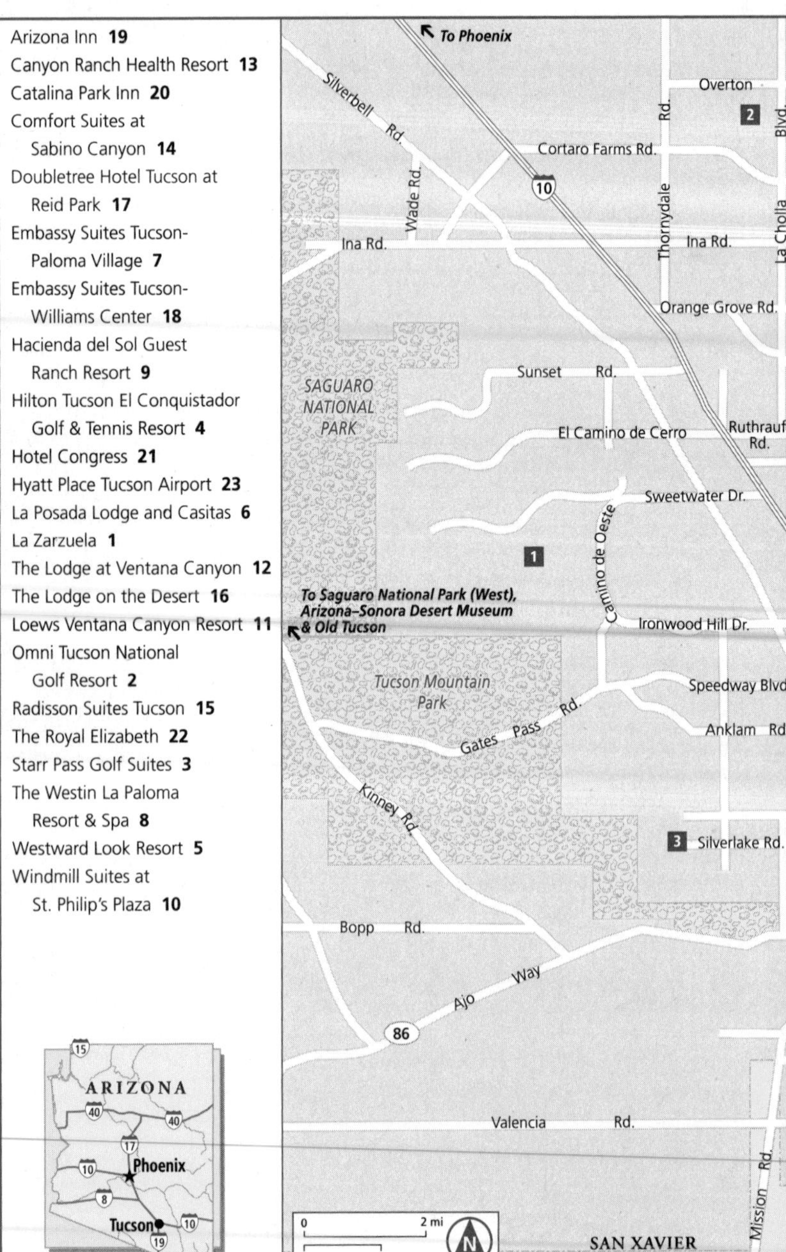
Arizona Inn 19
Canyon Ranch Health Resort 13
Catalina Park Inn 20
Comfort Suites at Sabino Canyon 14
Doubletree Hotel Tucson at Reid Park 17
Embassy Suites Tucson-Paloma Village 7
Embassy Suites Tucson-Williams Center 18
Hacienda del Sol Guest Ranch Resort 9
Hilton Tucson El Conquistador Golf & Tennis Resort 4
Hotel Congress 21
Hyatt Place Tucson Airport 23
La Posada Lodge and Casitas 6
La Zarzuela 1
The Lodge at Ventana Canyon 12
The Lodge on the Desert 16
Loews Ventana Canyon Resort 11
Omni Tucson National Golf Resort 2
Radisson Suites Tucson 15
The Royal Elizabeth 22
Starr Pass Golf Suites 3
The Westin La Paloma Resort & Spa 8
Westward Look Resort 5
Windmill Suites at St. Philip's Plaza 10
To Phoenix
Silverbell Rd.
Overton
Rd.
Blvd.
Cortaro Farms Rd.
Wade Rd.
10
Thornydale
La Cholla
Ina Rd.
Ina Rd.
Orange Grove Rd.
Sunset Rd.
SAGUARO NATIONAL PARK
El Camino de Cerro
Ruthrauff Rd.
Sweetwater Dr.
Camino de Oeste
To Saguaro National Park (West), Arizona–Sonora Desert Museum & Old Tucson
Ironwood Hill Dr.
Tucson Mountain Park
Speedway Blvd.
Gates Pass Rd.
Anklam Rd.
Kinney Rd.
Silverlake Rd.
Bopp Rd.
Ajo Way
86
Valencia Rd.
Mission Rd.
0
2 mi
0
2 km
N
SAN XAVIER INDIAN RESERVATION
15
ARIZONA
40
40
17
10
Phoenix
8
Tucson
10
19

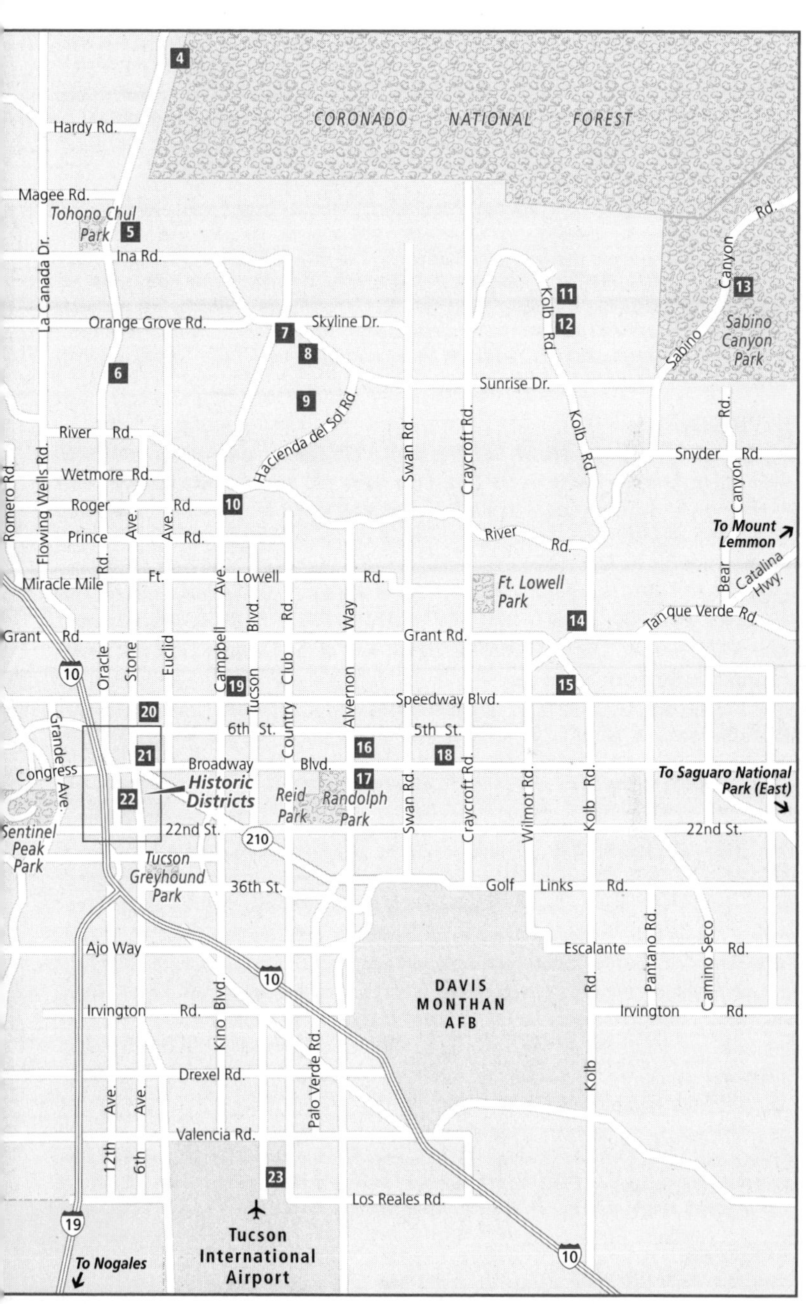
CORONADO NATIONAL FOREST
Hardy Rd.
Magee Rd.
Tohono Chul Park
Ina Rd.
La Canada Dr.
Orange Grove Rd.
Skyline Dr.
Sunrise Dr.
Hacienda del Sol Rd.
Swan Rd.
Craycroft Rd.
Kolb Rd.
Sabino Canyon Rd.
Sabino Canyon Park
Snyder Rd.
Bear Canyon Rd.
River Rd.
Wetmore Rd.
Roger Rd.
Prince Rd.
Romero Rd.
Flowing Wells Rd.
Miracle Mile
Ft. Lowell Rd.
Ft. Lowell Park
To Mount Lemmon
Catalina Hwy.
Tanque Verde Rd.
Grant Rd.
Oracle Rd.
Stone Ave.
Euclid Ave.
Campbell Ave.
Tucson Blvd.
Country Club Rd.
Alvernon Way
Speedway Blvd.
6th St.
5th St.
Grande Ave.
Congress
Broadway Blvd.
Historic Districts
Reid Park
Randolph Park
Wilmot Rd.
To Saguaro National Park (East)
Sentinel Peak Park
22nd St.
Tucson Greyhound Park
36th St.
Golf Links Rd.
Ajo Way
Escalante Rd.
Pantano Rd.
Camino Seco Rd.
DAVIS MONTHAN AFB
Irvington Rd.
Kino Blvd.
Drexel Rd.
Palo Verde Rd.
12th Ave.
6th Ave.
Valencia Rd.
Los Reales Rd.
Tucson International Airport
To Nogales
10
19
210
4
5
6
7
8
9
10
11
12
13
14
15
16
17
18
19
20
21
22
23

first congresswoman, the inn is still family owned and operated, and is imbued with Old Arizona charm. Play a game of croquet, take high tea in the library, or lounge by the pool, and you may start to feel as if this is your second home. Guest rooms vary in size and decor, but most have a mix of reproduction antiques and original pieces made for the inn years ago by World War I veterans with disabilities. Some units have gas fireplaces, and most suites have private patios or enclosed sun porches. The inn's main dining room (p. 366) is a casually elegant space. Fragrant flowering trees and vines surround the small pool.

2200 E. Elm St., Tucson, AZ 85719. ✆ **800/933-1093** or 520/325-1541. Fax 520/881-5830. www.arizonainn.com. 95 units. Mid-Jan to mid-Apr from $319 double, from $469 suite; mid-Apr to May from $229 double, from $369 suite; June to mid-Sept from $179 double, from $289 suite; mid-Sept to mid-Dec from $229 double, from $369 suite; mid-Dec to mid-Jan $259 double, from $359 suite. Summer rates include full breakfast and complimentary evening ice-cream fountain. Children 12 and under stay free in parent's room. AE, MC, V. **Amenities:** 3 restaurants; 2 lounges; babysitting; bikes; concierge; exercise room; heated outdoor pool; room service; saunas; 2 Har-Tru clay tennis courts. *In room:* A/C, TV/DVD, fridge, hair dryer, Internet.

Expensive

The Lodge on the Desert ★ Dating from 1936 and set amid neatly manicured lawns and gardens, the Lodge on the Desert is a classic old Arizona resort that was completely remodeled and expanded in 2009. The relaxing retreat looks a bit like a Mexican village, with narrow pathways winding between buildings. Guest rooms are in both hacienda-style adobe buildings tucked amid cactuses and orange trees and newly constructed adobe-style two-story buildings. Rooms feature a mix of contemporary and Southwestern furnishings; many units have beamed ceilings or fireplaces, and some have patios and tile floors. The small pool has a good view of the Catalinas. The new casitas are definitely the nicest rooms here.

306 N. Alvernon Way, Tucson, AZ 85711. ✆ **800/978-3598** or 520/325-3366. Fax 520/327-5834. www.lodgeonthedesert.com. 100 units. Jan–Apr $259–$449 double; May to early Sept $119–$199 double; early Sept to Dec $159–$279 double. Children 13 and under stay free in parent's room. AE, DC, DISC, MC, V. Pets accepted ($50 deposit, plus $25 per night). **Amenities:** Restaurant; lounge; concierge; access to nearby health club; outdoor pool; room service. *In room:* A/C, TV, hair dryer, Wi-Fi.

The Royal Elizabeth ★★ A block from the Temple of Music and Art, the Royal Elizabeth is an 1878 Victorian adobe mansion that features an unusual combination of architectural styles that makes for a uniquely Southwestern-style inn. In classic 19th-century Tucson fashion, the old home looks thoroughly unpretentious from the outside, but inside you'll find beautiful woodwork and gorgeous Victorian-era antique furnishings. Guest rooms (which are as gorgeous as the rest of the house, with high ceilings, beautiful antiques, and hardwood floors) open off a large, high-ceilinged central hall. The immediate neighborhood doesn't have a lot to offer, but art galleries, the Tucson Museum of Art, and several good restaurants are within walking distance. The inn also has a separate 1905 brick bungalow that it rents out.

204 S. Scott Ave., Tucson, AZ 85701. ✆ **877/670-9022** or 520/670-9022. Fax 928/833-9974. www.royalelizabeth.com. 7 units. $185–$245 double; $285 house. Rates include full breakfast. Children 9 and under stay free in parent's room. AE, DISC, MC, V. **Amenities:** Concierge; access to nearby health club; Jacuzzi; outdoor heated pool. *In room:* A/C, TV/VCR/DVD, fridge, hair dryer, Wi-Fi.

Moderate

Catalina Park Inn ★★ Close to downtown and overlooking a shady park, this 1927 home has been lovingly restored by owners Mark Hall and Paul Richard. From the outside, the inn has the look of a Mediterranean villa, while many interesting and playful touches enliven the classic interior. The huge Catalina Room in the basement is one of my favorites. Not only does it conjure up the inside of an adobe, but it also has a whirlpool tub in a former cedar closet. Two upstairs rooms have balconies, while two units in a separate cottage across the garden offer more contemporary styling than the rooms in the main house.

309 E. First St., Tucson, AZ 85705. ✆ **800/792-4885** or 520/792-4541. www.catalinaparkinn.com. 6 units. $139–$189 double. Rates include full breakfast. AE, DISC, MC, V. No children 9 or under. **Amenities:** Concierge. *In room:* A/C, TV/DVD, hair dryer, Wi-Fi.

Doubletree Hotel Tucson at Reid Park ★ This in-town high-rise hotel, with its pleasant orange-tree-shaded pool area, is midway between the airport and downtown Tucson, and is something of an in-town budget resort (the Randolph Park municipal golf course is right across the street). Guest rooms boast bright colors and bold contemporary designs, and there's a big exercise room by the pool. Although the hotel does a lot of convention business and sometimes feels crowded, the gardens, with their citrus trees (feel free to pick the fruit) and lawns, are always tranquil. Guest rooms are divided between a nine-story tower that offers views of the valley (even-numbered rooms face the pool, odd-numbered rooms face the mountains) and a two-story building with patio rooms overlooking the garden and pool area.

445 S. Alvernon Way, Tucson, AZ 85711. ✆ **800/222-TREE** [8733] or 520/881-4200. Fax 520/323-5225. www.dtreidpark.com. 295 units. Jan–May $139–$329 double, $349–$439 suite; June–Aug $89–$139 double, $179–$299 suite; Sept–Dec $149–$259 double, $259–$359 suite. Children 17 and under stay free in parent's room. AE, DC, DISC, MC, V. Pets accepted ($50 fee). **Amenities:** 2 restaurants; 2 lounges; concierge; exercise room; Jacuzzi; outdoor pool; room service; 3 tennis courts. *In room:* A/C, TV, hair dryer, Wi-Fi.

Inexpensive

Hotel Congress (Finds) Located in the heart of downtown Tucson, the Hotel Congress, built in 1919 to serve railroad passengers, once hosted John Dillinger. Today, it operates as a budget hotel and youth hostel and attracts young globe-trotters. Although the place is utterly basic, the lobby has loads of Southwestern elegance. Guest rooms remain true to their historical character, with antique telephones and old radios, so don't expect anything fancy (like TVs). Most bathrooms have tubs or showers, but a few have both. The classic little Cup Cafe is just off the lobby (think Edward Hopper meets Gen X), as is the tiny Tap Room bar. At night, the hotel's Club Congress (p. 396) is a popular (and loud) dance club (pick up earplugs at the front desk).

311 E. Congress St., Tucson, AZ 85701. ✆ **800/722-8848** or 520/622-8848. Fax 520/792-6366. www.hotelcongress.com. 40 units. $79–$119 double (lower rates in summer). AE, DISC, MC, V. Pets accepted ($10 per night). **Amenities:** Restaurant; bar; nightclub. *In room:* Wi-Fi.

EAST TUCSON

Expensive

Embassy Suites Tucson-Williams Center ★ (Kids) With its red-tile roof, cactus gardens, and colonial Mexican furniture in the lobby, this all-suite hotel feels as if it could be in Mexico, which makes it one of my favorite east Tucson lodgings. You'll surely feel like you're on vacation when you're here, even if you are in the middle of a business district. Guest rooms are two-room suites, which makes this place great for families, and the courtyard pool area, although not very large, provides plenty of opportunities for soaking up the sun on warm days.

 5335 E. Broadway Blvd., Tucson, AZ 85711. ✆ **800/EMBASSY** [362-2779] or 520/745-2700. Fax 520/790-9232. www.tucsonwilliamscenter.embassysuites.com. 142 units. Feb–Apr $199–$249 double; May–Jan $129–$149 double. Rates include full breakfast and evening social hour. Children 17 and under stay free in parent's room. AE, DC, DISC, MC, V. **Amenities:** Exercise room; Jacuzzi; outdoor pool; room service. *In room:* A/C, TV, fridge, hair dryer, Wi-Fi.

Moderate

Radisson Suites Tucson ★★ Value With large and very attractive rooms, this all-suite hotel is a good choice for both those who need plenty of space and those who want to be in the east-side business corridor. The five-story brick building is arranged around two long garden courtyards, one of which has a large pool and whirlpool. In fact, the pool and gardens are among the nicest at any nonresort hotel in Tucson and are the best reasons to stay here. Some rooms have Sleep Number® beds, and rooms on the fourth and fifth floors on the east side have nice mountain views.

6555 E. Speedway Blvd., Tucson, AZ 85710. ✆ **888/201-1718** or 520/721-7100. Fax 520/721-1991. www.radissontucson.com. 299 suites. Oct–May $149–$239 double; June–Sept $119–$149 double. Children 17 and under stay free in parent's room. AE, DC, DISC, MC, V. Pets accepted ($50 fee). **Amenities:** Restaurant; lounge; concierge; exercise room & access to nearby health club; Jacuzzi; outdoor pool; room service. *In room:* A/C, TV, fridge, hair dryer, Wi-Fi.

Inexpensive

Comfort Suites at Sabino Canyon Although it looks rather stark from the outside and shares a parking lot with a shopping center, this Comfort Suites is surprisingly pleasant inside. Built around four tranquil and lushly planted garden courtyards, the hotel has (for the most part) large rooms, some of which have kitchenettes. This is a good economical choice close to Sabino Canyon, the Mount Lemmon Highway, and Saguaro National Park's east unit.

7007 E. Tanque Verde Rd., Tucson, AZ 85715. ✆ **800/424-6423** or 520/298-2300. Fax 520/298-6756. www.choicehotels.com. 90 units. $90–$150 double. Rates include full breakfast and evening social hour. Children 18 and under stay free in parent's room. AE, DC, DISC, MC, V. Pets accepted ($25 per night). **Amenities:** Access to nearby health club; Jacuzzi; small outdoor pool. *In room:* A/C, TV, fridge, hair dryer, Wi-Fi.

THE FOOTHILLS

Very Expensive

The Lodge at Ventana Canyon ★★ This boutique golf resort shares the same two Tom Fazio–designed golf courses as Loews Ventana Canyon Resort. Stay here, though, and you'll get more personal service. The Lodge at Ventana Canyon is part of a gated country club community at the base of the Santa Catalina Mountains, so when you stay here you feel more like a resident than just another hotel guest. Because this is such a small resort, it has a more relaxed feel than the Hilton Tucson El Conquistador Resort or the Omni Tucson National Resort. Accommodations are in spacious suites, most of which have mission-style furnishings, small kitchens, large bathrooms with oversize tubs, and walls of windows facing the mountains. A few units have balconies, cathedral ceilings, and spiral stairs that lead to sleeping lofts. The third hole of the resort's Mountain Course is one of Tucson's most photographed holes.

6200 N. Clubhouse Lane, Tucson, AZ 85750. ✆ **800/828-5701** or 520/577-1400. Fax 520/577-4065. www.thelodgeatventanacanyon.com. 50 units. Jan to early Apr $289–$599 1-bedroom suite, $459–$739 2-bedroom suite; early Apr to mid-May $189–$419 1-bedroom suite, $359–$619 2-bedroom suite; mid-May to early Sept $109–$175 1-bedroom suite, $189–$275 2-bedroom suite; early Sept to Dec $179–$399 1-bedroom suite, $349–$599 2-bedroom suite. Rates do not include $24 nightly service charge. Children

17 and under stay free in parent's room. AE, DC, DISC, MC, V. Pets accepted ($50 fee). **Amenities:** Restaurant; lounge; snack bar; children's programs; concierge; 2 acclaimed 18-hole golf courses; exercise room; 2 Jacuzzis; outdoor pool; room service; full-service spa; 11 tennis courts. *In room:* A/C, TV, hair dryer, kitchen, Wi-Fi.

Loews Ventana Canyon Resort ★★★ Kids For breathtaking scenery, distinctive architecture, and superb resort facilities (including two Tom Fazio golf courses, a full-service spa, and lots of options for kids), no other Tucson resort can compare. The Santa Catalina Mountains rise behind the property, and flagstone floors in the lobby lend a rugged but luxurious appeal. Guest rooms have balconies that overlook city lights or mountains. Bathrooms include tubs for two, and some rooms have fireplaces. The Ventana Room (see review, p. 370) is one of the best restaurants in Tucson, and has great views. The lobby lounge serves afternoon tea before becoming an evening piano bar. In addition to numerous other amenities, there are jogging and nature trails and a playground.

7000 N. Resort Dr., Tucson, AZ 85750. ✆ **800/234-5117** or 520/299-2020. Fax 520/299-6832. www.loewshotels.com/hotels/tucson. 398 units. Early Jan to late May $289–$429 double, from $760 suite; late May to early Sept $160–$295 double, from $295 suite; early Sept to early Jan from $289–$429 double, from $700 suite. Children 17 and under stay free in parent's room. AE, DC, DISC, MC, V. Pets accepted ($25 fee). **Amenities:** 6 restaurants; 3 lounges; babysitting; children's programs; concierge; 2 acclaimed 18-hole golf courses; exercise room & access to nearby health club; 2 Jacuzzis; 2 outdoor pools; room service; full-service spa; 4 tennis courts. *In room:* A/C, TV, fridge, hair dryer, minibar, Wi-Fi.

The Westin La Paloma Resort & Spa ★★ Kids If grand scale is what you're looking for, this is the place. Everything about the Westin La Paloma is big—big portico, big lobby, big pool area—and from the resort's sunset-pink mission-revival buildings, there are big views. While adults will appreciate the resort's tennis courts, exercise facilities, and poolside lounge chairs, kids will love the 177-foot water slide. Guest rooms are in 27 low-rise buildings surrounded by desert landscaping. Couples should opt for the king rooms (ask for a mountain or golf course view if you don't mind spending a bit more). French-inspired Southwestern cuisine is the specialty at the on-site restaurant Janos (p. 370), which is one of Tucson's finest restaurants. The resort's spa is a Red Door Spa by Elizabeth Arden.

3800 E. Sunrise Dr., Tucson, AZ 85718. ✆ **800/WESTIN-1** [937-8461] or 520/742-6000. Fax 520/577-5878. www.westinlapalomaresort.com. 487 units. Jan to late May $249–$479 double, from $445 suite; late May to mid-Sept $119–$169 double, from $245 suite; mid-Sept to Dec $209–$279 double, from $375 suite. Rates do not include $15 daily service fee. Children 12 and under stay free in parent's room. AE, DC, DISC, MC, V. Valet parking $15. Pets accepted. **Amenities:** 7 restaurants; 3 lounges; babysitting; children's programs; concierge; 27-hole golf course; health club & full-service spa; 4 Jacuzzis; 5 pools (1 for adults only); room service; 10 tennis courts. *In room:* A/C, TV, hair dryer, minibar, Wi-Fi.

Expensive

Embassy Suites Tucson-Paloma Village ★ Kids Situated at the intersection of Skyline Drive and Campbell Road, this hotel is surrounded by upscale shopping centers and is close to some of Tucson's best restaurants. Although the suites here are small by Embassy Suites standards, you will still get two rooms, which makes this hotel a good choice for families on a budget. Some suites have mountain views, while others overlook the dense desert vegetation of a dry wash. The pool area has limited mountain views. The full breakfast and afternoon snacks and drinks can help you save on meal costs.

3110 E. Skyline Dr., Tucson, AZ 85718. ✆ **800/EMBASSY** [362-2779] or 520/352-4000. Fax 520/352-4001. www.tucsonpalomavillage.embassysuites.com. 119 units. Jan–Apr $169–$260 double; May and Sept–Dec $139–$180 double; June–Aug $89–$140 double. Rates include full breakfast and evening social hour. Children 17 and under stay free in parent's room. AE, DC, DISC, MC, V. **Amenities:** Exercise room; Jacuzzi; outdoor pool. *In room:* A/C, TV, fridge, hair dryer, Internet.

Hacienda del Sol Guest Ranch Resort ★★ Finds With its colorful Southwest styling, historical character, mature cactus gardens, and ridge-top setting, Hacienda del Sol is one of Tucson's most distinctive getaways. The lodge's basic rooms, set around flower-filled courtyards, are evocative of old Mexican inns and have a rustic and colorful character, with a decidedly artistic flair. If you prefer more modern, spacious accommodations, ask for a suite (several of which were redone in 2009); if you want loads of space and the chance to stay where Katharine Hepburn and Spencer Tracy may have stayed, ask for a casita. With large terraces for alfresco dining, the Grill (p. 369) is one of Tucson's best restaurants. During the day, you can lounge by the small pool or go for a horseback ride.

5601 N. Hacienda del Sol Rd., Tucson, AZ 85718. ✆ **800/728-6514** or 520/299-1501. www.haciendadelsol.com. 30 units. Early Jan to May $175–$280 double, $345–$355 suite, $395–$495 casita; June–Sept $109–$164 double, $175–$195 suite, $195–$310 casita; Oct to early Jan $165–$260 double, $330–$340 suite, $370–$495 casita. 2-night minimum stay weekends and holidays. AE, DC, DISC, MC, V. Pets accepted ($50 fee). **Amenities:** Restaurant; lounge; babysitting; access to nearby health club; Jacuzzi; small outdoor pool; room service; spa. *In room:* A/C, TV, fridge, hair dryer, minibar, Wi-Fi.

Westward Look Resort ★★ Value This reasonably priced resort, with the desert at its doorstep and a nature trail through the cactuses, is a favorite of mine. Built in 1912 as a private estate, Westward Look is the oldest resort in Tucson, and although it doesn't have a golf course, it has horseback riding stables, an excellent spa, and plenty of tennis courts. The large guest rooms have a Southwestern flavor and private patios or balconies with city views. For the ultimate in Southwest luxury, opt for one of the stargazer spa suites, which have outdoor hot tubs. The Gold Room, the resort's main restaurant, utilizes herbs and vegetables grown on-site. If you aren't a golfer but do enjoy resort amenities, this is one of your best bets in Tucson. By 2010, a $10-million renovation should be complete.

245 E. Ina Rd., Tucson, AZ 85704. ✆ **800/722-2500** or 520/297-1151. Fax 520/297-9023. www.westwardlook.com. 244 units. Jan–Apr $179–$395 double; May $149–$199 double; June–Sept $89–$189 double; Oct–Dec $169–$295 double. Rates do not include $12 daily resort fee. Children 17 and under stay free in parent's room. AE, DC, DISC, MC, V. Pets accepted ($75 fee). **Amenities:** 2 restaurants; lounge; concierge; exercise room & access to nearby health club; 3 Jacuzzis; 3 pools; room service; full-service spa; 8 tennis courts. *In room:* A/C, TV, fridge, hair dryer, Wi-Fi.

Moderate

Windmill Suites at St. Philip's Plaza Value Located on the edge of the foothills in the St. Philip's Plaza shopping center, this hotel offers both a great location and a good value. Best of all, you can walk to several restaurants and upscale shops right across the parking lot. Bikes are available to guests, and out the hotel's back door is a paved pathway along the Rillito River (which, by the way, is usually bone-dry). Accommodations are spacious and have double vanities, wet bars, and two TVs—basically, everything you need for a long, comfortable stay.

4250 N. Campbell Ave., Tucson, AZ 85718. ✆ **800/547-4747** or 520/577-0007. Fax 520/577-0045. www.windmillinns.com. 122 units. Jan–Mar $140–$170 double; Apr–May and Oct–Dec $108–$134 double; June–Sept $83–$93 double. Rates include continental breakfast. Children 17 and under stay free in parent's room. AE, DC, DISC, MC, V. Pets accepted. **Amenities:** Bikes; exercise room and access to nearby health club; Jacuzzi; outdoor pool. *In room:* A/C, TV, fridge, hair dryer, Wi-Fi.

Inexpensive

La Posada Lodge and Casitas ★ Value Although this hotel fronts busy Oracle Road, once you check in and park yourself on your patio overlooking the pool or the grassy courtyard, you'll forget all about the traffic out front. There are several different types of rooms here, but my favorites are the "Western"-style rooms, which have a sort of retro south-of-the-border decor that includes headboards painted with classic Mexican scenes. Casitas, which are the largest and most expensive rooms here, have a similar decor. There are also some fun rooms with a 1950s retro feel. The attractive rooms, pleasant pool area, and on-site Mexican restaurant together make this an excellent and economical choice.

5900 N. Oracle Rd., Tucson, AZ 85704. ✆ **800/810-2808** or 520/887-4800. Fax 520/293-7543. www.laposadalodge.com. 72 units. $89–$149 double. Rates include continental breakfast. Children 17 and under stay free in parent's room. AE, DC, DISC, MC, V. Pets accepted ($50 fee). **Amenities:** Restaurant; lounge; exercise room; Jacuzzi; outdoor pool. *In room:* A/C, TV, fridge, hair dryer, Wi-Fi.

WEST TUCSON, ORO VALLEY & MARANA

Expensive

Hilton Tucson El Conquistador Golf & Tennis Resort ★★ Kids Although this large resort is a bit out-of-the-way, the view of the Santa Catalina Mountains rising behind El Conquistador makes this northern foothills resort one of my favorites in Tucson. Sunsets are truly spectacular! Most guest rooms are built around a central courtyard with manicured lawns and a large oasis of swimming pools, one of which has a long water slide. The pool area and the resort's horseback-riding stables make the Hilton an excellent choice for families. All rooms feature Southwestern-influenced contemporary furniture, spacious marble bathrooms, and balconies or patios. Be sure to ask for a mountain-view room. Golf on the resort's three courses is the favorite pastime here, but this is not so exclusively a golf resort as such places as the Lodge at Ventana Canyon or the Omni Tucson National Resort.

10000 N. Oracle Rd., Tucson, AZ 85704. ✆ **800/325-7832** or 520/544-5000. Fax 520/544-1222. www.hiltonelconquistador.com. 428 units. Jan to late May $209–$319 double, from $359 suite; late May to early Sept $119–$209 double, from $179 suite; early Sept to Dec $149–$259 double, from $239 suite. Rates do not include $10 daily service fee. Children 18 and under stay free in parent's room. AE, DC, DISC, MC, V. Valet parking $11. Pets accepted ($50 fee). **Amenities:** 4 restaurants; 2 lounges; babysitting; seasonal children's programs; concierge; 1 9-hole and 2 18-hole golf courses; health club; 3 Jacuzzis; 4 pools; room service; saunas; spa; 31 tennis courts. *In room:* A/C, TV, hair dryer, minibar, Wi-Fi.

La Zarzuela ★★ If you want to stay in the middle of the desert and not the middle of the city, then this is the place for you. La Zarzuela sits high on a hill surrounded by saguaros and is just down a dirt road from Tucson Mountain Park, which is every bit as beautiful as Saguaro National Park. The inn has four colorfully decorated guest rooms spread around the sprawling modern Santa Fe–style building. The pool and hot tub are built on the edge of the desert, while courtyards and patios have splashes of colorful flowers in their landscaping. It's all very Southwestern, the perfect place to stay if you want to explore the desert.

455 N. Camino de Oeste (P.O. Box 86030), Tucson, AZ 85754. ✆ **888/848-8225.** www.zarzuela-az.com. 5 units. $275–$325 double. Rates include full breakfast and evening wine and hors d'oeuvres. 2-night minimum. DISC, MC, V. Closed June 15–Sept 15. No children 17 or under. **Amenities:** Concierge; access to nearby health club; Jacuzzi; outdoor pool. *In room:* A/C, TV/DVD, fridge, hair dryer, Internet.

Omni Tucson National Resort ★★ Golf is the name of the game at this boutique resort, which though a bit out of the resort mainstream is looking good after a major makeover. The spacious rooms here, with their warm contemporary styling and balconies or patios, are now some of the finest and most luxurious in town, and most cling to the edges of the golf course. The golf course here is far more forgiving than those shared by the Lodge at Ventana Canyon and Loews Ventana Canyon, which makes this a good choice for golfers not up to the challenge of desert-style golf.

2727 W. Club Dr. (off Magee Rd.), Tucson, AZ 85742. ✆ **800/THE-OMNI** [843-6664] or 520/297-2271. Fax 520/297-7544. www.omnihotels.com. 167 units. Jan–Apr $209–$459 double; May $199–$349 double; June–Aug $129–$259 double; Sept–Dec $239–$389 double. Rates do not include $12 nightly service charge. Children 17 and under stay free in parent's room. AE, DC, DISC, MC, V. Valet parking $10. Pets accepted ($50 fee). **Amenities:** 2 restaurants; lounge; concierge; 2 18-hole golf courses; health club; 2 Jacuzzis; large pool; room service; sauna; full-service spa; 4 tennis courts; Wi-Fi. *In room:* A/C, TV, hair dryer, minibar, Internet.

Moderate

Casa Tierra Adobe Bed & Breakfast Inn ★ If you've come to Tucson to be in the desert, then this secluded B&B west of Saguaro National Park is another good choice. Built to look as if it has been here since Spanish colonial days, the modern adobe home is surrounded by cactus and paloverde trees. There are great views across a landscape full of saguaros to the mountains, and sunsets are enough to take your breath away. Guest rooms, which have wrought-iron sleigh beds, open onto a central courtyard surrounded by a covered seating area. The two outdoor hot tubs make perfect stargazing spots, and there are a couple of telescopes on the property.

11155 W. Calle Pima, Tucson, AZ 85743. ✆ **866/254-0006** or 520/578-3058. www.casatierratucson.com. 4 units. Dec–Apr $165–$195 double, $215–$325 suite; May and Oct–Nov $150–$175 double, $195–$275 suite; June–Sept $135–$150 double, $165–$225 suite. Rates include full breakfast. 2-night minimum stay. AE, DISC, MC, V. Closed June 15–Aug 16. **Amenities:** Concierge; exercise room; Jacuzzi. *In room:* A/C, fridge, hair dryer, Wi-Fi.

Wingate by Wyndham Oro Valley/North Tucson Although this is primarily a business hotel, it has breathtaking views of the Santa Catalina Mountains from its east-facing rooms and is located across the highway from Catalina State Park. For these two reasons, I think it's a great bet for anyone looking for a moderately priced modern hotel close to good hiking. Guest rooms are large and very comfortable. Oro Valley, a suburb of Tucson, has been booming in recent years and now has some decent restaurants, so you won't have to drive too far for a good dinner.

11075 N. Oracle Rd., Oro Valley, AZ 85737. ✆ **800/228-1000** or 520/544-2100. Fax 520/544-2113. www.wingatehotels.com. 104 units. Jan–Apr $145 double, $199–$239 suite; May and Oct–Dec $125 double, $135–$239 suite; June–Sept $92 double, $110–$239 suite. Rates include continental breakfast. Children 17 and under stay free in parent's room. AE, DC, DISC, MC, V. **Amenities:** Excercise room; Jacuzzi; outdoor pool. *In room:* A/C, TV, fridge, hair dryer, Wi-Fi.

Inexpensive

Starr Pass Golf Suites ★ Located 3 miles west of I-10, Starr Pass is the most economically priced golf resort in the city. It's a condominium resort, however, which means you shouldn't expect the sort of service you get at other resorts. Accommodations are in privately owned Santa Fe–style casitas rented as two-bedroom units, master suites, or standard hotel-style rooms. The small hotel-style rooms are a bit cramped and not nearly as lavishly appointed as the master suites, which are more comfortable and have fireplaces, full kitchens, balconies, and a Southwestern style throughout. The desert-style

27-hole golf course is one of the best courses in the city. There are also hiking/biking trails on the property.

3645 W. Starr Pass Blvd., Tucson, AZ 85745. ✆ **800/503-2898** or 520/670-0500. Fax 520/670-0427. http://shellhospitality.com. 80 units. $76–$149 double, $102–$189 suite, $250–$350 casita. Children 17 and under stay free in parent's room. AE, DC, DISC, MC, V. **Amenities:** Restaurant; lounge; 27-hole golf course; exercise room; Jacuzzi; outdoor pool; 2 tennis courts; Wi-Fi. *In room:* A/C, TV/DVD/VCR, fridge, hair dryer, Internet.

NEAR THE AIRPORT

Moderate

Hyatt Place Tucson Airport The airport location is none too appealing and this is primarily a business-travelers' hotel, but the Hyatt Place is just so pretty and well-designed that you should consider it. The suites all have separate sitting and sleeping areas, with 42-inch flat-panel TVs that can be angled to either area. Unusual features include electronic self-service check-in kiosks, continental (free) or hot (charge) breakfasts, and a tiny lounge area to one side of the lobby. You can even get a light meal here if you don't feel like going out to a restaurant for dinner. Another reason to stay here? It's close to the Pima Air & Space Museum and Mission San Xavier del Bac.

6885 S. Tucson Blvd., Tucson, AZ 85756. ✆ **800/492-8847** or 520/295-0405. Fax 520/295-9140. www.hyattplace.com. 120 units. $99–$249 double. Rates include continental breakfast. Children 17 and under stay free in parent's room. AE, DC, DISC, MC, V. **Amenities:** Restaurant; lounge; free airport transfers; exercise room; outdoor pool. *In room:* A/C, TV, fridge, hair dryer, Wi-Fi.

NORTH OF TUCSON

Across the Creek at Aravaipa Farms ★★ (Finds) Located 60 miles north of Tucson on Aravaipa Creek, this B&B is a romantic getaway near one of the state's most spectacular desert-wilderness areas. Because the inn is 3 miles up a gravel road and then across a stream (high-clearance vehicles recommended), it's a long way to a restaurant. Consequently, innkeeper Carol Steele provides all meals. Guests entertain themselves hiking in the Aravaipa Canyon Wilderness, bird-watching, and cooling off in the creek. The casitas are eclectically decorated with a mix of folk art and rustic Mexican furnishings, and have tile floors, stone-walled showers, and shady verandas. For a romantic weekend or a vigorous vacation, this inn makes an ideal base. Carol also rents out a three-bedroom house that sleeps up to six people.

89395 Aravaipa Rd., Winkelman, AZ 85292. ✆ **520/357-6901.** www.aravaipafarms.com. 5 units. Oct–May $345 double, $750 house; June–Sept $250 double, $600 house. Rates include all meals. 2-night minimum stay weekends and holidays. AE, MC, V. Children by prior arrangement. **Amenities:** Dining room; outdoor pool. *In room:* Fridge, no phone.

SPAS

Canyon Ranch Health Resort ★★★ Canyon Ranch, one of America's premier health spas, offers the sort of complete spa experience that's available at only a handful of places around the country (and then only if you have both money and fat to burn). On staff are doctors, nurses, psychotherapists and counselors, fitness instructors, massage therapists, and tennis and golf pros. Services offered include health and fitness assessments; health, nutrition, exercise, and stress-management evaluations; fitness classes; massage therapy; therapeutic body treatments; facials, manicures, pedicures, and haircuts; makeup consultations; cooking demonstrations; and art classes. Guests stay in a variety of spacious and very comfortable accommodations. Three gourmet, low-calorie meals are served daily. If you're serious about getting healthy or looking younger, this is your place in the sun.

8600 E. Rockcliff Rd., Tucson, AZ 85750. ✆ **800/742-9000** or 520/749-9000. Fax 520/239-8535. www.canyonranch.com. 185 units. Sept to early June 4-night packages from $3,770 double; early June to Aug 4-night packages from $2,760 double. Rates include all meals and a variety of spa services and programs. AE, DC, DISC, MC, V. Pets accepted. No children 13 or under (with exception of infants in the care of personal nannies). **Amenities:** 2 dining rooms; free airport transfers; bikes; concierge; 7 exercise rooms; 8 Jacuzzis; 3 outdoor pools & 11,000-sq.-ft. aquatic center; room service; saunas; huge spa complex; 7 tennis courts. *In room:* A/C, TV/DVD, hair dryer, Internet.

Miraval Life in Balance Resort and Spa ★★★ Miraval, Tucson's other world-class destination spa, emphasizes stress management, self-discovery, and relaxation. To this end, activities at the all-inclusive resort include meditation, yoga, art classes, and a variety of confidence-building activities; more active types can go hiking, mountain biking, and rock climbing. Of course, there are also plenty of more traditional spa offerings such as massages, wraps, scrubs, facials, manicures, and pedicures. The spa also offers a variety of lifestyle-management workshops, fitness/nutrition consultations, exercise classes, and an "equine experience" program. The spa's main pool is a gorgeous three-tiered leisure pool surrounded by waterfalls and desert landscaping. Guest rooms, many of which have views of the Santa Catalina Mountains, are done up in a Southwestern style. Miraval has LEED-certified sustainable rooms, and its dining room uses local and organic ingredients as much as possible.

5000 E. Via Estancia Miraval, Tucson, AZ 85739. ✆ **800/232-3969.** Fax 520/825-5163. www.miravalresorts.com. 118 units. Mid-Jan to late May and mid-Oct to Dec $998–$1,938 double; late May to mid-Oct $798–$1,658 double. Rates do not include 17.5% service charge. Rates include all meals, classes, and a $125 per-person per-day credit for spa service, a round of golf, or private consultation. AE, DC, DISC, MC, V. No children. **Amenities:** 2 restaurants; lounge; snack bar; free airport transfers; bikes; concierge; superbly equipped exercise room; 5 Jacuzzis; 5 pools; room service; saunas; one of the most extensive spas in Arizona; 2 tennis courts. *In room:* A/C, TV/DVD, hair dryer, Wi-Fi.

GUEST RANCHES

Tanque Verde Ranch ★★ Want to spend long days in the saddle but don't want to give up resort luxuries? Then Tanque Verde Ranch, which was founded in 1868 and still has some of its original buildings, is for you. This is far and away the most luxurious guest ranch in Tucson. With Saguaro National Park and the Coronado National Forest bordering the ranch, there's plenty of room for horseback riding. There are also nature trails and a nature center, and at the end of the day, the spa provides ample opportunities to recover from too many hours in the saddle. Guest rooms are spacious and comfortable, with fireplaces and patios in many units. Some of the large casitas are among the most luxurious accommodations in the state. The dining room, which overlooks the Rincon Mountains, sets impressive buffets.

14301 E. Speedway Blvd., Tucson, AZ 85748. ✆ **800/234-DUDE** [3833] or 520/296-6275. Fax 520/721-9426. www.tanqueverderanch.com. 74 units. Late Dec to Apr $420–$720 double; May–Sept $330–$520 double; Oct to late Dec $370–$515 double. Rates include all meals and ranch activities. Children 3 and under stay free in parent's room. AE, DISC, MC, V. **Amenities:** Dining room; lounge; free airport transfers w/4-night stay; bikes; children's programs; exercise room; 2 Jacuzzis; 2 pools (indoor & outdoor); saunas; small spa; 5 tennis courts. *In room:* A/C, fridge, hair dryer, Internet.

White Stallion Ranch ★ (Kids Set on 3,000 acres of desert, the White Stallion Ranch is perfect for those who crave wide-open spaces. Operated since 1965 by the True family, this spread has a more authentic feel than any other guest ranch in the area. A variety of horseback rides are offered Monday through Saturday, and a petting zoo keeps kids entertained. There are also nature trails, guided nature walks and hikes, hayrides, weekly rodeos, and team cattle penning. Guest rooms vary considerably in size and comfort, from tiny, Spartan single units to deluxe two-bedroom suites. Renovated rooms are worth requesting.

9251 W. Twin Peaks Rd., Tucson, AZ 85743. ✆ **888/977-2624** or 520/297-0252. Fax 520/744-2786. www.wsranch.com. 42 units. Sept $254–$294 double, $316–$358 suite; Oct to mid-Dec, Jan to mid-Feb, and late Apr to mid-June $320–$372 double, $396–$454 suite; mid-Dec to Jan 1 and mid-Feb to late Apr $374–$454 double, $480–$550 suite. Rates do not include 15% service charge. Rates include all meals. 4- to 6-night minimum stay in winter. Children 2 and under stay free in parent's room. AE, DISC, MC, V. Closed mid-June to Aug. **Amenities:** Dining room; lounge; free airport transfers; bikes; children's programs; concierge; exercise room; Jacuzzi; small outdoor pool; sauna; small spa; tennis court. *In room:* A/C, hair dryer, no phone, Wi-Fi.

4 WHERE TO DINE

Variety, they say, is the spice of life, and Tucson certainly dishes up plenty of variety (and spice) when it comes to eating out. Tucson is a city that lives for spice, and in the realm of fiery foods, Mexican reigns supreme. There's historical Mexican at both El Charro Café and El Minuto Cafe, *nuevo* Mexican at Café Poca Cosa and J Bar, and family-style Mexican at El Minuto. So if you like Mexican food, you'll find plenty of places in Tucson to get all fired up.

On the other hand, if Mexican leaves you cold, don't despair—there are plenty of other restaurants serving everything from the finest French cuisine to innovative American, Italian, and Southwestern food. The last of these is almost as prevalent in Tucson as Mexican food, and you should be sure to dine at a Southwestern restaurant early in your visit. This cuisine can be brilliantly creative, and after trying it, you may want *all* your meals to be Southwestern.

Foodies fond of the latest culinary trends will find plenty of spots to satisfy their cravings. Concentrations of creative restaurants can be found along East Tanque Verde Road and at foothills resorts and shopping plazas. On the other hand, if you're on a tight dining budget, look for early-bird dinners, which are quite popular with retirees.

DOWNTOWN

Moderate

Café Poca Cosa ★★ Value CONTEMPORARY MEXICAN The cuisine served at this stylish downtown restaurant is the creation of owner/chef Suzana Davila and has been compared to the dishes dreamed up in *Like Water for Chocolate.* Although ostensibly Mexican, this food is not just *any* Mexican food; it's imaginative and different and is served in a bold and angular space that belies the location on the ground floor of a parking garage. Expect such creations as grilled beef with a jalapeño chili and tomatillo sauce, and chicken with a dark *mole* sauce made with Kahlúa, chocolate, almonds, and chiles. The menu is posted on portable blackboards, so you never know what you might find on any given day. Opt for the *plato* Poca Cosa, a trio of dishes chosen by the chef that provides you with good idea of what the food here is all about.

110 E. Pennington St. ✆ **520/622-6400.** www.cafepocacosainc.com. Reservations highly recommended. Main courses $13–$16 lunch, $18–$26 dinner. DISC, MC, V. Tues–Thurs 11am–9pm; Fri–Sat 11am–10pm.

Anthony's in the Catalinas **14**
Arizona Inn **26**
Beyond Bread **24**
Blanco Tacos + Tequila **15**
Brooklyn Pizza Company **4**
Café à la C'Art **2**
Café Poca Cosa **3**
Candela Restaurant **12**
The Dish Bistro & Wine Bar **28**
El Charro Café **1**, **10**, **30**, **31**, **36**
El Corral Restaurant **18**
El Guero Canelo **20**
Feast **29**
The Grill **17**
HiFalutin Rapid Fire Western Grill **9**
Janos **16**
JAX Kitchen **8**
J Bar **16**
Kingfisher Bar & Grill **25**
Little Anthony's Diner **32**
Lovin' Spoonfuls **22**
McMahon's Prime Steakhouse **35**
Miguel's **11**
Pastiche Modern Eatery **21**
Pinnacle Peak Steakhouse **33**
Teresa's Mosaic Café **5**
Tohono Chul Tea Room **6**
Tucson Tamale Company **27**
Ventana Room **37**
Vivace Restaurant **19**
Wildflower **7**
Yoshimatsu Healthy Japanese Eatery **23**
Zona 78 **13**, **34**

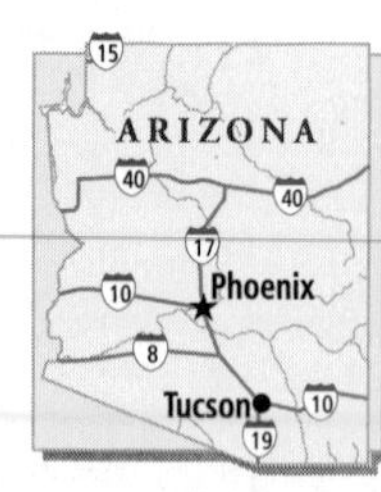

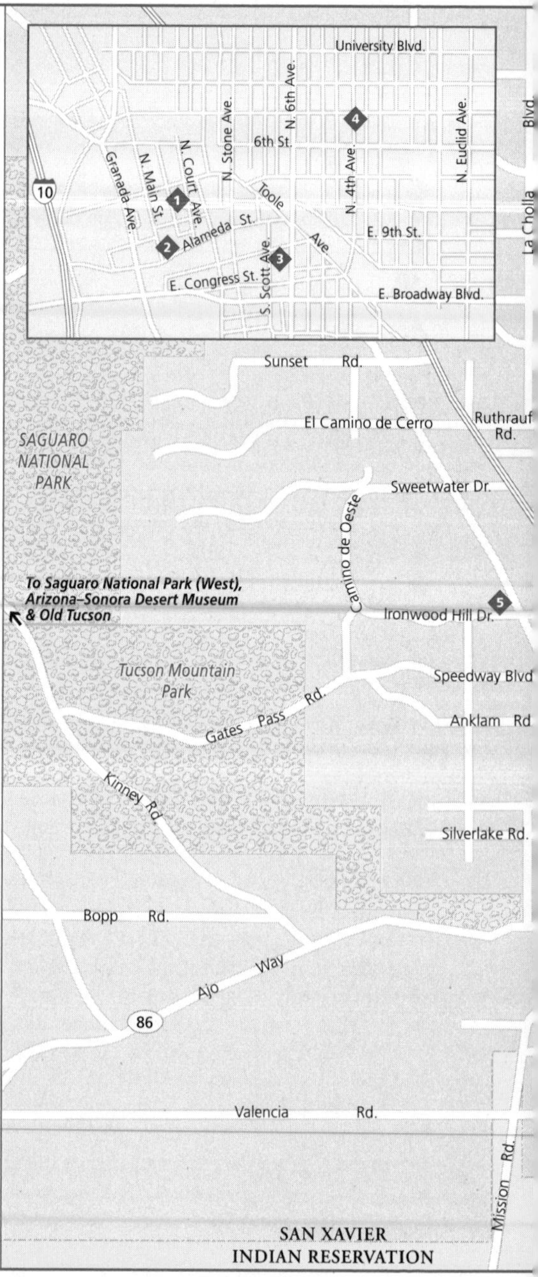

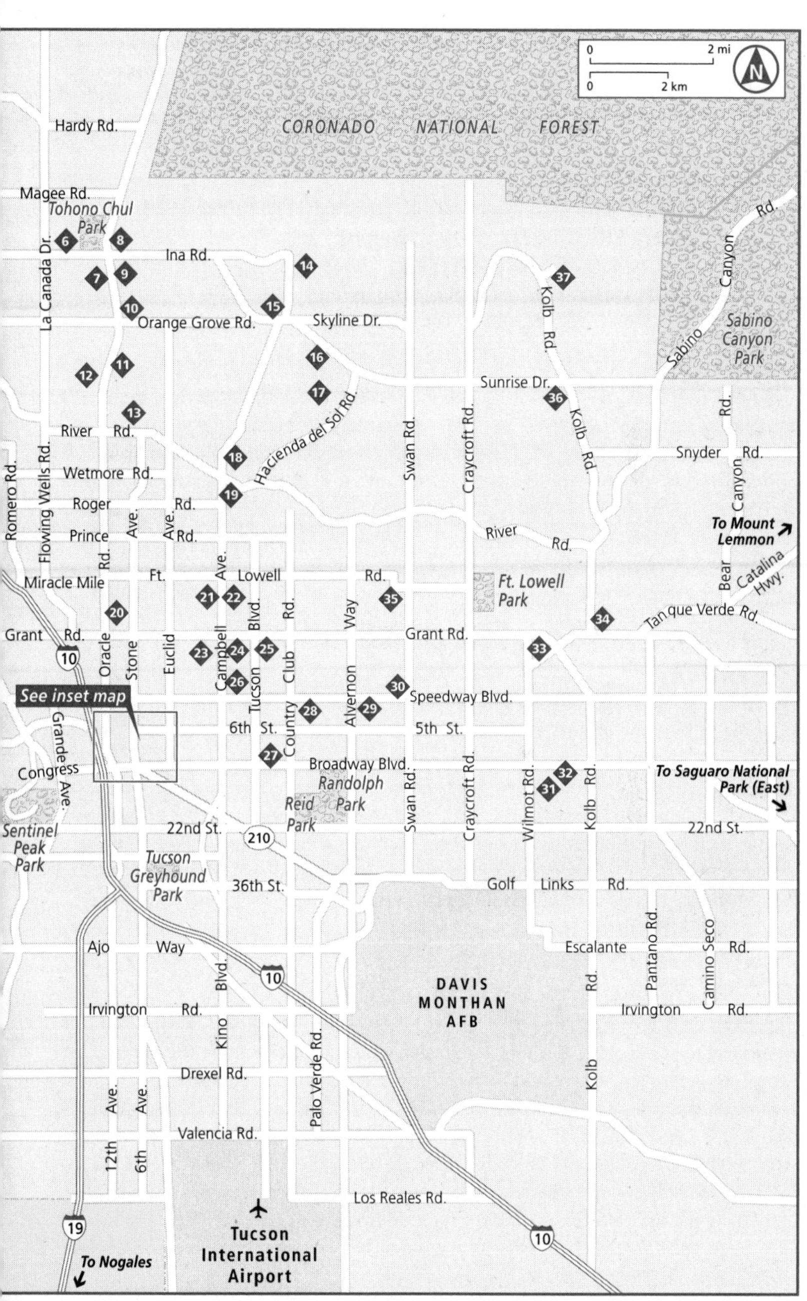
0
2 mi
0
2 km
N
CORONADO NATIONAL FOREST
Hardy Rd.
Magee Rd.
Tohono Chul Park
Ina Rd.
La Canada Dr.
Orange Grove Rd.
Skyline Dr.
Kolb Rd.
Sabino Canyon Rd.
Sabino Canyon Park
Sunrise Dr.
Hacienda del Sol Rd.
River Rd.
Wetmore Rd.
Roger Rd.
Prince Rd.
Romero Rd.
Flowing Wells Rd.
Swan Rd.
Craycroft Rd.
Snyder Rd.
Bear Canyon Rd.
To Mount Lemmon
Catalina Hwy.
Miracle Mile
Ft. Lowell Rd.
Ft. Lowell Park
Tanque Verde Rd.
Grant Rd.
Oracle Rd.
Stone Ave.
Euclid Ave.
Campbell Ave.
Tucson Blvd.
Country Club Rd.
Alvernon Way
Speedway Blvd.
See inset map
Grande Ave.
Congress
6th St.
5th St.
Broadway Blvd.
Randolph Park
Reid Park
Wilmot Rd.
To Saguaro National Park (East)
Sentinel Peak Park
22nd St.
210
Tucson Greyhound Park
36th St.
Golf Links Rd.
Ajo Way
Escalante Rd.
Pantano Rd.
Camino Seco Rd.
10
Kino Blvd.
DAVIS MONTHAN AFB
Irvington Rd.
Drexel Rd.
Palo Verde Rd.
12th Ave.
6th Ave.
Valencia Rd.
Los Reales Rd.
19
To Nogales
Tucson International Airport

El Charro Café ★ SONORAN MEXICAN El Charro, housed in an old stone building in El Presidio Historic District, is Tucson's oldest family-operated Mexican restaurant and is legendary around these parts for its unusual *carne seca,* a traditional air-dried beef that is a bit like shredded beef jerky. To see how they make *carne seca,* just glance up at the restaurant's roof as you approach. The large metal cage up there is filled with beef drying in the desert sun. You'll rarely find *carne seca* on a Mexican menu outside of Tucson, so indulge while you're here.

The adjacent **¡Toma!** (p. 397), a colorful bar/cantina, is under the same ownership. There are other El Charro locations at 6310 E. Broadway (✆ **520/745-1922**); 4699 E. Speedway Blvd. (✆ **520/325-1922**); 6910 E. Sunrise Dr. (✆ **520/514-1922**); and 7725 N. Oracle Rd., Oro Valley (✆ **520/229-1922**).

311 N. Court Ave. ✆ **520/622-1922.** www.elcharrocafe.com. Reservations recommended for dinner. Main courses $6.25–$19. AE, DISC, MC, V. Daily 11am–9pm.

Inexpensive

Café à la C'Art LIGHT FARE Located in the courtyard on the grounds of the Tucson Museum of Art, this cafe serves up tasty sandwiches and makes a good lunch spot if you're downtown wandering the Presidio neighborhood or touring the museum. Try the gingered apricot-almond chicken-salad croissant or the Cuban sandwich, which is made with roasted pork and ham. Wash it all down with some fresh lemonade, and be sure to save room for dessert.

150 N. Main Ave. ✆ **520/628-8533.** www.tucsonmuseumofart.org/visit/cafe.php. Reservations not accepted. Sandwiches and salads $7.50–$9.50. MC, V. Mon–Fri 11am–3pm; 1st Sun of each month noon–3pm.

CENTRAL TUCSON & THE UNIVERSITY AREA

Expensive

Arizona Inn–Main Dining Room ★ FRENCH/AMERICAN The dining room at the Arizona Inn, one of the state's first resorts, is consistently excellent. The pink-stucco pueblo-style buildings are surrounded by neatly manicured gardens that have matured gracefully, and the courtyard and the bar patio overlooking the colorful gardens make for romantic dining spots. The menu changes regularly, but includes plenty of classic dishes such as vichyssoise, bouillabaisse, and boeuf bourguignon and a handful of Southwestern-inspired offerings. Presentation is artistic, and fresh ingredients are emphasized. The homemade ice creams are fabulous. On weekends, you might catch some live music.

2200 E. Elm St. ✆ **520/325-1541.** www.arizonainn.com. Reservations recommended. Main courses $12–$25 lunch, $30–$44 dinner; tasting menu $65 ($85 with wine). AE, DC, MC, V. Daily 7–10am, 11:30am–2pm, and 5:30–10pm.

The Dish Bistro & Wine Bar ★★ NEW AMERICAN Located inside the Rumrunner wine-and-spirits shop, this tiny, minimalist restaurant is brimming with urban chic. On a busy night, the space could be construed as either cozy or crowded, so if you like it more on the quiet side, come early or late. The chef has a well-deserved reputation for artfully presented dishes that can be both creative and comforting at the same time. On a recent visit, the grilled pork tenderloin was just such a dish. Although the pork tenderloin was familiar enough, the accompaniments—black-pepper caramel sauce, shallot-and-fig confit, and yam *fonduta* (Italian for fondue)—were deliciously exotic. Naturally, because this place is associated with a wine shop, the wine list is great. Despite what the address says, the Dish is right on Speedway Boulevard.

3131 E. First St. ✆ **520/326-1714.** www.dishbistro.com. Reservations recommended. Main courses $18–$34. AE, DISC, MC, V. Tues–Sat 5–9pm.

Moderate

Kingfisher Bar & Grill ★ SEAFOOD If you're serious about seafood, Kingfisher is definitely one of your best bets for a memorable meal in Tucson. The freshest seafood, artfully blended with bright flavors and imaginative ingredients, is deftly prepared as appetizers, sandwiches, and main dishes. You may have difficulty deciding whether to begin with Hama Hama oysters, house-smoked trout, or scallop ceviche—so why not tackle them all and call it a meal? By the way, the warm cabbage salad is a must—delicious! The atmosphere is upscale and lively, the bar and late-night menu are a hit with night owls, and there's live jazz and blues on Monday and Saturday nights.

2564 E. Grant Rd. ✆ **520/323-7739.** http://kingfishertucson.com. Reservations recommended. Main courses $9.50–$14 lunch, $17–$28 dinner. AE, DC, DISC, MC, V. Mon–Fri 11am–midnight; Sat–Sun 5pm–midnight.

Pastiche Modern Eatery ★ NEW AMERICAN Located in a little shopping plaza that has lots of Tucson character, this high-energy bistro serves such an eclectic variety of dishes that it has long been a Tucson favorite. The colorful artwork and vibrant contemporary food fairly shout *trendy,* but the restaurant manages to appeal to a broad spectrum of the population. From a Southwest burger to thyme-crusted sea bass, there's enough here to keep everyone at the table happy. Light eaters can get half-orders of many entrees. The crowded bar is a popular watering hole that turns out tasty margaritas. There's also an adjacent wine shop.

3025 N. Campbell Ave. ✆ **520/325-3333.** www.pasticheme.com. Reservations recommended. Main courses $10–$26. AE, DC, DISC, MC, V. Mon–Fri 11:30am–midnight; Sat–Sun 4:30pm–midnight.

Inexpensive

Beyond Bread AMERICAN/BAKERY Although ostensibly a bakery, this place is really a bustling sandwich shop that also sells great breads and pastries. You can also get a hot breakfast or a selection from the pastry case. The sandwich list is long, with both hot and cold varieties, and they all come on the great bread that's baked on the premises. Most of the sandwiches are so big that you could split them between two people if you weren't too hungry.

There's another Beyond Bread on the east side of town at Monterey Village, 6260 E. Speedway Blvd. (✆ 520/747-7477).

3026 N. Campbell Ave. ✆ **520/322-9965.** www.beyondbread.com. Reservations not accepted. Main courses $4.75–$10. AE, MC, V. Mon–Fri 6:30am–8pm; Sat 7am–8pm; Sun 7am–6pm.

Brooklyn Pizza Company PIZZA Solar-powered pizza? That's what the sign says, and if you look on the roof of the building housing this little pizza joint, you'll see dozens of photovoltaic panels. While the pizzas themselves are baked in a gas-fired oven, everything else in the restaurant runs on the power of the sun. Now that's eco-friendly! There are lunch, late-night, and happy hour specials, plus house-made gelatos.

534 N. Fourth Ave. ✆ **520/622-6868.** www.brooklynpizzacompany.com. Reservations not accepted. Main courses $6–$17. AE, DISC, MC, V. Mon–Sat 11am–11pm; Sun noon–10pm.

El Guero Canelo (Finds) MEXICAN At El Guero Canelo, famous for its Sonoran hot dogs, just about everything in the restaurant is painted in the colors of the Mexican flag (green, white, and red) and mariachi bands sometimes play on the weekends. The hot dog, wrapped in bacon and slathered with beans and salsa, is good, but it isn't nearly as memorable as the restaurant scene itself. For a slice of authentic Tucson culture, this place is not to be missed. The original El Guero Canelo is at 5201 S. 12th Ave. (✆ **520/295-9005**).

2480 N. Oracle Rd. ✆ **520/882-8977.** www.elguerocanelo.com. Reservations not accepted. Main courses $2.50–$6.50. AE, DC, DISC, MC, V. Mon–Sat 7am–midnight; Sun 7:30am–midnight.

Lovin' Spoonfuls VEGAN Chili dogs, turkey sandwiches, tuna melts, bacon cheeseburgers. The menu at this casual little place may not sound too interesting until you realize that not one of those dishes actually has meat in it. This is a vegan restaurant, so there are no eggs or dairy products to be seen (or tasted). If you're already a vegetarian or vegan, you may not want to eat anywhere else while you're in Tucson. Oh, and there are organic beers and wines to accompany your meal.

2990 N. Campbell Ave., Ste. 120. ✆ **520/325-7766.** www.lovinspoonfuls.com. Main courses $5.75–$11. DISC, MC, V. Mon–Sat 9:30am–9pm; Sun 10am–3pm.

Tucson Tamale Company (Finds) MEXICAN Tamales, stuffed cornmeal dumplings steamed in corn husks, are a staple among the Southwest's Hispanic population, but the owners of this restaurant are hoping to take tamales to a broader audience. To that end, the tamales here are made without lard and sometimes include some very nontraditional ingredients. There are vegan tamales (one with spinach and mushrooms), as well as a grilled Wisconsin-cheese tamale. However, the more traditional offerings made with pork loin and green chilies, chicken and tomatillos, and beef sirloin and chipotle peppers are all hard to resist.

2545 E. Broadway. ✆ **520/305-4760.** www.tucsontamalecompany.com. Reservations not accepted. Main courses $3–$6.50. DISC, MC, V. Mon and Sat 10am–5pm; Tues–Fri 10am–6pm.

Yoshimatsu Healthy Japanese Eatery ★ JAPANESE Not only does this restaurant have a long menu of health-conscious Japanese dishes, but the decor in this ultracasual place is also truly outrageous, with little glass cases displaying all manner of Japanese toys and action figures. The *okonomiyaki,* sort of a Japanese pizza, is unusual, delicious, and filling. The green-tea milkshakes are also tasty. There's a stylish little sushi bar attached to the restaurant.

2660 N. Campbell Ave. ✆ **520/320-1574.** www.yoshimatsuaz.com. Reservations not accepted. Main courses $7.50–$17. MC, V. Sat–Thurs 11:30am–2:30pm and 5–9pm; Fri 11:30am–2:30pm and 5–10pm.

EAST TUCSON

Moderate

Zona 78 ★ (Finds) PIZZA Maybe it's the big stone oven they use or maybe it's all the locally grown organic produce, but whatever it is, this place does pizza right. Try the Tuscany, which is covered with Italian sausage, mozzarella, kalamata olives, fennel, garlic, onions, and mushrooms. This pie is just bursting with flavors. To really get the most out of a visit to Zona 78, you need to bring enough people so that you can order the big antipasti plate or the cheese-and-fruit plate, which has lots of great imported cheeses. If you're not that hungry, try the Tuscan bean-and-spinach soup.

There's a second Zona 78 on the west side at 78 W. River Rd. (✆ **520/888-7878**).

7301 E. Tanque Verde Rd. ✆ **520/296-7878.** www.zona78.com. Reservations accepted only for parties of 8 or more. Main courses $9–$20. AE, DISC, MC, V. Daily 11am–10pm.

Inexpensive

Feast ★ Finds INTERNATIONAL Feast is not only a casual sit-down restaurant, but also a gourmet to-go place, which makes it the perfect spot to pick up food for a sunset picnic dinner at Sabino Canyon Recreation Area or Saguaro National Park. The menu changes regularly, but you may find a seared salmon sandwich made with kalamata olive tapenade; saddle of rabbit stuffed with chicken livers, pancetta, artichoke hearts, and leeks; or pork tenderloin served with a warm salad of sunchokes, pancetta, and Brussels sprouts.

4122 E. Speedway Blvd. ✆ **520/326-9363** or 520/326-6500. www.eatatfeast.com. Reservations not accepted. Main courses $8.50–$22. AE, DC, DISC, MC, V. Tues–Sun 11am–9pm.

Little Anthony's Diner Kids AMERICAN This place is primarily for kids, although lots of big kids enjoy the 1950s music and decor. The menu includes such offerings as a Jailhouse Rock burger and Chubby Checker triple-decker club sandwich. Daily specials and bottomless soft drinks make feeding the family fairly inexpensive, and a video-game room will keep your kids entertained while you finish your milkshake. If you want to make a night of it (and you make a reservation far enough in advance), you can take in an old-fashioned melodrama next door at the Gaslight Theatre. Together, these two places make for a fun night out with the family.

7010 E. Broadway Blvd. (in back of the Gaslight Plaza). ✆ **520/296-0456.** www.littleanthonysdiner.com. Burgers and sandwiches $4.75–$9. MC, V. Mon 11am–9pm; Tues–Thurs 11am–10pm; Fri 11am–11pm; Sat 7:30am–11pm; Sun 7:30am–9pm.

THE FOOTHILLS

Expensive

Anthony's in the Catalinas ★★ NEW AMERICAN/CONTINENTAL From the moment you drive up and let the valet park your car, Anthony's, housed in a modern Italianate building overlooking the city, exudes Southwestern elegance. The waiters are smartly attired in tuxedos, and guests (the cigar-and-single-malt foothills set) are nearly as well dressed. In such a rarefied atmosphere, you'd expect only the finest meal and service, and that's exactly what you get. The house-smoked salmon and scallops Rockefeller are both fitting beginnings, followed by the likes of Chateaubriand with béarnaise sauce. Wine is not just an accompaniment, but also a reason for dining out at Anthony's; with more than 1,700 wines, the wine list may be the most extensive in the city.

6440 N. Campbell Ave. ✆ **520/299-1771.** www.anthonyscatalinas.com. Reservations highly recommended. Main courses $30–$49. AE, DC, DISC, MC, V. Daily 5:30–10pm.

The Grill ★★ REGIONAL AMERICAN Great food, historical Southwest character, views, live jazz—this place has it all. Located in a 1920s hacienda-style building at a former foothills guest ranch, the Grill is one of Tucson's best restaurants, so don't leave town without having at least one meal here. The menu changes regularly and always manages to keep up with the latest culinary trends. For a starter, you might be able to have some house-cured gravlax (salmon) or an artichoke-and truffle soup. Despite the price, the dry-aged New York strip steak is deservedly the most popular entree on the menu and is big enough for two people to share. Sunday brunch here is a real treat. The main patio overlooks the Catalinas and the fairways of the Westin La Paloma's golf course. Thursday through Sunday, the restaurant's Terraza del Sol bar has live music.

At the Hacienda del Sol Guest Ranch Resort, 5601 N. Hacienda del Sol Rd. ✆ **520/529-3500.** www.haciendadelsol.com. Reservations recommended. Main courses $16–$34; Sun brunch $32. AE, DC, DISC, MC, V. Daily 5:30–10pm; Sun brunch 10am–1:30pm.

Janos ★★★ SOUTHWESTERN/REGIONAL AMERICAN Janos Wilder, Tucson's most celebrated chef, is not only a world-class chef, but a real sweetheart, too. Should you happen to bump into him while dining here, he'll make you feel as though you've been a regular at his restaurant for years. It is this conviviality—which spills over into all aspects of a meal here—that makes this one of the most memorable restaurants in the state. Consequently, this luxuriously appointed restaurant, which is just outside the front door of the Westin La Paloma (p. 357), should be your top choice for a special-occasion dinner while in Tucson. The menu changes both daily and seasonally, but always features complex dishes that seamlessly meld Southwestern flavors with classic culinary traditions.

No other restaurant in Tucson does as much to promote local and indigenous ingredients as Janos, which works closely with Tucson's Native Seeds/SEARCH organization (p. 393).

At the Westin La Paloma, 3770 E. Sunrise Dr. ✆ **520/615-6100.** www.janos.com. Reservations highly recommended. Main courses $28–$50; 5-course tasting menu $75 ($115 with wine). AE, MC, V. Mon–Thurs 5:30–9pm; Fri–Sat 5:30–9:30pm.

McMahon's Prime Steakhouse ★ STEAK/SEAFOOD If a perfectly done steak is what you're craving, then McMahon's is the place. This restaurant serves some of the best steaks in Tucson, and with a decidedly modern opulence, McMahon's boasts an atmosphere calculated to impress (a large glass-walled wine room dominates the main dining room). You can drop a bundle on dinner here, but no more than you'd spend at such high-end restaurants as Janos or the Ventana Room. The main difference is that your choices at McMahon's are simpler: steak, seafood, or steak and seafood. You'd be wasting a night out, though, if you didn't order a steak. There's a separate piano lounge and cigar bar.

2959 N. Swan Rd. ✆ **520/327-7463.** www.metrorestaurants.com. Reservations recommended. Main courses $9–$18 lunch, $24–$55 dinner. AE, DISC, MC, V. Mon–Thurs 11:30am–10pm; Fri 11:30am–10:30pm; Sat 5–10:30pm; Sun 4–9pm.

Miguel's ★ NUEVO LATINO If you're staying at one of the foothills resorts and just can't get enough Mexican food, this is another good bet for upscale south-of-the-border cuisine. Be sure to start your meal with the guacamole or the lobster "cigars." The bacon-wrapped shrimp and the grilled pork chop with orange-ancho-chile sauce are favorites of mine, but there are also flavorful steaks and lots of seafood dishes. The tequila selection here is one of the best in Tucson, and the margaritas are delicious. If you can, eat before the sun goes down, as there are views of the Santa Catalinas and the city.

At La Posada, 5900 N. Oracle Rd. ✆ **520/887-3777.** www.miguelstucson.com. Reservations recommended. Main courses $16–$34. AE, DISC, MC, V. Daily 3–10pm.

Ventana Room ★★★ NEW AMERICAN The Ventana Room is Tucson's poshest and most classically elegant restaurant, as you'll immediately guess from the wall of wine bottles just inside the door. *Ventana* means "window" in Spanish, and the views through the windows of this restaurant are every bit as memorable as the food. Be sure you make an early dinner reservation so that you can catch the sunset. Although you may have trouble concentrating on your food, do try; you wouldn't want to miss any of the subtle nuances. The tasting menus are designed to provide you with a delicious variety of flavors and textures. Ingredients are flown in from all over the world, so you never know what may show up on the menu. In the restaurant's rarefied atmosphere, you'll be pampered by a bevy of waiters providing professional and unobtrusive service. For superb French-inspired cuisine and gorgeous views, this restaurant just can't be beat.

At Loews Ventana Canyon Resort, 7000 N. Resort Dr. ✆ **520/615-5494.** www.ventanaroom.com. Reservations highly recommended. Jackets recommended for men. Prix-fixe $95 ($175–$250 with wine). AE, DC, DISC, MC, V. Tues–Thurs 6–9pm; Fri–Sat 6–10pm. Closed early June to mid-Sept.

Moderate

Blanco Tacos + Tequila ★ MEXICAN The retro Swedish-modern decor at this restaurant is about as far as you can get from the usual perpetual-fiesta styling of most Mexican restaurants. However, Blanco is far from an average Mexican restaurant. The food here doesn't break any new ground, but the fish tacos are some of the best in Tucson. Dishes are made with fresh ingredients, and even the rice and vegetables that come with meals are well done. Service is friendly and there are great views from the deck. There's a great tequila list, and the bar makes some fun cocktails.

In La Encantada Center, 2905 E. Skyline Dr., Ste. 246. ✆ **520/232-1007.** www.foxrc.com. Reservations not accepted. Main courses $10–$19. AE, DISC, MC, V. Sun–Thurs 11am–10pm; Fri–Sat 11am–11pm.

JAX Kitchen ★ NEW AMERICAN With everything from steamed mussels with *frites* and a brioche grilled cheese to duck-leg confit and tuna niçoise, JAX Kitchen seems like the ultimate French bistro. However, most of the dishes here get a bit of an American or Southwestern spin. The mussels are steamed with chorizo sausage, the tuna is pan-seared for the niçoise, and duck-leg confit might be served in a salad with citrus, strawberries, goat cheese, and spicy almonds. Think of it as comfort food with a French accent, and the ultimate comfort dish here is the whole salt-crusted roast chicken, which takes an hour to prepare. Order it as soon as you walk in. There's a good selection of wines by the glass, and prices tend to be reasonable.

7286 N. Oracle Rd. ✆ **520/219-1235.** www.jaxkitchen.com. Reservations recommended. Main courses $9–$13 lunch, $11–$21 dinner. AE, DISC, MC, V. Tues–Thurs 11:30am–2:30pm and 5–9pm; Fri 11:30am–2:30pm and 5–10pm; Sat 5–10pm.

J Bar ★★★ SOUTHWESTERN The mouthwatering culinary creations of celebrity chef Janos Wilder at half-price? Sounds impossible, but that's pretty much what you'll find at this casual bar and grill adjacent to the famed foothills restaurant. Ask for a seat out on the heated patio, and with the lights of Tucson twinkling in the distance, dig into the best nachos you'll ever taste—here made with chorizo sausage and chile con queso. No matter what you order, you'll likely find that the ingredients and flavor combinations are most memorable. Who can forget spicy jerked pork with cranberry-habanero chutney or Yucatán-style plantain-crusted chicken with green coconut-milk curry? You won't want to miss sampling one of the *postres* (desserts). The dark-chocolate–jalapeño sundae may sound unusual, but it's delicious.

At the Westin La Paloma, 3770 E. Sunrise Dr. ✆ **520/615-6100.** www.janos.com. Reservations highly recommended. Main courses $15–$28. AE, DC, MC, V. Mon–Sat 5–9:30pm.

Vivace Restaurant ★★ NORTHERN ITALIAN With a beautiful Tuscan-inspired setting, this restaurant serves reasonably priced, creative dishes. The atmosphere is lively and the food down-to-earth. For starters, consider indulging in the luscious antipasto platter for two, containing marinated vegetables, prosciutto, roasted red peppers, grilled asparagus, and herbed goat-cheese mousse. Pasta dishes, such as penne with sausage and red pepper–tomato sauce, come nicely presented and in generous portions. But it's the crab-filled chicken breast that is most memorable. The wine list has plenty of selections, many fairly reasonably priced.

At St. Philip's Plaza, 4310 N. Campbell Ave. ✆ **520/795-7221.** Reservations recommended. Main courses $9–$20 lunch, $16–$32 dinner. AE, DC, DISC, MC, V. Mon–Thurs 11:30am–9:30pm; Fri–Sat 11:30am–10pm.

Wildflower ★ NEW AMERICAN Stylish comfort food in large portions is the order of the day at this chic and casually elegant north-Tucson bistro. A huge wall of glass creates minimalist drama, and large flower photographs on the walls enhance the bright and airy decor. The heaping plate of fried calamari with mizuna greens is a good bet for a starter, and entrees run the gamut from a comforting meatloaf to herb-crusted rack of lamb. Pasta and salmon also both show up in reliable guises. With so many tempting, reasonably priced dishes to sample, Wildflower is a foodie's delight.

At Casas Adobes Shopping Plaza, 7037 N. Oracle Rd. (at Ina Rd.). ✆ **520/219-4230.** www.foxrc.com. Reservations recommended. Main courses $9–$17 lunch, $14–$29 dinner. AE, DC, DISC, MC, V. Mon–Thurs 11am–9pm; Fri–Sat 11am–10pm; Sun 5–9pm.

Inexpensive

Candela Restaurant ★ *Finds* PERUVIAN/LATIN AMERICAN It's easy to miss this nondescript little restaurant, which is tucked into an older shopping plaza on Oracle Road south of Ina. However, keep looking. When you find it, you're in for a real treat if you enjoy trying new cuisines. As soon as you sit down, you'll be brought a basket of salty banana chips and a spicy dipping sauce. Make sure you order at least one dish with quinoa, a tiny South American grain. If you see *chicha morada* on the menu, try it. It's an unusual purple corn drink that tastes much better than it sounds.

5845 N. Oracle Rd. ✆ **520/407-0111.** Reservations recommended on weekends. Main courses $7–$10 lunch, $14–$25 dinner. AE, DISC, MC, V. Mon–Fri 11am–2:30pm and 5–9pm; Sat–Sun noon–9pm.

HiFalutin Rapid Fire Western Grill AMERICAN This place knows how to set the Wild West mood, and the restaurant comes through with tasty comfort food with a Western twist. Get anything with the marinated flank steak, and you won't be disappointed. You can get it tossed with pasta, in a salad, or just plain straight up. Wash it all down with one of the great margaritas they serve, and you'll definitely have a highfalutin kind of meal.

6780 N. Oracle Rd. ✆ **520/297-0518.** www.hifalutintucson.com. Reservations recommended. Main courses $8–$11 lunch, $9–$25 dinner. AE, DC, DISC, MC, V. Sun–Thurs 11am–9pm; Fri–Sat 11am–10pm.

Tohono Chul Tea Room REGIONAL AMERICAN Located in a brick territorial-style building in Tohono Chul Park (p. 378), this is one of the most tranquil restaurants in the city, and the garden setting provides a wonderful opportunity to experience the desert. Before or after lunching on grilled raspberry-chipotle chicken or tortilla soup, you can wander through the park's desert landscaping and admire the many species of cactuses. The patios, surrounded by natural vegetation and plenty of potted flowers, are frequented by many species of birds. The adjacent gift shop offers Mexican folk art, nature-themed toys, household items, T-shirts, and books.

7366 N. Paseo del Norte (1 block west of the corner of Ina and Oracle rds. in Tohono Chul Park). ✆ **520/797-1222.** www.tohonochulpark.org. Reservations accepted only for parties of 8 or more. Main courses $7–$11. AE, MC, V. Daily 8am–5pm.

(Kids) Cowboy Steakhouses

Cowboy steakhouses are family restaurants that generally provide big portions of grilled steaks and barbecued ribs, as well as entertainment such as live country music. They tend to be touristy, but they're generally a big hit with the kids.

Located in Trail Dust Town (p. 383), a Wild West–themed shopping, dining, and family entertainment center, **Pinnacle Peak Steakhouse,** 6541 E. Tanque Verde Rd. (© **520/296-0911**), specializes in family dining in a fun cowboy atmosphere. Stroll the wooden sidewalks past the opera house and saloon to the grand old dining rooms of the restaurant. Once through the doors, you'll be surprised at the authenticity of the place, which really does resemble a dining room in Old Tombstone or Dodge City. Be prepared for crowds—this place is very popular with tour buses. Oh, and by the way, wear a necktie into this place and it will be cut off! Main courses run $8 to $20.

Owned by the same folks who run Tucson's Pinnacle Peak Steakhouse, **El Corral Restaurant,** at 2201 E. River Rd. (© **520/299-6092**), is another inexpensive and atmospheric steakhouse. Good prime rib and cheap prices have made this place hugely popular with retirees and families. The restaurant doesn't accept reservations, so expect long lines. Inside, the hacienda building has a genuine old-timey feeling, with flagstone floors and wood paneling that make it dark and cozy. You'll pay $9 to $19 for a complete dinner here.

WEST TUCSON, ORO VALLEY & MARANA

Expensive

Harvest Restaurant ★★ NEW AMERICAN This restaurant, affiliated with both the Grill at Hacienda del Sol and Tucson's two Zona 78s, emphasizes fresh, local, seasonal ingredients and is a good bet if you are staying in the northwest foothills area. The empanadas, which have a lusciously flaky crust and come with a tangy *chimichurri* sauce, are absolutely delicious. Likewise, if you want a great burger, this is the place. Keep an eye out for unusual fish entrees such as pan-seared arctic char with toasted orzo. The attention to ingredients also extends to the cocktail menu, which features seasonal drinks made with fresh-squeezed juices.

10355 N. La Cañada Dr., Ste. 141. © **520/731-1100.** www.marketrg.com. Reservations recommended. Main courses $9–$14 lunch, $15–$29 dinner. AE, DISC, MC, V. Mon–Thurs 5–9pm; Fri 5–10pm; Sat–Sun 11:30am–3pm and 5–10pm.

McClintock's ★★ NEW AMERICAN For classic western ranch atmosphere, there simply is no place else in Arizona to compare with this restaurant inside the exclusive Saguaro Ranch housing development. When you arrive at the development gate, you'll even be escorted through the development to the restaurant. Be sure to make a reservation that will let you sit on the restaurant's veranda and watch the sun go down over the rugged saguaro-covered hills. The view is gorgeous. As often as possible, dishes are made with natural or organic ingredients, and the pastas and steaks are highlights. You'll find McClintock's at the north end of Thornydale Road (north of Tangerine Rd.).

In Saguaro Ranch, 3755 W. Conrads Way, Marana. ✆ **520/579-2100.** www.mcclintocks-restaurant.com. Reservations required. Main courses $17–$45. AE, DISC, MC, V. Sun–Thurs 5–10pm; Fri–Sat 5–11pm.

Inexpensive

Teresa's Mosaic Café ★ Finds MEXICAN A mile or so west of I-10, this casual Mexican restaurant, with colorful mosaic tile tables, mirror frames, and a kitchen counter, is hidden behind a McDonald's on the corner of Grant and Silverbell roads but is well worth finding for breakfast or lunch. Try the *chilaquiles* or chorizo and eggs for breakfast, and don't pass up the fresh lemonade or *horchata* (spiced rice milk). This is an especially good spot for a meal if you're on your way to the Arizona–Sonora Desert Museum, Old Tucson, or Saguaro National Park's west unit.

2456 N. Silver Mosaic Rd. ✆ **520/624-4512.** Reservations recommended on weekends. Main courses $5–$16. DISC, MC, V. Mon–Sat 7:30am–9pm; Sun 7:30am–2pm.

5 SEEING THE SIGHTS

Go west, young man (and woman). That's what you'll need to do if you're visiting Tucson and want to immerse yourself in the desert Southwest or the cinematic Wild West. Out past the western outskirts of Tucson, where the cactus grows and the tumbleweed blows, you'll find not only the west unit of Saguaro National Park (with the biggest and best stands of saguaro cactus), but also the Arizona–Sonora Desert Museum (one of the nation's top zoological parks) and Old Tucson Studios (film site over the years for hundreds of Westerns). Put these three attractions together for one long day of getting to know Tucson, and you have the city's best family outing (and you can bet the kids will be beat by the end of the day).

TUCSON AREA'S (MOSTLY) NATURAL WONDERS

Arizona–Sonora Desert Museum ★★★ Kids Don't be fooled by the name. This is a zoo, and it's one of the best in the country. The Sonoran Desert of central and southern Arizona and parts of northern Mexico contains within its boundaries not only arid lands, but also forested mountains, springs, rivers, and streams. To reflect this diversity, exhibits here encompass the full spectrum of Sonoran Desert life—from plants to insects to fish to reptiles to mammals—and all are on display in very natural settings. Coyotes and javelinas (peccaries) seem very much at home in their compounds, which are surrounded by fences that are nearly invisible and that make it seem as though there is nothing between you and the animals. You'll also see black bears and mountain lions, tarantulas and scorpions, prairie dogs and desert bighorn sheep. One walk-in aviary is devoted exclusively to hummingbirds.

The grounds here are quite extensive, so wear good walking shoes; a sun hat of some sort is also advisable. Don't be surprised if you end up staying here hours longer than you had intended. If you get hungry, there are two excellent dining options—the cafeteria-style Ironwood Terraces and the more upscale Ocotillo Café. You'll find this zoological park 14 miles west of downtown.

2021 N. Kinney Rd. ✆ **520/883-2702.** www.desertmuseum.org. Admission Sept–May $13 adults, $4.25 children 6–12; June–Aug $9.50 adults, $2.25 children 6–12. Oct–Feb daily 8:30am–5pm; Mar–Sept daily 7:30am–5pm. From downtown Tucson, go west on Speedway Blvd., which becomes Gates Pass Rd., and follow the signs.

Moments Driving the Catalina Highway

Within a span of only 25 miles, the Catalina Highway climbs roughly 1 mile in elevation from the lowland desert landscape of cactuses and ocotillo bushes to forests of ponderosa pines. Passing through several different life zones, this route is the equivalent of driving from Mexico to Canada. When you look at it this way, the $5 use fee is small compared to what a flight to Canada would cost (and that fee will also get you into Sabino Canyon). Along the way, there are numerous overlooks, some of which are nauseatingly vertiginous. Other spots are particularly popular with rock climbers. There are numerous hiking trails, picnic areas, and campgrounds along the route. For more information, contact the **Coronado National Forest Santa Catalina Ranger District,** 5700 N. Sabino Canyon Rd. (✆ **520/749-8700;** www.fs.fed.us/r3/coronado).

Sabino Canyon Recreation Area ★★ At the base of the Santa Catalina Mountains on the northeastern edge of the city, Sabino Canyon is a desert oasis and, with its impressive desert scenery, hiking trails, and stream, is a fabulous place to commune with the desert for a morning or an afternoon. The chance to splash in the canyon's waterfalls and swim in natural pools (water conditions permitting) attracts many visitors, but it is just as enjoyable simply to gaze at the beauty of crystal-clear water flowing through a rocky canyon guarded by saguaro cactuses. There are numerous picnic tables in the canyon, and many miles of hiking trails wind their way into the mountains from here, making it one of the best places in the city for a day hike.

A narrated tram shuttles visitors up and down the lower canyon throughout the day, and between April and November (but not July or Aug), there are moonlight tram rides three times each month (usually the nights before the full moon). The Bear Canyon tram is used by hikers heading to the picturesque Seven Falls, which are at the end of a 2.5-mile trail.

Another good way to experience the park is by bicycling up the paved road during the limited hours when bikes are allowed: Sunday through Tuesday, Thursday, and Friday before 9am and after 5pm. This is a strenuous uphill ride for most of the way, but the scenery is beautiful.

5900 N. Sabino Canyon Rd. ✆ **520/749-8700,** 520/749-2861 for shuttle information, or 520/749-2327 for moonlight shuttle reservations. www.fs.fed.us/r3/coronado or www.sabinocanyon.com. Parking $5 (also good for driving the Catalina Hwy.). Sabino Canyon tram ride $8 adults, $4 children 3–12; Bear Canyon tram ride $3 adults, $1 children 3–12. Park daily dawn–dusk. Sabino Canyon tram rides daily 9am–4:30pm (July to mid-Dec Mon–Fri 9am–4pm, Sat–Sun and holidays 9am–4:30pm); Bear Canyon tram rides daily 9am–4:30pm. Take Grant Rd. east to Tanque Verde Rd., continuing east; at Sabino Canyon Rd., turn north and watch for the sign.

Saguaro National Park ★★★ Saguaro cactuses are the quintessential symbol of the American desert and occur naturally only here in the Sonoran Desert. Sensitive to fire and frost, and exceedingly slow to mature, these massive, treelike cactuses grow in great profusion around Tucson but have long been threatened by both development and plant collectors. In 1933, to protect these desert giants, the federal government set aside two large tracts of land as a saguaro preserve. This preserve eventually became Saguaro National Park. The two units of the park, one on the east side of the city (Rincon Mountain

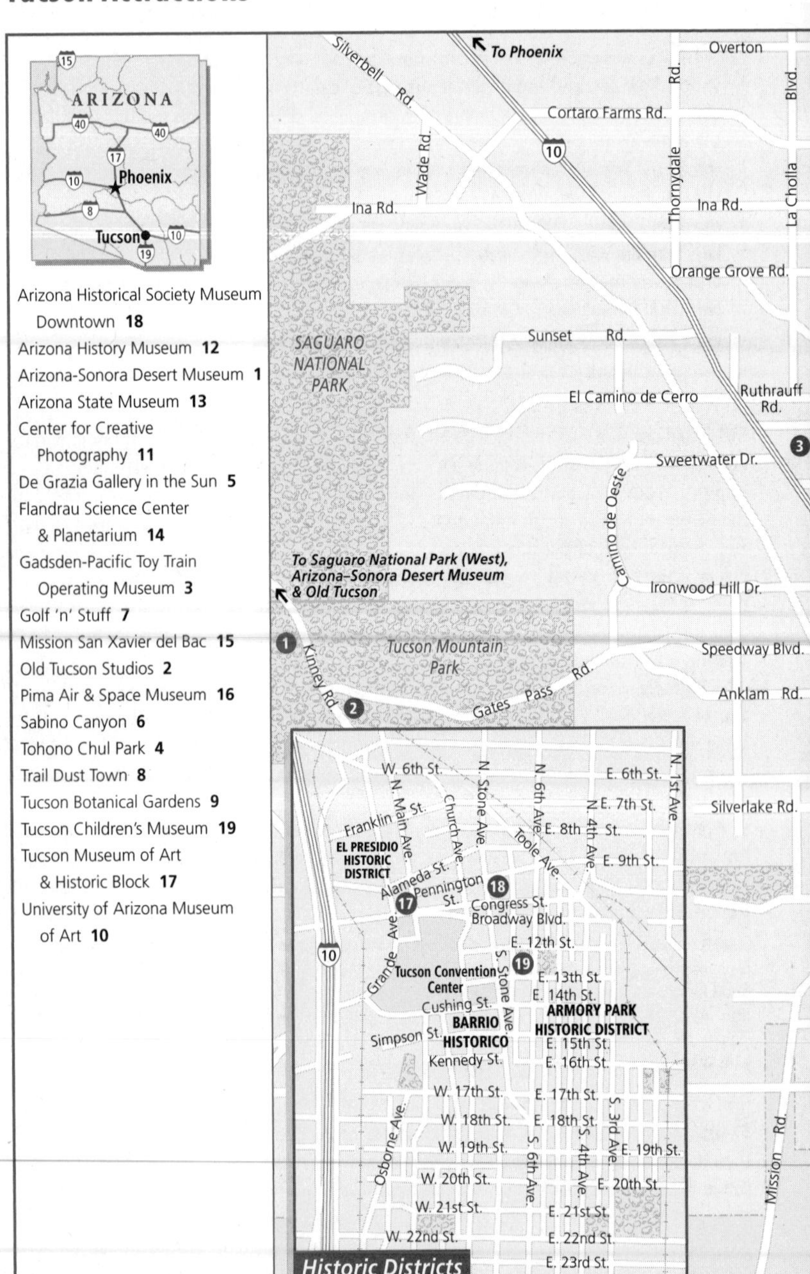
ARIZONA
Phoenix
Tucson
Arizona Historical Society Museum Downtown 18
Arizona History Museum 12
Arizona-Sonora Desert Museum 1
Arizona State Museum 13
Center for Creative Photography 11
De Grazia Gallery in the Sun 5
Flandrau Science Center & Planetarium 14
Gadsden-Pacific Toy Train Operating Museum 3
Golf 'n' Stuff 7
Mission San Xavier del Bac 15
Old Tucson Studios 2
Pima Air & Space Museum 16
Sabino Canyon 6
Tohono Chul Park 4
Trail Dust Town 8
Tucson Botanical Gardens 9
Tucson Children's Museum 19
Tucson Museum of Art & Historic Block 17
University of Arizona Museum of Art 10
To Phoenix
Silverbell Rd.
Overton
Cortaro Farms Rd.
Thornydale Rd.
La Cholla Blvd.
Wade Rd.
Ina Rd.
Orange Grove Rd.
SAGUARO NATIONAL PARK
Sunset Rd.
El Camino de Cerro
Ruthrauff Rd.
Sweetwater Dr.
Camino de Oeste
To Saguaro National Park (West), Arizona–Sonora Desert Museum & Old Tucson
Ironwood Hill Dr.
Tucson Mountain Park
Speedway Blvd.
Kinney Rd.
Gates Pass Rd.
Anklam Rd.
W. 6th St.
N. Main Ave.
N. Stone Ave.
N. 6th Ave.
E. 6th St.
N. 1st Ave.
Church Ave.
E. 7th St.
N. 4th Ave.
Silverlake Rd.
Franklin St.
E. 8th St.
EL PRESIDIO HISTORIC DISTRICT
Toole Ave.
E. 9th St.
Alameda St.
Pennington St.
Congress St.
Broadway Blvd.
Grande Ave.
E. 12th St.
S. Stone Ave.
Tucson Convention Center
E. 13th St.
E. 14th St.
Cushing St.
ARMORY PARK HISTORIC DISTRICT
BARRIO HISTORICO
Simpson St.
E. 15th St.
Kennedy St.
E. 16th St.
W. 17th St.
E. 17th St.
Osborne Ave.
W. 18th St.
E. 18th St.
S. 3rd Ave.
S. 4th Ave.
W. 19th St.
E. 19th St.
S. 6th Ave.
W. 20th St.
E. 20th St.
Mission Rd.
W. 21st St.
E. 21st St.
W. 22nd St.
E. 22nd St.
E. 23rd St.
Historic Districts

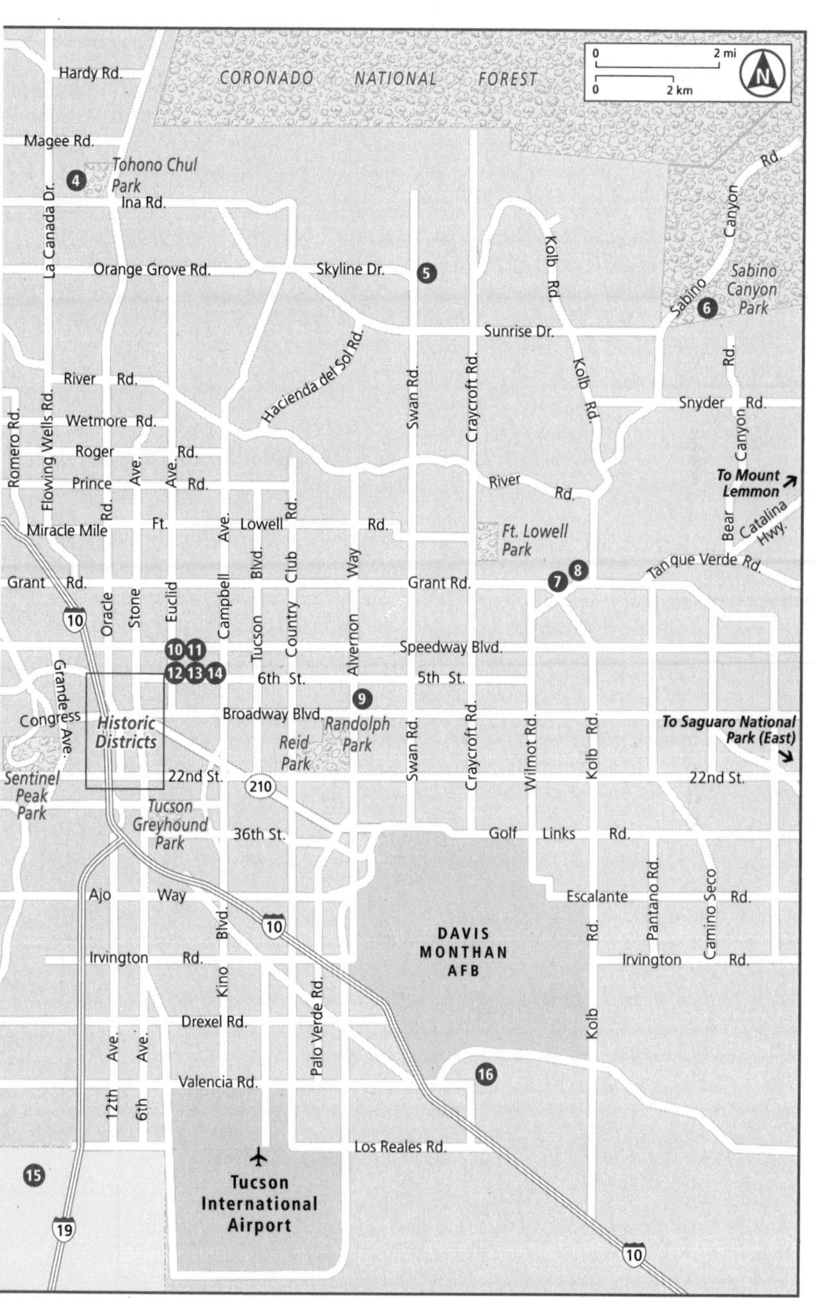

CORONADO NATIONAL FOREST
0
2 mi
0
2 km
N
Hardy Rd.
Magee Rd.
Tohono Chul Park
Ina Rd.
La Canada Dr.
Orange Grove Rd.
Skyline Dr.
Kolb Rd.
Sabino Canyon Rd.
Sabino Canyon Park
Sunrise Dr.
Hacienda del Sol Rd.
Swan Rd.
Craycroft Rd.
River Rd.
Wetmore Rd.
Roger Rd.
Prince Rd.
Romero Rd.
Flowing Wells Rd.
Snyder Rd.
Bear Canyon Rd.
To Mount Lemmon
Catalina Hwy.
Miracle Mile
Ft. Lowell Rd.
Ft. Lowell Park
Tanque Verde Rd.
Grant Rd.
Oracle Rd.
Stone Ave.
Euclid Ave.
Campbell Ave.
Tucson Blvd.
Country Club Rd.
Alvernon Way
Speedway Blvd.
6th St.
5th St.
Grande Ave.
Congress
Historic Districts
Broadway Blvd.
Randolph Park
Reid Park
Wilmot Rd.
To Saguaro National Park (East)
Sentinel Peak Park
22nd St.
210
Tucson Greyhound Park
36th St.
Golf Links Rd.
Ajo Way
Escalante Rd.
Pantano Rd.
Camino Seco
Kino Blvd.
DAVIS MONTHAN AFB
Irvington Rd.
Drexel Rd.
Palo Verde Rd.
12th Ave.
6th Ave.
Valencia Rd.
Los Reales Rd.
Tucson International Airport
10
19

Moments **Sunset on Signal Hill**

A hike to Signal Hill, located off the Bajada Loop Drive in Saguaro National Park's west unit and only a quarter-mile walk from the parking area, will reward you with not only a grand sunset vista away from the crowds at Gates Pass, but also the sight of dozens of petroglyphs.

District) and one on the west (Tucson Mountain District), preserve not only dense stands of saguaros, but also the many other wild inhabitants of this part of the Sonoran Desert. Both units have loop roads, nature trails, hiking trails, and picnic grounds.

The west unit of the park, because of its proximity to both the Arizona–Sonora Desert Museum and Old Tucson Studios, is the more popular area to visit (and your best choice if you're trying to do a lot in a short amount of time). This also happens to be where you'll see the most impressive stands of saguaros. Be sure to take the scenic Bajada Loop Drive, where you'll find good views and several hiking trails (the Hugh Morris Trail involves a long, steep climb, but great views are the reward). To reach the west unit of the park, follow Speedway Boulevard west from downtown Tucson (it becomes Gates Pass Blvd.).

The east section of the park contains an older area of saguaro "forest" at the foot of the Rincon Mountains. This section is popular with hikers because most of it has no roads. It has a visitor center, a loop scenic drive, a picnic area, and a trail open to mountain bikes (the paved loop drive is a great road-bike ride). To reach the east unit of the park, take Speedway Boulevard east, then head south on Freeman Road to Old Spanish Trail.

Rincon Mountain District visitor center: 3693 S. Old Spanish Trail. ✆ **520/733-5153.** Tucson Mountain District visitor center: 2700 N. Kinney Rd. ✆ **520/733-5158.** www.nps.gov/sagu. Entry fee $10 per car, $5 per hiker or biker. Daily 7am–sunset; visitor centers daily 9am–5pm; open to hikers 24 hr. a day. Visitor centers closed Christmas.

Tohono Chul Park ★ Although this park covers less than 50 acres, it provides an excellent introduction to the plant and animal life of the desert. You'll see a forest of cholla cactuses as well as a garden of small pincushion cactuses. From mid-February to April, the wildflower displays here are gorgeous (if enough rain has fallen in the previous months). The park also includes an ethnobotanical garden; a garden for children that encourages them to touch, listen, and smell; a demonstration garden; natural areas; an exhibit house for art displays; a tearoom that's great for breakfast, lunch, or afternoon tea; and two very good gift shops. Park docents lead guided tours throughout the day. There are also bird walks and many other special events throughout the cooler months of the year.

7366 N. Paseo del Norte (off Ina Rd., west of the intersection with Oracle Rd.). ✆ **520/742-6455.** www.tohonochulpark.org. Admission $7 adults, $5 seniors, $3 students, $2 children ages 5–12. Grounds daily 8am–5pm (visitors may remain until sunset). Exhibit house daily 9am–5pm. Tearoom daily 8am–5pm. Buildings closed New Year's Day, Memorial Day, July 4th, Thanksgiving, and Christmas (free admission to grounds on most of these days).

Tucson Botanical Gardens **Kids** Set amid residential neighborhoods in midtown Tucson, these gardens are an oasis of greenery and, though small, are well worth a visit if you happen to be interested in desert plant life, landscaping, or gardening. On the 5½-acre grounds, there are a dozen different gardens that not only have visual appeal, but also are educational. You can learn about creating a garden for birds or for butterflies, and then see what sort of crops the Native Americans of this region have traditionally grown. A sensory garden stimulates all five senses. A toy train layout and a tropical butterfly house (open fall through spring) make this a surprisingly good place to bring the kids.

2150 N. Alvernon Way. ✆ **520/326-9686.** www.tucsonbotanical.org. Admission $7 adults, $3 children 4–12. Daily 8:30am–4:30pm. Closed New Year's Day, July 4th, Thanksgiving, and Dec 24–25. Bus: 9 or 11.

HISTORIC ATTRACTIONS BOTH REAL & REEL

Mission San Xavier del Bac ★★★ Called the White Dove of the Desert, Mission San Xavier del Bac, an active Roman Catholic church serving the San Xavier Indian Reservation, is a blindingly white adobe building that rises from a sere, brown landscape. Considered the finest example of mission architecture in the Southwest, the beautiful church was built between 1783 and 1797, and incorporates Moorish, Byzantine, and Mexican Renaissance architectural styles. The church, however, was never actually completed, which becomes apparent only when the two bell towers are compared. One is topped with a dome, while the other has none.

Colorful murals cover the interior walls, and behind the altar are elaborate decorations. To the left of the main altar, in a glass sarcophagus, is a statue of St. Francis Xavier, the mission's patron saint, who is believed to answer the prayers of the faithful. A visit to San Xavier's little museum provides a bit of historical perspective and a chance to explore more of the mission. To the east of the church, atop a small hill, you'll find not only an interesting view of the church, but also a replica of the famous grotto in Lourdes, France. There are often food stalls selling fry bread in the parking lot in front of the church.

1950 W. San Xavier Rd. ✆ **520/294-2624.** www.sanxaviermission.org. Free admission; donations accepted. Daily 8am–5pm. Take I-19 S. 9 miles to exit 92 and turn right.

Old Tucson Studios ★ Kids Despite the name, this is not the historical location of the old city of Tucson—it's a Western town originally built as the set for the 1939 movie *Arizona.* In the years since, Old Tucson has been used during the filming of John Wayne's *Rio Lobo, Rio Bravo,* and *El Dorado;* Clint Eastwood's *The Outlaw Josey Wales;* Kirk Douglas's *Gunfight at the O.K. Corral;* Paul Newman's *The Life and Times of Judge Roy Bean;* and, more recently, *Tombstone* and *Geronimo.*

Today, however, Old Tucson is far more than just a movie set. In addition to serving as a site for film, TV, and advertising productions (call ahead to find out if any filming is scheduled), it has become a Wild West theme park with diverse family-oriented activities and entertainment. Throughout the day, there are staged shootouts in the streets, stunt demonstrations, a cancan musical revue, and other performances. Train and kiddie rides, restaurants, and gift shops round out the experience.

201 S. Kinney Rd. ✆ **520/883-0100.** www.oldtucson.com. Admission $17 adults, $11 children 4–11. Daily 10am–4pm. Closed Thanksgiving, Dec 24–25, and occasional special events. Take Speedway Blvd. west, continuing in the same direction when it becomes Gates Pass Blvd., and turn left on S. Kinney Rd.

ART MUSEUMS

Center for Creative Photography Have you ever wished you could see an original Ansel Adams print up close, or perhaps an Edward Weston or a Richard Avedon? You can at the Center for Creative Photography. Originally conceived by Ansel Adams, the center now holds more than 80,000 master prints by more than 2,000 of the world's best photographers, making it one of the best and largest collections in the world. The center mounts fascinating exhibits year-round and is also a research facility that preserves the photographic archives of more than 50 photographers, including Adams. While the main gallery is open on a regular basis, you must make an appointment to view images from the archives.

University of Arizona campus, 1030 N. Olive Rd. (east of Park Ave. and Speedway Blvd.). ✆ **520/621-7968.** www.creativephotography.org. Admission by donation. Mon–Fri 9am–5pm; Sat–Sun 1–4pm. Closed major holidays. Bus: 1, 4, 5, or 6.

De Grazia Gallery in the Sun Southwestern artist Ettore "Ted" De Grazia was a Tucson favorite son, and his home, a sprawling, funky adobe building in the foothills, is a city landmark and now serves as a museum for this prolific artist. De Grazia is said to be the most reproduced artist in the world because many of his images of big-eyed children were used as greeting cards during the 1950s and 1960s. Today De Grazia's images seem trite and maudlin, but in his day he was a very successful artist. This gallery is packed with original paintings, so it may surprise you to learn that, near the end of his life, De Grazia burned several hundred thousand dollars' worth of his paintings in a protest of IRS inheritance taxes. The gift shop has lots of reproductions and other objects with De Grazia images.

6300 N. Swan Rd. ✆ **800/545-2185** or 520/299-9191. www.degrazia.org. Free admission. Daily 10am–4pm. Closed New Year's Day, Easter, Thanksgiving, and Christmas.

Tucson Museum of Art & Historic Block ★ This museum complex includes galleries housed in historic adobe homes, a courtyard frequently used to display sculptures, and a large modern building that often mounts the most interesting exhibits in town. The *Palice Pavilion—Art of the Americas* exhibit, which consists of a large collection of pre-Columbian art that represents 3,000 years of life in Mexico and Central and South America, is a highlight of the museum. This collection is housed in the historic Stevens/Duffield House, which also contains Spanish colonial artifacts and Latin American folk art. The noteworthy Goodman Pavilion of Western Art comprises an extensive collection that depicts cowboys, horses, and the wide-open spaces of the American West. The museum has preserved a total of five historic homes on this same block, and all are open to the public. See "History Museums & Landmark Buildings," below, for details.

140 N. Main Ave. ✆ **520/624-2333.** www.tucsonmuseumofart.org. Admission $8 adults, $6 seniors, $3 students, free for children 12 and under; free on 1st Sun of each month. Tues–Sat 10am–4pm; Sun noon–4pm. Closed major holidays. All downtown-bound buses.

The University of Arizona Museum of Art ★★ With European and American works dating from the Renaissance up to the 20th century, the art collections at this museum are even more extensive and diverse than those of the Tucson Museum of Art. Tintoretto, Rembrandt, Picasso, O'Keeffe, Warhol, and Rothko are all represented. Another attraction, the *Retablo of Ciudad Rodrigo,* consists of 26 paintings from 15th-century Spain that were originally placed above a cathedral altar. The museum also has an extensive collection of 20th-century sculpture that includes more than 60 clay and plaster models and sketches by Jacques Lipchitz.

University of Arizona campus, 1031 N. Olive Rd. (at Park Ave. and Speedway Blvd.). ✆ **520/621-7567.** www.artmuseum.arizona.edu. Free admission. Tues–Fri 9am–5pm; Sat–Sun noon–4pm. Closed major holidays. Bus: 1, 4, 5, or 6.

HISTORY MUSEUMS & LANDMARK BUILDINGS

In addition to the attractions listed below, downtown Tucson has a couple of historic neighborhoods that are described in the box "Architectural Highlights," below. Among

Value Passport to Tucson

The **Tucson Attractions Passport** is a great way to save money on admissions to many of the city's top attractions. The passport, available at the downtown Visitors Center, 100 S. Church Ave. (✆ **800/638-8350** or 520/624-1817; www.tucson passport.com), costs $15 and gets you two-for-one admissions to the Arizona–Sonora Desert Museum, Old Tucson Studios, Biosphere 2, the Pima Air & Space Museum, Tohono Chul Park, the Tucson Museum of Art, Kartchner Caverns State Park, and many other attractions in Tucson and across southern Arizona.

the more interesting buildings are those maintained by the Tucson Museum of Art and located on the block surrounding the museum. A map and brochures are available at the museum's front desk, and guided tours of the historic block and Corbett House are available (free with admission to the museum).

Arizona Historical Society Downtown Museum If you want to learn more about the history of Tucson, this is the museum to visit. Exhibits cover Spanish presidio days, American army days, merchants, and schools. Through the use of artifacts and old photos, these exhibits help bring the city's past to life. One of the most curious exhibits focuses on the gangster John Dillinger, who was arrested here in Tucson.

140 N. Stone Ave. ✆ **520/770-1473.** www.arizonahistoricalsociety.org. Admission $3 adults, $2 seniors and students ages 12–18, free for children 11 and under; free on 1st Sat of each month. Tues–Fri 10am–4pm. Closed major holidays. All downtown-bound buses.

Arizona History Museum As the state's oldest historical museum, this repository of all things Arizonan is a treasure-trove for the history buff. If you've never explored a real mine, you can do the next best thing by exploring the museum's full-scale reproduction of an underground mine tunnel. You'll see an assayer's office, miner's tent, stamp mill, and blacksmith's shop in the mining exhibit. A transportation exhibit displays stagecoaches and the horseless carriages that revolutionized life in the Southwest, while a range of temporary exhibits give a pretty good idea of what it was like back then.

949 E. Second St. ✆ **520/628-5774.** www.arizonahistoricalsociety.org. Admission $5 adults, $4 seniors and students ages 12–18, free for children 11 and under; free for all 1st Sat of each month. Mon–Sat 10am–4pm. Closed major holidays. Bus: 1, 4, 5, or 6.

Arizona State Museum This museum, which is the oldest anthropological museum in the Southwest, houses *Paths of Life: American Indians of the Southwest,* one of the state's most interesting exhibits on prehistoric and contemporary Native American cultures of the Southwest. The exhibit focuses on 10 different tribes from around the Southwest and northern Mexico, not only displaying a wide range of artifacts, but also exploring the lifestyles and cultural traditions of Indians living in the region today. In addition, the museum showcases a collection of some 20,000 ceramic pieces. This pottery spans 2,000 years of life in the desert Southwest.

University of Arizona campus, 1013 E. University Blvd., at Park Ave. ✆ **520/621-6302.** www.statemuseum.arizona.edu. Admission $3 suggested donation. Mon–Sat 10am–5pm. Closed major holidays. Bus: 1, 4, 5, or 6.

Biosphere 2 Overrated For 2 years, beginning in September 1991, four men and four women were locked inside this airtight, 3-acre greenhouse in the desert 35 miles north of Tucson near the town of Oracle. During their tenure in Biosphere 2 (earth is considered Biosphere 1), they conducted experiments on how the earth, basically a giant greenhouse, manages to support all the planet's life forms. Today there are no longer any people living in Biosphere 2, and the former research facility is operated more as a tourist attraction than as a science center. Tours take visitors inside the giant greenhouse and into the mechanisms that helped keep this sealed environment going for 2 years. The strangest sight is the giant "lung" that allowed for the expansion and contraction of the air within Biosphere 2. Although the building, which is in the middle of desert hill country, is an impressive sight, the tours are something of a letdown.

32540 S. Biosphere Rd., Oracle (off Ariz. 77, at mile marker 96.5). ✆ **520/838-6200.** www.bio2.com. Admission $20 adults, $18 seniors, $13 children 6–12. Daily 9am–4pm. Closed Thanksgiving and Christmas. Take Oracle Rd. north out of Tucson and continue north on Ariz. 77 until you see the sign.

Flandrau: The University of Arizona Science Center Kids Located on the University of Arizona campus, Flandrau Planetarium is the most convenient place in Arizona to do a little stargazing through a professional telescope. As such, it should be on the itinerary of anyone coming to Tucson (unless it happens to be cloudy). The planetarium theater presents a variety of programs on the stars, and the exhibit halls contain a large mineral collection and hands-on science exhibits. However, the best reason to visit is to gaze through the planetarium's 16-inch telescope.

University of Arizona campus, 1601 E. University Blvd., at Cherry Ave. ✆ **520/621-7827.** www.flandrau.org. $5–$7.50 adults, $3–$5 children 4–9, free for children 3 and under; telescope viewing free. Thurs 9am–3pm; Fri 9am–3pm and 6–9pm; Sat noon–9pm; Sun noon–5pm. Telescope viewing (weather permitting) Wed–Sat 7–10pm. Closed major holidays. Bus: 1, 3, 4, 9, 15, or 20.

The International Wildlife Museum This castlelike building (modeled after a French Foreign Legion fort), located on the road that leads to the Arizona–Sonora Desert Museum, is a natural-history museum filled with stuffed animals in lifelike poses and surroundings. Animals from all over the world are displayed, and there are exhibits of extinct animals, including the Irish elk and the woolly mammoth. Among the more lifelike displays are the predator-and-prey exhibits. There are also fascinating exhibits of butterflies and other unusual insects.

4800 W. Gates Pass Rd. ✆ **520/629-0100.** www.thewildlifemuseum.org. Admission $7 adults, $5.50 seniors and students, $2.50 children 4–12. Mon–Fri 9am–5pm; Sat–Sun 9am–6pm. Closed Thanksgiving and Christmas. Take Speedway Blvd. W., continuing in the same direction when it becomes Gates Pass Blvd. The museum is 5 miles west of I-10.

Pima Air & Space Museum ★ Kids Located just south of Davis Monthan Air Force Base, the Pima Air & Space Museum houses one of the largest collections of historic aircraft in the world. On display are more than 275 aircraft, including a mock-up of an X-15A-2 (the world's fastest aircraft), an SR-71 Blackbird, several Russian MIGs, a "Superguppy," and a B-17G "Flying Fortress." Tours are available.

The museum also offers guided tours of Davis Monthan's AMARG (Arizona Maintenance and Regeneration Group) facility, which goes by the name of the Boneyard. Here, thousands of mothballed military planes are lined up in neat rows under the Arizona sun. Tours, offered Monday through Friday, last about 90 minutes and cost $7 for adults and $4 for children 12 and under.

Kids All Aboard!

If you've got kids who idolize Thomas the Tank Engine, then you'd better schedule your Tucson visit for the second or fourth Sunday of the month. On those days (with a few exceptions), the **Gadsden-Pacific Division Toy Train Operating Museum,** 3975 N. Miller Ave. (✆ **520/888-2222;** http://gpdtoytrainmuseum.com/toytrains), sends out little engines that think they can. The trains chug around a variety of layouts built in different model-railroad gauges. On the two days each month that it is open, the museum's hours are from 12:30 to 4:30pm. Admission is free. In July and August, the museum is closed.

6000 E. Valencia Rd. ✆ **520/574-0462.** www.pimaair.org. Admission Nov–May $16 adults, $13 seniors and military, $9 children 7–12; June–Oct $14 adults, $12 seniors and military, $8 children 7–12. Daily 9am–5pm. Closed Thanksgiving and Christmas. Take the Valencia Rd. exit from I-10 and drive east 2 miles to the museum.

Titan Missile Museum ★ If you've ever wondered what it would be like to have your finger on the button of a nuclear missile, here's your opportunity to find out. This deactivated intercontinental ballistic missile (ICBM) silo is now a museum—and is the only museum in the country that allows visitors to descend into a former missile silo. There's a huge Titan missile on display, and, even without its nuclear warhead, it is a terrifying sight. The guided tours do a great job of explaining not only the ICBM system, but also what life was like for the people who worked here. Operated by the Pima Air & Space Museum, this museum is located 25 miles south of Tucson near the community of Green Valley. On the first and third Saturday of each month, there are Beyond the Blast Door tours, which take visitors into areas not on the normal tour. There are also special tours on Tuesdays. It is even possible to spend the night in the silo. Contact the museum for details.

1580 W. Duval Mine Rd., Sahuarita (exit 69, off I-19). ✆ **520/625-7736.** www.titanmissilemuseum.org. Admission $9.50 adults, $8.50 seniors, $6 children 7–12; Beyond the Blast Door Tour $18 adults, $16 seniors, $9.95 children 8–12. Daily 8:45am–5pm. Closed Thanksgiving and Christmas. Take I-19 south to Green Valley; take exit 69 west a half-mile to main entrance.

ESPECIALLY FOR KIDS

In addition to the museums listed below, two of the greatest places to take kids in the Tucson area are the Arizona–Sonora Desert Museum and Old Tucson Studios. Kids will also get a kick out of the Sabino Canyon tram ride, the Reid Park Zoo, Flandrau Science Center & Planetarium, and the Pima Air & Space Museum. All are described in detail earlier in this chapter.

They'll also enjoy **Trail Dust Town,** 6541 E. Tanque Verde Rd. (✆ **520/296-5442;** www.traildusttown.com), a Wild West–themed shopping and dining center. It has a full-size carousel, a miniature train to ride, a museum dedicated to the horse soldiers of the West, shootout shows, and a family steakhouse. Basically, it's a sort of scaled-down Old Tucson. If the kids are into miniature golf, take them to **Golf n' Stuff,** 6503 E. Tanque Verde Rd. (✆ **520/296-2366;** www.golfnstuff.com), which is right next door to Trail Dust Town. Not only is there a miniature golf course, but there are also bumper boats, go-karts, batting cages, laser tag, a climbing wall, and a video-game arcade. Between these two side-by-side attractions, you've got plenty to keep the family entertained for hours.

Architectural Highlights

Tucson has a long and varied cultural history, which is most easily seen by strolling through the downtown historic neighborhoods. Start your explorations in El Presidio Historic District, which is named for the Presidio of San Augustín del Tucson (1775), the Spanish garrison built here to protect the San Xavier del Bac Mission from the Apaches. For many years the presidio was the heart of Tucson, and although no original buildings are still standing, there are numerous structures from the mid–19th century. Some of my favorites are listed below.

- **La Casa Cordova,** at 175 N. Meyer Ave., dates from about 1848 and is one of the oldest buildings in Tucson. It's been restored to look as it might have in the late 1800s. Each year from November to March, this building exhibits a very elaborate *nacimiento,* a Mexican folk-art nativity scene.
- **Corbett House,** a restored Mission Revival–style building located at 180 N. Main Ave., was built in 1907. The house, which is set back behind a green lawn, is strikingly different from the older, Sonoran-style adobe homes on this block. The Tucson Museum of Art offers guided tours of this house.
- **Fish House,** at 120 N. Main Ave., was built in 1867 on the site of old Mexican barracks. Named for Edward Nye Fish, a local merchant, it now houses the art museum's Western-art collection.
- **Julius Kruttschnidt House,** at 297 N. Main Ave., dates from 1886 and now houses a bed-and-breakfast inn. Victorian trappings, including a long veranda, disguise the adobe origins of this unique and beautifully restored home.
- **Steinfeld House,** at 300 N. Main Ave., was built in 1900 in California Mission Revival style and was designed by Henry Trost, Tucson's most noted architect. It served as the original Owl's Club, a gentlemen's club for some of Tucson's most eligible turn-of-the-20th-century bachelors.
- **Owl's Club Mansion,** at 378 N. Main Ave., was built in 1902 and designed by Henry Trost in the Mission Revival style, albeit with a great deal of ornamentation. It replaced the Steinfeld House as home to the bachelors of the Owl's Club.
- Built in 1928, the **Pima County Courthouse,** located at 115 N. Church Ave., incorporates Moorish, Spanish, and Southwestern architectural features, including a colorful tiled dome.
- **Sosa-Carillo-Frémont House,** located at 151 S. Granada Ave., on the grounds of the Tucson Convention Center, was built in the 1850s and later served as the home of territorial governor John C. Frémont.
- **The Barrio Histórico District** is another worthwhile area to explore, especially the northern (and more restored) section. With 150 adobe row houses, this neighborhood contains the largest collection of 19th-century Sonoran-style adobe buildings in the United States.

Tucson Children's Museum (Kids) This museum, in the historic Carnegie Library in downtown Tucson, is filled with fun and educational hands-on activities. Exhibits include a farmers' market, an enchanted rainforest, an ocean discovery center, and an electricity gallery. Expect to find such perennial kid favorites as a firetruck, a toy train, and dinosaur sculptures. Activities are featured daily.

200 S. Sixth Ave. ✆ **520/792-9985.** www.tucsonchildrensmuseum.org. Admission $7 adults, $5 seniors and children 2–18; free 1 day each month (call for date). Tues–Sat 10am–5pm; Sun noon–5pm. Closed Thanksgiving and Christmas. All downtown-bound buses.

6 ORGANIZED TOURS

Learning Expeditions, a program run by the **Arizona State Museum,** occasionally offers scholar-led archaeological tours. For information, contact the marketing department at the museum (✆ **520/626-8381;** www.statemuseum.arizona.edu).

For a look at a completely different sort of excavation, head 15 miles south of Tucson to the **ASARCO Mineral Discovery Center,** 1421 W. Pima Mine Rd., Sahuarita (✆ **520/625-7513;** www.mineraldiscovery.com), where you can tour a huge open-pit copper mine and learn about copper mining past and present. The center is open Tuesday through Saturday from 9am to 5pm; admission is free. The 1-hour mine tours are offered five times a day (call for summer days and hours). These tours cost $8 for adults, $6 for seniors, and $5 for children 5 to 12. To get here, drive south from Tucson on I-19 and take exit 80. You might want to combine this tour with a visit to the nearby Titan Missile Museum.

The ballooning season in Tucson runs September to June. **Balloon America** (✆ **520/299-7744;** www.balloonridesusa.com) offers flights over the foothills of the Santa Catalina Mountains ($249). **Fleur de Tucson Balloon Tours** (✆ **520/529-1025;** www.fleurdetucson.net) offers rides over the Tucson Mountains and Saguaro National Park. Rates are $250 per person, including brunch and a champagne toast.

7 GETTING OUTSIDE

BICYCLING Tucson is one of the best bicycling cities in the country, and the dirt roads and trails of the surrounding national forest and desert are perfect for mountain biking. At **Fair Wheel Bikes,** 1110 E. Sixth St. (✆ **520/884-9018;** www.fairwheelbikes.com), bikes rent for $45 to $65 per day.

If you'd rather confine your pedaling to paved surfaces, there are some great options around town. The number-one choice in town for cyclists in halfway decent shape is the road up **Sabino Canyon** (p. 356). Keep in mind, however, that bicycles are allowed on this road only 5 days a week and then only before 9am and after 5pm (the road is closed to bikes all day Wed and Sat). For a much easier ride, try the **Rillito River Park path,** which is paved for 12 miles between Craycroft Road and I-10. The trail parallels River Road and the usually dry bed of the Rillito River. Another option close to downtown is the 7-mile **Santa Cruz River Park path,** which runs along both sides of the usually dry Santa Cruz River and extends from West Grant Road to 29th Street and from Ajo Way to Irvington Road.

There are lots of great mountain bike rides in the Tucson area, too. For an easy and very scenic dirt-road loop through forests of saguaros, head to the west unit of Saguaro National Park (p. 375and ride the 6-mile **Bajada Loop Drive.** You can turn this into a 12-mile ride (half on paved road) by starting at the Red Hills Visitor Center.

BIRD-WATCHING Southern Arizona has some of the best bird-watching in the country, and although the best spots are south of Tucson, there are a few places around the city that birders will enjoy seeking out. Call the **Tucson Audubon Society's Rare Bird Alert** (✆ **520/798-1005;** www.tucsonaudubon.org) to find out which birds have been spotted in the area lately.

The city's premier birding spot is the **Sweetwater Wetland,** a man-made wetland just west of I-10 and north of Prince Road. These wetlands were created as part of a wastewater treatment facility and now have an extensive network of trails that wind past numerous ponds and canals. There are several viewing platforms and enough different types of wildlife habitat that the area attracts a wide variety of bird species. To find the wetlands, take I-10 south to the Prince Road exit, and at the end of the exit ramp, turn right onto Sweetwater Drive. If you're driving west on Prince Road, go to the end of the road, turn right on Business Center Drive, turn left on River Park Road (which becomes Commerce Dr.), take the first left (probably unmarked), and then turn left again on Sweetwater Drive.

Roy P. Drachman Agua Caliente Regional Park, 12325 E. Roger Rd. (off N. Soldier Trail), in the northeast corner of the city, is another great place to do some birding. The year-round warm springs here are a magnet for dozens of species, including waterfowl, great blue herons, black phoebes, soras, and vermilion flycatchers. To find the park, follow Tanque Verde Road east 6 miles from the intersection with Sabino Canyon Road and turn left onto Soldier Trail. Watch for signs.

Other good places include **Sabino Canyon Recreation Area** (p. 375), the path to the waterfall at **Loews Ventana Canyon Resort** (p. 357), and the **Rillito River path** between Craycroft and Swan roads.

The best bird-watching anywhere in the immediate Tucson area is at **Madera Canyon ★**, which is in **Coronado National Forest** (✆ **520/281-2296;** www.fs.fed.us/r3/coronado), about 40 miles south of the city. Because of the year-round water here, Madera Canyon attracts a surprising variety of bird life. Avid birders from around the country flock to this canyon in hopes of spotting more than a dozen species of hummingbirds and an equal number of flycatchers, warblers, tanagers, buntings, grosbeaks, and many rare birds not found in any other state. However, before birding became a hot activity, this canyon was popular with families looking to escape the heat down in Tucson, and the shady picnic areas and trails still get a lot of use by those who don't carry binoculars. If you're heading out for the day, arrive early—parking is very limited. To reach Madera Canyon, take the Continental Road/Madera Canyon exit off I-19; from the exit, it's another 12 miles southeast. The canyon is open daily from dawn to dusk for day use; there is a $5 day-use fee. There's also a campground (Bog Springs Campground; $10 per night; reservations not accepted).

GOLF Although there aren't quite as many golf courses in Tucson as in Phoenix, this is still a golfer's town. For last-minute tee-time reservations, contact **Standby Golf** (✆ **800/655-5345;** www.discountteetimes.com). No fee is charged for this service.

In addition to public and municipal links, numerous resort courses allow nonguests to play. Perhaps the most famous of these are the two 18-hole courses at **Ventana Canyon**

Golf and Racquet Club ★★, 6200 N. Clubhouse Lane (✆ **520/577-4015;** www.ventanacanyonclub.com). These Tom Fazio–designed courses offer challenging desert target-style play that is nearly legendary. The 3rd hole on the Mountain Course is one of the most photographed holes in the West. In winter, the greens fee is $195 ($120 for twilight play). You'll spend a bit less if you're staying at Loews Ventana Canyon Resort or the Lodge at Ventana Canyon.

As famous as the Ventana Canyon courses is the 27-hole **Omni Tucson National Resort** ★, 2727 W. Club Dr. (✆ **520/575-7540** or 297-2271; www.tucsonnational.com), a traditional course that is perhaps more familiar to golfers due to the fact that it was for many years the site of the annual Tucson Open. One of the 9-hole courses here is a desert-style target course, which makes this a good place for an introduction to desert golfing. If you are not staying at the resort, greens fees are $185 in winter, $70 in summer.

El Conquistador Country Club, 10555 N. La Cañada Dr., Oro Valley (✆ **520/544-1800;** www.elconquistadorcc.com), with two 18-hole courses and a 9-hole course, offers stunning (and very distracting) views of the Santa Catalina Mountains. Greens fees are $109 to $129 in winter ($69 for twilight play).

At the 27-hole Arnold Palmer–designed course at **Starr Pass Country Club & Spa,** 3645 W. Starr Pass Blvd. (✆ **520/670-0400;** www.starrpass.com), the fairways play up to the narrow Starr Pass, which was once a stagecoach route. The greens fee is $215 in winter ($120 for twilight play).

There are many public courses around town. The **Arizona National,** 9777 E. Sabino Greens Dr. (✆ **520/749-3636;** www.arizonanationalgolfclub.com), incorporates stands of cactuses and rocky outcroppings into the course layout. Greens fees are $145 to $175 in winter. The **Golf Club at Vistoso,** 955 W. Vistoso Highlands Dr. (✆ **877/548-1110** or 520/797-9900; www.vistosogolf.com), has a championship desert course, with fees of $105 to $150 in winter. **Heritage Highlands at Dove Mountain,** 4949 W. Heritage Club Blvd., Marana (✆ **520/579-7000;** www.heritagehighlands.com), is a championship desert course at the foot of the Tortolita Mountains; greens fees are $99 in winter.

Tucson Parks and Recreation operates five municipal golf courses, of which the **Randolph** and **Dell Urich,** 600 S. Alvernon Way (✆ **520/791-4161**), are the premier courses. The former has been the site of Tucson's LPGA tournament. Greens fees for 18 holes at these two courses are $42 to $70 in winter. Other municipal courses include **El Rio,** 1400 W. Speedway Blvd. (✆ **520/791-4229**); **Silverbell,** 3600 N. Silverbell Rd. (✆ **520/791-5235**); and **Fred Enke,** 8251 E. Irvington Rd. (✆ **520/791-2539**). This latter course is the city's only desert-style golf course. Greens fees for 18 holes at these three courses are $36 to $50 in winter. For general information and tee-time reservations for any of the municipal courses, visit **www.tucsoncitygolf.com**.

HIKING Tucson is nearly surrounded by mountains, most of which are protected as city and state parks, national forest, or national park, and within these public areas are hundreds of miles of hiking trails.

Saguaro National Park (✆ **520/733-5153;** www.nps.gov/sagu) flanks Tucson on both the east and the west, with units accessible off Old Spanish Trail east of Tucson and past the end of Speedway Boulevard west of the city. In these areas, you can observe Sonoran Desert vegetation and wildlife, and hike among the huge saguaro cactuses for which the park is named. For saguaro-spotting, the west unit is the better choice. See p. 375 for details.

Tucson Mountain Park, at the west end of Speedway Boulevard, is adjacent to Saguaro National Park and preserves a similar landscape. The parking area at Gates Pass, on Speedway, is a favorite sunset spot.

Sabino Canyon (p. 356), off Sabino Canyon Road, is one of Tucson's best hiking areas, but is also the city's most popular recreation area. A cold mountain stream here cascades over waterfalls and forms pools that make great swimming holes. The 5-mile round-trip **Seven Falls Trail** ★, which follows Bear Canyon deep into the mountains, is the most popular hike in the recreation area. You can take a tram to the trail head or add extra miles by hiking from the main parking lot.

With the city limits pushing right to the boundary of the Coronado National Forest, there are some convenient hiking options in Tucson's northern foothills. The **Ventana Canyon Trail** begins at a parking area adjacent to the Loews Ventana Canyon Resort (off Sunrise Dr. west of Sabino Canyon Rd.) and leads into the Ventana Canyon Wilderness. A few miles west, there's the **Finger Rock Trail,** which starts at the top of the section of Alvernon Road accessed from Skyline Drive. There are actually a couple of trails starting here, so you can hike for miles into the desert. Over near the Westward Look Resort is the **Pima Canyon Trail** ★, which leads into the Ventana Canyon Wilderness and is reached off Ina Road just east of Oracle Road. Both of these trails provide classic desert canyon hikes of whatever length you feel like (a dam at 3 miles on the latter trail makes a good turnaround point). Just south of the Hilton Tucson El Conquistador Golf & Tennis Resort, you'll find the **Linda Vista Trail,** which begins just off Oracle Road, on Linda Vista Boulevard. This trail lies at the foot of Pusch Ridge and winds up through dense stands of prickly-pear cactus. Higher up on the trail, there are some large saguaros. Because this trail is shaded by Pusch Ridge in the morning, it's a good choice for a morning hike on a day that's going to be hot.

Catalina State Park, 11570 N. Oracle Rd. (✆ **520/628-5798;** www.azstateparks.com/Parks/CATA/index.html), is on the rugged northwest face of the Santa Catalina Mountains, between 2,500 and 3,000 feet in elevation. Hiking trails here lead into the Pusch Ridge Wilderness; however, the park's best day hike is the 5.5-mile round-trip to **Romero Pools,** where small natural pools of water set amid the rocks are a refreshing destination on a hot day (expect plenty of other people on a weekend). This hike involves about 1,000 feet of elevation gain. Admission to the park is $6 per vehicle. Adjacent to the park are horseback-riding stables, and within the park is a Hohokam ruin.

One of the reasons Tucson is such a livable city is the presence of the cool (and, in winter, snow-covered) pine forests of 8,250-foot Mount Lemmon. Within the **Mount Lemmon Recreation Area,** at the end of the Catalina Highway, are many miles of trails, and the hearty hiker can even set out from down in the lowland desert and hike up into the alpine forests (although it's easier to hike from the top down). For a more leisurely excursion, drive up onto the mountain to start your hike. However, be aware that in winter, there can be snow atop Mount Lemmon. There is a $5-per-vehicle charge to use most of the sites within this recreation area, so you'll need to stop at the roadside ticket kiosk at the base of the mountain and pay your fee. For more information, contact the **Coronado National Forest Santa Catalina Ranger District,** 5700 N. Sabino Canyon Rd. (✆ **520/749-8700;** www.fs.fed.us/r3/coronado).

HORSEBACK RIDING If you want to play cowboy or just go for a leisurely ride through the desert, there are plenty of stables around Tucson where you can saddle up. In addition to providing guided trail rides, some of the stables below offer sunset rides with cookouts. Although reservations are not always required, they're a good idea. You can also opt to stay at a guest ranch and do as much riding as your muscles can stand.

Pusch Ridge Stables, 13700 N. Oracle Rd. (© **520/825-1664;** www.puschridgestables.com), is adjacent to Catalina State Park and Coronado National Forest. Rates are $35 for 1 hour, $55 for 2 hours, and $45 for a sunset ride.

Over on the east side of Tucson, there's **Spanish Trail Outfitters** (© **520/749-0167;** www.spanishtrailoutfitters.com), which leads rides into the foothills of the Santa Catalina Mountains off Sabino Canyon Road. Rates are $35 for a 1-hour ride, $55 for a 2-hour or sunset ride.

WILDFLOWER-VIEWING Bloom time varies from year to year, but April and May are good times to view native wildflowers in the Tucson area. While the crowns of white blossoms worn by saguaro cactuses are among the most visible blooms in the area, other cactuses are far more colorful. **Saguaro National Park** (p. 375) and **Sabino Canyon** (p. 356) are among the best local spots to see saguaros, other cactus species, and various wildflowers in bloom. If you feel like heading farther afield, the wildflower displays at **Picacho Peak State Park** (p. 463), between Tucson and Casa Grande, are the most impressive in the state.

8 SPECTATOR SPORTS

BASEBALL The **Colorado Rockies** (© **800/388-ROCK** [7625] or 520/327-9467) pitch spring-training camp in March at Hi Corbett Field, 3400 E. Camino Campestre, in Reid Park (at Randolph Way and E. Broadway). Tickets are $4 to $17. The **Arizona Diamondbacks** have their spring-training camps and exhibition games at Tucson Electric Park, 2500 E. Ajo Way (© **866/672-1343** or 520/434-1367; www.kinosportscomplex.com), on the south side of the city near the airport. Tickets range from $5 to $25.

Tucson Electric Park is also where you can watch the **Tucson Sidewinders** (© **520/434-1021;** www.tucsonsidewinders.com), the AAA affiliate team of the Arizona Diamondbacks. The season runs May through early September; tickets are $6 to $9.

GOLF TOURNAMENTS The **World Golf Championships–Accenture Match Play Championship** (© **866/942-2672;** www.pgatour.com), Tucson's main PGA tournament, is held in late February at the Gallery Golf Club at Dove Mountain. Daily tickets are $25 to $45.

9 DAY SPAS

If you'd prefer a massage to a round on the links, consider spending a few hours at a spa. While full-service health spas can cost $400 to $500 or more per day, for under $100 you can avail yourself of a spa treatment or two (massages, facials, seaweed wraps, salt scrubs, and the like) and maybe even get to spend the day lounging by the pool at some exclusive resort. Spas are also great places (for both men and women) to while away an afternoon if you couldn't get a tee time at that golf course you wanted to play or if it happens to be raining.

The **Elizabeth Arden Red Door Spa** ★, at the Westin La Paloma Resort & Spa, 3666 E. Sunrise Dr. (© **520/742-7866;** www.reddoorspas.com), focuses on skin-care services, but there are plenty of body wraps and massages available as well. With a 50-minute treatment (mostly $115–$145), you can use the spa's facilities for the day. However, unlike other spas in town, the Red Door is more about relaxation than staying fit, so you won't find aerobics classes or a pool here. Spa packages range in price from $215 to $575.

For a variety of services and a gorgeous location, you just can't beat the **Lakeside Spa at Loews Ventana Canyon Resort,** 7000 N. Resort Dr. (✆ **520/529-7830;** www.loewslakesidespa.com), which is wedged between the rugged Santa Catalinas and the manicured fairways of one of the most fabled golf courses in the state. Soothed by the scent of aromatherapy, you can treat yourself to herbal wraps, mud treatments, massage, facials, complete salon services, and much more. Fifty-minute treatments run $110 to $140. With any 50-minute body treatment, you get use of the spa's facilities and pool and can attend any fitness classes being held that day.

With six locations around the Tucson area, **Gadabout Salon Spas** (www.gadabout.com) offers the opportunity to slip a relaxing visit to a spa into a busy schedule. Mud baths, facials, and massages as well as hair and nail services are available, and body treatments and massages range from about $60 for a 50-minute massage to $400 for a full day at the spa. You'll find Gadabout at the following locations: St. Philip's Plaza, 1990 E. River Rd. (✆ 520/577-2000); 6393 E. Grant Rd. (✆ 520/885-0000); 3207 E. Speedway Blvd. (✆ 520/325-0000); 6960 E. Sunrise Dr. (✆ 520/615-9700); and 8303 N. Oracle Rd. (✆ 520/742-0000). There's also Gadabout Man, 2951 N. Swan Rd. (✆ 520/325-3300).

10 SHOPPING

Although the Tucson shopping scene is overshadowed by that of Scottsdale and Phoenix, Tucson does provide a respectable diversity of merchants. Tucsonans have a strong sense of their place in the Southwest, and this is reflected in the city's shopping opportunities. Southwestern clothing, food, crafts, furniture, and art abound (and often at reasonable prices), as do shopping centers built in a Southwestern architectural style.

The city's population center continues to move steadily northward, so it is in the northern foothills that you'll find most of the city's large enclosed shopping malls as well as the more tasteful small shopping plazas full of boutiques and galleries.

In downtown Tucson, on Fourth Avenue, between Congress Street and Speedway Boulevard, more than 50 shops, galleries, and restaurants make up the **Fourth Avenue historic shopping and entertainment district.** The buildings here were constructed in the early 1900s, and the proximity to the University of Arizona helps keep this district bustling. Many of the shops cater primarily to student needs and interests. Through the underpass at the south end of Fourth Avenue is Congress Street, the heart of the **Downtown Arts District,** where there are still a few art galleries (most, however, have moved to the foothills). Both areas are primarily hangouts for college students.

El Presidio Historic District around the Tucson Museum of Art is the city's center for crafts shops. This area is home to Old Town Artisans and the Tucson Museum of Art shop. The city's **"Lost Barrio"** district, on the corner of Southwest Park Avenue and 12th Street (a block off Broadway), is a good place to look for Mexican imports and Southwestern-style home furnishings at good prices.

ANTIQUES & COLLECTIBLES

Eric Firestone Gallery ★★ Collectors of Stickley and other Arts and Crafts furniture will not want to miss this impressive gallery, which is located in one of the historic buildings at Joesler Village shopping plaza. In addition to the furniture, there are period paintings and accessories. At Joesler Village, 4425 N. Campbell Ave. ✆ **520/577-7711.** www.ericfirestonegallery.com.

Michael D. Higgins & Son Located next door to the Eric Firestone Gallery, this little shop specializes in pre-Columbian artifacts but also carries African, Asian, and even ancient Greek and Roman pieces. At Joesler Village, 4429 N. Campbell Ave. ✆ **520/577-8330.** www.mhiggins.com.

Morning Star Antiques In a shop that adjoins Morning Star Traders (see "Native American Art, Crafts & Jewelry," below), Morning Star Antiques carries an excellent selection of antique Spanish and Mexican furniture, as well as other unusual and rustic pieces. 2020 E. Speedway Blvd. ✆ **520/881-2112.** www.morningstartraders.com.

Primitive Arts Gallery This is the best gallery in Tucson for pre-Columbian art, with an eclectic mix of ancient artifacts focusing on ceramics. You'll also find a smattering of other artifacts, from Greek urns to Navajo rugs. At Broadway Village, 3026 E. Broadway. ✆ **520/326-4852.**

ART

Tucson's gallery scene is not as concentrated as that in many other cities. Many Tucson galleries have in the past few years abandoned downtown in favor of the foothills and other more affluent suburbs. The current art hot spot is the corner of Campbell Avenue and Skyline Drive, where you'll find **Gallery Row,** a stylishly modern Southwestern shopping plaza that has several contemporary art galleries. Behind this complex, at 6420 N. Campbell Ave., is a small courtyard complex that is home to **Sanders Galleries** (✆ **520/299-1763;** www.sandersgalleries.com) and **Settlers West Galleries** (✆ **520/299-2607;** www.settlerswest.com), both of which specialize in Western art, as well as **Gallery West** (✆ **520/529-7002;** www.indianartwest.com), which specializes in American Indian art.

El Presidio Gallery Long one of Tucson's premier galleries, El Presidio deals primarily in traditional and contemporary paintings of the Southwest, and is located in downtown's El Presidio historic district. The contemporary works shown here tend toward the large and bright, and are popular decorations in foothills homes. In Old Town Artisans, 186 N. Meyer Ave. ✆ **520/299-1414.** www.elpresidiogallery.com.

Etherton Gallery For more than 25 years, this gallery has been presenting some of the most distinctive art to be found in Tucson, including contemporary and historical photographs. A favorite of museums and serious collectors, Etherton Gallery isn't afraid to present work with strong themes. A smaller location is at the Temple of Music and Art, 330 S. Scott Ave. (✆ **520/624-7370**). 135 S. Sixth Ave. ✆ **520/624-7370.** www.etherton gallery.com.

Medicine Man Gallery/Mark Sublette Modern ★★★ This gallery has the finest and most tasteful traditional Western art you'll find just about anywhere in Arizona. Artists represented include Ed Mell, Maynard Dixon, and Howard Post, and most of the gallery's artists have received national attention. There's an excellent selection of Native American crafts as well; see "Native American Art, Crafts & Jewelry," below, for more details. The gallery also houses a small Maynard Dixon Museum. At Santa Fe Square, 7000 E. Tanque Verde Rd. © **800/422-9382** or 520/722-7798. www.medicinemangallery.com.

Philabaum Contemporary Art Glass For more than 25 years, this gallery has been exposing Tucson to the latest trends in contemporary glass art. The gallery is full of lovely and colorful pieces by Tucson's own Tom Philabaum and more than 100 other artists from around the country. 711 S. Sixth Ave. © **520/884-7404.** www.philabaumglass.com.

BOOKS

Chain bookstores in the Tucson area include **Barnes & Noble,** 5130 E. Broadway Blvd. (© **520/512-1166**), and 7325 N. La Cholla Blvd., Ste. 100, in the Foothills Mall (© **520/742-6402**); and **Borders,** 4235 N. Oracle Rd. (© **520/292-1331**), and 5870 E. Broadway Blvd., at the Park Place Mall (© **520/584-0111**).

Bookmans This big bookstore, housed in a former supermarket, is crammed full of used books and recordings, and has long been a favorite of Tucsonans. There are other Bookmans stores at 6230 E. Speedway Blvd. (© **520/748-9555**) and 3733 W. Ina Rd. (© **520/579-0303**). 1930 E. Grant Rd. © **520/325-5767.** www.bookmans.com.

Clues Unlimited If you forgot to pack your vacation reading, drop by this fun little store. Not only can you shop for the latest Carl Hiassen or other mystery, but you can also say hi to Sophie and Emily, the resident potbellied pigs. Broadway Village, 123 S. Eastbourne St. © **520/326-8533.** www.cluesunlimited.com.

CRAFTS

Details Art & Design If you enjoy highly imaginative and colorful crafts with a sense of humor, you'll get a kick out of this place. Unexpected objets d'art turn up in the forms of clocks, ceramics, glass, and other media. At Gallery Row, 3001 E. Skyline Dr., Ste. 103. © **520/577-1995.** www.detailsart.com.

Obsidian Gallery Contemporary crafts by nationally recognized artists fill this gallery. You'll find luminous glass art, unique and daring jewelry, imaginative ceramics, and much more. At St. Philip's Plaza, 4320 N. Campbell Ave. (at River Rd.). © **520/577-3598.** www.obsidian-gallery.com.

Old Town Artisans ★ Housed in a restored 1850s adobe building covering an entire city block of El Presidio Historic District, this unique shopping plaza houses half a dozen different shops brimming with traditional and contemporary Southwestern designs. There's also free Wi-Fi in the courtyard here. 201 N. Court Ave. © **800/782-8072** or 520/623-6024. www.oldtownartisans.com.

Skyline Gallery At this foothills fine-crafts gallery, you'll find display cases full of gorgeous, colorful jewelry, art glass, and ceramics. There are also exquisite works in wood. In Paloma Village Center, 6360 N. Campbell Ave., Ste. 150. © **520/615-3800.** www.skylinegallerytucson.com.

Tucson Museum of Art Shop The Tucson Museum's gift shop offers a colorful and changing selection of Southwestern crafts, mostly by local and regional artists. 140 N. Main Ave. © **520/624-2333.** www.tucsonarts.com.

FASHION

See also the listing for the Beth Friedman Collection under "Jewelry," below. For cowboy and cowgirl attire, see "Western Wear," below.

Dark Star Leather If you're in the market for a distinctive leather jacket, belt, or purse, be sure to stop by this little locally owned shop in Plaza Palomino. Exotic leathers are used in the one-of-a-kind designs. You can sometimes find great deals on sale items. At Plaza Palomino, 2940 N. Swan Rd. ✆ **520/881-4700.** www.darkstarleather.com.

Maya Palace This shop features ethnic-inspired but sophisticated women's clothing in natural fabrics. The friendly staff helps customers of all ages put together a Southwestern chic look, from casual to dressy. Shops can also be found at El Mercado, 6332 E. Broadway Blvd. (✆ **520/748-0817**), and at Casas Adobes Plaza, 7057 N. Oracle Rd. (✆ **520/575-8028**). At Plaza Palomino, 2960 N. Swan Rd. ✆ **520/325-6411.** www.mayapalacetucson.com.

Rochelle K Fine Women's Apparel With everything from the latest in the little black dress to drapey silks and casual linens, Rochelle K attracts a well-heeled clientele. You'll also find beautiful accessories and jewelry here. At Casas Adobes Plaza, 7039 N. Oracle Rd. ✆ **520/797-2279.** www.rochellek.com.

GIFTS & SOUVENIRS

DAH Rock Shop If you can't make it to Tucson for the annual gem and mineral shows, don't despair. At this cluttered shop, you can pick through shelves crammed with all manner of rare minerals and exotic stones. 3401 N. Dodge Blvd. ✆ **520/323-0781.** www.dahrockshop.com.

Native Seeds/SEARCH ★★ Gardeners, cooks, and just about anyone in search of an unusual gift will likely be fascinated by this tiny shop, which is operated by a non-profit organization dedicated to preserving the biodiversity offered by native Southwest seeds. The shelves are full of heirloom beans, corn, chiles, and other seeds from a wide variety of native desert plants. There are also gourds and inexpensive Tarahumara Indian baskets, bottled sauces and salsas made from native plants, and books about native agriculture. 526 N. Fourth Ave. ✆ **520/622-5561.** www.nativeseeds.org.

Picánte Designs The plethora of Hispanic-themed icons and accessories here include *milagros,* Day of the Dead skeletons, Mexican crosses, jewelry, greeting cards, and folk art from around the world. This is a great place to shop for distinctive south-of-the-border kitschy gifts. 2932 E. Broadway. ✆ **520/320-5699.**

Tohono Chul Museum Shops ★ The two shops here are packed with Mexican folk art, nature-themed toys, household items, T-shirts, and books. These shops are an absolute must after a visit to surrounding Tohono Chul Park, which is landscaped with desert plants. Add a meal at the park's tearoom, and you've got a good afternoon's outing. For a description of the park, see p. 378. 7366 N. Paseo del Norte (1 block west of the corner of Ina and Oracle rds. in Tohono Chul Park). ✆ **520/742-6455.** www.tohonochulpark.org.

JEWELRY

In addition to the stores mentioned below, see the listing for the Obsidian Gallery under "Crafts," above.

Beth Friedman Collection This shop sells a well-chosen collection of jewelry by Native American craftspeople and international designers. It also carries some extravagant cowgirl get-ups in velvet and lace, as well as contemporary women's fashions. At Joesler Village, 1865 E. River Rd., Ste. 121. ✆ **520/577-6858.** www.bethfriedmanonline.com.

MALLS & SHOPPING CENTERS

Plaza Palomino Built in the style of a Spanish hacienda with a courtyard and fountains, this little shopping center is home to some of Tucson's most interesting specialty shops, as well as galleries and restaurants. There's a farmers' market here on Saturday mornings. Southeast corner of North Swan and Fort Lowell rds. ✆ **520/320-6344.** www.plazapalomino.com.

St. Philip's Plaza This upscale Southwestern-style shopping center contains a couple of good restaurants, a beauty salon/day spa, and numerous shops and galleries. On Saturday and Sunday mornings, there is a farmers' market. Makes a great one-stop Tucson shopping outing. 4280 N. Campbell Ave. (at River Rd.). ✆ **520/529-2775.** www.stphilipsplaza.com.

NATIVE AMERICAN ART, CRAFTS & JEWELRY

Bahti Indian Arts Family owned for more than 50 years, this store sells exquisitely made Native American crafts—jewelry, baskets, sculpture, paintings, books, weavings, kachina dolls, Zuni fetishes, and much more. At St. Philip's Plaza, 4330 N. Campbell Ave., Ste. 73. ✆ **520/577-0290.** www.bahti.com.

Gallery West Located right below Anthony's in the Catalinas restaurant, this tiny shop specializes in very expensive Native American artifacts (mostly pre-1940s) such as New Mexico Pueblo pots, Apache and Pima baskets, 19th-century Plains Indian beadwork, Navajo weavings, and kachinas. There is also plenty of both contemporary and vintage jewelry. 6420 N. Campbell Ave. (at Skyline Dr.). ✆ **520/529-7002.** www.indianartwest.com.

Medicine Man Gallery/Mark Sublette Modern This shop has the best and biggest selection of old Navajo rugs in the city, and perhaps even in the entire state. There are also Mexican and other Hispanic textiles, Acoma pottery, basketry, and other Indian crafts, as well as artwork by cowboy artists. At Santa Fe Square, 7000 E. Tanque Verde Rd., Ste. 16. ✆ **800/422-9382** or 520/722-7798. www.medicinemangallery.com.

Morning Star Traders ★★★ With hardwood floors and a museumlike atmosphere, this store features Native American crafts of the highest quality, including antique Navajo rugs, kachinas, furniture, and a huge selection of old Native American jewelry. This just may be the best store of its type in the entire state. An adjoining shop, Morning Star Antiques, carries an impressive selection of antique furniture (see "Antiques & Collectibles," above). 2020 E. Speedway Blvd. ✆ **520/881-2112.** www.morningstartraders.com.

Silverbell Trading Not your run-of-the-mill crafts store, Silverbell specializes in regional Native American artwork, such as baskets and pottery, and carries unique pieces that the shop owner handpicks. Items such as stone Navajo corn maidens, Zuni fetishes, and figures carved from sandstone are among the highlights. At Casas Adobes Plaza, 7119 N. Oracle Rd. ✆ **520/797-6852.** www.silverbelltrader.com.

WESTERN WEAR

Arizona Hatters Arizona Hatters carries the best names in cowboy hats, from Stetson to Bailey to Resistol, and the shop specializes in custom-fitting hats to the customer's head and face. 2790 N. Campbell Ave. ✆ **520/292-1320.**

Boot Barn If you want to put together your Western-wear ensemble under one roof, this is the place. It's the largest such store in Tucson and can outfit you and your kids in the latest cowboy fashions, including hats and boots. In Northwest Plaza, 3719 N. Oracle Rd. (at Prince Rd.). ✆ **520/293-1808.** www.bootbarn.com.

Stewart Boot Manufacturing Co. Boots that fit so well you don't even need socks. That's how a Tucson friend described the custom-made cowboy boots turned out by this South Tucson boot maker. You'll have to wait for your boots, though, since all the boots sold here are made to order. 30 W. 28th St. ✆ **520/622-2706.**

11 TUCSON AFTER DARK

Tucson after dark is a much easier landscape to negotiate than the vast cultural sprawl of the Phoenix area. Rather than having numerous performing-arts centers all over the suburbs as in the Valley of the Sun, Tucson has a more concentrated nightlife scene. The **Downtown Arts District** is the center of the action, with the Temple of Music and Art, the Tucson Convention Center Music Hall, and several nightclubs. The **University of Arizona campus,** a mile away, is another hot spot for entertainment.

The free *Tucson Weekly* contains thorough listings of concerts, theater and dance performances, and club offerings. The entertainment section of the *Arizona Daily Star* ("Caliente") and the *Tucson Citizen*'s "Calendar" both come out each Thursday and are good sources of information for what's going on around town.

THE CLUB & MUSIC SCENE

Country

Cactus Moon Café A 20- to 40-something crowd frequents this large and glitzy nightclub, which features primarily country music (with dance lessons several nights each week). Keep in mind, though, that rock instead of country may be played on some nights. Check the schedule before putting on your boots. 5470 E. Broadway Blvd. (at Craycroft Rd.). ✆ **520/748-0049.** www.cactusmoon.net. Cover free to $5.

The Maverick: King of Clubs The Maverick, in different incarnations and different locations around town, has been Tucson's favorite country-music dance club since 1962. Currently it's located in a modern space out in east Tucson and is open Tuesday through Saturday nights, with live country music every night. 6622 E. Tanque Verde Rd. ✆ **520/298-0430.** www.mavericktucson.com. Cover free to $5.

Dance Club

El Parador Restaurant Tropical decor sets the mood for live Latin dance music and salsa lessons on Friday nights. The music starts at 10pm and dance lessons start at 10:15pm. On Saturday, DJs spin more salsa music, and every other Saturday night there's a live band. Customers of this "all ages" club range from 20- to 60-somethings. 2744 E. Broadway. ✆ **520/881-2744.** www.elparadortucson.com. Cover $7.

Jazz

To find out what's happening on the local jazz scene, contact the **Tucson Jazz Society** (✆ **520/903-1265;** www.tucsonjazz.org). This organization's website lists various jazz nights at restaurants all over Tucson, including **Old Pueblo Grill Alvernon,** 60 N. Alvernon Way (✆ **520/326-6000;** www.metrorestaurants.com), with live jazz on Sunday nights; and **Acacia at St. Philip's,** 4340 N. Campbell Ave. (✆ **520/232-0101;** www.acaciatucson.com), with live jazz Wednesday through Saturday nights, plus a jazz brunch on Sunday.

The Grill ★★ No other jazz venue in Tucson has more flavor of the Southwest than this restaurant/lounge, perched high on a ridge top overlooking the city. There's live music (mostly jazz) Thursday through Sunday nights. At Hacienda del Sol Guest Ranch Resort, 5601 N. Hacienda del Sol Rd. ✆ **520/529-3500.** www.haciendadelsol.com.

Mariachi

Tucson is the mariachi capital of the United States, and no one should visit without spending at least one evening listening to some of these strolling musicians. In addition to the restaurants listed here, you can hear mariachi bands during Sunday lunch at downtown's **El Charro Café** (p. 366) and occasionally on weekends at **El Guero Canelo** (p. 367). At the **St. Augustine Cathedral,** 192 S. Stone Ave. (✆ **520/623-6351;** www.staugustinecathedral.com), there is a mariachi mass every Sunday at 8am.

Guadalajara Grill Located just west of N. Campbell Avenue, this large Mexican restaurant is convenient to several of the foothills resorts, which makes it a great place to catch an evening of lively mariachi music. The musicians perform nightly from 6 to 9pm. 1220 E. Prince Rd. ✆ **520/323-1022.** www.ggrill.com.

La Fuente ★ La Fuente is one of the largest Mexican restaurants in Tucson and serves up good food, but what really draws the crowds is the live mariachi music. If you just want to listen and not have dinner, you can hang out in the lounge. The mariachis perform Thursday through Sunday. 1749 N. Oracle Rd. ✆ **520/623-8659.** www.lafuenterestaurant.com.

Rock, Blues & Reggae

Chicago Bar Transplanted Chicagoans love to watch their home teams on the TVs at this neighborhood bar, but there's also live music nightly. Sure, blues gets played a lot, but so do reggae and rock and about everything in between. 5954 E. Speedway Blvd. ✆ **520/748-8169.** www.chicagobartucson.com. Cover $5.

Club Congress Just off the lobby of the restored Hotel Congress (now a budget hotel catering to younger travelers), Club Congress is Tucson's main alternative-music venue. There are usually a couple of nights of live music each week, and, over the years, such bands as Nirvana, Dick Dale, and the Goo Goo Dolls have played here. More recently, the club has tended to book primarily local and regional acts. 311 E. Congress St. ✆ **520/622-8848.** www.hotelcongress.com. Cover free to $15.

The Rialto Theatre This renovated 1919 vaudeville theater, although not a nightclub, is now Tucson's main venue for performances by bands that are too big to play across the street at Club Congress (Indigo Girls, Taj Mahal, Blues Traveler). 318 E. Congress St. ✆ **520/740-1000.** www.rialtotheatre.com. Tickets $13–$58.

THE BAR, LOUNGE & PUB SCENE

Armitage Wine Lounge If you're a wine lover and are staying at a foothills resort, be sure to check out this stylish wine bar at the corner of Skyline and Campbell. In addition to having more than 30 wines available by the glass, they also have a long cocktail menu. In La Encantada shopping center, 2905 E. Skyline Dr. ✆ **520/682-9740.** www.armitagewine.com.

Audubon Bar If you're looking for a quiet, comfortable scene, the piano music in this classic lounge at the Arizona Inn is sure to soothe your soul. The Audubon has a timeless feel, and before or after drinks, you can stroll the resort's beautiful gardens. 2200 E. Elm St. ✆ **520/325-1541.** www.arizonainn.com.

Barrio Brewing Co. Located in a warehouse district southeast of downtown and a few blocks south of Broadway, this big brewpub, which is affiliated with Gentle Ben's Brewing Co., isn't easy to find, but it is definitely worth searching out. Grab a seat on the loading-dock patio and sip a stout as the sun goes down. 800 E. 16th St. (at E. Euclid Ave. and Toole St.). ✆ **520/791-2739.** www.barriobrewing.com.

Cascade Lounge ★ This is Tucson's ultimate piano bar. With a view of the Catalinas, the plush lounge is perfect for romance or relaxation at the start or end of a night on the town. Sunday through Thursday nights, there's live piano music or a jazz band, and on Fridays and Saturdays, there's a DJ and dancing. At Loews Ventana Canyon Resort, 7000 N. Resort Dr. ✆ **520/299-2020.** www.loewshotels.com.

Cushing Street Bar & Restaurant Located on the edge of the Barrio Histórico district just south of the Tucson Convention Center, this restaurant/bar is in a historic 1860s adobe building and has loads of old Tucson character. There's also live jazz on Saturday nights and occasionally other nights in the month. 198 W. Cushing St. ✆ **520/622-7984.** www.cushingstreet.com.

The Kon Tiki With a Polynesian luau theme, this joint is not some modern-day designer's idea of what the 1950s were like; this is the real thing. Tiki lovers rejoice, but be careful, those sweet tropical cocktails can pack a Hawaiian punch! 4625 E. Broadway Blvd. ✆ **520/323-7193.** www.kontiki-tucson.com.

Nimbus Brewing ★ Located in a warehouse district on the south side of Tucson, this brewpub is basically the front room of Nimbus's brewing and bottling facility. The beer is good, and there's live blues, rock, folk, and reggae on a regular basis. Hard to find, and definitely a local scene. 3850 E. 44th St. (2 blocks east of Palo Verde Rd.). ✆ **520/745-9175.** www.nimbusbeer.com.

Thunder Canyon Brewery This big brewpub is a convivial and convenient place to down a pint if you're staying at a foothills resort. There are always plenty of different brews on tap. At Foothills Mall, 7401 N. La Cholla Blvd. (at Ina Rd.). ✆ **520/797-2652.** www.thundercanyonbrewery.com.

¡Toma! ★ This bar, in El Presidio Historic District and owned by the family that operates El Charro Café next door, has a fun and festive atmosphere complete with a Mexican hat fountain/sculpture in the courtyard. Drop by for cheap margaritas during happy hour (Mon–Fri 3–6pm). 311 N. Court Ave. ✆ **520/622-1922.**

Sports Bars

Famous Sam's With 10 branches around the city, Famous Sam's keeps a lot of Tucson's sports fans happy with its cheap prices and large portions. Other locations include 7930 E. Speedway Blvd. (✆ **520/290-9666**) and 2320 N. Silverbell Rd. (✆ **520/884-7267**). 1830 E. Broadway Blvd. ✆ **520/884-0119.** www.famoussams.net.

Gay & Lesbian Bars & Clubs

To find out about other gay bars around town, keep an eye out for the *Observer* (✆ **520/622-7176;** www.tucsonobserver.com), Tucson's newspaper for the gay, lesbian, and bisexual community. You'll find it at **Antigone Books,** 411 N. Fourth Ave. (✆ **520/792-3715;** www.antigonebooks.com), as well as at the bars listed here.

Ain't Nobody's Bizness Located in a small shopping plaza in midtown, this bar has long been *the* lesbian gathering spot in Tucson. There are pool tables, a dance floor, and a quiet, smoke-free room where you can duck out of the noise. This bar also has nights for gay men as well, so check the schedule. 2900 E. Broadway Blvd., Ste. 118. ✆ **520/318-4838.** www.thebiztuc.com.

IBT's Located on funky Fourth Avenue, IBT's has long been the most popular gay men's dance bar in town. The music ranges from 1980s retro to hip-hop, and regular drag shows add to the fun. There's always an interesting crowd. 616 N. Fourth Ave. ✆ **520/882-3053.**

THE PERFORMING ARTS

Tucson's performing arts scene is just as lively as Phoenix's, and three of Tucson's major companies—the Arizona Opera Company, Ballet Arizona, and the Arizona Theatre Company—spend half their time in Phoenix. This means that whatever gets staged in Phoenix also gets staged in Tucson. Tucson also has its own symphony and manages to sustain a diversified theater scene. Tickets to Tucson Convention Center events (but not the symphony or the opera) and other venues around town may be available by calling **Ticketmaster** (✆ **520/321-1000;** www.ticketmaster.com) or by stopping by the **TCC box office,** 260 S. Church Ave. (✆ **520/791-4101;** www.cityoftucson.org/tcc).

Outdoor Venues & Series

Weather permitting, Tucsonans head to Reid Park's **DeMeester Outdoor Performance Center,** at Country Club Road and East 22nd Street (✆ **520/791-4873**), for performances under the stars. This amphitheater stages live theater performances, as well as frequent concerts (many of which are free).

The **Tucson Jazz Society** (✆ **520/903-1265;** www.tucsonjazz.org), which manages to book a few well-known jazz musicians each year, sponsors different series at various locations around the city. Tickets are usually between $15 and $35.

Classical Music, Opera & Dance

Both the **Tucson Symphony Orchestra** (✆ **520/882-8585** or 520/792-9155; www.tucsonsymphony.org), which is the oldest continuously performing symphony in the Southwest, and the **Arizona Opera Company** (✆ **520/293-4336** or 520/321-1000; www.azopera.org), the state's premier opera company, perform at the Tucson Convention Center Music Hall. Symphony tickets run mostly $20 to $51; opera tickets are $25 to $100.

Theater

Tucson doesn't have a lot of theater companies, but what few it does have stage a surprisingly diverse sampling of both classic and contemporary plays. **Arizona Theatre Company** (✆ **520/622-2823;** www.aztheatreco.org), which performs at the Temple of Music and Art, splits its time between Tucson and Phoenix, and is the state's top professional theater company. Each season sees a mix of comedy, drama, and Broadway-style musical shows; tickets cost $26 to $64. The **Invisible Theatre,** 1400 N. First Ave. (✆ **520/882-9721;** www.invisibletheatre.com), a tiny theater in a converted laundry building, has been home to Tucson's most experimental theater for more than 35 years (it does off-Broadway shows). Tickets run about $22 to $42.

The West just wouldn't be the West without good old-fashioned melodramas, and the **Gaslight Theatre,** 7010 E. Broadway Blvd. (✆ **520/886-9428;** www.thegaslighttheatre.com), is where evil villains, stalwart heroes, and defenseless heroines pound the boards. You can boo and hiss, cheer and sigh as the predictable stories unfold on stage. It's great

Performing-Arts Centers & Concert Halls

Tucson's largest performance venue is the **Tucson Convention Center (TCC) Music Hall,** 260 S. Church Ave. (✆ **520/791-4101;** www.cityoftucson.org/tcc). It's the home of the Tucson Symphony Orchestra and where the Arizona Opera Company usually performs when it's in town.

The centerpiece of the Tucson theater scene is the **Temple of Music and Art,** 330 S. Scott Ave. (✆ **520/622-2823**), a restored historic theater dating from 1927. The 605-seat Alice Holsclaw Theatre is the Temple's main stage, but there's also the 90-seat Cabaret Theatre.

University of Arizona Centennial Hall, 1020 E. University Blvd. at Park Avenue (✆ **520/621-3341;** www.uapresents.org), on the UA campus, is Tucson's other main performance hall. It stages performances by touring national musical acts, international companies, and Broadway shows.

Originally opened in 1930, downtown Tucson's **Fox Theatre,** 17 W. Congress St. (✆ **520/624-1515** or 520/547-3040; www.foxtucsontheatre.org), is a restored 1930s movie palace that is now the city's most beautiful place to catch live music, a play, or even a classic or independent film.

The **Center for the Arts Proscenium Theatre,** Pima Community College (West Campus), 2202 W. Anklam Rd. (✆ **520/206-6986**), is another good place to check for classical music performances. It offers a wide variety of shows.

fun for kids and adults, with plenty of pop-culture references. Tickets are $18 for adults, $16 for students and seniors, and $8 for kids 12 and under. Performances are held Tuesday through Sunday, with two shows nightly Friday and Saturday, plus a Sunday matinee. Tickets often sell out a month in advance.

13

Phoenix & the Valley of the Sun

Forget the stately cactuses. Forget the cowboys riding off into the sunset. Think Los Angeles without the Pacific. While the nation has carefully nurtured its image of Phoenix as a desert cow town, this city in the Sonoran Desert has rocketed into the 21st century and become the fifth-largest city in the country. Sprawling across more than 500 square miles of what once was cactus and creosote bushes, the greater Phoenix metropolitan area, also known as the Valley of the Sun (or, more commonly, just the Valley), is now a major metropolitan area replete with dozens of resort hotels, fabulous restaurants, excellent museums, hundreds of golf courses, world-class shopping, four pro sports teams, and a red-hot nightlife scene.

Sure, it also has traffic jams and smog, but at the end of the day, it can usually claim to have had beautiful sunny weather. Sunshine and blue skies, day after day after day, have made this one of the most popular winter destinations in the country. When Chicago weather forecasts call for snow and subzero temperatures, you can have a hard time getting a tee time on a Phoenix-area golf course. Phoenicians may get the summertime blues when temperatures hit the triple digits, but from September to May, the climate here can verge on perfect—warm enough in the daytime for lounging by the pool, cool enough at night to require a jacket.

With green lawns, orange groves, swimming pools, and palm trees, it's easy to forget that Phoenix is in the middle of the desert. Water channeled in from distant reservoirs has allowed this city to flourish like a desert oasis. However, if you find yourself wondering where the desert is, you need only lift your eyes to one of the many mountains that rise amid the suburban sprawl. South Mountain, Camelback Mountain, Mummy Mountain, Piestewa Peak, Papago Buttes, Pinnacle Peak—these rugged, rocky summits have been preserved in their natural states, and it is to these cactus-covered uplands that the city's citizens retreat when they've had enough asphalt and air-conditioning. From almost anywhere in the Valley, you're no more than a 15- or 20-minute drive from a natural area where you can commune with cactuses while gazing out across a bustling, modern city.

Best of all, at the end of the day, you can retreat to a comfortable bed at one of the country's top resorts.

1 ORIENTATION

ARRIVING

BY PLANE Centrally located 3 miles east of downtown Phoenix, **Sky Harbor International Airport,** 3400 E. Sky Harbor Blvd. (✆ **602/273-3300;** www.phxskyharbor.com), has three terminals, with a free 24-hour shuttle bus offering frequent service between them. For information on airlines serving Phoenix, see chapter 3.

Tips A Name Change

In 2003, the official name of Phoenix's Squaw Peak was changed to Piestewa Peak (pronounced Pie-*ess*-too-uh) to honor PFC Lori Ann Piestewa, a member of the Hopi tribe and the first female soldier killed in the Iraq War. The peak in north Phoenix has long been a popular hiking destination. If you hear people referring to both Squaw Peak and Piestewa Peak, it's one and the same place. Ditto for the Squaw Peak Parkway, which is now Piestewa Freeway.

There are two entrances to the airport. The west entrance can be accessed from either the Papago Freeway (I-10) or 24th Street, while the east entrance can be accessed from the Hohokam Expressway (Ariz. 143) or the Sky Harbor Expressway (Ariz. 153), which is an extension of 44th Street. If you're headed to downtown Phoenix, leave by way of the 24th Street exit and continue west on Washington Street. If you're headed to Scottsdale, Tempe, or Mesa, head east out of the airport and follow signs for Ariz. 202 Loop.

SuperShuttle (✆ **800/BLUE-VAN** [258-3826] or 602/244-9000; www.supershuttle.com) offers 24-hour door-to-door van service between Sky Harbor Airport and resorts, hotels, and homes throughout the Valley. Per-person fares average $14 to $16 to the downtown and Tempe area, $16 to downtown Scottsdale, and $24 to $42 to north Scottsdale.

Taxis can be found outside all three terminals and cost only slightly more than shuttle vans. You can also call **AAA Cab** (✆ **602/437-4000**) or **Discount Cab** (✆ **602/200-2000;** www.discountcab.com). Taxis from the airport charge $5 for turning on the meter, a $1 airport surcharge, $2 per mile, and a minimum fare of $15. A taxi from the airport to downtown Phoenix will cost around $15; to Scottsdale, between $20 and $35.

Metro (✆ **602/253-5000;** www.valleymetro.org), the valley's light-rail line, connects Phoenix Sky Harbor Airport with the cities of Phoenix, Tempe, and Mesa. Metro runs daily every 15 to 20 minutes, between 5am and midnight. To take the light-rail, you'll first need to ride the free airport shuttle to the light-rail station at the corner of Washington and 44th streets. The ride from the light-rail station to downtown takes about 15 minutes and costs $1.25. There is no Metro service to Scottsdale, so you'll first need to go to Tempe and then transfer to a northbound Valley Metro bus.

BY CAR Phoenix is connected to Los Angeles and Tucson by I-10 and to Flagstaff via I-17. If you're headed to Scottsdale, the easiest route is to take the Red Mountain Freeway (Ariz. 202) east to US 101 N. This latter freeway loops all the way around the east, north, and west sides of the Valley. The Superstition Freeway (U.S. 60) leads to Tempe, Mesa, and Chandler.

BY TRAIN There is no passenger rail service to Phoenix. **Amtrak** (✆ **800/872-7245;** www.amtrak.com) will sell you a ticket to Phoenix, but you'll have to take a shuttle bus from either Flagstaff or Tucson. The scheduling is so horrible on these routes that you'd have to be a total masochist to opt for Amtrak service to Phoenix.

VISITOR INFORMATION

You'll find **tourist information desks** in all three terminals at Sky Harbor Airport. The city's main visitor center is the **Greater Phoenix Convention & Visitors Bureau,** 125 N. Second St., Ste. 120 (✆ **877/225-5749** or 602/254-6500; www.visitphoenix.com;

Mon–Fri 8am–5pm), across from the main entrance of the Hyatt Regency in downtown Phoenix. There's also a small visitor information center at the Biltmore Fashion Park shopping center, 2502 E. Camelback Rd., Ste. 101 (✆ **602/955-1963;** Mon–Wed 10am–7pm, Thurs–Fri 10am–8pm, Sat 10am–6pm, and Sun noon–6pm).

The **Visitor Information Line** (✆ **602/252-5588**) has recorded information about current events in Phoenix and is updated weekly.

If you're staying in Scottsdale, you can get information at the **Scottsdale Convention & Visitors Bureau Visitor Center,** Galleria Corporate Center, 4343 N. Scottsdale Rd., Ste. 170 (✆ **800/782-1117** or 480/421-1004; www.scottsdalecvb.com; Mon–Fri 8am–5pm).

CITY LAYOUT

MAIN ARTERIES & STREETS **US Loop 101** forms a loop around the east, north, and west sides of the Valley, providing freeway access to Scottsdale from I-17 on the north side of Phoenix and from US 60 in Tempe.

I-17 (Black Canyon Fwy.), which connects Phoenix with Flagstaff, is the city's main north-south freeway. This freeway curves to the east just south of downtown (where it is renamed the **Maricopa Fwy.** and merges with I-10). **I-10,** which connects Phoenix with Los Angeles and Tucson, is called the **Papago Freeway** on the west side of the Valley and as it passes north of downtown; as it curves around to pass to the west and south of the airport, it merges with I-17 and is renamed the Maricopa Freeway. At Tempe, this freeway curves to the south and heads out of the Valley.

North of the airport, **Ariz. 202 (Red Mountain Fwy.)** heads east from I-10 and passes along the north side of Tempe, providing access to downtown Tempe, Arizona State University, Mesa, and Scottsdale (via US Loop 101). On the east side of the airport, **Ariz. 143 (Hohokam Expwy.)** connects Ariz. 202 with I-10.

At the interchange of I-10 and Ariz. 202, northwest of Sky Harbor Airport, **Ariz. 51 (Piestewa Fwy.)** heads north through the center of Phoenix to US Loop 101 and is the best north-south route in the city.

South of the airport off I-10, **US 60 (Superstition Fwy.)** heads east to Tempe, Chandler, Mesa, and Gilbert. **US Loop 101** leads north from US 60 (and Ariz. 202) through Scottsdale and across the north side of Phoenix to connect with I-17. US 60 and US Loop 101 provide the best route from the airport to the Scottsdale resorts. US Loop 101 also heads south through Chandler to connect with I-10. This section is called the Price Freeway. The section of this freeway north through Scottsdale is called the Pima Freeway.

Secondary highways in the Valley include the **Beeline Highway (Ariz. 87),** which starts at the east end of Ariz. 202 (Red Mountain Fwy.) in Mesa and leads to Payson, and **Grand Avenue (US 60),** which starts downtown and leads west to Sun City and Wickenburg.

Phoenix and the surrounding cities of Mesa, Tempe, Scottsdale, and Chandler, and even those cities farther out in the Valley, are laid out in a grid pattern with major avenues and roads about every mile. For traveling east to west across Phoenix, your best choices (other than the above-mentioned freeways) are Camelback, Indian School, and McDowell roads. For traveling north and south, 44th Street, 24th Street, and Central Avenue are good choices. Hayden Road is a north-south alternative to Scottsdale Road, which gets jammed at rush hours.

FINDING AN ADDRESS **C Central Avenue,** which runs north to south through downtown Phoenix, is the starting point for all east-and-west street numbering. **Washington Street** is the starting point for north and south numbering. North-to-south numbered *streets* are to be found on the east side of the city, while north-to-south numbered *avenues* will be found on the west. For the most part, street numbers advance by 100 with each block. Odd-numbered addresses are on the south and east sides of streets, while even-numbered addresses are on the north and west sides of streets.

For example, if you're looking for 4454 E. Camelback Rd., you'll find it 44 blocks east of Central Avenue between 44th and 45th streets on the north side of the street. If you're looking for 2905 N. 35th Ave., you'll find it 35 blocks west of Central Avenue and 29 blocks north of Washington Street, on the east side of the street. Just for general reference, Camelback Road marks the 5000 block north. Also, whenever you're getting directions, ask for the cross street closest to where you're going.

2 GETTING AROUND

BY CAR

Phoenix and the surrounding cities that together make up the Valley of the Sun sprawl across more than 400 square miles, so if you want to make the best use of your time, it's essential to have a car. Outside downtown Phoenix, there's almost always plenty of free parking wherever you go (although finding a parking space can be time-consuming in Old Scottsdale and at some of the more popular malls and shopping plazas). If you want to feel like a local, opt for the ubiquitous valet parking (just be sure to keep plenty of small bills on hand for tipping the parking attendants).

Because Phoenix is a major tourist destination, good car-rental rates are often available. However, taxes and surcharges on rentals at Sky Harbor Airport now run 50% or more, which pretty much negates any deal you might get on your rate. Expect to pay anywhere from $160 to $250 per week ($240–$375 with taxes) for a compact car in the high season. See chapter 3 for general tips on car rentals.

All major rental-car companies have desks at Sky Harbor Airport's Rental Car Center, which is separate from the airport terminals and is served by a free shuttle bus. Be sure to leave time in your schedule to get from the Rental Car Center to the correct terminal for your flight. There are also plenty of other car-rental offices in Phoenix and Scottsdale. Rental-car companies at the airport include the following: **Advantage** (© 800/777-5500 or 602/244-0450), **Alamo** (© 800/462-5266 or 602/244-0897), **Avis** (© 800/331-1212 or 602/261-5900), **Budget** (© 800/527-0700 or 602/261-5950), **Dollar** (© 800/800-3665 or 866/434-2226), **Enterprise** (© 800/261-7331 or 602/225-0588), **Fox** (© 800/225-4369 or 602/275-9700), **Hertz** (© 800/654-3131 or 602/267-8822), **National** (© 800/227-7368 or 602/275-4771), **Payless** (© 800/729-5377 or 602/681-9589), and **Thrifty** (© 800/847-4389 or 602/244-0311).

BY PUBLIC TRANSPORTATION

The free **Downtown Area Shuttle (DASH)** provides bus service within the downtown area Monday through Friday from 6:30am to 6:30pm. These buses serve regular stops every 12 minutes; they're primarily for downtown workers, but attractions along the route include the state capitol and Heritage and Science Park. In Tempe, **FLASH** buses provide a similar service on a loop around Arizona State University, including Mill Avenue and Sun Devil Stadium, from Monday through Friday from 7am to 6pm; another loop operates Monday through Thursday from 7am to 1am and Friday from 7am to 10pm. For information on both DASH and FLASH, call © **602/253-5000.**

In Scottsdale, you can ride the **Scottsdale Trolley** (✆ **480/421-1004;** www.scottsdale trolley.com) shuttle buses between Scottsdale Fashion Square, the Fifth Avenue shops, the Main Street Arts district, and the Old Town district. These buses run daily from 11am to 9pm, with service every 10 minutes. Between mid-January and mid-April, free shuttles serve many of the area's resorts, including, among others, Camelback Inn, Sanctuary on Camelback, InterContinental Montelucia Resort & Spa, and Renaissance Scottsdale Resort. These trolleys operate daily from 9am to 6pm, with service every 30 minutes, and will take you to Scottsdale Fashion Square. From there you can take the Scottsdale Trolley to other shopping districts.

The area's most useful public-transit alternative is Valley Metro's **METRO light-rail system,** which runs along Central Avenue, through downtown Phoenix, and east to Tempe and Mesa. Attractions along or close to the line include the Heard Museum, Phoenix Art Museum, Historic Heritage Square, Phoenix Museum of History, Arizona Science Center, Pueblo Grande Museum and Archaeological Park, Desert Botanical Garden, Phoenix Zoo, Hall of Flame Firefighting Museum, Tempe's Mill Avenue shopping district, and the Arizona State University Art Museum. There is also a free airport shuttle that connects the 44th Street/Washington Street stop to the airport. For more information, contact Valley Metro (✆ **602/253-5000;** www.valleymetro.org).

BY TAXI

Because distances in Phoenix are so great, the price of an ordinary taxi ride can be quite high. However, if you don't have your own wheels or you had too much to drink and the bus isn't running because it's late at night or the weekend, you won't have any choice but to call a cab. **Yellow Cab** (✆ **602/252-5252;** www.aaayellowaz.com) charges $2.50 for the first mile and $2 per mile thereafter. **Discount Cab** (✆ **602/200-2000;** www. discountcab.com) charges $2.95 for the first mile and $1.95 per mile after that.

FAST FACTS

The Banner Good Samaritan Medical Center, 1111 E. McDowell Rd., Phoenix (✆ **602/ 239-2000**), is one of the largest hospitals in the valley. For a doctor referral, call the Banner Health Physician & Resource Line (✆ **602/230-2273**); for a dentist referral, call the Dental Referral Service (✆ **866/639-7444**).

State sales tax is 5.6% (plus variable local taxes, so expect to pay around 8%). Hotel room taxes vary considerably by city but are mostly between 10% and 11%. The total taxes and surcharges when renting a car at Sky Harbor Airport add up to more than 50%.

3 WHERE TO STAY

The Phoenix area has the greatest concentration of resorts in the continental United States. However, sunshine and spring training combine to make it hard to find a room on short notice between February and April. If you're planning to visit during these months, make your reservations as far in advance as possible. Also keep in mind that in winter, the Phoenix metro area has some of the highest room rates in the country.

With the exception of valet-parking services and parking garages at downtown convention hotels, parking is free at almost all Phoenix hotels. If there is a parking charge, I have noted it. You'll find that all hotels have nonsmoking rooms and all but the cheapest have wheelchair-accessible rooms.

Most resorts offer a variety of weekend, golf, and tennis packages, as well as off-season discounts and corporate rates (which you can often get just by asking). I've given only the official "rack rates," or walk-in rates, below, but it always pays to ask about special discounts or packages. Don't forget your AAA or AARP discounts if you belong to one of these organizations. Business hotels downtown and near the airport often lower their rates on weekends, and many hotels offer website-only specials.

BED & BREAKFASTS While most people dreaming of a Phoenix vacation have visions of luxury resorts dancing in their heads, there are some bed-and-breakfasts around the Valley. **Mi Casa Su Casa** (✆ **800/456-0682** or 480/990-0682; www.azres.com) can book you into dozens of different homes in the Valley of the Sun, as can **Arizona Trails Travel Services** (✆ **888/799-4284** or 480/837-4284; www.arizonatrails.com), which also books tour and hotel reservations.

SCOTTSDALE

Scottsdale is the center of the Valley's resort scene. Because Scottsdale is also the Valley's prime shopping and dining district, this is the most convenient place to stay if you're here to eat and shop. However, traffic in Scottsdale is bad, the landscape at most resorts is flat, and you don't get much of a feel for the desert.

Very Expensive

Camelback Inn, A JW Marriott Resort & Spa ★★★ Kids Set at the foot of Mummy Mountain and overlooking Camelback Mountain, the Camelback Inn, which opened in 1936, is one of the grande dames of the Phoenix hotel scene and abounds in traditional Southwestern character. Forget the glitz of the Phoenician (see below); this legendary retreat gives you old-school luxury with 21st-century enhancements. The two 18-hole golf courses are a magnet for golfers, and the spa is among the finest in the state. An extensive pool complex appeals to families. Guest rooms, which are spread over the sloping grounds, are decorated with Southwestern furnishings and art, and all have balconies or patios. Some rooms even have private pools. This is an old-money getaway that seamlessly melds tradition with modern amenities. A $50-million renovation was completed in late 2008.

5402 E. Lincoln Dr., Scottsdale, AZ 85253. ✆ **800/24-CAMEL** [242-2635] or 480/948-1700. Fax 480/951-8469. www.camelbackinn.com. 453 units. Jan to early June $299–$549 double, $570–$2,500 suite; early June to early Sept $179–$199 double, $260–$900 suite; early Sept to Dec $349–$459 double, $595–$1,700 suite. Children 17 and under stay free in parent's room. AE, DC, DISC, MC, V. Small pets accepted (fee varies). **Amenities:** 7 restaurants; 3 lounges; babysitting; bikes; children's programs; concierge; 2 18-hole golf courses; health club; 5 Jacuzzis; 2 pools; room service; full-service spa; 6 tennis courts. *In room:* A/C, TV, hair dryer, kitchenette, minibar, MP3 docking station, Wi-Fi.

Hotel Valley Ho ★★ This Scottsdale hotel dates back to the 1950s, but in 2005, it got a complete face-lift. What a looker she is now. The Valley Ho is one of my favorite Scottsdale hotels; it's hip and convenient, and has loads of outdoor space for soaking up the sun. I just love the big rooms, which are done in a bold contemporary style. The studio rooms are my favorites; they have curtains to partition off the vanity area and an ultracool free-standing tub. Big balconies and patios provide plenty of space for lounging outdoors. When it's time to get even more relaxed, grab one of the plush, circular lounge chairs at the pool. For a totally retro experience, there's even a Trader Vic's Polynesian restaurant here.

6850 E. Main St., Scottsdale, AZ 85251. ✆ **866/882-4484** or 480/248-2000. Fax 480/248-2002. www.hotelvalleyho.com. 193 units. Jan–Apr $319–$389 double, $449–$1,700 suite; May and Sept $199–$279

Phoenix & the Valley of the Sun Accommodations

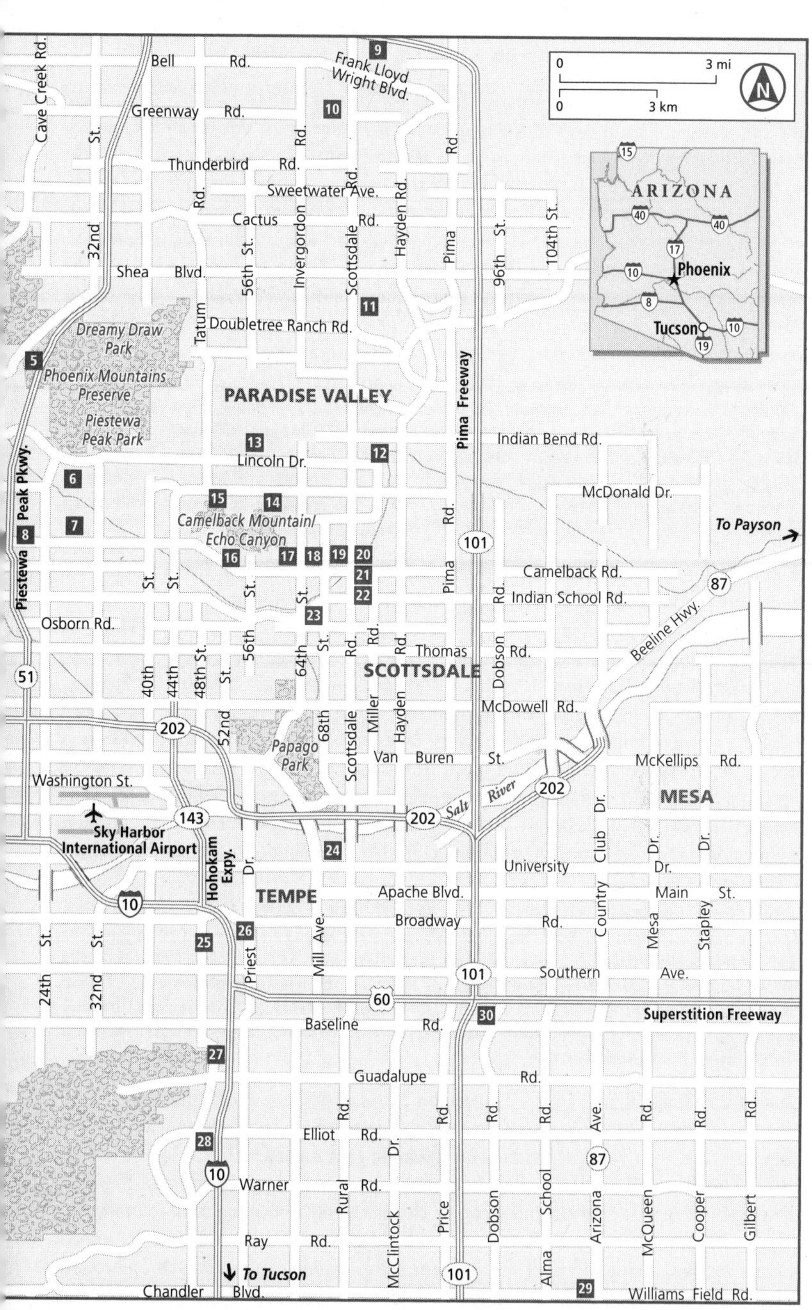

0 3 mi
0 3 km
N
ARIZONA
Phoenix
Tucson
Bell Rd.
Greenway Rd.
Thunderbird Rd.
Sweetwater Ave.
Cactus Rd.
Shea Blvd.
Frank Lloyd Wright Blvd.
Cave Creek Rd.
32nd St.
Tatum Rd.
56th St.
Invergordon Rd.
Scottsdale Rd.
Hayden Rd.
Pima Rd.
96th St.
104th St.
Doubletree Ranch Rd.
Dreamy Draw Park
Phoenix Mountains Preserve
Piestewa Peak Park
PARADISE VALLEY
Pima Freeway
Indian Bend Rd.
Lincoln Dr.
McDonald Dr.
Piestewa Peak Pkwy.
Camelback Mountain/ Echo Canyon
To Payson
Camelback Rd.
Indian School Rd.
Beeline Hwy.
Osborn Rd.
Thomas Rd.
SCOTTSDALE
40th St.
44th St.
48th St.
52nd St.
56th St.
64th St.
68th St.
Miller Rd.
Dobson Rd.
McDowell Rd.
Papago Park
Van Buren St.
McKellips Rd.
Washington St.
Salt River
MESA
Sky Harbor International Airport
Hohokam Expy.
University Dr.
Country Club Dr.
Mesa Dr.
Stapley Dr.
TEMPE
Apache Blvd.
Main St.
Broadway Rd.
Mill Ave.
Priest Dr.
24th St.
32nd St.
Southern Ave.
Superstition Freeway
Baseline Rd.
Guadalupe Rd.
Elliot Rd.
Rural Rd.
McClintock Dr.
Price Rd.
Dobson Rd.
Alma School Rd.
Arizona Ave.
McQueen Rd.
Cooper Rd.
Gilbert Rd.
Warner Rd.
Ray Rd.
To Tucson
Chandler Blvd.
Williams Field Rd.

double, $299–$1,000 suite; June–Aug $149–$179 double, $249–$699 suite; Oct–Dec $279–$299 double, $359–$1,000 suite. Children 17 and under stay free in parent's room. AE, DC, DISC, MC, V. Valet parking $12. Pets accepted. **Amenities:** 2 restaurants; 3 lounges; babysitting; bikes; concierge; exercise room; 2 Jacuzzis; pool; room service; full-service spa. *In room:* A/C, TV, hair dryer, minibar, Wi-Fi.

Hyatt Regency Scottsdale Resort & Spa at Gainey Ranch ★★★ Kids From the colonnades of palm trees to the lobby walls that slide away, this luxurious resort is designed to impress and continues to be my favorite Scottsdale resort. It's relatively close to downtown Scottsdale and has interesting architecture, beautiful grounds, and a large spa. What's not to love? A 2½-acre water playground serves as the resort's focal point, and the extravagant complex of 10 swimming pools includes a water slide, sand beach, and a huge whirlpool spa. Guest rooms are luxurious and were recently redesigned. The resort's Alto ristorante e bar features after-dinner gondola rides. The resort's Native American and Environmental Learning Center provides a glimpse into Sonoran Desert culture and ecology. Children's programs make this a super choice for families.

7500 E. Doubletree Ranch Rd., Scottsdale, AZ 85258. ✆ **800/55-HYATT** [554-9288] or 480/444-1234. Fax 480/483-5550. www.scottsdale.hyatt.com. 492 units. Jan to mid-May $399 double, from $999 suite and casita; mid-May to mid-Sept $169 double, from $429 suite and casita; mid-Sept to Dec $359 double, from $899 suite and casita. Children 18 and under stay free in parent's room. AE, DC, DISC, MC, V. Valet parking $27. Pets accepted ($50 fee). **Amenities:** 3 restaurants; 3 lounges; babysitting; bikes; children's programs; concierge; executive-level rooms; 27-hole golf course; health club; Jacuzzi; 10 pools; room service; spa; 4 tennis courts. *In room:* A/C, TV, fridge, hair dryer, MP3 docking station, Wi-Fi.

InterContinental Montelucia Resort & Spa ★★★ With architecture inspired by Spain's fabled Alhambra and the red rocks of Camelback Mountain looming overhead, this resort, which opened in late 2008, is one of Arizona's prettiest getaways. There are splashing fountains, a restaurant serving excellent Mediterranean cuisine, and a spa inspired by the *hammams* (public baths) of Morocco. Guest rooms continue the Spanish/Moroccan themes and are divided into different "villages." If you like peace and quiet, ask for a room in the Bocce Garden Village (and have a bocce court right outside your door). Night owls should opt for a room in the Kasbah Village, which is close to the open-air lounge and the main pool. Throughout the property, you'll see fascinating antiquities from Spain, including two giant amphorae in the entry courtyard and huge wooden doors that lead to the resort's ballroom. Not too big, not too small, Montelucia is just right.

4949 E. Lincoln Dr., Paradise Valley, AZ 85253. ✆ **888/627-3010** or 480/627-3200. www.icmontelucia.com. 293 units. Jan–Apr $395–$845 double, $695–$4,000 suite; May to mid-June and mid-Sept to Dec $245–$625 double, $545–$3,000 suite; mid-June to mid-Sept $145–$425 double, $345–$2,000 suite. Rates do not include $24 daily resort fee. Children 17 and under stay free in parent's room. AE, DC, DISC, MC, V. Valet parking $26. Pets accepted ($100 fee). **Amenities:** 4 restaurants; 2 lounges; snack bar; children's programs; concierge; exercise room; 2 Jacuzzis; 3 pools; room service; full-service spa. *In room:* A/C, TV, hair dryer, MP3 docking station, Wi-Fi.

The Phoenician ★★★ Kids Situated on 250 acres at the foot of Camelback Mountain, this palatial getaway is one of the world's finest resorts. So, if you must stay at the very best, this is it. Polished marble and sparkling crystal abound in the lobby, but the view through a wall of glass is what commands most guests' attention when they first arrive. The resort has a classic, international character, and service is second to none. The pool complex, with its water slide for the kids, is irresistibly seductive, and the resort's Centre for Well Being offers all the spa pampering anyone could ever want. There are also 27 holes of golf. The luxurious guest rooms have large patios and sunken tubs for two. For the ultimate in luxury, book a room in the Canyon Suites, a separate boutique hotel within the resort. The Phoenician's steakhouse is operated by Jean-Georges Vongerichten.

6000 E. Camelback Rd., Scottsdale, AZ 85251. ✆ **800/888-8234** or 480/941-8200. Fax 480/947-4311. www.thephoenician.com. 643 units. Jan–May from $529 double, from $1,150 suite; June to mid-Sept from $199 double, from $475 suite; mid-Sept to Dec from $489 double, from $1,100 suite. Children 17 and under stay free in parent's room. AE, DC, DISC, MC, V. Valet parking $26. Pets accepted ($150 deposit). **Amenities:** 3 restaurants; 5 lounges; 4 snack bars/cafes; babysitting; bikes; children's programs; concierge; executive-level rooms; 27-hole golf course; health club; 2 Jacuzzis; 9 pools; room service; spa; 11 tennis courts. *In room:* A/C, TV, CD player, hair dryer, Internet, minibar.

Sanctuary on Camelback Mountain ★★★ This visually breathtaking place was the Valley's first hip resort, and I still like the contemporary rooms here better than those at other hip hotels around town. Located high on the northern flanks of Camelback Mountain, the lushly landscaped property has unforgettable views across the Valley, especially from its restaurant and two bars. The extremely spacious guest rooms are divided between the more conservative deluxe casitas and the boldly contemporary spa casitas. With their dyed-cement floors, L-shaped couches, and streamline-modern cabinetry, these latter units are absolutely stunning. Bathrooms are huge, and some have private outdoor soaking tubs. The resort's spa is gorgeous.

5700 E. McDonald Dr., Paradise Valley, AZ 85253. ✆ **800/245-2051** or 480/948-2100. www.sanctuaryoncamelback.com. 105 units. Jan to mid-May and late Dec $520–$725 double, $650–$1,580 suite; mid-May to mid-Sept $235–$415 double, $340–$935 suite; mid-Sept to mid-Dec $395–$620 double, $545–$1,370 suite. Children 16 and under stay free in parent's room. AE, DC, DISC, MC, V. Pets accepted. **Amenities:** Restaurant; 2 lounges; babysitting; bikes; concierge; exercise room & access to nearby health club; 2 Jacuzzis; 4 pools; room service; full-service spa; 5 tennis courts. *In room:* A/C, TV/DVD, hair dryer, minibar, Wi-Fi.

Westin Kierland Resort & Spa ★★★ (Kids) A convenient location and distinct sense of place make this one of my favorite Phoenix-area resorts. Located just off Scottsdale Road adjacent to the Kierland Commons shopping center, the resort features artwork by Arizona artists, numerous interpretive plaques, and historical photos that provide insight into Arizona's cultural and natural history. Guest rooms all have balconies or patios, and although the bathrooms aren't all that large, this minor inconvenience is compensated for by Westin's Heavenly Beds, which have incredibly comfortable pillow-top mattresses. Excellent Nuevo Latino cuisine is served at deseo, and there's a great cowboy-style bar as well. The main pool area includes a long tubing river, a water slide, and a beach area.

6902 E. Greenway Pkwy., Scottsdale, AZ 85254. ✆ **800/WESTIN-1** [937-8461] or 480/624-1000. Fax 480/624-1001. www.kierlandresort.com. 732 units. Jan–Apr $379–$699 double; May–June $189–$489 double; July to mid-Sept $179–$349 double; mid-Sept to Dec $279–$529 double. Children 17 and under stay free in parent's room. AE, DISC, MC, V. Valet parking $24. Pets accepted. **Amenities:** 8 restaurants; 4 lounges; babysitting; children's programs; concierge; 27-hole golf course; health club; 3 Jacuzzis; 4 pools; room service; full-service spa; 2 tennis courts. *In room:* A/C, TV, hair dryer, minibar, Wi-Fi.

Expensive

FireSky Resort & Spa ★★ An exceptional location in the heart of the Scottsdale shopping district, a dramatic Southwestern contemporary styling (the focal point of the lobby is an impressive sandstone fireplace), and a small but well-designed pool area are the main reasons I like this little resort. Set in a lushly planted courtyard are a small lagoon-style pool, complete with sand beach and waterfall, and a second pool with flame-topped columnar waterfalls. An artificial stream and faux sandstone ruins add up to a lush desert fantasy landscape (although not on the grand scale to be found at some area resorts). The guest rooms are quite comfortable, and there's a pretty little spa on the premises.

4925 N. Scottsdale Rd., Scottsdale, AZ 85251. ✆ **800/528-7867** or 480/945-7666. Fax 480/946-4056. www.fireskyresort.com. 204 units. Jan to mid-Apr $289–$365 double, $799 suite; mid-Apr to May $219–$280 double, $499 suite; June–Aug $119–$184 double, $299 suite; Sept–Dec $249–$334 double, $549 suite. Children 17 and under stay free in parent's room. AE, DISC, MC, V. Pets accepted. **Amenities:** Restaurant; lounge; babysitting; concierge; exercise room; Jacuzzi; 2 pools; room service; full-service spa. *In room:* A/C, TV, hair dryer, minibar, Wi-Fi.

Hyatt Place Scottsdale/Old Town ★ With a great location in the heart of downtown Scottsdale, this hip business hotel is well worth choosing even if you're in town on vacation. The guest rooms are all spacious suites done in a homey, contemporary style with separate sitting and sleeping areas and 42-inch wall-hung flat-panel TVs that can be angled to either area. Unusual features include electronic self-service check-in kiosks, continental (free) or hot (charge) breakfasts, and a tiny lounge area to one side of the lobby. You can even get a light meal here if you don't feel like going out to a restaurant for dinner.

7300 E. Third Ave., Scottsdale, AZ 85251. ✆ **888/492-8847** or 480/423-9944. Fax 480/423-2991. www.hyattplace.com. 127 units. $99–$329 double. Rates include continental breakfast. Children 17 and under stay free in parent's room. AE, DC, DISC, MC, V. **Amenities:** Restaurant; lounge; exercise room & access to nearby health club; outdoor pool. *In room:* A/C, TV, fridge, hair dryer, MP3 docking station, Wi-Fi.

Moderate

Hotel Indigo ★ In the heart of downtown Scottsdale's nightlife district, this stylish hotel is a great choice for anyone in town to party. Guest rooms are distinctively different from those of most hotels in that they have wood floors and area rugs. The rooms are designed in a Scandinavian-modern aesthetic and have absolutely gorgeous bathrooms. Clock radios have MP3 jacks, and the beds have halogen reading lamps. Seasonal fragrances scent the air; and photo-murals of, among other things, northern Arizona's famous sandstone formation "the Wave" make the Indigo a feast for the senses.

4415 N. Civic Center Plaza, Scottsdale, AZ 85251. ✆ **888/554-6344** or 480/941-9400. Fax 480/675-5240. www.scottsdalehiphotel.com. 126 units. Jan–Apr $129–$299 double; May–Sept $89–$129 double; and Oct–Dec $129–$249 double. Children 17 and under stay free in parent's room. AE, DC, DISC, MC, V. Pets accepted. **Amenities:** Restaurant; lounge; exercise room; small outdoor pool; room service. *In room:* A/C, TV, hair dryer, MP3 docking station, Wi-Fi.

Scottsdale Resort & Athletic Club ★★ Fitness fanatics, rejoice; this club's for you. If you can't stand the thought of giving up your workout just because you're on vacation, book a stay at this little boutique hotel (and timeshare resort) just off busy Scottsdale Road and adjacent to the Silverado Golf Course. With standard rooms and huge one-, two-, and three-bedroom "villas," this place is plenty comfortable; but the main reason I like this hotel is that it's affiliated with the Scottsdale Athletic Club, a large workout facility that emphasizes its tennis program. The basic rooms are a real steal for Scottsdale, and while the villas are quite a bit more expensive, they're gigantic and have fireplaces, DVD players, full kitchens, and washers and dryers. On top of all this, you get a view of Camelback Mountain.

8235 E. Indian Bend Rd., Scottsdale, AZ 85250. ✆ **877/343-0033** or 480/344-0600. Fax 480/344-0650. www.scottsdaleresortandathleticclub.com. 85 units. Late Dec to mid-Apr $149 double, $179–$599 suite or villa; mid-Apr to May and mid-Sept to Dec $129 double, $159–$569 suite or villa; June to mid-Sept $79 double, $99–$249 suite or villa. Children 11 and under stay free in parent's room. AE, DISC, MC, V. **Amenities:**

Restaurant; lounge; babysitting; children's programs; concierge; health club; 2 Jacuzzis; 3 pools; room service; sauna; full-service spa; 11 tennis courts. *In room:* A/C, TV/DVD, CD player, fridge, hair dryer, Internet.

Inexpensive

Despite the high-priced real estate, Scottsdale does have a few relatively inexpensive chain motels, although during the winter season, prices are higher than you might expect. For location alone, your best choice would be the **Motel 6–Scottsdale,** 6848 E. Camelback Rd. (✆ **480/946-2280**), which has doubles for $76 to $86 during the high season.

Days Inn Scottsdale Resort at Fashion Square Mall Kids Value This is one of the last economical hotels in the Old Town Scottsdale area, and its location adjacent to the Scottsdale Fashion Square Mall makes it a great choice for shopaholics. The Days Inn may be just an aging chain motel, but its green lawns, pool, tall palm trees, and a convenient downtown location all make it worth recommending, particularly for families.

4710 N. Scottsdale Rd., Scottsdale, AZ 85251. ✆ **800/329-7466** or 480/947-5411. Fax 480/946-1324. www.scottsdaledaysinn.com. 167 units. Jan–Mar $85–$140 double; Apr–Dec $60–$100 double. Rates include continental breakfast. Children 17 and under stay free in parent's room. AE, DC, DISC, MC, V. **Amenities:** Seasonal poolside bar; Jacuzzi; small outdoor pool. *In room:* A/C, TV, fridge, hair dryer, Wi-Fi.

NORTH SCOTTSDALE, CAREFREE & CAVE CREEK

North Scottsdale is the brave new world for Valley of the Sun resorts. Situated at least a 30-minute drive from downtown Scottsdale, this area boasts the newest resorts, the most spectacular hillside settings, and the best golf courses.

Very Expensive

The Boulders Resort ★★★ Set amid a jumble of giant boulders 45 minutes north of downtown Scottsdale, this was the first luxury golf resort in the north Valley's rugged foothills. The adobe buildings blend unobtrusively into the desert, and the two golf courses epitomize the desert golf course experience. When not golfing, you can lounge around the small pool, play tennis, relax at the resort's Golden Door Spa, or try your hand at rock climbing. The lobby is in a Santa Fe–style building with tree-trunk pillars and a flagstone floor, and the guest rooms continue the pueblo styling with stucco walls, beehive fireplaces, and beamed ceilings. For the best views, ask for one of the second-floor units. Bathrooms are large and luxuriously appointed, with tubs for two and separate showers. In a commitment to being more eco-friendly, the Boulders is now emphasizing organic ingredients in its restaurants and has planted an organic herb-and-vegetable garden.

34631 N. Tom Darlington Dr. (P.O. Box 2090), Carefree, AZ 85377. ✆ **888/579-2631** or 480/488-9009. Fax 480/488-4118. www.theboulders.com. 215 units. Late Dec to May $299 double, from $899 villa; May to early Sept $149 double, from $499 villa; early Sept to late Dec $299 double, from $699 villa. (For all rates, there is an additional $29–$33 nightly service charge.) Children 16 and under stay free in parent's room. AE, DC, DISC, MC, V. Pets accepted ($100). **Amenities:** 6 restaurants; 3 lounges; babysitting; bikes; concierge; exercise room; 2 18-hole golf courses; 3 Jacuzzis; 4 pools; room service; full-service spa; 8 tennis courts. *In room:* A/C, TV, hair dryer, Internet, minibar, MP3 docking station (in some).

CopperWynd Resort and Club ★★ Value Tucked away on a ridge top on the northeastern edge of the Valley, this little boutique resort overlooking the town of Fountain Hills is one of the most luxurious resorts in the area. Best of all, the resort boasts some of the most picturesque mountain vistas in the Valley. CopperWynd also has a fabulous tennis facility, an impressive health club, and a spa, and, although there is no golf course on the premises, there are four highly regarded courses nearby. The resort's

Jacuzzi, tucked into a rocky hillside, is as romantic as they come. All guest rooms have great views and feature European deluxe decor. Balconies provide plenty of room for taking in the vista. There's also an excellent restaurant, Alchemy.

13225 N. Eagle Ridge Dr., Fountain Hills, AZ 85268. ✆ **877/707-7760** or 480/333-1900. Fax 480/333-1901. www.copperwynd.com. 40 units. Late Dec to late Apr $379–$429 double, $825–$925 villa; late Apr to mid-May and late Sept to late Dec $269–$329 double, $750–$900 villa; mid-May to late Sept $169–$209 double, $550–$650 villa. Children 17 and under stay free in parent's room. AE, DC, DISC, MC, V. **Amenities:** 2 restaurants; 2 lounges; concierge; health club; 2 Jacuzzis; 2 pools; saunas; full-service spa; 9 tennis courts. *In room:* A/C, TV, fridge, hair dryer, Wi-Fi (in some).

Fairmont Scottsdale ★★★ Kids With its royal palms, tiled fountains, and waterfalls, the Fairmont offers an exotic atmosphere that will delight anyone in search of a getaway that doesn't entail learning Spanish or spending Euros. A water playground (with two water slides) and a kids' fishing pond also make this resort a hit with families. The resort, a 20-minute drive from Old Town Scottsdale, is home to the FBR Open golf tournament, which means the fairways here are top-notch. Guest rooms are done in contemporary Southwestern style, and bathrooms have double vanities and separate showers and tubs. All units have private balconies. For stepped-up amenities, opt for a room in the Gold wing. There's also the Willow Stream spa (p. 449), and the resort offers an eco-education program that includes guided hikes.

7575 E. Princess Dr., Scottsdale, AZ 85255. ✆ **800/344-4758** or 480/585-4848. Fax 480/585-0091. www.fairmont.com/scottsdale. 649 units. $149–$589 double; $319–$3,800 suite. Children 17 and under stay free in parent's room. AE, DC, DISC, MC, V. Valet parking $23. Pets accepted ($25 per night). **Amenities:** 3 restaurants; 3 lounges; children's programs; concierge; executive-level rooms; exercise room; 2 18-hole golf courses; Jacuzzi; 5 pools; room service; full-service spa; 7 tennis courts; Wi-Fi. *In room:* A/C, TV, hair dryer, Internet, minibar, MP3 docking station (in some).

Four Seasons Resort Scottsdale at Troon North ★★★ In the foothills of north Scottsdale adjacent to (and with privileges at) the legendary Troon North golf course, the Four Seasons is even more impressive than the nearby Boulders Resort. This superluxurious resort may not feel as expansive as the Boulders, but in every other aspect it is superior. With casita accommodations scattered across a boulder-strewn hillside, the Four Seasons boasts one of the Valley's most dramatic settings, and with a hiking trail to nearby Pinnacle Peak Park, the resort is a good choice for anyone who wants to explore the desert on foot. Guest rooms and suites are among the most lavish you'll find in Arizona. If you can afford it, opt for one with a private plunge pool and an outdoor shower—a luxury usually found only in tropical resorts.

10600 E. Crescent Moon Dr., Scottsdale, AZ 85262. ✆ **888/207-9696** or 480/515-5700. Fax 480/515-5599. www.fourseasons.com/scottsdale. 210 units. Jan–May $475–$645 double, $825–$5,500 suite; June–Aug $195–$250 double, $500–$3,000 suite; Sept–Dec $295–$595 double, $500–$5,000 suite. Children 17 and under stay free in parent's room. AE, DC, DISC, MC, V. Valet parking $26. Small pets accepted. **Amenities:** 3 restaurants; 2 lounges; babysitting; children's programs; concierge; 2 18-hole golf courses; health club; Jacuzzi; 3 pools (including large 2-level pool); room service; sauna; spa; 2 tennis courts. *In room:* A/C, TV/DVD, hair dryer, minibar, MP3 docking station (in some), Wi-Fi.

Expensive

Radisson Fort McDowell Resort & Casino ★★ In the Scottsdale area, you just can't stay any closer to the desert than at this beautiful resort northeast of Fountain Hills. Although the Radisson is a 30-minute drive from downtown Scottsdale, the location is hard to beat if you've come to the area to experience the desert. The resort is on the Fort McDowell Yavapai Nation, and the tribe's Fort McDowell Casino is a big draw for many guests. However, the two 18-hole courses at the adjacent We-Ko-Pa Golf Club are also major draws here. Personally, I like the resort best for its creative Native American styling and its great desert and mountain views. For families, there's a children's water-play area, and horseback riding, and, in summer, float trips down the nearby Verde River can be arranged.

10438 N. Fort McDowell Rd., Fountain Hills, AZ 85264. ✆ **800/333-3333** or 480/789-5300. Fax 480/789-5333. www.radisson.com/ftmcdowellaz. 246 units. Jan–Mar $269–$299 double; Apr $199–$210 double; May, Sept, and Dec $139–$159 double; June–Aug $109–$139 double; Oct–Nov $219–$239 double. Children 11 and under stay free in parent's room. AE, DC, DISC, MC, V. Pets accepted. **Amenities:** Restaurant; lounge; snack bar; babysitting; concierge; exercise room; 2 18-hole golf courses; 2 Jacuzzis; outdoor pool; room service; full-service spa. *In room:* A/C, TV, hair dryer, minibar, Wi-Fi.

CENTRAL PHOENIX & THE CAMELBACK CORRIDOR

This area is the heart of the upscale Phoenix shopping and restaurant scene and is home to the prestigious Arizona Biltmore resort. Old money and new money rub shoulders along the avenues here, and valet parking is de rigueur. Located roughly midway between Old Scottsdale and downtown Phoenix, this area is a good bet for those intending to split their time between the downtown Phoenix cultural and sports district and the world-class shopping and dining in Scottsdale.

Very Expensive

Arizona Biltmore Resort & Spa ★★★ Kids For more than 80 years, this resort has been the favored Phoenix address of celebrities, politicians, and old money, and the distinctive cast-cement blocks inspired by a Frank Lloyd Wright design make it a unique architectural gem. However, it's the historical character and timeless elegance that really set this place apart. With wide lawns, colorful flower gardens, and views of Piestewa Peak, this is a resort for outdoor lounging. While the two golf courses and expansive spa are the main draws, the children's activities center and lawn games make this a popular choice for families. Of the several different styles of accommodations, the "resort rooms" are quite comfortable and have balconies or patios. Those rooms in the Paradise Wing are also good choices. Afternoon tea is served in the lobby Thursday through Sunday. For extra pampering, book a room in the resort's exclusive Ocatilla at Arizona Biltmore wing.

2400 E. Missouri Ave., Phoenix, AZ 85016. ✆ **800/950-0086** or 602/955-6600. Fax 602/381-7600. www.arizonabiltmore.com. 738 units. Jan to mid-May $595–$805 double, from $855 suite; mid-May to early Sept $279–$359 double, from $379 suite; early Sept to Dec $465–$585 double, from $615 suite. Rates do not include $28 daily service fee. Children 11 and under stay free in parent's room. AE, DC, DISC, MC, V. Valet parking $27; self-parking $12. Pets under 50 lb. accepted in cottage rooms ($100 deposit, $50 nonrefundable). **Amenities:** 4 restaurants; lounge; bikes; children's programs; concierge; executive-level rooms; 2 18-hole golf courses; health club; 2 Jacuzzis; 8 pools; room service; saunas; full-service spa; 7 tennis courts. *In room:* A/C, TV, fridge, hair dryer, Internet, minibar.

Royal Palms Resort and Spa ★★ This gorgeous little hideaway has the feel of a Spanish villa that was transported to Arizona and is so romantic and beautiful that the moment you set foot in the first cloistered garden, you might imagine that you hear flamenco guitar. Located midway between Old Town Scottsdale and Biltmore Fashion Park, the Royal Palms was constructed more than 50 years ago by Cunard Steamship executive Delos Cooke and is done in Spanish mission style. Giving the resort the tranquil feel of a Mediterranean monastery are lush walled gardens where antique water fountains splash. The most memorable guest rooms are the designer casitas, each with a distinctive decor ranging from opulent contemporary to classic European. However, all the rooms are beautiful and have superplush beds. T. Cook's restaurant is one of the city's most romantic restaurants (see "Where to Dine," later in this chapter).

5200 E. Camelback Rd., Phoenix, AZ 85018. ✆ **800/672-6011** or 602/840-3610. Fax 602/840-6927. www.royalpalmsresortandspa.com. 119 units. Jan–May $439–$579 double, $459–$2,599 suite; June to mid-Sept $169–$299 double, $189–$1,599 suite; mid-Sept to Dec $369–$509 double, $389–$2,599 suite. Rates do not include daily service fee of $22. Children 17 and under stay free in parent's room. AE, DC, DISC, MC, V. Pets accepted ($300 deposit, $100 nonrefundable). **Amenities:** Restaurant; poolside grill; lounge; babysitting; bikes; concierge; exercise room; Jacuzzi; outdoor pool w/cabanas; room service; full-service spa. *In room:* A/C, TV, CD player, hair dryer, minibar, Wi-Fi.

Expensive

Embassy Suites Biltmore ★ Located across the parking lot from the Biltmore Fashion Park shopping center, this hotel makes a great base if you want to be within walking distance of half a dozen good restaurants. The atrium is filled with interesting tile work, tropical greenery, waterfalls, and ponds filled with koi (colorful Japanese carp). In the atrium, you'll also find a romantic lounge with huge banquettes shaded by palm trees. All in all, this hotel is a good value, especially when you consider that rates include both breakfast and afternoon drinks.

2630 E. Camelback Rd., Phoenix, AZ 85016. ✆ **800/EMBASSY** [362-2779] or 602/955-3992. Fax 602/955-6479. www.phoenixbiltmore.embassysuites.com. 232 units. Jan to late May $239–$409 double; late May to early Sept $119–$219 double; early Sept to Dec $239–$329 double. Rates include full breakfast and afternoon drinks. Children 17 and under stay free in parent's room. AE, DC, DISC, MC, V. Parking $6. Pets accepted ($40). **Amenities:** Restaurant; lounge; concierge; exercise room & access to nearby health club; Jacuzzi; outdoor pool; room service. *In room:* A/C, TV, fridge, hair dryer, Wi-Fi.

Moderate

Maricopa Manor Centrally located between downtown Phoenix and Scottsdale, Maricopa Manor is just a block off busy Camelback Road and has long been Phoenix's best B&B. The inn's main building, designed to resemble a Spanish manor house, was built in 1928, and the orange trees, palms, and large yard all lend an Old Phoenix atmosphere. All guest rooms are large, comfortable suites, many with Arts and Crafts touches. One suite has a sunroom and another has an eat-in kitchen, while two others have two separate sleeping areas. Breakfast is delivered to your door, and you can eat in your room or at tables in the garden.

15 W. Pasadena Ave., Phoenix, AZ 85013. ✆ **800/292-6403** or 602/274-6302. Fax 602/266-3904. www.maricopamanor.com. 7 units. Late Dec to Apr $189–$239 double; May–June and Nov to late Dec $149–$179 double; mid-Sept to Oct $139–$169 double; July to mid-Sept $129 double. Rates include extended continental breakfast. Children 17 and under stay free in parent's room. AE, DISC, MC, V. **Amenities:** Access to nearby health club; Jacuzzi; seasonal outdoor pool. *In room:* A/C, TV/DVD/VCR, CD player, fridge, hair dryer, Wi-Fi.

Inexpensive

Extended Stay Deluxe Phoenix-Biltmore Billing itself as a temporary residence and located just north of Camelback Road not far from Biltmore Fashion Park, this hotel consists of studio-style apartments and offers discounts for stays of 7 days or more. Although designed primarily for corporate business travelers on temporary assignment in the area, this lodging makes a good choice for families as well. All units have full kitchens, big bathrooms, and separate sitting areas. Keep in mind that you only get maid service if you pay $5 to $10 extra per day or stay for a week or more.

5235 N. 16th St., Phoenix, AZ 85016. ✆ **800/398-7829** or 602/265-6800. Fax 602/265-1114. www.extendedstaydeluxe.com. 112 units. $70–$115 double. Children 16 and under stay free in parent's room.

AE, DC, DISC, MC, V. Pets accepted ($25 per night, $150 maximum). **Amenities:** Exercise room; Jacuzzi; small outdoor pool. *In room:* A/C, TV, hair dryer, kitchen, MP3 docking station, Wi-Fi.

NORTH PHOENIX

Some of the Valley's best scenery is in north Phoenix, where several small mountains have been protected as parks and preserves; the two Pointe Hilton resorts claim great locations close to these parks. So, if you're looking for quick access to desert trails, the resorts here are good choices. However, the Valley's best shopping and dining, as well as most major attractions, are all at least a 30-minute drive away.

Very Expensive

JW Marriott Desert Ridge Resort & Spa ★★ This is the largest resort in the state and it stays crowded with conference and convention groups. Because it is miles from any other resorts, high-end shopping areas, or concentrations of good restaurants, Desert Ridge is primarily a place to stay put and spend your days sitting in the sun drinking margaritas by the pool. To this end, there are 4 acres of water features and pools (including a tubing "river"). At the resort's grand entrance, desert landscaping and rows of palm trees give the resort a sense of place, and the lobby's roll-up walls let plenty of balmy desert air in during the cooler months. Guest rooms have balconies and hints of Mediterranean styling. Be sure to ask for a room with a view to the south; these rooms look out to several of Phoenix's mountain preserves.

5350 E. Marriott Blvd., Phoenix, AZ 85054. ✆ **800/835-6206** or 480/293-5000. Fax 480/293-3600. www.jwdesertridgeresort.com. 950 units. Jan–Apr $449–$529 double; May to mid-June $259–$339 double; mid-June to early Sept $199–$269 double; early Sept to late Sept $229–$389 double; Oct–Dec $409–$529 double. Children 17 and under stay free in parent's room. AE, DC, DISC, MC, V. Valet parking $25; self-parking $10. **Amenities:** 5 restaurants; 2 snack bars/cafes; 5 lounges; babysitting; bikes; children's programs; concierge; 2 18-hole golf courses; health club; 3 Jacuzzis; 5 pools; room service; sauna; full-service spa; 8 tennis courts. *In room:* A/C, TV, hair dryer, Internet, minibar.

Expensive

Pointe Hilton Squaw Peak Resort ★★ Kids At the foot of the Phoenix Mountains, this lushly landscaped resort makes a big splash with its 4-acre Hole-in-the-Wall River Ranch aquatic playground, which features a tubing "river," water slide, waterfall, sports pool, and lagoon pool. An 18-hole putting course and shopping arcade also help make it a great family-vacation spot. The resort is done in the Spanish villa style, and most of the accommodations are large suites. For a family vacation, this place is hard to beat. However, I prefer the nearby Pointe Hilton Tapatio Cliffs Resort for its dramatic hillside setting and location adjacent to the hiking trails of the North Mountain Recreation Area.

7677 N. 16th St., Phoenix, AZ 85020. ✆ **800/876-4683** or 602/997-2626. Fax 602/997-2391. www.pointehilton.com. 563 units. Jan to mid-May $169–$399 double; mid-May to mid-Sept $109–$209 double; mid-Sept to Dec $139–$299 double, year-round $1,500 grande or palacio suite. Children 17 and under stay free in parent's room. AE, DC, DISC, MC, V. Pets accepted ($75 fee). **Amenities:** 3 restaurants; 2 snack bars; 5 lounges; babysitting; children's programs; concierge; 18-hole golf course (4 miles away by shuttle); health club; 6 Jacuzzis; 8 pools; room service; saunas; small full-service spa; 3 tennis courts. *In room:* A/C, TV, hair dryer, Internet, minibar.

Pointe Hilton Tapatio Cliffs Resort ★★ Value If you love to lounge by the pool, then this resort is a great choice. The Falls, a 3½-acre water playground, includes two pools, a 138-foot water slide, 40-foot cascades, a whirlpool tucked into an artificial grotto, and rental cabanas. If you're a hiker, you can head out on the trails of the adjacent

North Mountain Recreation Area. All rooms are spacious suites with Southwest-inspired furnishings; corner units are particularly bright. This resort has steep walkways, so you need to be in good shape to stay here. At the top of the property is Different Pointe of View, a continental restaurant with one of the finest views in the city. This resort is more adult-oriented than the Pointe Hilton Squaw Peak Resort, but it is otherwise similar.

11111 N. Seventh St., Phoenix, AZ 85020. ✆ **800/876-4683** or 602/866-7500. Fax 602/993-0276. www.pointehilton.com. 584 units. Jan to mid-May $169–$399 double; mid-May to mid-Sept $109–$209 double; mid-Sept to Dec $139–$299 double; year-round $1,500 grande suite. Children 17 and under stay free in parent's room. AE, DC, DISC, MC, V. Pets accepted ($75 fee). **Amenities:** 5 restaurants; 2 poolside cafes; 5 lounges; babysitting; seasonal children's programs; concierge; exercise room; golf course; 8 Jacuzzis; 8 pools; room service; sauna; small full-service spa; 2 tennis courts. *In room:* A/C, TV, hair dryer, Internet, minibar.

Moderate/Inexpensive

Among the better moderately priced chain motels in north Phoenix is the **Best Western InnSuites Phoenix Biltmore/Scottsdale,** 1615 E. Northern Ave., at 16th Street (✆ **800/780-7234** or 602/997-6285; http://phoenix.innsuites.com), charging high-season rates of $108 to $180 double.

DOWNTOWN, SOUTH PHOENIX & THE AIRPORT AREA

Unless you're a sports fan or are in town for a convention, there's not much to recommend downtown Phoenix. This 9-to-5 area can feel like a ghost town at night. For the most part, south Phoenix is one of the poorest parts of the city. However, it does have a couple of wealthy enclaves that are home to exceptional resorts, and Phoenix South Mountain Park is one of the best places in the city to experience the desert.

Very Expensive

Arizona Grand Resort ★★ Kids This sprawling resort, which just underwent a $52-million makeover, abuts the 17,000-acre South Mountain Park and is one of the best choices in the Valley for families. If you want to score big points with your kids, stay here and let them spend every day playing in the wave pool, tubing "river," twisty water slide, and two free-fall-style water slides. Stables at the resort allow you and the kids to ride into the sunset on South Mountain, and there are numerous children's programs. The guest rooms, all suites, feature contemporary Southwestern furnishings and lots of space. Rustler's Rooste, the resort's fun cowboy steakhouse, serves rattlesnake appetizers (see "Where to Dine," below) and is a favorite with families.

8000 S. Arizona Grand Pkwy., Phoenix, AZ 85044. ✆ **866/267-1321** or 602/438-9000. Fax 602/431-6535. www.arizonagrandresort.com. 640 units. Jan–Apr from $399–$449 double; May to early Sept from $139–$189 double; early Sept to Dec from $179–$289 double. Rates do not include $30 daily resort fee. Children 17 and under stay free in parent's room. AE, DC, DISC, MC, V. **Amenities:** 5 restaurants; 4 lounges; babysitting; bikes; children's programs; concierge; 18-hole golf course; health club; 9 Jacuzzis; 11 outdoor pools (including 7-acre water park); room service; full-service spa. *In room:* A/C, TV, hair dryer, minibar, Wi-Fi.

Sheraton Wild Horse Pass Resort & Spa ★★★ Named for the area's wild horses, this resort is located 20 minutes south of Phoenix Sky Harbor International Airport on the Gila River Indian Reservation, and because the resort looks out across miles of desert, it has a pleasantly remote feel. Throw in horseback riding, a full-service spa featuring desert-inspired treatments, two golf courses, a nature trail along a 2½-mile-long artificial river, a pool with a water slide, the Rawhide Wild West theme park, and a nearby casino, and you'll find plenty to keep you busy. The resort is owned by the

Maricopa and Pima tribes, who go out of their way to share their culture with resort guests. Guest rooms have great beds, small patios, and large bathrooms. The menu in Kai, the main dining room, focuses on indigenous Southwestern flavors.

5594 W. Wild Horse Pass Blvd., Chandler, AZ 85226. ✆ **888/218-8989** or 602/225-0100. Fax 602/225-0300. www.wildhorsepassresort.com. 500 units. Early Jan to late May $329–$495 double, $650–$1,400 suite; late May to mid-Sept $189–$289 double, $600–$950 suite; mid-Sept to early Jan $289–$495 double, $650–$1,400 suite. Children 17 and under stay free in parent's room. AE, DISC, MC, V. Valet parking $18. Pets accepted. **Amenities:** 6 restaurants; 4 lounges; concierge; 2 18-hole golf courses; health club; 5 Jacuzzis; 4 outdoor pools; room service; full-service spa; 2 tennis courts. *In room:* A/C, TV, hair dryer, Internet, minibar.

Expensive

The Buttes, A Marriott Resort ★★ Just 3 miles from Sky Harbor Airport, this resort makes the most of its craggy hilltop location, and although some people complain that the nearby freeway ruins the view, the rocky setting is quintessentially Southwestern. The only other resorts in the area with as much desert character are the far more expensive Boulders and Four Seasons. From the cactus garden and waterfall *inside* the lobby to the circular restaurant and free-form swimming pools, this resort is calculated to take your breath away. Guest rooms are stylishly elegant. The city-view rooms are a bit larger than the hillside-view rooms, but second-floor hillside-view rooms have patios. Unfortunately, most bathrooms have only three-quarter-size tubs. The Top of the Rock restaurant has great views.

2000 Westcourt Way, Tempe, AZ 85282. ✆ **888/867-7492** or 602/225-9000. Fax 602/438-8622. www.marriott.com/phxtm. 353 units. Jan to mid-Apr $179–$329 double, from $475 suite; mid-Apr to mid-May $149–$289 double, from $475 suite; mid-May to early Sept $99–$199 double, from $375 suite; early Sept to Dec $149–$279 double, from $475 suite. Children 18 and under stay free in parent's room. AE, DC, DISC, MC, V. Parking $10. **Amenities:** 3 restaurants; 3 lounges; babysitting; concierge; exercise room; 4 Jacuzzis; 2 pools; room service; full-service spa; 2 tennis courts. *In room:* A/C, TV, hair dryer, minibar, Wi-Fi.

Moderate

Clarendon Hotel & Suites ★ (Finds If you're looking for a stylish yet casual place in downtown Phoenix, the Clarendon is a great choice. Having had an extreme makeover, it's now a hip hangout for young, style-conscious travelers and attracts a surprising number of celebrities. Guest rooms are done in a sort of budget contemporary that will appeal to young and artistic travelers. In the hotel's central courtyard, there's a 50-person hot tub and a gorgeous pool with gold- and platinum-coated tiles, dozens of fountains that spray water into the pool, and underwater speakers. Definitely a see-and-be-seen pool scene. The restaurant and cocktail bar are designed to appeal to young nightclubbers and fashionistas, and there's a rooftop lounge for sunset cocktails.

401 W. Clarendon Ave., Phoenix, AZ 85013. ✆ **602/252-7363.** Fax 602/274-9009. www.goclarendon.com. 105 units. Oct–May $109–$399 double; June–Sept $89–$199 double. Children 17 and under stay free in parent's room. AE, DC, DISC, MC, V. Pets accepted ($50 fee). **Amenities:** Restaurant; lounge; concierge; exercise room & access to nearby health club; Jacuzzi; room service. *In room:* A/C, TV, fridge, hair dryer, minibar, Wi-Fi.

Inexpensive

Grace Inn (Value Located just off I-17 about 15 minutes south of Sky Harbor Airport, this older high-rise hotel is slowly undergoing a renovation, and while the new rooms are definitely worth requesting, the older rooms are a great value for the Phoenix area. The location is convenient to South Mountain Park and Rawhide, which makes the

Grace Inn a good bet for a budget family vacation. The hotel is also popular with fans of the Los Angeles Angels, who have their spring-training facility at the nearby Tempe Diablo Stadium. Be sure to check the hotel's website for hot deals.

10831 S. 51st St., Phoenix, AZ 85044. ✆ **800/843-6010** or 480/893-3000. Fax 480/496-8303. www.graceinn.com. 160 units. $59–$259 double; $99–$299 suite. Children 17 and under stay free in parent's room. AE, DC, DISC, MC, V. **Amenities:** Restaurant; lounge; access to nearby health club; Jacuzzi; outdoor pool; room service; small spa; 2 tennis courts. *In room:* A/C, TV, fridge, hair dryer, Internet.

TEMPE, MESA & THE EAST VALLEY

Tempe, which lies just a few miles east of the airport, is home to Arizona State University and consequently supports a lively nightlife scene. Along Tempe's Mill Avenue, you'll find one of the only neighborhoods in the Valley where locals actually get out of their cars and walk the streets. Tempe is also convenient to Papago Park, which is home to the Phoenix Zoo, the Desert Botanical Garden, a municipal golf course, and hiking and mountain-biking trails.

Expensive

Tempe Mission Palms Hotel ★ With a great location on Tempe's lively Mill Avenue and guest rooms decorated in a wild combination of bold colors and modern geometric patterns, this is the perfect choice for a fun-filled weekend in Tempe. Sure, this is a business hotel (ergonomic desk chairs), but with a rooftop pool, tennis court, and Mill Avenue's nightlife right out the front door, it's also a great choice for active travelers. Come in the spring and you won't want to leave the courtyard, which is scented by the flowers of citrus trees.

60 E. Fifth St., Tempe, AZ 85281. ✆ **800/547-8705** or 480/894-1400. Fax 480/968-7677. www.missionpalms.com. 303 units. Jan–Apr $199–$299 double, $399 suite; May–June $139–$179 double, $279 suite; July–Aug $99–$169 double, $269 suite; Sept–Dec $159–$229 double, $339 suite. Rates do not include $11 daily hospitality fee. Children 17 and under stay free in parent's room. AE, DC, DISC, MC, V. Pets accepted ($100 deposit, $25 fee). **Amenities:** 2 restaurants; 2 lounges; bikes; concierge; exercise room & access to nearby health club; 2 Jacuzzis; outdoor pool; room service; tennis court. *In room:* A/C, TV, hair dryer, Wi-Fi.

Moderate

Crowne Plaza San Marcos Golf Resort ★ Built in 1912, the San Marcos is the oldest golf resort in Arizona and has a classic mission-revival styling. I love the timeless feel of this resort's palm-shaded courtyards, and I'm sure you will, too. Guest rooms are simply furnished, nothing special, but they have been kept up-to-date. You'll want to spend your time splashing around in the pool when you aren't playing tennis or golf. Downtown Chandler, where the San Marcos is located, has been undergoing a renaissance in recent years. There are now art galleries and some decent restaurants on the plaza just outside the resort's front door. Although the San Marcos is out of the tourist mainstream, the rates make it a real bargain.

One San Marcos Place, Chandler, AZ 85225. ✆ **800/528-8071** or 480/812-0900. Fax 480/899-5441. www.sanmarcosresort.com. 295 units. $100–$190 double; $136–$240 suite (lower rates in summer). Children 17 and under stay free in parent's room. AE, DC, DISC, MC, V. Pets accepted ($50 fee). **Amenities:** 2 restaurants; 2 lounges; concierge; exercise room; 18-hole golf course; Jacuzzi; outdoor pool; room service; 2 tennis courts. *In room:* A/C, TV, CD player, hair dryer, Internet.

Gold Canyon Golf Resort ★ Value Golfers willing to stay way out on the eastern outskirts of the Valley of the Sun (a 30- to 45-min. drive from the airport) will be thrilled by the economical room rates and great golf at this resort. At the foot of the Superstition

Mountains, Gold Canyon is a favorite of golfers for its exceedingly scenic holes. The spacious guest rooms are housed in blindingly white pueblo-inspired buildings; some have fireplaces, while others have whirlpools. The deluxe golf-course rooms are definitely worth the higher rates. If you're here primarily to play golf and don't have a fortune to spend, this is *the* place to stay.

6100 S. Kings Ranch Rd., Gold Canyon, AZ 85218. ✆ **800/827-5281** or 480/982-9090. Fax 480/983-9554. www.gcgr.com. 85 units. $135–$260 double. Children 15 and under stay free in parent's room. AE, DC, DISC, MC, V. Pets accepted ($75 fee). **Amenities:** 2 restaurants; lounge; bikes; seasonal children's programs; concierge; exercise room; 2 18-hole golf courses; Jacuzzi; pool; small full-service spa. *In room:* A/C, TV, hair dryer, minibar, Wi-Fi.

Inexpensive

Apache Boulevard in Tempe becomes Main Street in Mesa, and along this stretch of road there are numerous old motels charging some of the lowest rates in the Valley. However, these motels are very hit-or-miss. If you're used to staying at nonchain motels, you might want to cruise this strip and check out a few places. Otherwise, try the chain motels in the area (which tend to charge $20–$40 more per night than nonchain motels).

Best Western Dobson Ranch Inn & Resort This aging budget resort may not be very luxurious, but it has just about everything a sun-starved winter visitor could ask for—green lawns, flower gardens, palm trees, and a big pool surrounded by lounge chairs. The location, right off US 60 at the junction with US 101, also makes this resort relatively convenient for exploring the Valley. Guest rooms were redone in 2009 and are looking quite modern, although they are more functional than fancy, but the grounds more than make up for the unremarkable rooms.

1666 S. Dobson Rd., Mesa, AZ 85202. ✆ **800/528-1356** or 480/831-7000. Fax 480/831-7000. www.dobsonranchinn.com. 213 units. $70–$150 double. Rates include full breakfast. Children 12 and under stay free in parent's room. AE, DC, DISC, MC, V. **Amenities:** Restaurant; lounge; exercise room; 2 Jacuzzis; large outdoor pool; room service. *In room:* A/C, TV, fridge, hair dryer, Internet.

Fiesta Resort Conference Center ★ **Value** Reasonable rates, green lawns, palm- and eucalyptus-shaded grounds, and a location close to the airport, ASU, and Tempe's Mill Avenue make this older, casual resort one of the best deals in the Valley. Okay, so it doesn't have the desert character of the Buttes resort across the freeway, and it isn't as stylish as the resorts in Scottsdale, but you can't argue with the rates. The large guest rooms have all been recently redone with pillow-top mattresses. You may not feel like you're in the desert when you stay here (due to the lawns and shade trees), but you'll certainly get a lot more for your money than at other area hotels in this price range.

2100 S. Priest Dr., Tempe, AZ 85282. ✆ **800/528-6481** or 480/967-1441. Fax 480/967-0224. www.fiestainnresort.com. 270 units. Jan–Apr $140–$221 double; May–Dec $120–$150 double. Children 17 and under stay free in parent's room. AE, DC, DISC, MC, V. **Amenities:** 2 restaurants; lounge; free airport transfer; concierge; exercise room; Jacuzzi; pool; room service. *In room:* A/C, TV, fridge, hair dryer, Wi-Fi.

WEST VALLEY

The Wigwam Golf Resort & Spa ★★ Located 20 minutes west of downtown Phoenix, this property opened its doors to the public in 1929 and remains one of the nation's premier golf resorts. It's a classic, with old-school gentility, but when the money all headed to Scottsdale, this place became an elegant oasis surrounded by tract houses. Like the Arizona Biltmore and the Camelback Inn, the Wigwam Golf Resort & Spa is an old-money sort of place, and the traditional-style golf courses are the main attractions. Most of the guest rooms are in adobe-style buildings, surrounded by green lawns and colorful gardens, and all of the spacious units feature contemporary Southwestern furniture and plush beds. Some units have fireplaces, but the rooms to request are those along the golf course. There's an Elizabeth Arden Red Door Spa and a golf school.

300 E. Wigwam Blvd., Litchfield Park, AZ 85340. ✆ **800/327-0396** or 623/935-3811. Fax 623/935-3737. www.wigwamresort.com. 331 units. Early Jan to mid-May $269–$799 double, from $329 suite; mid-May to early Sept $119–$259 double, from $159 suite; early Sept to early Jan $199–$449 double, from $249 suite. Children 16 and under stay free in parent's room. AE, DC, DISC, MC, V. Valet parking $15. Pets accepted. **Amenities:** 3 restaurants; 3 lounges; children's programs; concierge; executive-level rooms; 3 18-hole golf courses; health club; 2 Jacuzzis; 2 pools; room service; full-service spa; 9 tennis courts. *In room:* A/C, TV, hair dryer, Internet, minibar.

4 WHERE TO DINE

As you would expect of any major metropolitan area with a population running into the millions, the Valley of the Sun boasts countless excellent restaurants. While there is hardly a corner of the Valley that doesn't have someplace good to eat, many of the best restaurants are concentrated in the Scottsdale Road, north Scottsdale, and Biltmore Corridor areas. If you want to splurge on only one expensive meal while you're here, consider a resort restaurant or someplace that offers a view of the city lights. If you've got the kids with you, you'll want to be sure to have dinner at one of the Valley's "cowboy" steakhouses. These family-oriented restaurants feature Wild West decor, live cowboy music, and lots of other fun entertainment.

Good places to go trolling for a place to eat include the trendy Biltmore Fashion Park shopping center, at Camelback Road and 24th Street (✆ **602/955-8400**), and Old Town Scottsdale. At the former, you'll find nearly a dozen restaurants. In downtown Scottsdale, within an area of roughly 4 blocks, you'll also find about a dozen good restaurants.

Phoenix is a sprawling city, and it can be a real pain to have to drive around in search of a good lunch spot. If you happen to be visiting the Phoenix Art Museum, the Heard Museum, or the Desert Botanical Garden anytime around lunch, stay put for your noon meal. All three of these attractions have cafes serving decent, if limited, menus.

SCOTTSDALE

Expensive

Cowboy Ciao ★★ SOUTHWESTERN/NEW AMERICAN Yee-ha, bambino, the food at this place beats all heck out of cowboy beans and deep-fried rattlesnake. It's better than spaghetti and pasta fazul, too. A fun, "cowboy chic" atmosphere and delicious food with a global influence make a meal here unforgettable. You absolutely must start your meal with the Stetson chopped salad; it's both a work of art and an explosion of flavors and textures. Other not-to-be-missed dishes include the exotic mushroom pan-fry and the daily soup. Whatever you decide on for an entree, think small; you want to save room for one of pastry chef Tracy Dempsey's legendary desserts. Cowboy Ciao is also notable for its wine list and bar. Located in downtown Scottsdale, the restaurant attracts a diverse crowd.

7133 E. Stetson Dr. (at Sixth Ave.). ✆ **480/WINE-111** [946-3111]. www.cowboyciao.com. Reservations recommended. Main courses $9–$20 lunch, $20–$36 dinner. AE, DC, DISC, MC, V. Sun–Thurs 11:30am–2:30pm and 5–10pm; Fri–Sat 11:30am–2:30pm and 5–11pm.

Eddie's House ★★ NEW AMERICAN Eddie Matney has been one of my favorite local chefs for two decades now, and here at his latest restaurant, he continues to dish up some of the best food the Valley has to offer. While this place has a glitzy facade, it's all warm and homey inside, with photos of Eddie's family all around the dining room. Don't-miss dishes include the toasted seafood wontons with raspberry-jalapeño sauce and the MoRockin' shrimp, which come with dough balls (simple and simply delicious) and a spicy chile-beer dipping sauce. After these two tasty starters, consider the perennially popular "What's in this?" steak (tenderloin wrapped in parmesan mashed potatoes), the bacon-infused meatloaf, or the seared diver scallops.

7042 E. Indian School Rd. ✆ **480/946-1622.** www.eddieshouseaz.com. Reservations recommended. Main courses $12–$29. AE, DC, DISC, MC, V. Mon–Sat 4–10pm.

Rancho Pinot ★★ NEW AMERICAN Rancho Pinot, hidden at the back of a nondescript shopping center adjacent to the upscale Borgata shopping plaza, combines a homey cowboy-chic decor with contemporary American cuisine, and has long been a favorite with Scottsdale and Phoenix residents. Look elsewhere if you crave wildly creative flavor combinations, but if you like simple, well-prepared food, Rancho Pinot is a great choice. For a tasty starter, try the grilled squid salad with preserved lemon; for an entree, you can always count on the handmade pasta or Nonni's chicken, braised with white wine, mushrooms, and herbs. As much as possible, Rancho Pinot uses organic, local produce, eggs, and dairy products.

6208 N. Scottsdale Rd., in Lincoln Village Shops (southwest corner of Scottsdale Rd. and Lincoln Dr.). ✆ **480/367-8030.** www.ranchopinot.com. Reservations recommended. Main courses $18–$29. AE, DISC, MC, V. Mon–Thurs 5:30–9pm; Fri–Sat 5:30–10pm. Summer hours may vary.

Roaring Fork ★ SOUTHWESTERN This restaurant, in one location or another, has been around for years and still serves some of the most creative Southwestern fare in the Valley. While no meal here is complete without a starter of the green-chile pork stew and a side of the green-chile macaroni and cheese, you'll probably also want an entree. Try the delicious duck breast with onion jam and sour-cherry mustard or the braised beef short ribs made with Dr. Pepper. If you can't get a table, dine in the saloon or on the saloon patio. Happy hour (Sun–Mon 4–10pm, Tues–Sat 4–7pm) is a good time for an early meal from the saloon menu, actually worth eating from just so you can order the "big ass burger," a 12-ounce patty with roasted green chiles. Wash it all down with a huckleberry margarita.

4800 N. Scottsdale Rd., Ste. 1700 (at the corner of Chaparral Rd.). ✆ **480/947-0795.** www.roaringfork.com. Reservations highly recommended. Main courses $13–$39. AE, DISC, MC, V. Daily 4–10pm.

Moderate

Arcadia Farms ★ NEW AMERICAN Long a favorite of the Scottsdale ladies-who-lunch crowd, this Old Town restaurant features well-prepared contemporary fare. Try the delicious raspberry goat cheese salad with jicama and candied pecans. The warm mushroom, spinach, and goat-cheese tart is another winner. Try to get a seat on the shady patio. This restaurant also operates cafes at the Heard Museum, the Heard Museum North, and the Phoenix Art Museum.

7014 E. First Ave. ✆ **480/941-5665.** www.arcadiafarmscafe.com. Reservations recommended. Main courses $12–$15. AE, MC, V. Daily 8am–3:30pm.

Bandera (Value) AMERICAN Once you've gotten a whiff of the wood-roasted chickens turning on the rotisseries in Bandera's back-of-the-building, open-air stone oven, you'll know exactly what to order when you finally get a seat at this popular spot in Old Town. What an aroma! The succulent spit-roasted chicken is the meal to have here, and

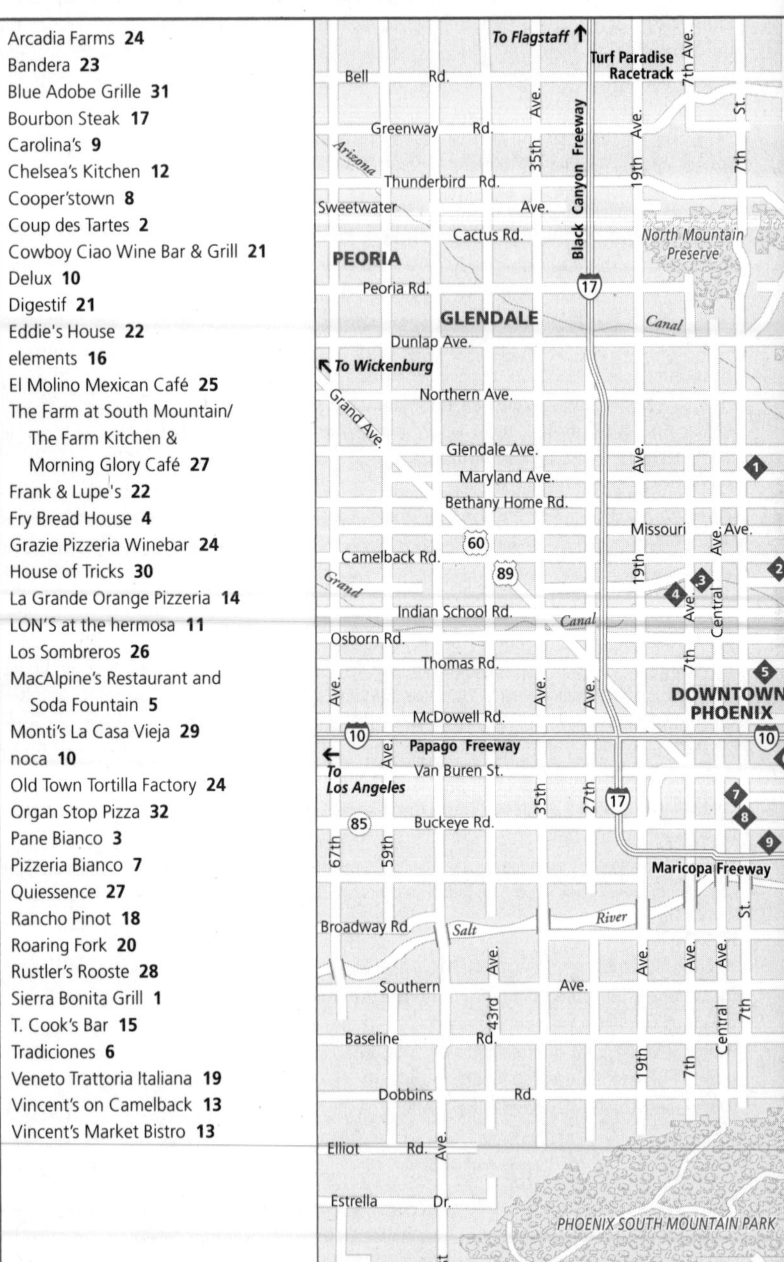
Arcadia Farms 24
Bandera 23
Blue Adobe Grille 31
Bourbon Steak 17
Carolina's 9
Chelsea's Kitchen 12
Cooper'stown 8
Coup des Tartes 2
Cowboy Ciao Wine Bar & Grill 21
Delux 10
Digestif 21
Eddie's House 22
elements 16
El Molino Mexican Café 25
The Farm at South Mountain/ The Farm Kitchen & Morning Glory Café 27
Frank & Lupe's 22
Fry Bread House 4
Grazie Pizzeria Winebar 24
House of Tricks 30
La Grande Orange Pizzeria 14
LON'S at the hermosa 11
Los Sombreros 26
MacAlpine's Restaurant and Soda Fountain 5
Monti's La Casa Vieja 29
noca 10
Old Town Tortilla Factory 24
Organ Stop Pizza 32
Pane Bianco 3
Pizzeria Bianco 7
Quiessence 27
Rancho Pinot 18
Roaring Fork 20
Rustler's Rooste 28
Sierra Bonita Grill 1
T. Cook's Bar 15
Tradiciones 6
Veneto Trattoria Italiana 19
Vincent's on Camelback 13
Vincent's Market Bistro 13
To Flagstaff
Turf Paradise Racetrack
Bell Rd.
Greenway Rd.
Arizona
Thunderbird Rd.
Sweetwater Ave.
Cactus Rd.
Black Canyon Freeway
35th Ave.
19th Ave.
7th Ave.
7th St.
North Mountain Preserve
PEORIA
Peoria Rd.
GLENDALE
Canal
Dunlap Ave.
To Wickenburg
Northern Ave.
Grand Ave.
Glendale Ave.
Maryland Ave.
Bethany Home Rd.
Missouri Ave.
Camelback Rd.
Grand
Indian School Rd.
Canal
Osborn Rd.
Thomas Rd.
Central Ave.
DOWNTOWN PHOENIX
McDowell Rd.
Papago Freeway
To Los Angeles
Van Buren St.
27th Ave.
Buckeye Rd.
67th Ave.
59th Ave.
Maricopa Freeway
Broadway Rd.
Salt River
Southern Ave.
43rd Ave.
Baseline Rd.
Dobbins Rd.
Elliot Rd.
51st Ave.
Estrella Dr.
PHOENIX SOUTH MOUNTAIN PARK
10
17
60
89
85
1
2
3
4
5
7
8
9

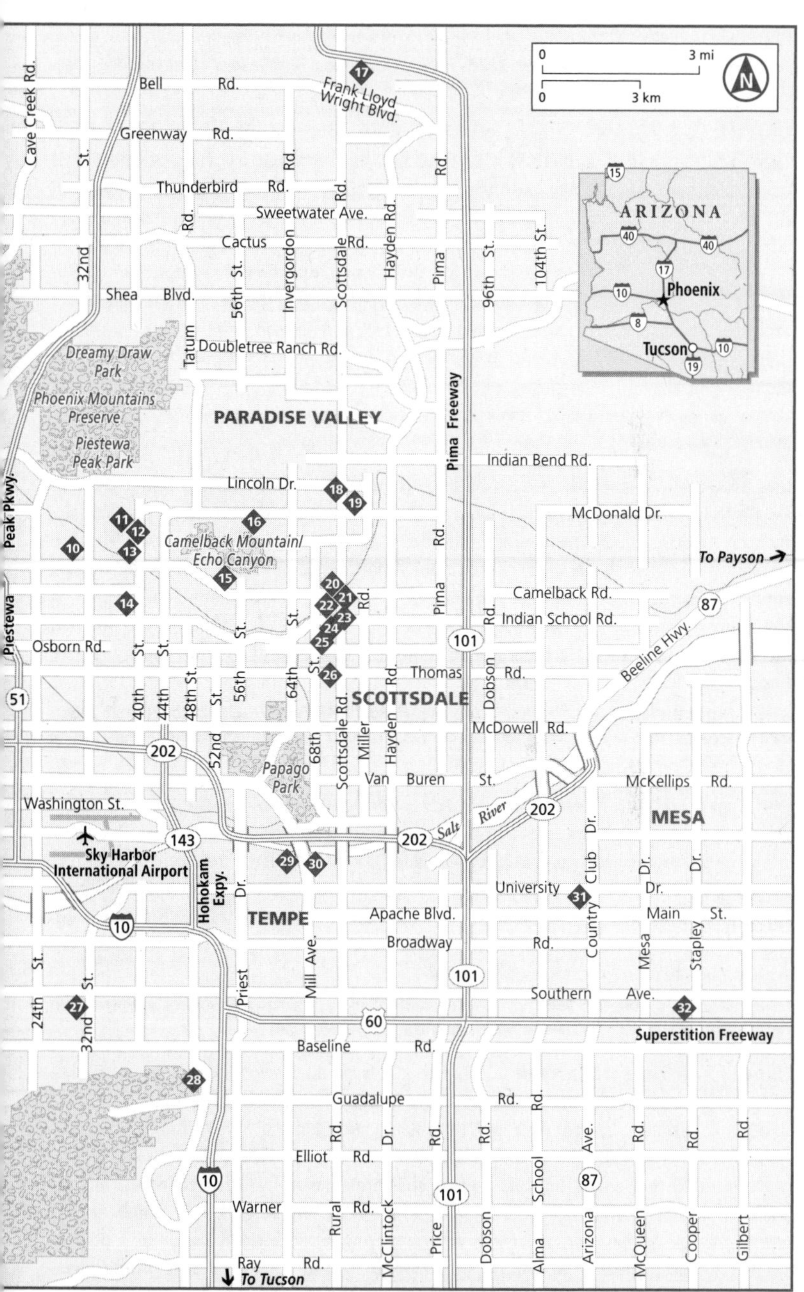
0 3 mi
0 3 km
N
ARIZONA
Phoenix
Tucson
15
40
17
10
8
19
Bell Rd.
Greenway Rd.
Thunderbird Rd.
Sweetwater Ave.
Cactus Rd.
Shea Blvd.
Doubletree Ranch Rd.
Frank Lloyd Wright Blvd.
Cave Creek Rd.
32nd St.
Tatum
56th St.
Invergordon Rd.
Scottsdale Rd.
Hayden Rd.
Pima Rd.
96th St.
104th St.
Dreamy Draw Park
Phoenix Mountains Preserve
Piestewa Peak Park
PARADISE VALLEY
Pima Freeway
Indian Bend Rd.
Lincoln Dr.
McDonald Dr.
Camelback Mountain/ Echo Canyon
To Payson
Camelback Rd.
Indian School Rd.
Beeline Hwy.
Piestewa Peak Pkwy.
Osborn Rd.
40th St.
44th St.
48th St.
52nd St.
56th St.
64th St.
68th St.
Thomas Rd.
Dobson Rd.
SCOTTSDALE
McDowell Rd.
Miller
Hayden
Scottsdale Rd.
Papago Park
Van Buren St.
McKellips Rd.
Washington St.
Salt River
MESA
Sky Harbor International Airport
Hohokam Expy.
Priest Dr.
TEMPE
University Dr.
Country Club Dr.
Mesa Dr.
Stapley Dr.
Apache Blvd.
Main St.
Broadway Rd.
Mill Ave.
24th St.
32nd St.
Southern Ave.
Superstition Freeway
Baseline Rd.
Guadalupe Rd.
Elliot Rd.
Warner Rd.
Ray Rd.
To Tucson
Rural Rd.
McClintock Dr.
Price Rd.
Dobson Rd.
Alma School Rd.
Arizona Ave.
McQueen Rd.
Cooper Rd.
Gilbert Rd.
51
202
143
10
101
87
60
10
11
12
13
14
15
16
17
18
19
20
21
22
23
24
25
26
27
28
29
30
31
32

make sure you get it with some of Bandera's great mashed potatoes or cornbread. Sure, you could order prime rib or seared ahi tuna, but you'd be a fool if you did. Stick with the chicken or maybe the barbecued ribs, and you won't go wrong.

3821 N. Scottsdale Rd. ✆ **480/994-3524.** www.hillstone.com. Reservations recommended. Main courses $11–$30. AE, MC, V. Sun–Thurs 4–10pm; Fri–Sat 4–11pm.

Digestif ★ ITALIAN Peter Kasperski, the restaurateur who gave Scottsdale Cowboy Ciao, Sea Saw, and Kazimierz World Wine Bar, has been hard at work expanding his culinary empire into the new SouthBridge development. This was his first restaurant in the new waterfront development, and as the name implies, *digestifs* (after-dinner drinks) are an essential part of a meal here. Sort of a reimagining of a basement Italian eatery in New York's Little Italy, this place is casual yet very hip. Don't miss the *bruschettone* (knife-and-fork *bruschetta*) with your choice of tasty toppings. For the day's freshest produce, order the "farm to sea to table" appetizer. Cheeses and various cured meats are on the menu for late-night noshing, and desserts are to die for. Whenever possible, local ingredients are used.

7114 E. Stetson Dr., Scottsdale. ✆ **480/425-WINE.** www.digestifscottsdale.com. Reservations recommended. Main courses $13–$28. AE, DISC, MC, V. Daily 11am–midnight.

Los Sombreros ★ Finds MEXICAN Although this casual Mexican restaurant is in an attractive old house, it doesn't look all that special from the outside. However, the menu is surprisingly creative and veers from the standard dishes served at most Mexican restaurants. Start with the chunky guacamole, which is some of the best in the city. Be sure to order the chicken *molé* or the *puerco en chipotle,* succulent, slow-roasted pork in tomatillo-chipotle sauce. Finish it all off with the flan, which will spoil you for flan anywhere else. For a real treat, get it with almond-flavored tequila. Unfortunately, service here can be slow.

2534 N. Scottsdale Rd. (at McKellips Rd.), Scottsdale. ✆ **480/994-1799.** www.lossombreros.com. Reservations accepted for 5 or more. Main courses $16–$21. AE, DC, DISC, MC, V. Sun and Tues–Thurs 5–9pm; Fri–Sat 5–10pm.

Old Town Tortilla Factory MEXICAN Located in an old house surrounded by attractive patios and citrus trees that bloom in winter and spring, this moderately priced Mexican restaurant has a great atmosphere, good food, and a lively bar scene (more than 80 premium tequilas). As you enter the restaurant grounds, you might even see someone making fresh tortillas, which come in two dozen different flavors. The rich tortilla soup and the tequila-lime salad make good starters. For an entree, try the pork chops crusted with ancho chile powder and raspberry sauce.

6910 E. Main St. ✆ **480/945-4567.** www.oldtowntortillafactory.com. Reservations not accepted. Main courses $14–$33. AE, DC, DISC, MC, V. Sun–Thurs 5–9pm; Fri–Sat 5–10pm.

Veneto Trattoria Italiana ★ ITALIAN This pleasantly low-key trattoria, specializing in the cuisine of Venice, serves satisfying "peasant food," including traditional pork-and-garlic sausages served with grilled polenta and braised savoy cabbage. *Baccala mantecato* (creamy fish mousse on grilled polenta, made with dried salt cod soaked overnight in milk) may sound unusual, but it's absolutely heavenly. Other good bets include the salad of thinly sliced smoked beef, shaved Parmesan, and arugula. For a finale, try the *semifreddo con frutta secca,* a partially frozen meringue, with dried fruits, in a pool of raspberry sauce. There's a welcoming bistro ambience and outdoor seating on the patio.

(Kids) Cowboy Steakhouses

Cowboy steakhouses are family restaurants that generally provide big portions of grilled steaks and barbecued ribs, outdoor and "saloon" dining, live country music, and various other sorts of entertainment.

At **Rustler's Rooste** ★ you can start your meal by scooting down a big slide from the bar to the main dining room. While the view north across Phoenix is entertainment enough for most people, there are also cowboy bands playing for those who like to kick up their heels. If you've got the appetite of a hard-working cowpoke, try the enormous cowboy "stuff" platter consisting of, among other things, steak kebabs, barbecued ribs, cowboy beans, fried shrimp, barbecued chicken, and skewered swordfish. You'll find Rustler's at the Arizona Grand Resort, 8383 S. 48th St., in Phoenix (✆ **602/431-6474;** www.rustlersrooste.com). Entrees range from $15 to $30.

Of the many cowboy steakhouses around the valley, **Rawhide Steakhouse,** 5700 W. North Loop Rd., Chandler (✆ **480/502-5600;** www.rawhide.com), at the Sheraton Wild Horse Pass Resort & Spa, is by far your best bet for a family dinner. Not only are the steaks some of the best you'll find at a family steakhouse, but there's an entire Western town mock-up surrounding the restaurant, so there's plenty to keep you and your kids entertained before and after dinner. If you feel adventurous, start your meal with some pan-fried rattlesnake. Cowboy bands keep the crowds entertained during dinner. From February to May and in October and November, there are also sundown cookouts ($45 adults, $19 children) that include a hayride, chuck-wagon dinner, live country music, and lots of other traditional Wild West entertainment.

In Hilton Village, 6137 N. Scottsdale Rd. ✆ **480/948-9928.** www.venetotrattoria.com. Reservations recommended. Main courses $11–$21 lunch, $15–$26 dinner. AE, DC, DISC, MC, V. Mon–Sat 11:30am–2:30pm and 5–10pm.

Inexpensive

El Molino Mexican Café (Finds) MEXICAN Located a bit out of the Old Town Scottsdale mainstream, this small Mexican joint is little more than a fast-food place, but it serves the best chimichangas in town. If you're among the few people still not familiar with what a chimichanga is, it's a deep-fried burrito. That said, the chimis here have crispy, light shells and are packed with tasty fillings. Try one with *machaca* (shredded and spiced beef) or green-chile beef, and I'm sure you'll become a convert. If fried food just doesn't do it for you, opt for a couple of green corn tamales, an Arizona specialty.

3554 N. Goldwater Blvd. ✆ **480/994-3566.** www.elmolinocafe.com. Reservations not accepted. Main courses $2.25–$14. AE, DISC, MC, V. Mon–Sat 9am–8pm.

Frank & Lupe's (Value) MEXICAN On the same street as some of Scottsdale's top contemporary art galleries, this casual Mexican restaurant is a welcome throwback to the days when Scottsdale was still a real cow town. Friends who have been eating here for years insist the only dish to get is the *carne adobada* burrito plate served enchilada style (smothered in a spicy red sauce). I have to agree. If at all possible, eat on the back patio; it feels so much like a restaurant patio in Mexico that you'll be shocked to find you're still in Scottsdale at the end of your meal.

4121 N. Marshall Way. ✆ **480/990-9844.** www.frankandlupes.com. Reservations not accepted. Main courses $7–$19. AE, DISC, MC, V. Daily 11am–10pm.

Grazie Pizzeria Winebar ★ (Finds) PIZZA This little neighborhood pizzeria is in downtown Scottsdale at the west end of Main Street near the Valley Ho resort and is a little gem of a place. It's also very popular on weekends, and the noise level can be deafening. Come on a weeknight or for lunch if you want to carry on a conversation without shouting. The weekend buzz aside, this is a great place to sip Italian wines and share a couple of designer pizzas from the wood-fired oven. Start your meal with the carpaccio bresaola, which is served with arugula, parmigiano-reggiano cheese, and a lemon vinaigrette; or a salad made with arugula, baby greens, parmigiano-reggiano, red onions, red bell peppers, and pine nuts. The pizzas here have paper-thin crusts, so don't worry about filling up before it's time to order the signature ice-cream calzone.

6952 E. Main St. ✆ **480/663-9797.** www.grazie.us. Reservations recommended Fri–Sat nights. Main courses $9–$15. AE, MC, V. Daily 11am–10pm.

NORTH SCOTTSDALE, CAREFREE & CAVE CREEK

Very Expensive

Binkley's ★★★ (Moments) NEW AMERICAN Foodies up on the latest trends in molecular gastronomy (the science of cooking) will want to make sure they have at least one meal at this astonishing little restaurant in Cave Creek. Utterly unpretentious yet sophisticated enough to hold its own with the finest restaurants in the world, Binkley's is the sort of place people dream of finding while on vacation. Every dish here is a work of art, and unexpected flavor combinations and presentations are the rule. Chef Kevin Binkley likes to leave his customers marveling at the meal they've just had. For the most enjoyable experience, opt for a four-, five-, or six-course tasting menu, which might include marlin with mango, avocado, and lotus root; a sweetbread sandwich; quail with truffles from Oregon, or escolar fish with kumquats and saffron-scented hearts of palm.

6920 E. Cave Creek Rd., Cave Creek. ✆ **480/437-1072.** www.binkleysrestaurant.com. Reservations highly recommended. Main courses $38–$44; tasting menus $65–$89 ($100–$134 with wine). AE, MC, V. Tues–Sat 5–9:30pm (plus Sun seasonally).

Bourbon Steak ★★★ STEAK This posh steakhouse from Chef Michael Mina, who in 2005 was named chef of the year by *Bon Appétit* magazine, is one of the Valley's best and most expensive restaurants. If you have an appreciation for lobster, caviar, and foie gras, then you'll be glad this restaurant is here. If you've never had beef tartare, this is the place to try it; and for a delicious twist on an old favorite, try the lobster potpie. Obviously, however, steaks are the thing here. If you're feeling flush, you could spring for the Japanese Kobe beef filet mignon for $150, but there are plenty of other less-expensive options. Steaks are served a la carte, and there are lots of tempting side dishes and accompaniments. How about some truffled macaroni and cheese, spinach soufflé, or roasted marrow bones to accompany your main dish?

At the Fairmont Scottsdale, 7575 E. Princess Dr. (about 12 miles north of downtown Scottsdale). ✆ **480/513-6002.** www.michaelmina.net. Reservations highly recommended. Main courses $22–$42; steaks $29–$150. AE, MC, V. Sun–Thurs 5:30–10pm; Fri–Sat 5:30–10:30pm.

Sassi ★★ ITALIAN If you've had to forego this year's vacation in Italy, then don't miss an opportunity to have a meal at this Tuscan villa transplanted to the Arizona desert. Every room in this beautiful, sprawling building is gorgeous and has a distinctive character of its own. The menu is not your standard southern Italian menu, so don't go looking for spaghetti and meatballs (although you might find an excellent *papparedelle* pasta with pork ragu or meatballs cooked in white wine). Instead, try the wood-oven shrimp with prosciutto or a dish with the house-made sausage. In fact, the best thing to do here is order a bunch of dishes and then share everything, as any good Italian family would.

10455 E. Pinnacle Peak Pkwy., Scottsdale. ✆ **480/502-9095.** www.sassi.biz. Reservations highly recommended. Primi $16–$25; secondi $24–$38. AE, DC, DISC, MC, V. Tues–Sun 5:30–9 or 10pm.

Expensive

Mosaic ★★★ (Finds) NEW AMERICAN The Pinnacle Peak area of north Scottsdale boasts one of the Valley's greatest concentrations of excellent, high-end restaurants, and this just may be the best of a very good bunch. Okay, so dinner here is going to set you back quite a bit, but the food is superb, and if you come before the sun goes down, you can soak up some of the best desert views in the Valley. Chef/owner Deborah Knight is one of the best chefs around and likes to show off her culinary creativity with a menu that changes regularly and is always provocative and daring. How about chilled pink-beet soup with prickly-pear puree or steak medallions with Navajo fry bread and a green chile and cheddar biscuit to start things out? For an entree, you might order a wild-game mixed grill with huckleberry-lingonberry sauce or grilled steelhead with fennel pollen and roasted fennel. You get the picture; this is a foodie's nirvana. There are also excellent and highly creative vegetarian dishes here.

10600 E. Jomax Rd., Scottsdale. ✆ **480/563-9600.** www.mosaic-restaurant.com. Reservations recommended. Main courses $26–$40; tasting menu $70–$90 ($110–$130 with wine). AE, DC, DISC, MC, V. Tues–Sat 5:30–9 or 10pm.

Moderate

Café Bink ★★ NEW AMERICAN This casual spinoff from the legendary Binkley's in Cave Creek is your best bet for lunch in Carefree. The menu is limited and a bit pricey at lunch, but the food is perfectly and beautifully prepared. There's a wonderful mushroom soup on the menu, and the corned beef, available as a Reuben sandwich at lunch and with cabbage and apples at dinner, is another good choice. If your tastes are simple, Amy's Bolognese is a good bet. If you've got expensive tastes but can't get a table at Binkley's, go ahead and order the foie gras terrine here at Café Bink.

36889 N. Tom Darlington Dr., Carefree. ✆ **480/488-9796.** www.cafebink.com. Reservations accepted only for 6 or more. Main courses $10–$23 lunch, $15–$23 dinner. AE, DISC, MC, V. Tues–Sun 11am–9pm.

Inexpensive

Greasewood Flat ★ (Finds) AMERICAN Burgers and beer are the mainstays at this rustic open-air restaurant in the Pinnacle Peak area of north Scottsdale. Located down a potholed gravel road behind Reata Pass steakhouse, Greasewood Flat is a desert party spot where families, motorcycle clubs, cyclists, and horseback riders all rub shoulders. Place your order at the window and grab a seat at one of the picnic tables. While you wait for your meal, you can check out the old farm equipment. This place is the antithesis of Scottsdale posh, and that's exactly why I love it. Only in Arizona could you find a place like this.

 27375 N. Alma School Pkwy., Scottsdale. ✆ **480/585-9430.** www.greasewoodflat.net. Main courses $3.75–$8. AE, DISC, MC, V. Daily 11am–1am.

CENTRAL PHOENIX & THE CAMELBACK CORRIDOR

Expensive

Chelsea's Kitchen ★ NEW AMERICAN Although this restaurant can seem a bit expensive for what you get, the setting, on the banks of a canal just a block off Camelback Road, is gorgeous. The patio, with a wood-burning fireplace, is nearly as large as the dining room and is where you should try to get a table. The sunsets can be absolutely unforgettable. Separating the dining room and patio is a fun indoor-outdoor bar. Under the same ownership as the nearby La Grande Orange Pizzeria and Postino wine bar, Chelsea's Kitchen features a menu of familiar comfort foods with a few more creative dishes thrown into the mix. The seasonal salads are usually a good choice, as are the fish tacos. Be sure to try the fried chicken and the short ribs.

5040 N. 40th St. ✆ **602/957-2555.** www.chelseaskitchenaz.com. Main courses $12–$27. AE, MC, V. Mon–Wed 11am–10pm; Thurs–Sat 11am–midnight; Sun 10am–9pm.

Coup des Tartes ★★ (Finds) COUNTRY FRENCH Chain restaurants, theme restaurants, restaurants that are all style and little substance: Sometimes in Phoenix it seems impossible to find a homey little hole in the wall that serves good food. Don't despair; Coup des Tartes is just the ticket. With barely a dozen tables and no liquor license (bring your own wine; $9 corkage fee), it's about as removed from the standard Phoenix glitz as you can get without boarding a plane and leaving town. Start your meal with pâté de campagne or the scrumptious brie brûlée, which is covered with caramelized apples. The entree menu changes regularly, but the Moroccan lamb shank with couscous is so good that it's always available. The filet mignon is another good choice. For dessert, you absolutely must have a tart. As often as possible, organic and local produce is used, as is wild-caught fish and naturally raised meat.

4626 N. 16th St. (a couple blocks south of Camelback Rd.). ✆ **602/212-1082.** www.nicetartes.com. Reservations recommended. Main courses $15–$36; brunch $10–$18. AE, DISC, MC, V. Tues–Thurs 5:30–10pm; Fri–Sat 5:30–11pm; Sun 9am–2pm.

LON's at the hermosa ★ NEW AMERICAN In a beautiful old adobe hacienda built by cowboy artist Lon Megargee and surrounded by colorful gardens, this restaurant is one of the most classically Arizonan places in the Phoenix area, and the patio, with its views of Camelback Mountain, is blissfully tranquil. Lunch on the patio is the meal to have here. Entrees are reliable, and if you peruse the menu closely, you'll turn up some interesting Southwestern ingredients, including prickly pear and Arizona-farmed shrimp. However, for the most part, you eat here more for the atmosphere than for gustatory epiphanies. The bar here has a cozy and romantic Wild West feel. Dishes often include herbs grown in the restaurant's own garden, and other ingredients are, as much as possible, from ecologically sound sources.

At the Hermosa Inn, 5532 N. Palo Cristi Rd. ✆ **602/955-7878.** www.lons.com. Reservations recommended. Main courses $11–$15 lunch, $22–$34 dinner. AE, DC, DISC, MC, V. Mon–Fri 11:30am–2pm and 5:30–10pm; Sat 5:30–10pm; Sun 10am–2pm (brunch) and 5:30–10pm.

noca ★★ NEW AMERICAN Self-confessed foodie Eliott Wexler hit on something Phoenix was craving when he opened noca—casual fine dining that incorporates the latest trends in molecular gastronomy and upscale comfort foods. The menu here is a foodie's dream come true. The melt-in-your-mouth *sous vide*–style house-made pastrami is prepared in a special slow cooker and should not be missed if it's on the menu. The menu is driven by the season, so you might start with cauliflower soup that's served with foie gras raviolini or duck confit on a huckleberry waffle. Among the pastas, the spinach *mezzaluna* is wonderfully fragrant, with herbs and a mix of cheeses. Entrees might include tuna au poivre with black rice or a rib-eye steak with salsify puree and exotic mushrooms. If you can resist the deconstructed cheesecake and the trio of doughnuts with mouth-watering dipping sauces, you have far more willpower than I.

3118 E. Camelback Rd. ✆ **602/956-6622.** www.restaurantnoca.com. Reservations highly recommended. Main courses $18–$36. AE, MC, V. Daily 5:30–10pm.

T. Cook's ★★★ MEDITERRANEAN Ready to pop the question? On your honeymoon? Celebrating an anniversary? This is the place for you. There just isn't a more romantic restaurant in the Valley. Located within the walls of the Mediterranean-inspired Royal Palms Resort and Spa, it's surrounded by decades-old gardens and even has palm trees growing right through the roof of the dining room. The focal point of the open kitchen is a wood-fired oven that turns out a fabulous spit-roasted chicken as well as an impressive platter of paella. T. Cook's continues to make big impressions right through to the dessert course.

At the Royal Palms Resort and Spa, 5200 E. Camelback Rd. ✆ **866/579-3636** or 602/808-0766. www.royalpalmshotel.com. Reservations highly recommended. Main courses $9–$16 lunch, $25–$42 dinner; tasting menu $75 ($110 with wine). AE, DC, DISC, MC, V. Mon–Sat 6–10am, 11am–2pm, and 5:30–10pm; Sun 6–10am, 10am–2pm (brunch), and 5:30–10pm.

Vincent's on Camelback ★★ SOUTHWESTERN Vincent's is a Phoenix bastion of Southwestern cuisine and has long enjoyed a devoted local following. The menu blends Southwestern influences with classic European dishes; and while there are plenty of delicious traditional dishes on the menu, if you're from outside the region, you should stick with Southwestern flavors. Among the appetizers, the duck tamale is perennially popular, and, for dessert, it's hard to beat the tequila soufflé. For an entree, the veal sweetbreads with blue cornmeal are an enduring favorite. Some of the same dishes served at dinner are available at lunch at more economical prices; and for a casual breakfast or lunch, try the attached Vincent's Market Bistro (see below).

3930 E. Camelback Rd. ✆ **602/224-0225.** www.vincentsoncamelback.com. Reservations highly recommended. Main courses $13–$18 lunch, $31–$36 dinner. AE, DC, DISC, MC, V. Mon–Fri 11:30am–2pm and 5–10pm; Sat 5–10pm.

Moderate

La Grande Orange Pizzeria PIZZA Good pizza and an off-the-beaten-tourist-path neighborhood location make this casual restaurant a good place to feel like a local. Best of all, La Grande Orange is convenient to both downtown Scottsdale and the pricey Camelback corridor. Gourmet pizzas are what this place is all about, but you should be sure to start with the orange-fennel salad or one of the other great salads. While you're here, check out the adjacent La Grande Orange gourmet grocery (great for stocking a picnic) and Arlecchino Gelateria (delightful on a hot day).

4410 N. 40th St. (at Campbell Ave.). ✆ **602/840-7777.** www.lagrandeorangepizzeria.com. Reservations not accepted. Main courses $11–$14. AE, MC, V. Daily 4–10pm.

Sierra Bonita Grill ★ SOUTHWESTERN This neighborhood restaurant is the sort of place you dream about finding—flavorful food, big portions, moderate prices. What's not to like? Well, it is a bit off the usual tourist routes, but don't let that scare you.

Start with the guacamole and the bacon-wrapped shrimp, and then maybe order the same thing again. Then, do not pass up the buttermilk chicken with the heavenly mashed sweet potatoes. If you're really hungry, opt for the pork *osso buco* (pork shank) with green chile sauce. The space is dark and a bit rustic, with a ranch feel and cowboy art on the walls.

6933 N. Seventh St. ✆ **602/264-0700.** www.sierrabonitagrill.com. Reservations recommended. Main courses $9–$28. AE, DC, MC, V. Sun–Mon 11am–9pm; Tues–Thurs 11am–10pm; Fri–Sat 11am–11pm.

Vincent's Market Bistro ★★ FRENCH Located in back of the ever-popular Vincent's restaurant, this casual place does a respectable job of conjuring up a casual backstreet bistro in Paris. It's quaint without being froufrou. This place stays packed on Saturday mornings when Vincent's farmers' market attracts crowds of shoppers in search of gourmet snacks and fresh produce. Be sure to order the coq au vin. You can also get great dinners to go.

3930 E. Camelback Rd. ✆ **602/224-3727.** www.vincentsoncamelback.com. Main courses $7–$16. AE, DC, DISC, MC, V. Mon–Fri 7am–8pm; Sat–Sun 7am–2pm (June–Sept closed Mon).

Inexpensive

Delux ★ AMERICAN With a sleek and stylish decor, a very limited menu (you'd better like burgers), and one of the best selections of draft beers in the Valley, this is the ultimate ultrahip burger-and-beer joint. The burgers get my vote for best burgers in the city, but it's the cute Barbie-size shopping carts full of crispy french fries that are the real reason to dine here. Talk about your guilty pleasures—it just doesn't get much better than a cart of fries and a pint of Old Rasputin imperial stout. If you're not a fan of burgers, don't despair; there are great salads and a few nonbeef sandwiches.

In the Biltmore Plaza, 3146 E. Camelback Rd. ✆ **602/522-2288.** www.deluxburger.com. Reservations not accepted. Main courses $6–$13. AE, DC, DISC, MC, V. Daily 11am–2am.

Pane Bianco ★ (Finds) LIGHT FARE Chris Bianco, owner of downtown's immensely popular Pizzeria Bianco (see below), has another winner on his hands with this casual counter-service bakery and sandwich shop not far from the Heard Museum. The menu consists of only four sandwiches and a couple of salads, but all the breads are baked on the premises in a wood-fired oven. The house-made mozzarella is exquisitely fresh and is served both as a caprese salad with tomatoes and basil and in a focaccia sandwich with the same ingredients. And that focaccia? The best in Phoenix.

4404 N. Central Ave. ✆ **602/234-2100.** www.pizzeriabianco.com. Reservations not accepted. Sandwiches and salads $8. AE, MC, V. Tues–Sat 11am–3pm.

DOWNTOWN, SOUTH PHOENIX & THE AIRPORT AREA

Expensive

Quiessence ★★ (Finds) NEW AMERICAN This place is as far from a typical Phoenix/Scottsdale dining experience as you can get without going to the airport and getting on a plane. Quiessence is set at the back of a shady pecan grove not far from South Mountain Park and is surrounded by organic vegetable gardens. These gardens, and the freshness of the ingredients they provide, is what makes the food here so wonderful; the rural setting is what makes Quiessence truly special. Fresh, seasonal ingredients are the rule here, so the menu changes often. Be sure to start your meal with the Chef's Spread, a platter of cheeses, terrines, and house-made salami.

6106 S. 32nd St. ✆ **602/276-0601.** www.quiessencerestaurant.com. Reservations recommended. Main courses $14–$18 lunch, $24–$32 dinner; 6-course sampling menu $75 ($120 with wine). AE, MC, V. Tues–Sat 11am–2pm and 5–9pm. Closed July.

Moderate

Alice Cooper'stown BARBECUE Owned by Alice Cooper himself, this sports-and-rock-themed restaurant/bar is downtown's premier eat-o-tainment center. Sixteen video screens (usually showing sporting events) are the centerpiece, but there's also an abundance of memorabilia, including guitars once used by the likes of Fleetwood Mac and Eric Clapton. The waitstaff even wears Alice Cooper makeup. Barbecue is served in various permutations, including a huge barbecue sandwich. If you're an Alice Cooper fan, or hope to spot some local pro athletes, this place is a must.

101 E. Jackson St. ✆ **602/253-7337.** www.alicecooperstown.com. Reservations accepted only for parties of 7 or more. Sandwiches/barbecue $8–$20. AE, DISC, MC, V. Sun–Thurs 11am–10pm; Fri–Sat 11am–11pm; Sun 9:30am–8pm.

Pizzeria Bianco ★ PIZZA Even though this historic brick building is in the heart of downtown Phoenix, the atmosphere is so cozy it feels like your neighborhood local. Best of all, the wood-burning oven turns out delicious rustic pizzas. Try the pie made with red onion, Parmesan, rosemary, and crushed pistachios; it's great. Don't miss the fresh mozzarella, either: Pizzeria Bianco makes its own, and it can be ordered as an appetizer or on a pizza.

At Heritage Sq., 623 E. Adams St. ✆ **602/258-8300.** www.pizzeriabianco.com. Reservations accepted for 6–10 people. Pizzas $10–$14. AE, MC, V. Tues–Sat 5–10pm.

Inexpensive

Carolina's (Finds) MEXICAN Located in a somewhat run-down neighborhood south of the US Airways Center and Chase Field, Carolina's is a Phoenix institution. As such you'll find everyone from Hispanic construction workers to downtown corporate types (men in suits, women in high heels and pearls). Everyone enjoys the down-home Mexican cooking here, but Carolina's flour tortillas are what really set this place apart. Order a burrito, perhaps with shredded beef in a spicy green sauce, and you'll be handed what feels like a down-filled pillow, so soft you'll want to lay your head on it. Or get the tortillas to go and use them as the basis for a fun Phoenician picnic.

There's a second Carolina's in north Phoenix, at 2126 E. Cactus Rd. (✆ **602/275-8231**).

1202 E. Mohave St. ✆ **602/252-1503.** www.carolinasmex.com. Main dishes $3–$7. AE, MC, V. Mon–Fri 7am–7:30pm; Sat 7am–6pm.

The Farm at South Mountain/The Farm Kitchen & Morning Glory Café ★ (Finds) (Kids) LIGHT FARE If being in the desert has you dreaming of shady trees and green grass, you'll enjoy the Farm Kitchen, an oasis reminiscent of a deep South pecan orchard. A rustic outbuilding has been converted to a counter-service lunch restaurant where you can order a filling sandwich or a delicious pecan turkey Waldorf salad. The grassy lawn, shaded by pecan trees, is ideal for a picnic. And you can let the kids run all over while you enjoy your salad or sandwich. At the back of the farm, you'll find the **Morning Glory Café** (✆ **602/276-8804**), a cozy little breakfast place.

6106 S. 32nd St. ✆ **602/276-7288.** www.thefarmatsouthmountain.com. Sandwiches and salads $10. AE, DC, MC, V. Mid-Sept to May Tues–Sun 10am–3pm. (If weather is inclement, call to be sure it's open.) Closed June to mid-Sept. Take exit 151A, off I-10, and go south on 32nd St.

Fry Bread House ★ Finds NATIVE AMERICAN Fry bread is just what it sounds like—fried bread—and it's a mainstay on Indian reservations throughout the West. Although you can eat these thick, chewy slabs of fried bread plain, salted, or with honey, they also serve as the wrappers for Indian tacos, which are made with meat, beans, and lettuce. If you've already visited the Four Corners region of Arizona, then you've probably had an Indian taco or two. Forget them—the ones here are the best in the state. Try one with green chile. If you still have room for dessert, do not miss the fry bread with chocolate and butter.

4140 N. Seventh Ave. ✆ **602/351-2345.** Reservations not accepted. Main courses $3.50–$6.75. DISC, MC, V. Mon–Sat 10am–9pm.

MacAlpine's Restaurant and Soda Fountain ★ Finds AMERICAN This is the oldest operating soda fountain in the Southwest, and it hasn't changed much since its opening in 1928. Wooden booths and worn countertops show the patina of age. Big burgers and sandwiches make up the lunch offerings and should be washed down with a root beer float, chocolate malt, or egg cream.

2303 N. Seventh St. ✆ **602/262-5545.** www.macalpinessodafountain.com. Reservations not accepted. Sandwiches/specials $4.75–$8. AE, DISC, MC, V. Sun–Thurs 11am–7pm; Fri–Sat 11am–8pm.

Tradiciones Finds MEXICAN Sort of a Disneyland of Mexican food, this restaurant not only serves great Mexican food, but also has strolling mariachis, courtyard dance performances, vendor stalls, and even clowns to entertain the kids. On top of all this, a large Hispanic supermarket is right next door. Anything from the courtyard grill is worth trying, especially the rotisserie chicken, but the "street vendors" tacos are deliciously authentic. For an unusual taste treat, try a cilantro margarita. On Sundays, there is a brunch from 9:30am to 1:30pm, and Tuesday through Friday, there's a good happy hour from 4 to 7pm. By the way, the adjacent supermarket has a great food court and is a good place to shop for unusual Mexican-cooking ingredients.

1602 E. Roosevelt St. ✆ **602/254-1719.** www.tradicionesrestaurant.com. Main courses $9–$17. AE, DISC, MC, V. Daily 11am–9pm.

TEMPE & MESA

Expensive

House of Tricks ★ NEW AMERICAN Despite the name, you'll find far more treats here than tricks. Housed in a pair of old Craftsman bungalows surrounded by a garden of shady trees, this restaurant seems a world away from the bustle on nearby Mill Avenue. This is a nice spot for a romantic evening and a good place to try some innovative cuisine. The garlicky Caesar salad and the house-smoked salmon with avocado, capers, and lemon cream are good bets for starters. Entrees change regularly, and lately there have been a lot of Mediterranean and Southwestern dishes on the menu. Try to get a seat on the grape-arbor-covered patio.

114 E. Seventh St., Tempe. ✆ **480/968-1114.** www.houseoftricks.com. Reservations recommended. Main courses $8–$12 lunch, $18–$34 dinner. AE, DISC, MC, V. Mon–Sat 11am–10pm.

Moderate

Blue Adobe Grille ★ Finds MEXICAN This restaurant looks like the sort of place you should drive right past. Don't! Despite appearances, this New Mexican–style restaurant serves deliciously creative Southwestern fare at very economical prices. To get an idea of what the food here is all about, try the Cruz Kitchen combination plate (a tenderloin

Moments Dining with a View

When you've got one of the best views around and some of the best patio dining, do you really have to serve good food? Probably not, but luckily **elements,** the stylish restaurant at the Sanctuary on Camelback Mountain resort doesn't try to slide by on looks alone. That said, the view is a big part of dinner here, so try to make a reservation so that you can catch the sunset light on Mummy Mountain. The menu changes regularly and includes influences from around the world. The restaurant is located at Sanctuary on Camelback, 5700 E. McDonald Dr., in Paradise Valley (✆ **480/607-2300;** www.elementsrestaurant.com). Main courses range from $13 to $24 at lunch and from $26 to $38 at dinner.

relleno and a smoked-pork tamale) or the lobster tamales with mango salsa and raspberry chipotle sauce. Of course, there are great margaritas, but there's also a surprisingly good wine list. This place is a hangout for Chicago Cubs fans and makes a good dinner stop on the way back from driving the Apache Trail.

There's a second Blue Adobe at 10885 N. Frank Lloyd Wright Blvd., Scottsdale (✆ **480/314-0550**).

144 N. Country Club Dr., Mesa. ✆ **480/962-1000.** www.blueadobegrille.com. Reservations recommended. Main courses $9–$20. AE, DC, DISC, MC, V. Mon–Thurs 11am–9pm; Fri–Sat 11am–10pm; Sun noon–8pm.

Monti's La Casa Vieja AMERICAN If you're tired of the Scottsdale glitz and are looking for Old Arizona, try this sprawling steakhouse. The adobe building was constructed in 1873 (*casa vieja* means "old house" in Spanish) on the site of the Salt River ferry, which operated in the days when the river flowed year-round. Today, local families know Monti's well and rely on the restaurant for solid meals and low prices—you can get a filet mignon for as little as $12. The dark dining rooms are filled with memorabilia of the Old West.

100 S. Mill Ave. (at Rio Salado Pkwy.), Tempe. ✆ **480/967-7594.** www.montis.com. Reservations recommended for dinner. Main courses $11–$26. AE, DISC, MC, V. Sun–Thurs 11am–10pm; Fri–Sat 11am–11pm.

Inexpensive

Organ Stop Pizza ★ Kids PIZZA The pizza here may not be the best in town, but the mighty Wurlitzer theater organ, the largest in the world, sure is memorable. This massive instrument, which contains more than 5,500 pipes, has four turbine blowers to provide the wind to create the sound, and with 40-foot ceilings in the restaurant, the acoustics are great. As you marvel at the skill of the organist, who performs songs ranging from the latest pop tunes to *The Phantom of the Opera,* you can enjoy simple pizzas, pastas, or snacks.

1149 E. Southern Ave. (at Stapley Dr.), Mesa. ✆ **480/813-5700.** www.organstoppizza.com. Reservations for large groups only. Pizzas and pastas $5.50–$19. No credit cards. Thanksgiving to mid-Apr Sun–Thurs 4–9pm, Fri–Sat 4–10pm; mid-Apr to Thanksgiving Sun–Thurs 5–9pm, Fri–Sat 5–10pm.

5 SEEING THE SIGHTS

THE DESERT & ITS NATIVE CULTURES

Deer Valley Rock Art Center ★ Located in the Hedgepeth Hills in the northwest corner of the Valley of the Sun, the Deer Valley Rock Art Center preserves an amazing concentration of Native American petroglyphs, some of which date back 5,000 years. Although these petroglyphs may not at first seem as impressive as those at more famous sites, the sheer numbers make this a fascinating spot. The drawings, which range from simple spirals to much more complex renderings of herds of deer, are on volcanic boulders along a .25-mile trail. An interpretive center provides background information on this site and on rock art in general.

3711 W. Deer Valley Rd. ✆ **623/582-8007.** www.asu.edu/clas/shesc/dvrac. Admission $7 adults, $4 seniors and students, $3 children 6–12. Oct–Apr Tues–Sat 9am–5pm, Sun noon–5pm; May–Sept Tues–Sun 8am–2pm. Closed major holidays. Take the Loop 101 hwy. west to 27th Ave., go north to Deer Valley Dr., and go west 2½ miles to just past 35th Ave.

Desert Botanical Garden ★★★ In Papago Park adjacent to the Phoenix Zoo, this botanic garden displays more than 20,000 desert plants from around the world, and its Plants and People of the Sonoran Desert Trail is the state's best introduction to Southwestern ethnobotany (human use of plants). Along this trail you can make your own yucca-fiber brush and practice grinding corn as Native Americans once did. On the Desert Wildflower Trail, you'll find colorful wildflowers. Each spring, there's usually a butterfly pavilion filled with live butterflies. If you come late in the day, you can stay until after dark and see night-blooming flowers and dramatically lit cactuses. A cafe here makes a great lunch spot; and during the cooler months, there are concerts. From late November to late December, during *Las Noches de las Luminarias,* the gardens are lit at night by luminarias (candles inside small bags).

In Papago Park, 1201 N. Galvin Pkwy. ✆ **480/941-1225.** www.dbg.org. Admission $15 adults, $14 seniors, $7.50 students 13–18, $5 children 3–12. Oct–Apr daily 8am–8pm; May–Sept daily 7am–8pm. Closed July 4th, Thanksgiving, and Christmas. Bus: 3. METRO light rail: Priest Dr./Washington St.

Heard Museum ★★★ The Heard Museum is one of the nation's finest museums dealing exclusively with Native American cultures and is an ideal introduction to the indigenous peoples of Arizona. From pre-Columbian to contemporary, if it's art created by Native Americans, you'll find it here. If you're interested in the Native cultures of Arizona, this should be your very first stop in the state. The ***Home: Native People in the Southwest*** exhibit examines the culture of each of the major tribes of the region. Included in this exhibit are more than 500 kachina dolls. In another gallery, you'll find fascinating exhibits of contemporary Native American art. Guided tours are offered daily. The annual **Guild Indian Fair and Market,** held the first weekend in March, includes arts, crafts, and traditional dances.

The museum also operates the **Heard Museum North,** 32633 N. Scottsdale Rd. (✆ **480/488-9817**), in Carefree. This gallery features changing exhibits and is open Monday through Saturday from 10am to 5pm, and Sunday from 11am to 5pm. Admission is $5 for adults, $4 for seniors, $2 for students, and free for children 5 and under (free for all on the second Sun of each month). A third museum—**Heard Museum West**—is in the city of Surprise at 16126 N. Civic Center Plaza (✆ **623/344-2200**). This museum is open Tuesday through Saturday from 10am to 5pm (free for all on the second Sat of each month). Admission is $5 for adults, $4 for seniors, $2 for students, and free for children 5 and under.

2301 N. Central Ave. ✆ **602/252-8848.** www.heard.org. Admission $10 adults, $9 seniors, $5 students, $3 children 6–12. Daily 9:30am–5pm. Closed major holidays. Bus: 0. METRO light rail: Encanto Blvd./ Central Ave.

Pueblo Grande Museum and Archaeological Park Located near Sky Harbor Airport and downtown Phoenix, the Pueblo Grande Museum and Archaeological Park houses the ruins of an ancient Hohokam village that was one of several villages along the Salt River between A.D. 300 and 1400. Sometime around 1450, this and other villages were mysteriously abandoned. Some speculate that drought and a buildup of salts from irrigation water reduced the fertility of the soil and forced the people to seek more fertile lands. The small museum here displays many of the artifacts that have been dug up at the site. Although these exhibits are actually more interesting than the ruins themselves, some furnished replicas of Hohokam-style houses give a good idea of how the Hohokam lived. The museum sponsors interesting workshops (some just for kids), demonstrations, and tours (including petroglyph hikes). The **Pueblo Grande Indian Market** in mid-December features more than 300 Native American artisans.

4619 E. Washington St. (btw. 44th and 48th sts.). ✆ **877/706-4408** or 602/495-0901. www.pueblogrande.com. Admission $5 adults, $4 seniors, $3 children 6–17. Oct–Apr Mon–Sat 9am–4:45pm, Sun 1–4:45pm; May–Sept Tues–Sat 9am–4:45pm. Closed major holidays. Bus: 1. METRO light rail: 44th St./Washington St.

ART MUSEUMS

Arizona State University Art Museum at Nelson Fine Arts Center ★ Although it isn't very large, this museum is memorable for its innovative architecture and excellent temporary exhibitions. With its colorful stucco facade and pyramidal shape, the stark, angular building conjures up images of sunsets on desert mountains. The entrance is down a flight of stairs that leads to a cool underground garden area. Inside are galleries for crafts, prints, contemporary art, and Latin American art, along with outdoor sculpture courts and a gift shop. The collection of American art includes works by Georgia O'Keeffe, Edward Hopper, and John James Audubon. It's definitely a must for both art and architecture fans. Across the street is the **Ceramics Research Center,** 10th Street and Mill Avenue (✆ **480/965-2787**), a gallery that showcases the university's extensive collection of fine-art ceramics. The latter gallery is open Tuesday through Saturday from 11am to 5pm.

10th St. and Mill Ave., Tempe. ✆ **480/965-2787.** asuartmuseum.asu.edu. Free admission. Tues 11am–8pm (11am–5pm in summer); Wed–Sat 11am–5pm; Sun 1–5pm. Closed major holidays. Bus: 66. METRO light rail: Mill Ave./Third St.

Phoenix Art Museum ★★ This is one of the largest art museums in the Southwest, and within its labyrinth of halls and galleries is a respectable collection that spans the major artistic movements from the Renaissance to the present. Exhibits cover decorative arts, historical fashions, Spanish colonial furnishings and religious art, and, of course, works by members of the Cowboy Artists of America. The collection of modern and contemporary art is particularly good, with works by Diego Rivera, Frida Kahlo, Pablo Picasso, Alexander Calder, Henry Moore, Georgia O'Keeffe, Henri Rousseau, and Auguste Rodin. The popular Thorne Miniature Collection consists of tiny rooms on a scale of 1 inch to 1 foot. Because this museum is so large, it frequently mounts traveling blockbuster exhibits. The cafe here is a good spot for lunch.

Phoenix & the Valley of the Sun Attractions

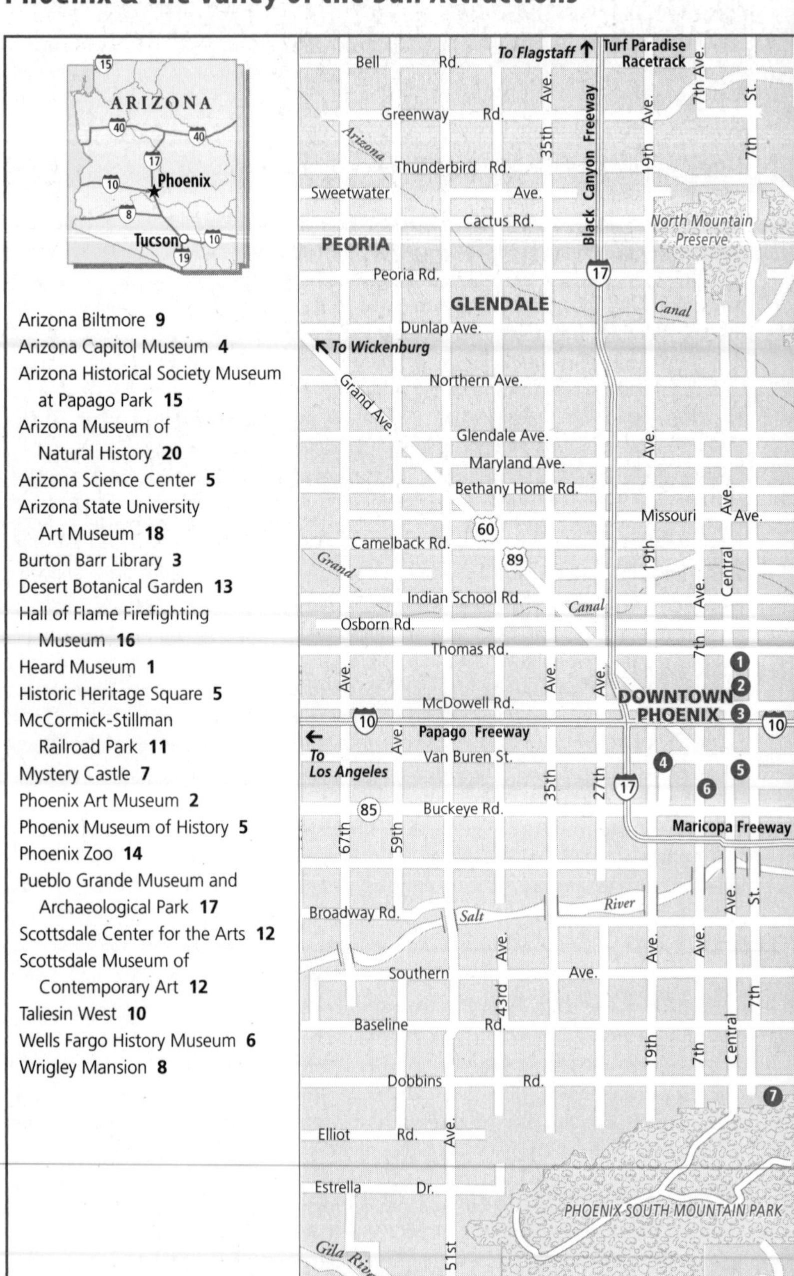

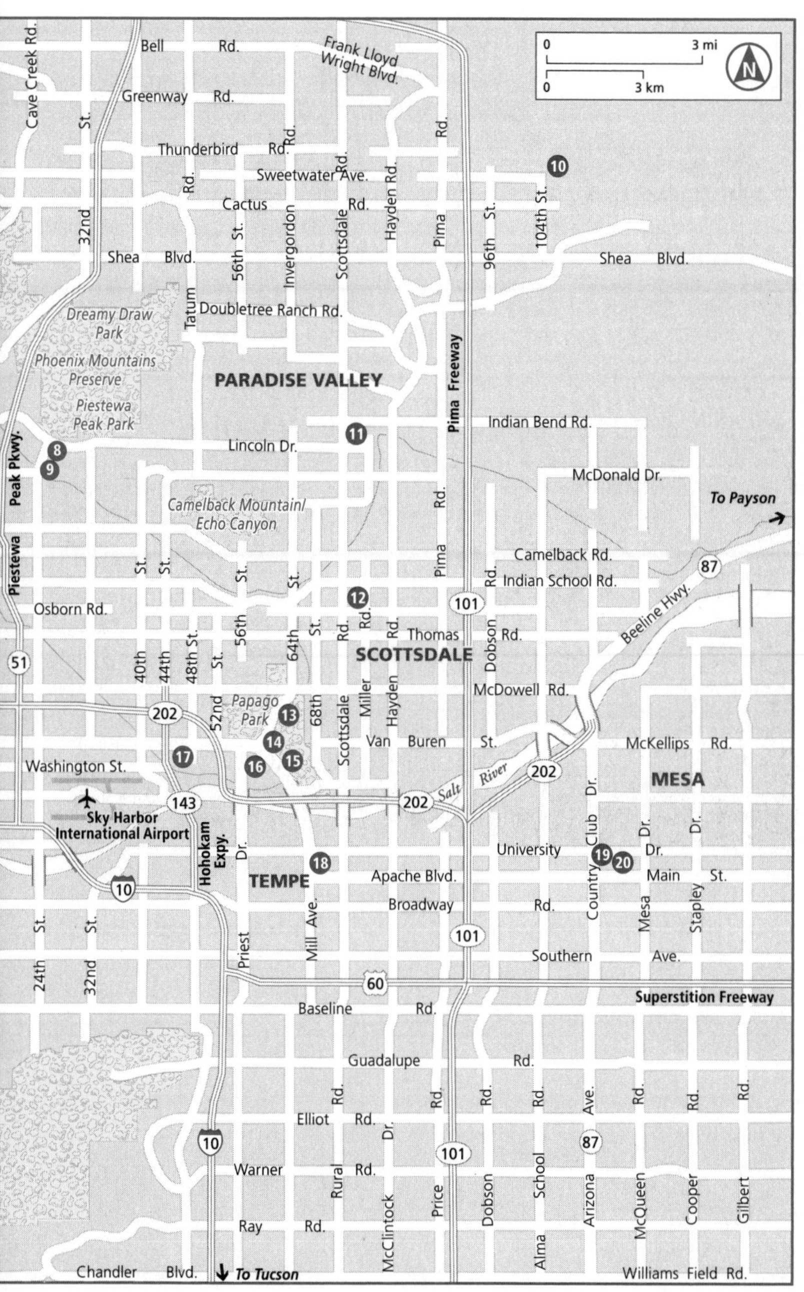

0
3 mi
0
3 km
N
Bell Rd.
Greenway Rd.
Thunderbird Rd.
Frank Lloyd Wright Blvd.
Sweetwater Ave.
Cactus Rd.
Shea Blvd.
Doubletree Ranch Rd.
Cave Creek Rd.
32nd St.
Tatum Rd.
56th St.
Invergordon Rd.
Scottsdale Rd.
Hayden Rd.
Pima Rd.
96th St.
104th St.
Dreamy Draw Park
Phoenix Mountains Preserve
Piestewa Peak Park
PARADISE VALLEY
Pima Freeway
Indian Bend Rd.
Lincoln Dr.
McDonald Dr.
To Payson
Piestewa Peak Pkwy.
Camelback Mountain/ Echo Canyon
Camelback Rd.
Indian School Rd.
Osborn Rd.
Thomas Rd.
Beeline Hwy.
SCOTTSDALE
40th St.
44th St.
48th St.
52nd St.
56th St.
64th St.
68th St.
Miller Rd.
Hayden Rd.
Dobson Rd.
McDowell Rd.
Papago Park
Van Buren St.
McKellips Rd.
Washington St.
Salt River
MESA
Sky Harbor International Airport
Hohokam Expy.
Priest Dr.
University Dr.
Country Club Dr.
Mesa Dr.
Stapley Dr.
TEMPE
Apache Blvd.
Main St.
Broadway Rd.
Mill Ave.
24th St.
32nd St.
Southern Ave.
Superstition Freeway
Baseline Rd.
Guadalupe Rd.
Elliot Rd.
Warner Rd.
Ray Rd.
Chandler Blvd.
To Tucson
Williams Field Rd.
Rural Rd.
McClintock Dr.
Price Rd.
Dobson Rd.
Alma School Rd.
Arizona Ave.
McQueen Rd.
Cooper Rd.
Gilbert Rd.
10
51
202
143
101
87
60

1625 N. Central Ave. (at McDowell Rd.). ✆ **602/257-1222.** www.phxart.org. Admission $10 adults, $8 seniors and students, $4 children 6–17; free for children 5 and under; free for all on Tues 3–9pm and first Fri of each month 6–10pm. Tues 10am–9pm; Wed–Sun 10am–5pm (also 6–10pm on first Fri of each month). Closed major holidays. Bus: 0. METRO light rail: McDowell Rd./Central Ave.

Scottsdale Museum of Contemporary Art ★★ Scottsdale may be obsessed with art featuring lonesome cowboys and solemn Indians, but this boldly designed museum makes it clear that patrons of contemporary art are also welcome here. Cutting-edge art, from the abstract to the absurd, fills the galleries, with exhibits rotating every few months. Don't miss James Turrell's skyspace *Knight Rise,* which is accessed from a patio off the museum shop and can be visited for free. By the way, the museum shop is full of beautiful items that will fit in your suitcase.

7374 E. Second St., Scottsdale. ✆ **480/994-ARTS** [2787]. www.smoca.org. Admission $7 adults, $5 students, free for children 14 and under; free for all on Thurs. Sept 1–May 27 Tues–Wed and Fri–Sat 10am–5pm, Thurs 10am–8pm, Sun noon–5pm; June–Aug Wed noon–5pm, Thurs 10am–8pm, Fri–Sat 10am–5pm, Sun noon–5pm. Closed major holidays. Bus: 41, 50, or 72. Also accessible via Scottsdale Trolley shuttle bus.

HISTORY MUSEUMS & HISTORIC LANDMARKS

Arizona Capitol Museum ★ In the years before Arizona became a state, the territorial capital moved from Prescott to Tucson, then back to Prescott, before finally settling in Phoenix. In 1898, a stately territorial capitol building was erected (with a copper roof to remind the local citizenry of the importance of that metal in the Arizona economy). Atop this copper roof was placed the statue *Winged Victory,* which still graces the old capitol building today. This building no longer serves as the actual state capitol, but has been restored to the way it appeared in 1912, the year Arizona became a state. Among the rooms on view are the senate and house chambers, as well as the governor's office. Exhibits provide interesting perspectives on early Arizona events and lifestyles. There are free guided tours Monday through Friday at 10am and 2pm.

1700 W. Washington St. ✆ **602/926-3620.** www.lib.az.us/museum. Free admission. Mon–Fri 8am–5pm; Sat 11am–4pm. Closed state holidays. Bus: 1 or DASH downtown shuttle.

Arizona Historical Society Museum at Papago Park ★ This museum, at the headquarters of the Arizona Historical Society, focuses its well-designed exhibits on the history of central Arizona. Temporary exhibits on the lives and works of the people who helped shape this region are always the highlights of a visit. An interesting permanent exhibit features life-size statues of everyday people from Arizona's past (a Mexican miner, a Chinese laborer, and so on). Quotes relate their individual stories, while props reveal what items they might have needed during their days in the desert.

1300 N. College Ave. (just off Curry Rd.), Tempe. ✆ **480/929-9499.** www.arizonahistoricalsociety.org. Admission $5 adults, $4 seniors and students 12–18, free for children 11 and under; free on 1st Sat of each month. Tues–Sat 10am–4pm; Sun noon–4pm. Bus: 66.

Historic Heritage Square The city of Phoenix was founded in 1870, but today few of the city's early homes remain. However, if you have an appreciation for old houses and want a glimpse of how Phoenix once looked, stroll around this collection of historic homes, which stand on the original town site. All of the buildings are listed on the National Register of Historic Places, and although most are modest buildings from the early 20th century, one impressive Victorian home was built in 1895. Today, the buildings house museums, restaurants, and gift shops. The Eastlake Victorian Rosson House, furnished with period antiques, is open for tours. The Stevens House features the Arizona

Doll & Toy Museum (see later in this chapter). The **Teeter House** (✆ **602/252-4682;** www.theteeterhouse.com) now serves as a Victorian tearoom (with cocktails and live jazz in the evening), the old Baird Machine Shop contains Pizzeria Bianco (see "Where to Dine," earlier in this chapter), and the Thomas House is home to Bar Bianco (see "Phoenix & Scottsdale After Dark," later in this chapter).

115 N. Sixth St., at Monroe. ✆ **602/262-5070.** www.rossonhousemuseum.org. Rosson House tours $5 adults, $4 seniors and students, $2 children 6–12. Wed–Sat 10am–4pm; Sun noon–4pm. Hours vary for other buildings; call for information. Closed Easter, July 4, mid-Aug to early Sept, Thanksgiving, Christmas, and New Year's. Bus: Red 0, 1, or DASH downtown shuttle. METRO light rail: Central Station.

Phoenix Museum of History ★ Located in the Heritage and Science Park in downtown Phoenix, this modern museum presents an interesting look at the history of a city that, to the casual visitor, might not seem to *have* any history. The modern design and interactive exhibits make this place much more interesting than your average local history museum. One unusual exhibit explores how "lungers" (tuberculosis sufferers) inadvertently helped originate the tourism industry in Arizona, while another exhibit looks at the once-popular occupation of ostrich farming.

105 N. Fifth St. ✆ **602/253-2734.** www.pmoh.org. Admission $6 adults, $4 seniors and students, $3 children 7–12, free for children 6 and under. Tues–Sat 10am–5pm. Closed major holidays. Bus: 0 or DASH downtown shuttle. METRO light rail: Central Station.

Wells Fargo History Museum ★ Finds Yes, this museum is small, and, yes, it's run by the Wells Fargo Bank, but the collection of artifacts here goes a long way toward conjuring up the Wild West so familiar from Hollywood movies. Not only is there an original Wells Fargo stagecoach on display, but there are also gold nuggets to ogle, old photos from the *real* Wild West, and plenty of artifacts and memorabilia from the days of stagecoach travel. There are also original paintings by N. C. Wyeth and bronze sculptures by Frederic Remington and Charles Russell.

145 W. Adams St. ✆ **602/378-1852.** www.wellsfargohistory.com. Free admission. Mon–Fri 9am–5pm. Closed major holidays. Bus: 0 or DASH downtown shuttle. METRO light rail: Central Station.

SCIENCE & INDUSTRY MUSEUMS

Arizona Museum of Natural History ★★ Kids This museum is one of the best museums in the Valley, and its wide variety of exhibits appeals to people with a range of interests. For the kids, there are animated dinosaurs on an indoor "cliff" with a roaring waterfall. Of course, there are also plenty of dinosaur skeletons. Also of interest are an exhibit on Mesoamerican cultures, a display on Arizona mammoth kill sites, some old jail cells, and a walk-through mine mock-up with exhibits on the Lost Dutchman Mine. There's also a mock-up of a Hohokam village.

53 N. MacDonald St. (at First St.), Mesa. ✆ **480/644-2230.** www.azmnh.org. Admission $9 adults, $8 seniors, $7 students, $5 children 3–12. Tues–Fri 10am–5pm; Sat 11am–5pm; Sun 1–5pm. Closed major holidays. Bus: 30.

Arizona Science Center ★ Kids So, the kids weren't impressed with the botanical garden or the Native American artifacts at the Heard Museum. Bring 'em here. They can spend the afternoon pushing buttons, turning knobs, and interacting with all kinds of cool science exhibits. In the end, they might even learn something in spite of all the fun they have. The science center also includes a planetarium and a large-screen theater, both of which carry additional charges.

Architectural Highlights

Architecture buffs will find plenty to gape at in Phoenix. Here's a list of my favorite buildings.

- **Arizona Biltmore** This resort hotel, although not designed by Frank Lloyd Wright, shows the famed architect's hand in its distinctive cast-cement blocks. It also displays sculptures, furniture, and stained glass designed by Wright. To learn more about the building, reserve ahead for a tour ($10 for nonguests, free for guests). The Biltmore is located at 2400 E. Missouri Ave. (✆ **602/955-6600**).
- **Burton Barr Library** This library is among the most daring pieces of public architecture in the city, and no fan of futuristic art or science fiction should miss it. The five-story cube is partially clad in enough ribbed copper sheeting to produce roughly 17,500,000 pennies. It's located at 1221 N. Central Ave. (✆ **602/262-4636;** www.phoenixpubliclibrary.org). Free admission.
- **Mystery Castle** ★ Built for a daughter who longed for a castle more permanent than those built in sand at the beach, Mystery Castle is a wondrous work of folk-art architecture. The 18-room fantasy has 13 fireplaces, parapets, and many other unusual touches. It's located at 800 E. Mineral Rd. (✆ **602/268-1581**). Admission $5 adults, $3 children 5–15. Closed June–Sept.
- **Taliesin West** ★★★ Frank Lloyd Wright fell in love with the Arizona desert and, in 1937, built Taliesin West as a winter camp that served as his home, office, and school. Today, the buildings of Taliesin West are the headquarters of the Frank Lloyd Wright Foundation and School of Architecture. Basic tours cost $27 adults, $23 students and seniors, and $10 for children (ages 6–12). Expanded Insight Tours ($32), behind-the-scenes tours ($60), guided desert walks ($33), apprentice shelter tours ($40), and night hikes ($43) are available at certain times of year. Call ahead for schedule information. Taliesen West is located at 12621 Frank Lloyd Wright Blvd. (at Cactus/114th St.), Scottsdale (✆ **480/860-8810** for information or 480/860-2700, ext. 494, for reservations; www.franklloydwright.org).

600 E. Washington St. ✆ **602/716-2000.** www.azscience.org. Admission $9 adults, $7 seniors and children 3–12. Planetarium and film combination tickets also available. Daily 10am–5pm. Closed Thanksgiving and Christmas. Bus: 0 or DASH downtown shuttle. METRO light rail: Central Station.

PARKS & ZOOS

Perhaps the most unusual park in the Phoenix metro area centers on **Tempe Town Lake,** 620 N. Mill Ave., Tempe (✆ **480/350-8625;** www.tempe.gov/lake), which was created in 1999 by damming the Salt River with inflatable dams. Tempe's 2-mile-long lake is lined with parks and bike paths on both the north and south shores. The best lake access is at Tempe Town Beach, at the foot of the Mill Avenue Bridge. Here you can rent kayaks and other small boats.

Among Phoenix's most popular parks are its natural areas and preserves. These include Phoenix South Mountain Park, Papago Park, Phoenix Mountains Preserve (site of Piestewa Peak), North Mountain Preserve, North Mountain Recreation Area, and Camelback Mountain–Echo Canyon Recreation Area. For more information on these parks, see "Bicycling," "Hiking," and "Horseback Riding" under "Outdoor Pursuits," below.

Phoenix Zoo ★ (Kids) Forget about polar bears and other cold-climate creatures; this zoo focuses its attention primarily on animals that come from climates similar to that of the Phoenix area (the rainforest exhibit is an exception). Most impressive of the displays are the African savanna and the baboon colony. The Southwestern exhibits are also of interest, as are the giant Galápagos tortoises and the exhibit featuring monkeys from Central and South America. All animals are kept in naturalistic enclosures, and what with all the palm trees and tropical vegetation, the zoo sometimes manages to make you forget you're in the desert. Families will enjoy *Zoolights,* an after-hours holiday-light display held late November to early January.

At Papago Park, 455 N. Galvin Pkwy. © **602/273-1341.** www.phoenixzoo.org. Admission $16 adults, $11 seniors, $7 children 3–12. Oct to early Nov and mid-Jan to May daily 9am–5pm; early Nov to mid-Jan daily 9am–4pm; June–Sept Mon–Fri 7am–2pm, Sat–Sun 7am–4pm. Closed Christmas. Bus: 3. METRO light rail: Priest Dr./Washington St.

ESPECIALLY FOR KIDS

In addition to the following suggestions, kids are likely to enjoy the Arizona Science Center, the Arizona Museum of Natural History, the Hall of Flame Firefighting Museum, and the Phoenix Zoo—all described in detail earlier in this chapter.

Arizona Doll & Toy Museum (Kids) This small museum is located in the historic Stevens House on Heritage Square in downtown Phoenix. The miniature classroom peopled by doll students is a favorite exhibit. With dolls dating from the 19th century, this is a definite must for doll collectors.

At Heritage Sq., N. Seventh and Monroe sts. © **602/253-9337.** Admission $3 adults, $1 children. Tues–Sat 10am–4pm; Sun noon–4pm. Closed Aug. Bus: 0, 1, or DASH downtown shuttle. METRO light rail: Central Station.

Arizona Museum for Youth (Kids) Using traditional displays and participatory activities, this museum allows children to explore the fine arts and their own creativity. It's housed in a refurbished grocery store, and the highlight is Artville, an arts-driven kid-size town. Exhibits are geared mainly toward toddlers through 12-year-olds, but all ages can work together to experience the activities.

35 N. Robson St. (btw. Main and First sts.), Mesa. © **480/644-2467.** www.arizonamuseumforyouth.com. Admission $5.50, free for children under 1. Tues–Sat 10am–4pm; Sun noon–4pm. Closed major holidays. Bus: 30.

Goldfield Ghost Town ★ (Kids) Over on the east side of the Valley, just 4 miles northeast of Apache Junction, you'll find a reconstructed 1890s gold-mining town. Although it's a bit of a tourist trap—filled with gift shops, an ice-cream parlor, and the like—it's also home to the **Goldfield's Historic Museum** (© **480/677-6463**), which has interesting exhibits on the history of the area. Of particular note is the exhibit on the Lost Dutchman gold mine, perhaps the most famous mine in the country, despite the fact that no one knows where it is. Goldfield Mine Tours provides guided tours of the gold mine beneath the town. The Superstition Narrow Gauge Railroad circles the town, and the **Goldfield Livery Stables** (© **480/982-0133**) offers horseback riding and carriage rides. If you're here at lunchtime, you can get a meal at the steakhouse/saloon.

4650 N. Mammoth Mine Rd. (4 miles northeast of Apache Junction on Ariz. 88). © **480/983-0333.** www.goldfieldghosttown.com. Museum admission $4 adults, $3 seniors, $1 children ages 5–12; train rides $6 adults, $5 seniors, $4 children 5–12; mine tours $7 adults, $6 seniors, $4 children 6–12; horseback rides $30 for 1 hr., $50 for 2 hr. Town daily 10am–5pm; museum, tour, and ride hours vary. Closed Christmas.

Hall of Flame Firefighting Museum ★ Kids This world's largest firefighting museum houses a fascinating collection of vintage firetrucks. The displays date from a 1725 English hand pumper to several classic engines from the 20th century. All are beautifully restored and, mostly, fire-engine red. In all, more than 90 vehicles are on display.

At Papago Park, 6101 E. Van Buren St. © **602/275-3473.** www.hallofflame.org. Admission $6 adults, $5 seniors, $4 students 6–17, $1.50 children 3–5, free for children 2 and under. Mon–Sat 9am–5pm; Sun noon–4pm. Closed New Year's Day, Thanksgiving, and Christmas. Bus: 3. METRO light rail: Priest Dr./Washington St.

McCormick-Stillman Railroad Park Kids If you or your kids happen to like trains, you won't want to miss this park. On the grounds are restored railroad cars and engines, two old railway depots, model railroad layouts, and, best of all, a 5/12-scale model railroad that takes visitors around the park. A 1929 carousel and a general store round out the attractions.

7301 E. Indian Bend Rd. (at Scottsdale Rd.), Scottsdale. © **480/312-2312.** www.therailroadpark.com. Train $2; carousel rides $1; museum admission $1 adults, free for children 2 and under. Hours vary with the season; call for schedule. Closed Thanksgiving and Christmas (museum closed June–Sept). Bus: 72.

Rawhide at Wild Horse Pass Kids Sure, Rawhide is a tourist trap, but this fake cow town is so much fun and such a quintessentially Phoenician experience that no family should get out of town without first moseying down its dusty streets. Those streets are lined with tourist shops and plenty of places for refreshments, including a steakhouse. Attractions and activities include stunt shows, gunfights, trick-roping demonstrations, a mechanical bull, gold panning, and stagecoach, burro, and train rides. February through May and October and November, there are Saturday sundown cookouts ($45 adults, $19 children) with hayrides, live music, and storytellers. Throughout the year, there are special events, including rodeos.

5700 W. North Loop Rd., Chandler. © **800/527-1880** or 480/502-5600. www.rawhide.com. Free admission (individual shows and rides $4; all-day ride/attractions pass $15). Hours vary with the seasons; call for details.

6 ORGANIZED TOURS & EXCURSIONS

The Valley of the Sun is a sprawling, often congested place, and if you're unfamiliar with the area, you may be surprised at the great distances between attractions. If map reading and urban navigation are not your strong points, consider taking a guided tour. Numerous companies offer tours of both the Valley of the Sun and the rest of Arizona. However, tours of the Valley tend to include only brief stops at highlights.

BUS TOURS **Gray Line Tours Phoenix** (© **800/777-3484** or 602/437-3484; www.graylinephoenix.com) is one of the largest tour companies in the Valley. It offers a 4-hour tour of Phoenix and the Valley of the Sun for $52; reservations are necessary. The tour points out such local landmarks as the state capitol, Heritage Square, Arizona State University, and Old Town Scottsdale. If you're looking for a simple overview of the city, these tours are fine, but you won't get more than a passing acquaintance with the various locales.

HOT-AIR BALLOON RIDES The still morning air of the Valley of the Sun is perfect for hot-air ballooning, and because of the stiff competition, prices are among the lowest in the country. **Over the Rainbow** (✆ **602/225-5666;** www.letsgoballooning.com) charges only $159 for a 1- to 1½-hour flight, while **Adventures Out West** (✆ **800/755-0935** or 480/991-3666; www.adventuresoutwest.com) charges $175 to $205 (or $195–$225 with transportation from your Scottsdale hotel) for a 1-hour flight.

JEEP TOURS After spending a few days in Scottsdale, you'll likely start wondering where the desert is. Well, it's out there, and the easiest way to explore it is to book a Jeep tour. Most hotels and resorts work with particular companies, so start by asking your concierge. Alternatively, you can contact one of the following companies. Most will pick you up at your hotel, take you off through the desert, and maybe even let you pan for gold or shoot a six-gun. Depending on how many people there are in your party and where you're staying, expect to pay around $75 to $85 for a 3-hour tour. Companies include **Arizona Desert Mountain Jeep Tours** (✆ **800/567-3619;** www.azdesertmountain.com) and **Arizona Bound Tours** (✆ **480/962-6620;** www.arizonabound.com).

If you want to really impress your friends when you get home, you'll need to try something a little different. How about a Hummer tour? Sure, a Hummer is nothing but a Jeep on steroids, but these off-road vehicles still turn heads. Contact **Desert Storm Hummer Tours** (✆ **866/374-8637** or 480/922-0020; www.dshummer.com), which charges $95 for a 4-hour tour ($75 for children 6–16); or **Stellar Adventures** (✆ **877/878-3552** or 602/402-0584; www.stellaradventures.com), which charges $135 for a basic 4-hour tour ($95 for children 10 and under) and $165 for its advanced tour. Both companies also offer night tours ($145–$165) that let you spot wildlife with night-vision equipment.

7 GETTING OUTSIDE

BICYCLING Although the Valley of the Sun is a sprawling place, it's mostly flat and has numerous paved bike paths, which makes bicycling a breeze as long as it isn't windy or, in the summer, too hot. In Scottsdale, **Arizona Outback Adventures,** 16447 N. 91st St., Ste. 101 (✆ **866/455-1601** or 480/945-2881; www.azoutbackadventures.com), rents road bikes for $50 to $85 per day, hybrid bikes for $35 per day, and mountain bikes for $35 to $85 per day. Mountain-biking trail maps are also available. This company also does half-day and full-day guided mountain-bike tours.

Among the best mountain-biking spots in the city are Papago Park (at Van Buren St. and Galvin Pkwy.), Phoenix South Mountain Park (use the entrance off Baseline Rd. on 48th St.), and North Mountain Preserve (off Seventh St., btw. Dunlap Ave. and Thunderbird Rd.). With its rolling topography and wide dirt trails, Papago Park is the best place for novice mountain bikers to get in some desert riding (and the scenery here is great). For hard-core pedalers, Phoenix South Mountain Park is the place to go.

There's also plenty of good road biking and mountain biking up in the Cave Creek area, where you can rent a bike for $45 a day at **Flat Tire Bike Shop,** 6149 E. Cave Creek

Rd. (✆ **480/488-5261;** www.flattirebikes.com). If you'd like a guide for some of the best biking in the desert, contact **Desert Biking Adventures** (✆ **888/249-BIKE** [2453] or 602/320-4602; www.desertbikingadventures.com), which leads 2-, 3-, and 4-hour tours (and specializes in downhill rides). Prices range from $80 to $100. In Old Town Scottsdale, you can rent a bike in Scottsdale at **Bicycle Haus,** 7025 E. Fifth Ave. (✆ **480/994-4287**), and head out on the gravel path beside the canal that flows through the heart of the Scottsdale Waterfront. Cruiser bikes rent for $40 per day or $30 for a half-day.

If you'd rather confine your cycling to a paved surface, there's no better route than Scottsdale's **Indian Bend Wash greenbelt,** a paved path that extends for more than 10 miles along Hayden Road (from north of Shea Blvd. to Tempe). The Indian Bend Wash pathway can be accessed at many points along Hayden Road. At the south end, the path connects to paved paths on the shores of Tempe Town Lake and provides easy access to Tempe's Mill Avenue shopping district.

GOLF With more than 200 courses in the Valley of the Sun, golf is just about the most popular sport in Phoenix and one of the main reasons people flock here in winter. Sunshine, spectacular views, and the company of coyotes, quails, and doves make playing a round of golf here a truly memorable experience.

However, despite the number of courses, it can be difficult to get a tee time on any of the more popular courses (especially during the months of Feb, Mar, and Apr). If you're staying at a resort with a course, be sure to make your tee-time reservations at the same time you make your room reservations. If you aren't staying at a resort, you might still be able to play a round on a resort course if you can get a last-minute tee time. Try one of the tee-time reservations services below.

The only thing harder than getting a winter or spring tee time in the Valley is facing the bill at the end of your 18 holes. Greens fees at most public and resort courses range from $100 to $185, with the top courses often charging $200 to $250 or more. Some municipal courses, on the other hand, charge less than $60. You can save money on many courses by opting for twilight play, which usually begins between 1 and 3pm.

You can get more information on Valley of the Sun golf courses from the **Greater Phoenix Convention & Visitors Bureau,** 125 N. Second St. (✆ **877/225-5749** or 602/452-6282; www.visitphoenix.com).

It's a good idea to make reservations well in advance. You can avoid the hassle of booking tee times yourself by contacting **Golf Xpress** (✆ **888/679-8246** or 602/404-GOLF [4653]; www.azgolfxpress.com), which can make reservations farther in advance than you could if you called the golf course directly, and can sometimes get you lower greens fees as well. This company also makes hotel reservations, rents golf clubs, and provides other assistance to golfers visiting the Valley. For last-minute reservations, call **Stand-by Golf** (✆ **800/655-5345;** www.discountteetimes.com).

The many resort courses are the favored fairways of valley visitors. Some of my favorites are listed below:

- **The Boulders ★★** For spectacular scenery, the two Jay Morrish–designed 18-hole courses at The Boulders, 34631 N. Tom Darlington Dr., Carefree (✆ **480/488-9028;** www.thebouldersclub.com), just can't be beat. Given the option, play the South Course, and watch out as you approach the tee box on the 7th hole—it's a real heart-stopper. You'll pay $215 to $285 for a round in winter.
- **Wigwam Golf and Country Club ★** Wigwam has, count 'em, three championship 18-hole courses. The Gold Course is legendary, but even the Blue and Red courses are worth playing. The club is in the city of Litchfield Park, on the far west side of the

valley, 300 Wigwam Blvd. (✆ **800/327-0396** or 623/935-9414; www.wigwamresort.com). In high season, greens fees are $129 on the Gold Course and $109 on the Blue and Red courses.

- **Gold Canyon Golf Resort** ★ This course, way over on the east side of the valley at the foot of the Superstition Mountains, has been rated the best public course in the state. It's located at 6100 S. Kings Ranch Rd., Gold Canyon (✆ **480/982-9449;** www.gcgr.com). Greens fees on the Dinosaur Mountain course range from $185 to $210 in winter. The Sidewinder course is more traditional and less dramatic, but much more economical. Greens fees are $95 to $115 in winter.
- **Phoenician Golf Club** Set at the base of Camelback Mountain (6000 E. Camelback Rd.; ✆ **800/888-8234** or 480/423-2449; www.thephoenician.com), this club has 27 holes that mix traditional and desert styles. Greens fees for nonresort guests are $200 in winter and spring; reservations can be made up to 30 days in advance.
- **Troon North Golf Club** ★★★ Of the valley's many daily-fee courses, the two 18-hole courses at this club garner the most local accolades. This is the finest example of a desert course that you'll find anywhere in the state. It's located at 10320 E. Dynamite Blvd., Scottsdale (✆ **480/585-7700;** www.troonnorthgolf.com). Greens fees are $245 to $295 in winter and spring.
- **Tournament Players Club (TPC) of Scottsdale** ★★ If you want to swing where the pros do, beg, borrow, or steal a tee time on the Tom Weiskopf and Jay Morrish–designed Stadium Course. The TPC's second 18, the Desert Course, is actually a municipal course. It's located at 17020 N. Hayden Rd. (✆ **888/400-4001** or 480/585-4334; www.playatpc.com). Stadium course fees top out at $272 in winter and spring, while Desert Course fees are a reasonable $130 in winter and spring.
- **Dove Valley Ranch Golf Club** If you want to take a crack at a desert-style course or two but don't want to take out a second mortgage, try this club at 33750 N. Dove Lakes Dr., Cave Creek (✆ **480/488-0009;** www.dovevalleyranch.com). Designed by Robert Trent Jones Jr., it was voted Arizona's best new public course when it opened in 1998. Greens fees are $99 to $109 in winter.
- **We-Ko-Pa Golf Club** This golf club is on the Fort McDowell Yavapai Nation, and the name is Yavapai for "Four Peaks," which is the mountain range you'll be marveling at as you play. Unlike at other area courses, fairways are bounded by desert, not luxury homes, so make sure you keep your ball on the grass. The two 18-hole courses are located off the Beeline Highway (Ariz. 87) in the northeast corner of the valley (18200 East Toh Vee Circle, Fort McDowell; ✆ **480/836-9000;** www.wekopa.com). Greens fees are $180 to $210 in winter. Reservations are taken up to 90 days in advance.
- **Papago Golf Course** One of the municipal courses in Phoenix, Papago offers fine views and a killer 17th hole. This is such a great course that it's used for Phoenix Open qualifying. It's located at 5595 E. Moreland St. (✆ **602/275-8428**), at the foot of the red sandstone Papago Buttes. In winter, greens fees are $115.

HIKING Several mountains around Phoenix, including Camelback Mountain and Piestewa Peak, have been set aside as parks and nature preserves, and these natural areas are among the city's most popular hiking spots. The city's largest nature preserve, **South Mountain Park/Preserve** ★ (✆ **602/495-0222;** www.phoenix.gov/PARKS/southmnt.html), covers 16,000 acres and is one of the largest city parks in the world. This park contains around 50 miles of hiking, mountain-biking, and horseback-riding trails, and the views of Phoenix (whether from along the National Trail or from the parking lot at the Buena Vista Lookout) are spectacular, especially at sunset. To reach the park's main entrance, drive south on Central Avenue, which leads right into the park. Once inside the park, turn left on Summit Road and follow it to the Buena Vista Lookout, which provides a great view of the city and is the trail head for the National Trail. If you hike east on this trail for 2 miles, you'll come to an unusual little natural tunnel that makes a good turnaround point.

Another place to get in some relatively easy and convenient hiking is **Papago Park,** Galvin Parkway and McDowell Road (✆ **602/261-8318;** www.phoenix.gov/PARKS/hikepapa.html), home to the Desert Botanical Garden, the Phoenix Zoo, and the fascinating Hole in the Rock (a red-rock butte with a large natural opening in it). There are both paved and dirt trails within the park; the most popular hikes are around the Papago Buttes (park on W. Park Dr.) and up onto the rocks at Hole in the Rock (park past the zoo, at the information center). During World War II, there was a German POW camp here.

Perhaps the most popular hike in the city is the trail to the top of **Camelback Mountain** ★, in the **Echo Canyon Recreation Area** (✆ **602/262-6575;** www.phoenix.gov/PARKS/hikecmlb.html), near the boundary between Phoenix and Scottsdale. At 2,704 feet high, this is the highest mountain in Phoenix and boasts the finest mountaintop views in the city. The 1.2-mile Summit Trail that leads to the top of Camelback Mountain is outrageously steep and gains 1,200 feet from trail head to summit. Yet on any given day there will be ironmen and ironwomen nonchalantly jogging up and down to stay fit. At times, it almost feels like a health club singles scene. To reach the trail head, drive up 44th Street until it becomes McDonald Drive, turn right on East Echo Canyon Parkway, and continue up the hill until the road ends at a parking lot, which is often full. Don't attempt this one in the heat of the day, and bring at least a quart of water. I also recommend wearing hiking boots.

At the east end of Camelback Mountain is the Cholla Trail, which, at 1.5 miles in length, isn't as steep as the Summit Trail (at least, not until you get close to the summit, where the route gets steep, rocky, and very difficult). The only parking for this trail is along Invergordon Road at Chaparral Road, just north of Camelback Road (along the east boundary of the Phoenician resort). Be sure to park in a legal parking space and watch the hours in which parking is allowed. There are great views down onto the fairways of the golf course at the Phoenician.

The 2,608-foot-tall **Piestewa Peak,** in the **Phoenix Mountains Park and Recreation Area/Dreamy Draw Recreation Area** (✆ **602/262-7901;** www.phoenix.gov/PARKS/hikephx.html), offers another aerobic workout of a hike and has views almost as spectacular as those from Camelback Mountain. The round-trip to the summit is 2.4 miles and gains almost 1,200 feet. Piestewa Peak is reached from Squaw Peak Drive off Lincoln Drive between 22nd and 23rd streets. Another section of this park, with much easier trails, can be reached by taking the Northern Avenue exit of Ariz. 51, and then driving east into Dreamy Draw Park.

Of all the popular mountain trails in the Phoenix area, the trail through **Pinnacle Peak Park,** 26802 N. 102nd Way (✆ **480/312-0990;** www.scottsdaleaz.gov/parks/pinnacle), in north Scottsdale, is my favorite. The trail through the park is a 3.5-mile round-trip hike and is immensely popular with the local fitness crowd. Forget about stopping to smell the desert penstemon; if you don't keep up the pace, someone's liable to knock you off the trail into a prickly pear. If you can find a parking space (arrive before 9am Sat–Sun) and can ignore the crowds, you'll be treated to views of rugged desert mountains (and posh desert suburbs). November through April, there are guided hikes Tuesday through Sunday at 10am. There are also wildflower walks, full-moon hikes, and astronomy evenings here. To find the park from central Scottsdale, go north on North Pima Road, turn right on East Happy Valley Road, left on North Alma School Parkway, left on East Pinnacle Peak Parkway, and left on North 102nd Way.

For much less vigorous hiking (without the crowds), try **North Mountain Park** (© **602/495-5458;** www.phoenix.gov/PARKS/nmvc.html), in North Mountain Preserve. This natural area, located on either side of Seventh Street, between Dunlap Avenue and Thunderbird Road, has more flat hiking than Camelback Mountain or Piestewa Peak. To orient yourself and get trail maps, stop by the **North Mountain Visitor Center,** 12950 N. Seventh St. (© **602/495-5540**).

The **Peralta Trail,** way out on the east side of the Valley in the impossibly steep and jagged Superstition Mountains, just might be my favorite hike in the entire state. Unfortunately, a lot of other people feel the same way, and on weekends, the trail is almost always packed with people. However, if you come early on a weekday, you can have this trail almost all to yourself. The route climbs steadily, though not too steeply, past huge old saguaros to a saddle with a view that will take your breath away. The view is an in-your-face look at Weaver's Needle, the Superstition Mountains' most famous pinnacle. The hike to the view at Fremont Saddle is 4.6 miles round-trip. To reach the trail head, drive east from Phoenix on US 60 past Apache Junction to Peralta Road, and then drive 8 miles north, mostly on gravel road, to the trail head. For information, contact the **Tonto National Forest's Mesa Ranger District,** 5140 E. Ingram St., Mesa (© **480/610-3300;** www.fs.fed.us/r3/tonto).

HORSEBACK RIDING Even in the urban confines of the Phoenix metro area, people like to play at being cowboys, and there are plenty of places around the Valley to saddle up your palomino. Because any guided ride is going to lead you through interesting desert scenery, your best bet is to pick a stable close to where you're staying. Keep in mind that most stables require or prefer reservations.

On the south side of the city, try **Ponderosa Stables,** 10215 S. Central Ave. (© **602/268-1261;** www.arizona-horses.com), which leads rides into South Mountain Park and charges $30 for a 1-hour ride or $50 for a 2-hour ride. These stables also offer fun dinner rides ($39) to a steakhouse, where you buy your own dinner before riding back under the stars. If you have time for only one horseback ride while you're in Phoenix, make it this latter ride. Breakfast rides are also offered.

On the north side of the Valley, **Cave Creek Outfitters,** off Dynamite Boulevard at 31313 N. 144th St. (© **888/921-0040** or 480/471-4635; www.cavecreekoutfitters.com), offers 2-hour rides for $65 ($80 with transportation to the stables).

WATER PARKS If you happen to be visiting during the hotter months, consider taking the family to one of the Valley's water parks for a day of keeping cool. At **Mesa Golfland Sunsplash,** 155 W. Hampton Ave., Mesa (© **480/834-8319;** www.golfland.com), you can splash in a wave pool and ride a water roller coaster. **Big Surf,** 1500 N. McClintock Rd., Tempe (© **480/947-2477;** www.golfland.com), has the country's original wave pool and all kinds of wild water slides. Both of these parks are generally open from Memorial Day weekend to Labor Day weekend (call for hours) and charge $26 for anyone taller than 48 inches, $20 for seniors and anyone under 48 inches, and $3 for children 2 and under. Mesa Golfland also has three slides that open at the start of spring break.

8 SPECTATOR SPORTS

Phoenix is nuts for pro sports and is one of the few cities in the country with teams for all four of the major sports (baseball, basketball, football, and hockey). Add to this baseball's spring training, professional women's basketball, golf and tennis tournaments, the annual Fiesta Bowl college football classic, and ASU football, basketball, and baseball, and you have enough action to keep even the most rabid sports fans happy. The all-around best month to visit is March, when you could feasibly catch baseball's spring training, the Suns, the Coyotes, and ASU basketball and baseball, as well as the Safeway International LPGA Tournament.

Call **Ticketmaster** (✆ **866/448-7849;** www.ticketmaster.com) for tickets to most of the events below. For sold-out events, try **Tickets Unlimited** (✆ **800/289-8497** or 602/840-2340; www.ticketsunlimitedinc.com) or **Ticket Exchange** (✆ **800/800-9811;** ticketexchangeusa.com).

BASEBALL The **Arizona Diamondbacks** (✆ **888/777-4664** or 602/514-8400; www.diamondbacks.com) have a devoted fan base and regularly pack downtown Phoenix's impressive Chase Field. The ballpark's retractable roof allows for comfortable play during the blistering summers and makes this one of only a few enclosed baseball stadiums with natural grass. Tickets to ballgames are available through the Chase Field ticket office and cost between $5 and $240. The best seats are in sections J and Q. If you'd like to get a behind-the-scenes look at Chase Field, you can take a guided tour. Tours cost $6 for adults, $4 for seniors and children ages 7 to 12, and $2 for children ages 4 to 6.

For decades, baseball's spring-training season has been immensely popular, especially with fans from northern teams, and don't think that the Cactus League's preseason exhibition games are any less popular just because the Diamondbacks play all summer. **Spring-training games** may rank second only to golf in popularity with winter visitors to the Valley. Thirteen major-league baseball teams have spring-training camps around the Valley in the month of March, and exhibition games are scheduled at nine different stadiums. Most tickets cost between $6 and $40. Get a schedule from a visitor center, check the *Arizona Republic* while you're in town, or check the website of the Cactus League (www.cactusleague.com). Games often sell out, especially on weekends, so be sure to order tickets in advance.

Teams training in the Valley include the **Chicago Cubs,** HoHoKam Park, 1235 N. Center St., Mesa (✆ 800/905-3315 or 480/964-4467; www.chicagocubs.com); the **Chicago White Sox,** Camelback Ranch, 10710 W. Camelback Rd., Phoenix (✆ 623/877-8585; www.chicagowhitesox.com); the **Cincinnati Reds,** Goodyear Ballpark, 1933 S. Ballpark Way, Goodyear (✆ 623/882-7525; www.cincinnatireds.com); the **Cleveland Indians,** Goodyear Ballpark, 1933 S. Ballpark Way, Goodyear (✆ 623/882-7525; www.clevelandindians.com); the **Kansas City Royals,** Surprise Stadium, 15960 N. Bullard Ave., Surprise (✆ 623/222-2222 or 480/784-4444; www.kcroyals.com); the **Los Angeles Angels of Anaheim,** Tempe Diablo Stadium, 2200 W. Alameda Dr. (48th St. and Broadway Rd.), Tempe (✆ 480/350-5205 or 480/784-4444 for tickets; www.angelsbaseball.com); the **Los Angeles Dodgers,** Camelback Ranch, 10710 W. Camelback Rd., Phoenix (✆ 623/877-8585; www.losangelesdodgers.com); the **Milwaukee Brewers,** Maryvale Baseball Park, 3600 N. 51st Ave., Phoenix (✆ 800/933-7890 or 623/245-5500; www.milwaukeebrewers.com); the **Oakland Athletics,** Phoenix Municipal Stadium, 5999 E.

A Day at the Spa

If you want truly spectacular surroundings and bragging rights, head north to the **Golden Door Spa at the Boulders,** 34631 N. Tom Darlington Dr., Carefree (✆ **480/595-3500;** www.goldendoorspas.com). This spa has tremendous name recognition, but it's not my favorite. The turquoise wrap, the spa's signature treatment, is a real desert experience.

Willow Stream–The Spa at Fairmont, 7575 E. Princess Dr. (✆ **800/908-9540** or 480/585-2732; www.fairmont.com), is my favorite valley spa. Designed to conjure up images of the journey to northern Arizona's Havasu Canyon, it includes a rooftop swimming pool and a large hot tub in a grotto below the pool.

Located high on the flanks of Mummy Mountain, the **Spa at Camelback Inn,** 5402 E. Lincoln Dr., Scottsdale (✆ **800/922-2635** or 480/596-7040; www.camelbackspa.com), is a deliciously tranquil place and has long been one of the valley's premiere spas. You just can't beat this spa for convenience and variety of treatments.

The **Centre for Well Being,** at the Phoenician, 6000 E. Camelback Rd., Scottsdale (✆ **800/843-2392** or 480/423-2452; www.centreforwellbeing.com), is one of the valley's most prestigious spas. Treatments include a botanical hydrating wrap and a shea butter wrap with honey-avocado foot therapy.

The historic setting and convenient location of the **Arizona Biltmore Spa,** 2400 E. Missouri Ave. (✆ **602/381-7632;** www.arizonabiltmore.com), make this facility an excellent choice if you're spending time along the Camelback Corridor. The spa menu includes dozens of different treatments.

Van Buren St., Phoenix (✆ 877/493-BALL [2255] or 602/392-0074; www.oakland athletics.com); the **San Diego Padres,** Peoria Sports Complex, 16101 N. 83rd Ave., Peoria (✆ 800/677-1227 or 623/773-8700; www.padres.com); the **San Francisco Giants,** Scottsdale Stadium, 7408 E. Osborn Rd., Scottsdale (✆ 877/473-4849 or 480/312-2586; www.sfgiants.com); the **Seattle Mariners,** Peoria Sports Complex, 16101 N. 83rd Ave., Peoria (✆ 800/677-1227 or 623/773-8700; www.seattlemariners.com); and the **Texas Rangers,** Surprise Stadium, 15960 N. Bullard Ave., Surprise (✆ 623/222-2222 or 480/784-4444; www.texasrangers.com).

BASKETBALL The NBA's **Phoenix Suns** play at the US Airways Center, 201 E. Jefferson St. (✆ **800/4-NBA-TIX** [462-2849] or 602/379-SUNS [7867]; www.suns.com). Most tickets cost between $10 and $250. Suns tickets are hard to come by; if you haven't planned ahead, try contacting the box office the day before or the day of a game to see if tickets have been returned. Otherwise, you'll have to try a ticket agency and pay a premium.

Phoenix also has a WNBA team, the **Phoenix Mercury** (✆ **602/252-9622** or 602/514-8333; www.phoenixmercury.com), which plays at the US Airways Center between late May and mid-August. Tickets cost $10 to $185.

FOOTBALL The **Arizona Cardinals** (✆ **800/999-1402** or 602/379-0102; www.azcardinals.com) play at the $450-million state-of-the-art University of Phoenix Stadium in the west Valley city of Glendale. This stadium has a retractable roof made of translucent fabric that lets lots of light in when the roof is closed. However, the stadium's most distinctive feature is its movable playing field, which is rolled out into the sun outside the stadium until a game is scheduled. This 2-acre, grass-covered tray is the first of its kind in North America. Most tickets cost $50 to $113, and single-game tickets for the entire season go on sale around mid-July.

GOLF TOURNAMENTS It's not surprising that, with more than 200 golf courses and ideal golfing weather throughout the fall, winter, and spring, the Valley of the Sun hosts some major golf tournaments. Late January's **FBR Open Golf Tournament** (✆ **602/870-0163;** www.fbropen.com) is by far the biggest. Held at the Tournament Players Club (TPC) of Scottsdale, it attracts more spectators than any other golf tournament in the world (more than 500,000 each year). The 18th hole has standing room for 40,000. Tickets start at $25 and are available through Ticketmaster (see above).

Each March, the **Phoenix LPGA International** (✆ **877/983-3300** or 602/495-4653; www.phoenixlpga.com) lures more than 100 of the top women golfers from around the world. Daily tickets are $16; weekly tickets are $64.

RODEOS, POLO & HORSE SHOWS Cowboys, cowgirls, and other horsy types will find plenty of the four-legged critters going through their paces most weeks at **WestWorld of Scottsdale,** 16601 N. Pima Rd., Scottsdale (✆ **480/312-6802;** www.scottsdaleaz.gov/westworld). With its hundreds of stables, numerous equestrian arenas, and a polo field, this complex provides an amazing variety of entertainment and sporting events. There are rodeos, polo matches, and horse shows.

9 SHOPPING

For the most part, shopping in the Phoenix area means malls. They're everywhere, and they're air-conditioned, which, I'm sure you'll agree, makes shopping in the desert far more enjoyable when it's 110°F (43°C) outside.

Scottsdale and the Biltmore District of Phoenix (along Camelback Rd.) are the Valley's main upscale shopping areas, with several high-end shopping centers and malls. The various distinct shopping districts of downtown Scottsdale are among the few outdoor shopping areas in the Valley and are home to hundreds of boutiques, galleries, jewelry stores, Native American crafts stores, and souvenir shops. The Western atmosphere of Old Town Scottsdale is partly real and partly a figment of the local merchants' imaginations, but nevertheless it's the most popular tourist shopping area in the Valley. With dozens of galleries in the Main Street Arts and Antiques District and the nearby Marshall Way Contemporary Arts District, it also happens to be the heart of the Valley's art market.

For locals, Scottsdale's shopping scene has been moving steadily northward over the past decade. Kierland Commons and the Shops at Gainey Village are both north of Old Town Scottsdale on North Scottsdale Road and are packed with women's fashion boutiques.

Shopping hours are usually Monday through Saturday from 10am to 6pm and Sunday from noon to 5pm; malls usually stay open until 9pm Monday through Saturday.

ANTIQUES & COLLECTIBLES

With more than 80 antiques shops and specialty stores, downtown Glendale (northwest of downtown Phoenix) is the Valley's main antiques district. You'll find the greatest concentration of antiques stores just off Grand Avenue between 56th and 59th avenues. A half-dozen times each year, the **Arizona Antique Shows** (✆ **602/717-7337;** www.azantiqueshow.com), Arizona's largest collectors' shows, are held at the Arizona State Fairgrounds, 19th Avenue and McDowell Road.

Ancient Arts Gallery ★★ Ancient ceramics pieces from around the Southwest are among the specialties at this amazing antiques store. There are lots of other pre-Columbian artifacts as well as Roman, Greek, and Egyptian pieces. These are museum-quality artifacts with prices to prove it. 7056 E. Main St., Ste. B, Scottsdale. ✆ **480/874-1007.** www.fortknoxartifacts.com.

Antique Trove If you love browsing through packed antiques malls searching for your favorite collectibles, then this should be your first stop in the Valley. With more than 100 dealers, it's one of the biggest antiques malls in the area. 2020 N. Scottsdale Rd., Scottsdale. ✆ **480/947-6074.** www.antiquetrove.com.

Arizona West Galleries ★★ Nowhere else in Scottsdale will you find such an amazing collection of cowboy collectibles and Western antiques. There are antique saddles and chaps, old rifles and six-shooters, sheriffs' badges, spurs, and the like. 7149 E. Main St., Scottsdale. ✆ **480/994-3752.**

Bishop Gallery for Art & Antiques ★ This cramped shop is wonderfully eclectic, featuring everything from Asian antiques to unusual original art. It's definitely worth a browse. 7164 E. Main St., Scottsdale. ✆ **480/949-9062.**

ART

In the Southwest, only Santa Fe is a more important art market than Scottsdale, and along the streets of Scottsdale's Main Street Arts and Antiques District and the Marshall Way Contemporary Arts District, you'll see dozens of galleries selling everything from monumental bronzes to contemporary art created from found objects. On Main Street, you'll find primarily cowboy art, both traditional and contemporary, while on North Marshall Way, you'll discover much more daring contemporary art.

In addition to the galleries listed here, you'll usually find a huge tent full of art along Scottsdale Road in north Scottsdale. The annual **Celebration of Fine Art** (✆ **480/443-7695;** www.celebrateart.com) takes place each year between mid-January and late March. Not only will you get to see the work of 100 artists, but on any given day, you'll also find dozens of the artists at work on the premises. Admission is $8 for adults and $7 for seniors. Call or check the website for location and hours of operation.

Cervini Haas Gallery This is Scottsdale's premier gallery of fine contemporary crafts, including furniture, ceramics, and jewelry. The works on display here often push the envelope of what's possible in any given medium. 7007 E. Fifth Ave., Scottsdale. ✆ **480/429-6116.** www.cervinihaas.com.

Lisa Sette Gallery If you aren't a fan of cowboy or Native American art, don't despair. Instead, drop by this gallery, which always mounts eclectic and fascinating shows. You might even catch a show by William Wegman, America's favorite dog photographer. 4142 N. Marshall Way, Scottsdale. ✆ **480/990-7342.** www.lisasettegallery.com.

Overland Gallery of Fine Art ★★ Traditional Western and Russian Impressionist paintings form the backbone of this gallery's offerings. The works on display here are museum-quality and prices sometimes approach $100,000. Definitely worth a look. The gallery also shows the angular Southwest landscapes of Ed Mell. 7155 Main St., Scottsdale. ✆ **800/920-0220** or 480/947-1934. www.overlandgallery.com.

Wilde Meyer Gallery Brightly colored and playful are the norm at this gallery, which represents Linda Carter Holman, a Southwestern favorite who does cowgirl-inspired paintings. There is another Wilde Meyer gallery at 7100 E. Main St., Scottsdale (✆ **480/947-1489**). 4142 N. Marshall Way, Scottsdale. ✆ **480/945-2323.** www.wildemeyer.com.

BOOKS

Major chain bookstores in the area include **Borders,** at Biltmore Fashion Park, 2402 E. Camelback Rd., Phoenix (✆ 602/957-6660), at the Waterfront, 7135 E. Camelback Rd., Scottsdale (✆ 480/423-0700), and at 4555 E. Cactus Rd., Phoenix (✆ 602/953-9699); and **Barnes & Noble,** 10235 N. Metro Pkwy. E., Phoenix (✆ 602/678-0088), in Kierland Commons, North Scottsdale Road and Greenway Road, Scottsdale (✆ 480/948-8551), 10500 N. 90th St., Scottsdale (✆ 480/391-0048), and Tempe Marketplace, 2000 E. Rio Salado Pkwy. (✆ 480/894-6954).

Guidon Books Whether you're already a student of Western and Civil War history or have only recently developed an interest in the past, this cramped little bookshop in Old Town Scottsdale should not be missed. Rare and out-of-print books are a specialty, but there are plenty of new books as well. Western Americana and the Civil War are the main focus here. 7117 W. Main St., Scottsdale. ✆ **480/945-8811.** www.guidon.com.

FASHION

In addition to the options mentioned below, there are lots of great shops in malls all over the city. Favorite destinations for upscale fashions include Scottsdale Fashion Square, Biltmore Fashion Park, the SHOPS Gainey Village, The Borgata of Scottsdale, and el Pedregal Shops & Dining at The Boulders. See "Malls & Shopping Centers," below, for details.

For cowboy and cowgirl attire, see "Western Wear," below.

Conrad Leather Boutique It may be hot when you visit Arizona, but remember, you have to go home where it's probably a whole lot cooler. If you need a new leather jacket or belt, there's no better place in the Valley to look than this north Scottsdale boutique. Beautiful leather jackets for both men and women fill the shop. In el Pedregal, 34505 N. Scottsdale Rd., Ste. E-7, Scottsdale. ✆ **480/488-2190.**

Electric Couture With its way-over-the-top supercluttered decor, this shop feels a bit like a cross between a drag queen's boutique and a bordello supply store. Got you curious? The clothes are sexy, that's for sure, and you have to be young and shapely to look good in anything they sell here. It's just such a fun shop, though—check it out even if you have no intention of buying. Also be sure to check out Electric Denim, 15435 N. Scottsdale Rd., Scottsdale (✆ **480/315-8184**), which is adjacent to a second Electric Couture (✆ **480/948-9341**). Scottsdale Fashion Square, 7014 E. Camelback Rd., Phoenix. ✆ **480/947-0651.** www.electriccouture.com.

Scottsdale Jean Company If you're searching for the latest high-fashion jeans, don't leave town without dropping by this shop in north Scottsdale. It has the biggest and best selection of jeans in the city. 14747 N. Northsight Blvd. (at Raintree Dr., on the northeast corner), Scottsdale. ✆ **888/255-9987** or 480/905-9300. www.scottsdalejc.com.

Stefan Mann Purses, purses, purses. Gorgeous leather purses, wallets, and luggage are to be had here at Stefan Mann, which has been in business for more than 25 years. If you're constantly on the prowl for a standout handbag, you'll certainly find something here. In el Pedregal, 34505 N. Scottsdale Rd., Ste. J-6, Scottsdale. ✆ **480/488-3371.** www.stefanmann.com.

GIFTS & SOUVENIRS

The Store @ Scottsdale Center for the Performing Arts ★ This gift shop on the downtown Scottsdale mall has a wonderful selection of fun, contemporary, and artistic gifts, including lots of jewelry. There's another gift shop next door at the Scottsdale Museum of Contemporary Art. 7380 E. Second St., Scottsdale. ✆ **480/874-4644.** www.scottsdaleperformingarts.com.

Two Plates Full It's worth wandering through this shop just to marvel at all the bright colors and fun designs. Featuring functional art and crafts, home accessories, and jewelry, this is a great place to shop for unique gifts. In the Borgata, 6166 N. Scottsdale Rd., Ste. 402, Scottsdale. ✆ **480/443-3241.** www.twoplatesfull.com.

JEWELRY

Cornelis Hollander Although this shop is much smaller and not nearly as dramatic as the nearby Jewelry by Gauthier store (see below), the designs are just as cutting edge. Whether you're looking for classic chic or trendy modern designs, you'll find plenty to interest you here. 4151 N. Marshall Way, Scottsdale. ✆ **800/677-6821** or 480/423-5000. www.cornelishollander.com.

Jewelry by Gauthier This elegant store sells the designs of the phenomenally talented Scott Gauthier. The stylishly modern pieces use precious stones and are miniature works of art. There's a second, much smaller shop in Kierland Commons, 15034 N. Scottsdale Rd., Ste. 120 (✆ **480/443-4030**). 4211 N. Marshall Way, Scottsdale. ✆ **888/411-3232** or 480/941-1707. www.jewelrybygauthier.com.

Sami This little jewelry store, northeast of Scottsdale in the town of Fountain Hills, specializes in amethyst from a mine in the nearby Four Peaks Mountains. The mine has been producing gemstones since Spanish colonial times, and the very best of the stones wind up at this shop. You'll also find Arizona peridot and "anthill" garnet jewelry here. 16704 Avenue of the Fountains, Ste. 100, Fountain Hills. ✆ **877/376-6323** or 480/837-8168. www.samifinejewelry.com.

MALLS & SHOPPING CENTERS

While locals don't want to call it a shopping center, the **Scottsdale Waterfront,** an ambitious mixed-use development along a canal at the corner of Camelback and Scottsdale roads, is essentially just that. There are shops, most of which are either national chains or satellites of popular local boutiques, restaurants (once again national and local chains), and high-rise residential towers. The only real difference between the Scottsdale Waterfront and the attached Scottsdale Fashion Square is that at the waterfront you actually have to (get to?) walk around outside. On the south side of the canal, you'll find the fun little boutiques of the **Mix Shops** (www.shopthemix.com), which is part of the **SouthBridge** development.

Biltmore Fashion Park ★ This open-air shopping plaza with garden courtyards is one of the most pleasant places to shop in Phoenix. Saks Fifth Avenue and Macy's are the two anchors, while smaller storefronts bear familiar names, including Tommy Bahama, Victoria's Secret, and Ralph Lauren. There are also nearly a dozen restaurants here. 2502 E. Camelback Rd. (at 24th St.). ✆ **602/955-8400.** www.shopbiltmore.com.

The Borgata of Scottsdale ★ Designed to resemble the medieval Italian village of San Gimignano, complete with turrets, stone walls, and ramparts, the Borgata is far and away the most architecturally interesting mall in the Valley. Within its walls, you'll find about 25 upscale boutiques, galleries, and restaurants. 6166 N. Scottsdale Rd. ✆ **602/953-6311.** www.borgata.com.

el Pedregal Shops & Dining at The Boulders ★ Adjacent to the Boulders resort 30 minutes north of Old Scottsdale, el Pedregal is the most self-consciously Southwestern shopping center in the Valley, and it's worth the long drive out just to see the neo–Santa Fe/Moroccan architecture. The shops offer high-end merchandise, fashions, and art. 34505 N. Scottsdale Rd., Carefree. ✆ **480/488-1072.** www.elpedregal.com.

Kierland Commons ★★ The urban-village concept of a shopping center—narrow streets, sidewalks, and residences mixed in with retail space—has taken off all over the country, and here in Scottsdale, the concept has taken on Texas-size proportions. However, despite the grand scale of this shopping center, it has a great feel. You'll find Tommy Bahama, Ann Taylor Loft, Crate & Barrel, and even a few local boutiques, including 42 Saint, which stocks fashions not found elsewhere. 15205 N. Scottsdale Rd. ✆ **480/348-1577.** www.kierlandcommons.com.

Scottsdale Fashion Square Scottsdale has long been the Valley's shopping mecca, and for years this huge mall has been the reason why. It now houses four major department stores—Nordstrom, Dillard's, Neiman Marcus, and Macy's—and smaller stores such as Coach, Eddie Bauer, J. Crew, and Louis Vuitton. 7014–590 E. Camelback Rd. (at Scottsdale Rd.), Scottsdale. ✆ **480/941-2140.** www.fashionsquare.com.

the SHOPS Gainey Village This upscale shopping center is much smaller than Kierland Commons farther up Scottsdale Road, but is no less impressive, especially after dark when lights illuminate the tall palm trees. There may not be a more impressive concentration of women's clothing stores anywhere in Scottsdale. 8777–8989 N. Scottsdale Rd. (at Doubletree Ranch Rd.). ✆ **602/953-6150.** www.theshopsgaineyvillage.com.

NATIVE AMERICAN ARTS, CRAFTS & JEWELRY

Bischoff's at the Park ★★ This museumlike store and gallery is affiliated with another Bischoff's right across the street (see "Gifts & Souvenirs," above). However, this outpost carries higher-end jewelry; Western-style home furnishings; and clothing, ceramics, sculptures, contemporary paintings, and books and music with a regional theme. 3925 N. Brown Ave., Scottsdale. ✆ **480/946-6155.**

Faust Gallery ★ Old Native American baskets and pottery, as well as old and new Navajo rugs, are the specialties at this interesting shop. It also sells Native American and Southwestern art, including ceramics, paintings, bronzes, and unusual sculptures. 7103 E. Main St., Scottsdale. ✆ **480/268-1260.** www.faustgallery.com.

Gilbert Ortega Gallery & Museum You'll find Gilbert Ortega shops all over the Valley, but this is the biggest and best. As the name implies, there are museum displays throughout the store. Jewelry is the main attraction, but there are also baskets, sculptures, pottery, rugs, paintings, and kachina dolls. 3925 N. Scottsdale Rd. ✆ **480/990-1808.**

Heard Museum Gift Shop The Heard Museum (see "Seeing the Sights," earlier in this chapter) has an astonishing collection of well-crafted Native American jewelry, art, and crafts of all kinds. This is the best place in the Valley to shop for Native American arts and crafts; you can be absolutely assured of the quality. Because the store doesn't have to charge sales tax, you'll also save a bit of money. Also be sure to check out the affiliated Berlin Gallery, which features contemporary Native American art. At the Heard Museum, 2301 N. Central Ave. ✆ **602/252-8344.** www.heard.org.

John C. Hill Antique Indian Art ★★ While shops selling Native American art and artifacts abound in Scottsdale, few offer the high quality available in this tiny shop. Not only does the store have one of the finest selections of Navajo rugs in the Valley, including quite a few older rugs, but there also are kachina dolls, superb pieces of Navajo and Zuni silver-and-turquoise jewelry, baskets, and pottery. 6962 E. First Ave., Ste. 104, Scottsdale. ✆ **480/946-2910.** www.johnhillgallery.com.

Old Territorial Shop ★★ Owned and operated by Alston and Deborah Neal, this is the oldest Indian arts-and-crafts store on Main Street, and it offers good values on jewelry, concho belts, kachina dolls, fetishes, pottery, and Navajo rugs. 7077 E. Main St., Ste. 7, Scottsdale. ✆ **480/945-5432.** www.oldterritorialshop.com.

River Trading Post If you are interested in getting into collecting Native American art or artifacts, this is a good place to get in on the ground floor. Quality is high and prices are relatively low. Not only are there high-quality Navajo rugs, but there are also museum-quality pieces of ancient Southwestern pottery. 7033 E. Main St., Scottsdale. ✆ **866/426-6901** or 480/444-0001. www.rivertradingpost.com.

WESTERN WEAR

Az-Tex Hat Company If you're looking to bring home a cowboy hat, this is the best place in Scottsdale to do your shopping. The small shop in Old Scottsdale offers custom shaping and fitting of both felt and woven hats. 3903 N. Scottsdale Rd., Scottsdale. ✆ **800/972-2116** or 480/481-9900. www.aztexhats.com.

Out West ★ If the revival of 1950s cowboy fashions and interior decor has hit your nostalgia button, then you'll want to high-tail it up to this eclectic shop. All things Western are available, and the fashions are both beautiful and fun (although fancy and pricey). 7003 E. Cave Creek Rd., Cave Creek. ✆ **480/488-0180.** www.outwestmercantile.com.

Saba's Western Stores Since 1927, this store has been outfitting Scottsdale's cowboys and cowgirls, visiting guest ranchers, and anyone else who wants to adopt the look of the Wild West. There's another Saba's around the corner, at 3965 N. Brown Ave. (✆ **480/947-7664**). Call or check the website for other locations around Phoenix. 7254 Main St., Scottsdale. ✆ **877/342-1835** or 480/949-7404. www.sabaswesternwear.com.

10 PHOENIX & SCOTTSDALE AFTER DARK

If you're looking for nightlife in the Valley of the Sun, you won't have to look hard, but you may have to drive quite a way. Although much of the nightlife scene is centered on downtown Scottsdale, Tempe's Mill Avenue, and downtown Phoenix, you'll find things going on all over.

The weekly *Phoenix New Times* tends to have the most comprehensive listings for clubs and concert halls. The Thursday edition of the *Arizona Republic* also lists upcoming events and performances. *Get Out,* published by the *East Valley Tribune,* is another tabloid-format arts-and-entertainment publication that is available free around Scottsdale, Phoenix, and Tempe. Other publications to check for abbreviated listings are *Arizona Key* and *Where Phoenix/Scottsdale,* both of which are free and can usually be found at hotels and resorts.

Tickets to many concerts, theater performances, and sporting events are available through **Ticketmaster** (✆ **866/448-7849;** www.ticketmaster.com), which has outlets at Macy's department stores and Fry's Marketplace grocery stores.

THE PERFORMING ARTS

Downtown Phoenix claims the Valley's greatest concentration of performance halls, but there are major performing-arts venues scattered across the Valley. Calling these many valley venues home are such major companies as the Phoenix Symphony, Scottsdale Symphony Orchestra, Arizona Opera Company, Ballet Arizona, Center Dance Ensemble, Actors Theatre of Phoenix, and Arizona Theatre Company. A wide variety of touring companies also stop in the Valley.

Outdoor Venues & Series

The **Cricket Pavilion,** 2121 N. 83rd Ave., Phoenix (✆ **602/254-7200;** www.cricketpavilion.com), west of downtown and a half-mile north of I-10, between 75th and 83rd avenues, is the city's top outdoor venue. This 20,000-seat amphitheater is open year-round and hosts everything from Broadway musicals to rock concerts.

The **Mesa Amphitheater,** at University Drive and Center Street, Mesa (✆ **480/644-2560;** www.mesaamp.com), is a much smaller amphitheater that holds a wide variety of concerts in spring and summer, and occasionally other times of year as well.

Throughout the year, the **Scottsdale Center for the Arts,** 7380 E. Second St., Scottsdale (✆ **480/994-2787;** www.scottsdaleperformingarts.org), stages outdoor performances in the adjacent Scottsdale Amphitheater on the Scottsdale Civic Center Mall. The Sunday A'fair series runs from January to April, with free concerts from noon to 4:30pm on selected Sundays of each month. Performances range from acoustic blues to zydeco.

Two perennial favorites of Valley residents take place in particularly attractive surroundings. The Music in the Garden concerts at the **Desert Botanical Garden,** 1201 N. Galvin Pkwy., in Papago Park (✆ **480/941-1225** or 480/481-8188; www.dbg.org), are held on Sundays between January and March. The season always includes an eclectic array of musical styles. Tickets are $20 for adults and $8 for children 3 to 12; garden admission is included. Between late March and late June, there are also Friday-night jazz concerts.

Classical Music, Opera & Dance

The **Phoenix Symphony** (✆ **800/776-9080** or 602/495-1999; www.phoenixsymphony.org), the Southwest's leading symphony orchestra, performs at Symphony Hall (tickets mostly run $22–$72).

Opera buffs will want to see what the **Arizona Opera** (✆ **602/266-7464;** www.azopera.org) has scheduled. Each season, this company stages up to five operas, both familiar and more obscure, and splits its time between Phoenix and Tucson. Tickets cost $25 to $144. Performances are held at Symphony Hall.

Ballet Arizona (✆ **602/381-1096;** www.balletaz.org) performs at both the Orpheum Theatre and Symphony Hall and stages both classical and contemporary ballets; tickets

Major Performing-Arts Centers

Symphony Hall, 75 N. Second St. (✆ **602/262-7272;** www.ci.phoenix.az.us/CIVPLAZA/stages.html#SYMPH), is home to the Phoenix Symphony and the Arizona Opera Company. It also hosts touring Broadway shows and various other concerts and theatrical productions.

The **Orpheum Theatre,** 203 W. Adams St. (✆ **602/262-7272**), is an elegant, historic Spanish-colonial baroque theater built in 1929.

Celebrity Theatre, 440 N. 32nd St. (✆ **602/267-1600;** www.celebritytheatre.com), seems to be booking lots of great performers these days, such as Taj Mahal or Ottmar Liebert.

The **Dodge Theatre,** 400 W. Washington St. (✆ **602/379-2800;** www.dodgetheatre.com), which seats from 2,000 to 5,000 people, books top names in entertainment as well as Broadway shows and international touring companies.

The Frank Lloyd Wright–designed **Grady Gammage Auditorium,** Mill Avenue and Apache Boulevard, Tempe (✆ **480/965-3434;** www.asugammage.com), on the Arizona State University campus, hosts everything from barbershop quartets to touring Broadway shows.

The **Scottsdale Center for the Arts,** 7380 E. Second St., Scottsdale (✆ **480/994-2787;** www.scottsdaleperformingarts.org), hosts a variety of performances and series, ranging from alternative dance to classical music.

run $15 to $117. The **Center Dance Ensemble** (✆ **602/252-8497;** www.centerdance.com), the city's contemporary dance company, stages several productions a year at the Herberger Theater Center. Tickets cost $24.

Theater

The **Herberger Theater Center,** 222 E. Monroe St. (✆ **602/254-7399;** www.herbergertheater.org), is the city's main venue for live theater. Its two Broadway-style theaters together host hundreds of performances each year, including productions by the Actors Theatre and the Arizona Theatre Company (ATC). **Actors Theatre** (✆ **602/253-6701** or 602/252-8497 for tickets; www.atphx.org) tends to stage smaller, lesser-known off-Broadway–type works; tickets go for $24 to $42. **ATC** (✆ **602/256-6995;** www.aztheatreco.org) is the state theater company of Arizona. Productions range from world premieres to classics. Tickets run $30 to $77.

Phoenix Theatre, 100 E. McDowell Rd. (✆ **602/254-2151;** www.phoenixtheatre.net), has its performance venue in the Phoenix Art Museum building. Musicals are the mainstays here; tickets to most shows are $25 to $53. If you're staying in Scottsdale and are looking for something to do with the entire family, the **Scottsdale Desert Stages Theatre,** 4720 N. Scottsdale Rd. (✆ **480/483-1664;** www.desertstages.com), stages primarily musicals and children's theater productions. Tickets range from $12 to $25.

THE CLUB & MUSIC SCENE

Even if it were not in the middle of the desert, the Scottsdale club scene would be red-hot. Packed into a few dozen blocks surrounding Old Town Scottsdale, near the corner of Camelback and Scottsdale roads, are dozens of trendy dance clubs and chic bars. This is where visiting celebrities, wealthy fashionistas, and wannabes all come to party. The crowd is young, affluent, and attractive, and with all the beautiful people cruising around in Porsches and limousines, it's easy to think you're in L.A. Cruise along **Stetson Drive,** which is divided into two sections (east and west of Scottsdale Rd.), to find the latest hot spots.

While Scottsdale is the nexus of nightclubbing for the fashion-conscious, the Valley has plenty of clubs and bars for those who don't wear Prada. Other nightlife districts include Tempe's Mill Avenue and downtown Phoenix. **Mill Avenue,** in Tempe, is a good place to wander around in search of your favorite type of music. Because Tempe is a college town, the crowd tends to be young and rowdy. Downtown Phoenix is home to Symphony Hall, the Herberger Theater Center, and several sports bars. However, much of the action revolves around sports events and concerts at US Airways Center and Chase Field.

Clubs come and go quickly, so to find out what's hot, get a copy of the *New Times.* Bars and clubs are allowed to serve alcohol until 2am.

Country

Buffalo Chip Saloon & Steakhouse Cave Creek is the Valley's last Wild West town and is full of cowboy bars. This barnlike place is a local favorite, especially with fans of the Green Bay Packers. There's live country music Thursday through Saturday nights, all-you-can-eat fish fries featuring walleye, and s'mores on the dessert menu. Currently, on the first Sunday of each month, there's cowboy-comedy dinner theater. 6811 E. Cave Creek Rd., Cave Creek. ✆ **480/488-9118.** www.buffalochipsaloon.com.

Handlebar-J This Scottsdale landmark is about as genuine a cowboy bar as you'll find in Phoenix, and cowpokes often stop by when they come in from the ranch. You'll hear live git-down two-steppin' music nightly; free dance lessons are given Wednesday, Thursday, and Sunday at 7pm. 7116 Becker Lane (1 block north of the northwest corner of Scottsdale Rd. and Shea Blvd.), Scottsdale. ✆ **480/948-0110.** www.handlebarj.com. Cover free to $5.

Rusty Spur Saloon A small, rowdy, drinkin'-and-dancin' place frequented by tourists, this bar is the oldest saloon in Scottsdale and is loads of fun, with peanut shells all over the floor, dollar bills stapled to the walls, and live country-music afternoons and evenings. If you're a cowboy or cowgirl at heart, this is the place to party when you're in Scottsdale. 7245 E. Main St., Old Scottsdale. ✆ **480/425-7787.** www.rustyspursaloon.com.

Dance Clubs & Discos

Axis/Radius If you're looking to do a bit of celebrity-spotting, Axis is one of the best places in town to keep your eyes peeled. For many years now, this has been one of Scottsdale's hottest dance clubs and liveliest singles scenes. The two-story glass box is a bold contemporary space with an awesome sound system. These twin clubs are open Thursday through Saturday. 7340 E. Indian Plaza (2 blocks east of Scottsdale Rd. and 1 block south of Camelback Rd.), Scottsdale. ✆ **480/970-1112.** www.axis-radius.com. Cover free to $10.

Barcelona It's big, it's beautiful, and it's busy. This is Scottsdale's premier supper club, and after the dinner crowd gives up its tables Thursday through Saturday nights, Barcelona becomes one of the city's top dance spots. The well-heeled crowd is primarily in their 30s to 50s. 15440 Greenway-Hayden Loop. ✆ **480/603-0370.** www.barcelonadining.com. Cover free to $15 (for men only).

Myst Always packed to the walls with the Valley's beautiful people, Myst is one of the top spots in Scottsdale to see and be seen. The atmosphere is lavishly ostentatious, with various themed rooms. The club is usually open Wednesday, Friday, and Saturday. 7340 E. Shoeman Lane, Scottsdale. ✆ **480/970-5000.** www.mystaz.com. Cover $7–$30.

Pepin Friday and Saturday starting at 10pm and Sunday beginning at 9pm, a DJ plays Latin dance music at this small Spanish restaurant located on the Scottsdale Mall. Friday and Saturday evenings, there are also live flamenco performances. 7363 Scottsdale Mall, Scottsdale. ✆ **480/990-9026.** www.pepinrestaurant.com. Cover $10.

Rock, Jazz & Blues

Char's Has the Blues You wouldn't think to look at this little cottage, but it really does have those mean-and-dirty, low-down blues. All of the best blues brothers and sisters from around the city and around the country make the scene here. 4631 N. Seventh Ave., 4 blocks south of Camelback Rd. ✆ **602/230-0205.** www.charshastheblues.com. Cover free to $10.

Geordie's at the Wrigley Mansion Open only on Friday and Saturday nights, this lounge is inside the historic Wrigley Mansion, which was built between 1929 and 1931 by chewing-gum magnate William Wrigley, Jr. The sprawling mansion is located on a hilltop adjacent to the Arizona Biltmore resort. 2501 E. Telawa Trail. ✆ **602/955-4079.** www.wrigleymansionclub.com.

The Rhythm Room This blues club, long the Valley's most popular, books quite a few national acts as well as the best of the local scene, and has a dance floor if you want to move to the beat. 1019 E. Indian School Rd. ✆ **602/265-4842.** www.rhythmroom.com. Cover free to $33.

THE BAR, LOUNGE & PUB SCENE

AZ88 Located across the park from the Scottsdale Center for the Arts, this sophisticated bar/restaurant has a hip, contemporary ambience that's just right for a martini or a basket of waffle fries before or after a performance. There's also a great patio area. 7353 Scottsdale Mall, Scottsdale. ✆ **480/994-5576.** www.az88.com.

Bar Bianco ★ Located downtown on Heritage Square, this little wine bar is in a restored historic home and is affiliated with Pizzeria Bianco (p. 431), the tiny and ever-popular designer-pizza place next door. This is a very romantic spot for a drink. 609 E. Adams St. ✆ **602/528-3699.** www.pizzeriabianco.com.

Four Peaks Brewing Company Consistently voted the best brewpub in Phoenix, this Tempe establishment, housed in a former creamery, brews good beers and serves decent pub grub. It's a favorite of ASU students. You'll find this pub south of East University Drive, between South Rural Road and South McClintock Drive. There's a second brewpub in north Scottsdale at the corner of Hayden Road and Frank Lloyd Wright Boulevard (✆ 480/991-1795). 1340 E. Eighth St., Tempe. ✆ **480/303-9967.** www.fourpeaks.com.

Hyatt Regency Scottsdale Lobby Bar ★★ The open-air lounge just below the main lobby of this posh Scottsdale resort sets a romantic stage for nightly live music (often flamenco or Caribbean steel drum music). Wood fires burn in patio fire pits, and the terraced gardens offer plenty of dark spots for a bit of romance. 7500 E. Doubletree Ranch Rd., Scottsdale. ✆ **480/444-1234.** www.scottsdale.hyatt.com.

Olive & Ivy ★ With a huge patio right on the canal in the Scottsdale Waterfront, the bar at this restaurant has become *the* place to see and be seen in Scottsdale. There are more than 45 wines available by the glass, and the bartenders mix decent drinks, too. Be sure to dress the part. 7135 E. Camelback Rd., Ste. 195, Scottsdale. ✆ **480/751-2200.** www.foxrestaurantconcepts.com.

T. Cook's Bar ★★ If you aren't planning on having dinner at this opulent Mediterranean restaurant, at least stop by for a cocktail in the bar. With its mix of Spanish colonial and 1950s tropical furnishings, this is as romantic a lounge as you'll find anywhere in the Valley. You can also snuggle with your sweetie out on the patio by the fireplace. At the Royal Palms Resort and Spa, 5200 E. Camelback Rd. ✆ **602/840-3610.** www.royalpalmshotel.com.

Wine Bars

Cave Creek Coffee Co. & Wine Bar Located way up north in the cow town of Cave Creek, this hip coffeehouse doubles as a lively wine bar that also happens to book some great music. Past performers have included Kelly Joe Phelps, Michelle Shocked, Richie Havens, and Rickie Lee Jones. 6033 E. Cave Creek Rd., Cave Creek. ✆ **480/488-0603.** www.cavecreekcoffee.com. Cover free to $60.

Kazimierz World Wine Bar ★ Sort of a spacious speakeasy crossed with a wine cellar, this place, which is associated with the nearby Cowboy Ciao restaurant (p. 420), offers the same wide selection of wines available at the restaurant. There are dozens of wines by the glass and live music several nights each week. The entrance is hard to find (look around back for the big wood door with a sign that says THE TRUTH IS INSIDE), but it's worth seeking out. 7137 E. Stetson Dr., Scottsdale. ✆ **480/946-3004.** www.kazbar.net. Cover $5 (after 8pm).

Postino ★★ This immensely popular wine bar is in the heart of the Arcadia neighborhood, south of Camelback Road, and is housed in a former post office. Casual yet stylish, the bar has garage-style doors that roll up to open the restaurant to the outdoors. Choose from a great selection of wines by the glass and a limited menu of European-inspired appetizers. There's a second Postino at 5144 N. Central Ave. (✆ **602/274-5144**). 3939 E. Campbell Ave. ✆ **602/852-3939.** www.postinowinecafe.com.

Cocktails with a View

The Valley of the Sun has more than its fair share of spectacular views. Unfortunately, most of them are from expensive restaurants. All these restaurants have lounges, though, where, for the price of a drink (and perhaps valet parking), you can sit back and ogle a crimson sunset and the purple mountains' majesty. Among the best choices are the bar at **Different Pointe of View,** at the Pointe Hilton Tapatio Cliffs Resort; **Rustler's Rooste,** at the Arizona Grand Resort; and both the cozy outdoors **edge** and the swanky **jade bar,** at the Sanctuary on Camelback Mountain.

Thirsty Camel Whether you've already made your millions or are still working your way up the corporate ladder, you owe it to yourself to spend a little time in the lap of luxury. You may never drink in more ostentatious surroundings than here at Arizona's most luxurious resort. The view is one of the best in the city. At the Phoenician, 6000 E. Camelback Rd. ✆ **480/941-8200.** www.thephoenician.com.

The Wright Bar & Squaw Peak Terrace Can't afford the lifestyles of the rich and famous? For the cost of a couple of drinks, you can sink into a seat here at the Biltmore's main lounge and watch the sunset test its color palette on Piestewa Peak. Alternatively, you can slide into a seat near the piano and let the waves of mellow jazz wash over you. At the Arizona Biltmore Resort & Spa, 2400 E. Missouri Ave. ✆ **602/381-7632.** www.arizonabiltmore.com.

Sports Bars

Alice Cooper'stown Sports and rock mix it up at this downtown restaurant/bar run by, you guessed it, Alice Cooper. Chase Field, where the Arizona Diamondbacks play ball, is only a block away. See p. 431 for more information. 101 E. Jackson St. ✆ **602/253-7337.** www.alicecooperstown.com.

Don & Charlie's Although this is primarily a steakhouse, it also has the best sports bar in Scottsdale. What makes Don & Charlie's such a great sports bar is not the size or number of its TVs, but rather all the sports memorabilia on the walls. 7501 E. Camelback Rd., Scottsdale. ✆ **480/990-0900.** www.donandcharlies.com.

Majerle's Sports Grill If you're a Phoenix Suns fan, you won't want to miss this sports bar located only a couple of blocks from US Airways Center, where the Suns play. Suns memorabilia covers the walls, and who knows, you just might bump into a team member or two while you're here. 24 N. Second St. ✆ **602/253-0118.** www.majerles.com.

Gay & Lesbian Bars & Clubs

Amsterdam/Club Miami/Malibu Beach Bar This downtown Phoenix nightclub complex may not look like much from the outside, but through the doors, you'll find a classy spot that's known across the Valley for its great martinis. There's usually a female impersonator 1 night of the week, and other nights, there's live music or DJ dance music. 718 N. Central Ave. ✆ **602/258-6122.** www.amsterdambar.com.

Charlie's If you're a cowpoke and want to do some boot scootin' while you're in town, head on over to Charlie's. This club is the home of the Arizona Gay Rodeo Association, and there's country music, clogging and line dance lessons, and an after-hours scene on the weekends. 727 W. Camelback Rd. ✆ **602/265-0224.** www.charliesphoenix.com. Cover free to $3.

Forbidden Night Club Forbidden, on the western edge of Old Town Scottsdale, is pretty much the only gay nightclub in a town packed with nightclubs for straights. So, if you're gay and you're staying in Scottsdale it's either this or a long drive into Phoenix (and back). 6820 E. Fifth Ave., Scottsdale. ✆ **480/994-5176.** www.forbiddenaz.com. Cover free to $5.

11 A SIDE TRIP: THE APACHE TRAIL ★★

There isn't a whole lot of desert or history left in Phoenix, but only an hour's drive to the east you'll find quite a bit of both. The **Apache Trail,** a narrow, winding, partially gravel road that snakes its way around the north side of the Superstition Mountains, offers some of the most scenic desert driving in central Arizona. Along the way are ghost towns and ancient ruins, saguaros and century plants, reservoirs and hiking trails. You could easily spend a couple days traveling this route, though most people make it a day trip. Pick and choose the stops that appeal to you, and be sure to get an early start. The gravel section of the road is well graded and is passable for regular passenger cars.

If you'd rather leave the driving to someone else, **Apache Trail Tours** (✆ **480/982-7661;** www.apachetrailtours.com) offers guided half-day and full-day tours along the Apache Trail. This company also offers off-road adventures in the Superstition Mountains and Four Peaks area. Tours range in price from $65 to $189.

To start this drive, head east on US 60 to the town of Apache Junction, and then go north on Ariz. 88. About 4 miles out of town is **Goldfield Ghost Town,** a reconstructed gold-mining town (see "Wild West Theme Towns" under "Seeing the Sights," earlier in this chapter). Allow plenty of time if you plan to stop here.

Not far from Goldfield is **Lost Dutchman State Park,** 6109 N. Apache Trail (✆ **480/982-4485;** www.azstateparks.com), where you can hike into the rugged Superstition Mountains and see what the region's gold seekers were up against. Springtime wildflower displays here can be absolutely gorgeous. Park admission is $5 per vehicle ($3 during the summer); the campground here charges $12 per site.

Continuing northeast, you'll reach **Canyon Lake,** set in a deep canyon flanked by colorful cliffs and rugged rock formations. It's the first of three reservoirs you'll pass on this drive. The lakes provide much of Phoenix's drinking water, without which the city would never have been able to grow as large as it is today. At Canyon Lake, you can swim at the Acacia Picnic Area or the nearby Boulder Picnic Area, which is in a pretty side cove. You can also take a cruise on the ***Dolly* steamboat** (✆ **480/827-9144;** www.dollysteamboat.com). A 90-minute jaunt on this reproduction paddle-wheeler costs $20 for adults and $12 for children 5 to 12. Lunch ($38) and dinner ($57 for adults and $38 for children) cruises are also available, and there's a lakeside restaurant at the boat landing. But if you're at all hungry, hold out for nearby **Tortilla Flat** (✆ **480/984-1776;** www.tortillaflataz.com), an old stagecoach stop with a restaurant, saloon, and general store. The ceiling and interior walls of this funky old place are plastered with thousands of dollar bills that have been left by previous customers. If it's hot out, be sure to stop in at the general store for some prickly-pear ice cream (guaranteed spineless).

A few miles past Tortilla Flat, the pavement ends and the truly spectacular desert scenery begins. Among the rocky ridges, arroyos, and canyons of this stretch of road, you'll see saguaro cactuses and century plants (a type of agave that dies after sending up its flower stalk, which can reach heights of 15 ft.). Next you'll come to **Apache Lake,** which is not nearly as spectacular as Canyon Lake, though it does have the **Apache Lake Marina and Resort** (✆ **928/467-2511;** www.apachelake.com).

Shortly before reaching pavement again, you'll see **Theodore Roosevelt Dam.** This dam, built in 1911, forms Roosevelt Lake and, despite its concrete face, is the largest masonry dam in the world.

Continuing on Ariz. 88, you'll next come to **Tonto National Monument** ★ (✆ **928/467-2241;** www.nps.gov/tont), which preserves some of the southernmost cliff dwellings in Arizona. These pueblos were occupied between about 1300 and 1450 by the Salado people and are some of the few remaining traces of this tribe, which once cultivated lands now flooded by Roosevelt Lake. The lower ruins are a half-mile up a steep trail from the visitor center, and the upper ruins are a 3-mile round-trip hike. The lower ruins are open daily year-round; the upper ruins are open November through April on guided tours (these tours are also offered on Sat mornings in May and Oct). Tour reservations are required (reserve at least 2 weeks in advance). The park is open daily (except Christmas) from 8am to 5pm (you must begin the lower ruin trail by 4pm); admission is $3.

Keep going on Ariz. 88 to the copper-mining town of **Globe.** Although you can't see the mines themselves, the tailings (remains of rock removed from the copper ore) can be

En Route to Tucson

Driving southeast from Phoenix for about 60 miles will bring you to the Casa Grande and Coolidge area, where you can learn about the Hohokam people who once inhabited this region, and, in spring, see desert wildflowers.

Casa Grande Ruins National Monument ★★, located outside Coolidge, preserves one of the most unusual Indian ruins in the state; an earth-walled structure built 650 years ago by the Hohokam people. Instead of using adobe bricks or stones, the people who built this structure used layers of hard-packed soil. Located 1 mile north of Coolidge on Arizona 87 (✆ **520/723-3172;** www.nps.gov/cagr). Admission is $5.

Alternatively, if you're heading to Tucson by way of I-10, consider a stop at **Picacho Peak State Park** ★★, 35 miles northwest of Tucson at exit 219 (✆ **520/466-3183;** www.azstateparks.com). Picacho Peak, which rises 1,500 feet above the desert, is a visual landmark for miles around. Hiking trails around the peak and up to the summit are especially popular in spring, when the wildflowers bloom. Admission is $6 per car ($3 in summer), for up to 4 adults.

seen piled high all around the town. From Globe, head west on US 60. Three miles west of Superior, you'll come to **Boyce Thompson Arboretum** ★★, 37615 US 60 (✆ **520/689-2811;** arboretum.ag.arizona.edu), dedicated to researching and propagating desert plants. This was the nation's first botanical garden established in the desert and is set in two small, rugged canyons. From the impressive cactus gardens, you can gaze up at sun-baked cliffs before ducking into a forest of eucalyptus trees that grow along a stream. September through April, the arboretum is open daily from 8am to 5pm, and May through August, it's open 6am to 3pm. Admission is $7.50 for adults and $3 for children 5 to 12. There are guided tours of the garden daily; call for a schedule.

14 Southern Arizona

In the southeastern corner of Arizona, the mile-high grasslands, punctuated by forested mountain ranges, have long supported vast ranches where cattle range across wide-open plains. It was also here that much of America's now-legendary Western history took place. Wyatt Earp and the Clantons shot it out at Tombstone's O.K. Corral, Doc Holliday played his cards, and Cochise and Geronimo staged the last Indian rebellions. Cavalries charged, and prospectors wandered the wilderness in search of the mother lode. Today, ghost towns litter the landscape of southeastern Arizona, but the past is kept alive by people searching for a glimpse of the Wild West.

The combination of low deserts, high plains, and even higher mountains has given this region a fascinating diversity of landscapes. Giant saguaros cover the slopes of the Sonoran Desert throughout much of southern Arizona, and in the western parts of this region, organ pipe cactuses reach the northern limit of their range. In the cool mountains, cactuses give way to pines, and passing clouds bring snow and rain. Narrow canyons and broad valleys, fed by the rain and snowmelt, provide habitat for hundreds of species of birds and other wildlife. This is the northernmost range for many birds usually found only south of the border. Consequently, southeastern Arizona has become one of the nation's most important bird-watching spots.

1 ORGAN PIPE CACTUS NATIONAL MONUMENT ★★

135 miles S of Phoenix; 140 miles W of Tucson; 185 miles SE of Yuma

Located roughly midway between Yuma and Tucson, Organ Pipe Cactus National Monument is a preserve for the rare cactus for which the monument is named. The organ pipe cactus resembles the saguaro cactus in many ways, but instead of forming a single main trunk, organ pipes have many trunks, some 20 feet tall, that resemble—you guessed it—organ pipes.

This is a rugged region with few towns or services. To the west lie the inaccessible Cabeza Prieta National Wildlife Refuge and the Barry M. Goldwater Air Force Range (a bombing range), and to the east is the large Tohono O'odham Indian Reservation. The only motels in the area are in the small town of Ajo, a former company town that was built to house copper mine workers. The downtown plaza, with its tall palm trees, covered walkways, and arches, has the look and feel of a Mexican town square. Be sure to gas up your car before leaving Ajo.

ESSENTIALS

GETTING THERE From Tucson, take Ariz. 86 west to Why, and turn south on Ariz. 85. From Yuma, take I-8 east to Gila Bend and drive south on Ariz. 85.

FEES The park entry fee is $8 per car.

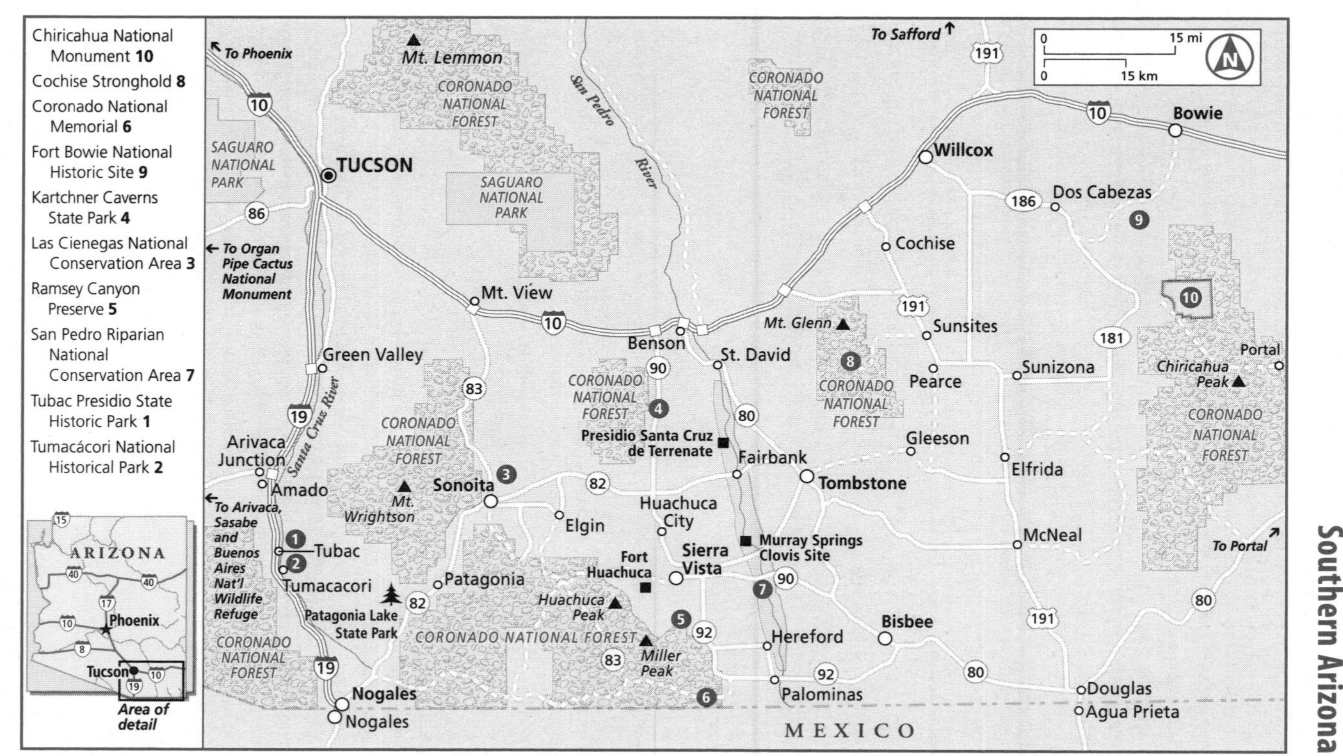
Chiricahua National Monument 10
Cochise Stronghold 8
Coronado National Memorial 6
Fort Bowie National Historic Site 9
Kartchner Caverns State Park 4
Las Cienegas National Conservation Area 3
Ramsey Canyon Preserve 5
San Pedro Riparian National Conservation Area 7
Tubac Presidio State Historic Park 1
Tumacácori National Historical Park 2
ARIZONA
Phoenix
Tucson
Area of detail
To Phoenix
To Organ Pipe Cactus National Monument
To Arivaca, Sasabe and Buenos Aires Nat'l Wildlife Refuge
To Safford
To Portal
0 15 mi
0 15 km
TUCSON
Mt. Lemmon
CORONADO NATIONAL FOREST
SAGUARO NATIONAL PARK
San Pedro River
Santa Cruz River
Mt. View
Benson
St. David
Willcox
Bowie
Dos Cabezas
Cochise
Mt. Glenn
Sunsites
Pearce
Sunizona
Portal
Chiricahua Peak
Gleeson
Elfrida
McNeal
Green Valley
Arivaca Junction
Amado
Tubac
Tumacacori
Mt. Wrightson
Sonoita
Elgin
Patagonia
Patagonia Lake State Park
Presidio Santa Cruz de Terrenate
Fairbank
Tombstone
Huachuca City
Sierra Vista
Fort Huachuca
Murray Springs Clovis Site
Huachuca Peak
Miller Peak
Hereford
Bisbee
Palominas
Douglas
Agua Prieta
Nogales
Nogales
MEXICO

VISITOR INFORMATION For information, contact **Organ Pipe Cactus National Monument** (✆ **520/387-6849;** www.nps.gov/orpi). The visitor center is open daily from 8am to 5pm, although the park itself is open 24 hours a day. The visitor center is closed Thanksgiving and Christmas.

EXPLORING THE MONUMENT

Two well-graded gravel roads lead through different sections of this large national monument, and many visitors are content to just drive through this unusual landscape. For the best scenery in the park, follow Ajo Mountain Drive, a 21-mile one-way loop, that meanders through the rugged foothills of the Ajo Mountains. Along this route, you can get out and hike the Arch Canyon, Estes Canyon, or Bull Pasture trails. Alternatively, if you are short on time, take Puerto Blanco Drive, a 5-mile route leading to the Pinkley Peak picnic area. Guides available at the park's visitor center explain natural features of the landscape along both drives. In the winter, there are guided van tours of Ajo Mountain Drive, as well as guided hikes. Much of the monument is now closed to the public due to safety concerns about the use of this area by illegal immigrants crossing the border from Mexico. Be sure to check with the national monument before planning any hikes.

WHERE TO STAY

There are two campgrounds within the park. Campsites are $8 in primitive **Alamo Campground** and $12 in the more developed **Twin Peaks Campground.** The nearest lodgings are in Ajo, with several old and very basic motels as well as a B&B. There are also plenty of budget chain motels in the town of Gila Bend, 70 miles north of the monument.

Guest House Inn Bed & Breakfast Built in 1925 as a guesthouse for mining executives, this B&B has attractive gardens in the front yard, a mesquite thicket off to one side, and a modern Southwestern feel to its interior decor. Guest rooms are simply furnished with reproduction antique and Southwestern furnishings. There are sunrooms on both the north and the south sides of the house.

700 Guest House Rd., Ajo, AZ 85321. ✆ **520/387-6133.** www.guesthouseinn.biz. 4 units. $89 double. Rates include full breakfast. Children 4 and under stay free in parent's room. MC, V. *In room:* A/C, fridge, hair dryer, Internet.

EN ROUTE TO TUCSON

If you're on your way from Organ Pipe Cactus National Monument to Tucson, you will pass through the large Tohono O'odham Indian Reservation. To learn more about this tribe, stop at the **Tohono O'odham Nation Cultural Center & Museum,** Fresnal Canyon Road, Topawa (✆ **520/383-0201**), south of the community of Sells. The museum is in a beautiful modern building with attractive gardens, and, although displays are designed primarily for tribal members, there is also plenty to interest anyone not from the reservation. A gift shop sells baskets, native wild foods, and other interesting gift items. The museum is open Monday through Saturday from 10am to 4pm; admission is free. To find the museum, drive 9 miles south from Sells on Indian Rte. 19 and watch for a water tower. Turn left here onto unpaved Fresnal Canyon Road and drive a quarter-mile.

2 TUBAC ★★ & ENVIRONS

45 miles S of Tucson; 21 miles N of Nogales; 84 miles W of Sierra Vista

Located in the fertile valley of the Santa Cruz River 45 miles south of Tucson, Tubac is one of Arizona's largest arts communities and home to a developing retirement community. Because the town's old buildings also house more than 80 shops selling fine arts, crafts, unusual gifts, and lots of Southwest souvenirs, Tubac is one of southern Arizona's most popular destinations.

After visiting Tubac Presidio State Historic Park and Tumacácori National Historical Park to learn about the area's history, you'll probably want to spend some time browsing through the shops. If you happen to be visiting between June and September, keep in mind that many of the local artists leave town during the summer and local shops tend to close on weekdays. During the busy season from October to May, however, shops are open daily.

ESSENTIALS

GETTING THERE The Santa Cruz Valley towns of Amado, Tubac, and Tumacácori are all due south of Tucson on I-19.

VISITOR INFORMATION For information on Tubac and Tumacácori, contact the **Tubac Chamber of Commerce** (✆ **520/398-2704;** www.tubacaz.com) or the **Tubac-Santa Cruz Visitor Center,** 4 Plaza Rd. (✆ **520/398-0007;** www.toursantacruz.com).

ART & HISTORY IN THE SANTA CRUZ VALLEY

Tubac Center of the Arts ★ Tubac is an arts community, and this Spanish colonial building serves as its center for cultural activities. Throughout the season, the center features workshops, traveling exhibitions, juried shows, an annual crafts show, and theater and music performances. The quality of the art at these shows is generally better than what's found in most of the surrounding stores. There is also a good little gift shop here.

9 Plaza Rd. ✆ **520/398-2371.** www.tubacarts.org. Admission by donation. Mon–Sat 10am–4:30pm; Sun 1–4:30pm. Closed mid-May to Labor Day and major holidays.

Tubac Presidio State Historic Park Although little remains of the old presidio (fort) other than buried foundation walls, this small park does a good job of presenting the region's Spanish colonial history. Park exhibits focus on Spanish soldiers, Native Americans, religion, and contemporary Hispanic culture in southern Arizona. Also on the grounds is the old Tubac School, built in 1885 and the oldest schoolhouse in the state. Living-history presentations are staged October through March on the first and third Sundays of the month between 1 and 4pm. Among the characters you'll meet are Spanish soldiers, settlers, and friars.

Presidio Dr. ✆ **520/398-2252.** www.azstateparks.com. Admission $3 adults, $1 children 7–13, free for children 6 and under. Thurs–Mon 9am–5pm. Closed Christmas.

Tumacácori National Historical Park ★ Founded in 1691 by Jesuit missionary and explorer Father Eusebio Francisco Kino, San José de Tumacácori mission was one of the first Anglo settlements in what is today Arizona. Father Kino's mission was to convert the Pima Indians, and for the first 60 years, the mission was successful. However, in 1751, during the Pima Revolt, the mission was destroyed. For the next 70 years, this mission struggled to survive, but during the 1820s, an adobe mission church was constructed. Today, the mission ruins are a silent and haunting reminder of the role that Spanish missionaries played in settling the Southwest. Much of the old adobe mission church still stands, and the Spanish architectural influences can readily be seen. A small museum contains exhibits on mission life and the history of the region. On weekends between October and April, Native American and Mexican craftspeople give demonstrations of indigenous crafts. February through April, there are tours to the nearby mission ruins of San Cayetano de Calabazas and Guevavi. These tours are by reservation (✆ **866/508-0094** or 520/398-2655) and cost $20 per person ($36 per person for living-history tours). **La Fiesta de Tumacácori,** a celebration of Indian, Hispanic, and Anglo cultures, is held the first weekend of December.

1895 E. Frontage Rd. ✆ **520/398-2341.** www.nps.gov/tuma. Admission $3 adults, free for children 15 and under. Daily 9am–5pm. Closed Thanksgiving and Christmas. Take I-19 to exit 29; Tumacácori is 3 miles south of Tubac.

SHOPPING

While tourist brochures like to tout Tubac as an artists' community, the town is more of a Southwest souvenir mecca. There are a few genuine art galleries here, but you have to look hard amid the many tourist shops to find the real gems.

Some of the better fine art in the area is at the **Karin Newby Gallery,** Mercado de Baca, 19 Tubac Rd. (✆ **888/398-9662** or 520/398-9662; www.karinnewbygallery.com), which also has a large sculpture garden. For traditional Western art, some by members of the prestigious Cowboy Artists of America, visit **Big Horn Galleries,** 37 Tubac Rd. (✆ **520/398-9209;** www.bighorngalleries.com).

If you want to take the flavor of the area home, stop in at the **Santa Cruz Chili & Spice Company** ★, 1868 E. Frontage Rd. (✆ **520/398-2591;** www.santacruzchili.com). At this combination store and packing plant near Tumacácori National Historical Park, you'll find all things hot (chiles, hot sauces, salsas) arranged on the shelves of one of the more genuine Tubac-area institutions. The shop is open Monday through Friday from 8am to 5pm and Saturday from 10am to 5pm.

BUENOS AIRES NATIONAL WILDLIFE REFUGE ★

If you're a bird-watcher, you'll definitely want to make the trip to **Buenos Aires National Wildlife Refuge,** P.O. Box 109, Sasabe, AZ 85633 (✆ **520/823-4251;** www.fws.gov/southwest/refuges/arizona/buenosaires/index.html), about 28 miles from Tubac. To get here, head north from Tubac on I-19 to Arivaca Junction, then drive west on a winding two-lane road. The refuge begins just outside of Arivaca.

Your first stop should be **Arivaca Cienega,** a quarter of a mile east of Arivaca. *Cienega* is Spanish for "marsh," and that is exactly what you'll find here. A boardwalk leads across this marsh, which is fed by seven springs that provide year-round water and consequently attract a wide variety of bird life. This is one of the few places in the United States where you can see a gray hawk, and vermilion flycatchers are quite common. Other good birding spots within the refuge include **Arivaca Creek,** 2 miles west of Arivaca, and **Aguirre Lake,** a half-mile north of the refuge headquarters and visitor center, which is off Ariz. 286, north of Sasabe.

The **visitor center** is a good place to spot one of the refuge's rarest birds, the masked bobwhite quail. These quail disappeared from Arizona in the late 19th century, but have been reintroduced in the refuge. Other birds you might spot outside the visitor center include Bendire's thrashers, Chihuahuan ravens, canyon towhees, and green-tailed towhees. The visitor center is open daily from 7:30am to 4pm (closed Thanksgiving, Christmas, New Year's Day, and summer weekends).

Other wildlife in the refuge includes pronghorn antelopes, javelinas, coatimundis, white-tailed deer, mule deer, and coyotes. Guided birding and other tours are offered weekends November through April. Call for details; some walks require reservations.

These roads also offer good mountain biking. If you're looking for a strenuous hike, try the **Mustang Trail,** which has its trail head 2 miles west of Arivaca. The trail climbs from Arivaca Creek into the surrounding dry hills and makes for a 5-mile round-trip hike.

GETTING OUTSIDE

Linking Tubac with Tumacácori is the 8-mile **de Anza Trail,** which follows the Santa Cruz River for much of its route and passes through forests and grasslands. This trail is part of the **Juan Bautista de Anza National Historic Trail,** which stretches from Nogales to San Francisco and commemorates the overland journey of the Spanish captain who, in 1775 and 1776, led a small band of colonists overland to California. These settlers founded what is now the city of San Francisco. Today, bird-watching is the most popular activity along the trail. The most convenient trail head is beside Tubac Presidio State Historic Park. **Rex Ranch** (✆ **520/398-2914;** www.rexranch.com) offers horseback rides starting at $40 per hour.

If golf is more your speed, you can play a round at the **Tubac Golf Resort & Spa** (✆ **520/398-2211;** www.tubacgolfresort.com), just north of Tubac off East Frontage Road. Greens fees range from $45 to $109 in the winter.

WHERE TO STAY

In Amado

The Inn at Amado Territory Ranch ★ This modern inn just off I-19 at the crossroads of Amado is built in the territorial style and has a bit of the feel of an old Arizona ranch house. Guest rooms are outfitted in a mix of Mexican rustic furnishings and reproduction East Coast antiques, much in the style in which homes would have been furnished in Arizona 100 years ago. Rooms on the second floor feature balconies with views across the farm fields of the Santa Cruz Valley, while those on the ground floor have patios.

3001 E. Frontage Rd. (P.O. Box 81), Amado, AZ 85645. ✆ **888/398-8684** or 520/398-8684. Fax 520/398-8186. www.amado-territory-inn.com. 9 units. Nov–June $130–$145 double, $250 suite; July–Oct $105–$115 double, $220 suite. Rates include full breakfast. AE, DC, DISC, MC, V. Children 13 and over welcome. Pets accepted. **Amenities:** Restaurant. *In room:* A/C, hair dryer, Wi-Fi, no phone.

The Rex Ranch ★ Finds With its classic Southwestern styling and location adjacent to the de Anza Trail, this place is truly a hidden getaway. Just getting to the remote property is something of an adventure, because you have to drive *through* the Santa Cruz River to reach the ranch. When you see the pink-walled mission-revival building in the middle of the desert, you'll know you've arrived someplace distinctly different. Although not all of the guest rooms are as attractively decorated as the public areas, the new rooms and the more recently renovated rooms are quite comfortable. The ranch offers horseback riding and a wide variety of spa treatments and massages.

131 Amado Montosa Rd. (P.O. Box 636), Amado, AZ 85645. ✆ **800/547-2696** or 520/398-2914. Fax 520/398-8229. www.rexranch.com. 30 units. $105–$125 double, $135–$165 suite, $205–$225 casita (lower rates July–Aug). AE, DISC, MC, V. 2-night minimum stay. **Amenities:** Restaurant; bikes; concierge; Jacuzzi; outdoor pool; spa; Wi-Fi. *In room:* A/C, fridge, no phone.

Starry, Starry Nights

Southern Arizona's clear skies and the absence of lights in the surrounding desert make the night sky here as brilliant as anywhere on earth. This fact has not gone unnoticed by the world's astronomers, and consequently, southern Arizona has come to be known as the Astronomy Capital of the World.

Many observatories are open to the public, but you'll need to make tour reservations well in advance. In addition to the ones listed below, the **Flandrau Science Center & Planetarium** (p. 382) in Tucson offers public viewings. In Flagstaff, there are public viewing programs at the **Lowell Observatory** (p. 558).

The **Fred Lawrence Whipple Observatory** (✆ **520/670-5707;** www.cfa.harvard.edu/facilities/flwo), atop 8,550-foot Mount Hopkins, is the largest observatory operated by the Smithsonian Astrophysical Observatory. Six-hour tours of the observatory are offered mid-March through November on Monday, Wednesday, and Friday, and cost $7 for adults, $2.50 for children 6 to 12; no children 5 or under are allowed. Reservations are required and should be made 4 to 6 weeks in advance. No food is available here, so bring a picnic lunch. The observatory's visitor center (Mon–Fri 8:30am–4:30pm; closed federal holidays) is located on Mount Hopkins Road, near Amado (take exit 56, off I-19, turn left under the freeway; then right on E. Frontage Rd. and drive south 3 miles; turn left on Elephant Head Rd., and then right on Mount Hopkins Rd.).

Located in the Quinlan Mountains atop 6,875-foot Kitt Peak, **Kitt Peak National Observatory** ★ (✆ **520/318-8732;** www.noao.edu/kpno) is the largest and most famous astronomical observatory in the region. This is the area's only major observatory to offer public nighttime viewing. Day visitors, however, must be content with a visitor center (daily 9am–3:45pm), museum, and guided tour. Tours are held at 10 and 11:30am, and 1:30pm. Admission to the visitor center is free; tours are $4 for adults ($7 all-day passes are also available) and $2.50 for children ages 6 to 12 ($4.50 for all-day pass). The observatory is 56 miles southwest of Tucson, off Ariz. 86 (allow 90 min. for the drive). Nighttime stargazing (reservations required, call ✆ **520/318-8726;** call 4–8 weeks in advance) costs $56 for adults; $41 for students and seniors. The visitor center is closed Thanksgiving, Christmas, and New Year's Day.

In Tubac

Tubac Golf Resort & Spa ★★ Value This economical golf resort is built on the Otero Ranch, which dates back to 1789 and is the oldest Spanish land-grant ranch in the Southwest. Today, with its green fairways, the resort is a lush oasis amid the dry hills of the Santa Cruz Valley and is luxurious enough to compete with many of Tucson's resorts. However, the Tubac Golf Resort has more a classic Southwestern ambience than most of the Tucson golf resorts, and because it is fairly small, it has a low-key feel that I like. The red-tile roofs and brick archways throughout the resort conjure up its Spanish heritage, while guest rooms are spacious and modern and set amid expansive lawns. Casitas have patios, beamed ceilings, and beehive fireplaces; newer rooms are worth requesting.

1 Otero Rd. (P.O. Box 1297), Tubac, AZ 85646. ✆ **800/848-7893** or 520/398-2211. Fax 520/398-9261. www.tubacgolfresort.com. 98 units. $189–$259 double; $239–$339 suite. Children 17 and under stay free in parent's room. AE, DC, DISC, MC, V. Pets accepted ($25 fee). **Amenities:** 3 restaurants; 2 lounges; babysitting; concierge; 27-hole golf course; exercise room; 2 Jacuzzis; outdoor pool; room service; full-service spa; tennis court. *In room:* A/C, TV, fridge, hair dryer, Internet.

WHERE TO DINE

In addition to the restaurants mentioned below, **Stables,** at the Tubac Golf Resort & Spa, serves good steaks.

Dos Silos ★ MEXICAN Set amid the green lawns and gardens of the Tubac Golf Resort, this restaurant takes its name from the two old silos that tower over the patio. Good Mexican food and a fun atmosphere make this my favorite area restaurant. The fish tacos and margaritas are both excellent and together make the perfect meal. There's also decent guacamole, and the ceviche is another good bet.

Tubac Golf Resort, 1 Ave. de Otero, Tubac. ✆ **520/398-3787.** Reservations only for parties of 8 or more. Main courses $10–$15 lunch, $15–$22 dinner. AE, DISC, MC, V. Daily 11am–9pm.

Shelby's Bistro AMERICAN Located behind a small shopping plaza and across a little footbridge, this casual place has a very pleasant patio and is a great spot for lunch. The lunch menu is a mix of pastas, salads, sandwiches, and pizzas; in the evening, there's prime rib, lobster, and steaks. Try the Sonoran spice-rubbed pork chop.

In Mercado de Baca, 19 Tubac Rd. ✆ **520/398-8075.** Reservations not necessary. Main courses $9.25–$33. AE, MC, V. Sun–Tues 11am–4pm; Wed–Sat 11am–4pm and 5–9pm.

Wisdom's Cafe (Finds) MEXICAN Located between Tubac and Tumacácori (look for the giant chicken statues out front), this roadside diner is a Santa Cruz Valley institution, in business since 1944. With a cement floor and walls hung with old cowboy stuff, it feels like a cross between a cave and an old barn. The short menu includes tostadas, tacos, and enchiladas made with turkey. Be sure to save room for a fruit burrito (Mexican fruit pie).

1931 E. Frontage Rd., Tumacácori. ✆ **520/398-2397.** www.wisdomscafe.com. Reservations not necessary. Main dishes $4.50–$16. AE, DC, DISC, MC, V. Mon–Sat 11am–3pm and 5–8pm.

3 PATAGONIA ★★ & SONOITA ★

Patagonia: 18 miles NW of Nogales; 60 miles SE of Tucson; 171 miles SE of Phoenix; 50 miles SW of Tombstone

A mild climate, numerous good restaurants, bed-and-breakfast inns, and a handful of wineries have turned the small communities of Patagonia and Sonoita into a favorite weekend getaway for Tucsonans. Sonoita Creek, one of the only perennial streams in southern Arizona, attracts an amazing variety of bird life and, consequently, also attracts flocks of bird-watchers from all over the country.

Patagonia and Sonoita are only about 12 miles apart, but they have decidedly different characters. Patagonia is a sleepy little hamlet with tree-shaded streets, quite a few old adobe buildings, and a big park in the middle of town. The town's main draw, especially for bird-watchers, is the Nature Conservancy preserve on the western edge of town. Sonoita, on the other hand, sits out on the windswept high plains and is really a highway crossroads, not a town. The landscape around Sonoita, however, is filled with expensive new homes on small ranches, and not far away are the vineyards of Arizona's wine country.

ESSENTIALS

GETTING THERE Sonoita is at the junction of Ariz. 83 and Ariz. 82. Patagonia is 12 miles southwest of Sonoita, on Ariz. 82.

VISITOR INFORMATION The **Patagonia Area Business Association Tourist Information Center,** 307 McKeown Ave. (✆ **888/794-0060;** www.patagoniaaz.com), is open Monday through Saturday from 10am to 5pm and Sunday from 10am to 4pm.

BIRD-WATCHING & WINE TASTING

Patagonia, 18 miles northwest of Nogales on Ariz. 82, is a historic mining and ranching town that is surrounded by the Patagonia Mountains. If the scenery here leaves you with a since of déjà vu, that is probably because you've seen this landscape in numerous movies and television shows. Over the years, this area has been a backdrop for such films as *Oklahoma!, Red River, A Star Is Born,* and *David and Bathsheba,* and such TV programs as *Little House on the Prairie* and *The Young Riders.* Today, however, bird-watching and tranquillity are the main draws.

The **Patagonia–Sonoita Creek Preserve** (✆ **520/394-2400;** www.nature.org) is owned by the Nature Conservancy and protects 2 miles of Sonoita Creek riparian (riverside) habitat, which is important to migratory birds. More than 300 species of birds have been spotted at the preserve, which makes it a popular destination with birders from all over the country. Among the rare birds that can be seen are 22 species of flycatchers, kingbirds, and phoebes, plus the Montezuma quail. A forest of cottonwood trees, some of which are 100 feet tall, lines the creek and is one of the best remaining examples of cottonwood-willow riparian forest in southern Arizona. At one time, such forests grew along all the rivers in the region. To reach the sanctuary, which is just outside Patagonia on a dirt road that parallels Ariz. 82, turn west on Fourth Avenue and then south on Pennsylvania Street, cross the creek, and continue about 1 mile. From April to September, hours are Wednesday through Sunday from 6:30am to 4pm; from October to March, hours are Wednesday through Sunday from 7:30am to 4pm. Admission is $5 ($3 for Nature Conservancy members). On Saturday, at 9am, there are naturalist-guided walks through the preserve; reservations are not required.

On your way to or from the Nature Conservancy Preserve, be sure to drop by **Paton's Birder's Haven,** which is basically the backyard of Marion Paton. Numerous hummingbird feeders and a variety of other feeders attract an amazing range of birds to the yard, making this a favorite stop of avid birders who are touring the region. If you're heading out to the Nature Conservancy preserve, watch for the BIRDER'S HAVEN sign at 477 Pennsylvania Rd. after you cross the creek.

Patagonia Lake State Park (✆ **520/287-6965;** www.azstateparks.com), about 7 miles south of Patagonia, off Ariz. 82, is a popular boating and fishing lake that was formed by the damming of Sonoita Creek. The lake is 2½ miles long and stocked in winter with rainbow trout. Other times of year, people fish for bass, crappie, bluegill, and catfish. Park facilities include a picnic ground, campground, and swimming beach. There is also good bird-watching here—elegant trogons, which are among the most beautiful of southern Arizona's rare birds, are often spotted here. The park day-use fee is $7. Campsites are $15 to $22; reservations are not accepted. Adjacent to the park, you'll find the **Sonoita Creek State Natural Area** (✆ **520/287-2791**), a 5,000-acre preserve along the banks of Sonoita Creek. During much of the year, the natural area operates boat tours several mornings each week. These tours focus on the birds and history of the area. There are also guided hikes and guided bird-watching outings.

Sonoita proper is little more than a crossroads with a few shops and restaurants, but surrounding the community are miles of rolling grasslands that are a mix of luxury-home "ranchettes" and actual cattle ranches, all of which have spectacular big-sky views. Out on those high plains, more than just deer and antelope play. Oenophiles roam, as well. With eight wineries between Sonoita and Elgin, this is Arizona's biggest little wine country (there are also concentrations of wineries to the east of here near Willcox and in the Sedona area of central Ariz.). Most of the wineries are located in or near the village of Elgin, which is 10 miles east of Sonoita. The following are my favorite area wineries. Remember that most area wineries will give you a discount on your tasting if you bring a glass from another area winery.

Right in Sonoita, you'll find **Dos Cabezas WineWorks,** 3248 Ariz. 82 (✆ **520/455-5141;** www.doscabezaswinery.com), which is located in the middle of town. The winery's tasting room is open Thursday through Sunday from 10:30am to 4:30pm ($7 tasting fee). Just west of Elgin, you'll find **Callaghan Vineyards** ★, 336 Elgin Rd. (✆ **520/455-5322;** www.callaghanvineyards.com), which is open for tastings Friday through Sunday from 11am to 3pm ($7 tasting fee). This winery produces by far the best wines in the region and, arguably, the best wines in the state. Next door to Callaghan is **Canelo Hills Vineyard & Winery,** 342 Elgin Rd. (✆ **520/455-5499;** www.canelohillswinery.com), a small winery with a casual tasting room in the winery itself. Owners Joan and Tim Mueller produce some excellent wines in the $20 to $30 range. The tasting room is open Friday through Sunday from 11am to 4pm. ($5 tasting fee). Next door to this winery is **Kief-Joshua Vineyards,** 370 Elgin Rd. (✆ **520/455-5582;** www.kj-vineyards.com), which boasts the most ostentatious tasting room in the area. It's open Friday through Sunday from 11am to 5pm ($5 tasting fee). As of 2009, all the wines here were being made with California grapes.

WHERE TO STAY

In Patagonia

Duquesne House B&B ★ This old adobe building 1 block off Patagonia's main street was built in 1898 as miners' apartments. The unusual little building, with its shady front porch, is your best choice for overnight accommodations in Patagonia. Each unit has its own entrance, sitting room, and bedroom, and is decorated in quintessentially Southwestern style. My favorite room has an ornate woodstove and claw-foot tub. At the back of the house, an enclosed porch overlooks the garden.

357 Duquesne Ave. (P.O. Box 162), Patagonia, AZ 85624. ✆ **520/394-2732.** www.theduquesnehouse.com. 4 units. $125 double. Rate includes full breakfast. No credit cards. *In room:* A/C, Wi-Fi, no phone.

In Sonoita

Xanadu Ranch GetAway To "B" or not to "B," that is the question at Xanadu Ranch, which calls itself a hybrid B&B. What this means is that you can opt for a breakfast basket or not, your choice. You can also opt to bring your own horse with you, if you wish, as this place is also a "horse motel." The ranch owners, Bernie and Karen Kauk, don't offer horseback riding, but they can put you in touch with people who do. Rooms are spacious and comfortable and the setting, on a hill south of town, provides great views and awesome sunsets. Despite the name, the Bunkhouse is both the nicest (and newest) room on the ranch.

92 S. Los Encinos Rd. (P.O. Box 345), Sonoita, AZ 85637. ✆ **520/455-0050.** www.xanaduranchgetaway.com. 4 units. $89–$124 double. AE, DISC, MC, V. Pets accepted ($5 per night). *In room:* AC, TV/DVD, fridge, Wi-Fi.

In Patagonia

For good coffee and pastries, check out **Gathering Grounds,** 319 McKeown Ave. (✆ **520/394-2097;** www.mygatheringgrounds.com), which also serves ice cream and has a deli.

Velvet Elvis Pizza Company ITALIAN This casual hangout sums up the unusual character of Patagonia's residents. Faux-finished walls ooze artiness, while paeans to pop culture include shrines to both the Virgin Mary and Elvis. The menu features a variety of pizzas heaped with veggies, cheeses, and meats, but if you can remember to plan a day in advance, you should call in an order for the Inca pizza (made with a quinoa-flour crust). Add an organic salad and accompany it with some fresh juice, microbrew, espresso, or wine.

292 Naugle Ave. ✆ **520/394-2102.** www.velvetelvispizza.com. Reservations not accepted. Pizzas $12–$45; other dishes $7.50–$10. MC, V. Thurs–Sun 11:30am–8:30pm.

In Sonoita

Grab good breads and pastries, hot breakfasts, and sandwiches at the **Grasslands Bakery & Café,** 3119 Ariz. 83 (✆ **520/455-4770;** www.grasslandsbakery.com), which is an outpost of organic foods. There are even tastings of organic wines and loads of house-made salsas, jams, and other items for sale. The bakery is open Friday and Saturday from 10am to 3pm and Sunday from 8am to 3pm.

Canela ★★ SOUTHWESTERN This little restaurant at the crossroads of Sonoita is the most upscale restaurant in the area and is an absolute must if you are in the area for a wine-country getaway. The menu changes frequently to take advantage of what's fresh and seasonal, but may include carrot soup with poblano chiles, bacon-wrapped quail, leg of lamb with saffron-braised fennel, or duck tamales. This is the quintessential Arizona wine-country restaurant. The Sunday brunch is a great way to begin an afternoon of wine tasting at area wineries.

3252 Ariz. 82. ✆ **520/455-5873.** www.canelabistro.com. Reservations recommended. Main courses $17–$25. AE, DISC, MC, V. Thurs–Sat 4–9pm; Sun 11am–3pm.

The Steak Out STEAK This is ranch country, and this big barn of a place is where the ranchers and everyone else for miles around head when they want a good steak. A classic cowboy atmosphere prevails—there's even a mounted buffalo head just inside the front door. The restaurant's name and the scent of a mesquite fire should be all the hints you need about what to order—a grilled steak, preferably the exceedingly tender filet mignon. Wash it down with a beer, and you've got the perfect cowboy dinner.

At intersection of Ariz. 82 and Ariz. 83. ✆ **520/455-5205.** www.azsteakout.com. Reservations recommended. Main courses $8–$36. AE, DISC, MC, V. Mon–Thurs 5–9pm; Fri 5–10pm; Sat–11am–10pm; Sun 11am–9pm.

4 SIERRA VISTA & THE SAN PEDRO VALLEY ★

70 miles SE of Tucson; 189 miles SE of Phoenix; 33 miles SW of Tombstone; 33 miles W of Bisbee

At an elevation of 4,620 feet above sea level, Sierra Vista is blessed with the perfect climate—never too hot, never too cold. This fact more than anything else has contributed to Sierra Vista becoming one of the fastest-growing cities in Arizona. Although the city itself is a modern, sprawling community outside the gates of the U.S. Army's Fort Huachuca, it is wedged between the Huachuca Mountains and the valley of the San Pedro River. Consequently, Sierra Vista makes a good base for exploring the region's natural attractions.

Within a few miles' drive of town are the San Pedro Riparian National Conservation Area, Coronado National Memorial, and the Nature Conservancy's Ramsey Canyon Preserve. No other area of the United States attracts more attention from birders, who come in hopes of spotting some of the 300 bird species that have been sighted in southeastern Arizona. About 25 miles north of town is Kartchner Caverns State Park, the region's biggest attraction.

ESSENTIALS

GETTING THERE Sierra Vista is at the junction of Ariz. 90 and Ariz. 92, about 35 miles south of I-10.

VISITOR INFORMATION The **Sierra Vista Convention & Visitors Bureau,** 3020 Tacoma St. (✆ **800/288-3861** or 520/417-6960; www.visitsierravista.com), can provide information on the area. To find the visitor center if you're coming from the north, take the Ariz. 90 Bypass, turn right on Coronado Drive, turn left on Tacoma Street, and continue to the Oscar Yrun Community Center.

ATTRACTIONS AROUND BENSON

Kartchner Caverns State Park ★★ These caverns are among the largest and most beautiful in the country, and because they are wet caverns, stalactites, stalagmites, soda straws, and other cave formations are still growing. Within the caverns are two huge rooms, each larger than a football field with ceilings more than 100 feet high. These two rooms can be visited on two separate tours. On the shorter Rotunda/Throne Room Tour, you'll see, in the Rotunda Room, thousands of delicate soda straws. The highlight, though, is the Throne Room, at the center of which is a 58-foot-tall column. The second, and longer, tour visits the Big Room and leads past many strange and rare cave formations. Within the park are several miles of aboveground hiking trails. A campground ($22 per night) provides a convenient place to stay in the area.

Because the caverns are a popular attraction and tours are limited, try to make a reservation in advance, especially if you want to visit on a weekend. However, it is sometimes possible to get same-day tickets for the Rotunda/Throne Room Tour if you happen to be passing by.

Off Ariz. 90, 9 miles south of Benson. ✆ **520/586-2283** for reservations or 520/586-4100 for information. www.azstateparks.com. Admission $5 per car; Rotunda/Throne Room Tour $19 adults ($17 Aug–Sept), $9.95 children 7–13 ($8.95 Aug–Sept), free for children 6 and under; Big Room Tour $23 adults, $13 children 7–13, children 6 or under not allowed. Park daily 7:30am–6pm; cave tours approx. every 20 min. 8am–5pm. Closed Christmas; no Big Room Tours Apr 16–Oct 14.

BIRDING HOT SPOTS & OTHER NATURAL AREAS

If you'd like to join a guided bird walk along the San Pedro River or up Carr Canyon in the Huachuca Mountains, an owl-watching night hike, or a hummingbird banding session, contact the **Southeastern Arizona Bird Observatory** (✆ **520/432-1388;** www.sabo.org), which also has a public bird-viewing area at its headquarters 2 miles north of the Mule Mountain Tunnel, on Ariz. 80, north of Bisbee (watch for Hidden Meadow Lane). Most activities cost $10 to $15, although some day trips are as much as $75. Workshops and tours are also offered.

Moments Hummingbird Heaven

If it's summer and you're looking to add as many hummingbirds to your life list as possible, take a drive up Miller Canyon (south of Ramsey Canyon) to **Beatty's Miller Canyon Guest Ranch and Orchard,** 2173 E. Miller Canyon Rd., Hereford (✆ **520/378-2728;** www.beattysguestranch.com), where a public hummingbird-viewing area is set up. A total of 15 species of hummers have been sighted here, and several times, 14 species have been seen in 1 day.

Serious birders who want to be sure to add lots of rare birds to their life lists might want to visit this area on a guided tour. Your best bet is **Mark Pretti Nature Tours** (✆ **520/803-6889;** www.markprettinaturetours.com), run by the former resident naturalist at Ramsey Canyon Preserve. A half-day birding tour costs $120 and a full-day tour costs $200 to $220. Melody Kehl's **Outdoor Adventures** (✆ **520/245-4085;** www.ebiz.netopia.com/outdoor) is another reliable local guide; her rates start at $20 per hour.

Coronado National Memorial About 20 miles south of Sierra Vista is a 5,000-acre preserve dedicated to Francisco Vásquez de Coronado, the first European to explore this region. In 1540, Coronado, leading more than 700 people, left Compostela, Mexico, in search of the fabled Seven Cities of Cíbola, said to be rich in gold and jewels. Sometime between 1540 and 1542, Coronado led his band of weary men and women up the valley of the San Pedro River, which this monument overlooks. At the visitor center, you can learn about Coronado's fruitless quest for riches and check out the wildlife observation area. Outside the visitor center, a trail leads three-quarters of a mile to 600-foot-long Coronado Cave. (You'll need to bring your own flashlight and get a permit at the visitor center if you want to explore this cave.) After stopping at the visitor center, drive up to 6,575-foot Montezuma Pass, which offers far-reaching views of Sonora, Mexico, to the south, the San Pedro River to the east, and several mountain ranges and valleys to the west. Along the .8-mile round-trip Coronado Peak Trail, you'll also have good views of the valley.

4101 E. Montezuma Canyon Rd., Hereford. ✆ **520/366-5515.** www.nps.gov/coro. Free admission. Daily 8am–4pm. Closed Thanksgiving and Christmas. Take Ariz. 92 south from Sierra Vista to S. Coronado Memorial Dr., and continue 5 miles to the visitor center.

Ramsey Canyon Preserve ★ Each year, beginning in late spring, a buzzing fills the air in Ramsey Canyon, but instead of reaching for the bug repellant, visitors reach for their binoculars. It's not the buzzing of bees or mosquitoes that fills the air, but rather the buzzing of hummingbirds. Over the years, 14 species of hummingbirds have been sighted here, and it is the whirring of these diminutive birds' wings that fills the air. Because Ramsey Creek, which flows through the canyon, is a year-round stream, it attracts a wide variety of wildlife, including bears, bobcats, and more than 170 species of birds. A short nature trail leads through the canyon, and a second trail leads higher up the canyon. April and May are the busiest times here, while May and August are the best times to see hummingbirds. Between March and October, guided walks are offered Tuesday, Thursday, and Saturday at 9am.

27 Ramsey Canyon Rd., off Ariz. 92, 5 miles south of Sierra Vista. ✆ **520/378-2785.** www.nature.org. Admission $5 ($3 for Nature Conservancy members); free on 1st Sat of each month. Feb–Oct daily 8am–5pm; Nov–Jan Thurs–Mon 9am–4pm. Closed New Year's Day, Thanksgiving, and Christmas.

San Pedro Riparian National Conservation Area ★ Over the past century, roughly 90% of Arizona's free-flowing year-round rivers and streams have disappeared due to human use of desert waters. These rivers and streams once supported riparian areas that provided water, food, and protection to myriad plants, animals, and even humans. You can get an idea of what such riparian areas were like by visiting this sprawling preserve, which is located 8 miles east of Sierra Vista. Don't expect a wide, rushing river when you visit the San Pedro; what you'll see here would be called a creek anywhere but Arizona. Still, the water attracts wildlife, especially birds (more than 350 species have been sighted here).

Also within the riparian area is the **Murray Springs Clovis Site,** where 16 spear points and the remains of a 13,000-year-old mammoth kill were found in the 1960s. Although there isn't much to see other than some trenches, there are numerous interpretive signs along the short trail through the site. It's just north of Ariz. 90, about 5 miles east of Sierra Vista.

For a glimpse of the region's Spanish history, visit the ruins of the **Presidio Santa Cruz de Terrenate,** about 20 miles northeast of Sierra Vista, off Ariz. 82, near the ghost town of Fairbank. This military outpost was established in 1775 or 1776 but was never completed due to the constant attacks by Apaches. Today only decaying adobe walls remain. To reach this site, take Ariz. 82 east from US 90, and drive north 1 3/4 miles on Ironhorse Ranch Road, which is at mile marker 60. It's a 1 1/4-mile hike to the site. To visit **Fairbank** ghost town, drive Ariz. 82 to the bridge over the San Pedro River. Here you'll find the remains of several buildings from the heyday of this former railroad town. Fairbank, which was founded in the 1880s to serve nearby silver-mining towns, once had a population of nearly 15,000 people. The old Fairbank School is now the **Fairbank Schoolhouse Museum and Store** (✆ **520/457-3062**) and is open Friday through Sunday from 9:30am to 4:30pm; admission is free. From Fairbank, several miles of hiking trails lead along the San Pedro River.

For bird-watching, the best place is the system of trails at the Ariz. 90 crossing of the San Pedro. Here you'll find the **San Pedro House,** a 1930s ranch that is operated as a visitor center and bookstore. It's open daily from 9:30am to 4:30pm and has information on guided walks and hikes, bird walks, bird-banding sessions, and other events that are scheduled throughout the year.

Ariz. 90. ✆ **520/439-6400.** www.blm.gov/az/st/en/prog/blm_special_areas/ncarea/sprnca.html. Free admission. Parking areas sunrise–sunset.

WHERE TO STAY

In Benson

Holiday Inn Express If you're looking for lodging close to Kartchner Caverns, try this off-ramp budget hotel in Benson. The hotel's lobby is done in Santa Fe style with flagstone floors and rustic Southwestern furniture. Guest rooms are strictly hotel modern, but they are roomy and reliable.

630 S. Village Loop, Benson, AZ 85602. ✆ **888/263-2283** or 520/586-8800. Fax 520/586-1370. www.bensonaz.hiexpress.com. 62 units. $85–$179 double. Rates include full breakfast. Children 19 and under stay free in parent's room. AE, DC, DISC, MC, V. **Amenities:** Exercise room & access to nearby health club; outdoor pool. *In room:* A/C, TV, fridge, hair dryer, Wi-Fi.

In Hereford

Casa de San Pedro ★ Built with bird-watching tour groups in mind, this modern inn is set on the west side of the San Pedro River on 10 acres of land. The inn is built in the territorial style around a courtyard garden and has large, comfortable hotel-style guest rooms and a large common room where birders gather to swap tales of the day's sightings. The inn also offers birding, cultural, and history tours. This is by far the most upscale inn in the region and is my favorite.

8933 S. Yell Lane, Hereford, AZ 85615. ✆ **888/257-2050** or 520/366-1300. Fax 520/366-0701. www.bedandbirds.com. 10 units. $155–$165 double. Rates include full breakfast. AE, DISC, MC, V. No children 11 or under. **Amenities:** Concierge; Jacuzzi; outdoor pool. *In room:* A/C, hair dryer, Wi-Fi.

Ramsey Canyon Inn Bed & Breakfast Adjacent to the Nature Conservancy's Ramsey Canyon Preserve, this inn is the most convenient choice in the area for avid birders who are here to see the canyon's famous hummingbirds. The property straddles Ramsey Creek, with guest rooms in the main house and housekeeping suites reached by a footbridge over the creek. In addition to the large gourmet breakfast, you'll also get pie in the afternoon. Book early during the birding season. With its on-demand water heaters, gray-water irrigation of the inn's orchard, and use of organic ingredients as often as possible, this inn is doing quite a bit to be eco-friendly.

29 Ramsey Canyon Dr., Hereford, AZ 85615. ✆ **520/378-3010.** www.ramseycanyoninn.com. 9 units. $135–$150 double; $150–$225 suite. Room rates include full breakfast (except in housekeeping suites). DISC, MC, V. No children 15 or under in inn, but children are accepted in suites. *In room:* A/C (in some), Wi-Fi, no phone.

WHERE TO DINE

Manda Le (Value) AMERICAN/SOUTHWESTERN Whether you're in the mood for a patty melt, a chimichanga, or lamb chops, this surprisingly stylish restaurant is the place. No place else in Sierra Vista compares, and the prices are so reasonable you can't help wishing there was someplace like this in Tucson or Phoenix. The prime rib and steaks are good bets. Manda Le tends to attract a younger crowd, and on Friday nights, a DJ spins dance tunes. You'll find Manda Le in a modern shopping plaza on the south side of Sierra Vista just off Ariz. 92.

3455 Canyon de Flores St. ✆ **520/803-9668.** Reservations recommended. Main courses $5–$22. AE, DISC, MC, V. Mon–Thurs 11am–8pm; Fri 11am–midnight; Sat–Sun 4–8pm.

The Mesquite Tree STEAK This casual steakhouse south of town (and not far from the mouth of Ramsey Canyon) has long been a favorite of locals. It's funky and dark, and the prices can't be beat. Although you can get chicken and fish dishes done in a variety of traditional Continental styles, most people come here for the steaks. Try the Vargas rib-eye, which is smothered with green chiles, jack cheese, and enchilada sauce—a real border-country original.

S. Ariz. 92 and Carr Canyon Rd. ✆ **520/378-2758.** Reservations recommended. Main courses $9.25–$30. AE, DISC, MC, V. Tues–Sat 5–9pm; Sun 5–8pm.

5 TOMBSTONE ★

70 miles SE of Tucson; 181 miles SE of Phoenix; 24 miles N of Bisbee

All it took was a brief blaze of gunfire more than 125 years ago to seal the fate of this former silver-mining boomtown. On these very streets, outside a livery stable known as the O.K. Corral, Wyatt Earp, his brothers Virgil and Morgan, and their friend Doc Holliday took on the outlaws Ike Clanton and Frank and Tom McLaury on October 26,

1881. Today, Tombstone, "the town too tough to die," is one of Arizona's most popular attractions, but we'll leave it up to you to decide whether it deserves its reputation (either as a tough town or as a legitimate tourist attraction).

Tombstone was named by Ed Schieffelin, a silver prospector who ventured into this area at a time when the region's Apaches were fighting to preserve their way of life. Schieffelin was warned that all he would find here was his own tombstone, so when he discovered silver, he named the strike Tombstone. Within a few years, the town of Tombstone was larger than San Francisco, and between 1880 and 1887, an estimated $37 million worth of silver was mined here. Such wealth created a sturdy little town, and as the Cochise County seat of the time, Tombstone boasted a number of imposing buildings, including the county courthouse, which is now a state park. In 1887, an underground river flooded the silver mines, and despite attempts to pump the water out, the mines were never reopened. With the demise of the mines, the boom came to an end and the population rapidly dwindled.

Today, Tombstone's historic district consists of original buildings (built after a fire in 1882 destroyed much of the town) and newer structures built in keeping with the architectural styles of the late 19th century. Most house souvenir shops and restaurants, which should give you some indication that this place is a classic tourist trap, but kids (and adults raised on Louis L'Amour and John Wayne) love it, especially when the famous shootout is reenacted.

ESSENTIALS

GETTING THERE From Tucson, take I-10 east to Benson and then Ariz. 80 south to Tombstone. From Sierra Vista, take Ariz. 90 north to Arizona 82, heading east.

VISITOR INFORMATION For more information once you hit town, stop by the **Tombstone Chamber of Commerce Visitor Center,** 395 E. Allen St. (✆ **888/457-3929** or 520/457-3929; www.tombstonechamber.com).

GUNSLINGERS & SALOONS: IN SEARCH OF THE WILD WEST

As portrayed in novels, movies, and TV shows, the shootout has come to epitomize the Wild West, and nowhere is this great American phenomenon more glorified than in Tombstone, where the star attraction is the famous **O.K. Corral,** 308 E. Allen St. (✆ **520/457-3456;** www.ok-corral.com), site of a 30-second gun battle that has taken on mythic proportions over the years. Inside the corral, you'll find not only displays on the shootout, but also an exhibit focusing on local photographer C. S. Fly, who ran the boardinghouse where Doc Holliday was staying at the time of the shootout. The O.K. Corral is open daily from 9am to 5pm, and admission is $5.50 (free for kids 5 and under); for $9, you can visit the corral and take in a shootout reenactment almost on the very site of the original gunfight.

When the smoke cleared in 1881, three men lay dead. They were later carted off to the **Boot Hill Graveyard** (✆ **520/457-3300**) on the north edge of town. The graves of Clanton and the McLaury brothers, as well as those of others who died in gunfights or by hanging, are well marked. Entertaining epitaphs grace the grave markers; among the most famous is that of Lester Moore—"Here lies Lester Moore, 4 slugs from a 44, No Les, no more." The cemetery is open to the public daily 7:30am to dusk. Enter through a gift shop on Ariz. 80.

When the residents of Tombstone weren't shooting each other in the streets, they were likely to be found in the saloons and bawdy houses that lined Allen Street. Most famous was the **Bird Cage Theatre,** Allen and Sixth streets (© **800/457-3423** or 520/457-3421), so named for the cagelike cribs (what most people would think of as box seats) suspended from the ceiling. These velvet-draped cages were used by prostitutes to ply their trade. For old Tombstone atmosphere, this place is hard to beat. Admission is $10 for adults, $9 for seniors, $8 for children 8 to 18; the theater is open daily from 8am to 6pm.

When it's time for a cold beer, Tombstone has a couple of very lively old saloons. The **Crystal Palace Saloon,** at 436 E. Allen St. (© **520/457-3611;** www.crystalpalacesaloon.com), was built in 1879 and has been completely restored. This is one of the favorite hangouts of the town's costumed actors and other would-be cowboys and cowgirls. **Big Nose Kate's,** 417 E. Allen St. (© **520/457-3107;** www.bignosekate.com), is an equally entertaining spot, full of Wild West character and characters.

Tombstone has long been a tourist town, and its streets are lined with souvenir shops selling wind chimes, dream catchers, and loads of cowboy souvenirs. There are also several small museums scattered around town. At the **Rose Tree Inn Museum,** at Fourth and Toughnut streets (© **520/457-3326**), you can see the world's largest rose tree. Inside are antique furnishings from Tombstone's heyday in the 1880s. The museum is open daily from 9am to 5pm (closed Thanksgiving and Christmas). Admission is $5 (free for children 13 and under).

Tombstone Courthouse State Park, 223 Toughnut St. (© **520/457-3311;** www.azstateparks.com), is the most imposing building in town and provides a much less sensationalized version of local history. Built in 1882, the courthouse is now a state historic park and museum containing artifacts, photos, and newspaper clippings that chronicle Tombstone's lively past. In the courtyard, you can still see the gallows that once ended the lives of outlaws. The courthouse is open Thursday through Monday from 9am to 5pm (closed on Christmas); the entrance fee is $4 for adults and $1 for children 7 to 13.

The **Tombstone Western Heritage Museum** ★, Fremont (Ariz. 80) and Sixth streets (© **520/457-3800;** www.thetombstonemuseum.com), a privately owned museum, holds the town's most fascinating collection of Tombstone artifacts and ephemera and should not be missed. Included in this impressive collection are artifacts that once belonged to Wyatt and Virgil Earp, rare photos of the Earps and the outlaws of Tombstone, and all kinds of original documents that date to the days of the shootout at the O.K. Corral. The museum is open Monday, Tuesday, and Thursday through Saturday from 9am to 6pm and Sunday from 12:30 to 6pm; admission is $5 for adults and $3 for children 12 to 18 ($13 for families).

WHERE TO STAY

Holiday Inn Express Tombstone On the northern outskirts of Tombstone, right next door to the older but slightly nicer Best Western, this is the newest hotel in Tombstone. The decor draws on a bit of Southwestern and Spanish colonial styling, but basically this is just a modern chain motel.

580 W. Randolph Way, Tombstone, AZ 85638. © **888/465-4329** or 520/457-9507. Fax 520/457-9506. www.hitombstone.com. 60 units. $104–$124 double. Rates include continental breakfast. Children 17 and under stay free in parent's room. AE, DISC, MC, V. **Amenities:** Outdoor pool; Jacuzzi; Wi-Fi. *In room:* A/C, TV, hair dryer, Internet.

Tombstone Boarding House Housed in two whitewashed 1880s adobe buildings with green trim, this inn is in a quiet residential neighborhood only 2 blocks from busy Allen Street. The main house was originally the home of Tombstone's first bank manager. Guest rooms are in an old boardinghouse. Accommodations are comfortable and clean, with country decor. Hardwood floors and antiques lend a period feel.

108 N. Fourth St. (P.O. Box 1700), Tombstone, AZ 85638. ✆ **877/225-1319** or 520/457-3716. www.tombstoneboardinghouse.com. 5 units. $99–$119 double. Rates include full breakfast. MC, V. Pets accepted ($10 per night). **Amenities:** Restaurant. *In room:* No phone.

WHERE TO DINE

Big Nose Kate's Saloon LIGHT FARE Okay, so the food here isn't all that memorable, but the atmosphere sure is. Big Nose Kate's dates back to 1880 and is primarily a saloon. As such, it stays packed with visitors who have come to revel in Tombstone's outlaw past. So, while you sip your beer, why not order a sandwich and call it lunch? You might even catch some live country music.

417 E. Allen St. ✆ **520/457-3107.** www.bignosekate.com. Reservations not accepted. Sandwiches $7–$16. AE, MC, V. Daily 11am–8pm.

The Lamplight Room ★ CONTINENTAL Located a few blocks off busy Allen Street, this restaurant serves the best food in Tombstone. The Lamplight Room is in the living room of an old 1880s home, which also lends this place more character than that of any other restaurant in town. The menu is short and includes lots of Mexican food, as well as grilled salmon, and a few other dishes from north of the border. On Friday and Saturday nights, there's live classical guitar music.

At the Tombstone Boarding House, 108 N. Fourth St. ✆ **520/457-3716.** www.tombstoneboardinghouse.com. Reservations recommended. Main courses $6–$17. MC, V. Fri–Sat 11:30am–3pm and 5–8:30pm; Sun 11:30am–3pm and 5–7pm.

6 BISBEE ★★

94 miles SE of Tucson; 205 miles SE of Phoenix; 24 miles NW of Douglas

Arizona has a wealth of ghost towns that boomed on mining profits and then quickly went bust when the mines played out, but none is as impressive as Bisbee, which is built into the steep slopes of Tombstone Canyon on the south side of the Mule Mountains. Between 1880 and 1975, Bisbee's mines produced more than $6 billion worth of metals. When the Phelps Dodge Company shut down its copper mines here, Bisbee nearly went the way of other abandoned mining towns, but because it's the Cochise County seat, it was saved from disappearing into the desert dust.

Bisbee's glory days date from the late 19th and early 20th centuries, and because the town stopped growing in the early part of the 20th century, it is now one of the best-preserved historic towns anywhere in the Southwest. Old brick buildings line narrow winding streets, and miners' shacks sprawl across the hillsides above downtown. Many artists call the town home, and aging hippies and other urban refugees have for many years been dropping out of the rat race to restore Bisbee's old buildings and open small inns, restaurants, and galleries. Between the rough edges left over from its mining days and this new cosmopolitan atmosphere, Bisbee is one of Arizona's most interesting towns. However, be aware that Bisbee is not for everyone. It appeals mostly to young, hip travelers who don't expect much from their accommodations and who like to stay up late partying. The rumble of motorcycles is a constant on Bisbee's streets.

ESSENTIALS

GETTING THERE Bisbee is on Ariz. 80, which begins at I-10, in the town of Benson, 45 miles east of Tucson.

VISITOR INFORMATION Contact the **Bisbee Visitor Center,** 2 Copper Queen Plaza (✆ **866/2-BISBEE** [224-7233] or 520/432-3554; www.discoverbisbee.com).

EXPLORING THE TOWN

At the Bisbee Visitor Center, in the middle of town, pick up walking-tour brochures that guide you past the town's most important historic buildings and sites. On the second floor of the **Copper Queen Library,** 6 Main St. (✆ **520/432-4232**), some great old photographs give a good idea of what the town looked like in the past century.

Don't miss the **Bisbee Mining & Historical Museum** ★, 5 Copper Queen Plaza (✆ **520/432-7071;** www.bisbeemuseum.org), housed in the 1897 Copper Queen Consolidated Mining Company office building. This small but comprehensive museum features exhibits on the history of Bisbee. It's open daily from 10am to 4pm; admission is $7.50 for adults, $6.50 for seniors, and $3 children 15 and under.

For another look at early life in Bisbee, visit the **Muheim Heritage House,** 207 Youngblood Hill (✆ **520/432-7698;** www.bisbeemuseum.org), which is reached by walking up Brewery Gulch. The house was built between 1898 and 1915 and has an unusual semicircular porch. The interior is decorated with period furniture. It's open Friday through Tuesday from 10am to 4pm; admission is $4.

O.K. Street, which parallels Brewery Gulch but is high on the hill on the southern edge of town, is a good place to walk for views of Bisbee. At the top of O.K. Street, there's a path that takes you up to a hill above town for an even better panorama of Bisbee's jumble of old buildings. Atop this hill are numerous small, colorfully painted shrines that are built into the rocks and filled with candles, plastic flowers, and pictures of the Virgin Mary. It's a steep climb on a rocky, very uneven path, but the views and the fascinating little shrines make it worth the effort.

Mining made this town what it is, so you should be sure to take an underground mine tour to find out what it was like to be a miner here in Bisbee. **Queen Mine Tours** ★ (✆ **866/432-2071** or 520/432-2071; www.queenminetour.com) takes visitors down into one of the town's old copper mines. Tours are offered daily between 9am and 3:30pm and cost $12 for adults and $5 for children 4 to 15. The ticket office and mine are just south of the Old Bisbee business district, at the Ariz. 80 interchange.

For an exploration of some of the steeper and narrower streets of Bisbee, take a 90-minute tour ($40) of old Bisbee with **Lavender Jeep Tours** (✆ **520/432-5369**). Several other tours are also available. For a walk on the dark side, sign up for the **Old Bisbee Ghost Tour** (✆ **520/432-3308;** www.oldbisbeeghosttour.com). These 90-minute tours are offered Friday through Sunday nights at 7pm and cost $13 for adults and $9 for children 11 and under.

Bisbee has lots of interesting stores and galleries, and shopping is the main recreational activity here. To get a look at some of the quality jewelry created from minerals mined in the area, stop by **Czar Jewelry,** 13 Main St. (✆ **520/432-3027**). Another good place to shop for jewelry is **Bisbee Blue,** at the Lavender Pit View Point, on Ariz. 80 (✆ **520/432-5511**), an exclusive dealer of the famous Bisbee Blue turquoise. Turquoise is associated with copper mines, and Bisbee's mines once produced some of the most famous turquoise in the country.

To protect your face from the burning rays of the sun (and make a fashion statement), visit **Optimo Custom Hat Works,** 47 Main St. (✆ **888/FINE-HAT** [346-3428] or 520/432-4544; www.optimohatworks.com), where owner Grant Sergot will custom fit your felt or Panama straw hat. (By the way, Panama hats actually come from Ecuador.)

WHERE TO STAY

Canyon Rose Suites ★ Value Located on the second floor of a commercial building just off Bisbee's main street, this property offers spacious suites with full kitchens, which makes it a good bet for longer stays. All units have hardwood floors and high ceilings, and the works by local artists and the mix of contemporary and rustic furnishings give the place plenty of Bisbee character. Constructed on a steep, narrow street, the building housing this lodging has an unusual covered sidewalk, making it one of the more distinctive commercial buildings in town.

27 Subway at Shearer St. (P.O. Box 1915), Bisbee, AZ 85603. ✆ **866/296-7673** or 520/432-5098. www.canyonrose.com. 6 units. $99–$210 double. Children 11 and under stay free in parent's room. AE, DISC, MC, V. *In room:* A/C, TV/DVD, hair dryer, kitchen, Wi-Fi.

Copper City Inn ★ Finds This inn is operated by Fred Miller, who has been the bartender at Bisbee's Cafe Roka for 16 years, and his wife, Anita Fox. The inn boasts some of the most attractive rooms in Bisbee. One room is done up with French antiques, while the other room has a modern Art Deco styling and is dedicated to early-20th-century hotel designer Mary Jane Colter. The suite has modern mission-style furnishings, tile floors, and a full kitchen. All the rooms have balconies overlooking Bisbee. Guests receive a complimentary bottle of wine upon check-in.

99 Main St., Bisbee, AZ 85603. ✆ **520/432-1418** or 520/456-4254. www.coppercityinn.com. 3 units. $110 double; $135 suite. Rates include continental breakfast. Children 10 and under stay free in parent's room. AE, DC, DISC, MC, V. **Amenities:** Access to nearby health club. *In room:* TV/DVD, fridge, hair dryer, Wi-Fi, no phone.

Copper Queen Hotel Built in 1902 by the Copper Queen Mining Company and right in the center of town, this is Bisbee's grande dame hotel and is the oldest continuously operating hotel in Arizona. The atmosphere is casual yet quite authentic with spacious halls that lead to guest rooms furnished with antiques. Unfortunately, the rooms vary considerably in size with the smallest being quite cramped. Be sure to ask for one of the renovated rooms, which are up-to-date and attractively furnished. The restaurant serves decent food, and out front is a terrace for alfresco dining. There's even a saloon and a resident ghost.

11 Howell Ave. (P.O. Drawer CQ), Bisbee, AZ 85603. ✆ **520/432-2216.** Fax 520/432-3819. www.copperqueen.com. 52 units. $89–$197 double. Children 16 and under stay free in parent's room. AE, DC, MC, V. **Amenities:** Restaurant; lounge; small outdoor pool. *In room:* A/C, TV, Wi-Fi.

Letson Loft Hotel ★★ Located up a flight of stairs, the Letson Loft Hotel feels a bit like an old Italian villa and has some of the prettiest rooms in town. High ceilings, old wood floors, Asian antiques, and plush beds with great linens all add up to comforts and class rarely seen in this funky town. Book one of the front rooms and you'll have a front-row seat for watching the Main Street action through bay windows. If you're a light sleeper, ask for a room at the back of the hotel or avail yourself of the bedside earplugs;

Bisbee can be a bit noisy at times. One of my favorite rooms has a huge skylight and another has a claw-foot tub. There's even a suite with a kitchen.

26 Main St. (P.O. Box 623), Bisbee, AZ 85603. ✆ **877/432-3210** or 520/432-3210. www.letsonlofthotel.com. 8 units. $120–$175 double; $140–$180 suite. Rates include continental breakfast. AE, DISC, MC, V. No children 11 or under. **Amenities:** Concierge. *In room:* A/C, TV/DVD, hair dryer, Wi-Fi.

Shady Dell Trailer Court *Finds* Yes, this really is a trailer court, but you'll find neither shade nor dell at the Shady Dell's roadside location just south of the Lavender Pit mine. What you will find are nine vintage trailers, a 1947 Airporter bus done in retro-Tiki style, and a 1947 Chris Craft yacht, all of which have been lovingly restored. Although some of the trailers don't have their own private bathrooms (a bathhouse is in the middle of the property), they do have all kinds of vintage furnishings—and recordings of period music and radio shows. In trailers that have vintage TVs, there are DVDs of old movies. **Dot's Diner** (see "Where to Dine," below), a 1957 vintage diner, is also on-site.

1 Old Douglas Rd., Bisbee, AZ 85603. ✆ **520/432-3567.** www.theshadydell.com. 11 units. $50–$145 per trailer (for 1–2 people). DISC, MC, V. No children 9 or under. **Amenities:** Restaurant. *In room:* A/C, kitchen, no phone.

WHERE TO DINE

Café Cornucopia, 14 Main St. (✆ **520/432-4820**), offers fresh juices, smoothies, and sandwiches. It's open Thursday through Sunday from 11am to 5pm. For good coffee and a mining theme (there's an old mining cart and photos of miners on the walls), check out the **Bisbee Coffee Co.,** Copper Queen Plaza, Main Street (✆ **520/432-7879;** www.bisbeecoffee.com). For gourmet picnic supplies, peruse the shelves of the **High Desert Market and Café,** 203 Tombstone Canyon Rd. (✆ **520/432-6775;** www.highdesertmarket.net), which has organic produce, imported cheeses, wine, and other assorted goodies for a great picnic. There is also a cafe here that is a great place for breakfast or lunch.

Bisbee Breakfast Club ★ *Finds* AMERICAN In the Lowell district on the far side of the Lavender Pit from old Bisbee, this huge diner is a locals' favorite. Big breakfasts (served all day) are the specialty here, and the cinnamon rolls are legendary around town. At lunch, try the coffee-charred breast of chicken salad; it'll really wake up your taste buds. The owners, Pat and Heather Grimm, are the couple who originally put Bisbee's diminutive Dot's Diner (see below) on the map.

75 Erie St. ✆ **520/432-5885.** www.bisbeebreakfastclub.com. Reservations not accepted. Main courses $5–$8. AE, MC, V. Thurs–Sun 7am–2pm; Mon 7am–noon.

Cafe Roka ★★ *Value* NEW AMERICAN The food at Cafe Roka is so good that it is reason enough for a visit to Bisbee. Casual and hip, this place is a real find in such an out-of-the-way town and offers good value as well as delicious and imaginatively prepared food. All meals include, for one fixed price, salad, soup, sorbet intermezzo, and your choice of entree (different entrees are priced differently). The grilled salmon with a Gorgonzola-dill crust and artichoke-and-portobello lasagna are two perennial favorites. The flourless chocolate cake with raspberry sauce is an exquisite ending. Local artists display their works, and on Friday nights there is live jazz.

35 Main St. ✆ **520/432-5153.** www.caferoka.com. Reservations highly recommended. Main courses $17–$27. AE, MC, V. Summer Fri–Sat 5–9pm; spring and fall Wed–Sat 5–9pm; winter Thurs–Sat 5–9pm. Closed mid-Jan to mid-Feb.

Dot's Diner ★ Finds AMERICAN At Dot's Diner, an original 1957 Valentine diner, you can take a step back into the Eisenhower years. This tiny diner has barely a half-dozen stools at the counter, which overlooks the kitchen and soda fountain area. As in the old days, meals are simple—filling breakfasts, basic sandwiches, and fresh house-made burgers.

At Shady Dell RV Resort, 1 Old Douglas Rd. ✆ **520/432-1112.** www.theshadydell.com. Reservations not accepted. Main courses $3.25–$6. DISC, MC, V. Fri–Tues 7:30am–2:30pm.

7 EXPLORING THE REST OF COCHISE COUNTY ★

Willcox: 81 miles E of Tucson; 192 miles SE of Phoenix; 74 miles N of Douglas

Although the towns of Bisbee, Tombstone, and Sierra Vista all lie within Cochise County, much of the county is taken up by the vast Sulphur Springs Valley, which is bounded by several mountain ranges. It is across this wide-open landscape that Apache chiefs Cochise and Geronimo once rode. Gazing out across this country today, it is easy to understand why the Apaches fought so hard to keep white settlers out.

While the Chiricahua and Dragoon mountains, which flank the Sulphur Springs Valley on the east and west respectively, are relatively unknown outside the region, they offer some of the Southwest's most spectacular scenery. Massive boulders litter the mountainsides, creating fascinating landscapes. The Chiricahua Mountains are also a favorite destination of bird-watchers, for it is here that the colorfully plumed elegant trogon reaches the northern limit of its range.

ESSENTIALS

GETTING THERE Willcox is on I-10, with Ariz. 186 heading southeast toward Chiricahua National Monument.

VISITOR INFORMATION The **Willcox Chamber of Commerce and Agriculture,** 1500 N. Circle I Rd. (✆ **800/200-2272** or 520/384-2272; www.willcoxchamber.com), can provide information.

SOUTHWEST OF WILLCOX

Scenic Landscapes

South of the community of Dragoon, which is known for its pistachio farms, lies a much less accessible area of the Dragoon Mountains known as **Cochise Stronghold** ★ (www.cochisestronghold.com). During the Apache uprisings of the late 19th century, the Apache leader Cochise used this rugged section of the Dragoon Mountains as his hideout and managed to elude capture for years. The granite boulders and pine forests made it impossible for the army to track him and his followers. Cochise eventually died and was buried at an unknown spot somewhere within the area. This rugged jumble of giant boulders is reached by a rough gravel road, at the end of which you'll find a campground, a picnic area, and hiking trails. For a short, easy walk, follow the .4-mile Nature Trail. For a longer and more strenuous hike, head up the Cochise Trail. The Stronghold Divide makes a good destination for a 6-mile round-trip hike. For more info, contact the **Coronado National Forest Douglas Ranger District,** 1192 W. Saddleview Rd., Douglas (✆ **520/364-3468;** www.fs.fed.us/r3/coronado).

A Memorable Museum in an Unlikely Locale

Amerind Foundation Museum ★★ It may be out-of-the-way and difficult to find, but this museum is well worth seeking out. Established in 1937, the Amerind Foundation has compiled one of the nation's finest private collections of Native American archaeological artifacts and contemporary pieces. There are exhibits on the dances and religious ceremonies of the major Southwestern tribes and cases full of archaeological artifacts amassed from the numerous Amerind Foundation excavations over the years. Fascinating ethnology exhibits include amazingly intricate beadwork from the Plains tribes, old Zuni fetishes, Pima willow baskets, old kachina dolls, 100 years of Southwestern tribal pottery, and Navajo weavings. The art gallery displays works by 19th- and 20th-century American artists, such as Frederic Remington.

2100 N. Amerind Rd., Dragoon. ✆ **520/586-3666.** www.amerind.org. Admission $5 adults, $4 seniors, $3 college students and children 12–18, free for children 11 and under. Tues–Sun 10am–4pm. Closed major holidays. Located 64 miles east of Tucson, btw. Benson and Willcox; take the Dragoon Rd. exit (exit 318) from I-10, and continue 1 mile east.

EAST OF WILLCOX

Chiricahua National Monument ★★ Sea Captain, China Boy, Duck on a Rock, Punch and Judy—these may not seem like appropriate names for landscape features, but this is no ordinary landscape. These gravity-defying rock formations—called "the land of the standing-up rocks" by the Apache and the "wonderland of rocks" by the pioneers—are the equal of any of Arizona's many amazing rocky landmarks. Rank upon rank of monolithic giants seem to have been turned to stone as they marched across the forested Chiricahua Mountains. Formed about 25 million years ago by a massive volcanic eruption, these rhyolite badlands were once the stronghold of renegade Apaches. If you look closely at Cochise Head peak, you can even see the famous chief's profile. If you're in good physical condition, don't miss the chance to hike the 7.5-mile round-trip **Heart of Rocks Trail ★★**. This trail leads through the monument's most spectacular scenery. A shorter loop is also possible. Also within the monument are a visitor center, a campground, a picnic area, and a scenic drive.

12856 E. Rhyolite Creek Rd. (off Ariz. 186). ✆ **520/824-3560.** www.nps.gov/chir. Admission $5 adults. Visitor center daily 8am–4:30pm. Closed Thanksgiving and Christmas. From Willcox, drive southeast on Ariz. 186 for 36 miles.

Fort Bowie National Historic Site ★ The Butterfield Stage, which carried mail, passengers, and freight across the Southwest in the mid-1800s, followed a route that climbed up and over Apache Pass, in the heart of the Chiricahua Mountains' Apache territory. In 1862, Fort Bowie was established near the mile-high pass to ensure the passage of the slow-moving stage as it traversed this difficult region. The fort was also used to protect the water source for cavalry going east to fight the Confederate army in New Mexico. Later, federal troops stationed at Fort Bowie battled Geronimo until, in 1886, the Apache chief finally surrendered. Today, little more than Fort Bowie's crumbling adobe walls remain, but the hike along the old stage route to the ruins conjures up the ghosts of Geronimo and the Indian Wars.

3203 S. Old Fort Bowie Rd. (off Ariz. 186). ✆ **520/847-2500.** www.nps.gov/fobo. Free admission. Visitor center daily 8am–4:30pm; grounds daily dawn–dusk. Closed Thanksgiving and Christmas. From Willcox, drive southeast on Ariz. 186; after about 20 miles, watch for signs; it's another 8 miles up a dirt road to the trail head. Alternatively, drive east from Willcox to Bowie and go 13 miles south on Apache Pass Rd. From the trail head, it's a 1.5-mile hike to the fort.

NEAR DOUGLAS

Slaughter Ranch Museum ★ Finds Down a dusty gravel road outside Douglas lies a little-known Southwestern landmark: the Slaughter Ranch. If you're old enough, you may remember a Walt Disney TV show called *Texas John Slaughter.* This was his spread. In 1884, former Texas Ranger John Slaughter bought the San Bernardino Valley and turned it into one of the finest cattle ranches in the West. Slaughter later went on to become the sheriff of Cochise County and helped rid the region of the unsavory characters who had flocked to the many mining towns of this remote part of the state. Today, the ranch is a National Historic Landmark and has been restored to its late-19th-century appearance. Surrounding the ranch buildings are wide lawns and a large pond that together attract a variety of birds, making this one of Arizona's best winter birding spots. For the-way-it-was tranquillity, this old ranch can't be beat.

6153 Geronimo Trail, about 14 miles east of Douglas. ✆ **520/558-2474.** www.slaughterranch.com. Admission $8 adults, free for children 13 and under. Wed–Sun 10am–3pm. Closed Christmas and New Year's Day. From Douglas, go east on 15th St., which runs into Geronimo Trail; continue east 14 miles.

BIRDING HOT SPOTS

At the **Willcox Chamber of Commerce,** 1500 N. Circle I Rd. (✆ **800/200-2272** or 520/384-2272; www.willcoxchamber.com), you can pick up several birding maps and checklists for the region.

To the east of Chiricahua National Monument, on the far side of the Chiricahuas, lies **Cave Creek Canyon,** one of the most important bird-watching spots in the United States. It's here that the colorful elegant trogon reaches the northern limit of its range. Other rare birds that have been spotted here include sulfur-bellied flycatchers, and Lucy's, Virginia's, and black-throated gray warblers. Stop by the visitor center for information on the best birding spots in the area. Cave Creek Canyon is just outside the community of Portal; in summer, it can be reached from the national monument by driving over the Chiricahuas on graded gravel roads. In winter, you'll likely have to drive around the mountains, which entails going south to Douglas and then 60 miles north to Portal or north to I-10, and then south 35 miles to Portal.

The **Cochise Lakes** (actually, the Willcox sewage ponds) are another great bird-watching spot. Birders can see a wide variety of waterfowl and shorebirds, including avocets and ibises. To find the ponds, head south out of Willcox on Ariz. 186, turn right onto Rex Allen, Jr. Drive at the sign for the Twin Lakes golf course, and go past the golf course.

Between October and March, as many as 30,000 sandhill cranes gather in the Sulphur Springs Valley south of Willcox, and in January, the town holds the **Wings Over Willcox** festival (www.wingsoverwillcox.com), a celebration of these majestic birds. Southwest of Willcox, on U.S. 191, near the community of Cochise and the Apache Generating Station electricity-generating plant, you'll find the **Apache Station Wildlife Viewing Area,** the area's best spot for viewing cranes. The Sulphur Springs Valley is also well known for its large wintering population of raptors, including ferruginous hawks and prairie falcons.

WHERE TO STAY

Near Willcox

Cochise Stronghold B&B ★★ Finds Set on 5 acres of private land within Coronado National Forest's Cochise Stronghold area, this remote and beautiful B&B is one of my favorites in the state. The inn is an energy-efficient, passive solar home with two housekeeping suites. It makes a superb base for hikes amid the area's fascinating rock formations and for excursions farther afield in Cochise County. Owners John and Nancy Yates are a great source of information both on solar-home design and on the preservation of the desert. In-room breakfast options include Southwestern dishes such as mesquite-cornmeal pancakes (made with mesquite flour). For a more adventurous experience, you can stay in a yurt.

2126 W. Windancer Trail (P.O. Box 232), Pearce, AZ 85625. ✆ **877/426-4141** or 520/826-4141. www.cochisestrongholdbb.com. $179–$209 double; $129 yurt. Rates include full breakfast. 2-night minimum stay. Children 8 and over welcome. AE, DC, DISC, MC, V. **Amenities:** Jacuzzi. *In room (but not in yurt):* A/C, TV/VCR, kitchenette, Wi-Fi.

Sunglow Guest Ranch ★★ (Value) Located in the western foothills of the Chiricahua Mountains, roughly 40 miles southeast of Willcox, this remote ranch is surrounded by Coronado National Forest and is one of the most idyllic spots in the state. There's great bird-watching both on the ranch and in the nearby hills, and guests can use the ranch's mountain bikes. The guest rooms are quite large, and decor includes rustic Mexican furnishings. More than half the units have wood-burning fireplaces. This guest ranch is different from others around the state, in that it doesn't offer horseback riding, but there is a stable nearby that will bring its horses to the ranch. The beautiful little dining hall/cafe here, built in classic Western-ranch style, serves some of the best food in this corner of the state. The ranch has also made numerous changes in the past couple of years to be more eco-friendly.

14066 S. Sunglow Rd., Pearce, AZ 85625. ✆ **866/786-4569** or 520/824-3334. www.sunglowranch.com. 9 units. $270–$375 double. Rates include breakfast and dinner (B&B rates also available). Children 5 and under stay free in parent's room. AE, DISC, MC, V. **Amenities:** Dining room; bikes; Wi-Fi. *In room:* Fridge, no phone.

In Portal

Portal Peak Lodge, Portal Store & Cafe This motel-like lodge, located behind the general store/cafe in the hamlet of Portal, has fairly modern guest rooms that face one another across a wooden deck. Meals are available in the adjacent cafe. If you're seeking predictable accommodations in a remote location, you'll find them here.

2358 Rock House Rd., Portal, AZ 85632. ✆ **520/558-2223.** Fax 520/558-2473. www.portalpeaklodge.com. 16 units. $75–$85 double. AE, DISC, MC, V. **Amenities:** Restaurant. *In room:* A/C, TV, no phone.

Southwestern Research Station, The American Museum of Natural History (Finds) Located in Cave Creek Canyon, this is a field research station that takes guests when the accommodations are not filled by scientists doing research. As such, it is the best place in the area for serious bird-watchers, who will find the company of researchers a fascinating addition to a visit. Guests stay in simply furnished cabins scattered around the research center. Spring and fall are the easiest times to get reservations and the best times for bird-watching.

P.O. Box 16553, Portal, AZ 85632. ✆ **520/558-2396.** Fax 520/558-2018. www.research.amnh.org/swrs. 12 units. Mar–Oct $160 double (rate includes all meals); Nov–Feb $70–$80 double (no meals provided). Children 3 and under stay free in parent's room. DISC, MC, V. **Amenities:** Dining room; outdoor pool. *In room:* No phone.

15

The Best of Central & Western Arizona

Between Phoenix and the Grand Canyon lies one of the most beautiful landscapes on earth—the red-rock country of Sedona. Decades ago, Hollywood came to Sedona to shoot Westerns; then came the artists and the retirees and the New Agers. Now it seems Hollywood is back, but this time the stars are building huge homes in the hills.

Central Arizona isn't just red rock and retirees, though. It also has the former territorial capital of Prescott, historic sites, ancient Indian ruins, an old mining town turned artists' community, even a few good old-fashioned dude ranches (now called "guest ranches") out Wickenburg way. There are, of course, thousands of acres of cactus-studded desert, but there are also high mountains, cool pine forests, and a fertile river valley. And north of Sedona's red rocks is Oak Creek Canyon, a tree-shaded cleft in the rocks with one of the state's most scenic stretches of highway running through it.

Also included in this chapter is Arizona's "west coast," 340 miles of Colorado River waters, most of which are impounded in three huge reservoirs—Lake Mead, Lake Mohave, and Lake Havasu—that provide water and electricity to sprawling Southwestern boomtowns such as Phoenix and Las Vegas.

As with any warm coastline, Arizona's West Coast is lined with lakefront resorts, hotels, RV parks, and campgrounds. Of course, watersports of all types are extremely popular here. For the most part, however, it's a destination for desert residents, so you won't find any hotels or resorts even remotely as upscale or expensive as those in Phoenix, Tucson, or Sedona.

1 WICKENBURG

53 miles NW of Phoenix; 61 miles S of Prescott; 128 miles SE of Kingman

Known a half century ago as the dude-ranch capital of the world, Wickenburg once attracted celebrities and families from all over the country. Those were the days when the West had only just stopped being wild, and spending the winter in Arizona was an adventure, not just a chance to escape snow and ice. Today, although the area has only a handful of dude (or guest) ranches still in business, Wickenburg still clings to its Wild West image. The guest ranches that remain range from rustic to luxurious, but a chance to ride the range is still the area's main attraction.

ESSENTIALS

GETTING THERE From Phoenix, drive north on I-17, then west on Ariz. 74, continuing west on US 60. From Prescott, take Ariz. 89. If you're coming from the west, take U.S. 60 from I-10. U.S. 93 comes down from I-40 in northwestern Arizona.

VISITOR INFORMATION Contact the **Wickenburg Chamber of Commerce,** 216 N. Frontier St. (✆ **800/942-5242** or 928/684-5479; www.outwickenburgway.com).

The visitor center is open Monday through Friday from 9am to 4:30pm, Saturday and Sunday from 10am to 2pm.

EXPLORING THE AREA

A Walk Around Town

While Wickenburg's main attractions remain the guest ranches outside of town, a walk around downtown also provides a glimpse of the Old West. Most of the buildings here were built between 1890 and the 1920s (although a few are older), and although not all of them look their age, there is just enough Western character to make a stroll worthwhile (if it's not too hot).

The old **Santa Fe train station,** on Frontier Street, is now the Wickenburg Chamber of Commerce, where you can pick up a map that tells a bit about the history of the town's buildings. The brick **post office,** almost across the street from the train station, once had a ride-up window providing service to people on horseback. Frontier Street is preserved as it looked in the early 1900s. The covered sidewalks and false fronts are characteristic of frontier architecture; the false fronts often disguised older adobe buildings that were considered "uncivilized" by settlers from back east. The oldest building in town is the **Etter General Store,** adjacent to the Homestead Restaurant. The adobe-walled store was built in 1864 and has long since been disguised with a false wooden front.

Two of the town's most unusual attractions aren't buildings at all. The **Jail Tree,** behind the convenience store at the corner of Wickenburg Way and Tegner Street, is an old mesquite tree that served as the local hoosegow. Outlaws were simply chained to the tree. Their families would often come to visit and have a picnic in the shade of the tree. The second, equally curious, town attraction is the **Wishing Well,** which stands beside the bridge over the Hassayampa. Legend has it that anyone who drinks from the Hassayampa River will never tell the truth again. How the well adjacent to the river became a wishing well is unclear.

Museums & Mines

Desert Caballeros Western Museum ★★ Wickenburg thrives on its Western heritage, and inside this museum you'll find an outstanding collection of Western art depicting life on the range, including works by Albert Bierstadt, Thomas Moran, Charles Russell, Frederick Remington, Maynard Dixon, and other members of the Cowboy Artists of America. The Hays "Spirit of the Cowboy" collection is an impressive display of historical cowboy gear that alone makes this museum worth a stop.

21 N. Frontier St. ✆ **928/684-2272.** www.westernmuseum.org. Admission $7.50 adults, $6 seniors, free for children 16 and under. Mon–Sat 10am–5pm; Sun noon–4pm. Closed Mon May–Aug, New Year's Day, Easter, July 4th, Thanksgiving, and Christmas.

The Vulture Mine (Kids) Lying at the base of Vulture Peak (the most visible landmark in the Wickenburg area), the Vulture Mine was first staked by Henry Wickenburg in 1863, fueling the small gold rush that helped populate this section of the Arizona desert. Today, the Vulture Mine has the feel of a ghost town, and though you can't go down into the old mine itself, you can wander around the aboveground shacks and mine structures on a self-guided tour. It's all mildly interesting for those who appreciate old mines, and it's fun for kids.

Vulture Mine Rd. ✆ **602/859-2743.** Admission $10, free for children 11 and under. Late Dec to mid-May daily 8am–4pm; mid-May to late Dec Fri–Sun 8am–4pm. Take U.S. 60 W. out of town, turn left on Vulture Mine Rd., and drive 12 miles south.

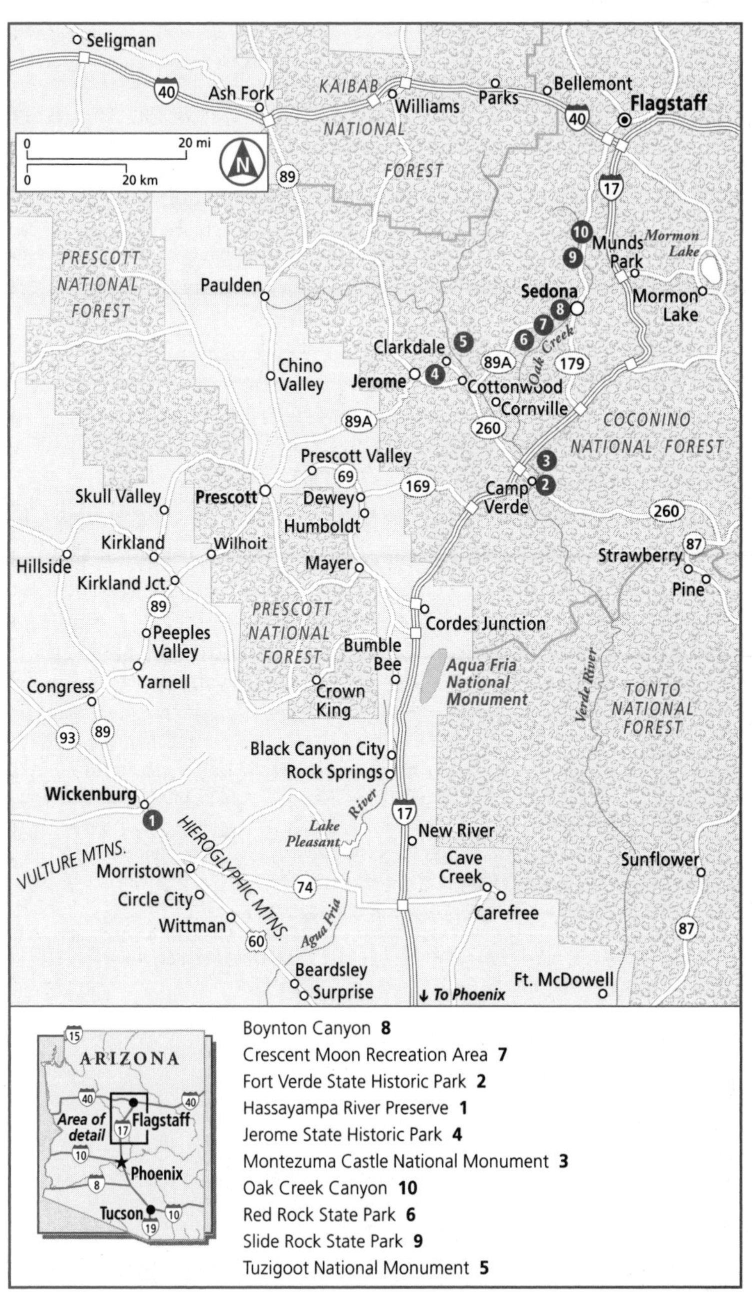
Seligman
Ash Fork
Williams
Parks
Bellemont
Flagstaff
KAIBAB NATIONAL FOREST
0 20 mi
0 20 km
N
PRESCOTT NATIONAL FOREST
Paulden
Munds Park
Mormon Lake
Sedona
Mormon Lake
Clarkdale
Chino Valley
Jerome
Cottonwood
Oak Creek
Cornville
COCONINO NATIONAL FOREST
Prescott Valley
Skull Valley
Prescott
Dewey
Humboldt
Camp Verde
Kirkland
Wilhoit
Hillside
Kirkland Jct.
Mayer
Strawberry
Pine
PRESCOTT NATIONAL FOREST
Cordes Junction
Peeples Valley
Yarnell
Bumble Bee
Crown King
Congress
Aqua Fria National Monument
Verde River
TONTO NATIONAL FOREST
Black Canyon City
Rock Springs
Wickenburg
HIEROGLYPHIC MTNS.
VULTURE MTNS.
Lake Pleasant
River
New River
Cave Creek
Sunflower
Morristown
Circle City
Wittman
Agua Fria
Carefree
Beardsley
Surprise
To Phoenix
Ft. McDowell
ARIZONA
Area of detail
Flagstaff
Phoenix
Tucson
Boynton Canyon 8
Crescent Moon Recreation Area 7
Fort Verde State Historic Park 2
Hassayampa River Preserve 1
Jerome State Historic Park 4
Montezuma Castle National Monument 3
Oak Creek Canyon 10
Red Rock State Park 6
Slide Rock State Park 9
Tuzigoot National Monument 5

Hassayampa River Preserve ★ The Nature Conservancy, a nonprofit organization dedicated to purchasing and preserving threatened habitats, owns and manages the Hassayampa River Preserve, which is one of the state's most important bird-watching sites (280 species of birds have been spotted here). Nature trails lead along the river beneath cottonwoods and willows, and past the spring-fed Palm Lake. On-site are a visitor center and bookshop. October through April, free naturalist-guided walks are offered on the last Saturday of the month at 8:30am (reservations required).

49614 U.S. 60 (mile marker 114, 3 miles southeast of Wickenburg). ✆ **928/684-2772.** www.nature.org. Suggested donation $5 ($3 for Nature Conservancy members). Mid-Sept to mid-May Wed–Sun 8am–5pm; mid-May to mid-Sept Fri–Sun 7–11am. Closed Thanksgiving, day after Thanksgiving, Christmas Eve, Christmas Day, New Year's Eve, and New Year's Day.

Getting Outside

If you're in the area for more than a day or just can't spend another minute in the saddle, you can go out on a Jeep tour and explore the desert backcountry, visit Vulture Peak, see some petroglyphs, or check out old mines. Call **B.C. Jeep Tours** (✆ **928/684-7901** or 928/231-1010; www.bcjeeptours.com), which charges $60 to $100 per person with a two-person minimum. However, if you've got time for only one Jeep tour on your Arizona vacation, make it in Sedona.

Los Caballeros Golf Club ★, 1551 S. Vulture Mine Rd. (✆ **928/684-2704;** www.loscaballerosgolf.com), has been rated one of the best courses in the state. Greens fees are $200 in the cooler months.

WHERE TO STAY

Flying E Ranch (Kids) This is a working cattle ranch with 20,000 high, wide, and handsome acres for you and the cattle to roam. In business since 1946, the Flying E attracts plenty of repeat business, with families finding it a particularly appealing and down-home kind of place. Accommodations vary in size, but all have Western-style furnishings and either twin or king-size beds. Three family-style meals are served in the wood-paneled dining room; but there's no bar, so you'll need to bring your own liquor. However, the main lodge does have a spacious lounge where guests like to gather by the fireplace. There are also breakfast cookouts, lunch rides, hay rides, and evening chuck-wagon dinners. Horseback riding costs an additional $40 to $60 per person per day.

2801 W. Wickenburg Way, Wickenburg, AZ 85390. ✆ **888/684-2650** or 928/684-2690. Fax 928/684-5304. www.flyingeranch.com. 17 units. $308–$392 double. Rates include all meals. 2- to 4-night minimum stay. MC, V. Closed May–Oct. Drive 4 miles west of town on U.S. 60. **Amenities:** Dining room; exercise room; Jacuzzi; outdoor pool; sauna; tennis court; Wi-Fi. *In room:* A/C, TV, fridge.

Kay El Bar Guest Ranch ★ This is the smallest and oldest of the Wickenburg guest ranches; its adobe buildings, built between 1914 and 1925, are listed on the National Register of Historic Places. The well-maintained ranch is quintessentially Wild West in style, and the setting, on the shady banks of the Hassayampa River (usually dry), lends the ranch a surprisingly lush feel compared with the arid surrounding landscape. While the cottage and the Casa Grande room are the most spacious, the smaller rooms in the adobe main lodge have original Monterey-style furnishings and other classic 1950s dude-ranch decor. I like this place because it's so small, you feel like you're on a friend's ranch. Guests can go out horseback riding twice a day, except on Sunday when there's a morning ride followed by an al fresco brunch.

Rincon Rd., off U.S. 93 (P.O. Box 2480), Wickenburg, AZ 85358. ✆ **800/684-7583** or 928/684-7593. Fax 928/684-4497. www.kayelbar.com. 11 units. $375–$465 double; $795–$895 cottage for 4. Rates do not include 15% service charge. Rates include all meals and horseback riding. 2- to 4-night minimum stay. Children 3 and under stay free in parent's room. MC, V. Closed May to mid-Oct. **Amenities:** Dining room; lounge; access to nearby health club; Jacuzzi; small outdoor pool. *In room:* Hair dryer, no phone.

Rancho de los Caballeros ★★ Located on 20,000 acres 2 miles west of Wickenburg, Rancho de los Caballeros is part of an exclusive country-club community and, as such, feels more like a resort than a guest ranch. However, the main lodge itself, with its flagstone floor, copper fireplace, and colorfully painted furniture, has a very Southwestern feel. Peace and quiet are the keynotes of a visit here, and most guests focus on golf (the golf course is one of the best in the state) and horseback riding ($35–$70 per ride). In addition, the ranch has a spa and offers skeet and trapshooting and guided nature walks. Guest rooms are filled with handcrafted furnishings, exposed-beam ceilings, Indian rugs, and, in some, tile floors and fireplaces. While breakfast and lunch are quite casual, dinner is more formal, with proper attire required.

1551 S. Vulture Mine Rd. (off U.S. 60 west of town), Wickenburg, AZ 85390. ✆ **800/684-5030** or 928/684-5484. Fax 928/684-9565. www.sunc.com. 79 units. Mid-Oct to mid-Dec and late Apr to early May $405–$508 double; mid-Dec to late Apr $462–$625 double. Rates do not include 15% gratuity charge. Rates include all meals. Children 4 and under stay free in parent's room. MC, V. Closed mid-May to mid-Oct. **Amenities:** Dining room; 2 lounges; babysitting; bikes; children's programs; concierge; 18-hole golf course; exercise room & access to nearby health club; small outdoor pool; full-service spa; 4 tennis courts. *In room:* A/C, TV, fridge, hair dryer, Wi-Fi.

2 PRESCOTT

100 miles N of Phoenix; 60 miles SW of Sedona; 87 miles SW of Flagstaff

Prescott, the former territorial capital, is an Arizona anomaly; it doesn't seem like the Southwest at all. With its stately courthouse on a tree-shaded square, its well-preserved historic downtown business district, and its old Victorian homes, Prescott wears the air of the quintessential small Midwestern town, the sort of place where the Broadway show *The Music Man* might have been staged. Prescott has just about everything a small town should have: an 1890s saloon (the Palace), an old cattlemen's hotel (the Hassayampa Inn), a burger shop (Kendall's), and a brewpub (the Prescott Brewing Company). Add to this several small museums, a couple of other historic hotels, the strange and beautiful landscape of the Granite Dells, and the nearby Prescott National Forest, and you have a town that appeals to visitors with a diverse range of interests.

Prescott has become an upscale retirement community, as much for its historic heritage as for its mild year-round climate. In summer, Prescott is also a popular weekend getaway for Phoenicians; it is usually 20° cooler here than it is in Phoenix.

ESSENTIALS

GETTING THERE Prescott is at the junction of Ariz. 89, Ariz. 89A, and Ariz. 69. If you're coming from Phoenix, take the Cordes Junction exit (exit 262) from I-17. From Flagstaff, the most direct route is I-17 to Ariz. 169, to Ariz. 69. From Sedona, just take Ariz. 89A all the way.

Shuttle "U" (✆ **800/304-6114** or 928/442-1000; www.shuttleu.com) provides service to Prescott from Sky Harbor Airport for $34 one-way, $56 round-trip.

VISITOR INFORMATION The **Prescott Chamber of Commerce** is at 117 W. Goodwin St. (✆ **800/266-7534** or 928/445-2000; www.prescott.org). The visitor center is open Monday through Friday from 9am to 5pm, and Saturday and Sunday from 10am to 2pm.

EXPLORING THE TOWN

A walk around **Courthouse Plaza** should be your first introduction to Prescott. The stately old courthouse in the middle of the tree-shaded plaza sets the tone for the whole town. The building, far too large for a small regional town such as this, dates from the days when Prescott was the capital of the Arizona territory. Under the big shade trees, you'll find several bronze statues of cowboys and soldiers.

Surrounding the courthouse and extending north for a block is Prescott's **historic business district.** Stroll around admiring the brick buildings, and you'll realize that Prescott was once a very important place. Duck into an old saloon or the lobby of one of the historic hotels, and you'll understand that the town was also part of the Wild West.

Phippen Museum ★ If you're a fan of classic Western art, you won't want to miss this small museum. Located on a hill a few miles north of town, the Phippen is named after the first president of the prestigious Cowboy Artists of America organization and exhibits works by established Western artists and newcomers alike. Also on display are artifacts and photos that help place the artwork in the context of the region's history. The **Phippen Museum Western Art Show & Sale** is held each year on Memorial Day weekend.

4701 U.S. 89 N. ✆ **928/778-1385.** www.phippenartmuseum.org. Admission $5 adults, $4 seniors and students, free for children 11 and under. Tues–Sat 10am–4pm; Sun 1–4pm.

Sharlot Hall Museum ★ Opened in 1928 in a log home that once served as the governor's mansion of the Arizona territory, this museum was founded by Sharlot Hall, who served as the territorial historian from 1909 to 1911. In addition to the governor's "mansion," which is furnished much as it might have been when it was built, several other interesting buildings can be toured. With its traditional wood-frame construction, the Frémont House, which was built in 1875 for the fifth territorial governor, shows how quickly Prescott grew from a remote logging and mining camp into a civilized little town. The 1877 Bashford House reflects the Victorian architecture that was popular throughout the country around the end of the 19th century. The Sharlot Hall Building houses exhibits on Native American cultures and territorial Arizona. Every year in early summer, artisans, craftspeople, and costumed exhibitors participate in the **Folk Arts Fair.**

415 W. Gurley St. ✆ **928/445-3122.** www.sharlot.org. Admission $5 adults, free for children 17 and under. May–Sept Mon–Sat 10am–5pm, Sun noon–4pm; Oct–Apr Mon–Sat 10am–4pm, Sun noon–4pm. Closed New Year's Day, Thanksgiving, and Christmas.

The Smoki Museum This interesting little museum, which houses a collection of Native American artifacts in a historic stone building, is named for the fictitious Smoki tribe. The tribe was dreamed up in 1921 by a group of non-Indians who wanted to inject some new life into Prescott's July 4th celebrations. Despite its phony origins, the museum contains genuine artifacts and basketry from many different tribes, mainly Southwestern. The museum also sponsors interesting lectures on Native American topics.

147 N. Arizona St. ✆ **928/445-1230.** www.smokimuseum.org. Admission $5 adults, $4 seniors, $3 students, free for children 12 and under. Tues–Sat 10am–4pm; Sun 1–4pm. Closed Easter, Thanksgiving, Christmas, and early Jan.

GETTING OUTSIDE

Prescott is situated on the edge of a wide expanse of high plains with the pine forests of **Prescott National Forest** at its back. Within the national forest are lakes, campgrounds, and many miles of hiking and mountain biking trails. My favorite hiking and biking areas in the national forest are Thumb Butte (west of town) and the Granite Mountain Wilderness (northwest of town).

Thumb Butte, a rocky outcropping that towers over the forest just west of town, is Prescott's most easily recognizable natural landmark. A 1.2-mile trail leads nearly to the top of this butte, and from the saddle near the summit, there's a panoramic vista of the entire region. The trail itself is very steep but paved much of the way. The summit of the butte is a popular rock-climbing spot. An alternative return trail makes a loop hike possible. To reach the trail head, drive west out of town on Gurley Street, which becomes Thumb Butte Road. Follow the road until you see the National Forest signs, after which there's a parking lot, picnic area, and trail head. The parking fee is $5.

The Granite Basin Recreation Area provides access to the **Granite Mountain Wilderness.** Trails lead beneath the cliffs of Granite Mountain, where you might spot peregrine falcons. For the best views, hike 1.5 miles to Blair Pass and then on up the Granite Mountain trail as far as you feel like going. To reach this area, take Gurley Street west from downtown, turn right on Grove Avenue, and follow it around to Iron Springs Road, which will take you northwest out of town to the signposted road for the Granite Basin Recreation Area (less than 8 miles from downtown). There is a $5 parking fee here.

Both of the above areas also offer mountain biking trails. Although the scenery isn't as spectacular as in the Sedona area, the trails are great. You can rent a bike and get maps and specific trail recommendations at **Ironclad Bicycles,** 710 White Spar Rd. (✆ **928/776-1755;** www.ironcladbicycles.com), which charges $24 to $48 per day for mountain bikes. This shop also rents bikes at **Encore Performance & Fabrication,** 2929 N. Ariz. 89 (✆ **928/778-7910**), near the Peavine Trail (see below).

For maps and information on these and other hikes and bike rides in the area, stop by the **Bradshaw Ranger Station,** 344 S. Cortez St. (✆ **928/443-8000;** www.fs.fed.us/r3/prescott).

North of town 5 miles, on Ariz. 89, is an unusual and scenic area known as the **Granite Dells ★★**. Jumbled hills of rounded granite suddenly jut from the landscape, creating a maze of huge boulders and smooth rock. In the middle of this dramatic landscape lies **Watson Lake,** the waters of which push their way in among the boulders to create one of the prettiest lakes in the state. On the highway side of the lake, you'll find **Watson Lake Park,** which has picnic tables and great views. Spring through fall (weather permitting), from 8am to 3pm Thursday through Sunday, you can rent **canoes and kayaks** ($15–$20 for the first hour and $10–$15 per hour after that) at the lake. Reservations aren't accepted, but you can call **Prescott Outdoors** (✆ **928/925-1410;** www.prescott outdoors.com) to make sure they'll be at the lake with their boats.

For hiking in the Watson Lake area, I recommend heading to the scenic **Peavine Trail ★★**, which is one of the most gratifying easy hikes in the state. To find the trail head, turn east onto Prescott Lake Parkway, which is between Prescott and the Granite Dells, and then turn left onto Sun Dog Ranch Road. This rails-to-trails path extends for several miles through the middle of the Granite Dells and is the best way to fully appreciate the Dells (you'll be away from both people and the highway). Although this is a fascinating, easy hike, it also makes a great, equally easy, mountain bike ride that can be extended 7.5 miles on the Iron King Trail. Also accessible from this same trail head is the

Watson Woods Riparian Preserve, which has some short trails through the wetlands and riparian zone along Granite Creek.

A couple of miles west of Watson Lake on Willow Creek Road, you can hike in **Willow Creek Park,** where several miles of trails lead through grasslands and groves of huge cottonwood trees adjacent to Willow Lake. The trails eventually lead to the edge of the Granite Dells. There's great bird-watching in the trees in this park, and there are even great blue heron and cormorant rookeries.

If you want to explore the area on horseback, try **Granite Mountain Stables,** 2400 Shane Dr. (✆ **928/771-9551;** www.granitemountainstables.com), which offers guided trail rides in the Prescott National Forest. A 1-hour ride is $35.

Reasonably priced golf is available at the 36-hole **Antelope Hills Golf Course,** 1 Perkins Dr. (✆ **800/972-6818** or 928/776-7888; www.antelopehillsgolf.com). Greens fees range from $32 to $60.

SHOPPING

Downtown Prescott is filled with antiques stores, especially along North Cortez Street, and is the best place in Arizona to do some antiques shopping. For Native American crafts and Old West memorabilia, be sure to stop in at **Ogg's Hogan,** 111 N. Cortez St. (✆ **928/443-9856**). In the Hotel St. Michael's shopping arcade, check out **Hotel Trading,** 110 S. Montezuma St. (✆ **928/778-7276**), which carries some genuine Native American artifacts at reasonable prices. Owner Ernie Lister also makes silver jewelry in the 19th-century Navajo style. In this same arcade, you'll find the **Old Sage Bookshop,** 110 S. Montezuma St. (✆ **928/776-1136**), a wonderful little used-book store selling primarily hardback editions. On the same block are both the **Arts Prescott Gallery,** 134 S. Montezuma St. (✆ **928/776-7717;** www.artsprescott.com), a cooperative of local artists; and **Van Gogh's Ear,** 156B S. Montezuma St. (✆ **928/776-1080;** www.vgegallery.com), which was founded by a splinter group from the co-op. Also on this block you'll find the **Newman Gallery,** 106-A S. Montezuma St. (✆ **928/442-9167;** www.newmangallery.net), which features the colorful Western-inspired pop-culture imagery of artist Dave Newman.

WHERE TO STAY

Expensive

Hassayampa Inn ★ Built as a luxury hotel in 1927, the Hassayampa Inn, which is listed on the National Register of Historic Places, evokes the time when Prescott was the bustling territorial capital. In the lobby, exposed ceiling beams, wrought-iron chandeliers, and arched doorways all reflect the place's Southwestern heritage. Unfortunately, guest rooms are not as impressive as the lobby. Rooms tend to be very small and have either original furnishings or antiques. Some suites are very oddly configured; you might find the shower in one converted closet and the commode in another. One room is said to be haunted; any hotel employee will be happy to tell you the story of the ill-fated honeymooners whose ghosts supposedly reside here.

122 E. Gurley St., Prescott, AZ 86301. ✆ **800/322-1927** or 928/778-9434. www.hassayampainn.com. 68 units. $99–$149 double; $169–$229 suite. Children 12 and under stay free in parent's room. AE, DISC, MC, V. **Amenities:** Restaurant; lounge; exercise room & access to nearby health club; room service. *In room:* A/C, TV, hair dryer, Wi-Fi.

Moderate

Hotel Vendome (Kids) Not quite as luxurious as the Hassayampa, yet not as basic as the St. Michael, the Vendome is a good middle-price choice for those who want to stay in a historic hotel. Built in 1917 as a lodging house, the restored brick building is only 2 blocks from the action of Whiskey Row, but far enough away that you can get a good night's sleep. Guest rooms are outfitted with modern furnishings, but some of the bathrooms still contain original claw-foot tubs. The two bedroom units, with an interconnected bathroom, are ideal for families. With any luck, your kids will be able to sleep in this haunted hotel. (Like a couple of other hotels in town, the Vendome has its own resident ghost.)

230 S. Cortez St., Prescott, AZ 86303. ✆ **888/468-3583** or 928/776-0900. www.vendomehotel.com. 20 units. $49–$109 double; $109–$149 2-bedroom unit. Rates include continental breakfast. AE, DISC, MC, V. **Amenities:** Lounge; concierge. *In room:* A/C, TV, hair dryer, Internet.

Rocamadour Bed & Breakfast for (Rock) Lovers ★★ The Granite Dells, just north of Prescott, is the area's most unforgettable feature. Should you wish to stay amid these jumbled boulders, there's no better choice than Rocamadour. Mike and Twila Coffey honed their innkeeping skills as owners of a 40-room château in France, and antique furnishings from that château can now be found throughout this inn. The most elegant pieces are in the Chambre Trucy, which also boasts an amazing underlit whirlpool tub. One cottage is built into the boulders and has a large whirlpool tub on its deck. The unique setting, engaging innkeepers, and thoughtful details everywhere you turn make this one of the state's must-stay inns.

3386 N. Hwy. 89, Prescott, AZ 86301. ✆ **888/771-1933** or 928/771-1933. 3 units. $149–$169 double; $219 suite. Rates include full breakfast. AE, MC, V. *In room:* A/C, TV/VCR, Wi-Fi.

Inexpensive

Hotel St. Michael (Value) Located right on Whiskey Row, this hotel, complete with resident ghost and the oldest elevator in Prescott, offers a historic setting at budget prices (don't expect the most stylish furnishings). All rooms are different; some have bathtubs but no showers. Its restaurant, the casual Caffe St. Michael, overlooks Courthouse Plaza.

205 W. Gurley St., Prescott, AZ 86301. ✆ **800/678-3757** or 928/776-1999. Fax 928/776-7318. www.hotelstmichael.net. 72 units. $59–$99 double; $89–$119 suite. Rates include full breakfast. AE, DC, DISC, MC, V. **Amenities:** Restaurant; access to nearby health club. *In room:* A/C, TV, Wi-Fi.

WHERE TO DINE

Moderate

El Gato Azul ★ MEDITERRANEAN Whether you're ravenous from a long day of hiking in the Granite Mountain Wilderness or still full from a huge breakfast at your B&B, this casual creekside restaurant in downtown Prescott is a great choice. You can have as few or as many *tapas* (small plates) as it takes to fill you up. If you want to pack in as many flavors as possible, order as many little appetizers as possible. Try the blackened scallops, the mint-pesto grilled shrimp, or the chicken *mole.* If you want something substantial, you can also order a nice big entree such as apricot duck or lamb with curry couscous. There's also a good selection of Spanish wines.

316 W. Goodwin St. ✆ **928/445-1070.** www.fourcornersrestaurants.com. Reservations recommended. Main courses $8–$15 lunch, $17–$24 dinner; *tapas* $4–$9. AE, DISC, MC, V. Mon–Thurs 11am–9pm; Fri–Sat 11am–10pm; Sun noon–3pm and 4–9pm.

129½ ★ NEW AMERICAN Prescott, a classic small-town-America sort of place, may seem an odd location for a classic New York–style jazz club, but this restaurant has it down. It may not be in a basement and it isn't smoky, but everything else has just the right feel. Best of all, the restaurant has great food. Steaks are the specialty and can be had with an assortment of delicious sauces, such as rosemary cream, mushroom ragout, and pinot and green peppercorn.

129½ N. Cortez St. ✆ **928/443-9292.** www.fourcornersrestaurants.com. Reservations recommended. Main courses $15–$26. DISC, MC, V. Tues–Thurs 4–9pm; Fri–Sat 4–10pm.

Inexpensive

Dinner Bell Café (Finds) (Kids) AMERICAN This casual little breakfast-and-lunch place is a big hit with local students and other people in the know who come to order either the waffles (served with a variety of toppings) or the thick, juicy burgers. The waffles are available at lunch, but people don't usually order burgers at breakfast. The Dinner Bell has a split personality. Up front, there's a classic old diner that's been in business since 1939; in back, there's a colorful modern space with walls that roll up. The setting, a block off Whiskey Row, makes this a great little hideaway for a quick, casual meal, and kids will want to wander along the creekside path nearby.

321 W. Gurley St. ✆ **928/445-9888.** Main courses $5.50–$9. No credit cards. Mon–Fri 6:30am–2pm; Sat–Sun 7am–2pm.

Sweet Tart ★ (Finds) BAKERY/LIGHT FARE/NEW AMERICAN This restaurant/patisserie makes some of the best pastries in Arizona, so before you walk through the door, make sure you're hungry enough for dessert—the pastry case here is absolutely irresistible. At breakfast, they have, among other treats, a variety of brioches, including blueberry and mixed-fruit, and fabulous almond croissants. On Saturday nights, there are four-course dinners that include the likes of French onion soup, sea bass in a jacket of thinly sliced potatoes, and wine-poached pears with mascarpone mousse; call for reservations.

125 N. Cortez St. ✆ **928/443-8587.** Reservations required for dinner. Main courses $7–$9; prix-fixe dinners $35. MC, V. Tues–Sat 7am–4pm; Sun 8am–3pm.

PRESCOTT AFTER DARK

Back in the days when Prescott was the territorial capital and a booming mining town, it supported dozens of rowdy saloons, most of which were concentrated along Montezuma Street on the west side of Courthouse Plaza. This section of town was known as **Whiskey Row,** and legend has it there was a tunnel from the courthouse to one of the saloons so lawmakers wouldn't have to be seen ducking into the saloons during regular business hours. On July 14, 1900, a fire consumed most of Whiskey Row. However, concerned cowboys and miners managed to drag the tremendously heavy bar of The Palace saloon across the street before it was damaged.

Today, Whiskey Row still has a few noisy saloons with genuine Wild West flavor. However, within a few blocks of Whiskey Row, you can hear country, folk, jazz, and rock at a surprisingly diverse assortment of bars, restaurants, and clubs.

If you want to see what this street's saloons looked like back in the old days, drop by **The Palace,** 120 S. Montezuma St. (✆ **928/541-1996;** www.historicpalace.com), which still has a classic bar up front.

If you want to drink where the ranchers drink and not where the hired hands carouse, head upstairs to the **Jersey Lilly Saloon,** 116 S. Montezuma St. (✆ **928/541-7854**), which attracts a more well-heeled clientele than the street-level saloons. On weekends, there is live music in a wide range of styles.

Two blocks away, you'll find the **Raven Café,** 142 N. Cortez St. (✆ **928/717-0009**), which is the most artsy and eclectic nightlife venue in town. Not only does the Raven have the best beer list in Prescott (with an emphasis on Belgian beers and American microbrews), but the entertainment lineup ranges from vintage movies on Tuesday nights to live jazz and salsa dancing.

3 JEROME

35 miles NE of Prescott; 28 miles W of Sedona; 130 miles N of Phoenix

Few towns anywhere in Arizona make more of an impression on visitors than Jerome, a historic mining town that clings to the slopes of Cleopatra Hill high on Mingus Mountain. The town is divided into two sections that are separated by an elevation change of 1,500 vertical feet, with the upper part of town 2,000 feet above the Verde Valley. On a clear day, the view from Jerome is stupendous—it's possible to see for more than 50 miles, with the red rocks of Sedona, the Mogollon Rim, and the San Francisco Peaks all visible in the distance. Add to the unforgettable views the abundance of interesting shops and galleries and the winding narrow streets, and you have a town that should not be missed.

ESSENTIALS

GETTING THERE Jerome is on Ariz. 89A, roughly halfway between Sedona and Prescott. Coming from Phoenix, take Ariz. 260 from Camp Verde.

VISITOR INFORMATION Contact the **Jerome Chamber of Commerce** (✆ **928/634-2900;** www.jeromechamber.com) for information.

EXPLORING THE TOWN

Wandering the streets, soaking up the atmosphere, and shopping are the main pastimes in Jerome. But before you launch yourself on a shopping tour, you can learn about the town's past at the **Jerome State Historic Park,** off Ariz. 89A, on Douglas Road, in the lower section of town (✆ **928/634-5381;** www.azstateparks.com). Located in a mansion built in 1916 as a home for mine owner "Rawhide Jimmy" Douglas, and as a hotel for visiting mining executives, the Jerome State Historic Park contains exhibits on mining as well as a few of the mansion's original furnishings. From its perch on a hill above Douglas's Little Daisy Mine, the mansion overlooks Jerome and, dizzyingly far below, the Verde Valley. The mansion was constructed of adobe bricks made on the site, and once contained a wine cellar, billiards room, marble shower, steam heat, and central vacuum system. Admission is $3, and the park is open daily (except Christmas) from 8:30am to 5pm. At press time, this park was temporarily closed, so be sure to call first to find out if it has reopened.

To learn more about Jerome's history, stop in at the **Jerome Historical Society's Mine Museum,** 200 Main St. (✆ **928/634-5477;** www.jeromehistoricalsociety.org), which has some small and old-fashioned displays on mining. It's open daily from 9am to 5pm; admission is $2 for adults, $1 for seniors, and free for children 12 and under. The second floor of the gift shop **Liberty Theatre & Gifts,** 110 Jerome Ave. (✆ **928/649-9016;** www.jeromelibertytheater.com), was a theater back in the town's heyday. The theater is now being slowly restored and is open to the public. Although small, the theater museum here is fun to wander through, and a film about the history of Jerome is usually playing in the old theater. For that classic mining-town tourist-trap experience, follow the signs up the hill from downtown Jerome to the **Gold King Mine** (✆ **928/634-0053;** www.goldkingmineghosttown.com), where you can see lots of old, rusting mining equipment and maybe even catch a demonstration. The mine is open 9am to 5pm daily, and admission is $5 for adults, $4 for seniors, and $3 for children ages 6 to 12.

Most visitors come to Jerome for the shops, which offer an eclectic blend of contemporary art, chic jewelry, one-of-a-kind handmade fashions, and unusual imports. Of course, there are now also the inevitable ice-cream parlors and shops full of tacky souvenirs.

WHERE TO STAY

Connor Hotel of Jerome Housed in a renovated historic hotel, this lodging has spacious rooms with large windows; views of the valley, however, are limited. Although a few of the rooms are located directly above the hotel's popular bar, which can be quite noisy on weekends, most rooms are quiet enough to provide a good night's rest. Better yet, come on a weekday, when the Harley-Davidson poseur crowd from the Scottsdale area isn't thundering through the streets on their hogs.

164 Main St. (P.O. Box 1177), Jerome, AZ 86331. ✆ **800/523-3554** or 928/634-5006. Fax 928/649-0981. www.connorhotel.com. 12 units. $90–$165 double. Children 11 and under stay free in parent's room. AE, DISC, MC, V. Pets accepted. **Amenities:** Bar. *In room:* TV, fridge, hair dryer, Wi-Fi.

Mile High Inn In classic European tradition, this inn is upstairs from a restaurant and is reached by a flight of stairs. Therein lies this inn's greatest charm. Although more than half the rooms have shared bathrooms, all the rooms are attractively decorated, some with antiques and some with more modern furnishings. Although the rooms are not very large, a couple do have king-size beds.

309 Main St. (P.O. Box 1311), Jerome, AZ 86331. ✆ **928/634-5094.** www.jeromemilehighinn.com. 7 units (3 with private bathroom). $85 double with shared bathroom; $120 double with private bathroom. Rates include full breakfast (except Mon–Wed in winter). 2-night minimum on holidays. MC, V. **Amenities:** Restaurant; lounge. *In room:* A/C, no phone.

WHERE TO DINE

The Asylum ★ **Finds** SOUTHWESTERN As the name would imply, this restaurant (inside a former hospital building high above downtown Jerome) is a bit out of the ordinary. The bedpan full of candy at the front desk and the odd little notes in the menu will also make it absolutely clear that this place doesn't take much, other than good food, seriously. Most recommendable are the distinctly Southwestern dishes, including the prickly-pear barbecued pork tenderloin with tomatillo salsa, and an unusual butternut-squash soup made with a cinnamon-lime cream sauce. Cocktails all get wacky loony-bin names, and there's also a superb, award-winning wine list.

200 Hill St. ✆ **928/639-3197.** www.theasylum.biz. Reservations recommended. Main courses $7.50–$13 lunch, $14–$28 dinner. AE, DISC, MC, V. Daily 11am–3pm and 5–9pm.

Flatiron Café LIGHT FARE The tiny Flatiron Café is a simple breakfast-and-lunch spot in, you guessed it, Jerome's version of a flatiron building. The limited menu includes the likes of lox and bagels, a breakfast quesadilla, black-bean hummus, smoked-salmon quesadillas, fresh juices, and espresso drinks. It looks as though you could hardly squeeze in here, but there's more seating across the street. It's definitely not your usual ghost-town lunch counter.

416 Main St. (at Hull Ave.). ✆ **928/634-2733.** Reservations not accepted. Most items $7.50–$12. MC, V. Wed–Mon 8am–3pm.

4 THE VERDE VALLEY

Camp Verde: 20 miles E of Jerome; 30 miles S of Sedona; 95 miles N of Phoenix

Named by early Spanish explorers who were impressed by the sight of such a verdant valley in an otherwise brown desert landscape, the Verde Valley has long been a magnet for both wildlife and people. Today, the valley is one of Arizona's richest agricultural and ranching region. The valley is also popular with retirees, and housing subdivisions now sprawl across much of the landscape. Cottonwood and Clarkdale, the valley's two largest towns, are old copper-smelting towns, while Camp Verde was an army post back in the days of the Indian Wars. All three towns have some interesting historic buildings, but it is the valley's two national monuments—Tuzigoot and Montezuma Castle—that are the main attractions.

These two national monuments preserve the ruins of Sinagua villages that date from long before the first European explorers entered the Verde Valley. By the time the first pioneers began settling in this region, the Sinaguas had long since moved on, and Apaches had claimed the valley as part of their territory. When settlers came into conflict with the Apaches, Fort Verde, now a state park, was established. Between this state park and the two national monuments, hundreds of years of Verde Valley history and prehistory can be explored. This valley is also the site of the most scenic railroad excursion in the state.

ESSENTIALS

GETTING THERE Camp Verde is just off I-17, at the junction with Ariz. 260. The latter highway leads northwest through the Verde Valley for 12 miles to Cottonwood.

VISITOR INFORMATION Contact the **Cottonwood Chamber of Commerce,** 1010 S. Main St., Cottonwood (✆ **928/634-7593;** www.cottonwood.verdevalley.com).

A RAILWAY EXCURSION

Verde Canyon Railroad ★★ When the town of Jerome was busily mining copper, a railway was built to link the booming town with the territorial capital at nearby Prescott. Because of the rugged mountains between Jerome and Prescott, the railroad was forced to take a longer but less difficult route north along the Verde River before turning south toward Prescott. Today, you can ride these same tracks aboard the Verde Canyon Railroad. The route through the canyon traverses both the remains of a copper smelter and unspoiled desert that is inaccessible by car and is part of Prescott National Forest. The views of the rocky canyon walls and green waters of the Verde River are quite dramatic, and if you look closely along the way, you'll see ancient Sinagua cliff dwellings. In late winter and early spring, nesting bald eagles can also be spotted. Although the Grand Canyon Railway travels to a more impressive destination, this is a more scenic excursion. Live music and an informative narration make the ride entertaining as well.

300 N. Broadway, Clarkdale. ✆ **800/320-0718.** www.verdecanyonrr.com. Tickets $55 adults, $50 seniors, $35 children 2–12; 1st-class tickets $80. Call or visit the website for schedule and reservations.

Fort Verde State Historic Park Just south of Montezuma Castle and Montezuma Well, in the town of Camp Verde, you'll find Fort Verde State Historic Park. Established in 1871, Fort Verde was the third military post in the Verde Valley and was occupied until 1891.

The state park, which covers 10 acres, preserves three officers' quarters, an administration building, and some ruins. The buildings that have been fully restored house exhibits on the history of the fort and what life was like here in the 19th century. With their gables, white picket fences, and shake-shingle roofs, the buildings of Fort Verde suggest that life at this remote post was not so bad, at least for officers. Costumed military reenactments are held here throughout much of the year; call for details.

125 E. Hollaman St., Camp Verde. ✆ **928/567-3275.** www.azstateparks.com. Admission $3 adults, $1 children 7–13, free for children 6 and under. Thurs–Mon 9am–5pm. Closed Christmas.

Montezuma Castle National Monument ★★ This Sinagua ruin is one of the best-preserved cliff dwellings in Arizona. The site consists of two impressive stone pueblos that were abandoned by the Sinagua people in the early 14th century.

The more intriguing of the two ruins is set in a shallow cave 100 feet up a cliff overlooking Beaver Creek. Construction on this five-story, 20-room village began sometime in the early 12th century. Because Montezuma Castle has been protected from the elements by the overhanging roof of the cave in which it was built, the original adobe mud that was used to plaster over the stone walls of the dwelling is still intact. Another structure, containing 45 rooms, stands at the base of the cliff. This latter dwelling is not nearly as well-preserved as the cliff dwelling.

Montezuma Well, located 11 miles north of Montezuma Castle, is a spring-fed sinkhole that was, for the Native peoples of this desert, a genuine oasis. This sunken pond was formed when a cavern in the area's porous limestone bedrock collapsed. Underground springs quickly filled the sinkhole, which today contains a pond measuring more than 360 feet across and 65 feet deep. Over the centuries, the presence of year-round water attracted first the Hohokam and later the Sinagua peoples, who built irrigation canals to use the water for growing crops. Some of these channels can still be seen. Sinagua structures and an excavated Hohokam pit house built around 1100 are clustered in and near the sinkhole. To reach Montezuma Well, take exit 293 off I-17.

Exit 289, off I-17. ✆ **928/567-3322.** www.nps.gov/moca. Admission $5 adults ($8 with Tuzigoot National Monument admission), free for children 16 and under; no charge to visit Montezuma Well. June–Aug daily 8am–6pm; Sept–May daily 8am–5pm. Closed Christmas.

Out of Africa Wildlife Park ★ Kids Lions and tigers and bears, oh my. And zebras and giraffes and wildebeests, oh yes. That's what you'll encounter at this sprawling wildlife park between Camp Verde and Cottonwood. The park includes both a "wildlife preserve" of large fenced predator enclosures and a "Serengeti Safari" area. In this latter area, you ride on a rugged safari vehicle through a vast enclosure populated by giraffes, zebras, ostriches, wildebeests, and other animals of the Serengeti. You may even get to feed a giraffe or zebra. The other half of the park is home to numerous lions, tigers, wolves, panthers, hyenas, and other large predators. All these carnivores are fed on Sunday, Wednesday, and Friday at 3pm, and following the feeders is one of the highlights of a visit to the park. One of the park's most popular attractions, especially with kids, is the Tiger Splash, in which big cats and their caretakers demonstrate predator-prey interactions in a large pool.

Verde Valley Justice Rd. (off Ariz. 260), Camp Verde. ✆ **928/567-2840** or 567-2842. www.outofafricapark.com. Admission $36 adults, $28 seniors, $20 children ages 3–12, free for children 2 and under. Wed–Sun 9:30am–5pm. Also open some holidays and during spring break. Closed Thanksgiving and Christmas.

Tuzigoot National Monument Perched atop a hill overlooking the Verde River, this small, stone-walled pueblo was built by the Sinagua people and was inhabited between 1125 and 1400. The Sinagua, whose name is Spanish for "without water," were traditionally dryland farmers who relied entirely on rainfall to water their crops. When the Hohokam, who had been living in the Verde Valley since A.D. 600, moved on to more fertile land around 1100, the Sinagua moved into this valley. Their buildings progressed from individual homes, called pit houses, to the type of communal pueblo seen here at Tuzigoot.

An interpretive trail leads through the Tuzigoot ruins, explaining different aspects of Sinaguan life, and inside the visitor center is a small museum displaying many of the artifacts unearthed here. Desert plants, many of which were used by the Sinagua, are identified along the trail.

Just outside Clarkdale, off Ariz. 89A. ✆ **928/634-5564.** www.nps.gov/tuzi. Admission $5 adults ($8 with Montezuma Castle National Monument admission), free for children 16 and under. Memorial Day weekend to Labor Day weekend daily 8am–6pm; rest of year daily 8am–5pm. Closed Christmas.

WHERE TO STAY

Hacienda de la Mariposa ★★ **Finds** This modern Santa Fe–style inn is set on the banks of Beaver Creek and is just up the road from Montezuma Castle National Monument. Guest rooms contain rustic Mexican furnishings, gas beehive-style fireplaces, small private patios, and lots of character. Bathrooms feature skylights and whirlpool tubs. With a patio overlooking the creek, the Mariposa Creekside room is my favorite. The little Casita de Milagros, a sort of cottage/massage room that serves as a gathering spot for guests, has a huge amethyst geode set into the ceiling. In a walled garden out back, you'll find a swimming pool only steps from the creek.

3875 Stagecoach Rd. (P.O. Box 310), Camp Verde, AZ 86322. ✆ **888/520-9095** or 928/567-1490. www.lamariposa-az.com. 5 units. $195–$235 double. AE, MC, V. **Amenities:** Jacuzzi; outdoor pool. *In room:* A/C, TV/DVD/VCR, hair dryer, Internet.

WHERE TO DINE

Blazin' M Ranch Chuckwagon Suppers **Kids** AMERICAN Located adjacent to Dead Horse Ranch State Park, the Blazin' M Ranch is classic Arizona-style family entertainment—steaks and beans accompanied by cowboy music and comedy. This place is geared primarily toward the young 'uns, with pony rides, farm animals, and a little cow town for the kids to explore. If you're young at heart, you might enjoy the Blazin' M, but it's definitely more fun if you bring the whole family. One of the highlights is the gallery of animated woodcarvings, which features humorous Western scenes.

Off 10th St., Cottonwood. ✆ **800/937-8643** or 928/634-0334. www.blazinm.com. Reservations recommended. Dinner $35 adults, $33 seniors, $25 children ages 3–12. AE, DISC, MC, V. Mon–Sat gates open at 5pm, dinner at 6:30pm, show at 7:30pm. Closed Jan.

Old Town Café **Finds** CAFE The almond croissants at this European-style cafe in downtown Cottonwood are among the best I've ever had. If that isn't recommendation enough for you, there are also good salads and sandwiches, such as a grilled panini of smoked turkey, spinach, and tomatoes.

1025 "A" N. Main St., Cottonwood. ✆ **928/634-5980.** Reservations not accepted. Salads and sandwiches $6–$9. MC, V. Tues–Sat 8am–3pm.

5 SEDONA & OAK CREEK CANYON ★★

56 miles NE of Prescott; 116 miles N of Phoenix; 106 miles S of the Grand Canyon

There is not a town anywhere in the Southwest with a more beautiful setting than Sedona. On the outskirts of town, red-rock buttes, eroded canyon walls, and mesas rise into blue skies. Off in the distance, the Mogollon Rim looms, its forests of juniper and ponderosa pine dark against the rocks. With a wide band of rosy sandstone predominating in this area, Sedona has come to be known as red-rock country, and each evening at sunset, the rocks put on an unforgettable light show that is reason enough for a visit. All this may sound perfectly idyllic, but if you lower your eyes from the red rocks, you'll see the flip side of Sedona—a sprawl of housing developments and strip malls. However, not even the proliferation of timeshare sales offices disguised as "visitor information centers" can mar the beauty of the backdrop.

With national forest surrounding the city (and even fingers of forest extending into what would otherwise be the city limits), Sedona also has some of the best outdoors access of any city in the Southwest. All around town, alongside highways and down side streets in suburban neighborhoods, there are trail heads. Trek down any one of these trails and you leave the city behind and enter the world of the red rocks.

Located at the mouth of Oak Creek Canyon, Sedona was first settled by pioneers in 1877 and named for the first postmaster's wife. Word of Sedona's beauty did not begin to spread until Hollywood filmmakers began using the region's red rock as backdrop to their Western films. Next came artists, lured by the landscapes and desert light (it was here in Sedona that the Cowboy Artists of America organization was formed). Although still much touted as an artists' community, Sedona's art scene these days is geared more toward tourists than toward collectors of fine art.

With its drop-dead gorgeous scenery, dozens of motels and resorts, and plethora of good restaurants, Sedona makes an excellent base for exploring central Arizona. Several ancient Indian ruins (including an impressive cliff dwelling), the "ghost town" of Jerome, and the scenic Verde Canyon Railroad are all within easy driving distance, and even the Grand Canyon is but a long day trip away.

ESSENTIALS

GETTING THERE Sedona is on Ariz. 179, at the mouth of Oak Creek Canyon. From Phoenix, take I-17 to Ariz. 179 north. From Flagstaff, head south on I-17 until you see the turnoff for Ariz. 89A and Sedona. Ariz. 89A also connects Sedona with Prescott.

Sedona Phoenix Shuttle (✆ **800/448-7988** in Ariz., or 928/282-2066; www.sedona-phoenix-shuttle.com) operates several trips daily between Phoenix's Sky Harbor Airport and Sedona. The fare is $50 one-way, $90 round-trip.

VISITOR INFORMATION The **Sedona Chamber of Commerce Visitor Center/Uptown Gateway Visitor Center,** 331 Forest Rd. (✆ **800/288-7336** or 928/282-7722; www.visitsedona.com), is at the corner of Ariz. 89A and Forest Road in uptown Sedona. The visitor center is open Monday through Saturday from 8:30am to 5pm, and Sunday and holidays from 9am to 3pm.

You can also get information, as well as a Red Rock Pass for parking at area trail heads, at the **Visitor Contact Center,** 8375 Ariz. 179, Village of Oak Creek (✆ **928/203-2900**), which is open daily from 8am to 5pm; or the **North Gateway Visitor Center,** Oak Creek Vista Overlook, Ariz. 89A (✆ **928/282-4119**), which is open March 1

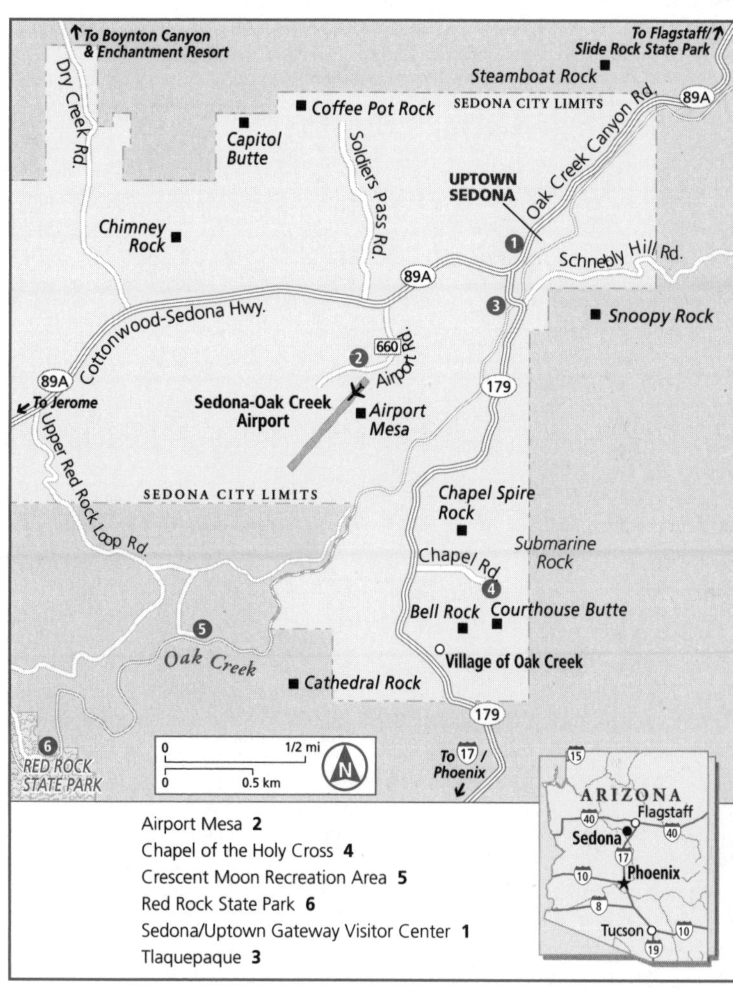

through November 1, weather permitting, daily from 9am to 4:30pm, and sometimes on weekends in other months.

GETTING AROUND Whether traveling by car or on foot, you'll need to cultivate patience when trying to cross major roads in Sedona. Traffic here, especially on weekends, can be some of the worst in the state. Also be prepared for slow traffic on roads that have good views; drivers are often distracted by the red rocks. You may hear or see references to the **"Y,"** which refers to the intersection of Ariz. 179 and Ariz. 89A between the Tlaquepaque shopping plaza and uptown Sedona.

Rental cars are available through **Enterprise** (© **800/261-7331** or 928/282-2052). You can also rent a Jeep from **Farabee Jeep Rentals** (© **877/970-JEEP** [5337] or

 928/282-8700; www.sedonajeeprentals.com), which charges $165 to $195 for 4 hours and $265 to $295 for 24 hours. Or you can get around Sedona on the **Sedona Roadrunner** (✆ **928/282-0938;** www.sedonaroadrunner.com), a free shuttle bus that operates every 10 minutes between uptown, Tlaquepaque, and the Hillside Sedona shopping plaza.

EXPLORING RED-ROCK COUNTRY

The Grand Canyon may be Arizona's biggest attraction, but there's actually far more to do in Sedona. If you aren't an active type, there's the obvious option of just sitting down and gazing in awe at the rugged cliffs, needlelike pinnacles, and isolated buttes that rise from the green forest floor at the mouth of Oak Creek Canyon. Want to see more but don't want to break a sweat? Head out into the red rocks on a Jeep tour or soar over the red rocks in a biplane. Want to go *mano a mano* with this wild landscape? Go for a hike, rent a mountain bike, or go horseback riding. (See "Organized Tours" and "Outdoor Pursuits," later in this chapter, for details.)

Although **Schnebly Hill Road,** which climbs into the red rocks east of Sedona, is a rough dirt road, it's a must for superb views. This road is best driven in a high-clearance vehicle or SUV, but depending on how recently it has been maintained, it can be passable in a regular car. To reach this scenic road, head south out of Sedona on Ariz. 179, turn left after you cross the bridge over Oak Creek (at the Tlaquepaque shopping center), and head up the road, which starts out paved but soon turns to dirt. As this road climbs to the top of the Mogollon Rim, each switchback and cliff-edged curve yields a new and more astonishing view. At the top, the Schnebly Hill overlook offers a view that just begs to be savored over a long picnic. If you don't feel comfortable doing this drive in your own vehicle, you can book a Jeep tour that heads up this way.

Just south of Sedona, on the east side of Ariz. 179, you'll see the aptly named **Bell Rock.** There's a parking area at the foot of this formation, and trails lead up to the top. Adjacent to Bell Rock is **Courthouse Butte,** and to the west stands **Cathedral Rock.** From the Chapel of the Holy Cross (see "Attractions & Activities Around Town," below) on Chapel Road, you can see **Eagle Head Rock** (from the front door of the chapel, look three-quarters of the way up the mountain to see the eagle's head), the **Twin Nuns** (two pinnacles standing side by side), and **Mother and Child Rock** (to the left of the Twin Nuns).

If you head west out of Sedona on Ariz. 89A and turn left onto Airport Road, you'll drive up onto **Airport Mesa,** which commands an unobstructed panorama of Sedona and the red rocks. About halfway up the mesa is a small parking area from which easy trails radiate, and at the top of the mesa is a huge parking area and viewpoint park that attracts large crowds of sunset gazers. The views from here are among the best in the region.

Boynton Canyon, located 8 miles west of the "Y," is a narrow red-rock box canyon and is one of the most beautiful spots in the Sedona area. This canyon is also the site of the deluxe Enchantment resort, but hundreds of years before there were luxury suites here, there were Sinagua cliff dwellings. Several of these cliff dwellings can still be spotted high on the canyon walls. **Boynton Canyon Trail** leads 3 miles up into this canyon from a trail head parking area just outside the gates of Enchantment. To get to the trail head, drive west out of Sedona on Ariz. 89A, turn right on Dry Creek Road, take a left at the first "T" intersection, and a right at the second "T."

On the way to Boynton Canyon, look north from Ariz. 89A, and you'll see **Coffee Pot Rock,** also known as Rooster Rock, rising 1,800 feet above Sedona. Three pinnacles,

Value The High Cost of Red-Rock Views

A **Red Rock Pass** will allow you to visit Palatki Ruins and the V Bar V Heritage Site (site of petroglyphs) and park at any national forest trail head parking areas. The cost is $5 for a 1-day pass, $15 for a 7-day pass, and $20 to $40 for a 12-month pass. Passes are good for everyone in your vehicle. If you plan to be in the area for more than a week and also want to visit Grasshopper Point (a swimming hole), Banjo Bill (a picnic area), Call of the Canyon (the West Fork Oak Creek trail head), and Crescent Moon (Sedona's top photo-op site), you'll want to buy the weekly pass. These sites each charge a $8 admission, so if you aren't planning on going to all of them, the pass won't save you anything. For more information on the Red Rock Pass, visit www.redrockcountry.org.

known as the **Three Golden Chiefs** by the Yavapai tribe, stand beside Coffee Pot Rock. As you drive up Dry Creek Road, on your right you'll see **Capitol Butte,** which resembles the U.S. Capitol.

To the west of Boynton Canyon, you can visit the well-preserved Sinagua cliff dwellings at **Palatki Heritage Site** (✆ **928/282-3854;** www.redrockcountry.org). These small ruins, tucked under the red cliffs, are the best place in the area to get a feel for the ancient Native American cultures that once lived in this region. Among the ruins, you'll see numerous pictographs (paintings) created by the past residents of Palatki. Before heading out to these ruins, be sure you make a reservation by calling the number above. To reach the ruins, follow the directions to Boynton Canyon, but instead of turning right at the second "T" intersection, turn left onto unpaved Boynton Pass Road (F.R. 152C), which is one of the most scenic roads in the area. Follow this road to another "T" intersection and go right onto F.R. 525, then veer right onto F.R. 795, which dead-ends at the ruins. You can also get here by driving west from Sedona on Ariz. 89A to F.R. 525, a gravel road leading north to F.R. 795. To visit Palatki, you'll need a Red Rock Pass (see "The High Cost of Red-Rock Views," below); the ruins are usually open daily from 9:30am to 3pm. The dirt roads around here become impassable to regular cars when they're wet, so don't try coming out here if the roads are at all muddy.

South of Ariz. 89A and a bit west of the turnoff for Boynton Canyon is Upper Red Rock Loop Road, which leads to **Crescent Moon Picnic Area** ★★, a national forest recreation area that has become a must-see for visitors to Sedona. Its popularity stems from a beautiful photograph of Oak Creek with **Cathedral Rock** in the background—an image that has been reproduced countless times in Sedona promotional literature and on postcards. Hiking trails lead up to Cathedral Rock. Admission is $8 per vehicle (unless you have previously purchased a weekly Red Rock Pass; see "The High Cost of Red-Rock Views," below). For more information, contact the **Red Rock Ranger District,** 8375 Ariz. 179, Village of Oak Creek (✆ **928/203-7500** or 928/282-4119; www.fs.fed.us/r3/coconino).

If you continue on Red Rock Loop Road, you will come to **Red Rock State Park,** 4050 Red Rock Loop Rd. (✆ **928/282-6907;** www.azstateparks.com), which flanks Oak Creek. The views here take in many of the rocks listed above, and you have the bonus of being right on the creek (though swimming and wading are prohibited). Park admission is $7 per car. The park offers lots of guided walks and interpretive programs.

South of Sedona, near the junction of I-17 and Ariz. 179, you can visit one of the premier petroglyph sites in Arizona. The rock art at the **V Bar V Heritage Site** (**© 928/282-3854;** www.redrockcountry.org) covers a small cliff face and includes images of herons and turtles. To get here, take the dirt road that leads east for 2²/₃ miles from the junction of I-17 and Ariz. 179 to the Beaver Creek Campground. The entrance to the petroglyph site is just past the campground. From the parking area, it's about a half-mile walk to the petroglyphs, which are open Friday through Monday from 9:30am to 3pm. To visit this site, you'll need a Red Rock Pass or another valid pass.

OAK CREEK CANYON

The **Mogollon Rim** (pronounced "*Mug*-ee-un" by the locals) is a 2,000-foot escarpment cutting diagonally across central Arizona and on into New Mexico. At the top of the Mogollon Rim are the ponderosa pine forests of the high mountains, while at the bottom the lowland deserts begin. Of the many canyons cutting down from the rim, Oak Creek Canyon is the most beautiful (and one of the few that has a paved road down through it). Ariz. 89A runs through the canyon from just outside Flagstaff to Sedona, winding its way down from the rim and paralleling Oak Creek. Along the way are overlooks, parks, picnic areas, campgrounds, and a variety of lodges and inns.

Approaching Oak Creek Canyon from the north, your first stop after traveling south from Flagstaff will be the **Oak Creek Canyon Vista,** which provides a view far down the valley to Sedona and beyond. The overlook is at the edge of the Mogollon Rim, and the road suddenly drops in tight switchbacks just south of here. You may notice that one rim of the canyon is lower than the other. This is because Oak Creek Canyon is on a geologic fault line; one side of the canyon is moving in a different direction from the other.

Although the top of the Mogollon Rim is a ponderosa pine forest and the bottom a desert, Oak Creek Canyon supports a forest of sycamores and other deciduous trees. There is no better time to drive scenic Ariz. 89A than between late September and mid-October, when the canyon is ablaze with red and yellow leaves.

In the desert, swimming holes are powerful magnets during the hot summer months, and consequently, **Slide Rock State Park,** 6871 N. U.S. 89A (**© 928/282-3034;** www.azstateparks.com), 7 miles north of Sedona on the site of an old homestead, is the most popular spot in Oak Creek Canyon during the summer. What pulls in the crowds of families and teenagers is the park's natural water slide and great little swimming hole. On hot days, the park is jammed with people splashing in the water and sliding over the algae-covered sandstone bottom of Oak Creek. Sunbathing and fishing are other popular pastimes. The park is open daily; admission is $8 per vehicle ($10 during the summer).

Within Oak Creek Canyon, several hikes of different lengths are possible. By far the most spectacular and popular is the 6-mile round-trip up the **West Fork of Oak Creek ★**. This is a classic canyon-country hike, with steep canyon walls rising from the creek. At some points, the canyon is no more than 20 feet wide, with walls rising up more than 200 feet. You can also extend the hike many more miles up the canyon for an overnight backpacking trip. The trail head for the West Fork of Oak Creek hike is 9.5 miles up Oak Creek Canyon from Sedona at the Call of the Canyon Recreation Area, which charges an $8 day-use fee per vehicle unless you have already purchased a weekly Red Rock Pass.

Stop by the Sedona Chamber of Commerce Visitor Center for a free map of area hikes. The **Coconino National Forest's Red Rock Ranger District,** 8375 Ariz. 179 (**© 928/203-2900;** www.redrockcountry.org), just south of the Village of Oak Creek on

Ariz. 179, is an even better source of hiking information. It's open Monday through Friday from 8am to 5pm.

ATTRACTIONS & ACTIVITIES AROUND TOWN

Sedona's most notable architectural landmark is the **Chapel of the Holy Cross** ★, 780 Chapel Rd. (✆ **928/282-4069;** www.chapeloftheholycross.com), a small church built right into the red rock on the south side of town. If you're driving up from Phoenix, you can't miss it—the chapel sits high above the road just off Ariz. 179. With its contemporary styling, it is one of the most architecturally important modern churches in the country. Marguerite Brunswig Staude, a devout Catholic painter, sculptor, and designer, had the inspiration for the chapel in 1932, but it wasn't until 1957 that her dream was finally realized. The chapel's design is dominated by a simple cross forming the wall that faces the street. The cross and the starkly beautiful chapel seem to grow directly from the rock, allowing the natural beauty of the red rock to speak for itself. It's open Monday through Saturday from 9am to 5pm and Sunday from 10am to 5pm; admission is free.

The **Sedona Arts Center,** 15 Art Barn Rd. (✆ **888/954-4442** or 928/282-3809; www.sedonaartscenter.com), near the north end of uptown Sedona, on Ariz. 89A, has a gallery that specializes in works by local and regional artists.

To learn a bit about the local history, stop by the **Sedona Heritage Museum,** 735 Jordan Rd. (✆ **928/282-7038;** www.sedonamuseum.org), in Jordan Historical Park. The museum, which is housed in a historic home, is furnished with antiques and contains exhibits on the many movies that have been filmed in the area. The farm was once an apple orchard, and there's still apple-processing equipment in the barn. Hours are daily from 11am to 3pm; admission is $3.

While Sedona isn't yet a resort spa destination on par with Phoenix or Tucson, it does have an ever-growing number of spas that can add just the right bit of pampering to your vacation. **Therapy on the Rocks,** 676 N. Hwy. 89A (✆ **928/282-3002;** www.myofascialrelease.com), with its creekside setting, is a longtime local favorite that offers massage, myofascial release, and great views of the red rocks. A half-day of pampering here will run you $350. For personal attention, try the little **Red Rock Healing Arts Center,** Creekside Plaza, 251 Hwy. 179 (✆ **888/316-9033;** www.redrockhealing.com), which is just up the hill from the Tlaquepaque shopping plaza and offers a variety of massages, wraps, scrubs, and facials. A 60-minute massage or other body treatment is only $85 to $90. In west Sedona, try **Sedona's New Day Spa,** 1449 W. Hwy. 89A (✆ **928/282-7502;** www.sedonanewdayspa.com), a beautiful day spa with a resortlike feeling. A 1-hour treatment will run you between $105 and $155. In the Village of Oak Creek, there's the **Hilton Spa,** at the Hilton Sedona Resort & Spa, 10 Ridge View Dr. (✆ **928/284-6900;** www.hiltonsedonaspa.com), offering a variety of treatments (try the Painted Desert clay wrap or Sedona stone massage). There are also exercise and yoga classes, a pool, and tennis courts. Most 60-minute treatments cost $139.

It may be a bit premature to start calling Sedona the next Napa Valley, but there are a few wineries in the area. Three of them, located in the community of Page Springs, about 20 minutes west of Sedona, are open to the public for tastings. To reach these wineries, drive west from Sedona on Ariz. 89A, and turn south on Page Springs Road. You'll first come to **Javelina Leap Vineyard & Winery,** 1565 Page Springs Rd. (✆ **928/649-2681;** www.javelinaleapwinery.com), where winemaker and owner Rod Snapp focuses on premium red wines. In 2009, the winery finally began releasing wines made with Arizona- and estate-grown grapes. The tasting room is open daily from 11am to 5pm. Right next door is **Oak Creek Vineyards and Winery,** 1555 Page Springs Rd. (✆ **928/649-0290;** www.oakcreekvineyards.net), which is across the street from the Page Springs Fish Hatchery. The tasting room here is open daily from 11am to 5pm. **Page Springs Cellars,** 1500 Page Springs Rd. (✆ **928/639-3004;** www.pagespringscellars.com), is the most impressive and reliable of the three wineries, although as of 2009, they were still making most of their wines with grapes from California, not from their own vineyards. Rhone varietals are the specialty here. The tasting room is open daily from 11am to 6pm.

ORGANIZED TOURS

For an overview of Sedona, take a tour on the **Sedona Trolley,** 276 N. Hwy. 89A (✆ **928/282-4211;** www.sedonatrolley.com), which leaves several times daily on two separate tours. One tour visits the Tlaquepaque shopping plaza, the Chapel of the Holy Cross, and several art galleries, while the other goes out through west Sedona to Boynton Canyon and Enchantment Resort. Tours are $12 for adults ($21 for both tours) and $6 for children 12 and under ($11 for both tours).

The red-rock country surrounding Sedona is the city's greatest natural attraction, and there's no better way to explore it than by four-wheel-drive vehicle. Although you may end up feeling like every other tourist in town, you quite simply should not leave Sedona without going on a Jeep tour. These tours will get you out onto rugged roads and 4×4 trails with spectacular views. The unchallenged leader in Sedona Jeep tours is **Pink Jeep Tours,** 204 N. Hwy. 89A (✆ **800/873-3662** or 928/282-5000; www.pinkjeep.com), which has been heading deep into the Coconino National Forest since 1958. It offers tours ranging in length from 1½ to 11 hours; however, the 2-hour "Broken Arrow" tour ($75 adults, $56 children 12 and under) is the most adventurous and is the tour I recommend. Pink Jeep Tours also offers tours to Grand Canyon National Park.

If a Jeep just isn't manly enough for you, how about a Hummer? Better yet, how about a Hummer that runs on enviro-friendly bio-diesel (have your quiche and eat it, too)? **Sedona Offroad Adventures,** 273 N. Hwy. 89A, Ste. C (✆ **928/282-6656;** www.sedonaoffroadadventures.com), will take you out in the red rocks in the ultimate off-road vehicle. One-hour tours run $39 to $49 ($29–$39 for children), and while there are 1½- and 2-hour tours, the 2½-hour "Jeep Eater Tour" for $99 ($89 for children) is the most fun.

How about a chance to play cowboy? **A Day in the West,** 252 N. Hwy. 89A (✆ **800/973-3662** or 928/282-4320; www.adayinthewest.com), has its own private ranch for some of its Jeep tours and horseback rides. There are cowboy cookouts, too. Prices range from $45 to $169.

For a tour of the Sedona area from a Native American perspective, contact **Way of the Ancients** (✆ **866/204-9243** or 928/204-9243; www.wayoftheancients.com), which offers 4-hour tours that cost $79 for adults and $69 for children. There are also excursions to the Hopi mesas ($159 for adults and $139 for children).

As spectacular as Sedona is from the ground, it is even more so from the air. **Red Rock Helicopter Tours** (✆ **800/TOO-RIDE** [866-7433] or 928/204-5939; www.sedonaairtours.com) offers short flights to different parts of this colorful region. A 25-minute tour costs $116 per person. This same company also operates **Sky Safari Air Tours** (✆ **800/TOO-RIDE** [866-7433] or 928/204-5939; www.sedonaairtours.com), which does a variety of flights in small planes. A 20-minute air tour will run you $69 per person (two-person minimum), while a 45-minute tour will cost $109 per person (three-person minimum). Flights as far afield as the Grand Canyon and Canyon de Chelly can also be arranged. However, my favorite Sedona air tours are those offered by the affiliated **Red**

Rock Biplane Tours (✆ **800/TOO-RIDE** [866-7433] or 928/204-5939; www.sedona airtours.com), which operates modern Waco open-cockpit biplanes. With the wind in your hair, you'll feel as though you've entered the world of Snoopy and the Red Baron. Tours lasting 20 to 60 minutes are offered; a 20-minute tour costs $99 per person, with a two-person minimum.

If something a bit slower is more your speed, how about drifting over the sculpted red buttes of Sedona in a hot-air balloon? **Northern Light Balloon Expeditions** (✆ **800/230-6222** or 928/282-2274; www.northernlightballoon.com) charges $195 per person. **Red Rock Balloon Adventures** (✆ **800/258-3754;** www.redrockballoons.com) also charges $195 per person, while the affiliated **Sky High Balloon Adventures** (✆ **800/551-7597;** www.skyhighballoons.com), which floats over the Verde Valley, charges $180 per person.

GETTING OUTSIDE

Hiking is the most popular outdoor activity in the Sedona area, with dozens of trails leading off into the red rocks. The only problem is that nearly everyone who comes to Sedona wants to go hiking, so finding a little solitude along the trail can be difficult. Not surprisingly, the most convenient trail heads also have the most crowded trails. If you want to ditch the crowds, pick a trail head that is *not* on Ariz. 179 or Ariz. 89A. That means that if you stop at any of the trail heads in Oak Creek Canyon or between the Village of Oak Creek and Sedona, you'll likely encounter lots of other people along the trail. You'll enjoy your Sedona hikes more if you start from a trail that begins down a side road. Among my personal favorites are the trails that originate at the end of Jordan Road, in uptown Sedona; the Cathedral Rock Trail, which starts in a housing development between Sedona and the Village of Oak Creek; and the trails off Boynton Pass Road. ***Note:*** Don't forget to get your Red Rock Pass before heading out for a hike.

This said, the most convenient place to get some red dust on your boots is along the **Bell Rock Pathway** ★, which begins alongside Ariz. 179 just north of the Village of Oak Creek. This trail winds around the base of Bell Rock and accesses many other trails that lead up onto the sloping sides of Bell Rock. Although this is one of the most popular hiking trails in the area and is always crowded, it is the single best introduction to hiking in Sedona's beautiful red-rock country. It's about 4 miles to go all the way around Bell Rock and the adjacent Courthouse Butte.

Among the most popular trails in the Sedona area are those that lead into **Boynton Canyon** (site of Enchantment Resort). Here you'll glimpse ancient Native American ruins built into the red-rock cliffs. Although the scenery is indeed stupendous, the great numbers of other hikers on the trail detract considerably from the experience, and the parking lot usually fills up early in the day. The 1.5-mile **Vultee Arch Trail,** which leads to an impressive sandstone arch, is another great hike. The turnoff for this hike's trail head is 2 miles up Dry Creek Road and then another $3^1/_2$ miles on a very rough dirt road. The **Devil's Bridge Trail,** which starts on the same dirt road, is a little easier to get to and leads to the largest natural sandstone arch in the area. This one is a 1.8-mile round-trip hike.

For the hands-down best views in Sedona, hike all or part of the **Airport Mesa Trail,** a 3.5-mile loop that circles Airport Mesa. With virtually no elevation gain, this is an easy hike. You'll find the trail head about halfway to the top of Airport Mesa on Airport Road. Try this one as early in the day as possible; by midday, the parking lot is usually full and it stays that way right through sunset.

For more information on hiking in Oak Creek Canyon (site of the famous West Fork Oak Creek Trail), see "Oak Creek Canyon," earlier in this chapter. For more information on all these hikes, contact the **Coconino National Forest's Red Rock Ranger District,** 8375 Ariz. 179, Village of Oak Creek (✆ **928/203-7500;** www.fs.fed.us/r3/coconino).

Sedona is rapidly becoming one of the Southwest's meccas for mountain biking. The red rock here is every bit as challenging and scenic as the famed slickrock country of Moab, Utah, and much less crowded. Using Sedona as a base, mountain bikers can ride year-round by heading up to Flagstaff in the heat of summer. One of my favorite rides is around the base of Bell Rock. Starting at the trail head parking area just north of the Village of Oak Creek, you'll find not only the easy Bell Rock Path, but also numerous more-challenging trails.

Another great ride starts above uptown Sedona, where you can take the Jim Thompson Trail to Midgely Bridge or the network of trails that head toward Soldier Pass. The riding here is only moderately difficult and the views are superb. To reach these trails, take Jordan Road to a left onto Park Ridge Road, and follow this road to where it ends at a trail head parking area. You can rent bikes from **Mountain Bike Heaven,** 1695 W. Hwy. 89A (✆ **928/282-1312;** www.mountainbikeheaven.com). Bikes rent for $40 to $65 per day. **Sedona Bike & Bean,** 6020 Hwy. 179, Village of Oak Creek (✆ **928/284-0210;** www.bike-bean.com), across the street from the popular Bell Rock Pathway and its adjacent mountain-bike trails, also rents bikes (and serves coffee). Bikes go for $40 to $70 for a full day. Any of these stores can sell you a good local trail map or Cosmic Ray's *Fat Tire Tales and Trails* guidebook to the best rides in Arizona. If you'd prefer to have a guide take you out on either a mountain-bike or road-bike tour, contact **Sedona MTB Adventures** (✆ **888/984-1246** or 928/284-1246; www.sedonamtbadventures.com).

If you'd rather saddle up a palomino than pedal a bicycle, you can book a horseback ride through **Sedona Red Rock Jeep Tours,** 270 N. Hwy. 89A (✆ **800/848-7728** or 928/282-6826; www.redrockjeep.com), which charges $99 for a 2-hour ride.

Surprisingly, Sedona has not yet been ringed with golf courses. However, what few courses there are offer superb views to distract you from your game. The **Oakcreek Country Club,** 690 Bell Rock Blvd. (✆ **888/703-9489** or 928/284-1660; www.oakcreekcountryclub.com), south of town, off Ariz. 179, has stunning views from the course. Greens fees are $45 to $99. The **Sedona Golf Resort ★★**, 35 Ridge Trail Dr. (✆ **877/733-6630;** www.sedonagolfresort.com), south of town, on Ariz. 179, offers equally breathtaking views of the red rocks. Greens fees are $59 to $105.

SHOPPING

Ever since the Cowboy Artists of America organization was founded in Sedona back in 1965 (at what is now the Cowboy Club restaurant), this town has had a reputation as an artists' community. Today, with dozens of galleries around town, it's obvious that art is one of the driving forces behind the local economy. Most of Sedona's galleries specialize in traditional Western, contemporary Southwestern, and Native American art, and in some galleries, you'll see works by members of the Cowboy Artists of America. You'll find the greatest concentration of galleries and shops in the uptown area of Sedona (along Ariz. 89A just north of the "Y") and at Tlaquepaque.

With more than 40 stores and restaurants, **Tlaquepaque,** 336 Hwy. 179 (✆ **928/282-4838;** www.tlaq.com), at the bridge over Oak Creek on the south side of Sedona, bills itself as Sedona's arts-and-crafts village and is designed to resemble a Mexican village. (It was named after a famous arts-and-crafts neighborhood in the suburbs of Guadalajara.) The maze of narrow alleys and courtyards, with its fountains, chapel, and bell tower, is worth a visit even if you aren't in a buying mood. Most of the shops here sell high-end art.

WHERE TO STAY

Sedona is one of the most popular destinations in the Southwest, with dozens of hotels and motels around town. However, across the board, accommodations here tend to be a bit overpriced for what you get. My advice is to save money elsewhere on your trip so you can afford a room with a view here in Sedona.

Very Expensive

El Portal Sedona ★★★ You just can't help but fall in love with this amazing inn. Owners Steve and Connie Segner have done everything right, and the overall experience here makes this one of the very best lodgings in the state. Located adjacent to the Tlaquepaque shopping center and built of hand-formed adobe blocks, El Portal is designed to resemble a 200-year-old hacienda and is a monument to fine craftsmanship. The inn is filled with Arts and Crafts–period antiques, and in the dining room the ceiling beams were salvaged from a railroad bridge. Each of the large guest rooms has its own distinctive character, from Arts and Crafts to cowboy chic. Most have whirlpool tubs, and many rooms have private balconies with red-rock views. Exquisite breakfasts and dinners are served. Guided hikes and Jeep tours can be arranged.

95 Portal Lane, Sedona, AZ 86336. ✆ **800/313-0017** or 928/203-9405. Fax 928/203-9401. www.elportalsedona.com. 12 units. Mar–May and Oct–Nov $250–$550 double; July–Aug $179–$359 double; Jan–Feb, June, Sept, and Dec $199–$450 double. Rates include afternoon hors d'oeuvres. 2-night minimum on weekends and holidays. AE, DISC, MC, V. Pets accepted. **Amenities:** Restaurant; concierge; access to nearby health club & adjacent resort pools; room service. *In room:* A/C, TV/DVD, fridge, hair dryer, minibar, Wi-Fi.

Enchantment Resort ★★★ (Kids) Located at the mouth of Boynton Canyon, this resort more than lives up to its name. The setting is breathtaking, and the pueblo-style architecture blends in with the landscape. The individual casitas can be booked as two-bedroom suites, one-bedroom suites, or single rooms, but it's worth reserving a suite just so you can enjoy the casita living rooms, which feature high-beamed ceilings and beehive fireplaces. All the rooms, however, have patios with dramatic views. Both the Yavapai Restaurant and a less formal bar and grill offer tables outdoors; lunch on the terrace should not be missed. Guests have access to the facilities at Mii amo spa, which is a separate entity within the resort (see review, below). With its great setting amid the red rocks, suites, croquet court, swimming pool, and children's programs, Enchantment is a great choice for families.

525 Boynton Canyon Rd., Sedona, AZ 86336. ✆ **800/826-4180** or 928/282-2900. Fax 928/282-9249. www.enchantmentresort.com. 220 units. $350–$450 double; $450–$550 junior suite; $750–$950 1-bedroom suite; $1,125–$1,425 2-bedroom suite. Rates do not include $22 resort fee. Children 12 and under stay free in parent's room. AE, DC, DISC, MC, V. **Amenities:** 2 restaurants; 2 lounges; babysitting; bikes; children's programs; concierge; putting green & 6-hole par-3 golf course; health club; 6 Jacuzzis; 7 pools; room service; full-service spa; 7 tennis courts. *In room:* A/C, TV/DVD/VCR, hair dryer, kitchen (in some), minibar, Wi-Fi.

Mii amo, a destination spa at Enchantment ★★★ This full-service destination spa inside the gates of the Enchantment Resort easily claims the state's best spa location. Designed to resemble a modern Native American–style pueblo, the spa backs up to the red-rock cliffs of Boynton Canyon and is shaded by cottonwood trees. Mii amo is well designed, with indoor and outdoor pools and outdoor massage cabanas at the foot of the cliffs. Guest rooms, which open onto a courtyard, have a bold, contemporary styling (mixed with Native American art and artifacts) that makes them some of the finest accommodations in the state. All units have private patios and gas fireplaces. Mii amo is a world unto itself in this hidden canyon, and no other spa in Arizona has a more Southwestern feel.

525 Boynton Canyon Rd., Sedona, AZ 86336. ✆ **888/749-2137** or 928/203-8500. Fax 928/203-8599. www.miiamo.com. 16 units. 3-night packages: Apr–May and Sept–Oct $4,470–$6,390 double; Nov–Jan $3,810–$5,730 double; Feb–Mar and June–Aug $4,140–$6,060 double. Rates include 3 meals per day, 2 daily spa treatments, and a variety of activities. AE, DC, DISC, MC, V. **Amenities:** Restaurant; bikes; concierge; exercise room; 3 Jacuzzis; 2 pools (indoor & outdoor); room service; full-service spa w/25 treatment areas & wide variety of body treatments. *In room:* A/C, TV, hair dryer, minibar, Wi-Fi.

Expensive

Adobe Village Graham Inn ★ A garden full of bronze statues of children greets you when you pull up to this luxurious inn in the Village of Oak Creek, 6 miles south of uptown Sedona. The inn lies almost at the foot of Bell Rock and features a variety of themed accommodations. The villas, the Sundance room, and the Sedona suite are the most impressive rooms here. My favorite is the Purple Lizard villa, which opts for a colorful Taos-style interior and an amazing rustic canopy bed. The Wilderness villa resembles a luxurious log cabin. The Lonesome Dove villa is a sort of upscale cowboy cabin with a fireplace, potbellied stove, and round hot tub in a "barrel." Can you say *romantic?* This inn also operates the Adobe Grand Villas in West Sedona.

150 Canyon Circle Dr., Sedona, AZ 86351. ✆ **800/228-1425** or 928/284-1425. Fax 928/284-0767. www.sedonasfinest.com. 11 units. $199–$319 double; $389 suite; $349–$479 villa. Rates include full breakfast and afternoon hors d'oeuvres. 2-night minimum weekends and holidays. AE, DISC, MC, V. **Amenities:** Concierge; Jacuzzi; outdoor pool; room service; spa services. *In room:* A/C, TV/DVD/VCR, hair dryer, kitchenette (in some), Wi-Fi (in some).

Amara Resort and Spa ★★ It's hip, it's convenient, and it's got drop-dead-gorgeous views. What's not to love about this hidden gem of a boutique hotel hidden behind the shops of uptown Sedona? Oh, did I mention the creekside setting shaded by grand old sycamores? There's even a swimming hole. How cool is that? This stylish hotel definitely offers the best of both worlds here in Sedona. The resort is hip and sophisticated, yet close to nature, and the minimalist decor and Zen-inspired style make Amara one of Sedona's most tranquil accommodations. From the outside, the hotel fits right in with the red-rock surroundings, while inside, bold splashes of color contrast with black-and-white photos. Guest rooms all have balconies or patios, wonderful pillow-top beds, and furnishings in black and red. The resort also has a full-service spa.

100 Amara Lane, Sedona, AZ 86336. ✆ **866/455-6610** or 928/282-4828. Fax 928/282-4825. www.amararesort.com. 100 units. $195–$299 double; from $285 suite. Rates do not include $20 resort fee. Children 16 and under stay free in parent's room. AE, DISC, MC, V. Pets accepted ($75 fee). **Amenities:** Restaurant; lounge; concierge; exercise room; Jacuzzi; outdoor saltwater pool; room service; sauna; full-service spa. *In room:* A/C, TV/DVD, fridge, hair dryer, Wi-Fi.

Briar Patch Inn ★★ (Value) If you're searching for tranquillity or a romantic retreat, this is the place. Located 3 miles north of Sedona on the shady banks of Oak Creek, this inn's cottages are surrounded by beautiful grounds, where bird songs and the babbling creek set the mood. The cottages date from the 1940s but have been attractively updated. A Western/rustic-Mexican style predominates. Most units have fireplaces and kitchenettes. In summer, breakfast is often served on a creekside terrace. There's also a swimming hole right here. Despite a lack of red-rock views, this inn offers a delightful combination of solitude and sophistication.

3190 N. Hwy. 89A, Sedona, AZ 86336. ✆ **888/809-3030** or 928/282-2342. Fax 928/282-2399. www.briarpatchinn.com. 19 units. $205–$395 double. Rates include full breakfast. Children 3 and under stay free in parent's room. AE, DISC, MC, V. **Amenities:** Concierge; access to nearby health club; spa services; Wi-Fi. *In room:* A/C, CD player, kitchen or kitchenette (in some), fridge, hair dryer.

Canyon Villa ★ In the Village of Oak Creek, 6 miles south of Sedona, this bed-and-breakfast offers luxurious accommodations and spectacular views of the red rocks. All rooms but one have views, as do the pool area, living room, and dining room. Guest rooms are varied in style—Victorian, Santa Fe, country, rustic—but no matter what the decor, the furnishings are impeccable. All rooms have balconies or patios, and several have fireplaces. Breakfast is a lavish affair meant to be lingered over, and in the afternoon there's an elaborate spread of appetizers.

40 Canyon Circle Dr., Sedona, AZ 86351. ✆ **800/453-1166** or 928/284-1226. Fax 928/284-2114. www.canyonvilla.com. 11 units. $199–$349 double (lower rates in off season). Rates include full breakfast. AE, DISC, MC, V. No children 10 or under. **Amenities:** Concierge; outdoor saltwater pool. *In room:* A/C, TV/DVD, hair dryer, Wi-Fi.

Garland's Oak Creek Lodge ★ (Kids) (Finds) Located 8 miles north of Sedona in the heart of Oak Creek Canyon, this may be the hardest place in the area to book a room. People have been coming here for so many years and like it so much that they reserve a year in advance (however, last-minute cancellations do occur). What makes the lodge so special? Maybe it's that you have to drive *through* Oak Creek to get to your log cabin. Maybe it's the beautiful gardens or the relaxing atmosphere of an old-time summer getaway. The well-maintained cabins, most of which have air-conditioning, are rustic but comfortable; the larger ones have fireplaces. Meals include organic fruits and vegetables grown on the property, and there's a yoga pavilion overlooking the creek. Kids can splash in the creek and play in the grass, which makes this a good choice for families.

P.O. Box 152, Sedona, AZ 86339. ✆ **928/282-3343.** www.garlandslodge.com. 16 units. $235–$290 double (plus 15% service charge). Rates include breakfast, afternoon tea, and dinner. 2-night minimum. Children 1 and under stay free in parent's room. MC, V. Closed mid-Nov to Mar and Sun year-round. **Amenities:** Dining room; lounge; babysitting; tennis court. *In room:* No phone.

L'Auberge de Sedona ★ Set on the banks of Oak Creek and shaded by towering sycamore trees, this luxurious boutique resort is a sort of French country retreat in the middle of the desert. L'Auberge's cottages, which are surrounded by colorful flower gardens and look like rustic log cabins from the outside, have a classic styling worthy of a luxury French country inn (leather couches, gorgeous beds, plush towels, wood-burning fireplaces). Although the large cottages have long been my favorite accommodations here, the resort underwent a $25-million expansion in 2009 that included 20 new hillside cottages that are among the largest and most luxurious accommodations in Sedona. Fabulous views and outdoor showers are just two features of these new cottages. The restaurant, which carries on the French theme in its decor and menu, has a creekside terrace during the summer.

301 L'Auberge Lane, Sedona, AZ 86336. ✆ **800/272-6777** or 928/282-1661. Fax 928/282-2885. www.lauberge.com. 76 units. $195–$400 double; $175–$375 cottage; $275–$535 2-bedroom cottage. Rates include continental breakfast and evening wine reception. Children 17 and under stay free in parent's room. AE, DISC, MC, V. Pets accepted ($35 fee). **Amenities:** Restaurant; lounge; babysitting; concierge; access to nearby health club; room service; small full-service spa. *In room:* A/C, TV, CD player, fridge, hair dryer, Wi-Fi.

The Lodge at Sedona ★★ Set amid pine trees a block off Ariz. 89A in west Sedona, this large inn is decorated in the Arts and Crafts/mission style, which makes it one of the more distinctive inns in Sedona. The best rooms are those on the ground floor. These tend to be large, and several are suites. Suites are only slightly more expensive than deluxe rooms, which makes the suites the best choices here. Second-floor rooms are more economical and tend to be fairly small. If you want views, book one of the small upstairs rooms or the Desert Trail, Copper Canyon, or Whispering Winds suite. Breakfasts are five-course affairs that can tide you over until dinner.

125 Kallof Place, Sedona, AZ 86336. ✆ **800/619-4467** or 928/204-1942. Fax 928/204-2128. www.lodgeatsedona.com. 14 units. $189–$339 double. Rates include full breakfast. 2-night minimum on most weekends. AE, DISC, MC, V. Dogs accepted ($35 per night). Children 11 and over welcome. **Amenities:** Concierge; access to nearby health club. *In room:* A/C, TV/DVD (in some), CD player, hair dryer, Wi-Fi.

Sedona Rouge Hotel & Spa ★★ This stylish boutique hotel is one of the most distinctive luxury hotels in Sedona, and although it is located right on busy U.S. 89A in west Sedona, I highly recommend it. Merging contemporary styling with North African details, the hotel manages to create an ambience that is very international in feel. Antique wrought-iron window grates from Tunisia decorate hallways, and guest rooms have Moroccan-inspired tables. Bathrooms, with dual, rainshower shower heads, are a real highlight. If you can, try to get a room on the third floor; these have vaulted ceilings that make the rooms seem larger. The tiny lobby is just off an enclosed courtyard with a splashing fountain. A rooftop patio has the best view at the hotel. This is a good pick for couples in a romantic mood.

2250 W. Hwy. 89A, Sedona, AZ 86336. ✆ **866/312-4111** or 928/203-4111. Fax 928/203-9094. www.sedonarouge.com. 77 units. Jan–Feb $169–$259 double; Mar–May and Sept–Oct $229–$289 double; June–Aug and Nov–Dec $199–$269 double. AE, DC, DISC, MC, V. Pets accepted ($100 deposit, $50 fee). **Amenities:** Restaurant; lounge; bikes; concierge; exercise room & access to nearby health club; Jacuzzi; outdoor pool; room service; full-service spa. *In room:* A/C, TV, fridge, hair dryer, Wi-Fi.

Moderate

Cedars Resort on Oak Creek Located right at the "Y" and set atop a 100-foot cliff, this motel has fabulous views across Oak Creek to the towering red rocks. Guest rooms are large and comfortable, and creekside rooms have private balconies. However, for the best views, ask for a king-size room. A long stairway leads down to the creek, and the shops of uptown Sedona are just a short walk away.

20 W. Hwy. 89A (P.O. Box 292), Sedona, AZ 86339. ✆ **800/874-2072** or 928/282-7010. Fax 928/282-5372. www.sedonacedarsresort.com. 38 units. $99–$149 double. Rates include continental breakfast. Children 12 and under stay free in parent's room. AE, DISC, MC, V. **Amenities:** Concierge; exercise room & access to nearby health club; Jacuzzi; small outdoor pool. *In room:* A/C, TV, fridge, hair dryer, Wi-Fi.

The Orchards Inn of Sedona For picture-perfect, in-your-face views of the red rocks, few Sedona hotels can compete with the Orchards. The red-rock views from the hotel's hillside setting above Oak Creek are simply spectacular. Best of all, every room here has a view, and glass patio doors to let you see plenty of the scenery. Don't be discouraged when you drive up to the front door; although the Orchards, which is more hotel than inn, is located amid the uptown tourist crowds, it seems miles away once you check into your room and gaze out at the red rocks. Rooms were completely remodeled in 2009 giving the hotel a fresh, contemporary look.

254 N. Hwy. 89A, Sedona, AZ 86336. ✆ **800/341-6075** or 928/282-2405. Fax 928/282-5710. www.orchardsinn.com. 41 units. $129–$249 double. Children 11 and under stay free in parent's room. AE, DISC, MC, V. **Amenities:** Restaurant; lounge; concierge; access to nearby health club; Jacuzzi; small outdoor pool; room service. *In room:* A/C, TV/DVD, fridge, hair dryer, Wi-Fi.

Inexpensive

Matterhorn Inn Located in the heart of the uptown shopping district, this hotel is convenient to restaurants and shops, and all of the attractively furnished guest rooms have excellent views of the red-rock canyon walls. Although the Matterhorn is set above a row of shops fronting busy Ariz. 89A, if you lie in bed and keep your eyes on the rocks, you'd never know there was so much going on below you.

230 Apple Ave., Sedona, AZ 86336. ✆ **800/372-8207** or 928/282-7176. www.matterhorninn.com. 23 units. Mar–Nov $89–$169 double; Dec–Feb $79–$159 double. Children 4 and under stay free in parent's room. AE, MC, V. Pets accepted ($10 per day). **Amenities:** Concierge; access to nearby health club; Jacuzzi; small outdoor pool. *In room:* A/C, TV, CD player, fridge, hair dryer, MP3 docking station, Wi-Fi.

Rose Tree Inn (Finds) This little inn, only a block from Sedona's uptown shopping district, is tucked amid pretty gardens (yes, there are lots of roses) on a quiet street. The property consists of an eclectic cluster of renovated older buildings. Each unit is furnished differently—one Victorian, one Southwestern, two with gas fireplaces. Four guest rooms have kitchenettes, making these rooms good choices for families.

376 Cedar St., Sedona, AZ 86336. ✆ **888/282-2065** or 928/282-2065. www.rosetreeinn.com. 5 units. $95–$149 double. Children 15 and under stay free in parent's room. AE, MC, V. **Amenities:** Concierge; access to nearby health club. *In room:* A/C, TV/VCR, kitchen (in some), fridge, hair dryer, Wi-Fi.

Sky Ranch Lodge ★ (Kids) This motel is located atop Airport Mesa and has the most stupendous vista in town. From here you can see the entire red-rock country, with Sedona filling the valley below. Although the rooms are fairly standard motel issue, some have such features as gas fireplaces, barn-wood walls, and balconies. Only the nonview units fall into the inexpensive category, but those great views are just steps away. With a pool and plenty of space for running around, this place will keep the kids happy. You can even walk up the road to watch planes and helicopters at the airport.

Airport Rd. (P.O. Box 2579), Sedona, AZ 86339. ✆ **888/708-6400** or 928/282-6400. www.skyranchlodge.com. 94 units. $80–$194 double. AE, MC, V. Pets accepted ($10 per night). **Amenities:** Jacuzzi; small outdoor pool. *In room:* A/C, TV, kitchenettes (in some).

Campgrounds

Within Oak Creek Canyon along Ariz. 89A, there are five national forest campgrounds. **Manzanita,** 6 miles north of town, is both the largest and the most pleasant (and the only one open in winter; $18 per night). Other Oak Creek Canyon campgrounds include **Bootlegger,** 9 miles north of town ($18 per night); **Cave Springs,** 13 miles north of town ($20 per night); and **Pine Flat,** 12 miles north of town ($20 per night). The **Beaver Creek Campground,** 3 miles east of I-17 on F.R. 618, which is an extension of Ariz. 179 (take exit 298 off I-17), is a pleasant spot near the V Bar V Heritage Site ($15 per night). For more information on area campgrounds, contact the **Coconino National Forest's Red Rock Ranger District,** 8375 Ariz. 179 (✆ **928/203-7500;** www.fs.fed.us/r3/coconino), which is located south of the Village of Oak Creek. Reservations can be made for Manzanita, Pine Flat, and Cave Springs campgrounds by contacting the **National Recreation Reservation Service** (✆ **877/444-6777** or 518/885-3639; www.recreation.gov).

Expensive

Cowboy Club Grille & Spirits Kids SOUTHWESTERN With its big booths, huge steer horns over the bar, and cowboy gear adorning the walls, this restaurant is Sedona's quintessential New West steakhouse. Start out with fried cactus strips with a prickly pear sauce or perhaps some deep-fried snake strips. For an entree, be sure to try the buffalo tenderloin, which is served with brandied peppercorn cream sauce. At lunch, try the buffalo burger. Service is friendly and can be slow during the peak tourist season. The adjacent Silver Saddle Room is a more upscale spin on the same concept, with similar menu prices. The kids should get a kick out of the cowboy decor and, who knows, you may even get them to taste your snake or cactus appetizer. It was in here in this building in 1965 that the Cowboy Artists of America organization was formed.

241 N. Hwy. 89A. ✆ **928/282-4200.** www.cowboyclub.com. Reservations recommended. Main courses $10–$45. AE, DISC, MC, V. Daily 11am–10pm.

El Portal Sedona ★★ NEW AMERICAN/SOUTHWESTERN Although El Portal is primarily a deluxe inn, it also serves superb dinners on Friday and Saturday nights. While many of the diners are guests at the inn, the meals are open to the public by reservation. These dinners provide anyone who is not staying at El Portal a chance to lounge around in the courtyard and living room/dining room, and get a sense for what it's like to stay here. The menu is short and usually includes about a half-dozen entrees and an equal number of appetizers and salads. Roast lamb loin with butternut squash ravioli and rack of elk with hazelnut griddle cakes are just two examples of the sorts of entrees you can expect. In the warmer months, there are Wednesday night barbecues ($29) in the courtyard.

95 Portal Lane. ✆ **800/313-0017** or 928/203-4942. www.elportalsedona.com. Reservations required. Main courses $34–$42. AE, DISC, MC, V. Fri–Sat 5:30–8pm.

The Heartline Café ★★ SOUTHWESTERN/INTERNATIONAL The heart line, from Zuni mythology, is a symbol of health and longevity; it is also a symbol for the healthful, creative food served here. To start with, don't miss the tea-smoked chicken dumplings with spicy peanut sauce or the Gorgonzola torte with caramelized pear. The must-have entree here is the heavenly pecan-crusted local trout with Dijon cream sauce. Those searching out variety in vegetarian choices will find it here. The beautiful courtyard and traditionally elegant interior are both good places to savor a meal. Lunch and gourmet takeout are available at the adjacent Heartline Gourmet Express & Market.

1610 W. Hwy. 89A. ✆ **928/282-0785** (cafe) or 928/282-3365 (Gourmet Express). www.heartlinecafe.com. Reservations recommended. Cafe main courses $17–$35; Gourmet Express main courses $5–$15. AE, DC, DISC, MC, V. Cafe daily 4:30–10pm; Gourmet Express daily 7am–4:30pm.

René at Tlaquepaque ★ CONTINENTAL/AMERICAN Although a formal dining experience and traditional French fare may seem out of place in a town that celebrates its cowboy heritage, René's makes fine dining seem as natural as mesquite-grilled steak and cowboy beans. Located in Tlaquepaque, the city's upscale south-of-the-border-themed shopping center, this restaurant is the best place in Sedona for a special meal. The house specialty is rack of lamb, and if you enjoy lamb, this dish should not be missed. More adventurous diners may want to try the excellent tenderloin of venison with whiskey–juniper berry sauce. Finish with a flambéed dessert. To save money, have lunch here instead of dinner.

At Tlaquepaque, 336 Hwy. 179, Ste. 118. ✆ **928/282-9225.** www.rene-sedona.com. Reservations recommended. Main courses $9–$19 lunch, $19–$45 dinner. AE, MC, V. Sun–Thurs 11:30am–2pm and 5:30–8:30pm; Fri–Sat 11:30am–2pm and 5:30–9pm.

Moderate

Café Elote ★ MEXICAN *Elote* is a Mexican preparation of corn on the cob that is made with freshly roasted corn that is slathered with spicy mayonnaise and sprinkled with white *cotija* cheese. Squirt on a little lime, and you have the ultimate south-of-the-border street food. Here at this treat's namesake restaurant, the *elote* is sliced from the cob and served as a sort of dip. This dish alone, maybe with a side of guacamole and a margarita, is reason enough to eat at this highly creative Mexican restaurant. For an entree, try the braised lamb in sweet-and-spicy ancho-chile sauce. This is a casual and colorful spot, and feels a bit like a Mexican beach bar.

At King's Ransom Sedona Hotel, 771 Hwy. 179. ✆ **928/203-0105.** www.elotecafe.com. Reservations only for 5 or more. Main courses $17–$21. AE, DISC, MC, V. Tues–Sat 5–9pm.

Cucina Rústica ★ MEDITERRANEAN/SOUTHWESTERN With its various distinct dining rooms and numerous antique doors, this sister restaurant to west Sedona's wonderful Dahl & DiLuca (see above) feels like a luxurious villa. One room here has a central dome that is lit by what appear to be thousands of stars, but for a genuine starlit dinner, you can ask for a seat on the patio. Start with the *bruschetta pomodoro,* a tomato-and-basil appetizer that tastes like a bite of summer; then, when it comes time to order an entree, just ask for the *gamberi del capitano.* These grilled prawns, wrapped in radicchio and prosciutto, are among the best prawns you'll ever taste—positively ambrosial.

7000 Hwy. 179, Village of Oak Creek. ✆ **928/284-3010.** www.cucinarustica.com. Reservations recommended. Main courses $12–$32. AE, MC, V. Sun–Thurs 5–10pm; Fri–Sat 5–11pm.

Dahl & DiLuca ★ ITALIAN A faux-Tuscan villa interior, complete with a bar in a grotto, makes this the most romantic restaurant in Sedona, and the excellent Italian food makes it that much more unforgettable. Be sure to start with some of the *pane romano,* which, as far as I'm concerned, is the best garlic bread west of New York's Little Italy. Pasta predominates here, and portions are big. The linguine Siciliana with calamari and mushrooms is a perennial favorite. The kitchen also serves deftly prepared seafood, chicken, and vegetarian dishes. The eggplant Parmesan and portobello *alla griglia* are real standouts. Keep in mind that during the high season (spring), this place stays packed with tourists and service can, at times, be brusque.

2321 W. Hwy. 89A (in west Sedona, kitty-corner from the Safeway Plaza). ✆ **928/282-5219.** www.dahl-diluca.com. Reservations recommended. Main courses $13–$31. AE, DISC, MC, V. Sun–Thurs 5–9pm; Fri–Sat 5–10pm.

Kurt's Main Street Café ★ NEW AMERICAN Although this restaurant is right in front of the Super 8 Motel, it is a sophisticated yet casual place serving some of the more creative food in Sedona. For a starter, try the green-corn tamale with chipotle cream sauce, and among the salads, the blue-corn chicken salad is a good bet. While there are plenty of southwestern dishes on the menu, there are also some well-prepared comfort foods, including a wonderful bacon-wrapped meatloaf and a chicken pot pie. At lunch, the ahi tuna club sandwich should not be missed, but you can also get the green-corn tamale as an entree.

2545 W. Hwy. 89A. ✆ **928/203-7878.** www.kurtsmainstcafe.com. Reservations recommended. Main courses $8.50–$13 lunch; $16–$29 dinner. AE, DISC, MC, V. Mon–Thurs 11am–2:30pm and 5–9pm; Fri 11am–2:30pm and 5–10pm; Sat 5–10pm.

Inexpensive

The Hideaway Restaurant (Kids) ITALIAN Hidden at the back of a shopping plaza near the "Y," this casual family restaurant is as popular with locals as it is with visitors. Basic pizzas, subs, sandwiches, salads, and pastas are the choices here. However, most people come for the knockout views. From the shady porch, you can see the creek below and the red rocks rising across the canyon. Lunch or an early sunset dinner is your best bet. The *paisano* (Sicilian sausage soup and a sandwich) lunch and antipasto salad are both good choices. Keep an eye out for hummingbirds and great blue herons.

Country Sq., 251 Hwy. 179. ✆ **928/282-4204.** Reservations accepted only for parties of 10 or more. Main courses $10–$12 lunch, $12–$15 dinner. AE, DISC, MC, V. Daily 11am–9pm.

Javelina Cantina MEXICAN Although Javelina Cantina is part of a chain of Arizona restaurants, the formula works, and few diners leave disappointed. Sure, the restaurant is touristy, but what it has going for it is good Mexican food, a lively atmosphere, decent views, and a convenient location in the Hillside shops. The grilled fish tacos are tasty, as is the pork adobo sandwich. The salmon tostadas are also worth trying. There are also plenty of different margaritas and tequilas to accompany your meal. Expect a wait.

At Hillside Sedona shopping plaza, 671 Hwy. 179. ✆ **928/203-9514.** www.javelinacantina.com. Reservations recommended. Main courses $9–$17. AE, DISC, MC, V. Daily 11:30am–9pm.

Tara Thai Cuisine THAI Friends who have a house in Sedona love this restaurant, and if you like Thai food, you probably will, too. Not only is the food packed with all those great, exotic Thai flavors, but also, in this overpriced tourist town, the reasonable menu prices are a welcome relief. The pad Thai is a good bet, and, if it's on the menu, be sure to try the mango sticky rice for dessert. You'll find Tara Thai tucked into a shopping center near the north end of the Village of Oak Creek.

34 Bell Rock Plaza, Village of Oak Creek. ✆ **928/284-9167.** Reservations recommended. Main courses $9–$19. AE, DC, DISC, MC, V. Mon–Sat 11am–3pm and 5–9pm; Sun noon–3pm and 5–9pm.

6 LAKE MEAD NATIONAL RECREATION AREA

70 miles NW of Kingman; 256 miles NW of Phoenix; 30 miles SE of Las Vegas, NV

This watersports playground straddles the border between Arizona and Nevada, boasting two reservoirs and a scenic, free-flowing stretch of the Colorado River. Throughout the year, anglers fish for striped bass, rainbow trout, channel catfish, and other sport fish, while during the hot summer months, lakes Mead and Mohave attract tens of thousands of water-skiers and personal watercraft riders.

The larger reservoir, Lake Mead, was created by Hoover Dam, which was constructed between 1931 and 1935. By supplying huge amounts of electricity and water to Arizona and California, the dam set the stage for the phenomenal growth the region experienced in the second half of the 20th century.

ESSENTIALS

GETTING THERE U.S. 93, which runs between Las Vegas and Kingman, crosses over Hoover Dam, and traffic backups at the dam have in the past been absolutely horrendous. However, now that trucks are prohibited from crossing the dam, the traffic jams have lessened somewhat. Several small secondary roads lead to various marinas on the

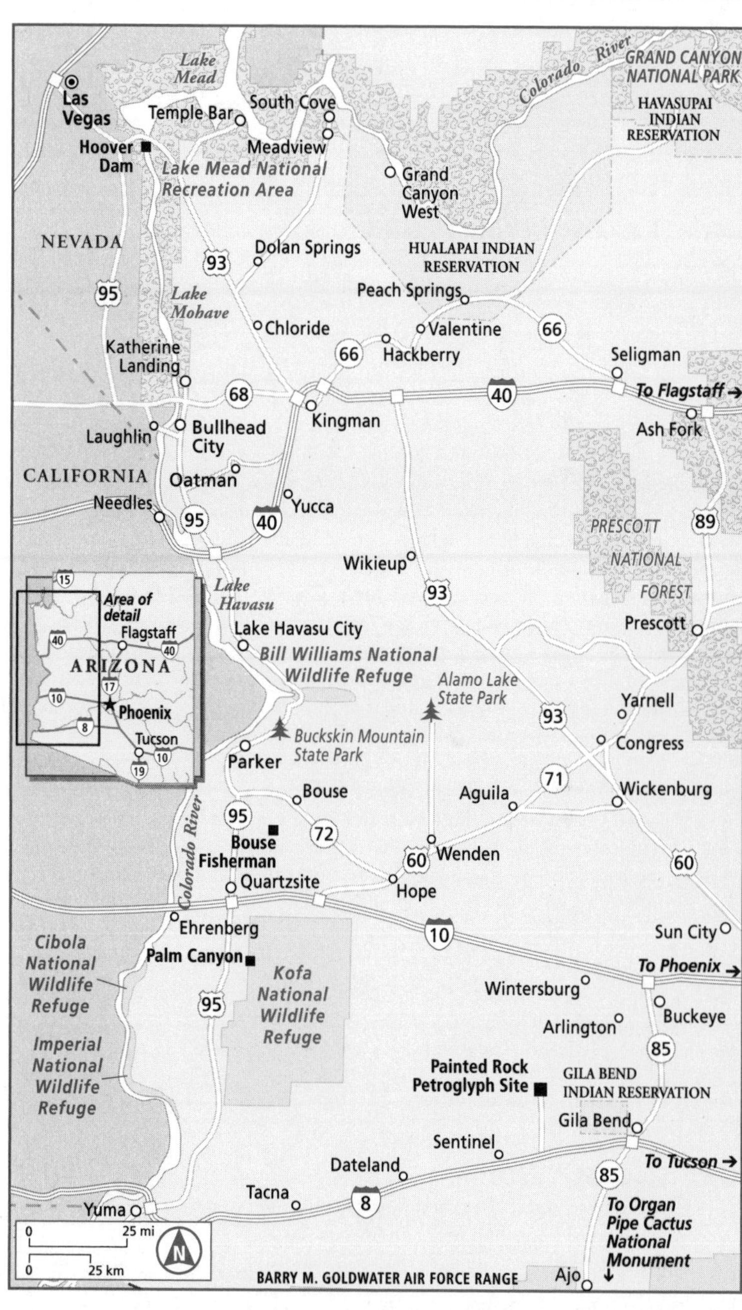

Lake Mead
Las Vegas
Temple Bar
South Cove
Meadview
Hoover Dam
Lake Mead National Recreation Area
Colorado River
GRAND CANYON NATIONAL PARK
HAVASUPAI INDIAN RESERVATION
Grand Canyon West
NEVADA
Dolan Springs
HUALAPAI INDIAN RESERVATION
Lake Mohave
Peach Springs
Chloride
Valentine
Hackberry
Katherine Landing
Seligman
To Flagstaff →
Kingman
Laughlin
Bullhead City
Ash Fork
CALIFORNIA
Oatman
Needles
Yucca
PRESCOTT NATIONAL FOREST
Wikieup
Lake Havasu
Area of detail
Flagstaff
ARIZONA
Phoenix
Tucson
Lake Havasu City
Bill Williams National Wildlife Refuge
Prescott
Alamo Lake State Park
Yarnell
Buckskin Mountain State Park
Congress
Parker
Bouse
Aguila
Wickenburg
Bouse Fisherman
Wenden
Quartzsite
Hope
Ehrenberg
Sun City
Cibola National Wildlife Refuge
Palm Canyon
Kofa National Wildlife Refuge
To Phoenix →
Wintersburg
Buckeye
Arlington
Imperial National Wildlife Refuge
Painted Rock Petroglyph Site
GILA BEND INDIAN RESERVATION
Gila Bend
Sentinel
Dateland
To Tucson →
Tacna
Yuma
To Organ Pipe Cactus National Monument ↓
0 25 mi
0 25 km
N
BARRY M. GOLDWATER AIR FORCE RANGE
Ajo

lake. There are also many miles of unpaved roads within the recreation area. If you have a high-clearance or four-wheel-drive vehicle, these roads can take you to some of the least visited shores of the two lakes.

VISITOR INFORMATION For information, contact the **Lake Mead National Recreation Area,** 601 Nevada Way, Boulder City, NV 89005 (© **702/293-8906;** www.nps.gov/lame), or stop by the **Alan Bible Visitor Center** (© **702/293-8990**), between Hoover Dam and Boulder City. The visitor center is open daily from 8:30am to 4:30pm (closed New Year's Day, Thanksgiving, and Christmas).

DAM, LAKE & RIVER TOURS

Standing 726 feet tall, from bedrock to the roadway atop it, and tapering from a thickness of 660 feet at its base to only 45 feet at the top, **Hoover Dam** (© **866/730-9097** or 702/494-2517; www.usbr.gov/lc/hooverdam) is the tallest concrete dam in the Western Hemisphere. Behind this massive dam lie the waters of **Lake Mead,** which at 110 miles long and with a shoreline of more than 550 miles is the largest artificial lake in the United States. To learn about the construction of Hoover Dam, stop in at the visitor center, which charges an $8 admission for anyone over age 3 and is open daily from 9am to 5pm (closed Thanksgiving and Christmas). Guided tours of the dam cost $11 for adults, $9 for seniors and children 4 to 16. Tickets, which include visitor center admission, can be purchased online. More extensive tours of the dam cost $30, and are offered only on a nonreservation basis. Parking is an additional $7. Including a tour, it takes about 2 hours to visit the dam.

If you'd like to tour the lake, call **Lake Mead Cruises** (© **702/293-6180;** www.lakemeadcruises.com) to book passage on the *Desert Princess* paddle-wheeler. These cruises leave from Lake Mead Cruises Landing, off Lakeshore Road on the Nevada side of Hoover Dam. Day tours, which go to the dam, last 1½ hours and cost $24 for adults and $12 for children 2 to 11. Other options include dinner cruises ($49 for adults, $25 for children) and brunch cruises ($39 for adults, $18 for children).

One of the most interesting ways to see remote parts of Lake Mohave is by sea kayak. **Desert River Outfitters** (© **888/KAYAK-33** [529-2533]; www.desertriveroutfitters.com) will rent you a boat and shuttle you and your gear to and from put-ins and take-outs. The trip through Black Canyon ($60 per person with a four-person minimum) starts at the base of Hoover Dam and is the most interesting route. (***Note:*** This trip requires advance planning because a permit is necessary.) You can also paddle past the casinos in Laughlin ($35), through the Topock Gorge ($50), or around Lake Mohave ($35). Raft trips through Black Canyon are offered by **Black Canyon River Adventures** (© **800/455-3490** or 702/294-1414; www.blackcanyonadventures.com). The 1-day rafting trips, on big motorized rafts, are an easy float through a scenic canyon and cost $83 for adults, $80 for children ages 13 to 15, and $51 for children ages 5 to 12. If you're not a paddler, this is a great way to see this remote stretch of river—it's definitely a highlight of a visit to this corner of the state. This company also has a marina where it rents a variety of motorboats.

GETTING OUTSIDE

Swimming, fishing, water-skiing, and powerboating are the most popular activities in Lake Mead National Recreation Area. On Arizona shores, there are swimming beaches at Lake Mohave's Katherine Landing (outside Bullhead City) and Lake Mead's Temple Bar (north of Kingman, off US 93). Picnic areas can be found at these two areas as well as

Willow Beach on Lake Mohave and more than half a dozen spots on the Nevada side of Lake Mead.

In Arizona, marinas can be found at Katherine Landing on Lake Mohave (just outside Bullhead City), near the north end of Lake Mohave at Willow Beach (best access for trout angling), and at Temple Bar on Lake Mead. At **Temple Bar Resort & Marina** (✆ **800/255-5561** or 928/767-3211), you can rent speedboats for $225 to $375 per day. At **Lake Mohave Resort** (✆ **800/752-9669** or 928/754-3245), you can rent ski boats, fishing boats, and patio boats for between $90 and $260 per day. Personal watercraft go for $350 per day at the former and $360 per day at the latter.

WHERE TO STAY

Seven Crown Resorts rents houseboats (see below) and runs a motel on Lake Mohave. For more information, contact Seven Crown Resorts (✆ **800/752-9669;** www.sevencrown.com). Lake Mohave Resort has huge rooms that are great for families ($60–$125 double). Temple Bar Marina, on Lake Meade, has a motel and a wonderfully remote setting with a beach right in front, great fishing nearby, and 40 miles of prime skiing waters extending from the resort. Rooms go for $70 to $125 double. For more information, contact Temple Bar Marina (✆ **928/767-3211;** www.templebarlakemead.com).

Houseboats

Seven Crown Resorts ★ (Kids) Why pay extra for a lake-view room when you can rent a houseboat that always has a 360-degree water view? There's no better way to explore Lake Mohave than on one of these floating vacation homes. You can cruise for miles, tie up at a deserted cove, and enjoy a wilderness adventure with all the comforts of home. Houseboats come complete with full kitchens, air-conditioning, and space to sleep up to 13 people. Bear in mind that the scenery here on Lake Mohave isn't nearly as spectacular as that on Lake Powell, Arizona's other major houseboating lake.

P.O. Box 16247, Irvine, CA 92623-6247. ✆ **800/752-9669.** www.sevencrown.com. $1,250–$4,250 per week. DISC, MC, V. Pets accepted. *In room:* A/C, kitchen, no phone.

Camping

In Arizona, there are campgrounds at Katherine Landing on Lake Mohave and at Temple Bar on Lake Mead. Both of these campgrounds have been heavily planted with trees, so they provide some semblance of shade during the hot, but popular, summer months. In Nevada, you'll find campgrounds at Cottonwood Cove on Lake Mohave and at Boulder Beach, Las Vegas Bay, Callville Bay, and Echo Bay on Lake Mead. Campsites at all campgrounds are $10 per night. For more information, contact **Lake Mead National Recreation Area** (✆ **702/293-8906** or 293-8990; www.nps.gov/lame).

7 LAKE HAVASU & THE LONDON BRIDGE

60 miles S of Bullhead City; 150 miles S of Las Vegas, NV; 200 miles NW of Phoenix

London Bridge is falling down, falling down, falling down. At least it was, until Robert McCulloch, founder of Lake Havasu City, hit upon the brilliant idea of buying the bridge and having it shipped to his undertouristed little planned community in the Arizona desert. More than 35 years later, London Bridge still attracts tourists by the millions.

Lake Havasu was formed in 1938 by the building of the Parker Dam, but it wasn't until 1963 that McCulloch founded the town of Lake Havasu City. In the town's early years, not too many people were keen on spending time in this remote corner of the desert, where summer temperatures are often over 110°F (43°C). It was then that McCulloch began looking for ways to attract more people to his little "city" on the lake. His solution proved to be a stroke of genius.

Today, Lake Havasu City attracts an odd mix of visitors. In winter, the town is filled with retirees. On weekends, during the summer, and over spring break, however, Lake Havasu City is popular with Arizona college students and the water-ski and personal-watercraft crowds. Expect lots of noise on weekends and holidays.

ESSENTIALS

GETTING THERE From Phoenix, take I-10 west to Ariz. 95 north. From Las Vegas, take U.S. 95 south, to I-40 east, to Ariz. 95 south.

The **Havasu/Vegas Express** (✆ **800/459-4884** or 928/453-4884; www.havasuvegasexpress.com) operates a shuttle van between Lake Havasu City and Las Vegas. Fares are $58 one-way and $104 round-trip ($53 and $95 for seniors).

VISITOR INFORMATION For more information on this area, contact the **Lake Havasu Convention & Visitors Bureau,** 314 London Bridge Rd. (✆ **800/242-8278** or 928/453-3444; www.golakehavasu.com), which has a visitor center (✆ **928/855-5655**) in English Village at the foot of the London Bridge. This visitor center is open Monday through Saturday from 9am to 5pm.

GETTING AROUND For car rentals, try **Avis** (✆ **800/331-1212** or 928/764-3001), **Enterprise** (✆ **800/261-7331** or 928/453-0033), or **Hertz** (✆ **800/654-3131** or 928/764-3994).

LONDON BRIDGE

Back in the mid-1960s, when London Bridge was sinking into the Thames River due to heavy car and truck traffic, the British government decided to sell the bridge. Robert McCulloch and his partner paid nearly $2.5 million for it and had it shipped 10,000 miles to Lake Havasu City. Reconstruction of the bridge was begun in 1968, and the grand reopening was held in 1971.

At the base of the bridge sits **English Village,** which is done up in proper English style and has shops, restaurants, and a waterfront promenade. You'll find several cruise boats and boat-rental docks here, as well as the chamber of commerce's visitor center.

Unfortunately, the London Bridge is not very impressive as bridges go, and the tacky commercialization of its surroundings makes it something of a letdown for many visitors. On top of that, over the years the jolly olde England styling that once predominated around here has been supplanted by a Mexican beach-bar aesthetic designed to appeal to partying college students on spring break.

LAND, LAKE & RIVER TOURS

Several companies offer different types of boat tours on Lake Havasu. **Bluewater Jet Boat Tours** (✆ **888/855-7171** or 928/855-7171; www.coloradoriverjetboattours.com) runs jet-boat tours that leave from the London Bridge and spend 2½ hours cruising up the Colorado River to the Topock Gorge, a scenic area 25 miles from Lake Havasu City. The cost is $38 for adults, $35 for seniors, and $20 for children 5 to 12. You can also go

Moments Canoeing the Colorado

Paddling down a desert river is an unusual and unforgettable experience. Both outfitters listed here provide boats, paddles, life jackets, maps, and shuttles to put-in and take-out points, but usually no guide. **Western Arizona Canoe and Kayak Outfitter** (© **888/881-5038** or 928/715-6414; www.azwacko.com) offers self-guided kayak or canoe trips through the beautiful and rugged Topock Gorge, where you can see ancient petroglyphs and possibly bighorn sheep. Trips take 5 to 6 hours, and the cost is $48 per person. **Jerkwater Canoe & Kayak Company** (© **800/421-7803** or 928/768-7753; www.jerkwatercanoe.com) offers a similar Topock Gorge excursion and also arranges other canoe and kayak trips of varying lengths. Jerkwater's Topock Gorge self-guided 5- to 6-hour trip is $46 per person in a canoe or $58 per person in a kayak.

out on the ***Dixie Belle*** (© **928/453-6776** or 928/855-0888), a small replica paddle-wheel riverboat, or the even smaller ***Kontiki.*** Cruises range from $15 to $25 for adults and $8 to $15 for children 4 to 12. The *Kontiki* goes to Copper Canyon, the narrow cliff-ringed cove that is the destination for college-age partiers each year during spring break.

GETTING OUTSIDE

GOLF **London Bridge Golf Club,** 2400 Clubhouse Dr. (© **928/855-2719;** www.londonbridgegc.com), with two 18-hole courses, is the area's premier course. High-season greens fees (with cart) top out at $75 on the Olde London course and $60 on the Nassau course. The **Havasu Island Golf Course,** 1040 McCulloch Blvd. (© **928/855-5585**), is a 4,012-yard, par-61 executive course with lots of water hazards. Greens fees are $24 to $29 if you walk and $32 to $39 if you ride. The 9-hole **Bridgewater Links,** 1477 Queens Bay Rd. (© **928/855-4777;** www.londonbridgeresort.com), at the London Bridge Resort, is the most accessible and easiest of the area courses. Greens fees for 9 holes are $9 to $18 if you walk and $15 to $24 if you ride.

Golfers won't want to miss the **Emerald Canyon Golf Course** ★, 7351 Riverside Dr., Parker (© **928/667-3366;** www.emeraldcanyongolf.com), about 30 miles south of Lake Havasu City. This municipal course is the most spectacular in the region and plays through rugged canyons and past red-rock cliffs, from which there are views of the Colorado River. One hole even has you hitting your ball off a cliff to a green 200 feet below! Greens fees are $35 to $55 in the cooler months, and tee-time reservations can be made a week in advance (farther out if you pay $10 per player). Also in Parker is the golf course at the **Havasu Springs Resort,** 2581 Ariz. 95 (© **928/667-3361**), which some people claim is the hardest little 9-hole, par-3 course in the state. It's atop a rocky outcropping with steep drop-offs all around. If you aren't staying here, greens fees are only $12 for 9 holes and $18 for 18 holes.

WATERSPORTS While the London Bridge is what made Lake Havasu City, these days watersports on 45-mile-long Lake Havasu are the area's real draw.

London Bridge Beach is the best in-town beach and is located in a county park, off West McCulloch Boulevard, behind the Island Inn. This park has a sandy beach, lots of palm trees, and views of both the London Bridge and the distant desert mountains. There are also picnic tables and a snack bar. Just south of the London Bridge on the "mainland" side, you'll find the large **Rotary Community Park,** which is connected to the bridge by a paved waterside path. Adjacent to the park is the **Lake Havasu Aquatic Center,** 100 Park Ave. (✆ **928/453-2687**), which has an indoor pool, 254-foot water slide, and lots of other facilities. There are more beaches at **Lake Havasu State Park** (✆ **928/855-2784;** www.azstateparks.com), 2 miles north of the London Bridge; and at **Cattail Cove State Park** (✆ **928/855-1223;** www.azstateparks.com), 15 miles south of Lake Havasu City. Both state parks charge a $10 day-use fee.

In English Village, at the foot of the London Bridge, you can go for a ride on the **London Bridge Gondola** (✆ **928/486-1891;** www.londonbridgegondola.com); the gondolier even sings in Italian as you cruise beneath the London Bridge. Ride prices range from $15 to $35. If kayaking or canoeing is more your style, contact **Western Arizona Canoe and Kayak Outfitter** (✆ **888/881-5038** or 928/855-6414; www.azwacko.com), which charges $25 to $40 per day for canoes and kayaks.

You can also rent your own boat from **Fun Time Boat Rentals,** 1685 Industrial Blvd. (✆ **800/680-1003** or 928/680-1003; www.funtimeboatrentals.com). Pontoon boats and ski boats equipped with water skis or knee boards both rent for $250 per day.

WHERE TO STAY

Hotels & Motels

Heat Hotel ★ Located at the foot of the London Bridge, this surprisingly stylish boutique hotel is by far the hippest hotel between Scottsdale and Las Vegas. Guest rooms are reminiscent of those at W hotels, although here you get much more room at a much lower price. Rooms are large and have balconies, and most overlook the bridge or the water. Platform beds, stylish lamps, and a sort of Scandinavian-modern aesthetic make this the most distinctive hotel on this side of the state. The Inferno Suites, with their Tempur-Pedic beds and Jacuzzi tubs, are my favorite rooms here. ***One caveat:*** The open-air bar directly across the channels plays loud music until 2am on warm nights (especially during spring break).

1420 McCulloch Blvd. N., Lake Havasu City, AZ 86403. ✆ **888/898-HEAT** [4328]. Fax 888/868-HEAT [4328]. www.heathotel.com. 23 units. $99–$239 double; $169–$389 suite. Children 12 and under stay free in parent's room. AE, DISC, MC, V. **Amenities:** Bar. *In room:* A/C, TV/DVD, hair dryer, Internet, minibar.

London Bridge Resort & Convention Center ★ Merry Olde England was once the theme at this timeshare resort, and Tudor half-timbers are jumbled up with towers, ramparts, and crenellations. However, England has given way to the tropics and the desert as the resort strives to please its young, partying clientele (who tend to make a lot of noise and leave the hotel looking much the worse for wear). Although the bridge is just out the hotel's back door, and a replica of Britain's gold state coach is inside the lobby, guests are more interested in the three pools and the tropical-theme outdoor nightclub. The one- and two-bedroom units are spacious, comfortable, and attractive, and those on the ground floor have double whirlpool tubs.

1477 Queens Bay, Lake Havasu City, AZ 86403. ✆ **866/331-9231** or 928/855-0888. Fax 928/855-5404. www.londonbridgeresort.com. 122 units. $119–$189 studio condo; $179–$299 1-bedroom condo. AE, DC, DISC, MC, V. **Amenities:** Restaurant; 2 lounges; babysitting; 9-hole golf course; exercise room; Jacuzzi; 3 pools; spa; tennis court. *In room:* A/C, TV/DVD/VCR, hair dryer, Internet, kitchenette.

Camping

There are two state park campgrounds in the Lake Havasu City area. **Lake Havasu State Park** (✆ **928/855-2784;** www.azstateparks.com) is 2 miles north of the London Bridge, on London Bridge Road, while **Cattail Cove State Park** (✆ **928/855-1223;** www.azstateparks.com) is 15 miles south of Lake Havasu City off Ariz. 95. The former campground charges $15 per night per vehicle, while the latter charges $19 to $30 per site. Reservations are not accepted.

WHERE TO DINE

Cha-Bones ★ AMERICAN Move over Scottsdale, Lake Havasu City is gettin' hip and crowdin' your turf. Well, sort of. This very stylish little restaurant, a few blocks north of the London Bridge, could hold its own in the big city, at least as far as the decor goes. The menu, on the other hand, sticks to familiar mesquite-grilled steaks, barbecued ribs, build-your-own burgers, and a few designer pizzas. Granted, the menu doesn't break any new ground, but the setting is unlike anything else in town.

112 London Bridge Rd. ✆ **928/854-5554.** www.chabones.com. Reservations not accepted. Main courses $7–$16 lunch, $11–$38 dinner. AE, DC, DISC, MC, V. Oct–Apr Sun–Thurs 11am–9pm, Fri–Sat 11am–10pm; May–Sept Sun–Thurs 11am–10pm, Fri–Sat 11am–11pm.

Javelina Cantina MEXICAN Located at the foot of the London Bridge on the island side, this large, modern Mexican restaurant is affiliated with Shugrue's on the other side of the street. As at Shugrue's, there is a great view of the bridge. In this case, it is from a large patio area that is kept heated during the cooler winter months. The bar has an excellent selection of tequilas, and margaritas are a specialty here. Accompany your libations with tortilla soup, fish tacos, or a salad made with blackened scallops, papaya, pecans, and bleu cheese.

1420 McCulloch Blvd. ✆ **928/855-8226.** www.javelinacantina.com. Reservations not accepted. Main courses $9–$17. AE, DISC, MC, V. Sun–Tues and Thurs 11:30am–9pm; Wed 11:30am–10pm; Fri–Sat 11:30am–9:30pm.

16 The Grand Canyon & Northern Arizona

The Grand Canyon attracts millions of visitors from all over the world each year. The pastel layers of rock weaving through the canyon's rugged ramparts, the interplay of shadows and light, the wind in the pines, California condors soaring overhead, and the croaking of ravens on the rim—these are the sights and sounds that transfix the hordes of visitors who gaze awestruck into the canyon's seemingly infinite depths.

Yet other parts of northern Arizona contain worthwhile, and less crowded, attractions. Only 60 miles south of the canyon stand the San Francisco Peaks, the tallest of which, Humphreys Peak, rises to 12,643 feet. These peaks, sacred to the Hopi and Navajo, are ancient volcanoes that today are popular with skiers, hikers, and mountain bikers.

Amid northern Arizona's miles of windswept plains and ponderosa pine forests stands the city of Flagstaff, home to Northern Arizona University. Born of the railroads and named for a flagpole, Flagstaff is now the main jumping-off point for trips to the Grand Canyon.

1 THE GRAND CANYON SOUTH RIM ★★★

60 miles N of Williams; 80 miles NE of Flagstaff; 230 miles N of Phoenix; 340 miles N of Tucson

Whether you merely stand on the rim gazing in awe, spend several days hiking deep in the canyon, or ride the roller-coaster rapids of the Colorado River, a trip to the Grand Canyon is an unforgettable experience. A mile deep, 277 miles long, and up to 18 miles wide, the canyon is so large that it is positively overwhelming in its grandeur, truly one of the great wonders of the world.

Layers of sandstone, limestone, shale, and schist give the canyon its colors, and the interplay of shadows and light from dawn to dusk creates an ever-changing palette of hues and textures. Formed by the erosive action of the Colorado River as it flows through the Kaibab Plateau, the Grand Canyon is an open book exposing the secrets of this region's geologic history. Geologists believe it has taken 17 million years for the Colorado River to carve the Grand Canyon, but the canyon's history extends much farther back in time. Written in the canyon's bands of stone are more than 2 billion years of history.

Millions of years ago, vast seas covered this region. Sediments carried by seawater were deposited and, over millions of more years, those sediments were turned into limestone and sandstone. According to the most widely accepted theory, the Colorado River began its work of cutting through the plateau when the ancient seabed was thrust upward to form the Kaibab Plateau. Today, 21 sedimentary layers, the oldest of which is more than a billion years old, can be seen in the canyon. Beneath all these layers, at the very bottom, is a stratum of rock so old that it has metamorphosed, under great pressure and heat, from soft shale to a much harder stone. Called Vishnu Schist, this layer is the oldest rock in the Grand Canyon, dating from 2 billion years ago.

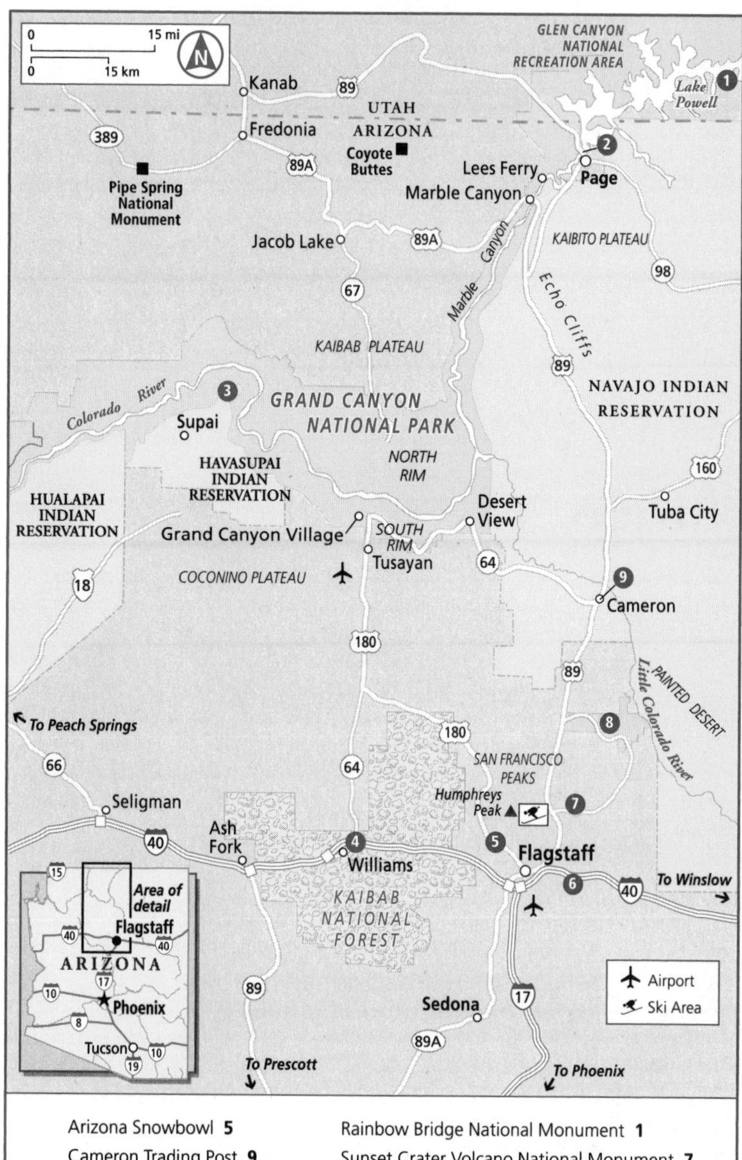

Arizona Snowbowl **5**
Cameron Trading Post **9**
Glen Canyon Dam **2**
Grand Canyon Railway **4**
Havasu Canyon **3**
Rainbow Bridge National Monument **1**
Sunset Crater Volcano National Monument **7**
Walnut Canyon National Monument **6**
Wupatki National Monument **8**

In the more recent past, the Grand Canyon has been home to several Native American cultures, including the Ancestral Puebloans (Anasazi), who are best known for their cliff dwellings in the Four Corners region. About 150 years after the Ancestral Puebloans and Coconino peoples abandoned the canyon in the 13th century, another tribe, the Cerbat, moved into the area. Today, the Hualapai and Havasupai tribes, descendants of the Cerbat people, still live in and near the Grand Canyon on the south side of the Colorado River. On the North Rim lived the Southern Paiute, and in the east, the Navajo.

However, there have been those in the recent past who regarded the canyon as mere wasted space, suitable only for filling with water. Upstream of the Grand Canyon stands Glen Canyon Dam, which forms Lake Powell, while downstream lies Lake Mead, created by Hoover Dam. The Grand Canyon might have suffered the same fate, but luckily the forces for preservation prevailed. Today, the Grand Canyon is the last major undammed stretch of the Colorado River.

All this popularity has taken its toll; with roughly four million people visiting the park each year, traffic during the summer months has become almost as bad at the South Rim as it is during rush hour in any major city, and finding a parking space is a challenge. But don't let these inconveniences dissuade you from visiting. Despite the crowds, the Grand Canyon more than lives up to its name and is one of the most memorable sights on earth.

ESSENTIALS

Getting There

BY CAR The South Rim of the Grand Canyon is 60 miles north of Williams and I-40 on Ariz. 64 and US 180. Flagstaff, the nearest city of any size, is 80 miles away. From Flagstaff, it's possible to take US 180 directly to the South Rim or US 89 to Ariz. 64 and the east entrance to the park. This latter route is my preferred way of getting to the canyon since it sees slightly less traffic. Be sure you have plenty of gasoline in your car before setting out for the canyon; there are few service stations in this remote part of the state and what gas stations there are charge exorbitant prices.

Long waits at the entrance gates, parking problems, and traffic congestion have become the norm at the canyon during the popular summer months, and even during the spring and fall there can be backups at the entrance gates and visitors can have a hard time finding a parking space. However, extra ticketing lanes built a few years ago have somewhat alleviated the congestion at the south entrance to the park.

BY PLANE The Grand Canyon Airport is in Tusayan, 6 miles south of Grand Canyon Village. **Scenic Airlines** (✆ **800/634-6801;** www.scenic.com) offers flights and overnight tours from the Boulder City Airport (near Las Vegas) and charges $299 to $399 round-trip. Alternatively, you can fly into Flagstaff and then arrange another mode of transportation the rest of the way to the national park (see "Flagstaff," later in this chapter, for details). See "Getting Around," below, for info on getting from the airport to your final destination.

BY TRAIN The **Grand Canyon Railway** operates excursion trains between Williams and the South Rim of the Grand Canyon. See "Williams," later in this chapter, for details.

For long-distance connections, **Amtrak** (✆ **800/872-7245;** www.amtrak.com) provides service to Flagstaff and Williams. From Flagstaff, it's then possible to take a bus directly to Grand Canyon Village. From Williams, you can take the Grand Canyon Railway excursion train to Grand Canyon Village. ***Note:*** The Amtrak stop in Williams is undeveloped and is on the outskirts of town. If you plan to take an Amtrak train to Williams, a shuttle from the Grand Canyon Railway Hotel will pick you up where the Amtrak train drops you off.

BY BUS Bus service between Phoenix, Flagstaff, Williams, and Grand Canyon Village is provided by **Open Road Tours** (✆ **800/766-7117** or 602/997-6474; www.openroadtours.com). Between Phoenix and Flagstaff, adult fares are $42 one-way and $76 round-trip ($30 and $52 for children); between Flagstaff and the Grand Canyon (by way of Williams), fares are $27 one-way and $54 round-trip ($19 and $38 for children).

Visitor Information

You can get advance information on the Grand Canyon by contacting **Grand Canyon National Park,** P.O. Box 129, Grand Canyon, AZ 86023 (✆ **928/638-7888;** www.nps.gov/grca).

When you arrive at the park, stop by the **Canyon View Visitor Center,** at Canyon View Information Plaza, 6 miles from the south entrance. Here you'll find exhibits, an information desk, and a shop selling maps, books, and videos. The center is open daily 8am to 5pm (9am–5pm in winter). Unfortunately, the information plaza, which is well designed for handling large crowds, has no adjacent parking, so you'll have to park where you can and then walk or take a free shuttle bus. The nearest places to park are at Mather Point, Market Plaza, park headquarters, and Yavapai Observation Station. If you're parked anywhere in Grand Canyon Village, you'll want to catch the Village Route bus. If you park at Yaki Point, you can take the Kaibab Trail Route bus. *The Guide,* a small newspaper full of useful information about the park, is available at both South Rim park entrances. Although smaller, the **Verkamp's Visitor Center,** near El Tovar hotel, is a much more convenient place to get park information. This visitor center is open daily from 8am to 5pm.

Orientation

Grand Canyon Village is built on the South Rim of the canyon and divided roughly into two sections. At the east end of the village are the Canyon View Information Plaza, Yavapai Lodge, Trailer Village, and Mather Campground. At the west end are El Tovar Hotel and Bright Angel, Kachina, Thunderbird, and Maswik lodges, as well as several restaurants, the train depot, and the trail head for the Bright Angel Trail.

Fees

The entry fee for Grand Canyon National Park is $25 per car (or $12 per person if you happen to be coming in on foot or by bicycle). Your admission ticket is good for 7 days (don't lose it, or you'll have to pay again).

Getting Around

As mentioned earlier, the Grand Canyon Village area can be extremely congested, especially in summer. If possible, you may want to use one of the transportation options below to avoid the park's traffic jams and parking problems. To give you an idea, in summer you can expect at least a 20- to 30-minute wait at the South Rim entrance gate just to get into the park. You can cut the waiting time here by acquiring an America the Beautiful–National Parks & Federal Recreational Lands Pass, before arriving. These passes are available as an Annual Pass ($80), a lifetime Senior Pass (available to U.S. citizens and permanent residents 62 or older for $10), and a lifetime Access Pass (available free to U.S. citizens and permanent residents with permanent disabilities). With pass in hand, you can use the express lane.

For **accessibility information,** check *The Guide* for park programs, services, and facilities that are partially or fully accessible. You can also get the Grand Canyon National Park *Accessibility Guide* at Canyon View Center, Yavapai Observation Station, Kolb Studio, Tusayan Museum, and Desert View Information Center. Temporary accessibility parking permits are available at the park entrances and the Canyon View Information Plaza, lodge transportation desks, Kolb Studio, and El Tovar concierge desk. The national park has wheelchairs available at no charge for temporary use inside the park. You can usually find one of these wheelchairs at the Canyon View Information Plaza. Wheelchair-accessible shuttle buses can be arranged by calling the national park (✆ **928/638-0591**) at least 48 hours in advance. Accessible tours can also be arranged by contacting any lodge transportation desk or by calling **Grand Canyon National Park Lodges** (✆ **928/638-2631**).

BY BUS Free shuttle buses operate on three routes within the park. The **Village Route** bus circles through Grand Canyon Village throughout the day with frequent stops at the Canyon View Information Plaza, Market Plaza (site of a general store, bank, laundry, and showers), hotels, campgrounds, restaurants, and other facilities. The **Hermit's Rest Route** bus takes visitors to eight canyon overlooks west of Bright Angel Lodge (this bus does not operate Dec–Feb). The **Kaibab Trail Route** bus stops at the Canyon View Information Plaza, Pipe Creek Vista, the South Kaibab Trailhead, and Yaki Point. There's also a morning Hikers' Express bus to the South Kaibab Trailhead. This bus stops at Bright Angel Lodge and the Back Country Information Office. Hikers needing transportation to or from Yaki Point when the bus is not running can use a taxi (✆ **928/638-2822** or 928/638-2631, ext. 6563).

Between mid-May and mid-October, **Trans Canyon** (✆ **928/638-2820;** www.transcanyonshuttle.com) offers shuttle-bus service between the South Rim and the North Rim. The vans leave the South Rim at 1:30pm and arrive at the North Rim at 6pm. The return trip leaves the North Rim at 7am, arriving back at the South Rim at 11:30am. The fare is $80 one-way and $150 round-trip; reservations are required.

BY CAR Service stations are outside the south entrance to the park in Tusayan, at Desert View near the east entrance (no cash sales in winter), and east of the park at Cameron. Because of the long distances within the park and to towns outside the park, fill up before setting out on a drive. Gas at the canyon is very expensive.

If you want to avoid parking headaches, try using the lot at the Market Plaza (the general store), which is up a side road near Yavapai Lodge and the Canyon View Information Plaza. From this large parking area, a paved hiking trail leads to the historic section of the village in less than 1.5 miles, and most of the route is along the rim. Another option is to park at the Maswik Transportation Center parking lot, which is served by the Village Route shuttle bus.

BY TAXI Taxi service is available to and from the airport, trail heads, and other destinations (✆ **928/638-2822** or 928/638-2631, ext. 6563). The fare from the airport to Grand Canyon Village is $10 for up to two adults ($5 for each additional person).

FAST FACTS

There's an ATM at the **Chase** bank (✆ **928/638-2437**) at Market Plaza, which is near Yavapai Lodge. The bank is open Monday through Thursday from 9am to 5pm and Friday from 9am to 6pm.

The **North Country Grand Canyon Clinic** (✆ **928/638-2551**) is on Clinic Drive, off Center Road (the road that runs past the National Park Service ranger office). The clinic is open daily from 8am to 6pm (shorter hours in winter). It provides 24-hour emergency service as well.

The **climate** at the Grand Canyon is dramatically different from that of Phoenix, and between the rim and the canyon floor there's also a pronounced difference. Winter temperatures at the South Rim can be below 0°F (–18°C) at night, with daytime highs in the 20s or 30s (minus single digits to single digits Celsius). Summer temperatures at the rim range from highs in the 80s (20s Celsius) to lows in the 50s (teens Celsius). The North Rim is slightly higher than the South Rim and stays a bit cooler. On the canyon floor, temperatures are considerably higher. In summer, the mercury can reach 120°F (49°C) with lows in the 70s (20s Celsius), while in winter, temperatures are quite pleasant with highs in the 50s (teens Celsius) and lows in the 30s (single digits Celsius).

DESERT VIEW DRIVE

The vast majority of visitors to the Grand Canyon enter through the south entrance, head straight for Grand Canyon Village, and proceed to get caught up in traffic jams. You can avoid much of this congestion and have a much more enjoyable experience if you enter the park through the east entrance. To reach the east entrance from Flagstaff, take US 89 to Ariz. 64. Even before you reach the park, you can stop and take in views of the canyon of the Little Colorado River. These viewpoints are on the Navajo Reservation, and at every stop you'll have opportunities to shop for Native American crafts and souvenirs at the numerous vendors' stalls that can be found at virtually every scenic viewpoint on the Navajo Reservation.

Desert View Drive, the park's only scenic road open to cars year-round, extends for 25 miles from Desert View, which is just inside the park's east entrance, to Grand Canyon Village, the site of all the park's hotels and most of its other commercial establishments. Along Desert View Drive, you'll find not only good viewpoints, but also several picnic areas. Much of this drive is through forests, and canyon views are limited; but where there are viewpoints, they are among the best in the park.

Desert View, with its trading post, general store, snack bar, service station, information center, bookstore, and historic watchtower, is the first stop on this scenic drive. From anywhere at Desert View, the scenery is breathtaking, but the very best perspective here is from atop the **Desert View Watchtower.** Architect Mary Elizabeth Jane Colter, who is responsible for much of the park's historic architecture, designed it to resemble the prehistoric towers that dot the Southwestern landscape, but the tower actually dates from 1932. Built as an observation tower and rest stop for tourists, the watchtower incorporates Native American designs and art. The curio shop on the ground floor is a replica of a kiva (sacred ceremonial chamber) and has lots of interesting souvenirs, regional crafts, and books. The tower's second floor features work by Hopi artist Fred Kabotie. Covering the walls are pictographs incorporating traditional designs. On the walls and ceiling of the upper two floors are additional traditional images by artist Fred Geary—this time, reproductions of petroglyphs from throughout the Southwest. From the roof, which, at 7,522 feet above sea level, is the highest point on the South Rim, it's possible to see the Colorado River, the Painted Desert to the northeast, the San Francisco Peaks to the south, and Marble Canyon to the north. Several black-mirror "reflectoscopes" provide interesting darkened views of some of the most spectacular sections of the canyon.

At **Navajo Point,** the next stop along the rim, the Colorado River and Escalante Butte are both visible, and there's a good view of the Desert View Watchtower. However, I suggest heading straight to **Lipan Point ★★**, where you get what I think is the South Rim's best view of the Colorado River. You can actually see several stretches of the river, including a couple of major rapids. From here you can also view the Grand Canyon supergroup: several strata of rock tilted at an angle to the other layers of rock in the canyon. The red, white, and black rocks of the supergroup are composed of sedimentary rock and layers of lava.

The **Tusayan Museum** (daily 9am–5pm) is the next stop along Desert View Drive. This small museum is dedicated to the Hopi tribe and the Ancestral Puebloan people who inhabited the region 800 years ago; inside are artfully displayed exhibits on various aspects of Ancestral Puebloan life. Outside is a short self-guided trail through the ruins of an Ancestral Puebloan village. Free guided tours are available.

Next along the drive is **Moran Point,** from which you can see a layer of red shale in the canyon walls. This point is named for 19th-century landscape painter Thomas Moran, who is known for his paintings of the Grand Canyon.

The next stop, **Grandview Point,** affords a view of Horseshoe Mesa, another interesting feature of the canyon landscape. The mesa was the site of the Last Chance Copper Mine in the early 1890s. Later that same decade, the Grandview Hotel was built and served canyon visitors until its close in 1908. The steep, unmaintained Grandview Trail leads down to Horseshoe Mesa from here. This trail makes a good less-traveled alternative to the South Kaibab Trail, although it is somewhat steeper.

The last stop along Desert View Drive is **Yaki Point,** which is no longer open to private vehicles. The park service would prefer it if you parked your car in Grand Canyon Village and took the Kaibab Trail Route shuttle bus from the Canyon View Information Plaza to Yaki Point. The reality is that people passing by in cars want to see what this viewpoint is all about and now park their cars alongside the main road and walk up the Yaki Point access road. The spectacular view from here encompasses a wide section of the central canyon. The large, flat-topped butte to the northeast is Wotan's Throne, one of the canyon's most readily recognizable features. Yaki Point is the site of the trail head for the South Kaibab Trail and consequently is frequented by hikers headed down to Phantom Ranch at the bottom of the canyon. The South Kaibab Trail is the preferred downhill hiking route to Phantom Ranch and is a more scenic route than the Bright Angel Trail. If you're planning a day hike into the canyon, this should be your number-one choice. Be sure to bring plenty of water.

GRAND CANYON VILLAGE & VICINITY

Grand Canyon Village is the first stop for the vast majority of the nearly four million people who visit the Grand Canyon every year (though I recommend coming in from the east entrance and avoiding the crowds). Consequently, it is the most crowded area in the park, but it also has the most overlooks and visitor services. Its many historic buildings add to the popularity of the village, which, if it weren't so crowded all the time, would have a pleasant atmosphere.

For visitors who have entered the park through the south entrance, that unforgettable initial gasp-inducing glimpse of the canyon comes at **Mather Point.** From this overlook, there's a short paved path to the Canyon View Information Plaza, but because you're allowed to park at Mather Point only for a maximum of 1 hour, you'll have to hurry if you want to take in the views and gather some park information.

Continuing west toward the village proper, you next come to **Yavapai Point,** which has the best view from anywhere in the vicinity of Grand Canyon Village. From here you can see the Bright Angel Trail, Indian Gardens, Phantom Ranch, and even the suspension bridge that hikers and mule riders use to cross the Colorado River near Phantom Ranch. Oh, yes, and of course you can also see the Colorado River. This viewpoint is a particularly great spot to take sunrise and sunset photos. Here you'll also find the historic **Yavapai Observation Station,** which houses a small museum and has big walls of glass to take in those extraordinary vistas. A paved pathway extends west from Yavapai Point for 3 miles, passing through Grand Canyon Village along the way. This trail also continues 2.5 miles east to the Pipe Creek Vista.

Continuing west from Yavapai Point, you'll come to a parking lot at park headquarters and a side road that leads to parking at the Market Plaza, which is one of the closest parking lots to the Canyon View Information Plaza.

West of these parking areas is Grand Canyon Village proper, where a paved pathway leads along the rim providing lots of good (though crowded) spots for taking pictures. The village is also the site of such historic buildings as **El Tovar Hotel** and **Bright Angel Lodge,** both of which are worth brief visits to take in the lodge ambience of their lobbies. Inside Bright Angel Lodge you'll find the **Bright Angel History Room,** which has displays on Mary Elizabeth Jane Colter and the Harvey Girls (see box "Fred Harvey & His Girls," on p. 98). Be sure to check out this room's fireplace, which is designed with all the same geologic layers that appear in the canyon. The **Hopi House Gift Store and Art Gallery,** across from El Tovar's front porch, dates to 1905 and was the first shop in the park. This store was built to resemble a Hopi pueblo and to serve as a place for Hopi artisans to work and sell their crafts. Today, it's full of Hopi and Navajo arts and crafts. **Verkamp's Visitor Center,** adjacent to the Hopi House, was originally a curio shop and also dates back to 1905. Today it is a small information center that houses displays on the history of Grand Canyon Village. Hours vary seasonally.

To the west of Bright Angel Lodge, two buildings cling precariously to the rim of the canyon. These are the Kolb and Lookout studios, both of which are listed on the National Register of Historic Places. **Kolb Studio** is named for Ellsworth and Emory Kolb, two brothers who set up a photographic studio on the rim of the Grand Canyon in 1904. The construction of this studio generated one of the Grand Canyon's first controversies—over whether buildings should be allowed on the canyon rim. Because the Kolbs had friends in high places, their sprawling studio and movie theater remained. Emory Kolb lived here until his death in 1976, by which time the studio had been listed as a historic building. It now serves as a bookstore, while the auditorium houses special exhibits. **Lookout Studio,** built in 1914 from a design by Mary Elizabeth Jane Colter, was the Fred Harvey Company's answer to the Kolb brothers' studio and incorporates architectural styles of the Hopi and the Ancestral Puebloans. The use of native limestone and an uneven roofline allow the studio to blend in with the canyon walls and give it the look of an old ruin. It now houses a souvenir store and two lookout points. Both studios are open daily; hours vary seasonally.

HERMIT ROAD

Hermit Road leads 8 miles west from Grand Canyon Village to Hermit's Rest, and mile for mile, it has the greatest concentration of breathtaking viewpoints in the park. Because it is closed to private vehicles March through November, it is also one of the most pleasant places to do a little canyon viewing or easy hiking during the busiest times of year: no traffic jams, no parking problems, and plenty of free shuttle buses operating along the route. Westbound buses stop at eight overlooks (Trailview, Maricopa Point, Powell Point, Hopi Point, Mohave Point, the Abyss, Pima Point, and Hermit's Rest); eastbound buses stop at only Mohave and Hopi points. December through February, you can drive your own vehicle along this road; but keep in mind that winters usually mean a lot of snow, and the road can sometimes be closed due to hazardous driving conditions.

Because you probably won't want to stop at every viewpoint along this route, here are some tips to help you get the most out of an excursion along Hermit Road. First of all, keep in mind that the earlier you catch a shuttle bus, the more likely you are to avoid the crowds (buses start 1 hr. before sunrise, so photographers can get good shots of the canyon in dawn light). Second, remember that the closer you are to Grand Canyon Village, the larger the crowds will be. So, I recommend heading out early and getting a couple of miles between you and the village before getting off the shuttle bus.

The first two stops are **Trailview Overlook** and **Maricopa Point,** both on the paved section of the Rim Trail and within 1½ miles of the village, and thus usually pretty crowded. If you just want to do a short, easy walk on pavement, get out at Maricopa Point and walk back to the village. From either overlook, you have a view of the Bright Angel Trail winding down into the canyon from Grand Canyon Village. The trail, which leads to the bottom of the canyon, crosses the Tonto Plateau about 3,000 feet below the rim. This plateau is the site of Indian Garden, where there's a campground in a grove of cottonwood trees. Because the views from these two overlooks are not significantly different from those in the village, I suggest skipping these stops if you've already spent time gazing into the canyon from the village.

Powell Point, the third stop, is the site of a memorial to John Wesley Powell, who, in 1869 with a party of nine men, became the first person to navigate the Colorado River through the Grand Canyon. Visible at Powell Point are the remains of the Orphan Mine, a copper mine that began operation in 1893. The mine went out of business because transporting the copper to a city where it could be sold was too expensive. Uranium was discovered here in 1951, but, in 1969, the mine was shut down; in 1987 the land became part of Grand Canyon National Park. Again, I recommend continuing on to the more spectacular vistas that lie ahead.

The next stop is **Hopi Point,** which is one of the three best stops along this route. From here you can see a long section of the Colorado River far below you. Because of the great distance, the river seems to be a tiny, quiet stream, but in reality the section you see is more than 100 yards wide and races through Granite Rapids. Because Hopi Point juts into the canyon, it is one of the best spots in the park for taking sunrise and sunset photos (remember, shuttle buses operate from 1 hr. before sunrise to 1 hr. after sunset).

The view is even more spectacular at the next stop, **Mohave Point.** Here you can see the river in two directions. Three rapids are visible from this overlook, and on a quiet day, you can sometimes even hear Hermit Rapids. As with almost all rapids in the canyon, Hermit Rapids are at the mouth of a side canyon where boulders loosened by storms and carried by flooded streams are deposited in the Colorado River. Don't miss this stop; it's got the best view on Hermit Road.

Next you come to the **Abyss,** the appropriately named 3,000-foot drop created by the Great Mojave Wall. This vertiginous view is one of the most awe-inspiring in the park. The walls of the Abyss are red sandstone that's more resistant to erosion than the softer shale in the layer below. Other layers of erosion-resistant sandstone have formed the free-standing pillars that are visible from here. The largest of these pillars is called the Monument. If you're looking for a good hike along this road, get out here and walk westward to either Pima Point (3 miles distant) or Hermit's Rest (4 miles away).

The **Pima Point** overlook, because it is set back from the road, is another good place to get off the bus. From here, the Rim Trail leads through the forest near the canyon rim, providing good views undisturbed by traffic on Hermit Road. From this overlook, it's also possible to see the remains of Hermit Camp on the Tonto Plateau. Built by the Santa

Fe Railroad, Hermit Camp was a popular tourist destination between 1911 and 1930 and provided cabins and tents.

The final stop on Hermit Road is at **Hermit's Rest,** which was named for Louis Boucher, a prospector who came to the canyon in the 1890s and was known as the Hermit. The log-and-stone Hermit's Rest building, designed by Mary Elizabeth Jane Colter and built in 1914, is on the National Register of Historic Places and is one of the most fascinating structures in the park. With its snack bar, it makes a great place to linger while you soak up a bit of park history. The steep Hermit Trail, which leads down into the canyon, begins just past Hermit's Rest.

HIKING THE CANYON

No visit to the canyon is complete without journeying below the rim on one of the park's hiking trails. Gazing up at all those thousands of feet of vertical rock walls provides a very different perspective than that from atop the rim. Should you venture far below the rim, you also stand a chance of seeing fossils, old mines, petroglyphs, wildflowers, and wildlife. However, because of the Grand Canyon's popularity, the park's main hiking trails are usually crowded.

That said, there is no better way to see the canyon than on foot (my apologies to the mules), and a hike down into the canyon will likely be the highlight of your visit. The Grand Canyon offers some of the most rugged and strenuous hiking anywhere in the United States, and for this reason anyone attempting even a short walk should be well prepared. Each year, injuries and fatalities are suffered by day hikers who set out without sturdy footgear or without food and adequate amounts of water. Even a 30-minute hike in summer can dehydrate you, and a long hike in the heat can necessitate drinking more than a gallon of water. So, carry and drink at least 2 quarts (2 liters) of water if you go for a day hike during the summer. Don't attempt to hike from the rim to the Colorado River and back in a day; there are plenty of hikers who have tried this and died. Also remember that mules have the right of way.

Day Hikes

There are no loop trails on the South Rim, but the vastly different scenery in every direction makes out-and-back hikes here as interesting as any loop trail could be. The only problem is that instead of starting out by slogging up a steep mountain, you let gravity assist you in hiking down into the canyon. With little negative reinforcement and few natural turnaround destinations, it is easy to hike so far that the return trip back up the trail becomes an arduous death march. Turn around *before* you become tired. On the canyon rim, the only hiking trail is the Rim Trail, while the Bright Angel, South Kaibab, Grandview, and Hermit trails all head down into the canyon.

For an easy, flat hike, your main option is the **Rim Trail,** which stretches from Pipe Creek Vista east of Grand Canyon Village to Hermit's Rest, 8 miles west of the village. Around 5 miles of this trail are paved, and the portion that passes through Grand Canyon Village is always the most crowded stretch of trail in the park. To the west of the village, after the pavement ends, the Rim Trail leads another 6.8 miles out to Hermit's Rest. For most of this distance, the trail follows Hermit Road, which means you'll have to deal with traffic noise (mostly from shuttle buses). To get the most enjoyment out of a hike along this stretch, I like to head out as early in the morning as possible (to avoid the crowds) and get off at the Abyss shuttle stop. From here it's a 4-mile hike to Hermit's Rest; for more than half of this distance, the trail isn't as close to the road as it is at the Grand Canyon Village end of the route. Plus, Hermit's Rest makes a great place to rest, and from here you can catch a shuttle bus back to the village. Alternatively, you could start hiking from Grand Canyon Village (it's just more than 8 miles from the west end of the village to Hermit's Rest) or any of the seven shuttle-bus stops en route, or take the shuttle all the way to Hermit's Rest and then hike back.

If you're looking for an easy hike and want to leave the crowds behind, then consider the short walk to **Shoshone Point.** The route to this secluded overlook (actually a reservable group picnic area) is along a flat dirt road that makes this a good bet for a family walk (just keep a tight rein on the kids once you get to the canyon rim, as there are no fences here). There are no signs for Shoshone Point, so you'll have to watch for the small dirt parking area and gate on the north side of the road at mile marker 246. You can't drive in without a permit, and if the gate is open, it usually means that a group is using the site. If this is the case, you'll probably want to skip this hike. You'll find the parking area 19 miles west of the Desert View entrance to the park and 2.3 miles east of the Grand Canyon Village end of Desert View Drive.

The **Bright Angel Trail,** which starts just west of Bright Angel Lodge in Grand Canyon Village, is the most popular trail into the canyon because it starts right where the greatest number of park visitors tend to congregate (near the ice-cream parlor and the hotels). It is also the route used by mule riders headed down into the canyon. Bear in mind that this trail follows a narrow side canyon for several miles and thus has somewhat limited views. For these reasons, this trail is worth avoiding if you're on foot. On the other hand, it's the only maintained trail into the canyon that has potable water, and there are four destinations along the trail that make good turnaround points. Both 1½ Mile Resthouse (1,131 ft. below the rim) and 3 Mile Resthouse (2,112 ft. below the rim) have water (except in winter, when the water is turned off). Keep in mind that these rest houses take their names from their distance from the rim; if you hike to 3 Mile Resthouse, you still have a 3-mile hike back up. Destinations for longer day hikes include Indian Garden (9 miles round-trip) and Plateau Point (12 miles round-trip), which are both slightly more than 3,000 feet below the rim. There is year-round water at Indian Garden.

The **South Kaibab Trail ★★★** begins near Yaki Point east of Grand Canyon Village and is the preferred route down to Phantom Ranch. This trail also offers the best views of any of the trails into the canyon, so should you have time for only one day hike, make it the South Kaibab Trail. From the trail head, it's 3 miles round-trip to Cedar Ridge and 6 miles round-trip to Skeleton Point. The hike is very strenuous, and no water is available along the trail.

If you're looking to escape the crowds and are an experienced mountain or desert hiker with good, sturdy boots, consider the unmaintained **Hermit Trail,** which begins at Hermit's Rest, 8 miles west of Grand Canyon Village at the end of Hermit Road. It's a 5-mile round-trip hike to Santa Maria Spring on a trail that loses almost all of its elevation (1,600–1,700 ft.) in the first 1.5 miles. Beyond Santa Maria Spring, the Hermit Trail descends to the Colorado River, but it is a 17-mile hike, one-way, from the trail head. Alternatively, you can do a 7-mile round-trip hike to Dripping Springs. Water from these two springs must be treated with a water filter, iodine, or purification tablets, or by boiling for at least 10 minutes, so you're better off just carrying sufficient water for your hike. March through November, Hermit Road is closed to private vehicles, so during these months, you'll need to take the free shuttle bus out to the trail head. If you take the first bus of the day, you'll likely have the trail almost all to yourself.

The **Grandview Trail,** which begins at Grandview Point 12 miles east of Grand Canyon Village, is another steep and unmaintained trail that's a good choice for physically fit hikers. A strenuous 6-mile round-trip hike leads down to Horseshoe Mesa, 2,600 feet below the trail head. No water is available, so carry at least 2 quarts. Just to give you an idea of how steep this trail is, you'll lose more than 2,000 feet of elevation in the first .8 mile down to Coconino Saddle.

Backpacking

Backpacking the Grand Canyon is an unforgettable experience. Although most people are content to simply hike down to Phantom Ranch and back, there are many miles of trails deep in the canyon. Keep in mind, however, that to backpack the canyon, you'll need to do a lot of planning. A **Backcountry Use Permit** is required of all hikers planning to overnight in the canyon, unless you'll be staying at Phantom Ranch in one of the cabins or a dormitory.

Because a limited number of hikers are allowed into the canyon on any given day, it's important to make reservations as soon as it is possible to do so. Reservations are taken in person, by mail, by fax (but not by phone), and online. Contact the **Backcountry Information Center,** Grand Canyon National Park, P.O. Box 129, Grand Canyon, AZ 86023 (✆ **928/638-7875** Mon–Fri 1–5pm for information; fax 928/638-2125; www.nps.gov/grca). The office begins accepting reservations on the first of every month for the following 5 months. Holiday periods are the most popular—if you want to hike over the Labor Day weekend, be sure you make your reservation on May 1. If you show up without a reservation, go to the Backcountry Information Center (daily 8am–noon and 1–5pm), adjacent to Maswik Lodge, and put your name on the waiting list. When applying for a permit, you must specify your exact itinerary, and once in the canyon, you must stick to this itinerary. Backpacking fees include a nonrefundable $10 backcountry permit fee and a $5 per-person per-night backcountry camping fee. Keep in mind that you'll still have to pay the park entry fee when you arrive at the Grand Canyon.

The *Backcountry Trip Planner* contains information to help you plan your itinerary. It's available through the Backcountry Information Center (see contact information, above). Maps are available through the **Grand Canyon Association,** P.O. Box 399, Grand Canyon, AZ 86023 (✆ **800/858-2808** or 928/638-2481; www.grandcanyon.org), and at bookstores and gift shops within the national park, including Canyon View Information Plaza, Verkamp's Visitor Center, Kolb Studio, Desert View Information Center, Yavapai Observation Station, Tusayan Museum, and, on the North Rim, Grand Canyon Lodge.

The best times of year to backpack are spring and fall. In summer, temperatures at the bottom of the canyon are frequently above 100°F (38°C), while in winter, ice and snow at higher elevations make footing on trails precarious (crampons are recommended). Plan to carry at least 2 quarts, and preferably 1 gallon, of water whenever backpacking in the canyon.

The Grand Canyon is an unforgiving landscape and, as such, many people might want a professional guide while backpacking through this rugged corner of the Southwest. To arrange a guided backpacking trip into the canyon, contact **Discovery Treks,** 28248 N. Tatum Blvd., Ste. B1-414, Cave Creek, AZ 85331 (✆ **888/256-8731** or 480/247-9266; www.discoverytreks.com), which offers 3- to 6-day all-inclusive hikes into the canyon with rates ranging from $795 to $1,995 per person.

OTHER WAYS OF SEEING THE CANYON

Bus Tours

If you'd rather leave the driving to someone else and enjoy more of the scenery, opt for a bus or van tour of one or more sections of the park. **Grand Canyon National Park**

Lodges (✆ **888/297-2757,** 303/297-2757, or, for same-day reservations, 928/638-2631; www.grandcanyonlodges.com) offers several tours within the park. These can be booked by calling or stopping at one of the transportation desks, which are at Bright Angel, Maswik, and Yavapai lodges (see "Where to Stay," below). Prices range from around $18 for a 1½-hour sunrise or sunset tour to around $50 for a combination of any two of the company's tours (Hermit's Rest, Desert View, sunrise, sunset).

Mule Rides ★

Mule rides into the canyon have been popular since the beginning of the 20th century, when the Bright Angel Trail was a toll road. After having a look at the steep drop-offs and narrow path of the Bright Angel Trail, you might decide this isn't exactly the place to trust your life to a mule. Never fear: Wranglers will be quick to reassure you they haven't lost a rider yet. Trips of various lengths and to different destinations are offered. The 1-day trip descends to Plateau Point, where there's a view of the Colorado River 1,300 feet below. This grueling trip requires riders to spend 6 hours in the saddle. Those who want to spend a night down in the canyon can choose an overnight trip to Phantom Ranch, where cabins and dormitories are available at the only lodge actually in the canyon. From November to March, a 3-day trip to Phantom Ranch is offered; other times of year, you'll ride down one day and back up the next. Mule trips range in price from $154 for a 1-day ride to $424 for an overnight ride to $593 for the 2-night ride. Couples get discounts on overnight rides.

Riders must weigh less than 200 pounds fully dressed; stand at least 4 feet, 7 inches tall; and speak and understand English fluently. Pregnant women are not allowed on mule trips.

Because these trail rides are very popular (especially in summer), they often book up 6 months or more in advance (reservations are taken up to 13 months in advance). For more information or to make a reservation, contact **Xanterra Parks & Resorts** (✆ **888/297-2757** or 303/297-2757; www.grandcanyonlodges.com). If, at the last minute (5 days or fewer from the day you want to ride), you decide you want to go on a mule trip, contact **Grand Canyon National Park Lodges** at its Arizona phone number (✆ **928/638-2631**) for the remote possibility that there may be space available. If you arrive at the canyon without a reservation and decide that you'd like to go on a mule ride, stop by the Bright Angel Transportation Desk to get your name put on the next day's waiting list.

The Grand Canyon Railway ★★

In the early 20th century, most visitors to the Grand Canyon arrived by train, and it's still possible to travel to the canyon along the steel rails. The **Grand Canyon Railway** (✆ **800/843-8724** or 928/773-1976; www.thetrain.com), which runs from Williams to Grand Canyon Village, uses 1950s diesel engines and, between Memorial Day and Labor Day, early-20th-century steam engines to pull vintage passenger cars. Trains depart from the Williams Depot, which is housed in the historic 1908 Fray Marcos Hotel and also contains a railroad museum, gift shop, and cafe. (Grand Canyon Railway also operates the adjacent Grand Canyon Railway Hotel.) At Grand Canyon Village, the trains use the 1910 log railway terminal in front of El Tovar Hotel.

Passengers have the choice of four classes of service: coach (which includes both Pullman and Budd cars), first class, observation dome (upstairs in the dome car), and luxury parlor class. Actors posing as cowboys provide entertainment, including musical performances, aboard the train. The round-trip takes 8 hours, including a 3¼- to 3¾-hour layover at the canyon. Fares range from $70 to $190 for adults, and $40 to $110 for children 2 to 12 (these rates do not include taxes or the park entry fee).

A Bird's-Eye View

Despite controversies over noise and safety (there have been a few crashes over the years), airplane and helicopter flights over the Grand Canyon remain one of the most popular ways to see this natural wonder. If you want to join the crowds buzzing the canyon, you'll find several companies operating out of Grand Canyon Airport in Tusayan. Air tours last anywhere from 30 minutes to about 2 hours.

Companies offering tours by small plane include **Air Grand Canyon** (✆ **800/247-4726** or 928/638-2686; www.airgrandcanyon.com) and **Grand Canyon Airlines** (✆ **866/235-9422** or 928/638-2359; www.grandcanyonairlines.com). This latter company has been offering air tours since 1927 and is the oldest scenic airline at the canyon. Fifty-minute flights cost $99 to $125 for adults and $89 to $99 for children.

Helicopter tours are available from **Maverick Airstar Helicopters** (✆ **888/261-4414** or 702/261-0007; www.airstar.com), **Grand Canyon Helicopters** (✆ **800/541-4537** or 928/638-2764; www.grandcanyonhelicoptersaz.com), and **Papillon Grand Canyon Helicopters** (✆ **888/635-7272** or 928/638-2419; www.papillon.com). Rates range from $125 to $165 for a 25- to 30-minute flight and from $179 to $225 for a 45- to 55-minute flight. Children sometimes receive a discount (usually around $20).

The Grand Canyon Field Institute

If you're the active type or would like to turn your visit to the Grand Canyon into more of an educational experience, you may want to consider doing a trip with the **Grand Canyon Field Institute** (✆ **866/471-4435** or 928/638-2485; www.grandcanyon.org/fieldinstitute). Cosponsored by Grand Canyon National Park and the Grand Canyon Association, the Field Institute schedules a wide variety of guided, educational trips, such as backpacking trips through the canyon and programs lasting anywhere from 1 day to more than a week. Subjects covered include wilderness studies, geology, natural history, human history, photography, and art.

Jeep Tours

If you'd like to explore parts of Grand Canyon National Park that most visitors never see, contact **Grand Canyon Jeep Tours & Safaris** (✆ **800/320-5337** or 928/638-5337; www.grandcanyonjeeptours.com), which offers three different tours that visit the park as well as the adjacent Kaibab National Forest. One tour stops at a lookout tower, while another visits an Indian ruin and site of petroglyphs and cave paintings. Prices range from $50 to $109 for adults and $40 to $89 for children 11 and under.

Rafting the Colorado River ★★★

Rafting down the Colorado River as it roars and tumbles through the mile-deep gorge of the Grand Canyon is the adventure of a lifetime. Ever since John Wesley Powell ignored everyone who knew better and proved that it was possible to travel by boat down the tumultuous Colorado, running the big river has become a passion and an obsession with adventurers. Today, anyone from grade-schoolers to grandmothers can join the elite group of people who have made the run. However, be prepared for some of the most furious white water in the world.

Most trips start from Lees Ferry near Page and Lake Powell. It's also possible to start (or finish) a trip at Phantom Ranch, hiking in or out from either the North or South Rim. The main rafting season is April through October, but some companies operate

A Shopping Break

Outside the east entrance to the park, the **Cameron Trading Post** (© **800/338-7385** or 928/679-2231; www.camerontradingpost.com), at the crossroads of Cameron where Arizona 64 branches off US 89, is the best trading post in the state. The original stone trading post, a historic building, now houses a gallery of Indian artifacts, clothing, and jewelry. The main trading post is a more modern building. Don't miss the beautiful terraced gardens in back of the original trading post.

year-round. Rafting trips tend to book up more than a year in advance, and some companies begin taking reservations as early as January for the following year's trips. Although it is possible to book a rafting trip for $250 or slightly less per day, the majority of trips fall in the $300 to $350 per day range, with rates depending on the length of the trip and the type of boat used.

The following are some of the companies I recommend checking out when you start planning your Grand Canyon rafting adventure:

- **Arizona Raft Adventures,** 4050 E. Huntington Rd., Flagstaff, AZ 86004 (© **800/786-7238;** www.azraft.com), offers 6- to 16-day motor, oar, and paddle trips. Although this is not one of the larger companies operating on the river, it offers lots of different trips, including those that focus on natural history and others that focus on tales from the canyon. They also do trips in paddle rafts that allow you to help navigate and provide the power while shooting the canyon's many rapids.
- **Canyoneers,** P.O. Box 2997, Flagstaff, AZ 86003 (© **800/525-0924** or 928/526-0924; www.canyoneers.com), has 3- to 7-day motorized-raft trips and 6- to 14-day oar-powered trips. Way back in 1938, this was the first company to take paying customers down the Colorado, and Canyoneers is still one of the top companies on the river.
- **Diamond River Adventures,** P.O. Box 1300, Page, AZ 86040 (© **800/343-3121** or 928/645-8866; www.diamondriver.com), offers 4- to 8-day motorized-raft trips and 5- to 13-day oar trips. This is the only women-owned and -managed rafting company operating in the Grand Canyon.
- **Grand Canyon Expeditions Company,** P.O. Box O, Kanab, UT 84741 (© **800/544-2691** or 435/644-2691; www.gcex.com), offers 8-day motorized trips and 14- and 16-day dory trips. If you've got the time, I highly recommend these dory trips—they're among the most thrilling adventures in the world.
- **Hatch River Expeditions,** HC 67 Box 35, Marble Canyon, AZ 86036 (© **800/856-8966;** www.hatchriverexpeditions.com), has 7- and 8-day motorized trips and 6- to 12-day oar trips. All of this company's trips, except their upper-canyon expedition, end with a helicopter flight out of the canyon. This company has been in business since 1929 and claims to be the oldest commercial rafting company in the U.S. With so much experience, you can count on Hatch to provide you with a great trip.
- **Outdoors Unlimited,** 6900 Townsend Winona Rd., Flagstaff, AZ 86004 (© **800/637-7238** or 928/526-4511; www.outdoorsunlimited.com), has 5- to 13-day oar and paddle trips. This company has been taking people through the canyon for nearly 40 years and usually sends them home very happy.

- **Wilderness River Adventures,** P.O. Box 717, Page, AZ 86040 (✆ **800/992-8022** or 928/645-3296; www.riveradventures.com), offers 4- to 8-day motorized-raft trips and 6-, 7-, 12-, 14-, and 16-day oar trips. The 4-day trips (actually 3½ days) involve hiking out from Phantom Ranch. This is one of the bigger companies operating on the canyon, and it offers a wide variety of trips, which makes it a good one to check with if you're not sure which type of trip you want to do.

For information on 1-day rafting trips at the west end of the Grand Canyon, see "Havasu Canyon & Grand Canyon West," later in this chapter.

WHERE TO STAY

Hotel rooms both within and just outside the park are in high demand. Make reservations as far in advance as possible, and don't expect to find a room if you head up here in summer without a reservation. There, is, however, one long-shot option. See "Inside the Park," below, for details.

Inside the Park

All hotels inside the park are operated by **Xanterra South Rim/Xanterra Parks & Resorts.** Reservations are taken up to 13 months in advance, beginning on the first of the month. If you want to stay in one of the historic rim cabins at Bright Angel Lodge, reserve at least a year in advance. However, rooms with shared bathrooms at Bright Angel Lodge are often the last in the park to book up, and although they're small and very basic, they're your best bet if you're trying to get a last-minute reservation.

To make reservations at any of the in-park hotels listed below, contact **Xanterra South Rim/Xanterra Parks & Resorts,** 6312 S. Fiddlers Green Circle, Ste. 600N, Greenwood Village, CO 80111 (✆ **888/297-2757** or 303/297-2757; www.xanterra.com or www.grandcanyonlodges.com). It is sometimes possible, due to cancellations and no-shows, to get a same-day reservation; it's a long shot, but it happens. Same-day reservations can be made by calling ✆ **928/638-2631.** Xanterra accepts American Express, Diners Club, Discover, MasterCard, and Visa. Children 16 and under stay free in their parent's room.

Expensive

El Tovar Hotel ★★ El Tovar Hotel, which first opened its doors in 1905, is the park's premier lodge. Built of local rock and Oregon pine by Hopi craftsmen, it's a rustic yet luxurious mountain lodge that perches on the edge of the canyon (although with views from only a few rooms). The lobby, entered from a veranda set with rustic furniture, has a small fireplace, cathedral ceiling, and log walls on which moose, deer, and antelope heads are displayed. Although guest rooms are comfortable and attractively decorated, the standard units are rather small, as are the bathrooms. For more legroom, book a deluxe unit. Suites, with private terraces and stunning views, are extremely spacious. El Tovar Dining Room (see "Where to Dine," below) serves a mix of continental and Southwestern cuisine and is the best restaurant in the village. Just off the lobby is a cocktail lounge with a view.

78 units. $174–$268 double; $321–$426 suite. **Amenities:** Restaurant; lounge; concierge; room service. *In room:* A/C, TV, fridge, hair dryer.

Thunderbird & Kachina Lodges If you want great views, these hotels are your best bets—but only if you get a room with a view. These two side-by-side hotels date from the 1960s and, with their dated exteriors, are a far cry from what you might imagine a national park hotel would look like. They do, however, have the biggest windows of any of the hotels on the canyon rim, and they also have the most modern rooms. If you get a second-story room on the canyon side of either hotel, you'll get some of the best views in the park (these rooms at the Kachina Lodge get the nod for having *the* best views). Book early—these two lodges are some of the park's most popular accommodations. Just remember, if it's not a view room, you'll be staring at the parking lot, and the lodge will not guarantee canyon-view rooms.

104 units. $170–$180 double. *In room:* TV, fridge, hair dryer.

Moderate

Maswik Lodge Set back a quarter-mile or so from the rim, the Maswik Lodge offers spacious rooms and cabins that have been comfortably modernized without losing their appealing rustic character. If you don't mind roughing it a bit, the 28 old cabins, which are available only in summer, have lots of character. These cabins have high ceilings and ceiling fans, and are my top choice away from the rim. If you crave modern appointments, lots of space, and predictably comfortable air-conditioned accommodations, opt for one of the large Maswik North rooms, which also have refrigerators and coffeemakers. Second-floor rooms have high ceilings and balconies, which makes them your most comfortable choice away from the rim.

278 units. $90–$170 double (winter discounts available); $90 cabin. **Amenities:** Restaurant; lounge. *In room:* TV, fridge.

Yavapai Lodge Located in several buildings at the east end of Grand Canyon Village (a 1-mile hike from the main section of the village, but convenient to the Canyon View Information Plaza), the Yavapai is the largest lodge in the park and thus is where you'll likely wind up if you wait too long to make a reservation. Unfortunately, it's also the least-appealing hotel in the park. There are no canyon views, which is why Yavapai is less expensive than the Thunderbird and Kachina lodges. If you must stay here, try for a room in the nicer Yavapai East wing, which is set under shady pines. Rooms in this wing have air-conditioning. However, I recommend that you plan ahead and try to stay at one of the lodges right on the rim.

358 units. $107–$153 double (winter discounts available). **Amenities:** Restaurant. *In room:* TV.

Inexpensive

Bright Angel Lodge & Cabins ★ Bright Angel Lodge, which began operation in 1896 as a collection of tents and cabins on the edge of the canyon, is the most affordable lodge in the park, and, with its flagstone-floor lobby and huge fireplace, it has a genuine, if crowded, mountain-lodge atmosphere. It also happens to offer the greatest variety of accommodations in the park. The best and most popular units are the rim cabins, which should be booked a year in advance. In fact, any rooms here should be booked as far in advance as possible. Most of the rooms and cabins feature rustic furnishings. The Buckey Suite, the oldest structure on the canyon rim, is arguably the best room in the park, with a canyon view, gas fireplace, and king-size bed. The tour desk, fireplace, museum, and restrooms account for the constant crowds in the lobby.

86 units (20 with shared bathrooms). $79 double with shared bathroom; $90 double with private bathroom; $111–$174 cabin; $138–$333 suite. **Amenities:** 2 restaurants; lounge, snack bar. *In room:* No phone.

Phantom Ranch ★ Built in 1922, Phantom Ranch is the only lodge at the bottom of the Grand Canyon, and it has a classic ranch atmosphere. Accommodations are in rustic stone-walled cabins or 10-bed gender-segregated dormitories. Evaporative coolers keep both the cabins and the dorms cool in summer. Make reservations as early as possible, and don't forget to reconfirm. (It's sometimes possible to get a room on the day of departure if there are any last-minute cancellations, though. To attempt this, you must put your name on the waiting list at the Bright Angel Lodge transportation desk the day before you want to stay at Phantom Ranch.)

Family-style meals must be reserved in advance. The menu consists of beef-and-vegetable stew ($25) and steak ($39). Breakfasts ($19) are hearty, and sack lunches ($12) are available as well. Between meals, the dining hall becomes a canteen selling snacks, drinks, gifts, and necessities. After dinner, it serves as a beer hall. There's a public phone here, and mule-back duffel transfer ($63) between Grand Canyon Village and Phantom Ranch can be arranged.

11 cabins, 40 dorm beds. $105 double in cabin; $39 dormitory bed. Mule-trip overnights (with all meals and mule ride included) $448 for 1 person, $791 for 2 people. 2-night trips available Nov–Mar. **Amenities:** Restaurant; lounge. *In room:* No phone.

In Tusayan (Outside the South Entrance)

If you can't get a reservation for a room in the park, this is the next closest place to stay. Unfortunately, this area can be very noisy because of the many helicopters and airplanes taking off from the airport. Also, hotels outside the park are very popular with tour groups, which during the busy summer months keep many hotels full. All of the hotels listed here are lined up along US 180/Ariz. 64.

Best Western Grand Canyon Squire Inn (Kids) If you prefer playing tennis to riding a mule, this may be the place for you. Of all the hotels in Tusayan, this one has the most resortlike feel because of its restaurants, lounges, and extensive recreational amenities. With so much to offer, it almost seems as if the hotel were trying to distract guests from the canyon itself. But even if you don't bowl or play tennis, you'll likely appreciate the large guest rooms with comfortable easy chairs and big windows. In the lobby, which is more Las Vegas glitz than mountain rustic, cases are filled with old cowboy paraphernalia. Down in the basement are an impressive Western sculpture, a waterfall wall, and even a bowling alley.

100 Ariz. 64 (P.O. Box 130), Grand Canyon, AZ 86023. ✆ **800/622-6966** or 928/638-2681. Fax 928/638-2782. www.grandcanyonsquire.com. 250 units. Mid-Mar to mid-Oct and late Dec $146–$206 double; mid-Oct to late Dec and Jan to mid-Mar $111–$136 double. Children 12 and under stay free in parent's room. AE, DC, DISC, MC, V. **Amenities:** 2 restaurants; 2 lounges; concierge; exercise room; Jacuzzi; seasonal outdoor pool; sauna. *In room:* A/C, TV, hair dryer, Wi-Fi.

Canyon Plaza Resort The setting behind the IMAX theater and surrounded by parking lots is none too pretty, but guest rooms, most of which were recently renovated with a bit of contemporary styling, are large and comfortable, and have balconies or patios. The hotel is built around two enclosed skylit courtyards, one of which houses a restaurant and the other a bar and whirlpool. Families will want to opt for one of the suites, which contain separate small living rooms. Unfortunately, the hotel is very popular with tour groups and can often feel crowded.

P.O. Box 520, Grand Canyon, AZ 86023. ✆ **866/698-2012** or 928/638-2673. Fax 928/638-9537. www.grandcanyonplaza.com. 232 units. $170–$190 double, $230 suite; Nov to mid-Mar $90–$120 double, $140–$160 suite. Rates include continental breakfast. Children 16 and under stay free in parent's room. AE, DC, DISC, MC, V. Pets accepted ($50 fee). **Amenities:** Restaurant; lounge; concierge; 2 Jacuzzis; outdoor pool. *In room:* A/C, TV, fridge (in some), hair dryer, Internet.

Grand Hotel ★ With its mountain lodge–style lobby, this modern hotel lives up to its name and is your best bet outside the park. There's a flagstone fireplace, log-beam ceiling, and fake ponderosa-pine tree trunks holding up the roof. Just off the lobby are a dining room (with evening entertainment ranging from Native American dancers to country-music bands), a small bar that even has a few saddles for bar stools, and an espresso stand. Guest rooms are spacious, with a few Western touches, and some have small balconies.

Ariz. 64 (P.O. Box 3319), Grand Canyon, AZ 86023. ✆ **888/634-7263** or 928/638-3333. Fax 928/638-3131. www.grandcanyongrandhotel.com. 121 units. $99–$229 double; $229–$339 suite. Children 12 and under stay free in parent's room. AE, DC, DISC, MC, V. **Amenities:** Restaurant; lounge; concierge; exercise room; Jacuzzi; indoor pool; Wi-Fi. *In room:* A/C, TV, hair dryer.

Holiday Inn Express Hotel & Suites–Grand Canyon (Kids) This hotel has modern, well-designed, and predictably clean and comfortable guest rooms. The hotel also includes a separate building that houses 32 large suites that are ideal for families. These suites are among the nicest accommodations inside or outside the park. Parents take note: In the main building, there are also "Kids' Suites" that have bunk beds, three TVs, and a video game machine.

Ariz. 64 (P.O. Box 3245), Grand Canyon, AZ 86023. ✆ **888/473-2269** or 928/638-3000. Fax 928/638-0123. www.gcanyon.com. 194 units. $74–$169 double; $84–$250 suite. Rates include continental breakfast. Children 17 and under stay free in parent's room. AE, DC, DISC, MC, V. **Amenities:** Jacuzzi; indoor pool. *In room:* A/C, TV, hair dryer, Wi-Fi.

Red Feather Lodge With more than 200 units, this motel is often slow to fill up, so it's a good choice for last-minute bookings. Try to get one of the newer rooms, which are a bit more comfortable than the older ones. In summer, the pool here makes this place a good bet for families.

106 Ariz. 64 (P.O. Box 1460), Grand Canyon, AZ 86023. ✆ **866/561-2425** or 928/638-2414. Fax 928/638-2707. www.redfeatherlodge.com. 216 units. $80–$175 double. Rates include continental breakfast. Children 17 and under stay free in parent's room. AE, DISC, MC, V. Pets accepted ($50 deposit plus $10 per night). **Amenities:** Restaurant; Jacuzzi; seasonal outdoor pool. *In room:* A/C, TV, Wi-Fi.

Other Area Accommodations

Cameron Trading Post Motel ★ (Finds) Located 54 miles north of Flagstaff on US 89 at the junction with the road to the east entrance of the national park, this motel offers some of the most attractive rooms in the vicinity of the Grand Canyon and is part of one of the best trading posts in the state. The motel, adjacent to the historic Cameron Trading Post, is built around the shady oasis of the old trading post's terraced gardens. The garden terraces are built of sandstone, and there's even a picnic table made from a huge slab of stone. Guest rooms feature Southwestern-style furniture and attractive decor. Most have balconies, and some have views of the Little Colorado River (which, however, rarely has much water in it). Don't miss the Navajo tacos in the dining room; the small ones are plenty big enough for a meal.

P.O. Box 339, Cameron, AZ 86020. ✆ **800/338-7385** or 928/679-2231. Fax 928/679-2501. www.camerontradingpost.com. 62 units. Jan–Feb $59–$69 double, $99–$129 suite; Mar–May $79–$89 double, $129–$159 suite; June to mid-Oct $99–$109 double, $149–$179 suite; mid-Oct to Dec $69–$79 double, $129–$159 suite. AE, DISC, MC, V. Pets accepted ($15 fee). **Amenities:** Restaurant. *In room:* A/C, TV.

Camping

Inside the Park

On the South Rim, there are two campgrounds and an RV park. **Mather Campground,** in Grand Canyon Village, has 327 campsites. Reservations can be made up to 6 months in advance and are highly recommended for stays between March and November (reservations not accepted for other months). Contact the National Recreation Reservation Service (✆ **877/444-6777** or 518/885-3639; www.recreation.gov). Between late spring and early fall, don't even think of coming up here without a reservation; you'll just set yourself up for disappointment. If you don't have a reservation, your next-best bet is to arrive in the morning, when sites are being vacated. Campsites are $18 per night ($15 per night Dec–Feb; reservations not accepted).

Desert View Campground, with 50 sites, is 25 miles east of Grand Canyon Village and open from May to mid-October only. No reservations are accepted. Campsites are $12 per night.

The **Trailer Village RV park,** with 79 RV sites, is in Grand Canyon Village and charges $30 per night (for two adults) for full hookup. Reservations can be made up to 13 months in advance by contacting **Xanterra South Rim/Xanterra Parks & Resorts,** 6312 S. Fiddlers Green Circle, Ste. 600N, Greenwood Village, CO 80111 (✆ **888/297-2757** or 303/297-2757; www.xanterra.com or www.grandcanyonlodges.com). For same-day reservations, call ✆ **928/638-2631.**

Outside the Park

Two miles south of Tusayan is the U.S. Forest Service's **Ten-X Campground.** This campground has 70 campsites, is open May through September, and charges $10. It's usually your best bet for finding a site late in the day.

You can also camp just about anywhere within the **Kaibab National Forest,** which borders Grand Canyon National Park. Several dirt roads lead into the forest from the highway, and although you won't find designated campsites or toilets along these roads, you will find spots where others have obviously camped before. This so-called dispersed camping is usually used by campers who have been unable to find sites in campgrounds. One of the most popular roads for this sort of camping is on the west side of the highway between Tusayan and the park's south entrance. For more information, contact the **Tusayan Ranger District,** Kaibab National Forest, P.O. Box 3088, Grand Canyon, AZ 86023 (✆ **928/638-2443;** www.fs.fed.us/r3/kai).

WHERE TO DINE

Inside the Park

If you're looking for a quick, inexpensive meal, there are plenty of options. In Grand Canyon Village, choices include **cafeterias** at the Yavapai and Maswik lodges and a **delicatessen** at Canyon Village Marketplace on Market Plaza. The **Bright Angel Fountain** serves hot dogs, sandwiches, and ice cream. At the west end of Hermit Road, there is the **Hermit's Rest Snack Bar.** The stone building that houses this snack bar was designed by Mary Elizabeth Jane Colter, who also designed several other buildings on the South Rim. At Desert View, there's the **Desert View Trading Post Cafeteria.** All of these places are open daily and serve meals for $10 and under.

The Arizona Room SOUTHWESTERN Because this restaurant has the best view of the three dining establishments right on the South Rim, it is immensely popular. Add to this the fact that the Arizona Room has a Southwestern menu almost as creative as that of El Tovar Dining Room, and you'll understand why there is often a long wait for a table here. To avoid the wait and take in the views, arrive early, which should assure you of getting a good table without too much of a wait. The pan-seared salmon with melon salsa and the baby back ribs with either the prickly pear or chipotle glaze are both good bets. Because this restaurant is open for lunch part of the year, you've got another great option for dining with a billion-dollar view.

At the Bright Angel Lodge. ✆ **928/638-2631.** Reservations not accepted. Main courses $7.75–$13 lunch, $17–$28 dinner. AE, DC, DISC, MC, V. Daily 4:30–10pm (Mar–Oct also lunch daily 11:30am–3pm). Closed Jan–Feb.

Bright Angel Restaurant Kids AMERICAN As the least expensive of the three restaurants right on the rim of the canyon, this casual Southwestern-themed coffeehouse in the historic Bright Angel Lodge stays packed with families throughout the day. Meals are simple and none too memorable, but if you can get one of the few tables near the windows, at least you get something of a view. The menu includes everything from burgers to fajitas to spaghetti (foods calculated to comfort tired and hungry hikers). The bread bowls full of chili and stew are particularly good. Wines are available, and service is generally friendly and efficient.

At the Bright Angel Lodge. ✆ **928/638-2631.** Reservations not accepted. Main courses $9.50–$27. AE, DC, DISC, MC, V. Daily 6:30–10pm.

El Tovar Dining Room ★★ CONTINENTAL/SOUTHWESTERN If you're staying at El Tovar, you'll want to have dinner in the hotel's rustic yet elegant dining room. But before making reservations at the most expensive restaurant in the park, be aware that few tables have views of the canyon. However, despite the limited views, the meals served here are the best in the park. The menu leans heavily to the spicy flavors of the Southwest, though plenty of milder, more familiar dishes are offered as well. The New York steak with crispy onion rings is a good bet, as is the wild salmon. Start your meal with the interesting little roulades (flavorful bite-size tortilla roll-ups). Service is generally quite good. Have a drink in the bar before dinner (you might even be able to snag a table with a view).

At El Tovar Hotel. ✆ **928/638-2631,** ext. 6432. Reservations highly recommended for dinner. Main courses $12–$20 lunch, $22–$36 dinner. AE, DC, DISC, MC, V. Daily 6:30–11am, 11:30am–2pm, and 5–10pm.

In Tusayan (Outside the South Entrance)

In addition to the restaurants listed below, you'll find a steakhouse and a pizza place, as well as familiar chains such as McDonald's, Pizza Hut, and Wendy's. If you need an espresso or a sandwich for a picnic on the South Rim, stop at **R.P.'s Stage Stop,** Ariz. 64 (✆ **928/638-3114**), which is located next door to the IMAX theater.

Canyon Star Restaurant and Saloon ★ AMERICAN/MEXICAN This place aims to compete with El Tovar Dining Room and the Arizona Room, and serves the most creative Southwestern fare this side of the park boundary, plus you'll have live entertainment while you eat. Try the barbecued buffalo brisket. Evening shows include performances of Native American songs and dances. This place is big, so there usually isn't too long a wait for a table; and even if there is, you can wait in the saloon where you can saddle up a bar stool (some of the stools have saddles instead of seats).

At the Grand Hotel, Ariz. 64. ✆ **928/638-3333.** Reservations not accepted. Main courses $9–$19 lunch, $14–$28 dinner. AE, DC, DISC, MC, V. Daily 6–10am, 11am–2pm, and 5–10pm.

Coronado Room CONTINENTAL/SOUTHWESTERN If you should suddenly be struck by an overpowering desire to have escargot for dinner, don't despair—head for the Best Western Grand Canyon Squire Inn (see above). Now, I'm well aware that Best Western and escargot go together about as well as the Eiffel Tower and rattlesnake fritters, but this place really does serve classic Continental fare way out here in the Arizona high country. You'll probably want to stick to the steaks, though (or the wild game such as elk tournedos). You might also want to try a few of the Southwestern appetizers on the menu. Be prepared for slow service.

At the Best Western Grand Canyon Squire Inn, Ariz. 64. ✆ **928/638-2681.** Reservations recommended. Main courses $22–$35. AE, DC, DISC, MC, V. Daily 5–10pm.

2 HAVASU CANYON ★★ & GRAND CANYON WEST

Havasu Canyon: 200 miles W of Grand Canyon Village; 70 miles N of Ariz. 66; 155 miles NW of Flagstaff; 115 miles NE of Kingman

Grand Canyon West: 240 miles W of Grand Canyon Village; 70 miles N of Kingman; 115 miles E of Las Vegas, NV

With traffic congestion and parking problems becoming the most memorable aspects of many people's visits to the Grand Canyon, you might want to consider an alternative to the South Rim. For most travelers, this means driving around to the North Rim; however, the North Rim is open only from mid-May to late October and itself is not immune to parking problems and traffic congestion.

There are a couple of lesser-known alternatives. A visit to Havasu Canyon, on the Havasupai Indian Reservation, entails a 20-mile round-trip hike or horseback ride similar to that from Grand Canyon Village to Phantom Ranch, although with a decidedly different setting at the bottom of the canyon. Grand Canyon West, home to the much-hyped Skywalk, is on the Hualapai Indian Reservation and is primarily a tour bus destination for vacationers from Las Vegas. This is also the only place where you can fly down into the canyon, which accounts for all the air traffic.

ESSENTIALS

HAVASU CANYON It isn't possible to drive all the way to Havasu Canyon's Supai village. The nearest road ends 8 miles from Supai at Hualapai Hilltop. This is the trail head for the trail into the canyon and is at the end of Indian Rte. 18, which runs north from Ariz. 66. The turnoff is 7 miles east of Peach Springs and 31 miles west of Seligman.

The easiest and fastest (and by far most expensive) way to reach Havasu Canyon is by helicopter from Grand Canyon Airport. Flights are operated by **Papillon Grand Canyon Helicopters** (✆ **888/635-7272** or 928/638-2419; www.papillon.com). The round-trip air-and-ground day excursion is $555; it's also possible to arrange to stay overnight. Lower rates are usually available on this company's website.

GRAND CANYON WEST The best route to Grand Canyon West is to head northwest out of Kingman on US 93. After 27 miles, turn right onto the Pearce Ferry Road (signed for Dolan Springs and Meadview). After 28 miles on this road, turn right onto Diamond Bar Road, which is signed for Grand Canyon West. Another 14 miles down this road brings you to the Hualapai Indian Reservation. A little farther along, you'll come to the Grand Canyon West Terminal (there's actually an airstrip here), where visitor permits and bus-tour tickets are sold.

VISITOR INFORMATION For information on Havasu Canyon, contact the **Havasupai Tourist Enterprises,** P.O. Box 160, Supai, AZ 86435 (✆ **928/448-2121** or 928/448-2141; www.havasupaitribe.com), which handles all campground reservations. For information on Grand Canyon West, contact **Destination Grand Canyon** (✆ **877/716-9378** or 702/878-9378; www.destinationgrandcanyon.com).

HAVASU CANYON ★★

Deep within the red sandstone walls of Havasu Canyon, a lush green riparian forest flanks the waters of a crystal-clear stream and waterfalls cascade into pools of turquoise water. The setting is spectacular and the colors are otherworldly, which is why Havasu Canyon is so popular with adventurous travelers. This canyon is the home of the Havasupai tribe, whose name not surprisingly means "people of the blue-green waters." For centuries, the Havasupai have called this idyllic desert oasis home. The waterfalls are the main attraction here, and most people are content to go for a dip in the cool waters, sun themselves on the sand, and gaze for hours at the turquoise waters.

Unfortunately, in August 2008, a massive flood roared through the canyon, gouging out a new creek channel that now completely bypasses one of the former waterfalls. The canyon was closed to the public for more than 8 months after the flood due to extensive damage to trails and bridges. However, floods have occurred here before, and the canyon is relatively quick to hide the scars caused by flooding.

The Havasupai entry fee is $35 per person to visit Havasu Canyon, and everyone entering the canyon is required to register at the tourist office in the village of Supai. Because it's a long walk to the campground, be sure you have a confirmed reservation before setting out from Hualapai Hilltop. It's good to make reservations as far in advance as possible, especially for holiday weekends.

If you plan to hike down into the canyon, start early to avoid the heat of the day. The hike is beautiful, but it's 10 miles to the campground. The steepest part of the trail is the first mile or so from Hualapai Hilltop. After this section, it's relatively flat.

Through **Havasupai Tourist Enterprises** (✆ **928/448-2121** or 928/448-2141; www.havasupaitribe.com), you can hire a horse to carry you or your gear down into the canyon from Hualapai Hilltop. Horse rental costs $70 to $94 each way. Many people who hike in decide that it's worth the money to ride out, or at least have their backpacks carried out. Be sure to confirm your horse reservation a day before driving to Hualapai Hilltop. Sometimes no horses are available, and it's a long drive back to the nearest town. There are also pack mules that will carry your gear into and out of the canyon.

If you'd like to hike into Havasu Canyon with a guide, **Arizona Outback Adventures,** 16447 N. 91st St., Ste. 101, Scottsdale, AZ 85260 (✆ **866/455-1601** or 480/945-2881; www.azoutbackadventures.com), leads 2- to 5-day hikes into Havasu Canyon and charges $1,297 to $1,748 per person. **Discovery Treks,** 28248 N. Tatum Blvd., Ste. B1, no. 414, Cave Creek, AZ 85331 (✆ **888/256-8731;** www.discoverytreks.com), offers similar 3-day trips for $895 to $1,165 per person.

GRAND CANYON WEST

Located on the Hualapai Indian Reservation on the south side of the Colorado River, **Grand Canyon West** (✆ **877/716-9378** or 702/878-9378; www.destinationgrandcanyon.com) overlooks the little-visited west end of Grand Canyon National Park. Although the view is not as spectacular as at either the South Rim or the North Rim, Grand Canyon West is noteworthy for one thing: It is one of the only places where you can legally take a helicopter ride down into the canyon. This is possible because the helicopters operate on land that is part of the Hualapai Indian Reservation. The tours are operated by **Papillon Helicopters** (✆ **888/635-7272** or 702/736-7243; www.papillon.com), which charges $135 to $204 per person for a quick trip to the bottom of the canyon and a boat ride on the Colorado River. ***Note:*** Lower rates may be available on their website.

Grand Canyon West is a self-styled major destination, with plans for a full-fledged resort and major airport in the future. The first phase of this development is called the **Skywalk,** but contrary to what you may have read about this Vegas-style attraction, the Skywalk is not over the Colorado River and is not in Grand Canyon National Park. The horseshoe-shaped glass observation platform juts over a side canyon of the Grand Canyon, and from the deck you can glimpse the Colorado River a short distance away and 4,000 feet below. However, you'll have to cough up $68 for the privilege of walking out on the Skywalk for a view that is only marginally better than the view from solid ground. For your $68, you'll also get to ride a **shuttle bus** along the rim of the canyon. Tours operate daily throughout the year and cost $38 per person (without the Skywalk); $68 with the Skywalk; $127 to $157 with a Hummer tour; $102 to $218 with a horseback ride; and $227 with a helicopter ride down into the canyon and a brief boat trip on the Colorado River. Reservations are recommended. If you're coming from Kingman, allow at least 2 hours to get here.

While I can recommend a trip out to Grand Canyon West only as a side trip from Las Vegas or for travelers who absolutely must fly down into the canyon, the drive out here is almost as scenic as the destination itself. Along Diamond Bar Road, you'll be driving below the Grand Wash Cliffs, and for much of the way, the route traverses a dense forest of Joshua trees.

OTHER AREA ACTIVITIES

If you long to raft the Grand Canyon but have only a couple of free days in your schedule to realize your dream, then you have just one option. Here, at the west end of the canyon, it's possible to do a 1-day rafting trip that begins on the Hualapai Indian Reservation. These trips are operated by **Hualapai River Runners** (✆ **888/255-9550** or 928/769-2219; www.destinationgrandcanyon.com), a tribal rafting company, and are offered between March and October. Expect a mix of white water and flat water (all of it very cold). One-day trips cost $328 per person.

Also in this area, you can visit **Grand Canyon Caverns** (✆ **928/422-3223;** www.grandcanyoncaverns.com), just outside Peach Springs. The caverns, which are accessed via a 210-foot elevator ride, are open from Memorial Day to October 15 daily from 9am to 5pm (sometimes until 6pm), and other months daily from 10am to 4pm. Admission is $15 for adults, $9.95 for children 4 to 12. "Explorers' Tours" ($45) head off into parts of the caverns that aren't seen on the regular tour.

WHERE TO STAY & DINE

In Peach Springs

Hualapai Lodge (Finds) Located in the Hualapai community of Peach Springs, this lodge offers by far the most luxurious accommodations anywhere in the region. Guest rooms are spacious and modern, with a few bits of regional decor for character. Most people staying here are in the area to visit Grand Canyon West, to go rafting with Hualapai River Runners, or to hike in to Havasu Canyon. The dining room is just about the only place in town to get a meal and serves some Native American dishes.

900 Rte. 66 (P.O. Box 538), Peach Springs, AZ 86434. ✆ **888/255-9550** or 928/769-2230. Fax 928/769-2372. www.destinationgrandcanyon.com. 57 units. $100–$110 double. Rates include full breakfast (Nov 1–Mar 15). Children 11 and under stay free in parent's room. AE, DC, DISC, MC, V. **Amenities:** Restaurant; concierge; exercise room; Jacuzzi; outdoor pool; room service. *In room:* A/C, TV, hair dryer, Wi-Fi.

In Havasu Canyon

Havasupai Lodge Located in Supai village, this lodge offers, aside from the campground, the only accommodations in the canyon. The two-story building features standard motel-style rooms that lack only TVs and telephones, neither of which is much in demand at this isolated retreat. The only real drawback of this comfortable though basic lodge is that it's 2 miles from Havasu Falls and 3 miles from Mooney Falls. The Havasupai Café, across from the general store, serves breakfast, lunch, and dinner. It's a very casual place, and prices are high for what you get because all ingredients must be packed in by horse.

P.O. Box 159, Supai, AZ 86435. ✆ **928/448-2111** or 928/448-2201. www.havasupaitribe.com. 24 units. $145 double. MC, V. *In room:* A/C, no phone.

3 THE GRAND CANYON NORTH RIM ★★★

42 miles S of Jacob Lake; 216 miles N of Grand Canyon Village (South Rim); 354 miles N of Phoenix; 125 miles W of Page/Lake Powell

Although the North Rim of the Grand Canyon is only 10 miles from the South Rim as the raven flies, it's more than 200 miles by road. Because it is such a long drive from population centers such as Phoenix and Las Vegas, the North Rim is much less crowded than the South Rim. Additionally, due to heavy snowfall, the North Rim is open only from mid-May to late October or early November. There are also far fewer activities or establishments on the North Rim than there are on the South Rim.

The North Rim is on the Kaibab Plateau, which is more than 8,000 feet high on average and takes its name from the Paiute word for "mountain lying down." The higher elevation of the North Rim means that instead of the mix of junipers interspersed with ponderosa pines of the South Rim, you'll see dense forests of ponderosa pines, Douglas firs, and aspens interspersed with large meadows. Consequently, the North Rim has a much more alpine feel than the South Rim. The 8,000-foot elevation—1,000 feet higher than the South Rim—also means that the North Rim gets considerably more snow in winter than the South Rim. The highway south from Jacob Lake is not plowed in winter, when the Grand Canyon Lodge closes down.

ESSENTIALS

GETTING THERE The North Rim is at the end of Ariz. 67 (the North Rim Pkwy.), reached from US 89A. **Trans Canyon** (✆ **928/638-2820;** www.trans-canyonshuttle.com) operates a shuttle between the North Rim and the South Rim of the Grand Canyon during the months the North Rim is open. The trip takes 5 hours; the fare is $80 one-way and $150 round-trip (reservations are required).

FEES The park entry fee is $25 per car and is good for 1 week. Remember not to lose the little paper receipt that serves as your admission pass.

VISITOR INFORMATION For information before leaving home, contact **Grand Canyon National Park,** P.O. Box 129, Grand Canyon, AZ 86023 (✆ **928/638-7888;** www.nps.gov/grca). At the entrance gate, you'll be given a copy of *The Guide,* a small newspaper with information on park activities. When you arrive at the park, stop by the **North Rim Visitor Center,** which is adjacent to the Grand Canyon Lodge and is open mid-May to mid-October daily 8am to 6pm.

Tips An Important Note

Visitor facilities at the North Rim are open only from mid-May to mid-October. From mid-October to November (or until snow closes the road to the North Rim), the park is open for day use only. The campground may be open after mid-October, weather permitting.

EXPLORING THE PARK

While it's hard to beat the view from a rustic rocking chair on the terrace of the Grand Canyon Lodge, the best spots for seeing the canyon are Bright Angel Point, Point Imperial, and Cape Royal. **Bright Angel Point** is at the end of a half-mile trail near the Grand Canyon Lodge, and from here you can see and hear Roaring Springs, which are 3,600 feet below the rim and are the North Rim's only water source. You can also see Grand Canyon Village on the South Rim.

At 8,803 feet, **Point Imperial** is the highest point on the North Rim. A short section of the Colorado River can be seen far below, and off to the east the Painted Desert is visible. The Point Imperial/Nankoweap Trail leads north from here along the rim of the canyon. However, this area was burned in a forest fire in 2000.

Cape Royal is the most spectacular setting on the North Rim, and, along the 23-mile road to this viewpoint, you'll find several other scenic overlooks. Across the road from the **Walhalla Overlook** are the ruins of an Ancestral Puebloan structure, and, just before reaching Cape Royal, you'll come to the **Angel's Window Overlook,** which gives you a breathtaking view of the natural bridge that forms Angel's Window. Once at Cape Royal, you can follow a trail across this natural bridge to a towering promontory overlooking the canyon.

Once you've had your fill of simply taking in the views, you may want to get out and stretch your legs on a trail or two. Quite a few day hikes of varying lengths and difficulty are possible. The shortest is the .5-mile paved trail to Bright Angel Point, along which you'll have plenty of company but also plenty of breathtaking views. If you have time for only one hike while you're here, make it down the **North Kaibab Trail.** This trail is 14 miles long and leads down to Phantom Ranch and the Colorado River. To hike the entire trail, you'll need to have a camping permit and be in very good physical condition (it's almost 6,000 ft. to the canyon floor). For a day hike, most people make Roaring Springs their goal. This hike is 9.5 miles round-trip, involves a descent and ascent of 3,000 feet, and takes 7 to 8 hours. You can shorten this hike considerably by turning around at the Supai Tunnel, which is fewer than 1,500 feet below the rim at the 2-mile point. For a relatively easy hike away from the crowds, try the Widforss Point Trail.

If you want to see the canyon from a saddle, contact **Grand Canyon Trail Rides** (**© 435/679-8665;** www.canyonrides.com), which offers mule rides varying in length from 1 hour ($40) to a full day ($165).

EN ROUTE TO OR FROM THE NORTH RIM

Between Page and the North Rim of the Grand Canyon, US 89A crosses the Colorado River at **Lees Ferry** in Marble Canyon. The original **Navajo Bridge** over the river here was replaced in 1995, and the old bridge is now open to pedestrians. From the bridge, which is 470 feet above the Colorado River, there's a beautiful view of Marble Canyon.

At the west end of the bridge, you'll find the Navajo Bridge Interpretive Center, which is operated by the National Park Service and is partly housed in a stone building built during the Depression by the Civilian Conservation Corps (CCC). At the east end of the bridge, which is on the Navajo Reservation, interpretive signs tell the story of Lees Ferry from the Native American perspective.

Lees Ferry is the starting point for raft trips through the Grand Canyon, and for many years it was the only place to cross the Colorado River for hundreds of miles in either direction. This stretch of the river is now legendary among anglers for its trophy trout fishing. Lees Ferry has a 54-site campground charging $12 per night. Reservations are not accepted.

Lees Ferry Anglers (✆ **800/962-9755** or 928/355-2261; www.leesferry.com), 11 miles west of the bridge at Lees Ferry, is fishing headquarters for the region. Not only does it sell all manner of fly-fishing tackle and offer advice about good spots to try your luck, but it also operates a guide service and rents waders and boats. A guide and boat costs $350 per day for one person, and $425 per day for two people.

Continuing west, the highway passes under the **Vermilion Cliffs,** so named for their deep-red coloring and now the namesake of the **Vermilion Cliffs National Monument** (✆ **435/688-3200;** www.blm.gov/az/st/en/prog/blm_special_areas/natmon/vermilion.html). At the base of these cliffs are huge boulders balanced on narrow columns of eroded soil. The balanced rocks give the area an otherworldly appearance.

Along this same stretch of road, you'll find the gravel road that leads north to the **Coyote Buttes** ★★★, which are among the most unusual rock formations in Arizona. Basically, these striated conical sandstone hills are petrified sand dunes, which should give you a good idea of why one area of the Coyote Buttes is called the Wave. The buttes are a favorite of photographers. You must have a permit ($7 per person) to visit this area, and only 20 people are allowed to visit each day (with a maximum group size of six people). Permits are issued by lottery, and applications must be submitted 4 months in advance. There's no actual trail to the buttes, so you have to navigate by way of the photos and map that you'll be sent when you receive your permit. For more information, contact the **Arizona Strip Interpretive Association,** 345 E. Riverside Dr., St. George, UT 84790 (✆ **435/688-3246;** www.az.blm.gov/az/asfo/paria/coyote_buttes/index.htm).

To learn more about the pioneer history of this remote region of the state (known as the Arizona Strip), continue west from Jacob Lake 45 miles on Arizona 389 to **Pipe Spring National Monument,** 406 N. Pipe Spring Rd., Fredonia (✆ **928/643-7105;** www.nps.gov/pisp), which preserves an early Mormon ranch house that was built in the style of a fort for protection from Indians. This "fort" was also known as Winsor Castle and occasionally housed the wives of polygamists hiding from the law. In summer, there are living-history demonstrations. The monument is open daily from 7am to 5pm June through August, and from 8am to 5pm the rest of the year (closed New Year's Day, Thanksgiving, and Christmas). Admission is $5 per adult.

WHERE TO STAY

Inside the Park

Grand Canyon Lodge ★★ Perched right on the canyon rim, this classic mountain lodge is listed on the National Register of Historic Places and is as impressive a lodge as any you'll find in a national park. The stone-and-log main building has a soaring ceiling and a viewing room set up with chairs facing a wall of glass, and on either side of this room are flagstone terraces furnished with rustic chairs. Accommodations vary from standard motel units to rustic mountain cabins to comfortable modern cabins. My favorites are the frontier cabins, which, although cramped and paneled with dark wood, capture the feeling of a mountain retreat better than the other options. Only a few units have views of the canyon. The dining hall has two walls of glass to take in the awesome canyon views.

Forever Resorts, 7501 E. McCormick Pkwy., Scottsdale, AZ 85258. ✆ **877/386-4383** or 480/337-1320. www.grandcanyonlodgenorth.com. 205 units. $112–$170 double. Children 15 and under stay free in parent's room. AE, DC, DISC, MC, V. Closed mid-Oct to mid-May. **Amenities:** 2 restaurants; lounge.

Outside the Park

North of the national park, the next-closest lodgings are the Kaibab Lodge and the Jacob Lake Inn. You'll also find lots of budget accommodations in Kanab, Utah, 37 miles west of Jacob Lake.

Jacob Lake Inn This is one of only two lodges outside the entrance to the North Rim of Grand Canyon National Park, and, because it is at the crossroads of Jacob Lake, it is always a busy spot in summer. While most of the units here are old cabins that tend to be cramped and old-fashioned, there are also two dozen modern motel-style rooms in a contemporary mountain-rustic lodge. It is these latter rooms, which are the inn's only rooms with TVs, telephones, and high-speed Internet access, that I recommend. Sure, they're more expensive than the cabins, but they are the nicest rooms in the area. Be sure to stock up on cookies at the inn's bakery.

Ariz. 67/US 89A, Jacob Lake, AZ 86022. ✆ **928/643-7232.** www.jacoblake.com. 69 units. $84–$106 cabin double; $110–$133 motel/lodge double. AE, DISC, MC, V. Pets accepted ($10 per night). **Amenities:** Restaurant. *In room:* TV (in some), Internet (in some).

En Route to the Park

Cliff Dwellers Lodge Affiliated with Lees Ferry Anglers, this motel is the area's de facto fly anglers' headquarters and tends to stay filled up with people who have come here to fish for the Colorado's huge rainbow trout. The newer, more expensive rooms here are standard motel units with tub/shower combinations, and are the best and most predictable rooms in the Vermilion Cliffs area. Older rooms, in an interesting stone-walled building, have knotty pine walls and showers only. If you're looking for comfort over character, these are the rooms for you. The lodge is close to some spectacular balanced rocks, and it's about 11 miles east to Lees Ferry. The views are unforgettable.

US 89A, MM 547 (H.C. 67, Box 30), Marble Canyon, AZ 86036. ✆ **800/962-9755** or 928/355-2261. Fax 928/355-2271. www.cliffdwellerslodge.com. 20 units. $80–$90 double (lower rates in winter). AE, DISC, MC, V. **Amenities:** Restaurant. *In room:* A/C, TV, no phone.

Lees Ferry Lodge at Vermilion Cliffs Located at the foot of the Vermilion Cliffs, $3^1/_2$ miles west of the Colorado River, Lees Ferry Lodge, built in 1929 of native stone and rough-hewn timber beams, is a small place with simple, rustic accommodations. However, the lodge's restaurant serves as a sort of de facto community center for area residents, and owner Maggie Sacher is usually on hand to answer questions and share stories. Also, the patio seating area in front of the lodge has fabulous views. The restaurant here has a great, old-fashioned atmosphere. With its rustic character and friendly feel, this is my favorite place to stay in the area.

US 89A (H.C. 67, Box 1), Marble Canyon, AZ 86036. ✆ **928/355-2231.** www.leesferrylodge.com. 10 units. $65–$80 double. Children 4 and under stay free in parent's room. AE, MC, V. Pets accepted. **Amenities:** Restaurant. *In room:* A/C, no phone.

Marble Canyon Lodge The Marble Canyon Lodge, built in the 1920s just 4 miles from Lees Ferry, is the closest lodge to the put-in spot for people rafting the Grand Canyon, and consequently this lodge is popular primarily with rafters. Accommodations are mostly in aging motel-style rooms that lack the modernity of the rooms at Cliff Dwellers Lodge or the character of the rooms at the Lees Ferry Lodge at Vermilion Cliffs. In addition to the restaurant, there's a general store that specializes in rafting supplies.

P.O. Box 6032, Marble Canyon, AZ 86036. ✆ **800/726-1789** or 928/355-2225. Fax 928/355-2227. www.leesferryflyfishing.com. 56 units. $65–$70 double; $134 apt. Children 11 and under stay free in parent's room. AE, DISC, MC, V. Pets accepted. **Amenities:** Restaurant; Wi-Fi. *In room:* A/C, TV, no phone.

Campgrounds

Just north of Grand Canyon Lodge, the **North Rim Campground** (✆ **928/638-7888**), with 83 sites and no hookups for RVs, is the only campground at the North Rim. It's open mid-May to mid-October. Reservations can be made up to 6 months in advance by calling the National Recreation Reservation Service (✆ **877/444-6777** or 518/885-3639; www.recreation.gov). Campsites cost $18 to $25 per night.

There are two nearby campgrounds outside the park in the Kaibab National Forest. The **DeMotte Campground** (May 15–Oct 15) is the closest to the park entrance, has 38 sites, and charges $17. **Jacob Lake Campground** (May 15–Nov 1) is 30 miles north of the park entrance, has 53 sites, and charges $12 per night. Neither campground takes reservations. You can also camp anywhere in the Kaibab National Forest as long as you're more than 200 feet from a main roadway or a quarter-mile from a water source. So if you can't find a site in a campground, simply pull off the highway in the national forest and park your RV or pitch your tent. Contact the North Kaibab Ranger District, 430 S. Main St. (✆ **928/643-7395;** www.fs.fed.us/r3/kai), for info.

The **Kaibab Camper Village** (✆ **800/525-0924,** 928/643-7804 May 15–Oct 15, or 928/526-0924 other months; www.kaibabcampervillage.com) is a privately owned campground in the crossroads of Jacob Lake, 30 miles north of the park entrance. It's open from mid-May to mid-October and has around 100 sites. Rates are $17 for tent sites, $34 for RV sites with full hookups. Make reservations well in advance.

WHERE TO DINE

Grand Canyon Lodge (see above) has a dining room with a splendid view. More casual choices at the lodge include a cafeteria and a saloon that serves light meals.

Your only choices for a meal outside the park are the **Kaibab Lodge** (✆ **928/638-2389;** www.kaibablodge.com), just north of the entrance, and the **Jacob Lake Inn** (✆ **928/643-7232;** www.jacoblake.com), 45 miles north at the junction with US 89A.

4 FLAGSTAFF ★★

150 miles N of Phoenix; 32 miles E of Williams; 80 miles S of Grand Canyon Village

With its wide variety of accommodations and restaurants, the great outdoors at the edge of town, three national monuments nearby, one of the state's finest museums, and a university that supports a lively cultural community, Flagstaff makes an ideal base for exploring much of northern Arizona.

The San Francisco Peaks, just north of the city, are the site of the Arizona Snowbowl ski area, one of the state's main winter playgrounds. In summer, miles of trails through these same mountains attract hikers and mountain bikers, and it's even possible to ride the chairlift for a panoramic vista that stretches 70 miles north to the Grand Canyon. Of the area's national monuments, two preserve ancient Indian ruins and the third is an otherworldly landscape of volcanic cinder cones.

It was as a railroad town that Flagstaff made its fortunes, and the historic downtown offers a glimpse of the days when the city's fortunes rode the rails. The railroad still runs right through the middle of Flagstaff, much to the dismay of many visitors, who find that most of the city's inexpensive motels (and even some of the more expensive places) are too close to the busy tracks to allow them to get a good night's sleep.

ESSENTIALS

GETTING THERE Flagstaff is on I-40, one of the main east-west interstates in the United States. I-17 starts here and heads south to Phoenix. Ariz. 89A connects Flagstaff to Sedona by way of Oak Creek Canyon. US 180 connects Flagstaff with the South Rim of the Grand Canyon, and US 89 connects the city with Page.

Pulliam Airport, 3 miles south of Flagstaff off I-17, is served by **US Airways** (© **800/428-4322**) from Phoenix and **Horizon Air** (© **800/547-9308;** www.horizonair.com) from Los Angeles. **Amtrak** (© **800/872-7245**) offers service to Flagstaff from Chicago and Los Angeles. The train station is at 1 E. Rte. 66.

VISITOR INFORMATION Contact the **Flagstaff Visitor Center,** 1 E. Rte. 66 (© **800/379-0065** or 928/774-9541; www.flagstaffarizona.org). The visitor center is open Monday through Saturday from 8am to 5pm and Sunday from 9am to 4pm.

GETTING AROUND Car rentals are available from **Avis** (© **800/331-1212**, 928/774-8421 at the airport, or 928/714-0713 downtown), **Budget** (© **800/527-0700,** 928/779-5235 at the airport, or 928/213-0156 downtown), **Enterprise** (© **800/261-7331** or 928/774-9407), **Hertz** (© **800/654-3131** or 928/774-4452 at the airport, or 928/226-0120 downtown), and **National** (© **800/227-7368** or 928/774-3321).

Call **A Friendly Cab** (© **800/853-4445** or 928/774-4444; www.afriendlycab.com) if you need a taxi. **Mountain Line Transit** (© **928/779-6624;** www.mountainline.az.gov) provides public bus transit around the city; the fare is $1.

GETTING OUTSIDE

Flagstaff is northern Arizona's center for outdoor activities. Chief among them is skiing at **Arizona Snowbowl** (© **928/779-1951;** www.arizonasnowbowl.com), on the slopes of Mount Agassiz, from which you can see all the way to the North Rim of the Grand Canyon. There are four chairlifts, 32 runs, 2,300 vertical feet of slopes, ski rentals, and a children's ski program. With an excellent mix of beginner, intermediate, and advanced slopes, and as the ski area that's most easily accessed from Phoenix, Snowbowl sees a lot of weekend traffic from the snow-starved denizens of the desert. Conditions are, however, very unreliable, and the ski area can be shut down for weeks on end due to lack of snow. All-day lift tickets are $49 to $53 for adults, $26 to $30 for children 8 to 12, $26 for seniors, and free for children 7 and under and seniors 70 and over. In summer, you can ride a chairlift almost to the summit of Mount Agassiz and enjoy the expansive views across seemingly all of northern Arizona. The round-trip lift-ticket price is $12 for adults, $8 for seniors and children 8 to 12. To get here, take US 180 N. from Flagstaff for 7 miles and turn right onto Snow Bowl Road.

If you'd like a short hike with a big payoff, hike to **Red Mountain.** This hike is only about 2.5 miles round-trip, but leads to a fascinating red-walled cinder cone that long ago collapsed to reveal its strange interior walls. To find the trail head, drive north from Flagstaff toward the Grand Canyon on US 180. At mile marker 247, watch for a forest road leading west for about a quarter-mile to the trail head parking area.

For information on other hikes in the Coconino National Forest, contact the **Peaks/ Mormon Lake Ranger District,** 5075 N. Hwy. 89, Flagstaff (✆ **928/526-0866;** www.fs.fed.us/r3/coconino).

SEEING THE SIGHTS

Downtown Flagstaff—along Route 66, San Francisco Street, Aspen Avenue, and Birch Avenue—is the city's **historic district.** These old brick buildings are now filled with shops selling Native American crafts, works by local artists and artisans, Route 66 souvenirs, and various other Arizona mementos such as rocks, minerals, and crystals. Don't miss **Jonathan Day's Indian Arts,** 21 N. San Francisco St. (✆ **928/779-6099;** www.traditionalhopikachinas.com), a small shop with what just might be the best selection of traditional Hopi kachinas in the state. **Puchteca Indian Art,** 20 N. San Francisco St. (✆ **928/774-2414**), is also worth a visit for its interesting Native American jewelry and pottery.

Lowell Observatory ★ This historic observatory is located atop aptly named Mars Hill and is one of the oldest astronomical observatories in the Southwest. Founded in 1894 by Percival Lowell, the observatory has played important roles in contemporary astronomy. Among the work carried out here was Lowell's study of the planet Mars and the calculations that led him to predict the existence of Pluto. It wasn't until 13 years after Lowell's death that Pluto was finally discovered almost exactly where he had predicted it would be.

The facility consists of outdoor displays, several observatories, and a visitor center with numerous fun and educational exhibits. While it can be interesting to visit during the day, the main attraction is the chance to observe the stars and planets through the observatory's 24-inch telescope. Keep in mind that the telescope domes are not heated, so if you come up to stargaze, be sure to dress appropriately. Also, there are no programs on cloudy nights.

1400 W. Mars Hill Rd. ✆ **928/774-3358** or 233-3211. www.lowell.edu. Admission $6 adults, $5 seniors and students, $3 children 5–17. Mar–Oct daily 9am–5pm (30-min. tours 10:15am–4:15pm); Nov–Feb daily noon–5pm (30-min. tours 1:15–4:15pm). Telescope viewings: June–Aug Mon–Sat 5:30–10pm; Sept–May Mon, Wed, and Fri–Sat 5:30–9:30pm. Closed Jan 1, Easter, Thanksgiving, and Dec 24–25.

Museum of Northern Arizona ★★ This small but surprisingly thorough museum is the ideal first stop on an exploration of northern Arizona. You'll learn, through state-of-the-art exhibits, about the archaeology, ethnology, geology, biology, and fine arts of the region. The cornerstone of the museum is an exhibit that explores life on the Colorado Plateau from 15,000 B.C. to the present. Among the other displays are a life-size kiva (ceremonial room) and a small but interesting collection of kachinas. The large gift shop is full of contemporary Native American arts and crafts, and during the summer special exhibits and sales focus on Hopi and Navajo arts and crafts.

3101 N. Fort Valley Rd. (3 miles north of downtown Flagstaff on US 180). ✆ **928/774-5213.** www.musnaz.org. Admission $7 adults, $6 seniors, $5 students, $4 children 7–17. Daily 9am–5pm. Closed New Year's Day, Thanksgiving, and Christmas.

Riordan Mansion State Historic Park ★ Built in 1904 for local timber barons Michael and Timothy Riordan, this 13,000-square-foot mansion—Arizona's finest example of an Arts and Crafts–era building—is actually two houses connected by a large central hall. Each brother and his family occupied half of the house (they had the rooflines constructed differently so that visitors could tell the two sides apart). Although the mansion appears to be built of logs, it's actually just faced with log slabs. Inside, mission-style furnishings and touches of Art Nouveau styling make it clear that this family was keeping up with the times. The west wing of the mansion holds displays on, among other things, Stickley furniture. Guided tours provide a glimpse into the lives of two of Flagstaff's most influential pioneers.

409 W. Riordan Rd. (off Milton Rd./Ariz. 89A, just north of the junction of I-40 and I-17). ✆ **928/779-4395.** www.azstateparks.com. Admission $6 adults, $2.50 children 7–13. May–Oct daily 8:30am–5pm; Nov–Apr daily 10:30am–5pm. Guided tours on the hour. Closed Christmas.

Sunset Crater Volcano National Monument ★ Dotting the landscape northeast of Flagstaff are more than 400 volcanic craters, of which Sunset Crater Volcano is the youngest. Taking its name from the colors of the cinders near its summit, Sunset Crater Volcano stands 1,000 feet tall and began forming in 1064. Over a period of 100 years, the volcano erupted repeatedly (creating the red-and-yellow cinder cone seen today) and eventually covered an area of 800 square miles with ash, lava, and cinders. A 1-mile interpretive trail passes through a desolate landscape of lava flows, cinders, and ash as it skirts the base of this volcano. If you want to climb to the top of a cinder cone, take the 1-mile Lenox Crater Trail. In the visitor center (at the west entrance to the national monument), you can learn more about the formation of Sunset Crater and about volcanoes in general. Near the visitor center is the 44-site Bonito Campground, which is open from early May to mid-October and charges $16 for a campsite.

14 miles north of Flagstaff off US 89. ✆ **928/526-0502.** www.nps.gov/sucr. Admission $5 adults, free for children 15 and under (admission also valid for Wupatki National Monument). Daily sunrise–sunset; visitor center daily May–Oct 8am–5pm, Nov–Apr 9am–5pm. Visitor center closed Christmas.

Walnut Canyon National Monument ★ The remains of 300 small 13th-century Sinagua cliff dwellings can be seen in the undercut layers of limestone in this 400-foot-deep wooded canyon east of Flagstaff. These cliff dwellings, though not nearly as impressive as the ruins at Montezuma Castle National Monument (50 miles to the south) or Wupatki National Monument (20 miles to the north), are worth a visit for the chance to poke around inside the well-preserved rooms, which were well protected from the elements (and from enemies). The Sinagua were the same people who built and then abandoned the stone pueblos in Wupatki National Monument, and it is theorized that when the land to the north lost its fertility, the Sinagua began migrating southward, settling for 150 years in Walnut Canyon.

A self-guided trail leads from the visitor center down 185 feet to a section of the canyon wall where 25 cliff dwellings can be viewed up close (some can even be entered). From Memorial Day to Labor Day three times each month, there are guided hikes into the monument's backcountry (reservations required).

7½ miles east of Flagstaff on Walnut Canyon Rd. (take exit 204, off I-40). ✆ **928/526-3367.** www.nps.gov/waca. Admission $5 adults, free for children 15 and under. May–Oct daily 8am–5pm; Nov–Apr daily 9am–5pm. Visitor center closed Christmas.

Wupatki National Monument ★★ The landscape northeast of Flagstaff contains hundreds of Native American habitation sites. The most impressive ruins are those left by the Sinagua (the name means "without water" in Spanish), who inhabited this area from around 1100 until shortly after 1200. The largest of the pueblos is Wupatki Ruin. Here the Sinagua built a sprawling three-story pueblo containing nearly 100 rooms. They also constructed what is believed to be a ball court, which, although quite different in design from the courts of the Aztec and Maya, suggests that a similar game may have been played in this region. Another circular stone structure just below the main ruins may have been an amphitheater or a dance plaza.

The most unusual feature of Wupatki, however, is a natural blowhole. A network of small underground tunnels and chambers here acts as a giant barometer, blowing air through the blowhole when the underground air is under greater pressure than the outside air. On hot days, cool air rushes out of the blowhole with amazing force.

Several other ruins within the national monument are easily accessible by car. Wukoki Ruin, built atop a huge sandstone boulder, is particularly picturesque. The visitor center is adjacent to the Wupatki ruins and contains interesting exhibits on the Sinagua and Ancestral Puebloan people.

33 miles north of Flagstaff, off US 89. ✆ **928/679-2365.** www.nps.gov/wupa. Admission $5 adults, free for children 15 and under (admission also valid for Sunset Crater Volcano National Monument). Daily sunrise–sunset. Visitor center daily 9am–5pm (closed Christmas).

WHERE TO STAY

Expensive

The Inn at 410 ★★ Situated only 2 blocks from historic downtown Flagstaff, this restored 1894 Craftsman home is one of the best B&Bs in Arizona, providing convenience, pleasant surroundings, comfortable rooms, and delicious breakfasts. Guests can lounge and enjoy afternoon tea on the front porch, in the comfortable dining room, or in the garden. Each guest room features a distinctive theme; my favorites are Canyon Memories and the Southwest Suite, which conjure up the inn's Western heritage. All rooms have fireplaces, and three have two-person whirlpool tubs. Some of the guest rooms are in an adjacent building, and these rooms are just as nice as those in the main house.

410 N. Leroux St., Flagstaff, AZ 86001. ✆ **800/774-2008** or 928/774-0088. Fax 928/774-6354. www.inn410.com. 10 units. $170–$300 double. 2-night minimum on weekends Apr–Oct. Rates include full breakfast and afternoon refreshments. MC, V. No children 4 or under. **Amenities:** Concierge; exercise room & access to nearby health club. *In room:* A/C, TV/DVD/VCR, fridge, hair dryer, no phone, Wi-Fi.

Moderate

England House Bed & Breakfast ★★ This B&B, just 3 blocks from Flagstaff's historic downtown, is a beautiful two-story Victorian red-sandstone house built in 1902. This old house was lovingly restored by owners Richard and Laurel Dunn, who are devoted to details. Consequently, the England House has a delightful period authenticity. The three large guest rooms are on the second floor and are furnished with 1870s French antiques. There's also a small guest room, called the Pantry (though it isn't really *that* small), on the ground floor. One room has a Tempur-Pedic® mattress, while another has a feather bed. Breakfasts are served in a bright sunroom just off the kitchen.

614 W. Santa Fe Ave., Flagstaff, AZ 86001. ✆ **877/214-7350** or 928/214-7350. www.englandhousebandb.com. 4 units. $129–$199 double. Rates include full breakfast. DISC, MC, V. No children 9 or under. **Amenities:** Concierge. *In room:* A/C, hair dryer, no phone, Wi-Fi.

Little America Hotel ★ Value Set on 500 acres of pine forest and with a trail that winds for 2 miles through the property, this hotel on the east side of Flagstaff might seem at first to be little more than a giant truck stop. However, on closer inspection, you'll find that behind the truck stop stands a surprisingly luxurious and economical hotel set beneath shady pines. The decor is dated but fun, with a sort of French Provincial style predominating. Rooms vary in size, but all have small private balconies.

2515 E. Butler Ave. (exit 198, off I-40), Flagstaff, AZ 86004. ✆ **800/865-1401** or 928/779-2741. Fax 928/779-7983. www.littleamerica.com/flagstaff. 247 units. $119–$189 double; $250–$350 suite. Children 17 and under stay free in parent's room. AE, DC, DISC, MC, V. **Amenities:** Restaurant; lounge; free airport transfers; concierge; exercise room; Jacuzzi; outdoor pool; room service; Wi-Fi. *In room:* A/C, TV, fridge, hair dryer, Internet.

Inexpensive

Historic Hotel Monte Vista This hotel is definitely not for everyone. Although it is historic, it is also a bit run-down and appeals primarily to young travelers who appreciate the low rates and the nightclub just off the lobby. So why stay here? In its day, the Monte Vista hosted the likes of Clark Gable, John Wayne, Carole Lombard, and Gary Cooper, and today, the hotel is supposedly haunted (ask at the front desk for the list of resident ghosts). Opened in 1927, the Monte Vista now has creatively decorated rooms that vary in size and decor. Although the hotel has plenty of old-fashioned flair, don't expect perfection. Check out a room first to see if this is your kind of place.

100 N. San Francisco St., Flagstaff, AZ 86001. ✆ **800/545-3068** or 928/779-6971. Fax 928/779-2904. www.hotelmontevista.com. 50 units (5 with shared bathrooms). May to early Nov $65 double with shared bathroom, $80–$130 double with private bathroom, $120–$175 suite; early Nov to Apr $50–$55 double with shared bathroom, $70–$110 double with private bathroom, $100–$140 suite. AE, DC, DISC, MC, V. Pets accepted ($25 deposit). **Amenities:** Restaurant; lounge. *In room:* TV, hair dryer.

WHERE TO DINE

Expensive

Brix ★★ NEW AMERICAN Although it's a bit hard to find (tucked into a corner of an old brick carriage house), Brix, Flagstaff's most contemporary restaurant, is well worth searching out. The menu relies on fresh, seasonal ingredients, so it changes regularly. However, any time of year, you'll find a great selection of artisanal cheeses, which make a good starter to a meal here. The chef's creativity shines through in such seasonal entrees as pork chops with mushroom spaetzle, chestnuts, and cranberries; duck breast with roasted pear; and winter squash ravioli with roasted mushrooms, apples, spiced pecans, and bleu cheese. There's an excellent wine list to accompany the food.

413 N. San Francisco St. ✆ **928/213-1021.** www.brixflagstaff.com. Reservations recommended. Main courses $10–$13 lunch, $23–$32 dinner. AE, DC, DISC, MC, V. Mon–Thurs 11am–2pm and 5–9pm; Fri–Sat 11am–2pm and 5–10pm.

Josephine's ★ REGIONAL AMERICAN Housed in a restored Craftsman bungalow with a beautiful stone fireplace and a wide front porch for summer dining, this restaurant combines a historical setting with excellent food that draws on a wide range of influences. The green-chile pork *osso buco* is a real winner. At lunch, try the crab-cake po' boy sandwich. There's a good selection of reasonably priced wines also. Be sure to save room for the molten chocolate cake or the unusual half-baked peanut butter–chocolate chip cookie.

503 N. Humphrey's St. ✆ **928/779-3400.** www.josephinesrestaurant.com. Reservations recommended. Main courses $9.25–$13 lunch, $20–$30 dinner. AE, DISC, MC, V. Mon–Fri 11am–2:30pm and 5–9pm; Sat–Sun 5–9pm.

Moderate

Pasto ★ ITALIAN Located in downtown Flagstaff, Pasto has a lively urban feel and serves some of the best food in town. It is always reliable, but be aware that it can get boisterous on the weekends. Casual yet sophisticated, Pasto is less formal than Brix, Cottage Place, or Josephine's, so if you don't feel like getting dressed up after a day at the canyon, come here. As the restaurant's name implies, the menu includes a good assortment of pastas; however, entrees here are so creative that you might want to start with a small order of pasta so you'll have room for the likes of seared scallops with mushroom risotto or spicy seafood stew.

19 E. Aspen St. ✆ **928/779-1937.** www.pastorestaurant.com. Reservations recommended. Main courses $17–$21. AE, DISC, MC, V. Tues–Sun 5–9pm.

Inexpensive

Beaver Street Brewery (Value) AMERICAN/PIZZA This big microbrewery, cafe, and billiards parlor on the south side of the railroad tracks serves up several good brews, and it also does great pizzas and salads. The Beaver Street pizza, made with roasted-garlic pesto, sun-dried tomatoes, fresh basil, and goat cheese, is particularly tasty. The Mongolian beef salad, served on a bed of greens with sesame-ginger dressing, is one of the best dishes on the menu. This place stays packed with college students, but a good pint of ale helps pass any wait quickly, especially if you can grab a seat by the woodstove. The brewery also operates the adjacent **Beaver Street Brews and Cues,** 3 S. Beaver St., which has pool tables and a vintage bar.

11 S. Beaver St. ✆ **928/779-0079.** www.beaverstreetbrewery.com. Reservations not accepted. Main courses $9.50–$15. AE, DISC, MC, V. Sun–Thurs 11:30am–11pm; Fri–Sat 11:30am–midnight.

Diablo Burger (Finds) AMERICAN If ever there were the quintessential hole in the wall, this is it. With little more than a small sign on the door of what looks to be an old silo but is actually a parking-garage support column, Diablo Burger may be hard to find, but it is definitely worth the search. Burgers are made from locally raised natural beef and, as often as possible, produce is local. The burgers are served on English muffins and come with some of the best fries in Arizona. The Blake burger, which is made with a roasted green chile, and the Vitamin B, with bacon, bleu cheese, and beets, are both delicious. To find Diablo Burger, look to the left of the Pesto Brothers restaurant on the plaza in downtown Flagstaff.

120 N. Leroux St. ✆ **928/774-3274.** www.diabloburger.com. Reservations not accepted. Main courses $6.50–$9.25. No credit cards. Mon–Wed 11am–9pm; Thurs–Sat 11am–11pm.

5 WILLIAMS

32 miles W of Flagstaff; 58 miles S of the Grand Canyon; 220 miles E of Las Vegas, NV

Although it's almost 60 miles south of the Grand Canyon, Williams is still the closest real town to the national park. Consequently, it has dozens of motels catering to those unable to get a room in or just outside the park. Founded in 1880 as a railroading and logging town, Williams also has a bit of Western history to boast about, which makes it an interesting place to explore for a morning or afternoon. Old brick commercial buildings dating from the late 19th century line the main street, while modest Victorian homes sit on the tree-shaded streets that spread south from the railroad tracks. In recent years, however, mid-20th-century history has taken center stage: Williams was the last town on historic Route 66 to be bypassed by I-40, and the town now plays up its Route 66 heritage.

Most important for many visitors, however, is that Williams is where you'll find the Grand Canyon Railway depot. The excursion train that departs from here not only provides a fun ride on the rails, but also serves as an alternative to dealing with traffic congestion in Grand Canyon National Park.

Named for famed mountain man Bill Williams, the town sits at the edge of a ponderosa pine forest atop the Mogollon Rim. Surrounding Williams is the Kaibab National Forest, and within the forest not far from town are good fishing lakes, hiking and mountain-biking trails, and even a small downhill ski area.

ESSENTIALS

GETTING THERE Williams is on I-40 just west of the junction with Arizona 64, which leads north to the South Rim of the Grand Canyon.

Amtrak (✆ **800/872-7245**) has service to Williams on its *Southwest Chief* line. There's no station, though—the train stops on the outskirts of town. However, a shuttle van from the Grand Canyon Railway Hotel will pick you up and drive you into town, and, because most people coming to Williams by train are continuing on to the Grand Canyon on the Grand Canyon Railway, this arrangement works well.

For information on the **Grand Canyon Railway** excursion trains to Grand Canyon Village, see "Exploring the Area: Route 66 & Beyond," below.

VISITOR INFORMATION For information on the Williams area, including details on hiking, mountain biking, and fishing, contact the **City of Williams/Forest Service Visitors Center,** 200 W. Railroad Ave. (✆ **800/863-0546** or 928/635-4707; www.williamschamber.com). The visitor center, which includes some interesting historical displays, is open daily from 8am to 5pm (until 6:30pm in the summer). The shop carries books on the Grand Canyon and trail maps for the adjacent national forest.

EXPLORING THE AREA: ROUTE 66 & BEYOND

These days, most people coming to Williams are here to board the **Grand Canyon Railway ★★**, Grand Canyon Railway Depot, 233 N. Grand Canyon Blvd. (✆ **800/843-8724** or 928/773-1976; www.thetrain.com), which operates vintage steam and diesel locomotives between Williams and Grand Canyon Village. Round-trip fares (not including tax or the national park entrance fee) range from $70 to $190 for adults, $40 to $110 for children 2 to 12. Although this is primarily a day-excursion train, it's possible to ride up one day and return on a different day—just let the reservations clerk know. If you stay overnight, be sure you have a reservation at one of the hotels right in Grand Canyon Village.

Route 66 fans will want to drive Williams's main street, which, not surprisingly, is named Route 66. Along this stretch of the old highway, you can check out the town's vintage buildings, many of which house shops selling Route 66 souvenirs. There are also a few antiques stores selling collectibles from the heyday of the famous highway.

Get Your Kicks on Route 66

About 65 miles west of Flagstaff begins the longest remaining stretch of old Route 66. Extending for 160 miles from Ash Fork to Topock, this lonely blacktop passes through some of the most remote country in Arizona (and goes right through the town of Kingman). In Seligman, at the east end of this stretch of the highway, you'll find the **Delgadillo's Snow Cap** (✆ **928/422-3291**), which serves up fast food amid outrageous decor. Next door at **Angel & Vilma Delgadillo's Route 66 Gift Shop & Visitor's Center,** 217 E. Rte. 66 (✆ **928/422-3352;** www.route66giftshop.com), owned by John's uncle Angel, you'll be entertained by one of Route 66's most famous residents and an avid fan of the old highway. The walls of Angel's old one-chair barbershop are covered with photos and business cards of happy customers. Today, Angel's place is a Route 66 information center and souvenir shop.

After leaving Seligman, the highway passes through such waysides as Peach Springs, Truxton, Valentine, and Hackberry. Before reaching Peach Springs, you'll come to **Grand Canyon Caverns,** once a near-mandatory stop for families traveling Route 66. In Hackberry, be sure to stop at the **Hackberry Store & Old Route 66 Visitor Center** (✆ **928/769-2605**), which is filled with Route 66 memorabilia as well as old stuff from the 1950s and 1960s. At Valle Vista, near Kingman, the highway goes into a 7-mile-long curve. Some claim it's the longest continuous curve on a U.S. highway.

After the drive through the wilderness west of Seligman, Kingman feels like a veritable metropolis; its bold neon signs once brought a sigh of relief to the tired and the hungry. Today, it boasts dozens of modern motels and is still primarily a resting spot for the road weary. Mr. D'z Route 66 Diner, a modern rendition of a 1950s diner (housed in an old gas station/cafe), serves burgers and blue-plate specials. Across the street at 120 W. Andy Devine Ave. is a restored powerhouse that dates from 1907 and is home to the **Historic Route 66 Association of Arizona** (✆ **928/753-5001;** www.azrt66.com), the **Historic Route 66 Museum** (✆ **928/753-9889;** www.kingmantourism.org), and the **Powerhouse Visitor Center.** Each year over the first weekend in May, Kingman is the site of the **Route 66 Fun Run,** which consists of a drive along 150 miles of old Route 66, between Topock and Seligman.

The last stretch of Route 66 in Arizona heads southwest out of Kingman through the rugged Sacramento Mountains and passes through the ghost town of Oatman.

WHERE TO STAY

Moderate

Grand Canyon Railway Hotel ★ This hotel is operated by the Grand Canyon Railway and combines modern comforts with the style of a classic Western railroad hotel. The high-ceilinged lobby features a large flagstone fireplace and paintings of the Grand Canyon. The very comfortable guest rooms feature Southwestern styling; ask for a unit in the wing with the fitness room, pool, and hot tub. The hotel's elegant lounge, which features a 100-year-old English bar, serves simple meals, and there's a buffet-style restaurant adjacent. This hotel also has a pet "resort."

233 N. Grand Canyon Blvd., Williams, AZ 86046. ✆ **800/843-8724** or 928/635-4010. Fax 928/773-1610. www.thetrain.com. 298 units. Mid-Mar to mid-Oct and holidays $169 double; mid-Oct to Dec $109 double; Jan to mid-Mar $109 double. Railroad/hotel packages available (mid-Mar to mid-Oct and holidays $225 per person; mid-Oct to mid-Mar $158 per person). Children 15 and under stay free in parent's room. AE, DC, DISC, MC, V. **Amenities:** 2 restaurants; lounge; exercise room; indoor pool. *In room:* A/C, TV, hair dryer, Wi-Fi.

The Red Garter Inn ★ Finds The Wild West lives again at this restored 1897 bordello, but these days the only tarts that come with the rooms are in the bakery downstairs. Located across the street from the Grand Canyon Railway terminal at the top of a steep flight of stairs, this B&B sports high ceilings, attractive wood trim, and reproduction period furnishings. Walls in a couple of rooms have graffiti written by bordello visitors in the early 20th century. The great historical atmosphere makes this my favorite place to stay in Williams.

137 W. Railroad Ave., Williams, AZ 86046. ✆ **800/328-1484** or 928/635-1484. www.redgarter.com. 4 units. $120–$145 double. Rates include continental breakfast. DISC, MC, V. No children 7 or under. **Amenities:** Restaurant. *In room:* TV, no phone, Wi-Fi.

Inexpensive

In addition to the following choices, there are numerous budget chain motels in Williams.

The Canyon Motel & RV Park ★ Kids Finds You'll find this updated 1940s Route 66 motor lodge on the eastern outskirts of Williams, tucked against the trees. While the setting and the rooms in 1940s flagstone cottages are nice enough, the real attractions are the railroad cars parked in the front yard. You can stay in one of two 1929 cabooses or a 1950s Pullman car, which makes this a fun place to overnight if you plan to take the excursion train to the Grand Canyon. I prefer the caboose rooms, which have a more authentic feel. An indoor pool, a horseshoe pit, a swing set, and nature trails provide plenty of entertainment for the entire family.

1900 E. Rodeo Rd., Williams, AZ 86046. ✆ **800/482-3955** or 928/635-9371. Fax 928/635-4138. www.thecanyonmotel.com. 23 units. $40–$79 double; $128–$139 caboose; $99–$116 Pullman double. Children 10 and under stay free in parent's room. DISC, MC, V. **Amenities:** Small indoor pool. *In room:* TV, fridge, no phone, Wi-Fi.

Camping

There are several campgrounds near Williams in the Kaibab National Forest. They include **Cataract Lake,** 1 mile northwest of Williams on Cataract Lake Road, with 18 sites; **Dogtown Lake,** 6½ miles southeast of Williams off Fourth Street/Perkinsville Road/F.R. 173, with 52 sites; **Kaibab Lake,** 4 miles northeast of Williams, off Ariz. 64, with 63 sites; and **Whitehorse Lake,** 19 miles southeast of Williams, off Fourth Street/Perkinsville Road/F.R. 173, with 94 sites. All campgrounds are first-come, first-served, and charge $14 to $18 per night.

WHERE TO DINE

Red Raven Restaurant ★ NEW AMERICAN A cheeseburger and a milkshake may be the meal of choice for most visitors to this Route 66 town, but here at the Red Raven, culinary horizons are a bit broader. Start your meal with Southwestern egg rolls that are served with a smoky chipotle dipping sauce. Then try the pork tenderloin with cranberry-pineapple salsa or the basil butter salmon with cranberry–pine nut couscous. There are also plenty of steaks. Although it is a fairly casual place, this is by far the most sophisticated restaurant in town.

135 W. Rte. 66. ✆ **928/635-4980.** www.redravenrestaurant.com. Reservations recommended. Main courses $6–$10 lunch, $10–$22 dinner. AE, DISC, MC, V. Tues–Sun 11am–2pm and 5–9pm (closed Tues–Wed in winter).

Southern Utah's National Parks

For many people, the best part of a Utah vacation is exploring the state's national parks, which offer spectacular red-rock scenery, deep green forests, rivers, historic sites, and numerous opportunities for hiking and other outdoor recreation.

Although visitation at some national parks has dropped from a peak in about 1999 or 2000, Utah's parks remain popular. Both **Zion** and **Arches** national parks broke visitation records in 2008.

For those trying to avoid the crowds, go in the off season. The parks are busiest in summer, when most children are out of school, so visit at almost any other time. Fall is usually best. Spring is okay, but often windy; and winter can be delightful but chilly.

1 ZION NATIONAL PARK ★★

Early Mormon settler Isaac Behunin is credited with naming his homestead "Little Zion" because it seemed to be a bit of heaven on earth. Today, 150 years later, Zion National Park casts a spell over you as you gaze upon its sheer multicolored walls of sandstone, explore its narrow canyons, hunt for hanging gardens of wildflowers, and listen to the roar of the churning, tumbling Virgin River.

Here you'll discover a smorgasbord of experiences, sights, sounds, and even smells, from massive stone sculptures and monuments to lush forests and rushing rivers.

Zion is home to an abundance of wildlife, with mammals ranging from pocket gophers to mountain lions, hundreds of birds (including golden eagles), lizards of all shapes and sizes, and a dozen species of snakes. Mule deer are common, and you may also see foxes, coyotes, ringtails, beaver, porcupines, and plenty of squirrels and bats. Practically every summer visitor sees lizards, often the colorful collared and whiptail varieties, and hears the song of the canyon wren and the call of the piñon jay.

ESSENTIALS

Located in southwest Utah, at elevations ranging from 3,666 feet to 8,726 feet, Zion National Park has several sections: **Zion Canyon,** the main part of the park, where everyone goes, and the less-visited **Kolob Terrace** and **Kolob Canyons** areas.

GETTING THERE **St. George** and **Cedar City** are the closest towns with airport service. From either airport, it's easy to rent a car and drive to Zion. Utah 9 crosses the park, giving the main section of the park two entry gates, south and east. The drive into Zion Canyon from I-15 on the park's western side—following Utah 9, or Utah 17 and Utah 9, to the south entrance at Springdale—is the more popular route.

From the east, a spectacularly scenic 24-mile drive leads from Mt. Carmel on Utah 9, reached from the north or south on US 89. However, be aware that this route into the park drops over 2,500 feet in elevation, passes through the mile-long Zion–Mt. Carmel Tunnel, and winds down six steep switchbacks. The tunnel is too small for two-way traffic that includes larger-than-standard passenger cars and pickup trucks. Buses, trucks, and most recreational vehicles must drive down the center of the tunnel, stopping all oncoming traffic. This applies to all vehicles over 7 feet 10 inches wide (including mirrors) or 11 feet 4 inches tall. These vehicles pay a $15 fee, good for two trips through the tunnel in a 7-day period. Contact park offices for details.

Kolob Terrace Road, with viewpoints and trail heads, is north off Utah 9 from the village of Virgin, about 15 miles west of the park's southern entrance. This road is closed in the winter. To reach the Kolob Canyons section, in the park's northwest corner, take the short Kolob Canyons Road, off I-15, exit 40.

VISITOR INFORMATION Contact **Zion National Park,** Springdale, UT 84767 (✆ **435/772-3256;** 435-772-0170 for the Backcountry Office; www.nps.gov/zion). You can order books, maps, and videos from the nonprofit **Zion Natural History Association,** Zion National Park, Springdale, UT 84767 (✆ **800/635-3959** or 435/772-3264; www.zionpark.org).

The **Zion Canyon Visitor Center,** near the south entrance, has outdoor exhibits, sells books and maps, and provides information. The smaller **Kolob Canyons Visitor Center,** in the northwest corner of the park off I-15, provides information, permits, books, and maps. The **Zion Human History Museum,** about 1 mile inside the south entrance, has museum exhibits, park information, and an orientation program, plus a bookstore. Both visitor centers and the museum are open daily (hours vary by season) except December 25.

FEES Entry to the park (for up to 7 days), including unlimited use of the shuttle bus (Apr–Oct), costs $25 per private vehicle, $12 per individual on foot, bicycle, or motorcycle.

Oversize vehicles pay an additional $15 for use of the Zion–Mt. Carmel Tunnel on the east side of the park (see "Getting There," above).

Backcountry permits, available at either visitor center, are required for all overnight hikes in the park as well as all slot canyon hikes. Permits cost $10 for 1 or 2 people, $15 for 3 to 7, and $20 for 8 to 12.

RANGER PROGRAMS A variety of free programs and activities are presented, mostly during the summer. Evening programs, which sometimes include a slide show, take place at campground amphitheaters and Zion Lodge. Topics vary but may include the animals or plants of the park, geology of the park, or perhaps some unique feature such as Zion's slot canyons. Rangers give short talks on similar subjects several times daily at the Zion Canyon Visitor Center and at other locations, and lead guided hikes and walks. Schedules are posted throughout the park. Children 6 to 12 can join the Junior Rangers to earn badges and patches.

SEEING THE HIGHLIGHTS

To get the most from your visit, your first stop should be the **Zion Canyon Visitor Center** (see "Visitor Information," above) for the orientation video and exhibits.

Then hop on the free **shuttle bus,** which takes you to the major roadside viewpoints. You'll be able to get off, look at the rock formations, take a short walk, then catch the next shuttle for a ride to the next stop. During the off season (Nov–Mar), you'll use your own vehicle.

We especially recommend stopping at the **Temple of Sinawava** and taking the easy 2-mile round-trip **Riverside Walk,** which follows the Virgin River through a narrow

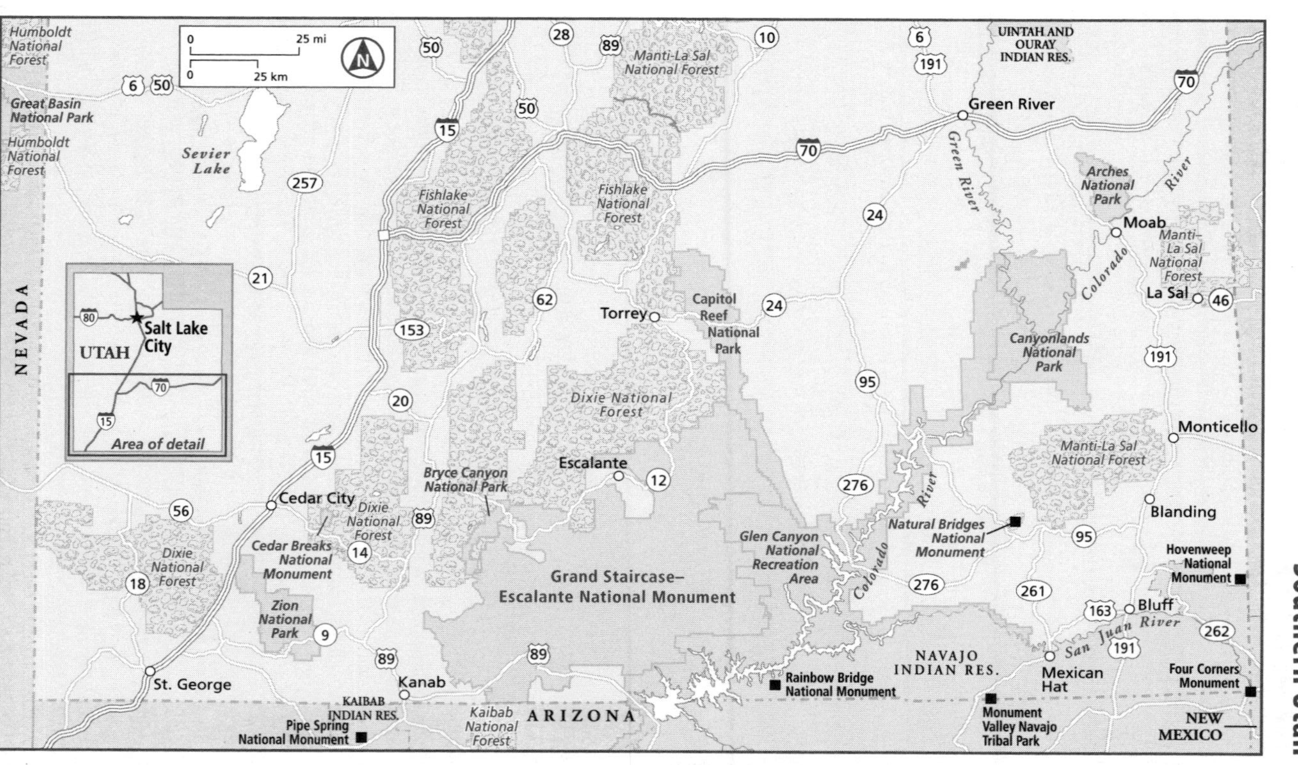

Humboldt National Forest
Great Basin National Park
Humboldt National Forest
NEVADA
Sevier Lake
25 mi
25 km
Salt Lake City
UTAH
Area of detail
Fishlake National Forest
Fishlake National Forest
Manti-La Sal National Forest
UINTAH AND OURAY INDIAN RES.
Green River
Green River
Arches National Park
River
Moab
Manti-La Sal National Forest
Colorado
La Sal
Capitol Reef National Park
Torrey
Canyonlands National Park
Dixie National Forest
Monticello
Manti-La Sal National Forest
Escalante
Bryce Canyon National Park
Cedar City
Dixie National Forest
Cedar Breaks National Monument
Dixie National Forest
Zion National Park
Blanding
Natural Bridges National Monument
River
Glen Canyon National Recreation Area
Colorado
Grand Staircase–Escalante National Monument
Hovenweep National Monument
Bluff
San Juan River
NAVAJO INDIAN RES.
Mexican Hat
Four Corners Monument
St. George
Kanab
KAIBAB INDIAN RES.
Pipe Spring National Monument
Kaibab National Forest
ARIZONA
Rainbow Bridge National Monument
Monument Valley Navajo Tribal Park
NEW MEXICO

canyon past hanging gardens. Then head back to the lodge (total time: 2–4 hr.). At the lodge, stop by the gift shop and perhaps have lunch in the excellent restaurant.

Near the lodge, you'll find the trail head for the **Emerald Pools.** Especially pleasant on hot days, this hike is discussed below under "Outdoor Pursuits." If you still have time and energy, head back to the south park entrance and stop at **Watchman** (east of Watchman Campground) for the 2-mile, 2-hour round-trip, moderately strenuous hike to a plateau with beautiful views of several rock formations and the town of Springdale.

OUTDOOR PURSUITS

Zion offers a wide variety of hiking trails, ranging from easy half-hour walks on paved paths to grueling overnight hikes over rocky terrain. Hikers with a fear of heights should be especially careful when choosing trails; many include steep drop-offs.

The **Weeping Rock Trail** ★, among the park's shortest hikes, is a .5-mile round-trip walk from the Zion Canyon Scenic Drive to a rock alcove with a spring and hanging gardens of ferns and wildflowers. Although paved, it's steep and not suitable for wheelchairs.

Another short hike, the **Lower Emerald Pools Trail** ★★, is an easy 1-hour walk. If you want to extend your trip to a moderately strenuous 2-hour hike, you can continue along the loop. A .6-mile paved path from the Emerald Pools parking area, suitable for those in wheelchairs with assistance, winds through a forest of oak, maple, fir, and cottonwood to a waterfall, a hanging garden, and the Lower Emerald Pool. From here, a steeper, rocky trail (not appropriate for wheelchairs) continues past cactus, yucca, and juniper another .5 mile to Upper Emerald Pool, with another waterfall. A third pool, just above Lower Emerald Pool, offers impressive reflections of the cliffs. The pools are named for the green color of the water, which is caused by algae.

A particularly scenic hike is the **Hidden Canyon Trail,** a 2-mile, moderately strenuous hike that takes about 3 hours. Starting at the Weeping Rock parking area, the trail climbs 800 feet through a narrow water-carved canyon, ending at the canyon's mouth. Those wanting to extend the hike can go another .6 mile to a small natural arch. Hidden Canyon Trail includes long, dizzying drop-offs.

For a strenuous 4-hour, 5-mile hike—one that's definitely not for anyone with even a mild fear of heights—take the **Angel's Landing Trail** ★ to a summit that offers spectacular views into Zion Canyon. But be prepared: The final .5 mile follows a narrow, knife-edge trail along a steep ridge, where footing can be slippery even under the best of circumstances. Support chains have been set along parts of the trail.

Hiking **The Narrows** ★★★ is not hiking a trail at all. It involves walking or wading along the bottom of the Virgin River, through a spectacular 1,000-foot-deep chasm that, at a mere 20 feet wide, definitely lives up to its name. Passing fancifully sculptured sandstone arches, hanging gardens, and waterfalls, this moderately strenuous 16-mile one-way hike can take anywhere from a day up to several days. The Narrows are subject to flash flooding and can be very treacherous, and park service officials remind hikers that they are responsible for their own safety and should check on current water conditions and weather forecasts. This hike is *not* recommended when rain is forecast. Permits are required for full-day and overnight hikes (check with rangers for details), but are not needed for short day hikes, which you can begin just beyond the end of the 2-mile **Riverside Walk.**

Zion is one of America's few relatively bike-friendly national parks. It permits bikes on the paved **Pa'rus Trail,** which runs several miles along the Virgin River. Bikes are also allowed on the park's established roads, except in the Zion–Mt. Carmel tunnel; from

April through October, **Zion Canyon Scenic Drive,** north of the Zion–Mt. Carmel Highway, is open only to shuttle buses, bicyclists, and hikers, plus tour buses and motorists going to Zion Lodge.

Guided horseback rides in the park are available from late spring through early fall from **Canyon Trail Rides,** P.O. Box 128, Tropic, UT 84776 (✆ **435/679-8665;** www.canyonrides.com), based near Zion Lodge. A 1-hour ride along the Virgin River costs $40, and a half-day ride on the Sand Beach Trail costs $75. Riders must weigh no more than 220 pounds. Children must be at least 7 years old for the 1-hour ride, and 10 years old for the half-day ride.

WHERE TO STAY IN & AROUND ZION

The only lodging in the park is Zion Lodge. The other properties listed here are in Springdale, at the park's south entrance.

For additional information on lodging, dining, and area attractions, contact the **Zion Canyon Visitors Bureau,** P.O. Box 331, Springdale, UT 84767 (✆ **888/518-7070;** www.zionpark.com).

Canyon Ranch Motel ★ Finds This series of two- and four-unit cottages set back from the highway looks old-fashioned on the outside, but inside you'll find modern motel rooms with a subdued Southwestern decor. Some units have showers only, while others have combination shower/tubs. Some units have kitchenettes. Room no. 13, with two queen-size beds, offers great views of the national park's rock formations; views from most other rooms are almost as good. There's a lawn with trees and picnic tables. All rooms are nonsmoking.

668 Zion Park Blvd. (P.O. Box 175), Springdale, UT 84767. ✆ **866/946-6276** or 435/772-3357. www.canyonranchmotel.com. 22 units. Apr–Oct $84–$99 double; Nov–Mar $59–$89 double; kitchenettes $10 more year-round. AE, DISC, MC, V. Pets accepted for $10 fee. **Amenities:** Outdoor pool; hot tub. *In room:* A/C, TV, fridge (most), hair dryer, Wi-Fi.

Cliffrose Lodge & Gardens ★★ With river frontage and 5 acres of lawns, shade trees, and flower gardens, the Cliffrose offers a beautiful setting just outside the entrance to Zion National Park. The architecture is Southwestern adobe style, with redwood balconies, and the outdoor rock waterfall Jacuzzi is a delight. The modern, well-kept rooms and suites have all the standard motel appointments, plus unusually large bathrooms with shower/tub combinations. Units accommodate from two to six people; most sleep four.

281 Zion Park Blvd., Springdale, UT 84767. ✆ **800/243-8824** or 435/772-3234. Fax 435/772-3900. www.cliffroselodge.com. 40 units. Apr–Oct and holidays $149–$199 per unit. Off-season discounts available. AE, DISC, MC, V. **Amenities:** Large heated outdoor pool; whirlpool tub. *In room:* A/C, TV/VCR, fridge, hair dryer, Wi-Fi.

Flanigan's Inn ★★ A mountain-lodge atmosphere pervades this attractive complex of natural wood and rock, set among trees, lawns, and flowers just outside the entrance to the park. Parts of the inn date from 1947, and all rooms have been beautifully renovated and have Southwestern decor, wood furnishings, and local art. All units are nonsmoking. A nature trail leads to a hilltop vista, and the inn has an excellent restaurant.

450 Zion Park Blvd., Springdale, UT 84767. ✆ **800/765-7787** or 435/772-3244. Fax 435/772-3396. www.flanigans.com. 34 units. Mid-Mar to mid-Nov and holidays $119–$159 double; $169–$289 suite. Off-season discounts available. AE, DISC, MC, V. **Amenities:** Restaurant (regional cuisine); heated outdoor pool; outdoor hot tub; Wi-Fi (in lobby). *In room:* A/C, TV, fridge (some).

Zion Lodge ★★ If you can afford it, this is the place to stay, and although somewhat pricey during the high tourist season, rates sometimes drop by half the rest of the year. Not only does Zion Lodge have the best location, but the units are quiet, comfortable, and well maintained, and you won't find a better staff. The motel units and cabins are a short walk from the main Zion Lodge, which contains the front desk, restaurants, and gift shop. Each charming cabin has a private porch, stone (gas-burning) fireplace, two double beds, pine-board walls, and log beams. The comfortable motel rooms each have two queen-size beds (a few have one king bed), a private porch or balcony, and most of the usual amenities except TVs and coffeemakers. Suites have one king bed, a sitting room, and a wet bar with a small refrigerator. All units are nonsmoking. The **Red Rock Grill** (see below) is a great spot to eat and enjoy the views.

Zion National Park, UT. ✆ **435/772-7700.** Information and reservations: Xanterra Parks & Resorts, Central Reservations, 6312 S, Fiddlers Green Circle, Ste. 600N, Greenwood Village, CO 80111. ✆ **888/297-2757** or 303/297-2757. Fax 303/297-3175. www.zionlodge.com. 121 units. Mid-Mar to Nov motel $159 double; cabin $173 double; suite $183 double. Winter discounts and packages available. AE, DISC, MC, V. **Amenities:** Restaurant. *In room:* A/C, hair dryer, Wi-Fi.

Camping

Both of Zion's main **campgrounds** have paved roads, well-spaced sites, and lots of trees. Facilities include restrooms with flush toilets but no showers, and a dump station. The fee is $16 per night for basic sites, $18 to $20 per night for sites with electric hookups.

South Campground has 127 sites and no hookups. It's usually open from March through October. Reservations are not accepted, and it often fills by early afternoon in summer. **Watchman Campground ★★** (✆ **877/444-6777** or www.recreation.gov for reservations, for an additional $10 fee) is our favorite campground here, mainly because of its fantastic views of the Watchman and other rock formations. It has 145 sites, with electric hookups at 63 sites. It is open year-round (reservations available spring to early fall only).

Lava Point, which has only six sites, is on the Kolob Terrace. It has fire grates, tables, and toilets, but no water, and there's no fee. Vehicles are limited to 19 feet. It's usually open from June through October.

If you can't get a site in the park, or if you prefer hot showers or complete RV hookups, several campgrounds are in the surrounding area. The closest, **Zion Canyon Campground & RV Park,** 479 Zion Park Blvd., Springdale, UT 84767 (✆ **435/772-3237;** www.zioncamp.com), is a half-mile south of the park entrance. It's open year-round and has 220 sites, many of which are shaded. Although it gets crowded in summer, the campground is clean and well maintained; in addition to the usual showers and RV hookups, you'll find Wi-Fi, a self-service laundry, dump station, convenience store, heated pool, playground, barbecue grills, and restaurant. Tenters are welcome; rates range from $30 to $35 for two people.

WHERE TO DINE IN & AROUND ZION

Red Rock Grill ★★ AMERICAN A mountain-lodge atmosphere prevails here, complete with large windows that face the park's magnificent rock formations. The menu changes periodically, but specialties often include excellent beef tenderloin tips and the very popular wild Alaskan salmon. There are also steaks, several chicken dishes, vegetarian items, and a very good soup and salad bar. At lunch, you'll usually find grilled salmon burgers, beef burgers, sandwiches, and salads; breakfasts consist of most of the usual offerings, including a good buffet, although those staying at the lodge for more than 2 or 3 days would appreciate a bit more variety on the buffet. Full liquor service is available. For something quick and cheap, Zion Lodge's **Castle Dome Café** serves burgers, deli sandwiches, hot dogs, pizza, and ice cream on an outdoor patio.

In Zion Lodge, Zion National Park. ✆ **435/772-7760.** www.zionlodge.com. Dinner reservations required in summer. Breakfast $5.50–$9.25, lunch $6.80–$9, dinner main courses $12–$20. AE, DC, DISC, MC, V. Late spring to early fall, daily 6:30–10am, 11:30am–3pm, and 5:30–9pm; slightly shorter hours the rest of the year.

Zion Park Gift & Deli ★ Value DELI This is our choice for a top-quality deli-style sandwich at an economical price. You can eat at one of the cafe-style tables inside or on the outdoor patio, or carry your sandwich off on a hike. All baked goods are made in-house. In typical deli style, you order at the counter and wait as your meal is prepared with your choice of bread, meats, cheeses, and condiments. Stop here at breakfast for fresh-baked cinnamon rolls, muffins, banana nut bread, and other goodies. Locally made candy, including excellent fudge, and 24 flavors of ice cream and frozen yogurt are also offered, along with espresso. No alcohol is served.

866 Zion Park Blvd., Springdale. ✆ **435/772-3843.** Main courses $5–$10. AE, DISC, MC, V. Summer Mon–Sat 8am–9pm; reduced hours in winter.

Zion Pizza & Noodle ★ Kids PIZZA/PASTA In a former Mormon church with a turquoise steeple, this casual place has small, closely spaced tables. Baked in a slate stone oven, the 12-inch pizzas are our favorites. You can get practically any type you want, including Southwestern burrito pizza and barbecue-chicken pizza. You can also design your own with a variety of toppings, from pepperoni to green chiles to pineapple. Options on the noodle side of the menu include such pastas as penne with grilled chicken, broccoli, carrots, fresh cream, and cheese. Calzones and stromboli are available. Beer is served inside and in the delightful year-round beer garden.

868 Zion Park Blvd., Springdale. ✆ **435/772-3815.** www.zionpizzanoodle.com. Reservations not accepted. Main courses $8.95–$15. No credit cards. Summer daily from 4pm; call for winter schedule.

2 BRYCE CANYON NATIONAL PARK ★★★

If you could visit only one national park in your lifetime, we'd suggest it be Bryce Canyon. Here you'll find magic, inspiration, and spectacular beauty. The main draw of the park is the thousands of intricately shaped hoodoos: Those silent rock sentinels and congregations gathered in colorful cathedrals, arranged in formations that invite your imagination to run wild.

Hoodoos, geologists tell us, are pinnacles of rock, often oddly shaped, left standing after millions of years of water and wind erosion. But perhaps the truth really lies in a Paiute legend. These American Indians told of a "Legend People" who lived here in the old days and because of their evil ways, were turned to stone by the powerful Coyote. Even today, they remain frozen in time.

Although the colorful hoodoos first grab your attention, it isn't long before you notice the deep amphitheaters that enfold them, with their cliffs, windows, and arches, all in shades of red, brown, orange, yellow, and white. Beyond the rocks are the other faces of the park: three separate life zones, each with its own unique vegetation; and a kingdom of animals, from the busy chipmunks and ground squirrels to the stately mule deer and their archenemy, the mountain lion.

The park is named for Mormon pioneer Ebenezer Bryce, who moved to the area in 1875 with his wife Mary and tried raising cattle. Although they stayed only a few years, Bryce left behind his name and his oft-quoted description of the canyon as "a helluva place to lose a cow."

ESSENTIALS

GETTING THERE The closest major towns with airports are **St. George** (130 miles southwest on I-15) and **Cedar City** (on I-15 about 80 miles west of the park).

From St. George, travel north on I-15 for 10 miles to exit 16, then head east on Utah 9 for 63 miles to US 89, north 44 miles to Utah 12, and east 13 miles to the park entrance road. The entrance station is 3 miles south of Utah 12. From Cedar City (I-15 exits 57, 59, and 62), follow Utah 14 west 41 miles to its intersection with US 89, and take US 89 north 21 miles to Utah 12, then east 17 miles to the park entrance road.

Utah 12 runs east-west across the park. The bulk of the park, including the visitor center, is accessible from Utah 63, which branches off from Utah 12 and goes south into the main portions of the park. Utah 89 runs north to south, west of the park, and Utah 12 heads east to Tropic.

VISITOR INFORMATION Contact **Bryce Canyon National Park,** P.O. Box 640201, Bryce, UT 84764-0201 (✆ **435/834-5322;** www.nps.gov/brca). You can order books, maps, and videos from the nonprofit **Bryce Canyon Natural History Association,** P.O. Box 640051, Bryce, UT 84764-0051 (✆ **888/362-2642** or 435/834-4602; www.brycecanyon.org).

The **visitor center,** at the north end of the park, has exhibits on the geology and history of the area, and a short introductory program. Rangers provide information and backcountry permits. The visitor center is open daily year-round except Thanksgiving and December 25.

FEES Entry to the park (for up to 7 days) costs $25 per private vehicle, $12 per individual on foot, bicycle, or motorcycle, which includes unlimited use of the park shuttle (when it's operating, usually late May to early Sept).

Backcountry camping permits, available at the visitor center, are required for all overnight trips into the backcountry. Cost is $5 per trip for one or two individuals, $10 for three to six people, and $15 for 7 to 15 campers. Groups of 7 to 15 can camp only in group sites.

RANGER PROGRAMS Evening talks, which may include a slide show, take place most nights at campground amphitheaters. Topics vary but may include such subjects as the animals and plants of the park, geology, and the role of humans in the park's early days. Rangers also give half-hour talks on similar subjects several times daily at various locations in the park. They also lead hikes and walks, including a moonlight hike (reservations required) and a wheelchair-accessible 1-hour canyon rim walk. Schedules are posted on bulletin boards at the visitor center, general store, campgrounds, and Bryce Canyon Lodge. During the summer, children under 13 can join the Junior Rangers, participate in a variety of programs, and earn badges and certificates.

SEEING THE HIGHLIGHTS

Because this is our favorite national park, we would be happy to spend our entire vacation here. But if you insist on saving time for the many other fascinating areas in the Southwest, there are ways to see a good deal of Bryce in a short amount of time.

Start at the **visitor center** and watch the short program that explains the area's geology. Then drive the 18-mile (one-way) dead-end **park road,** stopping at viewpoints to gaze down into the canyon. An alternative is to take the free **shuttle,** which will take you to most of the main viewpoints.

Whichever way you choose to get around, make sure you spend at least a little time at **Inspiration Point,** which offers a splendid (and, yes, inspirational) view of **Bryce Amphitheater** and its hundreds of statuesque pink, red, orange, and brown hoodoo stone sculptures.

After seeing the canyon from the top down, it's time to get some exercise. Walk at least partway down the **Queen's Garden Trail.** If you can spare 3 hours, hike down the Navajo Loop and return to the rim on the Queen's Garden Trail, as discussed below. An alternative is to take an easy walk along the **Rim Trail,** which provides spectacular views into the canyon. It's especially gorgeous about an hour before sunset.

OUTDOOR PURSUITS

One of the things we like best about Bryce Canyon is that you don't have to be an advanced backpacker to really get to know the park. However, all trails below the rim have at least some steep grades, so wear hiking boots with a traction tread and good ankle support to avoid ankle injuries. During the hot summer months, you'll want to hike either early or late in the day, carry plenty of water, and keep in mind that the deeper you go into the canyon, the hotter it gets.

The **Rim Trail** ★★, which does not drop into the canyon but offers splendid views from above, meanders along the rim for over 5 miles. Overlooking Bryce Amphitheater, the trail allows excellent views along most of its length. An easy to moderate walk, it includes a .5-mile section between two overlooks—Sunrise and Sunset—that is suitable for wheelchairs. This trail is a good choice for an after-dinner stroll, when you can watch the changing evening light on the rosy rocks below.

Your best bet for getting down into the canyon and seeing the most with the least amount of sweat is to combine two popular trails—**Navajo Loop** and **Queen's Garden** ★★★. The total distance is just under 3 miles, with a 521-foot elevation change. Most hikers take 2 to 3 hours to complete the trek. It's best to start at the Navajo Loop trail head at Sunset Point and leave the canyon on the less-steep Queen's Garden Trail, returning to the rim at Sunrise Point, .5 mile to the north. The Navajo Loop section is fairly strenuous; Queen's Garden is moderate. Along the Navajo Loop you'll pass Thor's Hammer and wonder why it hasn't fallen, then ponder the towering skyscrapers of Wall Street. Turning onto the Queen's Garden Trail, you'll see some of the park's most fanciful formations—including the trail's namesake, majestic Queen Victoria—and Gulliver's Castle.

Those looking for more of a challenge might consider the **Hat Shop Trail,** a strenuous 3.8-mile round-trip with a 900-foot elevation change. Leaving from the Bryce Point Overlook, you'll drop quickly to the Hat Shop, so named because it consists of hard gray "hats" perched on narrow reddish-brown pedestals. Allow 4 hours.

For die-hard hikers who don't mind rough terrain, Bryce has two backcountry trails, usually open in summer only. The **Under-the-Rim Trail** runs for some 23 miles, providing an excellent opportunity to see the park's spectacular scenery. **Riggs Spring Loop Trail,** 8.8 miles long, offers splendid views of the pink cliffs in the southern part of the park. The truly ambitious can combine the two trails for a weeklong excursion. Permits are required for all overnight trips.

To see Bryce Canyon the way the early pioneers did, you need to view the landscape from the back of a horse. **Canyon Trail Rides,** P.O. Box 128, Tropic, UT 84776 (✆ **435/679-8665;** www.canyonrides.com), offers a close-up view of Bryce's spectacular rock formations from the relative comfort of a saddle. The company has a desk inside Bryce Canyon Lodge (see below). A 2-hour ride to the canyon floor and back costs $50 per person, and a half-day trip farther into the canyon costs $75 per person. Rides are offered April through November. Riders must be at least 7 years old for the 2-hour trip, at least 10 for the half-day ride, and weigh no more than 220 pounds.

Bryce is beautiful in winter, when the snow creates a perfect white frosting on the red, pink, orange, and brown rock statues. **Cross-country skiers** will find several marked, ungroomed trails (all above the rim), including the Fairyland Trail, which leads 1 mile through a pine and juniper forest to the Fairyland Point Overlook. From here, you can take the 1-mile Forest Trail back to the road, or continue north along the rim for another 1.2 miles to the park boundary. **Snowshoes** may be used above the rim, but not on cross-country ski tracks.

WHERE TO STAY IN & AROUND BRYCE CANYON

Note that room taxes add about 11% to the total cost.

Best Western Ruby's Inn ★★ (Kids) This large Best Western provides most of the beds used by tired park visitors. The lobby is among the busiest places in the area, with an ATM, liquor store, beauty salon, 1-hour film processor, and activities desks where you can book excursions of all sorts, from horseback rides to helicopter tours. Off the lobby are a restaurant, an art gallery, a post office, and a huge general store. Outside are car rentals and a gas station.

Spread among nine buildings, the modern motel rooms feature wood furnishings, art showing scenes of the area, and shower/tub combinations; some have whirlpool tubs. Rooms at the back of the complex are a bit quieter, but you'll have to walk farther to the lobby. All rooms are smoke-free. **Cowboy's Buffet & Steak Room** (p. 578) is a good place to dine.

1000 S. Utah 63 (at the entrance to Bryce Canyon), Bryce, UT 84764. ✆ **866/866-6616** or 435/834-5341. Fax 435/834-5265. www.rubysinn.com. 368 units. June–Sept $135–$199 double, $195 suite; Oct–May $70–$140 double, $145 suite. AE, DC, DISC, MC, V. Pets accepted. **Amenities:** Restaurant; 2 indoor pools; 1 indoor and 1 outdoor whirlpool tub; courtesy transportation from Bryce Canyon Airport, on Utah 12 several miles from the park entrance; general store; liquor store. *In room:* A/C, TV, hair dryer, Wi-Fi.

Bryce Canyon Country Cabins ★ There's something special about staying in a log cabin during a national park vacation, but there's also something very appealing about hot showers and warm beds. Bryce Canyon Country Cabins offers the best of both worlds, with modern log-style cabins and a historic two-room pioneer cabin, set on a 20-acre farm. The grounds surrounding the cabins are nicely landscaped, and you get views out over the national park, although we wish the units were farther back from the highway. The intriguing part of the facility, though, is the farm behind the buildings, where cattle graze in the fields and the chickens think they own the place.

The comfortable modern cabins have knotty pine walls and ceilings, exposed beams, and ceiling fans. Each has two queen-size beds, a table with two chairs, a private porch, and outdoor barbecues. Bathrooms have showers only. The historic cabin, built in 1905, has two spacious rooms with country-style decor, each with its own entrance. Each of the rooms has two queen-size beds and a full bathroom. The historic cabin's two rooms can be rented together or individually.

320 N. Utah 12 (P.O. Box 141), Tropic, UT 84776. ✆ **888/679-8643** or 435/679-8643. www.brycecountry cabins.com. 13 units. Summer $95–$125 double; lower rates at other times. AE, DC, MC, V. *In room:* A/C, TV, fridge, hair dryer, microwave, Wi-Fi.

Bryce Canyon Lodge ★★★ Location is what you're paying for here, and there's no denying that this is the perfect place to stay while visiting Bryce Canyon. The handsome sandstone and ponderosa-pine lodge, opened in 1924, contains a busy lobby, with information desks for horseback riding and other activities, and a well-stocked gift shop.

The lodge suites are luxurious, with ceiling fans and separate sitting rooms. The motel rooms are simple; although the outside of the building looks like a hunting lodge, the guest units are pleasant, modern, and quite spacious, with two queen-size beds and either a balcony or a patio. However, we'd choose the "rustic luxury" of one of the cabins. They're fairly small, with tall ceilings that give a feeling of spaciousness, stone (gas-burning) fireplaces, two double beds, and log beams. It's the right place to stay in a beautiful national park setting like Bryce Canyon. All units are smoke free. The **restaurant** (p. 578) offers a good dining option right in the park.

Bryce Canyon National Park, UT. ✆ **435/834-5361.** Information and reservations: Xanterra Parks & Resorts, Central Reservations, 6312 S, Fiddlers Green Circle, Ste. 600N, Greenwood Village, CO 80111. ✆ **888/297-2757** or 303/297-2757. Fax 303/297-3175. www.brycecanyonlodge.com. 114 units (110 in motel rooms and cabins; 3 suites and 1 studio in lodge). $165–$175 double motel and cabins; $130–$179 lodge units. AE, DISC, MC, V. Closed Nov–Mar. **Amenities:** Restaurant.

Bryce View Lodge (Value) This basic modern American motel gets our vote for the best combination of economy and location. It consists of four two-story buildings, set back from the road and grouped around a large parking lot and attractively landscaped area. The simply decorated rooms are comfortable and quiet. Guests have access to the amenities at Best Western Ruby's Inn, across the street.

991 S. Utah 63 (P.O. Box 64002), Bryce, UT 84764. ✆ **888/279-2304** or 435/834-5180. Fax 435/834-5181. www.bryceviewlodge.com. 160 units. Summer $80–$110 double, rest of the year $60–$85 double. AE, DC, DISC, MC, V. Pets accepted. **Amenities:** See Best Western Ruby's Inn, p. 576. *In room:* A/C, TV.

Camping

Typical of the West's national park campgrounds, the two campgrounds at Bryce offer plenty of trees for a genuine "forest camping" experience, easy access to trails, and limited facilities. **North Campground ★★** has 107 sites and is open year-round; **Sunset Campground ★** has 96 sites and is open May through September only. We prefer North Campground because it's closer to the Rim Trail—making it easier to rush over to catch those amazing sunrise and sunset colors—but we would gladly take any site in either campground. Both campgrounds have modern restrooms with running water, but no RV hookups or showers. Reservations are available for some sites in North Campground (✆ **877/444-6777;** www.recreation.gov) for an additional fee from early May through late September. Camping at Sunset Campground is first come, first served; get there early to claim a site. Cost at both campgrounds is $15 per night.

Pay showers, a coin-operated laundry, a snack bar, food and camping supplies, and souvenirs are available in the summer at the **General Store** (for information, contact Bryce Canyon Lodge ✆ **435/834-5361**), which is a healthy walk from either campground. The park service operates an RV dump station ($2 fee) in the summer.

Those seeking a commercial campground with hot showers, RV hookups, and all the usual amenities won't do any better than **Ruby's Inn RV Park & Campground ★★**, 1280 S. Utah 63, Bryce, UT 84764 (✆ **866/866-6616** or 435/834-5301; www.rubys inn.com), right outside the park along the park's shuttle-bus route. Many of the 200 sites are shaded and there's an attractive tent area. Facilities include a pool, two coin-op laundries, a game room, horseshoes, barbecue grills, and a store with groceries and RV supplies. Also on the grounds are several camping cabins ($55 double) and tepees ($33 double), which share the campground's bathhouse. Campsite rates for two people are $33 to $39 for RV sites and $24 for tent sites. The campground is open from April through October.

WHERE TO DINE IN & AROUND BRYCE CANYON

Bryce Canyon Lodge ★★ AMERICAN We would come here just for the mountain-lodge atmosphere, with two large stone fireplaces and large windows looking out on the park. But the food's good, too, and quite reasonably priced considering the location. The menu changes periodically, but may include dinner specialties such as the cherry-glazed pork chops and the grilled trout, which is dusted with a seasoned mix and topped with toasted pumpkin seeds. The menu also offers steaks—including a wonderful New York strip and a grilled flat iron steak prepared with an Italian marinade and topped with marinated peppers plus chicken and several vegetarian selections. At lunch, you'll find sandwiches, burgers, salads, and other lighter items. Breakfasts offer the usual American standards and an excellent buffet. The restaurant has full liquor service.

Bryce Canyon National Park. ✆ **435/834-8760.** www.brycecanyonlodge.com. Reservations required for dinner. Main courses $3.95–$9.95 breakfast and lunch, $13–$24 dinner. AE, DC, DISC, MC, V. Daily 6:30–10:30am, 11am–3pm, and 5–10pm. Closed Nov–Mar.

Cowboy's Buffet & Steak Room STEAK/SEAFOOD The busiest restaurant in the Bryce Canyon area, this place moves 'em through with buffets at every meal, plus a well-rounded menu and friendly service. The breakfast buffet offers more choices than you'd expect, and at the lunch buffet you'll find country-style ribs, fresh fruit, salads, soups, and vegetables. The dinner buffet features charbroiled rib-eye steak and other meats, pastas, potatoes, and salads. Regular menu dinner entrees include prime rib, steaks, ribs, grilled Utah trout, burgers, and salads. In addition to the large, Western-style dining room, a patio is open in summer. There is full liquor service.

At the Best Western Ruby's Inn (see above), 1000 S. Utah 63, Bryce. ✆ **435/834-5341.** www.rubysinn.com. Reservations not accepted. Breakfast and lunch $6.95–$16, dinner main courses and buffets $8.95–$26. AE, DC, DISC, MC, V. Summer daily 6:30am–10pm; winter daily 6:30am–9pm.

Foster's Family Steak House STEAK/SEAFOOD The simple Western decor here provides the right atmosphere for a family steakhouse. Locally popular for its slow-roasted prime rib and steamed Utah trout, Foster's also offers several steaks (we like the 14-oz. T-bone), sandwiches, a soup of the day, and homemade chili with beans. All the pastries, pies, and breads are baked on the premises. Bottled beer is available with meals.

At Foster's motel (see above), 1150 Utah 12, about 1½ miles west of the park entrance road. ✆ **435/834-5227.** www.fostersmotel.com. Most breakfast and lunch items $3.95–$9.95, dinner main courses $8.95–$25. AE, DISC, MC, V. Mar–Nov daily 7am–10pm; call for winter hours.

3 CAPITOL REEF NATIONAL PARK ★★★

A wonderful and relatively little-known gem, Capitol Reef National Park offers loads of that spectacular southern Utah scenery, but with a unique twist and a geologic personality all its own. You'll see the aptly named Hamburger Rocks, sitting atop a white sandstone table; the silent, eerie Temple of the Moon; and the commanding Castle. The colors of Capitol Reef's canyon walls are spectacular, which is why Navajos called this "The Land of the Sleeping Rainbow."

But Capitol Reef is much more than brilliant rocks and barren desert. The Fremont River creates a lush oasis in an otherwise unforgiving land, with cottonwoods and willows along its banks. The area is also rich in history, with thousand-year-old rock art, historic buildings, and other traces of the past.

ESSENTIALS

GETTING THERE The park straddles Utah 24, which connects with I-70 to the northeast and northwest. Those coming from Bryce Canyon National Park can follow Utah 12 northeast to its intersection with Utah 24, and continue east into Capitol Reef. If you're approaching from the Four Corners area, follow Utah 276 or Utah 95 (or both) north to the intersection with Utah 24, where you'll then go west into the park.

VISITOR INFORMATION Contact **Capitol Reef National Park,** HC 70 Box 15, Torrey, UT 84775 (© **435/425-3791,** ext. 111; www.nps.gov.care).

The **visitor center** is on the park access road at its intersection with Utah 24. It's open daily in summer from 8am to 6pm, with shorter hours at other times, and closed on several major holidays. It has exhibits on the area's geology and history, and provides information and backcountry permits.

FEES Entry to the park (for up to 7 days) costs $5 per vehicle or $3 each for individuals. Free permits, available at the visitor center, are required for all overnight hiking trips into the backcountry.

RANGER PROGRAMS Rangers present a variety of free programs and activities from spring through fall. Campfire programs take place most evenings at the outdoor amphitheater next to Fruita Campground. Topics vary but may include animals and plants, geology, and human history in and of the area. Rangers also lead hikes and walks and give short talks on history at the pioneer Fruita Schoolhouse and the Mormon homestead. Schedules are posted on bulletin boards at the visitor center and campground. Kids can become Junior Rangers or Junior Geologists; they'll learn to map ancient earthquakes, inspect water bugs, and so on.

SEEING THE HIGHLIGHTS

Start at the **visitor center,** where you will learn about the park's geology and early history. From there, the paved 25-mile round-trip **Scenic Drive** leads south into the park, offering good views of its dramatic canyons and rock formations. Pick up a free copy of the Scenic Drive brochure at the entrance station and set out, stopping at viewpoints to gaze out at the array of colorful cliffs and commanding rocks.

If the weather's dry, drive down the gravel **Capitol Gorge Road** (5 miles round-trip), at the end of the paved Scenic Drive, for a look at what many consider the best backcountry scenery in the park. If you're up for a short walk, the relatively flat 2-mile (round-trip) **Capitol Gorge Trail,** which starts at the end of Capitol Gorge Road, takes you to the historic **Pioneer Register,** a rock wall where traveling pioneers "signed in."

HISTORIC SITES

In the park, you'll find evidence of human presence through the centuries. The **Fremont** people lived along the river as early as A.D. 700, and their petroglyphs (images carved into rock) and pictographs (images painted on rock) are visible on the canyon walls.

Prospectors and other travelers passed through **Capitol Gorge** in the late 1800s, leaving their names on a wall of rock that came to be known as the **Pioneer Register.** You can reach it on a 2-mile loop; see below under "Outdoor Pursuits."

Mormon pioneers established the appropriately named community of **Fruita** when they discovered that this was a good spot to grow fruit. The tiny 1896 **Fruita Schoolhouse** ★ served as a church, social hall, and meeting hall, in addition to being a one-room schoolhouse. The school closed in 1941, and it has been restored and furnished with old wood-and-wrought-iron desks, a wood stove, a chalkboard, textbooks, and even the hand bell that used to call students to class. Nearby, the **orchards** planted by the settlers continue to flourish, tended by park workers who invite you to sample the "fruits" of their labors.

The historic **Gifford Farmhouse,** built in 1908, is a typical early-20th-century Utah farmhouse. It offers displays of period objects and often schedules demonstrations of pioneer skills, such as quilting and rug making. Park across the road at the picnic area; a short path leads to the farmhouse.

OUTDOOR PURSUITS

This is the real Wild West; little has changed from the way cowboys, bank robbers, settlers, and gold miners found it in the late 1800s. Among the last areas in the continental United States to be explored, many parts of Capitol Reef National Park are still practically unknown, perfect for those who want to see this rugged country in its natural state. Several local companies offer guide and shuttle services. They include **Hondoo Rivers and Trails,** 90 E. Main St. (P.O. Box 98), Torrey, UT 84775 (✆ **800/332-2696** or 435/425-3519; www.hondoo.com); and **Wild Hare Expeditions,** 116 W. Main St. (P.O. Box 750194), Torrey, UT 84775 (✆ **888/304-4273** or 435/425-3999; www.color-country.net/~thehare).

Those who strike out on their own will find the park's hiking trails offer panoramic views of colorful cliffs and soaring spires, eerie journeys through desolate steep-walled canyons, and cool oases along the tree-shaded Fremont River. Watch for petroglyphs and other reminders of this area's first inhabitants.

Among the best short hikes is the 2.5-mile round-trip **Capitol Gorge Trail** ★★. It's easy, mostly level walking along the bottom of a narrow canyon, but looking up at the tall, smooth walls of rock conveys a strong sense of what the pioneers must have seen and felt 100 years ago, when they moved rocks and debris to haul their wagons up this canyon. Starting at the end of the dirt Capitol Gorge Road, the hiking trail leads past the **Pioneer Register** ★, where prospectors and other early travelers carved their names. The earliest legible signatures were made in 1871 by J. A. Call and "Wal" Bateman.

A more strenuous hike is the 3.5-mile round-trip **Cassidy Arch Trail.** This route offers spectacular views as it climbs steeply from the floor of Grand Wash to high cliffs overlooking the park. From the trail, you'll see Cassidy Arch, a natural stone arch named for outlaw Butch Cassidy, who is believed to have used the Grand Wash as a hideout. The trail is off the Grand Wash dirt road, which branches off the east side of the highway about halfway down the park's Scenic Drive.

As in most national parks, **bikes and four-wheel-drive vehicles** must stay on established roads, but Capitol Reef has several so-called roads—actually little more than dirt trails—that provide exciting opportunities for those using 4WD or pedal-power. ATVs are not permitted. Both the Grand Wash and Capitol Gorge roads, plus several much longer dirt roads, are open to mountain bikes as well as to four-wheel-drive vehicles. Details are available at the visitor center.

WHERE TO STAY IN & AROUND CAPITOL REEF

There are no lodging or dining facilities in the park; the town of **Torrey,** just west of the park entrance, can take care of most needs. Room tax adds just over 10% to lodging bills.

Austin's Chuckwagon Motel This attractive family-owned and -operated motel offers a wide range of options. The well-maintained property includes modern motel rooms, which have Southwestern decor, phones, and two queen-size beds; and a family suite with a large living room, fully equipped kitchen, and three bedrooms that sleep six. Our choice here, however, is one of the plush but still Western-style cabins. Measuring 576 square feet, each cabin has two bedrooms (each with a queen-size bed), a living room with a queen-size sofa bed, a complete kitchen, a full bathroom, a covered porch, and a small yard with a barbecue grill and a picnic table. The grounds are attractively landscaped, with a lawn and large trees; also on the property is a grocery store/bakery with a well-stocked deli that prepares hot and cold sandwiches. All rooms are smoke-free.

12 W. Main St. (P.O. Box 750180), Torrey, UT 84775. ✆ **800/863-3288** or 435/425-3335. Fax 435/425-3434. www.austinschuckwagonmotel.com. 24 units. Motel rooms $75 double (lower rates Mar and Nov); cabins $135 for up to 4; family suite $150 double. AE, DISC, MC, V. Closed Dec–Feb. **Amenities:** Deli; outdoor pool; whirlpool. *In room:* A/C, TV, Wi-Fi.

Capitol Reef Inn & Cafe (Value) This older, Western-style motel—small, beautifully landscaped, and well maintained—offers homey, comfortable guest rooms with solid wood furnishings, not fancy but completely adequate. One unit has a shower/tub combination; the rest have showers only. Facilities include a playground and a lovely desert garden. The book and gift shop offers American Indian crafts, guidebooks, and maps. The **Cafe** (see below) offers some of Utah's best locally grown and healthful cuisine.

360 W. Main St. (Utah 24), Torrey, UT 84775. ✆ **435/425-3271.** www.capitolreefinn.com. 10 units. $53 double. AE, DISC, MC, V. Closed Nov–Mar. **Amenities:** Restaurant; large hot tub. *In room:* A/C, TV, fridge.

SkyRidge Inn Bed & Breakfast ★★★ A B&B and an art gallery, this place offers a delightful alternative to the standard motel. Rooms in the three-story Territorial-style inn are distinctively decorated with an eclectic mix of antiques and contemporary art. Two have private decks with hot tubs; another has a two-person whirlpool tub inside and a private deck. The inn sits on 75 acres, with hiking trails and spectacular views. Full breakfasts include homemade granola, fresh-baked coffeecake or muffins, and a hot entree such as pecan griddlecakes served with maple breakfast sausage. Smoking is not permitted.

950 E. Utah 24 (P.O. Box 750220), Torrey, UT 84775. ✆ **800/448-6990** or 435/425-3222. www.skyridgeinn.com. 6 units. Apr–Oct $129–$175 double; Nov–Mar $119–$152 double. Rates include breakfast and evening hors d'oeuvres. AE, MC, V. **Amenities:** Whirlpool tub. *In room:* A/C, TV/VCR, CD player, hair dryer, Wi-Fi.

Camping

The 71-site **Fruita Campground ★★**, open year-round, is delightful, with plenty of trees and a forest atmosphere. It offers modern restrooms, drinking water, picnic tables, fire grills, and an RV dump station (open in summer only), but no showers or RV hookups. It's along the main park road, 1 mile south of the visitor center. Water may be turned off in winter, leaving only pit toilets. Camping costs $10; reservations are not accepted.

The park also has two **primitive campgrounds,** free and open year-round on a first-come, first-served basis. Both have tables, fire grills, and pit toilets, but no water. Check for directions and road conditions before going, because unpaved roads may be impassable in wet weather.

Backcountry camping is permitted in much of the park with a free permit, available at the visitor center. Fires are forbidden in the backcountry.

For a commercial campground with hot showers and RV hookups, we especially like the **Sandcreek RV Park,** 540 Utah 24 (P.O. Box 750276), Torrey, UT 84775 (✆ **435/425-3577,** or 407/363-1622 in winter; www.sandcreekrv.com). Five miles west of the park entrance, this 24-site campground has an open, grassy area, numerous young trees, and great views. Facilities include a large, clean bathhouse; horseshoe pits; a gallery; a dump station; and coin-op laundry. Rates are $13 for tents and $17 to $21 for RVs. It's open April through mid-October.

WHERE TO DINE AROUND CAPITOL REEF

Cafe Diablo ★★★ SOUTHWESTERN Among the West's finest restaurants, Cafe Diablo offers innovative beef, pork, chicken, seafood, and vegetarian selections, many created with a Southwestern flair. The menu varies but could include pumpkin seed–crusted local trout served with cilantro-lime sauce and wild-rice pancakes; Utah lamb marinated with sage and rosemary; and baby-back pork ribs, slow roasted in chipotle, molasses, and rum glaze. Pastries and ice creams, all made on the premises, are spectacular. Beer, wine, and cocktails are served.

599 W. Main St., Torrey. ✆ **435/425-3070.** www.cafediablo.net. Main courses $21–$29. MC, V. Daily 5–10pm. Closed mid-Oct to early Apr.

Capitol Reef Cafe ★★ (Finds) AMERICAN/VEGETARIAN This local favorite offers fine, fresh, healthful cuisine that's among the best you'll find in Utah. Known for its locally raised trout, the cafe is equally famous for the 10-vegetable salad served with all dinner entrees. Vegetables are grown locally, and several dishes—such as spaghetti and excellent fettuccine primavera—can be ordered vegetarian or with meat or fish. Steaks and chicken are also served. The atmosphere is casual, with comfortable seating, American Indian crafts, and large windows. The restaurant offers wine and beer.

360 W. Main St, Torrey. ✆ **435/425-3271.** www.capitolreefinn.com. Main courses $4.95–$12 breakfast and lunch, $8.95–$21 dinner. AE, DISC, MC, V. Daily 7am–9pm. Closed Nov–Mar.

4 ARCHES & CANYONLANDS NATIONAL PARKS ★★

Massive sandstone spires and arches that seem to defy gravity, all colored by iron and other minerals in shades of orange, red, and brown, define these two national parks. On opposite sides of the town of Moab, the parks offer numerous opportunities for hiking, mountain biking, and four-wheeling.

No lodging facilities, restaurants, or stores are inside either national park; most visitors stay and eat in Moab. For lodging, camping, and restaurant information for Moab, see "A Base Camp in Moab" (p. 587).

Moab is on US 191, 30 miles south of I-70 (take exit 180, at Crescent Junction) and 53 miles north of Monticello.

ARCHES NATIONAL PARK

Natural stone arches and fantastic rock formations, which look as if they were sculpted by an artist's hand, are the defining features of this park, and they exist in remarkable numbers and variety. Best of all, the formations here seem more accessible and less forbidding than the spires and pinnacles at nearby Canyonlands National Park. Arches is visitor-friendly, with relatively short, well-maintained trails leading to most of the park's major attractions.

Some people think of arches as bridges, but to geologists there's a big difference. Bridges are formed when a river slowly bores through solid rock. The often bizarre and beautiful contours of arches result from the erosive force of rain and snow, which freezes and thaws, dissolving the "glue" that holds sand grains together and chipping away at the stone, until gravity finally pulls a chunk off.

Essentials

GETTING THERE From Moab, drive 5 miles north on US 191.

VISITOR INFORMATION Contact **Arches National Park,** P.O. Box 907, Moab, UT 84532 (© **435/719-2299;** www.nps.gov/arch). **Canyonlands Natural History Association,** 3015 South US 191, Moab, UT 84532 (© **800/840-8978** or 435/259-6003; www.cnha.org), sells books, maps, and videos.

The **visitor center,** just inside the park entrance gate, provides maps, brochures, and information. It's open daily April through October from 7:30am to 6:30pm, and 8am to 4:30pm the rest of the year (closed Dec 25).

FEES Entry to the park (for up to 7 days) costs $10 per vehicle, $5 per person on foot, bicycle, or motorcycle.

RANGER PROGRAMS From March through October, rangers lead guided hikes on the Fiery Furnace Trail twice daily (see "Outdoor Pursuits," below), as well as daily nature walks at various park locations. Evening campfire programs (Apr–Oct) cover topics such as rock art, geological processes, and wildlife. A schedule of events is posted at the visitor center. Kids between 6 and 12 can pick up a Junior Ranger booklet at the visitor center. After completing the activities in the booklet and participating in several programs, they'll earn a badge.

Seeing the Highlights

Arches is the easiest of Utah's national parks to see in a day, if that's all you can spare. An 18-mile (one-way) **scenic drive ★★** offers splendid views of countless natural rock arches and other formations, and several easy hikes reveal additional scenery. Allow 1½ hours for the round-trip drive, adding time for optional hikes. Start by viewing the short program at the **visitor center** to get a feel for what lies ahead. Then drive north along the scenic drive, stopping at viewpoints and for occasional short walks. The scenic drive ends at the often-crowded parking area for the **Devils Garden Trailhead.** From here, you can hike to some of the park's unique arches, including **Landscape Arch,** which is among the longest natural rock spans in the world. From the trail head parking lot, it's 18 miles back to the visitor center.

Outdoor Pursuits

Most of the hiking trails here are short and relatively easy. Because of the hot summer sun and lack of shade, it's wise to carry water on even the shortest hike.

One easy walk is to **Sand Dune Arch,** a good place to take kids who want to play in the sand. It's only .3 mile (round-trip), but you can add 1.2 miles by continuing to Broken Arch. Sand Dune Arch is hidden among and shaded by rock walls, with a naturally created giant sandbox below the arch. Those continuing to Broken Arch should watch for mule deer and kit foxes along the way. Allow about 30 minutes to Sand Dune Arch and back; to Broken Arch, 1 hour.

From the **Devils Garden Trail** ★ you can see about 15 to 20 arches on a fairly long, strenuous, and difficult hike, or view some exciting scenery by following only part of the route. We suggest taking at least the easy to moderate 1.6-mile round-trip hike to **Landscape Arch** ★, a long, thin ribbon of stone that's one of the most beautiful arches in the park. Watch for mule deer along the way, and allow about an hour. Past Landscape Arch, the trail becomes more challenging, but it offers numerous additional views, including panoramas of the curious Double O Arch and a large, dark tower known as Dark Angel. From the section of the trail where Dark Angel is visible, you are 2.5 miles from the trail head. If you turn back at this point, the round trip will take about 3 hours.

Considered by many to be the park's most scenic hike, the 3-mile round-trip **Delicate Arch Trail** ★ is a moderate-to-difficult hike, with slippery slickrock, no shade, and some steep drop-offs along a narrow cliff. Hikers are rewarded with a dramatic and spectacular view of Delicate Arch. Allow 2 to 3 hours.

The **Fiery Furnace Guided Hike** is a strenuous 2-mile round-trip naturalist-led hike to some of the most colorful formations in the park. Guided hikes venture into this restricted area twice daily from spring through fall, by reservation, and last 2¼ to 3 hours. The cost is $10 for adults, $5 for children 6 to 12.

Camping in the Park

At the north end of the park's scenic drive, **Devils Garden Campground** is Arches's only developed camping area. The 52 well-spaced sites nestle among rocks, with plenty of piñon and juniper trees. From March through October, the campground accepts reservations (✆ **877/444-6777;** www.recreation.gov), with a $10 additional booking fee. In summer, the campground fills early, often by 9am, with people trying to garner the 24 first-come, first-served sites; make reservations or get to the campground early, often by 7:30am. Sites cost $20 per night. There are no showers or RV hookups.

CANYONLANDS NATIONAL PARK

Utah's largest national park is not for the sightseer out for a Sunday afternoon drive. Instead, it rewards those willing to spend time and energy—*lots* of energy—exploring the rugged backcountry. Sliced into districts by the Colorado and Green rivers, this is a land of extremes: vast panoramas, dizzyingly deep canyons, dramatically steep cliffs, broad mesas, and towering spires.

The most accessible part of Canyonlands is the **Island in the Sky District,** in the northern section of the park. A paved road leads to sites such as Grand View Point, which overlooks some 10,000 square miles of rugged wilderness.

The **Needles District,** in the southeast corner, offers only a few viewpoints along the paved road, but it boasts numerous possibilities for hikers, backpackers, and high-clearance four-wheel-drives. Named for its tall red-and-white-striped rock pinnacles, this diverse district is home to impressive arches, including 150-foot-tall Angel Arch, as well as grassy meadows and the confluence of the Green and Colorado rivers.

Most park visitors don't get a close-up view of the **Maze District;** they see it off in the distance. That's because it's practically inaccessible. You'll need a lot of endurance and at

Moments A Bird's-Eye View of Canyonlands

Canyonlands is beautiful, but many of its most spectacular sections are difficult to get to—to say the least. One solution is to take to the air. **Slickrock Air Guides, Inc.** (✆ **866/259-1626** or 435/259-6216; www.slickrockairguides.com), offers 1-hour scenic flights over Canyonlands National Park and nearby areas for $140 per person; 2½-hour flights that take in Canyonlands and Monument Valley cost $260 per person.

least several days to see even a few of its sites, such as the appropriately named Lizard Rock and Beehive Arch.

Essentials

GETTING THERE To reach the Island in the Sky Visitor Center, 34 miles west of Moab, take US 191 north to Utah 313, and follow it south into the park. To reach the Needles Visitor Center, 75 miles southwest of Moab, take US 191 south to Utah 211, and follow it west into the park. Getting to the Maze District is a bit more interesting. From I-70 west of Green River, take Utah 24 south. Watch for signs and follow two- and four-wheel-drive dirt roads east into the park.

VISITOR INFORMATION Contact **Canyonlands National Park,** 2282 SW Resource Blvd., Moab, UT 84532 (✆ **435/719-2313;** www.nps.gov/cany). Books, very useful maps, and videos are available from the nonprofit **Canyonlands Natural History Association,** 3031 South US 191, Moab, UT 84532 (✆ **800/840-8978** or 435/259-6003; www.cnha.org).

Island in the Sky Visitor Center, in the northern part of the park, and **Needles Visitor Center,** in the southern section, provide maps, free brochures on hiking trails, and, most important, advice from rangers. Both are open 9am to 4:30pm daily, with expanded hours in summer.

We cannot overemphasize how brutal the terrain at Canyonlands can be. It's important to know not only your own limitations but also those of your vehicle and other equipment.

FEES Entry to the park (for up to 7 days) costs $10 per vehicle, $5 per person on foot, bike, or motorcycle.

Permits, available at visitor centers, are required for all overnight stays except at the established campgrounds. Call ✆ **435/259-4351** or check the park website (see "Visitor Information," above) for rates and reservations.

RANGER PROGRAMS On summer evenings at Squaw Flat and Willow Flat campgrounds, rangers offer campfire programs on various aspects of the park. Short morning talks take place in summer at the Island in the Sky Visitor Center and at Grand View Point.

Seeing the Highlights

Canyonlands is not an easy place to see in a short time. In fact, if your schedule permits only a day or less, we suggest skipping the Needles and Maze districts entirely and going directly to the **Island in the Sky Visitor Center.** After looking at the exhibits, drive to several of the overlooks, stopping along the way for a short hike or two. Make sure you stop at the **Grand View Point Overlook,** at the south end of the paved road. Hiking the **Grand View Trail,** which is especially scenic in the late afternoon, literally gives you the "Grand View" of the park. Allow about 1½ hours for the easy 2-mile walk. We also recommend the **Upheaval Dome Overlook Trail,** which should take about half an hour and will bring you to a mile-wide crater of mysterious origins.

Outdoor Pursuits

Canyonlands has little shade and no reliable water sources, and temperatures soar to 100°F (38°C) in summer. Rangers strongly advise that hikers carry at least a gallon of water per person per day, along with sunscreen, a hat, and all the usual hiking and emergency equipment. If you expect to do serious hiking, try to plan your trip for the spring or fall, when conditions are much more hospitable. Because some trails may be confusing, hikers attempting the longer ones should carry good topographic maps.

In the Island in the Sky District, the **Mesa Arch Trail** provides the casual visitor with an easy .5-mile (round-trip) self-guided nature walk among piñon and juniper trees, cactus, and a plant called Mormon tea, from which Mormon pioneers made a tealike beverage. The loop trail's main scenic attraction is an arch, made of Navajo sandstone, that hangs precariously on the edge of a cliff, framing a spectacular view of nearby mountains. Allow about a half-hour.

An easy 2-mile hike, especially pretty at sunset, is the **Grand View Trail ★**, which follows the canyon rim from Grand View Point and shows off numerous canyons and rock formations, the Colorado River, and distant mountains. Allow about 1½ hours.

A bit more strenuous is the 5-mile **Neck Spring Trail,** which starts about .5 mile south of the Island in the Sky Visitor Center. Allow 3 to 4 hours for this hike, which follows old paths to two springs. You'll see water troughs, hitching posts, rusty cans, and the ruins of an old cabin. Climb to the top of the rim for a great view of the canyons and the Henry Mountains, some 60 miles away.

In the Needles District, one relatively easy hike is the **Roadside Ruin Trail,** a short (.3-mile), self-guided nature walk that takes about a half-hour round-trip. It leads to a prehistoric granary, probably used by the Anasazi (Ancestral Puebloans), some 700 to 1,000 years ago, to store corn, nuts, and other foods.

For a bit more of a challenge, try the **Slickrock Foot Trail,** a 2.4-mile loop that leads to several viewpoints and takes 2 or 3 hours. Slickrock—a general term for any bare rock surface—can be slippery, especially when wet. Viewpoints show off the stair-step topography of the area, from its colorful canyons and cliffs to its flat mesas and striped needles.

From **Elephant Hill Trailhead,** you can follow several interconnecting trails into the backcountry. The road to the trail head is gravel, but it is graded and drivable in most two-wheel-drive passenger cars; those in large vehicles such as motor homes, however, will want to avoid it. The 11-mile round-trip **Elephant Hill–Druid Arch hike ★** can be done in 4 to 6 hours and is moderately difficult, with some steep drop-offs and quite a bit of slickrock. But the views are well worth it. You hike through narrow rock canyons, past colorful spires and pinnacles, and on to the huge Druid Arch, which somewhat resembles the stone structures at Stonehenge.

The **Confluence Overlook Trail ★★**, an 11-mile round-trip day or overnight hike, leads to a spectacular bird's-eye view of the confluence of the Green and Colorado rivers and the 1,000-foot-deep gorges they've carved. The hike is moderately difficult, with steep drop-offs and little shade, but it splendidly reveals the many colors of the Needles District, as well as views into the Maze District of the park. Allow 4 to 6 hours.

Unlike most national parks, where all motor vehicles and mountain bikes are restricted to paved roads, Canyonlands has miles of rough roads for four-wheel-drive vehicles. Four-wheelers must stay on designated 4WD roads, but keep in mind that the term "road" can mean anything from a graded, well-marked, two-lane gravel byway to a pile of loose rocks.

Mountain bikes are also allowed on these roads, but they share space with motor vehicles and occasional hikers and horseback riders. Because some of the four-wheel-drive roads have spots of deep sand—which can turn into quicksand when wet—mountain biking may not be as much fun here as you'd expect.

The best four-wheel-drive adventure in the Island in the Sky District is the **White Rim Road** ★★. It winds some 100 miles through the district and affords spectacular views, from broad panoramas of rock and canyon to close-ups of red and orange towers and buttes. A high-clearance 4WD is necessary. Allow 2 to 3 days for the entire trip. There are primitive campgrounds along the way, but reservations and backcountry permits are needed. Mountain bikers also enjoy this trail, especially when accompanying a four-wheel-drive support vehicle with supplies.

Four-wheel-drive fans going into the Needles District will find one of their ultimate challenges on the **Elephant Hill Jeep Road,** which begins at a well-marked turnoff near Squaw Flat Campground. Although most of the 10-mile trail is only moderately difficult, the stretch over Elephant Hill itself (near the beginning of the drive) can be a nightmare. It has steep, rough slickrock, drifting sand, loose rock, and treacherous ledges. Coming down the hill, you'll reach one switchback that requires you to back to the edge of a steep cliff. This road is also a favorite of mountain bikers, although bikes will have to be walked on some stretches because of the abundance of sand and rocks. The route offers views of numerous rock formations, plus panoramas of steep cliffs and rock "stairs." Allow 8 hours to 3 days. Backcountry permits are needed for overnight trips.

For a spectacular view of the Colorado River, the **Colorado River Overlook Road** in the Needles District can't be beat. This 14-mile round-trip is popular with four-wheelers, backpackers, and mountain bikers. Considered among the park's easiest 4WD roads, the first part, accessible by high-clearance two-wheel-drives, is very easy indeed. But the second half has a few rough and rocky sections that require four-wheel-drive. The road features numerous panoramic vistas and a spectacular 360-degree view of the park and the Colorado River, some 1,000 feet below.

Camping in the Park

The park has two developed campgrounds, both first come, first served. In the Island in the Sky District, **Willow Flat Campground** has 12 sites, picnic tables, fire grates, and vault toilets, but no drinking water; camping is $10. In the Needles District, **Squaw Flat Campground** has 26 sites, fire grates, picnic tables, flush toilets, and drinking water; the fee is $15 per night. Both campgrounds are best suited to RVs not more than 28 feet long.

A BASE CAMP IN MOAB

Most visitors to Arches and Canyonlands national parks stay in Moab, which offers easy access to both parks, plenty of other opportunities for outdoor recreation, and an abundance of places to sleep and eat. For information, contact the **Moab Area Travel Council,** P.O. Box 550, Moab, UT 84532 (✆ **800/635-6622** or 435/259-8825; www.discovermoab.com). When you arrive, stop by the **Moab Information Center,** at the corner of Main and Center streets.

Where to Stay

Moab has most of the major chains, located on Main Street. Our favorite of the franchises here is the somewhat pricey but attractive and very well maintained **La Quinta Inn ★★**, 815 S. Main St., Moab, UT 84532 (✆ **435/259-8700;** www.laquintamoab.com), which is pet friendly and has summer rates of $126 to $151 double, with lower off-season rates. Moab's room tax of about 12.25% applies.

Aarchway Inn ★★ Two miles from the entrance to Arches National Park, this well-maintained modern motel has large rooms with great views, all of which are decorated in Southwestern style. Photos on the walls depict the area's scenic attractions. Rooms contain two queen beds or one king, and eight family units also have queen-size sofa beds. The suites have whirlpool tubs. Facilities include a courtyard with barbecue grills, covered and locked bike storage, conference rooms, and a gift shop. The entire property is smoke free.

1551 N. US 191, Moab, UT 84532. ✆ **800/341-9359** or 435/259-2599. Fax 435/259-2270. www.aarchwayinn.com. 97 units. Mar–Oct $139–$159 double, from $159 suite. Off-season discounts available. Rates include continental breakfast. AE, DC, DISC, MC, V. **Amenities:** Exercise room; indoor Jacuzzi; large heated outdoor pool. *In room:* A/C, TV, fridge, microwave, hair dryer, Wi-Fi.

Bowen Motel This family-owned and -operated motel offers fairly large, comfortable, basic rooms with attractive wallpaper, a king- or one or two queen-size beds, and shower/tub combinations. Refrigerators and microwaves are available. Two family rooms sleep up to six persons each. All units are smoke free.

169 N. Main St., Moab, UT 84532. ✆ **800/874-5439** or 435/259-7132. Fax 435/259-6641. www.bowenmotel.com. 40 units. $74–$99 double. Off-season discounts available. Rates include continental breakfast. AE, DC, DISC, MC, V. Pets accepted. **Amenities:** Heated outdoor pool. *In room:* A/C, TV, Wi-Fi.

Red Stone Inn (Value) This centrally located motel is comfortable and quiet, and offers quite a bit for the price. The exterior gives the impression that these are cabins, and the theme continues inside, where colorful posters and maps of area attractions decorate attractive knotty pine walls. Rooms are a bit on the small side, although perfectly adequate and spotlessly maintained. All units have kitchenettes with microwaves, coffeemakers (with coffee supplied), and refrigerators. Three rooms accessible to travelers with disabilities have combination shower/tubs; the rest have showers only. There's a covered picnic area with tables and gas barbecue grills, and a mountain-bike work stand and bike wash. Guests have free access to the pool at a motel across the street.

535 S. Main St., Moab, UT 84532. ✆ **800/772-1972** or 435/259-3500. Fax 435/259-2717. www.moabredstone.com. 52 units. Summer $80–$85 double; lower rates in winter; prices higher in Sept and during special events. AE, DISC, MC, V. Pets accepted ($10 fee). **Amenities:** Access to heated outdoor pool (across street); indoor hot tub. *In room:* A/C, TV, kitchen.

Sunflower Hill Luxury Inn ★★★ This country-style retreat is our top choice in Moab for a relaxing escape. Located 3 blocks off Main Street on a quiet dead-end road, it offers elegant rooms and lovely outdoor areas. The rooms are individually decorated—for instance, the Summer House Suite boasts a colorful garden-themed mural—and have handmade quilts. Deluxe rooms have jetted tubs and private balconies. The grounds are grassy and shady, with fruit trees and flowers in abundance, plus a swing, picnic table, and barbecue. There's also locked, covered bike storage. The substantial breakfast buffet includes homemade breads and fresh-baked pastries, honey-almond granola, fresh fruits, and a hot entree such as a garden vegetable frittata, blueberry pancakes, or asparagus quiche. All units are smoke-free.

185 N. 300 East, Moab, UT 84532. ✆ **800/662-2786** or 435/259-2974. Fax 435/259-3065. www.sunflowerhill.com. 12 units. Mid-mar to Oct and holidays $165–$235 double; Nov to early Mar $125–$185 double. Rates include full breakfast and evening refreshments. AE, DISC, MC, V. Children under 10 are usually not accepted. **Amenities:** Heated outdoor pool; hot tub. *In room:* A/C, TV/VCR, CD player, hair dryer, no phone, Wi-Fi.

Camping

A number of commercial campgrounds in Moab offer hot showers, RV hookups, and other amenities. Among those we especially like are **Archview Resort,** US 191, at the junction with US 313, 9 miles north of town (P.O. Box 938), Moab, UT 84532 (✆ **800/813-6622** or 435/259-7854; www.archviewresort.com). It has 60 sites as well as great views into Arches National Park. For two people, tent sites cost $19 and full-hookup RV sites cost $29 to $36. Rates for cabins start at $40 for two people. Another good choice, especially for those who want to be downtown, is **Canyonlands Campground & RV Park,** 555 S. Main St., Moab, UT 84532 (✆ **800/522-6848** or 435/259-6848; www.canyonlandsrv.com). This quiet, shady campground has 138 sites. For two people, it charges $22 to 25 for tent sites, $33 to $37 for RV sites, and $52 for cabins. Rates for both of these campgrounds include Wi-Fi.

Where to Dine

Buck's Grill House ★★ AMERICAN/SOUTHWESTERN This popular restaurant is our top choice in Moab for steak. The dining room's subdued Western decor is accented by exposed wood beams and local artwork. The attractive patio, away from the road, has trees and a delightful rock waterfall. Especially good is the grilled 14-ounce rib-eye, either plain or rubbed with the restaurant's "cowboy" spices. We also recommend buffalo meatloaf, with black onion gravy and mashed potatoes. Southwestern dishes include duck tamales with adobo and cilantro sauce. Buck's offers full liquor service and a good wine list, and serves a variety of Utah microbrews.

1393 N. US 191, about 1½ miles north of town. ✆ **435/259-5201.** www.bucksgrillhouse.com. Main courses $9–$32. DISC, MC, V. Daily 5:30pm–closing.

Eddie McStiff's ★ AMERICAN This bustling, noisy brewpub is part family restaurant and part tavern, with a climate-controlled garden patio as well. You'll find Southwest decor in the dining room, and the tavern looks just as a tavern should—long bar, low light, and lots of wood. The menu includes a good variety of charbroiled meats, excellent pizzas, and a selection of pasta dishes. Specialties include grilled wild Alaskan salmon and slow-smoked barbecued ribs. About a dozen fresh-brewed beers are on tap. Mixed drinks, wine, and beer are sold in the dining room with food only; the tavern sells beer with or without food. (You must be at least 21 to enter the tavern.)

In McStiff's Plaza, 57 S. Main St. (just south of the information center). ✆ **435/259-2337.** www.eddiemcstiffs.com. Main courses $7–$21. DISC, MC, V. Mon–Fri 5pm–midnight, Sat–Sun noon–midnight.

Moab Diner Kids AMERICAN/SOUTHWESTERN Breakfast—among the best in town—is served all day here. It features all the usual egg dishes, biscuits and gravy, and a spicy breakfast burrito. The decor is definitely diner-esque, but the place does have lots of green plants (real, not plastic). Hamburgers, sandwiches, and salads are the offerings at lunch. For dinner, there are steak, shrimp, and chicken, plus liver and onions. In addition to ice cream, you can get malts and shakes. No alcoholic beverages are served.

189 S. Main St. (2 blocks south of Center St.). ✆ **435/259-4006.** Main courses $4.95–$17. MC, V. Daily 6am–10pm. Closed Jan 1, Thanksgiving, and Dec 25.

18

Las Vegas

Las Vegas is a true original; there is nothing else like it in the world. In other cities, hotels are built near the major attractions. Here, the hotels *are* the major attractions. What other city has a skyline made up of buildings from other cities' skylines? You can also enjoy great works of art, world-renowned chefs, and rock clubs and arenas that attract major acts.

But Vegas is first and foremost a gambling destination. And though the hotels aren't undercharging for everything anymore in an effort to lure you into gambling round the clock, they still do their best to separate you from your cash. The cheap buffets and meal deals still exist, as do some cut-rate rooms, but both are likely to prove the old adage about getting what you pay for. Nevertheless, free drinks are handed to anyone lurking near a slot, and if show tickets aren't in the budget, you won't lack for entertainment. Free lounge shows abound, and the people-watching opportunities alone never disappoint.

Depending on which areas of the southwest you plan to visit, Las Vegas might make a convenient beginning or ending point to your vacation. Because it's such a popular destination, you can often find bargains on airfare and car-rental rates. And in its own way, Vegas is as amazing as the nearby Grand Canyon and every bit as much a must-see. It's one of the Seven Wonders of the Artificial World. And everyone should experience it at least once—you might find yourself coming back for more.

1 ESSENTIALS

GETTING THERE

BY PLANE Almost every major domestic airline, and some international airlines, fly into **McCarran International Airport** (✆ **702/261-5211;** TDD 702/261-3111; www.mccarran.com), just a few minutes' drive from the southern end of the Strip.

Bell Trans (✆ **800/274-7433;** www.bell-trans.com) runs 20-passenger minibuses daily between the airport and all major Las Vegas hotels and motels all day (7:45am–midnight). The cost is $6.50 per person each way to Strip area hotels ($12 round-trip), $8 to $12 to Downtown or other Off-Strip properties.

Even less expensive are **Citizen's Area Transit (CAT)** buses (✆ **702/CAT-RIDE;** www.rtcsnv.com). The no. 108 bus departs every 15 minutes from the airport and takes you to the Stratosphere, where you can transfer to the no. 301, which stops close to most Strip- and Convention Center–area hotels. The no. 109 bus goes from the airport to the Downtown Transportation Center (at Casino Center Blvd. and Stewart Ave.). The fares for buses on Strip routes are $3 one way; Downtown costs $1.75.

Taxis are also plentiful, and a ride to the Strip costs $15 to $20.

BY CAR The main highway connecting Las Vegas with the rest of the country is I-15 from the northeast (Salt Lake City) and southwest (Los Angeles and San Diego). Lots of folks drive up from Los Angeles, and, thanks to the narrow two-lane highway, it can get

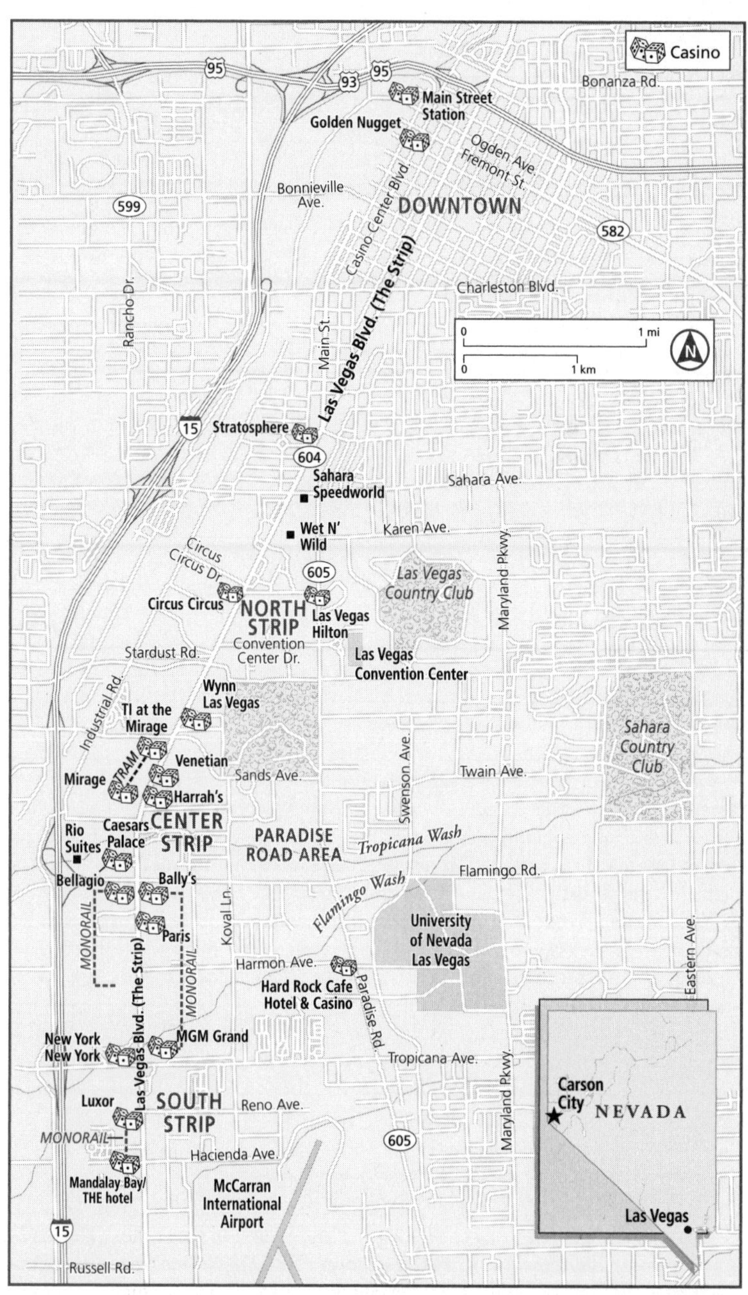
Casino
Bonanza Rd.
Main Street Station
Golden Nugget
Ogden Ave.
Fremont St.
Bonnieville Ave.
Casino Center Blvd.
DOWNTOWN
Charleston Blvd.
Rancho Dr.
Main St.
Las Vegas Blvd. (The Strip)
1 mi
1 km
Stratosphere
Sahara Speedworld
Sahara Ave.
Wet N' Wild
Karen Ave.
Circus Circus Dr.
Las Vegas Country Club
Maryland Pkwy.
Circus Circus
NORTH STRIP
Las Vegas Hilton
Stardust Rd.
Convention Center Dr.
Las Vegas Convention Center
Industrial Rd.
Wynn Las Vegas
TI at the Mirage
Sahara Country Club
Venetian
TRAM
Mirage
Sands Ave.
Swenson Ave.
Twain Ave.
Harrah's
Rio Suites
Caesars Palace
CENTER STRIP
PARADISE ROAD AREA
Tropicana Wash
Flamingo Rd.
Bellagio
Bally's
Flamingo Wash
MONORAIL
Koval Ln.
University of Nevada Las Vegas
Paris
Harmon Ave.
Hard Rock Cafe Hotel & Casino
Paradise Rd.
Eastern Ave.
MGM Grand
New York New York
Tropicana Ave.
Luxor
SOUTH STRIP
Reno Ave.
Carson City
NEVADA
Hacienda Ave.
Mandalay Bay/ THE hotel
McCarran International Airport
Las Vegas
Russell Rd.
95
93
599
582
15
604
605

very crowded on Friday and Sunday afternoons. Other major routes are US 93 from the southeast (Phoenix) and US 95 from the northwest (Reno).

VISITOR INFORMATION

For advance information, call or write the **Las Vegas Convention and Visitors Authority,** 3150 Paradise Rd., Las Vegas, NV 89109 (✆ **877/VISIT-LV** [847-4858] or 702 892-7575; www.visitlasvegas.com). Or stop by when you're in town. They're open daily from 8am to 5pm. Another excellent information source is the **Las Vegas Chamber of Commerce,** 6671 Las Vegas Blvd., S. Ste. 300, Las Vegas, NV 89119 ✆ **702/735-1616;** www.lvchamber.com). They're open Monday through Friday from 8am to 5pm.

GETTING AROUND

BY CAR We highly recommend that visitors rent a car. The Strip is too spread out for walking, and public transportation is often ineffective in getting you from Point A to Point B. All the major hotels offer free parking.

BY BUS & TROLLEY The no. 301 bus, operated by **CAT** (✆ **702/CAT-RIDE** [228-7433]; www.rtcsnv.com), plies a route between the Downtown Transportation Center (at Casino Center Blvd. and Stewart Ave.) and a few miles beyond the southern end of the Strip. The fare is $2 for adults, 60¢ for seniors 62 and older and children 6 to 17, and free for those under 6. For $4, you can get an all-day pass. CAT buses run 24 hours a day and are wheelchair-accessible. Exact change is required.

The Regional Transportation Commission (RTC) recently launched a service called **The Deuce** (✆ **702/CAT-RIDE** [228-7433]; www.rtcsouthernnevada.com/deuce), a fleet of modern double-decker buses that run the length of the Strip into Downtown and near the airport. A one-way ride is $2 for adults, $1 for seniors 62 and older and children 6 to 17, and free for those under 6. For a remarkably low $4, you get an all-day pass that lets you get on and off as many times as you like and also lets you ride all the other RTC buses all day. They even provide recorded color commentary as you sit in the mind-numbing traffic-jams that plug up the Strip most of the time. Exact change is required.

Las Vegas Strip Trolley (✆ **702/382-1404;** www.striptrolley.com) operates a classic streetcar replica that runs northward from Hacienda Avenue, stopping at all major hotels en route to the Sahara, and then looping back via the Las Vegas Hilton. They do not, however, go to the Stratosphere Casino Hotel & Tower or Downtown. Trolleys run about every 15 minutes daily between 9:30am and 1:30am. The fare is $2.50 for a single one-way ride or $4.25 (free for children under 5) for an all-day pass, and exact change is required.

There are also a number of free transportation services, courtesy of the casinos. A free monorail connects Mandalay Bay with Luxor and Excalibur, and a free tram shuttles between The Mirage and TI at the Mirage. Given how far apart even neighboring hotels can be, thanks to their size, and how they seem even farther apart on really hot (and cold and windy) days, these are blessed additions.

BY TAXI Cabs line up in front of all major hotels. They charge $3.30 at the meter drop and 20¢ for each additional 1/12 mile (or $2.40 per mile). A taxi from the airport to the Strip will run you $15 to $20, from the airport to Downtown $18 to $25, and between the Strip and Downtown about $10 to $15. Up to five people can ride for the same fare.

If you want to call a taxi, any of the following companies can provide one: **Desert Cab Company** (✆ **702/386-9102**), **Whittlesea Blue Cab** (✆ **702/384-6111**), or **Yellow/Checker Cab/Star Company** (✆ **702/873-2000**).

For minor problems, try the **Harmon Medical Urgent Care Center,** the closest to the Strip, with doctors and X-ray machines; it's located at 105 E. Harmon at Koval, near the MGM Grand (✆ **702/796-1116;** www.harmonmedicalcenter.com). It's open 24 hours. Emergency services are available 24 hours a day at **University Medical Center,** 1800 W. Charleston Blvd., at Shadow Lane (✆ **702/383-2000;** www.umc-cares.org). **Sunrise Hospital and Medical Center,** 3186 Maryland Pkwy., between Desert Inn Road and Sahara Avenue (✆ **702/731-8080**), also has a 24-hour emergency room. There's a 24-hour **Walgreens** (which has a 1-hr. photo service) at 3765 Las Vegas Blvd. S. (✆ **702/895-6878**), almost directly across from the Monte Carlo.

The sales tax on meals, goods, and some services is 7.75%. Clark County hotel room tax is 9%, and in Henderson it's 10%.

2 WHERE TO STAY

If there's one thing Vegas has in spades, it's hotels. Big hotels. The hotels here are the city's biggest tourist attraction, and they pack in the crowds accordingly. A last-minute Vegas vacation can turn into a housing nightmare, so make reservations in advance.

First-time visitors will most likely stay on the Strip, although Downtown is a lot nicer than it used to be, and the rates there are cheaper. The **Las Vegas Convention and Visitors Authority** runs a room reservations hot line (✆ **877/VISIT-LV** [847-4858] or 702/892-0711; www.visitlasvegas.com) that can be helpful.

Vegas does have hotels that eschew the theme scheme. Unlike many of the casino hotels, they are far more likely to cater to kids, making them good choices for families. One of two great selections is the luxurious **Four Seasons** (✆ **877/632-5000** or 702/632-5000; www.fourseasons.com), inside the Mandalay Bay, although it has its own entrance and facilities. The **Residence Inn by Marriott,** 3225 Paradise Rd., Las Vegas, NV 89109, between Desert Inn Road and Convention Center Drive (✆ **800/331-3131** or 702/796-9300; www.marriott.com), offers clean apartmentlike accommodations with full kitchens and sitting rooms.

All the usual budget chains, including Motel 6, Days Inn, Howard Johnson, Fairfield by Marriott, and Econo Lodge, are in Las Vegas.

VERY EXPENSIVE

Bellagio ★★ This $1.6 billion luxury resort is a big, grand, state-of-the-art Vegas hotel. Here you'll find fabulous fountains, classical gardens, an art gallery, and the best collection of restaurants in town. There is even an 8-acre Lake Como stand-in out front, complete with a dazzling choreographed water ballet extravaganza. Rooms are nicely decorated and the roomy bathrooms are even more luxurious. Service is surprisingly good given the size of the place. The pool area is exceptional and the spa is marvelous, if overpriced.

3600 Las Vegas Blvd. S. (at the corner of Flamingo Rd.), Las Vegas, NV 89109. ✆ **888/987-6667** or 702/693-7111. Fax 702/693-8546. www.bellagio.com. 3,933 units. $159 and up double. Extra person $35. AE, DC, DISC, MC, V. Free self- and valet parking. **Amenities:** 14 restaurants; nightclub; casino; concierge; large health club & spa; 6 outdoor pools; room service; executive-level rooms; showrooms; wedding chapel. *In room:* A/C, TV w/pay movies, hair dryer, Wi-Fi (for a fee).

Caesars Palace ★★ Caesars is the spectacle that every Vegas hotel should be. A combination of Vegas luxury and a good dose of camp, the hotel is graced by Roman colonnades, marble fountains, and staff members attired in gladiator outfits and togas. But the hotel has a confusing layout, and it takes forever to get anywhere. Accommodations occupy five towers; art in the rooms keeps to the Greco-Roman theme. The newest rooms are handsome, if not as giggle-inducingly overwhelming as the classic ones, and have floor-to-ceiling windows that offer a hypnotizing panoramic view. You'll likely enjoy a lavish bathroom with marble floor, European fixtures, and oversize marble tubs (about half are whirlpools). The **Garden of the Gods** pool area is a tasteful masterpiece.

3570 Las Vegas Blvd. S. (just north of Flamingo Rd.), Las Vegas, NV 89109. ✆ **877/427-7243** or 702/731-7110. Fax 702/697-5706. www.caesarspalace.com. 3,348 units. $150 and up double; $549 and up suite. Extra person $30. AE, DC, DISC, MC, V. Free self- and valet parking. **Amenities:** 25 restaurants; nightclub; casino; concierge; health club & spa; 4 outdoor pools; room service; executive-level rooms; 4 wedding chapels. *In room:* A/C, TV w/pay movies, hair dryer, robe/slippers, Wi-Fi (for a fee).

Hard Rock Hotel & Casino ★★ The hip flock to the Hard Rock, drawn by the cool 'n' rockin' ambience that pervades the place, from the piano-shaped roulette tables to the "backstage pass" room keys. The new and newly updated rooms are still a bit too '60s-futuristic hip to come off as posh, but they're certainly less immediately drab than the older versions, and they're more comfortable. Bathrooms are a big step forward—bigger, brighter, shinier. On warm days and nights the Hard Rock's beach-party pool is *the* hangout scene. ***Note:*** At press time, it was announced that $750 million worth of new hotel towers, including one that is all suites for VIPs, would open in September 2009.

4455 Paradise Rd. (at Harmon Ave.), Las Vegas, NV 89109. ✆ **800/473-ROCK** (7625) or 702/693-5000. Fax 702/693-5588. www.hardrockhotel.com. 657 units. $119 and up double; $250 and up suite. Extra person $75. Children 12 and under stay free in parent's room. AE, DC, MC, V. Free self- and valet parking. **Amenities:** 6 restaurants; concierge; casino; small health club & spa; 2 outdoor pools w/lazy river and sandy-beach bottom; room service; executive-level rooms; showroom. *In room:* A/C, TV w/pay movies, hair dryer, high-speed Internet access (for a fee).

Las Vegas Hilton ★★ This classy hotel is magnificent, from its lobby, glittering with massive chandeliers and gleaming marble, to its 8-acre recreation deck. The Hilton's location next to the convention center makes it the preferred choice of business travelers, and its Star Trek attraction—with its own space-themed casino—beams in the leisure crowd. The comfortable rooms have bathrooms with large marble tubs; some rooms offer views of an adjacent golf course. The lobby and older casino areas have been completely remodeled, giving the whole place a much more modern feel.

3000 Paradise Rd. (at Riviera Blvd.), Las Vegas, NV 89109. ✆ **888/732-7117** or 702/732-5111. Fax 702/732-5805. www.lvhilton.com. 3,174 units. $59 and up double; $275 and up suite. Extra person $35. Children 17 and under stay free in parent's room. AE, DC, DISC, MC, V. Free self- and valet parking. **Amenities:** 8 restaurants; casino; health club & spa; outdoor pool; room service; executive-level rooms; showrooms; 6 night-lit tennis courts. *In room:* A/C, TV w/pay movies, hair dryer, high-speed Internet access (for a fee).

Paris Las Vegas Casino Resort ★ *Sacre bleu!* The City of Light comes to Sin City in this Strip fantasy hotel. It's theme-run-amok time again, and we are so happy about it. You can stroll down a mini Rue de la Paix, ride an elevator to the top of the Eiffel Tower, stop at an overpriced bakery for a baguette, take your photo by several very nice fountains, and snicker at dubious French signage ("le car rental"). Rooms are disappointingly uninteresting, with furniture that only hints at mock French Regency, and with small but pretty bathrooms that have deep tubs. Try to get a Strip-facing room so you can see the

Bellagio's fountains across the street. Overall, not a bad place to stay but a great place to visit.

3655 Las Vegas Blvd. S., Las Vegas, NV 89109. ✆ **888/BONJOUR** (266-5687) or 702/946-7000. www.parislv.com. 2,916 units. $110 and up double; $530 and up suites. Extra person $30. Children 17 and under stay free in parent's room. AE, DC, DISC, MC. V. Free self- and valet parking. **Amenities:** 12 restaurants; casino; concierge; health club & spa; outdoor pool; room service; executive-level rooms; showrooms; 2 wedding chapels. *In room:* A/C, TV w/pay movies, hair dryer, high-speed Internet access (for a fee).

The Venetian ★★ The Venetian falls squarely between an outright adult Disneyland experience and the luxury resort sensibility of other Vegas hotels. The hotel impressively re-creates the city of Venice, including the outrageous prices. Rooms are the largest and probably the most handsome in town. They are all "suites," with a good-size bedroom giving way to steps down to a sunken living area, complete with pullout sofa bed. Bathrooms feature glassed-in showers, deep soaking tubs, double sinks, fluffy towels, and lots of space. A branch of the famous Canyon Ranch Spa is on the premises. If there's a weak point, it's the hotel's pool area, which is disappointing and bland.

3355 Las Vegas Blvd. S., Las Vegas, NV 89109. ✆ **888/2-VENICE** (283-6423) or 702/414-1000. Fax 702/414-4805. www.venetian.com. 4,027 units. $169 and up double. Extra person $35. Children 12 and under stay free in parent's room. AE, DC, DISC, MC, V. Free self- and valet parking. **Amenities:** 18 restaurants; casino; concierge; health club & spa; 6 outdoor pools; room service; executive-level rooms; showroom; 3 wedding venues. *In room:* A/C, TV w/pay movies, fax, fridge, hair dryer, high-speed Internet access (for a fee).

EXPENSIVE

The Flamingo Las Vegas ★ Gradually, all the Flamingo's dated rooms are getting upgraded. Rushing headlong into the Dean Martin/Rat Pack retro vibe, they are kicky candy modern, with hot pink accent walls, hot pink lights in the bathroom where you can also find TV screens embedded in the mirror, candy striped wallpaper, black and white photos of the Flamingo from its early days, squishy white beds with chocolate accents and vinyl padded headboards, huge flat screens with HDTV, iPod docking stations, and more. Two-bedroom suites scream classic playboy bachelor pad. The Flamingo's exceptional pool area encompasses fishponds, two water slides, five swimming pools, two whirlpools, waterfalls, and a flamingo enclave—plus its spa and tennis courts are a big draw.

3555 Las Vegas Blvd. S. (btw. Sands Ave. and Flamingo Rd.), Las Vegas, NV 89109. ✆ **800/732-2111** or 702/733-3111. Fax 702/733-3353. www.flamingolv.com. 3,517 units. $70 and up double; $130 and up suite. Extra person $30. Timeshare suites available. AE, DC, DISC, MC, V. Free self- and valet parking. **Amenities:** 8 restaurants; casino; health club & spa; 5 outdoor pools; room service; executive-level rooms; showrooms; 3 night-lit tennis courts; 6 wedding venues. *In room:* A/C, TV w/pay movies, hair dryer, high-speed Internet access (for a fee).

Golden Nugget ★★ The Grande Dame of Downtown got some much-needed attention, with new restaurants, remodeled rooms and public spaces, a big new pool, and even an entire new hotel tower going in across the street (or more specifically, on the street—they got permission to take over a small, rarely used lane just to the north of the existing property). The completed phases look terrific; a new color scheme has given it a rich, deep look that is most posh and fresh. Everything feels brighter, lighter, and more spacious. Rooms are comparable to midrange on the Strip, which makes them quite good for Downtown. You don't have to walk through the casino to get to your room, but you do have to walk a distance to get to the pool, which has an aquarium where you can get up close and personal with various marine life (with only a glass wall separating you). The presence of the pool, and general overall quality, makes this the best hotel Downtown for families.

129 E. Fremont St. (at Casino Center Blvd.), Las Vegas, NV 89101. ✆ **800/846-5336** or 702/385-7111. Fax 702/386-8362. www.goldennugget.com. 1,907 units. $59 and up double; $209 and up suite. Extra person $20. AE, DC, DISC, MC, V. Free self- and valet parking. **Amenities:** 5 restaurants; casino; health club & spa; outdoor pool; room service; executive-level rooms; showroom. *In room:* A/C, TV w/pay movies, hair dryer, high-speed Internet access (for a fee), robe/slippers.

Harrah's Las Vegas ★ There is much to like here, and occasional quite good rates might make the so-so bits worth overlooking. Make sure to ask for a newly renovated room. The rooms have undergone some cosmetic fluffing to the tune of good new mattresses and those white bed covers now more or less standard in most local hotels. Dark masculine decor is an odd choice for such a festive place. The rooms aren't flashy, but they are reliable for what is ultimately a gamblers' hotel. The hotel's health club is one of the best on the Strip, but its pool is underwhelming.

3475 Las Vegas Blvd. S. (btw. Flamingo and Spring Mountain roads), Las Vegas, NV 89109. ✆ **800/HARRAHS** (427-7247) or 702/369-5000. Fax 702/369-5283. www.harrahs.com. 2,526 units. $70 and up double; $110 and up minisuite. Extra person $30. AE, DC, DISC, MC, V. Free self- and valet parking. **Amenities:** 9 restaurants; casino; concierge; health club & spa; outdoor pool; room service; executive-level rooms; showrooms. *In room:* A/C, TV w/pay movies, hair dryer, high-speed Internet access (for a fee).

Mandalay Bay ★★ Kids Mandalay Bay is one of our favorite hotels. It doesn't really evoke Southeast Asia, but the Mandalay Bay actually looks like a resort hotel rather than just a Vegas version of one. You don't have to walk through the casino to get to any of these public areas or the guest room elevators, the pool area is spiffy, and the whole complex is less overwhelming than some of the neighboring behemoths. Rooms are perhaps the finest on the Strip, spacious and subdued in decor. The large bathrooms, stocked with a host of fabulous amenities, are certainly the best on the Strip and maybe the best in Vegas. The hotel's highly touted wave pool isn't very surf friendly, but it does offer a nice afternoon's relaxation. Note that a topless swimming area opened in 2003.

3950 Las Vegas Blvd. S. (at Hacienda Ave.), Las Vegas, NV 89119. ✆ **877/632-7000** or 702/632-7000. Fax 702/632-7228. www.mandalaybay.com. 3,309 units. $90 and up double; $130 and up suite. Extra person $30. Children 15 and under free in parent's room. AE, DC, DISC, MC, V. Free self- and valet parking. **Amenities:** 22 restaurants; aquarium; casino; concierge; health club & spa; Jacuzzi; 4 outdoor pools w/lazy river & wave pool; room service; executive-level rooms; sauna; watersports equipment/rentals; 1,700-seat performing-arts theater; 2 wedding chapels. *In room:* A/C, TV w/pay movies, hair dryer, Wi-Fi (for a fee).

MGM Grand Hotel/Casino ★★ Kids We've grown very fond of this hotel. Although the original standard rooms in the main tower with their 1930s-era Hollywood glam styling have been replaced by somewhat more blandly upscale decor, they are generously proportioned and equipped with pretty much everything you might need. A second section of the tower is now known as the West Wing, and it is here that you'll find the memorable accommodations. These rooms are smaller (a rather tiny 350 sq. ft.) but full of the trendy touches we are complete suckers for. There is no counter space in the open bathroom plan, but frosted green glass doors preserve privacy. DVD and CD players, TVs in the bathroom mirrors, and fluffy bedding, plus liberal use of electronic "gee whiz" moments like lamps that turn on and off if you touch them, while all lights in the rooms are controlled by the insertion of your room key. The Lion Habitat and fabulous pool area make this place popular with families.

3799 Las Vegas Blvd. S. (at Tropicana Ave.), Las Vegas, NV 89109. ✆ **800/929-1111** or 702/891-7777. Fax 702/891-1030. www.mgmgrand.com. 5,034 units. $120 and up standard double; $145 and up suite. Extra person $35. Children 13 and under stay free in parent's room. AE, DC, DISC, MC, V. Free self- and valet parking. **Amenities:** 15 restaurants; nightclub; casino; concierge; Lion Habitat; large health club & spa; Jacuzzi; 5 outdoor pools w/lazy river; room service; executive-level rooms; showroom; cabaret theater; 2 wedding chapels. *In room:* A/C, TV w/pay movies, hair dryer, high-speed Internet access (for a fee).

The Mirage ★★ You walk into the Mirage and breathe the faintly tropically perfumed air, and it's just a different experience from most Vegas hotels. The hotel, fronted by waterfalls and tropical foliage, centers on a very "active" volcano that erupts every 15 minutes after dark. Inside, you'll find a verdant rainforest. The rooms have been redone and while the results are not distinctive, they are handsome. The overall effect is more beach than Caribbean. Super-deluxe rooms have whirlpool tubs. The staff is genuinely helpful; any problems that may arise are quickly smoothed out. The pool is one of the nicest in Vegas.

3400 Las Vegas Blvd. S. (btw. Flamingo and Spring Mountain roads.), Las Vegas, NV 89109. ✆ **800/627-6667** or 702/791-7111. Fax 702/791-7446. www.mirage.com. 3,044 units. $109 and up double; $350 and up suite. Extra person $30. AE, DC, DISC, MC, V. Free self- and valet parking. **Amenities:** 11 restaurants; casino; concierge; health club & spa; beautiful outdoor pool & Jacuzzi; room service; executive-level rooms; showrooms. *In room:* A/C, TV w/pay movies, hair dryer, high-speed Internet (for a fee).

Monte Carlo Resort & Casino ★ This European-style hotel casino is not as theme-intensive as its Strip brethren—a nice change of pace from the usual Vegas kitsch. Its pool area, once the very last word in local pool fun, is now put to shame by better versions at Mandalay Bay and the MGM Grand. We love that the guest rooms are accessible without going through the casino, but we don't really love the rooms themselves, which are unimaginatively decorated and smaller than what we've grown accustomed to, especially in terms of bathroom square-footage.

3770 Las Vegas Blvd. S. (btw. Flamingo Rd. and Tropicana Ave.), Las Vegas, NV 89109. ✆ **800/311-8999** or 702/730-7777. Fax 702/730-7250. www.montecarlo.com. 3,002 units. $90 and up double; $140 and up suite. Extra person $25. AE, DC, DISC, MC, V. Free self- and valet parking. **Amenities:** 7 restaurants plus a food court; casino; concierge; health club & spa; Jacuzzi; outdoor pool w/wave pool & lazy river; room service; executive-level rooms; watersports equipment/rentals; showroom; wedding chapel. *In room:* A/C, TV w/pay movies, hair dryer, high-speed Internet access (for a fee).

New York–New York Hotel & Casino ★★ (Kids) A visit to this spectacular hotel, which looks like the New York City skyline (complete with a roller coaster running through it) is a must. Subtle it isn't. You can gamble in a casino done up as Central Park or play games in the Coney Island arcade. Recently redecorated rooms come in 64 different styles, with the original Deco-inspired decor having been replaced by something they call '40s inspired. Light sleepers should request a room away from the roller coaster. If you're a pool person, go elsewhere—the one here is pretty mediocre.

3790 Las Vegas Blvd. S. (at Tropicana Ave.), Las Vegas, NV 89109. ✆ **800/693-6763** or 702/740-6969. Fax 702/740-6920. www.nynyhotelcasino.com. 2,023 units. $90 and up double; suite $190 and up. Extra person $30. AE, DC, DISC, MC, V. Free self- and valet parking. **Amenities:** 9 restaurants plus a food court; casino; concierge; small health club & spa; Jacuzzi; outdoor pool; room service; executive-level rooms; showrooms. *In room:* A/C, TV w/pay movies, hair dryer, high-speed Internet access (for a fee).

Planet Hollywood Resort & Casino ★ Those looking for the pop kitsch sensibility of the Planet Hollywood restaurants will be disappointed; it's actually kind of classy and design intensive. What it really offers that's different are the rooms. Each has a movie or entertainment theme. Beds have purple velour padded headboards and the beds themselves are the Sheraton Four Comforts pillow-top thing. Bathrooms are larger than the standard bathroom but neither the largest on the Strip nor special enough to match the sleeping areas. The hotel also has its own arena, the **Center for the Performing Arts,** which attracts big names. Finally, there is the **Mandera spa ★★★**, maybe aesthetically our hands-down local favorite.

3667 Las Vegas Blvd. S., Las Vegas, NV 89109. ✆ **877/333-9474** or 702/785-5555. Fax 702/785-5558. www.planethollywood.com. 2,600 units. $99 and up double; 1-bedroom suite $599. Extra person $30 (no charge in 1-bedroom suite). AE, DC, DISC, MC, V. Free self- and valet parking. **Amenities:** 19 restaurants; 7 bars/lounges; babysitting; casino; chapel; concierge; health club & spa; 2 Jacuzzis; 2 outdoor pools; room service; executive-level rooms; performing-arts theater; showroom. *In room:* A/C, TV w/pay movies, hair dryer, high-speed Internet access (for a fee), free bottle of alcohol for each night's stay.

Rio All Suite Hotel & Casino ★ Although it's not on the Strip, the Rio Suite has a carnival atmosphere that packs in the crowds—and the accompanying noise. In addition to its tropically themed resort, the Rio has an immensely popular 41-story tower and Masquerade Village that simulate a European village, complete with shops, restaurants, and a bizarre live-action show in the sky. The "suites" are actually one rather large room with a sofa and coffee table. Rooms feature amenities such as fridges, and floor-to-ceiling windows offer views of the Strip. Note that the hotel actively discourages guests from bringing children.

3700 W. Flamingo Rd. (just west of I-15), Las Vegas, NV 89103. ✆ **888/752-9746** or 702/777-7777. Fax 702/777-7611. www.riolasvegas.com. 2,582 units. $70 and up double-occupancy suite, upper floors. Extra person $30. AE, DC, MC, V. Free self- and valet parking. **Amenities:** 12 restaurants, plus additional sports-book dining; casino; concierge; health club & spa; 4 outdoor pools; golf course; room service; executive-level rooms; showrooms. *In room:* A/C, TV w/pay movies, fridge, hair dryer, high-speed Internet (for a fee).

TI at the Mirage ★★ Huh? What happened to Treasure Island? What happened to the pirates? Why, Vegas grew up, that's what. Originally the most modern family-friendly hotel, the former Treasure Island was a blown-up version of Disneyland's Pirates of the Caribbean. But that's all behind them now, and the name change is there to make sure you understand this is a grown-up, sophisticated resort. What remains, after they stripped the pirate gilt, are good-size rooms in modified French Regency style that are much nicer than most in their price range. The pool is not that memorable, however.

3300 Las Vegas Blvd. S. (at Spring Mountain Rd.), Las Vegas, NV 89177-0711. ✆ **800/944-7444** or 702/894-7111. Fax 702/894-7446. www.treasureisland.com. 2,891 units. $69 and up double; $99 and up suite. Extra person $25. Inquire about packages. AE, DC, DISC, MC, V. Free self- and valet parking. **Amenities:** 11 restaurants; casino; concierge; health club & spa; outdoor pool; room service; executive-level rooms; showrooms. *In room:* A/C, TV w/pay movies, fax, hair dryer, Wi-Fi (for a fee).

MODERATE

Luxor Las Vegas ★★ (Kids It would be hard to miss the Luxor's 30-story pyramid, even without the 315,000-watt light beam at the top. The hotel is, despite outward appearances, inviting, classy, and functional. The Egyptian Revival lobby has been redone in marble and cherrywood and is one of the nicest lobbies in town. The pyramid rooms cross Egyptian kitsch with Art Deco stylings, including gleaming inlaid wood furniture and a hilarious hieroglyphic bedspread. Marvelous views are offered through the slanted windows (the higher up, the better, of course), but the bathrooms are shower-only, no tubs. Tower rooms are even heavier on the Egyptian motif, pleasing in a campy way but not as aesthetically successful. High-speed "inclinator" elevators run on a 39-degree angle, making the ride up to the Pyramid rooms a bit of a thrill. Two notable attractions here are **Titanic: The Artifact Exhibition** and **Bodies . . . The Exhibition.** Another child-pleaser is the 18,000-square-foot Games of the Gods Arcade.

3900 Las Vegas Blvd. S. (btw. Reno and Hacienda aves.), Las Vegas, NV 81119. ✆ **888/777-0188** or 702/262-4000. Fax 702/262-4478. www.luxor.com. 4,400 units. $55 and up double; $125 and up suite. Extra person $30. Children 11 and under stay free in parent's room. AE, DC, DISC, MC, V. Free self- and valet parking. **Amenities:** 7 restaurants plus a food court; casino; concierge; health club & spa; nightclub; 5 outdoor pools; room service; executive-level rooms; showrooms. *In room:* A/C, TV w/pay movies, hair dryer, high-speed Internet access (for a fee).

Stratosphere Casino Hotel & Tower ★ Kids At 1,149 feet, the Stratosphere is the tallest building west of the Mississippi; it's also in the middle of nowhere on the Strip, which explains the lack of crowds (and lower prices). The panoramic views available from the top of the tower and some amazing thrill rides (see "What to See & Do," later in this chapter) are the big attractions here. The smaller-size rooms here are basically motel rooms—really nice motel rooms, but with that level of comfort and style. Then again, you can often get such a room for around $50 a night. Perfect if you are coming to Vegas with no plans to spend time in your room except to sleep (if even that). Other elements to like include an area with kiddie-oriented rides, a pool with a view, and some of the friendliest, most accommodating staff in town. You can still ride the following incredible thrill rides (provided the wind isn't blowing too hard that day) on top of the tower: the **Big Shot,** a fabulous free-fall ride that thrusts passengers up and down the tower at speeds of up to 45 mph; **X-Scream,** a giant teeter-totter-style device that gives you the sensation of falling off the side of the building; and **Insanity: the Ride,** a whirly-gig contraption that spins you around more than 900 feet above terra firma.

2000 Las Vegas Blvd. S. (btw. St. Louis and Baltimore aves.), Las Vegas, NV 89104. ✆ **800/99-TOWER** (998-6937) or 702/380-7777. Fax 702/383-5334. www.stratospherehotel.com. 2,444 units. $60 and up double; $160 and up suite. Extra person $20. Children 12 and under stay free in parent's room. AE, DC, DISC, MC, V. Free self- and valet parking. **Amenities:** 9 restaurants, plus several fast-food outlets; casino; concierge; large pool area w/great views of the Strip; room service; executive-level rooms; showrooms; wedding chapel; free Wi-Fi in coffee shop in casino. *In room:* A/C, TV w/pay movies, hair dryer, high-speed Internet access (for a fee).

INEXPENSIVE

Circus Circus Hotel/Casino ★ Kids Circus Circus, once the epitome of kitsch, is trying to be taken more seriously. The bright primary colors and garish trims have vanished in favor of subtle, muted tones and high-rent touches that appeal more to the Cirque du Soleil crowd. Nevertheless, the world's largest permanent circus and indoor theme park are still here, and kids will love it. Tower rooms have newish, just slightly better-than-average furnishings; the Manor section comprises five white three-story buildings out back. These rooms are usually among the least expensive in town, but you get what you pay for. A renovation of these rooms added a coat of paint and some new photos on the wall, but not much else. The hotel also has its own RV park.

2880 Las Vegas Blvd. S. (btw. Circus Circus and Convention Center drives), Las Vegas, NV 89109. ✆ **877/434-9175** or 702/734-0410. Fax 702/734-5897. www.circuscircus.com. 3,774 units. $50 and up double. Extra person $15. Children 16 and under stay free in parent's room. AE, DC, DISC, MC, V. Free self- and valet parking. **Amenities:** 7 restaurants and several fast-food outlets; casino; circus acts; midway-style carnival games; 2 outdoor pools; room service; executive-level rooms; wedding chapel. *In room:* A/C, TV w/pay movies, hair dryer, high-speed Internet access (for a fee).

Main Street Station ★★ Finds The Main Street Station, one of the best bargains in the city, is just 2 short blocks away from Fremont Street in Downtown, barely a 3-minute walk. The overall look is turn-of-the-20th-century San Francisco, and the details, from the ornate chandeliers to the wood-paneled lobby, are outstanding. The long and narrow rooms are possibly the largest in Downtown, decorated with French provincial furniture. A 2005 overhaul gave them positively modern furnishings, new carpet and wall coverings, and updated fixtures in the bathrooms. The bathrooms are small but well appointed. If you're a light sleeper, request a room on the south side.

200 N. Main St. (btw. Fremont St. and I-95), Las Vegas, NV 89101. ✆ **800/465-0711** or 702/387-1896. Fax 702/386-4466. www.mainstreetcasino.com. 406 units. $40 and up double; $100 and up suite. $10 for extra person. Children 13 and under stay free in parent's room. AE, DC, DISC, MC, V. Free self- and valet parking. **Amenities:** 3 restaurants; casino; access to outdoor pool at nearby California Hotel; free Wi-Fi available in lobby. *In room:* A/C, TV w/pay movies.

3 WHERE TO DINE

The dining scene in Las Vegas is a melting pot of midnight steak specials, cheap buffets, and gourmet rooms that rival those found in New York or Los Angeles. One word of warning: You can eat well in Vegas, and you can eat cheaply in Vegas, but it's hard to do both at the same time.

Theme restaurant buffs can chow down at **House of Blues,** in Mandalay Bay, 3950 Las Vegas Blvd. S. (✆ 702/632-7605); the **Hard Rock Cafe,** 4475 Paradise Rd., at Harmon Avenue (✆ 702/733-7625); **ESPN,** in New York–New York, 3790 Las Vegas Blvd. S. (✆ 702/933-3776); the **Harley-Davidson Cafe,** 3725 Las Vegas Blvd. S., at Harmon Avenue (✆ 702/740-4555); the **Rainforest Café,** in MGM Grand, 3799 Las Vegas Blvd. S. (✆ 702/891-8580); or Jimmy Buffett's **Margaritaville,** in The Flamingo, 3555 Las Vegas Blvd. S. (✆ 702/733-3302).

For those wanting to sample one of the many hotel buffets, some of the better bets include **Luxor's Pharaoh's Pheast Buffet,** 3900 Las Vegas Blvd. S. (✆ 702/262-4000); **Mirage Cravings Buffet,** 3400 Las Vegas Blvd. S. (✆ 702/791-7111); **Rio's Carnival World Buffet,** 3700 W. Flamingo Rd. (✆ 702/252-7777); **Le Village Buffet,** in Paris Las Vegas, 3665 Las Vegas Blvd. S. (✆ 888/266-5687); **Golden Nugget Buffet,** 129 E. Fremont St. (✆ 702/385-7111); and **Main Street Station Garden Court,** 200 N. Main St. (✆ 702/387-1896). The best Sunday brunch buffet in Vegas is **Bally's Sterling Sunday Brunch,** 3645 Las Vegas Blvd. S. (✆ 702/967-7999), which costs $85 per person.

VERY EXPENSIVE

Aureole ★★★ NOUVELLE AMERICAN This branch of a New York City fave is noted for its glass wine tower. It's four stories of probably the finest wine collection in Vegas. The menu is a three-course prix fixe, though if you are winsome enough, they might send out luxurious extras like pâté on brioche topped with shaved truffles. Expect marvels such as a tender roasted lamb loin and braised shoulder. Everything demonstrates the hand of a true chef in the kitchen, someone paying close attention to his work and to his customers. Service is solicitous; desserts are playful, including a bittersweet chocolate soufflé with blood-orange sorbet. There is also an excellent cheese plate.

In Mandalay Bay, 3950 Las Vegas Blvd. S. ✆ **877/632-1766.** www.aureolelv.com. Reservations required. Fixed-price dinner $75; tasting menu $95. AE, DISC, MC, V. Sun–Thurs 6–10:30pm, Fri–Sat 5:30–10:30pm.

Picasso ★★★ FRENCH Madrid-born Chef Julian Serrano's cooking stands proudly next to the $30 million worth of Picassos that pepper the dining room's walls, making a meal here a truly memorable experience. This may well be the best restaurant in Vegas. The menu changes nightly and is always a choice between a four- or five-course fixed-price dinner or tasting menu. We were bowled over by roasted Maine lobster with a "trio" of corn—kernels, sauce, and flan. Hudson Valley foie gras was crusted in truffles and went down smoothly. And finally, the lamb rôti was an outstanding piece of lamb, crusted with truffles—just hope it's on the menu the night you're there. For dessert, a molten chocolate cake leaves any other you may have tried in the dust.

In Bellagio, 3600 Las Vegas Blvd. S. ✆ **866/259-7111.** Reservations recommended. Fixed-price 4-course dinner $113; 5-course dégustation $123. AE, DC, DISC, MC, V. Wed–Mon 6–9:30pm.

EXPENSIVE

Border Grill ★★★ MEXICAN For our money, here's the best Mexican food in town. This big cheerful space houses a branch of the much lauded L.A. restaurant, conceived and run by the Food Network's "Two Hot Tamales," Mary Sue Milliken and Susan Feniger. This is truly authentic Mexican home cooking. Consequently, don't expect precisely the same food you would encounter in your favorite corner joint, but do expect fresh and fabulous food, arranged as brightly on the plates as the decor on the walls. Don't miss the dense but fluffy Mexican chocolate cream pie (with a meringue crust).

In Mandalay Bay, 3950 Las Vegas Blvd. S. ✆ **702/632-7403.** www.bordergrill.com. Reservations recommended. Main courses $15–$28. AE, DC, DISC, MC, V. Sun–Thurs 11:30am–10pm; Fri–Sat 11:30am–11pm.

Canaletto ★★ ITALIAN Come here for solid, true Italian fare—and that means less sauce-intensive than the red-checked-tablecloth establishments of our American youths. Here, the emphasis is on the pasta, not the accompaniments. This place is all the more enjoyable for being perched on the faux St. Mark's Square; in theory, you can pretend you are sitting on the edge of the real thing, a fantasy we don't mind admitting we briefly indulged in. On our last visit, we had a risotto of porcini, sausage, and white-truffle oil that was full of strong flavors, while the wood-fired roast chicken was perfectly moist. You know, a properly roasted chicken should be a much-celebrated thing, and that alone may be a reason to come here.

In The Venetian Grand Canal Shoppes, 3377 Las Vegas Blvd. S. ✆ **702/733-0070.** Reservations recommended for dinner. Main courses $14–$36. AE, DC, MC, V. Sun–Thurs 11:30am–11pm; Fri–Sat 11:30am–midnight.

Rosemary's Restaurant ★★★ NOUVELLE AMERICAN A 15-minute (or so) drive down Sahara is all it takes to eat what the *Vegas-Review Journal* calls the best food in Las Vegas. Rosemary's cuisine covers most regions of the U.S., though Southern influences dominate. Seared foie gras with peach coulis, candied walnuts, and vanilla bean–scented arugula is like a quilt, with distinct flavors that all hang together nicely. Interesting sides include ultrarich bleu-cheese slaw, slightly spicy crispy fried tortilla strips, and perfect cornmeal jalapeño hush puppies. On a recent visit we had the crispy striped bass, among the better fish dishes we've ever had. Desserts are most pleasant. We also recommend trying some of the restaurant's beer suggestions.

8125 W. Sahara. ✆ **702/869-2251.** www.rosemarysrestaurant.com. Reservations strongly recommended. Lunch $14–$17; fixed-price 3-course lunch $28; dinner $24–$39; fixed-price 3-course dinner $55. AE, MC, V. Mon–Fri 11:30am–2:30pm and 5:30–10:30pm; Sat–Sun 5:30–10:30pm.

Second Street Grill ★ Finds INTERNATIONAL/PACIFIC RIM One of the better-kept secrets of Las Vegas, this Downtown jewel is a lovely bit of romantic, cozy class with excellent food to boot. You are probably best off with grill dishes, though here might be your best ratio of quality to price for lobster tail. Play around with the Hunan pork and beef lettuce wrap appetizers, and the Peking duck and shrimp tacos. The waist-conscious will be very pleased with the bamboo-steamed snapper in a nice broth, while others may want to try the grilled salmon with goat cheese Parmesan crust. Desserts are disappointing, unfortunately. Overall, a nice place for a family-event dinner Downtown, and certainly more affordable than fancy places on the Strip.

In Fremont Hotel & Casino, 200 E. Fremont St. ✆ **702/385-3232.** Reservations recommended. Main courses $17–$30. AE, DC, DISC, MC, V. Sun–Mon and Thurs 5–10pm; Fri–Sat 5–11pm.

MODERATE

Grand Wok ★★ Value ASIAN No longer thoroughly pan-Asian but still a solid choice for sushi and, more importantly, budget fare in the form of the combo soup full of noodles and different kinds of meat. It's particularly nice and more affordable than the usual hotel restaurant—and the primarily Asian clientele clearly agrees. Note that soup portions are most generous; four people could easily split one order and have a nice and very inexpensive lunch, an unexpected bargain option for the Strip.

In MGM Grand, 3799 Las Vegas Blvd. S. ✆ **702/891-7777.** Reservations not accepted. Main courses $9–$19; sushi rolls and pieces $4.50–$15. AE, DC, DISC, MC, V. Restaurant Sun–Thurs 11am–10pm, Fri–Sat 11am–1am; sushi bar Mon–Thurs 5–10pm, Fri–Sat 11am–1am, Sun 11am–10pm.

INEXPENSIVE

Capriotti's ★★★ DELI It looks like a dump but there's a reason that Capriotti's is one of the fastest growing businesses in town. They roast their own beef and turkeys on the premises and stuff them (or Italian cold cuts, or whatever) into huge sandwiches—the "large" is 20 inches, easily feeding two for under $10 total. And deliciously so; the "Slaw B Joe" (roast beef, coleslaw, and Russian dressing) is fabulous. They even have veggie varieties. We never leave town without a stop here, and you shouldn't, either.

322 W. Sahara Ave. (at Las Vegas Blvd. S.). ✆ **702/474-0229.** www.capriottis.com. Most sandwiches under $10. No credit cards. Mon–Fri 10am–5pm; Sat 11am–5pm.

Rincon Criollo CUBAN Located beyond the wedding chapels on Las Vegas Boulevard, Rincon Criollo has all the right details for a good, cheap ethnic joint: It's full of locals and empty of frills. It's not the best Cuban food ever, but it gets the job done. The main courses (featuring Cuban pork and chicken specialties) are hit-or-miss; try the marinated pork leg or, better still, ask your server for a recommendation. Paella is offered, but only for parties of at least five people (and starts at $25). The side-course *chorizo* (a spicy sausage) is excellent, and the Cuban sandwich (roast pork, ham, and cheese on bread, which is then pressed and flattened out) is huge and tasty. For only $3.50, the latter makes a fine change-of-pace meal.

1145 Las Vegas Blvd. S. ✆ **702/388-1906.** Reservations not accepted. Main courses $7.50–$13; paella (for 5) $25. AE, DISC, MC, V. Tues–Sun 11am–9:30pm.

Tiffany's ★★ Value DINER This decidedly unflashy soda fountain/lunch counter was Las Vegas's first 24-hour restaurant, and it has been going strong for 60 years. Plunk down at the counter and watch the cooks go nuts trying to keep up with the orders. The menu is basic comfort food: standard items (meatloaf, ground round steak, chops, and so on), fluffy cream pies, and classic breakfasts served anytime—try the biscuits and cream gravy at 3am. But the best bet is a half-pound burger and "thick, creamy shake," both about as good as they get. At around $6, this is half what you would pay for a comparable meal at the Hard Rock Cafe. Places like this are a vanishing species—it's worth the short walk from the Stratosphere. Note, however, that the neighborhood remains stubbornly rough in appearance, and that can be a turnoff. Stay alert if you come here at night.

1700 Las Vegas Blvd. S. (at East Oakey Blvd.). ✆ **702/444-4459.** Reservations not accepted. Most items under $8. No credit cards. Daily 24 hr.

4 WHAT TO SEE & DO

You can't sit at a slot machine forever. (Or maybe you can.) In any event, it shouldn't be too hard to find ways to fill your time between poker hands. Many of the hotels offer free entertainment in the form of light shows, animal-filled parks, and strolling musical performers. Can't-miss shows include the **Bellagio's dancing fountains,** a musical ballet of water and light that is the best free show in town; the **talking statues in Caesars' Forum Shops;** and the **Mirage's exploding "volcano."** Couch potatoes can watch the MGM Grand's 80-foot outdoor video screens, while adventurers head for a roller coaster celebrating that most daredevil of drivers—the New York cabbie. (This last one's not free, but that only heightens the reality of the experience.)

Nevertheless, when you finally tire of Strip-gazing (or your brain shuts down from the overload), there are plenty of other things to see and do in Las Vegas.

The Arts Factory ★★ (Finds Believe it or not, Las Vegas has a burgeoning art scene (what some would consider soul-crushing is what others consider inspirational), and this complex, located in the Gateway district, is the place to find proof. It features a few galleries and a number of work spaces for local artists. Several of the spaces are closed to the public. On the first Friday of each month, they have a party event (unimaginatively named "First Friday") showcasing local artists and arts-oriented businesses, with live music, street performances, and other entertainment and activities. Visit their website for further details.

101–107 E. Charleston Blvd. ✆ **702/676-1111.** www.theartsfactory.com. Free admission. Hours vary by gallery.

Fremont Street Experience ★★ The Fremont Street Experience in the heart of Downtown Vegas is a 5-block open-air pedestrian mall, a landscaped strip of outdoor cafes, vendor carts, and colorful kiosks purveying food and merchandise. Overhead is a 90-foot-high steel-mesh "celestial vault"; at night, it's the **Viva Vision,** a high-tech light-and-laser show enhanced by a concert-hall-quality sound system that takes place five times nightly. The canopy also cools the area through a misting system in summer and warms you with radiant heaters in winter. It's a place where you can stroll, eat, or even dance to the music under the lights. The crowd it attracts is more upscale than in years past, and of course, it's a lot less crowded than the hectic Strip.

Fremont St. (btw. Main St. and Las Vegas Blvd.), Downtown. www.vegasexperience.com. Free admission. Shows nightly.

Las Vegas Mini Gran Prix ★★★ (Kids Part arcade, part go-kart racetrack, this is exactly what you want to help your kids (and maybe yourselves) work their ya-ya's out. The arcade is well stocked, with a better quality of prizes than one often finds, but we suggest not spending too much time in there and instead hustling outside to the slide, the little roller coaster, and best of all, the four go-kart tracks. The staff is utterly friendly, and the pizzas at the food court are triple the size and half the price of those found in your hotel. The one drawback: It's far away from main Strip action—here's where you'll need that rental car, for sure. ***Note:*** Kids have to be at least 36 inches tall to ride any of the attractions.

1401 N. Rainbow Rd., just off US 95 N. ✆ **702/259-7000.** www.lvmgp.com. Ride tickets $6.50 each, $30 for 5. Mon–Fri 11am–9pm; Sat–Sun 10am–9pm.

Liberace Museum ★★★ (Moments) You can keep your Louvres and Vaticans and Smithsonians; *this* is a museum. Housed in a strip mall, this is a shrine to the glory and excess that was the art project known as Liberace. You've got your costumes (bejeweled), your many cars (bejeweled), your many pianos (bejeweled), and many jewels (also bejeweled). The museum is now better than ever, thanks to a costly renovation. Unless you have a severely underdeveloped appreciation for camp or take your museum-going very seriously, you shouldn't miss it. The museum is $2^1/_2$ miles east of the Strip on your right.

1775 E. Tropicana Ave. (at Spencer St.). ✆ **702/798-5595.** www.liberace.org. Admission $15 adults, $10 seniors over 65 and students with valid school ID. Free for children 10 and under. Free for Nevada citizens 2nd Sun of month. $2 discount on admission for those who arrive by taxi or bus and present valid receipt. Admission includes 1-hr. guided tour (call ahead for tour hours). Tues–Sat 10am–5pm; Sun noon–4pm. Closed Mon, New Year's Day, Thanksgiving, and Christmas.

MGM Grand Lion Habitat ★★ (Kids) Hit this attraction at the right time—when the crowds aren't here—and it's one of the best freebies in town. It's a large, multilevel glass enclosure, in which lions frolic throughout the day. In addition to regular viewing spots, you can walk through a glass tunnel and get a worm's eye view of the underside of a lion (provided one is in position); note how very big Kitty's paws are. Multiple lions share show duties, so what you observe is definitely going to depend on who is in residence when you drop by.

In MGM Grand, 3799 Las Vegas Blvd. S. ✆ **702/891-7777.** Free admission. Daily 11am–7pm.

Secret Garden & Dolphin Habitat ★★★ (Kids) Get up close and personal with white tigers, lions, and plain old gray elephants here at this minizoo; or better still, watch dolphins frolic in the neighboring Dolphin Habitat. There is nothing quite like the kick you get from seeing a baby dolphin play. Ask the staff to play ball with the dolphins; they toss large beach balls into the pools, and the dolphins hit them out with their noses, leaping out of the water cackling with dolphin glee.

In The Mirage, 3400 Las Vegas Blvd. S. ✆ **702/791-7111.** www.mirage.com. Admission $15 adults, $10 children 4–12, free for children 3 and under if accompanied by an adult. Mon–Fri 11am–7pm; Sat–Sun and major holidays 10am–7pm. Hours subject to change and vary by season.

Speed: The Ride/Las Vegas Cyber Speedway ★★ This popular stop has two attractions. The first is a remarkable 8-minute virtual-reality ride, **Cyber Speedway,** featuring a three-quarter-size replica of a NASCAR race car. **Speed: The Ride** is a new roller coaster that blasts riders out through a hole in the wall by the new NASCAR Cafe, then through a loop, under the sidewalk, through the hotel's marquee, and finally straight up a 250-foot tower. At the peak, you feel a moment of weightlessness, and then you do the whole thing backwards! Not for the faint of heart.

In the Sahara, 2535 Las Vegas Blvd. S. ✆ **702/737-2111.** www.nascarcafelasvegas.com. $23 for all-day pass on both rides. Cyber Speedway (simulator) $10 (you must be at least 54 in. tall to ride); SPEED: The Ride (roller coaster) $10 for single ride. Daily noon–10pm; hours may vary.

Stratosphere Thrill Rides ★★ (Kids) Atop the 1,149-foot Stratosphere Tower are three marvelous thrill rides. The **Big Shot** is a breathtaking free-fall ride that thrusts you 160 feet in the air along a 228-foot spire at the top of the tower, and then plummets back down again. Amping up the terror factor is **X-Scream,** a giant teeter-totter-style device that propels you in an open car off the side of the 100-story tower and lets you dangle there weightlessly before returning you to relative safety. And now they have the aptly named **Insanity,** a spinning whirly-gig of a contraption that straps you into a seat and twirls you around 1,000 feet or so above terra firma. Insanity is right. ***Note:*** The rides are shut down in inclement weather and high winds.

Atop Stratosphere Las Vegas, 2000 Las Vegas Blvd. S. ✆ **702/380-7777.** Admission: Big Shot $13; X-Scream $12; Insanity $12; plus fee to ascend Tower: $14 for adults; $10 for locals, seniors, and hotel guests; $8 children. Multiride and all-day packages also available for varying costs. Sun–Thurs 10am–1am; Fri–Sat 10am–2am. Hours vary seasonally. Minimum height requirement for Big Shot is 48 in.; minimum height requirement for X-Scream and Insanity are 52 in.

WHERE TO ROLL THE DICE

What? You didn't come to Las Vegas for the Liberace Museum? We are shocked. *Shocked.*

Yes, there are gambling opportunities in Vegas. Let's not kid ourselves; gambling is what Vegas is about. You should casino-hop at least once to marvel (or get dizzy) at the decor/spectacle and the sheer excess of it all. Beyond decoration, there isn't too much difference. All the casinos have slot and video poker machines and offer games such as blackjack, roulette, craps, poker, Pai Gow, keno, and baccarat. If you're a novice, many casinos offer free gambling lessons that include low stakes games, so you won't lose much while you learn.

Some notable places to gamble include the **MGM Grand,** the largest casino (you will get lost); **New York–New York,** where the change carts look like yellow cabs; the light and airy **Mandalay Bay;** the tasteful **Venetian;** the **Las Vegas Hilton,** where the space-themed casino has light beam–activated slots; **Harrah's,** where the "party pits" offer the most fun in town; **Paris Las Vegas,** where you'll find a kitschy Disneyesque atmosphere; and **Binion's,** where all serious gamblers head, thanks to low minimum bets and single-deck blackjack.

Downtown, stakes are lower, pretensions are nonexistent, and the clientele are often friendlier. You don't have to be a high roller. You would not believe how much fun you can have with a nickel slot machine. You won't get rich, but neither will most of those guys playing the $5 slots.

5 LAS VEGAS AFTER DARK

THE SHOWS

You won't go wrong seeing one of **Cirque du Soleil**'s productions—they're among the best in town. ***O,*** at the Bellagio (✆ **888/488-7111**), is a breathtaking mix of artistry and acrobatics over a 1.5-million-gallon pool; ***Mystère,*** at TI at the Mirage (✆ **800/288-7206**), is a sophisticated and surreal circus extravaganza. ***Folies Bergère,*** at the Tropicana, is the longest-running production show in town and has recently undergone a "sexier than ever" face-lift. The **Blue Men Group** at the Venetian is performance art for the masses, but don't let that prevent you from going and laughing your head off (✆ **702/**

Nighttime Is the Right Time

For a great selection of nightlife on the Strip, head for Mandalay Bay; **Aureole, Red Square,** and the **House of Blues** are all popular. You might also check out the incredible nighttime view at the bar atop the **Stratosphere**—nothing beats it.

414-9000). And if you want to see a classic Vegas topless revue—oh, why not?—check out ***Jubilee!,*** at Bally's (✆ **800/237-7469** or 702/739-4567).

Magic fans will love **Lance Burton: Master Magician,** at the Monte Carlo (✆ **877/386-8224**), whose sleight-of-hand tricks are extraordinary.

THE CLUB & BAR SCENE

Most Las Vegas bars and clubs don't even get going until close to midnight. **Body English,** in the Hard Rock Hotel, 4455 Paradise Rd. (✆ **702/693-5000;** www.bodyenglish.com), is one of the hottest clubs in town. **Jet,** in The Mirage, 3400 Las Vegas Blvd. S. (✆ **702/792-7900**), a three-dance-floor, four-bar club, opened in 2006. **Bank,** at the Bellagio, 3600 Las Vegas Blvd. S. (✆ **702/693-8300**), is a grown-up nightclub that caters to the silver spoon crowd but has a party atmosphere that doesn't feel exclusive.

Country music fans might want to wander on over to **Toby Keith's I Love This Bar & Grill,** Harrah's, 3475 Las Vegas Blvd. S. (✆ **702/369-5084**), which offers live music Wednesday through Saturday.

The Buffalo, 4640 Paradise Rd. (at Naples Dr.; ✆ **702/733-8355**), is a leather/Levi's gay bar, while **Gipsy,** located nearby at 4605 Paradise Rd. (✆ **702/731-1919;** www.gipsylv.net), is the gay dance club that draws the biggest crowds.

Some good comedy clubs on the Strip are **Bobby Slayton Room,** in the Tropicana, 3801 Las Vegas Blvd. S. (✆ **800/829-9034**); **The Improv,** at Harrah's, 3475 Las Vegas Blvd. S. (✆ **800/392-9002**); and **Comedy Club,** in The Riviera, 2901 Las Vegas Blvd. S. (✆ **877/892-7469**).

19

Fast Facts: American Southwest

AREA CODES The area code in Phoenix is 602. In Scottsdale, Tempe, Mesa, and the east valley, it's 480. In Glendale and the west valley, it's 623. The area code for Tucson and southeastern Arizona is 520. The rest of the state is area code 928. New Mexico has two area codes: The northwest, including Albuquerque and Santa Fe, have the 505 code, while the rest of the state it's 575. The area code for southwestern Colorado is 719 and for southern Utah, 435. Las Vegas's code is 702.

AUTOMOBILE ORGANIZATIONS Motor clubs will supply maps, suggested routes, guidebooks, accident and bail-bond insurance, and emergency road service. The **American Automobile Association** (**AAA**; ✆ **800/222-4357**; www.aaa.com) is the major auto club in the United States. If you belong to a motor club in your home country, inquire about AAA reciprocity. You may be able to join AAA even if you're not a member of a reciprocal club (call AAA). AAA has a nationwide emergency road service telephone number (✆ **800/AAA-HELP** [222-4357]).

BUSINESS HOURS The following are general hours. Banks are open Monday through Friday from 9am to 5pm (some also on Sat 9am–noon). Stores are open Monday through Saturday from 10am to 6pm and Sunday from noon to 5pm (malls usually stay open until 8 or 9pm Mon–Sat). Bars generally open around 11am and close between 1 and 2am, depending on the state.

DRINKING LAWS The legal age for purchase and consumption of alcoholic beverages is 21; proof of age is required and often requested at bars, nightclubs, and restaurants, so it's always a good idea to bring ID when you go out.

Each of the states in the region has its own restrictions on when and where you can buy alcohol. Arizona, New Mexico, and Colorado have pretty standard laws, which allow purchase from morning to 1 or 2am in licensed stores on most days, with some time restrictions on Sundays. Utah's laws are stricter; you can buy beer, wine, and hard liquor every day except Sunday, when the state-owned liquor stores are closed. You can buy 3.2% beer, which has less alcohol, 7 days a week. Note that some Native American reservations (including the Navajo reservation) prohibit alcohol within the reservation.

Do not carry open containers of alcohol in your car or any public area that isn't zoned for alcohol consumption. The police can fine you on the spot. Don't even think about driving while intoxicated.

DRIVING RULES See "Getting There & Getting Around," p. 40.

ELECTRICITY Like Canada, the United States uses 110 to 120 volts AC (60 cycles), compared to 220 to 240 volts AC (50 cycles) in most of Europe, Australia, and New Zealand. Downward converters that change 220 to 240 volts to 110 to 120 volts are difficult to find in the United States, so bring one with you.

EMBASSIES & CONSULATES All embassies are located in the nation's capital, Washington, D.C. Some consulates are located in major U.S. cities, and most nations have a mission to the United Nations in New York City. If your country isn't listed below, call for directory information in Washington, D.C. (✆ **202/555-1212**) or check **www.embassy.org/embassies.**

The embassy of **Australia** is at 1601 Massachusetts Ave. NW, Washington, DC 20036 (✆ **202/797-3000;** usa.embassy.gov/au).

The embassy of **Canada** is at 501 Pennsylvania Ave. NW, Washington, DC 20001 (✆ **202/682-1740;** www.canadianembassy.org). Other Canadian consulates are in Buffalo (New York), Detroit, Los Angeles, New York, and Seattle.

The embassy of **Ireland** is at 2234 Massachusetts Ave. NW, Washington, DC 20008 (✆ **202/462-3939;** www.irelandemb.org). Irish consulates are in Boston, Chicago, New York, San Francisco, and other cities. See the website for complete listing.

The embassy of **New Zealand** is at 37 Observatory Circle NW, Washington, DC 20008 (✆ **202/328-4800;** www.nzembassy.com). New Zealand consulates are in Los Angeles, Salt Lake City, San Francisco, and Seattle.

The embassy of the **United Kingdom** is at 3100 Massachusetts Ave. NW, Washington, DC 20008 (✆ **202/588-7800;** www.britainusa.com). British consulates are in Atlanta, Boston, Chicago, Cleveland, Houston, Los Angeles, New York, San Francisco, and Seattle.

EMERGENCIES In case of emergency, dial ✆ **911.**

GASOLINE (PETROL) In the past year the cost of gasoline has fluctuated wildly. In the Southwest, prices run a little above the national average. Taxes are already included in the printed price. One U.S. gallon equals 3.8 liters or .85 imperial gallons.

HOLIDAYS Banks, government offices, post offices, and many stores, restaurants, and museums are closed on the following legal national holidays: January 1 (New Year's Day), the third Monday in January (Martin Luther King, Jr., Day), the third Monday in February (Presidents' Day), the last Monday in May (Memorial Day), July 4 (Independence Day), the first Monday in September (Labor Day), the second Monday in October (Columbus Day), November 11 (Veterans' Day/Armistice Day), the fourth Thursday in November (Thanksgiving Day), and December 25 (Christmas). The Tuesday after the first Monday in November is Election Day, a federal government holiday in presidential-election years (held every 4 years, and next in 2012). For more information on holidays see "Calendar of Events," on p. 31.

HOSPITALS See the "Fast Facts" section in the major city chapters.

INSURANCE For information on traveler's insurance, trip cancellation insurance, and medical insurance while traveling, please visit www.frommers.com/planning.

INTERNET ACCESS Although you will find the some cybercafes in the Southwest, they are not as common as in more populated regions. Your best bet, other than using access provided by your hotel or resort, is to head to the nearest public library or copy shop, such as FedEx Kinko's. To find a cyber cafe in your city, try www.cybercafe.com. Also see the "Fast Facts" sections in individual chapters.

LEGAL AID If you are "pulled over" for a minor infraction (such as speeding), never attempt to pay the fine directly to a police officer; this could be construed as attempted bribery, a much more serious crime. Pay fines by mail, or directly into the hands of the clerk of the court. If accused of a more serious offense, say and do nothing before consulting a lawyer. Here the burden is on the state to prove a person's guilt beyond a reasonable doubt, and everyone has the right to remain silent, whether he or she is suspected of a crime or actually arrested. Once arrested, a person can make one telephone call to a party of his or her choice. International visitors should call your embassy or consulate.

MAIL At press time, domestic postage rates were 28¢ for a postcard and 44¢ for a letter. For international mail, a first-class letter of up to 1 ounce costs 98¢ (75¢ to Canada and 79¢ to Mexico); a first-class postcard costs the same as a letter. For more information go to **www.usps.com**.

If you aren't sure what your address will be in the United States, mail can be sent to you, in your name, c/o General Delivery at the main post office of the city or region where you expect to be. (Call ✆ **800/275-8777** for information on the nearest post office.) The addressee must pick up mail in person and must produce proof of identity (driver's license, passport, and so on). Most post offices will hold your mail for up to 1 month, and are open Monday to Friday from 8am to 6pm, and Saturday from 9am to 3pm.

NEWSPAPERS & MAGAZINES National newspapers include the *New York Times, USA Today,* and the *Wall Street Journal.* National newsweeklies include *Newsweek, Time,* and *U.S. News and World Report.* In large cities, most newsstands offer a small selection of the most popular foreign periodicals and newspapers, such as the *Economist* and *Le Monde.* The ***Albuquerque Journal,*** New Mexico's largest daily newspaper, circulates throughout the central and northern parts of the state. The ***El Paso Times*** is favored in southern New Mexico. The state's favorite magazine is ***New Mexico*** (www.nmmagazine.com), a colorful monthly published by the State Tourism and Travel Division since 1923. Check out the "King of the Road" column in the magazine, for some interesting off-the-beaten-track destinations. The ***Arizona Republic*** is Arizona's largest daily newspaper and can be found throughout central and northern Arizona. In the southern part of the state, you are more likely to find Tucson's ***Arizona Daily Star,*** a morning daily. ***Arizona Highways*** is a vivid and informative photo-driven monthly magazine published by the Arizona Department of Transportation. Both Phoenix and Tucson have a number of glossy monthly lifestyle magazines that are worth picking up for their monthly events listings.

PASSPORTS See **www.frommers.com/planning** for information on how to obtain a passport. See "Embassies & Consulates," above, for whom to contact if you lose yours while traveling in the U.S. For other information, please contact the following agencies:

For Residents of Australia Contact the **Australian Passport Information Service** at ✆ **131-232,** or visit the government website at **www.passports.gov.au**.

For Residents of Canada Contact the central **Passport Office,** Department of Foreign Affairs and International Trade, Ottawa, ON K1A 0G3 (✆ **800/567-6868;** www.ppt.gc.ca).

For Residents of Ireland Contact the **Passport Office,** Setanta Centre, Molesworth Street, Dublin 2 (✆ **01/671-1633;** www.irlgov.ie/iveagh).

For Residents of New Zealand Contact the **Passports Office** at ✆ **0800/225-050** in New Zealand or 04/474-8100, or log on to **www.passports.govt.nz**.

For Residents of the United Kingdom Visit your nearest passport office, major post office, or travel agency or contact the **United Kingdom Passport Service** at ✆ **0870/521-0410,** or search its website at **www.ukpa.gov.uk**.

For Residents of the United States To find your regional passport office, either check the U.S. Department of State website or call the **National Passport Information Center** toll-free number (✆ **877/487-2778**) for automated information.

POLICE In most of the region, phone ✆ **911** for emergencies. If 911 doesn't work, dial 0 (zero) for the operator and state your reason for calling.

SMOKING Arizona, New Mexico, and Colorado prohibit smoking in all indoor public places, including restaurants and bars. In Utah smoking is prohibited in restaurants but not private clubs, lounges, or taverns. Las Vegas prohibits smoking in most public places except casinos and bars that don't serve food.

TAXES Combined city and state sales taxes vary from place to place but usually range from 6% to 9% for purchases, 9% to 13% for lodging. The United States has no value-added tax (VAT) or other indirect tax at the national level. Every state, county, and city may levy its own local tax on all purchases, including hotel and restaurant checks and airline tickets. These taxes will not appear on price tags.

TELEPHONES See "Staying Connected," on p. 50.

TIME The continental United States is divided into **four time zones:** Eastern Standard Time (EST), Central Standard Time (CST), Mountain Standard Time (MST), and Pacific Standard Time (PST). Alaska and Hawaii have their own zones. For example, when it's 9am in Los Angeles (PST), it's 7am in Honolulu (HST), 10am in Denver (MST), 11am in Chicago (CST), noon in New York City (EST), 5pm in London (GMT), and 2am the next day in Sydney.

Daylight saving time is in effect from 1am on the second Sunday in March to 1am on the first Sunday in November, except in Arizona, Hawaii, the U.S. Virgin Islands, and Puerto Rico. Daylight saving time moves the clock 1 hour ahead of standard time.

The American Southwest is in the Mountain Time Zone, 1 hour ahead of the West Coast and 2 hours behind the East Coast. Note that Arizona does not observe daylight saving time, so time differences between Arizona and the rest of the country vary with the time of year. The Navajo Reservation observes daylight saving time. The Hopi Reservation, which is surrounded by the Navajo Reservation, does not.

TIPPING In hotels, tip **bellhops** at least $1 per bag ($2–$3 if you have a lot of luggage) and tip the **chamber staff** $1 to $2 per day (more if you've left a disaster area for him or her to clean up). Tip the **doorman** or **concierge** only if he or she has provided you with some specific service (for example, calling a cab for you or obtaining difficult-to-get theater tickets). Tip the **valet-parking attendant** $1 every time you get your car.

In restaurants, bars, and nightclubs, tip **service staff** and **bartenders** 15% to 20% of the check, tip **checkroom attendants** $1 per garment, and tip **valet-parking attendants** $1 per vehicle.

Tip **cab drivers** 15% of the fare; **skycaps** at airports at least $1 per bag ($2–$3 if you have a lot of luggage); and **hairdressers** and **barbers** 15% to 20%.

TOILETS You won't find public toilets or "restrooms" on the streets in most U.S. cities but they can be found in hotel lobbies, bars, restaurants, and so forth. Large hotels and fast-food restaurants are often the best bet for clean facilities.

VISAS For information about U.S. Visas go to **http://travel.state.gov** and click on "Visas." Or go to one of the following websites for the countries listed below.

Australian citizens can obtain up-to-date visa information from the **U.S.**

Embassy Canberra, Moonah Place, Yarralumla, ACT 2600 (© **02/6214-5600**) or by checking the U.S. Diplomatic Mission's website at **http://usembassy-australia.state.gov/consular**.

British subjects can obtain up-to-date visa information by calling the **U.S. Embassy Visa Information Line** (© **0891/200-290**) or by visiting the "Visas to the U.S." section of the American Embassy London's website at **www.usembassy.org.uk**.

Irish citizens can obtain up-to-date visa information through the **Embassy of the USA Dublin,** 42 Elgin Rd., Dublin 4, Ireland (© **353/1-668-8777**), or by checking the "Visas to the U.S." section of the website at **http://dublin.usembassy.gov**.

Citizens of **New Zealand** can obtain up-to-date visa information by contacting the **U.S. Embassy New Zealand,** 29 Fitzherbert Terrace, Thorndon, Wellington (© **644/472-2068**), or get the information directly from the website at **http://wellington.usembassy.gov**.

VISITOR INFORMATION For information on Arizona, contact the **Arizona Office of Tourism Visitor Center,** 125 N. Second St., Phoenix, AZ 85004 (© **866/275-5816;** www.arizonaguide.com). For suggested driving tours along Arizona's scenic roads, also check out the Arizona Office of Tourism's website, **www.arizonascenicroads.com**. The Visitors Information Center for the **New Mexico Department of Tourism** is at 491 Old Santa Fe Trail, Santa Fe, NM 87501 (© **800/545-2070** or 505/827-7400; www.newmexico.org).

For Colorado, contact the **Colorado Tourism Office,** 1625 Broadway, Denver, CO 80202 (© **800/COLORADO** [265-6723]; www.colorado.com), for a free copy of the official state vacation guide, which includes a state map and describes attractions, activities, and lodgings throughout Colorado. Another good source for Colorado information is the website of the *Denver Post,* the state's major daily newspaper (www.denverpost.com). For information on Utah as well as an official state map, contact the **Utah Office of Tourism,** Council Hall/300 N. State St., Salt Lake City, UT 84114 (© **800/200-1160** or 801/538-1030; www.utah.com).

For information about Las Vegas, contact the **Las Vegas Convention and Visitors Authority,** 3150 Paradise Rd., Las Vegas, NV 89109 (© **877/VISIT-LV** [847-4858] or 702/892-0711; www.visitlasvegas.com). Another excellent information source is the **Las Vegas Chamber of Commerce,** 3720 Howard Hughes Pkwy., No. 100, Las Vegas, NV 89109 (© **702/735-1616;** www.lvchamber.com). Request the *Visitor's Guide,* which contains extensive information about accommodations, attractions, excursions, children's activities, and more. The staff can answer all your Las Vegas questions, including those about weddings and divorces.

Addresses, telephone numbers, and Internet addresses for convention and visitors bureaus and chambers of commerce appear in the appropriate chapters in this book. Members of **AAA** can get a map and guidebook covering Arizona and New Mexico. You can also request the club's free *Southwestern CampBook,* which includes campgrounds in Arizona, Utah, Colorado, and New Mexico.

Some regional **websites** that might be of help include the following:

- www.desertusa.com
- http://phoenix.about.com
- http://gosw.about.com/od/southwestmiscelaneous/a/blogs.htm
- www.santafe.com
- www.taosplaza.com
- www.southernnewmexico.com

Some new general **blogs** that might help in planning your trip include the following:

- www.azreporter.com
- www.gridskipper.com
- www.travelblog.org
- www.worldhum.com
- www.writtenroad.com

1 AIRLINES

MAJOR AIRLINES

Aeroméxico
www.aeromexico.com

Alaska Airlines/Horizon Air
www.alaskaair.com

American Airlines
www.aa.com

Continental Airlines
www.continental.com

Delta Air Lines
www.delta.com

Frontier Airlines
www.frontierairlines.com

Hawaiian Airlines
www.hawaiianair.com

JetBlue Airways
www.jetblue.com

Midwest Airlines
www.midwestairlines.com

Northwest Airlines
www.nwa.com

United Airlines
www.united.com

US Airways
www.usairways.com

BUDGET AIRLINES

AirTran Airways
www.airtran.com

Frontier Airlines
www.frontierairlines.com

JetBlue Airways
www.jetblue.com

Southwest Airlines
www.southwest.com

WestJet
www.westjet.com

2 MAJOR HOTEL & MOTEL CHAINS

Best Western International
www.bestwestern.com

Clarion Hotels
www.choicehotels.com

Comfort Inn
www.ComfortInn.com

Courtyard by Marriott
www.marriott.com/courtyard

Crowne Plaza Hotels
www.ichotelsgroup.com/crowneplaza

Days Inn
www.daysinn.com

Doubletree Hotels
www.doubletree.com

Econo Lodges
www.choicehotels.com

Embassy Suites
www.embassysuites.com

Fairfield Inn by Marriott
www.fairfieldinn.com

Four Seasons
www.fourseasons.com

Hampton Inn
http://hamptoninn1.hilton.com

Hilton Hotels
www.hilton.com

Holiday Inn
www.holidayinn.com

Howard Johnson
www.hojo.com

Hyatt
www.hyatt.com

InterContinental Hotels & Resorts
www.ichotelsgroup.com

La Quinta Inns and Suites
www.lq.com

Loews Hotels
www.loewshotels.com

Marriott
www.marriott.com

Motel 6
www.motel6.com

Omni Hotels
www.omnihotels.com

Quality
www.QualityInn.com

Radisson Hotels & Resorts
www.radisson.com

Ramada Worldwide
www.ramada.com

Red Roof Inns
www.redroof.com

Renaissance
www.renaissancehotels.com

Residence Inn by Marriott
www.marriott.com/residenceinn

Rodeway Inns
www.RodewayInn.com

Sheraton Hotels & Resorts
www.starwoodhotels.com/sheraton

Super 8 Motels
www.super8.com

Travelodge
www.travelodge.com

Vagabond Inns
www.vagabondinn.com

Westin Hotels & Resorts
www.starwoodhotels.com/westin

Wyndham Hotels & Resorts
www.wyndham.com

3 CAR-RENTAL AGENCIES

Advantage
www.advantage.com

Alamo
www.alamo.com

Avis
www.avis.com

Budget
www.budget.com

Dollar
www.dollar.com

Enterprise
www.enterprise.com

Hertz
www.hertz.com

National
www.nationalcar.com

Payless
www.paylesscarrental.com

Rent-A-Wreck
www.rentawreck.com

Thrifty
www.thrifty.com

INDEX